KU-168-866

# WILKINSON'S

# ROAD TRAFFIC OFFENCES

# WILKINSON'S

# ROAD TRAFFIC OFFENCES

*Twelfth Edition*

## VOLUME 1

PATRICK HALNAN
*Metropolitan Stipendiary Magistrate*

JOHN SPENCER
*of the Inner Temple, Barrister*
*Clerk to the Bridport, Dorchester, Sherborne, and Weymouth and Portland Justices*

Longman Professional

ISBN 2 Vols: 0 85121 073 2
Vol 1: 0 85120 980 7
Vol 2: 0 85121 101 1

*First published* 1953
*Twelfth edition* 1985

Published by:
Longman Professional and Business Communications Division
21–27 Lamb's Conduit Street
London WC1N 3NJ
ENGLAND

Associated offices:

Longman Professional Publishing (Pty) Limited
130 Phillip Street
Sydney
NSW 2000
AUSTRALIA

Longman Group (USA)
500 North Dearborn Street
Chicago, Illinois 60610
USA

Longman Group (Far East) Limited
Cornwall House, 18th Floor
Tai Koo Trading Estate
Tong Chong Street
Quarry Bay
HONG KONG

Longman Singapore Publishers (PTE) Limited
25 First Lok Yang Road
SINGAPORE 2262

Longman Malaysia Sdn Bhd
Wisma Damansara/Tingkat 2
5 Jalan Semantan
Peti Surat 63
Kuala Lumpur 01–02
MALAYSIA



Printed in Great Britain by
Butler & Tanner Ltd, Frome and London

# Contents

## Chapter 2 Procedure and Evidence

## Chapter 3 Notices of Intended Prosecution



## Chapter 4 Drink/Driving Offences

## Chapter 6 Driver Offences

## Chapter 7 Accidents and Furnishing Information



## Chapter 8 Vehicle Offences

## Chapter 9 Protection of Drivers and Passengers



## Chapter 10 Insurance

## Chapter 11 Driving Licences

## Chapter 12 Excise and Trade Licences

## Chapter 13 Goods and Passenger Vehicles

## Chapter 14 Drivers' Hours and Records

## Chapter 15 Theft, Taking Conveyances and Criminal Damage

## Chapter 16 Forgery, Fraudulent Use and False Statements



## Chapter 17 Fixed penalties

## Chapter 18 Custodial and Other Penalties

## Chapter 19 Endorsement and Penalty Points



## Chapter 20 Disqualification

## Chapter 21 Special Reasons and Mitigating Circumstances

## Chapter 22 Appeals



## Appendix 1 Drink/Driving



## Appendix 2 Endorsement and Sentence Codes



## Appendix 3 Suggestions for Assessing Penalties

# Preface

**The law is as stated on 1 February 1985** both as to the text and as to the source material in Volume 2. We have, however, been able to incorporate into the text the surprising number of important cases relating to road traffic that have been reported since that date and up to the beginning of May, together with the new suggested penalties issued in May by the Magistrates' Association.

The last edition was published in November 1982. This edition was delayed in the expectation of Part II of the Transport Act 1982 being brought into force and for this reason a second cumulative supplement had to be issued. The amount of material is now such that a new edition can be delayed no longer. Moreover, as it has been announced that Part III of the Transport Act 1982 will be brought into force 'not later than April 1986' it was thought worthwhile to include this. Part III of the Transport Act 1982 is an extremely complex piece of legislation designed to improve the existing fixed penalty system and, at the same time, to bring within the scope of the system a greater number of trivial offences such as speeding as well as the existing 'stationary' parking and excess ticket offences. Because speeding is an endorsable offence the statutory provisions as to endorsement and penalty points disqualification have had to be allowed for in the legislation. We hope that the legislation will achieve the desired result of removing a substantial number of trivial traffic cases from magistrates' courts and that the fixed penalty system will be more effective (as long ago as 1978 only one in ten of those who should have been prosecuted for not paying parking tickets in London was in fact prosecuted). The complexity of the new system is such that we have our doubts as to whether it will work satisfactorily. The system is set out and discussed in Chapter 17 with flow charts provided to show the bewildered reader a path through the statutory jungle.

The opportunity has been taken to improve further the general lay-out of *Wilkinson*. This edition follows the same basic pattern as earlier editions: definitions, practice and procedure, discussion of particular offences, sentencing, special reasons and finally appeals. However, instead of having one enormous chapter in which almost all the offences are to be found, the number of chapters has been increased to allow one chapter for each group of offences.

The opportunity has also been taken to split sentencing into three chapters, the first (Chapter 18) dealing with custodial and other penalties with separate chapters on orders of endorsement (Chapter 19) and orders of disqualification (Chapter 20).

We are conscious of the fact that the sheer volume of text is such that it has sometimes been difficult for the unaccustomed reader to find his way. As well as increasing the number of chapters and often re-ordering the text in the chapter into a more logical sequence, we have at the same time introduced a system of paragraph numbering. Regular *Wilkinson* users will notice also that the work is now contained in two volumes. This development is as much a response to coping with the continuing expansion of road traffic law as it is an expedient to ensure the usefulness of the work. The publishers believe that it will sometimes be helpful for users to refer to the text of Volume 1 simultaneously with the corresponding statutory authority in Volume 2. The effect of the change in format and the reorganisation of the text, together with the detailed contents list on pp v–xxvi, should be to enable readers to find exactly the information they need in the shortest possible time.

Such was the impact of the introduction of the new evidential Intoximeter and Camic breath test machines in 1983 that some have overlooked the fact that this introduction coincided with a completely fresh statutory text being substituted in place of the former sections. Because of the necessity to prevent cases on the former law being wrongly applied to the new statutory provisions, it has been found necessary to rewrite completely the drink/driving offences chapter (Chapter 4). As anticipated, there has been both a sustained attack on the new evidential breath test devices and an endeavour to find as many loopholes in the new statutory provisions as were found in the old. A trio of cases, *Fox* v *Gwent*, *Anderton* v *Royle* and *Bunyard* v *Hayes* (page 184), has decided that the police no longer have to prove a lawful arrest before evidence of analysis of excess alcohol can be admitted. The Camic and Intoximeter devices have been held to have been properly approved even though the Home Secretary jumped the gun in doing so (*Hayward* v *Eames* etc page 227). Defendants have been debarred from fishing expeditions to see if the Intoximeter was working properly (*R* v *Skegness Magistrates' Court* etc on page 230). (In this connection we hope that the practice of the metropolitan police in giving defendants access to Intoximeter records will be made uniform throughout all police forces.) We anticipate further development of the law as to when the police may or may not require blood or urine samples instead of breath in accordance with s 8(3)(*a*) or (*b*), see *Horrocks* v *Binns* page 222 and *Cotter* v *Kamil* and *Morgan* v *Lee* on page 223.

One of the most important developments in the law has been in the field of procedure, particularly three House of Lords cases: *Clayton* v *Chief Constable of Norfolk* (page 104) which lays down guidelines as to when there should be one joint magistrates' court trial where there are a number of defendants similarly charged or where one defendant faces a number of separate charges; *Hill* v *Anderton* (page 82) which decided that proceedings are begun when the information is laid; and *Re Daley* (page 81) which decided that whether a 17 year old has a right of trial by jury depends on his age at the time the juvenile court decided the mode of trial. Cases on causing death by reckless driving and careless and reckless driving continue to be reported. Notable among them are the 'guideline' sentencing cases of *R* v *Boswell* etc (page 308) and *R* v *Krawec* (page 310) which provide helpful guidance to magistrates facing the difficult task of sentencing a driver who has caused death but has only been charged with careless driving.

Substantial alterations in the text have had to be made to take account of the Transport Acts of 1981 and 1982, the Criminal Justice Act 1982 and the Road Traffic Regulation Act 1984 which consolidated all the former statutory provisions relating to traffic regulation. Although the provisions of the Police and Criminal Evidence Act 1984 which concern road traffic are not expected to be brought into force until April of next year, we have indicated where these will have an effect.

Government departments have been as active as ever in issuing subordinate legislation. Most notable among the new regulations are the Road Vehicle Lighting Regulations 1984 which replace all existing lighting regulations and introduce new provisions (Chapter 8 therefore contains a completely rewritten section on lighting). Also covered are the consolidating Motor Vehicles (Type Approval) (Great Britain) Regulations 1984.

The importance of the EEC is again recognised and the Agreement on the International Carriage of Passengers by Road by means of Occasional Coach and Bus Services (ASOR) has been added to the International Agreements section in Volume 2. The harmonisation of drivers' hours and records throughout the EEC has resulted in cases being increasingly decided not only in accordance with the appropriate EEC regulation but also by the European Court (see for example *R* v *Thomas Scott* deciding the meaning of 'specialised vehicle' on page 604).

Thanks are once again extended to Paul Niekirk who is responsible for sources in Volume 2. In this edition we are also particularly grateful to Peter Wallis who has written the chapter on the new fixed penalty procedure (Chapter 17) and has devised the accompanying flow charts.

Patrick Halnan
John Spencer
London
*2 May 1985*

# Table of Cases

# Table of Statutes

# Table of Statutory Instruments

# Table of European Provisions

**EEC Regulations**

**International Agreements**

# Abbreviations

| | |
|---|---|
| Archbold | Archbold's *Criminal Pleading, Evidence and Practice* |
| E & E Dig | *English and Empire Digest* |
| Halsbury | *Halsbury's Laws of England* |
| Stone | *Stone's Justices' Manual* |
| RTLB | *Road Traffic Law Bulletin* |

# Chapter 1

# Definitions

## 1.1 General

In this book various terms are used which, unless the context otherwise requires, will generally be used in the sense given in this chapter. It should be remembered that the meaning of some terms, notably 'to permit' and 'to use', varies according to the context of the section of the particular statute in which they appear. Furthermore, definitions of the same word may vary as between the Road Traffic Acts and the Vehicles (Excise) Act 1971.

The terms immediately below should, in particular, be noted as they are used throughout this book.

*'Magistrates' court'*

'Magistrates' court' includes a juvenile court, but not the Crown Court, except in so far as the powers of the Crown Court on appeal are limited to those of a magistrates' court.

*'The 1972 Act' etc*

References to 'the 1972 Act' are to the Road Traffic Act 1972, and earlier Road Traffic Acts are mentioned similarly. The Road Traffic Act 1972 consolidated most of the Road Traffic Act 1960, most of the Road Traffic Act 1962, the whole of the Road Safety Act 1967, all the Road Transport Lighting Acts, together with the Road Traffic (Driving of Motor Cycles) Act 1960, the Road Traffic (Driving Instruction) Act 1967, the Road Traffic (Disqualification) Act 1970, and the Motor Vehicles (Passenger Insurance) Act 1971. It incorporated those provisions of the Vehicle and Driving Licences Act 1969 not already incorporated in the Vehicles (Excise) Act 1971, which is sometimes referred to as 'the 1971 Act'.

The Road Traffic Regulation Act 1984 (which consolidated with amendments the like-named 1967 Act), the Transport Act 1968, the Public Passenger Vehicles Act 1981 and the Transport Act 1981 are the other major enactments relating to road traffic. They are, together with all other Acts, generally referred to by their full titles.

The Road Traffic Act 1974 made extensive and unrelated amendments to the Road Traffic Acts 1960 and 1972, and the Transport Act 1968. The Road Traffic (Drivers' Ages and Hours of Work) Act 1976 amended the Road

Traffic Act 1972, the Transport Act 1968, and the European Communities Act 1972.

Where the 1974 Act or the 1976 Act has amended provisions relating to the 1972 Act or the Transport Act 1968 it has normally done so by inserting new sections. These may be detected by the use of capital letters (eg s 22A of the 1972 Act).

The Public Passenger Vehicles Act 1981 consolidated the provisions of Part III of the Road Traffic Act 1960, Part I of the Transport Act 1980, the Minibus Act 1977 and the Passenger Vehicles (Experimental Areas) Act 1977.

The Transport Act 1981 made major alterations in the law of disqualification generally and in the drink/driving laws and introduced a system of penalty points.

The Transport Act 1982, Part III (ss 27–51 inclusive) when in force will greatly extend the fixed penalty provisions. Fixed penalties will apply to a wider range of offences including many which carry endorsement.

## Motor Vehicles

### 1.2 'Motor vehicle'

'Motor vehicle' is defined by s 190 of the 1972 Act for the purposes of that Act and regulations made thereunder. Section 190(1) defines a 'motor vehicle' as a mechanically propelled vehicle intended or adapted for use on roads. The Road Traffic Regulation Act 1984, s 136, is in similar terms.

This definition does not necessarily apply under the Vehicles (Excise) Act 1971, but for many purposes it will be the same. Under the Vehicles (Excise) Act 1971 a motor vehicle need not be 'intended or adapted for use on a road' (see 12.2): that Act uses the term 'mechanically propelled vehicle' only. It follows that a motor vehicle may require an excise licence when it is kept or used on a public road even though it is not subject to the 1972 Act because it is not intended or adapted for use on a road (eg a stock car, a scrambling motor bicycle, a dumper or works truck or a digging machine). As to vehicle excise licences for dumper trucks, works and digging machines see 12.13.

A motor vehicle does not cease to be 'used' as a motor vehicle when it is towed by another (*Cobb* v *Whorton* [1971] RTR 392, 1.79).

It should be emphasised that, 'vehicle' and 'motor vehicle' are differently defined for the purpose of drivers' hours and records and tachographs when EEC Regulations 543/69 and 1463/70 as amended apply (see arts 1 and 2 of the respective regulations).

Section 196(2) of the 1972 Act and s 142(3) of the Road Traffic Regulation Act 1984 provide that references in the Act to a class of vehicle or traffic shall be construed as references to a class defined or described by reference to any characteristics of the vehicles or to any other circumstances whatsoever.

The definitions of other terms relating to motor vehicles and classes thereof (which are discussed below) are principally contained in s 190(2)–(8) of the 1972 Act and ss 136 and 137 of the Road Traffic Regulation Act 1984.

## 1.3 'Motor car'

Section 190(2) of the 1972 Act (as amended by the Road Traffic Acts 1960 and 1972 and Road Traffic Regulation Act 1967 (Metrication) and (Metrication) (No 2) Regulations 1981) (SI 1981 Nos 1373 and 1374)) defines 'motor car' as follows:

> In this Act 'motor car' means a mechanically propelled vehicle, not being a motor cycle or an invalid carriage, which is constructed itself to carry a load or passengers and the weight of which unladen—
>
> (*a*) if it is constructed solely for the carriage of passengers and their effects, is adapted to carry not more than seven passengers exclusive of the driver, and is fitted with tyres of such type as may be specified in regulations made by the [Secretary of State for Transport], does not exceed [3050 kilograms];
>
> (*b*) if it is constructed or adapted for use for the conveyance of goods or burden of any description, does not exceed [3050 kilograms], or [3500 kilograms] if the vehicle carries a container or containers for holding for the purpose of its propulsion any fuel which is wholly gaseous at [17.5 degrees Celsius] under a pressure of [1.013 bar] or plant and materials for producing such fuel;
>
> (*c*) does not exceed [2540 kilograms] in a case falling within neither of the foregoing paragraphs.

The definition in s 136(2) of the Road Traffic Regulation Act 1984 is similar.

Section 190 of the 1972 Act and s 136 of the Road Traffic Regulation Act 1984 further define the meanings of 'heavy motor car', 'motor carriage', 'motor tractor', 'light locomotive' and 'heavy locomotive'.

## 1.4 'Hovercraft'

A 'hovercraft' within the meaning of the Hovercraft Act 1968 is a motor vehicle, whether or not it is adapted or intended to be adapted for use on roads, but is treated as not being a vehicle of any of the classes or descriptions specified in s 190(2)–(8) of the 1972 Act (s 192(1)). Regulations may modify any of the provisions of the 1972 Act in relation to hovercraft (s 192(2)). Like provisions are in the Road Traffic Regulation Act 1984, s 139.

## 1.5 'Invalid carriage'

An 'invalid carriage' is defined by s 190(5) of the 1972 Act as follows:

> In this Act 'invalid carriage' means a mechanically propelled vehicle the weight of which unladen does not exceed [254 kilograms] and which is specially designed and constructed, and not merely adapted, for the use of a person suffering from some physical defect or disability and is used solely by such a person.

The definition in the Road Traffic Regulation Act 1984, s 136(5), is similar save that curiously the expression 'physical default' is used in place of 'physical defect'.

For the purposes of all parts of the Road Traffic Act 1972 and Road Traffic Regulation Act 1984 and of the Motor Vehicles (Construction and Use) Regulations (save the 10 cwt exception below), a carriage for invalids exceeding 254 kg in unladen weight is not classified as an 'invalid carriage' but is a motor car or, if it has three or less wheels and does not exceed 410 kg, a motor cycle; it will also require third-party insurance, though one of 254 kg or less does not (s 143(3)). Otherwise a carriage for invalids over 254 kg is again not an 'invalid carriage' but comes within whatever category is appropriate for the particular vehicle and these Acts and regulations thereunder will apply, in particular as to insurance, etc.

The weight limit is increased to 10 cwt from 254 kg for the purposes of Part III of the 1972 Act and regulations thereunder only. For this purpose a motor vehicle of 10 cwt or under which is otherwise a carriage for invalids is to be treated as an invalid carriage even though it exceeds 254 kg. Part III relates to driving licences and driving tests (Motor Vehicles (Driving Licences) Regulations 1981, reg 25 (SI 1981 No 1952)). (In this regulation the metric weight has not yet been introduced.) A person may drive an invalid carriage at the age of sixteen (s 96 of the 1972 Act as amended) and for this purpose the altered definition will apply.

Invalid carriages not exceeding 250 lbs and incapable under their own power of exceeding 4 mph and complying with regs 2–6 of the Use of Invalid Carriages on Highways Regulations 1970 (SI 1970 No 1391) are treated for the purposes of the 1972 Act and the Road Traffic Regulation Act 1984 as not being motor vehicles (s 20 of the Chronically Sick and Disabled Persons Act 1970). These invalid carriages may also use footways and bridlepaths and only need to show the lights set out in Sched 1 to the 1970 Regulations.

There is an exemption from vehicle excise duty under the Vehicles (Excise) Act 1971 for certain vehicles for disabled people under the Finance Act 1972, s 7. This exemption is not limited to vehicles which are 'invalid carriages'. For the requirements for exemption see the wording of the section.

## 1.6 'Motor cycle'

A 'motor cycle' is defined by s 190(4) of the 1972 Act as a mechanically propelled vehicle, not being an invalid carriage, with three wheels or less and the weight of which unladen does not exceed 410 kg. The definition in s 136(4) of the Road Traffic Regulation Act 1984 is similar. This definition may therefore include three-wheelers, motor bicycles, mopeds and certain mowing machines and pedestrian controlled vehicles.

### *A Three-wheeler cars*

A three-wheeler car not exceeding 410 kg comes within the definition of 'motor cycle'. By s 190(2) of the 1972 Act (and s 136(2) of the Road Traffic Regulation Act 1984), a motor vehicle which is a motor cycle is not a motor car (see 'Motor car' 1.3, above). There are special rules relating to three-wheelers as to learner drivers (see 11.9). Various other provisions apply specifically to three-wheelers.

For certain purposes 'motor cycle' is differently defined in the Motor Vehicles (Construction and Use) Regulations (see regs 31B(5) (noise) and 116C (silencers)). The definition is an EEC definition, namely any *two-wheeled* vehicle with or without a sidecar fitted with an engine, intended for use on a road and having a design speed of more than 50 km per hour.

*B 'Motor bicycle'*

A motor bicycle is not defined in the 1972 Act or the Road Traffic Regulation Act 1984. As the prefix implies, a motor bicycle is a form of motor cycle but with two wheels. It is perhaps obvious that the wheels of a side car are to be excluded. Otherwise a bicycle with a side car could not be a bicycle as eg under the 1980 Regulations below. Again there are special rules relating to learner drivers and such vehicles (see 11.7–9). There is a special definition of a motor bicycle in the Motor Cycles (Protective Helmets) Regulations 1980 (SI 1980 No 1279) reg 4 as amended. Under this a bicycle is a bicycle with or without a side car and in certain circumstances may include a vehicle with additional wheels. These regulations apply only to such bicycles.

*C 'Sidecar'*

There is no definition of a sidecar (that is, a side carriage) as such. A sidecar is part of the motor cycle itself and not of its equipment *Higgins* v *Feeney* (1954) 88 ILTR 152. Under the 1972 Act, s 190(1) and the Road Traffic Regulation Act 1984, s 137, if the sidecar complies with the specified conditions, which are to be found in reg 129 of the Motor Vehicles (Construction and Use) Regulations, it is part of the vehicle and if not it is a trailer. A number of consequences follow. The various restrictions on the use of trailers will apply to trailers and the speed limit for the class of vehicle will be governed accordingly by Sched 6 of the Road Traffic Regulation Act 1984. See also 11.7–9 as to the learner driver provisions.

A flat tubular framework attached to a motor bicycle with a wheel on an axle welded to that framework was held not to be a sidecar under the learner driver provisions (*Cox* v *Harrison* [1968] 3 All ER 811). It was said obiter there that a sidecar must be capable of carrying a passenger. In *Keen* v *Parker* [1976] RTR 213 the defendant rode a 500 cc motor bicycle with a tubular steel framework attached, designed for the carriage of goods. The framework was roadworthy with a properly sprung wheel. It was held that a roadworthy attachment for the carriage of goods was just as much a 'sidecar' as one designed for the carriage of a passenger. The obiter dictum of Ashworth J in *Cox* v *Harrison* above was disapproved.

Sidecars are again becoming popular because the learner driver provisions are favourable for such vehicles. Magistrates' courts have held quite small wheeled containers to be sidecars because they can carry goods, even though the wheel is sprung and not in contact with the road at all times.

*D 'Standard motor cycle'*

A 'standard motor cycle' is defined for the purposes of reg 46 of and Sched 12 to the Motor Vehicles (Construction and Use) Regulations 1978 as a motor cycle which is not a moped. This definition will include some three-wheelers. Motor cycles not exceeding 150 cc first used on or after 1 August 1977 are required to display plates in accordance with this regulation and schedule. In addition, under reg 46 and Sched 12A (as amended by SI 1981 No 915) motor cycles not exceeding 125 cc first used on or after 1 January 1982 are required to be equipped with a plate giving different information. Both types of plate must show whether the cycle is a 'standard motor cycle' or a 'moped'. For this purpose 'moped' means a moped first used on or after 1 August 1977 (see below). The plates must also give other information designed to show whether the vehicle is a moped (see below) and to enable learner drivers to be restricted to less powerful vehicles. Mowing machines and pedestrian controlled vehicles are not required to carry plates (see reg 46(1)(*b*) and (*c*)). It seems that a cycle is still within the definition of standard motor cycle where appropriate even if the plate is not exhibited.

*E 'Learner motor cycles'*

These are defined by s 88(2A) of the 1972 Act as inserted by s 23(2) of the Transport Act 1981. They are either electric motor cycles or those which do not exceed 125 cc, whose maximum engine power output does not exceed 9 kW and whose power to weight ratio does not exceed 100 kW per metric ton. This basic definition is supplemented by certain details in the section.

*F 'Moped'*

A moped comes within the definition of 'motor cycle' but is specifically defined in reg 3 of the Motor Vehicles (Driving Licences) Regulations 1981 as being *either* a cycle with a cubic capacity not exceeding 50 cc equipped with pedals capable of propelling the moped first used before 1 August 1977 *or* a cycle first used on or after that date which has a design speed not exceeding 30 mph, a kerbside weight not exceeding 250 kg and an engine (if an internal combustion engine) not exceeding 50 cc. It should be noted that the latter is still termed a moped even though it is not required to be equipped with pedals. It is required to carry a plate (see under 'Standard motor cycle' above—the latter definition of a moped in reg 46 is also adopted in reg 116C (it sets out some but not all silencer offences: see 8.31)). It seems that a cycle is still within the definition of moped even if the plate is not exhibited.

In *G* v *Jarrett* [1981] RTR 186 a juvenile was riding a motor cycle which had no foot rest on the nearside pedal shaft. Whether it was a moped depended inter alia on whether it was equipped with pedals capable of being propelled. His appeal to the Divisional Court against two convictions stemming from the vehicle being regarded as a motor cycle and not a moped was successful: the vehicle remained a moped.

## 1.7 Other motor vehicles

'Dual-purpose vehicle', 'land locomotive' and 'land tractor' are defined in the Motor Vehicles (Construction and Use) Regulations 1978, reg 3. See also 6.30*D* as to 'dual-purpose vehicle', 6.30*A* as to 'passenger vehicles', 6.30*B* as to 'goods vehicle', and 12.5 as to 'works truck'.

## 1.8 'Pedal cycles'

Pedal cycles fall into three categories: motor vehicles, certain electrically assisted pedal cycles which despite the motor assistance are excluded from being motor vehicles, and pedal cycles not propelled by mechanical power.

A pedal cycle is defined by the Pedal Cycles (Construction and Use) Regulations 1983 (SI 1983 No 1176) for those regulations as either a pedal cycle not propelled by mechanical power or an electrically assisted pedal cycle.

## 1.9 Electrically assisted pedal cycles (including the Sinclair C5)

By s 193(1) of the 1972 Act and s 140(1)(*c*) of the Road Traffic Regulation Act 1984, an electrically assisted pedal cycle as defined is not to be treated as a motor vehicle for the purposes of the 1972 and 1984 Acts. Such pedal cycles are defined by the Electrically Assisted Pedal Cycles Regulations 1983 (SI 1983 No 1168). They must be bicycles or tricycles. They must be fitted with pedals by means of which they are capable of being propelled. Their electric motor must not be able to propel the vehicle when travelling at more than 15 mph. If a bicycle (other than a tandem) it must have a kerbside weight not exceeding 40 kg and an electric motor not exceeding 0.2 kW. If a tandem bicycle or a tricycle (including a tandem tricycle) it must have a kerbside weight not exceeding 60 kg and an electric motor not exceeding 0.25 kW. A tandem bicycle is defined as a bicycle which is designed to carry two or more persons at least two of whom can propel the vehicle at the same time. Reference should be made to the Regulations for the full provisions.

The Sinclair C5 fulfils the requirements of an electrically assisted pedal cycle. As the motor vehicle provisions of the 1972 and 1984 Acts do not apply, the driver does not require a driving licence, insurance or a test certificate and does not have to wear a helmet. A Bow Street stipendiary magistrate held on 10 April 1985 that a C5 was not a 'cycle' under s 19 of the 1972 Act (cycling under the influence of drink or drugs). It is submitted that the wheel mechanism is in cycle form. The s 196 definition links the meaning of 'cycle' to wheel cycles. See also the definitions in 1.6 and *Floyd* v *Bush* and the other cases at 1.14. If s 19 applies to the C5, the following provisions of the 1972 Act will also apply: reckless cycling (s 17), careless or inconsiderate cycling (s 18), and racing on highways (s 20). These sections refer to cycles and are not restricted to pedal cycles. The Motor Vehicles (Construction and Use) Regulations do not apply but the Pedal Cycles (Construction and Use) Regulations 1983 do (see further 8.21 and 8.49). Provisions of the 1972 and 1984 Acts will apply if they apply to *vehicles* (eg s 22 of the 1972 Act: failing to conform to traffic directions).

As to the offence where such a vehicle is driven by a person under 14, see 11.14. Although not motor vehicles for the purposes of the 1972 Act, they are mechanically propelled (see 1.14). Such electrically propelled vehicles do not however require vehicle excise licences (see 12.1). As to taking an electrically assisted pedal cycle without consent, see 15.3.

## 1.10 Goods vehicles

Note that by s 190(2) of the 1972 Act goods vehicles are 'motor cars' if (in most cases) they do not exceed 3050 kg in unladen weight (see 1.3).

The distinction between heavy and light locomotives and motor tractors on the one hand, and heavy motor cars and motor cars on the other, is that the former are not constructed to carry any load (see further 'Loose equipment', 1.32). In *Thornton* v *Proudlock* (1952) unreported, Queen's Bench Division, 29 May, it was held that a tractor with a transport box is a vehicle 'adapted for use for the conveyance of goods'. This case was apparently under what is now the Vehicles (Excise) Act 1971 and would not necessarily apply under the 1972 Act. A locomotive or motor tractor permanently fitted with a crane, dynamo, etc, does not thereby become a goods vehicle (see s 190(10)); combine harvesters which are self-propelled would be tractors or locomotives (see *William Gwennap Agricultural Ltd* v *Amphlett* [1957] 2 All ER 605).

For other cases on the term 'goods vehicle' see 6.30*B* and 12.7.

## 1.11 'Heavy commercial vehicles'

'Heavy commercial vehicle' in s 138 of the Road Traffic Regulation Act 1984 for the purposes of that Act and in s 36A of the 1972 Act (prohibition of parking of heavy goods vehicles on verges and footways) means any goods vehicle which has an operating weight exceeding 7.5 tonnes. There are identical supplementary provisions in both Acts to which reference should be made. Under s 36A and under the 1984 Act there are transitional provisions up to 31 December 1989 and this should be borne in mind when relevant orders are considered.

## 1.12 'Constructed' and change of use

Where the use of a vehicle is not immediately apparent, the burden of proof to show that the vehicle is exempt from a construction and use regulation requirement is on the defendant (*Wakeman* v *Catlow* [1977] RTR 174). The fact that a vehicle is licensed as an 'exempt' vehicle is insufficient evidence by itself (ibid: jeep licensed as a 'land tractor' used on a road with defective tyre; neither prosecution nor defence gave evidence as to whether or not it was a land tractor).

A mini-car fitted with only one seat but designed with space for another seat which could easily be added was held to be constructed for the carriage of more than one person (*Vincent* v *Whitehead* [1966] 1 All ER 917). A vehicle was held to be equipped with means for reversing although the reverse gear was not usable because it had been blanked off (*Baldwin* v *Worsman* [1963] 2 All ER 8).

'Constructed' in a speed limit case was interpreted as meaning 'as originally constructed' (*Hubbard* v *Messenger* [1937] 4 All ER 48) but a motor vehicle can be reconstructed so that it joins another class (*Keeble* v *Miller* [1950] 1 All ER 261: heavy motor car converted to light locomotive). 'Constructed' in s 190(7) of the 1972 Act means 'constructed as at the time of the offence' not 'originally constructed'. The vehicle in *Keeble* v *Miller* was permanently fitted with a fairground lighting plant. 'Constructed' usually means 'as constructed when completed' (*Millard* v *Turvey* [1968] 2 All ER 7: a case on a motor vehicle chassis).

Generally it would seem that there must be a major reconstruction before a vehicle changes from one type to another (*Burrows* v *Berry* (1949) 113 JP Jo 492). The fact that a vehicle happens to be defective does not alter its design and construction unless the defect continues so long that it can be inferred that the defect is intended to remain or there is evidence that a part has been deliberately removed (*G* v *Jarrett* [1981] RTR 186). Whether there has been a change of type may depend on the circumstances. As is pointed out in a commentary on this case at [1980] Crim LR 652, it may not be possible to discover the type of vehicle by inspecting it. The moped in this case had no footrest on the nearside pedal shaft. Nevertheless it remained a moped.

*'Adapted'*

Where the word 'adapted' is used disjunctively as an alternative to 'constructed' it means 'altered so as to make fit' but where it is used on its own, the context will often show that 'adapted' means 'fit and apt' for a purpose without alteration as well as 'altered'.

Whether a vehicle is 'adapted' is a question of fact. 'Adapted' in speed limits legislation was held to mean suitable for the carriage of eight or more passengers whether by original construction or subsequent alteration (*Maddox* v *Storer* [1962] 1 All ER 831). It was also held to mean 'fit and apt for the purpose' not merely 'altered so as to be apt', although, *semble*, it can include both vehicles originally constructed to be fit and apt and those subsequently altered so that they then are fit and apt.

In *Taylor* v *Mead* [1961] 1 All ER 626 (a vehicle excise case) the defendant's saloon car was fitted in the rear part of the interior with rails from which dresses were hung, he himself having put in those rails and the screws for their support. When dresses were not hung inside, passengers could sit in the back seats in the normal way. On the question whether the car was adapted for use for conveying goods, the High Court refused to interfere with a finding of magistrates that the car had not been so adapted but did not say whether they (the judges) would have come to the same conclusion. Lord Parker CJ said that 'constructed or adapted' meant 'originally constructed or where the structure is subsequently altered' and approved two earlier cases on the Customs and Inland Revenue Act 1888, s 4, holding that adapting meant some amount of alteration of the original construction. Making a small fitting or attachment involving the boring of holes for screws in the structure would not be altering the structure but fitting stronger springs and widening the wheels would be (ibid).

A van adapted for the carriage of passengers with no shelves for goods and used only to carry samples to the owner's place of business was held not to be a goods vehicle in *Tait* v *Odhams Press* (1937) 26 Traff Cas 80, where certain exempting regulations were also in point. This was a case on goods vehicle licensing. Where a passenger vehicle has been altered to carry goods, the test whether the vehicle is a goods or passenger one is whether it would, if it had been constructed in its altered condition, still be regarded as a vehicle used to carry passengers and their effects (*Flower Freight Co* v *Hammond* [1962] 3 All ER 950). Passengers' effects are not goods and the addition of a luggage rack to a passenger vehicle, if not so big as to be out of keeping with the number of passengers, and so long as it does not involve interference with the structure, does not convert it to a goods vehicle (ibid).

A coach converted to carry six passengers, kitchen equipment and a stock car was held to be a goods vehicle (*Plume* v *Suckling* [1977] RTR 271). The justices had held that it was a passenger vehicle on the ground that the kitchen equipment and stock car were part of the personal effects of the defendant. Eveleigh J stated that 'Passenger effects are things which one would readily and normally recognise as accompanying a passenger. A stock car is not such' (ibid, at p 275 J).

In *Westacott* v *Centaur* [1981] RTR 182 four out of eleven seats on a minibus were rendered unusable: two double seats had been placed upside down to block four seats off. A finding of fact by the justices that the minibus was not adapted to fill the additional seats and that therefore the vehicle was not a public service vehicle was upheld. Certain reservations were expressed in the judgment. It was emphasised that the question of permanence did not necessarily arise, but that the primary consideration was the situation at the moment the vehicle was stopped. It was preferable to concentrate on the word 'adapted' rather than substituting 'suitable'. This is clearly a reference to earlier cases such as *Maddox* v *Storer* [1962] 1 All ER 831 and *Wurzal* v *Addison* [1965] 1 All ER 20, where the expression 'suitable' was used to interpret 'adapted'.

The conclusions to be drawn from the various road traffic authorities on the meaning of 'adapted' were set out in *Backer* v *Secretary of State for the Environment* [1983] 2 All ER 1021, a town and country planning case. The court pointed out that 'adapted' in the phrase 'constructed or adapted for use . . . solely for the conveyance of any goods' in the context of vehicle licensing was held to mean 'altered' in *French* v *Champkin* [1920] 1 KB 76 and *Taylor* v *Mead* [1961] 1 All ER 626. In the former case, Lord Reading CJ said (at p 79): 'The justices seem to have treated the word "adapted" as if it were synonymous with "suitable" or "apt", whereas it must be construed as meaning altered so as to make the vehicle apt for the conveyance of goods.'

In two other cases it was held that where the word 'adapted' appeared by itself it meant merely apt, fit or suitable (*Maddox* v *Storer* [1962] 1 All ER 831 and *Wurzal* v *Addison* [1965] 1 All ER 20). In *Burns* v *Currell* [1963] 2 All ER 297, it was said obiter that 'adapted' in the phrase 'intended or adapted for use on roads' means merely 'apt or fit'.

The court held in *Backer* that as 'adapted' was used in conjunction with 'designed', adapted in the context meant 'altered'.

See also 'Removable containers', 1.33.

## 1.13 'Vehicle'

The term 'vehicle' usually means one vehicle, not two linked together (*Dixon* v *BRS (Pickfords) Ltd* [1959] 1 All ER 449).

A poultry shed can be a vehicle (see *Garner* v *Burr* [1950] 2 All ER 683), and in *Boxer* v *Snelling* [1972] RTR 472 a moveable stall with tyred wheels was also held to be a 'vehicle' for the purposes of what is now the Road Traffic Regulation Act 1984. Where there is no statutory definition of the word 'vehicle' a court should consider in a 'borderline' case not only the construction or nature or function of the contrivance but also the circumstances in which it is used (ibid).

## 1.14 'Mechanically propelled'

In order that a motor vehicle can be held to come within the definition in s 190 of the 1972 Act or s 136 of the Road Traffic Regulation Act 1984, the vehicle must be 'mechanically propelled'. The same expression is used in the Vehicles (Excise) Act 1971.

The term includes not only petrol-driven and oil-driven vehicles, but also, it seems, steam-driven and electrically driven ones (see *Waters* v *Eddison Steam Rolling Co* (1914) 78 JP 327, where the term interpreted was 'locomotive' and the vehicle a steam-roller, and *Elieson* v *Parker* (1917) 81 JP 265, where an electrically propelled bath chair was held to be a vehicle propelled by mechanical power). Section 38(3) of the Vehicles (Excise) Act 1971 makes special provision as to electric vehicles. Electrically assisted pedal cycles as defined are presumably to be regarded as mechanically propelled but are to be treated as not motor vehicles for the purposes of the 1972 Act and the Road Traffic Regulation Act 1984 (see further 1.9). Subject to this, where a pedal cycle is fitted with an auxiliary engine and the engine is connected up, it is a motor vehicle whether the engine is running or not (*Floyd* v *Bush* [1953] 1 All ER 265).

The leaving or keeping of broken-down vehicles on a public road frequently gives rise to prosecutions for offences relating to test certificates, vehicle excise licences, insurance, or defective tyres, brakes or steering. In such cases the question is raised as to whether the particular vehicle can still be said to be mechanically propelled. The test to be followed by a court in deciding the case is whether the vehicle has reached such a stage that it can be said 'there is no reasonable prospect of the vehicle ever being made mobile again' (*Binks* v *Department of the Environment* [1975] RTR 318, approving Lord Parker CJ in *Law* v *Thomas* (1964) 62 LGR 195, 196 and also *Smart* v *Allan* [1962] 3 All ER 893). A brief description of the various cases follows.

In *Newberry* v *Simmonds* [1961] 2 All ER 318 it was held that a motor car from which the engine had been removed did not thereby cease to be a mechanically propelled vehicle if the evidence admitted the possibility that the engine might shortly be replaced and the motive power restored. Different considerations might apply if the mechanical means of propulsion had been permanently removed; it would be a question of fact and degree in which both the extent to which the power unit and transmission have been removed and the permanence of the removal are matters for consideration (ibid). *Semble*, the onus of proof that a vehicle had ceased to be mechanically propelled would lie on the defence so long as it resembled an ordinary motor vehicle. See in this connection the parallel argument as to 'use' in *Hewer* v *Cutler* (as explained by *Eden* v *Mitchell*, 1.79).

In *Lawrence* v *Howlett* [1952] 2 All ER 74, the cylinder, piston and connecting rod had been removed temporarily from the engine of an auto-assisted cycle; it was held that it was a pedal cycle, not a motor vehicle. This case is distinguishable from *Floyd* v *Bush*, above, on the ground that an auto-assisted cycle is capable of use either as a cycle or as a motor vehicle and, on the special facts, it was not only being used as a pedal cycle but was then incapable of use as a motor vehicle; and in *R* v *Tahsin* [1970] RTR 88 a defendant pedalling a moped was held to be rightly convicted under what are now ss 5(1) and 6(1) of the 1972 Act. *Floyd* v *Bush* was applied and on p 92 it was explained that the true test by Lord Goddard CJ in that case as to whether a vehicle is mechanically propelled is 'Is the vehicle constructed so that it can be mechanically propelled?' *not* 'Has it an engine which is in working order at the relevant time?' *Newberry's* case was distinguished in *Maclean* v *Hall* (1962) 77 Sh Ct Rep 161.

*Smart* v *Allan* [1962] 3 All ER 893 (vehicle without gear box, or with engine in such state that no prospect of vehicle being made mobile, held not motor vehicle) should be contrasted with *Law* v *Thomas* (1964) 62 LGR 195 (broken-down car capable of repair in a matter of minutes is still a mechanically propelled vehicle). A car is still a motor vehicle though incapable of being started because of a flat battery (*R* v *Paul* [1952] NI 61).

In *McEachran* v *Hurst* [1978] RTR 462 the defendant was pedalling a moped to a friend's house for repair. It was not taxed and there was no current test certificate. The justices held that it was not a mechanically propelled vehicle, on the grounds that it was being used as a pedal cycle, the engine did not work and there was no petrol in the tank. The Divisional Court, reversing the justices, held that the test to be applied to determine whether a moped was mechanically propelled was the same as that for any other motor vehicle, namely, on its construction. If it was constructed as a motor vehicle, it remained a mechanically propelled vehicle unless it could be said (applying the test in *Binks* v *Department of the Environment* above) that there was no reasonable prospect of it again being mechanically mobile.

For the purpose of the Refuse Disposal (Amenity) Act 1978, which relates to the removal of abandoned vehicles, the term 'motor vehicle' includes those which are in an unfit as well as in a fit state for use on the road and a chassis or body of a motor vehicle with or without wheels and trailers in similar condition (see s 11).

## 1.15 'Intended or adapted for use on roads'

The definition of a motor vehicle contained in s 190 of the 1972 Act and s 136 of the Road Traffic Regulation Act 1984 requires the vehicle to be 'intended or adapted for use on roads'. The use of the word 'or' implies that the words are disjunctive. For 'adapted' see 1.12, above. The test as to whether a vehicle is intended or adapted for use on roads is an objective one. It depends neither on the owner's intention nor, unless there is evidence of regular use on roads, on its particular use at the time. The cases indicate that 'intended' may mean no more than suitable or apt for use on roads.

*Go-carts, racing cars etc*

A motor go-cart was held not to be a motor vehicle where there was no evidence of regular use on the road, but it might be otherwise if there was such evidence; the test is whether a reasonable man looking at it would say that one of its uses would be a road use (*Burns* v *Currell* [1963] 2 All ER 297). This test was applied by juvenile court justices in *O'Brien* v *Anderton* [1979] RTR 388 when they held an 'Italjet' two-wheeled vehicle resembling a motor cycle with a seat and handlebars but with an engine capacity of only 22cc was a motor vehicle. The justices' decision was affirmed: they had applied the proper test.

In *Nichol* v *Leach* [1972] RTR 476 a mini-car rebuilt solely for 'auto cross' racing was held to have retained its original intended road use character even though the owner never intended it to be used on roads. *Brown* v *Abbott* (1965) 109 SJ 437, where the magistrates' finding that a Ford Anglia adapted for stock car racing was not a mechanically propelled vehicle intended or adapted for use on roads was upheld with reluctance by the High Court, was not cited to the court in *Nichol* v *Leach*. It is submitted that *Nichol* v *Leach* is the better authority as its reasoning follows that of *Burns* v *Currell*, above, and in particular *Daley* v *Hargreaves*, below, in that the intention of the owner was disregarded.

A high-powered racing car designed for use only on a race track would not normally be intended or adapted for use on roads on this basis whereas a racing car designed also for ordinary use would be.

The same principles would apply to motor cycles used for scrambling. Convictions have been successful in magistrates' courts where they have been used on roads even though they were not originally intended for such use. The convictions arise from the actual use and the understandable inference that the intended use is there. The courts also seem to take the view that despite the differences the vehicles are sufficiently close to an ordinary motor bicycle for them to be regarded as adapted for use on roads. The nature of the machine, the degree of adaptation necessary and the extent of the use are factors which have been taken into account. The various cases noted above suggest that such decisions might well be upheld by the Divisional Court depending on the actual facts. Scrambling motor bicycles are sometimes at present used for this purpose on public byways and bridleways. It should be remembered that such byways and bridleways are public highways and such byways are also public roads. See further 1.66–8.

An agricultural tractor can be a vehicle intended or adapted for use on roads (*Woodward* v *Young* [1958] SLT 289). So can a 'Hyster' grab fitted with an engine and rotating arms in front for picking up goods (*Furdson* v *McGovern* [1954] ALR 450: the Australian statutory definition was much the same).

*Dumper trucks, excavators etc*

A diesel dumper used solely for road construction work and not intended to be driven along the parts of the highway open to the public was held not to be a motor vehicle for insurance purposes (*MacDonald* v *Carmichael* [1941] SC(J) 27). Where there was no evidence whether some dumpers were suitable for being driven on the road in transit or to carry material from one site to another, the High Court, following *MacDonald* v *Carmichael*, held that they were not intended or adapted for use on the road, but it was said that the High Court might have found differently had there been evidence of such suitability (*Daley* v *Hargreaves* [1961] 1 All ER 552). It was also said that it might be that the legislature had no particular person's intention in view—manufacturer, seller, owner or user—as to 'intended' for use on the road; 'intended' may mean no more than suitable or apt for use.

In *Chalgray Ltd* v *Aspley* (1965) 109 SJ 394, a dumper used on a site was from time to time driven on the adjoining road for short distances. It was held that it was not a motor vehicle as there was no proof of general use on roads as opposed to occasional use. The driver's action could not make, in the absence of further evidence, a dumper into a motor vehicle. The fact that a dumper might emerge on the highway did not alone make it a motor vehicle. On the other hand, in *Childs* v *Coghlan* (1968) 112 SJ 175, a Euclid earth scraper which was too big to be transportable and the primary uses of which were to dig up earth on building sites and carry that earth to places away from those sites under its own power was held to be intended for use on roads. There was evidence that it could go at 45 mph. It was said that a machine, albeit its primary use was not on roads, which regularly went on roads from one site to another was clearly intended to be used on roads, especially if it had to go under its own power from one site to another. The facts that a dumper could go at a fairly fast speed and that the driver had good forward vision did not make that particular dumper into a motor vehicle in *MacLean* v *McCabe* [1964] SLT (Sh) 39: the vehicle had no horn or driving mirror.

Dumpers and excavators are specially dealt with for excise licence purposes under the Vehicles (Excise) Act 1971.

## 1.16 Miscellaneous vehicles

By s 193 of the 1972 Act an implement for cutting grass controlled by a pedestrian and not capable of being used or adapted for any other purpose shall, for the purposes of the Act, be treated as not being a motor vehicle. By virtue of s 193(2) the implement must either be constructed or adapted for use only under the control of a pedestrian or, if it is constructed so that it can be controlled either by a pedestrian or someone carried on it, the implement can only be treated as not being a mechanically propelled vehicle so long as it is controlled on foot. This definition must be borne in mind as there are a number of domestic motor mowers on the market with seats for the driver and the verge outside a private home will often be part of the road. Section 140 of the Road Traffic Regulation Act 1984 is in like terms to the 1972 Act. Any other pedestrian-controlled motor vehicle otherwise remains a motor vehicle, unless exempt by regulations.

The term 'goods vehicle' is discussed at 6.30*B* and 12.7.

The term 'articulated vehicle' is discussed in relation to 'Trailer' below. See also s 190(9) of the 1972 Act.

Trolley vehicles are within the Road Traffic Act for some purposes, but not for others (see s 198). Very few provisions apply to tramcars (ibid). In the case of both trolley vehicles and tramcars, s 198 applies only to those operated under statutory powers, as defined in s 198(7), and the Road Traffic Act 1972 applies in full to those not so operated. Trolley vehicles, trams, bicycles, horse-drawn carts and hand carts are generally vehicles and carriages within the meaning of most other Acts (see 210 LT News 201) and motor vehicles are carriages within the meaning of the Highways, Town Police Clauses, Public Health and other Acts and by-laws (Road Traffic Act 1972, s 195).

A bicycle is a vehicle (*Ellis* v *Nott-Bower* (1896) 60 JP 760) and also a carriage (*Corkery* v *Carpenter* [1950] 2 All ER 745).

**1.17–20 'Recovery vehicle', 'breakdown vehicle', 'disabled vehicle'**

Such expressions are used in various statutory provisions; see for example the Vehicles (Excise) Act 1971, s 16(8) ('recovery vehicle' as there defined) and regulations made under that section (see the Road Vehicles (Registration and Licensing) Regulations 1971 as amended and in particular reg 35(4)(*l*)), the Goods Vehicles (Operators' Licences) (Qualifications and Fees) Regulations 1984, Sched 1, which in effect applies the s 16(8) definition and the Goods Vehicle (Plating and Testing) Regulations 1982, Sched 2 ('breakdown vehicle' as defined in reg 3). It was observed in *Universal Salvage Ltd* v *Boothby* [1984] RTR 289 at p 300 that the definition of 'breakdown vehicle' in Sched 2 of the 1982 Regulations was for all material purposes identical with the definition of 'recovery vehicle' in s 16(8), the extra words in the former definition being of no materiality.

It was held in the *Universal Salvage* case that Parliament in the definitions deliberately distinguished between the singular and the plural and this showed a contrary intention nullifying the presumption in the Interpretation Act 1978 that the singular includes the plural with the result that only one disabled vehicle could be recovered or at most two—one up and one behind—because the definition allowed one disabled vehicle to be raised or carried and another to be drawn. A breakdown vehicle was ordinarily a vehicle which went to the assistance of a broken-down vehicle although for larger breakdown vehicles their most important function might be recovery. Carriage of a substantial number of broken-down vehicles would ordinarily be understood to be a form of transport rather than attending upon or recovering broken-down or disabled vehicles (ibid). A similar meaning was determined in the *Universal Salvage* case for a 'specialised recovery vehicle' under the EEC Regulations 543/69 as amended (drivers' hours and records) and 1463/70 (tachograph) (see 14.4).

A new motor car from which the rotor arm has been removed is not a 'disabled vehicle'. Disabled vehicles suffer some disability other than simply having the rotor arm removed (*Robertson* v *Crew* [1977] RTR 141).

The court in the *Universal Salvage* case above also confirmed the decision in *Gibson* v *Nutter* [1984] RTR 8 that a scrap vehicle is not a broken-down or disabled vehicle. This must be read in the light of the Finance Act 1984, s 4(*b*) which has amended the Vehicles (Excise) Act 1971, s 16(8) by inserting a definition that 'disabled vehicle' includes a vehicle which has been abandoned or is scrap. This amendment throws the *Universal Salvage* decision into slight disarray because it has not altered the definition of breakdown or recovery vehicle as interpreted in that case while it has extended the meaning of broken-down vehicles which may be recovered. It will still be a question of fact whether a vehicle is recovered or transported. The number of vehicles is still restricted to one up and one behind. The alteration applies to s 16, and therefore to the 1971 Regulations (see reg 35(4)(*l*)) and the 1984 Regulations, but not to the 1982 Regulations so that while no operator's licence is required vehicles recovering abandoned or scrap vehicles may still be required to be tested and plated unless otherwise exempt.

One of the purposes for which a recovery vehicle may be operated under a trade licence is the carrying of a disabled vehicle from the place where it broke down (or from where it was subsequently taken) to a place of repair (see the Road Vehicles (Registration and Licensing) Regulations 1971, reg 35(4)(*l*)). In *Squires* v *Mitchell* [1983] RTR 400, the Divisional Court held that reg 35(4)(*l*) was not apt to describe the carriage (by such a recovery vehicle) of the chassis of an old lorry attached to which were the axles, wheels, steering box and steering wheel, braking system and petrol tank; the lorry had been stripped down by its owner before renovation and restoration, and the parts carried on the recovery vehicle at the relevant time had been treated by sand-blasting and were to be taken elsewhere for further repair. It is made clear that the apparatus for raising the vehicle does not have to be mounted on the recovery vehicle, but it may be drawn. Indeed it would now appear that the definition is so wide as to enable practically any vehicle which carries a jack to be used as a recovery vehicle, and in *E Pearson & Son (Teeside) Ltd* v *Richardson* [1972] RTR 522 a vehicle equipped with heavy duty lifting jacks but not capable of suspended towing was held to be a 'recovery vehicle'. On the true construction of s 16(8) there are two sub-categories of vehicle, those equipped for drawing and those so equipped that they were only able to raise a disabled vehicle wholly or partly from the ground (ibid). The effect of the *Pearson* case is to make it clear that a vehicle is to be classed as a recovery vehicle if it falls into either sub-category or both sub-categories of vehicle as set out in s 16(8).

In *Hunter the Bakers Ltd* v *Hills* [1973] RTR 361, *Pearson* was followed and applied. It was held that a platform lorry with a detachable rigid tow bar with a bracket for it, four 4 cwt concrete ballast slabs, ropes and a 5-ton hydraulic jack was a recovery vehicle albeit that it was neither equipped with a crane or winch nor capable of suspended towing.

The definition in s 16(8) requires the recovery vehicle not to be used 'for the conveyance of goods other than a disabled vehicle wholly raised by that apparatus'. A 15-ton tracked shovel climbed on to a low loader under its own power and was then secured by a winch. It was held that as the tracked shovel had climbed on to the low loader under its own power, the tracked shovel was not wholly raised by that apparatus and the low loader could therefore not be classed as a 'recovery vehicle' (*Scott* v *Gutteridge Plant Hire Ltd* [1974] RTR 292).

## 'Trailer'

### 1.21 Meaning

A 'trailer' is defined in s 190(1) of the 1972 Act as a vehicle drawn by a motor vehicle. It is doubtful whether a trailer can be said to be so drawn if it has been detached, particularly if the detachment is for a substantial period of time (cf the discussion at 1.52–3 as to what is meant by 'driving').

A 'trailer' is differently defined for the purpose of drivers' hours and records when Regulation 543/69/EEC as amended applies (see art 1 of that regulation).

The term 'trailer' includes an empty poultry shed being drawn along by a tractor (*Garner* v *Burr* [1950] 2 All ER 683), and a hut used as an office so drawn (*Horn* v *Dobson* [1933] SC(J) 1). The Motor Vehicles (Construction and Use) Regulations give certain exemptions for trailers forming part of an articulated vehicle (see below) or being a land implement (as defined in reg 3 (1) of the Regulations). There are also a number of exemptions under the Construction and Use Regulations for trailers manufactured before certain dates. A poultry shed is not a land implement (*Garner* v *Burr*, above). Nor does a four-wheeled vehicle being towed with two wheels in the air thereby become a two-wheeled trailer (*Carey* v *Heath* [1951] 2 All ER 774). In *Baker* v *Esau* [1972] Crim LR 559 the justices were held to be 'plainly right' in holding that a racing car rigidly placed on a two-wheeled 'ambulance trailer' so that its front wheels remained on the road together constituted one trailer, not two. A vehicle and trailer closely coupled together do not thereby become one vehicle (*Dixon* v *BRS* (*Pickfords*) *Ltd* [1959] 1 All ER 449). A mobile car jack, ie a long tow bar with two wheels on a short axle at right angles to the tow bar, is a trailer (*Wilkinson* v *Barrett* (1958) 122 JP 349). This case is modified to some extent by reg 4 (12) of the Construction and Use Regulations. In *Jenkins* v *Deane* (1933) 103 LJKB 250 an insurance policy excepted use of the insured vehicle 'whilst it has a trailer attached thereto'. Towing a broken-down lorry was held not to be within the exception. This case was not cited in the other cases given in this paragraph. Quarter sessions have held that a van inhabited by a family can be a trailer ([1962] Jo Crim L 21). In *Boxer* v *Snelling* [1972] RTR 472 a moveable stall with wheels was held in the circumstances of the case to be a 'vehicle'. It was said to be a 'borderline' case. Where there is no statutory definition of 'vehicle', a court should consider in a borderline case not only the construction or nature of the contrivance but also the circumstances in which the contrivance is used (ibid).

A motor vehicle which is being towed by another motor vehicle both remains a motor vehicle and becomes for the time being a trailer also (*Milstead* v *Sexton* [1964] Crim LR 474), and there is nothing in the Vehicles (Excise) Act 1971 to exempt a mechanically propelled vehicle which is being towed and is for the time being a trailer (*Cobb* v *Whorton* [1971] RTR 392). The vehicle is 'used' for the purposes of insurance while stationary (*Elliott* v *Grey* [1959] 3 All ER 733). A mechanically propelled vehicle does not cease to be 'used' on a road when it is towed by another vehicle (*Cobb* v *Whorton* above; *Nichol* v *Leach* [1972] RTR 476). The use of the towed vehicle must therefore be covered by insurance, it must be taxed, and it must comply with the Construction and Use Regulations both as a motor vehicle and as a trailer. It would be a trailer only, however, if it had ceased to be mechanically propelled, eg if it was a wreck, or if it was not intended or adapted for use on roads, eg a high-powered racing car designed for use only on a race track (but not a racing car designed also for ordinary use or even a Mini rebuilt for use in 'auto cross' events: see *Nichol* v *Leach*, above). Even the high-powered racing car would be liable to excise duty, however, when on a public road, as the Vehicles (Excise) Act applies to 'mechanically propelled vehicles used on public roads' without requiring that they be intended or adapted for such use.

A car supported on roller skates so that its wheels did not touch the road surface was held, nevertheless, to be kept 'on' a road for the purposes of s 8 of the Vehicles (Excise) Act 1971 (*Holliday* v *Henry* [1974] RTR 101), nor would it appear to be 'on' a trailer (ibid).

## 1.22 'Semi-trailer' etc

A 'semi-trailer' is defined in reg 3(1) of the Construction and Use Regulations as a trailer which is constructed or adapted to form part of an articulated vehicle.

A 'composite trailer' is defined by the same regulation as a combination of a converter dolly (see below) and a semi-trailer. For the purpose of certain Construction and Use regulations only a 'composite trailer' is to be treated as one trailer (not being a semi-trailer converter dolly) only (see reg 6A).

A 'converter dolly' is defined fully in reg 3(1) but broadly speaking is a wheeled chassis between the drawing vehicle and the semi-trailer. It is also a trailer.

## 1.23 'Articulated vehicle'

An 'articulated vehicle' is still treated as a vehicle and a trailer for the purposes of the 1972 Act, the Road Traffic Regulation Act 1984 and the Public Passenger Vehicles Act 1981 (see the 1972 Act, s 191). The only exception is the articulated passenger vehicle referred to in s 191(2). These are distinguished from articulated vehicles generally by specified structural characteristics. They are classified instead as single motor vehicles thus making them eligible to be treated as public service vehicles. Buses of this type, looking rather like long caterpillars, are occasionally to be encountered on roads.

The drawing unit of an articulated vehicle is a motor car or heavy car, according to its unladen weight without including the trailer's weight (Road Traffic Act 1972, s 190(9)). In *Turberville* v *Wyer*, *Bryn Motor Co Ltd* v *Wyer* [1977] RTR 29 the Divisional Court declined to decide whether the load-carrying part of an articulated lorry which was carrying an insecure load should be described in an information as a trailer. If it was wrongly described in the information, the justices were entitled to ignore the defect under s 123 of the Magistrates' Court Act 1980 (ibid).

As to lamps and indicators on drawing vehicles on trailers, see the Road Vehicles Lighting Regulations and in particular 8.79 (exemptions from the regulations).

The effect of *A Stevens & Co (Haulage) Ltd* v *Brown* [1970] Crim LR 103 (which decided that in measuring the overall length of an articulated lorry with a projecting load the length of the tractor should be excluded) was reversed by the Motor Vehicles (Construction and Use) Regulations (see reg 140 of the 1978 Regulations).

An 'articulated vehicle', as defined by reg 3(1) of the Construction and Use Regulations 1978, is a heavy motor car or motor car with a trailer so attached to the drawing vehicle that part of the trailer is superimposed upon the drawing vehicle, and when the trailer is uniformly loaded, not less than 20 per cent of the weight of its load is borne by the drawing vehicle. There is a like definition for goods vehicle tractor units in the Vehicles (Excise) Act 1971, Sched 4. Under the Construction and Use Regulations articulated buses are excluded. (If the towed vehicle is not superimposed on the drawing vehicle, there is not an 'articulated vehicle' (*Hunter* v *Towers* [1951] 1 All ER 349).)

For the purposes, however, of speed limits governing certain classes of goods vehicles set out in Sched 6 to the 1984 Act 'articulated vehicle' is as defined by the Construction and Use Regulations. Under these regulations articulated buses are excluded but in any event the expression 'articulated vehicles' is used in Sched 6 only in relation to goods vehicles.

An 'articulated goods vehicle' is defined in s 110(1) of the 1972 Act as amended by the 1976 Act for the purposes of driving licences as follows:

'articulated goods vehicle' means a motor vehicle which is so constructed that a trailer designed to carry goods may by partial superimposition be attached thereto in such a manner as to cause a substantial part of the weight of the trailer to be borne by the motor vehicle, and 'articulated goods vehicle combination' means an articulated goods vehicle with a trailer so attached.

This definition also applies in respect of heavy goods vehicle licences (see s 124 of the 1972 Act as amended by the Road Traffic (Drivers' Ages and Hours of Work) Act 1976). This definition is also repeated in the Heavy Goods Vehicles (Driving Licences) Regulations as amended.

## 1.24 Drawing of trailers

Regulations 129–137 of the Motor Vehicles (Construction and Use Regulations) 1978 restrict the number of trailers which can be drawn by locomotives, motor tractors, heavy motor cars, motor cars and motor cycles. As to the difference between sidecars and trailers, see 'Sidecars', 1.6*C*.

The trailers which may be drawn by motor cycles are set out in reg 130. As to the meaning of a 'sidecar', see 1.6*C*. No motor cycle (whether three-wheeler, combination or motor bicycle) may draw more than one trailer. No motor cycle may draw a trailer carrying a passenger (save trailers which are certain broken-down motor cycles with one passenger). No motor cycle may draw a trailer with an unladen weight exceeding 254 kg or an overall width exceeding 1.5 m. This prohibition applies to drawing broken-down motor cycles of such a size.

A solo motor bicycle without a sidecar and with an engine capacity of 125 cc or less may not draw a trailer at all apart from a broken-down motor cycle. If such a solo motor bicycle exceeds 125 cc it may draw a trailer providing certain conditions are fulfilled. These conditions are that (i) the trailer has an overall width not exceeding 1 m, (ii) the distance between the rear axle of the motor bicycle and the rearmost part of the trailer does not exceed 2.5 m, (iii) the motor cycle is clearly and indelibly marked in a conspicuous and readily accessible position with its kerbside weight, (iv) the trailer is similarly marked with its *unladen* weight, and (v) the *laden* weight of the trailer must not exceed 150 kg or two-thirds the kerbside weight of the motor bicycle whichever is the greater. Presumably a chalk mark would not suffice. Curiously it is the *laden* weight of the trailer which must not exceed 150 kg but the *unladen* weight which must be marked on it. 'Kerbside weight' is defined in reg 46(4).

The provisions are relaxed for trailers which are broken-down motor cycles not exceeding 254 kg or 1.5 m in width. All motor cycle three-wheelers, combinations and those motor bicycles without sidecars which do not exceed 125 cc may draw such broken-down motor cycles.

Curiously, while the other conditions do not apply, conditions (i) and (ii) still apply to solo motor bicycles exceeding 125 cc when drawing a broken-down motor cycle. It means for instance that a solo motor bicycle of 125 cc or less may draw a broken-down motor cycle of between 1 m and 1.5 m in width whereas a solo motor bicycle over 125 cc is restricted to drawing broken-down motor cycles of 1 m in width or less only.

An invalid carriage or a straddle carrier may not tow a trailer (reg 132). No trailer may be used to convey passengers for hire or reward (reg 133) except for breakdowns as allowed by the regulation. (See, however, s 191 of the 1972 Act as amended by the Transport Act 1980 under which certain passenger vehicles with trailers are classified as single motor vehicles.) Regulation 135 (as amended by SI 1981 No 261) provides that no trailer may be drawn by a public service vehicle except where such a vehicle is drawing another to meet the circumstances of an emergency and both are empty of passengers, or where the drawing of the trailer and the means by which the trailer is attached to the drawing vehicle have been approved in writing by a certifying officer (as defined by s 7(1) of the Public Passenger Vehicles Act 1981). No trailer may be drawn by an articulated bus.

The permitted length of a combination of vehicles (towing vehicle and trailer or trailers) is indicated by reg 136.

The rearmost trailer must exhibit the drawing vehicle's number, with minor exceptions for works trucks and certain agricultural and other vehicles used on the road to a limited extent (Road Vehicles (Registration and Licensing) Regulations 1971, reg 22).

Where a trailer is drawn solely by a rope or chain and the drawing vehicle is a motor vehicle the length of the rope or chain must be such that the nearest points between the vehicles cannot exceed 4.5 m (reg 128). In effect the measurement is taken between the nearest points on the vehicles (ignoring attachment fittings: see reg 128(3)) when the rope or chain is taut. If the distance between the nearest points of the vehicles (whatever the means of attachment) exceeds 1.5 m, steps must be taken to render the means of attachment clearly visible to other road users within a reasonable distance from either side of the vehicle (reg 128(2)). A method commonly used is to tie a piece of cloth to the rope or chain.

In cases under the Construction and Use Regulations affecting trailers, the regulations themselves should be carefully considered for their definitions and exemptions as to trailers and in particular the definitions of 'composite trailer', 'converter dolly', 'semi-trailer' and 'articulated vehicle'.

A sidecar is part of the motor cycle itself, not of its equipment (*Higgins* v *Feeney* (1954) 88 ILTR 152). See also the proviso to s 190(1) of the 1972 Act.

The view is advanced at 126 JP Jo 247 that a motor cyclist who allows a cyclist to hold his shoulder is drawing a trailer.

### 1.25–30 Attendants on trailers

By s 34(1) of the 1972 Act, where a heavy or light locomotive is drawing a trailer or trailers on a highway (the term 'road' is not used), one or more persons, in addition to the two required in the driving cab, must be employed for the purpose of attending to the trailer or trailers at the rate of one such additional person for each trailer in excess of one. This requirement does not apply to road rollers while rolling. By s 34(2), where any motor vehicle other than a heavy or light locomotive is drawing a trailer or trailers on a highway, one person, in addition to the driver of the vehicle, must be carried on the vehicle or on a trailer for the purpose of attending to the trailer or trailers.

Under s 34, 'trailer' does not include a vehicle used solely for carrying water for the purposes of the drawing vehicle or an agricultural vehicle not constructed to carry a load. 'Agricultural vehicle' is not defined but 'agricultural trailer' is defined in reg 3(1) of the Construction and Use Regulations 1978 as a trailer the property of a person engaged in agriculture which is not used on a road for the conveyance of any goods or burden other than agricultural produce or articles required for the purposes of agriculture.

Section 34 must, however, never be referred to without at the same time referring in any particular case to reg 138 of the Construction and Use Regulations 1978 which modifies the effect of s 34 and provides a long list of exemptions.

Section 34 applies to Crown vehicles (s 188(1)) (other than those specifically exempted by reg 138) and to vehicles of visiting forces (SI 1965 No 1536). Attendants under s 34 qualify as attendants under Sched 8, para 2, to the Regulations (see 8.23).

The Motor Vehicles (Authorisation of Special Types) Order 1979 (8.34) may also require attendants in certain circumstances. See art 24(2) and (3) as to the number of attendants required where two motor vehicles are engaged in transporting a wide load.

## 'Weight'

### 1.31 Meaning

The provisions of the law relating to weight distinguish between laden and unladen weight. The distinction is relevant because there are prohibitions on the total weight which a laden vehicle may transmit to the road surface, while both laden and unladen weights form the criteria by which maximum speed and excise licence duty are computed.

The Road Traffic Act 1972, ss 190 and 194, and the Motor Vehicles (Construction and Use) Regulations 1978 provide the code in relation to matters arising under the 1972 Act and those regulations. Section 190 of the 1972 Act classifies motor vehicles by their unladen weight into heavy and light locomotives, motor tractors, heavy motor cars, motor cars, motor cycles and invalid carriages. Section 194 indicates the method of calculating unladen weight for the purposes of the 1972 Act, of the Road Traffic Regulations Act 1984, of the Vehicles (Excise) Act 1971, Sched 4 (duty on light goods vehicles), and also for the purposes of any enactment relating to the use of other motor vehicles or trailers on roads and as if a reference to the propulsion of the vehicle were a reference to the propulsion of any vehicle by which the trailer is drawn (Transport Act 1968, s 145(4)). The relevant Construction and Use Regulations are regs 42–46A, 49, 80, 82–89, 89A, 90–96, and 150, and Scheds 6 and 7. A prosecution under reg 97 for overloading etc is not an offence relating to a description of weight (*Hudson* v *Bushrod* [1982] RTR 87).

Vehicle excise duty under the Vehicles (Excise) Act 1971 is based both on unladen and gross weight and for this purpose the 1972 Act definitions of the Ministry plated weight and (where the Ministry plated weight is not yet shown) the manufacturer's plate are used.

The terms 'laden weight', 'gross weight' (or 'maximum gross weight'), 'axle weight' and 'train weight' are used in the Motor Vehicles (Construction and Use) Regulations 1978 and also in the Goods Vehicles (Plating and Testing) Regulations 1982. They are generally not there defined and speak for themselves, but there may be partial definitions in particular provisions (see for example the description of 'maximum gross weight' in relation to trailers in reg 46A of the Construction and Use Regulations for the purposes of that regulation). They may be described as follows:

'gross weight': the sum of the weights transmitted to the road surface by all the wheels of a vehicle;

'axle weight': the total weight transmitted to the road surface by all the wheels of an axle;

'train weight': the maximum laden weight of a vehicle together with any trailer or trailers drawn by it.

There are statutory definitions in s 110(1) of the 1972 Act of 'maximum gross weight', 'maximum train weight', 'permissible maximum weight', 'relevant maximum weight', and 'relevant maximum train weight' for the purposes of the provisions of Part III of the 1972 Act relating to driving licences (inserted by the Road Traffic (Drivers' Ages and Hours of Work) Act 1976). See also the Goods Vehicles (Ascertainment of Maximum Gross Weights) Regulations 1976 (SI 1976 No 555).

For the purposes of EEC Regulations 543/69 (drivers' hours) and 1463/70 (tachographs) 'permissible maximum weight' means the maximum authorised operating weight of a vehicle fully laden (art 1 of Regulation 543/69). There is a similar but differently worded definition in the AETR agreement.

Section 64(1) of the 1972 Act provides that in any proceedings for an offence under s 40(5) of the Act (which includes proceedings for an offence under the Construction and Use Regulations relating to weight which are made under this subsection) if any question arises as to a weight of any description specified in the plating certificate for a goods vehicle and a weight of that description is marked on the vehicle, it shall be assumed unless the contrary is proved that the weight marked on the vehicle is the weight so specified.

By s 160 as amended persons authorised by highway authorities and police officers authorised on behalf of such authorities by a chief officer of police may cause vehicles and trailers to be weighed. By reg 45 of the Road Vehicles (Registration and Licensing) Regulations 1971 licensing authorities are also given power to require proof of the unladen weight of a vehicle.

The weight of a vehicle which has been registered as being in a heavier class remains at the registered weight in the eyes of the law until it is re-registered as being in another class, though it may be used with a detachable body which, on removal, brings it in fact into that other class (*Scott* v *Dickson* (1939) 83 SJ 317).

## 1.32 'Loose equipment'

As will be seen from the definitions of 'motor tractor', 'light locomotive' and 'heavy locomotive' in the 1972 Act, s 190, 'loose equipment' is excluded from those definitions. Moreover s 194 (see above) requires the weight of 'loose equipment' to be excluded in any calculation of the unladen weight of a vehicle or trailer. What comprises 'loose equipment' is primarily a question of fact: the test is the nature of the superstructure, the use to which it would be put, and the character of its attachment to the vehicle (*Blaikie* v *Morrison* [1957] SLT 290).

'Loose equipment' does not include loose boards fitted in slots at the side of a lorry and used to enable it to carry a heavier load of coal (*Lowe* v *Stone* [1948] 2 All ER 1076) nor a heavy iron block used for ballast (*London County Council* v *Hay's Wharf Cartage Co* [1953] 2 All ER 34), but does include movable shelves fitted to slide on brackets in a baker's van and used to facilitate the delivery of goods to customers (*Darling* v *Burton* [1928] SC (J) 11, approved in *Lowe* v *Stone*). Planks and poles to load oil drums on a vehicle fitted with a diesel lighting plant are 'loose tools and equipment' (*Keeble* v *Miller* [1950] 1 All ER 261). Side, tail and front boards which, when in use, were fitted inside the vehicle's sides and secured to posts let into the body were held not to be 'loose equipment'.

## 1.33 Removable containers

A motor lorry, used to carry cattle and sheep, had superimposed on it a removable 'float' or large box secured by ropes, not adapted for use on the lorry alone as a separate body but only in conjunction with the lorry's fixed body. It was held that the float was neither an alternative body nor a part necessary to, or ordinarily used with, the lorry, and should therefore not be included in computing the unladen weight of the vehicle (*M'Cowan* v *Stewart* [1936] SC (J) 36). In *Cording* v *Halse* [1954] 3 All ER 287 the Queen's Bench Division came to a like conclusion in respect of a similar vehicle. In *Mackie* v *Waugh* [1940] SC (J) 49 it was held that a container for transporting sheep, held on a lorry by its own weight and by projections fitted over the platform, removed by a block and tackle and used on the lorry three days a week, was not to be included in its unladen weight. In *Paterson* v *Burnet* [1939] SC (J) 12, however, the court upheld a finding that a liftable container with roof, sides and floor, secured by bolts and rope cleats, was constructed primarily as an additional body and was not a receptacle, and distinguished *M'Cowan's* case. *M'Cowan's* case may be compared with *Patterson* v *Redpath Brothers Ltd* [1979]

2 All ER 108. This case was on the question of the meaning of an abnormal indivisible load. The Divisional Court held that a container was a container and not a load. The cases were reviewed in *Brindley* v *Willett* [1982] RTR 19 where it was held that a container was capable in law of being part of the vehicle. It was immaterial that the container could not be bolted on as it should have been because it had become warped. *Patterson* v *Redpath Brothers Ltd* and *Brindley* v *Willett* were followed in *Hawkins* v *Harold A Russett Ltd* [1983] 1 All ER 215 where O'Connor LJ at p 218 adopted the following test: 'Is this vehicle fitted with a body? The body of a vehicle does not cease to be a body because it can be detached with ease, laden or unladen and fitted to a sister chassis. This does not make the body "a receptacle on or attached to the vehicle . . . ": it is part of the vehicle.'

A decision of the High Court in Eire on weight as including a container is *A-G (de Burca)* v *Murtagh* (1961) 95 ILTR 56. The cases cited at 8.17 under 'Overhang and overall length' may be of some relevance.

## 1.34 Weight generally

By reg 80 of the Construction and Use Regulations, the unladen weight must be painted on the nearside of locomotives, motor tractors and heavy motor cars where the unladen weight is not shown on the Ministry plate. This does not apply to heavy motor cars not registered under the Vehicles (Excise) Acts. By reg 46A every unbraked trailer must have its maximum gross weight (in kilograms) on its near side. There are certain restrictions on the laden weight of an unbraked trailer and the drawing vehicle. (See reg 136A.)

The Motor Vehicles (Construction and Use) (Track Laying Vehicles) Regulations 1955 and the Motor Vehicles (Authorisation of Special Types) General Order 1979 indicate the maximum lawful weights for vehicles to which they apply. Where excess weight may be allowed under the Special Types Order, all the conditions as to attendants etc must be fulfilled; if one of them is not, an offence arises under the appropriate regulations of the Construction and Use Regulations (*Siddle C Cook Ltd* v *Holden* [1962] 3 All ER 984).

## 1.35 Plated weights

Weights may be shown on the manufacturer's plate or on the Ministry plate issued after testing or on the plate to be fixed in fourteen days on new vehicles subject to the compulsory type approval scheme.

Regulation 42(1)(*a*) of the Motor Vehicles (Construction and Use) Regulations 1978 requires all heavy motor cars and motor cars first used on or after 1 January 1968 (not being passenger vehicles—save as below—or dual-purpose vehicles, land tractors, works trucks or pedestrian-controlled vehicles), and every trailer manufactured on or after that date exceeding 1020 kg in weight unladen (save the exceptions mentioned in reg 42(1)(*c*)) to be equipped with a plate securely affixed to the vehicle in a conspicuous and readily accessible position and containing the particulars required by Sched 2, including maximum axle, gross and train weights for vehicles.

Large passenger carrying vehicles (whether or not articulated buses) manufactured on or after 1 October 1981 and first used on or after 1 April 1982 must also be equipped with such plates (reg 41(1)(*aa*)). Under reg 42(1)(*b*) there is a similar requirement for locomotives and motor tractors manufactured on or after 1 October 1972 and first used on or after 1 April 1973 (not being land locomotives, land tractors, industrial tractors, works trucks, engineering plant or pedestrian controlled vehicles).

Regulation 42(1)(*d*) extends the plate requirement to a 'converter dolly' trailer manufactured on or after 1 January 1979 even though it would not otherwise be classified as a trailer needing a plate. In particular therefore a 'converter dolly' trailer of 1020 kg or less unladen requires a plate. By an apparent oversight the exceptions in reg 42(1)(*c*) do not apply to such small trailers. Converter dollies are becoming quite common. They are trailers with two or more wheels enabling a semi-trailer to move without any part of its weight being directly superimposed on the drawing vehicle. The converter dolly must not itself be part of the drawing vehicle or semi-trailer.

Regulation 42 as amended by SI 1978 No 1235 provides that alternative plates may be affixed (see reg 42(2)(*b*)and (*c*)).

All such locomotives, heavy motor cars, motor cars and trailers are still subject to the weight limits laid down in regs 82–95.

Section 64 of the 1972 Act provides that where any proceedings are brought under s 40(5) of that Act and any question arises as to a weight of any description specified in the plating certificate for a goods vehicle and a weight of that description is marked on the vehicle, there is a presumption unless the contrary is proved that the weight marked on the vehicle is the weight so specified. Save in so far as provision is made by s 64 as to this presumption, there is nothing to make the weights marked on a plate affixed *pursuant to reg 42* being evidence of the permissible weights. Possibly the plate might be deemed to be an admission at common law by the vehicle owner as to the permitted weights, but this is doubtful as the weights are those fixed by the manufacturer and the owner is merely saying on the plate what the manufacturer has said and this is hearsay. If this evidence were admissible by itself the special provisions of s 64 would be unnecessary. The prosecutor should seemingly prove his case by evidence of the actual weight and type of vehicle, though the marking of the unladen weight on a locomotive, tractor or heavy motor car under reg 80, being done by the owner, is presumably an admission by him.

Where a goods vehicle has a 'Ministry plate' issued under Part II of the 1972 Act and the Goods Vehicles (Plating and Testing) Regulations 1982 (SI 1982 No 1478) following a test, s 64(1) of the Act of 1972 provides that if in proceedings for an offence under the Construction and Use Regulations under s 40(5) any question arises as to a weight of any description specified in a plating certificate for a goods vehicle and a weight of that description is marked on the vehicle in the Ministry plate, it shall be assumed, unless the contrary is proved, that the weight marked on the vehicle is the weight so specified.

A plating certificate has the meaning assigned to it by s 45(1) (1972 Act, s 196). Section 45(1) of the 1972 Act refers to the plated particulars under the

Goods Vehicles (Plating and Testing) Regulations 1982. Plated particulars are those shown on a Ministry plate as defined in the Construction and Use Regulations. Under those regulations a Ministry plate is a plate issued or *having effect as if issued* as specified in the regulations. This seems wide enough for a compulsory type approval certificate plate to be treated as a Ministry plate but possibly not wide enough for such a certificate to be treated as a plating certificate.

By reg 150 of the Construction and Use Regulations the certified weights, which may be less than those allowed by regs 85–94, must not be exceeded and so evidence that the actual weight exceeded the plated weight will suffice. It was held in *William Hampton Ltd and Another* v *Bryan Dixon* (1973) unreported 22 May, that s 40(5) of the Act obviated any necessity for the prosecution to serve a notice on the defendant to produce the plating certificate. Once the prosecution have proved the weight shown on the Ministry plate on the vehicle, it is at once assumed by virtue of s 40(5), in the absence of evidence to the contrary, that the plating certificate shows the same figure (ibid). The court also held that the weighbridge ticket was admissible under the Criminal Evidence Act 1965 as a trade or business record. See s 64(2) above as to proof of date of manufacture.

In *Wurzal* v *Reader Bros Ltd and Another* [1973] Crim LR 640 justices were held to be wrong in dismissing an information under what is now reg 150 of the 1978 Regulations because the traffic examiner did not produce his authority when requiring the vehicle to proceed to a weighbridge under s 224 of the 1960 Act. It was held that production of authority was only a prerequisite of prosecutions under what is now s 160 of the 1972 Act and it did not prevent prosecution for an overweight vehicle under what is now reg 150.

## 1.36 'Description of weight'

This expression is to be found in various places in the 1972 Act. See for example s 40(2) (regulations), s 40(6) (weight defences) and Sched 4 (penalties, see 8.43. It is not defined in the Act. It is not defined in the Construction and Use Regulations.

Goods vehicles have the advantage for 'description of weight' offences contrary to s 40(5) (construction and use requirements) of the s 40(6) defence but the disadvantage of an increased maximum fine. The increased penalty also applies to certain passenger vehicles but without the s 40(6) defence.

Some of the Motor and Vehicle (Construction and Use) Regulations require the weight or other relevant information to be displayed and others require the specified weight or weight ratio not to be exceeded. In one sense both are descriptions of weight. All that *Hudson* v *Bushrod* [1982] RTR 87 decided conclusively was that a Construction and Use reg 97 offence (overloading etc) was not an offence relating to a description of weight.

It is submitted that exceeding the description of weight regulations is within the definition but it is doubtful whether the weight marking regulations are. Some of the regulations require other information to be marked as well as the weight. The linking of 'descriptions of weight' to excess in s 40(2)(*a*) seems to be deliberate. The s 40(6) defence seems designed for where the wrong weight is carried rather than for where the wrong weight is marked.

### 1.37 Transmission and ascertainment of weight

The words 'the weight transmitted to the road surface by any two wheels in line transversely' occur in regs 82, 84, 85 and 86 of the Construction and Use Regulations. 'Transversely' does not mean 'obliquely' or 'diagonally' and the wheels concerned are (for a four-wheeled vehicle) the two front or the two back wheels, and the measurement is from nearside back to offside back wheel (or nearside front to offside front wheel) and not from offside front to nearside back wheel (*Thomas* v *Galloway* [1935] SC (J) 27). Regulation 85 indicates in respect of heavy motor cars and motor cars not being public service vehicles the maximum weights which may be transmitted to the road surface (*a*) by any one wheel where no other wheel is in the same line transversely, (*b*) by any two wheels in line transversely, and (*c*) by all the wheels. Breach of (*a*) or (*b*) or (*c*) is in itself an offence and, in a charge in respect of the weight transmitted by two wheels in line transversely, the prosecution need not also show that a forbidden weight was transmitted by all the wheels (*Martin* v *Robertson* (1949) 93 SJ 19).

The regulations, in limiting the weight transmitted to the road surface, make no exception with regard to the place at which, or the gradient on which, the weight was ascertained. When a weighing was done on ground which was uneven because of the camber of the road and it was considered by the magistrates that a different weight might be shown on a flat surface, it was nevertheless held by the High Court that, if the weighing on the camber showed an illegal weight, an offence had been committed under what is now reg 85 (*Prosser* v *Richings* [1936] 2 All ER 1627). But a weighing done with the engine still running and on an incline was held not to have been properly done (*McMillan* v *Caledonian Omnibus Co* (1938) 26 Traff Cas 374). In *Thurrock Borough Council* v *William Blyth & Co Ltd* [1977] RTR 301 it was held to be an unsatisfactory method of weighing an articulated goods vehicle for the tractor and trailer to be weighed separately but while remaining coupled, ie tractor weighed on the weighbridge and then driven forward bringing the trailer on to the weighbridge to be weighed separately.

However, many weighbridges will not weigh the whole of large vehicles and the practice is to 'double weigh', ie to weigh separately front and back and add the totals together. The advised method of cross-checking is by testing a 'sample' vehicle and then weighing it on a long weighbridge where it can be weighed in a single operation. The usual error for vehicles over 20 tonnes is less than half of one per cent. In view of this summonses should state that the maximum is exceeded, with the actual alleged overload being given in evidence or the statement of facts.

Prosecutors, advocates and their clients should ensure that this cross-check has been carried out. They should also check that the handbrake was off at the time of the test and that the approach surfaces were reasonably level as these factors may affect the test. Application of the brakes during the test may also affect the result.

Double weighing was used in *William Hampton Ltd and another* v *Bryan Dixon* (see 1.35) but the double weighing system was not in issue there.

Dynamic axle weighing machines are now in use enabling the axle weights of a motor vehicle or trailer to be ascertained. The limits of presumed accuracy of such machines, the manner in which they are to be used and the form of certificate when used are specified in the Weighing of Motor Vehicles (Use of Dynamic Axle Weighing Machines) Regulations 1978 (SI 1978 No 1180).

Where in any proceedings in Scotland for a road traffic offence any question arises as to a weight of any description in relation to a goods vehicle, a certificate of, or oral evidence by an inspector of weights and measures as to, the accuracy of the weighbridge or weighing machine used is sufficient evidence of the fact (1972 Act, s 64(4)). If such evidence is not produced, its lack may be fatal to the prosecution (*Grierson* v *Clark* [1958] SLT 112). This case would not necessarily be followed in England, however, as evidence of mechanical devices is acceptable without proof of their accuracy if the court think fit and the excess weight shown is considerable (cf *Nicholas* v *Penny* [1950] 2 All ER 89). In any proceedings for an offence under Part II of the 1972 Act other than ss 44 and 60, the date marked on the vehicle under regulations as the date of manufacture is evidence, in England, and sufficient evidence, in Scotland, that it was manufactured on the date so marked (Road Traffic Act 1972, s 64(2)).

## 1.38 Weight prosecutions

The question whether there can be offences simultaneously of excess axle weight and excess overall weight has been determined by *Theobald (Hounslow) Ltd* v *Stacey* [1979] RTR 411. The defendants were before the court for exceeding the overall gross weight, for exceeding the maximum weight on the first axle and for exceeding the maximum weight on the second axle. It was unsuccessfully argued that the three summonses were oppressive. The Divisional Court confirmed that convictions could be recorded on each summons. *Martin's* case (see 1.37) also seems to be in point. All overloading offences may affect the steering and the braking power and cause damage to the road surfaces. It should be remembered that while the regulations prohibiting excess axle weight are designed primarily to prevent damage to the surfaces and foundations of roads, the regulations prohibiting excess overall weight are designed to ensure that a vehicle does not exceed the weight for which it is designed and constructed to carry loads and is able to pull up within the distance for which its brakes were designed. The Magistrates' Association recommends that a separate penalty should be imposed on each charge (see Appendix 3).

## 1.39–45 Defences to weight prosecutions

Section 40 (6) of the 1972 Act reads:

In any proceedings for an offence under subsection (5) above in which there is alleged a contravention of or failure to comply with a construction and use requirement relating to any description of weight applicable to a goods vehicle, it shall be a defence to prove either—

(*a*) that at the time when the vehicle was being used on the road it was proceeding to a weighbridge which was the nearest available one to the place where the loading of the vehicle was completed for the purpose of being weighed, or was proceeding from a weighbridge after being weighed to the nearest point at which it was reasonably practicable to reduce the weight to the relevant limit without causing an obstruction on any road; or

(*b*) in a case where the limit of that weight was not exceeded by more than five per cent, that that limit was not exceeded at the time the loading of the vehicle was originally completed and that since that time no person has made any addition to the load.

A prosecution brought under reg 97 of the Motor Vehicles (Construction and Use) Regulations (overloading etc) is not an offence relating to a description of weight; *Hudson* v *Bushrod* [1982] RTR 87. It follows that the defence in s 40(6) does not apply to reg 97 offences. See also 1.36.

The 'nearest' weighbridge is the nearest in road distance that the particular vehicle can go (*Lovett* v *Payne* [1980] RTR 103). From a transcript of the judgment it may be noted that the test 'nearest weighbridge to which the lorry can go' should be applied in a practicable and sensible sense, ie a route would not be the nearest if it involved the lorry going on a road which was not suitable or practicable for that lorry. The 'practicable and sensible' test does not allow the choice of another weighbridge which is more convenient or which involves no element of danger. The vehicle must proceed to the nearest if it is available (*Halliday* v *Burl* [1983] RTR 21).

The burden of proof of establishing a defence under s 40(6) is upon the defendant and the standard is that of a balance of probabilities. Thus in *Thurrock D C* v *L A A Pinch Ltd* [1974] RTR 269 a magistrates' court was held to be wrong in dismissing charges on the ground that, because they were in doubt whether or not the vehicles were proceeding to a weighbridge to be weighed, the defendant was entitled to the benefit of that doubt. Local knowledge as to the location of weighbridges may be important in cases under s 40(6)(*a*). *Semble,* if the paragraph is interpreted literally, a defendant driver who is on his way to a weighbridge which he genuinely believes to be the nearest one, but which in fact is not, will be unable to set up the defence, but there is obvious mitigation. The weighbridge to which a driver is proceeding must be the 'nearest available' one and it is submitted that, when the driver leaves the place of loading, he must, to avail himself of the defence, believe that there is a weighbridge open within a reasonable distance. A driver who starts on a long journey late in the evening, when the weighbridges are all shut, should not be able to say in his defence that he is on the way to the nearest available weighbridge which is perhaps 150 miles and several hours' driving away. If he does and it is shown that he could not reasonably have believed that there was a weighbridge open within a reasonable distance, on this argument he could be convicted. The standard of proof on him is, no doubt, that of balance of probabilities. When he is coming from the weighbridge after being weighed and found overweight, he must, to avail himself of the defence under the second part of s 40(6)(*a*), be going to the nearest practicable unloading point. Often, there may be no such place available, eg because the yard where he loaded is shut for the evening. It is suggested that he may not then proceed on his journey but should take the vehicle off the highway, or, at least, stop driving until the yard opens or some of the excess load can be put into other vehicles.

The '5 per cent addition' under s 40(6)(*b*) was enacted primarily to deal with cases where snow or petrol etc have increased the weight, but the plain words of the subsection are not so limited (see eg *Thurrock Borough Council* v *William Blythe & Co Ltd* [1977] RTR 301). By s 57(7) of the 1972 Act, powers of immediately prohibiting the use on the road of overweight vehicles are conferred; and by s 64(3), if any question arises whether a weight has been reduced to the permitted limit in proceedings under s 57(7), the burden of proof is on the accused. (Section 57 of the 1972 Act has been amended by the Heavy Commercial Vehicles (Controls and Regulations) Act 1973 and by s 9 of and Sched 3 to the Transport Act 1978.) Where the burden of proof lies on a defendant, the standard of proof is only on a balance of probabilities (*R* v *Carr-Briant* [1943] KB 607).

As to penalties, see 8.41–60 and in particular 8.43.

## 'Accident'

### 1.46–50 Meaning

The word 'accident' is to be found in several places in the 1972 Act, notably in the drink/driving provisions (ss 5–12), particularly s 7(2) (administration of the breath test following an accident); s 25 (failing to stop and failing to report an accident); and s 179 (warning of intended prosecution: see Chapter 3). The equivalent of s 7(2) before the amendment by s 25 of and Sched 8 to the Transport Act 1981 was s 8(2).

In *R* v *Morris* [1972] RTR 201 (a case under s 8(2)) an 'accident' was said by Sachs LJ to mean 'an unintended occurrence which has an adverse physical result' and it was held that an accident had occurred where two car bumpers had become interlocked accidentally while one car was pushing the other. In *Chief Constable of West Midland Police* v *Billingham* [1979] RTR 446 (another case under s 8) it was stated that this attempted definition should be understood in relation to the particular facts of the case.

In *Billingham* the Divisional Court pointed out that there was no definition of the word 'accident' in the 1972 Act and both judges expressed themselves hesitant to attempt to define the word when Parliament had refrained from doing so: it had different meanings in different statutes according to the mischief against which the Act was aimed. Instead of attempting to give a definition, both judges preferred to suggest that a court, when having to decide whether there was an accident within the meaning of the 1972 Act, should ask itself the question 'Would an ordinary man in the circumstances of the case say there had been an accident?' Applying this test the Divisional Court reversed the justices who had followed *Morris* and held that there had been an accident. In *Billingham* a police motor vehicle had been damaged as a result of a deliberate act of mischief by someone setting the car in motion so that it ran downhill and collided with a telegraph pole.

*Billingham* was followed in *Chief Constable of Staffordshire* v *Lees* [1981] RTR 506 (again under s 8) where the defendant deliberately drove at a locked kissing gate, smashing it. Bingham J said:

It would be an insult to commonsense if a collision involving a motor car arising from some careless and inadvertent act entitled a constable to exercise his powers under the Act but a similar result caused by a deliberate anti-social act did not. Previous cases have made it clear that one should look at the ordinary meaning of the word 'accident', and it is relevant to note that in the *Oxford English Dictionary*, among other meanings, is to be found 'an unfortunate event, a mishap', which definition, it seems to me, is wide enough to include an event not occurring in the ordinary course, of such a nature as in this case. I might perhaps add that in speaking of 'moving accidents by flood and field' Othello [I iii 134] was, I think, referring to intentional as well as fortuitous events of which he had been the unhappy subject.

It is clear from *Billingham* and *Lees* that there is no need for any other vehicle to be involved. See also *R* v *Pico* [1971] Crim LR 599, where a car hit a bank and a gate post injuring the defendant driver and damaging the gate, and *R* v *Harling* [1970] RTR 441 (no other vehicle apparently involved).

# 'Driver'

## 1.51 Meaning

'Driver' (except for the purposes of s 1 (causing death by reckless driving)), where a separate person acts as steersman of a motor vehicle, includes that person as well as any other person engaged in the driving of the vehicle, and the expression 'drive' is construed accordingly (Road Traffic Act 1972, s 196). A similar definition is in the Road Traffic Regulation Act 1984, s 142(1). By s 34(1) of the 1972 Act two persons must be employed in driving or attending to a heavy or light locomotive whilst it is being driven on a highway (the term 'road' is not used) but only one need be so employed where no trailer is being drawn, with exceptions (see 'Attendants on trailers', 1.25).

Two people may be held to be actually driving the same car at the same time. In *Tyler* v *Whatmore* [1976] RTR 83 (following *Langman* v *Valentine* below) it was held that a girl in the passenger seat leaning across the person in the driver's seat with both her hands on the wheel, steering the car, with the ignition switch and handbrake within her reach, was 'actually driving'. Her companion in the driving seat whose view she obstructed and who was controlling the propulsion of the car but could not control the steering was also driving (ibid). The degree of control of a passenger must, however, be such as to amount to driving in the ordinary sense of the word (*Jones* v *Pratt* [1983] RTR 54). In *Jones* v *Pratt* the Divisional Court held that the front seat passenger in a moving car who momentarily grabbed the steering wheel, pushing it in a clockwise direction, causing the car to leave the road, could not properly be described as driving the car in the ordinary sense of the word and could not be convicted of driving with excess alcohol or without due care. A learner driver, sitting in the driving seat, is a driver, although the instructor who retains simultaneous control of the car may also be a driver (*Langman* v *Valentine* [1952] 2 All ER 803; see also *R* v *Wilkins* (1951) 115 JP

443, QS). In *Langman's* case the instructor had his hands on the brake and steering wheel. Where a licensed person merely sat beside a young boy, who was in the driving seat and, though able to reach the steering wheel and foot-brake, apparently did not have a hand on the wheel, he was held not to be a driver as he was not in control of the car (*Evans* v *Walkden* [1956] 3 All ER 64).

**1.52 'Driving'**

There are a number of cases on whether a person can be said to be 'driving'. Some are not easy to reconcile.

In *Saycell* v *Bool* [1948] 2 All ER 83 a person who sat in the driving seat, released the brake and let the vehicle run a hundred yards downhill was held to 'drive it' although there was no petrol in the tank and the engine was not started. In *Ames* v *MacLeod* [1969] SC 1 the High Court of Justiciary in Scotland held that a person 'drove' his car which had run out of petrol when he steered it by placing his hand on the wheel while walking beside it as it coasted down a slight incline in the road. In *R* v *Munning* [1961] Crim LR 55 a magistrates' court held that pushing a motor scooter was not driving. In *R* v *Roberts* (*No 2*) [1965] 1 QB 85 releasing the brake of a lorry parked on a hill and putting the vehicle in motion so that it ran down the hill was held not to be 'driving'. In *R* v *Kitson* [1955] 39 Cr App R 66 a passenger awoke to find the driver gone and the car moving. He steered it for 200 yards until he could safely stop. He was held to be a 'driver'.

In *Blayney* v *Knight* [1975] RTR 279 a taxi driver left his taxi which had automatic transmission with the engine running. The defendant, who had no intention of driving, sat in the driver's seat. In the course of a struggle with the taxi driver the defendant's foot touched the accelerator causing the taxi to drive along the road, mount the pavement and swerve back to the offside. The defendant was held not to be 'driving'.

In *R* v *MacDonagh* [1974] RTR 372, it was held that a person who pushed a car along a road with both feet on the ground with one arm in the car to control the steering wheel was not 'driving' the car and could not be therefore convicted of driving while disqualified.

It will be noted that the facts of *Ames* v *MacLeod* and *R* v *MacDonagh* are virtually indistinguishable. *R* v *MacDonagh* must be taken as representing the law in England and Wales. The conflict between the two cases may be the reason for a court of five judges in the latter case. A reading of the judgment of Lord Widgery CJ in *MacDonagh* leads, it is submitted, to the following conclusions:

(1) The primary consideration as to whether a person is 'driving' is essentially a question of fact, dependent on the degree and extent to which the person has control of the direction and movement of the vehicle.

(2) One test is whether the accused was 'in a substantial sense controlling the movement and direction of the car' (*Ames* v *MacLeod*). A person cannot be said to be 'driving' unless he satisfies this test.

(3) The fact that a person satisfies the test of control in *Ames* v *MacLeod* is not necessarily exhaustive. It has still to be considered whether the activity in

question could fall within the ordinary meaning of the word 'driving' in the English language. (See also *McQuaid* v *Anderton* and *R* v *Roberts* below.)

Further tests to determine whether a person is driving have been established by *Burgoyne* v *Phillips* [1983] RTR 49 and *Jones* v *Pratt*, 1.51 above.

(4) The essence of driving is the use of the driver's control in order to direct the movement of the vehicle however the movement is produced (*Burgoyne* v *Phillips*). (This is in effect a reiteration of (1) and (2).)

(5) Whether the defendant himself deliberately sets the vehicle in motion is an important factor (*Burgoyne* v *Phillips*).

(6) In borderline cases, it is important to consider the length of time the steering wheel or other control was handled (*Jones* v *Pratt*).

Applying principles (1), (2) and (3) in *MacDonagh* it was held that the defendant was 'pushing' rather than 'driving'. Similarly it was suggested that a person pushing a broken-down motor cycle and walking beside it could not be said to be 'driving'. On the other hand it was suggested that it would be possible to find as a fact that a person was driving if a motorist pushing the vehicle had one foot in the car in order to make more effective use of the controls.

In *Burgoyne* v *Phillips* the defendant was sitting behind the steering wheel of his car. Assuming he still had the keys in the ignition, he let the car roll forward to drive off carefully. He realised he had no keys and put the brakes on quickly. The steering wheel was locked and the engine was not running. The car rolled a distance of thirty feet by gravity and collided with another vehicle. The Divisional Court held that the defendant was driving as opposed to attempting to drive and was rightly convicted of driving with excess alcohol.

The facts of *Burgoyne* v *Phillips* do not altogether tally with the test used (ie test (4) above). The defendant had only limited scope for control. He apparently merely released the handbrake. Releasing the handbrake was held not to be driving in *R* v *Roberts*. However, unlike the person in that case he was behind the steering wheel and intended to drive. The facts of *Burgoyne* v *Phillips* are similar to those in *Saycell* v *Bool* save that *Burgoyne* v *Phillips* seems to be the first conviction for driving (apart from the 'continuing' cases noted below) where there was no control of the steering.

Whether a steersman in a motor vehicle towed by a rope or chain can be said to be driving has now been decided by *McQuaid* v *Anderton* [1980] 3 All ER 540. The defendant sat in the driver's seat of a motor car while it was being towed by means of a tow rope connected to another vehicle. He steered the towed car and was able to use its brakes as and when required. It was held that he was rightly convicted of driving whilst disqualified contrary to s 99(*b*) of the Road Traffic Act 1972. The decision was subsequently applied in the similar case of *Caise* v *Wright* [1981] RTR 49.

Lord Widgery CJ in *McQuaid* v *Anderton* said that the law hereafter on these points is that laid down in *R* v *MacDonagh* and justices will be well advised to apply that authority and no other.

Heilbron J quoted certain comments of Lord Widgery CJ in that case with approval. He had referred to the infinite number of ways in which a person might control the movement of a motor vehicle apart from the orthodox one of sitting in the driving seat and using the engine for propulsion. Although the word 'driver' must be given a wide meaning, the courts must be alert to see that the net is not thrown so widely that it includes activities which cannot be said to be driving a motor vehicle in any ordinary use of that word in the English language. Lord Widgery CJ had also said:

> The [1972] Act does not define the word 'drive' and in its simplest meaning we think that it refers to a person using the driver's controls for the purpose of directing the movement of the vehicle. It matters not that the vehicle is not moving under its own power or driven by the force of gravity, or even that it is being pushed by other well-wishers. The essence of driving is the use of the driver's controls in order to direct the movement, however that movement is produced.

Heilbron J also drew attention to the two factors to which Lord Parker CJ referred in *R* v *Roberts* [1964] 2 All ER 541: first that the alleged driver must be in the driving seat, or in control of the steering wheel, and secondly that his activities were nevertheless not to be held to amount to driving unless this came within the ordinary meaning of that word.

The case does not decide the position of a vehicle being towed with a rigid towbar, but it is submitted that applying the specified tests a person in the driver's seat of such a car would probably be held not to be driving.

In *R* v *Shaw (Kenneth)* [1975] RTR 160, a conviction under s 6(1) of the 1972 Act was set aside when the recorder did not leave to the jury the question of whether the steersman of a towed vehicle was 'driving'.

Driving a towing vehicle in such a way that the towed one snakes dangerously about the road can be dangerous driving (*Anderson* v *Transport Board* [1964] NZLR 881). This decision may still be relevant even though there is now no offence of dangerous driving.

Pedalling an auto-assisted cycle without starting the engine is 'driving away' (*Floyd* v *Bush* [1953] 1 All ER 265; *R* v *Tahsin* [1970] RTR 88, where a defendant pedalling a moped with the engine out of action was held to be driving; see also *Lawrence* v *Howlett* [1952] 2 All ER 74; and see 1.14 in relation to these cases). In *Crank* v *Brooks* [1980] RTR 441 Waller LJ said that if a person had been using a pedal cycle as a scooter by having one foot on the pedal and pushing herself along she would not have been a foot passenger. There is no reason why the same principle should not be applied to a motor bicycle. If so, if such a person is not a pedestrian he would appear to be driving. (See also 'Pushing and driving', 1.56 below.)

In Part VI of the Transport Act 1968, which relates to drivers' hours, s 95(3) refers to 'employee-drivers' and 'owner-drivers' and s 103(3) declares that references to a person driving a vehicle are references to his being at the driving controls of the vehicle for the purpose of controlling its movement, whether it is in motion or stationary with its engine running.

In *Collyer* v *Dring* [1952] 2 All ER 1004 a young girl entered a motor car parked in a private forecourt off the road, intending to drive it round the forecourt only and not to go on the road. Through her inexperience she engaged reverse gear and the car went on to the road. On being charged with careless driving and with uninsured use, she contended that she was not driving 'on the road' inasmuch as she was on it involuntarily and also that she was not using the car on the road. Her conviction on both charges was upheld by the Queen's Bench Division.

### 1.53 Continuing driving

The principles given in 1.52 only determine whether a person is driving. Once it has been determined that a person is driving, the driving may still continue even though the tests laid down by Lord Widgery CJ in *McQuaid* v *Anderton* cannot be fulfilled. A person may still be driving when he is buying a newspaper or changing a wheel (examples given in *Pinner* v *Everett* [1969] 3 All ER 257 (HL)) or when he is walking across the forecourt of a garage to take instructions (*Regan* v *Anderton* [1980] RTR 126). These cases were based on the former s 8(1) of the 1972 Act, since repealed and, if the issue arises whether a person is continuing to drive, it may be helpful to refer to these and other cases in the 11th Edition of this work at p 170 et seq. Section 8(1) was a section which had special features in that it was impossible to take it literally. Nevertheless the cases have a wider significance—see 11.27.

In *Stevens* v *Thornborrow* [1969] 3 All ER 1487 the following propositions were extracted from *Pinner* v *Everett*:

(1) Whether a person is 'driving or attempting to drive' is a question of fact.

(2) It is far easier to find as a fact that a motorist is driving if he is still at the wheel, more difficult if he has dismounted.

(3) The overriding principle, whether or not he is at the wheel, is whether he is doing something connected with driving.

The principles of *Pinner* v *Everett* and other cases were summarised (so far as still relevant) in *Edkins* v *Knowles* [1973] RTR 257 as follows:

(1) The vehicle does not have to be in motion; there will always be a brief interval of time after the vehicle has been brought to rest and before the motorist has completed those operations necessarily connected with driving, such as applying the hand-brake, switching off the ignition and securing the vehicle, during which he must still be considered to be driving.

(2) When a motorist stops before he has completed his journey he may still be driving; an obvious example is when he is halted at traffic lights. Each case will depend upon its own facts, but generally the following questions will be relevant: (*a*) What was the purpose of the stop? If it is connected with the driving, and not for some purpose unconnected with the driving, the facts may justify a finding that the driving is continuing although the vehicle is stationary. (*b*) How long was he stopped? The longer he is stopped the more difficult it becomes to regard him as still driving. (*c*) Did he get out of the vehicle? If he remains in the vehicle it is some though not a conclusive indication that he is still driving.

(3) If a motorist is stopped and an appreciable time lapses it will be a question of fact and degree whether the motorist is still to be considered as driving at that time.

(4) When a motorist has arrived at the end of his journey then subject to the brief interval referred to in (1) above he can no longer be regarded as driving.

(5) When a motorist has been effectively prevented or persuaded from driving he can no longer be considered to be driving.

### 1.54 Continuing driving: production of licences

The decision in *Edkins* v *Knowles* would still seem to be applicable (see 11.3).

### 1.55 'Use' and 'driving'

The distinction between 'use' and 'driving' was emphasised in *Samuelson* v *National Insurance and Guarantee Corporation Ltd* [1984] 3 All ER 107 (a civil case). The plaintiff was covered for the *use* of a vehicle whilst in the custody or control of a member of the motor trade for its upkeep or repair. He was not covered for *driving* by another person. It was held that he was not covered under the policy when the car was stolen whilst being *driven* by the motor trade repairer to buy spares.

### 1.56 Pushing and driving

Proceedings are sometimes brought against persons who have been disqualified from driving or have no driving licence when they have been caught pushing a car or motor cycle, with the engine not running, or against persons pushing a car with someone else at the steering wheel. In the former case the defendant would be 'driving' if he was in the driving seat or otherwise in control of the steering and had something to do with the propulsion, eg if he was engaged in a common design with his friends who were pushing, if not actually pushing himself (*R* v *Roberts* [1964] 2 All ER 541). If neither he nor his accomplices had any control over the steering, they would not appear to be driving. In the other case (the accomplices pushing from behind or at the side but with no personal control of the steering), it is submitted that they would be aiding and abetting (see 1.86–7) the one in control of the steering if they were all engaged in a common design and could therefore properly be charged (*Shimmell* v *Fisher* [1951] 2 All ER 672). These cases suggest that pushing motor vehicles with control of the steering would be 'driving', although sometimes the facts would point also to an attempt to drive. In almost all cases it would be 'using' (see 1.79) by those engaged in the common design whether there was 'driving' or not.

The position has now been clarified by the decision of *R* v *MacDonagh* [1974] RTR 373. The primary test of whether a person drives (see 1.52) is one of fact whether the person is substantially controlling the movement and direction of the vehicle, but even if the activity of the person satisfies this test, it is not necessarily exhaustive. It has still to be considered whether the activity in question can fall within the ordinary meaning of the word 'driving', in the English language. Thus if a person who pushed a car with two feet on the ground and one arm in the car on the steering wheel could not be said to be 'driving', he would be pushing (*R* v *MacDonagh*). It was also said that it mattered not how the vehicle was propelled, whether it was moving under its own power, driven by the force of gravity or even pushed by others, but there must be a distinction between 'pushing' and 'driving'. It was said a person pushing a broken-down motor cycle could not be said to be 'driving' even though he is in full control of its steering and possibly brakes. It was observed that cases such as these are near the borderline. If, for example, the defendant in *R* v *MacDonagh* also had had one foot in the car to control the brakes, he might well be properly convicted. In *R* v *Munning* [1961] Crim LR 55 a magistrates' court held that pushing a motor scooter was not driving. The decision is not binding but is in principle similar to that in *MacDonagh*. On the other hand in *Crank* v *Brooks* [1980] RTR 441 Waller LJ said that if a person had been using a pedal cycle as a scooter by having one foot on the pedal and pushing herself along she would not have been a foot passenger. There is no reason why the same principle should not be applied to a motor bicycle. If so, such a person would appear to be driving.

It may be worth remarking that *MacDonagh* and *Munning* are the first cases in which the more current meaning of the word 'driving' is relied upon. The conception of the term 'driving' goes back before the invention of the mechanically propelled vehicle—as do 'carriage' and 'carriageway' (see eg the Town Police Clauses Act 1847 and s 35 of the Offences against the Person Act 1861). A driver (or 'drover') drove or steered by using reins, by pushing or goading or by otherwise guiding. He might be behind the animal, in or on a vehicle drawn by it or on the animal. Seemingly if it were recalcitrant he might be in front of it.

For the purpose of reporting accidents under s 25 of the 1972 Act, 'driver' means the person who takes the vehicle on the road, and he remains the driver whilst in the car, although he may have stopped the car and engine (*Jones* v *Prothero* [1952] 1 All ER 434). In *Hamilton* v *Jones* [1926] 42 TLR 148 a demand for production of a driving licence made several hours after the accused had been seen driving was held to have been made to 'the driver' (but see also *Boyce* v *Absalom* [1974] RTR 248, 11.3).

## 1.57 'Taking a conveyance'

The offence under s 12 of the Theft Act 1968 involves 'taking' a conveyance. It was held in *R* v *Bogacki and Others* [1973] RTR 384 that 'taking' should not be equated with 'using': the word 'takes' requires not only an unauthorised taking of possession or control of the vehicle but also some movement of the vehicle however small. Thus taking control of a bus and unsuccessfully trying to start the engine so that the bus did not move could not justify a conviction for 'taking' the bus contrary to s 12, only for attempting to do so (ibid). However, the conveyance does not have to be moved in its own element for an offence to be committed. *P* was convicted of 'taking' a rubber dinghy by putting it on a road trailer and driving the trailer away (*R* v *Pearce* [1973] Crim LR 321).

The earlier legislation now repealed used the expression 'taking and driving away' and certain cases on the meaning of this may still be helpful. Where one man held the steering wheel and two others pushed, without the engine being started, all were held to be taking and driving away (*Shimmell* v *Fisher* [1951] 2 All ER 672). Pedalling an auto-assisted cycle without starting the engine was 'driving away' (*Floyd* v *Bush* [1953] 1 All ER 265). Releasing a vehicle's brake at the top of an incline and then quitting it, so that it ran downhill unattended, was not taking and driving it away since there cannot be driving unless the defendant is in the driving seat or in control of the steering wheel and also has something to do with the propulsion of the vehicle (*R* v *Roberts* [1964] 2 All ER 541).

### 1.58 'Rider'

The expression 'rider' is used in a number of statutory provisions. It will include a pedal cyclist. See, for example, the Theft Act 1968, s 12 (5) (riding a pedal cycle knowing it to have been taken without consent) and the Highway Act 1835, s 72 (wilfully riding on any footpath or causeway by the side of any road). It is an expression which will normally include the passenger who also rides. For instance, such passengers will require protective headgear on motor cycles (see 'Motor Cycle Helmets', 9.11).

As to what is meant by riding, see *Crank* v *Brooks* [1980] RTR 441 and the law as discussed in paragraphs 1.52 and 1.53. Subject to the issue of continuance (see 1.53) and a person stationary in traffic etc, riding implies movement. There may be a distinction in this respect between a horse and a vehicle. A horse is not used to serve the purpose of an armchair but a vehicle seat may be. The *Concise Oxford Dictionary* defines 'ride' as 'sit on and be carried by' including 'sit or go or be on something as on a horse especially astride'. A magistrates' court (see [1982] Jo Crim L 1) has held a person using a motor bicycle as a seat with the engine off not to be riding. Similarly a girl talking to her boyfriend (or a boy to his girlfriend) may have other things in mind and not be riding even though sitting astride the machine. The issue will be one of fact in each case.

### 1.59 Passenger

A crucial element of the definition of 'public service vehicle' in s 1(1) of the Public Passenger Vehicles Act 1981 is the number of passengers for which the vehicle is adapted. The specified number of passengers is nine as the section refers to 'more than eight'. The criterion in s 1(1)(*a*) is whether the vehicle is adapted to carry nine or more passengers, not the number in fact carried. Similar expressions are used in many other statutory provisions.

Whether the driver should be counted among the passengers is not clear. In Parts I and III of Sched 1 to the Public Passenger Vehicles Act 1981 'driver' is contrasted with 'passenger'. In Sched 5 to the Road Traffic Regulation Act 1967 (now repealed) the term 'passengers' exclusive of the driver was used, which suggests that there he was regarded as otherwise a passenger. In the equivalent part of the Road Traffic Regulation Act 1984 (Sched 6) the reference is merely to 'more than eight passengers' and the definition is now the same as in the 1981 Act. See also s 95(2) of the Transport Act 1968 where again the reference is merely to 'passengers'. Paragraph 1 of art 4 of EEC Regulation 543/69 (exceptions) refers to 'carrying not more than nine persons including the driver'. This exception also applies to EEC Regulation 1463/70 (see art 3). The *Concise Oxford Dictionary* defines 'passenger' as 'traveller in . . . public . . . conveyance'. A driver in a public conveyance is someone who conveys the traveller on a passage from A to B without wishing to arrive permanently at B himself: it would not be logical to regard Charon, the legendary ferryman over the Styx to Hades, as himself a passenger on a journey to Hell. In *Wurzal* v *Addison* [1965] 1 All ER 20, a finding of magistrates that a Volkswagen minibus seating six passengers behind and with a bench seat seating the driver and two passengers in front was not adapted to carry eight passengers was upheld because the gear lever was in the central position. This implies the driver is not to be included. Lord Parker CJ said that, in other cases involving similar vehicles, magistrates would, on proper evidence, be almost bound to find that they were adapted to carry eight passengers. (Note that the relevant number is now nine.) It is submitted that eight persons *plus* the driver may be carried before the limit is reached: ie the driver is *not* to be regarded as a passenger.

### 1.60–5 Automatism

The person sitting in the driving seat when the car is in motion is deemed to be the driver and the onus is on him to show that he was incapable of controlling the car by reason of having an epileptic fit or being in a coma or being knocked unconscious by a stone or being under attack by a swarm of bees. Unless he can show that he was temporarily incapable through some such circumstances, he is responsible as the driver (*Hill* v *Baxter* [1958] 1 All ER 193). Automatism connotes in law no wider concept than involuntary movement of a person's body or limbs (*Watmore* v *Jenkins* [1962] 2 All ER 868). There must be evidence to raise a reasonable doubt whether the driver's bodily movements which turned his car hither and thither and kept it moving at a fairly steady speed were wholly uncontrolled and uninitiated by any function of conscious will (ibid). That was a case of dangerous driving where the defendant, a diabetic, was in a state of confusion through his illness but, as he had driven for five miles in that state, a conviction was directed.

As to the burden of proof where a defence of automatism is raised or suggested, see also *R* v *Budd*, *Stevenson* v *Beatson* and *Cook* v *Atchison* at 5.29, and *R* v *Sibbles* at 5.29 as to a driver who knows that he is subject to dizzy spells.

In *R* v *Isitt* [1978] RTR 211 (a case of dangerous driving) the defendant was in a state of hysterical fugue. This was described as a grey area between automatism and insanity. It was nevertheless held that the defendant's mind was working sufficiently to the extent that his driving was purposeful to get away from the accident. The defendant's mind went with the acts alleged to be criminal. He was therefore rightly convicted.

After reviewing the earlier authorities it was held in a civil action for negligent driving that the defendant was unable to escape liability because of automatism or any similar ground unless his actions had been wholly beyond his control (*Roberts* v *Ramsbottom* [1980] 1 All ER 7). The defendant had suffered a stroke. Alternatively he was liable on the ground that he had continued to drive when he was unfit to do so and should have been aware of his unfitness. Neill J said that a similar approach to the defence should be applied in civil and criminal cases.

A similar approach to the second ground in *Roberts* v *Ramsbottom* was adopted in *Moses* v *Winder* [1981] RTR 37. The defendant was a diabetic who drove home even though he felt the onset of a diabetic coma and was involved in an accident. The Divisional Court directed a conviction. Roskill LJ said that he failed to take the precautions he ought to have taken. He emphasised that it was for the defence to show facts which could raise the defence of automatism. Justices needed to be extremely cautious before accepting the defence of automatism without medical evidence. The court quoted with approval Lawson LJ in *R* v *Quick* [1973] QB 910 when he said at p 922G:

A self-induced incapacity will not excuse . . . nor will one which could have been reasonably foreseen as a result of either doing, or omitting to do something, as, for example, taking alcohol against medical advice after using certain prescribed drugs, or failing to have regular meals while taking insulin. From time to time difficult cases are likely to arise.

An article on automatism at [1980] Crim LR 350 quotes a number of cases where a defence of automatism has been successful.

Where a person commits an offence under the influence of epilepsy the strict jury verdict should be 'not guilty by reason of insanity' (*R* v *Sullivan* [1983] 3 WLR 123 (HL)). Cases concerning epilepsy must be treated accordingly if tried on indictment.

In *R* v *Bailey* [1983] 2 All ER 503, the Court of Appeal decided that diabetes (unlike intoxication from alcohol or drugs) could provide a defence not only to crimes of specific intent but also crimes of basic intent. The court added that the question was whether the Crown had proved the necessary element of recklessness. Similar principles would appear to apply to epilepsy cases. It is submitted that there can be no defence to a charge of reckless or careless driving if the defendant knew of the risks of epilepsy or knew that he was a diabetic and was aware of the risks of too much or too little insulin.

## 'Road'

### 1.66 Roads and highways generally

'Road' means any highway *and any other road to which the public has access* and includes bridges over which a road passes (1972 Act, s 196). This definition is the same as in s 121 of the Road Traffic Act 1930 and s 257 of the Road Traffic Act 1960. The definition in the Road Traffic Regulation Act 1984, s 142(1) is the same save that it refers to 'any length of highway or of any other road' etc. It is submitted that the use of the word 'length' is unlikely to make any material difference.

The Vehicles (Excise) Act 1971 affects vehicles on 'public roads' (ie those repairable at the public expense—see s 38) and certain of the Motor Vehicles (Construction and Use) Regulations 1978 only apply to vehicles on highways (see reg 4).

'Road' has the same meaning under Parts V and VI of the Transport Act 1968 (see ss 92(1) and 103(1)) as in s 196 of the 1972 Act.

Generally it may be said to be a matter of fact and degree whether it is a 'road' or 'public place'. The onus is on the prosecution to prove that a road is one within the Act (*Williams* v *Boyle* (1962) 106 SJ 939), and also to prove that it is a 'public place' (*Pugh* v *Knipe* [1972] Crim LR 247).

The *Concise Oxford Dictionary* defines 'road' as a line of communication for use of foot passengers and vehicles. In *Oxford* v *Austin* [1981] RTR 416 a 'road' was said to be a definable right of way for passage between two points.

In *Randall* v *Motor Insurers' Bureau* [1969] 1 All ER 21 a vehicle was deemed on a road when it was partly on the road and partly on private land, and in *Holliday* v *Henry* [1974] RTR 101 a vehicle was held to be 'on' a road when, because a roller skate was interposed between each wheel and the surface of the road, it could not be said to be in actual physical contact with the road.

In relevant cases the test in *Hawkins* v *Phillips* [1980] RTR 197 may assist. The decision did not relate to a road as such but to a 'main carriageway'. It was held that a slip or filter road was part of the main carriageway because any vehicle going on to the slip road was committed to proceeding on to the trunk road. This is clearly not sufficient to turn a purely private access drive into a road within the meaning of the 1972 and 1984 Acts. A lay-by was held part of a public road though not maintained by the highway authority as such (*McNeill* v *Dunbar* [1965] SLTN 79).

Normally, a right of way extends to the whole space between the fences, and a grass verge between the pavement and the fence was held to be part of a road in *Worth* v *Brooks* [1959] Crim LR 855. In *A-G* v *Beynon* [1969] 2 All ER 263, it was held that the mere fact that a road ran between fences or hedges did not give rise by itself to a presumption. It was first necessary to decide whether the fences were put up by reference to the highway or for some other reason. If it would appear that the fences were put up with reference to the highway, a rebuttable presumption of law then arose that the highway extended to the whole space between the fences and was not confined to such part as had been made up.

A highway remains a highway though temporarily roped off (*McCrone* v *Rigby* (1952) 50 LGR 115; *Norton* v *Hayward* (1968) 112 SJ 767, 1.70).

The term 'road' can include a road to which the public of a foreign country has access in relation to proceedings against a serviceman for committing a civil offence outside Great Britain (*Cox* v *Army Council* [1962] 1 All ER 880).

The detailed definitions of 'road' and 'public place' in an Irish statute were considered in *A-G* v *Farrel* (1954) 88 ILTR 174, a case on a road in hospital grounds.

A footpath and a bridleway (defined below) would not normally be roads under the Road Traffic Act etc, save as indicated at 1.68, even though highways. In this respect 'highway' in the Road Traffic Act etc must be regarded as limited by its juxtaposition to 'any other road'. The reference in s 36 of the 1972 Act to 'any road being a footpath or bridleway' is not overlooked, but it is submitted that it does not make a place unsuited for vehicles into a road, especially as s 36 is not a definition section. As indicated by the *Concise Oxford Dictionary* a road is for vehicles and riders as well as foot passengers. The result is that 'road' offences are not committed by vehicles such as motor bicycles on footpaths and bridleways which are not roads. A 'cycle lane', may, like a footway, be part of a road set aside for the purpose. It seems that on this basis a separate cycle track (see the definition below) may similarly not be a road as it is restricted to cycles, and riders of animals are excluded. The consequence would be surprising as s 17 of the 1972 Act (reckless cycling), s 18 (careless and inconsiderate cycling) and s 21 (restriction on carriage of persons on bicycles) all apply only on roads and bridleways.

## 1.67 'Highway'

The term 'highway' is discussed in Jowett's *Dictionary of English Law*, and it is narrower than 'road' under the Road Traffic Acts. A *full* highway or cartway provides the public with a right of way on foot, riding or accompanied by a beast of burden or with vehicles and cattle (*Suffolk County Council* v *Mason* [1979] 2 All ER 369 (HL) at p 371). The term 'highway' therefore includes public footpaths, public bridleways, public driftways, public carriageways and public footways. See, however, under 'Roads and highways generally', 1.66.

### A *'Bridleway'*

A 'bridleway' is a highway over which the public has the following but no other rights of way:

(*a*) a right of way on foot;
(*b*) a right of way on horseback;
(*c*) a right of way leading a horse (including in the 1980 and 1981 Acts a pony, ass or mule);
(*d*) in some cases, a right to drive animals of any description along the way (a drove or driftway); and
(*e*) a right to ride a pedal cycle providing the cyclist gives way to pedestrians and to persons on horseback, providing also that there is no local authority order or by-law to the contrary.

(Road Traffic Act 1972, s 196; Highways Act 1980, s 329; Road Traffic Regulation Act 1984, s 142(1); Wildlife and Countryside Act 1981, s 66(1).)

### B *'Carriageway'*

A 'carriageway' is a way constituting or comprised in a highway, being a way (other than a cycle track) over which the public have a right of way for the passage of vehicles (Highways Act 1980, s 329).

### C *'Dual-carriageway'*

A dual-carriageway is defined for the purpose of speed limits for certain classes of vehicles by the Road Traffic Regulation Act 1984, Part IV, Sched 6, as a road part of which consists of a central reservation to separate the carriageways. This definition suggests that the dual-carriageway does not begin with the hatching markings but only with the physical central reservation itself, because hatching markings are not completely reserved and can be crossed in certain circumstances (see 6.12). Such dual-carriageways may be highways or any other road including a private road to which the public has access. This definition should be contrasted with the definition of a carriageway in the Highways Act 1980, s 329, which is limited to part of a highway.

*D 'Cycle track'*

A 'cycle track' is a way over which the public has a right of way on pedal cycles other than pedal cycles which are motor vehicles under the 1972 Act with or without a right of way on foot (Highways Act 1980, s 329 as amended by the Cycle Tracks Act 1984, s 1(1)).

*E 'Footpath'*

A 'footpath' is a highway over which the public has a right of way on foot only (Highways Act 1980, s 329; Road Traffic Act 1972, s 196; Road Traffic Regulation Act 1984, s 142; Wildlife and Countryside Act 1981, s 66(1)). All but the 1972 and 1984 Acts make clear that footways are excluded. See 6.75.

*F 'Footway'*

A 'footway' is a way (usually a pavement) comprised in a highway (which also comprises a carriageway) with a public right of way on foot only (Highways Act 1980, s 329).

*G 'Walkway'*

A 'walkway' is a way through, over or under a building created by agreement in accordance with s 35 of the Highways Act 1980 or its earlier equivalent (s 18 of the Highways Act 1971); it may be dedicated by the agreement as a footpath (Highways Act 1980, s 35).

*H 'Public path'*

A 'public path' is a highway being a footpath or a bridleway (Wildlife and Countryside Act 1981, s 66(1)).

*J 'Byway open to all traffic'*

A 'byway open to all traffic' is defined in the Wildlife and Countryside Act 1981 and for the purposes of s 127 of the Road Traffic Regulation Act 1984 (see below) as a highway over which the public have a right of way for vehicular and all other kinds of traffic, but which is used by the public mainly for the purpose for which footpaths and bridleways are so used. The expression was not previously defined in any of the Acts quoted above. There has been a progression in the terms used, from 'cartway' in the earlier Traffic Signs Regulations and General Directions to 'road used as a public path' and finally to 'byway open to all traffic'. These terms have all been attached to similar signs and seem to have similar meanings.

The Department of Transport signs are to be found in the Traffic Signs Regulations and General Directions 1981. The sign 'By-way to Ambridge' is sign No 737.1 in Sched 1, Part III (directional informatory signs). The title to the sign reads 'Direction to a place which can be reached by a by-way open to all traffic'.

The 1984 Act has effect in relation to any footpath, bridleway or byway as if any reference in the Act to traffic included foot passengers and persons driving, riding or leading horses or other animals of draught or burden and any reference in ss 2(3) and 14 to foot passengers included such persons also (s 127).

## 1.68 Determining the existence of a highway

A bridleway is a road for the purposes of the offences of reckless, careless or drunken cycling and carrying two persons on a bicycle (Road Traffic Act 1972, ss 18–21).

Section 328 of the Highways Act 1980 includes bridges and tunnels over or through which a highway passes as part of the highway for the purposes of that Act unless the context otherwise requires. The statement at 19 Halsbury (3rd ed) 13 that public bridges are highways so far as the right of passage is concerned is not repeated in the 4th edition, which merely refers to s 328, but it is submitted that it is still good law.

There should be some evidence of permanent dedication of a highway to the public. The maxim is 'once a highway, always a highway' and that would not apply to some of the ways held to be 'roads'.

Any court before determining whether a way has been dedicated as a highway must take into consideration any map, plan, local history or other document tendered in evidence, attaching such weight thereto as it thinks proper (Highways Act 1980, s 32). Such maps are not evidence of the boundaries of the highway (*Webb* v *Eastleigh Borough Council* (1957) 56 LGR 124). Part III of the Wildlife and Countryside Act 1981 concerns the ascertainment of public rights of way. Under s 56 of the Act certain facts may be established conclusively by the definitive map and statement. Where a footpath is shown, it is conclusive evidence that it was at the relevant date a highway with footpath rights without prejudice to the question of any other rights. Where a bridleway or a road used as a public path is shown, this is conclusive evidence that it was at the relevant date a highway with rights of way on foot and on horseback and leading a horse without prejudice to the question of any other rights such as a right to drive vehicles or other animals. If a 'byway open to all traffic' is shown, that is conclusive evidence that it was at the relevant date a highway with a public right of way for vehicles and all other kinds of traffic. 'Relevant date' means the date specified in the statement or order (s 56(2)). Section 56 reverses *Suffolk CC* v *Mason* [1979] AC 705 on the result of showing a footpath on the definitive plan. Section 53 of the 1981 Act provides for a duty to keep the definitive map and statement under continuous review.

The 1981 Act contains special provisions for roads used as public paths which must be redesignated. Under s 54 the surveying authority as soon as reasonably practicable is to carry out a review of the definitive map and statement as to roads used as public paths and to modify the map and statement as follows. Every road used as a public path is to be shown as a byway open to all traffic, or a bridleway, or a footpath (s 54(2)).

(1) If a public right of way for vehicular traffic has been shown to exist, it is to be shown as a byway open to all traffic.

(2) If (1) does not apply and public bridleway rights have not been shown not to exist, it is to be shown as a bridleway (note the double negative).

(3) If neither (1) nor (2) exists it is to be shown as a footpath (s 54 (3)).

All three (ie byways, bridleways and footpaths) are from the operation of the modification order deemed to be highways maintainable at the public expense and each way which under para 9 of Part III of Sched 3 to the Countryside Act 1968 was so shown shall continue to be so maintainable.

The position and width, if specified, of a road used as a public path and any specified conditions or limitations affecting the public rights of way may be established by the definitive map and statement.

The absence of a footpath, road or bridleway from the definitive map does not mean that there is not a right of way. Again, as indicated in s 56, where limited rights such as a footpath are shown, further rights may be established. It is always possible for evidence to be called as to the existence of a right of way when it is material in the proceedings.

Under s 56(4) a certified copy of or of any part of a definitive map or statement is receivable in evidence and is deemed unless the contrary is shown to be such a copy.

## 1.69 Public access

The definition of 'road' in s 196 of the 1972 Act and s 142(1) of the Road Traffic Regulation Act 1984 includes not only highways but roads other than highways 'to which the public have access'. The first question is whether it is a road, and the second whether the public have access (*Oxford* v *Austin* [1981] RTR 416). A road is a definable way for passage between two points (ibid). The majority of cases as to whether a road comes within this definition turn on the second question of whether the public have access to it.

Assuming that the way in question has the nature of a road (see 'Car parks and forecourts', 1.70) a prosecutor will usually have to prove only two things: first, that the general public, and not merely a special class of the general public, has access to the road; and secondly, that the public has access at least by the tolerance of the owner or proprietor of the road in question (*Deacon* v *AT* (*A Minor*) [1976] RTR 244). The test as to whether the public may be said to have access by the tolerance of the owner was said by Lord Sands in *Harrison* v *Hill* [1932] SC(J) 13, at p 17, to be as follows:

> Any road may be regarded as a road to which the public have access upon which members of the public are to be found who have not obtained access either by overcoming a physical obstruction or in defiance of prohibition express or implied.

This *dictum* of Lord Sands has been approved and applied in *Houghton* v *Scholfield* [1973] RTR 239, *Deacon* v *A T* (*A Minor*) [1976] RTR 244, and *Cox* v *White* (*Note*) [1976] RTR 248. In *Cox* v *White* Lord Widgery CJ, at p 251, stated: 'I think that in ninety-nine cases out of a hundred that direction [ie that of Lord Sands] is all the justices need for current purposes.'

Applying the test of Lord Sands, it is generally a matter of fact and degree whether the public in general have access (*R* v *Shaw* [1974] RTR 225; *Blackmore* v *Chief Constable of Devon and Cornwall* (1984) *The Times*, 6 December).

The public generally must be shown to have access: it is not sufficient to show that a restricted class only of the public has access. Thus in *Deacon* v *AT*, above, the prosecution failed because the prosecutor had not shown that the general public used the road (a housing estate road; there was no proof that it was used by persons other than residents or only visitors to the estate). Lord Clyde, the Lord Justice-General, said in *Harrison* v *Hill*, above, at p 17:

I think that, when the statute speaks of 'the public' in this connection, what is meant is the public generally, and not the special class of members of the public who have occasion for business or social purposes to go to the farmhouse or to any part of the farm itself; were it otherwise, the definition might just as well have included all private roads as well as all public highways.

In *Harrison* v *Hill* a road leading off the public road to a farmhouse was held to be a road to which the public had access. The road had no gate and was maintained by the farmer, who sometimes turned away people using it, but at other times it was used by people with no business at the farm at all.

The test in *Harrison* v *Hill* was again adopted in *Adams* v *Commissioner of Police* [1980] RTR 289 at p 297. The residents of a private estate sought a declaration that the private road, Aberdeen Park, London N5, was a road to which the public had access within the meaning of s 196(1). The purpose of the proceedings was to secure the enforcement of the road traffic laws. There was evidence of substantial use and the judge agreed with the plaintiffs although he did not consider a declaration appropriate. It was emphasised at p 298 that signs must be considered as part of the whole picture. Jupp J also pointed out at p 295 that it did not matter whether the public had access as pedestrians or drivers of motor vehicles as the Act was intended to protect all road users. He quoted *Harrison* v *Hill* and *R* v *Shaw* in support of this principle.

In Scotland, the private drive leading to a house has been held to be a road (*Davidson* v *Adair* 1934 SC (J) 37), but this case will not be followed in England (*Knaggs* v *Elson* (1965) 109 SJ 596) and it was doubted in *Hogg* v *Nicholson* 1968 SLT 265, at p 268. In *Harrison* v *Hill*, a road to a farmhouse from the public road was held to be a road. In *Hogg* v *Nicholson* a road marked 'private road' on an estate served a few houses but was used by police cars, visitors and delivery vans. A sub-post office to which people on the estate and from a village a mile away had access as of right was on the road. It was held to be a road to which the public had access. 'Private' notices are thus not conclusive. Where there were substantial businesses with premises and no restriction on the public in general coming to those businesses, that was sufficient to show that the public did have access; *Blackmore* v *Chief Constable of Devon and Cornwall* (1984) *The Times*, 6 December. *Harrison* v *Hill* was distinguished in *R* v *Beaumont* [1964] Crim LR 665, where an occupation road led to a farm, to a site for 200–250 caravans on that farm, and to a river where anglers went by leave of the farmer and which was also used by picnickers. At the entrance there was an ever-open gate, a 10 mph speed limit sign and two 'trespassers will be prosecuted' signs. It was held that there was no evidence that the general public used the road and the fact that a large number of persons in a particular class of people used it did not make it a road. In *Knaggs* v *Elson* above a cul-de-sac led to thirty-six houses. There was no gate but there were notices reading 'Private Property—No Parking'. There was evidence that a motorist not living there had turned his car round there, but this was held to be insufficient to show that the cul-de-sac was a road used by the public in general. Again in *Kreft* v *Rawcliffe* (1984) *The Times*, 12 May, use by a police constable, tradesmen, postmen, visitors to a wholesalers and (rarely) members of the public were not sufficient to make a lane a road. It was necessary to look at the actual access. If only a restricted class of the public is admitted, it is not a road; if only a restricted class is excluded, it will be a road (cf *R* v *Waters* (1963) 47 Cr App R 149, 4.30). In *Houghton* v *Scholfield* [1973] RTR 239 a justices' finding that a cul-de-sac behind some shops was part of a road was upheld because the public had been found there and there was no physical obstruction or prohibition express or implied.

In *Bugge* v *Taylor* (1940) 104 JP 467 a forecourt of an hotel was private property and the public had no access as of right but there was no obstruction of any kind separating the forecourt from High Street, Sutton, and members of the public had in fact used the forecourt not only to reach the hotel but also as a short cut from High Street to another street. On occasions vehicles had been along it. The forecourt was held to be a road. In *R* v *Shaw*, above, a lane on a council estate frequently used by pedestrians as a short cut between two public roads was held to be a road to which the public had access. The footway as well as the carriageway is included in the definition of 'road' in the Road Traffic Act (*Bryant* v *Marx* (1932) 96 JP 383). But a place is not necessarily a road, even if it is not separated by a wall or rail from the highway, and the forecourt of a shop not separated from the street pavement but used only by the customers and not habitually used by the public was held not to be a road (*Thomas* v *Dando* [1951] 1 All ER 1010). Contrast *White* v *Cubitt* (1930) 94 JP 60 and the other cases discussed at 4.30, as to 'public place'. In *Baxter* v *Middlesex County Council* [1956] Crim LR 561 a forecourt was held on the facts not to be part of the highway.

A cul-de-sac can be a road (*Bass* v *Boynton* [1960] Crim LR 497). Nor does it matter if the road is not made up (ibid). In *Griffin* v *Squires* [1958] 3 All ER 468 on the facts a car park was held not to be a road. But a conviction was upheld where a jury, on a proper direction, had found a market place to be a road (*R* v *Waterfield* (1964) 48 Cr App R 42 is the only report on this point). In *Chapman* v *Parlby* (1964) 62 LGR 150 a road led from the public highway to a Government depot and had a solid white line half-way across it from about half-way along. It was held that the part betweeen the highway and the white line was a road, there being no obstacle or prohibition, express or implied, to any member of the public till he reached the white line, and the road being available to the public.

A road in the docks, to which the general public does not have access, either by right or tolerance of the docks authority, is not a road under the Road Traffic Acts (*Buchanan* v *Motor Insurers' Bureau* [1955] 1 All ER 607). However, see the British Transport Commission Act 1961 and s 160(7) of the 1972 Act (which includes within the definition of road any 'harbour' for the purposes of that section) under 'Dock, airfield and Crown roads', 1.71. A road inside a factory, which only passholders may enter through gates guarded by the police, is not a road to which the public has access (*O'Brien* v *Trafalgar Insurance Co* (1945) 109 JP 107). In *Harrison* v *Co-operative Insurance Co Ltd* (1968) 118 NLJ 910, a road inside factory premises was used by the public to gain access to a weighbridge and to avoid congested highways. A 'private road' sign had been removed some time previously. It was held to be a road to which the public had access. A quayside where the public were free to walk or motor and where there was no notice or hindrance to stop them was held to be a road in *Newcastle Corporation* v *Walton* [1957] Crim LR 479.

### 1.70 Car parks and forecourts

There must be a mode of communication which can be described in ordinary speech as a road and the mere possibility of vehicular access is not enough: one must first find a road and then ask if it is a road to which the public has access (*Purves* v *Muir* 1948 SC(J) 122; *Oxford* v *Austin* [1981] RTR 416). In a case concerning a car park a 'road' was described as a definable right of way for passage between two points (*Oxford* v *Austin*). In *Griffin* v *Squires* [1958] 3 All ER 468 a car park was held not to be a road: the fact that the public have access to it does not of itself make a place a road. Streatfield J said that no one in the ordinary acceptance of the word 'road' would think of a car park as a road. Contrast *R* v *Waterfield* at 1.69 (market place as a 'road'). A courtyard leading off a highway to serve private premises was held not to be a road (*Henderson* v *Bernard* 1955 SLT(Sh) 27), and in *Heath* v *Pearson* [1957] Crim LR 195 a yard serving several houses was held on the facts not to be a road. A drive-in theatre can be a highway 'open to or used by the public' (*Dobell* v *Petrac* [1961] VR 70 (Aus)). A cul-de-sac may be a road (*Bass* v *Boynton* [1960] Crim LR 497). A justices' finding that a cul-de-sac behind some shops adjoining a road leading to a multi-storey car park was part of a road was upheld in *Houghton* v *Scholfield* [1973] RTR 239. See also *Bugge* v *Taylor*, *Thomas* v *Dando* and *Baxter* v *Middlesex County Council* (all 1.69 above) as to forecourts and *Newcastle Corporation* v *Walton* (1.69) as to a quayside. The fact that an area is private land does not prevent it from being part of a road (*Norton* v *Hayward* (1968) 112 SJ 767).

### 1.71–5 Dock, airfield and crown roads

Section 26(1) of the British Transport Commission Act 1961 (as amended by the Transport Act 1962 and the 1972 Act) together with the Port of London Act 1968, s 199, applies various sections of the Road Traffic Act 1972 to 'dock roads' within the jurisdiction of the British Transport Commission or Port of London Authority. 'Dock road' is defined in both Acts as 'any road, pier, wharf, quay, bridge, work or land . . . (not being a road as defined by s 196 of the Road Traffic Act 1972)'. The sections of the Road Traffic Act 1972 which are applied to 'dock roads' of the Docks Board, Waterways Board and Railways Board are ss 1, 2, 3, 5, 17, 18, 19, 21, 22, 23, 24, 25, 29, 30, 84, 99, 143, 159, 161, 162 and 166. In *Botwood* v *Phillips* [1976] RTR 260 it was suggested that the definition could not be read literally as it would then include premises such as the dock superintendent's office. It was suggested that the definition meant those parts of the premises listed in the definition where vehicles from time to time go under mechanical power. *Botwood* v *Phillips* was applied in interpreting a similarly worded provision to s 26(1) in

*R* v *Murray (Gerrard)* [1984] RTR 203. A private car park in the dock area was held to be a place where vehicles were moving around and therefore within the extended definition of a road.

Section 160(7) of the Act of 1972 (inserted by s 14 of the Act of 1974), which relates to the weighing of motor vehicles (see 1.31), defines a road for the purpose of that section as including any land forming part of a harbour or adjacent to a harbour and occupied wholly or partly for the purpose of harbour operations.

The Airports Authority Act 1975, s 13, applies the enactments relating to road traffic, including the lighting and parking of vehicles, and statutory instruments made thereunder, to roads within aerodromes owned or managed by that authority subject to any modifications made by order of the Secretary of State in respect of a particular airport road. Any road or place within an aerodrome in the Metropolitan Police District is deemed to be a street or place under s 35 of the London Hackney Carriage Act 1831. Section 37 of the Civil Aviation Act 1982 applied all enactments relating to road traffic, including lighting and parking, to roads on state and local authority airports subject to any modifications made by order of the Secretary of State in respect of a particular airport road. The state or local authority airport must have been designated for the purpose of s 37 by an order made by the Secretary of State.

A Crown road is defined in s 131 of the Road Traffic Regulation Act 1984 as a 'road, other than a highway, to which the public has access by permission granted by the appropriate Crown authority, or otherwise granted by or on behalf of the Crown'. Generally, therefore, a Crown road would come within the definition of 'road' within the meaning of the Road Traffic Act 1972, s 196, and the Road Traffic Regulation Act 1984, s 142(1). Section 149(1) of the Transport Act 1968 enables the road traffic enactments to be applied by order to Crown roads. The purpose of the section, it is understood, is to enable provisions to be applied to particular Crown roads which, because they might affect the status of the Crown road, could not otherwise be made. It is, therefore, submitted that statutory provisions which apply on roads generally and relate to vehicles and persons and which do not affect the interests of the Crown adversely will apply on Crown roads as they do elsewhere. Thus, it is submitted, a member of the public charged for example with reckless or careless driving or a drink/driving offence cannot escape liability because the offence took place on a Crown road. This view is strengthened by the judgment in *Kellett* v *Daisy* [1977] RTR 396, where it was held that the prosecution do not have to prove that the Act creating the offence (s 3 of the 1972 Act) of careless driving which occurred on a Crown road applies to Crown roads. The question is not whether the road was bound by the Act, but whether the defendant was (which he was) (ibid). It would be different (subject to s 188 of the 1972 Act) if a question arose whether the Act had affected the Crown or a Crown servant (ibid). It would therefore appear that once the Crown road appears to come within the definition of 'road' contained in s 196 (above) any member of the public may be prosecuted.

A statute will necessarily bind the Crown if it is apparent that the Act would be wholly frustrated unless the Crown were bound (*Province of Bombay* v *Bombay Corporation* [1947] AC 58, at p 63). As to the application of road traffic legislation to vehicles and persons in the service of the Crown, see 2.8.

## 'To cause', 'to permit', 'to use'

### 1.76 Meaning

'One may obtain some help from cases in which the construction of similar words in other statutes has had to be considered, but particular care must be taken' (per Edmund Davies LJ in *Sopp* v *Long* [1970] 1 QB 518, at p 524). The truth of this dictum is particularly apparent when one has to consider the meaning of the phrases 'to cause', 'to permit' and 'to use'. Not only has one to construe words in the context of the statute in which they appear but one may have to consider the mischief which the statutory provision is aimed at preventing.

It will be seen that where the statutory provisions create offences by reason of the words 'using', 'causing' or 'permitting to be used' appearing in juxtaposition, as for example in s 40(5)(*b*) of the 1972 Act (contravention of Construction and Use Regulations and the Road Vehicles Lighting Regulations) and ss 44 (test certificates) and 143 (third-party insurance) of the same Act, the words are construed differently where all three phrases do not appear together, eg 'uses or keeps' in s 8 of the Vehicles (Excise) Act 1971 (see 12.2), and 'causes to be kept' in s 98 of the Transport Act 1968 (drivers' records: see 14.61). Where these three phrases are used in juxtaposition, 'to cause' or 'to permit' generally require the prosecution to prove mens rea, while the words 'to use' will create an offence of absolute liability. Both the employer and the employee-driver may be convicted of 'using' the contravening vehicle if it is used on the employer's business. Where the prosecution is in doubt as to whether a corporate defendant should be charged with 'causing' or 'permitting' on the one hand or 'using' on the other, it should lay charges in the alternative (*Ross Hillman Ltd* v *Bond* [1974] RTR 279, at pp 285 and 290). Similarly, as to Scotland see *Smith of Maddiston Ltd* v *Macnab* 1975 SLT 86, (1.78).

In *Ferrymasters Ltd* v *Adams* [1980] Crim LR 187 (see 1.78) the report states the defendant was charged with 'causing or permitting' contrary to s 84(2) of the 1972 Act, as amended. The report is erroneous and in fact the defendant company were charged with 'permitting' only.

### 1.77 'To cause'

The offence of 'causing' unlawful use requires proof of mens rea in knowledge of the facts rendering the user unlawful: in the case of a limited company such knowledge has to be of someone exercising a directing mind over the company's affairs (*James & Son Ltd* v *Smee* [1955] 1 QB 78; *Ross Hillman Ltd* v *Bond* [1974] RTR 279).

In *Ross Hillman Ltd* v *Bond*, in which most of the cases cited in the seventh edition of this book were reviewed, the defendant company was summoned for 'causing' one of its vehicles to be used on a road with excess rear axle weight contrary to s 40(5)(*b*) of the 1972 Act. Those responsible for the direction of the company's affairs did not know of the overloading of the vehicle. Following *James & Son Ltd* v *Smee* above it was held that where the statute makes it an offence to 'cause' or 'permit' a contravening vehicle to be used on a road as well as the offence of actually 'using' the vehicle, the words 'cause' or 'permit' require proof of mens rea on the part of the defendant and in the case of a corporate defendant, following *Hill & Sons (Botley & Denmead) Ltd* v *Hampshire Chief Constable* [1972] RTR 29, such guilty knowledge must be knowledge of someone exercising a directing mind over the company's affairs. It was pointed out in *Ross Hillman* that *F Austin (Leyton) Ltd* v *East* [1961] Crim LR 119 should not be cited as authority that a company can be convicted of unlawfully causing a motor vehicle to be used in a dangerous condition without proof of mens rea as the point in issue was never argued in that case.

'To cause' involves some express or positive mandate from the person 'causing' to the other person, or some authority from the former to the latter, arising in the circumstances of the case (*McLeod* v *Buchanan* [1940] 2 All ER 179, at p 187). The general manager of five depots, at each of which there is a vehicle superintendent, is not guilty of causing a vehicle to be on a road in a dangerous condition where he has no knowledge that it is on the road (*Rushton* v *Martin* [1952] WN 258). In *Shave* v *Rosner* [1954] 2 All ER 280 a van was left in a garage for repairs but the garage staff negligently failed to tighten hub nuts on a wheel. The owner of the van then drove the van on the road with the wheel in this defective condition. It was held that the garage proprietor was not guilty of causing the van to be used in a defective condition, as the term 'cause' involves some degree of control and direction. Once he had delivered the van to its owner, he ceased to have control and dominion over it and had done nothing which was the active cause of the owner driving it on the road. The owner of a vehicle causes it to be used when he drives it himself as well as when it is driven by another person on his orders (*Baker* v *Chapman* [1963] 61 LGR 527). Towing a motor vehicle is causing it to be used (*Milstead* v *Sexton* [1964] Crim LR 474).

Where, however, the statute makes it an offence only to 'cause or permit' the contravention, without the use of the word 'use', an offence of absolute liability without proof of mens rea may be created. Reference was made in *Mounsey* v *Campbell* [1983] RTR 36 to two river pollution cases on the meaning of causing—*Price* v *Cromack* [1975] 2 All ER 113 and a House of Lords case, *Alphacell Ltd* v *Woodward* [1972] 2 All ER 475. Even where 'causing' does not import mens rea it was held in *Price* v *Cromack* that it requires some positive act and not merely a passive looking on.

In another pollution case, *FJH Wrothwell Ltd* v *Yorkshire Water Authority* [1984] Crim LR 43, the Divisional Court emphasised that 'cause' was to be given its ordinary commonsense meaning. The director of the defendant company was held to have caused the pollution in the stream when he deliberately poured the toxic material into drains even though he believed that the drains would carry the material to the public sewerage works and not to the stream. The case again shows that although a positive act is required, mens rea may not be necessary.

In *Mounsey* v *Campbell* the defendant parked his van right up against the bumper of a car. The car could have been moved at that time but it was subsequently penned in by a car parked two feet behind. The defendant refused to move his van and was convicted of causing unnecessary obstruction. He argued that he should have been charged with 'permitting' as he had not caused the unnecessary obstruction originally. It was held that he had been rightly convicted. On the facts the van caused an obstruction from the moment it was first parked. There was a positive act by the defendant. Ormrod J said at p 41 'His subsequent refusals to move it could just as well be described as causing an unnecessary obstruction because he could have removed it. It does not seem to me to be properly described, in those circumstances, as "permitted".'

Where the statute requires an employer or other person 'to cause' something to be done, it may be also held that an absolute offence without proof of mens rea is created. An employer whose driver keeps incorrect records is guilty of failing to cause correct records to be kept, though he had no chance of correcting the entries (*Cox* v *Sidery* (1935) 24 Traff Cas 69). An employer whose driver enters his records in advance is guilty of failing to cause current records to be kept (*Nelson* v *Coventry Swaging Co* (1936) 25 Traff Cas 68). These cases are now modified by s 98(4) of the Transport Act 1968 (see 14.63), which allows a defence to an employer charged with failing to cause records to be kept where he can prove he gave proper instructions to the driver and took reasonable steps to secure his instructions were carried out. Section 84(2) of the 1972 Act makes it an offence 'to cause or permit' an unlicensed driver to drive (see *Ferrymaster Ltd* v *Adams*, 1.78).

Where the owner of a vehicle is not the employer of the driver as, for example, where the owner hires out a defective vehicle, the owner cannot be said to be 'using' the vehicle. In such a case, however, the owner may be charged with 'causing' or 'permitting' and may be convicted on proof of mens rea (see *Crawford* v *Haughton*, 1.79), Similarly, where a vehicle is owned by a partnership, a partner who is not the driver cannot be convicted of using (see *Garrett* v *Hooper*, 1.79), but on proof of mens rea he may be convicted, it is submitted, of 'causing' or 'permitting' the unlawful use. If uncertain as to whether to charge 'causing' or 'permitting' on the one hand or 'using' on the other, prosecutors should prefer alternative charges (*Ross Hillman Ltd* v *Bond* above). This advice was repeated in *R* v *Newcastle JJ, ex parte Bryce* [1976] RTR 325.

## 1.78 'To permit'

*Meaning*

'To permit' is a vaguer term than 'to cause'. It may denote an express permission, general or particular, as distinguished from a mandate. The other person is not told to use the vehicle in a particular way, but he is told that he may do so if he desires. The word also includes cases in which permission is merely inferred. If the other person is given the control of the vehicle, permission may be inferred if the vehicle is left at the other person's disposal in such circumstances as to carry with it a reasonable implication of a discretion or liberty to use it in the manner in which it was used (*McLeod* v *Buchanan* [1940] 2 All ER 179, at p 187). The statement in *Goodbarne* v *Buck* [1940] 1 All ER 613, at p 616, that the only person who can permit the use of a car, in that he can forbid another person to use it, is the owner, is incorrect: any person who has control on the owner's behalf, eg a chauffeur or a manager of a company, can permit its use (*Lloyd* v *Singleton* [1953] 1 All ER 291; *Morris* v *Williams* (1952) 50 LGR 308). Permission is not necessarily revoked by the grantor's death (*Kelly* v *Cornhill Insurance Co* [1946] 1 All ER 321, HL).

'Permitting' means getting someone else to do something and it is wrong to charge a man with permitting himself to do something (*Waddell* v *Winter* (1967) 202 EG 1225, a planning case; *Keene* v *Muncaster* [1980] RTR 377). In *Keene* v *Muncaster* [1980] RTR 377 Lord Lane CJ said that the ordinary use of the word 'permit' in what is now reg 123 of the Motor Vehicles (Construction and Use) Regulations 1978 plainly envisages that the person requesting permission should request it from another and that a policeman could not therefore give himself permission. A person cannot be said to have permitted a vehicle to be used subject to an express prior condition unless and until that condition is complied with: permission given subject to such a condition which is unfulfilled is no permission (*Newbury* v *Davis* [1974] RTR 367).

The following propositions as to what constitutes 'permitting' are submitted:

(1) The context of the statutory provisions requires examination together with the mischief at which the prohibition is aimed. This may result in stricter liability under some statutory provisions than others, eg for insurance offences.

(2) A distinction should normally be drawn between knowledge of the use of the vehicle and knowledge of the unlawfulness of its use. Knowledge of the former kind is an essential ingredient of permitting, knowledge of the latter kind may or may not be an essential ingredient.

(3) Normally such knowledge of the unlawfulness of the vehicle's use is required to be proved. 'Permitting to be used' in contradistinction to 'using' imports mens rea. *Aliter* in the case of insurance offences, where knowledge that the vehicle's use was uninsured does not have to be proved.

(4) Where mens rea is an essential element of the offence of permitting, a limited company can only be convicted if the mens rea can be imputed to the 'brains' rather than 'hands' of the company.

(5) Mens rea can consist not only of actual knowledge but also of constructive knowledge in the sense that the person concerned wilfully shuts his eyes to the obvious or deliberately refrains from making proper inquiry. Possibly, a failure on the part of an employee can be 'permitting' on the part of the employer if it can be shown that the employer left duties to the employee without adequate supervision and in the knowledge that the employee would be employed on work for which he was unskilled.

(6) A prosecutor who is uncertain of being able to prove mens rea may prefer alternative charges of 'causing' or 'permitting' or 'using' (*Ross Hillman Ltd* v *Bond* at 1.77, *R* v *Newcastle JJ, ex parte Bryce* [1976] RTR 325). A sum-

mons for 'permitting' may be amended to a charge of 'using' even though the six-month period for the laying of an information imposed by s 127 of the Magistrates' Courts Act 1980 has expired (see *R* v *Newcastle JJ, ex parte Bryce*, above; see also 2.21). 'Using' does not, generally, require proof of mens rea (see 1.79 and *Green* v *Burnett* and *Ross Hillman Ltd* v *Bond*), but only the employer or employee driver can be convicted and the former may be appropriate for owners who are not the driver's employers (see *Carmichael & Sons Ltd* v *Cottle* and *Crawford* v *Haughton*, 1.79).

*Cases*

A leading case on 'permitting' is *James* v *Smee* [1954] 3 All ER 273. A vehicle belonging to a company had been sent on the road by the company in good condition but, while away from the control of any of the responsible officers of the company, the brakes became defective through the negligence of the vehicle's crew (also company employees) in coupling up the trailer. It was held that the company was not guilty of 'permitting' the use of the vehicle with defective brakes contrary to the Construction and Use Regulations, as there was no evidence of any permission *by a responsible officer*, and that the position would be the same whether the owner was a company or an individual. It must be proved that some person for whose criminal act the owner is responsible permitted it, said the court, but this statement, it seems, does not extend to every servant (cf *John Henshall (Quarries) Ltd* v *Harvey* [1965] 1 All ER 725, where a company was held not guilty of aiding and abetting where the illegal action had been done by a minor servant). Knowledge to constitute permitting can include shutting one's eyes (*semble*, in the case of a company, the eyes of responsible officers) to the obvious or allowing a servant to do something in circumstances where a contravention is likely, not caring whether it takes place or not (*James* v *Smee*, above, at p 278). *Goldsmith* v *Deaken* below, *Prosser* v *Richings* (1936) 100 JP 390 and *Churchill* v *Norris* (1938) 158 LT 255 were all cited in support of the latter view. In *Grays Haulage Co Ltd* v *Arnold* [1966] 1 All ER 896, it was said that the essence of permitting the commission of an offence is knowledge and, where there was no question of actual knowledge in the defendants, knowledge could not be imputed to them in the absence of prima facie evidence from which it could be said that they had shut their eyes to the obvious or had allowed something to go on not caring whether an offence was committed or not. Even where there has been recklessness in a member of the staff in allowing a vehicle to go on the road in a defective condition, the employing company may not be liable even though it has handed over responsibility to that person: the company is not criminally liable in the absence of knowledge of the facts constituting the offence for the failure of a servant to whom it has delegated a task, for the servant is not 'the brains of the company' and his knowledge cannot be imputed to a director (*Magna Plant Ltd* v *Mitchell* (1966) 110 SJ 349). This case together with *James* v *Smee* and *Grays Haulage Co Ltd* v *Arnold* (both above) were all considered in *Hill & Sons (Botley & Denmead) Ltd* v *Hampshire Chief Constable* [1972] RTR 29. The defendant company was convicted of permitting one of its haulage vehicles to be used with inefficient brakes. Quarter sessions upheld the conviction on the grounds that the managing director was reckless in not ensuring that the vehicle was lubricated more frequently than once every four weeks and also in not ensuring that the four-weekly lubrications were properly carried out. The company's conviction was set aside on the grounds that there was nothing to justify quarter sessions' finding that a four-week interval for lubrication was reckless, nor was it reckless (although it might be negligent) for the managing director not to check up on the foreman fitter, a man of long experience, who was responsible for overseeing the lubrication. Lord Widgery CJ expressly affirmed *Magna Plant Ltd* v *Mitchell*, above, in that it requires one to look at the minds of those officers of the company who can be described as its 'brains' rather than 'hands' and that if an employee of the company is shown to be reckless it is not sufficient to impute knowledge of that recklessness unless that person is one who can be fairly described as the 'brains' of the company.

It seems that, to make a company liable for permitting, a member of the directing staff should generally know what is happening, but it is submitted that a company may still be liable for permitting if it has delegated, through its directors, duties relating to vehicle maintenance etc to a subordinate employee, whom it knows to be unskilled and uninstructed in those duties, eg allowing a junior typist to say if a lorry shall go on the road. In such a case could it not be said that 'the brains' of the company were reckless in so doing? In *Dixon Bool Transport Ltd* v *Forsyth* [1967] Crim LR 52, a conviction for permitting was upheld where the company knew that its drivers had been breaking the law by driving for excessive periods and had not taken steps to remedy this or to acquaint them with the law. *Browning* v *Watson* [1953] 2 All ER 775 is distinguishable. There a company was guilty of permitting a breach of the law on a motor-coach in the charge of a driver because the company failed to take adequate precautions by instructing its staff by other means to see that the law was not broken. The decision in *Hutchings* v *Giles* [1955] Crim LR 784 is not correctly reported. The prosecution need not prove actual knowledge and it may suffice if constructive knowledge is shown, eg shutting one's eyes to the obvious (*Wilson* v *Bird* (1962) 106 SJ 880, where there was evidence of actual knowledge). Knowledge is an essential element in permitting and knowledge is not imputed by mere negligence but by something more, such as recklessly sending out a car not caring what would happen (*Fransman* v *Sexton* [1965] Crim LR 556). In that case the defendant owner had previously hired his car to a mechanical engineer who told him, on returning it, that the brakes had been tested and were operating efficiently. In fact they were not and it was held that in those circumstances the owner was not negligent in failing to take the only steps which would have revealed the defects.

An employer charged with permitting his driver to drive for an excessive period contrary to s 73 of the 1960 Act (now repealed) may be guilty although the driver may have had orders from him not to drive for a longer period than the law allows (*Sidcup Building Estates* v *Sidery* (1936) 24 Traff Cas 164; *Forsyth* v *Phillips* (1964) 108 SJ 36; see *Grays Haulage Co* v *Arnold* [1966] 1 All ER 896, at p 898H). In the first two cases the defendant had left to his staff, or his wife, the duty of collecting from the drivers their log books which showed that they had been driving excessive hours and had thus shut his eyes, through his responsible officers, to their breaches of the law. Compare *Griffiths* v *Studebakers* [1924] 1 KB 102 (see 1.79), where the master was convicted of using, though the driver had disobeyed his orders. Sections 96(11B) and 98(4) of the Transport Act 1968 now provide special statutory defences for employers and others charged with breaches of the law relating to drivers' hours and keeping records.

In *Macdonald* v *Wilmae Concrete Co* 1954 SLT (Sh) 33, a company was held not guilty of causing and permitting use with defective brakes when no responsible official knew of the defect.

Following *Ross Hillman*, 1.77, the Scottish High Court of Justiciary held that knowledge was essential for a company to be convicted of 'causing' or 'permitting' the use of a vehicle contrary to s 40 of the 1972 Act (*Smith of Maddiston Ltd* v *Macnab* 1975 SLT 86). Again, where auctioneers had sold a car and, unknown to them, their servants had given a bogus cover note to the buyer, who then drove the car uninsured, the auctioneers did not cause or permit such use by him (*Watkins* v *O'Shaughnessy* [1939] 1 All ER 385). Assistance in a fraud on an insurance company by the car owner does not necessarily render the aider liable for permitting uninsured use (*Goodbarne* v *Buck* [1940] 1 All ER 613).

In some contexts, eg permitting a vehicle to be used without third-party insurance, the statute imposes an absolute prohibition without proof of mens rea and it suffices to convict the defendant if he is shown to have permitted use, irrespective of whether he knew if the vehicle was insured or not (*Tapsell* v *Maslen* [1976] Crim LR 53, following *Lyons* v *May* [1948] 2 All ER 1062; *Morris* v *Williams*, see in 'Meaning', above. These cases were not cited to or apparently considered by the Divisional Court in *Davies* v *Warne* [1973] RTR 217 where, nevertheless, a conviction of permitting the use of an uninsured vehicle was upheld where both the user and permitter genuinely and reasonably believed that the user's use of the vehicle was covered by insurance.

A person who permits another to use his vehicle on the express condition that the user first insures the vehicle cannot be convicted of the offence of permitting because he has not permitted the vehicle to be used while uninsured: permission given subject to a condition which was unfulfilled is no permission (*Newbury* v *Davis* [1974] RTR 367). *Newbury* v *Davis* was followed and applied in *Baugh* v *Crago* [1975] RTR 453. The defendant, believing him to hold a driving licence, permitted another person to drive his vehicle which was insured for any driver on condition that the driver held a driving licence. The justices were directed to convict: an honest, albeit mistaken, belief that the driver had a licence is no defence.The defendant had not made it a condition of his allowing the vehicle's use by the driver that he was the holder of a licence.

The offence under s 84(2) of the 1972 Act used to be to 'employ' an unlicensed driver and it was generally held to be an absolute offence. The Road Traffic (Drivers' Ages and Hours of Work) Act 1976 substituted the words 'cause or permit' for the word 'employ'. In *Ferrymasters Ltd* v *Adams* [1980] Crim LR 187 the conviction of the employer for 'permitting' his employee driver to drive unlicensed was upheld on the ground that the employer had failed to adopt any system with a view to ensuring that reasonable checks on the employees' driving licences were made and had permitted him to drive, following *Baugh* v *Crago*. (For a criticism of the case see [1980] Crim LR 187; in addition, see 11.5.)

In *Sheldon Deliveries Ltd* v *Willis* [1972] RTR 217 a car delivery firm was held not to have permitted the uninsured use of a car when its delivery driver, contrary to his express instructions, used it on a Sunday and without trade plates. Although the judgments imply that the car delivery firm should not be convicted because knowledge of the fact that the vehicle was uninsured could not be imputed to the company, it was pointed out in *Newbury* v *Davis* above, at p 371, that the true ratio decidendi in *Sheldon's* case was lack of knowledge that the vehicle was to be used on the journey in question. Knowledge that a vehicle is used in contravention of the statute is a different matter from knowledge that a vehicle is to be used. The latter is an essential ingredient of permission (ibid).

The court ought to look at the object of the statute and see whether the principal might be held responsible for the conduct of his agent, though himself unaware of the statute being infringed. If the principal in effect hires out his coach, putting his servant in charge of it and at least leaving it to chance whether it would be used as a stage carriage or not, he permits it to be used as a stage carriage without a licence (*Goldsmith* v *Deakin* (1933) 98 JP 4; *Clydebank Co-operative Society* v *Binnie* 1937 SC(J) 17); *a fortiori* where he has been warned that it may be so used (*Osborne* v *Richards* (1933) 96 JP 377; *Webb* v *Maidstone, etc Services* (1934) 78 SJ 336). *Browning* v *Watson* above is in accord with these cases as, there, no adequate precautions in instructing the staff or in seeing that the law was obeyed had been taken. But where the owner has no reason to know that his vehicle may be used without the necessary licence, or there are no circumstances which ought either to have aroused his suspicion or put him on his guard, he is not guilty of permitting use without a licence for express carriages (*Newell* v *Cook* [1936] 2 All ER 203). Nor is he guilty of permitting use as a stage carriage if he does not know that such use is proposed and does not deliberately refrain from making inquiries or shut his eyes to the obvious (*Evans* v *Dell* [1973] 1 All ER 349). An owner may be liable for permitting overcrowding on a bus when he has appointed a young and inexperienced conductor and has given him no instructions (cf *Gough* v *Rees* (1929) 94 JP 53), provided that the regulations justify the use of the word 'permit' in the context.

In *Ross Hillman Ltd* v *Bond*, 1.77 above, the defendant company could not be convicted of 'causing' its vehicle to be used with excess axle weight because the prosecution was unable to prove guilty knowledge on the part of an officer responsible for directing the company's business. It was said that such mens rea was a necessary ingredient both of the offence of 'causing' and of 'permitting'. *Ross Hillman* was followed and applied in *P Lowery & Sons* v *Wark* [1975] RTR 45 where a conviction (under s 40) of the defendant company for 'permitting' their vehicle to be used with a dangerously insecure load was set aside where there was no proof of mens rea on behalf of a person controlling the company.

A corporation can permit an offence for which disqualification is a punishment though not disqualifiable itself (*Briggs* v *Gibson's Bakery* [1948] NI 165).

While a person may be guilty of permitting if he fails to take proper steps to prevent something, he is not guilty if he merely fails to take unreasonable steps to prevent it (*Test Valley Investments Ltd* v *Tanner* [1964] Crim LR 62, a case under another Act).

A person supervising a learner driver does not necessarily permit the driving. Where the learner was also the owner of the vehicle, the supervisor was not in a position to forbid the use of the vehicle to the owner (*Thompson* v *Lodwick* [1983] RTR 76). A conviction for permitting no insurance was quashed. While valuable, the test adopted in that case of forbidding the use is a negative one and may not therefore supply an answer in every case.

### 1.79–80 'To use'

*Meaning*

Many charges are brought for offences of 'using' a motor vehicle without third-party insurance or in breach of the Motor Vehicles (Construction and Use) Regulations 1978. The term in such cases usually imports absolute liability (unless there is some special statutory defence such as that given by s 143(2) of the Road Traffic Act 1972 for employees using their master's vehicle in ignorance of the lack of insurance cover) and those responsible for the use of the vehicle can be prosecuted, eg the driver and his employer, if the journey was made on the employer's business. An employer may thus find himself charged with an offence of which he himself was quite ignorant and which may have been committed hundreds of miles from his office. It was said in *Hart* v *Bex* [1957] Crim LR 622, however, where a defect in a braking system (a case of absolute liability) arose unexpectedly and suddenly and the driver was not under a duty to inspect the brakes, that the police should refrain from prosecuting him and, if he was charged, he should be given an absolute discharge. This advice from the High Court, it is submitted, should be considered by all prosecutors and defending advocates in cases where the driver or the owner of the vehicle appears to be morally guiltless and has not been guilty of negligence in relation to the causes of the defect or in carrying on after it has developed.

The following propositions are submitted:

(1) Absolute liability for use is imposed by certain statutes and regulations, eg use without third-party insurance or without most licences or contrary to most of the Construction and Use Regulations, and the fact that the person using is quite unaware of the breach of the law and has not been negligent is immaterial. It is a question of construction in each case whether absolute liability is imposed. (Note the paragraph above as to uninsured employees. There is also a special defence as to speedometers: see 8.19.)

(2) A master may be liable for use by his servant on the master's business and, if the statute or regulation imposes an absolute prohibition, lack of knowledge or of negligence on the master's part is no defence, though it may be mitigation. Again, it is a question of construction whether absolute liability for his employee's acts is imposed on the employer. In *Strutt* v *Clift*

(1911) 74 JP 471 a master entrusted a van to his servant to use legally on his (the master's) business, but the servant illegally used it for his own pleasure. The master was held liable in a Revenue prosecution. On the other hand, in *Phelon* v *Keel* (1914) 78 JP 247 'use' in the then regulations relating to trade plates was held to mean use by or on behalf of the holder and not unauthorised use by a trespasser. It is suggested that the very strict liability laid down in *Strutt* v *Clift* does not necessarily apply in road traffic cases and that it will often be a question of fact whether an employee's deviation from his duty and instructions is sufficiently gross to show that the use of a vehicle was no longer on the employer's business (but see *Richardson* v *Baker* [1976] RTR 56).

(3) Where the statute creates the offence of 'causing' or 'permitting' as well as 'using', only the driver, a person in the vehicle controlling the driver, a person engaged in a joint enterprise with the driver and the driver's employer, while it is being used on the employer's business, 'use' it. An aider and abettor, and an accessory before the fact, should be charged with 'permitting' or 'causing'. Where the only offence is 'using' and there is no offence of 'causing' or 'permitting', as in the Vehicles (Excise) Act 1971, then it may be possible for the owner of a vehicle to be charged with using if he caused it to be used by another on his behalf.

(4) Where an employee is driving a vehicle on behalf of a partnership it is normally being used by all the partners (*Passmoor* v *Gibbons* [1978] Crim LR 498), but it is being used otherwise if it is driven by one of the partners, because one partner is not the employer or employee of another partner (*Garrett* v *Hooper* [1973] RTR 1; *Bennett* v *Richardson* [1981] RTR 358).

(5) Where a vehicle and the vehicle's driver is hired out, the person hiring out the vehicle will not normally be held to be 'using' the vehicle (although he may be 'causing' or 'permitting' it to be used) because he is not the employer of the driver (see *Mickleborough* v *BRS (Contracts) Ltd* [1977] RTR 389 and other cases below).

(6) The cases indicate that a person *driving* a vehicle will normally be *using* it. A person may *use* it by having custody or control of it without *driving* it. There may however be a distinction between 'use' and 'driving' as was emphasised in *Samuelson* v *National Insurance and Guarantee Corporation Ltd* [1984] 3 All ER 107 (a civil case). The plaintiff was covered for the use of the vehicle whilst in the custody or control of a member of the motor trade for its upkeep or repair. He was not covered for driving by another person. It was held that he was not covered under the policy when the car was stolen whilst being driven by the motor trade repairer to buy spares.

*Cases*

A person does not use a motor vehicle under s 143 (insurance) of the 1972 Act unless there is an element of controlling, managing or operating the vehicle as a vehicle (cited with approval in *Nichol* v *Leach* [1972] RTR 476); nor does a passenger who is ignorant of the lack of insurance cover and does not procure the making of a journey (*D* v *Parsons* [1960] 2 All ER 493), nor a person sitting in the driving seat, drunk, when the car is stationary and the ignition-key and insurance are held by the owner also present in the car

(*Fisher* v *Kearton* (1964) 108 SJ 258). Passengers have, however, in two insurance cases, been held to be using a motor vehicle when they procured the journey (*Cobb* v *Williams* [1973] RTR 113) or engaged in a joint enterprise (*Leathley* v *Tatton* [1980] RTR 21). These cases should be compared with the situation where the passenger has no power of control over the driver and is therefore not using the vehicle (see further 10.16–17). See also *Hamilton* v *Blair and Meechan*; *Windle* v *Dunning & Son Ltd*; *Carmichael & Sons* v *Cottle*; *Crawford* v *Haughton*; and *Cobb* v *Williams* (all below).

A driver of a vehicle may be convicted of using it with his load improperly secured, contrary to the Construction and Use Regulations, although the loading was done under the supervision of the hirer's servant and the driver took no part in it (*Gifford* v *Whittaker* 1942 1 All ER 604). A driver who ought to have known his brakes were defective was also convicted of using his vehicle with defective brakes (*Adair* v *Donaldson* 1935 SC(J) 23). A trade licence issued to a company forbade the carrying of an excessive number of passengers in a vehicle. The company drew its drivers' attention to the licence and ordered them to observe that term. A car driven by an employee carried an excessive number of passengers. The company was convicted of using it and it was said that it would make no difference if the employer had been an individual (*Griffiths* v *Studebakers* [1924] 1 KB 102). However, where a vehicle was used without licence as an express carriage and the illegality arose through the action of some people who were not the vehicle owner's servants or agents, which action was unknown to him, he should not be convicted of using: a person is not guilty if he does an act lawful in itself but which has become unlawful, unbeknown to him, through the actions of such people (*Reynolds* v *Austin* [1951] 1 All ER 606).

A leading case on 'using' is *Green* v *Burnett* [1954] 3 All ER 273. In this case, an employee used a vehicle with defective brakes. There was some evidence of negligence by the owner's servant in maintaining the brakes but the owner had given him general instructions to take the vehicle to motor engineers whenever he felt it needed maintenance or some defect manifested itself. The vehicle was used on the owner's business and it was held that he (the owner) was guilty of 'using', as the Construction and Use Regulations (with a few exceptions) impose an absolute prohibition on use in breach of them, although the owner was quite unaware of the defect. Liability for contravention of an absolute prohibition depends on the fact of contravention and not upon the intention to contravene. Neither mens rea in its true sense of importing a blameworthy mind nor negligence in the form of a failure to take reasonable steps to prevent the offence is relevant save on the question of punishment.

For the purposes of Part V of the Transport Act 1968 (carriage of goods by road, operators' licences etc), the driver of a vehicle if he owns it or possesses it under a loan or hire-purchase agreement is deemed to use the vehicle, and in any other case the person whose servant or agent the driver is is the user of the vehicle (Transport Act 1968, s 92(2)). This is, it is submitted, essentially a question of fact. Thus where justices found as a fact that a driver who had been provided for a haulage company by the defendant employment agency was employed by the haulage company and not by the employment agency, the justices' decision of fact could not be impugned (*Alderton* v *Richard Burgon Associates Ltd* [1974] RTR 422). Nor was the justices' finding reversed when they came to an opposite conclusion, viz that an employment agency employed the driver and not the company to whom the driver was supplied (*Howard* v *G T Jones & Co Ltd* [1975] RTR 150).

An owner who hired a vehicle out was held not to be a user of it whilst the hirer had it, and the hirer also, when not in the vehicle, was held not to be using it (*Hamilton* v *Blair and Meechan* 1962 SLT 69). It was agreed that passengers, including possibly the hirer, were not users in breach of what is now the Public Passenger Vehicles Act 1981. In *Windle* v *Dunning & Son Ltd* [1968] 2 All ER 46, the defendants hired vehicles from a firm of haulage contractors; the drivers, although they spent a lot of time on the defendant's work, were paid by the contractors, and the defendant's servants loaded the vehicles and directed the drivers where to go. The defendant's servants sent them out with overloaded vehicles and it was held that only the drivers and not the defendants were using them as opposed to causing them to be used. 'Using' might also cover, it was said, an employer where the driver was about that employer's business.

Where works contractors hired a vehicle plus driver from another company, it was held that the contractors could not be said to be 'using' the vehicle which was in contravention of various Construction and Use Regulations, Lighting Regulations and s 22 of the Vehicles (Excise) Act 1971 (*Balfour Beatty & Co Ltd* v *Grindley* [1975] RTR 156). The defendant company could have been convicted of causing or permitting the use of the vehicle in contravention of the Construction and Use Regulations (ibid). Similarly it was held in *Howard* v *G T Jones & Co Ltd* (above) a company could not be held to be 'using' a motor vehicle contravening a construction and use regulation if the driver was not employed by the company charged with 'using'. In *Mickleborough* v *BRS (Contracts) Ltd* [1977] RTR 389, *Hamilton* v *Blair and Meechan*, above, was distinguished firstly on the grounds that it related to a different provision relating to express carriages and secondly that there was no evidence in that case that the driver was the employee of the owner defendant. In *Mickleborough* the owner was held responsible because the driver was acting in the course of his employer's business, namely that of hiring out motor lorries. The test was stated by Boreham J to be as follows:

> ['Using'] applies on the authorities to the driver of the vehicle. It ['using'] applies to the owner of the vehicle provided, first, the driver is employed under a contract of service, in the other words there is a relationship of master and servant between the owner and the driver; and secondly, that at the material time the driver was driving on his employer's business.

Where an owner lends his car to a friend on condition that he renews the licence when it expires, the owner does not use the car after expiry of the licence (*Abercromby* v *Morris* (1932) 96 JP 392). It is doubtful, indeed, if a person who lends his car to a friend for social purposes, abandoning all control, uses it at all but, if he knows of defects, he might be liable for aiding and abetting the friend. An unreported case (*Stone* v *Horton* (1935)) is mentioned at 113 JP Jo 674, however, in which an owner was held to be 'using' where he had hired or lent his car to a customer. Apparently, this case was under what is now the Vehicles (Excise) Act and the courts often take a stricter view in Revenue prosecutions than they do in criminal cases (cf *Strutt* v *Clift* (1911) 74 JP 471, and see *Hamilton* v *Blair and Meechan*, above). A further distinction between 'using' a vehicle without a licence contrary to the Vehicles (Excise) Act and 'using' a vehicle without insurance (s 143) or in contravention of a Construction and Use Regulation (s 40(5)) is that there is no offence of 'causing' or 'permitting' the use of an untaxed vehicle contrary to s 8 of the Vehicles (Excise) Act (see *Carmichael & Sons* v *Cottle* and *Crawford* v *Haughton*, below). A garage company which lent a car to a customer while his car was being repaired was not guilty of using the lent car when he later drove it with defective tyres, *semble*, even though they may have been defective when the company handed it over (*L F Dove Ltd* v *Tarvin* (1964) 108 SJ 404). See also *Strutt* v *Clift* and *Phelon* v *Keel* (1914) 78 JP 247 as to use without authority.

A vehicle is in use when it is stationary on a road for loading or unloading (*Andrews* v *Kershaw* [1951] 2 All ER 764) and is in use and requires to be insured even where it has been left immobile with an engine which does not work and without petrol or battery, so long as it can be moved, eg by pushing or releasing the brake (*Elliott* v *Grey* [1959] 3 All ER 733). Where a vehicle had been left in a gateway of a rural road (but, *semble*, on the road) for so long that the green grass grew all around, it was held that it was still used on the road for insurance and test certificate purposes (*Another* v *Howard*, JP Jo Supp, 11 June 1968). A person who had abandoned a car in a lay-by 'uses' it and requires a policy of insurance (*Williams* v *Jones* (1969) WLR, 7 March, 'Recent Points'). It might be that user in breach of other provisions would not necessarily be established in like circumstances. Also, the court said in *Another* v *Howard* that their finding might be otherwise if the car was totally immobilised by removal of its wheels, ie that the vehicle might have ceased to be a 'motor vehicle', and, indeed, in *Hewer* v *Cutler* [1974] RTR 155, for these reasons *Elliott* v *Grey* was not applied in a case of 'using' a motor vehicle without a current test certificate contrary to s 44 of the 1972 Act: it was held that a totally immobilised vehicle left on a road could not be said to be 'used' for the purposes of s 44. It was doubted, *obiter*, whether the test as to whether a vehicle is 'used' is the same in s 44 as in s 143: in *Elliott* v *Grey* it was said that 'use' for the purpose of s 143 was equivalent to 'have the use of the vehicle on the road'. But in *Eden* v *Mitchell* [1975] RTR 425, a car had two defective tyres and was left parked on a road. The owner did not intend to drive it while it had two defective tyres. For this reason the justices dismissed the two charges of using the car with a defective tyre contrary to reg 107 of the Construction and Use Regulations and s 40(5) of the 1972 Act. Reversing the justices, the Divisional Court said that 'use' (as in *Elliott* v *Grey*) meant 'having the use of' and as the car was capable of being used the justices were directed to convict. *Hewer* v *Cutler* was explained as being a case where the facts were that the car had been mechanically immobilised and was thus incapable of being driven. It was said that the true test that should be applied in cases of this nature is whether or not steps had been taken to make it impossible for anyone to drive the vehicle. The intention of the defendant as to whether he would drive it is immaterial. *Elliott* v *Grey* was also followed in *D (A Minor)* v

*Yates* (1984) JP 455 (a case on using a CB radio without a licence) where again 'use' was held to mean 'have the use of' or 'have available for use'.

For excise duty purposes, a motor vehicle kept on a public road is chargeable with duty while not used thereon, as well as when used (Vehicles (Excise) Act 1971, s 1(1)). See 'Vehicle excise licences', 12.2, as to 'keeping'.

The driver of a towing vehicle causes the towed vehicle to be used and presumably therefore the towed vehicle is also 'used' (*Milstead* v *Sexton* [1964] Crim LR 474). In *Cobb* v *Whorton* [1971] RTR 392 it was held that a van which was on tow on a road was 'used' and if it was untaxed the user, who was in charge of and responsible for the van, was guilty of an offence under s 7 of the Vehicles (Excise) Act 1962 (now s 8 of the 1971 Act). It was pointed out that it was inconsistent for the justices, having come to the conclusion that the van was 'used' while stationary, then to hold that it ceased to be used the moment it began to be towed (at p 395). *Cobb* v *Whorton* was applied in *Nichol* v *Leach* [1973] RTR 476. It was held that both the driver of a vehicle being towed by another vehicle and the driver of the towing vehicle could be convicted of 'using' whilst uninsured (contrary to s 201 of the 1960 Act, now s 143 of the 1972 Act) and without an excise licence contrary to s 8 of the Vehicles (Excise) Act 1971. A vehicle does not have to be driven under its own power to be 'used' on a road (ibid).

Employers can be convicted of 'using', contrary to what is now s 40 of the 1972 Act, a vehicle which contravenes a Construction and Use regulation when the vehicle is being driven as directed by police or a vehicle examiner (*Drysdale and Others* v *Harrison* [1973] RTR 45). Use of a vehicle by the employer does not cease through an incident of driving such as a police direction to the driver to stop or to take a certain course, or an examiner directing the vehicle to proceed to a weighbridge to be weighed (ibid). An employer is guilty of 'using' an unlicensed vehicle contrary to s 8 of the Vehicles (Excise) Act 1971 if the vehicle is used on his business. It is no defence that he did not authorise his employee to take the unlicensed vehicle if in fact the employee used it on the employer's business (*Richardson* v *Baker* [1976] RTR 56).

In *Carmichael & Sons Ltd* v *Cottle* [1971] RTR 11 a company hired out one of their cars to a hirer who was found driving it with a badly worn tyre contrary to what is now reg 107 of the Construction and Use Regulations (and what is now s 40 of the 1972 Act). The company was convicted of 'using' the vehicle in contravention of the regulation but the conviction was set aside on the ground that the only person who could be said to be 'using' the vehicle was the driver. It was argued before the Divisional Court that the company could be convicted as an accessory because the tyre must have been in a poor condition when the car was first hired out. This argument was dismissed on the ground that it had not been raised before the justices, but in the course of his judgment Lord Parker CJ suggested (supported by Ashworth J) that the argument could also be dismissed on the ground that where the words in a statute creating the offence are 'using or causing or permitting' the latter words provide for the offences of being an aider and abettor or an accessory and that if the defendant is an accessory or aider and abettor he should be specifically charged with 'causing' or 'permitting' the user and not with 'using'. This latter approach was specifically adopted by the Lord Chief

Justice, Lord Widgery, in *Crawford* v *Haughton* [1972] 1 All ER 535, where the owner of a stock car had been convicted by the magistrates' court of using the vehicle in contravention of seven separate Construction and Use Regulations, using it whilst uninsured, using it without a vehicle excise licence and using it displaying trade plates without being the holder of the trade licence. The convictions were set aside on the ground that he should have been charged with 'permitting'. Where the statute provides alternative offences of 'causing or permitting' the only persons who can be convicted of 'using' are the driver or an employer if the vehicle was being driven on the employer's business by his employee. The Divisional Court refused to extend the meaning of 'using' to include the owner where the person driving the vehicle was not his employee even though that person was driving at his specific request on a specific journey. Note that the convictions under the Vehicles (Excise) Act for using the vehicle without an excise licence and displaying trade plates were also set aside, because no distinction had been made in the magistrates' court between these offences and the remainder. Lord Widgery suggested that different considerations might apply if these two offences had been considered in isolation, as the sections creating the offence do not contain the alternatives of 'causing or permitting' the use. It is submitted that, at any rate so far as an offence under s 8 of the Vehicles (Excise) Act is concerned, where a vehicle is driven on behalf of the owner by another on a journey at his request and on his business, the owner may be found guilty of 'using'. Not only is the Vehicles (Excise) Act a taxation statute where a stricter view is often adopted by the courts, but more importantly there is no offence of 'causing' or 'permitting' the use of an unlicensed vehicle. Moreover an 'aider and abettor' or accessory may be convicted as a principal (Magistrates' Courts Act 1980, s 44; *Du Cros* v *Lambourne* (1907) 70 JP 525). The purpose of the Vehicles (Excise) Act is to tax the person who uses or keeps a vehicle on a road; the Act is silent and uncaring as to who is the driver.

The court applied *Crawford* v *Haughton*, above, and again refused to extend the category of person who can be said to be 'using' to a partner when the other partner was driving the vehicle (*Garrett* v *Hooper* [1973] RTR 1). A partner who is not the driver cannot be said to 'use' the vehicle driven by his partner because one partner is not the employee of the other (ibid). *Garrett* v *Hooper* was followed and applied in *Bennett* v *Richardson* [1981] RTR 358. A blind partner was sitting in the back of a van with no insurance, inefficient brakes, inefficient steering, dangerous rear suspension and defective windscreen washers, driven by the blind defendant's partner. The justices' dismissal of the charges against the defendant because one partner does not 'employ' another partner was upheld. (On the other hand if a vehicle belonging to a partnership is driven by an employee of the partners on their business, seemingly each and every partner can be said to be 'using'.) But in *Cobb* v *Williams* [1973] RTR 113 it was explained that *Crawford* v *Haughton* and the other cases supporting it were cases of vicarious liability; a restricted meaning of 'use' had been adopted in those cases where the defendant was not himself driving the car. Where a defendant is himself a passenger in his own car driven by a friend directly for the defendant's own purposes, then the defendant is 'using' and may be convicted of using the vehicle whilst not insured contrary to s 143 of the 1972 Act (*Cobb* v *Williams*, above). *Cobb* v *Williams* was applied and extended in *Leathley* v *Tatton* [1980] RTR 21 to a passenger who jointly with another wrongfully took a vehicle.

Employers are often prosecuted for offences under the Construction and Use Regulations because of the defective condition of the vehicle or its load (note the special defences as to speedometers) and the defence that there is a proper system of maintenance is advanced. Can it prevail? One can only refer to the various cases cited: some of them certainly lean strongly towards absolute liability, eg in *Gifford* v *Whittaker* [1942] 1 All ER 604, above, the vehicle had been loaded by experienced men and yet the driver, who had had no hand in it, was convicted. In *Cornish* v *Ferry Masters Ltd and Another* [1975] RTR 292 a drum fell off a lorry because the pallet upon which it was loaded collapsed due to some extraordinary, unexplained, inherent defect. Both the lorry's owner and driver were directed to be convicted of 'using' even though neither was negligent nor at fault. Cases on other (but not all) parts of the Road Traffic Act establish absolute liability on the employer, and in *Griffiths* v *Studebakers* (see the paragraph below) the convicted employers seem to have done all that could reasonably be expected of them to ensure compliance with the law. These regulations can certainly be said to be for the protection of the public and, if there is evidence that a vehicle was sent out on the road by the company's employees in an unlawful condition, the company is liable (*Provincial Motor Cab Co* v *Dunning* (1909) 73 JP 387). In *Churchill* v *Norris* (1938) 158 LT 255 and *Prosser* v *Richings* (1936) 100 JP 390 (both on these regulations), the facts showed that the convicted employers took some risk of the driver's accepting an excessive load, ie, both could be called slight cases of mens rea. It should also be noted that Parliament has recognised that 'using' a vehicle contrary to a Construction and Use regulation may be an offence of absolute liability by enacting column 5 of the entry relating to s 40(5) in Part I of Sched 4 to the 1972 Act, which provides that a person's driving licence shall not be endorsed in respect of construction and use offences relating to brakes, tyres and steering, dangerous condition and insecure load if that person proves that the facts of the case were such that he did not know and had no reasonable cause to suspect that an offence would be committed (see 8.46).

Whatever the position may be in law, it is submitted that the justices should inquire carefully into the facts. Rust, loose bolts and other defects are not usually things that come about in a moment, in the twinkling of an eye; they point to defective maintenance. If so, surely the employer is liable, however good he may have imagined his system of maintenance to be (*Provincial Motor Cab Co* v *Dunning* above). Even if a vehicle goes out in perfect condition and a defect occurs suddenly, eg a rod snaps through a fault in the metal, *Griffiths* v *Studebakers* [1924] 1 KB 102 suggests that the employer is still using the vehicle while it continues to be driven on the road although he may have told his drivers to take vehicles off the road immediately such a defect occurs. Indeed, it is hinted at 113 JP Jo 472 that it is difficult to defend a charge of 'using' under the regulations and *Green* v *Burnett* [1954] 3 All ER 273 reinforces that view. Whether there should in fact be a prosecution, however, is another matter (see *Hart* v *Bex* [1957] Crim LR 622, noted above).

Is an employer who duly authorises his driver to drive the firm's vehicle on the firm's business liable for using if the driver, without permission, lets some other person drive it on the firm's business? It was submitted, with hesitation, in the eighth edition that the owner was not liable when an act was done by a trespasser and in those circumstances would not be liable under s 143 if the insurance policy did not cover the unauthorised driver. This view may not now be correct. In *Richardson* v *Baker* [1976] RTR 56 an employer was held to have used an unlicensed vehicle contrary to s 8 of the Vehicles (Excise) Act when it was used on his business despite the fact that the employer had not authorised the particular lorry to be used anywhere other than in the employer's yard. The judgment of Lord Widgery in the case seems sufficiently wide to support the proposition that whenever a vehicle is used on the employer's business, the employer should be convicted of 'using' even if he had not specifically authorised the employee to undertake such use (per Lord Widgery at p 60). *Aliter* if it were used by a servant 'on a frolic of his own' or by a thief (ibid).

A special defence for employees charged with using a vehicle without insurance is given by the Road Traffic Act 1972, s 143(2) (see 'Insurance', 10.25).

It should be noted that there is no offence of 'using' a vehicle without a number plate contrary to s 22 of the Vehicles (Excise) Act 1971. A conviction for this was quashed (*Balfour Beatty & Co Ltd* v *Grindley* [1975] RTR 156). Section 22 of the 1971 Act makes it an offence only to 'drive' or 'keep'.

In accordance with s 9(4) of the 1974 Act the Road Vehicles Lighting Regulations 1984 (SI 1984 No 812) have effect as if made under s 40 of the 1972 Act. Persons may be prosecuted for 'using' a vehicle in contravention of any of the Lighting Regulations under s 40 of the 1972 Act and the law applicable to 'causing', 'permitting' or 'using' contrary to s 40 applies in the same way to a contravention of all the Lighting Regulations as to a contravention of the Construction and Use Regulations.

The owner is deemed to have been using the vehicle in the absence of contrary evidence (*Watson* v *Paterson*, noted at 121 JP Jo 336; *Ende* v *Cassidy* (1964) 108 SJ 522; but see the qualifications given at 2.87). On the other hand ownership or proof of ownership is not essential either for proof of 'using' a vehicle without being insured under s 143 of the 1972 Act or 'using' it without an excise licence contrary to s 8 of the 1971 Act (*Napthen* v *Place* [1970] RTR 248).

Quarter sessions have held that it is not 'using' a licence with intent to deceive to send it to the council for renewal; such use must be in connection with the driving or attempted driving of a motor vehicle (*R* v *McCardle* [1958] Crim LR 50), but the language of what is now s 169 of the 1972 Act does not seem to contain any such restriction on the meaning of 'use' in that section. In *R* v *Howe* [1982] RTR 45 CA, however, a conviction was quashed where the licence was handed over to police officers but not used for driving purposes. The mere handing over on request did not amount to 'use'.

See 5.43 and *Pawley* v *Wharldall* [1965] 2 All ER 757 as to persons 'using the road' under s 3 of the 1972 Act (driving without reasonable consideration).

# 'Agriculture'

## 1.81–5 Meaning

Some statutes and regulations refer to vehicles used 'in the business of agriculture' or some such phrase. The Road Traffic Act 1972 and the Road Traffic Regulation Act 1984 contain no general definition; the Vehicles (Excise) Act 1971 defines 'agricultural machine' in Sched 3, Part II (see *Bullen* v *Picking,* 12.5 and the other cases quoted there). There is a definition in s 75 of the Road Traffic Act 1972 which is applicable to that section only, and there is a definition in s 103(1) of the Transport Act 1968. 'Agricultural trailer' and 'land' implements, locomotives and tractors are defined by reg 3 of the Construction and Use Regulations.

The relevant definition should be consulted in every case, but there have been these decisions. Unprocessed hides imported from abroad are 'agricultural produce' (*Scarr* v *Wurzal* [1951] 1 All ER 1014). Taking a pony to a show is not use for hauling agricultural produce (*Henderson* v *Robson* (1949) 113 JP 313). A wholesale greengrocer who buys crops growing in a field does not use a vehicle sent to take them away in the business of agriculture (*Leach* v *Cooper* (1950) 48 LGR 526). A vehicle licensed as a farm goods vehicle and used to carry furniture from a sale room to a farm worker's cottage is not used solely for the conveyance of articles required for the purposes of agricultural land (*M'Boyle* v *Hatton Estate Co* 1951 SLT (Sh) 101. Certain relevant cases cited are mentioned at [1952] Jo Crim L 170).

Bricks and a fireplace for installation at a farm worker's cottage are not 'articles required for the farm' under what is now the Vehicles (Excise) Act 1971, Sched 3, Part II (*Brook* v *Friend* [1954] Crim LR 942). Nor is manure produced from racing stables after being produced on a farm as straw (*McKenzie* v *Griffiths Contractors (Agricultural) Ltd* [1976] RTR 140); nor animal carcasses being taken from a slaughter house to a butcher after being similarly produced on a farm (*Cambrian Land Ltd* v *Allan* [1981] RTR 109). A market gardener taking vegetables in his car to retail customers uses it in the business of agriculture (*Manley* v *Dobson* [1949] 2 All ER 578). *Fillingham* v *Hall* (1935) unreported, deciding that agriculture does not include selling and distributing milk by retail, may be compared so far as farmers so doing are concerned. Moving agricultural implements and furniture from one farm to another is use in the business of agriculture (*Flatman* v *Poole* [1937] 1 All ER 495). See also 117 JP Jo 18 where a decision of a Crown Court is noted accepting that moving furniture to a farm worker's cottage was within the terms of an insurance policy covering agricultural purposes. However, in a Scottish case a policy covering use 'solely for agricultural or forestry purposes including the hauling of . . . articles required for agriculture' did not cover use of a tractor to convey household furniture of a newly engaged farm servant to the farm (*Agnew* v *Robertson* 1956 SLT (Sh) 90). See also *Bruce* v *Odell* (1939) 27 Traff Cas 135, and [1954] Jo Crim L 57.

'Agriculture' seems to include chicken and livestock farming as well as cultivating the soil (*J M Knowles Ltd* v *Rand* [1962] 2 All ER 926) and hatching eggs can be articles required for agricultural land (ibid). See also *London*

*County Council* v *Lee*, and the other cases quoted at 12.9. Turf can be an agricultural product (*A-G* (*McCloskey*) v *East* [1964] Jo Crim L 123).

## 'Aiding, abetting, counselling and procuring'

### 1.86 Generally

A person who aids, abets, counsels or procures the commission by another person of an offence commits the like offence although he may be subject to a different penalty. See 19.10 as to the endorsement of licences and penalty points and 20.30 as to disqualification of aiders and abettors. Aiding etc, a summary offence, should in the information be stated to be contrary to s 44 of the Magistrates' Courts Act 1980 which governs the procedure for summary offences. The words aid, abet, counsel and procure do not indicate different offences, but a person cannot be convicted of aiding and abetting alone unless he was present when the offence was committed. It is for this reason preferable to use the complete phrase. Aiding etc requires proof of mens rea or guilty intent. Conspiracy to aid and abet is not an offence known to law (*R* v *Hollinshead* (1985) *The Times*, 3 January).

A person cannot be guilty of aiding and abetting a crime if it be shown that no crime was committed (*Thornton* v *Mitchell* [1940] 1 All ER 339), but this case is distinguishable where *A* is charged with aiding and abetting the commission of an offence by *B* and it is shown that the offence was committed though not by *B*; cf *R* v *Anthony* [1965] 1 All ER 440 and *R* v *Humphreys* [1965] 3 All ER 689. It seems that a person charged as a principal can be convicted although the evidence shows that he only aided and abetted (*Du Cros* v *Lambourne* (1907) 70 JP 525; *Cooper* v *Leeke* (1968) 112 SJ 46).

It is possible to aid and abet an attempt (*R* v *Dunnington* [1984] 1 All ER 676) although s 1(4) of the Criminal Attempts Act 1981 prevented the creation of the separate offence of attempting to aid and abet the commission of an indictable offence (including an 'either way' offence) contrary to s 1(1).

Under s 33A(3) of the 1972 Act *only* the person actually breaking the seat belt law is to be guilty notwithstanding any enactment or rule of law (eg aiding and abetting) to the contrary. This provision does not apply to s 33B (drivers to be responsible for the wearing of seat belts or restraining devices by children under fourteen in certain circumstances).

### 1.87–90 Cases

Reference to cases may be helpful. It was suggested by Lord Parker CJ obiter, with Ashworth J expressing his agreement, that where the statute creating the offence employs the words 'using or causing or permitting' the latter two verbal nouns provide for the offences of being an accessory or aiding and abetting and in such cases the aider and abettor or accessory should be more properly charged with 'permitting' or 'causing' (*Carmichael & Sons Ltd* v *Cottle* [1971] RTR 11, at pp 14, 15). Although Lord Parker remarked that he did not wish to come to a conclusion to this effect, this reasoning of

Lord Parker and Ashworth J was specifically approved in *Crawford* v *Haughton* [1971] RTR 11, 1.79.

If a person knows all the circumstances and those circumstances constitute an offence and he helps in the actions which constitute the offence, that may be enough to convict him of aiding and abetting, although he does not realise that those circumstances constitute an offence (*Ackroyds* v *DPP* [1950] 1 All ER 933). A person who carried on the business of a transport clearing house, hiring lorries to carry goods for other firms, should have inquired whether the A or B licence held by the lorry owner so engaged entitled him to carry the goods in question. If he fails in his duty to see whether the lorry owner can lawfully carry those goods, he abets the lorry owner in failing to comply with a condition of his licence should it be infringed by so carrying the goods (*Carter* v *Mace* [1949] 2 All ER 714). A man who does not know of the essential matters constituting an offence does not aid and abet its commission (*Johnson* v *Youden* [1950] 1 All ER 300). In *Ferguson* v *Weaving* [1951] 1 All ER 412 it was held on the facts that knowledge to constitute aiding and abetting could not be imputed to an employer because his servants know, and in *Cassady* v *Reg Morris (Transport) Ltd* [1975] Crim LR 3989 an employer was held to be rightly acquitted by justices of aiding and abetting his driver to fail to return his record book sheets to him where there was no evidence that the employer had encouraged his driver's failure. *Carter* v *Mace*, above, was distinguished in *Davies, Turner & Co* v *Brodie* [1954] 3 All ER 283. There the defendant had made proper inquiries as to whether goods could be carried in another firm's lorry without contravening the terms of an A licence, but had been given false information. It was held that the defendant was not guilty of aiding and abetting the other firm in the illegal use of the vehicle. In *Smith* v *Jenner* (1968) 112 SJ 52 a driving instructor was shown his pupil's then valid driving licence and he told him to renew when necessary. The instructor gave lessons without further inquiry and was charged with aiding and abetting the pupil to drive when unlicensed, the licence having expired. It was held that the instructor should not be convicted. See also *Stanton & Sons Ltd* v *Webber* (1972) 116 SJ 667 (firm acquitted where there was no actual knowledge that the employee was a learner driver). In *Bateman* v *Evans* (1964) 108 SJ 522, where the defendant allowed a disqualified person to drive his car in the belief that he was not disqualified, it was held that he was not guilty but would be if he shut his eyes to the obvious or perhaps refrained from making the inquiries a reasonably sensible man would make. Deliberate abstention from obtaining knowledge can be aiding and abetting (*Poultry World* v *Conder* [1957] Crim LR 803).

A person may be guilty of aiding and abetting where he is under a legal duty to act to prevent an offence and he remains passive (*Rubie* v *Faulkner* [1940] 1 All ER 285). A supervisor can be convicted of aiding and abetting the learner driver to drive with excess blood alcohol. He cannot escape conviction by arguing that he cannot know that the learner driver is above the limit unless and until the blood alcohol level has been scientifically determined (*Crampton* v *Fish* (1969) 113 SJ 1003). The learner driver and supervisor had been out drinking together that evening; the vehicle had hit the bank on three occasions and had been swerving from side to side. In *Carter* v

*Richardson* [1974] RTR 314, a supervisor of a learner driver was similarly convicted of aiding and abetting the learner driver to drive with alcohol in excess of the prescribed limit. It was held that it suffices if the aider and abettor was aware that the principal had had an excessive amount of alcohol or was reckless whether he had done so. The aider and abettor does not have to know the precise amount (ibid). The supervisor attempted to deceive the police that he had been driving and not his pupil. The justices were entitled to infer from that deception that he knew or believed his pupil had too much alcohol in his blood (per Mackenna J on p 318, ibid).

As to the liability of a master for his employees' acts, contrast *John Henshall (Quarries) Ltd* v *Harvey* [1965] 1 All ER 725 with *National Coal Board* v *Gamble* [1958] 3 All ER 203, where a private firm's lorry went to a Coal Board depot and was loaded with coal there. The Board's servant weighed the loaded lorry at a weighbridge of which he was in charge and found that the laden weight exceeded that allowed by the Construction and Use Regulations. Nevertheless he gave the weight ticket to the driver, who knew of the overweight. It was held, on a charge against the Board of aiding and abetting the use by the firm of an overweight lorry, that the crime of aiding and abetting was committed on proof of a positive act of assistance voluntarily done and a knowledge of the circumstances constituting the offence and that the question of motive was irrelevant. The handing of the weight ticket by the attendant at the weighbridge to the driver with knowledge that an offence was going to be committed made the Board aiders and abettors. A special feature of this case is that the Board called no evidence. In the *Henshall* case it was held that the knowledge of a subordinate employee, who was under the general supervision of a manager, was not enough to make his employer guilty of aiding and abetting an illegal act contributed to by the employee and unknown to the manager: to make the master, whether a company or an individual, liable the employee should be a responsible officer, part of the 'brains' of the company. It might be otherwise if the master had handed over the effective management to an employee.

In *Pope* v *Minton* [1954] Crim LR 711, the defendant knew that his friend had been disqualified from driving, but told him that he could use his (defendant's) car if he wanted. Defendant was not present when the friend used the car, nor (*semble*) did he do any more to assist him to take and use it. It was held that the defendant was guilty of aiding and abetting the friend to drive while disqualified, but it would be otherwise if the car owner was genuinely unaware of the disqualification (*Bateman* v *Evans* (1964) 108 SJ 522). A bus owner who put an inexperienced conductor in charge of the bus without proper supervision was held guilty of aiding and abetting the conductor in allowing overcrowding (*Gough* v *Rees* 1929 94 JP 53). A lorry driver employed by a Scottish company set off on a long journey into England with a dangerously worn front offside tyre the condition of which he knew. The state of the tyre was also known to the managing director of the Scottish company. The tyre burst and the lorry crashed into a motor car, killing its occupants. It was held that the company and the managing director were guilty of counselling and procuring the offence of causing death by dangerous driving because the managing director knew of the dangerous state of the tyre (*R* v

*Robert Millar (Contractors) Ltd and Robert Millar* [1970] 1 All ER 577). Moreover, as the crime of the lorry driver was committed in England, and as counselling and procuring was not a crime on its own account but rather participating in a crime, they could be tried in England; an alternative reason for trial in England was that the counselling and procuring was a continuous act and continued as long as the driver drove the lorry with the dangerous tyre.

Evidence that a person charged as an aider and abettor has previously been warned about the same matters is admissible to show that he knew what might be going on (*Duxley* v *Gilmore* (1959) 123 JP Jo 331). Merely riding in a vehicle, without more, does not show that the rider is aiding and abetting its illegal use: there should be some evidence of a joint enterprise (*D* v *Parsons* [1960] 2 All ER 493). In *Smith* v *Baker* [1972] Crim LR 25 a passenger in a stolen car was held not to be guilty of aiding and abetting its uninsured use when he had not assisted in its use in any way even though he had 'a fair idea it was stolen' and ran away when the police arrived.

Surreptitiously lacing a motorist's drink knowing that he will then drive with excess alcohol as a result is 'procuring' (*Attorney General's Reference No 1 of 1975* [1975] RTR 473).

## 'Attempt'

### 1.91–5 Generally

Motoring cases on attempt are discussed under the individual topics to which they relate: see 4.12 and 4.26 in relation to drink/driving 15.9 in relation to theft and taking conveyances and 11.28 in relation to driving while disqualified.

The Criminal Attempts Act 1981 abolished the common law doctrine that an attempt to commit an offence is itself an offence. By s 1(1) of the 1981 Act it is an offence to attempt to commit an indictable offence (including an 'either way' offence). An attempt is defined as with intent doing 'an act which is more than merely preparatory to the commission of the offence' (s 1(1)).

There is no general statutory provision enabling a person to be convicted of an attempt to commit a purely summary offence. It would seem, therefore, unless the wording of the summary offence itself includes attempts within its ambit (eg 'driving or attempting to drive' with excess blood-alcohol under s 6(1) of the 1972 Act), it is not an offence to attempt to commit a purely summary offence. Section 3 provides that for specific statutory offences of attempt a person is guilty of attempt if with intent he does an act more than merely preparatory to the commission of the full offence (s 3(3)).

It should be emphasised that under the Criminal Attempts Act 1981, s 1(1) and under s 3(3) the defendant must *intend* to commit the relevant full offence. It is submitted that this imports the full mens rea of intent and that recklessness is insufficient. The matter is discussed at [1983] Crim LR 365 and [1984] Crim LR 25.

A person may be guilty of attempt under s 1 (indictable offences) or s 3 (special statutory offences) even though the facts are such that the commission of the full offence is impossible (s 1(2) and s 3(4)). A person will still have the intent for the purposes of s 1 or s 3 in certain circumstances despite a misconception as to the facts (s 1(3) and s 3(5)). This was confirmed in *Anderton* v *Ryan* [1985] 1 All ER 138 (attempting to handle stolen goods—goods not stolen) and *R* v *Shivpuri* [1985] 1 All ER 143 (attempting drug offences—not diamorphine or heroin but snuff). There may be an appeal in these cases to the House of Lords.

There is still no offence if there is a misconception as to law.

Where an unfit driver had no ignition key, but was sitting in the driver's seat attempting to insert other keys into the ignition, the Divisional Court held that he was properly convicted of attempting to drive while unfit through drink or drugs, contrary to s 5(1) of the 1972 Act (*Kelly* v *Hogan* [1982] RTR 352). The court added that the position was the same as a burglar carrying a jemmy of the wrong size; the facts fell within the fourth category of offences described in *R* v *Smith (Roger)* [1975] AC 476.

Under the earlier law a person charged with attempting to commit an offence could be convicted even though in law he committed the full offence (*Webley* v *Buxton* [1977] 2 All ER 595). This still seems to be the law.

The mode of trial for offences under s 1(1) seems to be the same as for the full offence. For the special rules in s 4(2) as to the joinder of certain attempts and other offences see 'Attempts', 2.39.

Under s 4 a person convicted of an attempt under s 1(1) incurs 'any penalty' to which he would have been liable for the full offence. The effect of s 4 thus seems to be that where the full offence is obligatorily endorsable and carries discretionary disqualification, the attempt to commit that offence under s 1(1) itself becomes endorsable and disqualifiable (eg an attempt to drive while disqualified). (Attempted theft or the attempted taking of a motor vehicle are specifically endorsable and disqualifiable: see Sched 4 to the 1972 Act.)

Section 1(1) does not apply to conspiracy, aiding, abetting, counselling or procuring the commission of an offence, nor to offences under s 4(1) or s 5(1) of the Criminal Law Act 1967 (s 1(4)). Although s 1(4) prevented the creation of the separate offence of attempting to aid and abet etc the commission of an indictable offence (including an 'either way' offence) it is possible to aid and abet an attempt (*R* v *Dunnington* [1984] 1 All ER 676).

Incitement is not affected by the Criminal Attempts Act 1981. The old law applies and it is not possible to incite the impossible if it is impossible (*R* v *Fitzmaurice* [1983] 1 All ER 189).

## 'Owner'

### 1.96 Meaning

The term 'owner', in relation to a vehicle which is the subject of a hiring agreement or hire-purchase agreement, means the person in possession under that agreement (1972 Act, s 196(1); Road Traffic Regulation Act 1984, s 142(1)). For the purposes of giving information as to insurance under ss 162(1) and 166 the term in relation to a vehicle which is the subject of a hiring agreement includes each party to the agreement (Road Traffic Act 1972, ss 162(4), 167(2); see 10.30 and 7.18).

'Owner' is not defined in the Vehicles (Excise) Act 1971, but the person who is required to be registered as the owner is the person by whom the vehicle is kept (reg 3(1) of the Road Vehicles (Registration and Licensing) Regulations 1971, as amended). The expression 'ownership' is to be construed similarly (ibid). 'Owner' for the purpose of the vehicle owner liability provisions of the 1974 Act is similarly defined (s 5(3) of the Road Traffic Act 1974) (see 17.2).

See also 'Evidence', 'Proof of ownership', 2.87.

# Chapter 2

# Procedure and Evidence

## Commencing Proceedings

### 2.1 Generally

The majority of road traffic prosecutions are begun by summons issued on an information laid before a magistrate or justices' clerk. The information may, however, be laid on behalf of the informant by an agent or solicitor or counsel (Magistrates' Courts Rules 1981, r 4(1)). It may be an abuse of the process of the court for a prosecutor to lay an information before deciding whether to prosecute (*R* v *Brentford JJ, ex parte Wong* [1981] Crim LR 339. See further 'Refusal to hear a case', 2.32.)

An information may be oral or in writing (see below, however, for the requirements where a warrant is sought). There is no prescribed form. It should identify the informant and also the defendant (by description if necessary) and give particulars of the offence and statute etc. See 2.2 'Form of summons'.

There is a distinction between laying an information, which is a ministerial act by the prosecutor, and issuing process, which is a judicial function for the magistrate or justices' clerk and cannot be delegated: *Hill* v *Anderton* [1982] 2 All ER 963 (HL) also reported under the name *R* v *Manchester Stipendiary Magistrate* at [1982] RTR 449. The information is laid when it is received at the office of the Clerk to the Justices for the relevant area (ibid). See also 'When "proceedings are begun"', 2.4.

Factual and legal items common to a number of informations such as the date and place may be set out in a single preamble and incorporated by reference (*Shah* v *Swallow* [1984] 2 All ER 528 (HL)).

See 20.42 as to removals of disqualification.

A magistrate (or justices' clerk) may not reconsider an application which has already been rejected by a fellow magistrate (or clerk) (*R* v *Worthing JJ* [1981] Crim LR 778). It is submitted that this does not preclude a further application at the discretion of the magistrate (or clerk) where there is fresh material.

The issue of a summons is a judicial act. Certain basic requirements should be fulfilled before the issue, namely that:

(*a*) the allegation is of an offence known to law and the essential ingredients of the offence are prima facie present;

(*b*) the offence alleged is not 'out of time';
(*c*) the court has jurisdiction; and
(*d*) the information has the necessary authority to prosecute.

A proposed defendant has no right to be heard at this stage; he may be heard only at the discretion of the court (*R* v *West London JJ, ex parte Klahn* [1979] 1 WLR 933).

Magistrates may refuse to issue a summons if they think fit on reasonable grounds. If a summons is unreasonably refused, there may be a judicial review to compel its issue. A facsimile rubber stamp signature may comply with what is now r 98 of the Magistrates' Courts Rules 1981 (*R* v *Brentford JJ* above).

By s 1(4) of the Magistrates' Courts Act 1980 a warrant to arrest a defendant aged seventeen or over in the first instance may not be issued for any offence unless it is indictable or an 'either way' offence, or punishable with imprisonment, or his address is not sufficiently established to enable a summons to be served on him. For such a warrant the information must be in writing and substantiated on oath (s 1(3)).

Under s 13(3) of the Magistrates' Courts Act 1980 a warrant may only be issued on non-appearance where the offence is punishable with imprisonment or the court, having convicted the defendant, proposes to disqualify him. There are certain further restrictions on the exercise of this power to issue a warrant on non-appearance which are set out in s 13 of the Magistrates' Courts Act 1980. The information must be substantiated on oath (s 13(1)). If the court has received evidence or convicted the defendant on his pleading guilty the court must think it undesirable to proceed in his absence by reason of the gravity of the offence (s 13(5)). It is submitted that evidence means evidence in the trial and not in respect of a preliminary matter. Any summons issued must have been served and served a reasonable time before the hearing. Apart from this a warrant may always be issued for a failure to answer bail (Bail Act 1976, s 7(1)).

The distinction between the position at first instance and following non-appearance will be noted. Some 'either way' offences are punishable with imprisonment only on indictment (eg forgery of driving licences, insurances etc contrary to s 169(1) of the 1972 Act). Although such offences might be regarded as remaining imprisonable after the decision to proceed to summary trial and when being dealt with summarily because of, eg, the power under s 38 of the Magistrates' Courts Act 1980 to commit for sentence, *R* v *Melbourne* at 16.19 implies the contrary.

Unless a statute otherwise requires, a prosecution may be commenced by any person. Exceptions are most prosecutions under Parts II and III of the Public Passenger Vehicles Act 1981 (see s 69), and prosecutions for most of the offences under the Vehicles (Excise) Act 1971 (see s 28), and (possibly) for driving to the common danger under the Public Health Act 1925, s 74, and obstruction and other offences under the Town Police Clauses Act 1847, s 28. The view that a constable who witnessed the offence may prosecute under s 28 is advanced by implication in Stone's *Justices' Manual*.

The proceedings may be continued notwithstanding the death of the informant prior to the hearing (*R* v *Truelove* (1880) 5 QBD 336), or prior to the appeal if a police informant (*Hawkins* v *Bepey* [1980] 1 All ER 797). The issue and the service of summonses and other documents on a Sunday and the sitting of a magistrates' court on that day are discussed at 3.7.

## 2.2 Form of summons

The power of a magistrate or clerk to the justices to issue a summons cannot be delegated: *Hill* v *Anderton* [1982] 2 All ER 963 (HL).

An irregularity or illegality in the mode of bringing a defendant before the court, if not objected to at the hearing, does not invalidate the conviction (*Gray* v *Customs Commissioners* (1884) 48 JP 343).

By r 98(3) of the Magistrates' Courts Rules 1981 a single summons can be issued on more than one information, and r 12 of the Magistrates' Courts Rules 1981 expressly provides that two or more informations may be set out in one document. The cases where more than one charge has been included in the information should be read with these provisions in mind. See also *Shah* v *Swallow*, 2.1 above. As to the particulars in the summons generally see the Magistrates' Courts Rules 1981, r 100, and Brian Harris, *Criminal Jurisdiction of Magistrates*. Examples of insufficient detail in summonses are found in *Stephenson* v *Johnson* [1954] 1 All ER 369 and *Cording* v *Halse* [1954] 3 All ER 287. The summons does not have to show the date of the laying of the information unless there is some question of its being out of time (see *R* v *Godstone JJ, ex parte Secretary of State for the Environment* [1974] Crim LR 110). It is perfectly proper for the signature to be affixed by a rubber stamp (*R* v *Brentford JJ, ex parte Catlin* [1975] 2 All ER 201).

Under r 100 every information and summons must contain with the description of the offence a reference to the section of the Act or the rule, order, regulation, byelaw or other instrument creating the offence. The 1981 rules are, however, directory and not mandatory because in so far as they conflict with the statute they have to be adapted to meet it (per Ormrod LJ in *Thornley* v *Clegg* [1982] RTR 405 at p 410). In *Simmons* v *Fowler* (1950) 48 LGR 623 DC (discussed at 115 JP Jo 322) it was held that the summons should indicate the Act and the regulation. For example in that case the summons should have indicated that it was contrary to s 3(1) of the Road Traffic Act 1930 and the particular regulation. The summons should specify the defects in the parts and accessories but does not need to specify whether the defects are in the parts or in the accessories (*Brindley* v *Willett* [1981] RTR 19).

A person cannot be convicted under a repealed statute even if it has been re-enacted with identical words (*Stowers* v *Darnell* [1973] Crim LR 528). However, the information may be amended. Again, where the statute has been omitted it is possible to amend by inserting it providing the defendant is not misled (*Thornley* v *Clegg* above, applying s 123 of the Magistrates' Courts Act 1980).

See 2.46 as to duplicity and charging alternative offences and 2.45 as to amending a summons.

## 2.3 Authority to prosecute

Where the authority of some person or body to prosecute is required, the justice or justices' clerk before whom the information is laid should satisfy himself that such authority has been duly given before issuing the summons: at the hearing the summons is presumed to have been duly authorised and the prosecutor need take no further steps unless the defence raises an objection. Such an objection should be taken before the prosecutor's case is closed (*Price* v *Humphries* [1958] 2 All ER 725). Where necessary, an adjournment should be granted. Where, however, the defence request proof of compliance with the statutory formalities it is for the prosecution to produce the necessary evidence. In default the justices are entitled to hold that there is no case to answer (*Anderton* v *Frost* [1984] RTR 106). That case was one of driving a heavy goods vehicle without an HGV licence. Only certain persons, specified in s 123 of the 1972 Act, may prosecute. The informations were laid in the name of the Chief Constable under a general authority issued by him to his Divisional Chief Officers. The defence required evidence that the informations had been laid by the Chief Constable and this was not forthcoming. Cf *Westminster Coaching Services* v *Piddlesden* (1933) 97 JP 185. The decision in that case was based on what is now s 69 of the Public Passenger Vehicles Act 1981. The statutory provisions were similar to s 123 but it was held that authorisation had been given. A police sergeant laid an information which was signed by an Assistant Commissioner of the Metropolitan Police and by a Superintendent and the Commissioner had given a general authorisation in writing to prosecute. There is an article at (1984) 148 JP 521 drawing attention to some of the difficulties inherent in s 69.

See also the cases noted at 7.17 and 12.26.

Where a certificate may be produced to establish consent and an incorrect certificate has been produced or seemingly has been overlooked, a correct certificate may be produced subsequent to the laying of the information where the lawfulness is challenged: *R* v *Clerkenwell Metropolitan Stipendiary Magistrate, ex parte DPP* [1984] 2 WLR 244. The certificate is not the consent but *evidence* (or if the Act so stipulates) *conclusive evidence* of the consent (ibid).

Where, however, the information has been laid by a person who has not been generally or specifically authorised, an authorisation given after the laying of the information would not, it seems, validate the proceedings.

## 2.4 Juveniles

Subject to the exceptions below, only a juvenile court may deal with an offence by a juvenile under seventeen. Again, subject to the exceptions below, the court cannot commit the juvenile for trial at the Crown Court even if the prosecution or the defence wish to have the charge tried before a jury (Magistrates' Courts Act 1980, s 24). (As to when a juvenile 'appears or is brought' before magistrates for the purposes of s 24 see below.)

A juvenile charged with 'homicide' must be committed for trial at the Crown Court if the case justifies it. Such a charge cannot be tried summarily (s 24(1)). Causing death by reckless driving is considered to be an offence of 'homicide' (see 5.12).

If the offence is punishable if committed by an adult with fourteen years' imprisonment or more (eg robbery) the court may at its discretion commit for trial a juvenile between the ages of fourteen and sixteen inclusive (s 24(1)(*a*)). In exercising its discretion, a court does not have to hear evidence (*R* v *South Hackney Juvenile Court* (1983) 77 Cr App R 294).

However, in the case of 'a charge made jointly' against a juvenile and an adult, the juvenile *must* be sent to a magistrates' court other than a juvenile court (Children and Young Persons Act 1933, s 46). There is some uncertainty as to what is meant by 'charged jointly'. It may be more restricted than 'charged with a joint offence', so that a juvenile who is charged with a joint offence but not charged jointly, because eg the adult has absconded or been dealt with, may nevertheless be dealt with in a juvenile court.

Provided the juvenile is charged jointly with an adult, the magistrates' court may commit them both for trial if the court considers it necessary in the interest of justice to do so and if the case justifies it (Magistrates' Courts Act 1980, s 24(1)(*b*)). The *South Hackney Juvenile Court* decision (above) was under s 24(1)(*a*) but the principle seems equally applicable to s 24(1)(*b*). The court in such a case may also commit the juvenile for trial for any other indictable offence with which he is charged at the same time (whether jointly with the adult or not) if that other offence arises out of circumstances which are the same as or connected with those giving rise to the *joint* offence (s 24(2)). This may still mean that the adult is committed for trial on indictable offences connected with other indictable offences with which the juvenile is charged but for which he cannot be committed for trial. It would be preferable if the juvenile could be committed on all indictable offences in these circumstances.

Where a juvenile is before a magistrates' court on an information jointly charging him with an adult in this way and:

(*a*) the court does not dispose of the juvenile's case by way of committal proceedings;
(*b*) the adult(s) jointly charged are dealt with by way of committal proceedings or are tried summarily and *plead* guilty;
(*c*) the juvenile pleads not guilty,

the magistrates' court may remit him to a juvenile court for trial (Magistrates' Courts Act 1980, s 29).

It will be noted that in s 29 the words 'information jointly charging him' is specific. They do not mean charged at the same time. It is necessary to watch carefully for the case where the adult has been convicted on an earlier occasion but did not plead guilty. There is no power to remit in these circumstances. This power to remit is not restricted to indictable or 'either way' offences.

A court committing a juvenile for trial may do so under s 6 of the Magistrates' Courts Act 1980 (s 24(1)) without consideration of the evidence.

As stated above, a juvenile charged jointly with an adult *must* be sent to the magistrates' court (other than a juvenile court) along with the adult in the first instance. In certain other cases he *may* be tried by a magistrates' court other than a juvenile court:

(*a*) if either the juvenile or the adult is a principal offender and the other is an aider or abettor of the offence;
(*b*) if the fact that the defendant is a juvenile only emerges in the course of the proceedings; or
(*c*) if the juvenile is charged with an offence arising out of the circumstances or connected with the circumstances giving rise to an offence for which an adult is charged

(Children and Young Persons Act 1933, s 46; Children and Young Persons Act 1963, s 18).

Section 7(8) of the Children and Young Persons Act 1969 provides that where a magistrates' court tries a person who at the time the proceedings in question were begun has not attained the age of seventeen and guilt is established, the magistrates' court is required to remit the offender to a juvenile court, unless the court deals with the case by exercising one or more of the following powers: absolute or conditional discharge, a fine or order for costs or damages, an order for his parent to enter into a recognisance, an order of disqualification or endorsement of a driving licence under s 93 or s 101 of the 1972 Act or s 19(1) of the Transport Act 1981.

It should be noted that the determining date of the age of the offender is for the purposes of s 7(8) of the 1969 Act the date when the proceedings *were begun* (see below) and *not* the date of the commission of the offence. If, for example, the magistrates' court wishes to send to a detention centre an offender who has since become seventeen he must be remitted to the juvenile court to be sentenced. On the other hand, if a fresh charge is preferred after the juvenile attains seventeen, *R* v *Chelsea JJ, ex parte DPP* [1963] 3 All ER 657 still seems to be authority for the proposition that a juvenile court cannot deal with the fresh charge if at the time of preferment it was known he was then seventeen.

In England a person attains an age on the day which is the anniversary of his birth (Family Law Reform Act 1969, s 9). See 1962 SLTN 16 as to Scotland. For presuming and determining age see s 99 of the Children and Young Persons Act 1933 and s 150(4) of the Magistrates' Courts Act 1980. The procedure under s 12 of the Magistrates' Courts Act 1980 whereby an offender may plead guilty by post does not apply to juvenile courts, but s 46(1A) of the Children and Young Persons Act 1933 has the effect of preserving a conviction under that Act of a juvenile if the magistrates' court had no reason to believe he was a juvenile.

See 2.50 as to disregarding findings of guilt while under fourteen against a person who has attained the age of twenty-one and *R* v *Blandford JJ* [1966] 1 All ER 1021 as to accepting pleas of guilty from juveniles.

*Attaining seventeen before the conclusion of proceedings*

Where proceedings in respect of a young person are begun and he attains seventeen before the conclusion of the proceedings, the court may deal with the case and make any order which it could have made if he had not attained that age (Children and Young Persons Act 1963, s 29). As to the meaning of when 'proceedings are begun' see below. Those who laid informations or charged juveniles who might soon become seventeen should take all reasonable steps to find out exactly when they would become seventeen to ensure they would be bailed or summoned to the correct court (*R* v *Amersham Juvenile Court* [1981] 2 All ER 315).

Section 29 affords the justice no discretion to overrule the mandatory provisions of s 19(1) or s 24(1) of the Magistrates' Courts Act 1980, in particular as to the right of election of jury for persons aged seventeen or over (*R* v *Amersham JJ* above) although this decision was overruled on another point in *Re Daley*. These sections and *Re Daley* are discussed further below.

The juvenile court may proceed if the defendant is found to be seventeen during the hearing (Children and Young Persons Act 1933, s 48(1)).

*When a juvenile 'appears or is brought' before magistrates*

The meaning of the expression 'appears or is brought' in s 24(1) of the Magistrates' Courts Act 1980 is different from that of 'when proceedings are begun' in s 7(8) of the Children and Young Persons Act 1969 (see below). 'Appears or is brought' in s 24(1) means the appearance when the court makes its decision as to the mode of trial (*Re Daley* [1982] 2 All ER 974 (HL)). See also 2.41.

*When 'proceedings are begun'*

Section 7 of the 1969 Act does not define the moment at which it may be said 'proceedings are begun' for the purpose of s 7(8) of the Children and Young Persons Act 1969. The meaning of the expression 'when proceedings are begun' may be relevant for purposes other than s 7. It is also to be found in s 29 of the Children and Young Persons Act 1963 (see above). The six-month limitation period in s 127 of the Magistrates' Courts Act 1980 expressly refers to when 'the information was laid' or 'the complaint made'. However, for example, s 180 of the 1972 Act gives an extended time limit for certain road traffic offences, the marginal note referring to the 'time within which summary proceedings . . . must be commenced' and the section itself stating that 'summary proceedings . . . may be brought'.

The meaning of the expression 'when proceedings are begun' is different from that of when a defendant 'appears or is brought' in s 24(1) of the Magistrates' Courts Act 1980 (see above). The generally held view was that it meant when the information was laid, whether it was for a summons or for a warrant of arrest. See for example the ninth edition of this book, p 61, and the note on s 7(8) in Harris, *Criminal Jurisdiction of Magistrates* (9th ed). As to laying an information, see 2.1.

The earlier cases supported this view. A good example is *Thorpe* v *Priestnall* [1896] 1 QB 159. The Act in issue prohibited the institution of a prosecution without the written consent of the Chief Constable. Similar prohibitions are present in a number of current statutes. The written consent was given between the laying of the information and the hearing. The conviction was quashed. It was stated by Wills J: 'I cannot see any reason why the laying of the information which started it is not the commencement of the prosecution; and I certainly think this has been the meaning of the phrase commonly accepted in the profession.' He added that no distinction could be drawn between the words 'institute' and 'commence'. The advantage of this decision is that all the facts are marshalled and formulated for the purpose of laying the information.

This view of the law was shaken by the decision in *R* v *Billericay JJ, ex parte Johnson* [1979] Crim LR 315, where the Divisional Court considered s 7(8) and held that 'proceedings are begun' when a summons is served. The decision is criticised at (1979) 143 JP Jo 556 where it is pointed out that various summonses may be issued off a single information. In *R* v *Leeds JJ, ex parte Hanson* [1981] 3 All ER 72 Griffiths LJ said at p 78 'Proceedings are commenced . . . when the information is laid: see *Brooks* v *Bagshaw* [1904] 2 KB 798.' The *Leeds* decision subsequently came before the House of Lords in *Hill* v *Anderton* [1982] 2 All ER 963 and the same view is implicit in that decision. In *R* v *South Western Magistrates' Court* [1980] RTR 35 an information was laid before the appointed day and another after, upon which the defendant appeared. It was held that the proceedings began after the appointed day. However, this appears to be no more than an example of restarting proceedings.

A person may be arrested and charged without an information being laid. In such a case the proceedings may be said to have begun either with the arrest and charge or with the presentation of the information (usually in the form of a charge sheet) to the court or with the first court appearance. In *R* v *Brentwood JJ, ex parte Jones* (1979) 143 JP 211 the Divisional Court chose the first alternative. However, the arrest and police station 'charge' is not a judicial proceeding as no court official is involved.

*R* v *Amersham Juvenile Court, ex parte Wilson* [1981] 2 All ER 315 was as noted above overruled in *Re Daley* on another point but it is still of value on the issue of when proceedings are begun. It was held in that case that proceedings were not begun for the purposes of s 29 of the Children and Young Persons Act 1963 until the person concerned had been brought to court for the first time in connection with the offence charged. Accordingly the Divisional Court quashed a decision of a juvenile court in respect of a defendant who was sixteen when charged at a police station and remanded on police bail to appear at a juvenile court on a later date, by which time he was seventeen.

The following conclusions are submitted:

(1) Where an information is laid, the proceedings are begun at that stage (*Hill* v *Anderton* [1982] 2 All ER 963; see above and 2.1).

(2) Where a person is arrested and charged without a prior information, the proceedings are begun when the defendant first appears before the court (*R* v *Amersham JJ*) or, if earlier, when the information is presented to the court or court office (see Lord Roskill's comments in *Hill* v *Anderton* at p 971C).

## 2.5 Commonwealth and foreign servicemen

Where the defendant is a serviceman of a Commonwealth or allied country, such as the USA, the Visiting Forces Act 1952 as extended by the International Headquarters and Defence Organisations Act 1964 will enable magistrates' courts to try him for a road traffic offence, generally speaking, unless it arose out of, and in the course of, his duty (see s 3). Thus, an American Army officer driving on manoeuvres would be acting in the course of his duty and would normally not be triable in an English court, but, if he were on a domestic shopping trip with his family, he would not be acting in the course of his duty and would be triable for a road traffic offence by an English court. The 1952 Act is discussed in the *Modern Law Review*, January 1953, at 103 LJ News 149, and at 119 JP Jo 99. It applies to American servicemen and those of the countries listed in Stone's opening notes to the Act. The Motor Vehicles (Construction and Use) Regulations 1978, reg 4(9), the Motor Vehicles (Construction and Use) (Track Laying Vehicles) Regulations 1955, reg 4, the Motor Vehicles (Variation of Speed Limit) (Amendment) Regulations 1954, the Road Vehicles Lighting Regulations 1984, reg 7, the Motor Vehicles (Tests) Regulations 1981, reg 6, and the various Motor Vehicles (Type Approval) (Great Britain) Regulations among others give certain exemptions for the vehicles of visiting forces. As to insurance, see 10.08 and excise licences, 12.13.

The Visiting Forces and International Headquarters (Application of Law) Order 1965 (SI 1965 No 1536) applies many provisions of the Road Traffic Act 1960 to vehicles of visiting forces and their drivers when on duty, but offences committed on duty would be tried by the service courts. The general position is that drivers and vehicles of visiting forces are subject to the same provisions of the Road Traffic Acts as persons and vehicles in the service of the Crown (see 2.8). The Interpretation Act 1978, s 17(2), applies the provisions of the Road Traffic Regulation Act 1984 and the 1972 Act, replacing those of the 1960 Act, to the relevant parts of the 1965 Order.

A civil court may not try for the same crime a person already tried by the service court of a visiting force and, where the civil court tries him for a different crime but he has already been tried by the service court wholly or partly for the acts or omissions in respect of which the civil court convicts him, the latter court must have regard to the sentence already passed (Visiting Forces Act 1952, s 4).

## 2.6 Drivers from abroad

Where a solicitor is instructed in a case relating to the duty payable on, the insurance cover for, or the application of the Construction and Use Regulations to a car brought from abroad or as to the driving licences of overseas visitors, he should refer, inter alia, to the Motor Vehicles (International Circulation) Act 1952 and the Motor Vehicles (International Circulation) Order 1975 (SI 1975 No 1208) as amended by SI 1980 No 1095. As to driving licences he should refer to 'Drivers from abroad' under 'Driving Licences' in Chapter 11. He may also wish to refer to the Road Vehicles Lighting Regulations 1984, reg 5; the Motor Vehicles (Construction and Use) Regulations 1978, reg 4(7); and the Goods Vehicles (Plating and Testing) Regulations 1982, Sched 2, para 24 as amended. As to the need for a driver from abroad to have a valid test certificate, see 'Test Certificates and Testing' in Chapter 8. For drivers' hours and records where the EEC international rules apply, see 'Drivers' Hours' and 'Drivers' Records' in Chapter 14. International passenger services are governed by the Road Transport (International

Passenger Services) Regulations 1984 (SI 1984 No 748). These regulations are made in implementation of EEC regulations.

## 2.7 Diplomatic privilege

By the Diplomatic Privileges Act 1964, Sched 1, arts 31 and 37, members of the diplomatic, administrative and technical staff of a mission and members of the family of such staff forming part of their household are exempt from criminal proceedings, and members of the domestic service staff enjoy like immunity in respect of acts performed in the course of their duties. All such immunities may be waived. Private servants of members of the mission, as opposed to those of the mission itself, are not exempt; nor are members of the family of the diplomatic staff and members of the administrative and technical staff and their families who are British nationals or permanently resident here. Where a person is a member of a diplomatic mission of a Commonwealth country or Eire or a private servant of such a person, and is a citizen both of that country and of the United Kingdom, he has the same privileges and immunities as he would have if he were not a citizen of the United Kingdom (Diplomatic Privileges (Citizens of the United Kingdom and Colonies) Order 1964 (SI 1964 No 2043)). Similar privilege may also exist under the International Organisations Act 1968. Consular officers and consular employees, as defined in art 1 of the Schedule to the Consular Relations Act 1968, are not subject to the jurisdiction of British courts in respect of acts performed in the course of consular functions but such immunity may be waived (arts 43, 45). Where any question of diplomatic or consular immunity arises a certificate should be obtained from the Secretary of State, which certificate is conclusive as to the person's entitlement to immunity.

The waiver of diplomatic privilege must be made by or on behalf of the representative of the country concerned and cannot be made by the defendant himself; until there is due waiver, proceedings are without jurisdiction and null and void (*R* v *Madan* [1961] Crim LR 253).

## 2.8 The Crown

Parts I, II, III, IV and VII of the 1972 Act apply, to the extent stated in s 188 thereof, to persons and vehicles in the public service of the Crown. Other Parts of the Act do not apply to the Crown (*Adair* v *Feist* 1936 SLT (Sh) 22). Where under the relevant Part an offence has been committed in connection with a vehicle in the public service of the Crown, proceedings may be brought in respect of the offence against a person nominated for the purpose on behalf of the Crown and the nominated person may be convicted as well as any person actually responsible for the offence (but without prejudice to proceedings against any person so responsible) (s 188(8)).

Although the nominated person may be convicted, the only order which can be made is a fine (s 188(9)). Such an order cannot be enforced and the conviction is to be disregarded for all other purposes except appeal (whether by way of case stated or otherwise).

As to penalty points see the note to Crown servants, 19.21.

Section 130 of the Road Traffic Regulation Act 1984 and s 102 of the Transport Act 1968 contain identical provisions.

The nominated person will now normally be John Doe, the fictitious litigant of the seventeenth century, resurrected in *Barnett* v *French* [1981] RTR 173. The nominated defendant in that case was responsible for 3,500 Crown vehicles and would have been at risk of becoming the citizen with the largest record of motoring convictions ever known. The Divisional Court suggested the use of the name John Doe instead. The name Doe is particularly appropriate in that it comprises the initial letters of the Department of the Environment.

Drivers of Crown vehicles (including British servicemen on duty) are therefore fully responsible for offences of bad or drunken driving, disobeying traffic signs, not reporting accidents, breaches of the Construction and Use and Pedestrian Crossings Regulations, speeding (with certain exceptions) and so on. The position as to insurance is mentioned under that heading in this work, 10.8. The nationalised industries are not Crown emanations (*Tamlin* v *Hannaford* [1949] 2 All ER 327) and the BBC is not a Crown department (*British Broadcasting Corporation* v *Johns* [1964] 1 All ER 923) nor is the British Airports Authority (Airports Authority Act 1975). The Post Office Corporation is not a Crown department (Post Office Act 1969, s 6(5)).

A British serviceman may be convicted by court-martial of committing a civil offence of a road traffic type abroad contrary to s 70 of the Army Act (*Cox* v *Army Council* [1962] 1 All ER 880). The offence in question was careless driving on a road in Germany and it was said that there may be offences under the Road Traffic and Highway Acts which cannot be committed abroad. The provisions of the Road Traffic Act 1972, ss 5 and 6, as to driving, etc, when unfit through drink or with alcohol above the prescribed limit are applied to servicemen in Great Britain and abroad (1972 Act, s 188). Where a person subject to the Naval Discipline Act 1957 is acquitted or convicted of an offence by a Naval tribunal, a civil court shall by s 129(1) be debarred from trying him subsequently for the same offence and by s 129(2) acquittal or conviction by a civil court bars subsequent trial by a Naval tribunal. By the Armed Forces Act 1966, s 25, substituting a new s 133 in the Army and the Air Force Acts 1955, where a person subject to military or Air Force law has been tried for an offence by a court-martial or by his commanding officer or had it taken into consideration at a court-martial, a civil court is debarred from trying him subsequently for an offence substantially the same as that offence.

See 11.23 as to disqualification.

*Enactments not specifically naming the Crown*

As stated, many of the provisions of the Road Traffic Acts apply to the Crown and its servants but the provisions of s 28 of the Road Traffic Regulation Act 1984 (stopping for school crossing patrols) are not mentioned in s 130 nor do the Highway Act 1835, the Town Police Clauses Act 1847 and the Highways Act 1980, s 137 (obstruction), contain provisions binding the Crown.

A statute which does not name the Crown does not bind it unless it is an enactment of paramount importance to public safety which requires that Crown servants should be responsible if, in performance of their duties and acting under orders, they contravene its terms (*Cooper* v *Hawkins* (1904) 68 JP 25). It is submitted that the provisions of s 28 of the Road Traffic Regulation Act 1984 and of s 78 of the Highway Act 1835 (relating to school crossing patrols and negligent opening of car doors respectively) are enactments of sufficient importance to public safety to override the rule that Crown servants acting on duty are not liable under them. Even if they do not override that rule, where there is a personal element in a charge against a man under a statute which does not bind the Crown or an individual act by a driver apart from the performance of his duty as a servant of the Crown (per Lord Alverstone CJ in *Cooper* v *Hawkins*), or an act by a driver which is his own personal act, eg, being drunk or in a condition or under circumstances 'in which he was not performing a public duty or acting in accordance with superior orders' (per Wills and Channell JJ ibid), it is submitted that the driver in such a case cannot claim the benefit of any Crown exemption. Although in *Cooper* v *Hawkins* above a conviction of an Army driver for exceeding a local speed-limit was quashed because he was acting under orders and it was necessary both in the particular circumstances and in the interests of the Army generally that a low speed limit should not be observed, the cited dicta of the judges in the case are, it is argued, sufficient authority for saying that Crown drivers are in the same position as civilian drivers in regard to obeying school crossing patrols and taking precautions before opening car doors, for these are personal matters in the driver's control and save, perhaps, in exceptional circumstances, in no way hinder the performance of the functions of any Crown department. Examples of exceptional circumstances in which a Crown servant might not be liable would be a policeman opening the door of his car as quickly as possible to save life or the driver of an RAF ambulance, under orders to get to a crashed aircraft without delay, ignoring a school crossing patrolman's signal. It is submitted that it is only if the driver's personal act is in direct performance of his public duty that the exemption applies. Accordingly, Crown drivers cannot, if this argument is right, claim any exemption for the acts and omissions mentioned above or others arising under the same statutes. See also *Salt* v *Macknight* at 10.8. Prosecutions for 'opening car doors' will generally now be brought under the Construction and Use Regulations, which apply to the Crown.

As regards obstruction, there is no exemption for the Crown under the Motor Vehicles (Construction and Use) Regulations, which relate to motor vehicles and trailers, but it might sometimes be necessary to prosecute Crown drivers and their superior officers under the Highways Act 1980, s 137. Here a defence that it was necessary to leave vehicles near a particular Government building for the department's work to be done more efficiently might be successful.

As regards school crossing patrols, it is submitted that the omission of s 28 from s 130 of the Road Traffic Regulation Act 1984, which specifies the provisions of that Act which bind the Crown, is not conclusive in showing that s 28 does not anyhow itself bind the Crown. Section 130 is a re-enactment of a provision previously in the Road Traffic Regulation Act 1967 and in the Road Traffic Act 1930 and s 28 is a re-enactment (via s 25 of the 1967 Act) of the original School Crossing Patrols Act 1953; the 1953 Act contained no reference to the Crown so that the omission of s 28 of the 1984 Act from s 130, it is argued, does not expressly mean that it does not bind the Crown but merely that the position under the 1953 Act, which may or may not have bound the Crown, is preserved.

Crown roads are subject to the general statutory provisions which apply to roads generally, it is submitted. Those particular statutory provisions which apply to roads only if particular steps are taken, as by the making of an order, may be applied to Crown roads by order under s 131 of the Road Traffic Regulation Act 1984, eg restricted waiting orders, pedestrian crossings, etc. See further 1.71.

### 2.9–15 Waiving summons

The court may deal with a defendant actually before it, though not in answer to a summons, unless he seeks time to prepare his defence (see the current edition of Stone, Part I under 'Irregularities in Process etc'). Sometimes, when a defendant has come in answer to a summons, the prosecution desire to prefer a further or alternative charge. The defendant may waive a summons for the new charge and declare himself ready to meet it then and there, and, if he does, the new charge can be proceeded with immediately (*Eggington* v *Pearl* (1875) 40 JP 56). But he is entitled to know exactly the charge and should be told of his right to an adjournment to consider the new charge. *Semble*, a defendant who contends that he has been wrongfully arrested or that his summons is defective may properly object to being tried until proper process summoning him has been issued (*Dixon* v *Wells* (1890) 54 JP 308, 725), but it was remarked in that case that it had been held by some of the judges in *R* v *Hughes* (1879) 4 QBD 614 and *R* v *Shaw* (1865) 29 JP 339 that, if the accused were present and the court had jurisdiction, his protest against any defect in process or wrongful arrest might be of no avail. *Semble*, a summons returnable forthwith, if the time limit had not expired, could be sought and issued by the magistrates but the defendant should be allowed time to prepare his defence if he wants it. Where the prosecution agree with the defence to 'accept a plea' to careless driving on a summons for reckless driving, the defendant may waive having the summons for the lesser charge, but the procedure to be followed in these particular cases is mentioned at 5.7.

An appearance simply to draw attention to an irregularity in service is not a waiver (*Pearks, Gunston & Tee Ltd* v *Richardson* (1902) 56 JP 119). It has long been accepted that a court cannot deal with a defendant who appears under protest, unless the protest be properly overruled. The court must, of course, in every case have jurisdiction to deal with the offence: see 'Venue' below.

## Venue

### 2.16–20 Generally

The venue for indictable offences is regulated, so far as magistrates' courts are concerned, by s 2 of the Magistrates' Courts Act 1980. By s 2(3) and (4) magistrates may try summarily an 'either way' offence, eg taking a conveyance, which has been committed by a person who appears or is brought before the court, although it has been committed outside their area, provided it is committed in England or Wales or otherwise within their jurisdiction. A magistrates' court for any area by which a person is tried for an offence shall have jurisdiction to try him for any summary offence for which he could be tried by a magistrates' court for any other area (Magistrates' Courts Act 1980, s 2(6)). It is submitted that he must lawfully have first come before the court for an offence in that court's area or be otherwise lawfully triable by it by issue of a summons or warrant for an offence within the court's jurisdiction before he can be dealt with for a summary offence committed outside it.

Otherwise, unless the statute which creates the offence provides differently, the venue for offences which can only be tried summarily is where the offence was committed. Thus, where a driving offence is committed by an unknown person in Brighton and the owner of the vehicle concerned refuses to give information, contrary to the Road Traffic Act 1972, s 168, when interviewed in Dover, the owner's offence is committed in Dover (but see the Magistrates' Courts Act 1980, s 1(2), below). Again, where a driver exceeds the speed limit on a Kent road, but is not stopped by his pursuers till he is one mile inside Sussex, and he then fails to produce his licence, the speeding is committed in Kent and the non-production offence in Sussex (see below as to offences within 500 yards of a boundary), but under s 2(6) he can be tried for both offences together in Sussex or in Kent.

The Magistrates' Courts Act 1980, s 1(2)(*b*), enables a person to be tried for his offences in the same court as some other person charged with some other offence, where a magistrate considers it expedient so to do, although the former's offence may have been outside the jurisdiction of the court which is trying the latter's, eg, a person who gave in London general permission to use a vehicle could be tried for permitting an illegal use in Brighton along with the user. Further, a person charged with aiding, abetting, counselling and procuring may be tried either in the same court as the principal offender or where the aiding, etc, took place (Magistrates' Courts Act 1980, s 44).

Proceedings against a second defendant under s 1(2)(*b*) may be brought where there is some *nexus* between his offence and the first defendant's, but a magistrate should consider the interests of a defendant living at a distance before issuing process under s 1(2)(*b*) (*R* v *Blandford* [1955] 1 All ER 681). It is submitted that there must be a special application to a magistrate under s 1(2)(*b*) before issuing a summons pursuant to it and that it cannot be relied on to give jurisdiction where there has not been such an application.

The criminal jurisdiction of county justices extends throughout their county (*R* v *Beacontree JJ* (1915) 79 JP 461), and so they can try offences committed in another petty sessional division of the same county. England and Wales are divided into 'commission areas'. 'Commission areas' are the London commission areas (as specified by s 2(1) of the Justices of the Peace Act 1979), the City of London and (at the time of writing) a commission area for each of the metropolitan and non-metropolitan counties in England and Wales (see Scheds 1 and 4 to the Local Government Act 1972). Section 2(1) of the Magistrates' Courts Act 1980 states that magistrates' courts for a county shall have jurisdiction to try all summary offences committed within the county. (It is submitted that 'county' for this purpose now means a metropolitan or non-metropolitan county in accordance with the Local Government Act 1972.) The footnote to s 2(1) in Stone states that the power of a justice of the peace to sit is not restricted to the magistrates' court in the county in which he ordinarily sits. A metropolitan stipendiary magistrate is a justice of the peace for Greater London and for Essex, Hertfordshire, Kent and Surrey (Justices of the Peace Act 1979, s 31).

As to offences under the Metropolitan Police Act 1839 see 108 JP Jo 203.

By the Magistrates' Courts Act 1980, s 3, where an offence is committed on the boundary of two or more local jurisdictions or within 500 yards of such boundary, or is begun in one jurisdiction and finished in another, the offence may be treated as having been committed in any of these jurisdictions. The measurement, under s 3, will be in a straight line on a horizontal plane (Interpretation Act 1978, s 8). An offence of demanding an excessive taxi fare at *A* for a journey begun at *B* cannot be tried at *B*, as the offence was not in any sense commenced at *B* (*Ely* v *Godfrey* (1922) 86 JP 82).

By s 3(3), where an offence has been committed on any person, or on or in respect of any property in or on a vehicle on a journey through two or more jurisdictions or along any road forming the boundary between two or more jurisdictions, the offence may be treated as having been committed in any of them. To give jurisdiction in respect of offences committed on a journey the offence must relate to a person or property carried in the vehicle, eg, theft or wilful damage; an illegal user of the vehicle for carrying goods, where nothing is done to the goods, did not give jurisdiction under this section in any place save where the goods were carried, although the vehicle was on a continuous journey and carried them during part of it (*Wardhaugh* v *Mace* [1952] 2 All ER 28).

Certain cases relating to carriers' licences may be helpful. It was held that a firm charged with failing to comply with the terms of a carrier's licence might properly be dealt with in the court in whose area its offices or headquarters are situate and at or from which it controls its drivers and to which the drivers have to hand in their reports although the contravention was elsewhere (*Entwhistle* v *Woodford* (1937) King's Bench Division, unreported). A stipendiary magistrate has held that, where an employee is charged with committing an offence and the employer with permitting it, the offences occur simultaneously in the place where the employee was at the time of the offence and *Entwhistle* v *Woodford* does not apply to give jurisdiction at the place where the employer's office is and where he first gave permission.

For a case where a Scottish managing director and Scottish limited company were found guilty of counselling and procuring in England, see *R* v *Robert Millar (Contractors) Ltd and Robert Millar* [1970] 1 All ER 577.

It would seem that the venue for an offence under the Road Traffic Act 1974, s 1(7) or s 2(7), of failing to furnish a statutory statement of ownership would be the magistrates' court in whose area is the place to which the notice has to be sent. Where proceedings are also brought at the same time for another offence in another court's area, s 2(6) of the Magistrates' Courts Act 1980 allows both proceedings to be brought in either court.

Special cases on venue are dealt with under 'Vehicle Excise Licences', 'Drivers' Records' and 'Drivers' Hours'.

*Trying cases together*

An important point on procedure was emphasised in *R* v *Bennett* [1980] Crim LR 447. It was stated that it was the obligation of solicitors, counsel and judges to ensure that as far as possible all charges against an individual should be dealt with at the same court by the same judge on a single occasion. Where a solicitor or counsel knows that a defendant is waiting to be dealt with on other charges, there should be an application for the matter to be put back or transferred to the Crown Court centre where the outstanding charges are being tried. This would avoid inconsistency in the sentencing of individuals and the waste of time and money which could result. On the face of it there is no reason why this recommendation should not apply equally to magistrates' courts. It suggests that the practice whereby some courts and some police forces are reluctant to agree to the combination of proceedings may be wrong. Obviously there must be limits. It may well be wrong to combine proceedings which will require witnesses to travel long distances for a disputed case. Again, a case may be so trivial as not to justify the effort.

## Limitation of Time

### 2.21 Generally

For all summary offences, except where expressly provided otherwise by the statute, the information must be laid within six calendar months of the offence (Magistrates' Courts Act 1980, s 127). Section 127 does not prevent a magistrates' court from directing a charge under s 3 of the 1972 Act to be preferred after dismissal of a charge under s 2 (*R* v *Coventry JJ, ex parte Sayers* [1979] RTR 22).

There is no limit of time in respect of indictable offences unless the statute otherwise provides. Proceedings under s 24(1) of the Magistrates' Courts Act 1980 and s 51 of the Administration of Justice Act 1970 may also be brought without limit of time. Section 127 of the 1980 Act similarly provides that indictable offences triable summarily ('either way' offences) may be dealt with summarily at any time subject only to any time limit for bringing proceedings for the offence on indictment.

Time runs from the commission of the offence, not from its discovery (*Teall* v *Teall* [1938] 3 All ER 349). Provided the information is laid within six months the hearing, the issue and service of the summons and the conviction may all be outside that period (*Abraham* v *Jutson* (1962) 106 SJ 880; *R* v *Fairford JJ, ex parte Brewster* [1975] 2 All ER 757). Nevertheless, justices may decline jurisdiction if they conclude the prosecutor was guilty of an abuse of the process of the court by laying an information without having decided whether to prosecute (*R* v *Brentford JJ, ex parte Wong* [1981] Crim LR 339). On the same principle it may be possible to refuse to hear proceedings because of inordinate delay. See 'Refusal to hear a case', 2.32. The date of the information need not be stated in the summons unless there was some question of its being out of time (*R* v *Godstone JJ, ex parte Secretary of State for the Environment* [1974] QB 445).

Laying an information is a ministerial act and it is sufficient to deliver it to the office of the clerk of the justices for the relevant area (*Hill* v *Anderton* [1982] 2 All ER 963).

Where there is doubt as to whether an information was laid in time, it is for the prosecutor to satisfy the court that it was and the court is entitled to dismiss the case if he fails to do so (*Lloyd* v *Young* [1963] Crim LR 703). A summons or warrant shall not cease to have effect by reason of the death of the justice or his ceasing to be a justice (Magistrates' Courts Act 1980, s 124). This provision would presumably apply to a summons issued by a justices' clerk by virtue of the Justices' Clerks Rules 1970 (SI 1970 No 231), because the wording of s 28(1) of the Justices of the Peace Act 1979 shows that the clerk's power is equated with that of a single justice for such purposes. The proceedings may be continued notwithstanding the death of the informant prior to the hearing (*R* v *Truelove* (1880) 5 QBD 336), or before the appeal (*Hawkins* v *Bepey* [1981] 1 All ER 797), at least in the case of a police informant.

Section 180 of the 1972 Act lays down a special time limit for certain offences under the Act. Proceedings may be brought within the period of six months from the date on which sufficient evidence to warrant the proceedings in the opinion of the prosecutor came to his knowledge; and such proceedings may not be brought more than three years after the commission of the offence. Who is the prosecutor for the purposes of s 180? The opinion has been given that it is the informant (see (1976) 140 JP Jo 675).

The main offences to which s 180 applies are s 89(3) (driving licence holder failing to surrender his licence and give particulars when particulars become incorrect), s 99 (obtaining a driving licence, or driving, while disqualified), s 143 (uninsured use of a motor vehicle), ss 169, 170, 171 (forgery, issuing and making false statements in relation to driving licences, test certificates, insurance certificates and certain other documents).

With minor alterations s 28 of the Vehicles (Excise) Act 1971 is identical in wording to s 180 of the 1972 Act and applies a similar time limit to specified offences under that Act, viz, s 8 (using and keeping a vehicle without an excise licence), s 16(7) (misuse of trade licences), s 18(4) (using a vehicle for a purpose attracting a higher rate of duty), s 26(1) or (2) (forgery of and false statements relating to licences and registration marks) and 'regulations made in pursuance of the Vehicles (Excise) Act'. Section 29 imposes a similar limitation for vehicle excise offences in Scotland. The extended time limits given by s 180 of the 1972 Act and s 28 of the 1971 Act are now otiose so far as prosecutions for 'either way' offences are concerned (eg driving whilst disqualified contrary to s 99(*b*) of the 1972 Act and fraudulent use of an excise licence contrary to s 26 of the 1971 Act), because under s 127 of the Magistrates' Courts Act 1980 there is no time limit for 'either way' offences. If an offence has a special time limit, the time limit applies to an aider and abettor of the offence whether the period be longer (*Homolka* v *Osmond* [1939] 1 All ER 154) or shorter (*Gould* v *Houghton* (1921) 85 JP 93).

Where persons have conspired together to evade a statute creating summary offences, they may be tried on indictment for conspiracy even though some of the acts of evasion were more than six months previously (*R* v *Blamires Transport Services Ltd* [1963] 3 All ER 170), unless the statute itself makes conspiracy to evade it a summary offence (*R* v *Barnett* [1951] 1 All ER 917).

## 2.22 Computing time

The day of the offence is excluded in computing the time (*Radcliffe* v *Bartholomew* (1892) 56 JP 262; *Stewart* v *Chapman* [1951] 2 All ER 613) unless the relevant statute expressly provides otherwise, as in *Hare* v *Gocher* [1962] 2 All ER 763. If an offence is committed at any hour on 1 January, the information may be laid at any hour up to 11.59 pm on 1 July. A month ends on the day on the next month corresponding in number to that from which the computation begins or, if there is no corresponding one, to the one next before it. Thus where four calendar months ran from midnight 30 September, the period expired at midnight on 30 January and an application made on 31 January was out of time (*Dodds* v *Walker* [1981] 2 All ER 609, a unanimous decision of the House of Lords in a landlord and tenant case).

A time limit expired on a Sunday when the office in question was closed. It was held in *Swainston* v *Hetton Victory Club Ltd* (1983) *The Times*, 11 February (CA) (a civil case) that Monday was too late. Where notice had to be given it was stated in *Griffiths* v *Secretary of State for the Environment* (1982) *The Times*, 28 January (CA) doubting certain earlier cases, that this meant when received and not when sent. The decision was reversed by the House of Lords [1983] 1 All ER but on different grounds.

## 2.23–5 Continuing offences

The subject of continuing offences is discussed at 107 JP Jo 183 and 93 SJ 671. Later cases are *R* v *Wimbledon JJ, ex parte Derwent* [1953] 1 All ER 390, *R* v *Chertsey JJ, ex parte Franks* [1961] 1 All ER 825 and *Tandridge DC* v *Powers* [1982] Crim LR 373 (the last two are planning cases).

Where there is a failure to do some act within a specified period, a continuing offence is created (*Penton Park Homes Ltd* v *Chertsey UDC* (1973) 72 LGR 115 and *Mitchell* v *Lepine-Smith* (1977) 141 JP 510).

The article at 107 JP Jo 183 referred to above contrasts the 'once for all' offence and the continuing offence. It is suggested there that failing to produce driving documents within a stipulated time limit is not a continuing offence; additional tests suggested in the article are whether offences are punishable in respect of one occasion only and are not qualified in any way as to duration.

The question may arise where a person neglects to give information as to the identity of a driver, and relevant considerations may be whether a penalty is provided for default after conviction and the absence of a provision declaring it to be a continuing offence (cf the Mines and Quarries Act 1954, s 163(5)). While 'maintaining' may be a continuing offence (*Edwards* v *Bull* (1956) 54 LGR 338), an offence of 'depositing and leaving' is not complete unless both the deposit and the leaving were within the limitation period

(*Vaughan* v *Biggs* [1960] 2 All ER 473). See 6.74 as to abandoning under the Refuse Disposal Amenity Act 1978, s 2.

Where a regulation requires an action to be done 'forthwith', eg signing a driving licence, generally this is not a continuing offence and the limitation period runs from the date of the issue of the licence (*A & E McLennan (Blairgowrie) Ltd* v *MacMillan* 1964 SLT 2). For the same reason offences of failing to notify forthwith a change of ownership, etc, under reg 12(1), (2)(*a*) and (*b*), of the Road Vehicles (Registration and Licensing) Regulations 1971 (SI 1971 No 450) appear not to be continuing offences. It should be noted, however, that the time limit for these offences is governed not by s 127 of the Magistrates' Courts Act 1980 but by s 28 of the Vehicles (Excise) Act 1971, as s 28 applies not only to various offences under the Vehicles (Excise) Act, but also to offences under regulations made in pursuance of that Act.

## Legal Aid

### 2.26 Grant of legal aid

The Lord Chancellor's Department is responsible for legal aid in criminal proceedings by the Transfer of Functions (Legal Aid in Criminal Proceedings and Costs in Criminal Cases) Order 1980 (SI 1980 No 705). Duty solicitor schemes may be set up and organised under s 1 of the Legal Aid Act 1982.

Legal aid is granted under Part II of the Legal Aid Act 1974. The procedure and the method of assessment is covered in the Legal Aid in Criminal Proceedings (General) Regulations 1968, as amended in particular by the like-named 1983 amendment regulations (SI 1983 No 1863). It is available for binding-over proceedings as well as for any criminal offence. Under s 2 of the 1982 Act there is power to make a 'through' legal aid order covering both the committal proceedings and the trial. It should generally be given to a person committed for trial or sentence even though a plea of guilty is expected and any doubt as to whether it should be granted or not is to be resolved in the defendant's favour (Legal Aid Act 1974, s 29(6)). Application for legal aid is made to the relevant court under s 28 and not to the Law Society.

In certain circumstances where legal aid has been first refused by a magistrates' court an application may be made to the area criminal legal aid committee for review (Legal Aid Act 1982, s 6 and reg 6E). There is a time limit of fourteen days. The following must apply before the application for review can be entertained.

(*a*) The offence or one of the offences charged must be indictable (including criminal damage offences and offences triable either way); and
(*b*) The application must have been refused on the ground of 'interest of justice' (presumably the Widgery criteria referred to below should still be used to determine this); and
(*c*) The original application for legal aid must have been made not later than twenty-one days before the date fixed for the trial or committal

proceedings if such a date has been fixed. It would seem that the fixed date of trial includes the date fixed for the operative hearing of a guilty plea leading to conviction.

Where the applicant is sixteen or over an assessment of capital and income is obligatory. The capital is the capital belonging to him on the date of assessment. If a contribution is due a legal aid contribution order will be made forthwith. Where the contribution is to be from income it will be payable by instalments over a twenty-six week period. If it is to be from capital, the legal aid order itself may be withheld until payment is received. There may be a revised assessment at any time if fresh circumstances come to light or if circumstances change in excess of certain limits over the twenty-six week income contribution period. Payments due under the Green Form Scheme are to be deducted from any contribution order figure (Legal Aid Act 1982, s 12(3)).

The powers of the court at the conclusion of the proceedings are now restricted to the remission of sums due to be paid by instalments *after* the conclusion and repayment only to a parent who has been ordered to contribute or generally on an acquittal (s 8(5)). The court could presumably invite immediate enforcement and then remit sums already due (in accordance with the powers given by s 35 and the third schedule of the 1982 Act and s 95 of the Magistrates' Courts Act 1980).

The contribution period for payments based on income ends automatically when the legally assisted person is sentenced to detention centre, youth custody or an immediate term of imprisonment (reg 25E).

In general a legal aid order is not retrospective and cannot be backdated (*R* v *Rogers* [1979] 1 All ER 693; *Welch* v *Redbridge JJ* (1984) *The Times*, 4 April). A legal aid application is determined when it is finally refused or granted and any subsequent application is a new application and not an appeal or extension of the previous application (*Welch* v *Redbridge JJ*, above).

Because legal aid is not retrospective it has become much more common to use the Green Form Legal Aid Scheme for pre-court work. The scheme is also available for parties to court proceedings but only with the approval of the court (Legal Aid Act 1974, s 2A(1) and (2) and reg 19 of the Legal Advice and Assistance Regulations (No 2) 1980). In court a standard application for legal aid may be preferable.

An applicant is entitled to the solicitor of his choice. Where the cases of two or more applicants are being heard together there may be assigned under the Legal Aid in Criminal Proceedings (General) Regulations 1968, reg 14 a single legal representative (providing he has been nominated by one of them) (*Baker* v *West Sussex JJ* (1984) 148 JP 129) unless the interests of justice require separate representation. In *R* v *O'Brien and Cliffe* (1984) *The Times*, 24 December it was said that there was no power to fetter the right of the solicitor to select a separate counsel.

## 2.27–30 Legal aid in road traffic offences

The Departmental Committee on Legal Aid under the chairmanship of Lord Widgery (1966) recommended that, so far as the offences in this book are concerned, legal aid should be considered for grant where the accused is in real danger of losing his liberty or livelihood, or suffering serious damage to his reputation, or there is a substantial question of law, or the accused has insufficient knowledge of English or is mentally disabled, or the nature of the defence involves the tracing of witnesses or expert cross-examination. It is understood that the Lord Chancellor's Department has issued a circular dated 14 November 1984 expanding on these criteria. Copies have been sent to the Area Secretaries of Criminal Legal Aid Committees. The criterion most frequently applicable to users of this book is the likelihood of a defendant losing his livelihood if he is disqualified for holding or obtaining a driving licence.

One of the Widgery criteria was adopted in *R* v *Brigg JJ, ex parte Lynch* (1983) *The Times*, 17 December when it was said that the fact that the applicant's livelihood would be threatened by a conviction ought without more to have led to a grant of legal aid, subject to means.

Before a decision is made on legal aid there must be adequate knowledge of the facts of the case. It may be desirable for information to be obtained from the prosecution for this purpose (*R* v *Highgate JJ, ex parte Lewis* (1978) 142 JP 78, per Lord Widgery at p 80). Information may also be sought from the defence. It may include details of previous convictions and details of the nature of the defence, in particular defences raising substantial points of law or requiring expert cross-examination. The defendant is not bound to disclose his defence beforehand. However, if he fails to do so he runs the risk of a refusal of legal aid because he fails to establish one of the Widgery criteria. Unless permission is given such advance information as to a defence should not be disclosed to the prosecution.

A magistrate who has been informed of previous convictions for the purpose of considering legal aid should not subsequently try the defendant on a not guilty plea or hear committal proceedings. Any breach of this would be contrary to natural justice (see also *R* v *Colchester JJ, ex parte North Essex Building Co Ltd* [1977] 3 All ER 567). It was said in *R* v *Winter* [1980] Crim LR 659 (CA) that a legal aid application should be seen by a trial judge only after conviction and only for the purpose of dealing with a legal aid application. Material which was not evidence in the case should not have been used to damage the credit of the defendant. *R* v *Winter* was followed in *R* v *Stubbs* [1982] 1 All ER 424.

## The Hearing

### 2.31 The court

The hearing must be in public. There are certain statutory exceptions. Otherwise courts should only depart from this practice if, by proceeding in open court, they would frustrate or render impracticable the administration of justice: *R* v *Reigate JJ* (1983) 147 JP 385 applying *Scott* v *Scott* [1913] AC 417. This is not a matter of discretion.

Wherever possible this course should be avoided, either by handing in an appropriate written statement or by the use of s 4 or s 11 of the Contempt of Court Act 1981 (see below). Examining justices taking depositions should sit in open court except where it appears to them as respects the whole or any part of the proceedings that the ends of justice would not be served by so sitting (Magistrates' Courts Act 1980, s 4(2)). Juvenile courts admit only the press. A single magistrate may sit as an examining justice to take depositions but, unless expressly provided otherwise by statute, at least two justices must sit to try a case summarily (Magistrates' Courts Act 1980, s 121(1)). Not more than seven justices may sit in an adult court and not more than three in the juvenile court. Metropolitan and other stipendiary magistrates may sit alone. If the justices are equally divided in their findings, the case may be reheard by other justices.

A bench of *three* justices who had heard all the evidence in a case were required to proceed to a decision and were not entitled to send the case for rehearing by another bench. If they felt unhappy about convicting a defendant, then their obligation was fairly to acquit: *R* v *Bromley JJ, ex parte Haymills (Contractors) Ltd* (1984) 148 JP 363. If necessary a majority decision prevails.

If any evidence is taken, the whole case must be heard by the same justices or two of them, and, if another magistrate joins them, the witnesses must be recalled and testify again (*R* v *Manchester JJ, ex parte Burke* (1961) 125 JP 387; Magistrates' Courts Act 1980, s 121(6)). It does not suffice to read their evidence over again to the witnesses who have already given evidence, unless it be a deposition (see the current edition of Stone under 'Magistrates', 'Part hearing by different justices', in Part I). Thus, if a hearing begins on Monday before three justices, the hearing of the same case on Tuesday must be before them or two of them (only one, though, if depositions are being taken); if another magistrate sits with the two or one who come again on Tuesday, witnesses called on Monday must be recalled and give their evidence again. A differently constituted court may sentence a person after he has been convicted by another court, provided there is full inquiry into the facts and circumstances of the case (Magistrates' Courts Act 1980, s 121(7)).

Under the Magistrates' Courts Rules various warnings have to be given to the defendant. There is sufficient conformity if the clerk gives the various warnings (*R* v *Horseferry Road JJ, ex parte Farooki* (1982) *The Times*, 29 October).

For contempt of court reference should be made to the Contempt of Court Act 1981. Magistrates' courts have certain powers under s 12 to deal with misbehaviour and wilful interruptions. Legal aid may be granted (s 13) and the criminal legal aid provisions are applied. Where there is a possibility of imprisonment, legal advice is desirable although not essential—see *R* v *Newbury JJ* (1984) 148 JP 248.

A court may order the postponement of publication of the proceedings or any part of them if it appears to be *necessary* for avoiding a substantial risk of prejudice to the administration of justice in those proceedings or in any other pending proceedings (s 4). The court should specify the extent of the postponement (see the wording of s 4). Where a court having power to do so allows a name or other matter to be withheld from the public in the proceedings before the court, the court may give necessary directions prohibiting the publication of that name or matter in connection with the proceedings (s 11). The court must first have allowed the name or matter to be withheld from the public during the proceedings or s 11 cannot apply (*R* v *Arundel JJ, ex parte Westminster Press Ltd* (1985) *The Times*, 15 February).

## 2.32 Refusal to hear a case

Magistrates' courts as well as the higher courts have inherent power to refuse or decline to hear a case on the ground that the proceedings are oppressive or an abuse of process (*R* v *Brentford JJ, ex parte Wong* [1981] Crim LR 339), or where there is some impropriety or mala fides (*R* v *Grays JJ* [1982] 3 All ER 653).

It was doubted by Viscount Dilhorne in *DPP* v *Humphreys* [1976] RTR 339 at 354G whether magistrates' courts had such a power. He gave no authority for his dictum other than remarking that the exercise of such a power would not be uniform, and the point was not argued before their Lordships. Magistrates' courts, unlike the Crown Courts, derive their power wholly from statute. Certain remarks in *R* v *Sang* [1979] 2 All ER 1222 (HL), particularly by Lord Scarman, tend to the same view. He distinguished between certain powers to exclude evidence and the absence of any judicial power to veto a prosecution. Section 9(2) of the Magistrates' Courts Act 1980 appears to be mandatory ('The court, after hearing the evidence and the parties shall convict the accused or dismiss the information'). Nevertheless, the remarks of Lord Dilhorne in *Humphreys* must be regarded as qualified in view of the subsequent cases.

Proceedings that are vexatious or an abuse of the court can be prohibited summarily by applying to the Divisional Court for judicial review (per *R* v *Manchester City Magistrates' Court, ex parte Snelson* [1977] Crim LR 423 and *R* v *Horsham JJ, ex parte Reeves* [1981] Crim LR 566, cases on committal proceedings; and *R* v *Cwmbran JJ, ex parte Pope* (1979) 143 JP 638). In the latter case a defendant was acquitted by a jury on an excess alcohol charge on the defence that he was not driving or riding a motor cycle but pushing it. Subsequent proceedings for careless driving were stopped by the Divisional Court on the grounds that the issue was the same and the proceedings would be oppressive. Lord Widgery said in *R* v *West London JJ, ex parte Klahn* [1979] 1 WLR 933 'the magistrate in considering an application for the issue of a summons may and indeed should consider whether the allegation is vexatious: see *R* v *Bros* (1901) 8 LT 581'.

In *R* v *Brentford JJ, ex parte Wong* [1981] Crim LR 339 informations were laid against the applicant on 28 July 1978 in respect of various offences arising out of an accident which had occurred on 30 January 1978. In October the applicant was told he would be prosecuted but summonses were not served until 7 December. At the hearing on 25 April 1979 it was submitted that it was an abuse of the process of the court for the prosecutor to lay informations just before the time allowed under s 104 in order to give him more time to decide whether to prosecute. It was held there was power to decline jurisdiction, the informations having been laid when no decision as to whether to prosecute had been made. See also *R* v *Newcastle JJ, ex parte Hindle* [1984] 1 All ER 770 below.

In *R* v *Grays JJ* above the alleged offences occurred in January 1980. There was an initial denial by the defendant. Twenty-nine informations, one of theft and twenty-eight of deception, were laid on 5 June 1981. On 7 July the justices decided the case was not suitable for summary trial. The prosecution were not ready on 5 August and when again they were not ready on 20 August the magistrates refused a further adjournment and the defendant was discharged. The prosecution commenced fresh proceedings in December. The defendant sought an order of prohibition but this was refused. The delay was not sufficient to render the proceedings vexatious or an abuse of process: as stated there must be some impropriety or mala fides.

This decision does seem to leave prosecutors with considerable scope for dillying and dallying but the seriousness of the offences, the existence of committal proceedings and an unrestricted time limit may have been factors. However, a different decision was reached and prohibition granted in *R* v *Oxford City JJ, ex parte Smith* [1982] RTR 201 (Lord Lane CJ, Woolf J and Stuart-Smith J) (two years between commission date and hearing and twenty-one months between laying of information and hearing) and *R* v *Watford JJ, ex parte Outrim* [1983] RTR 26 (Donaldson LJ as he then was and McCullough J) (twenty-two months between commission date and hearing). In these cases there was no impropriety on the part of the police but there was negligence. Both cases were summary charges of excess alcohol. The two cases emphasise that the decision to refuse to hear is one for the justices.

The *Grays* decision was the later one and it is unfortunate that the court was apparently not referred to the *Oxford* and *Watford* cases. The authorities were reviewed in *R* v *Canterbury and St Augustine's JJ, ex parte Turner* (1983) 147 JP 193 (a case on committal proceedings). McNeill J said that the decided cases do not show that delay alone is an abuse of process. Drake J said that one could imagine very extreme cases of delay where delay of itself might constitute an abuse of process. He added that in the decided cases delay had been accompanied either by some deliberate exercise of bad faith or inefficiency or, at its lowest (as in the *Watford* case), by an inference that something had gone wrong with the prosecution process.

It was said in *R* v *Guildhall JJ* (1984) 148 JP 392 that where the prosecution's delay in committal proceedings had been truly excessive, examining justices did have power to require the prosecution to disclose a prima facie case on pain of refusing an application for further adjournment.

In *R* v *Ashton-under-Lyne JJ, ex parte Potts* (1984) *The Times*, 29 March the defendant was prosecuted in September and October 1980 for fifteen motoring offences. On 12 August 1981 these were adjourned sine die pending Crown Court proceedings. He was finally sentenced by the Crown Court in May 1982 to fifteen months' imprisonment and two years' disqualification. The adjourned sine die motoring summonses were reinstated in May 1983 and finally came before the court in September 1983. There was no suggestion of bad faith and the justices decided that the prosecution was not responsible for the delay in that the defendant had left prison in August 1982 with no forwarding address. They therefore decided to continue the hearing. The

Divisional Court stated that it would not interfere unless it was satisfied either that the justices had not properly directed themselves in law or that they had acted perversely.

In *R* v *West London Stipendiary Magistrate, ex parte Anderson* (1984) 148 JP 683 the charge was refusing to supply a laboratory specimen. The defendant was charged on 28 October 1979 and arrested on warrant on 10 December 1982. The magistrate considered that the defendant had made no subsequent inquiries and the police had not acted in bad faith. He decided that the delay did not constitute an abuse of the process of the court. The Divisional Court reversed his decision and prohibited continuance of the proceedings. Substantial delay might be caused by a deliberate act or by inefficiency on the part of the prosecution, and where the defendant had not caused or contributed to it. If the defendant was shown to have suffered prejudice or even if such prejudice was to be inferred from the delay, the justices might exercise their discretion to stop the proceedings. The longer the delay, the more readily might the justices draw the inference of prejudice. Where substantial delay had occurred and that delay could be attributed in part to the prosecution's inefficiency and in part to the defendant's conduct, the justices had to decide whether the substantial delay resulted from the inefficiency of the prosecution and if the defendant had been prejudiced by the delay.

This point was again taken up in *R* v *Derby JJ, ex parte Brooks* (1984) 148 JP 609 where it was said that the ultimate objective is to ensure a fair trial according to law, which involves fairness both to the defendant and the prosecution. As to that case, see further below.

*Conclusions*

The following conclusions are submitted.

(1) If an information is properly laid, disclosing an offence for which the magistrates' court has jurisdiction, the magistrates are required to deal with it, and if they decline, they may be compelled to do so by judicial review (Magistrates' Courts Act 1980, s 9(2)).

(2) Magistrates may refuse to hear a case if the proceedings are vexatious or otherwise an abuse of process (*R* v *Brentford JJ, ex parte Wong* [1981] Crim LR 339 and the other cases referred to above) or there is some impropriety or mala fides (*R* v *Grays JJ*). It may be an abuse of process if the prosecution have manipulated or misused the process of the court so as to deprive the defendant of a protection provided by the law or to take unfair advantage of a technicality (*R* v *Derby JJ*).

(3) In extreme cases, delay itself may amount to an abuse of process if on the balance of probability the defendant has been, or will be prejudiced in the preparation or conduct of his defence by delay on the part of the prosecution which is unjustifiable: for example, not due to the complexity of the inquiry and preparation of the prosecution case, or to the action of the defendant or his co-accused, or to genuine difficulty in effecting service (*R* v *Derby JJ*).

(4) Substantial delay may amount to an abuse of process if accompanied by some deliberate exercise of bad faith or inefficiency or, at its lowest (as in the *Watford* case) by an inference that something has gone wrong with the

prosecution process (*R* v *Canterbury and St Augustine JJ*).

(5) Where there is substantial delay which is due in part to the inefficiency of the prosecution and in part to the conduct of the defence the justices have to consider whether the substantial delay resulted from the prosecution's inefficiency and whether the defendant has been prejudiced thereby (*R* v *West London Stipendiary Magistrate*).

(6) Justices should exercise their discretion in these cases judicially, not dismiss them out of hand (*R* v *Birmingham JJ, ex parte Lamb* (1983) 147 JP 75).

(7) Where the justices exercise their discretion judicially the Divisional Court will not interfere unless the justices have not directed themselves properly in law or they have acted perversely (*R* v *Ashton-under-Lyne JJ*).

(8) The Divisional Court (and a fortiori the magistrates' court) has no right to inquire as to the regularity of the proceedings under which a fugitive has been apprehended and given over into custody; see *R* v *Plymouth JJ, ex parte Driver* (1985) *The Times*, 19 April, where the authorities are reviewed.

(9) Finally there is power to refuse to hear a case where there are mutually exclusive informations. It was stated in *R* v *Newcastle JJ, ex parte Hindle* [1984] 1 All ER 770 that it would be an abuse of the process to allow the prosecution to proceed with two mutually exclusive cases. The two cases were driving with excess alcohol and obstructing a police constable in the execution of his duty. Neither information could be pursued without necessarily relying on facts which were diametrically opposed. The prosecutor could not justify both informations under s 1 of the Magistrates' Court Act 1980.

## 2.33 Proof of service; attendance of defendant

A summons may be served personally, by leaving it with some person at the defendant's usual or last known place of abode or by post addressed to such place of abode (Magistrates' Courts Rules 1981, r 99). The court may proceed in the defendant's absence only if he was served personally a reasonable time before the hearing, unless satisfied, eg, by a letter from him, that the summons has come to his knowledge though served in one of the other ways specified. However, where the summons is for a purely summary offence, the fact that the summons came to his knowledge need not be proved if it was served personally or by recorded delivery or registered post or left with someone else at his abode. This means that where summonses have been served by ordinary post, an acknowledgement is always necessary before the court can proceed in the defendant's absence.

By s 14(1) of the Magistrates' Courts Act 1980 the defendant may have the proceedings or an adjudication set aside if he makes a statutory declaration that the summons had not come to his notice until a date specified in the declaration, and within twenty-one days of that date, the declaration is served on the clerk to the justices. The Act also allows a justice (or justices' clerk), on application by the defendant, to accept service of a statutory declaration outside the twenty-one day period if he thinks it unreasonable to have expected the defendant to have served the declaration within that period. The declaration sets aside the penalty including any disqualification or endorsement, but a fresh summons may be issued on the original information.

A summons may be served on a corporation by leaving it at, or sending it by ordinary post to, the registered office, if such office is in England or Wales; if there is no such office in England or Wales, it may be so served at any place in England or Wales where the corporation trades or conducts its business.

Summonses may be served for offences in England on persons who are in Scotland or the Isle of Man under the Summary Jurisdiction (Process) Act 1881. Warrants may also be so issued and executed (Magistrates' Courts Act 1980, s 126). If any such person is in any part of Northern Ireland, the Isle of Man or the Channel Islands a warrant may be executed but a summons may not be served under these provisions (ibid). So far as process between England, Wales, Scotland and Northern Ireland is concerned, these provisions have been largely superseded by ss 38 and 39 of the Criminal Law Act 1977. A summons for an offence may be served in Scotland or Northern Ireland for the person to appear before a court in England or Wales (s 39). The Magistrates' Courts Rules 1981, r 99, now provides accordingly. Similar provisions under r 99 also apply to corporations. A warrant issued in England or Wales for the arrest of a person charged with an offence may also be executed in Scotland or Northern Ireland (s 38). Under the same sections similar provisions are applied vice versa for Scotland and Northern Ireland.

If a person is outside the British Isles just named, he cannot be summoned or arrested by warrant save in so far as the procedure relating to fugitive offenders and extradition applies.

As to certain powers of reopening where the court has convicted or sentenced the defendant through mistake or inadvertence either on the part of the court or on the part of the defendant, see 2.44. This may well be preferable to the expense of an appeal (see *R* v *Maidstone JJ* there cited).

## 2.34 Adjournment

A single magistrate may adjourn a case and, subject to the consent of both parties, a clerk to the justices may further adjourn a case (Justices' Clerks Rules 1970 (SI 1970 No 231)).

A refusal to grant an adjournment making it impossible for the defendant to call a witness was insufficient to justify a judicial review of the decision unless it could be shown that the defendant had been denied in all the circumstances of the case a reasonable opportunity to present his case (*R* v *Grays JJ, ex parte Ward* (1982) *The Times*, 5 May). Yet generally the court will be well advised to grant an adjournment to allow such an opportunity. See *R* v *Thames JJ, ex parte Polemis* [1974] 2 All ER 1219 where it was said that a longer adjournment ought to have been granted to a defendant from abroad.

The defendant must have adequate notice of the adjournment in accordance with s 10(2) of the Magistrates' Courts Act 1980 and with the Magistrates' Courts Rules as to service (*R* v *Seisdon JJ, ex parte Dougan* (1983) 147 JP 177). The full transcript of the judgment makes it clearer that providing it is established that the notice has been properly *served* it is only necessary to establish that the notice has been *received* where required by the rules.

Where a person is convicted in his absence due to his belief that the case is to be adjourned to a later day, the High Court will not generally quash his conviction by a judicial review but will intervene only if it is clear that he had done everything in his power to make sure he was not required to attend on the first day and that any mistake about a possible adjournment was due solely to the court or the prosecution (*R* v *Pembroke JJ, ex parte Perrins* (1961) *The Guardian*, 26 October); the defendant should appeal to quarter sessions (ie now the Crown Court) (ibid). Where a defendant has been notified that a case is to be adjourned to a certain date, the case should not be heard in his absence on an earlier date without his being given notice of the change, even though he has told the court that he will not be attending (*R* v *Haverfordwest JJ, ex parte George* (1964) 108 SJ 199).

## 2.35 Binding authorities

An article by the editor of the *Criminal Law Review*, assisted by the advice of Professors Sir Rupert Cross and JCS Smith, at [1980] Crim LR 402, may be summarised as follows:

(1) One Crown Court ruling does not bind another Crown Court: even if the ruling is that of a High Court judge sitting in the court, it has no more than persuasive authority.

(2) A Crown Court ruling is not a precedent which binds magistrates' courts but is merely of persuasive authority.

## 2.36 Preliminary points

Preliminary points can be of several kinds. Normally a preliminary point as to jurisdiction, ie that the justices cannot try the case because it is outside their jurisdiction on grounds of venue, or because the information is out of time, should be raised at the outset, but nevertheless can be dealt with at any time. On the other hand if there is a point of law or fact in the case which may be decisive (eg, whether a constable had offered a defendant a part of the specimen of blood in accordance with s 10(6) of the 1972 Act) it is usually inappropriate for it to be dealt with as a preliminary point (per Lord Widgery CJ in *Williams* v *Mohamed* [1977] RTR 12, at p 16).

## 2.37 Trial within a trial

In a case before a judge and jury, the jury are asked to leave the court while an issue is tried on a matter with which the jury at that stage has no concern, such as the admissibility of evidence, because if the evidence is held to be inadmissible the jury would hear matters which they had no business to hear. In such a case admissions made in a voir dire should not be used against a defendant in the trial (*R* v *Brophy* [1981] 2 All ER 705 (HL)). Issues of excessive delay may well be best determined at the outset of the trial. Where, however, the abuse of the court's process is alleged to stem from the conduct of the prosecution, there is no general duty on a judge to conduct a pre-trial enquiry (*R* v *Heston-Francois* [1984] 1 All ER 785).

In proceedings before magistrates, there is no quesion of a trial within a trial because magistrates are judges both of fact and law and determine questions of admissibility as well as guilt and innocence (*F (An Infant)* v *Chief Constable of Kent* [1982] Crim LR 682). Incidental matters in magistrates' courts should be decided as separate issues and not as trials within trials and consequently there is no need for evidence to be repeated after the issue of admissibility has been determined. The *Brophy* principle does not therefore apply in magistrates' courts. It is quite impossible to lay down rules as to when magistrates should announce their decision on this type of point. Each case is different and the object of magistrates is to ensure that what is done is fair to the defendant and just to the prosecution (ibid).

## 2.38 Plea of guilty

A corporation or limited company may enter a plea by a representative appointed pursuant to s 33(6) of the Criminal Justice Act 1925 (Magistrates' Courts Act 1980, Sched 3). He need not be a solicitor or barrister but the section is silent on whether the representative may examine and cross-examine witnesses or, indeed, address the court. The extent to which he may do so is, it is submitted, at the discretion of the court (*O'Toole* v *Scott* [1965] 2 All ER 240). Where the defendant appears, s 9 of the Magistrates' Courts Act 1980 requires the court to *ask* him his plea. A plea of guilty by a solicitor on behalf of his client without the question having been put was, for this reason, quashed in *R* v *Wakefield JJ, ex parte Butterworth* [1970] 1 All ER 1181 and, similarly, where there was doubt as to whether the charge was properly put, the case was remitted back to the justices for rehearing (*R* v *Gowerton JJ, ex parte Davies* [1974] Crim LR 253), but it was said that if the charge had been properly put, there would be no objection to the plea being given by the solicitor and further that such pleas would be valid even if not justified by the solicitor's instructions if the client did not show dissatisfaction with the pleas at the time. A magistrates' court may allow a defendant to change his plea at any stage up to the moment sentence is pronounced (*S* v *Manchester City Recorder* [1969] 3 All ER 1130). Where a defendant has been committed for sentence the case may be remitted by the Crown Court back to the magistrates' court with a direction to enter a plea of not guilty, and unless the Crown Court has exceeded its jurisdiction the magistrates' court may not decline to do so (*R* v *Camberwell JJ, ex parte Slope* (1979) 123 SJ 49). The position is otherwise on appeal against sentence (ibid). See 2.54 for pleas in writing.

## 2.39 Hearing charges together

The law as to whether a number of charges against a single defendant or similar charges against two or more defendants can be heard together is now clearer. (As to the desirability of bringing together charges against an individual from different courts and from different occasions, see 'Trying cases together', 2.16.) There are special provisions relating to Juveniles (see 'Juveniles', 2.4). In criminal cases cross summonses cannot be heard together (*R* v *Epsom JJ, ex parte Gibbons* (1984) 148 JP 78).

Separate counts can be joined in one indictment and a judge has a discretion as to whether or not they should be severed. Whether the judge should sever counts depends on whether there is a nexus between the offences (*R* v *Ludlow* [1971] AC 29). *If there is no connection, counts should not be joined* (*R* v

*Bell (Peter)* [1984] Crim LR 360). It was held in *R* v *Bogdal* [1982] RTR 395 that there was insufficient nexus between a dangerous driving charge and a charge of using a driving licence with intent to deceive. The offences were committed on different occasions but in the same car. The judge should have ordered the counts to be severed. They were not a 'series of offences of a similar character' within the meaning of r 9 of the 1971 Indictment Rules.

In *Clayton* v *Chief Constable of Norfolk* [1983] 1 All ER 984 (HL), Lord Roskill at pp 990–992 set out the principles to be followed when deciding whether there should be a joint trial of defendants or informations. He pointed out that in *R* v *Assim* ([1966] 2 QB 249), a five-judge Court of Appeal considered at length the circumstances in which it was proper to join separate offenders charged on separate counts in the same indictment. That court had drawn back from laying down exhaustive rules. He quoted at length from Sachs J at p 261. Part of his quotation is as follows:

> As a general rule it is of course no more proper to have tried by the same jury several offenders on charges of committing individual offences that have nothing to do with each other, than it is to try before the same jury offences committed by the same person that have nothing to do with each other. Where however the matters which constitute the individual offences of the several offenders are upon the available evidence so related, whether in time or by other factors, that the interests of justice are best served by their being tried together, then they can properly be the subject of counts in one indictment and can, subject always to the discretion of the court, be tried together.

Lord Roskill stated in the *Clayton* case that the practice in magistrates' courts should henceforth be analogous to the practice prescribed in *Assim* for trial on indictment. In the interests of justice as a whole magistrates should have a discretion.

Where the facts were connected, there was no reason why the justices should not try the informations together if they thought fit. When the question arose, the justices would be well advised to inquire of both the prosecution and the defence if there were any objections to hearing the informations together. If consent was forthcoming on both sides there was no problem. If it was not, the justices should consider the rival submissions and, under any necessary advice from their clerk, rule as they thought right in the overall interests of justice. If the defendant was absent or not represented, the justices should seek the views of the prosecution, and again if necessary the advice of their clerk, and then make a ruling in the same way.

Lord Roskill considered that absence of consent, either express or where it was necessarily brought about by the absence of the defendant or the absence of representation, should no longer in practice be regarded as a complete and automatic bar, where the facts were sufficiently closely connected to justify joint trial and there was no risk of injustice to defendants by its adoption.

It was impossible to lay down general rules applicable to every case, but if justices always asked themselves the single question—what was the fairest thing to do in all the circumstances in the interests of everyone concerned?—they would be unlikely to err in their conclusion.

The principles to be applied were set out in *R* v *McGlinchey* (1984) 148 JP

73 for trials on indictment and they would seem to be similarly applicable to magistrates' courts in view of the *Clayton* decision. They are as follows:

(1) Two offences may constitute a series.

(2) Rule 9 does not mean that joinder of offences can only be sanctioned if they arise out of the same facts or are part of a system of conduct.

(3) A sufficient nexus must exist between the offences.

(4) A sufficient nexus will exist if evidence of one offence would be admissible on the trial of the other, but the rule is not confined to such cases.

(5) All that is necessary to satisfy the rule is that the offences should exhibit such similar features that they can conveniently be tried together in the general interest of justice, including those of the defendants, the Crown, the witnesses and the public.

(6) The manifest intention of the Indictments Act 1915 is that charges which either are founded on the same facts or relate to a series of offences of the same or similar character properly can, and normally should, be joined in one indictment and a joint trial of the charges will normally follow, although the judge has a discretionary power to direct separate trials under s 5(3) of the 1915 Act.

(7) The judge has no duty to direct separate trials under s 5(3) unless in his opinion there is some special feature of the case which would make a joint trial of several counts prejudicial or embarrassing to the accused and separate trials are required in the interests of justice. In some cases the offences charged may be too numerous and complicated so that a joint trial of all the counts is likely to cause confusion and the defence may be embarrassed or prejudiced. In the other cases objection may be taken to the inclusion of a count on the ground that it is of a scandalous nature and likely to arouse in the minds of the jury hostile feelings against the accused.

Where two defendants are charged with separate offences, eg, one with using and the other with permitting the use of the same vehicle on the same occasion, and are not tried together, the whole of the relevant evidence must be given in each case, even though most of it is repetition from the first hearing (*Taylor's Central Garages* v *Roper* (1951) 115 JP 445).

Where two defendants are being tried together on different charges, eg, for careless driving in a cross-roads collision, should the court allow the solicitor defending the one to cross-examine the other or the witnesses called for that other's defence? The defending solicitor may undoubtedly do so where there is a joint charge and the other accused's evidence is unfavourable to his client (*R* v *Hadwen* (1902) 66 JP 456; *Rigby* v *Woodward* [1957] 1 All ER 391), and even if it is not unfavourable (*R* v *Hilton* [1971] 3 All ER 541). (In *R* v *Hadwen* (above) it was said that evidence for one defendant might incriminate the other and become tacked, as it were, to the case for the prosecution.) In *R* v *Hilton* it was also stated in that case that one co-defendant may cross-examine another even if the co-defendant has given no evidence adverse to him. On this authority it is submitted that, where two defendants are tried together on separate charges, each should be allowed to cross-examine the other and his witnesses. The main justification for this opinion is that, if one defendant is not allowed to cross-examine the other, notwithstanding that the latter's evidence helps the prosecutor, a serious injustice may result; support for it may be found in *Lord* v *Colvin* (1855) 24 LJ Ch 517, and *Dryden* v *Surrey CC* [1936] 2 All ER 535 (both civil cases) and in *Murdoch* v *Taylor* [1965] AC 574 and *R* v *Rowson* (1985) *The Times*, 8 March.

In *Hedley* v *Sparrow* (1964) NI 72; (1965) Jo Crim L 210, a Northern Ireland case, Lord McDermott CJ said that trials together, while allowable, should not allow the admission of evidence not otherwise permitted. The court would be well advised to seek co-defendants' agreement as to the order of speeches. See also the fifth edition of Cross on *Evidence* p 256, section 3 as to mutual cross-examination and cross-examination as to character. The general question of hearing charges of dangerous or careless driving against *two defendants* together, eg in a cross-roads collision, is discussed at 120 JP Jo 38, where the view is advanced that they should be heard separately, but there is cited a dictum of Lord Hewart CJ that it is the proper course that they should be heard together.

The further question of trying charges against *one defendant* of reckless and careless driving together is discussed at 112 JP Jo 226 and 305, and 113 JP Jo 201. If the magistrates convict on both charges and impose penalties on both, their decision might be open to challenge as being equivalent in effect to punishing a person for both murder and manslaughter; if they convict on both and impose a penalty for reckless driving only, the defendant, on appeal to the Crown Court against the conviction for reckless driving, escapes all penalties if his appeal succeeds. Such charges are sometimes heard together. Magistrates might think it best to convict for reckless driving only and mark the other charges 'adjourned'. Obviously, a safe course for the prosecution is to prefer a charge of reckless driving only and let the court reduce it, if thought fit, under Sched 4, Part IV, para 4. And see *R* v *Hawarden JJ* at 5.7. Where there is a charge of reckless driving and the prosecution agree with the defence to accept a plea of guilty to careless driving only and not to proceed with the graver charge, it is submitted that the proper course is for the facts to be related by the prosecuting solicitor to the magistrates and their approval of this course obtained before applying to withdraw the charge of reckless driving and before any plea is taken. In *R* v *Bedwellty JJ, ex parte Munday* [1970] Crim LR 601 the prosecution agreed with the defence not to offer evidence on a dangerous driving charge if the defendant pleaded guilty to the lesser charge of careless driving. The transcript of the judgments of the Divisional Court shows that the consent of the prosecution to this course was given subject to the court's consent. The magistrates' court insisted on hearing an outline of the facts and after hearing the facts refused to accept the dismissal of the dangerous driving charge. Their insistence was upheld by the Divisional Court, but the magistrates were directed to allow the defendant to elect trial by jury on the dangerous driving charge as he had only consented to summary trial on the basis that he would have the charge dismissed. If there is a charge of reckless driving only, the court cannot reduce the charge under the 1972 Act, Sched 4, Part IV, para 4, until the 'hearing' has begun, though there would be no objection to a summons for careless driving (returnable forthwith) being preferred if in time. Where charges for reckless and careless driving are preferred together, it is argued at 112 JP Jo 226 that a plea of 'guilty' to careless driving may bar proceedings for reckless driving, but a defendant who agrees to two charges being heard together cannot say that the court cannot convict and punish him on both (*Williams* v *Hallam* (1943) 59 TLR 287).

In England and Wales a charge on indictment of 'motor' manslaughter should not be joined with a charge of causing death by reckless driving: *R* v *Seymour* [1983] RTR 455 (HL). The prosecution should be required to elect. See also *R* v *Newcastle JJ* under 'Refusal to hear a case', 2.32.

A charge of driving while disqualified should not be heard along with other charges under the Road Traffic Act because of the possible prejudice to the defendant (*R* v *Pomeroy* (1935) 25 Cr App R 147). But a contrary view is argued at [1961] Crim LR 275 in respect of magistrates' courts. Some magistrates' clerks get over the difficulty by omitting the charge of driving whilst disqualified from the court list put before the magistrates, until the defendant has pleaded guilty or been found guilty on the other charges. However, an indictment may properly be drawn containing a count for this offence and one for another offence and, if the defence is that the accused was not driving at all, he would not (according to the Court of Appeal) be prejudiced by the jury's knowing of his conviction for the offence for which he was disqualified. The defendant may always apply for separate trials. Where the issue was whether the defendant was the driver, counts of dangerous driving and driving while disqualified were heard together at a Crown Court (unreported) notwithstanding *R* v *Pomeroy* above.

Where charges against the same defendant are heard separately, the justices should convict or acquit on the first charge before starting on the second, but may postpone sentence (*Hamilton* v *Walker* (1892) 56 JP 583; *R* v *Fry* (1898) 62 JP 457). It is submitted that even where it is proper to announce a finding in one case before proceeding to the next 'linked' case it may be proper to postpone sentence and instead sentence everyone when all the cases are concluded. Where two defendants are being tried separately on charges arising out of the same facts, eg, careless driving and causing an accident, the magistrates should announce their finding in the first case before staring to hear the second (*R* v *Chambers* (1939) 83 SJ 439). Where the charge is a joint one, they hear both defendants before coming to a decision (cf *R* v *Hadwen* at 2.39). Where defendants on separate charges are being tried together the facts and evidence will normally be so intermingled as to make it desirable to defer any announcement as to findings of guilt or innocence until both defendants have concluded their cases. Where the same defendant is concerned in two cases heard successively it may be proper to offer trial before a different bench in the second case because of the possibility of not approaching the matter in a proper and impartial manner. This is essentially a matter for the discretion of the justices. In *R* v *Sandwich JJ, ex parte Berry* [1982] RTR 332 the defendant had been charged with sixteen road traffic offences alleged to have been committed on six different days. He chose separate trials on each of the six sets and then applied for each set to be tried by a different bench, renewing his application at the end of each hearing. The justices refused on each occasion and were upheld by the Divisional Court. It was right that the justices should review their discretion after hearing each case and they had done so.

*Attempts*

Section 4(2) of the Criminal Attempts Act 1981 contains special provisions enabling certain informations for attempt to be tried together summarily with certain other informations at the discretion of the magistrates and without the defendant's consent. In view of the House of Lords' decision in *Clayton* v *Chief Constable of Norfolk* above there should be little need to use these provisions. In theory it might occasionally be possible to use the provisions to join certain offences which are not linked but this is unlikely in practice. The provisions in s 4(2) are complicated and were discussed fully in the 11th Edition.

## 2.40 Categories of cases

Under the Magistrates' Courts Act 1980 (and as defined in Sched 1 to the Interpretation Act 1978) there are now only three categories of cases:

(*a*) those triable only on indictment;
(*b*) those triable 'either way', ie either on indictment or summarily; and
(*c*) those triable only summarily.

The offences with which this book is mainly concerned are categorised as follows:

*Triable only on indictment*: manslaughter and causing death by reckless driving (s 1 of the 1972 Act).

*Triable 'either way'*: reckless driving (s 2 of the 1972 Act); criminal damage where, generally, the damage exceeds £400 (Criminal Damage Act 1971; see further 'Criminal damage', 15.28); theft and the taking of conveyances (s 1 and s 12 of the Theft Act 1968); driving while disqualified (s 99(*b*) of the 1972 Act); forging, etc, of licences and certain other documents (s 169 of the 1972 Act).

*Triable only summarily*: almost every other offence under the 1972 Act, the Road Traffic Regulation Act 1984 or the Transport Act 1968 comes within this category. A defendant cannot elect trial by jury for any summary offence even if punishable with more than three months' imprisonment.

## 2.41 Mode of trial procedure

The restrictions on publicity (see 2.42) apply equally to the mode of trial procedure (Magistrates' Courts Act 1980, s 8(8)). The mode of trial procedure for 'either way' offences is set out in ss 18–23 of the 1980 Act. It applies to persons of seventeen and over (s 18(1)). The procedure may be before a single justice (s 18(5)) and there may be an adjournment. On such adjournments the defendant must be remanded if he has been previously bailed or remanded or been in custody for the offence (s 18(4)).

The procedure must be 'done before any evidence is called' (s 18(2)). It is submitted that this only refers to trial evidence and not evidence on preliminary matters such as bail. Nor does it preclude a change of election for good reason on a retrial. It is submitted that such a change is still possible despite the evidence taken at the previous trial.

There are indications in *Re Daley* [1982] 2 All ER 974 (HL) that the formal mode of trial decision should be taken *immediately* before plea and trial if the decision is for summary trial. Lord Diplock stated at p 979D:

> Section 9 [of the 1980 Act] provides for a summary trial of an information to begin with the court's stating to the accused the substance of the information and asking him whether he pleads guilty or not guilty; and, if he pleads not guilty, the court then proceeds to hear the evidence. It is immediately before that happens that it is contemplated by section 20(3) the decision as to mode of trial of offences triable either way falls to be made.

The comment is somewhat at odds with s 18(4) which allows the court proceeding under ss 19–23 to adjourn the proceedings at any time.

The decision in *Daley* was considered in *R* v *Lewes Juvenile Court, ex parte T* (1984) 149 JP 186, and it was held that the mode of trial procedure was valid even though the defendant attained seventeen subsequently and before the trial and he did not have a right of election. McNeill J suggested that in such cases the register should be marked 'remanded for summary trial'.

The court must first ensure that the charge is written down and read to the defendant. It must then give the prosecutor and the defendant an opportunity to make representations as to whether summary trial or trial on indictment is more suitable (s 19(2)). A note should be made that the defendant was asked if he wished to make representations and of his reply (or that he made no representations) (*R* v *Horseferry Road Magistrates' Court* [1981] Crim LR 504). The same principle presumably applies to the special mode of trial provisions for criminal damage. It may be unjust and wrong to add a charge triable only on indictment to ensure trial at the Crown Court (*R* v *Brooks* (1985) *The Times*, 6 March).

If the prosecution is being carried on by the Attorney-General, the Solicitor-General or the DPP and he applies for committal proceedings, the court must accede (s 19(4)). The court next announces its decision as to the mode of trial. If the court decides on summary trial, the defendant must be cautioned as to the right to commit for sentence under s 38 on conviction (see 2.57). The full wording is in s 20(2). The defendant then has a formal right to consent to summary trial or elect trial by jury. In *R* v *Warrington JJ* [1981] Crim LR 629 the defendant elected trial merely to obtain sight of the witness statements. He then applied to revert to summary trial. The justices refused to agree and the Divisional Court disapproved of the defendant's tactics and upheld the justices.

There are special provisions as to criminal damage (see 15.28) and juveniles (see 2.4). The mode of trial procedure may take place without the defendant if he is legally represented, if the court considers there is a good reason (s 23(1)). The main difference where the defendant is not present is that the s 20 caution is not given (s 23(4)) and any consent is signified by the person representing him.

In *R* v *Southampton JJ, ex parte Robins* [1980] Crim LR 440, it was held that the justices had a discretion to allow a defendant who had elected summary trial to change his mind at an adjourned hearing and elect trial by jury instead.

The cases on change of election were reviewed in *R* v *Birmingham JJ, ex parte Hodgson* [1985] Crim LR 226. The defendant's state of mind at the time is crucial and he should not lightly be deprived of the right to trial by jury. The fact that a defendant was originally unrepresented and did not understand the nature of the election was taken into account in *R* v *Highbury Corner JJ, ex parte Weekes* (1984) *The Times*, 22 December. It is not relevant to the *defendant's election* whether the magistrates' court considered itself capable of trying the case (ibid). This is only relevant for the earlier decision whether summary trial is suitable.

The provisions of ss 18–23 governing the mode of trial are mandatory, and failure to comply will lead to the proceedings being quashed as a nullity (*R* v *Tottenham JJ, ex parte Arthur's Transport Services* [1981] Crim LR 180; *R* v *Horseferry Road JJ* (above)).

## 2.42 Committal for trial proceedings

Save where s 6(2) of the Magistrates' Courts Act 1980 applies (see below), evidence on a committal for trial may be wholly oral or a mixture of oral and written or wholly written; the latter usually happens in the case where the defence wishes to submit that even the unchallenged evidence for the prosecution discloses no case. Written evidence, by s 102 of the Act, must contain the declarations, etc, indicated in s 102(2) and (3) and should be read aloud at the hearing, unless the court directs that an account shall be given orally of it; the court of its own motion or on the application of any party may require the maker of the statement to attend and give oral evidence. Admissions made in court pursuant to s 10 of the Criminal Justice Act 1967 should be written down and signed by the person making them (Magistrates' Courts Rules 1981, r 71). By s 102(2)(*d*) also a party may object to a particular written statement given in evidence, in which case the witness must attend. It suffices if a written statement is given in advance to the defending solicitor but there must be a copy for each defendant whom he represents (*R* v *Bott* [1968] 1 All ER 1119). The Magistrates' Courts Rules 1981, r 70, further deals with written evidence. Though no minimum time for the defendant to see the written statements is laid down, obviously it must be long enough to enable proper consideration to be given to them. The Attorney-General has issued guidelines on the disclosure of information to the defence in cases to be tried on indictment (see *Practice Note* [1982] 1 All ER 734). All unused material should normally be made available to the defence solicitor if it has some bearing, as soon as possible before committal. If it may cause delay and is unlikely to influence the committal, it should be done as soon as possible. The guidelines also mention certain exceptions to the general rule.

Under s 6(2) of the Magistrates' Courts Act 1980, where the defendant or all the defendants, if more than one, are legally represented and all the evidence for the prosecution has been tendered to the defence before the hearing, the defence may consent to a committal for trial without the court considering the evidence; this course may not be taken when any one of the defendants is not legally represented or does not consent.

The Magistrates' Courts Act 1980, s 24(1), allows a juvenile to be committed for trial under s 6(2) without consideration of the evidence if it is in the interests of justice. In reaching a decision under s 24(1) as to summary trial or trial on indictment the court is not obliged to hear evidence: *R* v *South Hackney Juvenile Court, ex parte RB (a minor) and CB (a minor)* (1983) 77 Cr App R 294.

Unless one of the defendants applies for the restrictions on publicity at the preliminary hearing to be lifted, the evidence will not be reported in the press prior to the trial on indictment, save where no defendant is committed for trial (s 8). By s 8(2A), as inserted by the Criminal Justice (Amendment) Act 1981, where there are two or more accused and one applies under s 8(1) for the lifting of restrictions and the other objects, the court must make the order lifting the restrictions if, and only if, it is satisfied, after hearing the representations of the accused, that it is in the interests of justice to do so.

It was said in *R* v *Ewing* [1983] 2 All ER 645 that 'satisfied' in a criminal case means satisfied to the criminal standard of proof. What would be 'in the interests of justice' in s 8(2A) was considered in *R* v *Leeds JJ, ex parte Sykes* [1983] 1 All ER 460. The court did not attempt a comprehensive definition but said that a paramount consideration was that the accused should have a fair trial. An order lifting reporting restrictions should be made only where a powerful case for reporting the proceedings was made out by the other co-accused.

An application was made by one accused to obtain publicity for what was alleged to be unfair action by the police in pursuing charges they had indicated would be dropped. The application was supported by a second accused but opposed by a third on the ground that his trial might be prejudiced. It was held that the applicant's ground was at the most of peripheral significance to the interests of justice and really of no weight when weighed against this belief of prejudice. This shows that 'the accused' includes all the accused, even those who have made no application and have not objected.

The principles of reopening (see 2.44) would seem equally to apply to committal proceedings. See *R* v *West London Stipendiary Magistrate, ex parte Kaminski* [1982] Crim LR 40 where there are dicta to this effect. In the committal proceedings in that case the prosecutor was allowed to reopen after a submission of no case and granted an adjournment for the purpose in order to adduce further evidence to clarify an ambiguity. The court added that r 7(6) of the Magistrates' Courts Rules 1981 was primarily a procedural rule. The same may be true of other similar rules of procedure in the 1981 Rules. See also comments to the same effect in *Thornley* v *Clegg* [1982] RTR 405 at p 410.

If the defendant gives evidence at the preliminary hearing before the magistrates, his deposition may be read to the jury at the trial before the close of the prosecution's case, even if he does not give evidence at the trial (*R* v *Boyle* (1904) 20 TLR 192), but he should be told of the prosecution's right (*R* v *Warren* (1909) 73 JP 359). Section 72 of the Criminal Justice Act 1982 abolished the right of the accused to make an unsworn statement in any criminal proceedings.

A person may be committed for trial either in respect of the offence for which he was charged, or for any other indictable offence disclosed in the committal proceedings even if he is not committed on the original charge.

Where the original charge or charges are 'either way' offences the court may revert to summary trial in accordance with s 25(3) of the 1980 Act but only after the inquiry has begun. This will be subject to the consent of the Attorney-General, Solicitor-General or DPP if prosecuting. This reversion is not possible if the original charge was triable only on indictment even if the court has determined that there is insufficient evidence to commit on that charge but only on an 'either way' offence; *R* v *Cambridge JJ, ex parte Fraser* (1984) 148 JP 720. A court cannot revert from summary trial to committal proceedings under s 25(2) once a conviction has been registered; *R* v *Dudley JJ, ex parte Gillard* (1984) 148 JP 577; *R* v *Grant* (1936) 26 Cr App R 8. It is submitted that this may not preclude a reversion if an equivocal plea of guilty is changed to not guilty.

If the evidence is insufficient for committal for trial for any indictable offence the defendant must be discharged under s 6(1), unless he is in custody for another matter. Where a defendant has been discharged under s 6(1) the prosecutor may bring fresh proceedings (*R* v *Manchester City Magistrates' Court, ex parte Snelson* [1977] Crim LR 423). Any unwarranted use of repeated committal proceedings could be prevented by judicial review (ibid). See also 'Refusal to hear a case', 2.32.

An error in the correct statute in a certificate of committal for trial did not invalidate the committal (*R* v *Hall* [1982] 1 All ER 75). The old and new statutes (Magistrates' Courts Acts 1952 and 1980) were in like terms and the actual committal in court was valid. Compare *R* v *Folkestone and Hythe Juvenile Court, ex parte R* [1981] 3 All ER 840 (a committal for sentence) at 2.57. Similarly in *R* v *Carey* [1983] Crim LR 111 the failure of the justice to sign the certificate of committal was held not to be fatal. The requirement in the Magistrates' Courts Rules to this effect was held to be directory only.

### 2.43 Speeches and no case to answer

The informant may conduct the case for the prosecution and cross-examine witnesses for the defence, and r 13 of the Magistrates' Courts Rules 1981 gives both the informant and the defendant in a trial the right to address the court. Where a defendant was denied her right to address a stipendiary magistrate, her conviction was set aside (*R* v *Great Marlborough Street Magistrate, ex parte Fraser* [1974] Crim LR 47). *R* v *Great Marlborough Street Magistrate* was followed in *R* v *Middlesex Crown Court, ex parte Riddle* [1975] Crim LR 731, where an appellant's application for certiorari quashing his conviction was granted because the Crown Court had refused to allow him a final speech after he had given evidence on his own behalf. But where a judge of the Crown Court and a lay justice retired to consider an appeal without giving the appellant an opportunity of a final speech, the appellant's application for certiorari was refused. Although a solicitor and a clerk to the justices, he had not protested when the judge retired nor when he returned, and the case was not one in which there was any injustice caused by lack of a final speech (*R* v *Knightsbridge Crown Court* [1976] Crim LR 463).

In many courts a senior police officer in fact conducts the case though he may not always be the informant; police advocacy was disapproved of in *May* v *Beeley* (1910) 74 JP 111, but in *O'Toole* v *Scott* [1965] 2 All ER 240 the Privy Council held that the New South Wales legislation (which is similar to s 122 of the Magistrates' Courts Act 1980) gave a discretion to a court of summary jurisdiction to allow the prosecutor or defendant to be represented by someone other than a barrister or solicitor. On the other hand the court is required to allow any party to proceedings in a magistrates' court to be represented by a solicitor or barrister (Magistrates' Courts Act 1980, s 122). See generally as to representation otherwise than by a lawyer, Harris, *Criminal Jurisdiction of Magistrates* (9th ed), 191.

Following the Report of the Royal Commission on Criminal Procedure (the Phillips Report) the Government has introduced a Prosecution of Offences Bill which will set up an independent prosecution system to take over responsibility for prosecutions from the police.

Where a solicitor appears to prosecute, he may make an opening speech, reply to points of law and intervene to correct misstatements of fact made by the defending solicitor. The defendant or the defending solicitor may address the court either at the end of the prosecution's case or at the end of his case; he may address the court a second time, if the court permits, but then the prosecution is entitled to a second speech, to be delivered prior to the second speech for the defence (Magistrates' Courts Rules 1981, r 13). It was held in *R* v *Wetwood*; *R* v *Watson* (1982) *The Times*, 20 January that there was nothing wrong in the prosecution addressing the jury twice even though the defendant gave no evidence. Rule 13 in fact gives these rights of address to the 'prosecutor' and the 'accused' and so apparently applies to those appearing in person and to prosecutors not legally qualified who are allowed to appear, eg under the Local Government Act 1972, s 223.

While the rules make no mention of submitting 'No case to answer', this is now a well-recognised procedure in magistrates' courts and in a criminal case the court should not put a defendant to his election whether to give evidence or rest on a submission of 'no case' (*Jones* v *Metcalfe* [1967] 3 All ER 205); evidence may be called if it is overruled. It is submitted that the prosecutor may reply to a submission that there is in law no case to answer but should not reply to a like submission on facts alone, eg that the witnesses have been so discredited that their evidence cannot be safely relied on. And see *Saunders* v *Johns* at 2.44.

Where the defence submit that there is no case to answer, the court should, before ruling, ask: 'Are you calling evidence?' so that there is no misunderstanding as to whether it is the final speech or a mere submission (*R* v *Birkenhead JJ, ex parte Fisher* [1962] 3 All ER 837; *R* v *Gravesend JJ, ex parte Sheldon* [1968] Crim LR 506). Where in reply to a submission of 'no case' the magistrates use words intended to amount to a conviction, their decision will be quashed (ibid, but see now *S* v *Manchester City Recorder*, below). But such words must be intended to amount to a conviction and if, through infelicity of expression, the chairman has announced a conviction in reply to a submission but his colleagues intended merely that he should announce that they overrule the submission, this verbal error can be corrected since it is a 'slip of the tongue' as in *R* v *Newcastle-upon-Tyne JJ, ex parte Swales* [1972] RTR

57. It is suggested that in such a case the prosecutor should immediately ask all the magistrates if it is the decision of the whole bench that there should be a conviction.

In a *Practice Direction* [1962] 1 All ER 448 (of which it has been said: 'All justices' clerks should keep on their table a copy and make a practice of putting it before the presiding justice for guidance on every submission of no case': per Lord Bridge in *Stoneley* v *Coleman* [1974] Crim LR 254), the Divisional Court stated that a submission that there is no case to answer may properly be made and upheld: (*a*) *when there has been no evidence to prove an essential element in the alleged offence; or* (*b*) *when the evidence adduced by the prosecution has been so discredited as a result of cross-examination or is so manifestly unreliable that no reasonable tribunal could safely convict on it.*

Apart from these two situations, the practice direction continues, a tribunal should not in general be called on to reach a decision as to conviction or acquittal until the whole of the evidence which either side wishes to tender has been placed before it. If, however, a submission is made that there is no case to answer, the decision should depend not so much on whether the adjudicating tribunal (if compelled to do so) would at that stage convict or acquit but on whether the evidence is such that a reasonable tribunal might convict. If a reasonable tribunal might convict on the evidence so far laid before it, there is a case to answer.

The nature of a submission of no case was further considered in *R* v *Galbraith* (1981) 145 JP 406 and discussed at (1981) 145 JP Jo 690. As suggested in the *Justice of the Peace*, it is submitted that *Galbraith* is not inconsistent with the practice direction but merely a restatement of the principles therein and that these principles are similar in both the Crown Court and the magistrates' courts. *Galbraith* prohibits the former practice in the Crown Court of founding such a submission on the ground that it would be unsafe or unsatisfactory (or both) for the case to go before the jury. It is pointed out in the *Justice of the Peace* that although the practice direction uses the word 'may', presumably the submission *should* be upheld if there is no case, and that the grounds '*discredited . . . or . . . manifestly unreliable*' are differently worded in *Galbraith* but that this may be no more than a difference of expression.

Convictions were quashed where submissions of no case were mistaken for final speeches in *R* v *Birkenhead JJ* and *R* v *Gravesend JJ*, above, but it is now submitted that if the court has not pronounced sentence, it may, as soon as it realises its mistake, adjourn the case to be reheard by a different bench. The House of Lords in *S* v *Manchester City Recorder* [1969] 3 All ER 1230 held that a magistrates' court is not functus officio until sentence is pronounced. The latter case allowed a defendant to change his plea after it had been accepted and the case adjourned. There is no difference in principle between a defendant being allowed to change his mind and a court being allowed to do so when the court has made a finding of guilt on a mistaken premise. The House of Lords in *S*'s case, above, held that magistrates have only one duty, that of carrying a case to its conclusion. This involves a conviction or finding of guilt followed by a further decision as to sentence. Therefore where a magistrates' court mistook a submission of no case for a final speech, announced conviction and did not pronounce sentence, it was held that the case could be reheard de novo by a differently constituted bench (*R* v *Midhurst JJ, ex parte Thompson* [1973] 3 All ER 1164). If it is argued that a fresh bench cannot hear the case because the defendant has already been convicted, the answer to such a plea of autrefois convict is that the conviction is a nullity because the defendant was given no opportunity of defending the case.

*S* v *Manchester City Recorder* was distinguished in *R* v *Maidstone JJ, ex parte Booth* (1980) 144 JP 452 on the ground that it did not expressly consider the question which arose in the latter case, namely whether a court had a like power to order a retrial where a person has been found guilty in his absence under what is now s 11(1) of the Magistrates' Courts Act 1980. It was held in *R* v *Maidstone JJ* that there was no such power in that situation. It was also stated that the position was now governed by the statutory provision for reopening in what is now s 142 of the 1980 Act. The decision is somewhat surprising in view of the wide terms used in *S*'s case. It is difficult to see how s 142 has brought to an end by implication any other pre-existing power to reopen. The court was apparently not referred to the remarks of Lord Widgery CJ in *R* v *Midhurst JJ, ex parte Thompson* which indicate that the *S* v *Manchester City Recorder* decision of the House of Lords gives the magistrates a discretion to reopen at any stage until sentence is passed. It is submitted that *R* v *Maidstone JJ* would not necessarily be followed should a similar case arise.

In *Lonnkuist* v *Lonnkuist* (1952) 96 SJ 135, a civil case, it was held that, when a defendant has begun to give evidence after an unsuccessful submission of 'no case', the court should not stop the case until his cross-examination is concluded. *Quaere*, whether this rule applies in criminal cases; it may be that it would be limited to cross-examination on the vital issue, eg, if the magistrates are satisfied that the defendant was not the driver in a s 2 case after he has been cross-examined on that issue, it seems pointless to continue cross-examining on any other issues.

The defendant or his advocate may further address the court on rejection of his submission of 'No case to answer' (*Disher* v *Disher* [1963] 3 All ER 933, a civil case). The magistrates may still dismiss a case after rejecting a submission of 'no case to answer' even though no evidence is given for the defence (*De Filippo* v *De Filippo* (1964) 108 SJ 56, a civil case; see also *Rabjohns* v *Burgar* [1972] Crim LR 46 where the justices' decision was overruled on other grounds).

## 2.44 Reopening

A sentence imposed, or other order made, by the Crown Court when dealing with an offender may be varied or rescinded by the Crown Court within the period of twenty-eight days beginning with the day on which the sentence or other order was imposed or made (Courts Act 1971, s 11(1)). This twenty-eight day period is the absolute maximum (*R* v *Menocal* [1979] 2 All ER 510).

Section 142 of the Magistrates' Courts Act 1980 enables a magistrates' court to reopen the case where the defendant has pleaded not guilty or has been convicted in his absence. The section also enables a court to vary or rescind any sentence or order made by the court, whether the defendant pleaded guilty or otherwise, but there is no power to reopen a case where the defendant has been acquitted (*R* v *Gravesend JJ, ex parte Dexter* [1977] Crim LR 298). The powers under the section are only exercisable within twenty-eight days beginning with the date of the hearing. Thus, if the mistake occurred on 1 January, the power under s 142 must be exercised before 29 January, and it would be too late to do so on 29 January. It should be noted that the section does not enable a court to reopen the case for the purposes of a re-trial where the defendant has pleaded guilty and has been sentenced. The twenty-eight day maximum period for the exercise of the power under s 142 cannot be extended by a letter from the clerk to the justices written within the period giving the defendant a later date upon which the court would reconsider their decision (*Bradburn* v *Richards* [1976] RTR 275).

The powers under s 142 must be exercised by the same justices as those who originally sat or, where there were three or more, a majority of them; see s 142(4) and *Morris* v *Grant* [1983] RTR 433. Similarly the variation or rescission of sentence or order under s 142(1) must be carried out by the same justices as those who originally sat or where there were three or more a majority of them. Where the court decides to reopen the case for rehearing under s 142(2) following a plea of not guilty or a conviction in the defendant's absence, the court must direct that the rehearing be before different justices and none of the same ones should therefore sit at the subsequent rehearing. While the power to direct a rehearing must be exercised in the twenty-eight day period it does not seem that the rehearing must take place within that period.

Some guidance on the principles to be applied when reopening under s 142 was given in *R* v *Camberwell Green Stipendiary Magistrate, ex parte Ibrahim* (1984) 148 JP 400. A failure to explain a late arrival should be no bar to the reopening of a serious charge particularly where the defendant was to be dealt with separately for breach of bail.

A defendant in a magistrates' court may have the proceedings or an adjudication set aside if he makes a statutory declaration that the summons had not come to his notice until a date specified in the declaration. The declaration must be made and served within a limited period. See further 2.33.

The prosecution may properly be allowed to reopen their case where some formal proof has not been given of, say, a statutory instrument or (subject to what is said below) to hear evidence which owing to mistake or accident or want of foresight has not been given; if the statutory instrument is not immediately available, the court should adjourn (*Duffin* v *Markham* (1918) 82 JP 281; *Palastanga* v *Solman* [1962] Crim LR 334). Justices have a discretion whether to allow a prosecutor to call evidence, after he has closed his case, to fill a gap and their discretion will not be interfered with by the High Court if they exercise it judicially (*Middleton* v *Rowlett* [1954] 2 All ER 277). In *Middleton's* case the magistrates refused to allow the prosecution to reopen the case to prove the identity of the driver on a charge of dangerous driving. As they had exercised their discretion judicially, their decision was upheld. *Middleton's* case was applied and approved in *Piggott* v *Sims* [1973] RTR 15, where on the other hand the justices had allowed the prosecution to reopen the case to adduce in evidence the certificate of the police surgeon as to the voluntary taking of blood from the defendant and the certificate of the analyst as to the blood-alcohol level. Melford Stephenson J emphasised that the justices have a discretion to allow the prosecution to reopen their case even if the evidence, as was the case, was a vital part of the prosecution's case and was no mere error of procedure on the prosecution's part. *Piggott's* case makes it clear that provided the justices exercise their discretion judicially, essential prosecution evidence can be admitted even if the evidence is more than of a formal or procedural nature. The justices' decision was 'abundantly justified' (per Melford Stephenson J on p 18). The justices were aware that copies of the certificates had already been tendered to the defence under (what is now) s 10(3) of the 1972 Act and had not been objected to by the defendant. The same principle as in *Piggott* was applied in *Matthews* v *Morris* (1981) 145 JP 262 (reopened to admit statement of owner of stolen property).

It was said in *Royal* v *Prescott-Clarke* [1966] 2 All ER 366 that magistrates should normally grant an adjournment to the prosecution after the close of their case to allow them to satisfy a formal requirement as to proof (though evidence should not be allowed merely to strengthen the case against the defendant) unless there is misconduct by the prosecutor or he elects to call no further evidence or there is potential prejudice to the defendant; in *Royal's* case evidence was allowed to prove that formal notice of the opening of the road as a motorway had been published even though the defence had given notice to the prosecution well in advance of the hearing that they would require proof of such formal requirements.

See further as to reopening under 'Irregularity' 2.47, and *Price* v *Humphries* [1958] 2 All ER 725, where the prosecutor was allowed to reopen to prove the consent to the prosecution. It was said there that cases can properly be reopened where there is an objection which goes only to procedure, but magistrates must be very careful about allowing the prosecution to call more evidence, after closing their case, to prove something which goes to the merits and upon which the guilt or innocence of the defendant depends. If, for instance, the necessary witness has been called and, through a slip of memory, the prosecutor has omitted to ask him the formal question 'Who was the driver?', it is submitted following the views of the judges both in *Middleton's* case and *Piggott's* case that it would be unfair and a wrong exercise of discretion not to allow him to reopen in such circumstances. If a prosecutor finds during the hearing that a vital matter is likely to be unproved through the non-appearance or hostility of witnesses, he should seek an adjournment. See also *Jones* v *Carter* at 2.86. However, in *Saunders* v *Johns* [1965] Crim LR 49, as explained in *Brake* v *Taylor* (1967) 1 June, unreported, Lord Parker CJ said that, on a submission of 'no case' because of failure to identify the defendant, the prosecutor or the court could have recalled the relevant witness as soon as the submission had been made and obtained evidence which would have completed the identification. In the *Saunders* case there had been a failure to state certain facts which would have identified the defendant. Although it was said in *Brake* v *Taylor*, above, that there had been several unreported cases which showed that it was only in the event of a technical omission in a prosecution case that the magistrates were under any obligation to permit the calling of further evidence, *Piggott's* case makes it clear that where there is no merit in the defence objection, essential evidence should be admitted where the defence are aware of the nature of that evidence and are not challenging it. In *R* v *Doran* (1972) 64 Cr App R 429, after two defence witnesses had been called, two of six other witnesses in court discovered their own capacity to contribute something to the trial. The judge's decision to allow the prosecutor to reopen his case was upheld.

Generally, the later the stage in the case and the more material the evidence is, the less desirable it becomes to permit reopening because of the prejudice to the defendant. The same principle applies to amendments of the information. Justices should be careful, in allowing the prosecution to reopen their case or to amend, not to appear to be leaning unduly towards the prosecution. Further evidence should not be admitted after both sides have completed their case and the magistrates have retired to consider their decision (*Webb* v *Leadbetter* [1966] 2 All ER 114), and a conviction was quashed where the justices, after retiring, returned and heard a prosecution witness whose evidence had already been given by the reading of her statement made by that witness under s 9 of the Criminal Justice Act 1967 (*French's Dairies (Sevenoaks) Ltd* v *Davis* [1973] Crim LR 630). Where a vital witness turns up at that stage, one course would be for the whole case to be adjourned for hearing by a different bench, but this cannot be done if the magistrates have announced the sentence.

Where a judge exercises his discretion to allow the defence to call further evidence after defence counsel's final speech, the defence have a right to sum up that evidence to the jury, pursuant to s 2 of the Criminal Procedure Act 1865 (*R* v *Cudwick* [1977] Crim LR 158). It would seem that following this case, a magistrates' court would be wise to allow a defendant or his advocate a similar opportunity to address the magistrates' court on the additional evidence where the magistrates' court has allowed additional evidence after the defence's final speech. It should also be borne in mind that r 13 of the Magistrates' Courts Rules 1981 allows either party with the leave of the court to address the court twice, but where one party is given leave the other party shall also have leave and where both parties address the court twice, the prosecutor is required to address the court for the second time before the defence does so.

The principle in *Royal* v *Prescott-Clarke* above is equally applicable to committal proceedings (*R* v *West London Stipendiary Magistrate, ex parte Kaminski* [1983] Crim LR 40). The prosecutor was allowed to reopen and was granted an adjournment for the purpose, after a submission of no case, in order to adduce further evidence to clarify an ambiguity.

## 2.45 Amending summonses

Under s 123 of the Magistrates' Courts Act 1980 no objection is allowed to any information or complaint, or to any summons or warrant to procure the presence of the defendant, for any defect in it in substance or in form, or for any variance between it and the evidence adduced on behalf of the prosecutor or complainant at the hearing of the information or complaint. If it appears to a magistrates' court that any variance between a summons or warrant and the evidence adduced on behalf of the prosecutor or complainant is such that the defendant has been misled by the variance, the court must, on the application of the defendant, adjourn the hearing.

This means in effect that the summons can be amended (per Byrne J in *Meek* v *Powell* [1952] 1 All ER 347). A crucial amendment cannot be made under s 123 on appeal (*Garfield* v *Maddocks* [1973] 2 All ER 303). However, in *Lee* v *Wiltshire Chief Constable* [1979] RTR 349, the defect in the original information was merely technical and could not mislead anybody and it was held that in such a case the Crown Court could not dismiss the appeal because the information was defective and could not be amended on appeal. A summons may, however, be amended even if it is outside the six months' time limit for laying an information imposed by s 127 of the Magistrates' Courts Act 1980 (*R* v *Newcastle JJ, ex parte Bryce* [1976] RTR 325). Justices should, however, exercise their powers under s 123 judicially and so as to do justice between the parties. (Limited company charged with *permitting* their vehicle to be used whilst overloaded, charge amended to the absolute offence of *using* their vehicle whilst so overloaded—held, justices were entitled to allow the amendment, the prosecutor was not introducing new facts.) Again, in an unlicensed sex establishment prosecution, an information was amended from 'neglect' to 'connivance' even though the amendment was more than technical and made outside the time limit. No injustice was caused (*R* v *Bow Street Acting Stipendiary Magistrate, ex parte Spiteri* (1984) *The Times*, 16 October). *R* v *Newcastle JJ, ex parte Bryce* was applied in *R* v *Sandwell JJ, ex parte West Midlands Passenger Transport Board* [1979] Crim LR 56 (see 8.25). The broad principle in *Garfield* v *Maddocks* and *R* v *Newcastle JJ, ex parte Bryce* was summed up by McCullough J in *Simpson* v *Roberts* (1984) *The Times*, 21 December, by stating that *an information which was good enough to enable a defendant to identify the misdoing alleged against him could be amended so long as it continued to allege the same misdoing*. In that case the misdoing was different and an appeal against conviction was allowed.

What is now s 123 was held to obviate the necessity for a summons to repeat the date upon which the information was laid (*R* v *Godstone JJ, ex parte Secretary of State for the Environment* [1974] Crim LR 110); *aliter* if there was any question as to the information being out of time. In *Atterton* v *Browne* (1945) 109 JP 25, magistrates were held entitled to dismiss the summons altogether for a serious defect, but apparently there were other grounds also for dismissing it. And see *Westminster City Council* v *Peart* [1968] Crim LR 504 for a case where a magistrate was justified in dismissing an insufficiently detailed summons. In *Wright* v *Nicholson* [1970] 1 All ER 12, it was held that the words of what is now s 123(1) of the Magistrates' Courts Act should not be read literally as meaning that there can be no attack on an information however fundamental the defect. Each case depends on its own merits and circumstances are infinitely variable. It depends in every case whether the variance is of such a character as to require amendment.

If the defendant has been misled or the variance is fundamental so that there might be injustice to an accused, an amendment is required. Once an amendment is required s 123(2) operates and requires the court to adjourn if the defence applies. If the defendant does not require an adjournment, the amendment may be made forthwith and the case proceeded with on the amended summons. Thus, where a defendant had been required to provide a specimen of breath by a constable 'who had reasonable cause to suspect him of having alcohol in his body', justices cannot convict him on the basis that the constable had reasonable cause to suspect him of having committed a moving traffic offence, without first informing the defendant of the charge and giving him the opportunity of applying for an adjournment under s 123(2) if he had been misled (*Morriss* v *Lawrence* (1977) 121 SJ 187).

The variance may be so trivial that no amendment at all is required. In *Darnell* v *Holliday* [1973] RTR 276 the defendant was charged on five informations with using a car in 'South Parade'. The justices dismissed the case on the grounds that the offences occurred not in South Parade but in an unnamed cul-de-sac opposite. The justices were directed to convict by the Divisional Court as no sort of injustice was suffered by the defendant because of the misnaming of the road. Similarly in *Taylor* v *Grey* [1973] RTR 281 a stipendiary magistrate was directed to hear and determine a case where the road was described as 'Princes' Street, London, W1' instead of 'Princess Street, London, W1', the Divisional Court again holding that no amendment was required; 'it was a simple typing error which could confuse nobody' (per Lord Widgery at p 289). In *Creek* v *Peck and Jones* (1983) 147 JP 537, the evidence established that the intention to steal a bicycle occurred not at Guildhall Street, Cambridge but at St Andrew's Green, one and a half miles away. A correction was directed and no amendment was necessary. In *Moulder* v *Judd* [1974] Crim LR 111 a defendant was charged with speeding on the M1 on an information that it was 'at Bushey . . . on the southbound carriageway of the M1'; on it being shown that no part of the speed check took place in the parish of Bushey, on a submission by the defendant the case was dismissed. The justices were ordered to continue the hearing—'it was inconceivable that the defendant was misled'. In *Cotterill* v *Johal* [1982] Crim LR 523 the defendant had an accident in Booth Street, Derby. He then returned to a party, had several more alcoholic drinks and drove away. He was stopped in Portland Street, Derby. The defendant was charged with an excess alcohol offence when driving in Booth Street. The prosecution sought an amendment to Portland Street but the justices refused. They considered that the Portland Street charge would be substantially different and unjust. The defence was unprepared. The justices were reversed on appeal to the Divisional Court which held that there was no injustice and it was an error which should have been anticipated. Justices were held to be entitled in *Turberville* v *Wyer* [1977] RTR 29 to apply what is now s 123 in respect of an insecure load carried on a 'motor lorry' without the necessity of formal amendment when the load was in fact carried on the trailer of an articulated motor lorry.

At the other extreme, one can have a defect that is so fundamental that, far from it being required to be cured by amendment, it is in fact incapable of being cured. Thus the summons cannot be amended to a different offence altogether (*Loadman* v *Cragg* (1862) 26 JP 743—from 'drunk and disorderly' to 'drunk'; *Lawrence* v *Fisher* (1947) Jo Crim L 356; *Atterton* v *Browne* (1945) 109 JP 25). Where a defendant is charged with an offence under a repealed statute he cannot be convicted unless the summons has first been amended, even if the statutes are word for word the same. Paragraph 3 of Sched 10 to the 1972 Act does not entitle a court to convict on the repealed statute (*Stowers* v *Darnell* [1973] RTR 459). An amendment has been allowed to insert a reference to a statute which had been omitted (*Thornley* v *Clegg* [1982] RTR 405).

It is proper to amend a summons, subject to the defendant's right to an adjournment if he has been deceived or misled, where the ownership of property maliciously damaged has been wrongly described (*Ralph* v *Hurrell* (1875) 40 JP 119); where the date of the offence has been wrongly stated so long as it is within the six-month period (*Exeter Corporation* v *Heaman* (1877) 42 JP 503); where the defendant appearing in court has been wrongly named in the summons (*Dring* v *Mann* (1948) 112 JP 270); by deleting superfluous words (*Rogerson* v *Stephens* [1950] 2 All ER 144) or where the defendant is charged under the wrong section and the charge is inadequately stated (*Hunter* v *Coombs* [1962] 1 All ER 904).

Where the defendant is the wrong limited company the summons cannot be amended to show the correct limited company (*Marco (Croydon) Ltd* v *Metropolitan Police* [1984] RTR 24). The judgment in the case makes it clear that where the correct defendant is summoned but is misnamed an amendment is possible (see for example *Allan* v *Wiseman* below) but where the incorrect defendant is summoned and the correct defendant does not appear in answer to the summons no amendment is possible.

On the other hand where a company had exchanged names an amendment to the correct name was allowed (applying *Allan* v *Wiseman*); *Tector Ltd* v *DHSS* (1983) *The Times*, 29 June. Both companies traded from the same address.

Section 123 can be used after conviction and before sentence (*Allan* v *Wiseman* [1975] Crim LR 37) (defendant convicted in the name of 'Jeffrey Thomas Loach'—real name 'Jeffrey Thomas Allan'—arrested—name amended to Allan on appearance for sentence). *Allan* v *Wiseman* was applied in *R* v *Eastbourne JJ, ex parte Kisten* (1984) *The Times*, 22 December (clerical error amended after conviction and before sentence). Where offences are charged in the alternative, the prosecutor must elect at the outset on which he will proceed and it is too late after that to amend the information (*Hargreaves* v *Alderson* [1962] 3 All ER 1019), but where justices convicted an employer of failing to cause a current record of driving to be kept between dates in August and dates in September, it was held that while an information bad for duplicity could not be cured on appeal, the circumstances of the justices' finding of guilt showed that they had found the offence to have been committed on the first date mentioned in the information and that the words 'between' and 'September 25' could be treated as mere surplusage (*Blakey Transport Ltd* v *Baggott* [1973] Crim LR 776). It was held that in a charge under s 9(3) of the 1972 Act (failing to provide a specimen of blood or urine) words alleging a defendant to be 'in charge' of a motor vehicle were 'mere surplusage' in view of the House of Lords' decision in *Commissioner of Police of the Metropolis* v *Curran*, 4.91 and no amendment under s 123 of the Magistrates' Courts Act 1980 was required (*Roberts* v *Griffiths* [1978] RTR 362).

See *R* v *Aylesbury JJ, ex parte Wisbey* [1965] 1 All ER 602 (a case concerning the Great Train Robbery) as to the amount of information to which a defendant is entitled prior to the hearing. Where the defence asks for further particulars, the prosecution would often be wise to supply them (*Robertson* v *Rosenburg* (1951) 115 JP 128). Justices are not deprived of jurisdiction because a summons is insufficiently detailed (*Neal* v *Devenish* (1894) 58 JP 246); contrast *Stephenson* v *Johnson* [1954] 1 All ER 369, where the particulars of the offence were so lacking that the justices 'should not have entertained it'. *Semble*, they could at their discretion have adjourned for further and better particulars to be given.

Generally, the later the stage in the proceedings and the more material the amendment, the less desirable it becomes to grant the amendment because of the prejudice to the defendant. One useful test for amending summonses may be to follow the comment of Ormrod LJ in *Thorney* v *Clegg* [1982] RTR 405 at p 410. This was that if the objection to amendment was an objection of substance and indicated some real injustice, or a risk of injustice being occasioned to the defendant, then the objection might well prevail.

Where the prosecutor does not avail himself of his chance to seek amendment of a defective information, a conviction on that information will be bad (*Hunter* v *Coombs*, above). A defendant who disputes the case on its merits is generally deemed to waive objection to unchallenged irregularities in the summons etc.

A defective summons can be withdrawn and a regular one issued in its place, if within the time limit and if there has been no adjudication on the first one.

## 2.46 Duplicity

Rule 12 of the Magistrates' Courts Rules 1981 provides that 'a magistrates' court shall not proceed to the trial of an information that charges more than one offence'. In *Hargreaves* v *Alderson* [1962] 3 All ER 1019 Lord Parker CJ indicated that this means before starting the trial. An information should charge one offence only and, if more than one offence is charged in one information in the alternative, eg, driving without due care and attention or without reasonable consideration, it is out of order; the court should call on the prosecutor to elect on which charge to proceed (*R* v *Surrey JJ, ex parte Witherick* (1932) 95 JP 219; *Fox* v *Dingley, Ware* v *Fox* [1967] 1 All ER 100).

The test for duplicity is whether the information alleges one or more than one illegal act.

In *Shah* v *Swallow* [1984] 2 All ER 528 (HL) substantial factual and legal material common to five informations was set out in a preamble and subsequently incorporated by reference. The document was held to be *not* bad for duplicity.

In *Kite* v *Brown* (1940) 104 JP 458; [1940] 4 All ER 295 supplying several kinds of rationed food was held to be one illegal act. In *Thomson* v *Knights* (1947) 111 JP 43; [1947] 1 All ER 112 an offence of driving whilst unfit through drink or drugs was held not to be bad for duplicity. In *Mallon* v *Allon* [1963] 3 All ER 843 admitting and allowing to remain in a betting shop was held to be bad for duplicity. In *Fox* v *Dingley, Ware* v *Fox* already referred to, using premises for smoking and/or dealing in cannabis was again held to be bad for duplicity.

The question has been raised whether it is one offence or more than one offence to fail to produce the various documents specified in paragraphs (i), (ii), (iii) in s 162 of the 1972 Act, namely the certificate of insurance, the test certificate and the goods vehicle test certificate, if applicable.

This matter was considered in a practical point at (1966) 130 JP 543. The answer given there was that this offence is in essence a failure to give to the police constable all the information to which he is entitled. In the answer reference was made to the words 'if he fails to do so' and it was stated that this has the natural meaning of 'if he fails to provide the information required by this section'.

Further support for the answer was also found in the wording of the proviso. It was considered that the use of the phrase 'offence under this subsection by reason only of failure to produce' supported the argument that there was only one offence committed however many items of information were withheld.

The answer was given in respect of the former section which was in similar terms, although the proviso is now contained in s 62(2).

The answer would still seem to be sensible and valid and indeed to the benefit of defendants with the result that only one offence is committed by the failure to produce one or more of the relevant documents.

Where there are different constituent elements of an offence such as an offence of theft, assault or careless driving, the various incidents may be included to constitute a single offence contained in a single information. Even though these are not bad for duplicity, there seems to be nothing to prevent the prosecutor including them in separate informations if each can, in its own right, constitute a separate offence.

An information alleging a single offence of driving without due care and attention was not bad for duplicity where the facts revealed two separate incidents separated by a ten minute interval and two miles in distance witnessed by two different police officers (*Horrix* v *Malam* [1984] RTR 112). *The test was whether the single count charged more than one activity even though the activity might involve more than one act.* The justices were entitled to take the view that the acts alleged constituted one, continuous, activity, taking into account the time and distance apart and that in each case the appellant was seen to be swerving erratically. A similar test was applied in *Heaton* v *Costello* (1984) 148 JP 688.

In *Edwards* v *Jones* [1947] 1 All ER 830 charges of dangerous and careless driving were wrongly included in one information. The prosecutor should have been asked to elect. The informations should be distinct even though set out in one document.

In *Cross* v *Oliver* (1964) 108 SJ 583 a defendant was charged with speeding in a road controlled as to part by 1957 regulations and as to part by 1958 ones. The speeding had occurred in both parts and the information alleged one offence of speeding contrary to both regulations. The prosecutor declined to elect to proceed for one offence against one of the regulations only and the conviction was quashed on the ground that the information was bad for duplicity as charging two offences. If a statute forbids the doing of act A or act B, it creates two offences and a conviction of both offences on one information is bad for uncertainty (*Field* v *Hopkinson* (1944) 108 JP 21, but contrast *Davis* v *Loach* (1886) 51 JP 118, where a by-law forbade the emission of 'smoke or steam' and a conviction for emitting 'smoke and steam' (they being mingled together) was upheld). But if there is one single incident *R* v *Clow* [1963] 2 All ER 216 is authority for allowing alternatives to be charged conjunctively. Thus in *Vernon* v *Paddon* [1972] 3 All ER 302 a charge under s 5 of the Public Order Act 1936 of insulting words and insulting behaviour was upheld where it arose out of a single incident. If a statute creates a duty to do either act A or act B, in order to constitute the offence there must be a failure to do both acts (*Field* v *Hopkinson*, above), and an information charging failure to do A or B is good. A charge of being unfit to drive through 'drink or drugs' is not bad for duplicity (*Thomson* v *Knights* [1947] 1 All ER 112), nor is one for 'wilfully or negligently' failing to comply with a condition under the now repealed s 134 of the 1960 Act (*G Newton Ltd* v *Smith* [1962] 2 All ER 19), nor one for drunken driving in 'a road or other public place' (*Montgomery* v *Loney* [1959] NI 171). An information bad for duplicity cannot be cured on appeal (see *Blakey Transport Ltd* v *Baggott* [1973] Crim LR 776). It is submitted that a charge of 'driving or attempting to drive' while unfit (s 5(1)) or with excess blood alcohol (s 6(1)) may be bad for duplicity.

## 2.47 Irregularity

Where an irregularity occurs during a trial, the court may start the hearing all over again on the same day (*R* v *Marsham* (1912) 76 JP 284) or permit the summons to be withdrawn and a fresh one issued, if in time (*Davis* v *Morton* (1913) 77 JP 223). If the irregularity prejudices the accused, eg, disclosure of previous convictions, the case should be adjourned to a fresh bench (see 2.50). Magistrates should not interview a witness privately, either before or after conviction (*R* v *Bodmin JJ* [1947] 1 All ER 109), nor allow an informant into their retiring room after retirement (*R* v *Stratford-upon-Avon JJ, ex parte Edmonds* [1973] Crim LR 241), nor a social worker in their retiring room (*R* v *Aberdare JJ, ex parte Jones* (1973) 137 JP 57).

## 2.48 Equivocal plea and change of plea

It is well established that courts must not accept an equivocal plea. See the notes in the current edition of Stone to s 9(1) of the Magistrates' Courts Act 1980. There is a clear distinction between the *obligation* not to accept an *equivocal* plea and the *discretion* to permit a change in an *unequivocal* plea of guilty at a later stage until the moment of sentence. This was emphasised in *R* v *South Tameside Magistrates' Court* [1983] 3 All ER 684, applying *S (an infant)* v *Recorder of Manchester* [1971] AC 481 and *P Foster (Haulage) Ltd* v *Roberts* [1978] 1 All ER 751.

On committal for sentence the Crown Court may remit a defendant to the magistrates' court for a plea of not guilty to be entered (*R* v *Camberwell JJ, ex parte Sloper* [1979] Crim LR 264). A Crown Court hearing an appeal has power, however, to investigate itself and should investigate a claim that a plea of guilty had been entered under duress even though the plea had been entered in the magistrates' court (*R* v *Huntingdon Crown Court, ex parte Jordan* [1981] Crim LR 641. The same principle applies on appeal where there has been an equivocal plea in the magistrates' court (*R* v *Rochdale JJ* [1981] 3 All ER 434). The Crown Court should only remit to the justices if it is satisfied that the original plea was equivocal.

The Crown Court should first make proper enquiry as to what happened in the magistrates' court (*R* v *Marylebone JJ, ex parte Westminster City Council* [1971] 1 All ER 1025; *R* v *Rochdale* above). A magistrates' court has a discretion to allow the defendant to withdraw his consent to summary trial (*R* v *Southampton City JJ, ex parte Briggs* [1972] 1 All ER 573).

A mistake in law by a defendant's solicitor does not automatically render a plea of guilty unequivocal and justices still have a discretion to allow a change of plea (*P Foster (Haulage) Ltd* v *Roberts*). The court indicated that applications at a late stage by defendants who have at all times been legally represented should be regarded with caution.

Certain earlier cases were disapproved by the House of Lords in the case of *S* v *Manchester City Recorder* in so far as those decisions held that a magistrates' court was functus officio as soon as a conviction or finding of guilt was announced. The House of Lords held that magistrates only have one officium, that of carrying a case to a conclusion. Where therefore a defendant pleads guilty and his plea is accepted and the case is adjourned, the defendant may change his plea to one of not guilty. The House of Lords' decision has, it is submitted, a much wider and more fundamental effect on the practice and procedure in magistrates' courts than may at first have been thought by commentators and other legal writers. It is submitted that, provided the court has not pronounced sentence, a magistrates' court may quite properly allow a defendant to change his plea of guilty at any stage of the proceedings. If prejudice is likely to be caused to the defendant by trial by the same justices (eg if evidence of previous convictions has been given) the case should be heard by a differently constituted bench. On the other hand, once the justices have pronounced sentence they are functi officio even if their sentence has not been entered in the court register. The entry in the court register is an administrative act recording the decision of the court. If the court has by a slip of the tongue announced the sentence wrongly, then, provided it is a slip of the tongue and not a change of mind, the sentence may be changed (*R* v *Newcastle-upon-Tyne JJ, ex parte Swales* [1972] Crim LR 111).

If the defendant is allowed to change his plea, the fact that he originally pleaded guilty may have some probative value and evidence of his original plea may be admitted on the trial of his not guilty plea; but before allowing such evidence, it should be decided by the judge whether it has any probative value, and if it has, whether its probative value would exceed the prejudice caused by its admission. If the charge is heard before a jury, the admissibility of the previous plea of guilty should be decided by the judge holding a 'trial within a trial' (*R* v *Rimmer* [1972] 1 All ER 604) (but this was held not to be essential in *R* v *Hetherington* [1972] Crim LR 703). Admissions made in a voir dire should not be used against the defendant in the trial (*R* v *Brophy* [1982] 2 All ER 705).

## 2.49 Autrefois acquit or convict and pleas in bar

Autrefois acquit or convict is a plea in bar on indictment and does not apply in a magistrates' court, but the same principle applies, viz: a defendant cannot be convicted twice of the same offence nor can he be again tried in respect of an offence for which he has been acquitted. The onus is, however, on the defendant to show that he has been previously acquitted (or convicted) of the offence. Thus, in *Iremonger* v *Vissenga and Another* [1976] Crim LR 524, it was held that before dismissing the case against defendants the justices must first hear evidence from the defendants that they had been convicted of a similar offence.

Issue estoppel has no application to the criminal law (*DPP* v *Humphrys* [1976] RTR 339) and in any event could not prevent a charge of perjury being brought where the original determination of the issue had been obtained by fraud (ibid). (Defendant acquitted of driving while disqualified, subsequently convicted of giving perjured evidence at the original proceedings that he had not driven at all in the year in question.) As to the extent to which courts have a discretion to refuse to hear a case because the proceedings are oppressive or an abuse of process see 2.32.

There is no double jeopardy where the earlier proceedings were a nullity and the prosecutor may successfully apply for judicial review even though there was a purported dismissal (*Harrington* v *Roots* [1984] 2 All ER 474; *Weight* v *McKay* [1984] 2 All ER 673).

Again, there is no double jeopardy by a foreign conviction unless there is a real risk or danger of punishment (*R* v *Thomas* [1984] 3 All ER 34). The plea of autrefois convict was held not available to a defendant who had been previously convicted of the same offences in Italy in his absence. He could not be extradited there and would almost certainly never be in jeopardy in that country.

A withdrawal of a summons does not bar subsequent proceedings (*Owens* v *Minoprio* [1942] 1 All ER 30), and in *R* v *Bedford and Sharnbrook JJ, ex parte Ward* (1973) 136 JP 40, justices were held to be entitled to hear a charge of driving with excess blood-alcohol against a Mr B C Ward who because he had been mistaken for a Colin Ward had been previously told that he would be required no further by the court. A conviction for causing death by reckless driving (or *semble* reckless driving) does not preclude a subsequent conviction for driving whilst unfit (or *semble* with excess alcohol) arising out of the same incident (*R* v *Coventry JJ, ex parte Wilson* [1982] RTR 177). A conviction for dangerous (now reckless) driving, where the justices have taken into consideration the defendant's speed, bars proceedings for speeding (*Welton* v *Tanebourne* (1908) 72 JP 419); *aliter*, it seems, an acquittal on the graver charge. A conviction or acquittal in Ireland on merits for driving in a dangerous manner barred subsequent proceedings for driving recklessly or at a dangerous speed (*R* v *Beattie* [1946] Ir Jur R 62). An acquittal on indictment for reckless driving used not to bar proceedings for careless driving, but different considerations now arise because a jury is now entitled as a result of the Criminal Law Act 1977 to bring an alternative verdict of careless driving.

As to the plea of autrefois acquit where there has been a dismissal without a hearing on merits, see 116 JP Jo 785.

The textbooks contain many other cases on these pleas (see Brian Harris, *Criminal Jurisdiction of Magistrates*, current edition, under this heading in the chapter on summary trial). The law generally was reviewed in *Connelly* v *Director of Public Prosecutions* [1964] 2 All ER 401. A dismissal without a hearing on the merits was held to allow a plea equivalent to autrefois acquit in *British Railways Board* v *Warwick* [1980] Crim LR 591 and *R* v *Swansea JJ, ex parte Purvis* (1981) 145 JP 252. The cases had been dismissed when the prosecution witnesses were not present. The test is not whether there has been a trial on the merits but 'whether the defendant has ever been in jeopardy' (ibid). An excess alcohol information in *Broadbent* v *High* (1984) *The Times*, 5 November, was defective in that it referred to a specimen of breath. A second correct information was laid referring to a specimen of blood. The prosecution had elected to proceed on the second correct information and the court had dismissed the first. The defendant unsuccessfully claimed double jeopardy on the authority of *Connelly* and *Purvis*. It was all part and parcel of the same process which resulted in the prosecutor being put to his election. The court indicated that it would have been preferable not to dismiss the first information until after the second had been disposed of. See also 'Convictions arising from the same incident', *The Magistrate*, November 1976. In *R* v *Burnham JJ, ex parte Ansorge* [1959] 3 All ER 505, it was said that where two informations, though alleging offences under different enactments, relate to the same facts and a plea of guilty to one information is accepted, the magistrates have jurisdiction to inquire into the matter but, if they find that the facts are the very facts which gave rise to the first conviction, they should proceed no further; if they did convict, appeal would lie. In that case the defendant had been charged with obstruction and breach of a 'no-waiting' order and both informations related to the same facts.

No person may be convicted of an offence if before proceedings are begun he has paid a fixed penalty under the Road Traffic Regulation Act 1984, Sched 12 (transitional fixed penalty and owner liability provisions). Similar provisions will apply when Part III of the Transport Act 1982 is in force. The Customs and Excise Commissioners have wide powers of imposing mitigated penalties under s 152 of the Customs and Excise Management Act 1979. The Secretary of State for Transport may also impose a mitigated penalty in respect of vehicle excise offences under s 3(3) of the Vehicles (Excise) Act 1971.

As to servicemen and members of visiting forces already dealt with by their own courts, see 2.5 and 2.8.

Where magistrates have adjudicated on a case on which they had no power to adjudicate, the case may properly be later heard before a court which can adjudicate upon it (*R* v *West* [1962] 2 All ER 624). If so, the second court has a discretion to allow the defendant to change his mind and elect trial by jury (*R* v *Coventry City JJ* [1981] Crim LR 787).

Where the right to recovery of a charge for towing away depends on the fact of an offence having been committed and the summons for that offence is dismissed without evidence having been offered, the charge cannot be recovered (*Commissioner of Police of the Metropolis* v *Meller* [1963] Crim LR 856).

Even if the defendant is discharged under s 6 of the Magistrates' Courts Act 1980, fresh proceedings against him for committal for trial may be taken (*R* v *Manchester City JJ, ex parte Snelson* [1977] Crim LR 423).

### 2.50 Defendant's previous convictions

When in force the Police and Criminal Evidence Act 1984, ss 73 and 75, will provide methods of proof of previous convictions and acquittals.

Section 42 of the Magistrates' Court Act 1980 prohibits a justice taking part in trying the issue of a defendant's guilt if the justice has been informed, for the purposes of determining bail, that the defendant has one or more previous convictions.

Previous convictions may not be put forward in the mode of trial procedure for the purpose of considering whether the case is more suitable for committal proceedings (*R* v *Colchester JJ, ex parte North Essex Building Co Ltd* [1977] 3 All ER 567).

Section 4 of the Rehabilitation of Offenders Act 1974 provides that a person shall be treated for all purposes as a person who has not committed, or been charged with, prosecuted for, convicted of, or sentenced for an offence for which he has become rehabilitated (a 'spent' offence). The Act does not apply to evidence in criminal proceedings (s 7(2)(*a*)). Nevertheless no oral evidence in a Crown Court should be given of such a 'spent' conviction without the authority of the judge who himself should make no reference to it unless it is necessary to do so for the purpose of explaining the sentence (*Practice Direction* [1975] Crim LR 520). Magistrates' courts are similarly enjoined to follow such a practice (Home Office circulars 98 and 130/75). When the Transport Act 1982 provisions as to fixed penalties are in force, unpaid penalties will be registered for enforcement as if on conviction. They will still not be previous convictions as such.

Where there was a reference to a previous conviction for dangerous driving during a hearing before magistrates but they announced that they would disregard such reference, and did disregard it, the conviction was upheld (*Cholerton* v *Copping* (1906) 70 JP 484; see also *Barker* v *Arnold* (1911) 75 JP 364). *Aliter* where the High Court are not satisfied that the previous conviction has been disregarded (*R* v *Grimsby Borough Quarter Sessions* [1955] 3 All ER 300). Where the defendant had been wrongly cross-examined as to a previous conviction, his conviction was quashed although the magistrates stated that their minds had not been in any way affected by the revelation of his previous court appearance; the cases of *Cholerton* v *Copping* and *Barker* v *Arnold*, above, were not apparently cited (*R* v *South Holderness JJ, ex parte Bonner* [1964] Crim LR 537). A certificate of conviction to prove a disqualification should mention only the offence (or, *semble*, one of the offences) for which the defendant was disqualified (*Stone* v *Bastick* [1965] 3 All ER 713). If an endorsed licence is used for this purpose, it is submitted that any other endorsements on it should be covered up before the magistrates see it. Generally, if an irregularity of this kind occurs during a trial and the justices feel that they cannot disregard it, they should adjourn the trial to a different bench (*Elkington* v *Kesley* [1948] 1 All ER 786). It seems to be the better opinion that, where the defendant is absent, previous convictions should not be mentioned on his being convicted unless, perhaps, he has clearly admitted them to a witness. If he is present, he should be asked if he admits them; if he denies them, they must either be strictly proved or ignored. The prosecution, however, may (save in juvenile courts) use s 104 of the Magistrates' Courts Act 1980. Under it, where a person is convicted by magistrates of a summary offence, then, if it is proved that he has been served personally or by registered post or recorded delivery with a list of previous convictions for summary offences (as defined by Sched 1 to the Interpretation Act 1978) not less than seven days previously, the court may in his absence take account of such convictions. This list, by virtue of the definition, can show previous traffic offences but not generally crimes of dishonesty. This procedure may be used whether the case has been established by a written plea of guilty under s 12 of the 1980 Act or by evidence in the defendant's absence. His attendance cannot be enforced by warrant, after he has been convicted in his absence, for the mere purpose of proving his record (*R* v *Montgomery* (1910) 74 JP 110). It should be noted that proof of previous convictions under the procedure set out in s 3 suffers from two defects from the point of view of the prosecutor for a road traffic endorsable offence. The notice under s 104 has to be served seven days previous to the conviction. If, therefore, a prosecutor becomes aware of previous convictions after the conviction, it is useless then to serve a notice under s 104. The other defect is that the notice cannot cite any previous convictions other than a summary offence. A summary offence for the purpose of all enactments unless the context otherwise requires means a purely summary offence (Interpretation Act 1978, Sched 1). Thus a notice under s 104 cannot cite many endorsable traffic offences, including causing death by reckless driving (s 1 of the 1972 Act), stealing a motor vehicle under the Theft Act, taking a motor vehicle (s 12 of the Theft Act 1968), and any 'either way' offence. To get over these difficulties the 1974 Act inserted a new subsection (2A) in s 182 of the 1972 Act in order that details of previous convictions for endorsable offences might be proved to a court in the absence of the defendant and after conviction, usually in the form of a certified computer print out. Section 182(2A) and in particular the period of notice required under it, is discussed further at 'Registration particulars and driving licence records', 2.80.

Particulars of an endorsement on the defendant's licence noted by the police prior to the hearing may be so given in evidence in his absence without a notice to produce it (*Martin* v *White* (1910) 74 JP 106). Where a conviction has to be proved by other means, it can be done by producing a record or extract of such conviction with proof of identity or by finger prints. It was suggested by the late author that s 16(2) of the Children and Young Persons Act 1963 requires previous findings of guilt whilst under fourteen to be disregarded where the defendant has attained the age of twenty-one. It is submitted that s 16(2) applies only where the defendant is examined as a witness as to his previous offences. If relevant, such previous findings of guilt can and should be contained in the defendant's antecedents prepared by the police, showing the defendant's history and previous offences; cf the *Practice Direction* at [1966] 2 All ER 929. Any doubts that existed as to whether a court is entitled to look at a driving licence have been resolved by s 101(4A) of the 1972 Act which provides that where a person is convicted of an obligatorily endorsable offence, the court may take into consideration particulars of any previous conviction or disqualification or penalty points endorsed on the licence when deciding what order to make in pursuance of the conviction.

The payment of a fixed penalty without prosecution under the Road Traffic Regulation Act 1984, Sched 12 (or the Transport Act 1982 when in force), or a mitigated penalty to a council under the Vehicles (Excise) Act 1971, does not count as a previous conviction and may not be included in a record of convictions submitted under the Magistrates' Courts Act 1980, s 104. Neither can constitute a previous conviction because neither penalty amounts to a conviction. An order of probation or conditional or absolute discharge is deemed not to be a conviction (Powers of Criminal Courts Act 1973, s 13) except for the purposes of discretionary or obligatory endorsement or disqualification (s 102 of the Act of 1972) or for the commission of a further offence during the period of conditional discharge or probation or for certain other limited purposes.

Magistrates should announce their decision to convict before inquiring into the defendant's record, but their failure to do so is not necessarily fatal, if they have actually so decided (*Davies* v *Griffiths* [1937] 2 All ER 671).

To prove guilty knowledge, previous convictions and even acquittals may in certain circumstances be mentioned and so may cautions (*Duxley* v *Gilmore* (1959) 123 JP Jo 331); this power should be used sparingly, however, and only where it is essential to prove a guilty state of mind and knowledge. When in force see the Police and Criminal Evidence Act 1984, s 74(3).

In giving the defendant's record after conviction, the police may, in addition to previous convictions, inform the court of matters, whether or not the subject of charges which are to be taken into consideration, which are not disputed by the defendant and ought to be known by the court (*R* v *Van Pelz* [1943] 1 All ER 36). This seems wide enough to allow them to mention undisputed cautions for motoring offences and also fixed penalty offences.

The Home Office after consultation considers it preferable as a general rule that cautions of juveniles should be cited in the juvenile court after a finding of guilt (see Home Office circular 49/1978, issued on 18 April 1978). In the circular it is stated that it is not normal to cite cautions administered to a juvenile in subsequent proceedings after he becomes of adult court age.

### 2.51 Cross-examination as to character

Evidence of the defendant's bad character and his cross-examination thereon is not permitted prior to conviction unless its admissibility falls within one of the recognised exceptions. One such exception is if the defendant 'has given evidence against any other person charged in the same proceedings' (Criminal Evidence Act 1898, s 1(*f*)(iii)). The words 'in the same proceedings' were substituted for the words 'with the same offence' by the Criminal Evidence Act 1979, thus reversing the effect of *R* v *Hills* [1978] 2 All

ER 1105 (HL). A defendant who merely says that he does not like driving at an excessive speed is not setting up his good character (*R* v *Beecham* (1921) 85 JP 276) and it is doubtful if he is setting it up if he says that he has driven for many years (see 125 JP Jo 774). If he merely makes imputations on the witnesses for the prosecution, evidence-in-chief of his bad character or previous convictions may not be given and the prosecution's rights are limited to cross-examining him if he chooses to give evidence (*R* v *Butterwasser* [1974] 2 All ER 415). Merely to deny in strong terms a witness's statement does not alone permit the prosecution to cross-examine the defendant as to his character (*R* v *Rouse* (1904) 68 JP 14) but they may do so, at the discretion of the court, if there are allegations of manufacturing evidence additional to those that the witness is not speaking the truth (*R* v *Clark* [1955] 3 All ER 29). The cases were reviewed in *Selvey* v *Director of Public Prosecutions* [1968] 2 All ER 497, where the House of Lords laid down that, where the defence attack the character of a prosecution witness, the court has an unfettered discretion to permit or exclude cross-examination of the defendant as to his record and that there is no general rule that it should not be allowed if the defence necessarily involves imputations against the character of a prosecution witness. Cross-examination of the defendant should not be so conducted as to induce him to attack the prosection witnesses' characters (*R* v *Baldwin* (1925) 89 JP 116). Where an unrepresented defendant in a magistrates' court begins to attack the character of a prosecution witness, the prosecutor should warn him of the risk of being himself cross-examined as to character; such warning should not be given in open court but an adjournment should be requested and the help of the magistrates' clerk enlisted to explain it all to the defendant in the magistrates' absence during the adjournment (*R* v *Weston-super-Mare JJ, ex parte Townsend* [1968] 3 All ER 225).

A defendant who has attained the age of twenty-one may not be cross-examined as to offences of which he was found guilty prior to his becoming fourteen (Children and Young Persons Act 1963, s 16(2)).

## 2.52 Presence of defendant

Minor cases are often dealt with in the absence of the defendant (Magistrates' Courts Act 1980, s 11(1)). However, the defendant must be present for committal proceedings unless the court orders otherwise, because of unruly behaviour or because he is ill and is legally represented and gives his consent (see s 4(4) of the 1980 Act). There are special rules for the mode of trial procedure (see 2.41). The defendant should always be given an adjournment, if he asks for it, when he has had the summons in insufficient time before the hearing. Save in cases where he is expressly required to be present by statute or bail, a party represented by solicitor or counsel is deemed not to be absent (Magistrates' Courts Act 1980, s 122). A corporation or limited company can plead by a representative or solicitor (see 2.38; the Magistrates' Courts Act 1980, Sched 3, makes provision as to election for summary trial by a corporation and its committal). A defendant cannot be sentenced to imprisonment or detention in his absence and he may not be disqualified if absent at the first hearing. In the latter case he must be given the chance to attend at an adjourned hearing; the notice to him of the adjournment should show the intention of the court to consider disqualification (Magistrates' Courts Act 1980, s 11(4)).

Save where the defendant is represented by a solicitor who pleads guilty on his behalf, the case must be proved by evidence, if he is absent, and letters to the court or police admitting the offence, if used at all to prove guilt, should only be used to supplement such evidence on proof that such letters are in the defendant's handwriting. No evidence need be given on a plea of guilty (Magistrates' Courts Act 1980, s 9(3)); although, where the defendant disputes the facts, magistrates may call for evidence. If evidence is given in the witness box by way of mitigation on a guilty plea, it follows that the person giving evidence is subject to cross-examination. It must make no difference that the person giving evidence in this way is the defendant himself. A defendant cannot be arrested on non-appearance, personally or by solicitor (where this suffices), unless the offence is punishable with imprisonment or, having convicted him, the magistrates propose to disqualify (Magistrates' Courts Act 1980, s 13(3)). There are special provisions in this respect relating to the mode of trial procedure—see s 26.

## 2.53 Final speech by or on behalf of defendant

In *R* v *Marylebone JJ, ex parte Yasmin Farrag* [1981] Crim LR 182, after the defendant had given evidence in chief, the chairman of the bench had stopped the prosecution's cross-examination and after consulting his colleagues had found the case proved. Counsel for the defendant had protested that no opportunity had been given to him to make a final speech and he had then been allowed to do so. The magistrates had then upheld the conviction explaining that they had considered the points in the speech but still stood by their original decision. It was held that the proceedings were a nullity and should be quashed. Once such a situation occurred, the only course was to order a retrial.

## 2.54 Pleading guilty in writing

As is well known the Magistrates' Courts Act 1980, s 12, enables pleas of guilty for summary offences (being neither indictable, nor 'either way' offences nor summary offences punishable with more than three months' imprisonment) to be received in writing in magistrates' courts, other than juvenile courts, in the absence of the defendant. With the summons the defendant is served an explanatory form and a statement of the facts of the offence. If he wishes to dispute the case, he or his solicitor should notify the court in order that a hearing can take place in the usual way with sworn oral evidence or statements under s 9 of the Criminal Justice Act 1967. The statement of facts prepared under s 12 may not be put in evidence at a trial and a witness cannot be cross-examined upon the statement (*Roper* v *Sullivan* [1978] RTR 181). If he does nothing, the prosecutor, on proof of service of the summons, may prove his case by oral evidence or s 9 statements. If the defendant or his solicitor writes to the court pleading guilty, then the statement of facts is read aloud to the court and his letter is also read aloud; no oral evidence is allowed to supplement the written statement of facts and the prosecutor may not add anything to the statement (*R* v *Malden JJ* [1966] Crim LR 387; *R* v *Liskerrett JJ, ex parte Child* [1972] RTR 141).

A corporation or limited company may plead guilty in writing signed by a director or secretary under s 12 (see Sched 3). The plea must clearly refer to all the offences charged (*R* v *Burnham JJ* [1959] 3 All ER 505). If the letter does not amount to a plea of guilty, oral evidence of the offence must be given at an adjourned court. Both the statement and the reply of the defendant must be read aloud (*R* v *Oldham JJ* [1958] 3 All ER 559); the onus of proving the contrary is on the defendant (*R* v *Davis, ex parte Brough* [1959] 1 WLR 59).

His licence may be ordered to be endorsed and penalty points assigned under the s 12 procedure but he may not be disqualified from driving in his absence, where he has pleaded guilty in writing pursuant to that procedure, unless and until the court has given him the opportunity of attending on an adjourned hearing (ss 12(2)(*a*) and 11(4); *R* v *Totton JJ* [1958] Crim LR 543; *R* v *Llandrindod Wells JJ, ex parte Gibson* [1968] 2 All ER 20). If a case under the s 12 procedure has been adjourned without a hearing and the accused has not been required to attend at the adjourned hearing, only the statement of facts served on him may be read out and no witness may be called by the prosecution at the adjourned hearing, unless the accused is present or represented (*R* v *Norham JJ* [1961] 1 All ER 455). A notice of adjournment should give the reason for it, eg where it is intended that the court will disqualify (ss 12(3) and 11(4)), and if the reason for adjournment was to consider disqualification and this was not stated, the disqualification will be quashed (*R* v *Mason* [1965] 2 All ER 308).

### 2.55 Conviction

To secure a conviction it is not necessary to prove each and every item or particular in a charge providing all the ingredients of the substantive offence are established (*R* v *Parker* [1969] 2 QB 248 and *Machent* v *Quinn* [1970] 2 All ER 255). These were cases of theft but it is submitted that the principle is of general application. It is submitted for instance that if a charge of careless driving contains two linked incidents of careless driving (as in *Horrix* v *Malam* [1984] RTR 112), perhaps in two different roads, it is still possible to convict even though only one incident is proved.

Where, following a plea of guilty, there is a sharp divergence on the facts the court must hear any submissions and, where there is a substantial conflict, either come down in favour of the defendant or call for evidence; *R* v *Newton* (1983) Cr App R 13; *R* v *Williams* (1984) 148 JP 375. The normal practice when sentencing co-defendants is to hear all the evidence and submissions relating to sentence in the presence of all of them before passing sentence on any one of them. This practice should only be departed from in exceptional circumstances (*R* v *Hall (ML)* (1982) 146 JP Jo 281(CA)).

### 2.56 Mitigation

Where justices have retired to consider whether to convict or acquit and have decided on the defendant's guilt, they should not on their return immediately announce their penalty. After they have announced a conviction, the prosecution should be given an opportunity of citing any previous convictions and making any application for costs, and the court, if it is an endorsable offence, should see the defendant's driving licence and, most importantly, the defendant or his solicitor or counsel should have an opportunity of putting forward any matter in mitigation. If justices find a case proved after a plea of not guilty and pronounce sentence without first giving the defence an opportunity to speak in mitigation of the sentence, their sentence may be set aside (*R* v *Southampton JJ, ex parte Atherton* [1974] Crim LR 108). (The justices decided on the defendant's guilt and immediately announced a fine of £100 without giving the defence counsel an opportunity to speak in mitigation. After remonstrations from the defence counsel they then heard him in mitigation and announced a reduced fine of £80 plus £21 costs. The sentence was quashed and the case was sent back by the Divisional Court for the sentence to be reconsidered by a different bench.) Similarly, a sentence was quashed where justices refused to hear counsel in mitigation after convicting the defendant and before sentencing him (*R* v *Billericay JJ, ex parte Rumsey* [1978] Crim LR 305).

It may be wise to support a plea in mitigation by evidence, particularly where the mitigation adduced is of an unusual nature or extraordinary character; in some cases, sworn evidence is essential: eg 'special reasons' for not endorsing or disqualifying (see 21.16). By giving sworn evidence a defendant renders himself subject to cross-examination. Where, however, such sworn evidence is required, a statement under s 9 of the Criminal Justice Act 1967 is admissible as evidence to the like extent as oral evidence (s 9(1)). Section 9 statements can be tendered by either party including the defendant. Admissions by the prosecutor may also be obtained (see 2.86).

### 2.57 Committals for sentence

The magistrates' court has the right to commit a defendant for sentence by the Crown Court for any 'either way' offence if 'having regard to his character or antecedents the magistrates' court is of the opinion he should receive greater punishment than the magistrates' court has power to inflict' (s 38 of the Magistrates' Courts Act 1980). When considering whether to commit a defendant to the Crown Court for sentence under s 38 and s 56 of the Criminal Justice Act 1967, justices should take account only of information which had come to their knowledge after they had decided that the case was suitable for summary trial; facts of which they had been aware when that decision had been taken were not subsequently to be considered when considering such a committal (*R* v *Guildhall JJ, ex parte Cooper* (1983) 147 JP 466).

There is a limited power for juvenile courts to commit fifteen and sixteen year olds under s 37 of the Magistrates' Courts Act 1980 (as amended) for a heavier sentence of youth custody than the juvenile court has power to impose. The age is the age on conviction and the offence must be punishable on indictment with imprisonment exceeding six months. Presumably this power also applies to those who attain seventeen after the proceedings are begun and before their conclusion in the juvenile court. Section 29 of the

Children and Young Persons Act 1963 empowers the juvenile court to deal with the case and make any order as if he were still sixteen.

An error as to the correct statute in a certificate of committal for trial did not invalidate the committal (*R* v *Hall* [1982] 1 All ER 75). The old and new statutes were in like terms and the actual committal in court was valid (cf *R* v *Folkestone & Hythe Juvenile Court, ex parte R* below, a committal for sentence). The magistrates' court, when committing the offender for sentence to the Crown Court under s 37 or s 38 of the Magistrates' Courts Act 1980, has no power to make any ancillary order, eg an order as to costs or compensation, other than an interim order of disqualification (see 20.33).

Where an offender is committed for sentence to the Crown Court, or for breach of parole (s 62(6) of the Criminal Justice Act 1967), or for committing an offence while subject to a suspended sentence imposed by a Crown Court (s 24(2) of the Powers of Criminal Courts Act 1973), or for being an incorrigible rogue under the Vagrancy Act 1824, or for being in breach of a probation order by the commission of a further offence, or for any suspended sentence in respect of which the court has power to deal with him, the magistrates' court may also commit the offender to the Crown Court for any other offence for which he has been convicted which is punishable with imprisonment or endorsable (s 56 of the Criminal Justice Act 1967), or if the committal for sentence is in respect of an 'either way' offence under the Magistrates' Courts Act 1980 he may be committed for any other offence whatsoever for which the committing court has power to deal with him and for which he has been convicted. Although a breach of a probation order by the commission of a further offence is included, by s 56 a similar breach of a conditional discharge is not.

An error as to the correct statute in a memorandum of conviction on a committal for sentence did not invalidate the committal (*R* v *Folkestone and Hythe Juvenile Court, ex parte R* [1981] 1 WLR 1501). The old and new statutes were in like terms and the actual committal in court was valid (cf *R* v *Hall*, a committal for trial, at 2.42).

Where an offender has been committed to the Crown Court for sentence under s 38 of the Magistrates' Courts Act 1980, the Crown Court's powers of punishment are the same as if the offender had been convicted on indictment before it. Where the offender has been committed for sentence under s 37 of the Magistrates' Courts Act 1980 the Crown Court, if it does not make a youth custody order, has only the same power of punishment as if that offender had been sentenced by the magistrates' court. The Crown Court has the same power of punishment as a magistrates' court in respect of offences committed under s 56 above.

## 2.58 Remitting to another magistrates' court for sentence

Section 39 of the Magistrates' Court Act 1980 enables one magistrates' court under certain circumstances to remit an offender to another magistrates' court for sentence. The offender must have been convicted of an imprisonable or disqualifiable offence by the remitting court and also have been convicted but not sentenced by the other magistrates' court. The remitting court must obtain the other court's consent to the offender being remitted. The remitting court may remand the offender on remitting him. There is no appeal against an order of remittal. The court to which he has been remitted further under s 39 may remit the offender back to the original court. The power under s 39 is exercisable only in respect of offenders aged seventeen or over. The section does not preclude the original court from making a restitution order under s 28 of the Theft Act 1968.

## 2.59 Withdrawal of proceedings

Under the Prosecution of Offences Regulations 1978 (SI 1978 No 1357) the clerk of the court is required to notify the DPP of any case which is wholly withdrawn or not pursued expeditiously and where the withdrawal or delay is not in good faith.

It was confirmed in *R* v *Redbridge JJ, ex parte Sainty* [1981] RTR 13 that the withdrawal of a summons in a summary case is at the discretion of the court. This does not, however, necessarily have the effect of putting to an end the ground of information or complaint. The principle was discussed in an article at (1979) 143 JP Jo 572 before this case was heard, and certain other cases are quoted there. Old informations were treated as spent and a new information approved in *R* v *South Western Magistrates' Court* [1980] RTR 35 (see 'When "proceedings are begun"', 2.4). This was doubted obiter in *R* v *Leigh JJ* [1981] Crim LR 628 but the other cases on withdrawal were apparently not quoted there.

In *R* v *Canterbury and St Augustine JJ, ex parte Klisiak*; *R* v *Ramsgate JJ, ex parte Warren* [1981] 2 All ER 129 it was held that the consent of the justices is not required for the withdrawal of committal proceedings although they had such a discretion in summary proceedings. In practice it is difficult to see any distinction between the two situations in this respect. The decision is criticised at (1980) 144 JP Jo 745.

It was held in *R* v *Straker (David)* (1983) *The Times*, 13 December that once an appellant had lodged a form abandoning his application for leave to appeal, that was treated as a refusal of leave by the full court and could not be withdrawn unless the appellant could subsequently show that it was a nullity because he had not taken a deliberate and informed decision to abandon the application.

It is submitted that the same principle should be applied to the withdrawal of proceedings once it has been accepted by the court.

Because of the power to award costs, courts should not allow proceedings to be withdrawn in the absence of the defendant unless satisfied that he has been notified of the proposal to withdraw. However, if proceedings have been marked 'withdrawn' without the defendant having been notified of the proposal, he may apply for costs later: *R* v *Bolton JJ* (1983) 147 JP 309.

## 2.60–5 Pardon

A pardon does not remove a conviction but merely removes all pains, penalties and punishments: *R* v *Foster* (1984) *The Times*, 31 March.

# Evidence

## 2.66 The Police and Criminal Evidence Act 1984

Part VIII of the 1984 Act will when in force codify certain laws of evidence in criminal proceedings and reference may be necessary accordingly.

## 2.67 Enforcing attendance

The attendance of witnesses and the production of documents may be secured by witness summons. Under the Magistrates' Courts Act 1980, s 97, application for a witness summons may be made without oath, but an oath is necessary for a warrant; a reasonable sum must be tendered to the witness for costs and expenses when he is served with the summons. Applications for a witness summons may be made to a justices' clerk, who may issue it (Justices' Clerks Rules 1970 (SI 1970 No 231)). Any witness may be committed for seven days (not fined any sum) if he refuses to be sworn, give evidence or produce a document, whether he attends on summons or not. Witness process granted when a witness is in England or Wales may be enforced by warrant in any other part of the British Isles under the Magistrates' Courts Act 1980, ss 125 and 126, if he goes there. See the current edition of Archbold, as to enforcing attendance of witnesses outside England and Wales, at the Crown Court. The attendance of a witness in prison may be obtained by Home Office order (Prison Act 1952, s 22).

The Criminal Procedure (Attendance of Witnesses) Act 1965 (as amended by the Courts Act 1971) regulates the procedure for the attendance of witnesses at the Crown Court.

Where documents are in the defendant's possession, he cannot be ordered to produce them, but should be given notice to produce them. If he has been given such notice and fails to produce them in court, secondary evidence may be given of their contents (see Stone (1984) Vol 1, Pt II, 459). Notice is unnecessary where the summons by its very character puts the accused on notice that a document will be required, eg, the certificate of insurance on a charge of uninsured driving (*Williams* v *Russell* (1933) 97 JP 128).

## 2.68 Best evidence

It was held in *Kajala* v *Noble* [1982] Crim LR 433 that the old rule that a party must produce the best evidence that the nature of the case would allow no longer applied except where the original document was available in the party's hands. The court was not confined to the best evidence but could admit all relevant evidence. The goodness or badness of it went to weight and not admissibility. The old rule was confined to written documents in the strict sense of the term and had no relevance to tape or films.

## 2.69 Evidence on oath or affirmation

It is the normal practice of a criminal court for all witnesses, whether witnesses for the prosecution or the defence, to be out of court during the hearing until called to give evidence. There is an exception in the case of expert witnesses. There may be other exceptions and it is for the court to decide (*R* v *Bexley JJ, ex parte King* [1980] RTR 49: cf *Tomlinson* v *Tomlinson* [1980] 1 All ER 593, a Family Division case) If, however, through inadvertence or any other reason the witness is in court, his evidence is admissible with the court making such deductions as to its weight as may be appropriate in the circumstances.

Witnesses in a trial or before examining justices must normally swear or affirm. The Magistrates' Courts Act 1980, s 98, provides that subject to the provisions of any enactment or rule of law (see below for examples) authorising the reception of unsworn evidence, evidence before a magistrates' court shall be given on oath. The words of the Oaths Act 1978 as to the methods of taking the oath are directory only. Although they should be complied with, failure to do so does not necessarily invalidate the taking of the oath. The efficacy of an oath depends on its being taken in a way binding, and intended to be binding, upon the conscience of the intended witness (*R* v *Chapman* [1980] Crim LR 42). In that case the witness failed to take the testament in his hand.

Where a child is of tender age, there should be an enquiry about the child's understanding of the nature of an oath. A note of the questions (and presumably the answers) should be kept in the transcript (or presumably by the clerk in a magistrates' court). What is a tender age will differ according to the child, but it will normally be under fourteen (see *R* v *Khan* [1981] Crim LR 330).

The evidence of a child of tender age who is not intelligent enough to understand the oath may be received unsworn in a criminal case (Children and Young Persons Act 1933, s 38; and by the Magistrates' Courts Act 1980, s 102, and the Criminal Justice Act 1967, s 9).

Where unsworn evidence of a child is admitted for the prosecution, the defendant must not be convicted unless that evidence is corroborated by some other material evidence in support implicating him (Children and Young Persons Act 1933, s 38). This section and the previous authorities were reviewed and considered by the House of Lords in *DPP* v *Hester* [1973] 3 All ER 1056. The unsworn evidence of a child can be supported by the sworn evidence of another child and they can be corroborative of each other, but this evidence must be weighed with special care. The sworn evidence of a child need not be corroborated in law, but although there is a risk in convicting on the child's evidence alone a court may do so if convinced that the child is telling the truth (ibid). The unsworn evidence of a child cannot be corroborated merely by the unsworn evidence of another child (ibid). Unsworn evidence of a child can be treated as corroboration of other evidence provided the court is satisfied that the child is a truthful witness (ibid).

Exhibits produced by a witness and views of the location are sometimes described as real evidence. Otherwise, all evidence (save where permitted in documentary form) must be given on oath (or affirmation, if oaths are contrary to the witness's religious belief or he has none or the Oaths Act 1978 is applied: see below), although a witness producing documents only need not be sworn (for other rare exceptions see Cross on *Evidence* (5th ed) 183). If a witness refuses to be sworn or to affirm or is of insufficient mental capacity to understand the oath, his evidence is not receivable. Magistrates, while entitled to convict on the sworn evidence of young children corroborating one another, should warn themselves of the risks of acting on such evidence (*R* v *Campbell* [1956] 2 All ER 272).

Under the Oaths Act 1978 affirmation in lieu of oath is permitted for any person who objects to being sworn. An affirmation is also permitted where it is not reasonably practicable without delay or inconvenience to administer an oath to a person in the manner appropriate to his religious belief. The Children and Young Persons Act 1963, s 28, prescribes the form of oath to be taken by all witnesses in juvenile courts and by juveniles in any court and enacts that the proper oath shall be deemed to have been taken although one of the forms prescribed by s 28 has been used instead of the other.

## 2.70 Sick witnesses

In the trial of a summary offence, the evidence of a witness who is too ill to come to court cannot be received in writing, on oath or not, even under s 9 of the Criminal Justice Act 1967, if the other side claims that the witness should attend; it may be received under s 9 if his attendance is not required. It is suggested at (1951) 95 SJ 178 that in such cases the place where a witness (on either side) lies ill should be designated an occasional court house and the magistrates and all the parties should attend at his bedside to hear his evidence; the rest of the case can be heard in the ordinary court house. Either way offences and civil complaints cannot be tried summarily in an occasional court house (Magistrates' Courts Act 1980, s 121). If the case is indictable, the witness's deposition may be taken by the magistrate who takes the other depositions at his bedside in the defendant's presence, provided the witness is either in the commission area for which the magistrate acts or in an adjoining commission area (*R* v *Bros, ex parte Hardy* (1911) 74 JP 483; Justices of the Peace Act 1979, s 66). Section 66 of the Justices of the Peace Act 1979 also enables a justice to act as such for his own commission area even though he is acting in an adjoining commission area.

Where an important witness is ill and unlikely to be well enough to attend a court within a reasonable time, in practice it is suggested that, if the case be indictable, it should be committed for trial, as his deposition is receivable (see below). Occasionally, in summary and indictable cases, the defendant's reply in the presence of the witness to the latter's statement might be usable in evidence as showing his acceptance of the truth of the statement. If it is desired to designate a place as an occasional court house, the procedure indicated in the Magistrates' Courts Act 1980, s 147, must be followed; licensed premises cannot be so designated.

In trials on indictment, the deposition of a witness for either side before the examining justices may be read if he is insane or too ill to attend (Criminal Justice Act 1925, s 13(3)). See the current edition of Archbold as to this provision.

By the Criminal Law Amendment Act 1867, s 6, and the Magistrates' Courts Act 1980, s 105, the evidence of a witness relating to an indictable offence may be taken at his bedside if he is dangerously ill and unlikely to recover. Reasonable notice must have been given to the defendant or prosecutor—for the procedure is available to both sides—so that he can be present and cross-examine, if he wishes. No one need actually have been charged but, if a charge is likely, the proposed defendant (if the witness is for the prosecution) or the chief constable (if he is a defence one) should be notified and given the chance to attend. The deposition so taken will then be available at the trial, if the witness is still ill or is dead, and at the preliminary hearing (Magistrates' Courts Act 1980, s 105; Magistrates' Courts Rules 1981, r 33). It is emphasised that the procedure can be used by both sides and relates not only to persons injured as a result of the offence, eg, a victim of reckless driving, but also to those seriously ill from other causes. The magistrate who takes the deposition need not be the one who commits the defendant for trial and the witness may be in his (the magistrate's) or an adjoining commission area. See the article by the first editor of this work at 118 JP Jo 726 as to the possibility of a wider jurisdiction. The procedure is commended to defending solicitors who have reserved their client's defence and then find a material witness in danger of dying. There is a useful article at 120 JP Jo 439 and 453 generally as to the depositions of sick witnesses. Written evidence may now be allowed under s 102 of the Magistrates' Courts Act 1980 or s 9 of the Criminal Justice Act 1967, but the 1867 Act does not require the consent of the other side.

Where the charge is one involving bodily injury to a juvenile under seventeen his evidence may be taken out of court (on notice to the defendant) if his attendance would endanger his health (Children and Young Persons Act 1933, s 42). This provision obviously applies to the offence of causing bodily harm to a juvenile by furious driving (Offences against the Person Act 1861, s 35) but it is doubtful if reckless and careless driving alone, contrary to ss 2 and 3 of the 1972 Act, are offences involving bodily injury, though a juvenile may have been injured in the accident. It was held in *R* v *Moore* [1954] 2 All ER 189 that arson of a house in which were some children (who were not injured by the fire) was not an offence 'involving bodily injury' to them and that those words referred to offences ejusdem generis with those set out in Sched 1 to the 1933 Act, which relates to assaults and other crimes of sex and violence.

It would seem that even in magistrates' courts the evidence of a witness who has already given evidence in proceedings on the same issue may be read at the second trial if he is too ill to attend, eg where careless driving is tried again because the magistrates could not agree (see Cross on *Evidence* (5th ed) 567). A transcript of evidence of a witness is admissible in evidence in a retrial of a defendant on the same charge when the witness is too ill to travel to court on the second trial (*R* v *Thompson* [1982] 2 WLR 603 (CA)). In the judgment Dunn LJ referred with approval to statements in Cross on *Evidence* (such evidence admissible if the witness was unable to attend through death or illness) and Phipson on *Evidence* (incapable of being called). But see *Bishop* v *Hosier* at 22.6. On a re-trial ordered under the Criminal Appeal Act 1968 evidence may, in the circumstances given in Sched 2, be read from the transcript.

## 2.71 Dead witnesses

The deposition of a witness for either side taken under the Criminal Law Amendment Act 1867, above, may be read at the trial or preliminary hearing, though he has since died (Magistrates' Courts Act 1980, s 105). The judge has a discretion whether or not to admit the deposition or statement depending on the circumstances (see *R* v *Blithing* (1983) 77 Cr App R 86) but should not do so if the admission as in that case would be unfair. It would seem that, if he died before his evidence was complete, the deposition would be inadmissible (cf *Waugh* v *R* [1950] AC 203). The deposition (or a written statement under the Magistrates' Courts Act 1980, s 102) of a witness for either side at the preliminary hearing before the justices may be read at the trial on indictment if he has died (Criminal Justice Act 1925, s 13(3); s 102(7) of the 1980 Act). See the notes in the current edition of Archbold on s 13(3). A dying declaration is admissible in homicide cases. 'Homicide' would seem to include causing death by reckless driving (see 5.12).

The evidence of a witness who has died cannot otherwise be brought before the court unless it comes within certain exceptions (given in the current edition of Phipson's *Manual of Evidence*, viz, declarations against interest, declarations in the course of duty and declarations as to public rights (see 115 JP Jo 599)). Also, where he has already given evidence in the same proceedings and they are begun again, his evidence to the court can be read (see Cross on *Evidence* (5th ed) 567). But see *Bishop* v *Hosier* at 22.6.

## 2.72 Witnesses abroad

The attendance of witnesses from Scotland, Ireland, the Isle of Man and the Channel Islands can be secured by process (see 2.67). The evidence of a witness outside the United Kingdom may be given before a British consul elsewhere and such depositions are admissible here (Merchant Shipping Act 1894, s 691). The section also permits such evidence to be given before a judge or magistrate in the British Empire. The defendant in a criminal case must be present at the examination of the witness and have the opportunity to cross-examine him; the statute seemingly requires the defendant's presence (but not the prosecutor's) even where the evidence is for the defence, but possibly this requirement would be construed to give a more sensible result. Section 691 applies to all criminal and civil proceedings and refers to a deposition 'previously' made; *quaere* whether this means previously to the commencement of the proceedings or to the hearing itself. Section 46(2) of the Criminal Justice Act 1972 enables statements made by witnesses outside the United Kingdom to be receivable under s 102 of the Magistrates' Courts Act 1952 in committal proceedings but not in respect of summary proceedings under s 9 of the Criminal Justice Act 1967. Statements made by witnesses in Scotland and Northern Ireland are, however, admissible in the same way as if they had been made in England or Wales (s 46(1) of the Criminal Justice Act 1972).

## 2.73 Spouses

The spouses of defendants may not be called for the prosecution in any road traffic cases save those of causing the death of, or bodily injury to, a juvenile under seventeen. The spouse is competent but not compellable in such cases (Children and Young Persons Act 1933, s 15). (See 2.70 as to whether this includes reckless and careless driving under ss 2 and 3 of the 1972 Act merely because a child has been injured.) The spouses of any defendants being tried jointly cannot be called for the prosecution even though their evidence does not relate to the particular defendant who is the husband or wife in question (*R* v *Mount* (1934) 24 Cr App R 135). This point should be watched where two defendants are being tried together on separate charges and the prosecution wish to call one defendant's spouse to prove facts against the other defendant. In *Parson* v *Tomlin* (1956) 120 JP 129, the evidence of a spouse was held inadmissible for the Crown in a dangerous driving charge involving a child's death. As her evidence was of no weight, the conviction was not quashed, but it would have been had her evidence been material (*R* v *Boucher* (1952) 36 Cr App R 152). Section 15 of the Children and Young Persons Act 1933, mentioned above, was not cited in *Parson* v *Tomlin* above.

May one spouse give evidence for the prosecution where the other has committed a road traffic offence deliberately directed against her? The point actually arose before a metropolitan magistrate when a husband was charged with failing to accord precedence to his wife on a pedestrian crossing, it being suggested that he was trying to frighten her. The magistrate did not allow her to give evidence. It is submitted that a spouse may testify for the prosecution in such circumstances only where a charge under the Offences Against the Person Act or for an attempt to commit an offence under that Act has been brought in respect of harm or threatened harm to her or binding-over is sought.

Spouses are competent witnesses for the defence but can only be called on the defendant's application—here again watch the point where two defendants are being tried together and it is desired to call the spouse of one to testify for the other defendant. Failure of a spouse to give evidence for the defence must not be made the subject of any comment by the prosecution; comment would seem to include such questions in cross-examination as, 'And yet your wife, who was sitting by you in the car, is not being called?' The Criminal Evidence Act 1898, s 1, which deals with the evidence of spouses, also provides that spouses are not compellable to disclose communications made to the witness-spouse by the other during marriage. This privilege (of non-disclosure of communications) does not extend to communications made by the witness-spouse to the other nor to evidence given by widows, widowers and divorced persons lawfully called (*Shenton* v *Tyler* [1939] 1 All ER 827). A communication privileged between spouses may be given in evidence by someone who overheard it or read it (*Rumping* v *Director of Public Prosecutions* [1962] 3 All ER 256). A divorced spouse cannot be called (save in the excepted cases) to testify against the other spouse in respect of any matters arising or conversations which passed during the marriage; the same rule applies where the marriage was voidable and has been annulled but not, *semble*, where it was void from the start (*R* v *Algar* [1953] 2 All ER 1381). Nor is the evidence of one spouse admissible in a road traffic prosecution against the other where they are judicially separated (*Moss* v *Moss* [1963]

2 All ER 829). If the prosecutor does comment on the failure of the defendant or his wife to give evidence the defendant shoud be offered an adjournment to a different bench (*R* v *Allerton* (1953) 117 JP Jo 421) but in *R* v *Hunter* (1969) 113 SJ 161, a conviction was upheld where a trial proceeded after the prosecution commented on the spouse not being called. The prosecutor may ask the defendant in cross-examination if his wife is at the trial so long as he does not comment on it (*R* v *Scales* in 'Recent Points' (1969) WLR, 7 March).

See generally, as to evidence of spouses in criminal cases, 99 SJ 551 and Cross on *Evidence* (5th ed) 173. When the Police and Criminal Evidence Act 1984, s 80, is brought into force the evidence of spouses will be governed by a statutory code.

## 2.74 Disclosure of previous convictions of prosecution witnesses

A conviction may be quashed if material previous convictions of prosecution witnesses (including 'spent' convictions) are not disclosed to the defence (*R* v *Paraskeva* [1983] Crim LR 186). Again, a conviction was quashed in *R* v *Knightsbridge Crown Court, ex parte Goonatilleke* (1985) *The Times*, 14 February, where the main prosecution witness deliberately contrived to keep the defendant in ignorance of his bad character and had thereby denied him a valuable plank in his defence.

## 2.75 Expert evidence

The opinion of a witness is inadmissible unless he is an expert giving an opinion on matters within his expertise for which he has special knowledge and experience. Taking account of information stemming from the work of others in the same field is an essential ingredient of the nature of expert evidence and is not hearsay (*R* v *Abadom* [1983] 1 All ER 364).

Where there is a conflict of evidence in a criminal case between the expert evidence put forward by the prosecution and the expert evidence put forward by the defence, the correct approach is as described in *R* v *Platt* [1981] Crim LR 332.

> The only safe way of directing the jury was either to tell them that before they accepted the opinion of the prosecution's [expert] they must feel sure that he was correct or else to tell them that they were to assume that the defence's [expert] was right and, therefore, to approach the case on the other evidence solely and not base their approach on the [expert's] evidence at all.

In that case the expert evidence was given by pathologists. This is an example of the general rule that the prosecution must prove a criminal case beyond reasonable doubt.

In *R* v *Oakley* [1979] RTR 417 the Court of Appeal upheld a trial judge who admitted a police constable's opinion on theories and conclusions about the accident based upon his considerable experience and expertise in accident investigations. *R* v *Oakley* was followed and applied in *R* v *Murphy* [1980] RTR 145.

The court may allow expert witnesses to remain in court while other evidence is given: an exception to the normal practice, discussed in *R* v *Bexley JJ, ex parte King* [1980] RTR 49.

## 2.76 Evidence by the defendant and unsworn statements

In a criminal case a defendant has two choices: to give evidence himself on oath or affirmation when he can be cross-examined (*R* v *Paul*; *R* v *McFarlane* [1920] 2 KB 183); or to say nothing (Criminal Evidence Act 1898, s 1). The general right to make an unsworn statement was abolished by the Criminal Justice Act 1982, s 72. This abolition would seem to apply equally to an unsworn statement in committal proceedings.

The general practice is that the defendant gives evidence before other defence witnesses and the court can insist on this. Rarely the court may consent to non-controversial evidence being called first (*R* v *Smith* [1968] 2 All ER 115). This practice will be codified in s 79 of the Police and Criminal Evidence Act 1984 when in force.

## 2.77 Witness statements

By s 102 of the Magistrates' Courts Act 1980 (committal proceedings) and s 9 of the Criminal Justice Act 1967 (summary proceedings) written evidence is permitted on the conditions there specified. In *Chapman* v *Ingleton* (1973) 137 JP 204 it was held that while it was vital for a statement under s 9 to contain the required declaration as to its truth, etc, it did not matter whether the declaration appeared at the head or foot of the statement. It would seem that a child under ten years of age cannot make a statement under s 102 or s 9, since a child under ten is not liable to prosecution. Statements under s 102 or s 9 would appear to fall within the definition of 'instruments' in the Forgery and Counterfeiting Act 1981. The preparation or use of a false statement therefore may constitute an offence under that Act. The use of s 9 statements to obviate the need for police officers to attend in minor cases was recommended in Home Office circular 56/81.

## 2.78 Statements generally

The law relating to confessions will be codified by the Police and Criminal Evidence Act 1984, ss 76 and 77 when in force.

The defendant's admission that he was driving will suffice to show that he was the driver. Statements by the defendant to the police are admissible in evidence without a caution having been administered and a constable may properly ask a person if he was driving on a particular occasion (*Hennell* v *Cuthbert* [1962] Crim LR 104). The person's answers will still be admissible provided that they were obtained without unfairness and that the constable had reasonable grounds for thinking that he had committed an offence (*Berry* v *Robson* (1964) 108 SJ 259). Similarly, in *Dilks* v *Tilley* [1979] RTR 459 justices were held to be wrong in refusing to admit in evidence the answers of the defendant to a constable who had arrived at the scene of an accident and had simply asked the defendant what had happened. The constable at that stage was simply asking for information and could not be thought to have reasonable grounds for suspecting the defendant had committed an offence and thus to be required to administer a caution by r II of the Judges' Rules (ibid). But if the defendant has been charged with or informed that he may be prosecuted for an offence or the constable has reasonable grounds for suspecting that he may have committed an offence, then he should first be cautioned. A statement by a defendant, which he had acknowledged but not signed, was held admissible in *The People* v *Wickham* [1949] Ir R 180, discussed at [1950] Jo Crim L 183. Indeed it is customary for all relevant remarks made by the defendant after an accident to be given in evidence anyhow. See generally the Judges' Rules. For r III(*a*) to apply, the defendant must actually have been charged or, though not arrested, be likely to be summoned; even where r III does not apply as above, no questioning after caution should take place if the constable concerned has enough evidence to prefer a charge (*R* v *Collier* [1965] 3 All ER 136). Arrest on suspicion does not necessarily mean that there is enough evidence to charge (ibid).

Where a statement is made without caution in circumstances where compliance with the Judges' Rules would necessitate a caution, it is for the judge or magistrates in exercise of their discretion to decide whether the statement should be admitted or not (*R* v *Ovenell* [1968] 1 All ER 933). The dictum in that case that the Rules are directed to the police alone overlooks r VI, which says that persons other than police officers charged with the duty of investigating offences shall, so far as practicable, comply with them; so the Rules may apply to Department of Transport examiners and government officers investigating excise licence offences. In Scotland it has been held that an admission by the defendant to a constable that he was the driver at the relevant time is not admissible if the constable had not been authorised by a chief officer of police to demand the information under what is now s 168(2) of the 1972 Act (*Foster* v *Farrell* 1963 SLT 182). The English decisions just cited suggest that this case would not be followed in England, and *Foster* v *Farrell* was distinguished in *Miln* v *Cullen* 1967 SLT 35, where it was held that the admission of the defendant at the scene of an accident in reply to a question by a constable whether he was the driver may be allowed in evidence if there is no unfairness to him. It was said obiter in *Berry* v *Robson*, above, that the question 'Are you the driver?' must be answered because of s 167 or s 168 but those sections apply only when the constable has been authorised to demand the information by or on behalf of a chief officer of police. It seems that statements made in breach of the Judges' Rules are anyhow admissible at the court's discretion (*Hennell* v *Cuthbert*, above).

Even though a judge or magistrates decide to admit a confession statement as voluntary, the defendant still has the right to challenge the confession statement during the course of the case. It is for the jury to decide whether the statement is true at the end of the case and if the jury consider that the statement was improperly induced it may affect their decision (*R* v *McCarthy* [1980] Crim LR 306). The judge or magistrates may reconsider their ruling later in the trial (*R* v *Watson* [1980] Crim LR 307).

The police should supply a copy of the defendant's statement to them to the defence on request (110 JP Jo 435) and the Home Secretary has said that it is the practice of the police to supply to the solicitor of an accused person on request copies of statements made by him, unless the police think that to do so would impede the course of justice (105 SJ 133). The police should supply to the defending solicitor, on his request, a list of the defendant's previous convictions, without waiting for the latter's permission. Abstracts of the police report of an accident will generally be supplied on payment of the appropriate charge unless a prosecution is pending. Charges are fixed, from time to time, for interviewing a police officer, for a copy of a witness's statement, a copy of a police report and for photographs. The *Law Society's Gazette*, August 1967, p 418, indicates the recommended police procedure for interviewing police officers and supplying statements, etc, for civil proceedings.

It is not customary for the police to supply copies of statements, made by witnesses who are to be called by them, to the defence in advance (*R* v *Bryant* (1946) 110 JP 267). See also *R* v *Warrington JJ* at 2.41. If the prosecution know of a credible witness who can speak of material facts which tend to show the defendant's innocence, his statement, if he is not to be called for the prosecution, should be made available to the defence (*Dallison* v *Caffery* [1964] 2 All ER 610). In *R* v *Leyland JJ, ex parte Hawthorn* [1979] 1 All ER 209 a conviction was quashed where the existence of available witnesses was not made known to the defence. A practice seems to have been growing up, however, at any rate at trials on indictment, of letting the defence see (*semble*, at the trial) the statements of witnesses called for the Crown, and how far this will extend to magistrates' courts is not clear (see *R* v *Hall* (1958) 43 Cr App R 29; *R* v *Fenn*, [1959] Jo Crim L 253). In the latter case Pilcher J said that, where a witness's evidence differs materially from that given in his statement to the police, that statement ought to be shown to the defence, so that there may be cross-examination on that issue, it being the prosecutor's duty to place all the facts before the court. See generally the current edition of Archbold on this point. See also 2.42 as to the guidelines issued by the Attorney-General on the disclosure to the defence (where possible, prior to the committal) of unused material in cases to be tried on indictment.

Witnesses or prospective witnesses may be interviewed before trial by either side, whether or not they have been seen already by the other side; once the defendant has been committed for trial, the defence may still interview the prosecution witnesses but the occasions when such a course is necessary must be rare and, if there is to be an interview after committal, the prosecutor should be invited to attend (*Law Society's Gazette*, February 1963). See also 118 NLJ 913. By Home Office circular 82/1969 (issued with the approval of the Lord Chief Justice and the judges of the Queen's Bench Division) witnesses for the prosecution are normally, though not in all circumstances, entitled, if they so request, to be supplied with copies of any statement taken from them by the police.

Statements in the defendant's presence are evidence against him of the truth of the matters stated so far as by words or conduct he has acquiesced in their contents (see *R* v *Chandler* [1976] Crim LR 308 and the cases there quoted). But where no admission can be reasonably inferred, it is in criminal cases a rule of practice that such statements should, in order to avoid prejudice to the prisoner, not be given in evidence at all (Phipson's *Manual of Evidence*). The working of this rule can be shown thus: Tate is charged with using a vehicle with defective brakes. In the presence of Tate and the police constable, a mechanic (not called as a witness) examines the brakes and mentions certain defects. If Tate then admitted the truth of the mechanic's remarks by words or conduct, the mechanic's statement and Tate's reply may be given in evidence; if Tate by words or conduct then denied their truth, the mechanic's remarks should not generally be given in evidence. Evidence of what has been said to the defendant by persons not called as witnesses may be given if relevant to show the defendant's state of mind (*Subramaniam* v *Public Prosecutor* [1956] 1 WLR 965; *R* v *Willis* [1960] 1 All ER 331), eg that what he had been told by a person not called as a witness induced in him a belief that the owner of a motor vehicle would have consented to his taking it.

A record of a police interrogation signed voluntarily by the accused may be put before the jury as an exhibit to oral evidence given by the police of the interview, notwithstanding that the document is not admissible otherwise as an aide-mémoire of a statement covered by r IV of the Judges' Rules (*R* v *Todd* [1981] Crim LR 611).

In *R* v *Martin (John)* (1983) *The Times*, 1 July, the court held that contemporaneous notes of an interview in which a defendant had largely remained silent or answered 'no' to questions asked, and of which only four questions and answers were relevant, ought not to have been admitted in evidence and exhibited.

*Editing statements*

Where a record of a police interview has been taken it should form part of the police report to the prosecuting solicitor and should then be included in instructions to prosecuting counsel. The police should not edit the record themselves (*R* v *Penfold* [1980] Crim LR 182). However, editing may be necessary if the police are conducting the prosecution themselves and it is appropriate to do so.

## 2.79 Refreshing memory

A witness may refresh his memory from any writing made or verified by himself contemporaneously with, and concerning, the facts to which he testifies. A pro forma witness statement made and signed contemporaneously by a doctor when asked by a constable for his consent to the patient supplying breath or blood samples can be used by him to refresh his memory (*Taylor* v *Armand* [1975] RTR 225) (see also *Groves* v *Redbart* at 6.27).

A constable was held to be entitled to refresh his memory from his notebook which he made up two hours later from brief jottings (*Attorney-General's Reference No 3 of* 1979 [1979] Crim LR 786). 'Contemporaneously' includes so shortly afterwards that the facts were fresh in the memory, eg a fortnight but not several weeks or more (see Cross on *Evidence* (5th ed) 228 as to this point). Thus, a witness may refresh his memory from police notes taken from his lips and signed by him (*R* v *Mullins* (1848) 12 JP 776). In *Gleed* v *Stroud* [1962] Jo Crim L 161, a witness had written a lorry's number on an envelope at the time of an offence by the lorry-driver. Two hours later, the witness made a statement to the police and included the lorry's number in it. When he gave evidence, the envelope had been lost. The High Court held that it was proper to allow him to refresh his memory of the number from his signed statement to the police. But where a witness wrote a car's number down at the request of someone who saw the car but the latter did not see what the witness wrote, it was held that the witness should not give evidence of the number which he wrote, for it was hearsay (*R* v *McLean* (1967) 111 SJ 925). And see *Jones* v *Metcalfe* at 2.86. It may, however, be possible to establish a 'chain' of evidence. In *R* v *Kelsey* [1982] RTR 135 (CA), a witness of an incident concerning a car was properly permitted to refresh his memory at a trial months later by referring to a note of the car number made by a police officer at the time of the incident in the witness's presence and at his dictation. The witness confirmed its accuracy at the time when it was read out by the officer although the witness did not actually examine the note when it was written. The police officer gave evidence that the note was the one he had made at the time. Taylor J, sitting with the Lord Chief Justice, Lord Lane, said that in their Lordships' view there was no magic in verifying by seeing as opposed to verifying by hearing. What had to be shown was that witness *A* had verified in the sense of satisfying himself while the matters were fresh in his mind (1) that a record had been made, and (2), that it was accurate. If *A* made a contemporaneous note himself, or if *A* read and adopted at the time a contemporaneous note made by *B*, *A* might refresh his memory from it without need of another witness. Where *A* dictated the number and heard it read back and confirmed its accuracy, although he saw it being made and did not read it, it was necessary for the officer to be called to prove that the note he produced was the one *A* saw him making and heard him read back.

A witness may also speak from records kept by him as part of his duty and say, 'I am satisfied I kept this record and that this or that happened as it is duly recorded', even though he may not actually remember the occurrence (*R* v *Bryant* (1946) 110 JP 267). Notes made with a view to subsequent litigation may be used to refresh memory and it is not necessary that the witness should have any independent recollection of the incident (*Buckeridge* v *Buckeridge* (1962) 10 SJ 471). A copy checked months later by the witness from an original record contemporaneously made by him may be used if the original be lost or even if its absence is not explained (*Talbot* v *Cusack* (1864) 12 LT 678). The record need not actually have been made by the witness provided he checked it contemporaneously (*Burrough* v *Martin* (1809) 2 Camp 12, NP). A witness may refresh his memory from a transcript of a contemporary note if it substantially reproduced the note (*R* v *Cheng* [1976] Crim LR 379).

On looking at his statement a witness may recall what was recorded. On the other hand he may merely confirm what was recorded without being able to recall it. Clearly the first is more valuable. In the Crown Court decision of *R* v *P and C* [1982] Crim LR 671 evidence in the second of these categories was held inadmissible. The evidence was of a car registration number. The position was complicated by the fact that the witness had also been reminded of the car number by her husband. The court relied on various statements in Cross on *Evidence* (see pp 1–2 and 5–6 in the 5th ed) that evidence in the second category above is not admissible.

The decision is a Crown Court one and is not binding (see 2.35). The court distinguished *R* v *Bryant* above on the ground that it was an exception limited to business records but there seems to be no justification for this. See also the other cases above indicating the contrary. The evidence is not well described as hearsay because it is the witness's own evidence and not heard from another. Evidence of conversations and other matters contemporaneously recorded is frequently allowed even though the witness cannot recall the details.

The matter is touched on in the Criminal Law Revision Committee Eleventh Report (Evidence) (Cmnd 4991) on pp 139 and 237. Compare s 2 of the Civil Evidence Act 1968.

The document, even if a confidential one, used to refresh memory must be made available to the other side (*Betts* v *Betts* (1917) 33 TLR 200), but, if no reference is made to any document to refresh memory, the other side cannot insist on seeing confidential documents, such as police notebooks (*Hinshelwood* v *Auld* 1926 SC(J) 4, but cf *R* v *Bass* [1953] 1 All ER 1064, where police notebooks should have been called for). Where a policeman before giving evidence had refreshed his memory from his notebook outside the court but had not used it in the witness box, the defendant was nevertheless entitled to examine it and cross-examine on relevant matters contained in it (*Owen* v *Edwards* (1983) 147 JP 245).

In *R* v *Richardson* [1971] 2 All ER 773 the Court of Appeal held that there could be no general rule that prosecution witnesses should not see their statements before going into court to give evidence. Such a rule could militate against the interests of justice if there has been lengthy delay in bringing the case to trial (ibid). Summary trials by their very nature are normally not subject to the same delay as trials on indictment (in *Richardson's* case the delay was eighteen months) and whether it is proper for prosecution witnesses to be shown their statements will depend on the length of the delay and the complexity and nature of their evidence. *R* v *Richardson* was followed and applied in *Worley* v *Bentley* [1976] Crim LR 310. The witness had refreshed her memory by reading immediately before the hearing her statement made to the police five months earlier. The justices dismissed the charge because the defence had not been informed of what had been done. Reversing the justices, the Divisional Court held that while it was desirable for the defence to be told that a witness had refreshed his memory by reading his statement before the hearing, it was not essential. Similarly in *R* v *Westwell* [1976] Crim LR 441 the defence was not told that immediately before the trial the prosecution witnesses had seen their statements which they had made to the police ten months before, and it was again held that although it was desirable that the defence should be told it was not essential.

By a Home Office circular, 82/1969, issued with the approval of the Lord Chief Justice and the judges of the Queen's Bench Division, witnesses for the prosecution are normally (though not in all circumstances) entitled, if they so request, to be supplied with copies of any statements taken from them by the police.

A tape recording may also be used to refresh memory (*R* v *Mills* [1962] 3 All ER 298). See further as to tape recordings 2.82.

## 2.80 Documentary evidence

By s 181 of the 1972 Act, in any proceedings for an offence under that Act specified in column 7 of Part I of Sched 4 to the Act, or under any other enactment relating to the use of vehicles on roads, a certificate in the form prescribed by the Evidence by Certificate Rules 1961 (SI 1961 No 248, as amended by SI 1962 No 2319), signed by a constable (or a traffic warden acting in discharge of functions authorised under the Functions of Traffic Wardens Order 1970) and certifying that a person specified in the certificate stated to him:

(*a*) that a particular motor vehicle was being driven or used by, or belonged to, that person on a particular occasion; or

(*b*) that a particular motor vehicle was used by, or belonged on a particular occasion to, a firm in which that person also stated that he was at the time of the statement a partner; or

(*c*) that a particular motor vehicle was used by, or belonged on a particular occasion to, a corporation of which that person also stated that he was at the time of the statement a director or officer or employee,

shall be admissible as evidence for the purpose of determining by whom the vehicle was being driven or used, or to whom it belonged, as the case may be, on that occasion. There are like provisions in s 113 of the Road Traffic Regulation Act 1984 in proceedings in England and Wales for any offence to which s 112 of that Act applies (save an offence under s 61(5)). Nothing in s 181 or s 113 shall be deemed to make such certificate admissible as evidence in proceedings for an offence except in a case where and to the extent to which oral evidence to the like effect would have been admissible in those proceedings. A copy of the certificate must have been served on the defendant in the manner indicated in r 3 of the Evidence by Certificate Rules 1961 not less than seven days before the hearing and the defendant may require, not later than three days before the hearing, the attendance of the constable who gives the certificate (see s 181(3) and s 113(3)). It would seem that, as leaving a vehicle on the road can be 'using' it (see *Andrews* v *Kershaw* [1951] 2 All ER 764 and other cases at 1.79), s 181 and s 113 apply to all charges of obstruction and parking. They apply to proceedings on indictment as well as before magistrates. The view is advanced at 122 JP Jo 131 that the certificate of a Scottish constable is admissible under (what is now) s 181 in England. Section 181 and s 113 apply only to motor vehicles and not to pedal cycles.

Offences under regulations made under any Act mentioned in s 181 are offences under that Act and s 181 applies to such offences (cf *Bingham* v *Bruce* [1962] 1 All ER 136; *Rathbone* v *Bundock* [1962] 2 All ER 257). The same principle would apply to s 113.

Note the limitations on the matters which can be stated in such certificates, eg, a constable can certify only that the person interviewed said he was driving a motor vehicle on a named occasion and not that that person said that some other person was driving. Although a certificate can be used to show that a particular person was driving, it cannot be used to prove that the vehicle was used or driven on the particular road or place alleged. Sections 181, 183, 113 and 114 are useful to prove ownership of a particular vehicle or to prove that the defendant admitted he was driving it, where the defendant or the owners are interviewed in a town a long way from the court, eg when a Durham lorry driver is summoned for an offence in Sussex and his firm, also in Durham, is summoned for permitting the offence. The evidence of the Durham constable who interviewed the defendant and the firm is thus receivable, without his (the constable's) attendance in Sussex, on the matters set out in the sections. It is submitted that the only person who can answer for a firm or company are those with sufficient authority to make admissions on its behalf.

Further powers of proving by writing that the defendant was the driver are given by the 1972 Act, s 183, and the Road Traffic Regulation Act 1984, s 114. On the summary trial of an information for an offence under the 1972 Act or any regulations made or continued thereunder to which s 183 is applied by virtue of column 7 of Part I of Sched 4 to the Act, or under any enactment relating to the use of vehicles on roads, if it is proved that a requirement under s 168(2) of the 1972 Act (see 7.16), to give information as to the identity of the driver of the particular vehicle on the particular occasion to which the information relates, has been served on the defendant by post and a statement in writing, purporting to be signed by the defendant, that he was the driver of the vehicle on that occasion, is produced to the court, that statement may be treated as evidence that he was the driver. Sections 183 and 114 do not apply to committal proceedings or to trials on indictment. It can be used only to prove that the defendant himself was the driver; it cannot be used to prove that he was the owner or that someone else was driving. Sections 183 and 114 apply to all types of vehicles and, it seems, to riders of cycles (cf s 168(2) of the 1972 Act). All the above powers are additional to the power to use written statements in evidence under s 102 of the Magistrates' Courts Act 1980 and s 9 of the Criminal Justice Act 1967.

*Registration particulars and driving licence records*

Section 31 of the Vehicles (Excise) Act 1971 and s 182 of the 1972 Act enable evidence as to registration particulars and driving licence records maintained by the Secretary of State for Transport with respect to vehicles to be given by certificate. The two sections read identically except that there is no provision in s 31 of the 1971 Act which corresponds to s 182(2A) of the 1972 Act. Section 182(2A) refers to a method of proving previous convictions of endorsable and disqualifiable offences. It is not therefore relevant to the 1971 Act. When a statement is produced to a magistrates' court in proceedings for an offence involving obligatory or discretionary disqualification within the meaning of Part III of the 1972 Act, for the purposes of s 182(2A) (establishing previous convictions), the procedure under subs (2A) must presumably be complied with if subs (2A) is to have any meaning. Apart from this instance, there is no procedural provision requiring the other party to be served with a copy of the certificate before the proceedings. As soon as the certificate is produced it proves itself. Moreover there is no limitation on the nature or type of proceedings for which a certificate may be used. It appears that the sections may be used for any civil or criminal proceedings and are not limited to proceedings under the 1971 Act and the 1972 Act. The only apparent limitation is that the matters for which evidence may be given are only those of a prescribed description (s 182(3) of the 1972 Act or s 31(3) of the 1971 Act) and that the evidence of any fact is admissible only to the same extent as oral evidence. If, therefore, the certificate contains inadmissible evidence, eg, hearsay, neither s 31 nor s 182 renders it admissible.

It will be noted that 'document' in s 31 (or s 182) has the same meaning as in s 10(1) of the Civil Evidence Act 1968 which provides that 'document' includes any photograph. A photograph of a fraudulent application for a vehicle's excise licence was held by a magistrates' court to be therefore admissible when certified in accordance with the section (see 'Practical Point' 2, 140 JP 508). Apparently application forms are photographed and subsequently destroyed when the licence is issued by the Department of Transport.

Reference should be made to reg 3 of the Vehicle and Driving Licences Records (Evidence) Regulations 1970 which prescribes the matters for which certificates may be given.

The purpose of s 182(2A) of the 1972 Act is to enable the prosecution to cite previous convictions for endorsable offences in the absence of the defendant. Although a defendant is required to produce his licence to a court on conviction of an endorsable offence and risks prosecution if he fails to do so, a magistrates' court frequently finds that a licence is not forthcoming even when the court has specifically adjourned sentence in order to obtain it. In the absence of a driving licence and in the absence of a notice under s 104 of the Magistrates' Courts Act 1980 (see 2.50), there was no way for a prosecutor to inform the court of a defendant's previous convictions in the absence of the defendant. Subsection (2A) enables a statement to be produced to the court specifying the previous endorsable convictions of the defendant in order that a court may take into account any previous convictions when sentencing the defendant in his absence. The statement normally takes the form of a computer print out and is commonly described as such. *Subsequent* convictions and in particular subsequent disqualifications cannot be quoted under subs (2A) however relevant they may be. If the notice discloses endorsable convictions so that s 19 of the Transport Act 1981 applies, it will be necessary for the court to adjourn the case further and serve notice on the defendant giving the reason for adjournment (see 2.52).

It should be noted that if a court convicts and adjourns sentence in order that the prosecution may have an opportunity of serving a notice under subs (2A), sufficient time must be given to enable the notice to be served 'not less than seven days before' the notice is produced, ie the notice must arrive in the ordinary course of post so that there are seven clear days between the date of service of the notice and the date of hearing at which the statement is produced. Justices may not adjourn after conviction for a period exceeding four weeks at a time (*R* v *Talgarth JJ* [1973] 2 All ER 717) (s 10(3) of the Magistrates' Courts Act 1980), but s 10(3) is directory, not mandatory (*R* v *Manchester City Justices, ex parte Miley and Dynan* (1977), unreported but discussed in (1977) 141 JP 248). Whether or not the seven-day notice has been served, there is no reason why the contents of a print out including convictions, disqualifications and endorsements should not be put to a defendant who appears and has been convicted.

*Weight tickets and timetables*

A weight ticket given under what is now s 160(3) of the 1972 Act was admitted by magistrates as showing weight, but their decision as to this was not mentioned by the High Court on appeal in *Churchill* v *Norris* (1938) 158 LT 255. See also *William Hampton Ltd and Another* v *Bryan Dixon* (1973) unreported but noted at 1.35. Obviously, it could be used to refresh the memory of someone who saw the weights shown on the dials.

Timetables, etc, are admissible against employers charged with procuring or inciting their drivers to exceed the speed limit (Road Traffic Regulation Act 1984, s 89(4)). Records of hours of driving kept by a firm's drivers are admissible against the firm on a charge of permitting them to drive for excessive periods contrary to what is now s 96 of the Transport Act 1968 (*Beer* v *Clench* [1936] 1 All ER 449; *Adair* v *Craighouse* 1937 SC(J) 89). The fact that the numbers on log sheets tally with the numbers of vehicles may suffice to relate the sheets to those vehicles (*Hogg* v *Burnet* 1938 SC(J) 160). Where letters are sent by a witness to a particular person on a particular matter and an answer is received in due course, there is a presumption that the answer has been written by the person in whose writing (or, *semble*, on whose headed letter-paper) it purports to be (see cases in 22 E & E Dig (Blue) 190).

*Manufacturers' records and computer evidence*

Sections 68 and 69 of the Police and Criminal Evidence Act 1984, when in force, deal with evidence from documentary and computer records respectively.

The Criminal Evidence Act 1965 provides that, where direct oral evidence of a fact would be admissible, any statement contained in a document and tending to establish that fact shall on production of the document be admissible as evidence of that fact if the document is, or forms part of, a record relating to any trade or business, compiled, in the course of that trade or business, from information supplied by persons who have or may reasonably be supposed to have personal knowledge of the matters dealt with in the information they supply, and the person who supplied that information is dead, abroad or ill, or has disappeared or, having regard to the lapse of time, cannot be reasonably expected to have any recollection of the matters dealt with in the information which he supplied. This Act reversed the decision in *Myers* v *Director of Public Prosecutions* [1964] 2 All ER 881 as to motor manufacturers' records. The admissibility of documents in evidence and the hearsay rule generally are discussed in that case.

The Act indicates the considerations to be applied in assessing the weight of such evidence. In *R* v *Jones* [1978] 2 All ER 718, it was held that single documents (bills of lading) could be records. In *R* v *Pettigrew* [1980] Crim LR 239 it was sought to adduce evidence under the Criminal Evidence Act 1965 from the automatic sorting process of a computer. The evidence was disallowed because it had not been within the personal knowledge or mind of anybody, as it was recorded purely by operation of the machine. The position might have been different had the operator had personal knowledge. It is submitted that the decision is correct on the strict interpretation of the statute but it should be compared with the common law position. In *R* v *Halpin* [1975] 2 All ER 1124 (CA), Lane J said that 'the common law should move with the times and recognise that officials in complicated times have no personal knowledge of the accuracy of the entries'. In that case, an extract from a company's returns entered in the Companies Registry under the Companies Act 1948 was admitted. In *R* v *Wood* [1982] Crim LR 668 a computer was used as a calculator and the evidence admitted. That case has been applied in cases on the Intoximeter 3000 breath specimen machine (see further the various cases at 4.80).

Section 1(4) provides that 'business includes any public transport, public utility, or similar undertaking carried on by a local authority and the activities of the Post Office'. In *R* v *Crayden* [1978] 2 All ER 700 the Court of Appeal held that 'business' had a commercial connotation and did not include the activities of the National Health Service and in particular medical records. The work of a Government department is not a trade or business (*R* v *Gwiliam* [1968] 3 All ER 821).

## 2.81 Plans, sketches and maps

Plans and sketches are frequently used in careless driving cases—some cases would be incomprehensible without them. It is a common practice not to draw plans to scale but to show distances from a specified location. The resulting sketch may mislead but it enables a correct plan to be drawn to scale if required. A map or plan prepared for the purpose of a trial ought not to contain any reference to transactions and occurrences which are the subject matter of the investigation before the court and were not existing when the survey was made; if it does *and objection is taken*, the court should not look at it (*R* v *Mitchell* (1852) 6 Cox CC 82). In *Tarbox* v *St. Pancras Borough Council* [1952] 1 All ER 1306 (a civil case), however, particulars of the place where the plaintiff said he was walking, the position of the defendant's servant and the position where the plaintiff fell were ordered to be put on a plan rather than in a statement of claim. If no objection is taken by the other side, a plan or sketch showing both things existing at the time it was made (eg, traffic lights, white lines, skid marks, piles of mud) and also things surmised by the artist (eg, the course of a car prior to stopping) can, it seems, be put in evidence, but the other side should first be given a sight of the drawing. Provided that it is made clear to the court that some of it is surmise, that it is for guidance only and that it must be carefully checked with the evidence, a plan or sketch not objected to, put in before the court for guidance only, seems to be no more inadmissible than a sketch made by a magistrate as the case unfolds. If a sketch not to a scale and showing only things existing and no presurmised tracks, etc, is objected to, it would seem that the person who prepared it can still put it in when called as a witness for what it is worth but, if it is such a bad sketch as to be completely out of proportion—as some are—it is submitted that the other side might successfully object to its being put in at all because it is so misleading. If it is a plan to scale, however, and shows only things existing when it is made, it must be admitted when the person who prepared it swears to it in the witness box. Further, by the Criminal Justice Act 1948, s 41 and regulations made thereunder, in any criminal proceedings a plan prepared by a constable, architect, chartered surveyor, civil engineer, municipal engineer or land agent and certified by him to be correctly drawn to a specified scale shall be evidence of the relative position of things shown thereon; the person who prepared the plan need not be called as a witness, but a copy of the plan and certificate must have been served on the defendant at least seven days before the hearing and, not less than three days before the hearing, the defendant can require that person to be called as a witness (see s 41(5)).

It was held in *Hogg* v *Clark* 1959 SC (J) 7 that a plan could be put by the defence to a prosecution witness although the plan had not at that time been proved.

Maps, such as the Ordnance Survey, are admissible as to matters deducible from them, such as whether a road is in existence, and distances. A rotameter may be used on a map to show distances travelled. In statutes passed after 1 January 1890 distance is measured in a straight line on a horizontal plane unless the contrary intention appears (Interpretation Act 1978, s 8). Ordnance maps are not in themselves evidence that a forecourt is part of the highway (*Baxter* v *Middlesex County Council* [1956] Crim LR 561), nor of the boundaries of the highway (*Webb* v *Eastleigh Borough Council* [1957] 56 LGR 124). The Highways Act 1980, s 32, however, allows maps, plans and local histories to be put in evidence as to the dedication of a highway. Moreover some Ordnance Survey maps show the footpaths, bridleways and roads used as public paths as on a 'definitive map' prepared under the National Parks and Access to the Countryside Act 1949 and now under Part III of the Wildlife and Countryside Act 1981 (see 1.68 as to the effect if a right of way is so shown on a definitive map).

## 2.82 Photographs, films, tapes and video tapes

Photographs are proved by the oath of the person who took them. They are commonly accepted without negatives, but if challenged the witness would be wise to produce any negatives at the same time. Photographs of the scene are often of assistance but it should be remembered that distances may appear foreshortened. The police will normally supply a copy of any photograph taken by them on payment of the appropriate fee.

It was stated in *R* v *Quinn* [1961] 3 All ER 88 that a film of a reconstruction of an accident or piece of driving would generally not be admissible. Accident investigation evidence is often based on reconstructions and is often accepted. Obviously such evidence must be approached with care as it is reconstruction only.

The High Court of Justiciary has admitted a tape recording in evidence (*Hopes* v *Lord Advocate* 1960 SLT 264) and a tape recording of an overheard conversation can be used to refresh the hearer's memory (*R* v *Mills* [1962] 3 All ER 298). The admissibility of video tape evidence was discussed in

*R* v *Fowden* [1982] Crim LR 588 (CA) and *R* v *Grimer* [1982] Crim LR 674 (CA) and approved in the latter case, where the evidence was admitted of a witness who identified someone pictured on video tape. The video tape had also been produced in evidence.

In *R* v *Maqsud Ali* [1965] 2 All ER 464 it was held that a tape recording of remarks made by a defendant is admissible if the recording can be properly proved and his voice identified; a properly proved transcript of the recording may be used to assist the court. In *R* v *Robson* [1972] 2 All ER 699, considering *R* v *Stevenson, Hulse and Whitney* [1971] 1 All ER 678 and *R* v *Maqsud Ali*, above, it was held that the prosecution must prove on the balance of probabilities that the recordings were original and authentic before they could be admitted as evidence.

In *Kajala* v *Noble* [1982] Crim LR 433 it was stated that the best evidence rule had no relevance to tape or films but applied only to documents where the original was available. On these authorities the film, tape, video tape or photograph must be proved as genuine but (on the authority of *Kajala* v *Noble*) need not be the original.

Section 71 of the Police and Criminal Evidence Act 1984 when in force will provide for the admissibility of enlargements of microfilm copies.

## 2.83 Exhibits

The best evidence rule applies to documents where the original is available but not to chattels generally (*Kajala* v *Noble* above; *R* v *Orrell* [1972] RTR 14 and *Tremlett* v *Fawcett* (1984) RTLB 68 at 4.80 and *Hockin* v *Ahlquist* [1943] 2 All ER 722). It is not essential to produce all exhibits (though some, such as statements, must be produced) but the absence of exhibits may be a matter for comment (*Hockin* v *Ahlquist*).

Under s 102 of the Magistrates' Courts Act 1980 and s 9 of the Criminal Justice Act 1967 (written statements in committal proceedings and summary trials respectively) any document or object referred to as an exhibit and identified in the statement is to be treated as if both produced and identified in court by the maker of the statement.

Exhibits when produced (or so treated as produced) are the responsibility of the court and the producer. This responsibility was considered in *R* v *Lambeth Stipendiary Magistrate, ex parte McComb* [1983] 1 All ER 460 where *R* v *Lushington* [1894] 1 QB 420 was applied. It is within the power of, and it is the duty of, constables to retain for use in court things which may be evidence of crime, and which have come into their possession without wrong on their part. When articles have been produced in court by witnesses it is right and necessary for the court, or the constable or person in whose charge they are placed, to preserve and retain them, so that they may be always available for the purposes of justice until the trial is concluded (*Lushington*). It may be right to release the exhibits temporarily for a proper purpose and if so it may be desirable to seek the permission of the court (*McComb*). Even if the exhibit is not produced or treated as produced it is submitted that the court may still have jurisdiction over it.

## 2.84 Local and specialised knowledge

Where it is a matter of notorious local knowledge that a journey of one and a half miles from point *A* to point *B* necessarily involved using several different public roads, the justices were held to be entitled to use this knowledge in rejecting a submission of no case and convicting the defendant where the prosecution had been unable to prove the precise route taken by the offending vehicle (*Borthwick* v *Vickers* [1973] RTR 390).

A judge hearing an appeal from magistrates was well acquainted with a road junction on the A25 and A20 and road works being carried on there. He informed the court of this knowledge. The hearing concerned a conviction for driving without reasonable consideration. The judge's use of his knowledge was unsuccessfully challenged in the Divisional Court. The Divisional Court held that local knowledge could not and should not be excluded from the court's mind in drawing inferences (*Chesson* v *Jordan* [1981] Crim LR 333). The use of local knowledge is implicit in the concept of local magistrates and local justice.

Justices had no direct evidence that a special constable who required a breath test was in uniform. Evidence was given that another special constable present was in uniform. The defence did not raise the issue in cross-examination. The justices, from their knowledge of the special constabulary, knew that there was no plain clothes department and the officer having stated that he was on duty they deduced he was in uniform. The Divisional Court held that there was circumstantial evidence whereby the justices could conclude that the officer must have been in uniform (*Richards* v *West* [1980] RTR 215).

A justice with specialised knowledge is entitled to use that knowledge in interpreting or assessing the evidence already before the court and can communicate his views to his fellow justices provided he does not thrust those views upon them. He must not, on the other hand, proceed to give evidence to his fellow justices contradicting the evidence given in court as it is not in open court nor subject to cross-examination (*Wetherall* v *Harrison* [1976] RTR 125).

In *Kent* v *Stamps* [1982] RTR 273 the justices used local knowledge of the location of a speed trap—round a bend and on an upward gradient (as well as an elderly lorry). The Divisional Court upheld with hesitation their rejection for these reasons of the result of the speed trap equipment.

## 2.85 Inspections

Where vehicles are near the court, the justices may inspect them provided they have sworn evidence as to whether they are in a different condition from that at the time of the offence (*Keeble* v *Miller* [1950] 1 All ER 261). Witnesses taking part in a view should be recalled for cross-examination, if desired (*Karamat* v *R* [1956] 1 All ER 415, where views generally are discussed). In *R* v *Knight* (1961) *The Times*, 14 June, the jury, in a case of taking and driving away a lorry, asked if they could inspect a similar lorry and were allowed to do so. The Court of Criminal Appeal said that applications for inspection should be regarded with great caution, especially when the conditions of the inspection differed. See also Cross on *Evidence* (5th ed) 12.

A conviction was quashed in *R* v *Lawrence* [1968] 1 All ER 579, where the jury inspected a vehicle after they had retired, but not quashed in *R* v *Nixon* [1968] 2 All ER 33, where the same had happened but defending counsel had said that he desired the jury to do so. Magistrates were held to be wrong when they took a tyre gauge with them when they retired and carried out a private test on a tyre. Lord Lane CJ said that the reason why they had carried out this test was objectionable: they were in breach of their duty to hear the whole case in open court (*R* v *Tiverton JJ* (1980) 144 JP 747).

See also 2.90.

## 2.86 Admissions

Admissions by either side before or at the hearing are allowed in the circumstances given in s 10 of the Criminal Justice Act 1967. A defendant may thus be asked to admit in court that he was the driver or what his reply to a constable was; his admission in a magistrates' court must be put in writing and signed by him (Magistrates' Courts Rules 1981, r 71) but no doubt the magistrates will control a prosecutor who tries to get the defendant to admit his case for him. Any admission made on behalf of an individual can only be made by a solicitor or barrister. An article on admissions under s 10 appears in [1969] Jo Crim L 285. Save so far as admissions are made in advance, each side should be ready to prove its case by ordinary evidence; an admission may only be withdrawn by leave of the court and the side relying on it would no doubt be granted an adjournment to call the necesssary evidence. In *R* v *Lewis* [1971] Crim LR 414, defending counsel admitted the facts as stated in the prosecutor's opening speech. The Court of Appeal said that it was a practice which should be adopted rarely and with extreme caution. A previous plea of guilty may or may not have some probative value, but before allowing a reference to such a plea it should first be considered whether such probative value as it had would exceed the prejudice induced by its admission (*R* v *Rimmer* [1972] 1 All ER 604).

## 2.87 Proof generally

The owner of a motor vehicle is presumed in law to be the user, in the absence of contrary evidence (*Watson* v *Paterson*, noted at 121 JP Jo 336). In *Barnard* v *Sully* (1931) 47 TLR 557, it was held that proof of a defendant being owner of a car was prima facie evidence that it was being driven at the material time by him or his servant or agent. This was a civil case and, in a reference to it in *Ende* v *Cassidy* (1964) 108 SJ 522, it was said that there would be a higher standard of proof in criminal cases, but it was held in *Ende's* case that ownership was some evidence that the defendant was responsible for an obstruction with his car, especially as it had been left outside a block of flats where he lived. *Barnard* v *Sully* was followed in *Baker* v *Oxford* at 4.44.

*Barnard* v *Sully* and *Ende* v *Cassidy* were again followed in *Elliott* v *Loake* [1983] Crim LR 36 where it was held that the justices were justified in finding that the owner of a car was the driver at a time an accident occurred. This prima facie inference was reinforced when the owner told lies. The owner had also not taken any steps to reply to the notice under s 168 of the 1972 Act asking him to state who the driver was and had given no satisfactory explanation for not doing so.

In *Stickings* v *George* [1980] RTR 237 justices were directed to continue the hearing of a case of careless driving which they had dismissed on upholding a submission of no case to answer on the ground that none of the prosecution witnesses had identified the defendant. The police had taken a statement from the defendant at the scene and the statement had been put in evidence. Moreover, the defendant, before pleading not guilty, had agreed that she was the person named in the information.

In *Scruby* v *Beskeen* [1980] RTR the defendant admitted owning a blue Range Rover and being at the place in question at the relevant time. The Divisional Court held that this was evidence upon which justices could find that the defendant was the driver of a blue Range Rover which had been driven carelessly at the place in question and upheld a conviction for careless driving.

It is difficult to say how far this line of cases will be taken. One has only to consider, as an example, whether a High Court judge would allow the conviction of a car owner for manslaughter where the sole evidence implicating him personally was that he owned the vehicle involved. In seeking proof as to the identity of a driver, the police should remember their powers of requiring the owner or any other person to give information as to this (see 7.16).

If the name and address of an offending motorist have been obtained from a driving licence produced by the offender at the time of the offence or if the offender has otherwise given a name and address to the constable, the appearance at court of a defendant of that name in answer to the summons is prima facie evidence that he is the driver. In *Cooke* v *McCann* [1974] RTR 131 it was held that justices were not entitled to hold there was no case to answer where a traffic warden was unable to identify the defendant as the driver he had seen driving the wrong way down a one way street when the person who had appeared in court bore the name and address he had obtained from the offender's driving licence. Appearance by counsel of a defendant is sufficient prima facie evidence of the identity of the defendant as the driver if the constable gives uncontradicted evidence that the speeding motorist when stopped by him gave the defendant's name and address (*Creed* v *Scott* [1976] RTR 485). There is no difference for the purpose of proving identity between taking the motorist's name and address from the driving licence produced by him (as in *Cooke* v *McCann*) and the motorist simply stating to the constable his name and address without production of the licence (ibid). Bean J in *Cooke* v *McCann* quoted with approval Lord Alverstone CJ in *Marshall* v *Ford* (1908) 72 JP 480, when he said: 'When in the course of his duty a constable acting under the Act gets the name of a person who afterwards appears in court that is evidence on which the magistrates may act.'

These cases were reviewed as well as a number of similar unreported cases from New Zealand in the New Zealand case of *Hays* v *MOT* [1982] 1 NZLR 25. *Marshall* v *Ford*, *Cooke* v *McCann*, *Creed* v *Scott* and *Hays* v *MOT* were all followed in *Allen* v *Ireland* (1984) 148 JP 545, where it was decided that the magistrate was entitled to take judicial notice of the ordinary processes of arrest, charge and bail so as to raise a prima facie case that the person surrendering to bail and answering was the same person who had been arrested, charged and bailed from a crowd of football supporters, although this inference could have been rebutted.

Where, however, a real question of identity arises, as, for example, where a constable sees a person driving the vehicle whom he believes he recognises as a disqualified driver, reference should be made to the appropriate paragraphs in Archbold and in particular *R* v *Turnbull* [1977] QB 224. The practitioner should be aware that in some traffic offence situations *Turnbull* will not necessarily apply fully, eg where the issue is whether the defendant or his passenger was the driver. In *McShane* v *Northumbria Chief Constable* [1980] RTR 406 the Divisional Court observed that *Turnbull* laid down (*a*) principles to be followed in summing up to a jury; and (*b*) a number of matters which could be put forward as being good advice for assistance to a tribunal of fact. Justices are not concerned with the first category but the matters of advice should be followed with great care and diligence. The Divisional Court dismissed an appeal by way of case stated in respect of a conviction upheld by the Crown Court on appeal where identification was in issue. The rider of a moped was seen by the constable with his head exposed in good light for some fifteen minutes and gave correctly the defendant's name and address but an incorrect date of birth. Six weeks later the constable identified the defendant as the rider of a moped when he was in a police station as the only civilian among constables present.

A registration document states that the registered keeper is not necessarily the legal owner. Such a document cannot be used in the ordinary course of business as proof of the possession or control of a car or authorising the possessor of the document to transfer the car. Its presence proves, or tends to prove, only the identity of the statutory 'keeper' (*Beverley Acceptances Ltd* v *Oakley* [1982] RTR 417 per Donaldson LJ at p 432—a civil case). The decision was by a majority with Lord Denning dissenting. It should be compared with *R* v *South Western JJ, ex parte Wandsworth LBC* (1983) *The Times*, 20 January (a Trade Descriptions Act case). There a vehicle had one owner but five hirers (and therefore registered keepers) under leasing agreements. It was held after reference to the Road Vehicles (Registration and Licensing) Regulations that a reference to one owner was a misleading trade description. It is submitted on these authorities that a person's name in the registration document and possession of the log book is capable of constituting some evidence of ownership, though it must be borne in mind that the registered keeper may well not be the owner. The registration document is not a document of title.

Where a witness observed a lorry and caused his wife to write down its number, she should be called to say what number she wrote down or the husband should produce and identify the piece of paper used as the one on which the number was written (*Grew* v *Cubitt* (1951) 49 LGR 650). This case was distinguished in *Jones* v *Metcalfe* [1967] 3 All ER 205, where it was held that, although an eye-witness had told the police the registration number of the defendant's vehicle and that it was the vehicle involved in an accident, there was no written evidence of the number or anything to identify the defendant. See also 2.79. In *Jones* v *Carter* [1956] Crim LR 275, an acquittal was directed in a careless driving case where the prosecutor had not proved that the defendant was driving, although there had been no cross-examination by the defence as to identity and the case had been conducted on the basis that the defendant (who did not testify) was driving. *Jones* v *Metcalfe* was applied in *Cattermole* v *Millar* [1978] RTR 258, where an acquittal was directed because of lack of evidence linking the defendant with the motor vehicle in question (prosecution witnesses referred to a 'white Vauxhall car'—defendant served with notice relating to car MPO 494J—one prosecution witness stated that she had noted down the number of the white Vauxhall but did not state the number in evidence—defendant agreed he had driven the vehicle at the relevant place and date as specified in the notice). The court may properly infer that traffic lights work correctly (*Wells* v *Woodward* (1956) 54 LGR 142). In *Farrell* v *Feighan* (1961) 76 Sh Ct Rep 141, the owner of a car was found in the road beside it, unconscious; it was held to be sufficient proof that he had been driving but not that he had been driving carelessly. See *Platt* v *Green* [1965] Crim LR 311 and *Dickens* v *Smith* [1965] Crim LR 312 for cases where the High Court refused to interfere with convictions in road traffic cases notwithstanding discrepancies in the evidence of identification. The defendant's appearance in court in answer to the summons is not an admission that he was the driver or user at the time of the offence (*Saunders* v *Johns* [1965] Crim LR 49).

Where several men are found together in a vehicle, which has been taken without the owner's consent, in suspicious circumstances, that may be prima facie evidence that they were acting in concert and they can all be properly charged with taking it and with using it without insurance (*Ross* v *Rivenall* [1959] 2 All ER 376). The presumption of guilt would be less strong, however, against a passenger where the circumstances were not suspicious (see 15.7). See also *R* v *Baldessare*, at 15.7.

In a case where the defendant was found to be driving a car seven miles from a town, it was presumed, in the absence of contrary evidence, that he was driving on the same journey and road when three miles from the town shortly before (*Beresford* v *St Alban's JJ* (1905) 22 TLR 1).

Where a car collided with a gatepost on private land adjacent to the public highway, it was held by the Divisional Court that it was as plain as a pikestaff that the collision could only have occurred because of the vehicle's presence on the road as it drove off either the road or the footpath which formed part of it (*Lewis* v *Ursell* (1983) *The Times*, 23 April).

The prosecution must prove their case. In some road traffic cases it suffices to show that the defendant did the forbidden act without any evidence of a guilty mind: see, for example, *Hawkins* v *Holmes* at 8.20 (failing to maintain brakes); in others, mens rea must be shown. In reckless and careless driving cases it is not sufficient to show an accident which may well have occurred through negligence; the defendant's guilt must be established by positive evidence (*Alexander* v *Adair* 1938 SC(J) 28); see further 5.30. But any exception, exemption, proviso, excuse or qualification for a defendant should be proved by him and need not be negatived by police evidence in opening (Magistrates' Courts Act 1980, s 101; see *Baker* v *Sweet* at 6.27). The defendant must prove facts peculiarly within his own knowledge, eg, that he has a licence (*R* v *Oliver* [1943] 2 All ER 800) or policy of insurance (*Leathley* v *Drummond*, below). Where it is an offence to do an act without lawful authority, the defendant must prove that he had such authority and the prosecution need not prove its absence (*Williams* v *Russell* (1933) 97 JP 128). On a charge of driving without a licence or insurance, it suffices if the prosecutor proves that the defendant drove a motor vehicle on a road on the day in question and, in law, no further evidence, eg, that he was asked for, and failed to produce his licence or insurance certificate, as the case may be, is required; the onus then shifts to the defendant to show that he had the licence (*John* v *Humphreys* [1955] 1 All ER 793) or insurance policy (*Leathley* v *Drummond* [1972] Crim LR 227). More proof, however, appears to be required in Eire (*A-G (McGowan)* v *Carville* (1961) 95 ILTR 41), but in *Tynan* v *Jones* [1975] RTR 465 *John* v *Humphreys* was again followed and was held to be still good law in England and Wales notwithstanding *A-G (McGowan)* v *Carville*. It would in fact be improper, however, to institute a prosecution on the sole ground that the defendant was seen to drive; the prosecutor should have some reason for thinking that no licence or insurance was in force. In *Howey* v *Bradley* [1970] Crim LR 223 the court left open the question of whether the onus is on the prosecution to prove that an otherwise valid insurance policy produced by the defendant does not cover the particular use of the vehicle. See 'Speed limits on restricted roads', 6.28, as to proof that a speed limit applies to a particular road. It should, however, be remembered that where the onus of proof lies upon the defendant, the onus is that of a balance of probabilities—a defendant does not have to prove the matter in question beyond a doubt based on reason (*R* v *Carr-Briant* [1943] 2 All ER 156).

Where two defendants each are separately charged with careless driving in a cross-roads collision or with certain other offences involving both, it seems that the prosecution can call one defendant to testify against the other, provided they are tried separately; the witness need not answer any questions tending to incriminate him (*A-G* v *Egan* [1948] Ir R 433; [1949] Jo Crim L 207). But a defendant jointly charged with another should not be called for the prosecution and, even where two defendants are charged with separate offences, it is suggested at 109 JP Jo 39 that one should not be called against the other if there is something linking the two offences, eg, using and permitting. But see *R* v *Norfolk Quarter Sessions, ex parte Brunson* [1953] 1 All ER 346. Any defendant may be called as a witness after he has been sentenced, acquitted or pardoned, or a *nolle prosequi* has been entered. There is no general rule that a defence witness should be sentenced on other pending charges before being called (*R* v *Coffey* [1977] Crim LR 45).

## 2.88 Proof in respect of companies, partnerships and employers

So far as companies are concerned the nature of the proof required will depend on whether the case is one of strict liability when the company will be vicariously liable. If, however, mens rea is required, it will be necessary to show that the requisite knowledge was possessed by the 'brains and nerve centre', in other words the directors and manager who represent the directing mind and will of the company and control what it does. The state of mind of these managers is the state of mind of the company and is treated by the law as such. The board of directors may delegate some part of their functions of management giving to their delegate full discretion to act independently of instructions from them. They thereby put such a delegate in their place so that within the scope of the delegation he can act as the company. The various authorities were reviewed in *Essendon Engineering Co Ltd* v *Maile* [1982] RTR 260, a case on s 171 of the Road Traffic Act 1972 (issue of a test certificate false in a material particular). See also *John Henshall (Quarries) Ltd* v *Harvey* at 1.87. This issue may also be relevant if a company is charged with causing, permitting or aiding and abetting (see Chapter 1). Again, in *Edwards* v *Brookes (Milk) Ltd* [1963] 3 All ER 62 it was held that admissions by employees may be used in evidence against their employer when there is prima facie evidence that they are the employer's agents and they have an ostensible status qualifying them to make statements on behalf of the employer; in that case the employee concerned was a depot manager and there was evidence to imply that he had authority. Admissions made by a subordinate employee, however, would not generally be allowed in evidence (*Roberts* v *Morris* [1965] Crim LR 46; here it was a lorry-driver). See 2.80 as to certificates of admission; it is submitted that the above rules apply to written admissions also. See generally the current edition of Cross on *Evidence*. *Watson* v *Paterson*, *Ende* v *Cassidy* and the other cases quoted in the previous section show that a vehicle-owner is presumed to be its user and evidence of ownership, if not obtained afrom the firm's directors, is obtainable from the Department of Transport and from the name and address painted on the vehicle itself (cf *Martin* v *White* (1910) 74 JP 106). A partner's admissions are evidence against the firm (Partnership Act 1890, s 15). Note also s 10 of the Criminal Justice Act 1967 at 2.86 which allows admissions before and at the hearing by a defendant or by the prosecution; where the defendant is an individual, only his lawyer may make them for him, prior to the hearing, under s 10. A corporation may make written admissions by its directors, manager, secretary or clerk under s 10.

## 2.89 Evidence illegally obtained

The exclusion of unfair evidence will be codified by s 78 of the Police and Criminal Evidence Act 1984 when in force.

Evidence (other than admissions or confessions) obtained by illegal means is generally admissible for the prosecution. Reference should now be made to the speeches of the law lords in *R* v *Sang* [1979] 2 All ER 1222. There is a useful commentary on the decision in [1979] Crim LR 656.

*R* v *Sang* was followed in *R* v *Trump* [1980] RTR 274, CA. In that case a defendant was wrongly arrested under s 5(5) of the 1972 Act because the requirements of the subsection then in force were not fulfilled. While at a police station he provided a blood specimen for analysis after having been warned in accordance with s 9(7) of the Act. The specimen was not obtained with the defendant's consent and was not therefore admissible under s 7(1) of the Act. The defendant was, however, charged with the s 5(1) offence of driving whilst unfit and applying *R* v *Sang* the Court of Appeal held that the judge had a discretion to admit evidence of the analysis and it would have been improper to exclude it. The court quoted Lord Diplock's statement in *Sang* that 'there is no discretion to exclude evidence discovered as the result of an illegal search but there is discretion to exclude evidence which the accused has been induced to produce voluntarily if the method of inducement was unfair'.

*R* v *Sang* was explained in *Morris* v *Beardmore* [1980] RTR 321. Lord Diplock emphasised that there was no general exclusionary discretion. It was confined to the two categories specified in *R* v *Sang* at [1979] 2 All ER 1231A, per Lord Diplock, namely:

> (1) A trial judge . . . has always a discretion to refuse to admit evidence if in his opinion its prejudicial effect outweighs its probative value.
>
> (2) Save with regard to admissions and confessions and generally with regard to evidence obtained from the accused after the commission of the offence, he has no discretion to refuse to admit relevant admissible evidence on the ground that it was obtained by improper or unfair means.

See also 4.4 and 'By or on behalf of a chief officer of police', 7.17.

## 2.90 Evidence generally

In many cases a view of the *locus* by the advocate is obviously helpful. Skid marks and other marks, damage, the visibility and obstructions at corners, the light, the state of the road at the time and mud or other indications where the point of impact was, are all things which may prove very significant at the hearing of a charge of reckless or careless driving and it should be remembered that the view of a driver from a low, long-bonneted car may differ from that of a tall policeman on foot. The observance or non-observance of the Highway Code may be relied on in any civil or criminal proceedings as tending to establish or negate liability (1972 Act, s 37; see further, however, at 5.46 where this provision is discussed in the light of recent cases). A table of braking distances taken, by permission, from the Highway Code appears at the end of this book, along with mileage per hour converted to feet per second. While the table of braking distances may be used in cross-examination to prove a breach of the Code, it is otherwise inadmissible by itself to prove speed as it is hearsay (*R* v *Chadwick* [1975] Crim LR 105). The Highway Code makes no reference to the question whether disc brakes are more efficient than other types. As to views generally, see 2.85.

While the court can call and recall witnesses itself, it was held in *R* v *Owen* [1952] 1 All ER 1040 (discussed at [1952] Jo Crim L 249) that this should not be done in jury cases after the summing-up, though this rule may be relaxed for the defence (*R* v *Sanderson* [1953] 1 All ER 485). But a witness may be recalled at a trial before justices or on appeal from such a trial where no shorthand note is taken, provided that the witness was recalled solely for the purpose of refreshing the court's memory (*Phelan* v *Back* [1972] Crim LR

104). It is submitted that justices should exercise such a power with extreme caution and should first endeavour to avoid having to do so by seeking agreement from the parties as to what the evidence was. And see the cases on inspecting vehicles at 2.85. Magistrates have a discretion to admit further evidence at least until the close of the case for the defence, but should not do so after they have retired save in very special circumstances (*Webb* v *Leadbetter* [1966] 2 All ER 114). In *Phelan* v *Back* [1972] 1 All ER 901 following *Webb* v *Leadbetter* a recorder hearing an appeal was upheld when he recalled a witness for the prosecution to refresh his memory as he had taken no note of his evidence. Justices should be careful not to call for any evidence which might fill a gap in the police case, but see *Saunders* v *Johns* and *Piggott* v *Simms*, as to calling evidence after a submission of 'no case', under 'Reopening', 2.44. On indictment the presiding judge has a discretion whether to recall a witness after a submission of 'no case' (*R* v *McKenna* (1956) 40 Cr App R 65).

Leading questions may not normally be asked in examination-in-chief save to prove introductory matters and contradiction but it is a common practice to allow a witness in a criminal case to be led as to matters not actually in controversy (see Cross on *Evidence* (5th ed) 226). A question may nevertheless be leading even if the witness is presented with a question in an alternative form. The primary test as to whether a question is leading is whether it suggests to the witness what the answer should be. The court also may relax the rule against asking leading questions if the court thinks it necessary in the interests of justice, although it is difficult to think of circumstances when the question could not be asked just as well in the alternative form. If the court exercises its discretion to allow leading questions, a higher court will not normally interfere (*Ex parte Bottomley* (1909) 73 JP 246). Cases where leading questions have been allowed are *Acerro* v *Petroni* (1815) 1 Stark 100 (witness said he could not remember the names of members of a firm but thought he would if they were read to him; reading them to him was allowed), *Rivers* v *Hague* (1837), cited in Phipson's *Manual of Evidence* (13th ed) (witness called to testify as to entries in the Bankruptcy List and the *Gazette* but mentioned only the List; the court allowed the question: 'Was anything said about the *Gazette*?') and *Courteen* v *Touse* (1807) 1 Camp 43 (witness, called to contradict another about the contents of a letter, which had been destroyed, was allowed to have the particular passage suggested to him after he had exhausted his memory). Failure to cross-examine a witness generally amounts to acceptance of his version (see the current edition of Cross on *Evidence*), but justices were held entitled to convict because they disbelieved the defence witnesses even though the evidence of the defendant and his witnesses had not been challenged (*O'Connell* v *Adams* [1973] RTR 150). Unlike professional judges, justices are under no obligation to test witnesses in respect of evidence they disbelieve (ibid). Leading questions should not be asked in re-examination.

As to corroboration in speeding cases, see 6.24. As to corroboration by defendant's own statements in court prior to the close of the Crown case, see 114 JP Jo 62. As to corroborating the evidence of children, see 2.69. It is desirable that the evidence of accomplices should be corroborated (see the current edition of Cross on *Evidence*).

See 5.32 as to giving evidence in reckless and careless driving cases when the defendant had been drinking.

Evidence of acts of driving some distance away may be given in certain circumstances (see 5.33).

As to exhibits, see 2.83 and *R* v *Orrell* [1972] RTR 14 and *Tremlett* v *Fawcett* (1984) 1 RTLB 68 at 4.80.

# Chapter 3

# Notices of Intended Prosecution

## 3.1 Generally

Section 179(2) of the Road Traffic Act 1972 requires that for certain offences:

(*a*) the defendant must have been warned at the time of the possibility of prosecution for the offence; *or*

(*b*) the defendant must have been served with the summons within fourteen days of the offence; *or*

(*c*) notice of the possibility of the prosecution must have been sent by the prosecutor within fourteen days of the offence either to the driver or to the registered keeper of the vehicle (or in cases under s 17 or s 18 (reckless or careless cycling) to the rider of the cycle).

## 3.2 Application of s 179

Section 179 applies to the following offences:

(i) driving a motor vehicle recklessly (s 2), without due care and attention or without reasonable consideration (s 3), at a speed exceeding a statutory speed limit or at a speed exceeding that lawful for vehicles of the particular type (s 89 of the Road Traffic Regulation Act 1984) or exceeding the speed limit on a motorway (whether punishable by virtue of s 89 or s 17 of the 1984 Act, or contravening a temporary speed limit imposed under s 88(7) of the 1984 Act (see 'Speeding' below));

(ii) reckless or careless riding by cyclists (ss 17 and 18) (in which case the notice is required to be sent to the alleged offender);

(iii) offences under s 22 and s 22A (disobeying certain traffic signs and police signals) and s 24 (leaving a vehicle in a dangerous position); in *Sulston* v *Hammond* [1970] 2 All ER 830 it was held that s 179 has no application to an offence under what is now s 25 of the Road Traffic Regulation Act 1984 of failing to comply with the requirement of a pedestrian crossing regulation;

(iv) aiding and abetting the commission of any of the above-named offences (*The People (A-G)* v *Carroll* [1950] Ir Jur R 20).

It does not apply to any of the offences (i), (iii) and (iv) above when committed by the driver of a tram or trolley vehicle operated under statutory powers (s 198(6)). It applies to horse-drawn vehicles and other vehicles other than motor vehicles under (iii). It does not apply to other road traffic offences by the driver of any vehicle (cf *Staunton* v *Coates* (1924) 88 JP 193). Nor does it apply to other road traffic offences even if they are similar in character to those enumerated in Sched 4, eg, pedestrian crossing offences (see *Sulston* v *Hammond*, above).

Failure to comply with s 179 means that there cannot be a conviction for the offences to which it applies. It suffices if any one of the requirements of s 179 is fulfilled, eg if the defendant was adequately warned at the time, there is no need for a notice (see also *Shield* v *Crighton* at 3.5). Many police forces, from abundant caution, do in fact send the notice in all cases although there may have been warning at the time. It will also be noted that, in the case of motor vehicles, the notice can be given to the driver or the registered keeper.

*Speeding*

Section 179 applies to all speeding offences 'punishable by virtue of s 89 of the Road Traffic Regulation Act 1984' (s 179(1)(*b*)) and also to offences under s 17(4) of that Act of failing to observe the speed limit on a motorway imposed by regulations under that section (s 179(1)(*aa*)). These provisions cover virtually all offences of speeding save those contrary to s 16 of the 1984 Act (temporary speed restrictions) which is not specified in s 179 (see 6.29 and 6.34 and in particular *Platten* v *Gowing* [1983] Crim LR 84).

In particular s 179 applies to speeding offences on motorways under both the Motor Vehicles (Variation of Speed Limits) Regulations 1984 (SI 1984 No 325) and the Motorways Traffic (Speed Limit) Regulations 1974 (SI 1974 No 502). The 1974 Regulations prohibit vehicles from exceeding the overall speed limit of 70 mph on motorways or 60 or 50 mph on certain lengths of particular motorways specified by the same regulations. The 1984 Regulations prohibit certain goods and passenger vehicles and vehicles drawing trailers from exceeding certain lower maximum speed limits on motorways.

Temporary speed limits imposed under s 88(1) (see 6.29) are subject to s 179 whether they be 'temporary' maximum speed limits (which have been continued 'indefinitely') or temporary minimum speed limits (s 179(1)(*b*)), but temporary speed restrictions under ss 14–16 of the 1984 Act are not.

*Offences causing death and courts-martial*

It will be noted that the offences of manslaughter and causing death by reckless driving do not require a warning or notice.

The presumed effect of para 5 of Part IV of Sched 4 to the 1972 Act is that a person charged on indictment with such an offence need not have received a warning or notice if the jury convict him in the alternative either of reckless driving or of careless driving. Where a charge of reckless driving under s 2 is reduced to careless driving or driving without reasonable consideration under s 3 pursuant to para 4 of Part IV of Sched 4, notice or warning of the substituted charge need not have been given (para 7). A like provision applies to cyclists.

Section 179 does not apply in favour of a soldier charged at a court-martial with committing a civil offence, viz careless driving contrary to the Army Act

1955, s 70, so that warning or notice need not have been given (*R* v *Jennings* [1956] 3 All ER 429).

*Waiver*

May a defendant waive a failure to comply with s 179 and submit to judgment? It is submitted that he may (Maxwell on *The Interpretation of Statutes* (11th ed) 377, citing *R* v *Hughes* (1879) 4 QBD 614; see also Craies on *Statute Law* (6th ed) 269).

### 3.3 Accidents

Section 179(3A) exempts the prosecution from complying with the requirements of s 179(2) if, owing to the presence on a road of the vehicle in respect of which the offence was committed, an accident occurred at the time of the offence or immediately thereafter.

It was held by the Inner London Crown Court in *Metropolitan Police* v *Scarlett* [1978] Crim LR 234 and confirmed in *Bentley* v *Dickinson* [1983] RTR 356 that a notice of intended prosecution *is* required if an accident occurs of which the defendant is *unaware* and that s 179(3A) only applies if the defendant is aware of the accident.

The primary purpose of the enactment of the subsection was to relieve the police of having to serve numerous notices of intended prosecution whenever a series of multiple accidents occurred on a motorway. The subsection clearly will apply, however, to any accident, no matter how trivial, and even if one vehicle only is involved. For the meaning of the expression 'accident' see Chapter 1. Notwithstanding the wide terms of the subsection many police forces continue to comply with s 179 in simple accident cases. It would seem that the fact that a prosecutor endeavoured to comply with the requirement of s 179 but failed to do so will not debar him subsequently from claiming exemption from the requirements of s 179 if the subsection applies. The subsection will also allow a defendant who has been summoned under s 2 or s 3 following an accident to apply for a cross-summons against the other party to the accident. In many cases in the past a defendant was unable to do so because he was outside the time limits imposed by s 179.

The subsection will chiefly apply to reckless driving under s 2 and to careless or inconsiderate driving under s 3 where accidents have occurred. It should be observed, however, that the subsection applies to all offences to which s 179 is otherwise applicable; accidents may occur, for example, as a result of an offence of failing to comply with a traffic signal (s 22) or causing or permitting a vehicle to remain at rest in a dangerous position, etc (s 24). The accident must occur 'owing to the presence on a road of the vehicle'. These words were considered in *Quelch* v *Phipps* [1955] 2 All ER 302 in respect of an offence of failing to report an accident (see 7.9). It was held that there must be some direct causal connection between the vehicle on the road and the occurrence of the accident. Difficulties of causation may arise in respect of an offending vehicle which is not itself involved in the resulting accident, eg a vehicle left in a dangerous position on a road as a result of which another vehicle has to pull out to overtake and collides with a vehicle coming in the opposite direction. It is submitted that as long as the accident occurs as a direct result of the offending vehicle's presence subs (3A) applies but not if the accident occurs only incidentally or indirectly. Section 24 itself requires the offending vehicle 'to cause danger' and it may therefore be difficult to envisage a conviction under s 24 if the vehicle only indirectly causes danger. The accident must occur 'at the time of the offence or immediately thereafter' (subs (3A)). In *R* v *Okike* [1978] RTR 489 (see 3.5) it was held that the words 'at the time of the offence' in s 2 (*a*) were a question of fact and degree. Particularly in the case of a s 24 offence difficulties of interpretation may arise. The offence under s 24 is committed if a person 'causes or permits' a vehicle 'to remain at rest' in a dangerous position, etc. If a vehicle is allowed to remain at rest in a dangerous position and the accident does not occur immediately after the vehicle was left on the road, the subsection may apply if a s 24 offence is regarded as a continuing offence. It would seem, however, that an offence under s 24 is complete as soon as the offender has caused or permitted the vehicle to remain at rest.

## 3.4 Presumption of conformity with s 179

As is clear from s 179(3), it is unnecessary for the prosecution to give any evidence that its requirements have been fulfilled. It is for the defence to allege that they have not, and to call evidence to that effect. This was confirmed in *Offen* v *Ranson* [1980] RTR 484 where it was emphasised that the burden of proof was on the defendant on the balance of probabilities. In that case the justices were doubtful whether the warning had been understood because it was given on a noisy road by an officer speaking rapidly through the window of a low-slung car. The Divisional Court held that that was the wrong approach. The defendent had not discharged the onus of proof but merely raised a doubt. He had at least to satisfy the justices that he probably did not hear the warning.

While it is a convenient practice to decide this issue as a preliminary point, the issue can be raised at any relevant stage of the proceedings (*R* v *Edmonton JJ, ex parte Brooks* [1960] 2 All ER 475). The defence must show that the driver and the registered 'keeper' of a motor vehicle have not had the notice under s 179(2)(*c*) and both the driver and the keeper should give evidence to that effect; it is not enough for the defendant alone, when he is not also the keeper, to give evidence that he has not had it (*Sanders* v *Scott* [1961] 2 All ER 403). If the defendant proves that neither he nor the registered 'keeper' has had the notice, it is for the prosecutor to prove its posting by registered or recorded delivery post, if he can, to the last-known address (*Archer* v *Blacker* (1965) 109 SJ 113). *Semble*, it would be unnecessary to call the 'keeper' if the police were to admit in evidence that no notice had been given to him. See under 'Service of notice', 3.7, as to non-receipt of a notice sent by post and under 'Reasonable diligence', 3.8, as to excusing non-compliance with s 179. Where a case is to be sent for trial on indictment, the magistrates should normally not deal with the issue whether s 179 had been complied with; that is a matter for the court of trial (*Card* v *Salmon* [1953] 1 All ER 324).

In *Rogerson* v *Edwards* (1951) 49 LGR 358, the owners of the vehicle concerned were Greenwoods (Contractors) Ltd, Bury Road, Ramsey, and there was another company named Greenwoods (Transport) Ltd in the same street. The police sent a notice addressed to 'Messrs. Greenwoods, Bury Road, Ramsey'. It was held that the defendant must show that the right company had not had the notice and, in the absence of evidence that Greenwoods (Contractors) Ltd had not received it, the case should proceed. It is submitted that, if it can be proved by evidence given for the prosecution or by the defendant's admission in cross-examination or prior to the hearing that he did receive a notice of intended prosecution within fourteen days of the offence, the proceedings should not be dismissed although there may have been mistakes in the addressing and stamping of the envelope or it came by ordinary post or it was left at the wrong house or with the wrong person; the defendant, however, should also have known, in the case of an incorrectly named or addressed notice, that he was in fact the person for whom it was intended (cf *Re Poyser and Mills' Arbitration* [1963] 1 All ER 612, at p 617, a case on another statute).

A similar provision to s 179 in Irish legislation has been interpreted more strictly than s 179 has in England. The Irish cases, which are reviewed at 88 ILTN 123 and 129, are therefore of little authority here, though some are cited in this chapter on points where there is no English or Scottish authority.

### 3.5 Warning at the time

A warning under s 179(2)(*a*) may be oral or written. Where an accident occurred at 11.45 am, the police arrived at 12.15 pm, and the defendant was given an oral warning at the scene of the accident at 12.20 pm, this was held to be 'warning at the time', it having been given at the earliest time reasonably possible after the arrival of the police and while the parties were still at the scene of the accident (*Jeffs* v *Wells* (1936) 100 JP Jo 406; see also *Shield* v *Crighton* below). A warning at 4 pm in respect of an offence at 8.30 am the same day is not a warning at the time (*Cuthbert* v *Hollis* [1958] SLT (Sh) 51; [1958] Crim LR 814). In *Jollye* v *Dale* [1960] 2 All ER 369, a driver was pursued by the police for 30 minutes after an act of dangerous driving and then arrested. An hour later he was medically examined and, very soon after, the first oral warning was given. It was held that the words 'at the time of the offence' were not limited to the point of time when the offence was committed and it was a question of fact whether there had been a warning at the time: the High Court refused to interfere with the magistrates' finding that there had been a proper warning under s 179. It was added, however, that where the earliest possible time for warning the driver was several hours later, this would not generally be a warning at the time. After an accident in the country, a car driver took the victim to two hospitals and did not report to the police until four hours after the accident; a warning then sufficed (*Sinclair* v *Clark* 1962 SLT 307). In *Shield* v *Crighton* [1974] Crim LR 605 it was held that the phrase 'at the time' had to be construed 'sensibly' and it was held that an oral warning was 'at the time the offence occurred' where the constable arrived at the scene of the accident giving rise to the offence ten minutes after it occurred and gave the oral warning only after having first taken a written statement from the defendant under caution. Whether a warning was given 'at the time the offence was committed' was again held to be a question of fact and degree (*R* v *Okike* [1978] RTR 489). The test is what is reasonable. It is for the defendant to show that a time lapse between the offence and the warning is unreasonable or unjustifiable and in the absence of evidence to that effect a conviction will stand (ibid). (The facts were that the defendant was arrested at 12.40 am and not warned until 3.05 am, during which time, it would appear, the police were investigating whether the defendant was the driver, he having admitted that he was the registered owner of the vehicle but having denied driving it.)

The test in *Okike* was applied in *R* v *Stacey* [1982] RTR 20. The defendant was arrested at 11.30 pm for driving whilst unfit. He was not charged with any offence relating to drink but just under three hours later he was charged with reckless driving. The subsequent conviction was upheld in the Court of Appeal. The court also applied the test in *Sinclair* v *Clark*: whether or not the chain of circumstances was unbroken and all that took place was connected with the accident.

The issue is one for the judge not the jury (*R* v *Stacey*).

The form of words necessary to constitute a warning has been the subject of many decisions, which are discussed at 213 LJ News 204; most of them were under an earlier Act which required that the defendant be 'warned of the intended prosecution'. The words, 'I think you are exceeding the limit but if (on checking) I find that I am wrong, you will hear no more about it', were held sufficient (*Jessopp* v *Clarke* (1908) 72 JP 358; and see *Taylor* v *Horn* 1929 SLT 600). Is it necessary to state for what offence or offences prosecution may be considered? In *Watt* v *Smith* 1942 SC(J) 109; [1942] Jo Crim L 293, it was held that the words, 'The circumstances of the accident will be reported to the fiscal for the purpose of considering a prosecution', were insufficient though they were spoken at the scene of the accident; they might have been thought to refer to a common-law offence or some other contravention of the Road Traffic Acts. It was also said that the constable need not select the particular offence for which there might be a prosecution, but he must so word his warning as to direct attention to ss 2 and 3. In *Alston* v *Nurse* (1933) unreported, the King's Bench Division upheld as a good warning the words, 'I will have to report the matter to my superior officer with a view to prosecution'; they gave, it was said, the information which s 179 intends the motorist to have. In *A-G* v *Foley* (1952) 86 ILTR 30, it was held to be unnecessary to specify for what offences the prosecution would be (see also [1953] Jo Crim L 170). In view of the infinite variety of warning formulae usable, every case must be decided on its facts. In *Parkes* v *Cole* (1922) 86 JP 122, however, it was held that warning of a charge of dangerous driving did not amount to a warning of a charge of exceeding the speed limit.

If a defendant has been orally warned at the time, can he say that the warning was ineffective because he did not or could not take it in? Defendants have successfully so pleaded in Ireland (see [1954] Jo Crim L 275) but here, it is submitted, it would be a question of fact, a heavy onus being on the defendant to show that the warning was ineffective. This submission was approved by Donaldson LJ in *Gibson* v *Dalton* [1980] RTR 411 at p 413. In that case it was held that the obligation on the prosecutor was to warn the motorist that the question of prosecution would be taken into consideration and not merely to address a warning to him or give a warning. Whether the motorist was in fact warned is a question of fact: prima facie a motorist is warned if on an objective view words addressed to him would be expected to be heard and understood by him, but it is still open to him to prove, if he can, that he did not understand or appreciate the words and therefore was not warned. In *Gibson* v *Dalton* itself the Crown Court found as a fact that the warning to the lady motorist did not get through to her and the Crown Court's decision was upheld.

Obviously, bawling formulae into the ear of an unconscious or seriously injured man is insufficient. *Gibson* v *Dalton* still leaves open the position where adequate and proper warning is given, as in that case, but does not get through because of the defendant's own hidden inadequacies of intellect or comprehension. Donaldson LJ said that the warning must be heard and understood by the person intended to take account of it. If the defendant is apparently in full possession of his faculties, can he plead that because of his own shortcomings or state of anxiety he failed to understand what the policeman said to him? In *Offen* v *Ranson* [1980] RTR 484 Ackner LJ said obiter that (if this stage had been reached in that case) there might well have been argument as to whether or not it was his fault he had not heard. In *Day* v *Harris* (1953) 117 JP 313, a civil case on a different statute, it was held that a provision requiring a notice to be read and explained was satisfied if this was done, although the listener was mentally incapable of understanding it. It might also be argued that a defendant who never took in an oral warning contributed to the failure to comply with s 179 by his own conduct in not listening properly. See also 126 JP Jo 262 and *Wheatley* v *Lodge* [1971] 1 All ER 173 as to stating the reason for arrest to a deaf person. In *A-G* v *Wallace* [1964] ILT 117, a notice written in a language which the defendant did not understand was held to be valid.

## 3.6 Service of summons

A drunken driver, on awaking from his stupor, will sometimes find himself charged with reckless driving without a summons being served on him. Does this suffice, for the purposes of s 179(2)(*b*), as being equivalent to a summons being served on him? Neither an information nor a charge sheet is a summons. It is submitted that, while he can insist on a summons, he can also waive having one and, as the charges are as fully apparent to him as if he had had a summons, s 179 is sufficiently complied with. But the police would be wise to serve a summons or notice all the same. Where the defendant was committed for trial on a charge of driving under the influence of drink, and a charge of reckless driving was added for the first time at sessions more than fourteen days after his arrest, the omission to comply with s 179 was fatal to the prosecution ([1953] Jo Crim L 22).

The effect of s 47 of the Magistrates' Courts Act 1980 and r 99(1) and (2) of the Magistrates' Courts Rules 1981 would appear to be that if the prosecutor has sent a summons by registered, recorded delivery or ordinary post which in the ordinary course of post should have arrived within fourteen days, he may, if the defendant fails to appear or if there is no other proof of due service as required, serve another summons within fourteen days of the return date of the original summons. Provided the second summons is validly served within fourteen days from the return date of the first summons it will be in compliance with s 179(2).

A summons for an offence under s 2 of the 1972 Act (reckless driving) is not a purely summary offence. If the defendant fails to appear, service of such a summons by leaving it for him with some person at his last known or usual place of abode or sending it in a letter addressed to him at his last known or usual place of abode (registered, recorded delivery or otherwise) is only to be treated as proved if it is proved that it came to his knowledge. The same rule applies for all other summonses for offences to which s 179 applies, and in addition as they are purely summary offences they may be treated as served *without proof of acknowledgement*, if they are served by registered or recorded delivery post, or left for him with some person at the last known or usual place of abode. Service by ordinary post is not sufficient without acknowledgement. This distinction between reckless driving and other s 179 offences must be kept in mind. If a summons is satisfactorily served as indicated in such a way as to arrive within fourteen days in the usual course of post the service would be sufficient to satisfy s 179(2). If, however, the summons is so served by post but the service is not validly established, use may be made of the time extension in s 47.

Section 179(2) does not specify any particular form of service. Summonses may also be validly served in other ways under r 99 but it may be preferable to use the postal service method to fulfil s 179(2) possibly in addition to attempting the other methods, as the time extension in s 47 applies only to instances where the postal method is used unsuccessfully.

## 3.7 Service of notice

The notice for the purposes of s 179(2)(*c*) must be in writing. If the notice was sent by registered post or recorded delivery service addressed to the defendant or the registered keeper of a motor vehicle at his last-known address, by s 179(2)(*c*) it is in effect due service under, and compliance with, s 179, notwithstanding that the notice was returned as undelivered or was for any other reason not received by him. The motorist cannot object if the notice arrives late if it has been sent on time. In *Groome* v *Driscoll* [1969] 3 All ER 1638 the offence occurred on 4 September and the notice of intended prosecution was posted by recorded delivery the following day but was not actually delivered until 21 September. The justices dismissed the case, apparently overlooking the proviso to s 179(2)(*c*), and the Divisional Court directed a conviction. Section 179 is, however, not complied with if a notice arrives outside the fourteen-day period because it was posted so late—eg, the fourteenth day—that the notice could not be expected to arrive within the fourteen days in the normal course of post (*Nicholson* v *Tapp* (1972) 116 SJ 527). In *Groome* v *Driscoll* the Divisional Court interpreted the proviso as if the words 'in time' were added to the end of the proviso and it was held in

*Nicholson* v *Tapp* that the proviso only applies if the notice was sent at such a time that it could be reasonably expected to arrive in time in the normal course of post. *Stewart* v *Chapman*, below, although decided before the proviso to s 179(2)(*c*) was inserted by the 1972 Act, would therefore still appear to be good law. It was held in *Layton* v *Shires* [1959] 3 All ER 587 that it was good service of a notice if it was sent by registered post to the defendant's address so that it arrived within fourteen days after the offence and was taken in there by some person authorised to receive letters on his behalf, eg, a member of his family or a domestic servant, even if the defendant did not see the notice till over a fortnight after the offence.

A notice may also be served personally, provided it is served within fourteen days of the offence. If the defendant and the registered keeper have no fixed abode, eg, they are gipsies, and dodge personal service, it seems that s 179(4) would apply to excuse the police from serving the notice, provided some effort had been made to reach them. Where the notice was handed by a constable to the defendant's wife, who was authorised to accept letters for him, this was held to be valid service (*Burt* v *Kircaldy* [1965] 1 All ER 741). Indeed, it is an irresistible inference that a wife living with her husband is fully authorised to take in and deal with mail addressed to her husband (*Hosier* v *Goodall* [1962] 1 All ER 30; in this case the defendant was in hospital at the time). In *Burt's* case, it was doubted whether delivery to a hall-porter would be sufficient. The case of *Martin* v *Brooman* (1909) 73 JP 484 was not cited in *Burt's* case; it was held there that it sufficed to leave a notice with a hall-porter under a statute which required the notice to be 'sent', not 'served'. *Martin's* case, however, is out of harmony with modern cases which suggest the test to be receipt by a person authorised to deal with a notice, although in *Layton* v *Shires* [1959] 3 All ER 587 receipt by a servant of the defendant's household was held valid. If a notice is validly served within fourteen days of the offence, it will not matter if the defendant does not see it until later.

If service of a notice has been by leaving it with an adult, para (*c*) of s 179(2) will not of itself apply to overcome its non-receipt, as para (*c*) in regard to non-receipt applies only to registered or recorded delivery postal service. In this respect the requirements for the service of the summons by this means for a summary offence are less onerous. The police would be wise always to serve personally or by registered post or recorded delivery, as, if the defendant proves that he did not himself get a notice left with an adult within fourteen days and it was not given to a person authorised to take in letters and other documents for him, such service does not comply with s 179: *Hosier* v *Goodall* above where the defendant was in hospital and the notice was sent to his home address and then taken in and was received on his behalf by his wife. This was held to be good service. In *Phipps* v *McCormick* [1971] Crim LR 541 it was argued (and accepted by the justices) that as the police knew the defendant had been taken to hospital following the accident, the hospital was the correct address for the purposes of s 179(2)(*c*) as this was his last address that the police knew and that notice should therefore have been sent to the hospital rather than to his home. The Divisional Court overruled the justices and held that 'his last known address' for the purposes of s 179 meant the place where the person concerned would normally expect to receive correspondence, an address which had some degree of permanence.

A notice may be served on a Sunday as, unlike a summons, it is not 'process' (*Maher* v *Predergast* [1948] Ir R 339) but this decision is now otiose in England as a summons may now be served on a Sunday as a result of the repeal of the Sunday Observance Act 1677 by s 1 of the Statute Law (Repeals) Act 1969. But the opinion has been advanced that the issue of a summons on a Sunday may be of doubtful validity on the ground that Sunday is a dies non for judicial acts (see 140 JP 40). The matter has now presumably been put right beyond doubt by s 153 of the Magistrates' Courts Act 1980 which permits a magistrates' court to sit on a Sunday. The view that following the repeal of the 1677 Act all forms of magistrates' court process may be both issued and executed on Sunday in England and Wales is held by the Home Office (see Home Office circular 274/1969). Where appropriate, however, reference should be made to the restrictions in the Rules of the Supreme Court.

Earlier cases on non-receipt of a notice because the defendant, being in hospital, did not receive a notice addressed to him at home were overruled in *Hosier* v *Goodall* above. The significance of the latter case is abrogated by the new provision of s 179 declaring that it suffices to post the notice to the driver or keeper by registered or recorded delivery post (see above); *Hosier's* case had held that the reasonableness of the police action in sending the notice to a particular address was no longer the test. It might still be held, however, that s 179 is not complied with if the prosecutor posts the notice to an address which he well knows is no longer the defendant's permanent address unless he had left no address and it is the only address to which the prosecutor can send. The address must be the 'last known' address, notwithstanding that this may differ from the one in the register or given to the police but 'last known' address should not be interpreted too literally and means, in effect, the last known permanent address at which he may be expected to receive correspondence (*Phipps* v *McCormick* above). In *Price* v *West London Investment Building Society Ltd* [1964] 2 All ER 318 a case on another statute, it was said that 'last known' place of abode means that last known to the person sending the notice and might include a place which the defendant had left if the change was unknown to the sender of the notice.

The notice, if sent by registered or recorded delivery post, should be posted within such a time that, in the ordinary course of post, it will reach the person to whom it is addressed within the fourteen days (*Stewart* v *Chapman* [1951] 2 All ER 613; *Nicholson* v *Tapp* above). The day of the offence is not counted in computing the fourteen days. Thus, if an offence occurs on 1 January, the notice should be posted so that it reaches the defendant's address not later than last post on 15 January. The state of the postal service near Christmas and the difference in the time of delivery between first-class and second-class mail should be remembered. A properly addressed letter sent by post will be deemed to have been received, unless the contrary is proved, when it would be delivered in the ordinary course of post (Interpretation Act 1978, s 7); *aliter*, where it is wrongly addressed (*Getreide etc Co* v *Contimar etc Co* [1953] All ER 223). In a case before a metropolitan magistrate, the envelope was postmarked so as to be outside the fourteen days but there was sworn evidence that it was posted on the ninth day. The magistrate accepted the sworn evidence but, as the envelope had been addressed to the defendant's son, and the defendant, who saw it sixteen days after the offence, had claimed that he did not realise it was meant for him (his son was aged three and a half years), the magistrate held that the notice had not been served on the defendant ([1965] Jo Crim L 153).

The prosecutor, in cases where non-receipt of a notice is put forward, should always make sure that a warning at the time of the offence was not given as, if it was, it will not matter when the notice was received. He should remember, too, to ask the defendant expressly, if he has the chance, when the notice was received as it may transpire that, notwithstanding wrong addressing or receipt by another, the defendant did have it within the fortnight. See 3.4 as to the need for the defendant to prove non-receipt by him and the keeper.

See under 'Reasonable diligence', below, as to the defendant's conduct contributing to the failure to comply with s 179.

Notice may be either to the defendant or to the person registered as keeper of the vehicle at the time of the offence, save that in cases of reckless or careless cycling it should be given to the defendant.

If given to the keeper, the notice need not specify the name of the person to be summoned (*R* v *Bolkis* (1932) 97 JP 10). The police should, it seems, and generally will, send it to the driver, where he is known; if they serve the keeper, they probably need not show that they did not know who the driver was (*Rogerson* v *Edwards* (1951) 49 LGR 358, at p 360). A notice sent to the owner stating that 'you' will be prosecuted for reckless driving of a lorry is good, although the intention is to prosecute the driver and not (now) the keeper (*Taylor* v *Campbell* [1956] Crim LR 342). See 3.9 as to errors in the notice. Delivery at the registered office of a company is good and valid service of a notice to the owner, if the company is the owner, but all that is necessary is that the notice should be in the hands of a responsible officer of the company within the fourteen days (*R* v *Bilton* (1964) 108 SJ 880). There, the notice had been brought to the manager at a local office, which was not the registered office; he accepted it after he had consulted the company's solicitors and the notice was in the hands of the assistant secretary and the solicitors within a fortnight of the offence. This was held to be good service.

Notice of intended prosecution was duly served on a defendant. The police then wrote to him saying that he would not be prosecuted. Later the police decided to prosecute him. It was held that cancellation of the notice did not affect the matter and that he was rightly convicted (*Lund* v *Thompson* [1958] 3 All ER 356).

The cases are reviewed at 104 SJ 397; those relating to owners would seem to be relevant to keepers.

## 3.8 Reasonable diligence

Section 179(4) provides that the police need not have complied with it if neither the driver's nor the registered keeper's identity could with reasonable diligence be ascertained in time for a summons or notice to be served or sent. A defendant drove on after an accident but his number was taken; it was held that, as the police actually ascertained the owner's identity in time for a notice to be sent to him, the fact that the driver's identity was unknown did not excuse them from so doing and, as no notices had been sent at all, the defendant was acquitted (*R* v *Bolkis* above). The question of reasonable diligence is for the judge, not the jury (ibid, confirmed obiter in *R* v *Stacey* [1982] RTR 20 at p 26). The position seems to be that, if the police have time to find out the identity of, and serve, either the driver or (if he is unknown) the keeper within fourteen days, the driver's conduct at the time of the offence does not contribute to their failure to do so. But, if the defendant drives away before his number can be taken, the provisions of subs (4) excuse the police from complying with the section unless they could have discovered his or the owner's identity with reasonable diligence, or, *a fortiori*, do discover it within fourteen days. It will not suffice if the defendant is interviewed and given an oral warning within that time; a summons must be served or written notice given when he was not warned at the time of the offence. Giving a false address or information or deliberately evading service is conduct contributing to the failure of the police to comply with s 179 and excuses them. Giving an address at which the defendant knows he will not be at the likely time is also such conduct ([1959] Jo Crim L 2) but not merely going away on holiday with no intent to evade service (*Beer* v *Davies* [1958] 2 All ER 255). A person who goes away without arranging for mail to be forwarded is not normally evading service (*Macleod* v *Anderson* 1961 SC(J) 32). See, however, now s 179(2)(*c*) which provides that posting a notice suffices.

Where the police made inquiry of the Motor Licences Department in good time but were given wrong information, it was held that they had shown reasonable diligence and their failure to send the notice to the correct person was in those circumstances no bar to conviction (*Clarke* v *Mould* [1945] 2 All ER 551; see also *Rogerson* v *Edwards*, above, and *Carr* v *Harrison* (1966) *The Times*, 18 November, the only report on this point, where it was held that the police in approaching the licensing authority in good time had shown reasonable diligence, though the authority had been slow in supplying the information).

Where the police were supplied with the wrong name of the registered keeper at the relevant time and accordingly sent the notice to the wrong person at the wrong address, this failure to send a notice to the registered keeper is no bar to conviction because they will have shown due diligence under s 179(4)(*a*) (*Haughton* v *Harrison* [1976] RTR 208). Once the police have established under s 179(4) that their failure to serve a notice is no bar to a conviction, the police are under no duty to serve any further notices as soon as they are told of the correct name and address of the registered keeper (ibid).

Notice addressed to a firm cannot be regarded as notice to every individual in a firm, and the fact that the owner had caused the vehicle to be registered in the firm's name was not conduct on his part contributing to the police failing to comply with s 179 (*Clarke* v *Mould* above). There the owner had actually received the notice and, though *Clarke's* case was mentioned in

*Rogerson* v *Edwards* above, it was not distinguished. Notice addressed to a limited company omitting the word 'Limited' is good (*Springate* v *Questier* [1952] 2 All ER 21). A notice addressed to 'O'Loughlin' was served on the defendant McLoughlin. He signed it and the policeman then put the correct name on it. It was held to be a good notice (*The State (McLoughlin)* v *The President of the Circuit Court* [1949] Ir R 439). If a notice is otherwise good and the defendant obviously knows to what incident it relates, a mistake in the number of his car is immaterial (*A-G (O'Gara)* v *Callaman* (1958) 92 ILTR 74). See also *Taylor* v *Campbell*, 3.7. A notice in the name 'Hornet' sent to a defendant Horne was held not to have misled him and the error was not sufficient to invalidate the notice (*Camp* v *Horne*, noted at [1965] Jo Crim L 153).

### 3.9 Errors in the notice

It was said in *Beresford* v *St. Alban's JJ* below that the notice for the purposes of s 179 (2) (*c*) is intended to give an idea of the offence of which the defendant will be accused and to guard against the possibility of his being taken unawares (see also *Pope* v *Clarke* [1953] 2 All ER 704), and in *Milner* v *Allen* (1933) 97 JP 111, that the test of the validity of the notice is whether the defendant is in any way prejudiced in his defence by the defect. In *R* v *Bilton* (1964) 108 SJ 880, it was said that the object of the notice is to ensure that the driver is not taken by surprise long after the offence, when his recollection is dulled and witnesses may be difficult to trace.

*Errors in the nature of the offence*

Where a charge of reckless driving is reduced to one under s 3 of the 1972 Act, pursuant to para 4 of Part IV of Sched 4 to the Act, the defendant may be convicted although s 179 has not been complied with as respects the new charge (para 7). A notice stating that the defendant would be reported for dangerous driving and specifying his conduct, eg, overtaking and cutting-in, is good although he is subsequently charged with careless driving only (*Milner* v *Allen* (1933) 97 JP 111). The view is advanced at 123 JP Jo 35 that a notice specifying a charge of careless driving would suffice for a prosecution for dangerous (now reckless) driving. A notice alleging driving without due care and attention but not specifying the acts of bad driving is good (*Percival* v *Ball* [1937] WN 106). So is a notice stating that it was intended to prosecute the defendant 'for an offence against s 12 of the Road Traffic Act 1930 [now s 3 of the 1972 Act] in that you did drive a motor car' at a specified time and place, despite the omission of the words 'without due care and attention' or of any alleged acts of bad driving (*Venn* v *Morgan* [1949] 2 All ER 562). In *Venn's* case the car's number was not given.

*Errors in date, time or place*

A notice referred in error to dangerous driving at '1.15 pm'; in fact, the accident from which the charge arose was at 11.15 am. It was held that the mere fact that the time was wrongly stated made no difference and the notice was valid, for the notice mentioned the place where the accident occurred and the defendant could have been under no doubt that the notice related to it; different considerations might apply where he had had two accidents on the same day or, *semble*, when the charge was speeding and he had been on the same road more than once that day without being accosted by the police (*Pope* v *Clarke* [1953] 2 All ER 704; *Carr* v *Harrison* [1967] Crim LR 54, where, although the notice referred to 8.40 pm instead of am, the defendant, having been interviewed about the incident and knowing all about it, was not prejudiced by the mistake). In *Walton* v *Hawkins* [1973] RTR 366 and 369 the Divisional Court approved the abandonment of a contention that a notice was bad in that the occurrence took place south of a junction when in fact the road ran east and west, citing *Pope* v *Clarke*, above. In *Goody* v *Fletcher* [1962] Crim LR 324, a mistake of one day in stating the date was held not to invalidate the notice; the time and place were correctly given in the notice and the defendant was in no doubt as to the incident referred to. A notice cannot be 'amended'; if time permits, a fresh notice should be served or sent in lieu of the defective one. It was said obiter in *R* v *Budd* [1962] Crim LR 49 that there can be a conviction for dangerous driving only if it occurred in the road named in the warning of intended prosecution. In *Shield* v *Crighton* [1974] Crim LR 605 a notice erroneously stated the name of a road some eighty yards distant from the road where the offence was committed; it was said obiter that a written document mis-stating the place could be misleading, but as an oral warning had been given at the scene at the time (see 3.5), s 179 had been complied with; *semble aliter* if the defendant had received no oral warning. *Shield* v *Crighton* is now more fully reported at [1978] RTR 494. It is submitted that where an error in the notice is as to the place, it is a question of fact and degree whether the defendant has been misled and that a misstatement is not ipso facto fatal if the defendant has not been misled by the mis-statement. The time, apparently, need not be mentioned in a summons. A notice alleging excessive speed 'between' two places more than ten miles apart was held good in *Beresford* v *St. Alban's JJ* (1905) 22 TLR 1, but the then statute did not require, as s 179 does, that the 'place' of offence be specified. In Ireland a notice alleging dangerous driving in a road a mile and a quarter long was held to be too vague; there had been no accident (*Duffy* v *Lovegrove* [1955] Jo Crim L 172). Likewise, in *Young* v *Day* (1959) 123 JP 317, a notice alleging dangerous driving by nearly colliding with a stationary car on the offside in 'the Hothfield to Bethersden road' was held insufficient; there had been no accident and the defendant had not been stopped. The High Court said that it was a question of fact for magistrates, using their local knowledge, to decide if a 'place' was sufficiently specified. The road named is about four miles long.

Chapter 4

# Drink/Driving Offences

## Introduction

### 4.1 The new law

Section 25 of and Sched 8 to the Transport Act 1981 (as amended by the Transport Act 1982) substantially amended the existing offences under s 5 of the Road Traffic Act 1972 (driving etc a motor vehicle while unfit to drive through drink or drugs) and wholly replaced the existing ss 6–12 of the 1972 Act. These sections contain virtually the whole of the statutory provisions relating to the offences of driving, attempting to drive, or being in charge of a motor vehicle with excess alcohol levels, together with the offences of failing to provide a specimen for a breath test or specimens for analysis. The new statutory provisions and amendment were together all brought into force on 6 May 1983.

Because the statutory provisions are, except for s 5, completely new it is not thought appropriate either to explain or to expound the former law. Nor will a case on the former statutory provisions be cited except in so far as it is considered one which can afford guidance to the interpretation of the new statutory provisions. Practitioners should be particularly careful not to apply a case on the former law to the new statutory provisions without first considering whether the case is relevant. The most important and least obvious difference between the new and old law is that conviction under s 6(1)(*a*) or (*b*) and s 8(7) (driving or being in charge with excess alcohol and refusing to supply laboratory specimens) no longer depends on the police having validly arrested the defendant or having complied with the road test procedure. The great majority of the cases on the former law depended on the police having to prove a valid arrest at the roadside. This is no longer so (see 4.4). Conviction for any one of the offences will generally simply depend on whether the police can prove, in the case of offences under ss 5 or 6, (*a*) whether the defendant was driving, attempting to drive or in charge of a motor vehicle on a road; and (*b*) whether the defendant was unfit to drive through drink or drugs or that the proportion of alcohol in his blood, breath or urine exceeds the prescribed limit.

For offences under s 8(7) (refusing to supply specimens of blood, breath or urine for analysis) the police will simply have to prove whether the defendant has validly been required to provide specimens and has failed or refused to do so without reasonable excuse. A summary of the offences is set out in 4.11–16.

Where a section of a statute is referred to without its statute being named, the reader may assume that it refers to the Road Traffic Act 1972 ('the 1972 Act') as amended by the Transport Acts 1981 and 1982.

## 4.2 Offences

The offences dealt with in this chapter are:

(1) Driving or attempting to drive a motor vehicle while unfit to drive through drink or drugs (s 5(1)).

(2) Being in charge of a motor vehicle while unfit to drive through drink or drugs (s 5(2)).

(3) Driving or attempting to drive a motor vehicle on a road or other public place after consuming so much alcohol that the proportion of it in the person's breath, blood or urine exceeds the prescribed limit (s 6(1)(*a*)).

(4) Being in charge of a motor vehicle on a road or public place after consuming alcohol so that the proportion of it in the person's breath, blood or urine exceeds the prescribed limit (s 6(1)(*b*)).

(5) Without reasonable excuse, failing to supply a specimen for a breath test (s 7(4)).

(6) Without reasonable excuse, failing to supply specimens of breath, blood or urine for analysis (s 8(7)).

A summary of these offences is set out in 4.11–16.

## 4.3 Differences between the new and old provisions

The first important difference between the new and old provisions is the least obvious and most important, *viz* that the principle of *Scott* v *Baker* [1969] 1 QB 659 will not apply to the new provisions. The effect is that the conviction on an excess alcohol offence will no longer depend on whether the police have strictly complied with the procedural requirements of the screening breath test. For this reason many of the former cases can no longer be relied upon even if the statutory provision is substantially the same as its replacement (see further 4.4).

The second difference between the former provisions and the new is that, while the screening breath test has been retained, the circumstances in which a motorist can be required to be breath tested have been greatly widened.

The third major difference is that normally the motorist will have no choice as to the type of specimen for analysis which will be required of him. Under the old law the motorist was first required to supply blood; if he failed or refused to do so, he was then asked to supply two specimens of urine in an hour; and if he failed or refused to supply these, he was again asked to supply blood. Now the motorist will normally only be required to supply one type of specimen, which will be blood or urine or, if at a police station, more usually breath. The motorist will not normally be given a choice: it will be for the police officer concerned, sometimes subject to medical advice, to decide which type of specimen has to be provided. Whichever type of specimen is required the motorist will commit an offence if, without reasonable excuse, he fails or refuses to provide the specimen, and if breath is required, he will commit the offence of failing to supply a specimen of breath if he fails to supply breath 'in such a way as to enable the objective of the analysis to be satisfactorily achieved'. As in the former offence the prosecution has to prove that he failed or refused to supply a specimen 'without reasonable excuse'.

The fourth major difference is that consumption of alcohol after committing the offence, but before providing a specimen for analysis, will no longer be a complete defence. The motorist will only escape the conviction if he is able to prove that but for the additional consumption of alcohol he would not have been above the limit or, if the charge is under s 5, he would have been fit to drive.

The fifth important feature of the new provisions is that the police in certain circumstances not only have power to arrest but also a power of entry either to arrest or to require a screening breath test.

Lastly it should be noted that the statutory provisions as to the provision of breath, blood or urine for analysis have been designed to enable the police to require the appropriate type of specimen for analysis if the motorist's impairment is suspected to be caused by drugs rather than alcohol.

Finally, although based on existing law, the Secretary of State for Transport, with effect from 6 May 1983, will refuse automatically to issue driving licences to 'high risk offenders' or 'problem drinkers', ie drivers who have twice been convicted in ten years of drink/driving offences where both offences show the blood-alcohol to have been over two and a half times the limit, or where both were for refusing to provide a specimen, or where one offence was for refusing to provide a specimen and the other for blood-alcohol over two and a half times the limit. Where a motorist comes within this 'high risk offender' category, he will not be able to obtain a driving licence unless he can satisfy the Secretary of State that his driving does not present a risk of danger to the public. There is a right of appeal against the Secretary of State's decision to the magistrates' court in whose area the offender resides.

## 4.4 Abolition of the principle in *Scott* v *Baker*

Before a certificate of analysis was admissible in law the defendant had, in accordance with the former s 9(1) to have been 'arrested under section 5(5) or 8'. Following *Scott* v *Baker* [1969] 1 QB 659 these words were held to mean *lawfully* arrested under s 5 or s 8; and in order to prove that the arrest was lawful, the police had to prove either that they had strictly complied with the procedural provisions of the screening roadside breath test under the former s 8, or that the defendant had been lawfully arrested under s 5 for driving whilst unfit.

In contrast to the former statutory provision (s 9) which only enabled an officer to require specimens for laboratory testing from 'a person who has been arrested under sections 5(5) or 8', the present law entitles a constable to require specimens of breath, blood or urine 'in the course of an investigation whether a person has committed an offence under section 5 or section 6' (s 8(1)). For this reason it has now been held in three separate cases in the

Divisional Court (*Fox* v *Gwent Chief Constable* [1984] RTR 402, *Anderton* v *Royle* [1985] RTR 91 and *Bunyard* v *Hayes* (1984) *The Times*, 3 November) that the fact that the arrest was unlawful (as in *Fox*) or that the officers had failed to prove a valid arrest (as in *Anderton* v *Royle*) is irrelevant provided that the specimen for analysis was obtained without inducement, threat (other than the statutory warning), trick or other impropriety. In *Bunyard* the defendant refused to supply evidential breath specimens at the police station after having been arrested on suspicion of being the driver involved in an accident (which he was not). It was again held following *Fox* that as there was no misconduct on the part of the police the defendant should be convicted under s 8(7) of refusing specimens for analysis.

Although the cases based on the former statutory provisions may be of help in deciding the meaning of a phrase where that phrase or a similar phrase is repeated in the new provisions, those cases based on the principle in *Scott* v *Baker* would seem now therefore only to be of relevance in respect of the offence of failing without reasonable excuse to provide the preliminary screening specimen of breath, contrary to s 7 (4).

It may be noted that even assuming that it should be held that the police have to prove compliance with the procedural provisions of s 7, it may be rare for the police to fail to be able to do so because of the very considerably widened powers of requiring a preliminary breath test in s 7.

### 4.5–10 Exclusion of evidence of analysis

The only ground upon which the evidence of analysis can be excluded is if there was deliberate bad faith or trickery on the part of the police. Mere illegality of arrest or of improper administration of the breath test or its requirement would seem insufficient. The only possible ground for exclusion is if the defence can show positive mala fides on the part of the police.

In *R* v *Sang* [1980] AC 402 it was held by the House of Lords that although a judge has a discretion to exclude evidence of admissions, confessions and evidence obtained from the accused after the commission of the offence, he has no discretion to refuse to admit relevant admissible evidence merely because it had been obtained by improper or unfair means. Analysis of blood, urine or breath is of course obtained only with the consent of the accused after commission of the offence. It was for this reason that the Divisional Court in *Fox* declared that, following *Sang*, the certificate was admissible in that it was obtained without inducement, threat (other than the statutory warning), trick or other impropriety.

The principles of *Sang* will be overtaken by statute when s 78 of the Police and Criminal Evidence Act 1984 is brought into force. This provides that in any proceedings the court may refuse to allow evidence on which the prosecution proposes to rely to be given if it appears to the court that having regard to all the circumstances including the circumstances in which the evidence was obtained, the admission of the evidence would have such an adverse effect on the fairness of the proceedings that the court ought not to admit it.

This statutory provision clearly can apply to statements produced by the

Intoximeter or Camic machines. The section states that the court has a discretion to exclude the unfairly obtained evidence in any proceedings ('proceedings' are defined as criminal proceedings including courts martial etc, s 82). The section would thus seem to be of general application. It will be noted that unlike the doctrine of law in the United States ('the fruit of the poisoned tree') the evidence will not be automatically excluded if obtained illegally or if obtained after an unlawful arrest; instead the court under s 78 has to consider whether the admission of the evidence would have such an adverse effect on the fairness of the proceedings that it ought not to be admitted having regard to all the circumstances including the circumstances in which it was obtained.

## Summary of Offences

### 4.11 Failing to supply a roadside specimen of breath (s 7 (4))

The offence is fully committed when a person fails (and failure includes refusal) to provide a specimen of breath for a breath test when required to do so. The circumstances in which a motorist can be required to do so are considerably wider than under the old law and are set out in 4.41–4. The person must have been either driving or attempting to drive (see 4.26) or in charge (see 4.27) of a motor vehicle (see 4.28) on a road (see 4.29) or other public place (see 4.30). For special provision for hospital patients, see 4.96–101. For procedure, trial and penalties, see 4.116–30.

### 4.12 Driving or attempting to drive a motor vehicle while unfit through drink or drugs (s 5(1))

It is an offence under s 5 (1) for a person to drive or attempt to drive (see 4.26) a motor vehicle (see 4.28) on a road (see 4.29) or other public place (see 4.30) while unfit to drive through drink or drugs (see 4.63 and 4.64). For procedure, trial and penalties, see 4.116–30. For hospital patients, see 4.96. For post-offence consumption of alcohol or drugs, see 4.106.

### 4.13 In charge of a motor vehicle while unfit through drink or drugs (s 5(2))

It is an offence under s 5(2) for a person to be in charge (see 4.27) of a motor vehicle (see 4.28) on a road (see 4.29) or other public place (see 4.30) while unfit through drink or drugs (see 4.63 and 4.64). It is a defence for the motorist to prove that there is no likelihood of his driving while unfit (see 4.111). For procedure, trial and penalties, see 4.116–30. For hospital patients, see 4.96–101.

### 4.14 Driving or attempting to drive a motor vehicle with excess alcohol (s 6(1)(*a*))

It is an offence under s 6(1)(*a*) for a person to drive or attempt to drive (see 4.26) a motor vehicle (see 4.28) on a road (see 4.29) or other public place (see 4.30) with excess alcohol (see 4.75) in his breath (see 4.72), blood or urine (see 4.73) as evidenced by a certificate of analysis or printout (see 4.80). It is not normally a defence that he has not been arrested or validly arrested (see 4.80) but it may be a defence if the level of alcohol is due to consumption of alcohol after the offence (see 4.106). For special provisions for hospital patients, see 4.96–101. For procedure, trial and penalties, see 4.116–30.

### 4.15 In charge of a motor vehicle with excess alcohol (s 6(1)(*b*))

It is an offence under s 6(1)(*b*) for a person to be in charge (see 4.27) of a motor vehicle (see 4.28) on a road (see 4.29) or other public place (see 4.30) with excess alcohol (see 4.75) in his breath (see 4.72) or in blood or urine (see 4.73) as evidenced by a certificate of analysis or statement (see 4.80). It is a defence for the motorist to prove that he would be unlikely to drive while above the limit (see 4.111). For post-offence consumption of alcohol, see 4.106. For special provisions for hospital patients, see 4.96–101. For procedure, trial and penalties, see 4.116–30.

### 4.16 Failing to provide a specimen for analysis (s 8(7))

It is an offence for a person who has been required to provide specimens for analysis (see 4.72 and 4.77) to fail without reasonable excuse to do so. The offender is liable to compulsory disqualification if he was driving or attempting to drive but if he was not driving or attempting to drive it is endorsable by 10 penalty points. The police do not have to prove that he was in charge of a motor vehicle (see 4.27). For procedure, trial and penalties generally, see 4.116–30.

### 4.17–25 Interaction of the offences

Although the offences under ss 5 and 6 are quite distinct, the two offences are closely inter-related because a person arrested under s 5 will usually have been required to provide a specimen for analysis. (Section 8(1) allows a constable to require specimens for analysis in the course of an investigation whether a person has committed an offence under s 5 or s 6.) For this reason it is usual for a person charged under s 5 to be additionally charged under s 6 if he provides a specimen over the prescribed limit or under s 8(7) (failing without reasonable excuse to provide specimens for analysis) if he fails or refuses to provide specimens. Further, it was held in *Duddy* v *Gallagher* (1984) *The Times*, 5 December that justices were entitled to convict both under s 8(7) and s 6(1) where the defendant gave only one specimen of breath (which was above the prescribed limit) but failed to provide the second specimen.

## Definitions

### 4.26 'Drives or attempts to drive'

The relevant words in the former s 8(1) as to who may be required by a police constable to supply a specimen of breath are 'driving or attempting to drive'. These words were the subject of intensive litigation and their meaning was settled by the leading case of *Pinner* v *Everett* [1969] 3 All ER 257, as finally illustrated and explained in *Edkins* v *Knowles* [1973] QB 748. These cases were concerned not with whether the motorist could be said to have been driving or attempting to drive: in every single case there was no dispute that the defendant at some moment of time had been driving. The cases were instead concerned with whether, at the particular time that the constable's suspicions were aroused, the motorist could at that moment in time still be said to be 'driving or attempting to drive'.

The case of *Pinner* v *Everett* as explained by *Edkins* v *Knowles* will not need to be referred to in respect of cases under the new drink/driving provisions. Section 7(1) is wider than the former s 8(1) and enables a constable to require a breath test not only from a person who *is* driving or attempting to drive but also a motorist who either *has been* driving or attempting to drive, or is or *has been* in charge of a motor vehicle.

It is submitted that the word 'drives' and the words 'attempts to drive' create two separate and alternative offences and that a summons or charge containing both is bad because of duplicity. The difference between driving and attempting to drive depends on whether the vehicle is ever actually put in motion on a road or public place. A metropolitan stipendiary magistrate dismissed a case where the motorist had been charged with driving. The breath test was administered in respect of a vehicle parked at the side of a road. The defendant started or attempted to start the vehicle's engine but the wheels of the vehicle were never put in motion.

It is submitted that the same principles must be applied to 'attempts to drive' as to any other criminal attempt, ie there must be an act sufficiently proximate to the commission of the full offence, in this case, driving.

A drunken person went to the front of a car and turned the starting handle; he then opened the offside door, leaned inside and appeared to touch the dashboard instruments. He returned to the starting handle and then sat in the driver's seat; the engine was heard to turn over, but failed to start. The court found that he had the immediate intention of driving and it was held that this was an attempt to drive (*The State* (*Prendergast*) v *Porter* [1961] Ir Jur Rep 15). In *Shaw* v *Knill* [1974] RTR 142 it was held that a motor cyclist could be convicted of attempting to drive while disqualified when he pushed a motor cycle six yards towards the entrance on to a public road where he was about to ride it. In *Harman* v *Wardrop* [1971] RTR 127 a motorist gave up his ignition keys to a person whom he mistakenly thought was a police constable. When he realised his mistake he asked for his keys back with the intention of driving the car. He was refused. Lord Parker doubted whether the motorist would ever be said to be attempting to drive if he merely asked for his keys, although where an unfit driver who had no ignition key sat in the driver's seat attempting to insert other keys into the ignition, he was held to be properly convicted of attempting to drive (*Kelly* v *Hogan* [1982] RTR 352).

A person was held to 'attempt to drive' even though due to a mechanical malfunction the vehicle could not be driven. In *R* v *Farrance* [1978] RTR 225 the defendant was held to be 'attempting to drive' when found revving the engine of a motor car which in fact could not be driven because the clutch had been burnt out.

It is not clear whether s 3 of the Criminal Attempts Act 1981 applies to attempted offences contrary to s 5 or s 6 of the 1972 Act: it is possible that it does not, as the wording of s 3 is obscure.

Whereas starting the engine without putting the car into motion may be said to be 'attempting to drive' the converse, ie putting the car into motion without starting the engine, has been held to be 'driving'. The essence of driving is the use of the driver's control to direct the movement of the vehicle however the movement was produced; the Divisional Court in *Burgoyne* v *Phillips* [1983] RTR 49 so held when confirming Plymouth Crown Court's decision, and dismissed an appeal where the defendant, thinking he had the key in the ignition deliberately let the car roll forward thirty feet by gravity, where it collided with another vehicle. The steering had locked and he had applied the brakes as soon as he realised he had no key. Similarly in *Saycell* v *Bool* [1948] 2 All ER 83, a person who sat in a driving seat, released the brake and let it run downhill for a hundred yards was held to 'drive it' even though there was no petrol and the vehicle was not started. The defendant must intend to put the car in motion; in *Blayney* v *Knight* [1975] RTR 279 the defendant, in the course of a struggle with a taxi driver who had left his automatic drive taxi with its engine running, accidentally touched the accelerator, causing the taxi to move. The defendant was not found to 'drive', as he had no intention of driving.

Other illustrations of the principle that if the vehicle is deliberately put in motion, and its movements are controlled by the motorist he may be said to 'drive' the vehicle albeit there is no motive power of the vehicle are *McQuaid* v *Anderton* [1980] 3 All ER 540 and *Caise* v *Wright* [1981] RTR 49. These two cases both decided that the steersman of a vehicle towed by another vehicle can be said to 'drive' the towed vehicle within the meaning of the 1972 Act.

However, it still has to be considered whether the activity in question can fall within the ordinary meaning of the word 'drives' in the English language, and the courts will not hold a person to be 'driving' a motor vehicle when his activity is better described as 'pushing' the vehicle (*R* v *McDonagh* [1974] RTR 372, where a person who pushed a car with both feet on the ground, with one arm in the car to control the steering wheel was held not to 'drive' the car, but to be merely pushing it). Nor was a front seat passenger said to 'drive' the car when he momentarily grabbed the steering wheel, causing the car to leave the road.

See further 'Driver', 1.52–6.

### 4.27 'In charge'

For there to be a conviction under s 5(2) (unfit through drink or drugs) or under s 6(1)(*b*) (exceeding prescribed limit of alcohol in breath, blood or urine) the prosecution have to prove that the defendant was 'in charge' of a motor vehicle. (It should be noted that the prosecution do not have to prove that the defendant was actually 'in charge' of a motor vehicle on a charge of refusing or failing without reasonable excuse to supply a specimen of breath, blood or urine for analysis—see 4.91–5.)

The words 'in charge' are not defined in the 1972 Act.

Whether or not a person is 'in charge' of a motor vehicle is a question of fact (see Lord Goddard CJ in *R* v *Harnett* [1955] Crim LR 793 and *R* v *Short* (1955) *The Times* 10 December). But the meaning of the phrase has given rise to considerable difficulty in the past; and there has been a difference in approach between the Scottish and English courts. In general, the Scottish courts have required a close connection between the defendant and the control of, or likelihood of driving, the motor vehicle. The English courts have tended to work from the presumption that someone must be 'in charge' of any motor vehicle which is parked on a road or public place, and, prima facie, that person will be the person with the keys.

An example of the Scottish courts' approach is *Crichton* v *Burrell* 1951 SLT 365. The owner of a car, who had a key of the car on him, was waiting by the car for another man, who had a duplicate key, to come and drive the car. The owner was arrested before the other man arrived. The owner's conviction was quashed by the High Court of Justiciary, which stated that 'in charge' meant 'in de facto control', in which, on a strict construction, the owner would appear to have remained. In view of the statutory defence now available (see 4.111) this approach would appear to be wrong, if and in so far as the concept of being 'in de facto control' is intended to include an element of likelihood of driving. For if it is, there would be no need for the statutory defence.

The English courts' approach can be seen in the case of *Woodage* v *Jones* (*No 2*) [1975] RTR 119. A driver was stopped by other motorists, and pulled off the road, drawing into a garage forecourt. When he learnt that the police had been called, he walked off, and was half a mile away when arrested. He was held to have been still 'in charge', as he had not put his vehicle into the charge of anyone else. In *Ellis* v *Smith* [1962] 3 All ER 954, a bus driver who left his bus on the road when he went off duty was still 'in charge' unless and until he handed the bus over to the charge of someone else.

The most robust statement of this principle is by Lord Goddard CJ in *R* v *Short* above: 'Somebody must be in charge of a car when it is on a road unless it has been abandoned altogether.' This suggests that a person will be 'in charge' of his car even, for example, whilst asleep in bed, and therefore vulnerable to prosecution in circumstances which might appear grotesque.

In the final analysis, a person whose blood-alcohol level is in excess of the prescribed limit will only be sure of avoiding a conviction for being 'in charge' of his motor vehicle if he has taken it off the road or public place, or has taken positive steps to place it in the charge of someone else.

The Scottish courts have held that the supervisor of a learner driver is 'in charge' of the motor vehicle (*Clark* v *Clark* 1950 SLT (Sh Ct) 68). In England and Wales supervisors have been charged with aiding and abetting (*Crampton* v *Fish* [1970] Crim LR 235) and cannot escape conviction on the ground that no-one can know whether a person's blood is above the limit until it is actually analysed (*R* v *Tinsley* [1963] Crim LR 520).

Two people can actually drive the same car at the same time. In *Langman* v *Valentine* [1952] 2 All ER 803 it was held that a supervisor who retains control may also be the driver. It is submitted that it is primarily a matter of degree of control as to whether a supervisor is a driver; the better view may be that as well as aiding and abetting an offence by the learner, a supervisor can safely be said to be 'in charge' if he himself is unfit or above the limit, as a supervisor's duty is to supervise the learner driver, and in an emergency to take control. In the ordinary sense of the word it would seem that the supervisor is 'in charge' of the motor vehicle and only 'drives' when he takes control of the car from the learner driver. (See also *Sheldon* v *Jones* (1969) 113 SJ 942, 4.111.)

### 4.28 'Motor vehicle'

Drink/driving offences under ss 5, 6, 7 and 8 can only be committed if committed in respect of a 'motor vehicle'. A motor vehicle is defined by s 190 as a mechanically propelled vehicle intended or adapted for use on roads, but by s 193(1), a grass cutting machine controlled by a pedestrian is not a motor vehicle provided that, if it is of the type that can carry a person, it is not in use under or proceeding under the control of the person carried on it. An electrically assisted pedal cycle of such a class as is prescribed is also not a motor vehicle for the purposes of the Act (s 193(1)(*e*)). The test as to whether a motor vehicle can be said to be 'mechanically propelled' for the purposes of s 190 depends not on whether it is, or is capable of becoming, mechanically propelled but whether 'there is any reasonable prospect of the vehicle being made mobile again' (*Binks* v *Dept of the Environment* [1975] RTR 318 approving Lord Parker CJ in *Law* v *Thomas* (1964) 62 LGR 195 at p 196). Where a pedal cycle is fitted with an auxiliary engine and the engine is connected up, it is a motor vehicle whether the engine is running or not (*Floyd* v *Bush* [1953] 1 All ER 265). In *R* v *Tahsin* [1970] RTR 88 a defendant pedalling a moped was held to be rightly convicted for driving a motor vehicle while unfit through drink or drugs and in *McRachran* v *Hurst* [1978] RTR 462 it was similarly held that a moped, being pedalled while the engine did not work and which was without petrol, remained (because it was constructed as a mechanically propelled vehicle) 'mechanically propelled' for the purpose of the Act. On the other hand, where a vehicle is constructed either as a pedal cycle or as a motor vehicle, as in the case of a pedal cycle fitted with an auxiliary motor, it was held that the temporary removal of essential parts of the engine (cylinder, piston and connecting rod) resulted in the vehicle reverting to its use as a pedal cycle (*Lawrence* v *Howlett* [1952] 2 All ER 74).

See further 'Motor vehicles', 1.2–12.

### 4.29 'Road'

'Road' is defined in s 196 of the 1972 Act as meaning 'any highway and any other road to which the public has access'.

A highway consists of a right of way which can be exercised as of right by the public with a right of way on foot, riding or accompanied by a beast of burden or with vehicles or cattle (*Suffolk County Council* v *Mason* [1979] 2 All ER 369, HL at p 371). At first sight therefore, public footpath and bridleway would seem to be included in the definition of s 196 but this would seem not to be the case because ss 18–21 each specifically provide that a public bridleway is a road for the purposes of each of the offences of reckless, careless or drunken cycling and carrying two persons on a bicycle. The onus of proving that a road is within the Act is on the prosecution (*Williams* v *Boyle* (1962) 106 SJ 939).

There is usually little dispute as to whether a particular road is a public highway. Whether or not a particular road is a highway is usually easily ascertainable. The decided cases chiefly centre on whether the road is 'any other road to which the public have access'.

The first question is whether it is a road and the second is whether the public have access (*Oxford* v *Austin* [1981] RTR 416). A road is a definable way for passage between two points (ibid) but it is not proposed to discuss the cases concerning whether eg a market place, forecourt or car park is or is not a road, because offences under ss 5–8 can be committed not only on a road, but also on any other public place.

If the road is not a highway, the prosecutor will usually have to prove only two things, first that the general public, and not merely a special class of the general public, has access to the road and secondly whether access is only by the tolerance of the owner or proprietor of the road in question (*Deacon* v *A T* (*A minor*) [1976] RTR 244). The test as to whether the public may be said to have access was said by Lord Sands in *Harrison* v *Hill* [132] SC(J) 13 at p 17 to be as follows:

> Any road may be regarded as a road to which the public have access upon which members of the public are to be found who have not obtained access either by overcoming a physical obstruction or in defiance of prohibition express or implied.

This dictum has been applied in numerous cases and in *Cox* v *White* [1976] RTR 248 at p 251 Lord Widgery stated:

> I think that in ninety-nine cases out of a hundred that direction [ie that of Lord Sands] is all the justices need for current purposes.

Normally a right of way extends throughout its boundaries. In *A-G* v *Beynon* [1969] 2 All ER 263 it was held that it is first necessary to look at whether the fences were put up with reference to the highway, or for some other reason. If it appears that the fences are put up with reference to the highway, a rebuttable presumption of law then arises that the highway extends to the whole area within the fences and is not confined to such part as has been made up. See further 'Road', 1.66–71.

## 4.30–40 'Or other public place'

The term 'or other public place' is not defined; it is discussed at (1955) Jo Crim L 12, in Stroud's *Judicial Dictionary* and Saunders' *Words and Phrases Legally Defined*, and at 127 JPN 563. It is a question of degree and fact whether a place is public or private; if only a restricted class of person is permitted or invited to have access, the case would fall on the side of the place being private, but if only a restricted class is excluded, the place would be public (*R* v *Waters* (1963) 47 Cr App R 149). It is for the prosecution to prove that a place is public (*Pugh* v *Knipe* below).

Magistrates may make use of their general local knowledge in deciding whether a car park is a public place under s 5 or s 6 (*Clift* v *Long* [1961] Crim LR 121). But knowledge of one magistrate only need not be accepted by the other magistrates, for the prosecution must prove that the place was a public place at the time of the offence: evidence that it is normally public may not suffice where it is not clear that at the time it was (*Williams* v *Boyle* (1962) 106 SJ 939).

A private field to which the public were temporarily invited to watch racing was held to be a public place under s 5, although it could be closed at any time and particular persons could be refused admission (*R* v *Collinson* (1931) 23 Cr App R 49). *Paterson* v *Ogilvy* 1957 SC(J) 42 is a case to like effect. Conversely, a car park attached to a public house may be regarded as a public place during general licensing hours but it may well be no longer a public place outside those hours. In *Sandy* v *Martin* [1974] Crim LR 258 justices were held to be entitled to acquit after the prosecution had failed to prove that the invitation to the public to use the car park extended one hour after closing time. In *Montgomery* v *Loney* [1959] NI 171, where a Northern Irish statutory definition of 'road' was considered, it was held that the forecourt of a petrol filling station, with carriageways with unobstructed entrances to, and exits from, the highway, was a 'road or public place'. It was said that although the forecourt was open only to those members of the public who wished to do business with the station owner, they were enough to show that the public had access. It was also said that an offence charged as being 'in a road or other public place' was not bad for duplicity. In *Elkins* v *Cartlidge* [1947] 1 All ER 829 there was at the side of an inn a well-defined parking ground from which an open gateway gave access to an enclosure. Cars went into this enclosure and parked there. The enclosure was held to be a public place, as being a place to which the public had access in fact; but a car park attached to a *club* can only be regarded as public if there is evidence of public use of the car park; a public house offers its services to the public but a private club does not (*Pugh* v *Knipe* [1972] RTR 286 distinguishing *Elkins* v *Cartlidge* above). A vacant piece of land used as an overflow parking ground was held to be a public place in *McDonald* v *M'Ewen* 1953 SLT (Sh) 26. In *White* v *Cubitt* (1930) 94 JP 60, a case under another statute, a piece of private ground adjoining an inn and separated from the highway only by a level row of stone setts was held to be a public place. The public did not have access to this ground save to enter the inn and it was not a car park.

A part of the grounds of a hospital into which visitors and their friends were permitted to enter was held to be a public place under the Prevention of Crime Act 1953, where 'public place' is defined as including any highway or place to which at the material time the public have or are permitted to have access whether on payment or otherwise (*R* v *Powell* [1963] Crim LR 511).

## Preliminary Breath Tests

### 4.41 Requirement to provide

The preliminary breath test is retained as part of the new system. As in the former provisions, the circumstances in which a constable may require a motorist to provide a preliminary test are dependent on whether the motorist, on the one hand, was committing a moving traffic offence or had alcohol in his body or on the other, was involved in an accident. The circumstances under which a breath test may be demanded have been widened to include motorists who are or were in charge of motor vehicles. In addition, the constable's suspicion no longer has to arise while the motorist is still driving or attempting to drive. The police may now require a breath test in respect of a motorist who *has been* driving.

The importance of the police complying with the statutory requirements as to the requirement of breath tests is considerably diminished. While a defendant would seem to be entitled to be acquitted of failing to supply a specimen for a breath test if it was wrongly required, the wrongful requirement of a breath test will no longer automatically entitle him to be acquitted of a subsequent drink/driving offence if he subsequently provides a specimen for analysis over the limit or refuses or fails to do so without reasonable excuse (see further 4.4: abolition of the principle in *Scott* v *Baker*).

It remains an offence to fail or refuse to supply a specimen of breath for breath testing (s 7(4)). The offence (unlike the former s 8(3) offence) is endorsable and an offender thus incurs 4 penalty points. Sentencing and the penalties for the offence are set out in 4.116–25.

## 4.42 Breath test on suspicion of alcohol or moving traffic offence: s 7(1)(*a*) and (*b*)

Under s 7(1)(*a*) a constable in uniform may require a breath test where he has reasonable cause to suspect a motorist to be driving or attempting to drive or in charge of a motor vehicle on a road or other public place with alcohol in his body or to have committed a traffic offence whilst the vehicle was in motion. Under s 7(1)(*b*) a constable has a similar power where the person *has been* driving or attempting to drive or in charge on a road or other public place and that that person still has alcohol in his body. Under s 7(1)(*c*) a constable may require a breath test where the motorist *has been* driving or attempting to drive or in charge of a motor vehicle and has committed a moving traffic offence while the vehicle was in motion.

### *A 'Road or other public place'*

The meaning of the term 'road or other public place' is discussed in 4.29 and 4.30. The terms 'motor vehicle', 'drives or attempts to drive' and 'in charge' are discussed in 4.28, 4.26 and 4.27 respectively.

### *B 'Breath test'*

'Breath test' is defined by the new s 12(2) to mean 'a preliminary test for the purpose of obtaining, by means of a device of a type approved by the Secretary of State, an indication whether the proportion of alcohol in a person's breath or blood is likely to exceed the prescribed limit'.

All the existing preliminary breath testing devices, the Alcotest 80 and 80A, the Alcolyser, the Alcolmeter and the Alert have continued to be used in respect of the new provisions. The Alcotests and Alcolyser consist of a plastic bag and a glass tube of yellow crystals showing a positive result if the green stain caused by the motorist's breath passes the indication on the tube. The Alcolmeter and Alert on the other hand are electronic devices in which a charge is generated proportionate to the amount of alcohol in the breath. Compliance with the manufacturer's instructions in respect of the devices is now of importance only in respect of an offence under s 7 (4) and the situation of a wrongly administered breath test is discussed under 4.45. As to approval of the devices by the Home Secretary, see 4.45.

*C 'Constable in uniform'*

As in the former s 8(1) the requirement under s 7(1)(*a*), (*b*), or (*c*) has to be made by a 'constable in uniform'.

A 'constable' in the section, it is suggested, must refer not to the rank of constable but to any constable of whatever rank and 'constable' must refer to any member of any police force within the jurisdiction, including special constables (Police Act 1964, s 19). If the constable omits to state that he was in uniform a court is entitled to assume that he was in uniform when he has stated that he was on duty as a motor patrol officer (*Cooper* v *Rowlands* [1971] RTR 291). The word 'constable' includes a special constable. In *Richards* v *West* [1980] RTR 215 the justices had no direct evidence that a special constable who required a breath test was in uniform. Evidence was given that another special constable present was in uniform. The defence did not raise the issue in cross-examination. The justices, from their knowledge of the special constabulary, knew that there was no plain clothes department and, the officer having stated that he was on duty, deduced he was in uniform. The Divisional Court held that there was circumstantial evidence whereby the justices could conclude that the officer must have been in uniform. Whether a constable is 'in uniform' is a question of fact. In *Wallwork* v *Giles* (1969) 114 SJ 36 it was held that a police constable who was not wearing a helmet but who otherwise was in his normal uniform was nevertheless 'in uniform'. It was said that the object of the provision was to ensure that the constable might be easily identified as a police constable.

In *Taylor* v *Baldwin* [1976] RTR 265 this general principle was followed. A police sergeant, wearing his ordinary raincoat over his uniform, driving his private car, was held to have been entitled to require a driver to provide a specimen of breath. It was further held that a constable does not have to be in uniform when the suspicion arises: it is only when the constable requires the specimen of breath that the Act requires him to be in uniform.

*D 'May require'*

The constable does not have to use any particular formula when he requires the motorist to take a breath test. The words 'I intend to give you a breath test' were held sufficient in *R* v *O'Boyle* [1973] RTR 445, and 'I wish to give you a breath test' were held sufficient in *R* v *Clarke* (*Christopher*) (1969) 113 SJ 428. As long as the language used can fairly be said to be capable of amounting to a requirement, it is purely a question of fact as to whether a constable 'required' a motorist to take a breath test (see *R* v *O'Boyle* above).

*E 'Driving or attempting to drive'*

The former s 8(1) only enabled a constable to make a requirement of a person who *is* 'driving or attempting to drive'. Whilst whether or not a person is driving or attempting to drive is a question of fact (*R* v *Guttridge* [1973] RTR 135), but because a literal interpretation would produce absurdity, considerable judicial energy and efforts were expended in making sense of the phrase. The difficulty faced by the courts was that the constable could only require a breath test of a person who *is* driving or attempting to drive; once the constable's suspicion arose after he had ceased to drive there was no power to require a breath test even if he was still in charge. These difficulties of interpretation do not now arise. It will have been noted that s 7 enables a constable to require a breath test of a person who either is *or has been* driving a motor vehicle or who is or *has been* in charge of a motor vehicle.

As to the meaning of 'driving or attempting to drive', see 4.26.

*F 'Reasonable cause to suspect'*

As in the former s 8(1), s 7(1) gives a constable power to require a breath test where he has reasonable cause to *suspect* a moving traffic offence or consumption of alcohol. By contrast, s 7(2) gives a constable power to require a breath test following an accident only where he has reasonable cause to *believe*. The distinction between suspicion and belief is a matter of degree and may be important. The circumstances for a constable to be said to have reasonable cause to believe clearly have to be more definite than the circumstances justifying mere suspicion (see *Johnson* v *Whitehouse*, 4.44*B*).

Whether a constable has or has not reasonable cause to suspect is a fact, and depends on the circumstances. The cases on the former statutory provisions as to what circumstances are or are not sufficient will be of help in deciding whether or not an offence under s 7(4) has been committed.

It is clear that the test is not whether the motorist has actually consumed alcohol or actually committed a traffic offence. What matters is whether the constable has reasonable cause to suspect consumption of alcohol or a moving traffic offence. It is for the prosecution to prove that the constable had reasonable cause to suspect but it may be no defence (nor is it a reasonable excuse) for failing to supply a specimen for analysis that in fact alcohol may not have been consumed (see *McNicol* v *Peters* 1969 SLT (J) 261). If a moving traffic offence is suspected then it is not a defence for failing to supply a specimen for laboratory testing for the defendant to believe that he had not committed a moving traffic offence. All that the prosecution must prove is that the constable had reasonable cause to suspect he had committed a traffic offence while the vehicle was in motion (*R* v *Downey* [1970] RTR 257).

Nor is it necessary for the constable's ground of suspicion to be first-hand. A constable has been held by the English High Court to have reasonable ground for suspecting a motorist of having consumed alcohol when his only source of knowledge is what he has been told by another constable (*Erskine* v *Hollin* [1971] RTR 199). The Scottish High Court came to a similar conclusion when it was held that a uniformed officer could have reasonable cause for suspicion when he has been called in for this purpose by plain-clothes police officers (*Copeland* v *McPherson* 1970 SLT 87). In *R* v *Moore* [1970] RTR

486 it was held that when a police constable received a radio message to the effect that the driver was believed to be drunk it was not possible for it to be argued that the constable had no reasonable cause to suspect alcohol and, although the judge should have left the matter to the jury, the Court of Appeal applied the proviso and dismissed the appeal. *Erskine* v *Hollin* was applied in *R* v *Evans* (*Terence*) [1974] RTR 232 where it was held that a police patrolman who had been informed by radio of a foot constable's suspicion of alcohol of a motorist seen driving erratically, could thereby himself have reasonable cause to suspect the motorist.

Can a constable have reasonable cause to suspect if his informant is not a police officer? It is submitted that this is primarily a question of fact, not law, and the answer in practice will depend entirely on who was the informant, the precise nature of the information given and all the surrounding circumstances. However, it would be customary for a constable to state the grounds of his suspicion to the motorist before making the requirement and if there is any truth in the allegation either the answer of the motorist or the manner in which the answer is given might well provide sufficient justification for the constable to confirm or negative his suspicions. The facts giving rise to the suspicion must, however, relate to the actual driving of the vehicle on the day in question. In *Monaghan* v *Corbett* (1983) *The Times*, 23 June neighbours told a constable at about midday that the motorist and his wife had been seen driving off that day and that they habitually went off to a public house at lunch-time on Sunday. The constable, who had smelt alcohol on the motorist's breath the day before, then went to the police station and collected Alcotest equipment, returned to the scene and made a request for a breath test when the motorist returned to his home at 2.30 pm. It was held that the policeman could not form a reasonable suspicion of alcohol at 2.30 pm on the basis that he had smelt alcohol the day before and the neighbours' information about the motorist's Sunday habits.

A 'U' turn in a road, wrong indicator and excess speed do not of themselves indicate a reasonable suspicion of alcohol and if these are the only facts the court will quash a conviction; these facts alone being held insufficient to constitute a suspicion of alcohol (*Williams* v *Jones* [1972] RTR 5). If it is a matter of fact primarily for the court, a conviction will only be quashed where the evidence as a matter of law could not support reasonable grounds for suspicion (*R* v *Fardy* [1973] RTR 268). In considering whether a constable had reasonable grounds for forming a suspicion, regard was to be had to all the circumstances, and the fact that the incident occurred at 3.30 am was not to be overlooked (ibid). In *R* v *McGall* [1974] RTR 216 it was again held that all the circumstances had to be considered as to whether a constable had reasonable cause to suspect a motorist of alcohol; abnormally slow driving for no apparent reasons late at night with a trafficator unjustifiably repeated after correction could give rise to reasonable suspicion.

In law a constable under the former s 8(1) either had to suspect alcohol *or* a moving traffic offence. In practice constables rarely require a breath test simply on suspicion of a moving traffic offence; they do so only when suspicion of alcohol arises as well. Usually, by definition, suspicion of a moving traffic offence will have arisen while the defendant was still driving but often the constable only begins to suspect alcohol after the defendant had ceased to drive. It was held in a number of cases that the constable was still entitled to require a breath test provided it was made clear that the constable was relying on suspicion of a moving traffic offence (*Timmins* v *Perry* [1970] RTR 477; *Rickwood* v *Cochrane* [1978] RTR 218). The alternative ground had to be clearly established on the evidence (*Clements* v *Dams* [1978] RTR 206) and if the prosecution ran the case on one ground of suspicion, justices were held not to be entitled to convict the defendant on the alternative basis of suspicion of a moving traffic offence (*Morriss* v *Lawrence* [1977] RTR 205). If justices were considering doing so the defendant should be informed and be allowed to apply for an adjournment if he had been misled.

While s 7(1)(*a*) is in similar terms to the former s 8(1), s 7(1)(*b*) enables a constable to require a breath test of a person who *has been* driving, attempting to drive or in charge of a motor vehicle if he has reasonable cause to suspect that he has been driving etc with alcohol in his body 'and still has alcohol in his body'. The circumstances relied upon must therefore be two-fold, namely that the constable has reasonable grounds for suspecting not only that he drove etc with alcohol in his body, but also that he has reasonable cause to suspect he still has alcohol in his body.

Section 7(1)(*c*) entitles a constable to require a breath test of a person who he has reasonable cause to suspect *has been* driving, attempting to drive or been in charge of a motor vehicle and *has* committed a traffic offence while the vehicle was in motion.

It should be noted that while s 7(1)(*b*) and (*c*) both refer to motorists who have been driving, it would seem clear that the police have no power of entry to demand a breath test. While the police may require a breath test 'off the road' there is no power of entry on to the defendant's property against his will except in the limited circumstances contained in s 7(6) (breath test following an accident causing personal injury); see further 4.52.

*G 'Traffic offence'*

A traffic offence is defined by s 7(8) (as amended by the Road Traffic Regulation Act 1984, Sched 13) as any offence under the 1972 Act except Part V (which relates to the registration etc of driving instructors), any offence under the Road Traffic Regulation Act 1984 or Part I of the Transport Act 1980. The definition also includes any offence under Part III of the Road Traffic Act 1960. Part III of the Road Traffic Act 1960 was replaced by the Public Passenger Vehicles Act 1981. There must be some doubt as to whether an offence under this latter Act therefore comes under the definition. While the former s 8(8) (which defined 'traffic offence' for the purpose of the former drink/driving provisions) was specifically amended by including a reference to the Public Passenger Vehicles Act 1981, the new s 7(8) has not been so amended. It may be difficult to argue that s 17(2) of the Interpretation Act 1978 saves the position because the Transport Act 1981 which substituted the new ss 6–12 of the 1972 Act was passed after the Public Passenger Vehicles Act 1981. Section 17(2) of the Interpretation Act 1978 does save the position for offences under the Road Traffic Regulation Act 1967, however.

The traffic offence must have been committed while the vehicle was in motion. Thus driving without lights justifies a test (eg *R* v *Price* [1968] 3 All ER 814) but not driving with an unilluminated rear number plate (as for example in *Pinner* v *Everett* [1969] 3 All ER 257) because this offence is contrary to regulations made under the Vehicles (Excise) Act 1971. It would seem, however, that offences under regulations made under the Acts within the definition are included (*Bingham* v *Bruce* [1962] 1 All ER 136, *Rathbone* v *Bundock* [1962] 2 All ER 257).

The offence of taking a motor vehicle (now contrary to s 175 of the 1972 Act) was replaced in England and Wales by the Theft Act 1968. It would seem doubtful whether an offence under s 12 of that Act comes within the definition. (Although using a motor vehicle without third party insurance contrary to s 143 is within the definition. A joy rider will not usually be insured in respect of the vehicle he has taken.)

*H 'There or nearby'*

The breath test under the former s 8(1) had to be made 'there or nearby'. This was held to be a matter of fact and degree in all the particular circumstances of the case and the High Court will regard itself as bound by a finding of fact (*Arnold* v *Kingston-upon-Hull Chief Constable* [1969] 3 All ER 636, where a police station 1½ miles away was held not to be 'there or nearby'). Similarly the Divisional Court refused to disturb a finding that 160 yards away was not 'there or nearby' (*Donegani* v *Ward* [1969] 3 All ER 636).

The new s 7(3) requires a breath test to be made 'at or near where the requirement is made'. This would seem, as in the former s 8(1), to be a matter of fact and degree and similarly, unless the magistrates' finding of fact is so perverse that no reasonable tribunal could come to such a conclusion, the magistrates' finding will not be reversed by the Divisional Court.

*J 'As soon as reasonably practicable'*

The former s 8(1) required a constable who had stopped a motorist for a breath test because of a traffic offence to administer the breath test 'as soon as reasonably practicable' after the commission of the traffic offence. The present s 7 now contains no such provision.

### 4.43 Random tests

There still remains much confusion amongst the public about random tests. The police have a general power to stop a motor vehicle pursuant to s 159 of the 1972 Act. This power was examined in *Beard* v *Wood* [1980] RTR 454, where it was held that there was nothing in the section which required the prosecutor to prove that a constable stopping a vehicle under s 159 was acting under a common law power: the constable's duty and power came from the section itself. Once a vehicle is stopped, it is possible then for the first time for a constable to suspect the motorist of consuming alcohol. Provided that at the time the constable's suspicions arose the motorist is still 'driving or attempting to drive', the constable is lawfully entitled to require the motorist to take a breath test even though the motorist was stopped at random. In *R* v *Needham* [1974] RTR 201, the Court of Appeal arrived at the same conclusion on this point, and specifically held there was nothing in the statutory provisions to prevent random stopping; they declined to introduce any further provision as to the circumstances of the stopping of the vehicle which could lead to a lawful demand for a breath test. Justices acquitted a motorist of a charge under s 6(1) because they found that the police officer had no reasonable grounds for believing a moving traffic offence had been committed, and that the sole purpose of the police officer in stopping the motor vehicle was to ascertain whether he had alcohol in his blood. The justices were directed to convict in the absence of a finding of malpractice on the part of the police (*Such* v *Ball* [1982] RTR 140). *Quaere* the position if the police had stopped a vehicle pretending a moving traffic offence had been committed in order to randomly stop a vehicle to administer a breath test (ibid). In *Steel* v *Goacher* [1983] RTR 98 Griffiths LJ doubted whether s 159 confers any power to stop a motorist but held that once he had stopped, the police could still administer a breath test despite a mistaken view as to the power to stop.

The matter may best be summarised by saying that the police may or may not be prohibited from random stopping, but the police are prohibited from requiring breath tests 'at random'. It is only if the constable has reasonable cause to suspect under s 7 of having alcohol or committing a traffic offence while the vehicle was in motion that the constable may lawfully require a breath test (for further authority supporting this view see *Harris* v *Croson* [1973] RTR 57, *R* v *Gaughan* [1974] RTR 195, *Adams* v *Valentine* [1975] Crim LR 238). In *Winter* v *Barlow* [1980] RTR 209 it was held that once the former s 8(1) had been complied with it was unnecessary to consider the legality of the police stopping the motorist under s 159, because s 8(1) is a safeguard against arbitrary requests for a breath test. In *Lodwick* v *Sanders* [1985] Crim LR 210 it was held that s 159 gave a power to a police constable to stop a vehicle and that he may detain the vehicle while he exercised any power he was entitled to exercise in the circumstances.

The power of constables to stop and search persons and vehicles will be regulated by statute when ss 1 and 2 of the Police and Criminal Evidence Act 1984 are in force. Section 4 of the same statute also makes provision for road checks. A road check under s 4 cannot be used for random checks to see if persons are driving with excess alcohol as these are 'traffic offences' and not 'serious arrestable offences'.

### 4.44 Breath test following an accident: s 7(2)

Under s 7(2) a constable may require a breath test of a motorist who he has reasonable cause to believe was driving or in charge of a motor vehicle owing to the presence of which an accident had occurred.

Section 7(2) is similar to the former s 8(2) except in two respects:

(1) the constable is no longer required to be 'in uniform' to breath test a motorist following an accident, and

(2) the constable may additionally breath test a person who he has reasonable cause to believe was 'in charge' of the vehicle at the time of the accident.

Other than these two differences, the wording of s 7(2) is identical to the wording of the former s 8(2).

*A 'Accident'*

The wording of the section is such that the police have to prove there has been an accident. It is not sufficient to show that the constable had reasonable cause to believe that there had been an accident (*R* v *Fardy* [1978] RTR 202; *Chief Constable of the West Midlands Police* v *Billingham* [1979] RTR 446).

The meaning of the word 'accident' was considered in *R* v *Morris* [1972] RTR 201. One vehicle was pushing another with its front bumper against the rear bumper of the leading vehicle. The bumpers became interlocked and damage was caused to both vehicles. It was held that there was an 'accident', which Sachs LJ defined as 'an unintended occurrence which had an adverse physical result'. It was, however, decided in *Billingham* above that it was inappropriate for a definition of the word to be, in effect, written into the 1972 Act when the Act itself did not define it. The meaning of the word 'accident' had different meanings in different statutes. The word in a particular Act should be looked at in the context of the statute and the mischief against which the Act was aimed. The test which should be applied to determine whether there had been an 'accident' within the meaning of the word in the 1972 Act was: 'Would an ordinary man conclude on the facts of the particular case that there had been an accident?' Applying this test it was held that there was an accident where damage was caused to a police motor vehicle because of a deliberate act of mischief, as a result of which it had rolled away colliding with a telegraph pole and carrying on down an embankment. It was stated that the attempt to define the word in *R* v *Morris* above must be understood in relation to the particular facts of the case. The test of what an ordinary man would conclude was also applied in *Chief Constable of Staffordshire* v *Lees* [1981] RTR 506 where it was held that an accident had occurred where the defendant had deliberately driven through a locked gate.

No other vehicle need be involved, as in *R* v *Pico* [1971] Crim LR 500, where the defendant's car hit the kerb and a gatepost, injuring the defendant and damaging the gate. Similarly in *R* v *Harling* [1970] RTR 441, no other vehicle was apparently involved. Where an accident occurs it is not necessary for the defendant's vehicle to be physically involved in the accident; it is only necessary for there to be a direct causal connection between the presence of the defendant's vehicle on the road, and the accident occurring (*Quelch* v *Phipps* below). So that where a car left the road, and collided with a gate pillar on private land, the accident occurred 'owing to' the presence of that car on the road (*Redman* v *Taylor* [1975] Crim LR 348). *Redman* v *Taylor* was applied in *M (A Minor)* v *Oxford* [1981] RTR 246, where it was held that damage caused by a lorry running off a road and colliding with a wall of a house occurred due to an accident 'arising out of the presence of a motor vehicle on a road'.

The words 'owing to the presence of a motor vehicle on a road' were first considered in *Quelch* v *Phipps* [1955] 2 All ER 302 where it was held that there must be some causal connection between the vehicle and the occurrence of the accident. The presence of a vehicle must be a sine qua non and an indirect connection is insufficient (eg a pedestrian stepping back to avoid a car and injuring another pedestrian).

Questions will now arise as to how far the presence of a stationary vehicle can be said to cause an accident. Unlike the former s 8(2), s 7(2) entitles a constable to breath test a person 'in charge' at the time of the accident. It would seem clear that a stationary car in the carriageway of a non-residential road might well be the cause of an accident, particularly if at night or unlit, but it would appear doubtful if the car is in a layby, or if the car was collided with as a result of a collision between two other vehicles.

*B 'Reasonable cause to believe'*

The constable may require a breath test solely on the fact that he has reasonable cause to believe that the motorist was involved in the accident, even if hours before. It is immaterial that the constable has no reason to believe the motorist had consumed alcohol, or had driven carelessly or recklessly or had committed any traffic offence. (He cannot, however, be arrested unless he either gives a positive breath test or if he fails to give a breath test and the constable has reasonable cause to suspect he has alcohol in his body (see 4.42*F*).)

The criteria of a lawful breath test following an accident are:

(*a*) that there has been in fact an accident owing to the presence of a vehicle on a road (see 'Accident' above); and
(*b*) that the constable had reasonable cause to believe that the defendant was driving or attempting to drive the vehicle at the time of the accident.

Where there had been an accident, and the constable had reasonable cause to believe that the defendant drove the vehicle at the time of the accident, and the defendant in fact drove the vehicle away from the scene of the accident, the conviction under s 6(1) was upheld notwithstanding there was doubt if he in fact drove the vehicle at the time of the accident (*R* v *Wedlake* [1978] RTR 529). An offence under s 6(1)(*a*) or s 6(1)(*b*) requires the prosecution to prove that the defendant drove or attempted to drive or, in the case of s 6(1)(*b*), was in charge of a motor vehicle. There is no such requirement in respect of a charge under s 8(7) for refusing specimens of breath, blood or urine. A conviction was accordingly directed where a defendant had been arrested because the police believed he had been the driver and had refused at the police station to provide specimens for analysis even though it was subsequently shown he was not the driver (*Bunyard* v *Hayes* (1984) *The Times*, 3 November (see further 4.91). In *Baker* v *Oxford* [1980] RTR 315 two men ran away from an abandoned car involved in an accident. One of the two admitted that he was the owner. The justices' finding that the policeman had reasonable cause to believe the defendant was the driver was based on the fact that not only did he admit he was the owner but also that the police computer showed that he was the registered keeper of the vehicle.

The court emphasised in *Baker* v *Oxford* that the justices appreciated the difference between the words 'suspect' and 'believe'. The circumstances must be stronger before it can be held that a constable has reasonable cause to 'believe'. Reasonable cause for suspicion alone is insufficient. It was held in *Johnson* v *Whitehouse* [1984] RTR 38 that the greater force of the word 'believe' than 'suspect' was an essential part of the law and a breath test following an accident could only be lawfully required if the constable had reasonable grounds for believing that the person concerned was driving at the time of the accident. Where, however, a constable inaccurately uses in evidence the word 'suspect' this will not invalidate the requirement for a breath test if in fact the evidence is such that he clearly had reasonable cause to believe the defendant to have been driving (ibid).

The breath test following an accident is required in accordance with s 7(3) to be administered 'either at or nearby' where the requirement is made (see 'There or nearby', 4.42*H*) or, if the constable thinks fit, at a police station specified by the constable.

## 4.45 Preliminary breath testing devices

Police forces in England and Wales have continued to use all the existing breath test devices, the Alcotest 80 and 80A, the Alcolyser, the Alcolmeter and the Alert. As in the former law, a preliminary breath test has to be on a device approved by the Secretary of State (see definition of 'breath test' in s 12(2)). No approval orders have been made since the new law came into force. In *Bentley* v *Northumbria Chief Constable* [1984] RTR at pp 280–1 (a case under the former law) it was observed that judicial notice could be taken that the Alcolyser had been approved by the Home Secretary despite the fact that the relevant approval order (the Breath Test Device (Approval) (No 2) Order 1979) was not cited. *Bentley* followed *R* v *Jones (Reginald Williams)* [1970] RTR 35 where it was similarly held that judicial notice of the Home Secretary's approval of the Alcotest could be taken. Can judicial notice be taken that the same devices have been approved by the Home Secretary for use under the new law? It would seem possible that the various approval orders enure for the benefit of the new law under s 17(2)(*b*) of the Interpretation Act 1978. It may also be possible to argue that because the same devices have continued to be used, judicial notice of their approval can continue to be taken. In any event no statutory order is strictly necessary. The reason why approval orders were made was to enable the prosecution to avoid having to call an official to give evidence that the Home Secretary had approved the device, production of the order under s 2 of the Documentary Evidence Act 1868 affording prima facie evidence of the Home Secretary's approval (*Hayward* v *Eames*; *Kirkpatrick* v *Harrigan* [1985] RTR 12 citing *R* v *Clarke* [1969] 2 QB 91).

The importance of the proper administration of the breath test devices is diminished. It is, of course, no offence to give a positive breath test result and it has never been so. If, however, the breath test was improperly given then any resulting analysis under the former s 9 was also invalid as would be a prosecution under s 9(3). The only effect now of an invalid breath test under the new provisions is that a prosecution under s 7(4) may fail (see 4.4).

The law on the administration of the Alcotest device was reviewed by the

House of Lords in *DPP* v *Carey* [1969] 3 All ER 1662. The justices found that the defendant (contrary to the manufacturer's instructions) had consumed alcohol within twenty minutes of the test, that he had smoked shortly before and neither police officer had instructed him to fill the bag in not less than ten nor more than twenty seconds and the question that arose in the case was 'How far does non-compliance with the manufacturers' instructions invalidate a breath test?' The House of Lords held:

(1) That the manufacturers' instructions supplied with the Alcotest formed no part of the device as approved by the Home Secretary.
(2) That the only manufacturers' instructions which necessarily had to be complied with were those as to the assembly of the device.
(3) That provided there was a bona fide use of the device by the constable subsequent proof of failure to comply with the other instructions would not invalidate the breath test, and in particular:
    (*a*) As to the instructions relating to recent consumption of alcohol, ie twenty minutes should elapse between consumption of alcohol and the test: if the constable had no knowledge of or reasonable cause to suspect the consumption of alcohol within twenty minutes preceding the test (if he had he should wait) or recent smoking it was a valid test even if the motorist had consumed alcohol within twenty minutes of the test. Moreover a police officer had no duty to inquire when a motorist last consumed alcohol.
    (*b*) As to the instructions relating to inflating the bag in not less than ten seconds or more than twenty seconds: a direction to the motorist to take a deep breath and blow in the bag was adequate: the officers could see for themselves whether or not the bag had been inflated in ten or twenty seconds (and see *A-G's Reference (No 1 of 1978)* [1978] RTR 377 below).
(4) (Per Lord Diplock) the only relevance of non-compliance with any of the instructions for the use of the Alcotest (other than those relating to its assembly) was that it might be evidence from which the mala fides of the constable could be inferred.

It is not proposed to discuss further the numerous previous cases on the improper administration of the breath test devices, save to point out that in law a breath test incorrectly assembled or defective device is not in law a breath test. Therefore if a constable realises that the equipment is defective or he has assembled it incorrectly he may reassemble the device or require the test on another device (eg *Price* v *Davies* [1979] RTR 204). The second point is that a constable has a discretion to administer a second test even if he could have arrested the defendant as a result of the first test. The motorist may be confused or anxious, misunderstand the procedure or make a poor showing on the first occasion (*R* v *Broomhead* [1975] RTR 558; *Revel* v *Jorden* [1983] RTR 497; *Hills* v *Nicholson* [1983] LSG 157).

A third reason as to why the cases on the former provisions no longer may apply is that s 12(3) now provides that the motorist must supply a specimen for a breath test 'in such a way as to enable the objective of the test . . . to be carried out'. This latter provision is discussed in the next section where the manufacturer's instructions for the case of the breath test devices are also set out.

## 4.46 Failing to supply a specimen of breath: s 7(4)

It is an offence contrary to s 7(4) to fail without reasonable excuse to provide a specimen of breath when required to do so in accordance with s 7.

For an offence to be committed the defendant must have failed to provide a specimen of breath 'when required to do so in pursuance of this section'. It would therefore appear that the test must have been provided in accordance with varying circumstances set out in s 7(1)–(3) (see 4.42 and 4.44).

A person may also not be convicted of failing to supply a specimen of breath if the police officers were trespassers (see *Fox* v *Gwent Chief Constable* [1984] RTR 402, and see further 4.52 below).

The Alert and Alcolmeter require a breath specimen to be delivered in a manner or at a pressure for which the machine is programmed. The manufacturers' instructions for the Alcotest require the measuring bag to be inflated by one single breath in not less than ten and not more than twenty seconds. The Alcolyser similarly requires the motorist to take a deep breath and blow steadily until the bag is fully inflated. The former s 12(3) stated that references to providing a breath test are references to providing a breath specimen in sufficient quantity to enable the test to be carried out. It was therefore held that if a person did not fully inflate the Alcotest measuring bag, but notwithstanding that the crystals gave a positive result, he had not 'failed' to supply a specimen of breath (*Walker* v *Lovell* [1975] RTR 377; *R* v *Holah* [1973] RTR 74). Similarly if the motorist fills the bag in short puffs and the crystals nevertheless turn green he has not 'failed' to supply a specimen of breath. In the case of the Alcolmeter apparently it may be capable of giving a positive result even if the motorist does not blow long enough to illuminate light B. Where this happened and the officer did not press the Read button it was held in *Fawcett* v *Tebb* [1984] Crim LR 175, following the same point as in *Walker* v *Lovell* above, that it could not be said that the defendant failed to supply a specimen of breath, and that the case should therefore be dismissed.

These and other similar cases may no longer apply because the present s 12(3) of the Act provides, as amended by s 59 of the Transport Act 1982, that not only does the motorist have to provide sufficient breath but that it must also be 'provided in such a way to enable the objective of the test or analysis to be satisfactorily achieved'. The manufacturers of the devices have given instructions as to how the devices should be used. It would seem, therefore, that (to quote s 12(3) as amended) 'the objective of the test will not be satisfactorily achieved' if the operating instructions are not sufficiently observed. Thus, for example, while the Alcolmeter is capable of giving a positive result even if light B is not illuminated, the analysis cannot normally be satisfactorily achieved until light B is illuminated. The instructions for the devices are as follows:

## 4.47 The Alcolmeter

The Home Secretary approved the Alcolmeter device for the purpose of taking breath tests by the Breath Test Device (Approval) (No 2) Order 1979 (as to approval of breath devices, see 4.45). The operating instructions for the Alcolmeter are as follows:

*Points to remember*

Each breath test must be preceded by a satisfactory READY CHECK.

Twenty minutes should elapse between the consumption of alcohol and the use of this instrument.

Use a new mouthpiece for every test and ensure that the subject blows through the lipped-edge, wide bore end.

Don't allow the subject to hold the instrument.

Don't allow tobacco smoke to be blown through the mouthpiece.

Store the unit with the SET button locked in the down position.

Avoid storing the unit in extremes of temperature.

Don't subject the instrument to severe mechanical shock.

*Subject breath test—operation checklist*

*Ready Check.* Press 'READ' button and hold down for 10 seconds. Observe display. Only green 'BAT' and 'READY' lights should come on. If amber light comes on depress and lock 'SET' button, wait 2 minutes, repeat Ready Check.

*Set.* Depress and lock 'SET' button.

*Attach mouthpiece.* Attach sampling port to hole in the side of a new mouthpiece. Ensure firm connection.

*Take sample.* Explain the test procedure to the subject. Request subject to fill his lungs and blow one continuous breath through lipped-edge, wide bore end of mouthpiece. He must blow strongly enough to bring on light A and long enough to bring on light B. When light B illuminates, press READ button. Tell subject to stop blowing. If light B does not illuminate, the subject has not provided a satisfactory sample.

*Observe reading.* To obtain an indication of the subject's blood-alcohol concentration, hold down 'READ' button and observe display lights as they rise to a maximum reading after approximately 40 seconds. Interpret according to table below.

*Reset.* Note final maximum reading, depress and lock 'SET' button.

*Wait.* If any light other than the green 'READY' light was illuminated as a result of the test, it may take a few minutes before a satisfactory READY CHECK can be obtained before re-use of the instrument.

*Interpretation of display*

The highest level shown on the display indicates the blood-alcohol level of the subject to be as follows:

| | |
|---|---|
| RED | blood-alcohol above 80 mg per 100 ml—POSITIVE TEST |
| RED–AMBER | blood-alcohol between 70 and 80 mg per 100 ml—NEGATIVE TEST |
| AMBER | blood-alcohol between 5 and 70 mg per 100 ml—NEGATIVE TEST |
| GREEN | blood-alcohol less than 5 mg per 100 ml—NEGATIVE TEST |

## 4.48 The Alert

The Home Secretary approved the Alert device for the purpose of taking breath tests by the Breath Test Device (Approval) (No 1) Order 1980 (as to approval of breath devices, see 4.45).

The operating procedure is as follows:

(1) Switch unit on—Note: if 'ON' light is not continuously illuminated, batteries need recharging.

(2) Fit a new mouthpiece to the unit.

(3) After approx 2 minutes, 'READY' light comes on. Test should commence within 15 sec of 'READY' light appearing. If this is not possible, switch unit off and start procedure again.

(4) Tell subject to blow hard and continuously into mouthpiece until instructed to stop. 'TEST' light should appear. If unit returns to 'ON' state, subject is not giving a satisfactory sample.

(5) After blowing satisfactorily for 6 sec, 'TEST' and 'READY' lights go out. Tell subject to cease blowing.

(6) Test results are displayed immediately by 'PASS'—'WARN'—'FAIL' lamps.

In both the Alert and Alcolmeter the system of lights shows (*a*) whether it is working properly, (*b*) whether sufficient breath has been given for the purpose of analysis, and (*c*) whether the subject has failed the test.

## 4.49 The Alcotest and Alcolyser

In each box of the Alcotest device (which contains ten ampoules) there is an instruction leaflet. In addition to the leaflet the manufacturers print short instructions on the lid of the box. (As to approval of breath devices, see 4.45.)

The short instructions are as follows (the words in italic are as underlined in the instructions):

At least 20 minutes should elapse between the consumption of alcoholic drinks and using the ALCOTEST 80. Smoking during or immdiately prior to the test should not be permitted.

(1) Scratch both ends of the tube on the built in ampoule saw and break off tips in the snap hole.

(2) Insert the green end of the tube into the collar of the empty measuring bag and the white end into the mouthpiece. Confirm correct assembly by observing that the arrow points towards the bag.

(3) The measuring bag must be fully inflated by *one single breath in not less than 10 and not more than 20 seconds.*

(4) The test is positive if a green stain shows past the yellow ring.

The booklet states (inter alia):

(1) *General*

The ALCOTEST 80 objectively determines whether or not the blood alcohol concentration of a tested person appears to exceed a prescribed limit. Provided the test is correctly carried out the ALCOTEST 80 indicates the order of the alcohol concentration in the blood at the time of the test. If the ALCOTEST 80 gives a positive result, the taking of a subsequent blood sample for legal purposes is justified . . .

(3) *How to use the ALCOTEST 80*

. . . The subject being tested must blow through the mouthpiece and tube into the bag until the latter is fully inflated. This should be done with *one single breath in not less than 10 and not more than 20 seconds.*

(4) *Evaluation of the results*

. . . The result is therefore limited to the one observation, ie *does the green reaction stain pass the yellow ring or not?*

* * *

Special points to be observed when testing:

*It is essential that at least 20 minutes should elapse between the drinking of alcohol and using the ALCOTEST 80. This delay should also be observed if mouth sprays have been used or aromatic drinks consumed.*

Immediately after the consumption of an alcoholic drink the alcohol remaining in the mouth and in the saliva will cause a falsely high indication which bears no relation to the true blood alcohol level. After 20 minutes the distorting influence of the mouth alcohol disappears, and the blood alcohol content is thus accurately indicated by the expired air.

A high concentration of tobacco smoke tends to colour the reagent brown. Smoking during or immediately prior to the test should not therefore be permitted.

(5) *General Remarks*

Packets of ALCOTEST 80 should always be kept closed and protected from strong light, excessive heat, damp or cold. In these conditions their shelf life is at least three years.

Before use the colour of the indicator reagent should be checked. This should be a clear yellow colour; any green discolouration indicates a possible leak in the tube, and such a tube should not be used for testing purposes . . .

On the box cover is written:

To be stored below 30°C (86°F).

Please protect from light

The Alcolyser is very similar to the Alcotest and consists of a box containing ten glass ampoules and mouthpieces together with a measuring bag. The instructions for use are as follows:

Wait 20 minutes after alcoholic drink before testing.

(*a*) Cut and break off each end of the tube in the saw aperture provided. Remove mouthpiece cap.

(*b*) Push red band end of the tube into the neck of the plastic bag, and insert the arrow end of the tube firmly into the exposed mouthpiece.

(*c*) Take a deep breath and blow steadily until the bag is fully inflated (blowing time 10–20 seconds).

## 4.50 Refusal to supply a specimen of breath

By section 12(2) the word 'fail' includes 'refuse'. A person who without reasonable excuse refuses to supply a specimen of breath for a breath test is therefore guilty of an offence under s 7(4).

It was held in *R* v *Ferguson* [1970] 54 Cr App R 410 that once a person had been given the opportunity to do something and did not do it, there was a 'failure' to do it. Thus where a motorist refused to wait until the Alcotest arrived and suddenly pushed the constable in the chest and knocked him against the side of the car and said, 'I am not waiting,' it was held by the Divisional Court in *R* v *Wagner* [1970] Crim LR 535 that he had refused the test and the constable was thus justified in arresting him. It was also said in the case that a time-lag will often occur between the requirement to take the breath test and its administration. The Alcotest or other approved device (as in *R* v *Wagner*) may not be immediately to hand or it may be necessary to wait because of the fact that the constable had reason to believe that the defendant had consumed alcohol less than twenty minutes before. If a defendant shows by his actions, either by running away or otherwise, that he is refusing the test, he may be arrested. If the Alcotest is not available, the time which a motorist can be required to wait is what is reasonable in all the circumstances of the case (*Ely* v *Marle* [1977] RTR 412). If the motorist did not wait a reasonable time, his action in not waiting amounted to a 'failure' to take the test because 'failure' indicates refusal (applying *R* v *Wagner* above).

Similarly in *Horton* v *Twells* (1983) *The Times*, 9 December a conviction under the former provisions was directed where a motorist refused to wait another ten minutes. He had told the constable that he had last consumed alcohol ten minutes beforehand, and the constable had arrested him and he refused to wait, knowing that the Alcolmeter should not be operated within twenty minutes of the consumption of alcohol. Where police officers were faced with a person who refused to wait they should consider proceeding to arrest for failing to provide a specimen of breath (ibid).

### 4.51 Defence of reasonable excuse

Although a person may be said to have 'failed' to supply a specimen of breath in accordance with s 12(3) when he does not provide breath in the manner or at a pressure for which the machine is programmed, a person cannot be convicted of an offence under s 7(4) if he has a reasonable excuse for failing to do so.

Once the defence of reasonable excuse is advanced, it is for the prosecution to negative the defence (*Roland* v *Thorpe* [1970] 3 All ER 195 at p 197). It is a question of fact as to whether there is a 'reasonable excuse' and the court must be satisfied beyond reasonable doubt that the defendant had no reasonable excuse (*R* v *Harling* [1970] RTR 441) but whether facts are capable of amounting to a reasonable excuse is a matter of law.

It would seem to be a reasonable excuse if a motorist is bronchitic, asthmatic or has a medical or physical condition resulting in loss of lung capacity and for this reason is unable to blow the bag in one continuous breath, or sufficiently hard to operate the Alert or Alcolmeter. In *R* v *Lennard* [1973] RTR 252 it was held that a reasonable excuse *must arise out of a physical or mental inability to provide (a specimen) or a substantial risk in its provision.*

It is not, however, a reasonable excuse for a defendant to believe that he is not 'in charge' of the motor vehicle (*Williams* v *Osborne* [1975] RTR 181) nor that he thought he had not committed a moving traffic offence (*R* v *Downey* [1970] Crim LR 287) nor that he had not consumed any alcohol (*McNicol* v *Peters* 1969 SLT(J) 261) nor that she was not the driver at the time of the accident (*McGrath* v *Vipas* [1984] RTR 58). These and other cases on 'reasonable excuse' are further discussed in 4.91*C*.

### 4.52 Powers of entry

The importance of cases on the former law as to whether the police were or were not trespassers when requiring the roadside breath test is largely diminished so far as offences under ss 5, 6 and 8(7) are concerned. In *Fox* v *Gwent Chief Constable*, below and at 4.4, it was held that where the police were trespassers and administered a breath test the conviction of the defendant under s 7(4) of refusing the preliminary breath test should be set aside, but that the conviction under s 6 of the defendant who had supplied specimens of breath at the police station on the Lion Intoximeter should be upheld. It is only where the evidence of the Intoximeter is obtained by a trick, oppression or inducement that it is possible for the evidence of the printout to be excluded and, normally, the fact that the arrest is unlawful is insufficient (see further 4.4). It would seem, therefore, that in practice the police will normally be able to obtain a conviction under ss 5, 6 or 8(7) even if it is shown that the police were trespassers and had no power of entry or arrest in the case in question. The relevance of whether or not the police have or have not properly exercised their powers under s 5 or s 7 will usually be confined in practice to offences of refusing the initial screening breath test under s 7(4).

It would seem that a constable may administer a breath test off the road provided that he is not trespassing on the defendant's own property and where the defendant is himself a trespasser.

In *Trigg* v *Griffin* (1969) 113 SJ 962 the conviction of the defendant was quashed by the Divisional Court on the ground that, although the defendant was a person 'driving or attempting to drive', he was not 'on a road or public place' because he had driven from the road onto a private forecourt of lock-up garages, one of which was used by him. In *R* v *Jones* (*EJM*) [1970] 1 All ER 209 the Court of Appeal disapproved of *Trigg* v *Griffin*. A motorist cannot, said the Court of Appeal, stultify police action by turning a few feet off the highway. As long as the police have reasonable suspicion of the driver having consumed alcohol or having committed a moving traffic offence, the police may pursue the driver in order to make a breath test requirement. Following the line of decisions relating to arrest and 'fresh pursuit', the Court of Appeal in *R* v *Jones* ruled that a driver cannot escape the requirement by driving into private property.

The question was raised in *Morris* v *Beardmore* [1980] RTR 321 whether, if the arresting officer was a trespasser at the time of the breath test requirement, the trespass renders the arrest and subsequent analysis unlawful. The facts were that the officers wished to interview the defendant in connection with an accident. They were let into his house by his son. He then indicated via his son that he was unwilling to discuss the matter and that they were to leave. They went to his bedroom and asked for a specimen of breath. He protested that they were trespassers and refused, whereupon he was arrested under the former s 8(5). As the constable was a trespasser the House of Lords unanimously held that the defendant's detention or arrest following his refusal to give a breath test was unlawful. If Parliament had intended to authorise the tortious act of a police officer, it would have done so expressly. Following on the decision of *Morris* v *Beardmore* the further question was raised, as to the position where after having properly requested the breath test at the defendant's door, either under the former s 8(1) or the former s 8(2), the constable is then refused entry and in the two cases heard together before the House of Lords, *Clowser* v *Chaplin*; *Finnigan* v *Sandiford* [1981] RTR 317 it was unanimously held that the constables effecting the arrests being trespassers at the time had no authority to arrest them under the former s 8(5). While the police have no power to arrest if they are trespassers on the defendant's own property, once a defendant has been lawfully arrested the police are entitled to enter the defendant's property to recapture him. A defendant was initially arrested outside his front door where the police had an implied licence to be; on arrest, a struggle took place with the defendant pulling the constable into the house. It was held that the police had acted lawfully; once an arrest had taken place they were entitled to enter the house to recapture him even if asked to leave (*Hart* v *Chief Constable of Kent* [1983] Crim LR 117).

The arrest or requirement for a breath test is still lawful until the constable becomes a trespasser. Constables, like the general public, have an implied licence to enter on a person's property on lawful business, and go from a person's gate to his front or back door. Until the implied licence is rebutted (eg by a notice saying 'No admittance to police officers') or revoked, the policeman is not a trespasser (see *Robson* v *Hallett* [1967] 2 QB 939, in particular Diplock LJ at p 953 and Parker LJ at p 951). Thus in *Pamplin* v *Fraser* [1981] RTR 494, the defendant, who had driven off the road into an alleyway on his own land, wound up the windows of the car and locked himself inside, was held to be rightly convicted of failing to supply a specimen of breath and of wilfully obstructing a police constable in the execution of his duty, because the constable's implied licence to enter had not been withdrawn. Instances where the implied licence to enter has been withdrawn as a result of which the breath test requirement and arrest became invalid may be found in *Lambert* v *Roberts* [1981] RTR 113 and *R* v *Allen* [1981] RTR 410. In *Snook* v *Mannion* [1982] RTR 321 it was held that the implied licence for police officers to enter the defendant's land between his gate and his front or back door must be expressly revoked. The defendant had said 'fuck off' to the officers when they caught up with him in his driveway. The justices came to the conclusion that his vulgarity was insufficient to revoke the licence. Their decision was upheld: from the decision in *Gilham* v *Breidenbach* [1982] RTR 328 it was clear that it was for justices to decide whether 'fuck off' was to be taken as terminating a licence to enter or was mere vulgar abuse. In *Faulkner* v *Willets* [1982] RTR 159 it was held that an invitation to enter private premises could be implied by conduct and need not be orally made. The conviction of refusing to supply a specimen for a laboratory test was upheld. The police officer had gone to the defendant's front door and had explained his reasons to the defendant's wife, whereupon she had opened the door fully and walked back into the house giving the officer the impression it was an implied invitation to follow her. At no time was the officer asked to leave the house.

When considering the new drink/driving law contained in the new ss 6–12, the effect of *Morris* v *Beardmore* and *Clowser* was considered by Parliament and express power of entry, if need be by force, was given by s 5(6) (see 4.65 and 4.66) and by s 7(6) below. It may be possible to argue that, except in the circumstances set out in s 5(6) and s 7(6) (where Parliament has given constables express power to enter land), constables, once they are trespassers, have no power to enter land either to breath test the defendant or to arrest him under s 7. This view is clearly correct where an officer is a trespasser on the defendant's own property. In *Fox* v *Gwent Chief Constable* [1984] RTR 402 it was held that the police were not entitled to enter the defendant's house under s 7(6) where the police had no information (and thus had no reason to suspect) that the accident involving the defendant's vehicle had caused any injury to the defendant's passenger, and, therefore, the conviction under s 7(4) of the defendant who had refused a breath test was set aside. While it is clear that the defendant can escape from the requirement of a breath test or arrest once he reaches his own property (except in the circumstances in s 5(6) and s 7(6)) it is still not clear that he can do so by leaving the highway and going on to someone else's private property upon which he as well as the police are trespassers. It is submitted, indeed, that the decision of *R* v *Jones ante* may apply in such circumstances. In *Morris* v *Beardmore* itself, every single one of their lordships stressed that their decision was limited to the case where the police officer was a trespasser on the defendant's own property. It was said by Lord Roskill [1980] RTR at p 339 'It by no means follows that a motorist who is himself a trespasser can take advantage of that fact to defeat the intentions of a police officer intent upon performing the duties required of him by statute.' Lord Scarman at p 337 said 'The House is not declaring that every roadside hedge signals to the fugitive motorist the presence of sanctuary from the pursuing officers of the law.' Lord Diplock stated: (at p 328) 'Very different considerations may apply to cases of . . . "hedge hopping", ie where the driver tries to dodge the constable by getting off the road onto adjacent property on which he is also a trespasser.'

The powers of entry in respect of suspected offences in England and Wales under ss 6–12 of the Act are contained in s 7(6). Section 7(7) provides that s 7(6) does not apply in Scotland and nothing in that subsection affects any rule of law in Scotland concerning the right of entry of a constable in Scotland.

Section 7(6) enables a constable to enter, if need be by force, any place where a person is, or where the constable with reasonable cause suspects him to be, either for the purpose of obtaining a breath test or to arrest him, but only where there has been an accident involving injury.

An analysis of the subsection imposes the following limitations on the power to enter for a breath test:

(1) There must actually have been an accident; it is not enough for the constable to have reasonable cause to believe there was an accident.
(2) The constable must have reasonable cause to 'believe' (not 'suspect')

that the person was driving or attempting to drive or was in charge of the motor vehicle owing to the presence of which the accident occurred.

(3) The constable must have reasonable cause to 'suspect' (not 'believe') that the accident involved injury to another person (ie not the person himself) (see *Fox* v *Gwent Chief Constable* above).

(4) The place entered must be where the person is or where the constable with reasonable cause 'suspects' (not 'believes') him to be.

Section 7(6) also enables a constable to enter by force for the purpose of arrest under s 7(5), ie if a breath test has proved positive or he has failed to provide a breath test after having been required to do so (see 4.53).

The power to require a breath test under s 7(1) and s 7(2) is subject to special provisions if the defendant is a patient at a hospital. The power of arrest under s 7(5) cannot be exercised in respect of a hospital patient (see Hospital Patients, 4.96–101). For this reason there is no power of entry under s 7(6) in order to effect an arrest.

## 4.53–60 Powers of arrest

Unlike the former provisions an arrest is not a condition precedent to a conviction under s 6 or s 8(7).

The powers of arrest in respect of offences under ss 6–12 are continued in s 7(5). Although a constable may arrest under s 7(5) he is not compelled to do so; the power of arrest is at his discretion. Indeed, it is to be deprecated that in the Metropolitan area and, it is believed, in the great majority of police areas, the individual policeman is not encouraged to use his discretion not to arrest a motorist where there is no apparent need to do so.

Section 7(5)(*a*) entitles a constable to arrest if as a result of a screening breath test the constable has reasonable cause to suspect the proportion of alcohol in the motorist's breath or blood exceeds the prescribed limit. Section 7(5)(*b*) alternatively entitles a constable to arrest a motorist who has been required to provide a specimen of breath for a breath test and has failed to do so *and* the constable has reasonable cause to suspect he has alcohol in his body. It will have been noted that a constable does not have to suspect either alcohol or the commission of a traffic offence to require a breath test from a motorist believed to have been driving at the time of an accident; under s 7(5), therefore, he cannot be arrested unless he subsequently provides a positive breath test or if, despite refusal of the test, the constable has reasonable cause to suspect he has alcohol in his body. It will also be noted that both in s 7(5)(*a*) and s 7(5)(*b*) the constable does not have to have reasonable cause to *believe*, only reasonable cause to *suspect*.

The power of arrest under s 7(5) cannot be exercised where the person is at a hospital as a patient (see 4.96–101).

The fact that the arrest is unlawful will not normally preclude a conviction under ss 5, 6 or 8(7) (see 4.4).

The power of arrest under s 7 is specifically preserved under the Police and Criminal Evidence Act 1984 and will not be affected when the Act comes into force (Police and Criminal Evidence Act 1984, s 26(2) and Sched 2).

## Driving or in Charge whilst Unfit

### 4.61 Statutory amendments

Unlike the former excess alcohol provisions, offences under s 5 have not been replaced by entirely new statutory provisions. The Transport Act has merely amended s 5(3) and substituted new subss (5)–(7) in place of the former s 5(5). The amendment to s 5(3) brings the statutory defence to an offence of being in charge while unfit (s 5(2)) in line with the statutory defence to being in charge with excess blood/urine/breath alcohol levels (s 6(2)) (see 4.111). The new subss (5)–(7) widen the power of arrest for offences under the section (see 4.65) and give a new and extensive power of entry for the purpose (see 4.66).

The provisions of the former s 7 as to the taking of specimens for analysis purely for offences under s 5 for being unfit, which pre-dated the obtaining of blood or urine specimens under the Road Safety Act 1967, have not been continued in the new ss 6–12 substituted by the Transport Act 1981. The requirement to provide specimens of breath, blood or urine under the new s 8 can be made of persons suspected of offences under s 5 in the same way as persons suspected of excess alcohol offences under s 6 (see 4.72–7). Certificates of analysis will be admissible to prove impairment (see 4.63). For the first time special provision has been made to obtain specimens of blood or urine for analysis where the impairment is suspected to be due to drugs rather than alcohol (see 4.64).

Although the offences under ss 5 and 6 are quite distinct in practice, the two offences are closely inter-related because a person arrested under s 5 will usually have been required to provide specimens for analysis. For this reason it is usual for a person charged under s 5 to be additionally charged under s 6 if he provides a specimen over the prescribed limit or under s 8 if he refuses to do so. Similarly if originally arrested under s 6 he may be charged under s 5, if there is evidence of impairment either because of drugs or a combination of drugs and alcohol.

A certificate of analysis of blood or urine, or a statement and certificate of breath is admissible both in respect of a charge under s 5 and under s 6.

Offences under s 5(1) (driving or attempting to drive while unfit) and s 5(2) (in charge while unfit) must be proved to have occurred on a 'road or other public place' in respect of a 'motor vehicle' and while the defendant was 'driving or attempting to drive' or 'in charge'. The meaning of these basic terms is discussed in detail in 4.26–30.

### 4.62 The offence: s 5(1) and (2)

It is an offence under s 5(1) to drive or attempt to drive a motor vehicle on a road whilst unfit to drive through drink or drugs. It is an offence under s 5(2) similarly to be 'in charge' of a motor vehicle.

As already noted, the offences under s 5 have not been replaced by new statutory provisions. The Transport Act 1981 has, however, amended s 5(3) and has substituted new subss (5)–(7) in place of the former subs (5).

The meaning of the terms 'driving or attempting to drive', 'in charge', 'motor vehicle' and 'road or other public place' are the same as for the other drink/driving offences and are discussed in detail at 4.26–30. The terms 'unfit to drive', 'drink' and 'drugs' are discussed at 4.63–4.

**4.63 Evidence of impairment**

Under s 5(4) a person shall be taken to be 'unfit to drive' if his ability to drive properly is for the time being impaired. The law before 1962 required that he should be under the influence of drink or drugs to such an extent as to be incapable of having proper control of a motor vehicle, and this is still the standard in respect of cyclists charged under s 19. The fact that the defendant had driven for 200 yards in a proper way did not create a presumption of sobriety which medical evidence could not displace in a charge under the old law (*Murray* v *Muir* 1950 SLT 41). In *R* v *Hunt* [1980] RTR 29 a jury was held to be entitled to infer that the defendant's driving was impaired from the facts that (*a*) he collided with a stationary van which should have been plainly visible to him and (*b*) his blood-alcohol analysis was nearly two and a half times the prescribed limit.

Impairment of ability to drive properly can be proved by evidence that a car was being driven erratically or had an accident at a spot where there was no hazard for a normal driver, provided, of course, that there is also evidence of drink or drugs. It can be assumed from evidence of the defendant's condition, eg frequently falling asleep or inability to stand or mental confusion, provided, again, that there is some evidence that his condition was due to drink or drugs and not to illness. It will be noted that the test is ability to 'drive properly' and that the prosecutor need only prove that the defendant could not drive properly. Impairment can also be shown by evidence of the amount of alcohol taken by the defendant as revealed by a test of his blood or urine, if the analysis shows a high blood-alcohol content. It was held in *MacNeill* v *Fletcher* 1966 SC(J) 18 that even a high blood/alcohol level may still be disregarded by a jury or court in a charge under s 5. It is now, however, submitted that there is increasing evidence, and public awareness, of the fact that a high blood/alcohol level normally will result in substantial impairment of a person's ability to drive properly. Evidence of analysis, whether above or below the limit always has to be taken into account now (s 10(2)), though the lower the result the more it favours the defence. There are a number of cases where the High Court has held that an analysis, although inadmissible in respect of a charge under the former s 6(1) or the former s 6(2), is nevertheless admissible in a charge under s 5(1) or s 5(2).

The 1965 *Report of a Special Committee of the British Medical Association* (which preceded the enactment of the Road Safety Act 1967) recommended that conversion tables should no longer be used to estimate the minimum amount of alcohol which must have been taken by the suspect, because, as is stated in the summary of the Report:

> the relationship between the amount of alcohol taken and the blood-alcohol concentration varies greatly, both as between different individuals, and in the same individual at different times. It is not possible to give the courts more than a very rough figure and this must often be a gross underestimate. Impairment of driving

ability depends primarily upon the concentration of alcohol in the body and not on the amount of alcohol taken, and we recommend that attempts to translate the blood-alcohol concentration into the quantity of alcohol consumed should be limited to the purpose of confirming or rejecting a plea that the suspect has taken little or no alcohol before he was detained. For this purpose detailed conversion tables are not necessary. All that need be said is that a male weighing 11st with a blood alcohol concentration of 50 mg/100 ml cannot possibly have taken less than 1½ pints of ordinary beer or 3 single whiskies, and that he has almost certainly had very much more.

By virtue of s 10(1) and (2) a certificate of analysis obtained under s 8 of the new provisions will be admissible where the person faces a charge under s 5. Section 8 enables the police to require the provision of blood, breath or urine for analysis 'in the course of an investigation whether a person has committed an offence under s 5 or s 6' (s 8(1)). The only situation, it is submitted, where a certificate of analysis may be treated as inadmissible is where the specimen for analysis was obtained improperly (see 4.4).

Section 10(2) provides not only that it shall be assumed that the proportion of alcohol at the time of the offence shall not be less than in the specimen, but also that in proceedings both for s 6 and s 5 offences the certificate 'shall be taken into account'. Section 10(2) does provide an exception if the defendant can show that he consumed alcohol after the offence (see 4.106).

Under the former provisions a person arrested under s 5 could either be required under s 9 to provide a specimen of blood or urine, with failure to do so giving rise to an offence under s 9(3), or he could be asked to provide a specimen under the former s 7 and if he refused his refusal could be treated as supporting the prosecution's evidence of impairment unless reasonable cause for the refusal was shown. The former s 7 has not been replaced. It was chiefly used where the defendant gave a negative breath test at the police station or where the impairment was thought to be due to drugs. This new s 8 is discussed later (see 4.72–7). Special provision is made where impairment is thought to be due to drugs and is discussed in 4.64.

It should be noted that it is usual for the police to charge an offence under s 5 together with an offence under s 6 if a specimen of blood, breath or urine is subsequently provided and is above the prescribed limit or together with an offence under s 8 if a specimen is refused without reasonable excuse. A court will often consent to a withdrawal either of the s 6 charge or the s 5 charge if a plea of guilty is tendered to one of the charges under s 5 or s 6. Courts may occasionally be more reluctant to agree to the withdrawal of a s 8(7) charge on a plea of guilty to the s 5 charge on the ground that s 8(7) of necessity includes an element of obstruction of criminal justice.

A witness who is not an expert can give his general impression as to whether a person has taken drink and must decide the facts on which he founds that impression (*R* v *Davies* [1962] 3 All ER 97; *Sherrard* v *Jacob* [1965] NI 151). He may not, merely because he is an experienced driver, give his impression as to whether such a person was fit to drive (ibid). Where the court has disregarded opinions as to unfitness to drive given by laymen, a conviction may be upheld (*R* v *Neal* [1962] Crim LR 698). Where a driver, before consenting to examination by the police surgeon, has been told that the results of the examination will not be given in evidence, evidence of those results should not be admitted (*R* v *Payne* [1963] 1 All ER 848). Now a doctor will usually be called to examine a person arrested under s 5. Where a defendant was found by the doctor to be very much under the influence of drink half an hour after his arrest, it was held that the charge should not have been dismissed merely because the doctor's evidence did not relate to the time of the arrest (*Dryden* v *Johnson* [1961] Crim LR 551).

The fact that the defendant drove for 200 yards in a proper way did not create a presumption of sobriety which medical evidence could not displace (*Murray* v *Muir* 1940 SC(J) 127). The evidence of a doctor who, in a proper manner, persuaded the accused, after protests, to be examined is admissible. (*Aliter* where a doctor told the motorist that the results of his examination would not be given in evidence: *R* v *Payne* [1963] 1 All ER 848.) The evidence of a doctor, police surgeon or not, should be treated as that of a professional man giving independent expert evidence with no other desire than to assist the court unless the doctor himself shows that it ought not to be (*R* v *Nowell* [1948] 1 All ER 794; *R* v *Lanfear* [1968] 1 All ER 683). In Scotland and Ireland, however, the rule is that the accused's voluntary submission to test and questioning must be proved (*Reid* v *Nixon* 1948 SC(J) 68; *Gallacher* v *HM Advocate* 1963 SLT 217; *The State* (*Sullivan*) v *Robinson* (1954) 88 ILTR 169).

## 4.64 Drugs

It was held in *Armstrong* v *Clark* [1957] 1 All ER 433 that a drug means a medicament or medicine, something given to cure, alleviate or assist an ailing body. In that case it was held that a diabetic who took a wrong dose of insulin and thereby became incapable of proper control of a car could be charged with driving under the influence of a drug. In *Bradford* v *Wilson* [1984] RTR 116 it was held that *Armstrong* v *Clark* was not an authority for saying a substance could only be a drug if it was a medicine; without giving a comprehensive definition, a substance taken into the body which was not a drink and not taken as a food which affected the control of the human body was capable of being a drug (ibid). Accordingly the defendant, who had inhaled toluene when glue-sniffing, was properly convicted under s 5 (ibid).

These two cases were decided under the former drink/driving provisions. 'Drug' is now defined by s 12 as including 'any intoxicant other than alcohol'. It would therefore seem that toluene would similarly be held to be a drug. 'Intoxicant' in s 12 would seem to mean any substance that affects the self-control of the human body.

It should be noted that certain drugs not only affect the human body but also increase the effect of alcohol. The words 'through drink or drugs' in an earlier statute (a predecessor of the 1972 Act) were held to be merely adjectival and accordingly a conviction on a charge of driving while 'unfit through drink or drugs' was upheld (*Thomson* v *Knights* [1947] KB 336).

Where the police are 'in the course of an investigation whether a person has committed an offence under s 5 or s 6' the police may require the person concerned to supply samples of blood, breath or urine for analysis (s 8(1): see, further, 4.72–7). The former statutory provisions and s 9 in particular were framed only to detect excess levels of alcohol. Special provision has accordingly been made in s 8 where impairment because of drugs is suspected.

The intention of the statutory provisions is to enable the police to obtain the provision of the appropriate type of specimen. Some drugs may be more easily detected in urine, others in blood. Neither the Lion Intoximeter nor the Camic Breath Analyser analyse the breath for anything other than alcohol levels and if the defendant is at a police station a requirement for a specimen of blood or urine cannot be made unless s 8(3)(*a*), (*b*) or (*c*) applies.

Section 8 (3)(*c*) accordingly provides that where the suspected offence is one under s 5 and the constable making the requirement has been advised by a medical practitioner that the person's condition might be due to some drug, the constable may require the provision of blood or urine. The constable may require such a specimen even though the person has already provided or been required to provide breath specimens (s 8(3)). Although advice from a medical practitioner is a condition precedent, it would seem that there is nothing in the statutory provisions to prevent a station officer who obtains a negative breath analysis from a motorist from obtaining the advice of a police surgeon if the officer then suspects drugs for the first time. If the doctor then advises the station officer to require the provision of specimens of blood or urine the officer is then legally entitled to do so. (Normally, though, the police will obtain a medical examination of the motorist where an offence under s 5 is suspected and the doctor would presumably at that stage advise the police officer that the motorist may be under the influence of drugs rather than alcohol and advise a requirement of blood or urine depending on the type of drug suspected.)

Under s 8(4) the police officer requiring a specimen of blood or urine normally decides for himself whether the specimen should be of blood or urine. If, however, he has been advised by the doctor that for medical reasons blood cannot or should not be provided, the police officer is required to ask the motorist to provide a specimen of urine (s 8(4)). Curiously, the Act does not provide the converse; the police can require urine even if the doctor advises that urine cannot or should not be provided. As will be seen from 4.77, however, the police pro forma which is used by most police forces envisages that the station officer will normally require blood under s 8(4) even though the Act gives the police officer requiring specimens of blood or urine under s 8(4) an otherwise complete discretion as to whether it should be blood or urine. (The reason for the pro forma advising the taking of blood specimens may be that it is not uncommon for a defendant who has been required to provide specimens of urine to be unable to provide the second specimen within an hour of the original requirement. If this occurs, a prosecution under s 8(7) will fail unless the police can prove that the defendant had no reasonable excuse for failing to give the second specimen.)

While a certificate of analysis relating to a drug shall be taken into account under s 10, there is no statutory assumption in the section that the proportion of a drug in the specimen is not less than at the time an offence is committed. It therefore appears necessary for the prosecution to relate the amount of drug shown in the certificate to the amount of drug that would have been shown if the specimen had been provided at the time of the offence. It will also be open to the defence to attack the certificate on the ground that the defendant ingested the drug after the arrest but before he provided the blood or urine sample.

## 4.65 Power of arrest

The legality or otherwise of an arrest is no longer an integral part of the proof of an offence. The requirement to provide specimens for analysis no longer depends on whether the person has been arrested nor upon whether he has been lawfully arrested (see 4.4). Moreover the power of arrest under s 5 (in contrast to the former s 6) has long been held not to require the constable's suspicion to arise while he was still driving or attempting to drive (*R* v *Roff* below, *Norman* v *Magill* [1972] RTR 81).

Nevertheless the power of arrest for an offence under the new s 5(5) is considerably wider than under the former subsection.

The new subs (5) enables a constable to arrest a person without warrant if he has reasonable cause to suspect that that person is or has been committing an offence under this section.

The former subsection enabled a constable to arrest a person who 'is committing' an offence. This was held to mean *apparently* committing. A subsequent acquittal did not render an arrest unlawful for a person apparently committing an offence even if he was subsequently acquitted (*Wiltshire* v *Barrett* [1966] 1 QB 312). The new subsection gives the constable power to arrest a person whom 'he has reasonable cause to suspect' of an offence. Parliament has not required the circumstances to be such as to justify *belief* on the part of the constable; reasonable cause for suspicion suffices (contrast s 7(2); see 4.44B). In *R* v *Roff* [1976] RTR 7 and in *R* v *Estop* [1976] RTR 493 it was held that the arrest must be contemporaneous with the offence, ie the power of arrest must be exercised whilst the offence is being committed, or very shortly afterwards. These decisions no longer seem to apply. The former subsection gave a power of arrest only to a person who 'is committing' an offence. The new subsection enables a constable to arrest a person whom he has reasonable cause to suspect is, or *has been*, committing an offence.

It should finally be noted that the power of arrest applies to 'an offence under this section'. The power therefore includes not only an offence of driving or attempting to drive under s 5(1) but also an offence under s 5(2) of only being 'in charge' of a motor vehicle.

The power of arrest for s 6 offences is discussed at 4.53.

The power of arrest under s 5 will not be repealed by the Police and Criminal Evidence Act 1984 and will not be affected when the Act is brought into force (Police and Criminal Evidence Act 1984, s 26(2) and Sched 2).

## 4.66–70 Powers of entry

In *Clowser* v *Chaplin* [1981] RTR 317 it was held by the House of Lords that a power of arrest given by statute does not give the constable power to enter on private premises to effect the arrest, unless the statute specifically gives such a power to the constable. There was therefore no power to enter premises to arrest under the former s 8(5). The new s 5(6) accordingly confers on a constable the power to enter (if need be by force) any place where that person is, or where the constable with reasonable cause suspects him to be, for the purpose of arresting a person under s 5(5). It may be noted that this power is draconian and wide: reasonable cause to *suspect* is sufficient. The power of entry conferred by s 5(6) is in material respects identical to the power of entry contained in s 2(6) of the Criminal Law Act 1967 in respect of 'arrestable offences' (offences, or attempts to commit such offences, which are punishable with five or more years of imprisonment). It may also be noted that s 3 of the Criminal Law Act 1967 enables the constable to use such force as is reasonable in the circumstances in effecting or assisting the lawful arrest of offenders. In *Swales* v *Cox* [1981] QB 849 it was held that the constable will have to prove that force was necessary before he can justify an entry in which he used force.

Powers of entry for s 6 offences are discussed at 4.52.

## Driving or in Charge above the Limit

### 4.71 The offence: s 6(1)(*a*) and (*b*)

Under s 6(1)(*a*) it is an offence if a person drives or attempts to drive a motor vehicle on a road or other public place after consuming so much alcohol that the proportion of it in his breath, blood or urine exceeds the prescribed limit.

The new offence, as with the former s 6(1), requires the offender to be 'driving or attempting to drive' a 'motor vehicle' on a 'road or other public place' and the courts will doubtless interpret these terms in the same way as under the former law. These are all discussed in detail in 4.26–4.30.

As indicated in the Introduction, unlike the position under the former s 6(1), strict compliance with the statutory procedure may not have to be proved (see 4.4).

The circumstances under which a person who is 'driving or attempting to drive' a motor vehicle may be required to provide a preliminary breath test are discussed at 4.41–4 and the circumstances under which he may subsequently be required to provide a specimen of breath, blood or urine for analysis are discussed below.

The 'prescribed limit' is defined by s 12(2) as 35 μg of alcohol in 100 ml of breath, 80 mg of alcohol in 100 ml of blood or 107 mg of alcohol in 100 ml of urine, or such other proportion as may be prescribed by regulations made by the Secretary of State. See further 4.75.

Analysis of blood or urine specimens will continue to be required to be made by an 'authorised analyst' and that definition is discussed in detail in 4.80.

The defendant may challenge the analysis if he proves that he consumed alcohol after the commission of the offence, but before the analysis (see 4.106).

Under s 6(1)(*b*) it is an offence if a person is in charge of a motor vehicle on a road or other public place after consuming so much alcohol that the proportion of it in his breath, blood or urine exceeds the prescribed limit.

As in the former s 6(2) the offence requires the offender to be 'in charge' of a 'motor vehicle' on a 'road or other public place' and the existing case law on these phrases will therefore be relevant. These are discussed in 4.26–4.30. The statutory defence to a charge under s 6(1)(*b*) is discussed at 4.111 along with the similar defence to a charge under s 5(2).

The provision of specimens at a police station (as to the provision of specimens at a hospital, see 4.96–101) under s 8 differs radically from the former s 9 in a number of respects. The main differences are as follows:

(1) On his arrival at the police station following a roadside breath test, the motorist need no longer be offered another screening breath test.

(2) A person may be required under s 8 to provide a specimen if the police are 'in course of an investigation whether a person has committed an offence under s 5 or s 6' (s 8(1)).

A conviction for a drink/driving offence based on an analysis or a conviction for refusing a specimen for analysis will therefore no longer depend on a lawful arrest following a lawfully required breath test (see 4.4). The defendant does not have to be arrested.

(3) The motorist will usually be asked only for one type of specimen for analysis ie breath, blood or urine. The motorist will not have a choice of the type of specimen; it will be decided by the station officer.

(4) Unless one of three statutory sets of circumstances (s 8(3)(*a*), s 8(3)(*b*) and s 8(3)(*c*)) exist, the police officer has no choice but to ask the motorist to provide specimens of breath for analysis on an approved evidential breath test machine which provides an instant printout which will be evidentially admissible.

(5) If the alcohol/breath level is 50 μg or below, the motorist can ask for his blood or urine to be analysed instead. If he provides a specimen for analysis the breath specimens are no longer used. (Where the level is above 50 μg, see Appendix 1, 'Blood or urine option experiment'.) The motorist will not have a choice as to whether he will provide blood or urine. This will be decided by the police officer.

It should be noted that when the Police and Criminal Evidence Act 1984 is brought into effect the provisions in the Act controlling, defining and restricting police powers in respect of persons detained at police stations do not affect the exercise of s 8 of the Road Traffic Act 1972 (Police and Criminal Evidence Act 1984, s 36(6)(*d*)).

## 4.72 Provision of breath specimens

The phrase 'the constable making the requirement' occurs in a number of places in s 8. Only selected police officers have been trained to operate the evidential breath testing machines, and the Lion Intoximeter cannot be operated until the officer keys his operator's number into the machine. There appears to be nothing in the phrase, however, to limit the making of a requirement to a constable who has been trained to operate the machine. It would seem to bear its ordinary meaning, namely the constable, whoever he may be, who makes a requirement under s 8. The only statutory requirement is that it must be a constable. This would seem to include any police constable of any rank including a special constable. There is no requirement for the constable to be in uniform. In practice the constable who usually makes the requirement is the station officer.

A motorist may only be required to provide *breath* specimens for analysis at a police station (s 8(2)). The police are compelled to ask for breath rather than blood or urine specimens at a police station, unless one of the three situations below exists (s 8(3)):

(*a*) the constable making the requirement has reasonable cause to *believe* that for medical reasons a specimen of breath cannot be provided or should not be required;
(*b*) at the time the requirement is made a device or reliable device of the type mentioned [the Lion Intoximeter or Camic Breath Analyser] is not available at the police station or it is for any other reason not practicable to use [the machine] there;
(*c*) the suspected offence is one under section 5 of this Act and the constable making the requirement has been advised by a medical practitioner that the condition of the person required to provide the specimen might be due to some drug.

It should be noted that the proviso at the end of s 8(3) 'but may then be made notwithstanding that the person required to provide the specimen has already provided or been required to provide two specimens of breath' applies not only to s 8(3)(*a*) but to s 8(3)(*a*) and (*b*). The statutory text is defective in this respect in some text books.

Under s 8(6), if the lower of the two breath specimens is no more than 50 $\mu$g the motorist may claim that it should be replaced by a specimen under s 8(4), ie a specimen of blood or urine: see (*d*) below. Where the specimen is above 50 $\mu$g a motorist may also from 16 April 1984 check the breath print-out by providing a specimen of blood or urine: see Appendix 1, 'Blood or urine option experiment'.

*Reasonable cause to believe that a specimen cannot be provided (s 8(3)(a))*

It will be seen from the wording of para (*a*) that although no doubt the constable will accept any medical advice obtainable, there is nothing to prevent the constable believing the motorist's statement that he is chronically short of breath or is bronchitic or asthmatic or for any other reason has not the necessary lung capacity to give two specimens of breath. Both machines, the Lion Intoximeter and the Camic Breath Analyser, require the subject to blow at a required pressure for the required length of time. If the motorist fails to blow at the pressure and for the length of time required the cycle of the machine will halt. At this stage the constable is in practice presented with a choice of action. He can immediately charge the motorist under s 8(7) with failing to provide specimens for analysis. On the other hand if he has reasonable cause to believe that for medical reasons the person was unable to provide specimens of breath on the machine, he can proceed to require a specimen of blood or urine under s 8(4). (It should be noted that the constable only has to have reasonable cause to believe that medical reasons exist. He does not have to obtain medical advice. If Parliament had intended for a constable to act under s 8(3)(*a*) and proceed under s 8(4) to require blood or urine only after obtaining medical advice, Parliament would no doubt have done so as in s 8(3)(*c*) below.) Where, however, the officer is in some doubt he will be wise to obtain medical advice; see *Horrocks* v *Binns* below.

It should be particularly noted that s 8(3)(*a*) requires the constable to have reasonable cause to *believe* that medical reasons exist that specimens of breath cannot or should not be provided. Belief imports a higher degree of certainty than mere suspicion, and the phrase 'reasonable cause to believe' has been contrasted with the phrase 'reasonable cause to suspect'. These phrases and the contrast between them as used in the former s 8(1) and s 8(2) (now repeated in s 7(1) and s 7(2)) have been the subject of judicial discussion (*Johnson* v *Whitehouse* [1984] RTR 38, *Baker* v *Oxford* [1980] RTR 315). Where a constable suspected that the defendant might be telling the truth when he said that he had a medical condition preventing his giving breath specimens, but believed that it was really a delaying tactic on the part of the defendant, a metropolitan stipendiary magistrate held that the constable was not entitled to require a blood specimen as he had no reasonable cause to 'believe' in accordance with s 8(3)(*a*). In *Horrocks* v *Binns* (unreported, the Divisional Court, 26 July 1984) it was similarly held that the station officer was not entitled to require a blood specimen where he did not believe the motorist's injury affected his ability to give breath specimens, but was prepared to give the motorist the benefit of the doubt since he felt that the motorist was the best judge of his own injuries. In *Horrocks* it was stated that if a station officer is genuinely in some doubt as to whether or not a driver can blow into the machine he can take the opinion of a doctor. It should be borne in mind that if the station officer is over hasty in charging a defendant under s 8(7) for failing to give specimens of breath, the prosecution will not succeed if it subsequently transpires that the defendant might for medical reasons have been unable to give specimens of breath at the pressure and the length of time required by the machine. It is for the prosecution to prove that a defendant charged under s 8(7) has no reasonable excuse to provide specimens for analysis; the onus is not upon the defendant to show that he has (see 'Reasonable excuse', 4.91*C*).

*Reliable device not available for use (s 8(3)(b))*

If the calibration check of the machine is not within the permissible limits or if the machine does not satisfactorily purge itself, it would seem that a 'reliable device' is not available. If this is the case, or if for any other reason it is not practicable to use the machine, the police constable may proceed to require a specimen of blood or urine under s 8(4). The police, however, are not bound to proceed to require specimens of blood or urine under s 8(4), and there seems nothing to prevent the police taking the motorist to another police station where another machine is available, and to require the motorist to provide specimens of breath there. (Thus if Limehouse Police Station has so many motorists brought in after positive breath tests on a Saturday night after closing time that it would take most of the rest of the night for the motorists to be tested, the police could take some of them to Leman Street or Bow Road Police Stations.)

Section 8(3)(*b*) entitles a station officer to require a specimen of blood or urine if at the time the requirement is made a device or a reliable device is not available or for any other reason it is not practicable to use such a device. It was held in *Cotter* v *Kamil* [1984] RTR 371 that the words 'at the time the requirement was made' refer to the time at which the subsequent requirement to provide blood or urine is made. It was therefore held that where the defendant had provided two specimens of breath on the Lion Intoximeter but before completion of its operation it reached a temperature at which analysis by the machine became unsatisfactory, the station officer in accordance with s 8(3)(*b*) was entitled to require a specimen of blood. In *Morgan* v *Lee* (1985) *The Times*, 17 April it was held that the failure of an Intoximeter to expel the printout did not entitle the officer to demand a specimen of blood under s 8(3)(*b*), as he could have read the analysis of breath and the calibration checks on the display panel and given evidence of what he saw.

Whether a person can blow into the machine is a question of objective fact, and if the machine is in working order it follows that it is practicable to use it (*Horrocks* v *Binns*, above). In *Slender* v *Boothby* (1984) *The Times*, 4 December it was held that 'reliable' in the phrase in s 8(3)(*b*) 'a reliable device . . . is not available' meant 'reliable' for the purposes of the Act. Parliament contemplated that the device should have the capacity to produce the correct date and time. Accordingly it was held that a 'reliable' device was not available on 29 February 1984 when the machine, because it had not been programmed to cope with a leap year, incorrectly showed the date as 1 March 1984. The station officer was held to be entitled to require the provision of a specimen of blood.

Other instances where the device is not reliable are where the calibration checks are outside the limits (see 4.76) or where the purge results are other than zero (for sample printouts, see Appendix 1).

*Condition of person giving specimen may be due to drugs (s 8(3)(c))*

Because this paragraph relates to an offence under s 5 (driving etc while unfit through drink or drugs) the paragraph is discussed in 4.64.

A person who is required to give breath is required to give two breath specimens (s 8(1)(*a*)). By virtue of s 8(6), of any two specimens of breath, that with the lower proportion is to be used and the other shall be disregarded. The breath specimens must be provided 'by means of a device of a type approved by the Secretary of State'. The two devices which have been approved are the Lion Intoximeter 3000 and the Camic Breath Analyser (see further 4.76).

## 4.73 Defendant's option to provide blood or urine specimens

If the lower of the two breath specimens is no more than 50 μg the person may claim under s 8(6) that it should be replaced by such a specimen as may be required under s 8(4). (Section 8(4) enables a constable to require a specimen of blood or specimens of urine. The defendant cannot choose whether it will be blood or urine, the choice is that of the constable alone; see further 4.77.)

Section 8(6) refers to 'no more than 50 microgrammes'. Neither the Lion Intoximeter and Camic Analyser give readings of breath in fractions of a microgramme; the readings are in whole numbers. As a result it would appear that a defendant is entitled to opt to give blood or urine instead where the lower of the two breath readings is 50 $\mu$g.

It was conceded in *Reeves* v *Enstone* (1985) *The Times*, 15 February that the Intoximeter could be inaccurate by two or three microgrammes either way. For this reason the motorist sought to argue that as his lower reading was 51 he was entitled to exercise the option under s 18(6). It was held that s 8(6) clearly contemplated the actual reading of the device to be the determining factor and that if the reading exceeded 50 the right to exercise the option did not arise.

If the defendant provides a specimen of blood or specimens of urine then s 8(6) provides that 'neither specimen of breath shall be used'. This seems to mean neither specimen of breath shall be used in evidence. For this reason a metropolitan stipendiary magistrate refused to accept a plea of guilty from a defendant who had provided two specimens of breath below 50 $\mu$g but above 35 $\mu$g whose sample of blood given after exercising his statutory option was on analysis stated to be 'not less than 80 milligrammes'. The proceedings were subsequently withdrawn on the advice of the Metropolitan Police Solicitor.

The statute does not expressly place an obligation on the police to inform the motorist of his statutory option, although all police pro formas remind the station officer to inform the motorist of his statutory option. In *Anderton* v *Lythgoe* [1985] Crim LR 158 it was held by the Divisional Court that a driver is entitled to be told of his statutory option under s 8(6) where his lower breath specimen was no more than 50 $\mu$g, and where the police had failed to advise a motorist of this right the justices had a discretion to exclude the evidence of the Intoximeter printout and dismiss the case.

If the defendant, after opting, fails to provide a specimen of blood or urine under s 8(4) he does not commit any offence, but if for whatever reason the defendant fails or refuses to provide the blood or urine, the breath specimen may still be used in evidence against him in respect of an offence under s 6 or s 5.

The Secretary of State can by regulation substitute another proportion of breath/alcohol in place of the 50 $\mu$g level (s 8(9)).

### 4.74 Blood or urine option experiment (16 April 1984)

On 26 March 1984 the Home Secretary announced that, from 16 April to 15 October 1984, motorists whose lower breath-alcohol readings exceed 50 $\mu$g on the Lion Intoximeter or Camic Analyser may choose to provide a sample of blood or urine. The sample will be analysed and the motorist may use it to challenge the accuracy of the breath test machine. The scheme is experimental and is not based on statute: the police will continue to rely on the printout to prove their case; and the defendant will merely be provided with an official analysis of the sample of blood or urine provided by him to use it to dispute the accuracy of the breath printout.

The circular makes it clear that the defendant will not have an option to provide blood or urine; the option is merely to provide a sample of blood or urine, and (as in the case of the statutory option where the reading is 50 μg or less), the police will decide whether he is to provide blood or urine.

If, because of the lapse of time between the time the motorist provides the breath specimen and the time he provides the sample of blood or a second specimen of urine, the subsequent official analysis is below the prescribed limit, the police will not prosecute. If, however, the certificate of analysis is above the prescribed limit, the defendant can attempt to challenge the accuracy of the Lion Intoximeter or Camic Analyser printout by production of the certificate.

On 26 September 1984 the Home Secretary announced a continuation of the blood or urine informal option beyond 15 October until the results of the monitoring of breath tests, where the option had been exercised during the six month period, had been published: this was likely to be in early 1985. The only change is that the results of the cases where the option is exercised will not be monitored after 15 October.

For further detail see Appendix 1, 'Blood or urine option experiment', which sets out the original Home Office Circular after editorial comment.

## 4.75 Alcohol levels

Section 12(2) lays down the following as the prescribed limits:

(*a*) 35 microgrammes of alcohol in 100 millilitres of breath; or
(*b*) 80 milligrammes of alcohol in 100 millilitres of blood; or
(*c*) 107 milligrammes of alcohol in 100 millilitres of urine.

(To convert μg alcohol per 100 ml of breath to equivalent of mg of alcohol per 100 ml of blood, multiply the breath/alcohol figure by 2.3 and round up or down to the nearest whole number; to convert to urine multiply by 3.06.) A conversion chart is set out in Appendix 1, 'Alcohol concentration'. The Secretary of State may by regulation alter the prescribed levels (s 12(2)).

The police are entitled therefore to proceed against a person under s 6 where the level is 36 μg in breath, 81 mg in blood and 108 mg in urine (s 6 states that the prescribed levels must be exceeded), and it was held in *Delaroy-Hall* v *Tadman* [1969] 2 QB 208 that it was not a special reason for not disqualifying the fact that the defendant's blood alcohol was 'not less than 81 mg'. In practice, however, a motorist whose breath reading is 39 μg or less will not be charged under s 6. Chief Constables are independent of the Home Office, but usually are careful to follow the advice given by the Home Office and in Home Office Circular 46/1983 it is stated:

> To cater for those occasions where the machine may be reading high, albeit within this range [ie 32–38 μg inclusive] the police will not proceed against the offender with a result less than 40 μg. This will ensure that the offender prosecuted will have a result in excess of the prescribed limit. This allowance is comparable with the allowance currently subtracted from specimens analysed in the laboratory.

(The allowance currently subtracted from specimens of blood analysed in the laboratory is 6 mg from all averages of 100 mg or less and 6 per cent from all averages exceeding 100 mg.)

Note that the Act requires the defendant's blood, breath or urine/alcohol level to 'exceed' the prescribed level. A metropolitan stipendiary magistrate refused to accept a plea of guilty where the defendant's blood had been analysed at 'not less than 80 milligrammes'. The Metropolitan Police Solicitor subsequently withdrew the proceedings.

*Back calculation*

Section 10(2) states that it shall be assumed that the proportion of alcohol in the accused's breath, blood or urine was 'not less' than in the specimen. This wording prevents a defendant challenging the analysis as being too high on the ground that because he had only recently imbibed alcohol, his breath, blood or urine/alcohol level had risen since the time he was stopped by the police.

On the other hand, the definition would seem to allow the police to call evidence that at the time of the commission of the offence, the defendant's alcohol level was higher than shown in the analysis or printout. This is most likely to occur where there has been a considerable lapse of time between the time of the offence and the time of the defendant's apprehension and subsequent provision of specimens for analysis. Depending on the rate of ingestion, the alcohol level will continue to rise for a short while after consumption but will thereafter decline. The rate of decline and the consequential back calculation depends on a great number of factors, all of which may have a major effect on the calculation; the factors include the individual's personal physiology, the time of day or night at which the alcohol was consumed, the rate at which it was consumed, whether the alcohol was on an empty stomach, or taken with a meal, and the amount and type of alcohol. The prosecution would additionally have to prove that the defendant had not consumed alcohol after the offence had occurred and before the provision of the specimen.

As regards such 'back calculation' the 1965 *Report of a Special Committee of the British Medical Association* noted:

> It is inevitable that some delay will occur between the time when the alleged offence was committed and the time when a sample is obtained for analysis. It takes between 15 and 90 minutes for the peak concentration in blood to be reached following a drink of alcohol, and in most cases little more than 30 minutes. If, as must generally be the case, the motorist is detained by the police after the peak concentration has been reached, the delay in obtaining a sample will be in his favour, as the sample will yield a lower concentration than when the offence was alleged to have been committed. In this connection we advise strongly against the court permitting any 'back calculation' to determine how much higher the blood alcohol concentration must have been at the material time. In fact the rate of elimination of alcohol, both between different individuals and in the same individual at different times, varies to some extent and an exercise of this kind cannot, in our opinion, be justified, although we are aware that it is the accepted practice in some other countries. Conversely, if the suspect is known to have taken alcohol just prior to being detained the possibility must be borne in mind that the blood alcohol concentration was still rising at the time the sample was taken.

The mean elimination rate in respect of blood-alcohol appears to be 11–21 mg per hour, but Dubowski ('Unsettled Issues and Practices in Chemical Testing for Alcohol' in *Alcohol and Road Traffic*, London, British Medical Association, 1963) states:

> Numerous recent studies confirm the extreme variability of the blood clearance rate . . . with most investigations disclosing significant numbers of individual clearance rates which exceeded or trailed the average by factors of 2–4, and some extremes differing by factors of 8.

## 4.76 Evidential breath test devices

Section 8(1)(*a*) requires a defendant to provide two specimens of breath on the approved device and s 8(6) provides that of any two such specimens that with the lower proportion of alcohol shall be used and the other disregarded. In *Howard* v *Hallett* [1984] Crim LR 565 the operator neglected to ask the motorist for a second specimen. On realising his mistake he restarted the machine and obtained two further specimens. The prosecution relied on the second printout of the two later specimens and on cross-examination it was admitted that the first breath specimen was lower than the second or third specimens. The Divisional Court held that on a proper construction of s 10(2) only evidence of the proportion of alcohol in a person's breath, blood or urine which had been obtained in accordance with the statutory procedure in s 8 was to be taken into account and accordingly directed the defendant's acquittal. In *Duddy* v *Gallagher* (1984) *The Times*, 5 December the defendant had provided one specimen of breath but had failed without reasonable excuse to provide the second specimen which he had been required to give. He was convicted both under s 8(7) of failing without reasonable excuse to provide two specimens of breath and also under s 6(1) on the evidence of the single specimen of breath which he had provided and which was above the prescribed limit. The convictions for both offences were upheld by the Divisional Court, there being nothing in the Act to prevent the justices properly convicting the defendant of both offences once evidence of the single specimen was properly adduced. It was further held that *Howard* v *Hallett* above was not authority for the proposition that evidence of a single specimen was inadmissible, but that the specimen had to be taken in accordance with the statutory procedure under the Act. The report of *Duddy* v *Gallagher* does not disclose whether s 8(6) was considered by the court. This states that the lower specimen shall be used and the other shall be disregarded. 'Specimen' in s 10(2) would therefore refer to the lower of two specimens of breath. How can one know which is the lower specimen of breath if only one specimen has been provided? It is no doubt for this reason that s 8 requires two specimens of breath to be provided and for it to be an offence if the motorist fails to do so.

Section 8(1)(*a*) requires the type of device to be approved by the Secretary of State. In order to avoid the police having to call evidence from someone on behalf of the Home Secretary the Lion Intoximeter and Camic Breath Analyser have been approved by the Home Secretary by the Breath Analysis Devices (Approval) Order 1983 made on 18 April 1983.

In *Hayward* v *Eames*; *Kirkpatrick* v *Harrigan* [1985] RTR 12 it was held that the terms of s 8(1) plainly implied that the Home Secretary had both the power and the duty to approve such type of device as he thought fit and the fact that his approval was given two weeks before the Act came into force did not mean the approval was ineffective. The approval order merely meant that the fact of the approval became a matter of easy proof under s 2 of the Documentary Evidence Act 1868 by simple production of the order.

Both devices may be used by any police force in England and Wales; it is understood that the Lion Intoximeter is used by the great majority of police forces, the Camic mainly being used in the North of England and in Scotland.

Both instruments are controlled by a microprocessor, which automates the sampling checking and recording procedures. Both work on the absorption of infra-red radiation to detect any ethyl/alcohol in the accused's breath. Both machines automatically correct the alcohol reading if acetone is also present due to diabetes or fasting; the Lion Intoximeter displays the presence of acetone, while the Camic does not. Both machines have a calibration check device consisting of a sealed jar containing a solution of alcohol at a given strength through which air is passed at a controlled temperature of 34° centigrade which should produce a vapour at the prescribed limit, ie 35 μg. Both devices provide for the operator to type on the machine's keyboard the name of the police station, the operator's name, the subject's name and, in the case of the Intoximeter only, his date of birth. Both machines are wired into the electricity mains and both give the time. (The time for both machines is Greenwich Mean Time. For this reason advocates should be careful not to be misled as to the actual time, and during British Summer Time, the date.)

Both devices check themselves against a simulated breath sample mechanically blown through the simulator (this should be within the range of 32–38 for the Camic and 32–37 for the Intoximeter) then both machines purge themselves (and the reading should therefore be zero). If the purge results are not zero, the machine would not appear 'reliable' within the meaning of s 8(3)(*b*). The subject then provides his first specimen of breath, after which each machine purges itself (the reading again should be zero); the subject then provides the second specimen of breath, and each machine again purges itself (the reading of which should again be zero) and finally, each machine again checks its calibration through the simulator (the reading should again be within the range 32–38 inclusive for the Camic, and 32–37 for the Intoximeter). The subject has some three or so minutes to provide a breath specimen. In the case of the Intoximeter he must blow at a sufficient rate for sufficiently long until a * appears (see Operator Instruction Card, Appendix 1). Up to five attempts can be made before the machine prints 'No sample'. The rate of flow of air into the machine is shown by blips on the screen, the greater the flow the greater the number of blips. When the machine prints 'No sample' the screen shows 'Aborted' on the test display panel.

It should be noted that the calibration check range for the Intoximeter was originally stated as being 32–38 by the initial Home Office circular to the courts. By Home Office circular 32/1984 it was made clear that the Lion Intoximeter readings always had to fall within the range of 32 to 37 μg.

While the Intoximeter will automatically abort if the initial calibration check is outside these limits, it will provide a printout if only the final calibration check is outside these limits. Advocates should be careful, therefore, to check the final calibration figure in case it is outside and has not been noticed by the police operator.

If the two check results are not within this figure or if the machine does not satisfactorily purge itself, the police are entitled in accordance with s 8(3)(*b*) (see above) to require blood or urine under s 8(4) (see 4.77).

Both machines produce at the conclusion of the sequence a print-out in triplicate incorporating the statement and certificate as defined by s 10(3)(*a*). (As to proof and production etc of the statement and certificate, see 4.80.) The certificate will be signed by the operator and the subject will also be invited to sign. The person is under no legal obligation so to sign; if he does not do so, the operator usually writes 'refused' in the space for the subject's signature, and makes a note in the appropriate place on the pro forma.

Set out in Appendix 1 are the operational instructions for both machines, together with specimen printouts from both.

Oral evidence by itself of the printout levels of the defendant's breath specimens is inadmissible unless it includes not only the breath/alcohol measurements of the breath specimens given by the defendant but also the results of the self-calibration of the device which are vital to establishing the reliability of the device (*Owen* v *Chesters* [1985] Crim LR 156 and see *Morgan* v *Lee* (1985) *The Times*, 17 April at 4.72).

It is believed that both machines contain a memory and for this reason it may be possible for a copy of an original printout to be obtained. Of the three copies which are initially produced, one is handed to the subject and the others stapled to the police pro forma. (If the accused refuses his copy the pro forma provides that this too should be stapled to the pro forma and a note made of the refusal.)

Both the Camic and Intoximeter devices prove themselves. Both are automatic measuring devices. In the absence of expert evidence challenging their reliability, the defendant can only challenge the printout by proving that he consumed alcohol after he ceased to drive or be in charge of the motor vehicle and before he provided the breath specimens for analysis (see 4.106). In *Anderton* v *Waring* (1985) *The Times*, 11 March where an Intoximeter did not record any sample, a conviction was directed by the Divisional Court; justices must assume the machine was in good working order unless the contrary is proved (ibid).

The breath printout will also not be used if the result was 50 μg or less and the defendant chose to provide blood or urine instead (see 4.73). Defendants can also check the printout by providing a sample even where the result is above 50 μg. (See Appendix 1, 'Blood or urine option experiment'.)

Where the accuracy of the analysis is challenged on the grounds of non-compliance with the instructions as to its use, it would seem that the onus will be on the defence to show that the instructions have not been complied with, and that, that being so, the non-compliance is unduly favourable to the prosecution (*A-G's Reference* (*No 1 of 1978*) [1978] RTR 377). In *Black* v *Bickmore* [1982] RTR 167 the principle of the *A-G's Reference* was applied to the

Alcolmeter and it would seem applicable to evidential breath test devices in the same way as to screening breath devices.

Defendants wishing to challenge the accuracy of the machine were denied by the High Court the use of witness summonses to investigate the Intoximeter log, service repair reports and test records. It was said that it was up to police forces to consider whether a more uniform practice was desirable and whether in the light of the Metropolitan Police experience a policy of voluntary disclosure should be more widely adopted. There was no discovery of documents in the magistrates' court or Crown Court and a witness summons must not be issued as a disguised attempt to obtain discovery (*R* v *Skegness Magistrates' Court, ex parte Cardy*; *R* v *Manchester Crown Court, ex parte Williams* [1985] RTR 49).

Even if expert evidence has been given that the Intoximeter was working erratically and unpredictably, if the effect of the defect is to make the readings too low, the justices are still entitled to rely on the printout as the error was entirely in the motorist's favour (*Wright* v *Taplin* (1985) *The Times*, 13 February).

It is possible in certain circumstances to show that, while the machine accurately recorded the breath/alcohol, the readings did not show the defendant's true breath/alcohol level but could have been affected by alcohol vapour directly blown into the machine by the defendant. One reported instance is where the defendant belched when blowing into the machine, so that the machine received the digestive alcoholic vapour in his stomach. In another case a metropolitan stipendiary magistrate disregarded the breath/alcohol reading where it might have been affected by the motorist using a 'Gold-Spot' aerosol for the prevention of bad breath at the time of his providing breath specimens; the defence bringing expert evidence to the effect that the aerosol vapour included alcohol and could have affected the machine's reading.

## 4.77 Provision of blood or urine specimens

A person may only be required to provide specimens of blood or urine at a police station or a hospital (s 8(3)). But a person may be required to provide blood or urine at a police station instead of breath only if one of the three situations set out in s 8(3)(*a*), (*b*) or (*c*) exist (see 4.72). If one of these situations exist, he may be required to provide blood or urine specimens notwithstanding that he 'has already provided or been required to provide two specimens of breath' (s 8(3)).

Under the former law the defendant had an option as to whether to provide blood or urine. Under s 8(4) only the police officer requiring a specimen of blood or urine decides whether to require the accused to provide a specimen of blood or specimens of urine, and he is under no obligation to consult the accused. His discretion is virtually absolute; whether it shall be blood or urine 'shall be decided by the constable making the requirement' (s 8(4)). If, however, a medical practitioner is of the opinion that for medical reasons a specimen of blood cannot or should not be taken, the constable is then, and only then, restricted to requiring urine (s 8(4)).

In practice, the officer under s 8(4) will almost invariably require blood. The police pro forma encourages him to do so and only suggests that he require urine when he is advised by a medical practitioner not to require blood. The reason for this may perhaps be that it is not uncommon for a person who has been required to provide specimens of urine to be unable to provide a second specimen of urine within one hour of requirement. In *Pine* v *Collacott* [1984] 41 LSG 3180 the Crown Court allowed an appeal against conviction under s 6(1) where the defendant had been required to provide a specimen of blood under s 8(4) because the constable had not applied his mind to whether he should require the provision of blood or of urine specimens from the defendant but had routinely followed the police pro forma not knowing that the Act gave him a discretion. In directing a conviction the Divisional Court held that it was sufficient for the purposes of s 8(4) if the constable decided on grounds of policy or for other reasons to be taken into account that blood should always be given.

*Blood specimens*

Section 10(4) lays down that a specimen of blood will be disregarded unless it is taken from the accused with his consent by a medical practitioner. Section 12(4) also states that a person provides a specimen of blood if and only if he consents to it being taken by a medical practitioner and it is so taken. It is not clear why Parliament found it necessary to repeat the same provision in different language.

Under the former law it was clear that if consent was obtained improperly the defendant could not be said to consent and a conviction would be quashed. In *R* v *Palfrey*; *R* v *Sadler* [1970] 2 All ER 12 the Court of Appeal made it clear that if there was some real substance in the assertion that the specimen of blood or urine was improperly taken against the will of the defendant or without his true consent, it was for the defendant to raise the issue, and show that there was some substance in it, and the court then had a discretion to exclude the results. The court referred to *R* v *Payne* [1963] 1 All ER 848 (a s 5 case) where the results of a medical examination were excluded after the defendant before consenting to a medical examination was told by the police surgeon that the results of the examination would not be given in evidence (see also 4.4 and 4.5).

It is for the doctor to say how the blood specimen should be taken. The defendant cannot insist on the blood being taken from a particular part of his anatomy selected by him (*Solesbury* v *Pugh* [1969] 2 All ER 1171) nor can he insist on giving capillary blood instead of intravenous blood (*Rushton* v *Higgins* [1972] Crim LR 440). Under the former law it was possible for the defence to establish the analysis to be incorrect because the sample of blood or urine was placed in a dirty or contaminated container, or a container not empty of material, or that a proper specimen was not taken. This is a matter of fact to be decided by the court. In *Rowlands* v *Harper* [1972] RTR 469 a police sergeant contrary to instructions assembled the syringe needle and capsules for the taking of the blood specimen. The justices had doubts as to whether a true specimen was taken. Upholding the justices' decision, the Court of Appeal said that the true ratio decidendi is that the prosecution have to prove beyond reasonable doubt that the sample has been properly taken.

Although the onus is on the prosecution if the defence have not required the presence of the analyst or medical practitioner, the burden of proof that it was properly taken is sufficiently discharged by the production of the certificates. Even where the doctor gives evidence, a court may infer the specimen was properly taken even where the evidence is very scanty. In *Braddock* v *Whittaker* [1970] Crim LR 112 the defendant was held to be rightly convicted, even though the sample produced in court was not identified by the doctor and the cups into which the samples of blood taken from the specimen were placed contained crystals which the doctor assumed contained anti-coagulant crystals without any evidence as to what the crystals actually were.

*Urine specimens*

The former s 9(5)(*b*) required the defendant to provide two specimens of urine within one hour of the request and the former s 9(6) provided that the first specimen was to be disregarded. The new s 8(5) states that 'a specimen of urine shall be required within one hour of the requirement for its provision being made and after provision of a previous specimen of urine'. It is difficult to see any practical difference between the former and present statutory provisions. The cases under the former law as to when a person provided or did not provide a specimen of urine would seem to continue to be relevant.

Where the defendant supplies a specimen of urine the analyst is not required under the former s 12(4) to make a further calculation to show what would be the equivalent blood/alcohol level: *McGarry* v *Chief Constable of Bedfordshire* [1983] RTR 172.

Although the former and present statutory provisions lay down that the requirement to provide a second specimen is to be made within one hour, in two cases on the former provisions it was held that analyses of second specimens obtained more than one hour after the first were admissible (*Roney* v *Matthews* [1975] RTR 273; *Standen* v *Robertson* [1975] RTR 329).

Unlike blood specimens, specimens of urine are not required to be taken by a medical practitioner. They are usually taken by the police officer who made the initial requirement, but the statutory provisions are silent as to who may take them. Occasionally the specimens may be taken by the police surgeon if he is present. Where the person is a woman the specimen will be taken either by the police surgeon or by a woman police officer.

There is nothing in the former or present statutory provisions requiring the person giving specimens to empty his bladder when giving the first specimen nor do the provisions require the first or second specimen to be of any particular quantity. A conviction was upheld in *R* v *Radcliffe* [1977] RTR 99 even though the defendant on the doctor's advice may not have fully emptied his bladder when giving the first specimen. Similarly where a defendant had of his own free will given a second specimen one minute after the first, a conviction was directed as it was clear that two distinct specimens had been given (*Over* v *Musker* [1985] RTR 84). But where a station officer initially took a specimen of the defendant's urine, told him to stop and then to 'continue urinating' the whole process taking no more than two minutes, justices were upheld in finding that the urine obtained was all one specimen and that the analysis was therefore inadmissible (*Prosser* v *Dickeson* [1982] RTR 96).

Evidence has to be given to prove that the correct specimen of urine was sent for analysis. If there is any doubt raised as to whether the analyst's certificate relates to the correct specimen, it is submitted that it is for the prosecution to prove that it was. See *Dickson* v *Atkins* [1972] RTR 209 and *R* v *Orrell* [1972] RTR 14.

As in the case of a blood sample (see *Rowlands* v *Harper* above), analysis of a urine sample may be successfully challenged if it is shown that the specimen as analysed may have been contaminated. Where an analyst stated that a urine sample was found to be contaminated by micro-organisms capable of producing alcohol but that it was unlikely that the organisms present would have significantly contributed to the alcohol in the specimen unless the defendant suffered from diabetes, it was held that in the absence of any evidence as to whether or not the defendant had diabetes, the court could not be satisfied so that they could be sure of the defendant's guilt (*Collins* v *Luckin* [1983] RTR 312).

### 4.78 Results of laboratory analysis

A defendant may properly challenge the accuracy of the analysis of blood or urine by giving evidence of the analysis of his sample and challenging the accuracy of the sample analysed by the forensic laboratory. In *R* v *Kershberg* [1976] RTR 526 the Court of Appeal quashed a conviction because of a lingering doubt as to the correctness of official analysis (official analysis of urine 108 mg, defendant's sample's analysis 70 mg—defendant gave a negative breath test after supplying specimen of urine). The analysis must 'exceed' the prescribed limit (s 6(1)).

The former s 6(1) required the defendant's blood/alcohol to be ascertained from the laboratory test and from no other source. High blood/alcohol could therefore be proved by no other method. Under the present law it would appear that a certificate of analysis is no longer a sine qua non to a successful prosecution under s 6, although the prosecution may have difficulty in proving the defendant's blood, breath or urine/alcohol level to be above the limit in the absence of a certificate or printout. Oral evidence of the lower breath reading on the visual display of the Intoximeter is not sufficient as it is vital to establish the machine was properly calibrated (*Owen* v *Chesters* [1985] Crim LR 156 and see also *Morgan* v *Lee* at 4.72).

It was held that the former law did not require the prosecution to prove beyond doubt a particular figure as to the blood or urine/alcohol level, only that the level exceeded the prescribed limit (*R* v *Coomaraswamy* [1976] RTR 21; dicta to different effect in *R* v *Boswell* [1974] RTR 273 were not followed).

If there is a dispute between the prosecution's and defendant's analysts, the court is entitled to prefer the prosecution's analyst in the same way as it is entitled to accept or reject any other evidence. The court is entitled to act on the opinion of one expert in preference to another; so long as it is satisfied beyond reasonable doubt that the expert it relies on is right, it does not have to explain the difference between the two opinions (*R* v *Elliott* [1976] RTR 308; *R* v *Sodo* [1975] RTR 357; *R* v *Marr* [1977] RTR 168). In *Walker* v *Hodgkins* [1983] Crim LR 555 the police analyst had followed the usual practice of deducting 6 mg for a margin of error while the defendant's analyst had not. The police analyst then gave a figure of 96 and the defendant's analyst 83. The justices were upheld in acquitting the defendant; it was held that they were entitled to have regard to the normal laboratory practice of deducting 6 mg, and had acted perfectly properly in deciding that they could not be satisfied beyond reasonable doubt that the defendant's blood/alcohol content exceeded the limit when the defence analyst had acted in good faith and used unimpeachable methods.

## 4.79 Supply of specimen of blood or urine to the defendant

The former s 10(5) required the accused to be supplied with a specimen or part of a specimen if he asked for one and the former s 10(6) required the constable to offer to supply the accused in a suitable container a specimen of blood or part specimen of blood or urine.

The former s 10(5) is substantially re-enacted as s 10(6) but the former s 10(6) has not been re-enacted. The position is therefore that while the accused has to be given a part of the specimen of blood or urine *if he asks for it* there is neither any obligation on the part of the constable to remind him when requesting a specimen of blood or urine that he is entitled to a sample, nor does that sample have to be offered to him in a 'suitable container'. It is unfortunate that the former s 10(6) has not been re-enacted. Defendants will in future have to rely on the standard police pro forma being followed. If the words of the statute are strictly followed the defendant cannot escape conviction on the ground that he was not reminded that he could ask to be supplied with a sample, nor can he argue that he was not supplied with a suitable container to contain his sample of blood or urine. However, in *Anderton* v *Lythgoe* [1985] Crim LR 158 it was held by the Divisional Court that a driver is entitled to be told of his statutory option to provide blood or urine where his lower breath specimen is no more than 50 $\mu$g, and where the police omitted so to inform him it was held that a court has a discretion to exclude evidence of the printout. By analogy, if the High Court are prepared to follow the reasoning of *Anderton*, it may be that the High Court may hold that there is a similar discretion to exclude the analysis of the blood or urine sample where the defendant is not told of his right to have a sample of his own for independent analysis, particularly if the official analysis is only just above the prescribed limit.

The present s 10(6) is similar to the former s 10(5) save that the specimen of blood is now required to be divided into two parts at the time it was provided, and the part not sent to the police laboratory supplied to the accused. It is no longer possible for two specimens of blood to be taken from the accused, one specimen being analysed by the laboratory and the other specimen supplied to the accused for analysis by him.

It should be noted that if s 10(6) is not complied with, the certificate is not admissible and a prosecution under s 6 will fail unless the prosecution can by other means show that the defendant's alcohol level was above the prescribed limit. It should be noted also that a certificate of analysis is also not admissible if the charge is one under s 5, and s 10(6) has not been complied with. As the section states that the certificate is not admissible it would seem that the court has no discretion and must exclude it, save that a defendant if properly advised may presumably waive the benefit of the subsection where it has been complied with and agree to evidence of the analysis being given.

Where the defendant intends to argue that s 10(6) has not been properly complied with, objection must be taken during the prosecution case to the admissibility of the prosecution's analysis (*Hudson* v *Hornsby* [1973] RTR 4).

Section 10(6) applies where the defendant asked for the sample at the time of the provision of the specimen, but not where he asks for it afterwards. Whether he has been supplied with it is a question of fact (*R* v *Jones* (*Colin*) [1974] RTR 117). While it is a wise and proper practice to supply the part of the specimen to the accused before he leaves the police station, it need not necessarily be supplied to him before he does so long as it is supplied within a reasonable time; the court should review all the circumstances, including the reason why the police did not give it to him before he left (eg he was too drunk to accept it) and the question whether he was prejudiced by the failure to get it when he left and whether the time when he did get it was within a reasonable time (*R* v *Sharp* [1968] 3 All ER 182).

In the former s 10(5) the words a 'single specimen' may appropriately refer to any aliquot part of the total quantity of blood which was in the syringe. It was further held that the totality of blood taken did not have to be divided into two parts. Where the contents of the syringe were divided into three parts, it was held that, in order to give the defendant one of the three, what is required is that the part of the specimen given to the defendant shall be capable of analysis (*Kidd* v *Kidd*; *Ley* v *Donegani* [1968] 3 All ER 226).

There were a large number of cases on whether, in accordance with the former s 10(5), the part of the specimen given to the defendant is adequate. The cases may be summarised as follows:

(1) Each part of the specimen including the part given to the defendant must be of a quality and quantity to be capable of analysis by the use of ordinary equipment and ordinary skill by a reasonably competent analyst (*Smith* v *Cole* [1971] 1 All ER 200, *Nugent* v *Hobday* [1972] Crim LR 569).

(2) The part when handed to the defendant must also be capable of remaining suitable for analysis within a reasonable time (*Thompson* v *Charlwood* (1969) 113 SJ 1004, *Ward* v *Keene* [1970] RTR 177, *R* v *Wright* (*John*) [1975] RTR 193).

(3) The adequacy of the sample is a question of fact, not law, and must be decided by the court on the evidence presented to it. The burden of proof of the adequacy of the sample is on the prosecution, although the fact that the prosecution's sample which was chosen at random was capable of analysis was evidence, but not conclusive evidence, that the defendant's was also capable of analysis (*Crankshaw* v *Rydeheard* (1969)

113 SJ 673; *Ward* v *Keene* and *Smith* v *Cole* above, *Kierman* v *Willcock* [1972] RTR 270).

Defendants anxious to obtain an analysis of the part specimen can obtain advice as to how to keep the sample, and where and to whom it should be sent for analysis, from the Royal Institute of Chemistry, 30 Russell Square, London WC1B 5DT, who also publish a leaflet.

### 4.80 Certificates of analysis and printouts etc

Evidence of the proportion of alcohol or a drug in a specimen of breath, blood or urine and that a specimen of blood was taken from the accused with his consent by a medical practitioner can be proved in proceedings for offences under ss 5 and 6 by the production in court of the following documents:

(1) a statement as to analysis of breath automatically produced by the Camic Breath Analyser or Lion Intoximeter with the certificate signed by the constable that the statement relates to a specimen provided by the accused at the date and time shown in the statement; and
(2) a certificate signed by an authorised analyst as to the proportion of alcohol or any drug found in a specimen of blood or urine identified in the certificate; and
(3) a certificate purporting to certify that a specimen of blood was taken from the accused with his consent by a medical practitioner purporting to be signed by a medical practitioner.

By virtue of s 10(5) a statement as to breath analysis produced by he Camic Breath Analyser or Lion Intoximeter with the accompanying certificate signed by the constable can *only* be produced if a copy of it either was handed to the accused when the document was produced by the machine, or was served on him not later than seven days before the hearing. If not served not later than seven days before the hearing the copy must be handed to the motorist. It is not sufficient to place copies on the counter of the station with no indication that one was for him to take away (*Walton* v *Rimmer* (1985) *The Times*, 11 February), but the Act could not be construed so that a defendant could render the copy inadmissible by refusing to take the document handed to him (ibid).

In *Chief Constable of Surrey* v *Wickens* (1984) *The Times*, 16 November, the constable signed the original certificate but had served an unsigned copy on the defendant. It was held that an unsigned copy was a copy for the purposes of s 10(5) and that if the legislature had intended the copy as well as the original to be signed it would have said so. There was no question in the present case of the defendant's interests having been prejudiced. Section 10(3) envisages that the certificate signed by the constable will either be a certificate separate from the printout or 'statement automatically' produced by the Camic Breath Analyser or Lion Intoximeter or on the printout itself. As will be seen from Appendix 1 both the Lion Intoximeter and Camic Breath Analyser automatically provide on the printout itself such a certificate to be signed by the police officer. Section 10(5) only requires the statement and certificate to be handed to the accused at the time the document was produced.

There is no requirement that the accused sign the printout nor is there any requirement that the accused need accept it when handed to him. The police pro forma used by most forces advises that the additional printout be stapled with the others in the space provided in the pro forma, and a note made as to whether the accused signed or refused to sign the printout and whether he accepted or refused to accept the printout when handed to him.

The prosecution must normally rely on the printout itself for evidence as to the measurement of the breath specimens provided by the motorist. It is inadmissible for the constable to give oral evidence of the defendant's breath specimens only because the printout also gives the result of the self-calibration checks which are vital to establishing the reliability of the device (*Owen* v *Chesters* [1985] Crim LR 156 and see *Morgan* v *Lee* (1985) *The Times*, 17 April, at 4.72).

In *Gaimster* v *Marlow* [1984] RTR 49 justices refused to admit in evidence the printout produced by a Lion Intoximeter, on the ground that the test record produced by the machine was unintelligible. The justices further held that they should refuse to allow the police operating the machine to explain its meaning. It was unanimously held by the Divisional Court presided over by the Lord Chief Justice that the whole of the document including the certificate signed by the constable was admissible and that the document which contained both the statement and the certificate should be construed as a whole. The test record was such a statement and if it was unintelligible, which their lordships doubted, it could be explained by the police officer provided the police officer is shown to be a trained operator of the machine. The court refused leave to appeal to the House of Lords and on 16 December 1983 refused to certify that a point of law of general public importance was involved in the decision to enable the defendant to petition the House of Lords for leave to appeal.

The offence in *Gaimster* v *Marlow* was an offence contrary to s 6(1). Section 10 only applies to proceedings for offences contrary to ss 5 and 6 (s 10(1)). Where a defendant is charged with an offence under s 8(7) of refusing without reasonable excuse to supply specimens for analysis, s 10 cannot be relied on as authority for the production of the printout. In *Castle* v *Cross* [1985] RTR 62, justices refused to admit the printout in evidence in proceedings for an offence under s 8(7) on the ground that the printout was a statement made by a machine akin to a computer, that the Intoximeter contributed to its own knowledge and that the printout was therefore inadmissible. Reversing the justices, the Divisional Court held that the printout was admissible. An Intoximeter was a tool, albeit sophisticated, operated by a police officer trained in its use. The printout was a product of the machine and fell into the category of real evidence as the recordings did in *The Statue of Liberty* [1968] 1 WLR 739. It should be observed that the Divisional Court in *Castle* v *Cross* specifically observed that there was no challenge in the particular case to the efficiency of the machine and no finding that it was defective. It would appear, therefore, that it is still open to the defence in an appropriate case to challenge the admissibility of the printout on the ground that the machine did not work or did not work properly or was unreliable. In *Duddy* v *Gallagher* (1984) *The Times*, 5 December, the defendant was charged both under s 6(1) of driving with excess alcohol and under s 8(7) with failing without reasonable excuse to provide two specimens of breath, he having given one positive breath specimen on the Intoximeter, but having failed to give a second breath specimen. Convictions for both offences were upheld by the Divisional Court, evidence of the single specimen being admissible if the statutory procedure of s 8 has been complied with (but *quaere* whether this is correct having regard to s 8(6); see further 4.76).

Section 10(5) provides that the other certificates (ie certificate of analysis or the taking of blood specimens by a medical practitioner) may only be produced in court in evidence if they have been served on the accused 'not later than seven days before' the hearing. If not 'handed' to the defendant at the time s 10(5) provides that the printout and certificate signed by the constable may also be admissible if it is served on the accused 'not later than seven days before the hearing'. 'Not later than seven days before' seems to mean seven clear days between the date of service and the date of hearing.

If the defendant is legally represented not only is service of the certificate etc on the solicitor most convenient, but it is legally untenable to hold that the document has not been properly served under s 10(5) because it has been served on the solicitor instead of the defendant personally: *Anderton* v *Kinnard* (1985) *The Times*, 13 February. The copies may be served personally or sent by registered post or recorded delivery (s 10(8)). Proof of proper service of the document either in person or by post may be proved by production of a certificate purporting to be signed by the person who posted to or served the certificate or document on the accused (Magistrates' Courts Rules 1981, r 67(2)).

Section 7 of the Interpretation Act 1978 provides that service will be deemed to have been effected when it would have arrived in the normal course of post.

The accused can secure the attendance at court of the person who signed any of the documents (ie the police officer who signed the certificate relating to the printout, the medical practitioner or the authorised analyst) if the accused has served the prosecutor personally by registered post or recorded delivery a notice to that effect 'not later than three days before the hearing or within such further time as the court may in special circumstances allow' (s 10(6)).

It would seem that if the prosecution has not complied with the requirements of s 10(5) they are entitled to call the person in question as a witness in court whether that person be the registered medical practitioner, the authorised analyst, or the police officer who certified the printout (as to oral evidence of the Intoximeter see *Owen* v *Chesters* above and *Morgan* v *Lee* at 4.72).

There have been a number of cases on the former s 10(1) (which corresponds to the present s 10(3)) as to whether or not a certificate of analysis can be proved to relate to the actual specimen blood or urine taken from the accused. It should be noted that both in the former s 10(1) and the present s 10(3) the specimen of blood or urine may be identified in the certificate. It is submitted that in practice the production of the certificate bearing on it the name of the accused, and the labelling of the specimen container of the sample of blood or urine with the time, date and place as to when and by whom the specimen was taken, is usually sufficient for a court to infer that the analysis is of the specimen taken from the accused. Moreover the police officer at the station is usually required to give corresponding evidence of the labelling of the specimen after referring to the standard police pro forma (Form 106). Difficulties can arise where there are typographical errors either on the certificate or in the labelling of the specimen. It is submitted that, as in *Dickson* v *Atkins* [1972] RTR 209, what it is necessary for the prosecution to prove is:

(*a*) that the specimen taken from the accused was sent to the analyst; and
(*b*) that the analyst's certificate refers to that specimen.

If the prosecution can satisfy the court on (*a*) and (*b*) above, it matters not that the certificate or label show typographical errors (ibid). Similarly in *R* v *Orrell* [1972] RTR 14 it was held by the Court of Appeal that it was sufficient for the prosecution to prove by written markings on the sample bottle of urine that the sample of urine taken from the defendant was that received by the laboratory and analysed by the analyst. In *Tremlett* v *Fawcett* (1984) 1 RTLB 68 it was held that there was no need for the prosecution to prove specifically that a sample of urine had been sent from the police to the laboratory for analysis. In that case the sample had been marked and placed in an envelope signed across the seal by the police officer with the envelope bearing the name of the defendant. The analyst had certified that he had received the specimen in a sealed container.

Analyses of blood or urine specimens are required to be made by an 'authorised analyst'. The definition of 'authorised analyst' in s 10(9) is identical to that contained in the former s 10(7), ie persons possessing the qualifications prescribed by regulations made under the Food and Drugs Acts for appointment as public analysts together with any other person authorised by the Home Secretary to make analyses for the purposes of s 10. Such latter authority has been given by the Home Secretary to various named persons at the police forensic laboratories. It was held in *R* v *Rutter* [1977] RTR 105 that although the certificate has to be given by the analyst, there is nothing in the section which requires the analysis to be made by the analyst himself; it suffices if the analysis was carried out under his control and supervision.

Section 10(2) provides that a defendant can rebut the assumption as to the level of alcohol in his blood, breath or urine as evidenced by the specimen provided by him if he proves that he consumed alcohol after he had ceased to drive, attempt to drive or be in charge and before he provided the specimen. This is dealt with and discussed in 4.106. The defendant is also entitled, if he asks for it, to a sample of any specimen of blood or urine provided by him. This has been dealt with in 4.79, above.

**4.81 Warning of prosecution**

Section 8(8) places a duty upon the constable when requiring a specimen of breath, blood or urine under s 8 to warn the defendant that failure to provide it may render him liable to prosecution. The former s 9(7) specifically empowered the court to dismiss a prosecution if the warning was not given. In *R* v *Dolan* [1970] RTR 43 it was pointed out that failure to give the warning would constitute a reasonable excuse for failing to provide a specimen. Although there is now no provision equivalent to the former s 9(7) which specifically empowers a court to dismiss a prosecution where no warning under s 8(8) is given, it would seem, as was pointed out in *Dolan*, that failure to give a warning would constitute a reasonable excuse for refusing to supply specimens.

Where the defendant provided specimens, despite the absence of a warning, the failure to give a warning would not seem to constitute a ground for acquittal of a charge under s 6. Even assuming that a court has a discretion to dismiss a charge under s 6 on this ground, it is likely that a court will wish to follow the observation made by the court in *R* v *Brush* [1968] 3 All ER 467 where it was stated that it was difficult to see how a motorist can be said to be prejudiced who gave a specimen notwithstanding that he was not warned of the consequences of his failing or refusing to do so.

It is a reasonable excuse for a defendant if he was unable to understand because of his limited command of English the purpose of a requirement to provide laboratory specimens, or to appreciate the penal consequences of a refusal (*Beck* v *Sager* [1979] Crim LR 257).

### 4.82–90 Detention at the police station

Section 11 provides that after a person has been required to provide a specimen of breath, blood or urine he may thereafter be detained at a police station until it appears to a constable that he would not be committing an offence under s 5 or s 6 of the Act if he were then to drive, but a person may not be detained if it appears to a constable that there is no likelihood of his driving or attempting to drive whilst his ability to drive properly is impaired or whilst the proportion of alcohol is above the prescribed limit. If there is any question of a person's ability to drive being affected through drugs, the constable is required to consult a doctor and act on his advice (s 11(*b*)).

These provisions replace the former s 11 which enabled a person to be detained until he gave a negative breath test. The new s 11 is silent on how a constable should form his opinion as to whether the defendant is or is not likely to be above the limit. In cases where the accused may still be suffering the effects of alcohol it is the practice in many police stations to detain the car rather than the driver and to allow the accused to be driven home by taxi or by a friend. The new section specifically recognises this practice and requires the constable to release him if it appears to the constable there is no likelihood of his driving while impaired or above the limit.

## Failing to Provide a Specimen

### 4.91–5 The offence: s 8(7)

A person who without reasonable excuse fails to provide a specimen when required to do so in pursuance of s 8 is guilty of an offence (s 8(7)). The wording of this section differs little from the former s 9(3).

In practice there are three differences between the former and present law: the first is that a person could only be required to provide a specimen for analysis under the former section if he 'had been arrested under s 5(5) or 8 of this Act'. This was interpreted to mean that:

(*a*) he had actually to be arrested; and
(*b*) the arrest had to be lawful.

This in turn meant that if he had been arrested under the former s 8, the police had to prove that he had been lawfully required to provide a roadside screening test, that he had given a positive result or had failed or refused to provide a breath specimen. Under the present s 8 this will no longer be the case. A person can be lawfully required to provide specimens of blood, breath or urine 'in the course of an investigation whether a person has committed an offence under section 5 or section 6' (s 8(1)). There is therefore no requirement for the person to have been arrested, nor will the legality of an arrest following a road-side breath test be an issue. In *Bunyard* v *Hayes* (1984) *The Times*, 3 November, it was held following *Fox* v *Gwent Chief Constable* that the fact that a person may possibly have been wrongly arrested does not preclude him being convicted of failing to provide specimens of breath.

The second difference lies in the fact that the defendant will normally only be required to provide one type of specimen, that of breath, blood or urine. Hitherto the defendant had to have 'a reasonable excuse' both for failing to supply blood and for failing to supply urine in order for there to be an acquittal. Now a reasonable excuse will only have to be advanced for the particular type of specimen required.

The third difference lies in the penalties for the offence of failing or refusing to provide specimens for analysis.

As in the former law, it would seem that in certain circumstances an offence can be committed of failing to supply specimens even if it subsequently transpires that the offender was neither driving nor attempting to drive nor in charge of a motor vehicle. It was held by the House of Lords in *Commissioner of the Metropolitan Police* v *Curran* [1976] RTR 61, that in accordance with the entry in Sched 4 relating to the former s 9(3) offence, the court were obliged to endorse the offender's licence, and could disqualify him but could not impose a fine or imprisonment as he was never in charge of a motor vehicle. The penalties for the offence under the former s 9(3) were different depending on whether at the 'relevant time' the offender was (*a*) driving or attempting to drive or (*b*) in charge of a motor vehicle or (*c*) (in accordance with *Curran*) neither driving nor attempting to drive nor in charge. For the new offence under s 8(7) there are only two sets of penalties, (*a*) where the offender was driving or attempting to drive, and (*b*) all other cases, ie where the offender was not driving or attempting to drive, whether or not he was in charge. Where the offender was driving or attempting to drive, the offence under s 8(7) is obligatorily disqualifiable. (It will be noted that the words 'at the relevant time' no longer appear in the entry relating to s 8(7) in Part I of Sched 4 of the 1972 Act, the statutory definition of these words contained in Sched 5 having been repealed at the same time as the coming into force of the new law.) Where the offence under s 8(7) is thus obligatorily disqualifiable it comes under Part I of Sched 7 of the Transport Act 1981. On the other hand, where the offender was not driving nor attempting to drive, the offence is no longer obligatorily disqualifiable (see para (*b*) in columns 4 and 5 of the entry relating to s 8(7) in Part I of Sched 4 of the 1972 Act) and an offender incurs 10 penalty points in accordance with the reference to s 8(7) in Part II of Sched 7 to the 1981 Act. No doubt in the majority of cases where the offender is not driving or attempting to drive it can be shown that he was in charge, but even if he is neither proved to be in charge nor driving or attempting to drive he will now be liable to the full range of penalties in accordance with (*b*) in columns 4 and 5 of the entry relating to Sched 4.

In *Bunyard* v *Hayes* (above) the defendant was held to be rightly convicted under s 8(7) where he refused without reasonable excuse to provide specimens of breath for analysis, the police officers having taken the defendant to the police station after forming the suspicion that he had been the driver of a vehicle involved in an accident, although it subsequently transpired that he was not the driver.

*A 'Fails'*

The cases on the former section show that a person cannot be convicted of failing to supply a specimen for analysis if he has consented to supply a specimen and provided it. Thus in *R* v *Rothery* [1976] RTR 550 a defendant was acquitted of failing to supply a specimen where after providing a specimen of urine he stole it before leaving a police station; he could only be convicted of theft (ibid). The defendant in *Ross* v *Hodges* [1975] RTR 55 was held not to have provided a specimen when the jar containing the specimen fell out of his hand as he handed it to the police officer. If the second specimen of urine is in fact so small as to be incapable of analysis, it cannot be said that the defendant has provided a specimen (*R* v *Coward* [1976] RTR 425).

Where an Intoximeter did not record any sample as having been provided by the defendant, the Divisional Court directed a conviction under s 8(7); justices must assume that the Intoximeter was in good working order in the absence of any evidence to the contrary (*Anderton* v *Waring* (1985) *The Times*, 11 March). It should be noted in this context that s 12(3), as amended by the Transport Act 1982, requires the specimen of breath 'to be provided in such a way as to enable the objective of the test or analysis to be satisfactorily achieved'.

*B 'Refuses'*

As in the former law the word 'fails' includes 'refuses' (s 12(2)), and the cases on the former law would appear relevant.

It was held in the former law that once the defendant has refused all three requests, blood, urine and then blood, the offence is complete. In *Procaj* v *Johnstone* [1970] Crim LR 110 the accused changed his mind before being charged, and it was held that it was then too late to do so. In *Muat* v *Thynne* (1984) *The Times*, 28 May, the defendant failed to supply specimens of blood or urine in accordance with the former s 9. His conviction under s 9 was upheld by the Divisional Court even though he subsequently supplied a blood sample for the purpose of determining whether an offence under s 5 had been committed. It would seem that in the present law once a defendant has been properly required to provide a specimen in accordance with the procedure under s 8 he can be charged even if he subsequently changes his mind.

If a defendant, after giving a lower breath specimen of 50 μg or less, opts to give a specimen of blood or urine instead under s 8(4), he cannot be convicted under s 8(7) of failing or refusing to supply a specimen if he then fails to provide a specimen. The only effect of his failure in such circumstances is that the original breath specimen cannot be used in evidence against him (see further 4.73).

*C 'Reasonable excuse'*

The offence is only committed if the defendant fails or refuses 'without reasonable excuse'. Once the defence of reasonable excuse is advanced it is for the prosecution to disprove it (*Rowland* v *Thorpe* [1970] 3 All ER 195, at p 197). It is a question of fact as to whether a defendant has a reasonable excuse and the court must be satisfied beyond reasonable doubt that the defendant had no reasonable excuse before he can be convicted (*R* v *Harling* [1970] RTR 441; *R* v *Knightley* [1971] 2 All ER 1041). But whether facts are capable of amounting to a reasonable excuse is a matter of law; if it is capable in law of amounting to a reasonable excuse, then it becomes a matter of fact and degree whether it does so or not, with the burden being on the prosecution to negative it (*Law* v *Stephens* [1971] RTR 358).

A mistaken or even genuine belief on the part of the defendant is usually incapable of amounting to a 'reasonable excuse'; eg that he had not consumed alcohol (*McNicol* v *Peters* 1969 SLT(J) 261); that he did not believe he had committed a moving traffic offence (*R* v *Downey* [1970] Crim LR 287); that he did not believe that he was 'in charge' of a motor vehicle (*Williams* v *Osborne* [1975] RTR 181); that he did not think the officer was acting bona fide (*McGrath* v *Vipas* [1984] RTR 58); that he thought he had not failed the breath test (*Mallows* v *Harris* [1979] RTR 404). An agreement subject to an unreasonable condition is treated as no acceptance and amounting to a refusal, eg an agreement only to provide a specimen when his solicitor was present (*Pettigrew* v *Northumbria Police Authority* [1976] RTR 177; *Payne* v *Diccox* [1980] RTR 83). Although the police have a discretion to allow a solicitor to be present, they are under a duty to end their concession if it appears to be a delaying tactic or creates too great a delay. Where the defendant's own doctor is present, the defendant will not be held to have refused if he consents to the blood specimen being taken only by his own doctor (*Bayliss* v *Thames Valley Police* [1978] RTR 328). The defendant cannot insist on the blood specimen being taken only from a particular part of his anatomy, or of capillary instead of intravenous blood. Once a doctor has asked to take a specimen in accordance with ordinary medical practice, an offer for it to be taken only in a different way is a refusal (*Solesbury* v *Pugh* [1969] 2 All ER 1171; *Rushton* v *Higgins* [1972] Crim LR 440; *R* v *McAllister* [1974] Crim LR 716).

A constable is justified in treating the refusal to sign a form of consent for a specimen of blood to be taken by a medical practitioner as a refusal where the defendant had previously refused to supply a blood specimen (*R* v *McAllister*).

A driver was however held *not* to have refused when he insisted on reading the consent form before signing it, although it appeared to the police to be a delaying tactic (*Hier* v *Read* [1978] RTR 114).

In *R* v *Harling* [1970] RTR 441 a defendant lost confidence in a doctor after three unsuccessful efforts to obtain blood, and it was observed that he might have had a reasonable excuse to refuse to supply blood. In *Roland* v *Thorpe* above the court may have been prepared to hold as a reasonable excuse for refusing to supply urine that there was no woman police officer present to take the specimen, as the defendant was a woman. Mental incapacity can amount to a reasonable excuse. In *R* v *Harding* [1974] RTR 325 a conviction was set aside where a jury might have found the defendant was so afraid of a hypodermic needle as to be incapacitated from submitting to it. In most cases, fear of providing blood must be supported by medical evidence (ibid). *Harding* was applied in *Alcock* v *Read* [1980] RTR 71 where justices were upheld in finding the defendant had a reasonable excuse because of an 'invincible repugnance' to giving blood. Evidence was given that he had twice passed out after giving blood and was terrified of blood being taken. Where the defendant threw an apparent fit when a doctor tried to obtain a blood specimen, the justices' finding that the fit could have been genuine was held to justify an acquittal. *R* v *Lennard* [1973] RTR 252 and *Harding* were applied in *Sykes* v *White* [1983] RTR 419 where it was held that fear of blood so that the defendant became light-headed and had to sit down and fear of fainting so that he could not provide urine could not amount to a reasonable excuse, nor could an irrational belief that discomfort at providing blood would be misinterpreted as incapacity to drive a motor vehicle.

It was said in *R* v *Lennard* that a reasonable excuse *'must arise out of a physical or mental inability to provide one or a substantial risk to health in its provision'*. Under the present law the prosecution are less likely to succeed in negativing a reasonable excuse based on a physical inability to provide a specimen, particularly where the specimens required to be provided are breath. Both the Camic and Lion breath evidential devices require the subject to blow for a given interval at a given pressure and under s 12(3) as amended by the Transport Act 1982 a specimen of breath has to be 'provided in such a way as to enable the . . . analysis to be satisfactorily achieved'. A defendant is therefore entitled to advance as a reasonable excuse that he had not the lung capacity or physical ability to blow sufficiently hard and long to provide a specimen which the Camic or Lion was able to analyse.

It would appear that a physical inability is clearly capable of a reasonable excuse, eg bronchitis or asthma if breath is demanded, or haemophilia if blood is required. The religious beliefs of a person precluding the giving of blood were held, however, *not* to amount to a reasonable excuse (*R* v *John* [1974] RTR 332). In *John*, while following *R* v *Lennard*, it was said that the language of *Lennard*, if construed too strictly, might result in an 'over rigid approach', but that a distinction must be drawn between some physical or mental condition of a person which might preclude the giving of specimens, and his beliefs, which although sincere could not preclude the giving of specimens.

One circumstance that may amount to a reasonable excuse is if the defendant does not understand the statutory warning that he will be prosecuted if he fails or refuses to supply specimens for analysis (*R* v *Dolan* [1970] RTR 43; see further 4.81). In *Beck* v *Sager* [1979] Crim LR 257 it was held to be a reasonable excuse that the defendant was unable to understand because of his limited command of English the purpose of the requirement to provide a laboratory specimen or to appreciate the penal consequence of a refusal.

## Hospital Patients

### 4.96 Introduction

The new law, like the former, contains special provisions for the protection of hospital patients.

Section 9 states that while a person is *at a hospital as a patient* he cannot be required to provide a breath test or specimens for analysis until *the medical practitioner in immediate charge of the case* has first been notified of the proposal to require a breath test. The medical practitioner may object either to the requirement or its provision (s 9(1)). The grounds upon which the doctor may object are that the requirement, the actual provision or the warning under s 8(8) would be prejudicial to the proper care and treatment of the patient.

### 4.97 'At a hospital'

'Hospital' is defined in s 12(2) as an institution which provides medical or surgical treatment for in-patients or out-patients. This definition is identical to the definition of the former law. Whether an institution is a hospital seems to be a simple question of fact. Both private and NHS hospitals come within the definition. The protection afforded by s 9(1) depends on whether the person is a patient 'at' the hospital. Under the former law, for this reason, someone in an ambulance on his way to hospital was held not to be 'at a hospital' (*Hollingsworth* v *Howard* [1974] RTR 58). A person is, however, 'at a hospital' if he is anywhere within the precincts of the hospital, eg the hospital car park (*A-G's Reference* (*No 1 of 1976*) [1977] RTR 284).

### 4.98 'As a patient'

A person may be at a hospital, but the protection of the statute only applies to a person who can be said to be at the hospital 'as a patient'. This is usually a simple question of fact. The word clearly includes both in-patients and out-patients in view of the definition of 'hospital' above. Hospitals usually have a strict routine as to the keeping of records and once a person is admitted as a patient he will be regarded by the hospital as a patient until discharged by a doctor or by himself. If he discharges himself against medical advice the hospital will normally record this fact. The purpose of the law was held to be the protection of patients and the avoidance of a collision between doctors trying to treat their patients and the police endeavouring to require a breath test. In the *A-G's Reference* (*No 1 of 1976*) [1977] RTR 284 it was held that where a person attended hospital to seek treatment he ceases to be a patient as soon as the treatment on the occasion of his visit is complete, even if he is required subsequently to return for further treatment (eg for the removal of stitches). It was also suggested that 'treatment' should be given a wide interpretation (eg if he was told 'sit down for half-an-hour before you go', then the subsequent half hour would be included).

### 4.99 'Medical practitioner in immediate charge of his case'

This phrase was also included in the former law. It was held that the police do not have to produce medical lists to prove that the person is a medical practitioner, nor do they have to call the doctor himself and check that no objection is made. In *Jones* v *Brazil* [1970] RTR 449 it was agreed that if the police said M appeared to be the casualty officer with nurses and others in attendance, this was sufficient to raise a prima facie case that M was the 'medical practitioner in immediate charge of his case'.

A constable may give evidence that the doctor did not object; this is not hearsay (*Burns* v *Kernohan* [1973] RTR 82).

### 4.100 Preliminary breath tests

The protection afforded to a patient at a hospital by s 9(1) is similar to those in the former s 8(2). The power to require a breath test following an accident under s 7(2) is expressly 'subject to section 9'.

While a person is at a hospital as a patient he cannot be required to provide a breath test until the doctor has been notified of the proposal and the doctor does not object. It was held in respect of a requirement under the former law that a patient did not have to be out of earshot of the doctor when the policeman is notifying the doctor of his proposal (*Oxford* v *Lowton* [1978] RTR 237).

The doctor may object not only to the provision of breath but also to 'the requirement'. The condition of a patient may be such that a doctor may consider it prejudicial to the proper care of his patient's treatment merely to be asked to provide a breath specimen.

In practice the doctor is frequently asked simultaneously by the constable if he objects to the requirement to provide a breath test, the provision of breath, the requirement to provide specimens of blood or urine, the actual provision of specimens and the accompanying warning of the consequence of failure to provide specimens for analysis; in *Ratledge* v *Oliver* [1974] RTR 394 it was held that there was no objection to such a course.

Once the requirement for a breath test is made the patient is guilty of an offence if he fails or refuses to provide a specimen of breath (see further 4.46). The breath must be provided 'at the hospital'; it cannot be provided elsewhere or, seemingly, at another hospital (s 9(1)(*a*)).

The patient, while a patient at the hospital, cannot be arrested whether or not he gives a positive breath test or fails or refuses to do so (s 7(5)).

### 4.101–5 Blood or urine specimens

Neither the Lion Intoximeter nor the Camic Breath Analyser can be used at a hospital. Section 8(2) only allows a requirement for specimen of breath for evidential purposes to be made at a police station.

Although in most cases the police will continue only to require the provision of blood or urine specimens after the patient has been required to give a breath test, the police can now apparently require the provision of blood or urine notwithstanding the fact that the patient has not been asked to undergo a breath test. Section 8 entitles a constable to require specimens for analysis 'in the course of an investigation whether a person has committed an offence under s 5 or s 6'. If, therefore, the doctor has objected to a breath test but does not object to the warning and the requirement for the provision of a blood or urine specimen, a specimen of blood or urine may be required.

The safeguards for the provision of a blood or urine specimen are similar to those of the former law. The doctor has to be notified of the proposal to make the requirement and may object if the requirement, the warning under s 8(8) or the provision of blood or urine would be prejudicial to the proper care and treatment of his patient.

Section 9(1)(*b*) states that if the doctor objects, 'the requirement shall not be made'. At first sight this would seem to preclude any requirement being made if the doctor raises a partial objection, eg an objection to blood but not to urine. The purpose of s 9 is the proper protection of patients and a strict and careful analysis does not seem to require s 9 to be interpreted in such a way that an objection to the taking of one type of specimen has the effect of forbidding the constable to require the taking of the other.

As in the former law the doctor may object not only to the requirement but also to the warning required to be given to the patient should he refuse or fail to give specimens for analysis. It was held in *Baker* v *Foulkes* [1975] RTR 509 that there was no obligation on the police to notify the doctor that the warning would be given or to obtain his consent to the warning; nor is there any obligation on the police to ensure that the patient is out of earshot when the police notify the doctor (*Oxford* v *Lowton* above). The warning required under s 8(8) is simply that 'failure or refusal to supply a specimen may render you liable to prosecution' and is thus less frightening and less likely to be objected to than the warning under the former law ('failure to provide a specimen may make you liable to imprisonment, fine and disqualification').

The requirement will be to provide specimens either of blood or urine. The patient will not have a choice: the constable making the requirement shall decide whether the specimen required shall be of blood or urine save that if a medical practitioner is of the opinion that for medical reasons a specimen of blood cannot or should not be taken the specimen shall be a specimen of urine (s 8(4)). The constable need not necessarily apply his mind as to the exercise of his discretion (see *Pine* v *Collacott*, 4.77).

Difficulties have arisen in the past where a person either ceases to be a patient at the hospital or absconds (*Bosley* v *Long* [1970] RTR 432; *Bourlet* v *Porter* [1973] RTR 293; *Cunliffe* v *Bleasdale* [1972] Crim LR 567; *Edwards* v *Davies* [1982] RTR 279), but in practice the new law does not seem to provide as many difficulties as the former law. Cases will no doubt arise where a patient absconds from hospital after being required to provide a breath test or having to provide blood or urine specimens. If he absconds after being required to provide a breath test, he can be dealt with under s 7, as he will by definition no longer be a patient at a hospital. If he absconds after being required to provide either a specimen of blood or of urine, he will have failed to provide a specimen as soon as he absconds, contrary to s 8(7). Section 8(7) no longer requires him to be given the triple choice of blood, urine, and then blood again.

Where the person does not abscond but ceases to be a patient at the hospital because his treatment is complete (see 4.98) s 9 does not require the person to remain a patient by the time he actually provides the specimen. The only requirement of s 9 is that if a person is a patient at a hospital, the specimen must be provided at the hospital. If the person concerned has not been required to provide a breath test before he ceases to be a patient, there seems no reason why he should not be required to provide a breath test under s 7(2) nor if he is still at the hospital does there seem to be any reason precluding the police from requiring him to provide blood or urine under s 8 for analysis.

## Post-offence Consumption of Alcohol or Drugs

### 4.106 Alcohol

Under the former provisions it was held by the House of Lords that as the certificate of analysis must relate to the defendant's alcohol when he was driving, consumption of alcohol after he had ceased to drive and before he provided the specimen of blood or urine rendered the subsequent certificate inadmissible (*Rowlands* v *Hamilton* [1971] 1 All ER 1089). This case will not apply to certificates obtained under the new drink/driving provisions.

A certificate of analysis obtained in accordance with the present s 8 shall be 'taken into account' in respect of offences under s 5 and s 6, and may be evidence of the proportion of alcohol or any drug in a specimen of breath, blood or urine (s 10). Section 10(2) further provides that it shall be assumed that the proportion of alcohol at the time of the offence is not less than that contained in the certificate of analysis.

It is also provided that this statutory assumption that his alcohol level was not less than that of the certificate will not apply if the accused proves that he (*a*) had consumed alcohol after he had ceased to drive, attempt to drive or be in charge, and before he provided the specimen and (*b*) that had he not done so the proportion of alcohol would not have been such as to impair his ability to drive properly or, in the case of s 6 offences, above the prescribed limit. It should be noted that the onus of proof that he consumed alcohol is on the defendant, and it is for the defendant to establish by properly admissible evidence that he had consumed alcohol after the relevant time. In *Patterson* v *Charlton* (1985) *The Times*, 26 February, there was evidence by admission that the defendant had driven the car but no evidence that he had driven it after drinking. The justices dismissed the case but were directed by the Divisional Court that once the sample showed excess alcohol s 10(2) operated to transfer the burden of proof on to the defendant to show that he consumed alcohol after he ceased to drive.

As the onus of proof is on the defence, it would seem that as in other criminal statutes where Parliament has placed an onus of proof on the defendant it will be held that the onus is only that of a balance of probabilities.

Where the offence is under s 5 the defendant merely has to show that but for the added alcohol, his ability to drive properly would not have been impaired. Where the offence is under s 6 the defendant has to show that his alcohol level would not have been above the prescribed limit. In this connection, the comments in the 1965 *Report of a Special Committee of the British Medical Association* as to the translation of blood-alcohol concentration into quantity of alcohol consumed should be noted (see 4.75).

Courts are advised to adopt a similar approach as in the 'laced drink' case of *Pugsley* v *Hunter* [1973] RTR 284, namely that unless it is obvious to a layman that the post-offence consumption of alcohol explained the excess, the defendant must call medical or scientific evidence to prove that he would not otherwise have been above the prescribed limit (*Dawson* v *Lunn* (1984) *The Times*, 13 December, where the dicta of Lord Widgery in *Pugsley* v *Hunter* were said to be equally applicable to the defence under s 10(2) where the facts were not obvious from the non-expert evidence).

In *Lloyd* v *Knight* (1985) *The Times*, 13 February, the Divisional Court refused to overturn an acquittal by virtue of s 10(2) where the justices had relied upon a forensic scientist's report with the consent of the prosecutor, even though, if the report had not been agreed and the scientist called, the examination and cross-examination of the scientist might have thrown some doubt on his evidence.

It should be noted that s 10(2) states that the level of alcohol as shown by the certificate shall be assumed to be not less than *'at the time of the offence'*. By contrast, s 10(2)(*a*) requires the defendant to show that he consumed alcohol 'after he had ceased to drive, attempt to drive or be in charge of a motor vehicle on a road or other public place'. It is submitted that the contrast between the moment of time specified in s 10(2) (ie 'time of the offence') and the time in s 10(2)(*a*) (ie 'after he had ceased to drive . . . or be in charge') may be deliberate. The Blennerhasset Committee recommended that post-accident consumption of alcohol should not be a defence if the added alcohol was taken in order to avoid a conviction. Parliament has not enacted this specific recommendation, but it would seem that one effect of the wording of s 10(2)(*a*) is that a person who consumes alcohol after he has ceased driving but before he ceases to be in charge cannot avail himself of the defence. The words in section 10(2)(*a*), it is submitted, require the defendant to show that he consumed the added alcohol not only after he had ceased to drive or attempt to drive but also after he had ceased to be in charge. Parliament may well have had in mind the necessity of discouraging a drunken driver who has alcohol in his car from taking a quick gulp in the hope that he can then argue that but for the added alcohol he would not have been above the limit.

### 4.107–10 Drugs

It should be noted that while a certificate of analysis showing the proportion of a drug in a specimen can be 'taken into account' under s 10(2), there is no statutory assumption in the section that the proportion of a drug in the specimen is not less than that at the time the offence is committed. Section 10(2) refers only to the proportion of *alcohol*. Moreover, the proviso in s 10(2)(*a*) and (*b*) also refers only to alcohol. It would therefore appear that it is firstly necessary for the prosecution to relate the amount of a drug shown in the certificate to the amount of the drug that would have been shown if the specimen had been provided at the time of the offence. Secondly, it will be open to the defence to attack the certificate of analysis on the ground that he had ingested the drug after the time of the offence, but before he provided the specimen of blood or urine.

## Defences to 'in charge' Offences

### 4.111–15 Defences under s 5(2) and s 6(2)

A person charged under s 5(2) with being in charge of a motor vehicle while unfit to drive through drink or drugs is deemed not to be in charge of a motor vehicle if he proves that at the material time the circumstances were such that there was no likelihood of his driving it so long as he remained unfit to drive through drink or drugs. Similarly s 6(2) gives a defence to a charge under s 6(1)(*b*) (in charge with excess alcohol level) if he proves that, at the time he is alleged to have committed the offence, the circumstances were such that there was no likelihood of his driving the vehicle whilst the proportion of alcohol in his breath, blood or urine remained likely to exceed the prescribed limit.

There are semantic differences between the two defences. In s 5 the person is deemed not to be in charge if he establishes the statutory defence, in the s 6 offence 'it is a defence' if he establishes the statutory defence; in s 5, the defendant has to establish the defence that there was no likelihood of his driving 'at the material time' while in s 6 the material time is described as 'the time he is alleged to have committed the offence'. It is submitted that these differences between the statutory defences (and indeed the difference between the former s 6(3) defence and the present s 6(2) defence) are purely semantic. It is difficult to discern a difference in meaning albeit slightly differing words are used.

The only material difference between the two defences is that in s 5 the defendant has to show there is no likelihood of his driving while unfit and in s 6 that there is no likelihood of his driving while above the prescribed proportion of alcohol in his body.

The onus of proof is on the defendant, but, as in other cases where the onus is on the defendant, the standard of proof is the balance of probabilities (see *Morton* v *Confer* [1963] 2 All ER 765 and *Neish* v *Stevenson* [1970] Crim LR 161).

It is submitted that in practice it may be easier to establish a defence under s 5 that there is no likelihood of his driving while unfit than to establish the defence under s 6. In *Northfield* v *Pinder* [1968] 3 All ER 854 the defendant was accused of being in charge with more than 80 mg of alcohol in his blood; the certificate of analysis showed that he had 240 mg. He was found by his car at 9.14 pm and the magistrates considered that he was at that time so hopelessly drunk as to be incapable of driving his car or even of finding it or walking to it, so they dismissed the charge. The High Court quashed their decision and directed a conviction, saying that he must show that there was no likelihood of his driving whilst his level exceeded 80 mg and that there had been no evidence that he would not have driven when the worst effects of the drink had worn off. Medical evidence would probably be needed to show when his level would decrease to 80 mg but other evidence such as arranging for someone else to drive it or taking a bedroom at a hotel nearby would prove the 'unlikelihood' better. A very material factor in almost every case will be the level of alcohol in the blood as found by the analyst. If the level is only just over the limit, the defendant's blood-alcohol level will comparatively quickly recede below 80 mg. If, on the other hand, the blood-alcohol level is grossly above the limit, medical evidence may be required even if the defendant can show that he had arranged overnight accommodation. It is perfectly possible for a person to be still over the prescribed limit the morning after the night before, particularly if the night before involved a very large amount of alcohol.

In *Pugsley* v *Hunter* it was held that it was only if it were obvious to a layman that the 'lacing' of the defendant's drink accounted for the defendant being above the limit that expert evidence is not required to be called by the defence. It is thought likely that a similar approach to this problem should be adopted to a defence under s 6. It should be noted that in *Dawson* v *Lunn* (1984) *The Times*, 13 December, the dicta of Lord Widgery in *Pugsley* v *Hunter* were held to be similarly applicable to a defence under s 10(2) (see 4.106).

The level at which a person's blood alcohol declines is normally in the region of 11–21 mg: see Back Calculation, 4.75. Defending advocates should be careful to have regard to the fact that there is usually a time interval between the time at which the offence occurred and the time at which the specimen for analysis was given.

Originally a defendant seeking to defend a s 5 offence had to show not only that he was unlikely to drive while unfit but also that he had not actually driven while unfit. This was removed by Parliament in order to encourage those who are responsible enough to appreciate that they have drunk too much, to stop driving in the expectation that even if they remain technically 'in charge' their good intentions will help them to establish that there was no likelihood of their driving thereafter whilst over the limit.

The defence under s 5(3) was amended by s 25 of the Transport Act 1981 by providing that a court in determining whether there was any likelihood of his driving whilst unfit *may* disregard any injury to him and any damage to his vehicle. This amendment to s 5(3) is in identical terms to a similar proviso to s 6(2).

It should be noted that the word *may* in both subsections imparts a discretion as to the exercise of which the Act gives no assistance. The intention would appear to prevent a driver from relying on the defence where, had it not been for the purely fortuitous intervention of an accident, he would have continued to drive or remained in charge.

A drunken supervisor of a learner driver may be held to be 'in charge' of the motor vehicle and in *Sheldon* v *Jones* (1969) 113 SJ 942, the prosecution sought to argue that it was impossible for a supervisor to establish that there was no likelihood of his driving since at any moment he might have to take over the driving. The justices found as a fact that there was no such likelihood, and the Divisional Court, although stating that they themselves might have come to a different conclusion, felt unable to disturb the justices' finding to that effect. It is, however, submitted that a supervisor will usually have a difficult task in proving that there was no likelihood of his driving. It is submitted that momentarily taking over control of the steering or of the engine may well amount to 'driving' as one of the main duties of a supervisor of a learner-driver is to take control of the car in an emergency.

## Sentencing, Procedure and Trial

### 4.116 Procedure and trial

All drink/driving offences under the new statutory provisions are triable only summarily. Offences contrary to s 5 are also only triable summarily (unless the proceedings for the offence were commenced before 17 July 1978). Where the offence is under s 8(7) (refusing or failing without reasonable excuse to provide a specimen) or under s 5(1) or (2) (driving or in charge while unfit), some police forces, following an arrest, immediately charge the offender and either bail him to appear at the magistrates' court under s 43 of the Magistrates' Courts Act 1980 or, if not bailed, produce him as soon as reasonably practicable. Some police forces similarly charge and bail where the police are able to rely on a statement as to the proportion of breath being above the limit. In all other cases the police either bail under s 43(3) to come back to the police station when the certificate of analysis of blood or urine is available or else proceed by way of summons.

In *R* v *McKenzie* [1971] 1 All ER 729 (a decision of first instance at Durham Assizes) it was held that the former provisions of the Act only allowed the arrest and detention of a motorist for the purpose of supplying a specimen of blood or urine for laboratory testing and that the police only had power to detain him thereafter under s 11. Therefore, it was held, the police had no power to require a recognizance under what is now s 43(3) and bail him to appear at the police station or court. The view is taken by many police forces and, it is believed, the Home Office that *McKenzie* applies to the present statutory provisions albeit that s 11 has been re-enacted in slightly different form. If this is the case the effect on a person charged and bailed would not be to set aside any subsequent conviction (the reading of the charge in court constitutes the laying of an information (*R* v *Brentford JJ, ex parte Catlin* [1975] 2 All ER 201)). The main effect is that any detention beyond the period set out in s 11 would appear unlawful and any subsequent proceedings under the Bail Act 1976 for failing to surrender to bail might fail. The Police and Criminal Evidence Act 1984 will remove the uncertainty caused by *R* v *McKenzie* and it would appear that a person arrested under the Police and Criminal Evidence Act 1984 may be bailed under s 38 of that Act because s 34(6) specifically provides that an arrest under s 7(5) constitutes an arrest for an offence.

[*Paragraph 4.117 follows on page 254.*]

## 4.118 Custodial sentences

As a result of the Criminal Law Act 1977 all drink/driving offences proceedings for which were begun on or after 17 July 1978 became triable only by magistrates. The policy of the Court of Appeal dealing with drink/driving offences committed before 1978 is, however, relevant. Four basic sentencing considerations seem relevant: first the circumstances of the offence (and 'circumstances are infinitely variable': *R* v *Nokes* below); secondly the record of the offender; thirdly his blood-alcohol level; and fourthly whether the offence is associated with an episode of bad or wicked driving. There is no principle of sentencing that a custodial sentence should not be imposed for a first drink/driving offence (*R* v *Nokes* [1978] RTR 101; six months' imprisonment upheld; 183 mg of alcohol; excess speed; bad behaviour on being analysed; resisting arrest; bad motoring record; previous custodial sentence). Where the blood-alcohol level is high, a sentence of imprisonment may not be upheld if this is the only factor (*R* v *Newman* [1978] RTR 107; *R* v *Beardsley* [1979] RTR 472; *R* v *Thomas* (*Colin*) (1973) 57 Cr App R 596), notwithstanding the dicta to the contrary by Scarman LJ in *R* v *Pashley* [1974] RTR 149 and Roskill LJ in *R* v *Tupa* [1974] RTR 153. What is clear is that, where there are repeated offences coupled with a bad record, the Court of Appeal is prepared to uphold a comparatively lengthy sentence (*R* v *McLaughlin* [1978] RTR 452; total of 30 months' imprisonment; three separate drink/driving offences; menace to road users because of a serious drink problem which he was not prepared to recognise). Lastly it may be said with confidence that where death or serious injury occurs as a result of reckless driving while the offender's blood-alcohol level was above the limit, an immediate custodial sentence will be imposed unless there are exceptional mitigating circumstances (*R* v *Eadie* [1978] RTR 292). In *R* v *Boswell* [1984] RTR 315, the 'guideline' sentencing case in respect of causing death by reckless driving, one of the aggravating sentencing factors was the amount of consumption of alcohol or drugs.

## 4.119 Detention in police custody

A magistrates' court having power to impose imprisonment or youth custody may, instead of so doing, order him to be detained for any period not exceeding four days 'in a place certified by the Home Secretary as suitable' (Magistrates' Courts Act 1980, s 134(1)). The Home Secretary under

## 4.117 Table of penalties etc

| *Offence* | *Section* | *Imprisonment* | *Fine** | *Disqualification* | *Penalty points* | *Endorsement code* | *Magistrates' Association's Suggestions* |
|---|---|---|---|---|---|---|---|
| Driving or attempting to drive while unfit | s 5(1) | 6 months | level 5* | Obligatory | (4)† | DR20 | £200 dis 12 months but 18 months over 150 mg blood, 66 μg breath, 200 mg urine; 2 yrs over 200 mg blood, 88 μg breath, 267 mg urine; 3 yrs over 250 mg blood, 110 μg breath, 333 mg urine‡ |
| Driving or attempting to drive with excess alcohol | s 6(1)(*a*) | 6 months | level 5* | Obligatory | (4)† | DR10 | |
| In charge while unfit | s 5(2) | 3 months | level 4* | Discretionary | 10 | DR50 | £100 and consider disqualification |
| In charge with excess alcohol | s 6(1)(*b*) | 3 months | level 4* | Discretionary | 10 | DR40 | |
| Refusing a roadside breath test | s 7(4) | — | level 3* | Discretionary | 4 | DR70 | £50 |
| Failing or refusing to supply an evidential specimen when 'driving or attempting to drive' | s 8(7) | 6 months | level 5* | Obligatory | (4)† | DR30 | £200 dis 18 months |
| Failing or refusing to provide an evidential specimen when not 'driving or attempting to drive' | s 8(7) | 3 months | level 4* | Discretionary | 10 | DR60 | £100 |

* As to the current levels of maximum fines, see 4.120 below.
† No points may be imposed when offender is disqualified (see further 4.123).
‡ For conversion of breath-alcohol to blood/urine-alcohol see Appendix 1, 'Alcohol concentration'.

s 134(2) may certify as suitable for detention police cells, bridewell, and any place or other place provided by him or a police authority.

This power was used at Christmas 1983 and since for persons convicted of drink/driving offences, particularly, but not exclusively, those committed in Essex. The requirements as to legal aid, the obtaining of social enquiry reports etc as set out in ss 20, 20A and 21 of the Powers of Criminal Courts Act 1973 or ss 1–3 of the Criminal Justice Act 1982 do not apply to orders of detention under s 134. The power under s 134 would not, however, appear to be available unless there are police cells certified by the Home Secretary. It is understood that no cells in the Metropolitan Police area have been approved as suitable; it is believed that this is so in some other police areas.

### 4.120 Fines etc

In order to keep the maxima of fines in line with inflation, the Home Secretary was empowered by s 143 of the Magistrates' Courts Act 1980 to make an order increasing the levels of fines. An order has been made increasing the levels as follows.

| *Levels on the scale* | *Previous maxima* | *New maxima* |
|---|---|---|
| 1 | £25 | £50 |
| 2 | £50 | £100 |
| 3 | £200 | £400 |
| 4 | £500 | £1,000 |
| 5 | £1,000 | £2,000 |

The order came into effect on 1 May 1984 and the new maxima only apply to offences committed on or after that date. No further order has been made under s 143 up to January 1985.

The Magistrates' Association's suggestions as to the appropriate starting points for fines are set out at 4.117. The suggestions are, however, only a starting point for an average first offence by a person of average means and must be read subject to 'How to Use the "Suggestions" ' which is set out in Appendix 3. In fixing the amount of the fine, a magistrates' court is required to take into consideration amongst other things the means of the offender so far as they are known to the court (Magistrates' Courts Act 1980, s 35). A court cannot claim to have had regard to the means of the offender merely by ordering payments by instalments over a long period of time (*R* v *Hewitt* (1971) 55 Cr App Rep 433).

It is suggested that the main factors governing the level of fine to be imposed should be the alcohol level, the circumstances surrounding the offence (including any other offence committed on the same occasion) the defendant's previous motoring convictions and his circumstances and means. Where the court is obliged to disqualify, or is considering doing so, the court may be reminded to consider the financial effect that any period of disqualification will have on the offender, as suggested by the Magistrates' Association. Even where he does not lose his livelihood on disqualification, an order usually leads to heavy additional financial burdens.

A court may not impose a fine in addition to an order of absolute or conditional discharge, nor to an order of probation, but s 102 of the 1972 Act requires a court to make orders of disqualification or endorsement notwithstanding the fact that the offender is placed on probation or given an absolute or conditional discharge.

### 4.121 Community service order

A community service order may not be combined with any other sentence eg a fine, but by s 14(8) a court may in addition to community service make orders as to costs, compensation, deprivation of property, restitution and disqualification. Although the power of endorsement is not specifically included in s 14(8) it is submitted that where an offender is sentenced to community service in respect of an endorsable offence, the court must make an order of endorsement including the appropriate number of penalty points.

### 4.122 Compensation

Although a magistrates' court may order an offender to pay up to £2,000 compensation resulting from an offence, no compensation can be ordered in respect of death or 'of injury, loss or damage due to an accident arising out of the presence of a motor vehicle on a road'. For this reason the court will normally have no power to award compensation in respect of a drink/driving offence. The question of compensation will in practice only arise where the offender is also convicted under the Theft Act 1978 of theft or an unlawful taking of the motor vehicle. In such a case the person convicted may be ordered to pay compensation in respect of damage to the owner's vehicle which occurred after the vehicle had been taken and before its recovery.

### 4.123 Obligatory disqualification

On conviction of an offence under s 5(1) (driving or attempting to drive while unfit), s 6(1)(*a*) (driving or attempting to drive with excess breath, blood, or urine/alcohol levels) or s 8(7) (failing to supply specimens for analysis when driving or attempting to drive) a court is obliged to disqualify for *at least* twelve months unless the court for *special reasons* orders him not to be disqualified or disqualifies him for a shorter period (see Chapter 21).

Section 11(4) of the Magistrates' Courts Act 1980 prohibits a court from disqualifying a person in his absence unless the court has previously adjourned under s 10(3) of the Magistrates' Courts Act 1980. The notice of adjournment must include notice of the reason for the adjournment (Magistrates' Courts Act 1980, s 11(4)). Where a magistrates' court, without first adjourning under (what is now) s 10(3) of the Magistrates' Courts Act 1980, convicted and disqualified a defendant in his absence for driving with excess blood-alcohol, the disqualification (but not the conviction) was quashed (*R* v *Bishop's Stortford JJ, ex parte Shields* [1969] Crim LR 201).

*Period of obligatory disqualification*

The Magistrates' Association's Suggestions recommend (see Appendix 3) that where the blood-alcohol level is over 150 mg the disqualification should be for eighteen months, where over 200 mg two years and where over 250 mg three years' disqualification. (The levels 150 mg, 200 mg and 250 mg in blood are equivalent to 200, 267 and 334 mg in urine and 65, 87 and 109 microgrammes in breath (see Appendix 1, 'Alcohol concentration').)

Support for these recommendations may be found in the consistent policy of the Court of Appeal to uphold periods of disqualification longer than the minimum twelve months where the level is considerably in excess of the limit or where the offence is accompanied by evidence of bad driving or behaviour. The courts have increasingly recognised that an order of disqualification is the chief penalty for most offenders, and have wished to show a distinction in the period of disqualification between an offender only slightly above the limit whose driving ability is only slightly impaired, if at all, and an offender whose alcohol level is greatly in excess of the prescribed limit and whose driving has clearly been affected by his consumption of alcohol. In *Sakhuja* v *Allen* [1972] RTR 315, Lord Hailsham LC in his speech in that case remarked:

> It may well be that circuit judges and recorders will do well to bear in mind that they have a discretion to impose longer periods of disqualification when bad driving and bad behaviour follow the drink. In this way they can differentiate between drivers whose excessive drinking is substantial . . . and those where the drinking is only slightly above the limit and has not been accompanied by bad driving or bad behaviour.

These remarks were followed and applied in *R* v *Slade* [1974] RTR 20 where a disqualification of thirty months was upheld. Despite the hardship caused by disqualification (living in remote area; wife unwell and not able to drive; daughter having to be driven to school; defendant driving 25,000 to 30,000 miles a year) the period of disqualification was 'wholly right' as the defendant's blood-alcohol level was 165 mg of alcohol in 100 ml of blood.

In *R* v *Yoxall* [1973] Crim LR 63 a period of three years' disqualification was upheld (236 mg of alcohol in 100 ml blood); in *R* v *Thomas* [1973] RTR 325 a two-year period was upheld (292 mg of alcohol in 100 ml of urine); in *R* v *Tupa* [1974] RTR 153 a period of five years was upheld (289 mg of alcohol in 100 ml of blood); in *R* v *Sharman* [1974] RTR 213 a period of two years was upheld (143 mg of alcohol in 100 ml of blood); in *R* v *Mills* [1974] RTR 215 a period of two years was upheld (118 mg of alcohol in 100 ml of blood: per Lord Widgery CJ at p 216; 'it is quite wrong to talk about the tariff disqualification being twelve months . . . It cannot be less than twelve months and it is a matter within the discretion of the court and a fairly wide discretion how long a disqualification is imposed'); in *R* v *Newton* (*David*) [1974] RTR 451 an eighteen months' period was upheld even though the defendant's drink had been laced.

On the other hand it is the policy of the Court of Appeal not to approve excessively long periods of disqualification particularly where there is a risk of the offender being thereby tempted to drive while disqualified and there are no considerations of public safety involved. In *R* v *Calhoun* [1974] Crim LR 436 a period of fifteen years' disqualification was reduced to the minimum of three years for this reason. In *R* v *Pashley* [1974] RTR 149 a sentence of twelve months' imprisonment was upheld but a disqualification of three years was reduced to twelve months because of the risk of the defendant being tempted to drive while disqualified on coming out of prison.

The Magistrates' Association suggest that eighteen months should be the normal period of disqualification for the offence of refusing to supply samples of breath, blood or urine for analysis when driving or attempting to drive at the relevant time. There is little judicial authority for this recommendation. The Act does not lay down a longer minimum period of disqualification for an offence under s 8(7) than for one under s 5(1) or s 6(1)(*a*). On the other hand, if it were to become the general policy of courts only to impose twelve months' disqualification for refusal, it would encourage drivers who had been drinking heavily to refuse to supply specimens for laboratory testing, rather than to supply them. In *R* v *Nicholls* [1977] Crim LR 685 a period of disqualification of eighteen months for refusing was upheld. It is submitted that whilst the court is by the very nature of the offence handicapped by not knowing the exact alcohol level of the defendant, the level of penalties and the period of disqualification should approximate as nearly as possible to the penalties which would have been imposed if the defendant had supplied a specimen and the analysis had shown a high blood-alcohol level. It may be difficult for a defendant who refuses to supply a specimen to persuade a court that his alcohol level would have been low, since he could have demonstrated that fact by supplying specimens for analysis. Of necessity he can only have committed the offence by failing to supply a specimen without reasonable excuse.

It is suggested that where alcohol levels are well above the limit so that the offender cannot plead that he did not know he was above the prescribed limit, one important mitigating factor will be the severity of the effect of the disqualification on the offender and his family. Where a court disqualifies an offender (whether or not the court was obliged to or merely had a discretion to do so) the licence is required to be endorsed but no penalty points may be imposed.

### 4.124 Penalty points disqualification

Although a court cannot order the imposition of penalty points when disqualifying an offender, the court is required to take into account the four penalty points in respect of an obligatorily disqualifiable offence. For this reason a court would seem to be under an obligation to impose an additional penalty points disqualification where the offender has eight points already endorsed on his licence.

The offences under s 5(2) and s 6(1)(*b*) of being in charge while unfit or with excess alcohol incur ten penalty points and the offence of refusing a preliminary breath test involves four penalty points.

For discussion as to endorsement of these penalty points and any resulting penalty points disqualification see 20.19.

### 4.125 Obligatory disqualification for at least three years

Where a defendant is convicted of driving or attempting to drive whilst unfit (s 5(1)) or with excess alcohol levels (s 6(1)(*a*)) or refusing to supply a laboratory specimen (s 8(7)) when driving or attempting to drive at the relevant time and has been previously convicted of any such offence within a period of ten years, the minimum period for which a court is obliged to disqualify is increased to three years (s 93(4)) of the 1972 Act as amended by Sched 9, para 3 of the Transport Act 1981 and Sched 5, para 13(1) of the Transport Act 1982).

Paragraph 13 of Sched 5 to the Transport Act 1982 has the effect of including previous convictions under the former s 6(1) (driving with excess alcohol) and convictions under the former s 9(3) (failing to supply specimens for analysis when driving or attempting to drive at the relevant time) as previous convictions for the purposes of s 93(4) providing, of course, such convictions are within the ten-year period.

Previous convictions under the present or former provisions of the Act of 1972 in respect of being *in charge* of a motor vehicle do not count as previous convictions for the purpose of increasing the obligatory disqualification to three years on conviction of a drink/drive offence. (Although it would seem that a person convicted of driving with excess alcohol or unfit who on the earlier occasion was not disqualified because of 'special reasons' will nevertheless be liable to the minimum period of three years' disqualification if he commits another such offence within the three year period; s 93(4) merely refers to a person being 'convicted'. It was, moreover, held in *Bolliston* v *Gibbons* (1984) *The Times*, 31 March, that a court can only take into account special reasons which relate to the later offence.)

It should be particularly noted that the wording of s 93(4) makes it clear that the ten-year period has to be calculated from the date of the *commission* of the subsequent offence back to the date of the *conviction* of the earlier offence. This has a number of consequences; a person appearing before a court charged with two offences committed on different dates is only liable to a minimum of twelve months on each as he will not necessarily have been convicted for the earlier offence when he committed the second offence. (It should also be noted in such an instance that the court cannot make the two orders of disqualification consecutive: *R* v *Bain* [1973] RTR 213.) Similarly if, for example, an offender commits an offence on 1 December 1984 of driving while unfit contrary to s 5(1), and commits an offence of driving with excess alcohol on 28 February 1985, he will not be liable to the minimum three-years' disqualification when he is dealt with for the 28 February offence unless he was convicted of the 1 December offence before 28 February.

The method of calculating the ten-year period in accordance with s 93(4) can, however, also work to the disadvantage of the defendant. Thus if the later offence occurred on 1 January 1985 and the earlier offence was committed in December 1974, for which the defendant was convicted on 1 February 1975, he is liable to the three-year compulsory disqualification. (*Quaere* in such a case whether the disqualification cannot be reduced to less than three years for 'special reasons'. It would seem not. To do so would seem to involve the proposition that the words of s 93(4) do not mean what they say.)

A motorist who has been disqualified for the three-year obligatory period may, despite the fact that it is a minimum period of three years, apply for removal of the disqualification under s 95 of the 1972 Act after two years: *Damer* v *Davison* [1976] RTR 45 (but see the remarks of Lord Widgery CJ in that case, noted at 20.41).

Where the two offences are both above two and a half times the limit, where one is an offence under s 8(7) and the other is above two and a half times, or where both offences are under s 8(7) the Secretary of State for Transport will not automatically issue a licence to the offender at the conclusion of the period of disqualification (see below).

### 4.126–30 Problem drinkers

The Committee on Drinking and Driving (the 'Blennerhasset Committee') in 1976 was concerned with the problem posed by those whom the committee referred to as 'high risk offenders'. Statistics show that there is a category of offender who repeatedly commits drink/driving offences with high blood-alcohol content—so high in fact that much expert evidence is of the opinion that such offenders usually are among the class of persons with an alcohol problem. The Government accordingly decided, with effect from 6 May 1983, to introduce special arrangements as to the issue of licences after the expiration of the court's order of disqualification in respect of offenders who come within one of the three following categories:

(1) Those disqualified twice within ten years for driving or attempting to drive when on both occasions their alcohol level was more than two and a half times the prescribed limit.
(2) Those disqualified twice within ten years, once for driving with more than two and a half times the prescribed limit, and once for failing to provide a specimen of breath, blood or urine for analysis when required to do so.
(3) Those disqualified twice within ten years for failing to provide a specimen for analysis where police evidence suggests that there are reasonable grounds for suspecting that the driver has an alcohol problem.

After a second conviction such an offender will be advised by the DVLC that when he re-applies for a licence on the expiry of the second period of disqualification, consideration will be given to whether the convictions indicate a medical disability and, if so, whether he has managed to bring the drinking problem under control. He will be advised to seek such help and advice during the period of disqualification.

Four months before the end of the disqualification the Medical Advisory Branch of the Department of Transport will send him an application form for renewal of his licence together with a letter explaining that his licence will not be renewed unless he can satisfy the Secretary of State that he does not have an alcohol problem.

Once an application is received at DVLC the offender will be invited to attend a special examination centre where he will be taken through an interview and given a medical examination. Following the interview the offender will be referred to a local hospital for a blood sample which will be analysed by the Isaac Wolfson Research Laboratory at Birmingham.

The results of the interview and blood analysis will determine the Secretary of State's decision as to whether or not to refuse to issue the licence. Borderline cases will be referred to a consultant psychiatrist specialising in alcohol problems.

*Legal position*

The powers of the Secretary of State to revoke or to refuse a licence are contained in s 87 of the 1972 Act and he has no choice but to refuse if on enquiry he is satisfied that the person concerned is suffering from a 'relevant disability'. These include not only the various diseases or disabilities set out in reg 22 of the Driving Licences Regulations 1981 as amended (see above) but also 'any other disability likely to cause the driving of a vehicle by him . . . to be a source of danger to the public' (s 87(1)(*a*) as amended by s 13 and Sched 3 of the Road Traffic Act 1974). Alcoholism is not one of the prescribed diseases or disabilities set out in reg 22 of the Driving Licences Regulations but there seems no doubt it comes within the statutory definition set out above. If after the enquiries set out above the Secretary of State refuses to issue a licence by virtue of s 87, the applicant has a right of appeal under s 90 of the 1972 Act to the magistrates' court acting for the petty sessions area in which he resides, or, if he resides in Scotland, to the sheriff within whose jurisdiction he resides. The decision of the court is binding on the Secretary of State.

On appeal to the magistrates' court it would seem to be a matter of fact for the court to decide in accordance with the medical and other evidence before it as to whether the applicant has or has not an alcohol problem so that it can be said he *is* suffering from a disability or disease 'likely to cause the driving of a vehicle by him to be a source of danger to the public'. It is relevant that a person can be cured of an alcohol problem and presumably the court when considering the appeal will have to decide not whether he *had* such a problem but whether the alcohol problem of the defendant is such that at the time of the hearing he still has an alcohol problem and therefore it *is* 'likely to cause the driving of a vehicle by him to be a source of danger to the public'.

## Other Offences involving Drink or Drugs

### 4.131 Riding a cycle whilst unfit

Section 19 (1) of the 1972 Act provides that it is an offence for a person to ride a bicycle, tricycle or cycle having four or more wheels, not being a motor vehicle, on a road (including a bridleway) or other public place, whilst unfit to ride it through drink or drugs. By s 19(4) 'unfit to ride' means being under the influence of drink or drugs to such an extent as to be incapable of having proper control. The offence is punishable with a fine of level 3 on the standard scale.

The police are given a power of arrest by s 19(3). Section 19(3) will be repealed as far as England and Wales are concerned by the Police and Criminal Evidence Act 1984 but although s 19 will thus no longer be an arrestable offence a constable can arrest if he has reasonable grounds for believing that an arrest of the cyclist is necessary to prevent the cyclist causing physical injury to himself or any other person (Police and Criminal Evidence Act 1984, s 25(2)(*d*)(i)). There are no provisions importing the procedures under ss 7, 8, 9 or 10 of the Act into offences involving cyclists; and the police have therefore no power to require a cyclist to provide a specimen of breath, blood or urine. Nor can the prosecution rely on any refusal by the cyclist to provide any specimen of blood or urine as support for its case. But if the cyclist in fact provides a specimen, its analysis will presumably be admissible.

The offence may be committed not only on a public highway, but also on footpaths or footways forming part of a road. It will also be committed upon a private road to which the public has access.

Section 19(2) exempts any person liable to be charged under s 19(1) from any charge under s 12 of the Licensing Act 1872 (see below) or the equivalent Scottish enactment. As this exemption only applies to a person liable to be charged with 'riding' a cycle, the appropriate charge for a person attempting to ride, or in charge of, a cycle whilst drunk may be under s 12 of the Licensing Act 1872.

**4.132 In charge of a carriage, horse or cattle, when drunk**

Section 12 of the Licensing Act 1872 makes it an offence to be in charge of any carriage, horse or cattle on any highway or other public place when drunk. The penalty is a fine of level 1 on the standard scale or one month's imprisonment. The section applies to cyclists (*Corkery* v *Carpenter* [1951] 1 KB 102) and, *semble*, barrows ([1939] Jo Crim L 338). 'Cattle' generally includes housed domestic animals, horses, asses, pigs and sheep.

The prosecution must establish that the defendant was not merely under the influence of drink, but 'drunk'.

# Chapter 5

# Reckless, Careless and Inconsiderate Driving etc

### 5.1 Introduction

The offences with which this chapter is mainly concerned are contained in ss 1–3 of the Road Traffic Act 1972, as amended by the Criminal Law Act 1977, and are as follows:

(*a*) causing death by reckless driving (s 1);
(*b*) reckless driving (s 2); and
(*c*) careless and inconsiderate driving (s 3).

This chapter also deals with the related offences of reckless, careless and inconsiderate cycling in ss 17 and 18 of the 1972 Act, and other related offences in the 1972 and other Acts, including 'motor manslaughter'. The penalties and sentencing for all the above offences are dealt with at 5.71–90.

The former offences of causing death by driving, and driving, in a manner dangerous or at a speed dangerous to the public were repealed, with effect from 1 December 1977, by s 50 of the Criminal Law Act 1977.

## Reckless Driving

### 5.2 The offence: s 2

Section 2 of the 1972 Act, as amended by the Criminal Law Act 1977, provides that 'a person who drives a motor vehicle on a road recklessly shall be guilty of offence'. Section 3 remains unaltered by the 1977 Act and provides that it is an offence for a person to drive a motor vehicle on a road 'without due care and attention, or without reasonable consideration for other persons using the road'.

Although many of the cases on the former offence of dangerous driving may be of relevance to cases of careless or inconsiderate driving, they will usually be of little relevance in deciding what amounts to reckless driving. The cases on the former offences of dangerous driving established that a person could be convicted of dangerous driving even if his fault consisted only of carelessness or incompetence. It is submitted that it is obvious that a person may not be convicted of reckless driving if he is only guilty of careless driving or lack of consideration for other road users.

Sections 2 and 3 apply to trolley vehicles but not to tramcars operated under statutory powers (s 198(1)), and all offences of reckless and careless driving (and cycling) apply to servants of the Crown (s 188).

Offences under ss 2 and 3 can be committed only on a 'road' (as defined in the 1972 Act: see Chapter 1).

To produce false evidence with a view to misleading a court and perverting the course of justice constitutes the common law offence of perverting the course of justice. It is also an offence to incite a person to do so (*R* v *Andrews* [1973] 1 All ER 857, where the defendant offered to make a false statement to the police regarding an accident in which *R* was involved in return for a reward from *R*).

## 5.3 What is reckless driving?

On a charge under s 2 the prosecution must prove that the defendant drove recklessly. The numerous reported cases on the former offences of driving in a manner dangerous or at a speed dangerous may not be of much relevance as to what is reckless driving, particularly as it has been held that a person could be convicted of dangerous driving even though he was only careless. Because it was easier to obtain a conviction before a jury of dangerous driving than of reckless driving, the very great majority of prosecutions under ss 1 and 2 were for driving in a dangerous manner or driving at a dangerous speed. With the elimination of these offences by s 50 of the Criminal Law Act 1977 it became necessary to define reckless driving. Although the law may seem to differ between Scotland (*Allan* v *Patterson* below) and England (*R* v *Lawrence* below), Lord Diplock in the latter case said, at [1981] RTR 227:

I do not think that, having regard to the likelihood that the jury will draw the inference to which I have referred, the practical result of approaching the question of what constitutes driving recklessly in the way that was adopted by the Lord Justice-General in *Allan* v *Patterson* is likely to be any different from the result of instructing a jury in some such terms as I have suggested [see Model Direction below]. The same Act applies to both countries; it would be unfortunate if the interpretation put upon it by the Scots courts differed from that put upon it by the courts in England and Wales.

*Scotland*

In *Allan* v *Patterson* [1980] RTR 97 the Scottish High Court of Justiciary held that the test as to whether a defendant has driven recklessly is as follows:

Section 2 as its language plainly, we think, suggests, requires a judgment to be made quite objectively of a particular course of driving in proved circumstances, and what the court or a jury has to decide, using its commonsense, is whether that course of driving in these circumstances had the grave quality of recklessness. Judges and juries will readily understand, and juries might well be reminded, that before they can apply the adverb 'recklessly' to the driving in question they must find that it fell far below the standard of driving expected of the competent and careful driver and that it occurred either in the face of obvious and material dangers which were or should have been observed, appreciated and guarded against, or in circumstances which showed a complete disregard for any potential dangers which might result from the way in which the vehicle was being driven. It will be understood that in reaching a decision upon the critical issue a judge or jury will be entitled to have regard to any explanation offered by the accused driver designed to show that his driving in the particular circumstances did not possess the quality of recklessness at the material time.

It should be noted that the judgment above requires the jury to find that the driving in question falls '*far* below' the standard of a competent and careful driver. The test of whether a person has driven without due care and attention is whether the prosecution can prove the driving is below that of a careful and competent driver. A jury, if not satisfied that a defendant is guilty of reckless driving, may bring in an alternative verdict of careless driving. Thus the test for careless driving is driving *below* the standard of a careful and competent driver and the test for reckless driving is driving *far below* that standard. The distinction between the two offences is further spelt out in the judgment of *Allan* v *Patterson* as follows:

In its context [reckless driving] plainly means a piece of driving which, judged objectively, is eloquent of a high degree of negligence—much more than a mere want of due care and attention—and supports the inference that material risks were deliberately courted or that these risks which ought to have been obvious to any observant and careful driver were not noticed by reason of gross inattention. Driving 'recklessly', accordingly, is driving which demonstrates a gross degree of carelessness in the face of evident dangers.

Finally, it should be noted from the first extract from the judgment that the jury must have regard to any explanation offered by the accused driver.

It would also seem that if the driving was caused by a mechanical failure or defect of which the defendant was not aware and of which it would not be reasonable to expect him to be aware, he is entitled to be acquitted (see *R* v *Spurge* at 5.34, a mechanical defect). On the other hand if he was aware of the defect or should have been aware of it, this will be very relevant as to whether he should be convicted (see eg *R* v *Millar* at 5.34). The established law as to automatism also still seems to apply (see 5.29).

*England and Wales*

The direction as to reckless driving as enunciated by the Court of Appeal in *R* v *Murphy* [1980] RTR 145 was held to be wrong by the House of Lords in *R* v *Lawrence* [1981] RTR 217 by a unanimous decision. The speeches in *R* v *Lawrence* were given immediately following those in *Commissioner of Police for the Metropolis* v *Caldwell* (1981) 73 Cr App R 13, where the House of Lords were concerned with 'recklessness' in the context of the Criminal Damage Act 1971. In that case the House of Lords, with the exception of Lord Edmund-Davies, held self-induced intoxication to be no defence to a crime in which recklessness is enough to constitute the necessary mens rea. In so doing it condemned the use of the labels 'subjective' and 'objective'. Where the mens rea of an offence consists of recklessness, it was held, applying its ordinary English meaning to the word, that a person is reckless when, doing an act creating an obvious risk, he either has not given any thought to the possibility of there being any such risk or has recognised that there is some risk involved and nonetheless goes on to do it. Accordingly, it was held that a proper direction in respect of a charge under s 1(1) of the Criminal Damage Act 1971 is to instruct the jury to convict if they are satisfied that (1) the defendant did an act which in fact created an obvious risk that property would be destroyed or damaged; and (2) when he did the act he either had not given any thought to the possibility of there being any such risks or had recognised that there was some risk involved and nonetheless had gone on to do it.

The House of Lords in *R* v *Lawrence* followed the reasoning of their decision in *Caldwell* as to the meaning of 'reckless'. There are only two speeches, those of Lord Hailsham and Lord Diplock, the former supporting the reasoning set out in the latter's speech. All the other members of the House of Lords, including the Scots Law Lord, Lord Fraser of Tullybelton, fully agreed with Lord Hailsham and Lord Diplock. It was held that the actus reus on a charge under s 1 or s 2 of the Road Traffic Act 1972 consists of driving the vehicle in such a manner as to create an obvious and serious risk of harmful consequences. The mens rea consists of the driver's being reckless, ie (following *Caldwell*) failing to give any thought to there being any possibility of any such risk or, having recognised that there is such a risk, nevertheless going on to do it.

*Model Direction to juries*

Lord Diplock suggested the following as an appropriate direction to a jury (and by implication a direction which magistrates should themselves apply in reaching a decision on a charge of reckless driving):

The jury must be satisfied of two things:

*First*, that the defendant was in fact driving the vehicle in such a manner as to create an obvious and serious risk of causing physical injury to some other person who might happen to be using the road, or doing substantial damage to property; and

*Second*, that in driving in that manner the defendant did so without having given any thought to the possibility of there being any such risk or, having recognised that there was some risk involved had nonetheless gone on to take it.

Lord Diplock further said:

It is for the jury to decide whether the risk created by the manner in which the vehicle was being driven was both obvious and serious and, in deciding this, they may apply the standard of the ordinary prudent motorist as represented by themselves. If satisfied that an obvious and serious risk was created by the manner of the defendant's driving, the jury are entitled to infer that he was in one or other of the states of mind required to constitute the offence and will probably do so; but regard must be given to any explanation he gives as to his state of mind which may displace the inference.

In *R* v *Madigan* [1983] RTR 198 it was held to be highly desirable that Lord Diplock's model definition of reckless driving should be given by the judge word for word when directing a jury.

## 5.4 Summary of reckless driving

The position as to reckless driving may thus be summarised as follows:

(1) A person is guilty of reckless driving (or if a death is caused, causing death by reckless driving: see 5.11) if the jury or magistrates are satisfied that:

(*a*) the defendant was driving the vehicle in such a manner as to create an *obvious* and *serious* risk of causing physical injury to some other person who might happen to be using the road or of doing *substantial* damage to property; and

(*b*) that in so driving he did so without having given any thought to the possibility of there being any such risk or, having recognised that there was some risk involved, nonetheless went on to take it.

(2) The jury or magistrates are entitled to infer that the defendant drove recklessly from the manner in which the vehicle was driven and the road conditions, but must have regard to and consider any explanation put forward as to the manner in which the vehicle was driven. If a reasonable explanation is put forward which amounts to a defence, it is for the prosecution to disprove it not for the defence to prove that it is true.

It should be added that the House of Lords in *R* v *Lawrence* above were only concerned with the manner of driving. It would seem that a defendant who drove a vehicle while having actual knowledge of a defect can also be convicted of reckless driving (see *R* v *Millar*, 5.34). Similarly it would seem that a defendant who drove with knowledge of a physical illness or disability which could result in an obvious and serious risk of causing physical injury to other road users could also be liable to a charge of reckless driving (see *R* v *Sibbles*, 5.29). Likewise where a defendant has taken alcohol in sufficient quantity that he knew or must have known his ability to drive was substantially impaired and that there was therefore a risk of his causing injury to other road users (see *R* v *Griffiths*, 5.32).

A useful article which analyses *R* v *Lawrence* will be found in the November 1981 issue of *Criminal Law Review* (Professor Edward Griew, 'Reckless Damage and Reckless Driving' [1981] Crim LR 743). Reference may also be made to another article in the *Criminal Law Review* by George Syrota ([1982] Crim LR 97).

## 5.5 Procedure

Reckless driving contrary to s 2 of the 1972 Act is an 'either way' offence within the meaning of the Magistrates' Courts Act 1980: the prosecution may request trial on indictment and the defence has a right to elect trial on indictment (see Chapter 2). Careless or inconsiderate driving contrary to s 3 may only be tried summarily (although a jury may convict a defendant of careless or inconsiderate driving if acquitted of a charge of causing death by reckless driving contrary to s 1 or of reckless driving contrary to s 2). If reckless driving is heard on indictment it is a Class 4 offence and thus will ordinarily be heard at the lowest tier Crown Court (see Directions of the Lord Chief Justice).

As juries are now permitted to bring in an alternative verdict of careless driving (see below) and the Crown Court on hearing an appeal against a charge under s 2 can direct a charge under s 3 to be preferred (*Killington* v *Butcher* [1979] Crim LR 458), the practice of some police forces of charging a defendant under both s 2 and s 3 now seems unnecessary and may attract the criticism of lending itself to undesirable or improper plea bargaining.

It was held in *R* v *McBride* [1962] 1 QB 167 that a charge of driving under the influence of drink might be tried along with one for dangerous or careless driving. It would seem that a s 5 or s 6 charge may similarly be tried along with reckless or careless driving (see *R* v *Thorpe* [1974] RTR 465) as there seems to be no distinction between the former offence of dangerous driving and reckless driving in this context. It should be noted, however, that the drink/driving offences under ss 5 and 6 can no longer be tried on indictment. It is submitted that evidence proving the commission of an offence under s 5 or s 6 may be admissible in a charge of reckless driving tried on indictment (see 5.32).

If a defendant charged with reckless driving elects to be tried by jury and the magistrates find no case to answer against him, the court (if consisting of two or more magistrates) may proceed to hear a charge for careless driving or some other lesser offence on the same facts if the defendant has been duly summoned or waives having a summons on such a charge. The evidence would all have to be given again, however, unless there was a plea of guilty. It may be, however, that para 4 of Part IV of Sched 4 (allowing preferment of a s 3 charge on failure of a s 2 one) would apply (see below), so that a charge of careless driving (but not of any other offence) could be heard without recalling the witnesses, unless requested.

Careless or inconsiderate driving can only be tried by magistrates. The consent of both sides should be obtained where more than one charge is being tried together even if both charges arise from the same incident, though such consent is often impliable (*R* v *Ashbourne JJ* (1950) 48 LGR 268; *Brangwynne* v *Evans* [1962] 1 All ER 446).

It is for the prosecutor, not the magistrates, to decide at the first instance whether the charge shall be under s 2 or s 3 and the magistrates should not refuse to issue a summons for careless driving if he applies for that only (*R* v *Nuneaton JJ* [1954] 3 All ER 251), but where the prosecution have preferred the offences under both s 2 and s 3 magistrates may refuse to consent to the withdrawal of the more serious charge (see *R* v *Bedwellty JJ*, 2.39).

See 2.39 as to trying together charges against separate defendants or a number of charges against one defendant.

A serviceman may properly be tried by court-martial for reckless or careless driving on a road abroad on a charge of committing a civil offence contrary to the Army Act 1955, s 70 (*Cox* v *Army Council* [1962] 1 All ER 880).

Warning of intended prosecution is required for offences under ss 2 and 3 unless an accident occurred (see Chapter 3).

A constable may arrest without a warrant a driver who within his view commits an offence under s 2 or s 3 unless he has given his name and address or produced his licence (1972 Act, s 164(2)). Section 164(2) will be repealed by the Police and Criminal Evidence Act 1984 when that Act is brought into force but s 25 of that Act will give a power of arrest where the person's name cannot be readily ascertained by the constable or he has reasonable grounds for doubting that the person has given his real name or that his address is not satisfactory for service of a summons.

Section 127(1) of the Magistrates' Courts Act 1980 requires an information for a s 3 offence to be laid within six months. This time limit does not apply to reckless driving because s 2 is an 'either way' offence and s 127(1) does not apply to indictable and 'either way' offences (Criminal Law Act 1977, ss 8 and 64(1)).

As to venue see Chapter 2.

## 5.6 Alternative verdicts: trial on indictment

Paragraph 3A of Part IV of Sched 4 to the 1972 Act (inserted by the Criminal Law Act 1977) allows juries to find a defendant guilty of a s 3 offence when acquitting him of an offence under s 1 or s 2. Paragraph 3A simply states:

where the jury finds him not guilty of the offence specifically charged they may (without prejudice to s 6(3) of the Criminal Law Act 1967) find him guilty

(*a*) if the offence so charged is an offence under section 1 or 2, of an offence under s 3.

A Crown Court normally has no jurisdiction to try a case of careless or inconsiderate driving and can only sentence a defendant acquitted of reckless driving after the jury, following an appropriate direction, have convicted him of careless driving as an alternative (see *R* v *Thompson*, 5.13). (For a discussion as to the difference between reckless and careless driving, see 5.26).

Section 3 creates two separate offences and a conviction for driving without due care or reasonable consideration is bad (*R* v *Surrey JJ* (1932) 95 JP 219). In *Hutton* v *Casey* (1952) 116 JP Jo 223, however, convictions under both limbs of s 3 not in the alternative were upheld in respect of an act of driving lasting only a few seconds. In Scotland, it seems, a charge under both limbs of s 3 in the alternative is good (*Archibald* v *Keiller* [1931] JC 34). As s 3 consists of two separate offences, it would seem necessary for a jury to be directed as to which of the two s 3 offences they should find the defendant guilty. It would seem that a person driving without reasonable consideration is also driving without due care. On the other hand a person driving without due care and attention is not necessarily driving without reasonable consideration for other road users (see 5.28). For this reason a direction to the jury that they may find the defendant guilty of driving without due care or attention if they find a charge under s 1 or s 2 not proved may usually be correct, but a direction to find him guilty of driving without reasonable consideration for other road users may not be if there is no evidence of lack of consideration for actual road users.

## 5.7–10 Preferral of s 3 charge: summary trial

Magistrates are empowered to direct a charge under s 3 to be preferred if they find a charge under s 2 not proved (1972 Act, Sched 4, Part IV, para 4). (For a discussion as to the difference between reckless and careless driving, see 5.26). It should be noted that, unlike a jury acting under para 3A (above) they may not immediately find the defendant guilty of a s 3 offence when dismissing a s 2 offence. It is necessary for the s 3 offence to be 'preferred' for the defendant to plead to the offence, and if necessary, for the evidence to be heard again (see below). By a majority it was held by the Divisional Court that magistrates may exercise their power for a charge under s 3 to be preferred notwithstanding six months having elapsed since the date of the offence (*R* v *Coventry JJ, ex parte Sayers* [1979] RTR 22).

By para 7 warning of intended prosecution need not have been given in such a case so far as the charge under s 3 is concerned.

No charge save one under s 3 can be preferred pursuant to this procedure: eg disobeying a traffic sign. Paragraph 4 does not apply to trials on indictment and it is, of course, unnecessary to apply it in a magistrates' court where a charge of careless driving has been tried simultaneously with the one under s 2. It is also not clear whether a magistrates' court, consisting of two or more magistrates, which has refused to commit a defendant for trial for reckless driving, may then apply the subsection and direct the preferment of a charge of careless driving, without recalling any of the prosecution witnesses, unless requested. The wording of para 4 does not seem to be limited to trials as opposed to committals, however.

If there is already a charge under s 3 before the magistrates to which a plea has not been taken, the prosecutor, if he chooses to proceed on that charge and not make use of para 4, must call his witnesses again, unless the defendant pleads guilty to careless driving. Where a reckless driving charge alone has been tried summarily and the magistrates decide to reduce it under para 4, it is submitted that the magistrates, besides giving the defence the chance of recalling prosecution witnesses for cross-examination and of adjourning, should allow, if desired, a further address by the defendant or his advocate and the recall of defence witnesses, in view of the words 'or otherwise' in para 4. *Semble*, on reducing a charge under para 4, the defendant should also be asked if he pleads guilty to the new charge. There is no power, on a charge under s 2, to convict under s 3 unless the procedure of para 4 has been followed or a charge under s 3 has been specifically tried before the court (cf *Ex parte Newsham* [1964] Crim LR 57). A person was charged with the former offence of dangerous driving under s 2 and, alternatively, with careless driving. The s 2 charge was then heard alone. After evidence had been heard on that dangerous driving charge, it was dismissed. The defendant had pleaded not guilty to careless driving, but the magistrates purported to convict him of it without hearing any more evidence. The conviction was quashed (*R* v *Hawarden JJ, ex parte Leo* (1966) *The Guardian*, 4 February). If a charge of careless driving has been heard simultaneously with one of reckless driving, the magistrates would be justified in dismissing the s 2 charge and convicting on the s 3 one at the end of the hearing; if the reckless driving charge had been heard alone, they should either use the procedure of para 4 on dismissing the reckless driving charge or rehear all the evidence when the careless driving charge is put, if there is a plea of not guilty to it (unless, as often happens, the defendant is represented and the advocate specifically allows the bench to adjudicate without hearing further evidence).

The Crown Court, when hearing an appeal from a magistrates' court may 'exercise any power which [the magistrates' court] might have exercised' (Supreme Court Act 1981, s 48(2)). For this reason it was held in *Killington* v *Butcher* [1979] Crim LR 458 that the Crown Court may exercise the power of a magistrates' court under para 4. On his pleading not guilty to the careless driving charge preferred at the Crown Court, he elected not to give evidence and was convicted.

Some police forces are known to prefer separate informations for charges under ss 2 and 3 together (as to hearing charges together see 2.39). It is submitted that such a practice of issuing a summons under both s 2 and s 3 simultaneously may now give rise to the criticism that it lends itself to improper plea bargaining.

## Causing Death by Reckless Driving

### 5.11 The offence: s 1

Section 1 of the 1972 Act, as amended by the Criminal Law Act 1977, provides that 'a person who causes the death of another person by driving a motor vehicle on the road recklessly shall be guilty of an offence'.

The statutory offence of causing death by reckless driving on a road is also manslaughter (see *R* v *Governor of Holloway, ex parte Jennings* [1983] AC 624, 5.20). Manslaughter will normally only be charged in a very grave case, see further 5.20. It should also be noted that it is not possible to charge a person with causing death by reckless driving if the offence was not on a 'road' or the vehicle was not a 'motor vehicle' within the meaning given to these words in the 1972 Act (see Chapter 1).

### 5.12 Evidence and procedure

The prosecution must prove that the defendant caused the death by driving recklessly. As to what amounts to reckless driving see 'What is reckless driving?', 5.3.

Some of the cases on dangerous driving (5.41) may or may not be relevant to charges of causing death by reckless driving under s 1. The cases at 5.33 as to driving in the period prior to the main accident would appear to be of some relevance. In *R* v *Spurge* [1961] 2 All ER 688 (see 5.34) a dangerous manoeuvre caused by a mechanical defect of which the defendant was aware was held to be dangerous driving. This principle, ie that a driver who, knowing of the defect, drives a defective vehicle, is guilty, where danger results, of dangerous driving, has been applied to the offence of causing death by dangerous driving: *R* v *Robert Millar (Contractors) and Robert Millar* [1970] 1 All ER 577. The defendant drove a lorry with a dangerously worn tyre which burst. The lorry as a result hit a motor car, killing the occupants. The defendant company and the managing director were also convicted of aiding and abetting the offence even though resident in Scotland. Aiding, abetting, counselling and procuring is a continuing offence and the company sent the vehicle into England knowing of the defective tyre. Although *Spurge* and *Millar* are both cases of dangerous driving, if the defect is of such a nature that the risk was obvious and known to the defendant who chose to ignore it (as, indeed, in *Millar*) it would seem that a defendant could be convicted of reckless driving and, if a death resulted, of causing death by reckless driving.

The prosecution must also prove that the defendant caused the death of another person, who may be a passenger in the defendant's vehicle. In *R* v *Curphey* [1957] Crim LR 191 (a case of causing death by dangerous driving) it was held that a jury might properly be directed to convict if they considered the defendant's driving was the *substantial* cause of death but not the sole one. In *R* v *Gould* [1963] 2 All ER 847 a jury were directed that they might convict if the defendant's dangerous driving was *a* substantial cause and not *the* substantial cause. These cases were reviewed by the Court of Appeal in *R* v *Hennigan* [1971] 3 All ER 133. The defendant's car was driven in a restricted area at estimated speeds of up to 80 mph. It crashed into another car which was astride the centre of the road having emerged from a minor road. The defendant was going dangerously fast but it might be held that the other driver was substantially to blame as she was clearly at fault in emerging from the minor road. The jury were directed that they could convict even if the defendant was only a little more than one-fifth to blame. The Court of Appeal ruled that this was an incorrect approach. The proper way for a jury to be directed is for them to be told to consider whether the defendant's driving is *a* cause, and it no longer has to be a *substantial* cause, Lord Parker CJ stated (p 135):

> the court would like to emphasise that there is nothing in the statute which requires the manner of the driving to be a substantial cause or a major cause or any other description of cause, of the accident. So long as the dangerous driving is *a* cause and something more than *de minimis*, the statute operates.

Questions of causation were raised in *R* v *Pagett* (1983) *The Times*, 4 February, and in *R* v *Mitchell* [1983] Crim LR 549. In the former case a conviction for manslaughter of a pregnant girl was upheld where the defendant who shot at armed police used the pregnant girl as a shield who was killed by the police. In the latter case the defendant hit an elderly man who fell against an elderly woman who subsequently died; his conviction for manslaughter of the elderly woman was also upheld. In *Pagett* Lord Justice Robert Goff said 'the question whether an accused person can be guilty of homicide . . . of a victim the immediate cause of whose death is the act of another person must be determined on the ordinary principles of causation'. These words were cited with approval in *Mitchell*. Causing death by reckless driving is a statutory form of manslaughter (see *R* v *Gail Anne Jennings*, 5.20). The statement of Lord Justice Parker in *R* v *Hennigan* above would seem to be in general accord with these two cases. If *A* drives recklessly as a result of which he collides with *B*'s vehicle which as a result then collides with *C*'s vehicle killing *C*, surely *A* can be convicted of causing death by reckless driving, of *C*?

Death—if the rule as to other forms of homicide applies—must occur within a year and a day.

For the purposes of s 1, 'driver' does not include a separate person acting as steersman (s 195(1)) but such a person might, if the facts warrant, be prosecuted for aiding and abetting an offence under s 1.

The offence can be committed only on a 'road' (as defined in the 1972 Act: see Chapter 1) and relates only to motor vehicles. Carters, drivers of 'fours in hand' and pony traps, and cyclists may be charged with manslaughter.

Spouses are competent witnesses in the Crown Court against each other where the victim was under seventeen years of age (Children and Young Persons Act 1933, s 15 and Sched 1) as 'bodily injury' must include a fatal injury.

By s 37 of the 1972 Act non-observance of the Highway Code may tend to establish liability for the offence (for a discussion of the Highway Code as to offences of reckless or careless driving, see Highway Code, 5.46).

In *R* v *Bogdal* [1982] RTR 395 it was held that a charge of dangerous driving and one of using a licence with intent to deceive were in the circumstances of the case not a 'series of offences of a similar character' within the meaning of r 9 of the 1971 Indictment Rules and should not have been tried together (20 October licence suspended and defendant ordered to produce his licence in seven days under s 101(4), 24 October seen driving by constable to whom he produced licence, 27 November seen by same constable driving dangerously).

It is no longer possible for a case of driving under the influence of drink or drugs (s 5(1) or with excess blood-alcohol (s 6(1)) to be tried on indictment, but it is submitted that evidence of drink is only admissible if 'the amount of drink taken was such as would adversely affect a driver or alternatively the driver was in fact adversely affected' (see *R* v *Thorpe* and other cases under 'Drink', 5.32). Self-induced intoxication would not seem a defence to a charge of causing death by reckless driving (*R* v *Caldwell* (1981) 73 Cr App R 13 and see also *R* v *Griffiths*, 5.32).

Causing death by reckless driving is triable only on indictment at the Crown Court. It was a Class 4 offence in accordance with the Directions of the Lord Chief Justice and was thus ordinarily triable at the lowest tier of Crown Court. The most recent direction does not specifically include the offence in Class 4. It would therefore now appear to be a Class 3 offence. Magistrates' courts must commit the offence, therefore, to a first- or second-tier Crown Court centre unless otherwise directed.

Warning of intended prosecution is not required for offences under s 1 nor does s 179 prevent a jury bringing in alternative verdicts under s 2 of reckless driving or s 3 of careless or inconsiderate driving (1972 Act, Sched 4, Part IV, para 5).

The proceedings will be commenced by summons or arrest, with remand on bail or in custody, to the magistrates' court where the defendant will in due course be committed for trial to the Crown Court (see Chapter 2).

A constable, on reasonable suspicion that an offence under s 1 has been committed, may arrest without warrant a person suspected by him with reasonable cause of having committed it (Criminal Law Act 1967, s 2). When the Police and Criminal Evidence Act 1984 is in force, s 2 of the Criminal Law Act 1967 will be repealed, but as the offence is punishable with five years' imprisonment, the offence becomes an 'arrestable' offence for which a person may be arrested without warrant (Police and Criminal Evidence Act 1984, s 24(1)(*b*)).

A juvenile court may not try homicide (Children and Young Persons Act 1969, s 6). The legal dictionaries define homicide as 'killing a person' and do not limit it to murder and manslaughter. Homicide thus includes any offence an essential element of which is that the accused caused the death of another person. Causing death by reckless driving contrary to s 1 of the 1972 Act satisfied this test as well as the more usual forms of homicide such as murder, manslaughter or infanticide. It is therefore submitted that a juvenile charged with causing death by reckless driving can only be tried at the Crown Court. Stone's *Justices' Manual* is of the same view.

The Prosecution of Offences Regulations 1978 (SI 1978 No 1357) as amended by SI 1978 No 1846 require chief officers of police to report to the Director of Public Prosecutions any homicide where a prima facie case appears to exist. This requirement does not apply to causing death by reckless driving (reg 6(*d*)), but the Director has required chief officers of police to report any offence of causing death by reckless driving where the deceased is a close relative of the accused (see Stone).

## 5.13 Alternative verdicts

Although s 2(2) of the Road Traffic Act 1960 was repealed by the Criminal Law Act 1967, it seems that under s 6(3) of the 1967 Act the jury on a charge under s 1 may convict the defendant of reckless driving under s 2 or, possibly, of causing bodily harm by furious driving under s 35 of the Offences against the Person Act (see 5.55). The jury may also alternatively convict the defendant of careless or inconsiderate driving contrary to s 3 (1972 Act, Sched 4, Part IV, para 3A). In *R* v *Thompson* [1980] RTR 387 the defendant pleaded not guilty to reckless driving but guilty to careless driving. The prosecution was not prepared to accept the plea and the matter proceeded to trial. The jury acquitted the defendant of reckless driving. The judge thereupon, on the basis of the original plea, sentenced the defendant for careless driving. The sentence was set aside as a complete nullity. The judge had not, as he could have done, directed the jury as to an alternative verdict of careless driving should they find the reckless driving not proved.

It is submitted that, in any event, a Crown Court can only sentence a defendant for careless driving after a jury have found him guilty of careless driving as an alternative to reckless driving, or when he is committed for sentence under s 56 of the Criminal Justice Act 1967, or on appeal, or in any other case where the Crown Court is given specific jurisdiction. Careless driving is a purely summary offence and cannot otherwise be dealt with by the Crown Court.

## 5.14–19 Inquests

Section 56 of and Sched 10 to the Criminal Law Act 1977 substituted a new s 20 of the Coroners (Amendment) Act 1926. The new section requires the coroner, in the absence of reason to the contrary, to adjourn the proceedings when he is notified by the clerk of the magistrates' court of a charge under s 1 or of manslaughter, murder, infanticide or aiding and abetting a suicide. The coroner is also similarly required to adjourn the proceedings where requested to do so by the Director of Public Prosecutions where a person has been charged with any offence other than those set out above committed in circumstances connected with the death of the deceased. The clerk of the magistrates' court is required to notify the coroner of the result of the committal proceedings, and the appropriate officer of the Crown Court the results of the proceedings before that court. Where the coroner has been requested by the Director of Public Prosecutions to adjourn the proceedings, the Director is required to notify the coroner of the offence selected by him and the result of the proceedings.

# Motor Manslaughter

## 5.20 Constituents of the offence

Manslaughter, whether committed by an adult or a juvenile, is a Class 2 offence (see Directions of the Lord Chief Justice) triable at the Crown Court. It need not have been committed on a road.

The offence is an obligatorily disqualifiable offence (Part II of Sched 4 to the 1972 Act). By s 37 of the 1972 Act non-observance of the Highway Code may tend to establish liability for the offence (for a discussion as to the effect of s 37(5) on careless and reckless driving offences, see 5.46.

By paragraph 1 of Part V of Sched 4 juries in Scotland may bring in an alternative verdict of causing death by reckless driving if they find a motorist not guilty of culpable homicide but in England and Wales the House of Lords in *R* v *Seymour (Edward)* [1983] RTR 455 has stated (Per Lord Roskill p 465L) that there should not be a joinder of the charges of manslaughter and causing death by reckless driving on a single indictment and if any such joinder should occur it is incumbent on the trial judge to require the prosecution to elect on which of the two counts they wish to proceed and not to allow the trial to proceed on both events (p 466A–B).

The House of Lords held that, while prosecuting authorities today would only prosecute for manslaughter 'in a very grave case' (per Lord Roskill (p 19G–H)), the offence of 'motor manslaughter' was not abolished by implication either by the creation of the offence of causing death by reckless or dangerous driving in 1956 or by the amendment of that offence (Criminal Law Act 1977, s 50) restricting it to a single offence of causing death by reckless driving (*R* v *Governor of Holloway, ex parte Jennings* [1983] RTR 1).

In *R* v *Seymour (Edward)* [1983] RTR 455 the defendant who had been convicted of 'motor manslaughter' appealed to the House of Lords from the Court of Appeal on the question 'where manslaughter is charged and the circumstances of the offence are that the victim was killed as a result of the reckless driving of the defendant on a public highway; should the trial judge give the jury the direction suggested in *R* v *Lawrence* [1981] RTR 217, 229C–G [see Model Direction to juries, 5.3], in its entirety; or should the direction be that only a recognition by the defendant that some risk was involved and he had nonetheless gone on to take it would be sufficient to establish the commission of the offence?'. It was unanimously held that the trial judge should give the model direction in *R* v *Lawrence* but that it is appropriate also to point out to the jury that in order to constitute the offence of manslaughter the risk of death being caused by the manner of the defendant's driving must be very high.

See 5.14 as to inquests and as to notifying the coroner of committal.

### 5.21–5 Hit-and-run drivers

It is submitted that there may be one other instance where manslaughter might possibly be committed by a motorist. One of the purposes of Parliament when enacting the duty to stop after an accident and to report that accident now contained in s 25 of the 1972 Act was, it was submitted, the saving of life. If therefore a motorist, knowing serious injury and the risk of death if not medically attended, fails to stop or fails to report the accident and as a result of that failure the person whom he has hit with his motor vehicle dies, it could be argued that his deliberate or reckless failure to comply with the positive duty placed upon him by s 25 might be sufficient to warrant a charge of manslaughter even if there is no evidence of the manner of the defendant's driving. It should be noted that the duty to stop means to stop sufficiently long to exchange particulars with anyone requiring the same (*Lee* v *Knapp*, 7.8). The duty of reporting an accident is required to be exercised 'as soon as reasonably practicable'. As was held in *Bulman* v *Bennett* [1974] RTR 1, this means exactly this; it does not mean that the motorist has twenty-four hours within which to report the accident.

## Careless and Inconsiderate Driving

### 5.26 The difference between reckless and careless driving

The House of Lords in *R* v *Lawrence* above judicially recognised that the purpose of the amendment of ss 1 and 2 of the Road Traffic Act 1972 by s 50 of the Criminal Law Act 1977 was to restore the difference in culpability between the offence under s 2, for which a defendant has the right to elect trial by jury, and the offence under s 3, for which he has no such right. The actus reus under 1 and 2 is driving in a manner which in fact creates a real and obvious risk of causing physical injury to someone else who happens to be using the road or of causing substantial damage to property. Lord Diplock stated that the damage must be more substantial than the kind of minor damage that may be caused by an error of judgment in the course of parking one's car. By contrast, the actus reus of a charge under s 3 is departing from the standard of a reasonable, prudent and competent driver in all the circumstances of the case: this may merely cause annoyance or show lack of consideration, with little risk of injury or substantial damage. The mens rea for offences under ss 1 and 2, ie 'recklessness', has already been set out. By contrast, the offence under s 3 is an offence which is absolute in the sense that it is unnecessary to show that the defendant's mind was conscious of the consequences of his actions; it is only necessary to show that he was conscious of what he was doing.

## 5.27 Summary of careless and inconsiderate driving

The prosecutor has to prove beyond reasonable doubt that the motorist is 'at fault', ie has departed from the standard of a reasonable, competent and prudent driver in all the circumstances of the particular case. This is primarily a question of objective fact. An acquittal by magistrates on the facts will normally not be set aside by the High Court unless the facts are such that no reasonable tribunal could possibly have acquitted. Normally the justices are the best judges as to the actual facts. The Highway Code is a good guide to whether the motorist has departed from the required standard of driving, but breach of the code is not necessarily conclusive. If the facts are such that in the absence of an explanation put forward by the defendant the only possible conclusion is that he was careless, he should be convicted. Unless there is evidence before them for it, magistrates should refrain from theorising and advancing an explanation for the behaviour of the defendant's vehicle. However, once a possible explanation is put forward the prosecution are required to prove it untrue beyond reasonable doubt. It is a defence that the vehicle had a sudden defect of which the defendant neither knew nor should have been expected to know. On the other hand, if a defendant drives knowing of the defect, he is ipso facto guilty of careless or, possibly, reckless driving. Similarly automatism is a defence, but if the defendant knows that he is suffering from an illness likely seriously to affect his control of the car and drives, he is ipso facto guilty. For an offence under s 3 (also ss 1 and 2) to be committed the prosecution must show that the defendant 'drove'. The meaning of the word is discussed in Chapter 1. In *Jones* v *Pratt* [1983] RTR 54 it was held that a front seat passenger was not 'driving' when he momentarily grabbed the steering wheel of the car causing it to go off the road when he saw a small animal running across the road.

## 5.28 The difference between careless and inconsiderate driving

Driving without due care and attention may be said to mean departing from the standard of driving which would be exercised by a reasonable, prudent, competent driver in all the circumstances of the particular case. It follows that a person who drives without reasonable consideration for other road users can be convicted of driving without due care and attention, because a reasonable, competent and prudent driver would not drive without reasonable consideration for others. However, the corollary does not apply. A person may be convicted of driving without reasonable consideration for other road users only, seemingly, if other road users were inconvenienced. There is no reference in s 3, as there was formerly in s 2, to persons who might be expected to be on the road.

It would seem that *Dilkes* v *Bowman Shaw* [1981] RTR 4 is authority for the proposition stated in the text that an actual road user must be inconvenienced before a person may be convicted of driving without reasonable consideration. The defendant was in the offside lane of the M1 behind two other vehicles. He drew into the nearside lane and overtook one or both of the vehicles and then when sealed up in the nearside lane drew in between those two vehicles. The justices acquitted the defendant because neither of the two drivers in the offside lane was inconvenienced, both having given evidence to that effect. It was corroborated by the evidence of the police officers that no one was in fact inconvenienced. The court found no ground for interfering with the acquittal. Per Ormrod LJ:

> One thing which should be made plain in this case is that it is no authority for passing on a motorway on the nearside lane. The decision we have made today is . . . on the material facts of the case and they are very unusual.

## 5.29 Objective standard of danger and care

The former offence under s 2 of driving in a manner dangerous contained an absolute prohibition in that the prosecution did not have to prove an intention on the part of the driver to drive dangerously. If the driver's defence was that he was in a state of automatism through a fit or had lost control because of an attack by bees, he had to bring evidence to show this (*Hill* v *Baxter* [1958] 1 All ER 193). In *Moses* v *Winder* [1980] Crim LR 232 the justices were directed to convict a defendant who had crossed to the wrong side of the road on a bend and collided with a car going in the opposite direction. The defendant who had suffered from diabetes for 20 years felt he was going into a diabetic coma and before driving had taken sugar sweets to delay the attack. The justices had acquitted on the ground that he was in a state of automatism. In directing the justices to convict, the court said that while medical evidence was not essential to prove automatism, the defence could rarely succeed without it. In this case the defendant has not taken all the precautions he ought to have taken to deal with the threat of diabetic coma. The court quoted with approval Lawson LJ in *R* v *Quick* [1973] QB 910 when he said at p 922G:

> A self-induced incapacity will not excuse . . . nor will one which could have been reasonably foreseen as a result of either doing, or omitting to do something, as, for example, taking alcohol against medical advice after using certain prescribed drugs, or failing to have regular meals while taking insulin. From time to time difficult cases are likely to arise.

Magistrates cannot theorise that a dangerous course of driving arose because the defendant had a black-out in the absence of any evidence to that effect (*Richards* v *Gardener* [1974] RTR 477). It would appear, however, that the offence of reckless driving connotes a state of mind, although the defendant's manner of driving would be evidence of his state of mind (see 'What is reckless driving?', 5.3). If an explanation of automatism is suggested and supported by evidence of sufficient substance to merit consideration, the onus on the prosecution (of proof of guilt) is not discharged unless the court or jury, having considered this explanation, are still left in no reasonable doubt of the driver's guilt (*R* v *Budd* [1962] Crim LR 49; see also the cases discussed below and under 'Automatism', 1.60). A civil case of negligence where automatism was not established is *Roberts* v *Ramsbottom* [1980] RTR 261. Reference may also be made to the Divisional Court case of *Moses* v *Winder* above.

It was held that if a man who knows that he is subject to dizzy spells or black-outs drives, it is no defence to charge of dangerous driving that his dangerous driving was caused by his having an attack (*R* v *Sibbles* [1959] Crim LR 660). Similarly, a man cannot plead the effect of high blood pressure bringing on a black-out and causing his car to be driven dangerously if he has aggravated his condition by drinking beforehand (ibid). Where a diabetic in a state of confusion through his illness had driven for five miles but there was no evidence to show that the movements of his body and legs in driving were involuntary and wholly uncontrolled and uninitiated by any function of conscious will, the High Court directed a conviction (*Watmore* v *Jenkins* [1962] 2 All ER 686). Where a diabetic's state of mind was caused by his taking too much insulin rather than by the disease itself, he is entitled to put forward a defence of automatism (*R* v *Quick* [1973] 3 All ER 347). The Court of Appeal in *Quick* approved the following direction to a jury in the Scottish case of *HM Advocate* v *Ritchie* [1926] SC(J) 45:

> Automatism is a defence to a charge of dangerous driving provided that a person takes reasonable steps to prevent himself from acting involuntarily in a manner dangerous to the public. It must be caused by some factor which he could not reasonably foresee and not by a self-induced incapacity.

It should, however, be noted that this may not be the law in Scotland as *Ritchie* was over-ruled in *HM Advocate* v *Cunningham* [1963] SC(J) 80. It should also be noted that *R* v *Quick* was apparently decided without *Cunningham* being cited to the Court of Appeal. It is, with respect, suggested that the distinction between impairment caused by the disease itself and impairment caused by too much insulin is unreal. In *Stevenson* v *Beatson* [1965] SLT(Sh) 11 there was a conviction where the defendant failed to prove that he had been in a state of automatism, and in *Cook* v *Atchison* (1968) 112 SJ 235, magistrates were directed to convict where a defendant gave evidence that he thought he must have had a mild black-out because of his inability to brake on seeing that the traffic lights were red but no medical evidence was called. The mere fact that the magistrates thought that his evidence was apparently credible was not a sufficient foundation for the defence of automatism.

In *R* v *Sullivan* [1983] Crim LR 740 the defendant attacked a friend while subject to an epileptic seizure. As he did not know what he was doing it was held that the strictly proper verdict should be the special verdict of 'not guilty by reason of insanity'. Whether a particular disorder amounts to 'a disease of the mind' within the meaning of *M'Naghten* is a matter of law (ibid). Cases on automatism must now be read subject to *Sullivan*. A person who drives knowing he is subject to fits may nevertheless be guilty of reckless or careless driving as the offence is then self-induced (see eg *R* v *Quick* and *R* v *Sibbles* above).

The court's duty under s 92 of the 1972 Act to notify the Secretary of State where a person may be suffering from a disease or disability (see 20.38) should always be borne in mind in such cases.

Overtaking in dangerous circumstances under the mistaken belief that one is in the proper lane in a dual carriageway has been held to be dangerous driving (*R* v *Johnson* [1960] Crim LR 430), but for it to be dangerous driving to do so, the defendant had nevertheless to be 'at fault' (see *R* v *Gosney* [1971] All ER 220). But a conviction for dangerous driving was quashed where there had been, in the words of the jury, 'a mere error of judgment' (*R* v *Howell* (1938) 103 JP 9, a case later said to lay down no principle of law).

Some of the above cases were for the former offence under s 2 of driving in a dangerous manner. They may still be of relevance in a charge of reckless driving. It is submitted that if a man is driving dangerously as a result of a medical condition of which he is aware, he may be convicted of reckless driving. It may be said to be reckless driving if he knows of the risk for him to drive because of his state of health or medical condition, and proceeds to drive notwithstanding the risk.

The test as to whether a defendant is guilty of careless driving is an objective one (*McCrone* v *Riding* below). What the prosecution have to prove is *that the defendant has departed from the standard of a reasonable, prudent and competent driver in all the circumstances of the case*. This is primarily a question of fact. The standard of care demanded by the criminal law cannot be higher than that demanded by the civil law of negligence (*Scott* v *Warren* [1974] RTR 104).

If the defendant fails to exercise due care, he is guilty whether or not his failure is due to his inexperience (*McCrone* v *Riding* [1938] 1 All ER 157: learner driver guilty) and whether or not it was a deliberate act or an error of judgment (*Taylor* v *Rogers* (1960) 124 JP 217). *McCrone* v *Riding* was followed in *R* v *Preston JJ ex parte Lyons* [1982] RTR 173, where the Divisional Court refused an order of mandamus requiring the justices to state a case. The applicant, an 'L' driver, had been instructed by his driving instructor to execute an emergency stop. He had not looked in his mirror and a motor cyclist had driven into the back of his vehicle. The justices convicted the defendant, ordered an absolute discharge and did not endorse his licence, holding the test of whether a person had driven carelessly to be objective. A criticism of the case is contained in an article by Martin Wasik [1982] Crim LR pp 411–418). The commentator to the report in the Criminal Law Review also criticised the case as unjust ([1982] Crim LR p 451). It is submitted that the underlying ratio of the decision, namely the necessity for an objective standard of driving to be maintained, is correct (see also the letter from the Prosecutor ([1982] Crim LR p 620)).

Nor is knowledge of the defendant's carelessness an essential element of careless driving. A lorry driver who was not aware that he had hit a stationary vehicle was held to be rightly convicted of careless driving, although his conviction for failing to report the accident was quashed because he did not know of the accident (*Hampson* v *Powell* [1970] 1 All ER 929).

If a driver does not exercise that degree of care and attention which a reasonably prudent man would exercise in the circumstances, he is guilty whether or not he is committing an error of judgment (*Simpson* v *Peat* [1952] 1 All ER 447, discussed at 102 LJ News 146; 213 LT News 176 and 121 JP Jo 591). Where magistrates had dismissed a charge of careless driving because they thought that the driver must have had a dizzy spell or been hit by a stone or a bird, there being no evidence before them to that effect, they were directed to convict, it being said that their doubt was fanciful and not reasonable (*Oakes* v *Foster* [1961] Crim LR 628). See also *Johnson* v *Fowler, Rabjohns* v *Burgar, Gubby* v *Littman* under 'Res ipsa loquitur' below. If the charge is one of driving without reasonable consideration for other road users, it is submitted that the test here would also be objective. One can have a situation where a whole enterprise was reckless and yet have an incident within the chain of reckless events which can properly be described as careless driving (*M (A Minor) and another* v *Oxford* [1981] RTR 246). It is submitted that a person is guilty of careless driving once it is proved that he has departed from the required standard of driving. It matters not whether this was due to his negligence, incompetence, inexperience, recklessness, or even his deliberate intent: the only mens rea required in a case of careless driving is (per Lord Diplock in *R* v *Lawrence* [1981] RTR 217 at p 220) 'simply to show that the prohibited physical act (actus reus) done by the accused was directed by a mind that was conscious of what his body was doing'.

In another sense the test as to what is careless driving is subjective. Although careless driving objectively depends on whether the defendant departed from the standard of what might be expected of a prudent, competent and reasonable driver in all the circumstances of the case, the particular circumstances of each case must be considered subjectively. What may amount to careless driving in one situation may be wholly prudent in a different situation. What may be careless driving on a road in the rush hour may not be at 10 o'clock on a Sunday morning. It is primarily a question of fact whether the particular circumstances of the case do, or do not, show that the defendant departed from the standard to be expected.

The best judges as to what is or what is not careless driving are the justices who know the district (see *Walker* v *Tolhurst* [1976] RTR 513). Each case is unique. Thus while a motorist who collides with a cyclist at night or collides when emerging from a side turning into a main road will usually be convicted, not all such cases invariably lead to a conviction because the facts and road situation in each case will differ (see some of the cases cited under 'Highway Code', 5.46).

A wrong action in the agony of the collision will not suffice alone to prove an offence under s 2 or s 3 (*Simpson* v *Peat* above), if the defendant had been driving properly beforehand and his actions prior to the time when the collision became imminent had been those of a prudent driver.

## 5.30 Res ipsa loquitur

Frequently the only evidence which the police are able to bring is evidence of the defendant's vehicle leaving the road and a collision occurring with a wall or a pole or the vehicle ending up in a ditch or upside down in a field. In the absence of any explanation by the defendant, if the only conclusion which it is possible to draw is that the defendant was negligent or had departed from what a reasonably prudent and competent driver would have done in the circumstances, a court should convict. The doctrine of res ipsa loquitur is a rule of evidence applicable to the tort of negligence and as such has no application to the criminal law. But the fact that res ipsa loquitur has no application to criminal law does not mean that the prosecution have to negative every possible explanation of a defendant before he can be convicted of careless driving where the facts at the scene of an accident are such that, in the absence of any explanation by the defendant, a court can have no alternative but to convict. Thus in *Rabjohns* v *Burgar* [1972] Crim LR 46 the defendant's car on a dry road collided with the concrete wall of a bridge on a fine clear day with no other vehicle apparently involved. There were two skid marks behind the car. There were no witnesses to the accident and the defendant gave no explanation as to how the accident occurred. The justices found that there was sufficient evidence for the defendant to be required to answer the prosecution's case but, on the defendant declining to give or call any evidence, ruled that there was insufficient evidence to convict. The Divisional Court held that the facts were so strong that the defendant should be convicted and pointed out that the prosecution did not have to show there was nothing wrong with the steering as the defendant had not raised the matter. A magistrates' court was directed to find that there was a case for the defendant to answer in *Watts* v *Carter* [1971] RTR 232, where the defendant's car was found to have hit a Post Office support pole two feet nine inches from the edge of the road and his suggestion that there was something wrong with the steering was shown to be wrong. This case was applied in *Wright* v *Wenlock* [1972] Crim LR 49, where the defendant's vehicle hit a telegraph pole near to the road's edge. In the absence of any explanation of the accident, the justices were directed by the Divisional Court to find that there was a case for the defendant to answer. Similarly in *Bensley* v *Smith* [1972] Crim LR 239 justices were directed to convict a defendant who had crossed a central white line and collided with a car coming in the opposite direction. Crossing a white line was itself evidence of careless driving and in the absence of explanation the justices must convict (ibid).

However, if an explanation, other than a fanciful explanation, is given by the defendant it is for the prosecution to disprove it and unless it is disproved the defendant is entitled to the benefit of the doubt (see *R* v *Spurge*, 5.34). Thus in *Butty* v *Davey* [1972] Crim LR 48 the defendant's car, after negotiating a sharp bend, failed to negotiate a slight left-hand bend and slid on to the wrong side of the road and collided with an oncoming lorry. The defendant contended that he could only have done so because of some unexpected slipperiness of the road due to rain. The justices were upheld in dismissing the case as the defendant's explanation was not fanciful. It was also said that it was not incumbent on a defendant in a criminal case to show that he had skidded without fault (although it should be noted that in this particular case the defendant had given an explanation which was upheld by the justices). In *Lodwick* v *Jones* [1983] RTR 273 the defendant skidded on an icy patch and collided with a motorcyclist. The justices dismissed the case on the ground that the prosecution had not proved that ice could reasonably have been expected on the road. It was held that the justices' conclusion was not shown to be perverse, although there was frost on the windscreen of the car when the defendant had set out that morning this did not give rise to an irresistible inference that there was ice on the road, moreover the motorcyclist had ridden on the road without difficulty. Where a vehicle takes a dangerous course and there is an accident, magistrates should refrain from theorising about its causes in the absence of any evidence and should not assume that the steering column must have broken just before the accident, when there is evidence that the vehicle was in good condition prior to the accident (*Johnson* v *Fowler*

[1959] Crim LR 463). In *Griffin* v *Williams* [1964] Crim LR 60 a conviction was directed where a car went out of control and there was no evidence of any defect. In *Hougham* v *Martin* (1964) 108 SJ 138, a car inexplicably veered off its course and collided with another vehicle: it was said that magistrates were not entitled to assume, without evidence, that, because it was a modern, mass-produced car, it was prone to mechanical defects. There must be properly admissible evidence of a mechanical defect. Justices dismissed a case of careless driving on the supposed ground that the defendant was unaware that brand new tyres do not have the holding qualities of ones which had run a few hundred miles, causing him to go onto the wrong side of the road when rounding a bend thus causing an accident. The evidence as to this supposed lack of holding qualities of brand new tyres consisted of a suggestion to this effect from an otherwise unqualified police officer who had interviewed the defendant and the production by the defendant's solicitor of a leaflet issued by the British tyre industry without either the leaflet's author being called or any expert evidence adduced to show any inherent risk involved when running in brand new tyres. The justices were directed to reconsider the case on the basis that there was no evidence of hazard in new tyres (*Gubby* v *Littman* [1976] RTR 476). See *Oakes* v *Foster*, 5.29.

On the other hand, it should perhaps be emphasised that the facts must be so strong that in the absence of any evidence of mechanical defect, illness or other explanation that is given, the facts must give rise to an inference that the defendant was guilty of careless or reckless driving. The facts have to be such as to show beyond reasonable doubt that the defendant's standard of driving was less than that required of a prudent and competent driver in all the circumstances of the case (see 5.46 and in particular *Scott* v *Warren*: following car hitting car in front which had made an emergency stop; and also *Jarvis* v *Fuller* colliding at night with cyclist without lights).

### 5.31 Falling asleep

A driver who allows himself to be overcome by sleep, so that the car mounts the pavement or goes to the wrong side, is guilty of dangerous or careless driving, for he should have stopped when he felt sleep overtaking him (*Kay* v *Butterworth* (1946) 110 JP 75; *Henderson* v *Jones* (1955) 119 JP 305). In the latter case, *Edwards* v *Clarke* (1951) 115 JP Jo 426 was explained as showing only that a driver's statement that he was asleep without other evidence of careless driving is insufficient for a conviction under s 3, for he had not said nor was it shown that he went to sleep while driving. There appear to be no reported cases as to whether it can be said to be reckless driving if a defendant falls asleep. It is submitted that a person cannot be convicted of reckless driving if he falls asleep unless it can be shown there is evidence that there was a risk of his falling asleep but he nevertheless, persisted in continuing to drive.

### 5.32 Drink

Where there is no charge of driving under the influence of drink and the accused is being tried for reckless or careless driving only, evidence that he was at the time adversely affected by drink is of probative value and admissible and its admissibility is not limited to rebuttal of such a defence as that he was not in control through no fault of his own. Such evidence must tend to show that the amount of drink taken was such as adversely to affect a driver or that he was in fact adversely affected, but the court has an overriding discretion to exclude such evidence where its prejudicial effect outweighs its probative value (*R* v *McBride* [1962] 2 QB 167). Ashworth J said that no general rule could be laid down as to the way in which the discretion could be exercised, as each case must be considered on its own particular facts, but, if such evidence is introduced, it should at least appear of substantial weight (ibid, at p 172). Cases where such evidence has been allowed are *R* v *McBride* above (enough drink taken to justify a charge of driving under the influence of drink); *R* v *Richardson* [1960] Crim LR 135 (visits to public houses before driving); and *R* v *Fisher* (ibid: practically the whole day spent in public houses prior to driving). In *R* v *Thorpe* [1972] RTR 118, following *R* v *McBride* above evidence that the defendant was guilty of an offence of having more than the prescribed blood-alcohol level contrary to s 6 of the 1972 Act was held to be admissible on a charge of causing death by dangerous driving because a blood-alcohol level of over 80 mg per 100 ml was such that it could tend to prove that it could affect a driver even if, for a particular driver, it might or might not affect his ability to drive. The test of whether evidence of drink is admissible was said in *R* v *Thorpe* to be (quoting Ashworth J in *R* v *McBride* above, at p 172, with approval) that 'such evidence must tend to show that the amount of drink taken was such as would adversely affect a driver or alternatively that the driver was in fact adversely affected'. Thus evidence merely that the driver's breath smelled of drink or that he had been in one bar for a short while would not, it is submitted, generally be of sufficient probative value to justify its admission. As stated, the court has a discretion to exclude any such evidence, and the test to be applied is that already quoted.

On the other hand, the amount of alcohol may be such that the defendant knew or must have known that his ability to drive was substantially impaired and that there was therefore a risk of his causing injury to other road users. If the defendant then chose to drive and the manner of his driving was such that it created an obvious serious risk of causing physical injury to some person who happened or might happen to be using the road or of doing substantial damage to property, he was guilty of reckless driving and, if his driving caused the death of another road user, guilty of causing death by reckless driving (*R* v *Griffiths (Rupert)* [1984] Crim L R 629).

It would seem that like principles might apply where it is alleged that the defendant's driving was affected by his having taken a drug or even by severe pain or emotional upset, if such evidence is of substantial weight.

A like rule as to admissibility of evidence of drinking applies in Scotland (*Burrell* v *Hunter* [1956] SLT (Sh) 75).

A charge of driving under the influence of drink or drugs may be tried along with one of reckless or careless driving (*R* v *McBride* above), provided that in a magistrates' court the parties consent.

Reckless driving and driving under the influence of drink or with excess blood-alcohol cannot now be tried together on indictment because charges under ss 5 and 6 are now only triable summarily. It would seem following *R* v *Caldwell* (1981) 73 Cr App R 13 that self-induced intoxication is not a defence to a charge under either s 1 or s 2.

The fact that reckless driving is caused by drink is an aggravating feature, see *R* v *Boswell*, 5.88.

## 5.33 Evidence of previous driving

Evidence of dangerous driving a few minutes before but two miles from the scene of the accident was held to be admissible in *Hallett* v *Warren* (1929) 93 JP 225; and in *R* v *Taylor* (1927) 20 Cr App R 71, evidence of reckless driving five miles away was given. It is submitted, however, that the evidence of the earlier acts of driving must have some relevance to those charged, eg fast driving in the Strand is not necessarily relevant on a charge of careless driving in Piccadilly if the only allegation in Piccadilly is that the defendant, while driving slowly was frequently glancing at shop windows as he drove. Indeed, evidence that the defendant was driving fast at a place where it was not unsafe to drive fast seems irrelevant and might be unfairly prejudicial, and it is submitted that only acts of reckless or careless driving within a reasonable distance and time should be allowed in evidence. It seems to be in order to charge the offence as having been committed in all the roads where the defendant drove recklessly or carelessly. If the charge relates to driving in the last road only and evidence is tendered of driving in other roads so that the defendant is misled or taken by surprise, he should be granted an adjournment, if he asks for it (*Hallett* v *Warren* above). That case suggested that, if dangerous driving within the jurisdiction was proved, the court should convict even if there was no proof of an offence on the road actually charged as the scene of the offence, eg a charge of dangerous driving in Piccadilly should not be dismissed even if there was no evidence of dangerous driving there, so long as there is proof of dangerous driving in Trafalgar Square and Lower Regent Street. The prosecutor, however, would be wise to name all the roads in his information, as *Hallett* v *Warren* above may yet be distinguished and it was said obiter in *R* v *Budd* [1962] Crim LR 49 that there can be a conviction for dangerous driving only if it occurred in the road named in the warning of intended prosecution under s 241 (now s 179 of the 1972 Act). In *Horrix* v *Malam* [1984] RTR 112 28 March a conviction for careless driving was confirmed. The Divisional Court held that the information was not bad for duplicity when it referred to two incidents of swerving separated by a ten minute interval and two miles in distance witnessed by two different police officers. The test in such a case is whether the charge or information involves only one activity even though that activity might involve more than one act (*R* v *Jones* [1974] ICR 310). It was, however, said in *Coles* v *Underwood* (1983) *The Times*, 2 November that evidence of previous driving may be admissible but justices must be extremely circumspect in having regard to what took place at some distance from the event which is the subject of the charge.

## 5.34–40 Mechanical defects

It is a defence to the former charge of dangerous driving and also to careless driving that the driver, without fault of his own, was deprived of control of his vehicle by a mechanical defect therein of which he did not know and which was not such as he should have discovered if he had exercised reasonable prudence and, once there is some evidence of such a defect, the accused should be acquitted if his explanation leaves a real doubt in the minds of the jury or magistrates (*R* v *Spurge* [1961] 2 All ER 688). It would also be a defence to a charge of reckless driving that the manner of his driving was caused by a mechanical defect of which he did not know, because reckless driving means taking an unjustifiable risk of which the defendant is aware and if the defendant did not know of the defect he could not know of the risk. In *Spurge* the conviction was upheld because, although a defect causing the car to pull to its offside was proved, the driver knew of this defect and yet continued to drive in a manner which was dangerous in those circumstances. Where a lorry driver knew that a tyre was dangerously worn and drove, his conviction for causing death by dangerous driving was upheld after the tyre had burst, causing the lorry to swerve and kill the occupants of an oncoming car (*R* v *Robert Millar (Contractors) Ltd and Robert Millar* [1970] 1 All ER 577, following and approving the principle of *R* v *Spurge*). The principle in *R* v *Spurge* is that if the danger was created by a sudden loss of control in no way due to any fault on the part of the driver, the defendant should be acquitted. Once there is evidence of a mechanical defect which the driver neither knew of nor ought to have known of, 'the onus of disproving [it] undoubtedly rests on the prosecution' (per Salmon J, at p 692, expressly cited with approval by the Court of Appeal in *R* v *Gosney* [1971] 3 All ER 220). Once it has been found as a fact that the motorist knows or ought to have known of the mechanical defect, he cannot avail himself of the defence even if the car has been subsequently serviced by a garage (*Haynes* v *Swain* [1975] RTR 40). Where a car has been serviced by a garage all that can be assumed is that the car has been serviced, nothing else (ibid). (If, however, the defendant in *Haynes* v *Swain* above had been charged with reckless driving he would have been acquitted if he was not reckless in thinking the defect had been put right by the garage when servicing his car.)

The converse of the principle that an unexpected mechanical defect is a defence is that if the motorist drives a car having a mechanical defect of which he knows or ought to know, and danger results, he should be convicted of careless driving. No reasonable, prudent and competent driver will knowingly drive a motor vehicle with a worn tyre, defective steering or defective brakes, and if a driver does so he is ipso facto departing from the standard of a prudent, reasonable and competent driver. Moreover, he is guilty of reckless driving if the defect is such that it (to quote from *R* v *Lawrence* [1981] RTR 217) creates an obvious and serious risk of causing physical injury to some other person who might be on the road, or doing substantial damage to property. *R* v *Spurge* was expressly upheld not only in *R* v *Gosney* above but also in *R* v *Atkinson* [1970] Crim LR 405, where a motorist's conviction was quashed when he had not even allowed to call evidence to rebut the prosecution's evidence that he should have known his brakes were defective.

The court should not assume, without evidence, that a vehicle must have developed defects: see *Rabjohns* v *Burgar*, *Johnson* v *Fowler*, *Bensley* v *Smith* and *Gubby* v *Littman*, 5.30.

## Cases on Dangerous and Careless Driving

### 5.41 Former offence of dangerous driving

The following cases on the former offence of dangerous driving are of relevance in deciding whether a driver may be convicted of careless driving but will not usually be helpful in deciding what is reckless driving. Moveover, many of the cases do not really lay down principles of law. Whether a particular situation or course of action gives rise to danger is primarily a question of fact and a slight variation in fact, eg the time of day or the traffic, may make a difference.

In *Troughton* v *Manning* (1905) 69 JP 207, it was held that the intention of the statute is to prevent misconduct in the management of the vehicle towards the people outside it on the highway, and not towards persons in the vehicle. It was said in *Pawley* v *Wharldall* [1965] 2 All ER 757 that the judgment of Kennedy J in *Troughton's* case went too far. Moreover, s 143 has now been amended to require motorists to insure against any liability to their passengers. See also *Pawley* v *Wharldall*, above and at 5.43. Potential danger, having regard to the traffic which might reasonably be expected to be on the road may suffice for a conviction, even though no other traffic was in fact endangered (*Bracegirdle* v *Oxley* [1947] 1 All ER 126: lorry going at more than twice the permitted speed along a road normally carrying heavy traffic, overtaking without a signal on a bend and 'charging at narrow bridges'). In *Marson* v *Thompson* (1955) *The Times*, 8 March, magistrates were directed by the High Court to convict a motorist under s 2 where he had 'cut in' in a dangerous way, ignoring a signal not to do so. Driving a motor cycle along an unrestricted road in a built-up area at 64 mph in heavy traffic and making a third line of traffic when overtaking a vehicle itself overtaking was held to be dangerous driving (*Baker* v *Williams* (1956) 54 LGR 197). Overtaking two lines of traffic at speed, when traffic is approaching from the other direction, can be dangerous driving (*Squire* v *Metropolitan Police Commissioner* [1957] Crim LR 817). Overtaking in dangerous circumstances under the mistaken belief that the driver is in one lane of a dual carriageway was held by a judge to be dangerous driving (*R* v *Johnson* [1960] Crim LR 430). In *Johnstone* v *Hawkins* [1959] Crim LR 854, the High Court refused to quash an acquittal for dangerous driving at 85 mph along a main road past a road junction controlled by a 'slow' sign, where the driver had a long view down the minor road when twenty yards from it, but it was said that passing a junction at that speed was prima facie dangerous driving. In *Tribe* v *Jones* (1961) 59 LGR 582 the High Court refused to interfere with an acquittal for driving at a dangerous speed where a car had been driven along a restricted road at speeds between 45 and 65 mph: it was a wide road, well surfaced and bounded by common land, the road was not busy at the time (7.20 am) and the visibility and weather were good. Momentary inattention, resulting in a failure to see traffic lights, can amount to dangerous driving (*R* v *Parker* (1957) 41 Cr App R 134). In a case noted on p 4 of *The Guardian* of 28 January 1966, magistrates were directed to convict a motor cyclist who had driven at a speed of 60 mph with his hands off the handlebars for four seconds, on a road with fairly heavy traffic. In *Anderson* v *Transport Board* [1964] NZLR 881, the driver of a towing vehicle drove it in such a manner that the trailer snaked dangerously about the road. He was convicted of dangerous driving.

### 5.42 Careless driving

It is again emphasised that the following cases of careless driving do not lay down principles of law but are of use principally in illustrating what facts can amount to careless driving. A slight variation in the facts of a particular case, eg visibility, amount of traffic or geography, may make a difference. Whether a person should be convicted of careless driving is primarily a question of fact not of law.

Mounting the verge and hitting a pole nearly three feet from the edge of the road is prima facie evidence of careless driving, unless explained, eg a skid (*Watts* v *Carter* (1959) *The Times*, 22 October). A driver who signals that he will turn right and then turns left without taking any precautions to see if anything is coming behind is guilty of careless driving (*Pratt* v *Bloom* [1958] Crim LR 817). Failing to stop and look at a 'T' junction was held to be careless driving in *Baker* v *Spence* (1960) *The Times*, 27 May. The driver's duty is not confined to making signals: he must see, so far as he can, that they have been understood and he may be guilty of careless driving if he drives on after making one without so seeing (*Sorrie* v *Robertson* [1944] SC(J) 95). The High Court reluctantly upheld a conviction of a motorist who edged from a park on to a road when his view of it was obstructed by parked vehicles (*O'Connel* v *Fraser* (1963) 107 SJ 95). A defendant who gave misleading signals that he was going to turn but did not in fact turn was held guilty of careless driving (*Another* v *Probert* [1968] Crim LR 564). It is submitted that this case is not necessarily an authority for the view that a driver who is, without negligence, unaware that his indicators are flashing is therefore guilty of careless or inconsiderate driving. A conviction was directed when a car was driven at 25 mph past an obscured halt sign, and though the driver must have seen the white lines to mark the junction, he failed to see a car on the main road (*Spencer* v *Silvester* (1963) 107 SJ 1024). Crossing a central white line is itself evidence of careless driving in the absence of an explanation (*Bensley* v *Smith* [1972] Crim LR 239). A metropolitan magistrate convicted a driver who was reading a newspaper and the case was likened to a driver who kept kissing his passenger ([1954] Jo Crim L 204). A driver of a bus who is reversing and relying on his conductor's signals must satisfy himself that the conductor is so positioned that he can see what he ought to see; if that person is not so positioned, the driver may be guilty of careless driving (*Liddon* v *Stringer* [1967] Crim LR 371).

## 5.43 Inconsiderate driving

Drivers have been prosecuted for driving without reasonable consideration for other road users where they have had brilliant headlights which they have not dipped for oncoming traffic, or they have driven through puddles at speed, drenching pedestrians (129 JP Jo 338). In *Saville* v *Bache* (1969) *The Times*, 28 February, a civil case, it was said by the Court of Appeal that, if a motorist drove with undipped headlights in circumstances where he should know that they might dazzle an oncoming driver, it was for the former motorist to disprove his prima facie negligence in doing so by giving evidence of a good reason for not dipping. See 5.57 as to driving with uncorrected defective eyesight. A conviction was directed where the only road users affected were passengers in the defendant's vehicle; 'other road users' include persons in or outside the vehicle (*Pawley* v *Wharldall* [1965] 2 All ER 757). *Semble*, it must be proved that there actually were other road users; there is no reference, as there was in the former offence of dangerous driving, to persons who might reasonably be expected to be on the road. The defendant in *Pawley's* case had driven a bus in a way which scared the passengers. It may be necessary on this charge to show that the defendant was knowingly acting without consideration for others; his acts or omissions will often establish a prima facie case to this effect. A motorist who kicked out at a pedal cyclist was held not guilty of this offence as there was no evidence that his machine came near enough to the pedal cycle to constitute the offence (*Downes* v *Fell* (1969) 113 SJ 387).

## 5.44 Civil cases

The standard of driving required by the criminal law cannot be greater than that imposed by the tort of negligence (*Scott* v *Warren* [1974] RTR 104).

A skid is not necessarily evidence of negligence (*Laurie* v *Raglan etc Co* [1941] 3 All ER 332), and in *Custins* v *Nottingham Corporation* [1970] RTR 365 a bus driver was found not to be negligent in allowing his bus to get out of control on an icy road. But in *Richley* v *Faull* [1965] 3 All ER 109 an unexplained and violent skid was said to be in itself evidence of negligent driving.

Stopping suddenly is not necessarily evidence of negligent driving (*Parkinson* v *Liverpool Corporation* [1950] 1 All ER 367). Automatic stop lights may not be in themselves sufficient warning to following traffic (*Croston* v *Vaughan* [1937] 4 All ER 249). Hitting an unlit obstruction in the road does not necessarily show that the driver is negligent (*Tidy* v *Battman* [1934] 1 KB 319), and in *Hill* v *Phillips* (1963) 107 SJ 890, it was said that persons driving along country roads with dipped headlights should keep an especially careful look-out, as the presence of unlit obstructions should be anticipated there. In *Grange Motors (Cwmbran) Ltd* v *Spencer* [1969] 1 All ER 340 it was held that a driver is not necessarily negligent in acting on the signals of another person, here a postman-driver as opposed to a casual onlooker. In *Clarke* v *Winchurch* [1969] 1 All ER 275 the Court of Appeal said that flashing headlights could mean 'come on', notwithstanding para 96 of the 1969 Highway Code, which said it means merely advising other road users of one's presence. If a driver is proceeding slowly and carefully where his view is obstructed, it is a counsel of perfection to require him to stop and look again when his bonnet is one foot out (ibid), but Russell LJ dissented where the situation was potentially dangerous. It should be noted that *Clarke* v *Winchurch* has twice been suggested as not to have been laying down any principle of law (*Garston Warehousing Company Ltd* v *O F Smart* [1973] RTR 377 and *Worsfold* v *Howe* [1980] RTR 131).

A driver on a major road must still take precautions as to traffic emerging from minor roads and take due care to avoid colliding with it or endangering it (*Lang* v *London Transport Executive* [1959] 3 All ER 609) and it is a question of fact whether he has been negligent in regard to it. While entitled to assume that drivers on the minor road will behave properly, he must take precautions if it is apparent they will not (*Browne* v *Central SMT Co* [1949] SC 9). It was said in *Butters* v *J H Fenner & Co* (1967) *The Times*, 6 February, that a driver on a major road must still watch minor roads. It may be negligent to enter another road without ensuring that there is no traffic hidden by other vehicles in that road (*Harding* v *Hinchliffe* (1964) *The Times*, 8 April).

It was a dark and stormy night and a lorry was being backed into a car park: it was at right angles to the carriageway and totally obstructed it and it showed no lights to the side. The plaintiff, driving along the road, collided with it and it was held that there was negligence by the lorry driver (*Barber* v *British Road Services* (1964) *The Times*, 18 November). Similarly in *Jordan* v *North Hampshire Plant Hire* [1970] RTR 212 the driver of an articulated lorry was held to be negligent to drive, in the dark, his 35-foot-long lorry out of a drive and across a fast stretch of road where there were double white lines and a gradual bend. It was said to be a most dangerous manoeuvre despite the fact that the sides of the lorry were not required by law to be lit. It is submitted that both in *Barber* and in *Jordan* either defendant could be charged with driving without reasonable consideration. If a driver is in doubt whether he has room to pass a stationary vehicle or obstruction, he should stop and check up (*Randall* v *Tarrant* [1955] 1 All ER 600). To drive a motor vehicle along a country road when the driver knows that the vehicle has no front light is negligent (*Dawrant* v *Nutt* [1960] 3 All ER 681). A motorist who disregards a white line at an uncontrolled road junction is not negligent (*Homewood* v *Spiller* (1962) 106 SJ 900) but per Pearson LJ it might indicate a junction where extra care is needed. Now, under reg 22(2) of the Traffic Signs Regulations and General Directions 1981, double broken lines at a road mouth mean that the driver must take precautions. It may therefore be that *Homewood* v *Spiller* is now of less authority. It is not necessarily negligent to drive at a very high speed on a motorway but the driver should not assume that all overtaken vehicles will invariably observe lane discipline (*Hurlock* v *Inglis* (1963) 107 SJ 1023). In *Quinn* v *Scott* [1965] 2 All ER 588 driving at a speed of 75 mph on a three-lane country road, when traffic was not heavy, was held not to be negligent in the circumstances. Driving at a speed of 25–30 mph in a quiet residential road on a Sunday and not sounding a horn or slowing down when passing a large coach parked on the nearside is not negligent (*Moore* v *Poyner* [1975] RTR 127). Deceleration without warning to following traffic is not an act of negligence, even on a motorway, but a driver should signal his intention to make a sudden heavy stop (*Jungnickel* v *Laing*

(1967) 111 SJ 19), and in *Goke* v *Willett and Another* [1973] RTR 422 a driver was held to be negligent in relying solely on his indicator and stop lights when slowing down in the centre lane of a three-lane busy trunk road to turn right into a service station.

## 5.45 Careless driving generally

It is emphasised again that reckless and careless driving are questions of fact, and decisions of the High Court will generally be of little value because it is the facts in the particular case before the magistrates which must be considered and, even if a High Court decision can be found to fit them, there will almost certainly be some material variation in weather, state of traffic or other matter. The test as to whether a driver charged with careless driving is 'at fault' may be said to be whether the prosecution have proved *that the defendant departed from the standard of care and skill that in the particular circumstances of the case would have been exercised by a reasonable, prudent and competent driver* (see 5.27).

Careless driving is primarily a question of fact. Each set of circumstances is unique. Careless driving is objective in the sense that the standard of driving demanded of a driver is an objective standard. A person is guilty of careless driving once it is proved that he has departed from the standard required. It matters not whether this was due to his negligence, incompetence, inexperience, recklessness, or even his deliberate intent: the only mens rea required in a case of careless driving is (per Lord Diplock in *R* v *Lawrence* [1981] RTR 217 at p 220) 'simply to show that the prohibited physical act (actus reus) done by the accused was directed by a mind that was conscious of what his body was doing'. In another sense, careless driving is subjective in that it is the particular circumstances of the particular case that have to be examined. The people primarily concerned to make the decision are the justices who know the district (per Lord Widgery in *Walker* v *Tolhurst* [1976] RTR 513, at p 515G). Before a decision of magistrates on a careless driving case can be reversed, the circumstances must be such that it is possible to say that the justices reached a conclusion which no reasonable bench could have reached (*Bracegirdle* v *Oxley* [1947] KB 349, applied in *Walker* v *Tolhurst*). It follows that a bench will sometimes come to a different conclusion in a particular case from that which would normally be made. Thus in *Walker* v *Tolhurst* the acquittal was upheld of a motorist seeking to emerge from a side turning into a main road who failed to see an approaching cyclist on his side of the road (the decision was 'bold' but not perverse). Similarly in *Hume* v *Ingleby* [1975] RTR 502 the Divisional Court refused to find justices perverse after they had acquitted a driver of careless driving who had entered his van parked off the main carriageway on an unlit road at night and in the process of driving away had reversed colliding with a car parked immediately behind him (see further below).

## 5.46 Highway Code

The best *guide* for those engaged in reckless and careless driving cases is the Highway Code itself; its non-observance can be relied on as tending to establish liability in such cases, but failure to observe a provision of the Highway Code will not of itself render that person liable to criminal proceedings of any kind (s 37(5) of the 1972 Act). The present edition of the Highway Code was approved by Parliament in 1977. It is more detailed than the former edition and in places, gives specific rather than general advice.

While the table of braking distances (reproduced at the end of this volume) may be used in cross-examination to prove a breach of the Code, it is otherwise inadmissible by itself to prove speed as it is hearsay (*R* v *Chadwick* [1975] Crim LR 105).

Prosecutions occasionally are brought on the basis that because a defendant is in breach of a provision of the Highway Code, he should automatically be convicted of careless driving in the absence of any other explanation. The facts of the case may, of course, be so overwhelming that in the absence of any explanation the defendant should be convicted (see 'Res ipsa loquitur', 5.30), but the mere breach of a provision of the Code by itself is not sufficient (s 37(5)). In *Scott* v *Warren* [1974] RTR 104 the defendant driving in a line of moving traffic was unable to avoid hitting a piece of metal which had fallen off a lorry in front of the van. The magistrates dismissed the case and it was suggested on the hearing of the case stated before the High Court that if a driver did not leave sufficient space between himself and the vehicle in front to avoid a collision then the defendant was prima facie guilty of careless driving as he would be in breach of rules 34 and 35 of the Highway Code. The Divisional Court disagreed, holding that whether a person has driven carelessly is primarily a matter of fact: the duty of a driver following another vehicle was, as far as reasonably possible, to take up such a position and to drive in such a fashion as to be able to deal with all traffic exigencies reasonably to be expected (applying *Brown and Lynn* v *Western SMT Co Ltd* [1975] SC 31). Another case where the justices' dismissal of a careless driving charge was upheld by the High Court where the defendant was in breach of the Highway Code is *Jarvis* v *Fuller* [1974] RTR 160. The defendant drove at 50 mph in drizzle at night with dipped headlights and failed to avoid hitting a pedal cyclist wearing dark clothing whose rear light was probably not working. The Divisional Court again emphasised that whether a defendant was driving carelessly is primarily a question of fact. *Jarvis* was followed in *Webster* v *Wall* [1980] Crim LR 186 where the High Court refused to disturb the justices' acquittal of careless driving of a motor cyclist who had collided at night with an unlit stationary vehicle on a wet road in conditions of poor visibility. It was impossible to say that the decision was perverse: the question was whether the justices' decision could have been reached by a reasonable bench of justices.

In *Hume* v *Ingleby* [1975] RTR 502 a defendant was acquitted of careless driving. He entered his van, which was parked off the main carriageway on an unlit road at night, he looked in his rear view mirrors, looked round as far as he could and reversed, thereby colliding with a car parked facing away from him and causing slight damage to the car and his van. The Divisional Court refused to hold that the acquittal of the motorist by the justices was perverse: a motorist who reverses and collides with something behind him is not ipso facto guilty of careless driving despite rule 108 of Highway Code

('Before you reverse make sure that there are no . . . obstructions . . . behind you').

It may be 'bold' for justices to acquit a motorist of careless driving who emerged into a high street with trafficators working and hit a cyclist riding along the high street. It was 5.50 pm on a dark January evening. The street lights were not lit and it was raining. The Divisional Court observed that, more often than not, colliding with another vehicle on the main road on emerging from a side road must amount to careless driving, but the decision of the justices must be a subjective one on the facts. The case was not strong enough for it to be said that the justices' decision was perverse (*Walker* v *Tolhurst* [1978] RTR 513). A breach of the Highway Code is, in accordance with s 37(5) of the 1972 Act, only evidential in its effect. On the other hand, the evidential effect of a failure to observe the Code may be strongly relied on to prove carelessness, reckless or potentially reckless driving. In *Trentham* v *Rowlands* [1974] RTR 164, the Divisional Court relied, inter alia, on rule 116 of the former edition of the Code ('overtake only on the right . . . never move to a lane on your left to overtake') in holding that it was potentially dangerous and thus dangerous driving for a motorist to overtake another on the outside lane at 70 mph by moving over to the inner lanes to do so, particularly having regard to the obligation imposed by rule 114 on the driver being overtaken to return to the inside lane. It should also be noted that under s 37(5) only a *failure* to observe the Code is of evidential value. The fact that a defendant or prosecution witness has complied with the Code does not mean that that person cannot have been careless or negligent. In *Goke* v *Willett and Another* [1973] RTR 422, a driver who gave no hand signal but relied only on his indicator and stop lights to show he was slowing in the middle lane of a three-lane trunk road to turn right, was held to be negligent even though the Highway Code can be read as indicating that if trafficators and stop lights are both fitted and are in good working order, hand signals need never be used. In so far as the Code indicated that hand signals need never be used, this is unwise advice (ibid, per Edmund Davies LJ, at p 425). Rule 35 of the most recent edition of the Code requires motorists only to use the correct signals, stop light signals and arm signals. Arm signals are for use when direction indicators are not used or when necessary to reinforce direction indicator signals and stop lights (p 49 of the Code). The facts of *Goke* v *Willett* seem to indicate a situation where arm signals are necessary in addition to indicator and stop lights.

## 5.47 Visibility

Where a driver finds himself unexpectedly blinded by headlights or the sun, or for any reason he cannot see properly or control the car, eg his dog suddenly jumps on his lap, then, unless the loss of vision or control immediately ceases, he should stop at once. If during the literal second or two while he has not proper vision or control an accident occurs which is due entirely to that loss of vision or control, it is submitted that he is not guilty of careless driving. But if the accident occurs more than two seconds after the loss of vision or control began and the driver has not done anything about reducing speed or stopping, he should, it is submitted, generally be found guilty of careless driving at least, not so much for running into something because he could not see it but rather for continuing to drive when he could not see or control the car properly. In *S* v *Lombard* [1964] (4) South African LR 346 it was held that if a horsefly or any insect which could perhaps cause trouble flies in at the window, a reasonable driver will immediately apply his brakes and stop. Again, the driver should keep his eyes on the road, but must occasionally look aside to watch his dashboard or pedestrians or police signals from the pavement or to observe direction signs. It is submitted that no criminal liability should attach to a driver for not keeping a proper look-out during the second or two while he necessarily glances away from the road ahead, provided he is driving at a reasonable speed. If he is travelling at a speed of 30 mph, a glance away for even four seconds may be dangerous; certainly gazing up at signposts while approaching a busy road junction could be, and a driver's failure to stop or slow down might amount to careless driving. The late author recalled a very experienced solicitor advising a driver to plead guilty to a charge of careless driving where the latter had reversed a few yards from a stationary position and collided with something because she had not made sure that the road behind was clear (in *Hume* v *Ingleby* the defendant looked in his mirrors—see 5.46). Somewhat similar cases are reported at [1954] Jo Crim L 120 and 121 JP Jo 421. A driver who intends to reverse and cannot see from the driving seat whether he safely can, should, it is submitted, alight and satisfy himself that the road will be clear. If there are children about, even that might not suffice, and he should wait until some reliable person can be found to signal him. It was held in *S* v *Lalla* [1964] (4) South African LR 320 that the reasonable driver who intends to reverse out of his garage or backyard where small children are or may be playing in close proximity to his line of travel knows that he must not begin to reverse before satisfying himself that no child has walked or crawled behind the car, for he is alive to that possibility and to the fact that he may not observe such a child by merely looking behind him from the driver's seat. (Reference should now be made to rr 108 and 109 of the current edition of the Code which require a motorist to ensure there is nothing behind him when reversing, and if he cannot see to get someone to guide him.)

### 5.48 Use of headlights

It is obviously reckless to drive at night with sidelights only on an unlit road, and by reg 22 of the Road Vehicles Lighting Regulations 1984 it is an offence if the street is not illuminated by street lamps. The Court of Appeal in *Hill* v *Phillips* (1963) 107 SJ 890 (a civil case) held that, when driving with dipped headlights in country roads, motorists should drive so that they could see unlighted obstructions the presence of which might be anticipated, eg cycles without lights or people in dark clothes. But whether the defendant who collides or fails to see something at night or in conditions of poor visibility is like any other case guilty of careless driving is primarily a question of fact (see *Jarvis* v *Fuller, Webster* v *Wall* and *Hume* v *Ingleby*, 5.47).

## 5.49 Two offences from one incident

The police sometimes charge a driver with both careless driving and disobedience to traffic lights or a 'stop' sign in respect of the same incident. It is submitted that it is proper to convict on the major charge only where there has been some carelessness over and above the disobedience to the sign, eg approaching the junction too fast or not keeping a proper look-out for approaching traffic; the other charge can be marked 'no adjudication' or 'adjourned sine die' if there is a conviction on the graver offence, so as to preserve, if desired, the position on appeal. Alternatively, if there is no likelihood of appeal or there has been a plea of guilty to the major charge, the lesser charge, it is submitted, may properly be dismissed. If the adjudication on the lesser charge has been adjourned, it may in any event be dismissed once the time for appeal has expired. Like principles would apply where there are charges of failing to accord precedence on a crossing and of careless driving from one incident or of crossing double white lines and careless driving from one incident. If there is nothing more to the case than disobedience to the red light (or other minor charge) and the driver has otherwise been careful, it is submitted that a conviction on the lights charge suffices and the careless driving one can properly be dismissed. Similarly, it is also submitted that if the only carelessness is to fail to observe the lights or traffic sign, conviction on the graver charge only is sufficient. *R* v *Parker* (1957) 41 Crim App R 134 is not overlooked, but it is submitted that to convict on both is oppressive, especially as it can lead to two endorsements and two penalties for one incident which might properly have been charged as a traffic light offence at the start. Cf *R* v *Burnham JJ* at 2.49.

The above paragraph was considered by the Divisional Court in *Theobald (J) (Hounslow) Ltd* v *Stacey* [1979] RTR 411 and given qualified approval (see Lord Widgery J, at p 416B–D). See also *Welton* v *Taneborne* at 2.49.

## 5.50 Aiders and abettors and supervisors

In *Du Cros* v *Lambourne* (1906) 70 JP 525, it was held that a person charged with dangerous driving could be convicted although the evidence might show only that he was aiding, abetting, counselling and procuring, and the actual driver had not been summoned (see also [1953] Jo Crim L 173). In that case the lower court had found it unnecessary to decide whether the defendant had been driving: he had been sitting in the front of the car, and, being its owner, could control the manner of its driving. Two persons pursuing a common purpose may be guilty of criminal negligence in driving, although only one of them drives (*R* v *Baldessare* (1930) 22 Cr App R 70). In that case the jury found that the passenger joined in responsibility with the driver for the way in which the vehicle was driven, but the doctrine of joint responsibility should not be applied indiscriminately where it is not clear who drove or that the passenger joined in responsibility for the way it was driven (*Webster* v *Wishart* [1955] SLT 243). A managing director of a haulage company, together with the haulage company in Scotland, were held to be rightly convicted of aiding and abetting causing death by dangerous driving in England where the defendant lorry driver had been sent on a journey from Scotland into

England when the managing director knew that the lorry had a dangerously worn tyre (*R* v *Robert Millar* [1970] 2 QB 54).

The supervisor of a learner driver may be found guilty of aiding and abetting careless driving by the learner if he has failed to supervise him properly (*Rubie* v *Faulkner* [1940] 1 All ER 285). He must not be passive where his supervisory duties require him to be active and he must advise the learner what to do to avoid accidents and risks (ibid). If he does so advise and takes other available steps to avoid danger, it is submitted that the supervisor should not be found guilty merely because there has nevertheless been an accident because of the learner's failure to heed his advice, or because of a sudden and unexpected action. Driving test examiners are there to observe the driver's mistakes and are not in the position of a driving instructor or supervisor (*BSM Ltd* v *Simms* [1971] RTR 190).

### 5.51 Public emergencies

There is no exemption for police, fire-engine or ambulance drivers from prosecution for reckless or careless driving and prosecutions are reported at 113 JP Jo 374; 114 JP Jo 54 and [1961] Jo Crim L 1. See also *R* v *Lundt-Smith* in 'Emergency', 21.8 and *R* v *O'Toole* (1971) 55 Cr App R 206 (two cases of ambulance drivers driving dangerously in an emergency). In *Gaynor* v *Allen* [1959] 2 All ER 644, a civil case, it was held that a police officer driving in the course of his duty owes the same duty as a civilian driver to the public to drive with due care, and in *Wardell-Yerburgh* v *Surrey County Council* [1973] RTR 462 it was held that the driver of a fire tender responding to an emergency call owed to the public the same duty of care as any other driver. In *Wood* v *Richards* [1977] RTR 201 the conviction of a police officer of driving without due care and attention was upheld for the same reason. Responding to an emergency, the police patrol driver drove along the hard shoulder of a motorway and collided with a stationary lorry. It was again held that it was impossible to say that a special standard should be applied to a police officer and in *Marshall* v *Osmond* [1983] 2 All ER 225 it was again emphasised that a police officer driving a vehicle in accordance with his duty owed the same duty of care as he owed to anyone else in all the circumstances of the case. The officer was pursuing someone who bore the appearance of someone enraged in an arrestable criminal activity and that fact was one of the circumstances of the case which must be borne in mind in deciding whether or not the constable had been negligent. Any sympathy with a police officer driving in such a situation is best expressed when the court comes to consider the penalty (*Wood* v *Richards*, above). See also Chapter 21 as to 'special reasons'.

### 5.52–4 Defence of necessity or duress

In *Wood* v *Richards* above it was held that the defence of necessity was not justified in that case. In *Buckoke* v *GLC* [1971] 2 All ER 254 there was no such defence available to a fireman who jumped a red light in order to attend an emergency.

Presumably, however, the defence may still remain as a possibility in an appropriate case. In was stated by three of the law lords in *Lynch* v *DPP* [1975] 1 All ER 913 that there is no logical distinction between the principles of necessity and duress. There must be a relationship between the need or the duress and the act, ie the need or duress must justify the act.

Where the defence of necessity or duress is not available or is not accepted the circumstances may still amount to special reasons for not endorsing or not disqualifying (see Chapter 21).

## Related Offences

### 5.55 Causing bodily harm by furious driving etc

Section 35 of the Offences against the Person Act 1861 is still occasionally used, particularly where the driving complained of did not take place on a road within the meaning of the 1972 Act. Section 35 reads as follows:

> Whosoever having the charge of any carriage or vehicle, shall, by wanton or furious driving or racing, or other wilful misconduct, or by wilful neglect, do or cause to be done any bodily harm to any person whatsoever, shall be guilty of an offence.

An offence under s 35 is only triable on indictment (unless committed by a juvenile). It should be noted that s 35 creates a number of separate offences. Section 35 applies to pedal cycles as well as to other vehicles (*R* v *Parker* (1859) 59 JP 793). Where the victim is a juvenile, spouses are competent witnesses for the prosecution against each other (Children and Young Persons Act 1933, s 15). Quarter sessions have held that, on a charge under s 35, the Crown must prove a degree of lack of care which would amount to dangerous driving: 'wanton driving' indicates a positive lack of care and 'wilful neglect' implies something of a negative nature ([1954] Crim LR 137). In *R* v *Philip Cooke* [1971] Crim LR 44 the charge under s 35 was that the defendant having charge of a motor vehicle caused bodily harm by 'wilful misconduct'. The jury at quarter sessions were directed that there was no need for the prosecution to prove an intention to cause injury or bodily harm. If the defendant's driving was intended it was 'wilful' and if it fell below the normal standard so that it could be called 'misconduct' it sufficed if the 'wilful misconduct' amounted to a substantial cause of the injury. Failure to have a light at night on a horse-drawn vehicle can be 'wilful neglect' under s 35 (*A-G* v *Joyce* (1956) 90 ILTR 47). A conviction under s 35 was upheld where the jury had found that the defendant was driving in a wanton way by reason of the amount of liquor he had taken; there was also evidence of reckless driving (*R* v *Burdon* (1927) 20 Cr App R 80). In *R* v *Mohan* [1975] RTR 337 the defendant drove his motor car at a police constable, who leapt out of his way and avoided being struck. He was charged with attempting by wanton driving to cause bodily harm to the constable. It was held that mens rea was an essential element of the common law offence of attempting to commit an offence under s 35 of the Offences against the Person Act 1861 and a specific intent on the part of the defendant to commit the offence had to be proved.

The only useful purposes of s 35 now seem to be for dealing with horse-drawn vehicles and cyclists and as a reserve charge for motorists who cannot be prosecuted for reckless driving either because notice of intended prosecution was not given or the offence was not committed on a road within the meaning of the 1972 Act.

Where, however, a motor vehicle is deliberately used as a weapon for the purpose of inflicting injury on another, although the defendant may be often charged with reckless driving it is submitted it would be more appropriate for him to be charged under s 18 of the Offences Against the Person Act 1861 (although he rarely is; see 'Motor Vehicles Used as Weapons of Offence', J.R. Spencer [1985] Crim LR 29).

## 5.56 Motor racing on highways

It is an offence to promote or take part in a race or trial of speed between motor vehicles on a public highway (s 14 of the 1972 Act).

The offence must be committed on a 'public highway'. This expression is not defined. It seems narrower than a 'road' within the meaning of s 196 (see 1.66), since the definition would seem to exclude a private road to which the public has access. At common law a highway is by definition public, ie it is a right of way upon which the public are entitled to pass and repass.

It would seem that time keepers, stewards and possibly passengers as well as promoters can be convicted under s 14: anyone who 'takes part in' a race or trial of speed commits a s 14 offence. It has been held by the Crown Court that an offence is committed even when different routes are taken by each vehicle starting from a common starting point to a finishing point. The offence must consist of a race or trial between vehicles. No offence is committed under this section where one vehicle races and is not in competition with another vehicle.

The offence is triable summarily only. For penalty see 5.71.

It is similarly an offence to promote or take part in a race or trial of speed between cycles unless authorised or conducted in accordance with regulations (s 20).

## 5.57 Driving with uncorrected defective eyesight or refusing to submit to an eyesight test

It is an offence under s 91(1) of the 1972 Act for a person to drive a motor vehicle on a road while his eyesight is such that he cannot comply with the prescribed requirement. The offence is committed if the defective vision either is not or cannot be sufficiently corrected by glasses. It is also an offence under s 91(2) for a driver to refuse to submit to an eyesight test when required to do so by a constable who suspects he may be committing an offence under s 91(1). The requirement as to eyesight mentioned in s 91 is that the driver, whether wearing glasses or not, can read a car's number plate at a distance of 75 feet in good daylight (45 feet for pedestrian-controlled vehicles) or, where the letters or figures are $3\frac{1}{8}$ inches in height instead of $3\frac{1}{2}$ inches, at a distance of 67 feet (40 feet for pedestrian-controlled vehicles) (Motor Vehicles (Driving Licences) Regulations 1981, Sched 4, para 1). Inability to comply with this requirement (with the aid of glasses if worn) is a prescribed disability preventing the holding of a driving licence (reg

22(1)(*f*)). There is a question to this effect on driving licence application forms and a person who knowingly makes a false answer to this quesion commits an offence under s 170 of the 1972 Act.

The Secretary of State for Transport, by virtue of s 87A(2)(*b*) of the 1972 Act, can require a licence holder or applicant for a licence whom he believes may have defective eyesight to submit to an examination. Section 91 makes it clear that, if he needs glasses to read the plate at 75 feet and he was not wearing them when he was driving, he is guilty and that he is to be tested in the same state as to wearing or not wearing them as when he was driving. It is submitted that the police may require the motorist under s 91(2) to take an eyesight test subsequent to the occasion which gave rise to the constable's suspicions. A person may be seen driving at night or in conditions of poor visibility and the prescribed test as to eyesight has to be taken in good daylight.

If the defendant's eyesight has not been corrected by spectacles or is incapable of being corrected by spectacles, a court would seem to be under a duty under s 92 to notify the Secretary of State with a view to the licence being revoked. Additionally, the court may consider disqualifying the defendant under s 93(7) until he passes a test.

For penalties for offences under s 91, see 5.71.

### 5.58–65 Driving to the common danger etc

Offences akin to dangerous and careless driving arise also under the Highway Act 1835, s 78, the Metropolitan Police Act 1839, s 54, the Town Police Clauses Act 1847, s 28, and the Public Health Act 1925, s 74. These Acts would apply to motor vehicles, cycles and horse-drawn vehicles and (except for s 28) to equestrians, mahouts, cameleers and outward-bound ladies from Riga (*Williams* v *Evans* (1867) 41 JP 151) but see 119 JP Jo 746. As to Crown drivers, see 2.8.

The only value of these Acts so far as cases against motorists and cyclists are concerned is that warning of intended prosecution need not have been given (see Chapter 3).

## Reckless, Careless and Inconsiderate Cycling

### 5.66–70 The offences: ss 17 and 18

Sections 17 and 18 of the 1972 Act contain provisions similar to those of ss 2 and 3 in respect of reckless or careless riding of bicycles, tricycles and (s 196) cycles having four or more wheels. The Criminal Law Act 1977, s 50, amended s 17 in the same manner as s 2: viz the offence of dangerous cycling was repealed.

It would seem that reckless cycling should be interpreted in the same manner as reckless driving, and similarly careless or inconsiderate cycling is interpreted in the same manner as careless or inconsiderate driving.

A road is defined for ss 17 and 18 as including a bridleway (see 1.67*A*).

An auto-assisted cycle may be a cycle for the purposes of ss 17 and 18 if its engine is disconnected and essential parts have been removed (*Lawrence* v *Howlett* [1952] 2 All ER 74). Otherwise, it is a motor vehicle whether the engine is running or not, and the definition of 'cycle' contained in s 196 specifically excludes cycles which are motor vehicles (but it may nevertheless be a pedal cycle for the purpose of s 12(5) of the Theft Act 1968, see 15.3).

The *Concise Oxford Dictionary* defines 'ride' as 'sit on and be carried by', including 'sit or go or be on something as on a horse, especially astride'. It is not clear whether a cyclist who is propelling himself by standing with one foot on the pedal and by touching the ground occasionally with the other 'rides': it can certainly be said that he is being 'carried by' his machine.

In *Crank* v *Brooks*, 6.42, it was observed obiter that a cyclist having one foot on the pedal was 'riding' if she was thereby using the cycle as a scooter. In that case the cyclist was pushing the cycle with both feet on the ground and was held to be a foot passenger for the purpose of the 'Zebra' Pedestrian Crossings Regulations. By contrast, s 22 of the 1972 Act (failing to conform to traffic directions or signs) refers to persons 'driving or propelling vehicles'.

Offences contrary to ss 17 and 18 are only triable summarily. (Even Parliament, as well as Homer, may nod: when inserting para 31A(1)(*b*) and (2) in Part IV of Sched 4 to the 1972 Act, it was overlooked that s 17 can never be tried by a jury.)

A constable may arrest without warrant a person who in his view commits an offence of reckless or careless cycling if he does not give his name and address (1972 Act, s 164(2)(*b*)). This power of arrest will be repealed by the Police and Criminal Evidence Act 1984 when brought into force. Section 25 of that Act will, however, give a general power of arrest if the constable cannot ascertain his name, or doubts whether the person has given his real name or suspects that his address for service of a summons is unsatisfactory.

The provisions of s 179 (notices of intended prosecution: see Chapter 3) apply to offences under ss 17 and 18.

Paragraph 4 of Part IV of Sched 4 allows a charge of reckless cycling to be reduced to one of careless or inconsiderate cycling (as it allows a charge of reckless driving to be reduced to one of careless driving: see 5.7). As in cases of reckless driving, it would seem that justices may direct a charge of careless cycling to be preferred notwithstanding six months have elapsed since the date of offence (see *R* v *Coventry JJ*, 5.7). Similarly the Crown Court would have power, on appeal from a reckless cycling charge, to direct a charge of careless cycling (see *Killington* v *Butcher*, 5.7).

It is an offence contrary to s 20 of the 1972 Act for a person to promote or take part in a race or trial of speed of cycles (not being motor vehicles) on public highways (note that the offence is confined to 'public highways'). This is a different definition from the definition of 'road' under s 196 (see Chapter 1). It would seem to include public paths, roads used as public paths and bridleways within the meaning of the Wildlife and Countryside Act 1981 but would seem not to include roads to which the public have access which are not public highways (see further Chapter 1).

For penalties for offences contrary to ss 17, 18 and 20, see 5.71.

# Penalties and Sentencing

## 5.71 Table of penalties

| *Offence* | *Mode of trial* | *Section* | *Imprisonment* | *Level of fine* | *Disqualification* | *Penalty points* | *Endorsement code* | *Mag. Assoc. Suggestions* |
|---|---|---|---|---|---|---|---|---|
| Manslaughter or, in Scotland, culpable homicide | Only on indictment | Common law | Life | Unlimited | Obligatory | 4* | DD60 | — |
| Causing death by reckless driving | Only on indictment | s 1 | 5 years (or before a Sheriff in Scotland 2 years) | Unlimited | Obligatory | 4* | DD70 | — |
| Reckless driving | (a) On indictment | s 2 | 2 years | Unlimited | Obligatory if committed within 3 years after a previous conviction otherwise discretionary (see 5.74) | 4* (if obligatory) otherwise 10 | DD70 | — |
| | (b) Summarily | | 6 months | Level 5† | | | | £300 and consider disqualification |
| Careless or inconsiderate driving | Summary | s 3 | — | Level 4 | Discretionary | 2–5 | CD10 careless driving CD20 inconsiderate driving | £60 but *always* consider degree of carelessness |

[*Table continued overleaf*]

## 5.71 Table of penalties *ctd*

| *Offence* | *Mode of trial* | *Section* | *Imprisonment* | *Level of fine* | *Disqualification* | *Penalty points* | *Endorsement code* | *Mag. Assoc. Suggestions* |
|---|---|---|---|---|---|---|---|---|
| Causing bodily harm by furious driving etc | Only on indictment | s 35 of the Offences against the Person Act 1861 | 2 years | Unlimited | — | — | — | — |
| Motor racing | Summary | s 14 | — | Level 4† | Obligatory | 4* | MS50 | — |
| Driving with uncorrected sight, or refusing to submit to an eyesight test | Summary | s 91(1)<br>s 91(2) | — | Level 3† | — | 2 | MS70<br>MS80 | — |
| Reckless cycling | Summary | s 17 | — | Level 3† | — | — | — | — |
| Careless or inconsiderate cycling | Summary | s 18 | — | Level 1† | — | — | — | — |

* No penalty points may be imposed if the offender is disqualified but four penalty points have to be taken into account in considering whether the court is obliged to disqualify under the Transport Act 1981, s 19.

† For current maxima for the standard levels of fine, see 18.6.

### 5.72 Causing death by reckless driving

The maximum penalty is five years' imprisonment (two years' imprisonment if convicted by a sheriff's court in Scotland). The defendant may also be fined to an unlimited amount.

Disqualification and endorsement is obligatory unless there are 'special reasons' (see Chapter 21). The disqualification must be at least twelve months. Unless special reasons for not endorsing are found the offender will also incur 4 points (see 19.25).

The endorsement code for the offence is DD 70.

A person convicted of the offence may also be disqualified under s 93(7) (see 20.32) until he passes a driving test.

The offence is endorsable and the offender may be liable to a penalty points disqualification, see 20.18–29.

### 5.73 Reckless driving

The maximum penalty on indictment is two years' imprisonment or a fine of an unlimited amount or both. When tried summarily the maximum penalty is six months' imprisonment and/or a level 5 fine. The justices have power to commit the offender for sentence by the Crown Court if they consider their powers of punishment are inadequate.

### 5.74 Second conviction for reckless driving

The offence is obligatorily endorsable, unless there are 'special reasons' (see Chapter 21), but disqualification is discretionary unless the offender has been convicted of another offence under s 1 or s 2 within three years of the commission of the offence. Where disqualification is obligatory, the court must disqualify unless there are 'special reasons' (see Chapter 21). Note that the disqualification is only obligatory if the offender is subsequently convicted of an offence *committed* within three years after the date on which he was previously *convicted*. Thus if the second offence occurred after the first offence, but at the time of commission of the second offence the defendant had not yet been convicted of the first offence, the court is not obliged to disqualify him (although, of course, in such a case it is thought that ordinarily a court would consider exercising its discretionary power to disqualify). On the other hand, disqualification may be obligatory even if the dates of the offences are more than three years apart (eg a person who committed an offence of reckless driving on 1 December 1981 for which he was convicted on 1 March 1982 must be disqualified if he is convicted of reckless driving which he committed on 1 February 1985).

The previous conviction may be either under s 1 (causing death by driving) or s 2 (reckless driving), or for aiding and abetting an offence under s 1 or s 2 (*Makeham* v *Donaldson* [1981] Crim LR 570, where it was held that a defendant convicted of a drink/driving offence should be disqualified for at least three years because he had been previously convicted of aiding and abetting a drink/driving offence). A previous conviction of motor manslaughter or culpable homicide within three years does not render a subsequent conviction for reckless driving obligatorily disqualifiable. If it is a first offence or the previous conviction was more than three years ago, the court has a discretion whether or not to disqualify. Offences under s 2 are offences to which s 19 of the Transport Act 1981 applies. A person convicted of an offence of reckless driving will incur on endorsement 10 penalty points if he is not disqualified. It therefore follows that on being convicted for a second time (provided that he was not disqualified for the earlier offence) the court will not only be obliged to disqualify for the offence but also will normally have to impose a concurrent penalty points disqualification under s 19 if the earlier offence is within the period for a penalty points disqualification (for calculation of the period for a penalty points disqualification see 20.21, this is different from the 'second conviction' period set up above). Any such disqualification is concurrent with a disqualification for the offence.

The endorsement code for reckless driving is DD 30.

If the justices consider that their powers of punishment (ie six months' imprisonment and/or a maximum fine of £2,000) are inadequate, the offender can be committed for sentence to the Crown Court under s 38 of the Magistrates' Courts Act 1980 (see 2.57).

The Magistrates' Association recommended as a starting point a fine of £300 'and consider disqualification' (see the Association's Suggestions in Appendix 3). (As to the application of the Association's Suggestions generally see 18.1.)

A person convicted of an offence under s 2 may be ordered under s 93(7) to be disqualified until he passes a driving test (see 20.32).

The offence is obligatorily endorsable with ten penalty points (see 5.71) unless there are 'special reasons' (see Chapter 21).

### 5.75 Careless or inconsiderate driving

The maximum penalty is a level 4 fine. Imprisonment cannot be imposed for the offence.

The endorsement code is CD 10 for driving without due care and attention, CD 20 for driving without reasonable consideration; CD 30 is used in Scotland for both offences.

The Magistrates' Association recommend as a starting point a fine of £60 but add 'but consider *always* degree of carelessness' (see the Association's Suggestions in Appendix 3). (As to the application of the Association's Suggestions generally see 18.1.)

The Crown Court, when sentencing an offender found guilty by a jury of careless or inconsiderate driving after an acquittal of a charge of causing death by reckless driving or reckless driving, has the same powers and duties as to sentencing as a magistrates' court (1972 Act, Sched 4, Part IV, para 3A(2)).

A person convicted under s 3 may be disqualified under s 93(7) (see 20.32) until he passes a driving test.

The offence is endorsable with two to five penalty points unless special reasons are found. For the penalty points system see 19.21. It is thought that the criterion for the number of penalty points is primarily the degree of carelessness or lack of consideration, see further 'Variable penalty points', 19.23.

## 5.76 Reckless, careless and inconsiderate cycling

The level of fine on the standard scale for reckless cycling is 3, and for careless or inconsiderate cycling, 1. Imprisonment may not be imposed for either offence.

## 5.77 Manslaughter

The maximum penalty for manslaughter is imprisonment for life and/or an unlimited fine.

Manslaughter, and culpable homicide in Scotland, if committed by the driver of a motor vehicle is obligatorily disqualifiable in the absence of 'special reasons' and endorsable (see Chapter 21). The period must be for at least twelve months.

The offender must be disqualified under s 93(7) (see 20.32) until he passes a driving test.

The offence is endorsable and the offender may incur a penalty points disqualification in addition to the disqualification for the offence (see 20.18).

The endorsement code for manslaughter, or in Scotland, culpable homicide, is DD 60.

## 5.78 Causing harm by furious driving etc

The offence is triable only on indictment and is punishable by a maximum term of imprisonment of two years and/or an unlimited fine.

No disqualification or endorsement may be ordered (but see s 44 of the Powers of Criminal Courts Act 1973, 20.31).

## 5.79 Motor racing on highways

The level of fine on the standard scale is 4. Imprisonment may not be imposed.

Disqualification for a period of at least twelve months together with endorsement is obligatory in the absence of 'special reasons' (see Chapter 21). For the penalty points system, see 19.21.

The offender may be disqualified under s 93(7) until he passes a driving test (see 20.32).

The endorsement code for the offence is MS 50.

The offence is obligatorily disqualifiable and endorsable and the offender must be disqualified for at least twelve months and will incur four penalty points and may thus be additionally disqualified for a penalty points disqualification (for the penalty points system, see 19.25).

## 5.80 Driving with uncorrected defective eyesight or refusing to submit to an eyesight test

Offences under s 91(1) and (2) are both punishable by a fine of level 3 on the standard scale. Imprisonment may not be imposed.

Disqualification is discretionary but endorsement of two penalty points is obligatory in the absence of 'special reasons' (see Chapter 21). For the penalty points system, see 19.21.

The offender may be disqualified under s 93(7) (see 20.32) until he passes a driving test.

The endorsement code for driving with uncorrected defective eyesight or for refusing to submit to an eyesight test are MS 70 and MS 80, respectively.

### 5.81–5 Driving to the common danger etc

The offences under s 78 of the Highway Act 1835 are punishable by a fine of level 1 on the standard scale; under s 74 of the Public Health Act 1925, by a fine of level 1 on the standard scale and under s 54 of the Metropolitan Police Act 1839, by a fine of level 2 on the standard scale.

Offences contrary to s 28 of the Town Police Clauses Act 1847 are punishable by a fine of level 3 on the standard scale.

Disqualification and endorsement cannot be ordered for these offences.

## Sentencing Guidelines

### 5.86 Drink

In *R* v *Eadie* [1978] RTR 292 the Court of Appeal considered the future position having regard to the changes made by the Criminal Law Act 1977. It was stated that drivers who have had too much to drink and cause accidents resulting in injury or death must expect to lose their liberty in the absence of exceptional mitigating circumstances. In *R* v *Midgley* [1979] RTR 1 a sentence of imprisonment of fifteen months for causing death by reckless driving was reduced to six months to run concurrently with a sentence of six months for driving with excess blood-alcohol. The defendant had a perfectly respectable record, but his counsel recognised that he could not expect anything short of an immediate prison sentence. In *R* v *Wright (Earnest)* [1979] RTR 15 for a 'disgraceful case' of causing death by dangerous driving while unfit to drive through drink a sentence of three years' imprisonment was upheld on appeal, despite the fact that the defendant was fifty years old, had never been in prison and had been ostracised in his small home town for nine months while awaiting trial. It was said that where the defendant is under the influence of drink a custodial sentence is generally necessary (*R* v *Worrell* [1965] Crim LR 561) even where the defendant is of previous good character and would lose his job as an airline pilot but had a blood-alcohol level of 292 mg per 100 ml (*R* v *Kashyap* [1972] Crim LR 257). See also *R* v *Sullivan* [1974] Crim LR 56 where a sentence of eighteen months was upheld even though the defendant's expectation of life was uncertain following an operation for cancer. In *R* v *Austin (Howard)* [1981] RTR 10, the defendant, suspected of having excess blood-alcohol, was chased by the police for some eleven miles in the course of which he drove recklessly. He finished up in a hedge where he was approached by policemen from front and rear. He thereupon reversed, causing one constable to jump clear, and then drove forward, causing another constable to dive on to the bonnet of his car falling to the road and sustaining injury. The defendant was charged with reckless driving and with causing bodily harm to the constable by wanton or furious driving contrary to s 35 of the Offences against the Person Act 1861. He pleaded guilty to the reckless driving and was convicted of the s 35 offence as well. He was sentenced to six months for the reckless driving and six months, to run consecutively, for the s 35 offence. His appeal was dismissed. The sentence was 'not a day too long': the eleven miles of reckless driving and the incident when he was stopped were two separate incidents.

A twenty year old with a blood-alcohol level of 125 mg was sentenced to four months' imprisonment for causing death by reckless driving. The Court of Appeal while holding it was clearly a case where immediate imprisonment was justified reduced to sentence to twenty-eight days (*R* v *Brown* [1982] Crim LR 242) and in *R* v *Lemmings* [1983] Crim LR 268 it was held that a partially suspended prison sentence of nine months, three months to be suspended, was proper (salesman plied with drinks at firm's best customer's premises—collides with and kills a cyclist—so drunk that he is not aware of the accident.)

It should be noted that a defendant cannot now be tried by the Crown Court for an offence of driving while unfit under s 5(1) or with excess alcohol under 6(1) even where he is also charged under s 1 with causing death by reckless driving or under s 2 with reckless driving. (In *Midgley* above the provision of the Criminal Law Act altering s 1 had come into force but the provision making s 5 and s 6 offences triable only summarily had not.) Evidence of the amount of drink taken may, however, be admissible (see 5.32).

Reference may also be made to sentencing for drink/driving offenders, 4.118. It should also be noted that drink has been said to be one of the aggravating sentencing features in *R* v *Boswell*, 5.88, below.

### 5.87 Imprisonment

In *R* v *Bibi* [1980] Crim LR 732 the Court of Appeal issued general guidelines on the use of imprisonment in the present day situation of prison overcrowding. In *R* v *Matthews* [1981] Crim LR 789 a sentence of six months for causing death by reckless driving was reduced to three months: 'in the climate of today's sentencing policy' it was unnecessary for a sentence as long as six months' imprisonment to be imposed for this particular offence. In *R* v *Taylor* [1981] Crim LR 423, also a case of causing death by reckless driving, the sentence was reduced from twelve months to six months. In neither case had the defendant been to prison before. These cases must, however, now be read in the light of *R* v *Boswell*, below, a guideline sentencing case.

### 5.88 Causing death by reckless driving and reckless driving

In *R* v *Guilfoyle* [1973] RTR 272 the Court of Appeal suggested guidelines for s 1 offences, and drew a distinction between 'those who have caused a fatal accident through a selfish disregard for the safety of other road users or their passengers, or who have driven recklessly' on the one hand, and those cases in which 'the accident has arisen through momentary inattention or misjudgement' on the other. It was considered that a custodial sentence may be appropriate for cases in the former category and a fine normally sufficient in the latter.

In *R* v *Boswell*, below, it was stated that because the former offence of causing death by dangerous driving was abolished in effect by the Criminal Law Act 1970 together with the consideration of the authoritative statement as to the meaning of the offence of causing death by reckless driving by the House of Lords in *R* v *Lawrence* [1981] RTR 217, it was clear that the present offence of causing death by reckless driving must come within the more serious category adumbrated in *Guilfoyle*.

In recent years the Court of Appeal has adopted the practice of using an appropriate case or cases to set out guidelines for Crown Court sentencers for a particular type or class of offence. Guidelines for Crown Court sentencing for the offence of causing death by reckless driving, together with the offence of reckless driving, are now set out in *R* v *Boswell*, *R* v *Elliott (Jeffrey)*, *R* v *Daley (Frederick)*, *R* v *Rafferty* [1984] RTR 315. After observing that courts had been much less severe than Parliament had intended, the Lord Chief Justice observed that a person convicted of the offence, particularly those who saw the risk, was *prima facie* deserving of severe punishment. Many cases should involve an immediate loss of liberty.

The Court then proceeded to list, amongst others, factors which aggravated the appropriate sentence and those factors which amongst others would go to mitigation of the sentence.

Some aggravating features were:

(1) The consumption of alcohol or drugs. This may range from a couple of drinks to a 'motorised pub-crawl'.

(2) A driver who races; competitive driving against another vehicle; grossly excessive speed; showing off.

(3) The driver who disregards warnings from his passengers.

(4) A prolonged, persistent and deliberate course of very bad driving.

(5) Other related offences committed at the same time, ie driving without ever having held a licence, driving whilst disqualified, driving while a learner while unsupervised and so on.

(6) Previous motoring convictions, particularly offences involving bad driving or excessive consumption of alcohol, ie a man who shows that he is determined to continue to drive badly despite past experience.

(7) Where several people have been killed as a result of the offence.

(8) Bad behaviour at the time of the offence, eg failing to stop, or worse, trying to throw the victim from his car bonnet in order to escape.

(9) Causing death in the course of reckless driving in an attempt to avoid detection or apprehension.

On the other hand, some mitigating factors were: (a) a 'one off' piece of reckless driving—momentary reckless error of judgement, briefly dozing at the wheel or failing to notice a pedestrian at a crossing; (b) a good driving record; (c) good character generally; (d) a plea of guilty would be taken into account in favour of the defendant; (e) the effect of the offence on the defendant, shocked or generally remorseful, particularly where the victim or a close friend or relation and the consequent emotional shock was likely to have been great.

Where no aggravating features were present a non-custodial sentence might be appropriate. Where aggravating features were present a custodial sentence would generally be necessary. In a serious case, a community service order or a wholly or partly suspended sentence would seldom be considered appropriate.

It was further stated that records showed that the general maximum term of imprisonment imposed was twelve to eighteen months. It was not easy to see why that should be so. Drivers, for example, who indulged in racing on the highway with reckless disregard for the safety of others after taking alcohol should understand that in bad cases they would lose their liberty for two years or more.

In *R* v *McLaren* [1984] RTR 126 where the defendant was given a fine of £100 and disqualified for five years for causing death by reckless driving the Court of Appeal said that a fine of £100 is totally inadequate to mark the gravity of the offence. It was stated that a fine of £500 represents the absolute minimum which should be imposed in such a case.

For further discussion of these cases, see the article 'Death and the Traffic Offender' by G.A. Walters, (1985) 2 RTLB 9.

### 5.89 Sentencing by magistrates for reckless and careless driving

The general sentencing criteria for magistrates for offences of reckless driving are the same as for the Crown Court. The main differences are that the maxima are different (six months' compared to two years' imprisonment on indictment and a fine of £2,000 compared to an unlimited fine).

The Magistrates' Association's suggested starting point for reckless driving is £300 'and consider disqualification', and for careless or inconsiderate driving '£60 but *always* consider degree of carelessness.' Careless driving cases vary more in their seriousness than practically any other road traffic offence dealt with by magistrates. As a result of the Criminal Law Act 1977 careless driving convictions will now include cases which formerly would have resulted in convictions for causing death by dangerous driving or at a dangerous speed and dangerous driving or driving at a dangerous speed. This fact gives additional emphasis to the Magistrates' Association's recommendation that when considering the starting point of £60 for careless driving the bench should consider the degree of carelessness. Some benches are known to impose a fine of £60 whatever the degree of carelessness; others are prepared to vary the £60 in accordance with the degree of carelessness, but only downward. It cannot be emphasised too strongly that the recommended figure of £60 is a starting point which should be varied both upwards and downwards in accordance with the particular circumstances of the case and of the offender. It is submitted that the degree of carelessness must be a primary consideration in fixing the amount of the fine. The degree of carelessness between one case and another varies enormously. A conviction under s 3 can include a slight bump between two vehicles caused by a minor error of judgment on the length of the vehicle when manoeuvring out of or into a parking space on a road, to a high speed collision on the open road.

Judicial support for the view that the starting point of £60 should not be applied rigidly but in accordance with the degree of carelessness is to be found in the cases of *R* v *Simpson* and *R* v *Krawec* noted below. It should be noted that the introduction to the Association's Suggestions (and in the body of the Suggestions it is reiterated that it is a misuse of the actual suggested figures not to follow the introduction) emphasises that the list is not a tariff and penalty in each case must be judicially assessed in accordance with the circumstances of the particular case and the particular offender. The various criteria are listed: gravity of offence, record and means of the offender, whether the offence was committed deliberately or inadvertently. The introduction specifically reminds benches that the seriousness of offences varies widely especially in cases of careless driving and that many road traffic offences are more hazardous when speeds are higher.

It is submitted that the consequences of an accident may sometimes have little relevance to the penalty that should be imposed. Sometimes a period of momentary inattention can have tragic results, while a piece of extreme bad or wicked driving can fortunately result in an offender escaping any accident. The actual culpability or degree of carelessness is the main criterion.

Magistrates are often faced with having to decide the proper penalty where careless driving has resulted in a death. It is submitted that it is wrong to attempt to punish an offender convicted of careless driving as if he had been convicted of causing death by reckless driving (see *The Magistrate*, October 1981, p 148, for an example). In *R* v *Simpson* [1981] Crim LR 650 a lorry driver was convicted of careless driving on an indictment for causing death by reckless driving, he was fined £200 and disqualified for twelve months. The Court of Appeal reduced the fine to £100 and the disqualification to three months. The facts were that the lorry driver knew that the lorry's brakes were not in perfect order, but did not know what would happen in an emergency stop. The employers were fined £350 and £200 by the magistrates' court for offences under the Construction and Use Regulations in respect of the lorry. The Court of Appeal had regard to the Magistrates' Association's suggested starting figure of £60, but as it was not a case of momentary inattention increased the fine to £100, at the same time reducing the disqualification from twelve months to three.

In *R* v *Krawec* [1985] RTR 1 the defendant had been acquitted by the jury of causing death by reckless driving but convicted of careless driving. In fining him £350 the trial judge stated that it was a serious case because death had resulted. In reducing the fine to £250, the Court of Appeal held that the unforeseen and unexpected results of carelessness were not in themselves relevant to penalty—the fact that the defendant failed to see the pedestrian until too late and collided with him was relevant, but that the fact that the pedestrian unfortunately died was not—and made reference to the Magistrates' Association's Suggestions and in particular the fact that the list is not a tariff and the seriousness of offences varies widely, especially in cases of careless driving.

See further, as to the Association's Suggestions, 18.1 and Appendix 3.

### 5.90 Disqualification

It was said in relation to offences under s 1 in *R* v *Guilfoyle* above that if the offender's driving record is good he should be disqualified for the minimum period, if indifferent, two to four years, and if bad, for a long time (per James LJ in *R* v *Lobley* [1974] RTR 550, at p 553: 'But let this be said, *R* v *Guilfoyle* was not laying down any rule of law but only guidelines, and in the end each case has to be visited with a period of disqualification which is appropriate to the facts of that particular case'). A period of disqualification should be fixed without regard to the right of a defendant to apply for its removal under s 95 of the Road Traffic Act 1972 (*R* v *Lobley* [1974] RTR 550). In *R* v *Gisbourne* [1977] Crim LR 299 (a case of causing death by dangerous driving described as 'simply inattention at a critical moment') the disqualification for three years of the eighteen-year-old defendant was reduced to twelve months.

Where the offender is young, the principle that young offenders should normally not be disqualified for very long periods applies to s 1 offences. Nevertheless, in an appropriately serious case a lengthy period of disqualification will be upheld (see eg *R* v *Marshall* [1976] RTR 483: an eighteen-year-old, 'showing off', driving at 50 mph in a 30 mph area, unable to avoid hitting an eighty-one-year-old; disqualification for five years upheld. On the other hand a young offender has less experience of driving and it is therefore more appropriate to order the offender to take a driving test at the end of a period of disqualification (*R* v *Guilfoyle*, where a period of disqualification for three years was reduced to one but the order under s 93(7) was upheld). It was further suggested in *R* v *Guilfoyle* that the longer a person is disqualified, the more important it is that he be ordered to undergo a driving test before he again obtains a full licence. In *R* v *Lobley* above an order under s 93(7) was imposed on apppeal by the Court of Appeal when reducing a period of disqualification from four to two years, because the facts of the case raised serious doubts as to his driving ability and qualifications. In *R* v *Rowe* [1975] Crim LR 245 an order to take a test was upheld on a man who would have been sixty-seven when his term of disqualification expired and where there were indications that his powers of concentration were declining. A fine of £250 was upheld, but although he was a man of means an order to pay prosecution costs of £1,500 as well was quashed. In *R* v *Farrugia* [1979] RTR 422 (a case of 'preventative disqualification') the defendant having a bad driving record was disqualified for seven years for a bad case of causing death by reckless driving. The Court of Appeal reduced the period of disqualification to five years: it was said a long sentence of disqualification can be counter-productive particularly for men in their twenties. In *R* v *Hudson* [1979] RTR 401 a period of disqualification was reduced from five years to three because of the defendant's loss of employment. In *R* v *Midgley* [1979] RTR 1 despite not having asked for a reduction, the period of disqualification of seven years was reduced to four.

In *R* v *Boswell*, 5.88, the Court of Appeal emphasised that a distinction should be drawn between cases of driving while disqualified and such like cases where there was no evidence of bad driving and cases such as the cases in *R* v *Boswell* where the essence of the offence was the actual manner of driving. Where a person in the latter category of case showed himself to be a menace on the road he should be disqualified for a substantial length of time, in the very worst cases seven to ten years would not be too long.

It may be appropriate to disqualify for a first offence of careless driving where it is something more than momentary inattention (*R* v *Simpson* [1981] Crim LR 650). In that case the defendant was driving a lorry with bad brakes, which he knew not to be in perfect order, lost control of the lorry, slid across the road colliding with a road sign and killing a motor cyclist coming in the opposite direction. The defendant was acquitted by the jury of causing death by reckless driving but convicted of careless driving. The Court of Appeal reduced the £200 fine to £100 and the twelve months' disqualification to three.

Chapter 6

# Driver Offences

## Signs and Signals

### 6.1 Generally

Offences against traffic signs and police signals are dealt with in ss 22, 22A, 23 and 159 of the 1972 Act. The use of traffic signs is regulated by ss 64–80 of the Road Traffic Regulation Act 1984.

The expression 'traffic sign' is defined in s 64 of the 1984 Act and the colour, size and type of traffic signs are prescribed by the Traffic Signs Regulations and General Directions 1981 (SI 1981 No 859). These have been amended by the Traffic Signs (Amendment) Regulations 1982 and 1983 (SI 1982 No 1879 and SI 1983 No 1088) and the Traffic Signs General (Amendment) Directions 1982 and 1983 (SI 1982 No 1880 and SI 1983 No 1086) and the Traffic Signs (Amendment) Regulations and General Directions 1984 (SI 1984 No 966). The power of the Secretary of State to add to or modify any of the directions (but not the regulations) in their application to any particular case must always be borne in mind.

Section 65 of the 1984 Act authorises the highway authority to place traffic signs on or near any road. In s 65, 'highway authority', by s 80 includes any person, not being a highway authority, responsible for the maintenance of a road and therefore includes persons responsible for private roads which are nevertheless roads within the definition of the 1984 Act (see Chapter 1). Section 66 of the same Act authorises constables, or any person acting under the instructions (general or specific) of a chief officer of police, to place on any highway or on any structure on a highway authorised signs relating to certain special traffic regulations, orders and directions.

By s 67 of the 1984 Act constables, or any person acting under the instructions (general or specific) of a chief officer of police, may place on a highway or on a structure on a highway authorised signs to prevent or mitigate congestion or obstruction of, or danger to or from traffic in consequence of extraordinary circumstances, but such signs by s 67(1) may not be maintained for longer than seven days.

The offences under ss 22 and 159 of the 1972 Act are considered below, and matters relating to particular signs are dealt with thereafter. Proceedings and penalties for the offences will be found at 6.16–19.

## 6.2 Failing to comply with a sign

It is an offence under s 22(1) and (2) of the 1972 Act to fail to comply with the indication given by a sign if it indicates a statutory prohibition, restriction or requirement or if it is expressly provided by or under any provisions of the Act that s 22 applies to that sign or type of sign. Section 22(2) is curiously worded in that it says that a sign shall not be deemed to have been 'lawfully placed' unless it indicates the statutory prohibition, etc, or it is expressly provided that s 22 applies to the sign; it does not expressly say that it is not an offence to disobey any other sign. The term 'statutory prohibition, restriction or requirement' means, it is submitted, one having effect pursuant to a public or local Act of Parliament and does not extend to signs, such as 'No Waiting', having effect under an order or regulation (see below): cf the meaning of 'enactment' in s 168 (see 7.17).

Regulation 7 of the Traffic Signs Regulations and General Directions provides that s 22 applies to the signs listed in that regulation, so that it is an offence under s 22 to fail to comply with such a sign. They are 'Stop' (at junctions of major road), 'Give Way' (at junction of major road or at certain open railway level crossings), 'Stop' (at road works), the straight arrow to indicate that traffic is to proceed in a particular direction, the diagonal arrow for 'keep left' or 'right', red traffic lights (including certain motorway flashing red signals and the flashing red lights at railway automatic level crossings), the double white lines (either both unbroken or continuous/broken line), the round red sign with the white band meaning 'No Entry' and the 'Drivers of Large or Slow Vehicles Must Phone' sign at automatic level crossings.

Temporary signs erected by the police in the exercise of the powers conferred on them by s 67 of the 1984 Act are expressly included in the category of signs to which s 22 applies by virtue of s 67(2). The signs most often used by the police when exercising their powers of placing temporary signs under s 67 in order to prevent obstruction at public events are 'no waiting' cones. The cones, as such, do not appear to be authorised by the 1981 Regulations; the opinion is held, however, that provided the cone bears the sign shown in diagram 636 and its dimensions are within the permissible limits, a motorist may be convicted under s 22 of failing to conform with the sign, as the structure upon which the sign is allowed to be displayed is not prescribed.

As to signs at census points, see 6.10.

Is it an offence under s 22 to fail to comply with any other sign prescribed by the regulations such as 'One Way Traffic', 'No Waiting', or 'No Right Turn'? It is submitted that disobedience to any such sign should be prosecuted under s 5(1), s 8(1) or s 53(5) or (6) of the 1984 Act in respect of the particular traffic regulation order whereby waiting in, entry to the street, etc, is forbidden and not under s 22. If any sign indicates a 'statutory prohibition, restriction or requirement' (see s 22(2)(*a*)), then reg 7 which sets out certain signs to which s 22 does apply, is completely unnecessary. The signs in reg 7 have effect under the Traffic Signs Regulations and General Directions 1981 just as other signs have effect under the 1981 Regulations and (usually) some other order as well. Indeed, if a person stopped to unload goods in a 'No Waiting' area where unloading was allowed, to charge him with contravention of the 'No Waiting' sign might be to deprive him of the benefit of the unloading exemption unless it can be said that the latter part of s 22(2) preserves his rights.

Although contravention of a sign which is not referred to in reg 7 can seemingly not be dealt with under s 22, such a contravention may amount to evidence of reckless, careless or inconsiderate driving, eg a driver who crosses from a minor into a major road disobeying double broken transverse lines at the junction. It has been suggested that such contraventions may be offences contrary to s 118 of the Road Traffic Regulation Act 1984 or s 178 of the 1972 Act. These are sections which provide generally, subject to certain exceptions, for a maximum fine of level 3 for contraventions of regulations made under the respective Acts where no offence is provided elsewhere. The 1981 Regulations are made under s 64 of the 1984 Act and it is submitted that any prosecution would be under this Act if at all. However, many of the signs are advisory or informatory and it is doubtful for similar reasons whether a contravention amounts to an offence under s 87 any more than under s 22 unless it is expressly specified to be one by virtue of reg 7 or otherwise. Penal provisions are construed strictly. If it were to be an offence merely to contravene the sign, the various exemptions might be lost.

*Cyclists, other vehicles and equestrians*

Section 22 applies to cyclists, trams, trolley vehicles, horse-drawn vehicles and hand carts as well as to motor vehicles, but not to equestrians. Section 22 applies to Crown vehicles. There is an experimental advanced stop line for cyclists in Oxford in the cycle lane at the junction of Broad Street (commonly called 'the Broad') and Parks Road with the result that Oxford undergraduates have a flying start.

As to persons pushing cycles, see 114 JP Jo 160. A person who pushed a lorry to try to make it start was held to be guilty of taking and driving it away (*Shimmell* v *Fisher* [1951] 2 All ER 672) and so it can be argued that persons pushing bicycles and hand carts are guilty of an offence if they disobey a traffic sign. On the other hand, there is the argument that 'Stop' signs and traffic lights do not apply to persons pushing pedal cycles and hand carts because, presumably, such signs are not meant to affect pedestrians, who can walk into main roads and against traffic signs at their pleasure. If a pedestrian can do that, cannot a pedestrian pushing a pram, or a child with a scooter, do the same? And if a pram-pusher can, why should not a cycle-pusher? A counter-argument is that the mischief aimed at by s 22 is to prevent any type of vehicle being in a major road in disobedience to the sign or going against the red light and that it is immaterial whether such a vehicle arrives there by mechanical or muscular power, the offence being 'driving or propelling' a vehicle. Compare *McKerrell* v *Robertson* at 6.43—woman and go-cart which she was pushing held to be one entity under the Pedestrian Crossings Regulations, and *Crank* v *Brooks* [1980] RTR 441. In the latter case, a cyclist pushing a cycle using both feet on the ground was held to be a foot passenger for the purpose of the 'Zebra' Pedestrian Crossings Regulations; *aliter* if the person had one foot on the pedal and was using the cycle as a scooter.

*Conformity of signs*

A traffic sign placed on or near a road shall be deemed to be of the prescribed size, colour and type or of another character authorised by the Secretary of State for Transport and to have been lawfully so placed, unless the contrary is proved (1972 Act, s 22(3)). See 6.13 as to defective signs. See also *Woodriffe* v *Plowman* at 6.4.

Traffic lights are presumed to be working properly (see *Wells* v *Woodward* at 6.4).

An order under s 1 of the Road Traffic Regulation Act 1984 may provide that a part of the road, or the times at which a part of the road is controlled, may be identified by the placing of a traffic sign. For the purposes of the order any such traffic sign is deemed to be lawfully placed unless the contrary is proved (s 4(1)).

Illumination of signs is dealt with below in respect of particular signs and by regs 15–19 of the Traffic Signs Regulations and General Directions 1981.

*Defences*

It is no defence that the defendant did not see the sign; mens rea is not essential (*Rees* v *Taylor* (1939), unreported, cited in Stone's *Justices' Manual* in the notes to s 22(1)(*b*); *Hill* v *Baxter* [1958] 1 All ER 193).

In *R* v *Spurge* [1961] 2 All ER 688 it was held that it is a defence to a charge of what was then dangerous driving if it occurred owing to a defect in the vehicle of which the driver did not know and which he could not previously have discovered by the exercise of reasonable prudence, and in *Burns* v *Bidder* [1966] 3 All ER 29 it was said that being pushed by another vehicle on to a crossing or a latent defect might afford a defence to a charge of not according precedence on a pedestrian crossing. The same principles presumably apply as defences to charges of disobeying police signals and traffic signs.

## 6.3 Neglecting or refusing to comply with directions given by police or traffic wardens

By the Police and Criminal Evidence Act 1984, Part I, when in force, the police will have powers to carry out searches including vehicle searches and road checks, but these will not apply to minor road traffic offences. No offence is created but there may be an obstruction of the constable in the execution of his duty contrary to s 51(3) of the Police Act 1964.

By s 22 of the 1972 Act it is an offence if any person driving or propelling a vehicle of any kind (including a pedal cycle) neglects or refuses to stop the vehicle or make it proceed in or keep to a particular line of traffic when directed so to do by a constable or traffic warden engaged in regulating traffic on a road; the vehicle itself need not be on a road. By s 159 of the 1972 Act, a person driving a motor vehicle and a person riding on a road a cycle (ie a bicycle, tricycle or any other form of cycle) shall stop on being so required by a constable in uniform.

It is an offence under s 23 of the 1972 Act for a pedestrian to fail to comply with a direction to stop given by a constable in uniform in the execution of his duty. Section 165 gives to constables (and traffic wardens) the right to require names and addresses from offenders against s 23.

*'Constable' and 'traffic warden'*

The Police Act 1964, s 19, allows a constable to act as such anywhere in England and a special constable to act as a constable in his own and adjoining areas. Under ss 23 and 159 of the 1972 Act, offences arise only if the constable is in uniform; under s 22 he need not be in uniform but, if he is not, it must be proved that the defendant knew him to be a constable. On the other hand, it can be argued that the liability under s 22 is absolute, so that it is unnecessary to prove that the defendant knew a person in plain clothes to be a constable and his ignorance is no defence: cf *Kenlin* v *Gardiner* [1966] 3 All ER 931, at p 934, where it was said that, on a charge of assaulting a police officer, knowledge that he was one is not necessary.

Traffic wardens appointed under the Road Traffic Regulation Act 1984 s 95 are not constables but by virtue of the Functions of Traffic Wardens Order 1970 (SI 1970 No 1958) and s 96 of the 1984 Act references to a constable in ss 22 and 23 include traffic wardens. If a motorist ignores a traffic warden's direction under s 22, he can thus be prosecuted and convicted exactly as if a constable had been on duty. Moreover the traffic warden is empowered (also by virtue of the Functions of Traffic Wardens Order and s 96) to demand the offending motorist's name and address under s 162(1). The traffic warden (unlike a constable) cannot, however, demand to see the offending motorist's driving documents, as reg 3(3) only applies s 162(1) so far as it relates to 'the furnishing of names and addresses'. A traffic warden can demand the production of a driving licence and require in the prescribed circumstances a statement of the date of birth (see reg 3(4)) in a different context (certain functions regarding the custody of vehicles, eg at a car pound). The functions prescribed for Scottish traffic wardens are set out in a like Scotland order (SI 1971 No 374).

A motorist failing to comply with a traffic warden's directions and contravening s 22 is liable to have his licence endorsed (see 6.18).

*'Engaged in the regulation of traffic'*

It will be noted that offences under s 22 arise only where the constable (or traffic warden) is engaged in regulating traffic, and there is no such limitation under s 159. The *Concise Oxford Dictionary* gives one definition of 'traffic' as 'coming and going of persons or goods by road' etc. This implies that for s 22 the *purpose* must be more than stopping a single vehicle even though only one vehicle may be stopped. Section 22 refers to 'regulation' and to various forms of traffic while s 159 refers only to stopping when required.

*'In the execution of his duty'*

In both ss 22 and 159, before an offence can be said to have been committed, the constable must have been acting in execution of his duty. Section 22(1)(*a*) explicitly so states and it was held in *R* v *Waterfield* [1963] 3 All ER 659 that s 159 does not confer statutory power on a police constable improperly to detain a vehicle where a constable would not have power under the common law to do so. *Waterfield* was distinguished in *Beard* v *Wood* below, a case also on s 159, but was applied to s 22 in *Hoffman* v *Thomas* [1974] RTR 182 where it was held that the power of a constable to regulate traffic in execution of his duty stems from the constable's duty and right at common law to act in protection of life and property and that a constable has no right to regulate traffic for personal motives or other extraneous reason; his right and duty solely arise because of the danger to life and limb which unregulated traffic can present. The conviction under s 22 of a motorist who refused to proceed to a census point in accordance with the direction of a constable who was engaged in selecting vehicles at random on a motorway and directing the selected vehicles to a census point was accordingly set aside. Conducting a traffic census is not part of a constable's duty to regulate traffic in execution of his right to protect life and property (ibid) (but see now s 22A and 'Census points', 6.10. *Hoffman* v *Thomas* was followed in *Johnson* v *Phillips* [1976] RTR 170, where a conviction for obstructing a policeman in the execution of his duty was upheld. The defendant refused to obey a constable who requested him to reverse his car the wrong way down a one-way street in order to avoid his car obstructing the removal of injured persons and the possible arrival of other ambulances. Each case depends on its own facts: a constable has no general discretion to disobey traffic regulations or to direct other persons to disobey them (ibid). However, in accordance with the special facts of the case the constable was entitled and indeed under a duty to give such instructions if it was reasonably necessary for the protection of life and property. Refusal to obey them in these circumstances was obstructing the constable in the execution of his duty.

*Waterfield* and *Hoffman* v *Thomas* were distinguished as invalid exercises of the power given by ss 159 and 122 in *Beard* v *Wood* [1980] RTR 454. In that case it was stated that the police constable derives his duty as well as his power to stop vehicles from the terms of s 159 itself. It was suggested that a different conclusion might have been reached if the constable had not been acting bona fide. In *Steel* v *Goacher* [1983] RTR 98, Griffiths LJ at p 103 doubted dicta of Ashworth J in *Waterfield* (adopted by Wien J in *Beard* v *Wood*) that what is now s 159 confers a power to stop drivers of motor vehicles. Griffiths LJ said that nothing in s 159 gives any power to a constable to stop a motorist. Once a motorist has stopped he can, thereafter, challenge the constable's right to stop him. Griffiths LJ pointed out however that under *Winter* v *Barlow* [1980] RTR 209 and *Such* v *Ball* [1982] RTR 140 the police could still proceed to administer a breath test despite a mistaken view as to the power to stop. See further 4.43.

The powers of the constable under s 159 were reviewed in the important case of *Lodwick* v *Sanders* [1985] 1 All ER 577. It was again stated that the authorities were inconsistent with the proposition that s 159 conferred upon a constable a power physically to detain a motor vehicle. It was also stated that the driver was under a duty to stop when required and having stopped was under a similar duty to remain at a standstill while the officer exercised whatever power he sought to exercise.

As to constables at census points, see 6.10.

*'Stop'*

See above and 7.8 for further cases on the meaning of 'stop'. It is suggested that 'stop' in these sections means both 'bring to a halt' and 'remain at rest'. The requirement to stop may be a verbal one as well as by hand signal.

Notwithstanding *R* v *Oliver* at 6.71 'Exemptions for loading etc' and the reference in s 28(2) of the Road Traffic Regulation Act 1984 to starting up again after being required to stop by a school crossing patrol, it is submitted that a driver who has stopped at a constable's signal may not start again until he has been signalled or otherwise permitted to proceed. If the constable is still holding up his hand, the driver offends in the second after he has started again by not stopping; in other cases, the constable will often in fact have made a second signal to him.

The Divisional Court has stated that the offence under s 22 is committed when a driver who has stopped then proceeds in defiance of a command to remain stationary. This does not mean that the driver has to remain stationary until ordered to proceed. Each case has to be decided on its merits. In this case there was no evidence that the driver was required to remain stationary by a traffic warden and the driver was acquitted although she had proceeded after stopping (*Kentesber* v *Waumsley* [1980] RTR 462).

*Defences*

Is it a defence that the defendant in any of the above cases never saw the constable's signal? In *R* v *Ellis* [1947] 1 WWR 717, a Canadian case, it was held that a driver could not be guilty of failing to stop at a junction when 'signalled' to do so by a policeman unless the signal was consciously received by him, although his failure to see it was due to the fact that he was not keeping a proper look-out in the direction in which he was going. In *R* v *Barber* [1963] 3 S African LR 700, a defendant who had not in fact seen the constable's signal was held to have been properly acquitted, after reference to English cases including *Harding* v *Price*, below. On the other hand, it may be thought that a signal can be made without necessarily being seen and it is no defence here that a driver failed to see a traffic sign (*Rees* v *Taylor* at 6.2). It can be argued, however, that traffic signs are placed in positions where they can easily be seen and at places, such as road junctions, where a driver would expect to find them, and it is a different matter where a driver without negligence and in conditions of bad visibility fails to see a policeman's signal from a crowded footpath or in an ill-lit street. There was once no offence in like circumstances under the Pedestrian Crossings Regulations (*Leicester* v *Pearson* [1952] 2 All ER 71: see 6.43) and the law does not call on persons to perform a duty on an event happening unless they know that the event has happened (*Harding* v *Price* [1948] 1 All ER 283 and cases there cited: see 7.7. Magistrates in a case reported at 119 JP Jo 659 dismissed a charge of failing to stop in response to a lamp signal given by a policeman at night where the motorist had not understood the meaning of the signal. In *Keane* v *McSkimming* (1883) SCCR 220 the police officer's signal to stop was not recognised by the driver. The charge was dismissed on a submission of no case to answer, implying that the onus is on the prosecution. The decision was upheld on appeal by the High Court. The view is advanced at [1956] Jo Crim L 192 that a defendant may be excused if he does not see a constable's signal through no fault of his own, but the onus of proving his lack of negligence lies on him. Dicta in *Harding* v *Price* also support this view.

See 'Absolute liability of a driver', 6.43 as to defects in the vehicle making compliance with a signal impossible.

*Horse riders*

The 1972 Act contains no provision requiring equestrians, mahouts and other riders of animals to obey police signals. If an accident occurs or might occur because of a horseman's disregard of a constable's signal, it might be that this would be obstructing the police in that an accident could be a breach of the peace (cf *Duncan* v *Jones* (1936) 99 JP 399). Also, he might be charged, if the facts warrant, with interrupting by negligence or by misbehaviour the free passage of another person or of a vehicle (Highway Act 1835, s 78; see *Baldwin* v *Pearson* at 6.77.

## 6.4 Traffic lights

Regulations 31–36 of the Traffic Signs Regulations and General Directions 1981 deal with light signals for traffic and pedestrians. Regulation 34(3) requires drivers passing signals to proceed with due regard for the safety of other road users and subject to the directions of any uniformed constable or other duly authorised person engaged in the regulation of traffic. Traffic wardens may regulate traffic and so be duly authorised persons (see 6.3).

In *Eva* v *Reeves* [1938] 2 All ER 115 (a civil case) it was held that a driver who has the green light in his favour owes no duty to traffic entering a crossing in disobedience to the lights save that, if he actually sees such traffic, he must take all reasonable steps to avoid a collision. (See, however, the terms of reg 34(3).)

The 1981 Regulations exempt a vehicle from compliance with traffic lights if the vehicle is being used for 'fire brigade, ambulance or police purposes' and the observance of the red light is 'likely to hinder the use of that vehicle for the purpose for which it is being used on that occasion'. Where for such a purpose a red light is disregarded the driver is required, in effect, to treat the red signal as a 'Give Way' sign, ie he must not enter the road in such a manner or at such a time as to be likely to cause danger to any other driver on the road or so as to necessitate a change of course or speed by that driver in order to avoid an accident. The ambulance, police or fire engine driver, etc, is also required not to endanger 'traffic which is not vehicular' (presumably this includes pedestrians, horses, etc). It may be observed that the regulation does not expressly require the vehicle to be an ambulance, fire engine or police vehicle. It would seem that any vehicle comes within the exemption conferred by the regulation if the vehicle is used for fire brigade, ambulance or police purposes and observance of the traffic lights would hinder the purpose for which the vehicle was used on 'that' occasion. The use of the demonstrative article 'that' seems to imply that the particular occasion must be looked at in every case.

By reg 34(1)(*c*) of the 1981 Regulations the amber-with-red signal shall not alter the prohibition conveyed by the red signal. By reg 34(1)(*e*) the amber alone signal shall convey the prohibition that traffic shall not proceed beyond the stop line or, if that line is not for the time being visible or there is no stop line, beyond the post or other structure on or in which the primary signals are mounted, except in the case of any vehicle which, when the signal first appears, is so close to the line, post or structure that it cannot safely be stopped before passing it. The reference to stop line, post or structure is the same as in reg 34(1)(*a*) (red light) and is discussed below. Regulation 7 does not provide that disobedience to the amber-alone signal is an offence against s 22. A metropolitan magistrate has dismissed a case under s 22 of crossing on amber alone ([1959] Jo Crim L 87). It is also doubtful whether there is an offence contrary to s 118 of the Road Traffic Regulation Act 1984. For the arguments see 'Failing to comply with a sign', 6.2. The driver might still be liable for careless driving. The position with regard to the amber alone signal may be compared with the steady amber light and flashing amber light provisions in the 'Pelican' Pedestrian Crossings Regulations etc 1969 (see 6.46).

Regulation 34(1)(*a*) of Part I of the 1981 Regulations describes the significance of the red light as follows:

> . . . the red signal shall convey the prohibition that vehicular traffic shall not proceed beyond the stop line on the carriageway provided in conjunction with the signals or, if that line is not for the time being visible or there is no stop line, beyond the post or other structure on or in which the primary signals are mounted.

The prohibition on passing over the stop line applies to any part of the vehicle when the red light is showing; if the front of a vehicle has already crossed that line when the light goes red, it is an offence under s 22 for it to proceed further (*Ryan* v *Smith* [1967] 1 All ER 611).

The 1981 Regulations substituted the words 'post or other structure on or in which the primary signals are mounted' for the word 'signals' (formerly in the 1975 Regulations) for the stopping point in those cases where there is no stop line or the stop line is invisible. Some structures may be quite large and the new definition may cause difficulties. The alteration makes it clear that it is not an offence for a vehicle to move if it has wholly passed the stopping point even though it has not yet passed the secondary light. Reference should be made to the definitions of 'primary' and 'secondary' signals in the regulations (see reg 34(6)).

Where lights have apparently stuck at red, a district justice has held that a driver who has waited a reasonable time for them to change in his favour may then proceed with caution against them ([1959] Jo Crim L 222). The case was heard in the Dublin District Court. In effect the justice held that a reasonable belief that the lights had failed would be a defence. This decision was criticised in [1959] Jo Crim L 222 at p 224. A prosecution against a careful driver in such circumstances would rightly be condemned but he might have no defence in particular in a civil case. It is submitted that if the lights have, in fact, failed a motorist may ignore the lights because the lights, having failed, no longer comply with the regulations. The onus is, however, on the defendant to show that the lights are out of phase.

There may be problems where some of the traffic signals are working and some are not. The situation is covered to some extent by reg 34(6)(*b*) which states that:

> any reference to light signals, to the signals or to a signal of a particular colour, is, where secondary signals have been erected as well as primary signals, a reference to the light signals, signals or particular signal displayed by both the primary signals and the secondary signals or by either the primary signals operating without the secondary signals, or by the secondary signals operating without the primary signals.

This implies that an offence may be committed where the secondary lights are working but the primary lights are not and vice versa. It is relevant only where secondary lights have been erected as well as primary lights. It leaves open the position where primary or secondary lights alone respectively are relied on and one of the sets is not working. The wording of reg 34(6)(*b*) seems to imply that either *both* the primary signals or *both* the secondary signals must be working where there is more than one. 'Primary' and 'secondary signals' are defined in reg 34(6)(*c*) and (*d*). The definitions make clear that both nearside and offside signals are included as appropriate but does not help further. It may still be the case therefore that no offence is committed where reliance is on the primary lights alone or the secondary lights alone and one of them is not working. It is always possible for the other working set to be obscured or hidden from view. The offence arises from the prohibition conveyed by the red light or possibly the amber light. Subject to the comments above about the interrelationship of the primary and secondary signals, if the relevant red light (or possibly amber light) is not working it is submitted that there can be no prohibition and no offence.

Portable lights are authorised by reg 33(1) in the following cases:

(*a*) where the width of the carriageway is restricted so that it will carry only one line of traffic provided that the length of road for which the lights are used is not joined anywhere along its length by any road for vehicular traffic; (As to whether a cycle track is a road, see 1.66.)

(*b*) at railway level crossings when work is being carried out; and

(*c*) during the progress of temporary schemes of traffic control, where the signals are under the control and regular supervision of the police and have been erected at a site approved in writing by the highway authority.

A temporary light signal for road works is, it seems, presumed to have been lawfully placed and it is not necessary to prove that it was lawfully maintained; s 67 of the Road Traffic Regulation Act 1984, relating to emergency signs, does not apply (*Woodriffe* v *Plowman* (1962) 60 LGR 183). Portable signals have to comply with the specifications applicable to permanent lights contained in reg 31(*a*), (*b*), (*c*), (*e*), (*f*) and (*g*). The main effect is that portable lights have to include an amber light, show the lights in the same sequence as permanent lights and be of the same dimensions save that the lenses may be closer together.

If the lights are showing green for east-west traffic, magistrates are entitled to infer, unless the contrary be shown, that they are red for north-south traffic (*Wells* v *Woodward* (1956) 54 LGR 142; *Pacitti* v *Copeland* [1963] SLT (Notes) 52). Intermittent red signals under reg 31(4) (which are for use at automatic level crossings) convey the prohibition that, subject to the vehicle not being so close when the signal first appears that it cannot safely be stopped before passing the line or signal, a vehicle shall not proceed beyond the stop line or if there is no stop line, or if it is not visible, the signals (reg 34(5)) (see also 6.9).

*Motorway traffic lights*

The four intermittent red signals under reg 31(3) displayed at the side of a motorway convey the prohibition that vehicular traffic shall not proceed beyond those lights. When placed over the motorway they operate similarly on the appropriate traffic lane (reg 34(4)). Vehicles being used for 'fire brigade, ambulance or police purposes' (for the meaning of this see above) are not within reg 34(4) and these intermittent red lights are to have no significance to them (ibid) (at least in law). As already indicated, it is an offence under s 22 to contravene these lights.

It is not an offence under s 22 to ignore a motorway 'red cross' closing a lane nor a motorway or hazard warning, because regs 36 and 38 are not included in reg 7. Proceedings may possibly arise for driving recklessly, carelessly or without consideration.

## 6.5 'Stop' signs at major roads

The octagonal 'Stop' sign is prescribed by diagram 601.1 in the 1981 Regulations and it is an offence under reg 7 to disobey it. The sign is required to be 750, 900 or 1200 mm in width (for tolerances see reg 8). By direction 18 the temporary 'Stop' signs may only be used where one way working is necessary owing to a temporary closure of one width of the carriageway. By direction 10 a 'Stop' sign may be used on a road only in conjunction with the road marking of solid transverse lines to indicate the position beyond which vehicles must not proceed (diagram 1002) and with the painted letters 'Stop' on the carriageway (diagram 1022), save where road works temporarily require their removal or the 'Stop' sign itself was erected temporarily because of road works. Other directions relating to 'Stop' signs are directions 5, 11 and 25. The post should be coloured grey, unless it is concrete or a temporary wooden post (direction 35). The back of the sign shall be grey (direction 36), but as the back of the sign is not the side designed to give the indication and guidance for which it was erected, presumably the High Court would hold that the sign would not be invalidated if it were painted a different colour (see *Sharples* v *Blackmore* [1973] RTR 249, where it was held that a speed limit sign was not invalidated by its back not being painted grey).

The requirement of this 'Stop' sign is that every vehicle shall stop before crossing the transverse line or, if that line is not clearly visible, before entering the major road and shall not proceed past that line or, if it is not clearly visible, enter the major road so as to be likely to cause danger to the driver of any other vehicle on the major road or to cause that driver to change the speed or course of his vehicle so as to avoid an accident (reg 11(1) item 1).

Presumably an offence is committed if any part of the vehicle stops on or over the line or enters the major road in breach of the regulation (cf *Ryan* v

*Smith* [1967] 1 All ER 611 at 6.4). There must be a likelihood (and not a mere possibility) of danger to the driver and not merely to the vehicle. Many cases are based on the second part (changing speed or course etc). The accident avoided need not necessarily be with the vehicle entering from the minor road.

The 'Stop' sign presumably requires that a vehicle subject to it be brought to a standstill; it was so held in relation to the former 'Halt' sign (*Tolhurst* v *Webster* [1936] 3 All ER 1020), where it was also said that the vehicle should stop (see reg 11(1)) at the major road or line provided and not the sign itself. Justices were directed to convict where a driver had stopped at the sign and not at the major road (*Brooks* v *Jefferies* [1936] 3 All ER 232).

For a case where the word 'Stop' painted on the carriageway was partially invisible, see *Skeen* v *Smith* at 6.13.

## 6.6 'Give Way' signs

The 'Give Way' sign is No 602 in the 1981 Regulations and it is an offence under reg 7 to disobey it. It is an inverted white triangle and its measurements are 600, 750, 900, 1200 or 1500 mm (for tolerances see reg 8); its borders are red and the lettering black and, by reg 14, the size of the letters is proportionate. By direction 10 the 'Give Way' sign may be used only in conjunction with the road marking of broken transverse lines (diagram 1003) and the triangle painted on the road (diagram 1023), save where road works temporarily require the removal of the lines and triangle. By reg 11(1) item 2 the requirement conveyed by the 'Give Way' sign is that no vehicle shall cross the transverse line nearest to the major road or, if that line is not clearly visible, enter that major road so as to be likely to cause danger to the driver of any other vehicle or to cause that driver to change the speed or course of his vehicle so as to avoid an accident.

As to this wording see the comments under ' "Stop" signs at major roads', 6.5. It may be noted that the regulation requires the emerging vehicle not to affect in the manner specified not only a vehicle on the near side of the main road but also a vehicle on the far side of it.

The wording under reg 11(1) item 3 is similar where a 'Give Way' sign is used at an open level crossing.

## 6.7 'One Way', 'No Right Turn', 'Access Only' etc orders

It is submitted that disobedience to signs having effect under traffic regulations or designation orders should be prosecuted under s 5(1), s 8(1), s 53(5) or (6) of the 1984 Act and not under s 22 (see 6.2).

Where defendants are charged under s 5, s 8, or s 53 with using a vehicle, or causing or permitting a vehicle to be used (for 'using, causing or permitting', see Chapter 1, 1.76–80) or for any other offence in contravention of a traffic regulation order, the defence may properly insist on production of the relevant order. If the order has not been published in accordance with regulations made under what is now Part III, Sched 9 of the 1984 Act no offence will have been committed (*James* v *Cavey* [1967] 1 All ER 1048). If the prosecution, even after notice from the defence, omits to prove proper publication, the court should normally grant the prosecution an adjournment to do so, it is submitted, as such evidence is of a formal nature (see *Royal* v *Prescott-Clarke* [1966] 2 All ER 366 where the High Court similarly interpreted comparable regulations made under s 72(5) of the 1967 Act in respect of motorways).

In *Wright* v *Howard* [1973] RTR 12 the High Court considered the effect of a 'no right turn' order. The relevant order prohibited motorists emerging from Turl Street, Oxford, to 'make a right hand turn into' High Street (commonly called 'the High'). The right hand kerb of Turl Street was in line with the left hand kerb of Alfred Street. The defendant therefore had to veer slightly to the right across High Street to enter Alfred Street. The Divisional Court held that no offence was committed; giving importance to the word 'into' it was held that making a right turn 'into' meant proceeding right 'into' High Street, not virtually going straight across High Street and veering slightly right to enter Alfred Street.

Whether a person turns right (or left) is a question of fact. Justices were entitled to find as a fact that a motorist did not turn right who drove a motor car along a lane, passed 'No Right Turn' signs before and at its junction with a bypass, and then turned *left* into the bypass and drove along it for some 60 yards before executing a 'U' turn and returning as if he had turned *right* (*Gouldie* v *Pringle* [1981] RTR 525).

One sign in common use is the sign prohibiting entry for motor vehicles save for access. Reference should in all cases be made to the relevant order as under many orders the access must be to adjacent premises. Under such an order a magistrates' court has convicted a person who entered to park in the road, and who did not visit any adjoining premises.

## 6.8 'Keep Left' signs and arrows

It is an offence under s 22 by virtue of reg 7 of the 1981 Regulations to disobey the white arrow on a blue circle, with white border (diagram 606—proceed in direction indicated by arrow) and the diagonal white arrow on a blue circle, with white border (diagram 610—keep left or right). The dimensions are 270, 300, 600, 750, 900, 1200 or 1500 mm (as to variations see reg 8(1)). Sign 606 may be used only on the central island of roundabouts, with the dual-carriageway sign (diagram 608) or to indicate the effect of an order, regulation, byelaw or notice. The illumination of signs 606 and 610 is prescribed by reg 15(2). By reg 18(2) both signs must otherwise be illuminated by reflecting material.

It is seemingly not an offence contrary to s 22 to contravene a requirement of diagram 609 (vehicular traffic must turn left (or right)) because reg 7 does not list this sign as one to which s 22 applies even though diagram 609 is somewhat similar to diagrams 606 and 610. See under 'Failing to comply with a sign', 6.2.

A roundabout bore a 'Keep Left' sign but a motorist approaching made a 'U' turn in the road sixty-two feet short of it. It was held that in those circumstances he had not committed an offence of disobeying the sign (*Brazier* v *Alabaster* [1962] Crim LR 173). *Semble*, if he had been very close to the sign, he would have had to obey it and go round the roundabout in order to turn back.

## 6.9 Automatic level crossings

The sign requiring drivers of abnormally large or slow vehicles (abnormal transport units) to telephone the railway signalman to obtain permission to cross at automatic railway level crossings is diagram 649.2 and is governed by reg 11(1) item 4 of the regulations. Note that the person who must telephone is the actual driver of the vehicle; if there is more than one driver, the driver of the foremost vehicle forming part of the vehicle must telephone. The railway signalman can impose terms on the driver before allowing the vehicle to cross and if the terms are not complied with the regulation is contravened (reg 11(1) item 4(*c*)). Note also the proviso at the end of the regulation which requires a driver who does not receive an answer to try for not less than two minutes to telephone the signalman unless the line is dead and only to cross the crossing during the times shown near the telephone during which trains do not normally travel. If no such times are exhibited, the driver has no alternative but to wait until the signalman answers the telephone and gives him permission to cross.

'Abnormal transport units' are defined as motor vehicles or vehicle combinations which, inclusive of any load, exceed 55 feet in length or 9 feet 6 inches in width or with a maximum gross weight exceeding 38 tonnes, or which are incapable of proceeding or unlikely to proceed over such crossings faster than 5 mph.

The approaches to many railway level crossings (whether or not they are automatic) are marked by double white lines. These double white lines are not part of the signs of an automatic level crossing. Regulation 23 governs all double white lines whether at railway level crossings or elsewhere, and prosecutions for failing to conform to double white lines at level crossings will be by virtue of that regulation and not reg 11(2). Similarly a driver who disobeys the red lights at the automatic level crossing will contravene reg 34(5) and not reg 11(2): the offence is contrary to s 22. The red lights consist of two horizontal red lights with an amber light below the centre point between the two red lights. The sequence of lights (amber followed by red), the flashing of the red lights (one must be on while the other is off), the rate of flashing and dimensions are set out in reg 31(4).

## 6.10 Census points

Section 22A of the 1972 Act was passed as a result of the decision in *Hoffman* v *Thomas* [1974] RTR 182 (see 6.3) where it was held that a constable was not acting in execution of his duty of regulating traffic in selecting vehicles at random from a motorway to go to a census point. A motorist who refused to comply with the constable's signal directing him to stop and proceed to the census point was not guilty of an offence under s 22. It was also held that the sign 'Stop at Census Point' was informatory only in its effect, and non-compliance with it could also not give rise to an offence contrary to s 22.

Section 22A reverses the decision of *Hoffman* v *Thomas*. The census signs (830, 830.1, 831: 'Stop at Census Point', 'Census Stop If Required', and 'Slow—Census Point') now appear to be mandatory by virtue of s 22A (1)(*b*). It is also made an offence by s 22A(1)(*a*) to fail to comply with traffic directions given by a constable for the purpose of a traffic census. Subsection (2) gives a wide definition of a 'traffic direction' for this purpose and subs (3) amends s 22(1)(*a*) for this purpose so that a motorist commits an offence not only if he neglects or refuses to stop or make the vehicle proceed in, or keep to, a particular line of traffic as directed but also if he fails 'to proceed to a particular point'. Parliament was anxious that motorists should not be compelled to give census information and that any information should only be given voluntarily. Not only is it not an offence to refuse to supply information for the purposes of a survey (see definition of 'traffic direction' in subs (3)), but also the power to give a traffic direction must, in accordance with subs (4), be exercised so as not to cause unreasonable delay to a person who indicates he is unwilling to participate in the census. Nevertheless it would seem that a motorist who is unwilling to participate in the census must comply with traffic directions unless and until he indicates he is unwilling to furnish information. On the other hand it would seem that a constable will not be acting in execution of his duty and a conviction under s 22 will be set aside if the power to give a traffic direction is exercised in contravention of subs (4) of s 22A. Although a traffic direction for the purpose of a traffic census is treated by virtue of s 22A(1)(*a*) as a direction by a police constable in the execution of his duty, a constable may not be said to be acting in execution of his duty if he acts in contravention of the wishes of Parliament as enacted in subs (4).

Contravention of a traffic direction for the purpose of a traffic census or of the sign is by virtue of s 22A an offence contrary to s 22 and is punishable accordingly.

The census signs (diagrams 830, 830.1, 831 and 832) may be used only for a traffic census approved by the highway authority and the chief constable and approved by or on behalf of the Secretary of State for Transport (direction 20).

## 6.11 Other signs

A portable sign of an authorised nature requiring a vehicle to stop must be obeyed although the person using it is not a policeman in uniform (*Langley Cartage Co* v *Jenks* [1937] 2 All ER 525). Such signs are now only the round red 'Stop' signs used at road works (diagram 603 in the 1981 regulations). Sign 603 may be used only where one way driving is necessary owing to temporary closure of a width of the carriageway of the road.

## 6.12 White lines and double white lines

By the Road Traffic Regulation Act 1984, s 64, lines or marks on roads may be traffic signs if they indicate a warning, prohibition, restriction or requirement prescribed or authorised under s 64. It had been held previously in *Evans* v *Cross* [1938] 1 All ER 751 that a white line on a bend or down the centre of a road was not a traffic sign. Single white lines, if disobeyed, create no offence under s 22, although a charge of careless driving may be justified for a central white line (see *Bensley* v *Smith*) at 5.30, but reg 22(2) specifically provides that the transverse lines at the mouth of a minor road (diagram 1003), where it enters a major road, whether or not used with the 'Give Way' sign (602), create the requirement that no vehicle shall pass them into the major road in such a manner or at such a time as is likely to cause danger to a vehicle on the major road or to cause it to change speed or course to avoid it. This is the old wording used in reg 11(1) and has not yet been changed to correspond (see 6.6). Note that the change of speed or course referred to in reg 22 must be to avoid the entering vehicle. A driver who disobeyed this requirement, however, would not seem to offend against s 22 where there was no 'Give Way' sign, as reg 7 does not apply s 22 to diagram 1003, only to the 'Give Way' sign, but he could properly be charged, if the facts warranted, with careless or reckless driving. It is doubtful whether he could be charged with disobeying reg 22(2) contrary to s 118 of the 1984 Act. For the arguments see under 'Failing to comply with a sign', 6.2.

*Double white lines*

Regulation 23 of the 1981 Regulations deals with the double white lines (diagram 1013.1). Double white lines consist either of two continuous white lines or one continuous white line together with a broken white line. Two continuous white lines require vehicles in either direction at all times to keep to the nearside of the nearest continuous line, and a broken line with a continuous white line requires a vehicle to keep to the nearside of the continuous white line when the continuous white line is the nearer of the two lines to his vehicle. In diagram 1013.1 five different methods of marking are indicated. The second of the five consists of two continuous white lines with hatching between them. It is not always appreciated that the double white line regulation (and thus s 22) applies to them. See below, however, as to the need for an approach arrow.

Regulation 7 applies so that contravention of the requirements of reg 23 (2) becomes an offence contrary to s 22.

It is an offence to stop on *either* side of a road within a double white line system, whether the lines are both continuous or only one of the two lines is continuous. It is also a requirement that the driver must keep his moving vehicle in a position on a road governed by a double white line system so that at all times the offside of the vehicle is on the nearside of the white lines while both white lines are continuous or where the nearside white line is continuous and the offside line is broken. On the other hand if the broken line of a double white line is nearest to the vehicle viewed in the direction of travel, the double line may be crossed if it is seen to be safe to do so (reg 23(5)); if it was crossed when unsafe, the charge should not be under s 22, for reg 7 does not apply to breach of reg 23(5), but careless driving. It is doubtful whether a breach of reg 23(5) contrary to s 118 of the Road Traffic Regulation Act 1984 could be charged (see 6.2). Stopping is permitted by reg 23(3) to enable a person to board or alight from the vehicle or to load or unload goods, for building operations, road and public utility works, for vehicles used for fire, ambulance or police purposes (as to this see the comments at 6.4 as to the traffic lights exemption), for pedal cycles without sidecars, whether or not auto-assisted, for exigencies of traffic, to avoid an accident or with the permission of a constable in uniform or when directed by a traffic warden. It is an offence to drive on the wrong side of double white lines when both lines are continuous or only the nearside is continuous even if it is perfectly safe to do so.

Defences are set out in reg 23(4). These allow a vehicle to cross or straddle the continuous line in order to obtain access to side roads or land or premises adjoining the road; to pass a stationary vehicle; to avoid an accident or in circumstances beyond the driver's control or under the direction of a uniformed police constable or traffic warden. In *R* v *Blything* (*Suffolk*) *JJ, ex parte Knight* [1970] RTR 218 the justices were advised by their clerk that reg 23(4) only gave a defence where the vehicle actually crossed or straddled the white lines and therefore the defendant, who was on the offside of the road before the double white lines began, could not avail himself of the defence contained in the regulations. It was held that this was wrong and that 'crossing or straddling' did not have this restricted meaning. On the facts the Divisional Court held that the defendant, who had commenced overtaking two vehicles before the double white lines, could not have a defence under reg 23(4). *R* v *Blything* was explained in the unreported case of *Hillyer* v *Hooper* heard in the Divisional Court on 20 March 1984. It was held in the latter case that the position depended on the facts as to whether the act or omission of a third party or parties enabled the person to bring himself within the defence of circumstances beyond the driver's control. The decision in *Blything* was that where in the circumstances a man chose to overtake and then for one reason or another—connected with the ordinary experience in the course of driving vehicles on the highway—found it impossible to get back, that was not a statutory defence.

The lines must, by reg 24(1), be white and, by reg 25(1), illuminated by reflecting material and studs incorporating reflectors between the two lines. The variations in dimensions allowed by reg 8(3) apply.

The lines must comply with the regulations and if they do not a person contravening them commits no offence even if the lines are readily recognisable as double white lines (*Davies* v *Heatley* [1971] RTR 145, where the lines were not in accordance with diagram 1013 under the 1964 regulations in so far as an intermittent white line had been placed between two continuous white lines and the continuous lines were too far apart). In *Walton* v *Hawkins* [1973] RTR 366 it was held that diagram 1013 of the 1964 Regulations was not one unit but consisted of three separate markings each having a different purpose and the sequence in which they were imposed was a matter for the highway authority to suit the requirements of the road in question. *Aliter*, seemingly, if the markings or the arrows have been correctly marked even though they are partially invisible (cf *Skeen* v *Smith* at 6.13), providing their meaning is clear.

A trivial departure from the requirements of regulations will not however provide immunity from prosecution (*Cotterill* v *Chapman* [1984] RTR 73). In that case for some 30 mm distance the gap between the double white lines was 87 mm instead of the 90 mm minimum. The error had arisen following repainting.

Under the 1981 Regulations a warning arrow (diagram 1014) is mandatory (see direction 42). More than one (in line) is permissible. The 1981 Regulations differ from the 1975 Regulations in that only one arrow is necessary, but there are no exceptions, and no approach distance is specified. It would seem that a prosecution for a failure to comply with a double white line system should fail if there is no such warning arrow.

### 6.13–15 Non-conforming and damaged signs

The colours, sizes, dimensions, proportions and forms of letters and numerals are dealt with by regs 9–14; illumination of signs by regs 15–19; and the variations by reg 8. The dimensions of all signs are metricated.

All existing permanent regulatory signs under the 1975 Regulations are preserved by reg 3(2). Certain other signs are preserved to 31 December 1985, 31 December 1989 and 31 December 1992 (see reg 3).

Where a 'no waiting' order or other traffic regulation order, eg a clearway, has been made, normally it must be indicated by traffic signs which conform with the 1981 Regulations, even though the local authority have a discretion whether to erect such signs. If it is not so indicated or the signs do not conform, *MacLeod* v *Hamilton* [1965] SLT 305 seems to be authority for the proposition that there might be no offence against the order. In *Power* v *Davidson* [1964] Crim LR 781 it was held in relation to former push button pedestrian crossing regulations of 1954 that where the studs were not in compliance with the regulations no offence was committed. *Davies* v *Heatley* [1971] RTR 145 is authority for the proposition that, because by s 64(2) of the Road Traffic Regulation Act 1984 traffic signs shall be of the size, colour and type prescribed by regulation, if a sign the contravention of which is an offence contrary to s 22 is not as prescribed by the regulation, no offence is committed if the sign is contravened even if the sign is clearly recognisable to a reasonable man as a sign of that kind (but see *Sharples* v *Blackmore* below). The facts of *Davies* v *Heatley* were that a single intermittent line had originally been placed in the centre of the road. Double white lines were subsequently placed on the road but the intermittent line was insufficiently defaced. Although the court might possible have been able to hold that the old line could be subtracted from the existing double lines and thus form no part of them, in any event the existing double lines were more widely spread than was permitted by the regulation.

A trivial departure however, from the regulation requirements will not provide immunity from prosecution (see *Cotterill* v *Chapman* [1984] RTR 73 under 'Double white lines'; 6.12).

In *Skeen* v *Smith* [1979] SLT 295 the 'Stop' sign on the pole was in order, but the word 'Stop' painted on the road was not fully visible. The Appeal Court directed the magistrates to convict. This was not a case of an initial and continuing failure to comply with the regulations: the markings had been in order at one time and were still partially visible.

In *Sharples* v *Blackmore* [1973] RTR 249 the Divisional Court held that the colour of the back of a speed limit sign was immaterial as it was the front of the sign which of course conveyed the warnings to the motorist. Where, therefore, a speed limit sign's back was painted black instead of grey, the sign was nevertheless held to be a sign prescribed under the Traffic Signs (Speed Limits) Regulations and General Directions 1969. It would seem that a sign not complying with direction 36 of the 1981 Directions which requires the back of signs to be grey (or black in the case of signs mounted on traffic lights) would, following *Sharples* v *Blackmore,* be held to comply with the 1981 Regulations and Directions, where the back of the sign is immaterial for its purpose of regulating traffic. *R* v *Priest* (1961) 35 CR 31, a decision of the Ontario Court of Appeal that a non-conforming stop sign was binding on the driver providing he could have seen it if he was keeping a proper lookout, was distinguished in *Davies* v *Heatley* on the ground that the Canadian legislation did not make it an offence to comply with a 'prescribed stop sign' but only with a stop sign.

## Signs and Signals: Proceedings and Penalties

### 6.16 Warning of intended prosecution

Warning of intended prosecution (see Chapter 3) is required for all offences under s 22 (1972 Act, s 179 and Sched 4), whether committed by the driver of a motor vehicle or by the rider or propeller of any other type of vehicle, including pedal cyclists and tricyclists, or by the driver of a horsedrawn vehicle, unless s 179(3A) applies in the particular case. In *Walton* v *Hawkins* [1973] RTR 366 at p 369, it was argued that the notice of intended prosecution did not comply with the statutory requirements in that the failure to observe double white lines according to the notice occurred south of a junction when in fact the road ran east and west; this contention was abandoned by the appellant with the approval of the court as the appellant had not been prejudiced by the error (following *Pope* v *Clarke* [1953] 2 All ER 704). In view of the wording of s 22A, offences under that section are committed under s 22 and thus s 179 applies.

### 6.17 Proceedings generally

An information under s 22 is not bad because it uses the word 'fail' instead of 'neglect' (*Pontin* v *Price* (1933) 97 JP 315).

Where a court has taken into consideration disobedience to traffic signs on convicting for reckless or careless driving, the conviction would seem to be a bar to further proceedings under s 22 (cf *Welton* v *Taneborne* (1908) 72 JP 419) but it would be otherwise if there had been an acquittal under s 2 or s 3. See 5.49 as to convicting for both offences.

## 6.18–19 Penalties

The penalty for an offence against s 22 of the 1972 Act is a fine of level 3. Disqualification may be ordered and endorsement is obliged to be ordered (in the absence of 'special reasons': see Chapter 21) on conviction for an offence under s 22 of failing to comply with a constable's traffic direction or with a specified sign (see below). Section 19 of the Transport Act 1981 (penalty points disqualification) applies to these specified offences under s 22 (see 20.18–21), which carry 3 penalty points. The court may also order the defendant to be disqualified until he passes a driving test under s 93(7) (see 20.32).

The signs, disobedience of which under s 22 carried optional disqualification and obligatory endorsement, are those set out in reg 7(2) (see Vol 2), namely the 'Stop' signs at major roads, red traffic lights (including motorway flashing red lights, the flashing red lights at automatic level crossings and the portable red lights at road works), any contravention of double white lines (whether by stopping within the system or driving a vehicle on the wrong side of double lines or the wrong side of a continuous line if it is on the nearside of the road) and failing to obtain permission for a large or slow vehicle to cross an automatic level crossing.

Neither disqualification nor endorsement may be ordered for any other offence under s 22 such as disobedience to a 'No Entry', 'Give Way' or 'Keep Left' sign or arrow, temporary traffic signs erected under s 67 of the Act of 1984, or any of the traffic census signs.

The decision in *Rumbles* v *Poole* [1980] RTR 499 that a motorist convicted of failing to conform to a traffic warden's directions is not liable to be disqualified nor is his licence liable to endorsement has now been reversed, as collumn 5 of Sched 4 now includes reference to 'traffic warden' as well as 'constable' (Transport Act 1981, Sched 9, para 22) in relation to s 22 offences.

The penalty for an offence against s 159 of the 1972 Act is a fine of level 3 (Sched 4, as amended). Disqualification, endorsement and penalty points may not be ordered.

Pedestrians disobeying police signals are liable by s 23 of the 1972 Act to a maximum fine of level 3.

Offences under ss 5, 8 and 53 of the 1984 Act are punishable by a maximum fine of level 3. Neither disqualification nor endorsement nor penalty points can be ordered.

The endorsement codes for traffic sign offences are as follows:

| | |
|---|---|
| Traffic lights signals | TS10 |
| Double white lines | TS20 |
| 'Stop' sign | TS30 |
| Police constable's traffic directions | TS40 |
| Any other sign | TS50 |

The Magistrates' Association's suggested penalty (see 18.1 and Appendix 3) is £40 for contravention of all traffic signs including traffic lights, double white lines and police signals.

# Speed Limits

## 6.20 Generally

Offences of exceeding the speed limit are contained in the Road Traffic Regulation Act 1984 and fall into four classes, viz:

(*a*) exceeding the limit on a road restricted to 30, 40 or 50 mph;
(*b*) exceeding the temporary limits of 70, 60 and 50 mph on roads other than motorways;
(*c*) exceeding on any road the limit applicable to the class of vehicle; and
(*d*) exceeding the limits of speed applicable to motorways only.

Heavy lorries, for example, are subject to speed limits under all four; ordinary passenger motor cars and motor cycles with pneumatic tyres, not drawing trailers, are subject to a limit only on a restricted road and to the overall maxima of 70 mph on dual carriageway roads and motorways, 60 mph on single carriageway roads, or such lesser speed as may be specified in respect of certain specified stretches of road under the Temporary Speed Limit Order.

The limit of 30 mph on restricted roads is imposed by the Road Traffic Regulation Act 1984, s 81; s 84 of that Act allows the proper authorities to fix other speed limits for designated roads in all areas.

The Road Traffic Regulation Act 1984, s 88, authorises certain temporary or experimental speed limits and minimum speed limits on specified roads. Temporary speed limit orders made under s 88 can be made in respect of all types of road other than motorways (s 88(6)). A temporary speed restriction may also be imposed under the Road Traffic Regulation Act 1984, s 14, where a speed restriction is required because of roadworks.

The offences in relation to the class of vehicle on all roads and on motorways fall under the Road Traffic Regulation Act 1984, s 86, and the limits for the various classes are indicated in Sched 6 to the 1984 Act.

There may also be some speed limits of local application, eg in Royal Parks. Section 199(4) of the Port of London Act 1968 has the effect of imposing a speed limit of 30 mph on all vehicles in the Port of London Authority area.

Offences of contravening speed limits are punishable under s 89 and Sched 7 of the Road Traffic Regulation Act 1984, except that contravening a motorway speed limit (other than the motorway speed limits for special classes of vehicle) is punishable under s 17(4) and Sched 7; offences against orders under s 88(1)(*b*)imposing minimum speed limits are punishable under s 88(7) and Sched 7 and offences against s 14 (temporary speed restrictions for road works etc.) are punishable under s 16(1) and Sched 7.

The four classes of offences are considered in more detail at 6.28–32 after evidential matters, and the proceedings and penalties for the offences will be found at 6.33–7.

## 6.21 Application

Speed limits under the above sections do not apply to tramcars or trolley vehicles operated under statutory powers (s 141). The sections apply only on roads and to motor vehicles (as defined in Chapter 1). Save as mentioned at 6.22, the limits apply to vehicles of the Crown and visiting forces.

The British Transport Commission Act 1956, s 27(4), relates to speed limits in the Commission's docks.

### 6.22 Exemptions

Vehicles being used for fire brigade, ambulance or police purposes are not subject to any speed limit either on a restricted road or by virtue of their class if observance of the limit would be likely to hinder their use for the purpose for which they are being used on that occasion (Road Traffic Regulation Act 1984, s 87), but are otherwise. A private person who is trailing a police car with a view to obtaining evidence to prosecute its driver for speeding cannot plead s 87 as a defence (*Strathern* v *Gladstone* [1937] SC (J) 11). If, in a particular case and a particular set of special circumstances, it is established that, solely in order to enable a police purpose to be performed, or solely to ensure that a police purpose requiring to be performed is not frustrated, use must be made of a vehicle and the use being made of it would be hindered by observance of the provisions restricting the speed at which vehicles can travel, then in such circumstances what is now s 87 excuses the offence of travelling too fast (*Aitken* v *Yarwood* [1964] 2 All ER 537). In that case, the car taking a policeman to court to give evidence broke down and it was held that in those circumstances he was entitled to exceed the limit in order to get to court in time. Normally, however, a constable should start for court in time to get there without exceeding the limit and it would only be in unforeseen circumstances, eg a breakdown or stopping to give first aid at an accident, that he would be entitled to exceed the limit. Like considerations apply to fire and ambulance vehicles; they may exceed the limit only if it would hinder the relevant use on the particular occasion, eg the chief fire officer in his car must obviously get to the fire as quickly as possible but there is no need to hurry home on going off duty. *Semble*, a car taking a casualty to hospital in an urgent case is being used for ambulance purposes but it is doubtful if a doctor hurrying to an urgent case is using his car for ambulance purposes; an ambulance, according to the *Oxford Dictionary*, is a vehicle for conveying the wounded.

The Motor Vehicles (Variation of Speed Limit) Regulations 1947 (SR & O 1947 No 2192), as amended by SI 1954 No 943, provide that what is now Sched 6 to the 1984 Act shall have effect as though it imposed no speed limits in relation to certain types of vehicles owned by the Secretary of State for Defence and used for naval, military or air force purposes or which are so used whilst being driven by persons subject to the orders of a member of the armed forces of the Crown. There is a similar exemption (by the 1954 Regulations) for like vehicles in the service of a visiting force (see 2.5). The types of vehicles so exempted are ones constructed or adapted for combative purposes or training in connection therewith, for conveyance of personnel, for use with or to carry or draw guns and machine guns, certain track-laying vehicles, fire tenders and ambulances. Vehicles used for salvage purposes pursuant to Part IX of the Merchant Shipping Act 1894 are also exempt from Sched 6 under the 1947 Regulations and so are vehicles used in the conduct of experiments or trials for road improvements (see Part IV, para 1 of Sched 6).

The 1947 Regulations only exempt the vehicles referred to therein from the provisions of Sched 6. The Regulations do not confer exemption on these vehicles in respect of roads subject to restricted speeds. Section 87 would seem to confer exemption from such restrictions in respect of service ambulances and fire brigade vehicles, and (possibly) service police vehicles if it can be argued that military, naval or air force police purposes come within 'police purposes' in s 87.

## 6.23 Driving at a dangerous speed

The offence under s 2 of the 1972 Act of driving at a dangerous speed was abolished by s 50 of the Criminal Law Act 1977. Reckless driving (s 2) and promoting or taking part in a race or speed trial between motor vehicles (s 14) are dealt with in Chapter 5.

## 6.24 Evidence and corroboration

By the Road Traffic Regulation Act 1984, s 89(2), a person prosecuted for driving a motor vehicle at a speed exceeding the limit imposed by or under any enactment shall not be convicted solely on the evidence of one witness to the effect that, in the opinion of the witness, the defendant was driving at a speed exceeding that limit. A like provision applies to offences of not attaining minimum speed limits (1984 Act, s 88(7)).

These corroboration requirements do not apply to motorway speeding offences contrary to s 17(4) of the 1984 Act (overall speed limit on motorways) as s 17(2) is specifically excluded from the effects of s 89 by s 89(3) but they do apply to the motorway speed limits for special classes.

The corroborative witness must speak as to speeding at the same moment of time as the first witness, so one police officer who saw the defendant on one part of the road did not corroborate another who saw him some moments later at a place further along the same road (*Brighty* v *Pearson* [1938] 4 All ER 127). Corroboration is usually provided nowadays by the speedometer of a police vehicle, radar equipment, or Vascar or by the speed testing device being used. In *Nicholas* v *Penny* [1950] 2 All ER 89 it was held that a person could be convicted on the evidence of one policeman supported by evidence by him of the reading of a speedometer or other mechanical means, even though there was no evidence that the speedometer had been tested. In that case the defendant was said to be going 10 mph in excess of the limit and the court commented on the amount of the excess; had the speed been only, say, 2 mph in excess of the limit, they might have called for evidence of the accuracy of the speedometer. In any case, it is in the discretion of the magistrates to accept or reject evidence tendered in speeding as in all other cases. Applying *Nicholas* v *Penny* it was held in *Swain* v *Gillett* [1974] RTR 446 that for the purposes of s 89(2) a speedometer reading was capable of amounting to corroboration of a police officer's opinion evidence about the speed of a vehicle without proof of testing of the accuracy of the speedometer. The magistrates, who had dismissed a case of speeding on accepting a submission of no case to answer on the ground that the officer's evidence as to speeding was not corroborated by a speedometer for which no evidence as to its accuracy had been produced, were directed to continue the hearing of the case.

Similarly a radar gun reading can amount to reliable or proper corroboration of the opinion of a police officer even though the gun has not been checked against the known speed of a vehicle fitted with a calibrated speedometer (*Collinson* v *Mabbott* (1984) *The Times*, 6 October).

The evidence of two police officers independently forming an opinion about the speed of an offending vehicle is sufficient as a matter of law to constitute corroboration as required by s 89(2), but it is for the magistrates as a tribunal of fact to consider how much weight should be attached to the evidence adduced.

In *Houston* v *Leslie* [1958] SLT 109; [1958] Crim LR 477, a variation between the evidence of two constables as to the vehicle's position behind another vehicle was held enough to justify a doubt as to the proving of the case, on its particular facts. In *Gillespie* v *Macmillan* [1957] SLT 283; [1957] Jo Crim L 341, a conviction was upheld where a constable, on a measured length of road, had started a stopwatch when a car passed; another constable further along the same length had started his watch when the car passed him and, on the watches being stopped when the car was stopped, a comparison of the two watches showed a speed of 52 mph.

## 6.25 Speed check equipment

The general approach to the use of speed check equipment is indicated by the comments of Ormrod J in *Kent* v *Stamps* [1982] RTR 273 at p 278 in relation to the Truvelo electronic trip wire equipment.

> The basic principle must be that the reading on the machine is evidence. It is very cogent evidence indeed, and in the vast majority of cases one would suppose that it was conclusive evidence. But we have not reached the stage when the reading on such a piece of apparatus as this has to be accepted as absolutely accurate and true, no matter what. There are all kinds of things in a case like this which might have gone wrong....The reading on the machine is, as I have said before, strong and should in most cases be conclusive evidence of the fact that the vehicle was travelling at a speed in excess of the limit. The justices would be, and should be, extremely reluctant to reject that finding, although there must be situations in which they are entitled to doubt it. They will be very few and far between, and the justices must be very careful not to allow somebody to run away with their judgment on these matters.

The decision in *Kent* v *Stamps* should be compared with that in *Burton* v *Gilbert* [1984] RTR 162. The court held that the mere opinion of a driver as to his speed provided no evidential basis to cast doubt on the reading provided by the speed testing equipment. The decision is not easy to follow in that the court apparently accepted a similar opinion by the police officer as to the speed and regarded the radar machine as corroborating it.

When in force s 90 of the 1984 Act will require radar speed check devices to be approved by the Secretary of State before the evidence from them can be used in prosecutions. Two reports on radar speed detection devices have been produced under the aegis of the Home Office. Reference has been made to them under the respective headings where these radar devices are considered. It is planned to implement s 90 of the Road Traffic Regulation Act 1984 during 1985.

*Radar speed meters*

These are discussed at 101 SJ 761, 765 and 820, in (1965) *The Times*, 21 April, and at 129 JP Jo 341 and 388, and there is an article by an electrical engineer at [1958] Crim LR 349.

The Home Office Scientific Research and Development Branch has produced a report on fixed radar speed detection devices. It is entitled *The Evaluation of the Gatso Radar Speedmeter* by R. J. Harris, D. S. Keen and S. J. Amos. The report makes certain recommendations and examines the value of the Gatso devices.

In *Farrell* v *Simpson* [1959] SLT (Sh) 23; [1959] Jo Crim L 278 there is a good example of the type of evidence given in a straightforward case. A sheriff convicted on the evidence of a reading of such a meter by two constables, who also gave their opinion that the car was exceeding 30 mph. The evidence showed that the road was straight and level for a long distance, that the car was the only vehicle about, that the meter had been tested that day and that the speed of 42 mph recorded on the meter had been shown thereon for over two and a half seconds.

Evidence of mechanical devices such as speedometers and stopwatches is acceptable in English courts (*Nicholas* v *Penny* [1950] 2 All ER 89) and, where radar is used, it is a question of fact for the magistrates whether or not its evidence on the particular facts before them should be accepted. Such cases and opinions as have been reported or given seem to show that meters are very accurate if working under good conditions and operated by experienced constables. Such cases as are dismissed by magistrates are almost invariably dismissed not because the magistrates are not satisfied as to the accuracy of the radar meter but because they are not satisfied as to the accuracy of the evidence of the police officers operating the radar trap. Instances have occurred where the police officer has been unable to satisfy the magistrates that either he had read the radar meter correctly or the meter reading he has given in evidence referred to the defendant's motor vehicle. Radar traps are usually operated so that one constable is stationed by the radar set observing the speed of the vehicle as it passes through the radar beam, and another constable is stationed considerably further down the road to stop an offending vehicle. The constable stopping an offending vehicle will usually be told by radio of that vehicle's registration number and the type of vehicle; occasionally magistrates have dismissed a case where they have not been satisfied that the correct vehicle was stopped, either because of a possible error on the part of the constable at the radar set in identifying the vehicle, or an error on the part of the constable responsible for stopping the vehicle.

The use of a device, 'Radatec', without a post office licence, to receive advance signals of a radar meter was held to constitute the commission of an offence under s 1(1) of the Wireless Telegraphy Act 1949 and the company selling the device were convicted of inciting the commission of such an offence by reason of an advertisement inserted in a magazine by them (*Invicta Plastics Ltd* v *Clare* [1976] RTR 251).

*Hand held radar guns*

Many police forces have now introduced hand held radar guns which also operate by means of a radar beam. Some forces have, however, refused to do so because of doubts about their accuracy. They may be operated by a single constable and the machine itself is capable of providing corroboration when required by law.

There are various types of gun in use: the Muni Quip, the Kustom and the MPH K-15. These machines all work on the doppler effect. The gun is pointed by the constable at the moving vehicle. A radar beam strikes the vehicle and the frequency of the beam reflected back to the gun is changed proportionate to the speed of the vehicle. The gun measures this change and gives the speed of the vehicle on a digital display which may be retained in the machine by pressing a button or similar mechanism. The guns have a range of 500 yards or more.

There are at least five ways the guns can give a false reading: through low batteries; poor contact through car lighter sockets; radio or similar interference; reflection of the beam off a metal object (such as a lamp-post or post-box) on to some other moving object; or measurement of the speed of some other object in the wide beam. One gun pointed at a bench of magistrates recorded a speed of 175 mph! A test on a smaller nearer vehicle might pick up a reflection from a larger more distant one behind. Usually in such instances the reading would not be steady and would jump from one vehicle to another. The Home Office study *Measurements on Police Hand Held Radar Speedmeters* (Home Office Publication 28/84) did not indicate any likelihood of false readings from aircraft, birds, insects, powerlines or a movement *behind* the radar gun.

The Muni Quip training manual warns against using a device within a quarter of a mile of powerful VHF radio or UHF TV transmitters; within 100 yards of high voltage overhead power cables; near large rotating fans or signs; near large rotating radar equipment; or within 30 yards of smaller transmitters.

A case before the Newport Crown Court already cited in numerous speeding cases in magistrates' courts (even though a Crown Court decision is binding neither on other Crown Courts nor on magistrates' courts: see 2.35), was reported in *The Times* on 25 March 1981 and concerns the proper use of these radar guns when proving a speeding offence. In that case the judge said that the evidence showed that the gun might have given false readings. He made certain recommendations. Before setting up a speed trap, police should test the gun against a vehicle travelling at a known speed, should test the site for possible sources of radio interference, and should make sure that their radio equipment is not being used near the gun. They should also take care that there is a suitable period before the figure shown on the gun is locked into the mechanism to give the final reading. It may be emphasised that the decision does not prohibit a successful radar gun prosecution and that it is a decision of the Crown Court only.

The procedure to be followed by police officers was recommended in the Home Office study to be as follows. A position by the road should be selected with a clear view. The battery indicator should be checked but if this is not fitted the later checks should confirm the battery state. The range switch should be pointed at the sky and turned slowly through 360°. During this test the display should be examined for several seconds to see that it is clear and there is no radio interference, and that the meter is working and the battery is not flat. This procedure should be repeated at intervals between speed measurements. Any test buttons should also be checked.

A tuning fork should then be struck and vibrated in front of the aerial. The reading on the machine should correspond with the reading on the fork. The checks recommended in the Newport Crown Court case should also be carried out. A written note should be kept of the speed of the vehicle used to test the radar gun.

The means of carrying out a radar check should be as follows. When, in the opinion of the officer, a vehicle is considered to be exceeding the speed limit, the speedmeter should be pointed at the vehicle and a reading taken. The reading should be observed for at least three seconds and during that period the reading should be steady. An erratic series of numbers would indicate that an erroneous reading had been taken, and that the measurement was invalid. If the reading is considered correct, the trigger in the handle of the meter can be squeezed, and the speed reading fixed on the display. The reading can then be shown to the offending motorist although there is no legal requirement to do so. When the button is squeezed again the reading is lost and the meter is ready to make another measurement.

In practice many courts have shown a reluctance to convict where these recommendations and procedures have not been carried out adequately, and a doubt is established as to the speed recorded. As with other radar equipment, if operated correctly, radar guns normally have a high standard of accuracy but it may be possible to challenge the accuracy of the police officer or suggest the radar beam struck the wrong vehicle or another object. In cases of doubt the defence representative should question the prosecution carefully on any of the points mentioned above which may have affected the accuracy of the reading, in particular enquiring whether there was a parked car or other metal object nearby.

*Vascar*

Some police forces have equipped traffic police vehicles with Vascar (visual average speed computer and recorder). Like radar meters, Vascar is technically extremely accurate. Unlike radar meters which record the vehicle's speed in the fraction of a second it takes a vehicle to pass through the radar beam, the Vascar device records the speed as averaged by the vehicle over the distance recorded; but like radar meters, it will usually be extremely difficult to obtain an acquittal on a charge of speeding on technical grounds where Vascar is used. The degree of training required of a police constable for the proper operation of Vascar is, if anything, rather more than that required for radar, and it is believed most forces require a constable to pass a stringent test programme before allowing the constable to operate the device for the purposes of prosecution. The proper operation of Vascar depends on the police constable accurately operating the switches and being able to satisfy the court that there has been no mistake in relation to the identification of the offending vehicle and no misjudgment of the exact moment the vehicle passed the relevant landmark used in its operation sufficient to render unreliable the speed as recorded by the device.

*Electric trip wire equipment*

The electronic equipment used by the police in *Kent* v *Stamps* [1982] RTR 273 is called Truvelo equipment. Two wires are stretched across the carriageway at a fixed distance apart, the distance being 1.5 m. It was stated in that case that the normal police practice is to set the wires 1.55 m apart so as to leave a margin of error in favour of the driver. The wires consist of co-axial cables which are sensitive to pressure. When a vehicle is driven over them first one and then the other, a pulse or electrical charge is created, and these pulses or charges are conveyed to a computer, which then calculates from the time taken to compress, first, one cable and then the other the actual speed in miles per hour of the vehicle.

In *Kent* v *Stamps* the justices rejected the result of the equipment even though they apparently accepted that it was in working order and had been checked and used correctly. The rejection was because of the age of the lorry and their knowledge of the location—round a bend and on an upward gradient. With some hesitation the Divisional Court agreed that they were entitled to wonder whether the machinery had worked accurately and to reach the decision they did.

*Warnings of speed traps: obstruction*

In *Bastable* v *Little* [1907] 1 KB 59 the defendant gave warnings of a speed trap. He was acquitted of obstruction on the ground that he was preventing offences because the drivers of other vehicles slowed down. The decision was strongly criticised in *Green* v *Moore* [1982] 2 WLR 671, where the Divisional Court said that until overruled it should be strictly confined to its own facts.

## 6.26 Accident investigation

Sometimes charges of speeding are brought following an accident. The estimate of speed is based on tyre marks and other factors and presumably the various technical factors involved must constitute corroboration of each other. For a report of a successful appeal against a speeding conviction on such evidence see (1977) 141 JP 403 in which the judge commented on the lack of safeguards for a defendant when presented with such technical evidence. Reference should also be made to a letter commenting on the report at ibid, p 463.

For the technical aspects of accident investigation use may be made of the *Manual of Road Accident Investigation* Vols 1 and 2 by R Byatt and R Watts published in 1980 by Pitman Publishing Ltd. There is also an article on the subject at (1976) 140 JP Jo 665.

### 6.27 Evidence generally

Timetables, schedules and directions issued by an employer may be produced as evidence in a prosecution of the employer for procuring or inciting his drivers to exceed a speed limit imposed under any enactment, where they show that the driver is bound to exceed the limit if he is to comply with the document issued to him (Road Traffic Regulation Act 1984, s 89(4); and see *Newman* v *Overington* (1928) 93 JP 46).

Measurement of a distance on a map by a rotameter, to show that the distances given in the driver's records could not be covered without exceeding the limit, was held admissible in *Morrison* v *M'Cowan* [1939] SC(J) 45.

The opinion of any witness as to speed is receivable (Cross on *Evidence*). Magistrates have convicted on the evidence of policemen on foot alone, without stopwatches or speedometers, in a case of exceeding the limit on a restricted road, for, while it is unwise to accept such evidence as to what a vehicle's speed was, it is relatively easy to accept that a vehicle which is going very fast is going in excess of 30 mph (118 JP Jo 105 and 104 SJ 20) but it is in their discretion whether or not to accept such evidence.

A person may refresh his memory from a contemporaneous record compiled by another provided it was checked at the time by him and adopted as his own. The constable who had observed the speed recorded by the radar meter of an offending vehicle checked and countersigned a record compiled by the constable responsible for later stopping the offending vehicle; he was held to be entitled to refresh his memory from the other constable's record of the offence (*Groves* v *Redbart* [1975] Crim LR 158). See further 2.79 as to refreshing memory.

In *Baker* v *Sweet* [1966] Crim LR 51 a temporary speed limit order restricted speeds on all roads save motorways and dual-carriageways; on the hearing of a charge of exceeding the limit, the order was not produced and no evidence was given that it applied to the road in question and it was held that it was for the defendant to show, pursuant to what is now s 101 of the Magistrates' Courts Act 1980, that the order did not apply to the road. As the order was not even published as a statutory instrument, this is an unsatisfactory decision in that magistrates seem to be expected to take their law from what they have read about speed limits in the newspapers or from the '*ipse dixit*' of the prosecutor.

### 6.28 Speed limits on restricted roads

The term 'built-up', which appeared in former Acts, is still an expression which is commonly used but it is not used in the Road Traffic Regulation Act 1984; s 81 of that Act makes it an offence to drive a motor vehicle on a 'restricted road' at a speed exceeding 30 mph. Where a limit had been imposed under s 84 of the 1984 Act (generally a limit other than 30 mph), such a road is not deemed to be a restricted road for the purposes of s 81 (s 84(3)). By s 82 a 'restricted road' is a road where there is provided a system of street lighting furnished by means of lamps placed not more than 200 yards apart or a road in respect of which the relevant authority has made a direction that it shall be a restricted road notwithstanding the absence of such street lighting. In the following paragraphs the term means roads subject to speed limits whether of 30 mph or otherwise.

In *Hood* v *Lewis* [1976] RTR 98 a speeding motorist failed to see the 30 mph signs as his vision of them was obscured by bushes and posts and a lorry which he was overtaking. Since street lamps not more than 200 yards apart were plainly to be seen, the justices were directed to convict. It was also said that it is no possible answer to prosecution on a charge of speeding if a motorist driving into a built-up area plain for all to see chooses to follow closely behind or overtake a lorry so that he fails to see the 30 mph signs (nor can it be a special reason for not endorsing if the 30 mph signs are obscured if there is a system of street lamps not more than 200 yards apart: see *Walker* v *Rawlinson*, at 21.11.

Where a lamp is temporarily missing, eg it has been knocked down, so that at one place two lamps are more than 200 yards apart, it is suggested that a 'system of street lighting' is still provided as above (see 114 JP Jo 627). Where there is a direction in force imposing a limit under what is now s 82 on a road without the requisite lamp-posts, the presence of the speed limit signs is prima facie evidence that the speed limit applies to that road, and the police need not call evidence to prove the direction unless the defence call evidence that the road is not restricted (*Boyd-Gibbins* v *Skinner* [1951] 1 All ER 1049). A conviction was upheld where a defendant had exceeded the limit on a road on which there were four lamps, two of which were 201½ yards apart and the others 200 yards apart (*Briere* v *Hailstone* (1968) 112 SJ 767); the 'de minimis' principle was applied. It might be otherwise if all or nearly all the lamps were more than 201 yards apart. Indeed, it is respectfully submitted that *Briere's* case was not really a correct application of the 'de minimis' rule; part of the road in question there had the relevant system of street lighting and it was thus relevant that the limit was also exceeded on a part where the lamps were more than the prescribed distance apart. It may also be pointed out that s 82 refers to a 'system' of street lighting furnished by lamps placed not more than 200 yards apart. If some of the gaps between lights are slightly more than 200 yards it is possible to argue that there is still a 'system' of street lighting if the number of lights is such that the gaps average less than 200 yards.

In *Roberts* v *Croxford* (1969) 113 SJ 269 magistrates, on inspecting a road, found that the system of street lighting was for lighting a promenade nearby and not for lighting the road; their action in inspecting and their finding that the road had not the necessary system was upheld.

By the Road Traffic Regulation Act 1984, s 85(4), if a road has the relevant system of street lighting, evidence of the absence of derestriction signs shall be evidence that it is deemed to be a road which is restricted. If the road has not the relevant system of street lighting but is restricted, a person shall not be convicted unless there are the necessary restriction signs (s 85(3)).

Where different lengths of one road are governed by different regulations applying to one length only, even though imposing the same limit, an information alleging an offence against both regulations is bad for duplicity; there should either be separate, fresh informations for each length or the prosecution should have elected on the original information to proceed in respect of one length only (*Cross* v *Oliver* (1964) 62 LGR 501).

The signs to indicate that a road is restricted are set out in the Traffic Signs (Speed Limits) Regulations and General Directions 1969 (SI 1969 No 1487) as amended by like-named amendment regulations of 1977 (SI 1977 No 952). The regulations allow for variations in the dimensions of the overall diameter of the signs, which is the only measurement prescribed. Speed limit signs should be illuminated by lighting or 'reflecting material' (see *Bursey* v *Barron*, below), unless the Department of Transport has agreed otherwise. The table at the end of the Directions indicates the maximum distances there must be between signs. There is a saving for signs which conform to previous regulations and directions, but note s 85(4) (above) as to roads which have not the necessary lamps. Where some lamps were more than 200 yards apart and there were no intermediate repeater signs as required by the relevant Traffic Signs (Speed Limits) Regulations and General Directions, a conviction for exceeding the limit was quashed (*Mackereth* v *Madge* (1968) 66 LGR 69). The erection of repeater signs in a 30 mph area governed by a system of street lighting is specifically prohibited by the 1969 regulations. It is submitted that where there are such illegal repeater signs, a conviction for exceeding 30 mph will not be invalidated. Only the converse applies (see s 85(3) and (4) of the 1984 Act).

It is a common complaint that there are no repeater signs indicating restricted roads. In fact the reference to the relevant system of street lighting is designed to obviate the need for such repeater signs. Were they to be used on some roads it would be argued that they should be used on all the vast number of restricted roads which have the relevant system of street lighting.

As special limit signs must, in accordance with s 85 and s 64(1), (2) and (3), be the 'prescribed' traffic signs it would appear that, if the sign is not in accordance with the regulations, the defendant is entitled to be acquitted unless the offence took place in an area restricted to 30 mph by reason of a system of street lamps not more than 200 yards apart. Under reg 4(4) of Part II of the regulations, signs not illuminated by external lighting must be illuminated by 'reflecting material', but by reg 4(6) no reflecting material is to be applied to any part of the sign coloured black. In *Bursey* v *Barron* (1971) 115 SJ 469 it was held that reflecting material in this context meant reflecting material designed to illuminate the sign, and a coat of varnish which had been applied to the black '50' of the sign and which reflected direct light was held not to invalidate the sign.

The only signs which are required to be illuminated are those 'terminal' signs erected on a trunk or principal road where there is an electrical street lamp within 50 m. Such 'terminal' signs are required either to be continuously illuminated through the hours of darkness, or illuminated while the street lamp is lit providing the sign is also illuminated by reflecting material (ie reflecting material designed to illuminate: see *Bursey* v *Barron* above). A 'terminal' sign is defined by reg 4 as those required at the beginning of the speed limit in accordance with directions 2(1), 2(2) and 4 but does not include speed limit signs at junctions or signs under directions 2(3) or 2(4). Where a terminal sign required to be illuminated under reg 4 was in such a condition that it could not be illuminated, justices dismissed a case of speeding during daylight hours on the ground that as the sign could not comply with reg 4 it did not comply with s 54(2) of the Road Traffic Regulation Act 1967. The justices were directed to convict where the speeding took place in daylight: the requirement that the sign should be illuminated was not contravened, as there was no requirement that during daylight hours the sign should be in a state fit for illumination in the dark (*Stubbs* v *Morgan* [1972] RTR 454).

Direction 9 requires the back of any speed limit sign to be grey. The justices dismissed a case of speeding where the back of a speed limit sign was painted black instead of grey because s 64(2) of the Road Traffic Regulation Act 1984 requires speed limit signs to be not only of the prescribed size and type but also of the prescribed colour. The High Court, in directing the justices to convict, held that the requirements of s 75 of the Road Traffic Regulation Act only apply to the front of the prescribed sign and the colour of the back of the sign is immaterial (*Sharples* v *Blackmore* [1973] RTR 249). The colour of the back of a sign (which no driver sees until he passes it and only then if he turns round) does not make an otherwise restricted road into an unrestricted road (ibid).

In *Burgess* v *West* [1982] RTR 269, the finding was that there was no 30 mph speed limit sign. The rightness of the conviction was not canvassed. The defendant believed he was in a 40 mph area. The absence of the sign was a fact and not a mere mistaken belief (see *Jones* v *Nicks* on 21.11). Because the belief was induced by the fact of the absence of the sign it was a reason special to the offence and the justices were entitled at their discretion to find it a special reason for not endorsing. See further 21.11.

Interestingly the actual speed was 46 mph. The defendant contended that the police would not have prosecuted for a 6 mph excess and the court did not comment on this—and did not use it as a ground for overturning the special reason finding. Clearly it is not a ground for an acquittal.

## 6.29 Temporary speed limits

Temporary maximum and minimum speed limits may be imposed by orders made under s 88(1)(*a*) and (*b*) respectively of the 1984 Act. Temporary speed restrictions may also be imposed by orders under s 14 of the 1984 Act because of road works.

### *Temporary maximum speed limits*

The 70 mph, 60 mph and 50 mph (Temporary Speed Limit) Order 1977 is deemed to be made under s 88 of the Road Traffic Regulation Act 1984 and applies to all roads other than motorways in England, Wales and Scotland. For motorway speed limits see 6.31. Unless a lower limit is specified for any particular road or stretch of road either by Sched 1 or 2 to the Order, as varied, unrestricted dual-carriageway roads are limited to 70 mph and all unrestricted single carriageway roads are limited to 60 mph. The order came into force on 1 June 1977. The 1977 Order would have ceased on 30 November 1978 but was continued indefinitely in force by SI 1978 No 1548.

The 1978 Order, other than continuing the 1977 Order in force as varied does not amend the 1977 Order in any way.

Section s 88(5) of the Road Traffic Regulation Act 1984 provides that where a temporary speed limit is imposed on all roads, on all roads of any class specified in the order or on all roads other than roads of any specified class, s 85 (which requires speed limit signs to be displayed) does not apply. The effect of s 88(5) of the Road Traffic Regulation Act 1984 seems to be that speed limit signs need not be displayed in respect of the overall limits of 70 and 60 mph. Those lengths of dual or single carriageway roads specified in Sched 1 to the order and limited to 50 mph together with the dual-carriageway roads specified in Sched 2 limited to 60 mph are required to have signs displayed.

See *Baker* v *Sweet* at 6.27 as to proof of the Temporary Speed Limit Order.

*Temporary minimum speed limits*

These may be imposed for specified roads by orders under the Road Traffic Regulation Act 1984, s 88(1)(*b*) and are punishable under s 88(7) and Sched 7, not s 89. By s 88(5) signs must be displayed where the limit is for a specific road. The relevant order, when made, should be consulted to see if it contains any exception allowing lower speeds for safety reasons.

*Temporary speed restrictions for road works etc*

A highway authority may impose a temporary speed restriction under the Road Traffic Regulation Act 1984, ss 14–16, because of road works or works near the road or because of the likelihood of danger to the public or of serious damage to the highway. Such restrictions cannot remain in force for longer than three months without the approval of the Secretary of State unless made by the Secretary of State or the Greater London Council. It is an offence to contravene, or use or permit the use of a vehicle in contravention of a restriction. As to 'use' and 'permit' see Chapter 1. Such a speed restriction may be imposed in respect of any road. This therefore includes a motorway, a view supported by a 'Question and Answer' at (1979) 143 JP 212. It was emphasised in *Platten* v *Gowing* [1983] Crim LR 184 that this is a speed *restriction* and not a speed *limit*. It is implied in that decision that notices of intended prosecution (see Chapter 3) are not required. Corroboration in accordance with s 89(2) is also not required as it is not specified in Sched 7 against s 16(1) (the penalty subsection). See the entry against s 89(1) (general speed limits) in Sched 7 where s 89(2) (corroboration) is specified. This conclusion is also supported by the fact that ss 14–16 provide for restrictions and not limits caught by s 89.

The section does not apply to tramcars and trolley vehicles operated under statutory powers (s 141(1) of the 1984 Act).

## 6.30 Speed limits applicable to particular classes of vehicle

Certain vehicles are restricted as to speed, whether on restricted roads or not, by the Road Traffic Regulation Act 1984, Sched 6; see Vol 2. There are different limits for motorways, dual-carriageway roads other than motorways, and other roads. A dual-carriageway is defined in Part IV of Sched 6 as a road part of which consists of a central reservation to separate the carriageways. This definition suggests that the dual-carriageway does not begin with the hatching markings but only with the physical central reservation itself.

There are special limits for trailers constructed as grass cutters and hedge trimmers, straddle carriers, land tractors used for threshing and reaping, hay and straw balers, vehicles for moving excavated material or for carrying abnormal indivisible loads and engineering plant and loads exceeding 14 feet in width (Motor Vehicles (Authorisation of Special Types) General Order 1979 (SI 1979 No 1198)). *Semble*, if a vehicle to which the Special Types Order applies exceeds its special limit under that order but keeps within the limit laid down by Sched 6 to the 1984 Act, no speeding offence is committed, but the driver may be prosecuted under the Construction and Use Regulations in respect of matters, such as width, length, etc, to which they apply, for the protection of the Special Types Order is lost when it is breached (see 8.34).

The terms 'light (and) heavy locomotive', 'motor tractor' and 'invalid carriage' used in this schedule are defined in s 136 of the Road Traffic Regulation Act 1984 in similar terms to s 190 of the 1972 Act. The definition of an 'articulated vehicle' where the expression is used in Sched 6 under 'goods vehicle' is the same as in the Motor Vehicles (Construction and Use) Regulations (see Chapter 1 and in particular *Hunter* v *Towers* at 1.23, and under 'Goods vehicles' below). The definitions of 'passenger vehicle', 'dual-purpose vehicle', 'industrial tractor' and 'works truck' are also as in those regulations.

See 1.12 as to 'constructed' and 'adapted'. A vehicle can be reconstructed so that it joins another class (*Keeble* v *Miller* [1950] 1 All ER 261). Adaptation, seemingly, is insufficient to change a goods vehicle to a passenger one, however; there must be a major reconstruction (*Fry* v *Bevan* (1937) 81 SJ 60). Fitting a different body could be a major reconstruction (*Burrows* v *Berry* (1949) 113 JP Jo 492). Fitting a container to a tractor or locomotive would not convert it to a goods vehicle and, in view of para 4, Part IV of Sched 6, it seems doubtful if such an adaptation would allow such vehicles to go at the same speed as goods vehicles. See *Plume* v *Suckling* below.

Weight is calculated pursuant to s 194 of the 1972 Act (see that section and Chapter 1), even though this may result in a vehicle being of a different unladen weight under the Vehicles (Excise) Act.

### A *Passenger vehicles and motor caravans*

Ordinary, ie passenger-carrying, motor cars of an unladen weight not exceeding 3.05 tonnes and motor cycles and motor cycle combinations, provided they are adapted to carry not more than eight passengers exclusive of the driver, and motor caravans are not subject to any special speed limit applicable to the class, unless drawing trailers. The speed limits for other passenger-carrying vehicles are indicated in Sched 6. Passenger vehicles, motor caravans and dual-purpose vehicles with an unladen weight exceeding 3.05 tonnes or adapted to carry more than eight passengers exclusive of the driver are subject to a 70 mph limit on motorways. At present this makes no material difference as this is the overall maximum. They are subject to a 60 mph limit on dual-carriageways and 50 mph on other roads. If they exceed 12 m in overall length they are subject as well to a 60 mph limit on motorways. Unlike goods vehicles and car derived vans the reference is to unladen weight.

If they are drawing one trailer they (and also car derived vans) are subject to a 50 mph limit on all roads including motorways and if more than one trailer to 40 mph on motorways and 20 mph on all other roads including dual-carriageways.

The distinction between a vehicle being used under a PSV operator's licence and a passenger vehicle being used otherwise has been abolished.

'Passenger vehicle' is defined by the Construction and Use Regulations for this purpose as a vehicle 'constructed solely for the carriage of passengers and their effects'. As to 'constructed', 'passenger' and 'trailer', see Chapter 1. A goods vehicle adapted to carry passengers is not so 'constructed'. Further, a vehicle must be constructed 'solely' to carry passengers and a utility vehicle made to carry passengers or goods is not constructed 'solely' to carry passengers even if goods are never in fact carried (*Hubbard* v *Messenger* [1937] 4 All ER 48). Unless, as will often be the case now, it is a dual-purpose vehicle, as defined in the Schedule, a utility vehicle will generally be classed as a goods vehicle; cf *Taylor* v *Thompson* [1956] 1 All ER 352.

In *Plume* v *Suckling* [1977] RTR 271 a coach adapted to carry six passengers, kitchen equipment and a stock car was held to be a 'goods vehicle' and restricted to 40 mph under what is now para 2(8). The defendant had converted the coach to carry his family, kitchen equipment and a stock car at weekends, which the justices had held to constitute 'passengers and their effects'. Eveleigh J stated that 'passenger effects are things which one would readily and normally recognise as accompanying a passenger. A stock car is not such' (ibid, at p 275J).

*B Goods vehicles*

Goods vehicles by Part IV of Sched 6 have the same meaning as in s 196(1) of the 1972 Act. They are therefore vehicles constructed or adapted for use for the carriage of goods or burden of any description. As to 'constructed or adapted', see 1.12 and also below. Car derived vans (see below) are treated separately and it is necessary therefore to check first that the goods vehicle is not a car derived van.

Goods vehicles (not drawing trailers) having a maximum laden weight of 7.5 tonnes or less are not subject to any special speed limits on motorways and may therefore travel at up to 70 mph. They are subject to a 60 mph limit on dual-carriageways and 50 mph on other roads.

All goods vehicles drawing one trailer where the maximum laden weight of goods vehicle and trailer together is 7.5 tonnes or less and all articulated vehicles of whatever weight up to 7.5 tonnes are subject to a 60 mph limit on motorways and to 50 mph on dual-carriageways as well as to 50 mph on other roads.

All goods vehicles (whether or not drawing a trailer with an aggregate maximum laden weight exceeding 7.5 tonnes and all articulated vehicles again with an aggregate maximum laden weight exceeding 7.5 tonnes are subject to a 60 mph limit on motorways, 50 mph on dual-carriageways and 40 mph on other roads. Goods motor vehicles carrying more than one trailer are subject to a 40 mph limit on motorways and 20 mph on all other roads including dual-carriageways.

There are special limits for vehicles which have a wheel or wheels not fitted with pneumatic tyres and for track-laying vehicles. Motor cycles with side-cars made to carry goods may be goods vehicles and therefore subject to goods vehicle limits when drawing a trailer. See also under 'car derived vans' below. Works trucks and industrial tractors are restricted to 18 mph on all roads. Other motor tractors, light locomotives and heavy locomotives are restricted (with or without one trailer) to 40 mph on motorways and 30 mph on all other roads including dual-carriageways, if they (including any trailer) have the springs and wings specified in Part IV of Sched 6. If not or if drawing more than one trailer, they are limited to 20 mph on all roads including motorways.

It will be seen that motor tractors are now subject to stringent limits including limits on motorways. A motor tractor is defined by s 136 of the Road Traffic Regulation Act 1984 as a motor vehicle which is not constructed itself to carry a load, other than excepted articles as there specified and of which the weight unladen does not exceed 7,370 kg.

The limits apply whether the vehicle is carrying goods or not and whether it has a goods vehicle licence or not and whatever its unladen weight, save that dual-purpose vehicles, as defined below, are treated in the same way as passenger vehicles. The speed limit for tower wagons, sound-recording vans, breakdown lorries and vehicles fitted with a special appliance or apparatus is discussed at 121 JP Jo 479; such items are by s 137(3) not goods or burden. Generally, such vehicles will carry goods also and can be found to be goods vehicles. A chassis, while remaining a motor vehicle, was held not to be subject to any limit, as it did not come within any of the types there specified (*Millard* v *Turvey* [1968] 2 All ER 7). This still seems to be the position. A vehicle constructed solely to carry passengers and their effects and not adapted to carry goods will remain a passenger vehicle and subject only to the limits (if any) prescribed for such vehicles even though it carries goods which are not the 'effects' of the passengers. Dual-purpose vehicles (below) are also treated on the same basis as passenger vehicles.

Goods vehicles must comply with speed limits at all times, whether or not they are carrying goods, because the test is not whether goods are actually carried but whether the vehicle is constructed or adapted for the carriage of goods or burden of any description, not including dual-purpose vehicles. In *Bryson* v *Rogers* [1956] 2 All ER 826, a farmer's Austin pick-up van, which did not conform to the definition of dual-purpose vehicle, as defined below, was held to be subject to a goods vehicle speed limit although it was not carrying goods. A van adapted to carry passengers and with no shelves for goods was held not to be a goods vehicle (see *Tait* v *Odhams Press*, a case on goods vehicles licensing, and the other cases noted at 13.7). In *Levinson* v *Powell* [1967] 3 All ER 796, a taxi was held not to be a goods vehicle, though it may be a dual-purpose one.

'Goods' is not confined to goods for sale or delivery; it includes a window-cleaner's ladders, rags and buckets (*Clarke* v *Cherry* [1953] 1 All ER 267) and effluent (*Sweetway Sanitary Cleansers* v *Bradley* [1961] 2 All ER 821); in *Bourne* v *Norwich Crematorium Ltd* [1967] 1 WLR 691, at p 695 (a tax case), it was held that corpses are not 'goods', though it was argued that coffins and shrouds might be and reference was made to a case where dogs were held to be goods.

*C Car derived vans*

The restrictions on goods vehicles do not apply to car derived vans. 'Car derived vans' by Sched 6, Part IV are goods vehicles which are constructed or adapted as a derivative of a passenger vehicle and which have a maximum laden weight not exceeding 2 tonnes. Strangely enough despite the use of the word 'van', this definition is wide enough to include a motor cycle constructed or adapted to carry goods. Although it will be a question of fact, such a vehicle might well be regarded as being derived from a passenger vehicle. The position will be relevant if a trailer is being drawn on a motorway and curiously the limit is lower (50 mph instead of 60 mph) if it is classified as a car derived van.

The only restrictions on these vehicles as a class are when drawing one trailer (50 mph on all roads including motorways) and when drawing more than one trailer (40 mph on motorways and 20 mph on dual-carriageways and other roads).

As to 'constructed' and 'adapted' see 1.12. It will be noted that the reference is to *laden* weight. Car derived vans have been omitted from item 1 in Sched 6. This would only be material in the unlikely event of a car derived van being both a goods vehicle and at the same time a vehicle adapted to carry more than eight passengers exclusive of the driver but not within the narrower definition of a dual-purpose vehicle. Such a car derived van would not be subject to the item 1 limits.

*D Dual-purpose vehicles*

'Dual-purpose vehicle' has the same meaning as in the Motor Vehicles (Construction and Use) Regulations, reg 3(1). All dual-purpose vehicles must not exceed 2,040 kg in unladen weight. The reference to unladen weight should be contrasted to goods vehicles where the position depends on maximum laden weight for the purposes of Sched 6. They must be 'constructed or adapted' etc and this expression is interpreted differently from and should be contrasted with the expression 'constructed solely' which is used in the definition of passenger vehicles, and to 'adapted' by itself used for dual-purpose vehicles in Sched 6, item 1. As to the meaning of 'constructed or adapted' see 1.12.

Dual-purpose vehicles are treated exactly the same in Sched 6 as passenger vehicles and motor caravans and not as goods vehicles regardless of whether or not they are carrying goods.

They are basically exempt from speed limits relating to the type of vehicle. In effect these limits will only apply if they are adapted to carry more than eight passengers excluding the driver or if they are drawing one or more trailers. As to 'passengers' see 1.59.

They include shooting brakes and utility vehicles. Vehicles so constructed or adapted that the driving power of the engine is, or by the appropriate use of the controls can be, transmitted to all the wheels are also included providing the unladen weight does not exceed 2,040 kg and there are an increasing number of such vehicles. Examples are Range Rovers, Land Rovers, Jeeps, certain similar Japanese vehicles and those designed to go over rough ground as well as on roads, not being track laying vehicles; and they are dual-purpose vehicles whether or not they comply with the conditions as to construction specified in the Construction and Use Regulations, eg rigid roofs, transverse seats, etc (*Kidson* v *Swatridge* [1957] Crim LR 193). Shooting brakes and utility vehicles without four-wheel drive must comply with those conditions to obtain the relevant exemptions from speed limits when not on restricted roads. A van had been adapted to be a 'dual-purpose vehicle' by adding windows, but its windows were covered by panels of wood screwed into the windows so as to obscure them entirely. It was held that the van had been adapted to become a dual-purpose vehicle and that is was not subject to any limit as a goods vehicle (*Popperwell* v *Cockerton* [1968] 1 All ER 1038). In *Levinson* v *Powell* [1967] 3 All ER 769 a taxi was held to be a dual-purpose vehicle, but each vehicle would have to be inspected to see if it did fall within the definition in the regulations.

Four-wheel-drive vehicles are excluded from the definition of 'dual-purpose vehicle' in respect of the Type Approval Regulations (see 8.6). This provision in the Type Approval Regulations does not appear to affect in any way the meaning of the expression in Sched 6 or the definition in the Construction and Use Regulations.

If a vehicle, though constructed or adapted to carry goods and passengers, does not come within the definitions given, eg because its unladen weight exceeds 2,040 kg or it has a non-rigid roof or its seats run lengthways and not transversely, it will under the regulations be a goods vehicle, whether or not it is carrying goods (*Bryson* v *Rogers* [1956] 2 All ER 826).

*E Articulated vehicles and trailers*

The lower limits laid down when a vehicle draws a trailer will be noted. The limits for these vehicles have been set out above under the various types. In effect while there are special provisions for goods vehicles, the requirements for passenger vehicles, motor caravans, dual-purpose vehicles and car derived vans are the same, ie, restricted to 50 mph on all roads including motorways when drawing one trailer. The need for a 50 mph trailer plate has been abolished.

The position should be contrasted with certain goods vehicles with one trailer and articulated goods vehicles with in each case an aggregate maximum laden weight of up to 7.5 tonnes. These may go faster (up to 60 mph) on motorways. Other goods vehicles and articulated goods vehicles have lower maximum speed limits depending on the circumstances.

Passenger vehicles, motor caravans, dual-purpose vehicles, car derived vans and goods vehicles (unless having a lower maximum limit) are all limited when drawing more than one trailer to 40 mph on motorways and 20 mph on other roads including dual-carriageways.

An articulated goods vehicle is defined for the purpose of Sched 6 by reg 3(1) of the Motor Vehicles (Construction and Use) Regulations and is not treated as a vehicle drawing a trailer but as a single vehicle. Articulated buses are excluded.

This definition is somewhat different from and less comprehensive than that in ss 190(9) and 191 of the 1972 Act and ss 137(2) and 136 of the 1984 Act and this could give rise to problems.

The only specific reference to articulated vehicles in Sched 6 is under goods vehicles and the definition in the Construction and Use Regulations applies to such goods vehicles. Other vehicles including buses may be articulated and the Construction and Use Regulations' definition of an articulated vehicle will not apply, and the definition in ss 137(2) and 136 will normally apply instead. Such vehicles are again treated as one vehicle.

A vehicle and trailer closely coupled together not being an articulated vehicle, do not thereby become one vehicle (*Dixon* v *BRS* (*Pickford*) *Ltd* [1959] 1 All ER 449). A car towing a two-wheeled caravan with the aid of a 'van-dolly', ie a small chassis with two wheels, is towing a four-wheeled trailer (*Brown* v *Dando* (1954) 118 JP Jo 319). A trailer and car amalgamated into one four-wheeled rigid unit is one trailer not two (*Baker* v *Esau* [1972] Crim LR 559).

Many caravans are drawn by passenger or dual-purpose vehicles and as trailers come under para 1.

### 6.31–2 Motorway speed limits

The motorway speed limits for certain classes of vehicle have been set out above, 6.30, under the various classes. See Sched 6 of the 1984 Act in Vol 2. Where there is an overall lower maximum motorway speed limit (see below) this lower maximum will apply instead.

For the vehicles which may lawfully travel on a motorway see 6.38.

The temporary speed limits of 50, 60 and 70 mph do not and could not apply to motorways as the enabling section of the Act under which the order was made does not apply to motorways (s 88 of the Road Traffic Regulation Act 1984). Vehicles not already subject to a lower speed limit by virtue of Sched 6 are subject to an overall maximum limit of 70 mph on motorways by virtue of the Motorways Traffic (Speed Limit) Regulations 1974 (SI 1974 No 502). These regulations provide for an overall motorway limit of 70 mph and also special overall limits of 50 and 60 mph on particular stretches of various motorways as set out in Schedules to the order as amended. The 1974 Regulations are not temporary or limited in time and are made by virtue of s 13 of the Act. See also 'Temporary speed restrictions for road works etc', 6.29.

## Speed Limits: Proceedings and Penalties

### 6.33 Warning of intended prosecution

Warning of intended prosecution is required for speeding offences 'punishable' by virtue of s 89 and s 17(4) of the Road Traffic Regulation Act 1984 and offences of failing to observe a minimum speed limit under s 88(7) (see

Chapter 3). Such a warning is not seemingly required for prosecutions for contravening temporary speed restrictions for road works etc (s 14 offences).

## 6.34 Temporary speed restrictions for road works etc

The court in *Platten* v *Gowing* [1983] Crim LR 184 drew a distinction between *temporary speed restriction* under ss 14–16 and the more *general speed limits*. A temporary speed restriction must always be lower than the relevant speed limit. If the speed limit is contravened as well a person will commit two offences and the prosecuting authorities may proceed for the contravention of the speed limit offence, if they so wish, provided a notice of intended prosecution has been given and corroborative evidence exists (ibid). Notices of intended prosecution (see Chapter 3) and corroboration (see s 89(2)) both relate to speed limit offences and as indicated in *Platten* v *Gowing* would not seem to be required for temporary restriction offences. Section 89(2) (corroboration) is not specified against s 16(1) (the penalty subsection) in Sched 7. Cf the entry against s 89(1) where it is specified.

As to two convictions from one incident see below.

## 6.35 Proceedings generally

In *Welton* v *Taneborne* (1908) 72 JP 419 a conviction for driving in a dangerous manner, where the court had taken into consideration the defendant's speed, was held to bar a subsequent prosecution for exceeding the speed limit. In that case both summonses had been preferred together, but the dangerous driving charge was heard first and upon the conviction being announced, the police desired to proceed on the speeding charge also. It would seem, however, that, if there had been an acquittal on the graver charge, this would not necessarily bar the speeding one. See also 'Two offences from one incident' at 5.49.

## 6.36–7 Penalties

The penalty for an offence of exceeding a speed limit punishable by virtue of s 89, ie imposed by or under the Road Traffic Regulation Act 1984 (except s 17(2) and (4) (ie except the 70 mph etc overall limit on motorways)), the Parks Regulation (Amendment) Act 1926, s 2, or any Act passed after 1 September 1960, is a fine of level 3 (s 89 and Sched 7). The offender's driving licence must be endorsed unless there are special reasons (see Chapter 21). The offence carries 3 penalty points. The offender may be disqualified for any period at the court's discretion. The court may also order the defendant to be disqualified until he passes a driving test (1972 Act, s 93(7)) (see 20.32). Section 19 of the Transport Act 1981 (penalty points disqualification) applies to endorsable offences of exceeding a speed limit (see 20.18–21 and Chapter 21 on 'Mitigating circumstances'). The same penalties apply to aiders, abettors and inciters.

The maximum penalty for exceeding the overall 70 mph etc limits on a motorway is a fine of level 4 (s 17(4) and Sched 7), but is a fine of level 3 in respect of goods and other vehicles exceeding the various limits for particular classes of vehicles on motorways in contravention of Sched 6 to the 1984 Act (s 89 and Sched 7). Both offences carry discretionary disqualification, obligatory endorsement and 3 penalty points (as above).

The maximum fine for offences of failing to observe a minimum speed limit is level 3 (s 88(7) and Sched 7). There is no power to order endorsement, disqualification or penalty points.

The penalty for failing to observe a temporary speed restriction for road works etc contrary to s 14 of the 1984 Act is a fine of level 3 (s 16(1) and Sched 7). The offence does not require corroboration or warning of intended prosecution, nor may the offender be disqualified or have his licence endorsed or receive penalty points. See 'Temporary speed restrictions for road works etc', 6.34 and the comments on *Platten* v *Gowing* discussed there.

The endorsement codes for speeding offences are as follows:

| | |
|---|---|
| Exceeding speed limit for type of vehicle | SP20 |
| Exceeding statutory limit on road | SP30 |
| Exceeding passenger vehicle speed limit | SP40 |
| Exceeding speed limit on a motorway | SP50 |

The Magistrates' Association's suggested penalties (see 18.1 and Appendix 3) for speeding offences read as follows: '£2 per mph over any limit. More for heavy vehicles. Consider disqualification if 30 mph over limit.'

## Motorways

### 6.38–9 Generally

The only vehicles which may lawfully use the motorways at all times are those in Classes I and II in Sched 4 to the Highways Act 1980 or Sched 2 to the Special Roads Act 1949. (The two schedules are in identical terms.)

Class I vehicles are heavy and light locomotives, heavy motor cars, motor cars and motor cycles with engine or cylinder capacity not less than 50 cc which comply with the Construction and Use Regulations and satisfy various conditions. Trailers drawn by such vehicles are also included in the class. Class II vehicles include motor vehicles and trailers authorised to carry abnormal indivisible loads; certain motor vehicles and trailers constructed for the purposes of the armed forces or defence purposes; and motor vehicles and trailers to which art 15, 16 or 19 of the Motor Vehicles (Authorisation of Special Types) General Order 1979 (SI 1979 No 1198) applies, which are authorised to be used and which are capable of attaining a speed of 25 mph on the level, unladen and when not drawing a trailer.

The remaining classes may only use a motorway in accordance with reg 15 of the Motorways Traffic (England and Wales) Regulations 1982 (SI 1982 No 1163) as amended by the like named Amendment Regulations (SI 1983 No 374 and SI 1984 No 1479) (emergencies, repairs etc). Class III consists of motor vehicles controlled by pedestrians and Class IV of all motor vehicles (other than invalid carriages and motor cycles less than 50 cc) not comprised in Classes I–III. 'Abnormal indivisible load' in Class II has the same meaning as in the Motor Vehicles (Authorisation of Special Types) General Order 1979.

Curiously a 50 cc motor cycle may be used on a motorway even though it may be classified as a moped (see 1.6*F*). As to invalid carriages, certain vehicles are treated as invalid carriages *for certain purposes* (see 1.5), eg carriages for invalids exceeding 254 kg but not exceeding 10 cwt are treated as invalid carriages for the purpose of Part III of the 1972 Act (driving licences and driving tests). As expressions in Sched 4 to the Highways Act 1980 have the same meaning as in the 1972 Act, it is submitted that such invalid carriages are *not* therefore excluded from motorways.

The use of a motorway by a vehicle of a class or type excluded from motorways is an offence contrary to s 17 of the Road Traffic Regulation Act 1984.

Special speed limits for certain classes of vehicles on motorways are prescribed by Sched 6 of the Road Traffic Regulation Act 1984 but the law relating to speed limits generally is otherwise applicable (see the previous section on Speed Limits).

Contravention of the red flashing motorway signs is dealt with in the section relating to traffic lights at 6.4, 'Motorway traffic lights'.

Certain of the cases in Chapter 5 relate to motorways (see notably *Trentham* v *Rowlands* at 5.46).

Where the prosecution omitted before closing their case to prove that a motorway was a 'special road' in accordance with the Special Roads (Notice of Opening) Regulations 1962, made under what is now s 17(2) of the Road Traffic Regulation Act 1984, and also to prove the regulations, the justices were directed that they had a discretion to allow the prosecution to re-open their case and should exercise their discretion in favour of the prosecution as the evidence was purely of a formal nature (*Royal* v *Prescott-Clarke* [1966] 2 All ER 366), despite the fact that the defence had given the prosecution notice prior to the hearing that formal proof of these matters would have to be given.

Standing on any part of a motorway is an offence contrary to reg 13 of the Motorways Traffic Regulations 1982, but in *Reed* v *Wastie* [1972] Crim LR 221 it was held that it was also wilful obstruction of a highway contrary to what is now s 137 of the Highways Act 1980, and that a constable could therefore lawfully arrest a person who was standing on the carriageway causing danger to himself and others and who had refused to move when requested to do so.

The Motorways Traffic Regulations 1982 contain many prohibitions and the regulations should in each particular case be referred to. The definitions include specific definitions of 'carriageway', 'hard shoulder' and 'verge'. Carriageway is no longer that part constructed with a surface suitable for the regular passage of motor vehicles, but that part provided for them. It has been suggested that the change is merely an acceptance of reality. The definitions are such that the hard shoulder is not part of the carriageway and is no longer part of the verge. The verge in turn means 'any part of a motorway which is not a carriageway, a hard shoulder, or a central reservation.'

Regulation 7 contains restrictions on stopping on carriageways, and where a vehicle has to stop on a motorway by reason of an emergency or other circumstances set out in reg 7(2), it is required to be driven or moved on to a hard shoulder. Regulation 9 makes it an offence for a vehicle to be driven or to stop on a hard shoulder unless the circumstances set out in reg 7(2) or (3) exist.

One of the grounds set out in reg 7(2) justifying a motorist stopping on the hard shoulder is 'by reason of any accident, illness or other emergency' (reg 7(2)(*b*)). A motorist, when a mile from a motorway, began to feel drowsy but reached the slip road to the motorway before he saw a place to park his car. Knowing that the next motorway intersection was ten miles further on he parked his car at the side of the slip road. It was held that the element of suddenness was not to be emphasised in the meaning of 'emergency' in reg 7(2)(*b*) but the emergency must arise after the defendant had entered the motorway system and he should therefore be convicted as he felt drowsy before he reached the motorway slip road (*Higgins* v *Bernard* [1972] RTR 304). The conviction of a defendant praying in the direction of Mecca who had stopped his vehicle on a motorway is reported in *The Times* on 8 February 1980.

Other offences contained in the regulations are reversing (reg 8), using the central reservation or verge (reg 10), driving by learner drivers (reg 11). The learner drivers excluded under reg 11 do not include HGV licence learners if they have passed the ordinary driving licence test.

Vehicles now excluded from the outside lane of a motorway with three or more operational lanes are listed in reg 12. The prohibited vehicles are goods vehicles with an operating weight exceeding 7.5 tonnes, passenger vehicles with an overall length exceeding 12 m, vehicles drawing a trailer and other vehicles (excluding passenger vehicles) which are heavy motor cars, motor tractors or light or heavy locomotives. See the Motorways Traffic Regulations in Vol 2 for the full wording. 'Goods vehicle' and 'operating weight' are as defined in s 138 of the 1984 Act and basically the operating weight is the maximum laden weight. The exclusion does not apply when it is necessary to use the outside lane to pass a vehicle carrying a load of exceptional width.

Regulation 15 allows vehicles otherwise excluded from the motorway to use it in the circumstances set out in the regulation and reg 16 contains exceptions and relaxations of the regulations for certain purposes or in certain circumstances.

## Motorways: Penalties

### 6.40 Generally

All offences under the Motorways Regulations and under s 17 of the Road Traffic Regulation Act 1984 (this includes the driving of excluded vehicles on motorways) are purely summary offences punishable under s 17(4) and Sched 7 of the Road Traffic Regulation Act 1984. All offences under s 17(4) are punishable with a fine of level 4. Offences committed in respect of motor vehicles subject to the exceptions below carry obligatory endorsement (in the absence of 'special reasons': see Chapter 21), optional disqualification and 3 penalty points.

The only motor vehicle offences which do not carry disqualification, endorsement or penalty points are specified in the relevant part of Sched 4 of the 1972 Act as unlawfully *stopping* or allowing the vehicle to *remain at rest* on a part of the motorway on which vehicles are in certain circumstances permitted to *rest*. Unlike the first part, the last part of this refers only to *resting* and not to *stopping*. Vehicles are permitted to rest in certain circumstances on the hard shoulder (see regs 7 and 9) and on the carriageway (see reg 7(4)). As the offence is unlawfully stopping or resting it must be something different from lawfully stopping or resting. Vehicles are prohibited from stopping or resting on the central reservation and on the verge by reg 10. On this basis reg 7(1) and 9 offences of unlawfully stopping or remaining at rest on a carriageway or hard shoulder respectively do not carry endorsement, disqualification or penalty points, but unlawfully *driving* on to a hard shoulder contrary to reg 9 and unlawfully stopping or remaining at rest on a verge or central reservation contrary to reg 10 do carry endorsement etc. In some cases a vehicle may be unlawfully driven on to a hard shoulder in order to stop or rest unlawfully. In other cases the initial driving on to the hard shoulder may be within the regulations and the stopping or resting offence committed subsequently.

Offences committed not in respect of a motor vehicle (eg reg 13) are not endorsable or disqualifiable but now attract the same penalty (level 4) as offences committed in respect of motor vehicles. Where a court is required to endorse the offender's licence the court may also disqualify, and, under s 93(7), order the offender to take a test. Section 19 of the Transport Act 1981 (penalty points disqualification: see 20.18–21) also applies to a conviction for an endorsable motorway offence.

The endorsement code for all motorway offences other than speed limits is MW 10. Exceeding a speed limit on a motorway is SP 50.

Motorway offences are included in the list of recommended penalties published by the Magistrates' Association (see generally 18.1 and items 43–52 in Appendix 3). It should be noted that the list no longer recommends heavier penalties for contravention of the Construction and Use Regulations committed on motorways.

## Pedestrian Crossings

### 6.41 Generally

Section 25 of the Road Traffic Regulation Act 1984 empowers the Secretary of State to make regulations as to pedestrian crossings.

There are two basic types of crossing created by regulations made under s 25: 'uncontrolled' crossings (now termed 'zebra' crossings) and controlled crossings, ie controlled by pedestrian-operated push buttons (now termed 'pelican' crossings).

There are special provisions as to pedestrians going on parts of the carriageway of certain streets in London. These are contained in the Controlled Areas (Pedestrians) Regulations 1965 (SI 1965 No 545). They are not, however, made by virtue of s 25 of the 1984 Act but under s 6 and are not relevant in this context.

By s 25(6) a crossing shall be deemed to be duly established and indicated unless the contrary be proved.

## 6.42 Uncontrolled or 'zebra' crossings

Zebra crossings are regulated by the 'Zebra' Pedestrian Crossings Regulations 1971 (SI 1971 No 1524). The regulations prescribe the road markings for the crossing, the controlled areas and the appropriate traffic signs together with the various offences (see Sched 2).

The regulations apply to the drivers of motor vehicles, trams, trolley vehicles and horse-drawn vehicles and to the riders of motor cycles and cycles (save as indicated in reg 12) but not to equestrians. Save as provided in reg 14, there is no exemption for fire engines, ambulances or police cars. The regulations apply to Crown vehicles (s 130 of the 1984 Act).

By reg 4 every crossing and its limits shall be indicated in accordance with the provisions of Sched 2. This means that every crossing shall be indicated by two lines of studs placed across the roadway in accordance with Part I of Sched 2. There the distances apart, the colour, size, shape and permitted projection of the studs are prescribed and by para 2 a crossing or its limits shall not be deemed to have ceased to be indicated by reason only of the discoloration or temporary removal or displacing of one or more studs in any line so long as the general indication of the line is not thereby materially impaired. Paragraph 1(2) and (3) save crossings which comply for the most part as respects the studs and distances apart.

The crossing must also be indicated by black and white stripes on the crossing (para 4). Paragraph 4(1) allows the omission of black painted stripes where the surface of the road provides a reasonable contrast to the white stripes. By para 4(3) the provisions as to the width and extent of the stripes shall be regarded as having been complied with though they may not have been so complied with as respects one or more of the stripes, and disregarding any imperfection, discoloration or partial displacement of one or more of the stripes, so long as the general appearance of the stripes is not materially impaired.

Paragraph 1 and para 2(1) of Part II of Sched 2 require the crossing also to be indicated by yellow globes mounted on posts or brackets. Although there must be a yellow globe at or near each end of the crossing, there need not be globes on any central reservation or street refuge but such globes *may* be placed there. If globes are not placed on a central reservation, the crossing would appear to be sufficiently indicated. The globes are required to be illuminated by flashing lights or, where so authorised by the Secretary of State for Transport, by a constant light. But by para 3 a crossing shall not cease to be properly indicated by reason only of the imperfection, discoloration or disfigurement of any of the posts, globes or brackets or the failure of the illumination of the globes. If, however, the illumination of *all* the globes fails, then the proviso to para 3(*b*) has the effect of removing the protection of para 3. Where therefore there is not at least one globe illuminated, the crossing is not indicated as required by the regulations and a motorist may not be convicted of failing to accord precedence. Paragraph 2(2) and (4) prescribe the limits of dimensions of the globes, their height above ground, and the alternate black and white horizontal stripes on the posts. Where a globe is mounted on a bracket, the bracket does not have to be striped. It is only posts specially provided for the purpose of bearing globes which are required to be painted black and white.

Schedule 3 contains provisions prescribing the manner in which the zebra controlled area and 'give way' lines are to be indicated. Regulation 5(3) enabled the appropriate authority to dispense with the necessity of a controlled area by the giving of a notice before 30 November 1973 to the Secretary of State for Transport. A broken white line (the 'give way' line) must be placed one metre each side of the crossing and two or more longitudinal white lines ('zig-zag' lines) must be placed on each side of the crossing indicating the controlled area. The schedule prescribes the dimensions of the signs and reg 6 prescribes the permitted variations in the dimensions. By para 7 of Sched 3 the controlled area and its limits are sufficiently indicated despite the imperfection, discoloration or displacement of any of the lines so long as the general indication of such line is not materially impaired.

There are various provisos in Scheds 2 and 3 whereby studs, lines etc comply 'so long as the general indication . . . is not materially impaired'; if it is, it is submitted that no offence can be committed (cf *Power* v *Davidson* (1964) 62 LGR 320 at 6.46–51 and see 'Non-conforming and damaged signs', 6.13).

The failure of the illumination of a lamp provided under reg 7 would not appear to invalidate the crossing because the regulation does not make it mandatory to provide such a lamp.

The Road Traffic Regulation Act 1984, s 25(4), allows special provisions to be made in regard to particular crossings (note also the provisions as to variation contained in paras 3 and 4 of Sched 3).

*The 'limits' of a zebra crossing*

The 'limits' of a zebra crossing referred to in reg 4 of the regulations are defined by the studs across the road on each side of the black and white stripes (Sched 2, Part I, para 1(1)), and a vehicle has not come 'within the limits of a crossing' under reg 4 if it has come within the zig-zag lines marking the approach to the crossing but has not reached the studs bordering the black and white stripes (*Moulder* v *Neville* [1974] RTR 53, a case on the 1971 Regulations, following *Hughes* v *Hall* [1960] 2 All ER 504, a similar decision on the 1954 Regulations). A pedestrian is seemingly outside the limits of the crossing if he is outside the studs but within the 'give way' line which is one metre away. It seems that the effect of the 'give way' line is not to extend the limits of the crossing but to indicate to the motorist where he should stop to accord precedence to a pedestrian who is on the black and white stripes of the crossing.

Note the provision in reg 8 as to the parts of a zebra crossing on each side of a street refuge or central reservation being treated as separate crossings for the purposes of that regulation.

## 6.43 According precedence at zebra crossings

This is dealt with by reg 8 of the 1971 Regulations. The definition of 'uncontrolled crossing' is in reg 3(1) and see *Wright* v *Hunt* below. If the crossing is for the time being controlled by a policeman in uniform or by a traffic warden the crossing ceases to be 'uncontrolled' and the provisions relating to pedestrians being accorded precedence and motorists being forbidden to overtake cease, but vehicles and pedestrians must obey the policeman's or traffic warden's signals (see further below) and failure to do so may result in prosecution under s 22, s 23 or s 159 of the 1972 Act.

Liability under reg 8 arises only if the pedestrian is on the carriageway within the limits of the crossing before the vehicle or any part of it has come on the carriageway within those limits, ie, the black and white striped area inside the innermost lines of studs. See above as to the 'limits' of a crossing. A pedestrian waiting on the kerb or walking along the roadway towards the crossing is thus not within reg 8. It is essential not to be confused between the 'limits' of the crossing and the 'zebra-controlled area', ie the area of carriageway, bordered by zig-zag lines both sides of the actual crossing (see 6.44 as to the zebra-controlled area). Justices who dismissed a case of failing to accord precedence under reg 8 because they were not certain whether the motorist reached the beginnings of the zebra-controlled area before the pedestrian stepped on the actual crossing were directed to convict the motorist (*Moulder* v *Neville* [1974] RTR 53); a case can only be dismissed under reg 8 if the prosecution fail to prove that the foot passenger stepped onto the actual crossing before the car reached the actual limits of the crossing, ie the black and white striped area.

Regulation 5(2) requires the motorist to stop at or before the 'give way' line, which is one metre from the limits of the crossing, in order to accord the pedestrian precedence, and he will offend against reg 8 if he does not do so.

Where there is a central reservation or street refuge in a crossing, the parts on each side of the reservation or refuge are treated as separate crossings (reg 8). A motorist approaching a crossing on the left hand side of a road thus owes no duty under reg 8 to a pedestrian who is walking from the right-hand kerb towards a central reservation.

If a zebra crossing is for the time being controlled by a police officer or traffic warden, again reg 8 will not apply, and the driver or rider of a vehicle must obey the police officer's signals. The reason for this provision seems to be that pedestrians who themselves disobey the warning gestures of a police officer thereby put themselves in peril, and to cast a double duty on a motorist of both obeying a police officer and according precedence to a pedestrian would be unfair. A High Court decision noted at (1966) 130 JP Jo 759 is that a crossing is not controlled by a police officer when the latter is standing on the pavement at the crossing but has not begun controlling the traffic, even if he is about to do so. A policeman was on a school crossing patrol at a pedestrian crossing. He only stopped the traffic when children or sometimes the elderly wanted to cross. When he did so other adults crossed the road. At other times he allowed the traffic to continue and a motorist driving across at this time was convicted of failing to accord precedence to a pedestrian. The motorist thought the pedestrian should have waited for the policeman to indicate that he should cross. A Crown Court judge sitting with justices at the Inner London Crown Court dismissed an appeal against conviction by magistrates but found special reasons for not endorsing as the motorist had been misled. The Crown Court held that the crossing was not controlled all the time and was not controlled when his vehicle passed. The decision is not binding: whether a crossing is controlled is very much a question of fact.

In *Kayser* v *LPTB* [1950] 1 All ER 231, a case on the pre-1951 regulations, it was held that, where a driver is satisfied that persons on the crossing are out of danger from him, he may proceed at a reasonable speed. Compare *Wishart* v *McDonald* below.

In *McKerrell* v *Robertson* [1956] SLT 290 it was held that precedence must be accorded to a woman pushing a go-chair when the go-chair is on the crossing, although she is still on the pavement: she and the go-chair are one entity. The case is discussed at 125 JP Jo 341 of a pedestrian on a crossing who does not wish to cross.

A magistrates' court has held that a child on roller-skates is not a 'foot passenger'. It is submitted that this decision is correct. In the absence of a definition a 'foot passenger' must mean someone on foot. Cyclists who push their cycles across uncontrolled pedestrian crossings are pedestrians (*Crank* v *Brookes* [1980] RTR 441). '[A person] with both feet on the ground, so to speak, is clearly a foot passenger. If for example she had been using [the bicycle] as a scooter by having one foot on the pedal and pushing herself along, she would not have been a foot passenger' (per Waller LJ at p 443).

*Absolute liability of driver*

Subject to the limited exceptions given in *Burns* v *Bidder*, below, the duty of the motorist, cyclist or other driver to accord precedence is absolute.

In *Neal* v *Reynolds* (1966) 110 SJ 353, it was said that magistrates should not approach these prosecutions on the basis whether the defendant driver was negligent or not. In *Burns* v *Bidder* [1966] 3 All ER 29, the cases were all reviewed again and James J said:

> Regulation 4 must be read 'subject to the principle of impossibility' . . . In my judgment the regulation does not impose an absolute duty come what may, and there is no breach [of it] in circumstances where the driver fails to accord precedence to a pedestrian solely because his control of the vehicle is taken from him by the occurrence of an event which is outside his possible or reasonable control and in respect of which he is in no way at fault. [He instanced the driver being stung by bees or having an epileptic fit or his vehicle being propelled forward by being hit from behind as illustrations of the vehicle's being taken out of the driver's control, so that his failure then to accord precedence would be no offence, and continued] . . . a sudden removal of control over the vehicle occasioned by a latent defect of which the driver did not know and could not reasonably be expected to know would render the resulting failure to accord precedence no offence, provided he is in no way at fault himself. But beyond that limited sphere, the obligation of the driver under the regulations can properly be described . . . as an absolute one.

This case settled the law fairly conclusively as to reg 4 of the 1954 Regulations. Regulation 8 of the 1971 Regulations does not differ materially from reg 4 and it is submitted that *Burns* v *Bidder* still expresses the law. Similar factors were mentioned in *R* v *Bell* (*David*) [1984] Crim LR 685 (a reckless driving case) and it was held that an excuse of being driven on by God was not in that category. Running out of petrol is not a latent defect (*Oakley-Moore* v *Robinson* at 6.44).

In *Gibbons* v *Kahl* [1955] 3 All ER 345 it was said that it is the duty of a driver to be able to stop before he gets to a crossing unless he can see that there is no one on it. If he cannot see if there is anybody on it; he must drive in such a way that he can stop if there is a person on it masked from him by other traffic. In *Gibbons'* case, the defendant overtook a bus, which had stopped at a crossing to allow pedestrians to proceed; the pedestrians were hidden from the defendant by the bus and he did not see them until they had passed in front of the bus. He was then too near the crossing to stop and he was held guilty of not according precedence. This case was followed in *Lockie* v *Lawton* (1960) 124 JP 24, where it was said that a driver approaching a crossing must drive in such a way that he can stop if there is a pedestrian on the crossing, although his view of the crossing may be blocked by other vehicles until he is right on it. In *Hughes* v *Hall* [1960] 2 All ER 504 it was said that there was an absolute duty under the regulations, and it is immaterial whether there is any evidence of negligence or failure to take care by the driver. In *Scott* v *Clint* (1960) *The Times*, 28 October, a driver was approaching a crossing at 15–20 mph and, when he was ten yards from it, two children stepped on it without looking. He swerved but could not avoid hitting one of them. It was held that he was guilty but that it was a proper case for an absolute discharge. The case of *Leicester* v *Pearson* [1952] 2 All ER 71, holding that a driver could be excused if he was driving reasonably and with care in bad visibility, no longer seems to be of authority. In *Hughes* v *Hall* above the driver was approaching the crossing at a proper speed and had passed or partly passed over the approach studs when a pedestrian stepped on the crossing without looking and walked nine or ten feet before being hit by the car, which was rapidly pulling up. As stated, the driver was held guilty, and unless the High Court is prepared to draw a distinction between the cases cited above and cases where a pedestrian steps practically in front of a slow-moving car when it is a foot or so from the crossing, it seems that the driver must always be found guilty if he had not in fact accorded precedence, although an absolute discharge is often justifiable, where the driver is not negligent, and 'special reasons' could be found.

The meaning of the term 'accord precedence' was considered by two metropolitan magistrates, whose views are reported at [1952] Jo Crim L 105 and 110, but should now be read in the light of the cases cited in the last paragraph. In one case the defendant drove between two pedestrians on a zebra crossing; he was driving cautiously and neither pedestrian was endangered. Sir Wilfred Bennett dismissed the charge, holding that 'according precedence' meant much the same as 'not interrupting the free passage of a pedestrian', the term in the pre-1951 regulations. He said that the new regulation required that a driver must not cause a pedestrian to stop once he has started to cross. The expression 'accord precedence' is still used in the current regulations. In the other case, the facts accepted were that the pedestrians were on the crossing but so far away from the defendant's car that he could not have interrupted their crossing. Mr T F Davis apparently did not agree that the law had not been altered and, save for 'suicide cases' (*semble*, people who stepped practically in front of a fast moving car) held that a motorist who could reasonably stop must stop if there are pedestrians on the crossing. In *Rhind* v *Irvine* [1940] 2 WWR 333, a Canadian case, it was held that the motorist's duty to 'yield the right of way' to a pedestrian on a crossing did not give a pedestrian a right to walk into or against an obstructing car or to walk over the crossing with his eyes shut. In *Wishart* v *McDonald* (1962) 78 Sh Ct Rep 3, a driver passed over a crossing while a blind pedestrian was walking over it, the pedestrian being neither impeded by the car nor even aware of it; the sheriff acquitted the driver of not according precedence. The sheriff rejected the view that the regulation means that the pedestrian shall go first over the crossing before the vehicle goes over it. Precedence, he said, means 'go before' or 'in front of' and the regulation means that the vehicle shall not prevent a foot-passenger from crossing; the issue of precedence would arise only where there was a likely encounter between vehicle and pedestrian. A New Zealand regulation required the motorist when approaching a pedestrian crossing to 'yield the right of way' to a pedestrian on it. It was held that a motorist approaching a crossing on which there was a pedestrian must surrender to the latter any priority in passage ahead which he might otherwise have had whether or not a collision might seem likely or however far the pedestrian might be on the crossing to his left and that a pedestrian who had begun to cross and then paused and stopped was still within the protection of the regulation (*Torok* v *Lake* [1964] NZLR 824). In *Kozimor* v *Adey* [1962] Crim LR 564, a civil case, Megaw J said that the only way a motorist can be certain of avoiding a breach of the regulations is to approach the crossing at such a low speed that he can stop in the event of any conceivable use of the crossing by any conceivable pedestrian except a suicidal one who deliberately walked in front of a car. If, therefore, a motorist driving in the centre of a wide street sees a pedestrian step off the kerb, the motorist, it is submitted, must stop if there is any reasonable possibility that the pedestrian might get in the car's path; the fact that the pedestrian is walking so slowly that it is unlikely that he will get in the car's path would not necessarily be an excuse, for he might panic and break into a run. If a pedestrian signals a car to come on and himself stops, it still seems that the driver should accord him precedence as a matter of strict law (*Neal* v *Bedford* [1965] 3 All ER 250), though no doubt it would be strong mitigation if the driver accepted the pedestrian's signal to him to proceed and then the pedestrian dashed forward. In that case pedestrians had stopped to allow a car ahead of the defendant's car to pass in front of them; they moved on when the first car had passed and the defendant's car also came on and struck one of them. The High Court said that reg 4 of the 1954 Regulations imposed an absolute duty to accord precedence and whether the defendant genuinely thought that the pedestrians would let him pass was irrelevant; they had not waived their precedence by signalling to him to pass but had started walking. A conviction was directed. However, in most cases it will turn out to be a question of fact and a motorist, even if he is held to have broken the law, may still have many matters to urge in mitigation of penalty. The question of liability under the 1954 Regulations is discussed in the *Criminal Law Review*, March 1967.

*Defence of mechanical failure etc*

See *Burns* v *Bidder* above, where it was said that it would be a defence if a vehicle went on to a crossing because of the driver's excusable loss of control, through being stung or being pushed forward by a vehicle behind or through a latent defect in the brakes of which the driver could not reasonably be expected to know, so long as he was in no way at fault himself. As to running out of petrol, see *Oakley-Moore* v *Robinson* below.

The 1971 Regulations are in a quite different form from the pre-1950 regulations and the decisions on the latter are not necessarily of any help in deciding points arising on the present law; the old cases were reviewed in *LPTB* v *Upson* [1949] 1 All ER 60. The latter case also deals with the question of a pedestrian's contributory negligence in a civil action.

### 6.44 Stopping in the zebra-controlled area

Regulation 9 relates to stopping on crossings: circumstances beyond the driver's control and stopping to avoid an accident are defences. The regulation also forbids pedestrians to loiter on the crossing. Regulation 12 forbids the driver of a vehicle to stop in the zebra controlled area. Note the definition of 'zebra controlled area' in reg 3(1). It is the area bordered by zig-zag lines as required by Parts I and II of Sched 3 and not for instance the crossing itself, a point emphasised in *Wright* v *Hunt* (1984) *The Times*, 12 May. Note Part I of Sched 3 and reg 6 as to variations and in particular para 7 of Part I of Sched 3 as to imperfections. Bicycles are exempted from the regulation even if additional means of propulsion are attached. The bicycle must not, however, have a sidecar. It should be noted that the controlled area normally extends to both sides of the crossing, and unlike the former regulations, it is an offence to stop on the further side of the crossing, as well as on its approach.

Regulations 14 and 15 contain various exemptions from reg 12: fire, ambulance, police and defence purposes, building works, road works, emergencies, etc. Stopping for the purpose of turning right or left is exempted. Public service vehicles are also exempted for the purpose of picking up or dropping passengers on the far side of the crossing but not on the approach to the crossing. Stopping for reasons beyond a driver's control or to avoid an accident is also exempted. In *Oakley-Moore* v *Robinson* [1982] RTR 74 a motorist brought his car to rest within the approach limits of a pelican crossing, thinking he had run out of petrol. He claimed that he was prevented from proceeding by circumstances beyond his control. The Divisional Court upheld the justices' finding that this was a matter within his control: it was not a latent defect. The same principle would seem to apply to a zebra pedestrian crossing. It was suggested (ibid) that the burden of proof regarding circumstances beyond the driver's control and stopping to avoid an accident remained on the prosecution throughout, although no doubt the defendant would raise the matter in the first instance. This suggestion must be treated with some reserve. It was accepted in the judgment but the point was not argued. The words 'nothing shall apply' etc in the regulation do seem to be an exception etc within the meaning of s 101 of the Magistrates' Courts Act 1980 as indeed the justices thought. The regulations forbidding stopping in the area controlled by a zebra crossing apply even if the zebra crossing is for the time being controlled by a policeman or traffic warden.

### 6.45 Overtaking in the zebra-controlled area

It is an offence when approaching a zebra crossing to overtake a moving motor vehicle (reg 10(*a*) or a stationary vehicle (reg 10(*b*)) in the area controlled by the crossing. It is not an offence to overtake a vehicle in the controlled area on the further side of the crossing. It is also not an offence where the passing vehicle is on the crossing itself at the moment at which it passed ahead of the foremost part of the other vehicle, because the passing vehicle had by then passed one of the limits of the crossing and because the crossing itself was not part of the controlled area (*Wright* v *Hunt* (1984) *The Times*, 12 May).

Regulation 10 is phrased in such a way that a vehicle 'overtakes' another once any part of the vehicle passes ahead of the foremost part of the other vehicle. It would appear, therefore, that an offence is committed even if the overtaking vehicle subsequently drops back. However, it is only an offence if the vehicle overtaken is either the only other vehicle on the approach to the crossing or, if there is more than one, it is the nearest vehicle to the crossing.

The vehicle being overtaken may be either moving or stationary, but if it is stationary the overtaking is only an offence if the vehicle overtaken 'has stopped for the purpose of complying with reg 8' (see reg 10(*b*)). It was held in *Gullen* v *Ford*; *Prowse* v *Clark* [1975] RTR 303 that 'stopped for the purpose of complying with regulation 8' did not mean that the stationary vehicle must have stopped because a pedestrian had a foot on the crossing and the driver would thus have committed an offence under reg 8 if the car had not stopped. Stopping for the purpose of reg 8 includes a car which had stopped out of courtesy only to a pedestrian who was waiting to cross but who had not actually placed his foot on the carriageway. It was said obiter by Lord Widgery CJ that he was concerned in the case of very long crossings when no danger was caused by reason of a technical breach of reg 10(*b*). He suggested that the prosecution in such a case should refrain from prosecuting on a purely technical charge when no danger of any kind was created. *Gullen* v *Ford* above was followed in *Connor* v *Paterson* [1977] DRTR 379. A mini had stopped at a crossing to give precedence to pedestrians using the crossing; the defendant's van had pulled alongside the mini and then passed in front of it over the crossing at a time when no pedestrians were using it. It was held that an offence contrary to reg 10 had been committed. 'Stopped for the purpose of complying with regulation 8' meant stopped not only when pedestrians were on the crossing, or likely to be there (as in *Gullen* v *Ford*, above) but also when the overtaken vehicle had stopped to allow pedestrians to move away, but had not moved after having stopped to allow them to cross.

A further distinction between the offence under reg 10(*a*) of overtaking a moving motor vehicle and under reg 10(*b*) of overtaking a stationary vehicle is that an offence is only committed in overtaking a moving vehicle if the vehicle which is overtaken is a motor vehicle. An offence under reg 10(*b*) on the other hand is committed if the vehicle overtaken is any type of vehicle including a bicycle (see 'Vehicle', 1.13 and also 1.16).

If the crossing is controlled for the time being by a policeman or traffic warden, the provisions forbidding overtaking do not apply (see under 'According precedence at zebra crossings', 6.43). Regulation 11 treats a crossing in a one-way street which has a central reservation as two separate crossings and allows a vehicle on one side of the crossing to overtake a vehicle which has stopped on the other side of the reservation to allow a passenger to cross.

## 6.46–51 Controlled or 'pelican' crossings

Pelican crossings are dealt with by the 'Pelican' Pedestrian Crossings Regulations and General Directions 1969 (SI 1969 No 888), as amended by SI 1979 No 401.

The crossings are controlled by traffic lights. The succession of lights is green, steady amber, steady red, flashing amber, then back to green and so on.

Regulations 6 and 7 are made under s 64 of the 1984 Act and regs 9 (stopping between approach studs), 10 (red light), 11 (flashing amber light), and 12 (stopping within limits) are made under s 25. The penalty (see 6.52) varies accordingly.

By regs 6(1)(*c*) and 10 the red light prohibits vehicles proceeding beyond the stop line or, if the latter is not visible, beyond the traffic light.

By reg 6(1)(*b*), when a steady amber light is showing vehicles must stop at the line unless the vehicle is so close to the stop line that it cannot safely stop; unlike the comparable provision in the Traffic Signs Regulations relating to the amber signal in ordinary traffic lights (see 6.4), non-compliance with the steady amber light seems clearly to be an offence under the regulations and s 64 of the 1984 Act. If a driver passes the stop line while there is a steady amber light, the driver commits an offence under s 64 unless he shows, on the balance of probabilities, that his vehicle cannot be safely stopped before passing the stop line or signal.

The flashing amber light allows vehicles to proceed across the crossing but requires the driver to accord precedence to any pedestrian on the crossing (regs 6(1)(*d*) and 11). Reg 6(1)(*d*) and reg 11 are in similar terms to reg 8 of the Zebra Crossing Regulations and the comments and cases cited on the Zebra Pedestrian Crossing Regulations as to according precedence appear apposite.

Regulation 9 prohibits the stopping of vehicles between the line of studs on the approach to a pelican crossing and the pelican crossing iself. This is in somewhat similar terms to reg 14 of the Zebra Crossing Regulations (see 6.44) but is restricted to the approach side. Again unlike the Zebra Crossing Regulations there is no prohibition on overtaking on the approach. These distinctions no doubt explain the differences in the road markings. It is sometimes suggested that the stopping prohibition would be clearer if the prohibition area were marked by zig-zag lines instead of studs, but as the legal requirements are different it is desirable for the road markings to be different also. In *Power* v *Davidson* (1964) 62 LGR 320, it was held in relation to the former push-button regulations of 1954, that where the studs did not comply with the regulations, no offence was committed. However, this case must be read subject to the various provisos in Sched 2 which are similar to those applying to zebra crossings (see 6.42 and also 6.13).

Regulation 12 forbids either vehicles or pedestrians to wait on the pelican crossing itself.

## Pedestrian Crossings: Proceedings and Penalties

### 6.52 Generally

Section 179 of the 1972 Act requiring warning of intended prosecution (see Chapter 3) does not apply to an offence in respect of a pelican crossing (*Sulston* v *Hammond* [1970] 2 All ER 830). It would appear that s 179 does not apply to an offence committed in respect of a zebra crossing either.

The penalty for a breach of the 1969 'Pelican' or 1971 'Zebra' Crossings Regulations is a fine of level 3 (Road Traffic Regulation Act 1984, s 25(5), and Sched 7). However the penalty for a breach of a regulation made under s 64 (eg the steady amber light) is by s 118 and Sched 7 a fine of level 3 also but without the power to endorse, disqualify or order penalty points.

Where the defendant is convicted under s 25 in respect of a motor vehicle, his driving licence must be endorsed unless there are special reasons (see Chapter 21); the offence carries 3 penalty points and the defendant may be disqualified for any period (1972 Act, s 93(2)).

Section 19 of the Transport Act 1981 (penalty points disqualification) applies (see 20.18–21). Mitigating circumstances justifying a court refraining from applying the penalty points disqualification are discussed in Chapter 21. The offender may be ordered to be disqualified until he passes a driving test (s 93(7) of the 1972 Act, where there is power to disqualify generally; see 20.32).

Section 112 of the 1984 Act (information as to identity of driver or rider), s 113 (evidence by certificate) and s 114 (proof of identity of driver) apply to s 25 offences but not to s 118 offences (see Sched 7). Section 25 applies to vehicles and persons in the public service of the Crown; so does s 64 but not the penalty section for s 64, s 118 (see s 130).

The endorsement codes in respect of pedestrian crossing offences are as follows:

| | |
|---|---|
| Undefined contravention of pedestrian crossing regulation (Scottish courts only) | PC 10 |
| Contravention of regulations with moving vehicle | PC 20 |
| Contravention of regulations with stationary vehicle | PC 30 |

The Magistrates' Association suggested penalties for pedestrian crossing offences are £20 for parking within the limits of a pedestrian crossing and '£40 and consider disqualification' for the other offences under the regulations. See 18.1 and Appendix 3.

### 6.53–5 Proceedings for other offences

It is not uncommon, particularly where a pedestrian has been injured on a zebra or pelican crossing, for the prosecution to bring proceedings for careless or even reckless driving in addition to the pedestrian crossing offence.

A conviction for the more serious offence, ie reckless or careless driving, together with the imposition of a penalty, would generally afford a good ground for not convicting or sentencing for the pedestrian crossing offence (see 'Two offences from one incident' at 5.49). An acquittal for the offence of careless or reckless driving would be no bar, however, to the proceedings in respect of the pedestrian crossing offence.

## School Crossings and Street Playgrounds

### 6.56 Generally

Sections 26–30 of the Road Traffic Regulation Act 1984 contain provisions as to school crossings and street playgrounds.

### 6.57 School crossings

Under s 26 of the Road Traffic Regulation Act 1984, authorities (principally the Commissioner of Police in the Metropolis and county councils outside the metropolitan police area) are empowered to arrange the patrolling of crossings used by children on their way to or from school or on their way from one part of a school to another. Section 28 of the Act lays down the circumstances under which vehicles can be required to stop and to remain stationary by the school crossing patrol.

A person required to stop by the school crossing patrol sign must 'cause the vehicle to stop before reaching the place where the children are crossing or seeking to cross and so as not to stop or impede their crossing' (s 28(2)(*a*)) and must not put it in motion again to reach that place while the sign continued to be exhibited (s 28(2)(*b*)). It should be noted that before a person may be convicted under s 28(2)(*a*) or s 28(2)(*b*) he must first have been required to stop in accordance with s 28(1).

In *Franklin* v *Langdown* [1971] 3 All ER 662 a party of children with two or three adults were crossing a road under the protection of a school crossing patrol sign. When the last of the children had passed over the crown of the road, the defendant drove out of a side turning and passed behind the last of the adults, causing her to hasten her steps. At the time of so doing, the sign continued to be exhibited. The magistrates' court dismissed the case because they were of the opinion that a conviction under what is now s 28(2)(*a*) could only be obtained if the motorist acted so as to stop or impede the children crossing. The justices were directed to convict and it was held that the words 'and so as not to stop or impede their crossing' were merely descriptive of the manner in which a motorist is required to stop (see further below). In *R* v *Greenwood* [1962] Crim LR 639 a motorist was acquitted where there were no children on the crossing and none, apparently, seeking to cross. This decision, which was criticised in *Franklin* v *Langdown*, above, may possibly be explained on the ground that the motorist in that case had not been lawfully required to stop under what is now s 28(1) because, when he was required to do so, there were no children crossing or seeking to cross and the patrolman could not therefore display his sign in accordance with the section. Nevertheless, the case was again criticised in *Wall* v *Walwyn* [1974] RTR 24, where following *Franklin* v *Langdown* justices were again directed to convict a motorist whom they had acquitted because the children had not been impeded. Lord Widgery in *Wall* v *Walwyn*, at p 27, repeated his view as to the duty of a driver as he expressed it in *Franklin* in the following terms:

> In my judgment the reference to 'and so as not to stop or impede their crossing' in s 25(1)(*a*) is merely descriptive of the manner in which the driver should stop. My reading of the section, therefore, is that once the sign has been properly exhibited in accordance with s 25(1) the driver must stop, unless indeed by the time he reaches the crossing the prescribed sign had already been removed. Of course, if he approaches slowly and the patrol had taken the sign down before the driver gets there, naturally he can proceed. But if the sign is still exhibited there is in my judgment an obligation to stop, which obligation cannot be released until s 25(2)(*b*) has been satisfied, namely, that the sign no longer continues to be exhibited.

Under the 1984 Act s 28 is in equivalent terms to s 25. It is submitted that the liability under s 28 is absolute and that a driver must stop even if it is very difficult for him to do so because of the lateness of the signal; compare the cases on according precedence at 6.43. Where it is desired to exempt drivers from an absolute duty to stop, the regulations say so, eg as to amber lights. The sign must be exhibited by the patrol in such a way that the approaching driver can see the words on the sign but it need not be full face to oncoming traffic (*Hoy* v *Smith* [1964] 3 All ER 670). The sign has been altered from 'Stop: Children Crossing' to 'STOP: Children', but *Hoy* v *Smith* seems as applicable to the new signs as to the old.

Section 28(2)(*b*) creates a separate offence of again putting the vehicle in motion so as to reach the place while the sign continues to be exhibited. It should be noted that this is a separate offence from s 28(2)(*a*) and that an information charging both offences would be bad for duplicity. It would appear that an offence can only be committed under s 28(2)(*b*) after the motorist has stopped. If he does not stop at all he should be charged with not stopping contrary to s 28(2)(*a*). It may also be noted that the vehicle may move sufficiently 'so as to reach the place in question', ie the place where children are crossing or seeking to cross, before having to stop.

By s 25(4) signs are presumed to be of the prescribed size, colour and type and to have been illuminated as prescribed.

The signs are prescribed by the Traffic Signs Regulations and General Directions 1981 (SI 1981 No 859) (see diagram 605.1, reg 37 and direction 36). Warning lights may be erected giving motorists advance warning of the school crossing patrol. The warning lights are governed by reg 37(2). The erection of warning lights is discretionary and it would seem that their absence or non-illumination would not affect a conviction under s 28. Of the directions only direction 36 (relating to the colour of the back of signs) appears to relate to school crossing patrols. It is submitted that even if the colour of the back of the sign were incorrect, this would not invalidate a conviction (see 6.28 and *Bursey* v *Barron* noted there).

By s 28(1) the patrolman must wear the approved uniform. The uniform worn is deemed to be approved by the Home Secretary unless otherwise proved (s 28(4)). No statutory instrument approving any uniform has been found, but by Home Office circular 123/76 the approved uniform for a school crossing patrol is a peaked cap, a black or navy blue beret or a yellow turban and a white raincoat, or other white coat. The coat may be covered on the upper half or any part by fluorescent material. It seems that this means that a fluorescent over garment may be worn or the fluorescence may be applied. Having regard to the presumption contained in s 28(5)(*b*), it is not necessary for the prosecution to prove that the Home Secretary's approval has been given to the uniform. The prosecution only has to prove that the school crossing patrol is wearing a uniform. *Semble* the defence would succeed if the school crossing patrol did not wear a white dust coat or macintosh, but it is submitted that the wearing of the cap or beret is not essential (see *Wallwork* v *Giles*, 4.42*C*, as to a police constable in 'uniform'). (As to traffic wardens acting at school crossings see below.)

'School' is not defined and the term seems to include private and nursery schools and Sunday schools as well as those of education authorities. Section 28(1) applies, however, only when children are crossing or seeking to cross and are on their way to or from school or from one part of a school to another. It does not apply where adults alone are crossing or children are shown not to be on the way to or from school or from one part of a school to another. Note that, by s 28(5)(*c*), unless the contrary is shown, there is a presumption that children at a crossing are on their way to or from school, if it is proved that a prescribed sign was exhibited by a patrol. It will be noted that s 28 applies only between 8 am and 5.30 pm.

On the analogy of *Burns* v *Bidder*, cited at 6.43, the inability of a motorist or cyclist to stop because of a latent defect in his brakes, undiscoverable on a reasonable examination, or because he was pushed forward by a vehicle colliding with his vehicle's rear, or because he lost control under attack by a swarm of bees, would probably be a defence.

'Road' has the same meaning as elsewhere in the 1972 Act (see Chapter 1).

Section 28 applies to all vehicles, including trams, trolley vehicles and cycles, but not seemingly to equestrians. See also *Crank* v *Brooks* at 6.43.

The term 'children' is not defined for the purposes of s 28. While a child under the Children and Young Persons Act 1933 means one under the age of fourteen, it is submitted that for the purposes of s 28 the definition should not exclude children of fourteen or above but should at least extend to all children of compulsory school age, and that it would be within the spirit and object of s 28 if it extended to all pupils at secondary schools, whether above or below compulsory school age. 'Child', in the context of s 28, it is submitted, means any child of any age who goes to school.

Sometimes the school crossing patrol displays his sign for the benefit of children cycling to school. There appears to be nothing in s 28(1) to limit the protection given by the school crossing patrol to children on foot only and it is submitted that a motorist can be lawfully required to stop whether the children are crossing the road on foot or on bicycles.

Traffic wardens appointed under the Road Traffic Regulation Act 1984, s 95, may act as school crossing patrols (see SI 1970 No 1958) and when so doing it is not essential for them to wear the white coat prescribed in the Home Office circular 122/76, but they must when so doing exhibit the prescribed sign and be wearing the approved traffic warden's uniform (see Home Office circular 110/1965 which was addressed to police authorities and chief constables only; presumably the Home Office will be prepared to supply a copy if applied to). A traffic warden may under para 1(5) of the Schedule to the 1970 Order be engaged in a school crossing patrol or by para 1(6) engaged in the general regulation of traffic. The corresponding prosecution will be under s 28 of the 1984 Act or s 22 of the 1972 Act respectively. The two main differences between s 28 and s 22 are the required exhibition of the sign under s 28 and the application of s 179 (notices of intended prosecution) to s 22 offences, but not to s 28 offences.

If the traffic warden is operating a school crossing patrol and has the sign, it is submitted that prosecutions should be brought under s 28 and he should exhibit the pole bearing the sign. He is presumably operating under para 1(5). Motorists would be watching the sign and might otherwise be seriously misled. If he does not have the sign the question arises whether he is operating incorrectly under para 1(5) or under para 1(6). This will be a question of fact and impression but it may be possible to regard him as operating under s 22.

Nothing in s 28 prevents proceedings being taken against motorists and all cyclists for reckless or careless driving or riding or against drivers or riders of any vehicles and equestrians for driving or riding to the common danger under the Public Health Act 1925, s 74, or under the Highway Act 1835 (but see 'Two offences from one incident' at 5.49).

Section 28 does not apply to vehicles and persons in the public service of the Crown. It is nevertheless submitted that a Crown vehicle driver may be prosecuted for reckless, careless or inconsiderate driving if he recklessly or negligently fails to observe a school crossing patrol's sign and endangers or inconveniences other road users or children as a result.

### 6.58–62 Street playgrounds

County councils are empowered by s 29 of the Road Traffic Regulation Act 1984 to make orders prohibiting or restricting roads from use by vehicles to enable them to be used as a street playground. Any such order is required to make provision for permitting reasonable access to premises on or adjacent to the street.

It is an offence by virtue of s 29(3) for a person to use, or cause or permit a vehicle to be used in contravention of a street playground order (for 'using', 'causing' or 'permitting' see Chapter 1).

The Common Council of the City of London together with London borough councils are similarly enpowered to make street playground orders in their areas by s 30 of the 1984 Act and a person who uses or causes or permits a vehicle to be used in contravention of a street playground order commits an offence (see s 30(5)).

Section 31 of the Act allows county councils, the City of London and London borough councils to make byelaws for street playgrounds.

Sections 29 and 30 do not apply to vehicles or persons in the public service of the Crown.

## School Crossings etc: Penalties

### 6.63–5 Generally

Offences of failure to comply with a school crossing patrol under s 28 or using, causing or permitting a vehicle to be used in contravention of a street playground order under s 29 or s 30 are triable summarily only and punishable by a maximum fine of level 3.

Endorsement must be ordered for all offences under ss 28, 29 and 30 committed in respect of motor vehicles unless there are 'special reasons' (see Chapter 21). The school crossing patrol offence carries 3 penalty points and the street playground offences carry 2 penalty points.

For offences under ss 28, 29 and 30 committed in respect of motor vehicles disqualification may be ordered on conviction (s 93(2)) and must be ordered if the penalty points disqualification under s 19 of the Transport Act 1981 applies: see 20.18–21 unless there are mitigating circumstances (see Chapter 21). Disqualification until the passing of a driving test may be ordered (s 93(7): see 20.32).

The endorsement code for a school crossing offence contrary to s 28 is TS 60, and for a street playground offence, MS 30.

The Magistrates' Association's suggested penalty for a school crossing offence (see 18.1 and Appendix 3) is '£40 and consider disqualification'. The association does not suggest a penalty for a street playground offence.

## Obstruction, Parking etc

### 6.66 Generally

Obstruction and parking offences are contained in a number of Acts including the Highway Act 1980, the Road Traffic Regulation Act 1984 and the 1972 Act. The 1984 Act regulates the provisions of parking places and the making of traffic regulation orders. The various offences are considered below and the penalties for the offences will be found at 6.85–86. Parking within the limits of a pedestrian crossing is considered under the section on 'Pedestrian Crossings' (see 6.44 and 6.46). The Highways (Road Humps)

Regulations 1983 (SI 1983 No 1087) have been made under the Highways Act 1980 as amended, and road humps may be set up on public roads.

### 6.67 Obstruction

Proceedings for obstructing the highway can be brought under the Highways Act 1980, s 137 (wilfully obstructing the free passage of a highway), the Town Police Clauses Act 1847, s 28 (wilfully causing an obstruction in any public footpath or public thoroughfare), and reg 122 of the Motor Vehicles (Construction and Use) Regulations 1978 (causing or permitting (see Chapter 1) a motor vehicle or trailer to stand on a road so as to cause any unnecessary obstruction thereof). The regulations extend to the whole of Great Britain and the Highways Act to England and Wales, including London (London Government Act 1963, s 16(2)). (See below as to the 1847 Act.) The law is discussed at 94 SJ 811 and, with particular reference to Irish cases, at [1953] Jo Crim L 78 and 168 and at 99 ILTN 181, 187, 197, 207, 217 and 227. Reference can also be usefully made to *Parking Law* by Charles Brandreth (published by David and Charles) particularly in relation to parking meter and 'yellow line' offences.

The regulations apply to a 'road' as defined in Chapter 1. The Highways Act applies to ways over which all members of the public are entitled to pass and repass. A decision of quarter sessions under s 31(1) of the National Parks and Access to the Countryside Act 1949, since repealed, was a judgment in rem and binding on a magistrates' court. An owner was held not to be able therefore to dispute the status of a public path declared to be such by quarter sessions when prosecuted under the Highways Act for wilful obstruction (*Armstrong* v *Whitfield* [1973] 2 All ER 546) (but see 1.66).

The Town Police Clauses Act 1847, s 28, other than the provisions relating to hackney carriages, seems now to apply to all districts, whether they were formerly boroughs, urban districts or rural districts (s 171 of the Public Health Act 1875 and para 23 of Sched 14 to the Local Government Act 1972). An obstruction under the Act must be shown to have been to the obstruction, annoyance or danger of the residents or passengers in the street.

The question as to who may prosecute under the Town Police Clauses Act is discussed at 119 JP Jo 746 and in Stone, where it is suggested that the constable who saw the offence should be the informant. A prosecution under the Highways Act or the regulations may be brought by any person.

Regulation 122 does not apply to trams and trolley vehicles (see s 198 of the 1972 Act), but otherwise applies to motor vehicles. The Acts apply to all vehicles.

The position as to the application of the Highways and Town Police Clauses Acts to Crown vehicles is discussed at 2.8. The regulations apply to Crown vehicles.

### 6.68 What amounts to obstruction?

Obstruction can be caused by actual physical obstruction of an essential line of traffic, eg taking up half of a narrow, busy road, so that single-line working has to be employed. Or it may be unreasonable use of the right of stopping even though there is plenty of room for other traffic to pass. An example of the former is *Wall* v *Williams* [1966] Crim LR 50, where a vehicle making a forbidden 'U' turn in a very crowded street held up the traffic for fifty seconds; the conviction under (what is now) reg 122 was upheld.

In *Mounsey* v *Campbell* [1983] RTR 36, the defendant parked his van right up against the bumper of a car. The car could have been moved at that time but it was subsequently penned in by a car parked two feet behind. The defendant refused to move his van and was convicted of causing unnecessary obstruction contrary to reg 122. He argued that he should have been charged with 'permitting' as he had not caused the unnecessary obstruction originally. It was held that he had been rightly convicted, because on the facts the van caused an unnecessary obstruction from the moment it was first parked.

The case does not cover the situation where the defendant parks his car a reasonable distance in front and the blockage is caused by the unreasonable way the car behind is parked subsequently (always assuming there is no refusal to move). There is clearly an obstruction but it is submitted it might be held to be neither 'wilful' nor 'unnecessary' on the part of the defendant.

Parking in a bus bay for five minutes was held not to be unnecessary obstruction in *Brown* v *Cardle* [1983] SLT 218 in the absence of any evidence of a bus trying to park during that time. The bus bay was held to be simply part of the road. The same principle would apply to parts of the road set aside similarly for other purposes. Obviously the position would be different if a bus had tried to park.

While there is obviously an offence if there is a serious obstruction in fact, unreasonable use of the highway calculated to obstruct and whereby persons might be obstructed may suffice for a conviction without evidence that anyone has actually been obstructed (*Gill* v *Carson* (1917) 81 JP 250, a case under the 1847 Act, s 28). In *Nagy* v *Weston* [1965] 1 All ER 78 parking a van for five minutes in a wide, busy street near a bus stop and refusing to move was held to be an obstruction under what is now s 137 of the Highways Act 1980. Lord Parker CJ said:

> While there must be proof of unreasonable use, whether or not user amounting to an obstruction was or was not unreasonable use was a question of fact, depending on all the circumstances, including the length of time the obstruction continued, the place where it occurred, the purpose for which it was done and whether it caused an actual as opposed to a potential obstruction.

These words were expressly approved by Ashworth J in *Evans* v *Barker* [1971] RTR 453, at p 456, where it was held, following *Solomon* v *Durbridge* below that leaving a car for a reasonable time, although amounting to an obstruction, did not amount to an unnecessary obstruction within the meaning of reg 122 of the Construction and Use Regulations. The facts were that the defendant had left his car on a Wednesday, which was the market day, between 2.45 pm and 4 pm in Welsh Walls, Oswestry, leaving 20 feet of the width of the road clear. The justices' finding that this was not an 'unnecessary' obstruction was upheld by the Divisional Court. It is primarily a question of fact, applying a test such as is adduced by Lord Parker as quoted, whether the circumstances in which a car is left are 'unreasonable'. If the obstruction is 'unreasonable' it would appear to be 'unnecessary' within the meaning of reg 122.

It was again emphasised in *Wade* v *Grange* [1977] RTR 417 that what amounts to obstruction is primarily a question of fact and that the Divisional Court is only concerned with correcting mistaken applications of the law.

The test of reasonableness or unreasonableness was applied in *Lewis* v *Dickson* [1976] RTR 431 where the defendant was charged with wilful obstruction under what is now s 137 of the Highways Act 1980. The defendant, who was a security officer on duty at a large factory, caused continuous lines of employees' vehicles to build up in both directions on the main road due to his stopping every vehicle at the factory gate to check it. The case was sent back to the justices who were directed that the proper test for them to apply in deciding the case was whether the defendant's action in all the circumstances at the time was a reasonable method of admitting the cars to the works. In *Nelmes* v *Rhys Howells Transport Ltd* [1977] RTR 266 the definition of obstruction (as quoted above in *Nagy* v *Weston*) was again followed in a case contrary to reg 122 where the defendants had used a road for parking four or five of their trailers for which they had no room in their yard. The justices found the defendants had no case to answer as the prosecution had adduced no evidence of actual obstruction. The case was sent back to the justices; in considering whether or not the obstruction was unreasonable, one of the factors is the purpose for which it was done, and it should be borne in mind when considering the purpose of the obstruction that the highway was intended to provide for the requirements of people in transit and that the highway was not a store (ibid). In *Absalom* v *Martin* [1974] RTR 145 a bill poster parked his van with two wheels on a footpath and the other two on the roadway while posting a bill. The justices found as a fact that the obstruction was not an unreasonable use of the highway and their dismissal of a charge under s 121(1) of the Highways Act 1959 was upheld by the High Court who again cited with approval the words of Lord Parker CJ in *Nagy* v *Weston* set out above. The court reserved for a future occasion whether it is more difficult to justify reasonable use when parking on a footpath rather than on the carriageway (see also *Worth* v *Brooks*, below). In *Pitcher* v *Lockett* (1966) 64 LGR 477 it was held that it was not a reasonable use of the highway to park a van on a busy road to sell hot dogs from it. It was said also that, normally, if what is done is nothing to do with the passage to and fro, this is not making a use of the highway which is reasonable, but that a milkman on his rounds was making a reasonable use of the road even though he might occasionally sell a bottle of milk. This view was applied in *Waltham Forest LBC* v *Mills* [1980] RTR 201 where it was held that selling refreshments from a parked mobile snack bar in a highway layby was an unreasonable use of the highway in itself and an offence contrary to what is now s 137. The decision is of considerable importance in view of the prevalence of the practice.

Whether particular facts amount to an unreasonable use would depend very much on the magistrates' local knowledge of the importance of the particular road; a long stay may not be out of order in a quiet residential side road, but it would be otherwise in a busy shopping street. An obstruction only comes into existence if there is an unreasonable use of the right of stopping (*Nagy* v *Weston* above), and it is a matter of degree (*Dunn* v *Holt* (1904) 68 JP 271). In *Gill's* case a vehicle had been left unattended for five minutes in such a position as to block one out of four lines of traffic in a street carrying a tram route, and the High Court held that those facts showed no evidence of unreasonable use of the highway; it added, however, that, had the vehicle been left for a long period, there would have been an obstruction. In *Dunn's* case, where there was an acquittal, no one was obstructed and the vehicle, though stationary for several hours, took up less than 3 feet in a carriageway 30 feet wide. It is doubtful how far *Dunn's* case is still of authority in relation to obstructions lasting several hours. In *Absalom* v *Martin*, where the nearest public car park was several hundred yards away, the defendant parked partly on the carriageway and partly on the footpath and was endeavouring to carry on his business of bill posting in such a way as to cause the least inconvenience to pedestrians and other road users. A defendant who sold fruit from a barrow for fifteen minutes, the barrow taking up 5 feet in a 24 foot road and customers causing further obstruction, was held to have been rightly convicted, as continuous selling does not mean that the barrow was not standing longer than was necessary (*Whiteside* v *Watson* [1952] SLT 367). In *Bego* v *Gardner* [1933] SLT 110 the conviction was upheld of a man who sold ices from his van parked in a cul-de-sac frequented by the public.

Leaving a car unattended for three hours, which was found to cause danger to the public and annoyance to the residents but which was not specifically found to cause an obstruction, was held to constitute the offence of leaving a car unattended for longer than was necessary to load or unload it (*Henderson* v *Gray* [1927] SC(J) 43). A motorist parked his car in a line of cars in a street and left it there for five hours. He argued that, as he parked in a line of cars, he was not causing an unnecessary obstruction. The High Court held that he clearly caused one (*Solomon* v *Durbridge* (1956) 120 JP 231). In *Gelberg* v *Miller* [1961] 1 All ER 291, at pp 295–296, it was said that to leave a car for the luncheon period in Jermyn Street, London, was plainly an obstruction. Parking for five hours on a grass verge between the footpath and the wall was held to cause an unnecessary obstruction in *Worth* v *Brooks* [1959] Crim LR 885, but in *Police* v *O'Connor* [1957] Crim LR 478, quarter sessions held that it was not an unreasonable use of the highway to park a large vehicle outside the driver's own house in a cul-de-sac. In *Worth's* case it was said that, if a car was immobile through a breakdown, the obstruction might be 'necessary'.

In *London Borough of Redbridge* v *Jacques* [1971] 1 All ER 260 it was held that the fact that a street trader had for many years sold from a fruit stall erected on the back of his stationary vehicle without objection from the local authority and without inconveniencing the public use of the highway was not a reason for dismissing a charge of wilful obstruction under what is now s 137 of the Highways Act 1980. This case was applied in *Cambridgeshire County Council* v *Rust* [1972] 3 All ER 2362, where it was held not to be a 'lawful excuse' for a person, prosecuted under what is now s 137 for setting up a stall on the highway, to believe he could lawfully do so because he made reasonable enquiries and had paid rates on the stall to the district council. Once a highway always a highway, and a council cannot grant a licence to perform an unlawful act.

It was held in *Arrowsmith* v *Jenkins* [1963] 2 All ER 210, a case of causing a crowd to collect, that, if a person intentionally by exercise of his will does something which causes an obstruction of a highway, this constitutes wilful obstruction under what is now s 137 and it is no defence that the person believes that he has genuine authority to do what he is doing if he has not lawful authority or reasonable excuse.

The judgment of the sheriff-substitute in *Macmillan* v *Gibson* [1966] SLT (Sh) 84 suggests that, when there is no actual physical obstruction, a conviction should follow only if it has been brought to the motorist's attention, eg, by a police warning or by a notice or sign, that there is a regulation against the stopping of vehicles in the particular street, ie, that the obligation imposed on the driver is not absolute but the prosecutor should show mens rea. That case concerned parking in breach of byelaws, not of reg 122, and *Watson* v *Ross* [1920] 1 SLT 65, on which reliance was placed, concerned a charge of standing longer than necessary.

In *Seekings* v *Clarke* (1961) 59 LGR 268, a case under what is now s 137 not involving a motor vehicle, it was said that anything which substantially prevented the public from passing over the whole of the highway (including the footway) and which was not purely temporary was an unlawful obstruction, subject to an exception on the de minimis principle. This case is discussed in *Wolverton UDC* v *Willis* [1962] 1 All ER 243.

The driver of a slow vehicle does not 'negligently interrupt the free passage' of overtaking vehicles merely because they have to go to the offside of the road to pass him (*Sleith* v *Godfrey* (1920) 85 JP 46). In a case noted at 85 JP Jo 500, the High Court upheld the conviction for obstruction where a lorry driver refused to draw into his nearside but drove along the centre of the road so that traffic could not overtake him. Obstruction of the footway can be an offence under the regulations (*Bryant* v *Marx* (1932) 96 JP 383). Other earlier cases on obstruction, mainly civil, are collected at E & E Dig, Repl vol 26, p 466 *et seq*. On a charge of having deposited without lawful authority or excuse anything on a highway in consequence whereof a user of the highway was injured or endangered, it is no defence that it was commercially convenient to do so (*Gatland* v *Metropolitan Police Commissioner* [1968] 2 All ER 100—hopper, 6 feet wide, left at night on 43 foot road, only place where it could conveniently be placed). Builders' skips have subsequently become subject to control by what are now ss 139 and 140 of the Highways Act 1980 (see 6.76).

The right of an occupier of premises abutting on a highway to make use of it for the purpose of obtaining access to his premises and of loading and unloading goods there is subject to the right of the public to use the highway (*Vanderpant* v *Mayfair Hotel Co* (1930) 94 JP 23, a civil case). In *Trevett* v *Lee* [1955] 1 All ER 406, a civil case, a landowner laid a small hosepipe across the road to other land; it was held that whether or not he was obstructing the highway was to be judged by reasonableness both from his point of view and from that of other members of the public. In *Marr* v *Turpie* [1949] Jo Crim L 416, the High Court of Justiciary upheld the conviction of a motorist who had left his car for thirty minutes outside his own premises in a narrow street. The question whether a moving vehicle can be said to 'stand' on a road within the meaning of reg 122 of the Construction and Use Regulations was raised but not decided in *Carpenter* v *Fox* (1929) 93 JP 239; Lord Hewart CJ thought, however, that it was not a very strong argument to say that a moving vehicle was not 'standing'. The fact that someone is left in charge of a vehicle does not prevent there being an offence of obstruction if there is in fact an obstruction (*Hinde* v *Evans* (1906) 70 JP 548).

An act which in fact causes an obstruction cannot be justified by the motive or purpose which inspires or induces its commission (*W R Anderson (Motors) Ltd* v *Hargreaves* [1962] 1 All ER 129). It is submitted, however, that to constitute an offence the obstruction must be unlawful, and whether or not obstruction is unlawful depends on whether the action of the person was, or was not, reasonable in all the circumstances at the time (see *Lewis* v *Dickson*, above).

When lorries were parked on a grass verge and the drivers went to a café to get meals, it was held that they did not obstruct the highway merely by a temporary call for a legitimate purpose provided that they did not stop in a place where the mere presence of a stationary vehicle would create an obstruction (*Rodgers* v *Ministry of Transport* [1952] 1 All ER 634). But to leave a large roller on the highway, even when it belongs to the owner of the land on each side, is not a reasonable use of the highway (*Wilkins* v *Day* (1883) 48 JP 6). (As to the parking of vehicles on verges now see s 36A and s 36B of the Road Traffic Act 1972, at 6.73). In *Baxter* v *Middlesex County Council* [1956] Crim LR 561, a forecourt was held on the facts not to be part of the highway; it was used as a display park for cars. A claim by an innkeeper for standing his guests' vehicles on the highway cannot be supported, even though it has been so used for more than twenty years (*Gerring* v *Barfield* (1864) 28 JP 615); once a highway always a highway see *Cambridgeshire CC* v *Rust* above. If a local authority has designated part of a street as a parking place under the Public Health Act 1925, s 68, or other legislation, no offence of unnecessary obstruction is committed by leaving vehicles in that part during the period allowed by the order and the motive in leaving them there, eg, to relieve congestion in the owner's premises, is irrelevant (*W R Anderson (Motors) Ltd* v *Hargreaves* [1962] 1 All ER 129); but it is submitted that if the vehicle is parked in such a way as to cause a physical obstruction in a busy street where proper parking would not cause it, then the offender could properly be charged notwithstanding the street's designation for parking. If a vehicle breaks down and causes an obstruction, there is no wilful obstruction, it seems, if the driver does his best to get it moved out of the way within a reasonable time (*Original Hartlepool Collieries* v *Gibb* (1877) 41 JP 660). A van driver who stops it to sell ices has not 'pitched a stall on the highway' contrary to what is now s 148 of the Highways Act 1980 (*Divito* v *Stickings* [1948] 1 All ER 207). *Divito* v *Stickings* was distinguished in *Waltham Forest LBC* v *Mills* [1980] RTR 201 where parking a mobile snack bar in a layby was held to be 'pitching a stall'. The snack bar was a 'stall' since it could be removed from the towing vehicle, and it had been 'pitched' on the layby, being always in the same place for extended periods. The defendant was convicted not only under what is now s 148 but also under what is now s 137. A bus driver who left a bus in the road and went off duty without giving its charge to any other person caused an obstruction under what is now reg 122 (*Ellis* v *Smith* [1962] 3 All ER 954).

### 6.69 Arrest

A constable may arrest without warrant any person whom he sees obstructing the highway contrary to s 137(2). An arrest of a lorry driver whose vehicle was standing on a motorway was upheld in *Reed* v *Wastie and Another* [1972] Crim LR 221. The Metropolitan Police have special powers of arrest of persons obstructing the highway by virtue of s 54 of the Metropolitan Police Act 1839. These powers of arrest in s 137(2) and s 54 are due to be repealed by s 119 of and Part I of Sched 7 to the Police and Criminal Evidence Act 1984 and replaced when in force by the powers of arrest in that Act.

### 6.70 Parking meters

The Road Traffic Regulation Act 1984, ss 45–56 deal with parking on the highway and parking meters. It is necessary to obtain information about orders designating parking areas locally from the police or local authority.

'Parking places' are provided on the highway, marked with lines, and some may accommodate several vehicles. Each driver, on putting the appropriate coin in the meter, may park there for a specified time but no longer; if the vehicle stays for longer than that time, an excess charge must be paid to the local authority. If it is there for more than four hours, an offence is committed. A motorist may not put more money in the meter to extend his period, unless the order permits. He may go to another 'parking place' but may not return to his original one or sometimes one within the same zone until he has been gone from it for a prescribed period. The cited provisions are taken from one particular order and other orders differ. The police or council may prosecute for offences.

Section 47(1) specifies a number of offences and s 47(2) makes the driver who first left the vehicle generally responsible. One example which has been quoted is a driver who was responsible even though it was his mother-in-law who by mistake put the money in the wrong meter. The spouse who drove the vehicle thus would be responsible even though it was the other spouse who arrived late to drive it away.

By s 48(1) acceptance of the excess charge bars proceedings for failing to pay an initial charge. A defendant accused of failing to pay an excess charge may in the circumstances given in s 47(6) be convicted of failing to pay an initial charge. An excess charge levied by a local authority for the non-payment or non-display of parking tickets or for overstaying in a car park is not unlawful or unreasonable even if it includes operating costs such as recovering excess charges from non-payers in civil proceedings (*Crossland* v *Chichester DC* [1984] RTR 181). In that case the district council had fixed £20 as the excess charge but had also fixed a lower sum of £8 by way of discount for prompt payment.

On and after 1 January 1963 parking meters first installed at a parking place in England or Wales must be of a design and type approved by the Minister of Transport (Parking Meters (Type and Design Approval) (Appointed Day) Order 1962 (SI 1962 No 947)). By s 47(5) a meter is presumed to be of the approved type and design.

Orders usually contain exemptions for loading and unloading. A case under an order of two vehicles parking in one space is reported at [1959] Jo Crim L 98.

An order regulating the use of a parking place may make provision for treating the indications given by a meter or ticket as evidence of such facts as may be provided by the order (s 46(2)).

By s 124(1)(*f*) and Sched 9, Part VI a designation order, setting aside parking places on the highway, may not be challenged in any legal proceedings, save that it allows a challenge in the High Court only for a period after the order has been made. These provisions are extended to certain other orders under the 1984 Act by the same Schedule.

If a motor vehicle is left in a parking bay, no time is allowed for delaying the insertion of the coin in the meter unless it be merely to alight from the car and walk to the meter. Payment must be made as soon as the car is left in the bay, whether the driver stays in it or not, and he must not go off looking for change if he has not the right coin on him. (*Strong* v *Dawtry* [1961] 1 All ER 926). In *Riley* v *Hunt* [1981] RTR 79 it was held that the latest time for paying the initial charge payable under the Mendip District Council (Off-street Parking Places in Street) Order 1976 was before the person parking his car left the car park. Justices were directed to convict the defendant who had arrived at the car park without the appropriate coin and had gone off shopping with the intention of returning and paying the charge afterwards. The relevant order should always be scrutinised, however, to see if it contains exemptions not in the order considered in *Strong's* case, where the High Court expressed surprise that a motorist who had left his car for only a minute or so to get change for the meter had been fined at all.

In *Roberts* v *Powell* (1966) 64 LGR 173 it was held, on the terms of a particular order, that where a meter had been temporarily suspended or removed by the local authority a prosecution under the order failed. *Roberts* v *Powell* was followed in *Wilson* v *Arnott* [1977] 2 All ER 5, where it was held that while the placing of a red bag over the meter suspended the bay from normal use, the bay nevertheless remained a designated parking place within the meaning of the local order and 'waiting' in the bay as distinct from 'using' the bay was not suspended. The conviction of the defendant was set aside as he was entitled under the local order to 'wait' in the parking bay for not more than thirty minutes for loading or unloading.

Where tickets were issued by a machine for use in an unattended car park and had to be fixed to the vehicle parked, the fact that the machine *might* be out of order was not a defence to a charge of not fixing a ticket (*Rawlinson* v *Broadley* (1969) 113 SJ 310).

'Bank holiday' in a parking order means an official public holiday, not a day when the banks have shut pursuant to a royal proclamation (*O'Neill* v *George* (1969) 113 SJ 128).

For an article on parking meters, see [1962] Crim LR 947.

### 6.71 'No Waiting' streets

'No Waiting' and other traffic regulation orders are made under ss 1–8 of the Road Traffic Regulations Act 1984. Offences against such orders are under s 5(1) and Sched 7 (outside Greater London) and s 8(1) and Sched 7 (Greater London). For the purpose of s 2(3) there is a widened definition of pedestrian in s 127.

By s 3(4) outside Greater London a traffic regulation order imposing restrictions on waiting shall not apply to a stage carriage, viz a bus or coach carring passengers at separate fares for other than certain long journeys (not one used to carry an employer's workmen free or, it seems, a bus company's bus not actually carrying passengers, eg returning empty to the depot). (For the full definition of stage carriage, see 13.27*A*.) A 'No Waiting' order presumably does not affect such a bus or coach in service to carry passengers for fares but does otherwise. There is no such exemption for express carriages. As to what is meant by an express carriage, see the definition at 13.27*B*. In addition, the exemption in s 3(4) relating to a stage carriage is not to operate within a trial area within the meaning of ss 38–41 of the Public Passenger Vehicles Act 1981. However, any order made, or having effect as if made, under s 1, s 9 or s 12 of the Road Traffic Regulation Act 1967 (the equivalent provisions are now ss 5, 9 and 14 of the 1984 Act) before 6 October 1980 and imposing a prohibition or restriction on waiting has effect as if the operation of s 39(3) of the 1981 Act had not taken place (Transport Act 1980 (Commencement No 2) Order 1980, art 27). In other words, express carriages (and stage carriages in trial areas) continue to be exempt as indicated under orders made before 6 October 1980. This, however, will be subject to any such traffic orders made after 26 October 1980 varying or revoking any such prohibition or restriction. Subject to this the exemption for express carriages (and for stage carriages in trial areas) has ceased. This does not appear to be altered by the consolidation of the relevant provisions of the Transport Act 1980 in the Public Passenger Vehicles Act 1981. Certain parts of Devon have been designated a trial area by the Devon Trial Area Order 1982 (SI 1982 No 1243).

Section 2(4) of the 1984 Act enables county councils to make orders specifying through routes for heavy commercial vehicles and prohibiting or restricting their use in specified zones or on particular roads. As to the definition of 'heavy commercial vehicles', see 1.11.

By s 3(1), relating to places outside Greater London, an order may not prevent access to premises adjoining the road at any time for persons on foot and for no more than eight hours out of every twenty-four in respect of vehicles; if it does, presumably it is ultra vires to that extent. 'Preventing access' in s 1(5) was held to mean precluding access and not merely hindering it (*Corfe Transport Ltd* v *Gwynedd County Council* [1984] RTR 79). Section 3(1) has to be read subject to s 3(2) which allows orders to restrict vehicle access provided that the order states that the highway authority is satisfied that such restriction is necessary to avoid danger, to prevent danger arising or damage to the road or buildings on or near it, to facilitate passage of vehicles on the road, or to preserve or improve amenity by restricting or prohibiting the use of heavy commercial vehicles.

There were formerly restrictions on prosecutions but these were removed as noted in earlier editions and any person or constable may bring such a prosecution.

*Signs*

If signs to indicate the effect of a 'No Waiting' order have not been erected or signs have been erected not conforming to s 64 of the Road Traffic Regulation Act 1984 and the Traffic Signs Regulations and General Directions 1981 (SI 1981 No 859), no offence against the 'No Waiting' order is committed (*MacLeod* v *Hamilton* [1965] SLT 305). See also *Davies* v *Heatley* at 6.13.

A single yellow line supplemented by the authorised indication of the duration of the prohibition is sufficient indication that parking is prohibited on a Sunday as well as working days, and a conviction will be directed if the local order so prohibits parking on a Sunday (*Derrick* v *Ryder* [1972] RTR 480). In *James* v *Cavey* [1967] 1 All ER 1048 a motorist parked at 6 am, when the sign indicated that parking was permitted under an 'alternative day waiting' order. At 9 am the sign was changed to forbid parking. It was held that, as the sign did not forbid parking when he left his car, he committed no offence under the order by waiting after 9 am.

The placing of signs to mark the effect of no parking orders was formerly discretionary in London and mandatory elsewhere. For this reason the absence of yellow lines on a street in the City of London was held not to be fatal to a prosecution (*Cooper* v *Hall* [1967] 111 SJ 928). The regulations relating to traffic orders in the Metropolis were brought into line with those applying outside London (see reg 18(1)(*f*) of the London Authorities Traffic Orders (Procedure) Regulations 1972 (SI 1972 No 729)). Although many if not all of the current London Traffic Orders were made before 1972, the absence of yellow lines in London may, it is submitted, notwithstanding *Cooper* v *Hall* above, afford a defence.

Direction 28 of the Traffic Signs Regulations and General Directions 1981 requires all parts of a controlled zone not allocated to parking bays to be marked with yellow lines. This obligation is now specific and in this respect differs from the former reg 28 of the 1975 Regulations.

In *Macmillan* v *Gibson* [1966] SLT (Sh) 84 a person parked his vehicle in breach of byelaws made under the Roads and Bridges Act 1878; as there were no notices to warn him of the byelaws and no evidence that he knew of them, he was acquitted.

In *Kierman* v *Howard* [1971] Crim LR 286 it was held that a local authority had erected signs near the road '. . . where parking was allowed' in accordance with reg 17(1)(*f*) of the Local Authorities' Traffic Orders (Procedure) (England and Wales) Regulations 1969 (SI 1969 No 463), when the only signs they had erected informing motorists of a disc parking scheme were at the entrances to and exits from the zone. 'Near' should be interpreted in the light of all the circumstances and in the case of a zone or area could be aptly treated as meaning at the entrance to the zone or area (ibid). (This case, presumably, will apply to London Traffic Orders, as reg 18(1)(*f*) of the London Authorities' Traffic Orders (Procedure) Regulations 1972 (SI 1972 No 729) is in similar terms.)

*Exemptions for loading etc*

Local Acts and orders sometimes permit vehicles to stop in 'No Waiting' streets while loading or unloading goods.The question was raised but not decided in *Kirkland* v *Cairns* [1951] SC (J) 61 whether the goods must be limited to those not sold from the vehicle; in that case fish and chips were sold from the vehicle. In *Whiteside* v *Watson* [1952] SLT 367 it was doubted if selling to customers is 'unloading'. 'Unloading' was held by a metropolitan magistrate to include taking a large sum of money from a car into a bank [1952] Jo Crim L 193). Money in bulk can be 'goods' (112 JP Jo 49, QS). It is not 'loading goods' to put a small parcel in a private car, but it might be if an object not easily portable was put in a car, eg, a laundry basket or several chairs (*Sprake* v *Tester* (1955) 53 LGR 194). In *Richards* v *McKnight* [1977] RTR 289 it was held by a majority that, in accordance with a local order in Manchester, a motorist was not exempted from parking restrictions when collecting £695 for his employees' wages which he was able to carry on his person. The exemption was held to cover the collection and delivery of goods *in a vehicle*. but not the mere collection and delivery of goods by a person who happens to be in a vehicle, ie if a vehicle is needed for collection or delivery of the goods, the vehicle is exempted; but otherwise if the goods to be collected can be carried on the driver's person eg a fountain pen or pair of shoes, or (as in *Boulton* v *Pilkington* [1981] RTR 87) a Chinese take-away meal. It is submitted that, on the authority of these cases, the need of a vehicle may depend on the physical capabilities of the persons in it.

A metropolitan magistrate has held that, where a van is left in a restricted street for eighteen minutes and during most of that time the driver is not engaged in loading or unloading, he is not within an exemption for delivering or loading, etc. The van must be engaged, as distinct from the driver, in loading or delivering during the whole time. Further, the regulations in question required the driver to be with the van all the time (102 SJ 358). In *McLeod* v *Wajkowska* [1963] SLT (Notes) 51 it was held that an exemption in an order for loading and unloading goods extended to taking goods from the vehicle into premises and depositing them there. Similarly, in *Bulman* v *Godbold* [1981] RTR 242 it was held permissible to unload frozen fish into a hotel refrigerator. Where an order permits waiting 'while loading', the defendant must show that his actions were covered by the latter words; if he had merely been asking customers if they had goods for loading but no goods had been loaded, he was not within the permission (*Holder* v *Walker* [1964] Crim LR 61). A metropolitan magistrate has held that waiting in expectation of a load is not within the exemption [1963] Crim LR 706). In *Chafen* v *Another*, Supplement to the *Justice of the Peace and Local Government Review*, 21 March 1970, it was held that an exemption for the loading or unloading of goods did not extend to leaving a vehicle for so long as might be necessary for the goods to be located. No criticism could be made of a finding that thirty-five minutes' parking was unreasonable.

It was held in *Hunter* v *Hammond* [1964] Crim LR 145 to be no defence to a charge of waiting for longer than the permitted period that the defendant was delayed by having to dry his coat, when coffee had been spilt upon it. Nor is it a defence to a charge of breach of a 'No Waiting' order that a taxi driver would otherwise find it very difficult to carry on his legitimate business (*Levinson* v *Powell* [1967] 3 All ER 796). Orders forbade waiting in roads *A* and *B* but exempted unloading; a driver unloaded goods outside premises in *A* and them moved to *B* to park there, as *B* was a wider road. He was held guilty, as the unloading was finished even though the business connected with it was not; on the facts the High Court recommended leniency (*Pratt* v *Hayward* [1969] 3 All ER 1094).

When an order in respect of a 'No Waiting' street forbade a vehicle to wait but continued an exemption for waiting for so long as may be necessary to enable any person to board or alight from the vehicle', it was held that this allowed a car to stop for only so long as necessary to allow someone to get in or out; taking parcels into a nearby house and returning, all within five minutes, was not within the exemption (*Clifford-Turner* v *Waterman* [1961] 3 All ER 974). In *Kaye* v *Hougham* (1964) 62 LGR 457 it was likewise held not to be within that exemption where a taximan went to get change for a £5 note from his fare at the end of the fare's journey, but it was said that prosecutions should not be brought in such circumstances. The relevant order should always be scrutinised to see the precise form of exemption.

For a case of a constable purporting to give herself permission to park in a no waiting area, see 131 JP 627. In *Keene* v *Muncaster* [1980] RTR 377 Lord Lane CJ said that the ordinary use of the word 'permit' in what is now reg 123 of the Motor Vehicles (Construction and Use) Regulations (parking after dark) plainly envisages that the person requesting permission should request it from another and that a policeman could not therefore give himself permission. The position would depend on the wording in the order and whether the word 'permit' is used. A constable who parked in a place reserved for disabled drivers in order to visit a nearby jewellers to take a statement as to a recent robbery was held to be performing a statutory power or duty in a police force vehicle and thus exempted by art 11 of the Borough of Reading (Parking Places for Disabled Drivers) Order 1955 (*George* v *Garland* [1980] RTR 77).

A byelaw prohibited 'stopping' in a street between 4 pm and 6 pm. A driver left his car there before 4 pm and it remained after that hour. It was held that he was not guilty as the byelaw made no reference to remaining at rest (*R* v *Oliver* (1958) 119 CCC 394, a Canadian case).

The prosecution need not show that the defendant's conduct in parking did not fall within any of the exemptions, such as unloading; it is for the defendant to establish that the waiting was for a permitted purpose (*Funnell* v *Johnson* [1962] Crim LR 488).

*Exemptions for disabled drivers*

Orange badges may be issued by local authorities under the Chronically Sick and Disabled Persons Act 1970 for motor vehicles driven by, or used for the carriage of, disabled persons (s 21). The Local Authorities Traffic Orders

(Exemption for Disabled Persons) (England and Wales) Regulations 1971 (SI 1971 No 1493), as amended by like-named 1975 Amendment Regulations (SI 1975 Nos 267 and 1562), provide that, broadly speaking, all limited waiting and (provided loading and unloading is permitted) no waiting traffic orders under ss 5, 8 and 11 of the Road Traffic Regulation Act 1984 and all parking place orders under ss 8, 35, 45, 46 and 50 of that Act must contain an exemption in respect of vehicles displaying these orange badges. The exemptions to be included in orders under these sections relate to parking on streets and highways and do not extend to off street parking. These are minimum exemptions which *must* be contained in the orders and all orders should be consulted as they may contain additional exemptions. Off street parking orders may also contain their own exemptions.

In the case of on street parking meters there is no charge or time limit. In the case of limited waiting orders there is no time limit. In the case of no waiting orders (where loading and unloading is permitted) the maximum waiting period for disabled persons is two hours, and the time disc issued for use with orange badges in such circumstances must also be set and displayed in addition for the exemption to apply.

It should be emphasised that the exemptions conferred on orange badge-holders are only in respect of orders made under the specific provisions of the 1984 Act and do not extend to other provisions of road traffic law, so that displaying the orange badge does not, for example, permit a person to cause an obstruction.

There are two situations in which the provisions of the 1970 Act operate: where the disabled person is the driver and where he is the passenger. If he is the passenger, it is immaterial whether he or his driver stays with the vehicle when it is parked, providing the vehicle 'is being used to convey him' (s 21(1) and (3)). There is no reason why the vehicle should not be used by an able bodied driver or passenger providing it is being used as indicated by the orange badge holder.

The orange badge must be displayed on the nearside of the front windscreen or, if there is no windscreen, in a conspicuous position. Under s 21(1) of the 1970 Act, an orange badge issued in one local authority area must be valid in other such areas subject to the provisions of the regulations. If the conditions relating to the badge, including its display and, where appropriate, the display of the time disc are not complied with, the driver and in certain circumstances the owner commit the underlying parking offence.

The 1971 Exemption Regulations do not apply to orders made by London local authorities other than the GLC or to any London orders in the cities of London and Westminster, the Royal Borough of Kensington and Chelsea or that part of the London Borough of Camden which is south of and includes Euston Road. These areas have their own regulations and exemptions, each individual to the area concerned.

Badges are issued in accordance with the Disabled Persons (Badges for Motor Vehicles) Regulations 1982 (SI 1982 No 1740). The badge being issued under the revised regulations is larger and square instead of round. The regulations prescribe the descriptions of persons to whom a badge may be issued and the cases where a local authority may refuse to issue a badge, or require its return. These cases include where in relation to a badge misuse on at least three occasions has led to a relevant conviction, or would give grounds for such a conviction. The expression would give grounds for such a conviction is in wide terms but may give rise to difficulties. For example, it seems wide enough to include the facts which give rise to a spent conviction. In addition there could not be a *conviction* if the limitation period had expired, but it may be that it could still be said that there would have been grounds for a conviction. Compare s 117(2) where the expression 'is guilty of an offence' is used and see the comments on this below.

'Relevant conviction' means:

(*a*) the conviction of either the holder of a disabled person's badge; or any other person using a disabled person's badge with the holder's consent, of an offence of using or causing or permitting a vehicle to be used arising—
  - (i) under ss 5(1), 8(1), 11 or 16(1) of the Road Traffic Regulation Act 1984 if the offence consisted of the unlawful parking of the vehicle, or
  - (ii) under s 35(4) (including its aggravated form—see Sched 7), s 35(5) and s 47(1) (including its aggravated form—see Sched 7) of the 1984 Act; and

(*b*) the conviction of any person other than the holder of a disabled person's badge of an offence under section 117 of the 1984 Act where the badge was displayed on the vehicle with the consent of the holder at any time during which the offence was being committed.

'Relevant conviction' is also deemed to include the equivalent fixed penalty liability. The regulations referred to sections in the 1967 Act and the equivalent sections in the 1984 consolidating Act have been incorporated instead.

Where a badge is refused or recalled because of misuse there is a right of appeal to the Secretary of State within twenty-eight days of the date on which the notice is issued. There is no right of appeal under the regulations for a refusal on other grounds. It will be noted that the relevant convictions may be of persons other than the badge holder and it is the use or display as appropriate of the badge with the holder's consent which is specified and not the commission of the offence with the holder's consent. Some of the appeals may turn on whether this consent to the use or display was in fact given.

The provisions in the regulations regarding misuse were made as a consequence of ss 21(7A–7E) of the Chronically Sick and Disabled Persons Act 1970 inserted by s 68 of the Transport Act 1982. See the provision in s 21(7B) as to the service of notices by post.

A person who improperly uses a disabled person's badge on a motor vehicle so that a disabled person's concession is available and who is guilty of an offence under the 1984 Act (including orders and regulations made thereunder), also commits an offence under s 117. See the provisions of that section in Vol 2.

Section 117 is in unusual terms. The defendant has to be guilty also of the first offence ie an offence under any provision of the 1984 Act other than s 117. It is submitted that this is not a form of double jeopardy if he has been *convicted* of the first offence, as s 117 constitutes a second and more serious offence. As noted above, unlike the regulations relating to misuse, there is no reference to a conviction. This implies that an actual conviction is not a pre-requisite providing the elements of the offence can be established. For instance the time limit for the first offence may well have expired by the trial date of the second offence under s 117. It is submitted that it could still be established that he was guilty of the first offence. In any event one would have regard to the position when the information for the second (s 117) offence was laid and not the time of its trial. For a contrary view, see (1984) 148 JP 560.

Offences against s 35(4) (breach of order as to off street parking or on street parking without payment) and against s 47(1) (contraventions relating to designated parking places) are committed in an aggravated form and carry a heavier maximum fine where the person parks in a place reserved for disabled persons' vehicles without qualifying (see the entries in Sched 7 referring to these offences). In the unanimous decision of the House of Lords in *R* v *Courtie* (1984) Cr App R 292, Lord Diplock said at p 300 (in relation to a different statute) that the much more suitable way is to put into separate counts in an indictment charges which include allegations of factual ingredients which attract different maximum punishments. It is suggested therefore that where the allegation is of an aggravated offence, this should be specified and set out in an information separate from that for an unaggravated offence.

## 6.72 Clearways

The Various Trunk Roads (Prohibition of Waiting) (Clearways) Order 1963 (SI 1963 No 1172), and the like London Order (SI 1963 No 1247) are made under ss 1 and 6 of the Road Traffic Regulation Act 1984 (see 6.71 as to the provisions of these sections). They forbid vehicles to stop on the main carriageways of certain named roads unless with police permission, for building, road or public utility works, fire, ambulance or police purposes, postal collections and deliveries, local authority cesspool and refuse vehicles, to close gates and barriers, to avoid accidents or in circumstances beyond the driver's control. 'Main carriageway' means any carriageway of that road primarily used by through traffic and excludes lay-bys. A slip way was held to be within the definition of 'main carriageway' in *Hawkins* v *Phillips* [1980] RTR 197 because any vehicle going on to the slip road was committed to go on the main road. It is submitted that parking on a grass verge is not included within the definition in that the verge is not a carriageway. A vehicle may not wait on a lay-by or verge of any such clearway for the purpose of selling goods from that vehicle unless they are at once delivered to premises adjacent to that vehicle. Other clearways orders have been made and the wording of each order should be referred to in each case.

## 6.73 Parking on verges, footpaths and central reservations

Section 36A of the 1972 Act prohibits the parking of heavy commercial vehicles on verges, footpaths or central reservations of roads, and s 36B prohibits the parking of vehicles other than heavy commercial vehicles on the verges, footpaths or central reservations of 'urban roads'.

For the definition of a heavy commercial vehicle, in s 36A, see 1.11. Under s 36A(9) the Secretary of State for Transport may by regulation amend this definition. Under s 36A(3A) the Secretary of State for Transport may exempt certain classes of vehicle from the provisions of s 36A or apply the section subject to specified conditions.

'Urban road' is defined by s 36B as a road subject to a speed limit not exceeding 40 mph imposed by s 81 or s 84 of the Road Traffic Regulation Act 1984 or any local Act. Local authorities can make orders either wholly exempting, or partially exempting at all times or during specified hours, specified roads in their area from the operation of s 36B.

The prohibition under s 36A or 36B applies to 'the verge' of the road, 'any land which is situated between two carriageways . . . ' of the road and any 'footway', ie a way over which the public have a right on foot only and which is comprised in a highway consisting of a carriageway (see s 329 of the Highways Act 1980).

Provided it is not left unattended, it is a defence to a charge under either section if the vehicle was parked for loading or unloading on the footway or verge and the loading or unloading could only be satisfactorily performed by being so parked. It is also a defence to either section if the vehicle was parked with police permission or for life saving, fire fighting or in a like emergency.

Evidence may be given by way of certificate under s 181 of the Act of 1972 (see 2.80) and proof of identity of the driver may be given by s 183 (see 2.80).

Subsections 36B(5)–(8) were brought into force on 31 October 1975. The remainder were not in force on 1 February 1985.

*Immobilisation of vehicles illegally parked*

The immobilisation of vehicles illegally parked is provided for by ss 104–106 of the Road Traffic Regulation Act 1984. The immobilisation is by means of a wheel clamp. It has been introduced in such areas as the Secretary of State specifies by order, initially on an experimental basis. Only one such order has been made—for the London Boroughs of Westminster, and Kensington and Chelsea (SI 1983 No 218, to be continued in force by SI 1985 No 464 until 15 May 1987). The device can only be fixed by or under the direction of a constable. With the device an appropriate notice must also be fixed to the vehicle. The notice includes information as to how the release of the vehicle may be secured. Subject to this, release may be obtained by payment of the prescribed charge (£19.50—SI 1983 No 220). The police still retain the power to remove such illegally parked vehicles. Interference with the notice is an offence (s 104(5)) carrying a maximum penalty of level 2. It is also an offence to remove or attempt to remove the device without authorisation; the maximum penalty for this is a fine of level 3 (s 104(6)).

There are exemptions for vehicles displaying a current disabled person's badge (s 105). However, under s 105(5) and (6) it is an offence for an able bodied person to use the badge illegally in the immobilisation area. The maximum penalty is a fine of level 3. It is also not possible to use the device on vehicles parked for up to two hours after the expiry of the initial parking meter charge (including 'borrowed time'). However, the device may be used where there have been other contraventions.

By s 72 of the 1982 Act, ss 53 and 54 apply to vehicles and persons in the public service of the Crown.

## 6.74 Abandoning vehicles

By s 2(1) of the Refuse Disposal (Amenity) Act 1978 any person who, without lawful authority, abandons on any land in the open air, or on any other land forming part of a highway, a motor vehicle or anything which formed part of a motor vehicle and was removed from it in the course of dismantling the vehicle on the land commits an offence. By s 2(2), a person who leaves anything on any land in such circumstances or for such a period that he may reasonably be assumed to have abandoned it or to have brought it to the land for the purpose of abandoning it there, shall be deemed to have abandoned it there or, as the case may be, to have brought it to the land for that purpose unless the contrary is shown. Proof of the contrary seems to be on the defendant. The offence may be prosecuted by any person, eg an aggrieved landowner. In view of the wording of s 2(2), it may be that the time limit for proceedings runs from the date of the leaving of the vehicle and that the offence is not a continuing one; cf *R* v *Boulden* (1957) 41 Cr App R 105; *Vaughan* v *Biggs* [1960] 2 All ER 473. 'Motor vehicle' is widely defined in s 11(1) of the Act as including trailers and contraptions which have ceased to be motor vehicles under the 1972 Act.

By ss 3 and 4 of the Act power is given to local authorities to remove vehicles appearing to have been abandoned on any land in the open air or on any other land forming part of a highway, to dispose of abandoned vehicles and to recover their expenses.

'Abandon', according to the *Concise Oxford Dictionary*, means to give up or forsake; it is not 'abandoning children in a manner likely to cause them unnecessary suffering' to leave them in Chatham Juvenile Court whilst in session (*R* v *Whibley* [1938] 3 All ER 777).

## 6.75 Driving on the footway and on common or private land

Under the Highway Act 1835, s 72, it is an offence wilfully to ride or drive on the footway, even though the driving may last for only a few seconds (*M'Arthur* v *Jack* [1950] SC(J) 29). The offence will apply to pedal and motor cyclists. Driving across the footway to get to a private park was held to be an offence in the absence of proof of long user or of its being a way of necessity (*Curtis* v *Geeves* (1930) 94 JP 71) but in *Vestry of St Mary, Newington* v *Jacobs* (1871) LR 7 QB 47 the owner of land adjoining the highway was held to be entitled to convey machinery on trolleys over the pavement into his premises. 'Wilfully' under this section means purposely; see *Fearnley* v *Ormsby* 43 JP 384, and a magistrates' court has acquitted a defendant who drove on the footway in ignorance that it was part of the footway. On the same principle a defendant who drove on the footway accidentally should be acquitted.

Section 28 of the Town Police Clauses Act 1847 also prohibits the drawing or driving of a carriage upon any footway of a street. Both the 1847 and the 1835 Acts refer to 'carriages', which expression includes motor vehicles and trailers (1972 Act, s 195). Not all police forces take active steps to enforce these sections, but many more are now doing so in order to prevent subsequent parking on the pavement. *Quaere* whether there is a common law right to divert on to the pavement in cases of necessity when the carriageway is blocked.

Section 36 of the 1972 Act prohibits the driving of motor vehicles on footpaths, bridleways, common land, moorland or other land not part of a road, with an exception for parking within fifteen yards of a road or for emergencies.

The effect of s 36, it is submitted, is that a motorist may drive on common or moorland off a public road for fifteen yards, so long as he intends to park; if he goes more than fifteen yards, he commits an offence whether he parks or not. If he goes on private land, he commits no offence so long as he parks there and does not go more than fifteen yards, although the landowner does not consent to the vehicle going on the land; the landowner should sue for trespass. If the motorist parks, say, twenty yards from the road on private land, he commits an offence under s 36 and he also commits an offence if he drives less than fifteen yards on private land for the purpose of turning his car round. *Quaere*, if a defence of de minimis could be raised for a move lasting four or five seconds only three feet up a private drive. It seems to be an offence to drive on private land under s 36, unless within the exceptions; consequently, motoring trespassers can be prosecuted if, say, they drive up the approach to a country house or a farm purely from motives of curiosity and with no intention of visiting the occupant. The motorists' passengers could be charged if aiding, abetting, counselling and procuring can be proved. Persons coming to a house on lawful business, however, have an implied licence to go through an unlocked gate (if motorists, perhaps not to open a closed gate) and up to the door (*Robson* v *Hallett* [1967] 2 All ER 407) but not, it is suggested, to deviate from a driveway or roadway on to grassland. The opinion is advanced that s 36 extends to any private land and that such land need not be ejusdem generis with a common or moorland—it could be a factory yard or private carpark as well as a field—the words 'other land of whatsoever description' being wide enough to exclude the ejusdem generis rule (Maxwell on the *Interpretation of Statutes*, 12th ed, pp 303–305 (general words construed generally).

The question is discussed at 125 JP Jo 251 whether s 36 applies to all footpaths, both those at the side of carriageways and those ways for pedestrians and cyclists only. It is submitted there, following earlier opinions cited, that s 36 is aimed at persons who drive motor vehicles on footpaths and bridleways which are not at the side of a carriageway and that the section applies to such ways for foot passengers and cyclists in towns as well as in the country but not those adjoining a carriageway. For a contrary view that s 36 applies also to footways adjoining a carriageway, see an article at (1981) 145 JP Jo 697. See 1.66–8 and in particular 1.67*A* as to offences by cyclists on bridleways and as to the meaning of that term. The Highway Act 1835, s 72, refers to footpaths at the side of a road.

Certain local authority vehicles are exempt (Public Health Act 1961, s 49; Vehicles (Conditions of Use on Footpaths) Regulations 1963 (SI 1963 No 2126) and 1966 (SI 1966 No 864)).

The Law of Property Act 1925, s 193(4), provides that any person who without lawful authority draws or drives upon any metropolitan common, manorial waste, common wholly or partly within a borough or urban district, or any land subject to rights of common to which the section may be applied under s 193(2), any carriage, cart, caravan, truck or other vehicle or who camps or lights a fire thereon commits an offence.

### 6.76 Depositing builders' skips on the highway

The Highways Act 1980, s 139(1) and (3), makes it an offence to be the 'owner' (see definition below) of a builder's skip which has been deposited on the highway without permission of the highway authority. It was said in *York City Council* v *Poller* [1976] RTR 37 that the Act does not contemplate blanket permits and any permission has to be in writing. It is also an offence for the owner to fail to comply with a condition imposed by the permission or to fail to secure that the skip is properly lighted at night, to fail to remove the skip as soon as practicable after it has been filled and to fail to secure that the skip is clearly and indelibly marked with his name and address or telephone number.

Section 139(11) defines a 'builder's skip' as a container designed to be carried on a road vehicle and to be placed on a highway or other land for the storage of builder's materials, or for the removal and disposal of builder's rubble, waste, household and other rubbish or earth. 'Owner' is defined as the hirer where the skip is hired for not less than one month or is hired under a hire purchase agreement.

The skip must under s 139(4) also comply with the marking regulations. The Builders' Skips (Markings) Regulations 1984 (SI 1984 No 1933) have been made. From 1 January 1986 each end of a builder's skip, part of which is placed on any part of a highway except a footway or verge, must be marked with a specified marking. Every such marking must be clean and efficient and clearly visible for a reasonable distance to persons using the highway. The only exception is a door required to be open for loading or unloading. Accidentally leaving the door open would not be an exception; the door must be required to be open for the purpose of loading or unloading.

The s 139(1) offence is wide enough to include leaving a skip for a number of days after permission had expired; *Craddock* v *Green* [1983] RTR 479. Under s 139(5) proceedings may be taken against any other person whose act or default resulted in the offence being committed whether or not proceedings are also taken against the owner (*PGM Buildings Co Ltd* v *Kensington LBC* [1982] RTR 107). It is only if some other person's act or default resulted in the offence that proceedings may be taken against a person other than the owner (see for example *York City Council* v *Poller* above).

It is a defence to a charge under s 139 that the commission of the offence was due to the act or default of another and that the defendant took all reasonable precautions and exercised all due diligence to avoid the commission of the offence (s 139(6)). For the nature of this defence, see 14.63. To avail oneself of the defence notice has to be given to the prosecutor seven clear days before the hearing of such information identifying or assisting in the identification of the other person as is then in one's possession (s 139(7)). It is not necessary to identify the other person if it is not possible to do so (*PGM Buildings Co Ltd* v *Kensington LBC* above). If notice has not been given or seven days' notice is not given, the defence may be relied on with the leave of the court. A defendant giving notice under s 139(7) identifying that other person has to give as full information as he was able honestly to provide in accordance with the facts in his possession at the time gave the notice (*Barnet London BC* v *S & W Transport Ltd* [1975] Crim LR 171). It was held in *Lambeth London BC* v *Saunders Transport Ltd* [1974] RTR 319 that the owner of a skip who had hired it out could avail himself of the defence as he had taken all reasonable precautions and had used due diligence to see that the hirers were aware of their duties as to lighting it. The purpose of s 139(6) was to provide a defence for owners of skips who were accustomed to hire out skips and took the necessary steps to see that the hirers complied with their duties such as lighting (ibid).

## 6.77 Negligent opening of car doors

It is convenient to mention here prosecutions of motorists and their passengers who suddenly open a car door and strike a passing cyclist or pedestrian. The position is now covered, so far as motor vehicles and trailers are concerned, by reg 125 of the Motor Vehicles (Construction and Use) Regulations 1978, discussed below. Prosecutions may still be brought under the Highway Act 1835, s 78, however, and persons on cycles and in horse-drawn vehicles who cause hurt can only be charged under that Act. They should not be charged under the limb of s 78 of the Highway Act 1835 which deals with drivers on the highway causing hurt by negligence; that limb is concerned with negligence in driving and not with things done after the vehicle has stopped (*Shears* v *Matthews* [1948] 2 All ER 1064). But the driver or any passenger who opens a car door in a negligent way may be convicted of interrupting by negligence the free passage of a person or vehicle on the highway under another limb of s 78 (*Watson* v *Lowe* [1950] 1 All ER 100). Where a defendant had taken precautions to see if traffic was coming and nevertheless an accident occurred when he opened the door, it was held on those facts that he should not be convicted of 'wilful obstruction' (*Eaton* v *Cobb* [1950] 1 All ER 1016). It may be that the 'interrupting by negligence' limb of s 78 covers cases where cigarette ash is carelessly flicked into a cyclist's face causing him to have an accident. 'Car door' accidents, if a person or animal is injured or another vehicle damaged, should be reported to the police by the driver where s 25 or s 166 of the 1972 Act applies (*Jones* v *Prothero* [1952] 1 All ER 434). See 7.8.

A passenger may properly be convicted of hindering the free passage of a person on the highway by negligently opening a car door (*Baldwin* v *Pearson* (1958) 122 JP 321).

Regulation 125 of the Motor Vehicles (Construction and Use) Regulations

1978 makes it an offence to cause or permit any door of a motor vehicle or trailer to be opened on a road so as to cause injury or danger to any person.

The regulation applies to any person, eg a commissionaire, as well as to people in the vehicle. It applies only on a road (see Chapter 1), and it is submitted, as 'trailer' is defined in s 190(1) of the 1972 Act as a vehicle drawn by a motor vehicle, that it applies to caravans and other trailers only whilst they are attached to a motor vehicle (see Chapter 1). This may be interpreted slightly more widely (see under 'Trailers' in Chapter 1).

In *R* v *Cowley* [1971] CLY 10145, a case at Middlesex Quarter Sessions, the words 'cause injury or danger' were held to be merely descriptive and the summons was thus not held to be bad for duplicity. *Quaere* whether the defendant is liable to conviction if he has not been negligent. While there is a presumption that mens rea is required for all offences, this can be displaced by the subject matter with which the regulation deals. Normally, unless mens rea is clearly or by necessary implication ruled out, proof of it is required (*Brend* v *Wood* (1946) 110 JP 317). On the other hand, it can be argued that it is the duty of every door opener to satisfy himself that no cyclist or other person can possibly be endangered and to make allowance for blind spots in his view behind, eg by using another door, so that an almost undischargeable burden is on the defendant; support for this strict view may come from the need to suppress the mischief at which reg 125 is obviously aimed, as decisions establishing absolute liability often arise from statutes which strike at an evil affecting the public welfare. But in *Sever* v *Duffy* [1977] RTR 429, justices dismissed a charge brought under reg 125 on the ground that there was an element of doubt whether the defendant caused danger to other road users in that they considered he had done all that was reasonable in all the circumstances and that the car overtook the defendant's stationary vehicle too closely. The justices' dismissal was upheld: this was a factual decision they were entitled to make (ibid). It was unnecessary to decide whether the offence involved an element of mens rea as it did not arise on the facts found by the justices (ibid). It would seem that justices are entitled to find as a fact that the act of opening a car door did not cause danger, if the driver of the stationary car took all reasonable precautions and the danger was caused by the overtaking vehicle.

See 2.8 as to drivers in Crown service committing these offences.

## 6.78 Leaving vehicle in dangerous position

Section 24 of the 1972 Act prohibits causing or permitting a vehicle or trailer to remain at rest on a road so as to be likely to cause a danger to other persons using the road. This includes not only leaving a vehicle just around a blind corner, but also leaving one in a position which is safe while it is at rest but dangerous if it moves (*Maguire* v *Crouch* (1940) 104 JP 445: driver leaving a vehicle without setting the brake so that it ran away).

Warning of intended prosecution (see Chapter 3) is required (1972 Act s 179) for all vehicles; s 24 applies to Crown vehicles, trams and trolley vehicles operated under statutory powers, cycles and carts as well as to motor vehicles on roads but not off them.

## 6.79 Parking or driving on cycle tracks

A person who drives or parks a motor vehicle wholly or partly on a cycle track without lawful authority commits an offence, contrary to s 2(1) of the Cycle Tracks Act 1984. For this purpose 'motor vehicle' is as defined in the 1972 Act (see 1.2) and 'cycle track' is as defined in the Highways Act 1980 (see also 1.67*D*). The offence does not apply to trailers. Electrically assisted pedal cycles as defined in Chapter 1 are allowed to use such tracks but pedal cycles which are motor vehicles under the 1972 Act are excluded.

## 6.80 Parking at night

By reg 123 of the Construction and Use Regulations 1978, no person shall cause or permit a motor vehicle to stand on any road during the hours of darkness otherwise than with its left or near side as close as may be to the edge of the carriageway. The main exceptions are (*a*) leave of a policeman in uniform, (*b*) fire, police, defence and ambulance vehicles but only in such circumstances that compliance with this regulation would hinder or be likely to hinder the use of the vehicle for the purpose for which it is being used on that occasion, (*c*) car parks, taxi stands and bus stops, (*d*) one-way streets, and (*e*) vehicles on building work, repair work or road work (see 118 JP Jo 101), or removing traffic obstructions.

A case is discussed at 131 JP Jo 627 of a policewoman in uniform purporting to give herself leave to park in a 'No Waiting' area; vehicles used for police purposes may be exempt under reg 123. It is submitted that it is primarily a question of fact whether a vehicle is used for police purposes. In *Keene* v *Muncaster* [1980] RTR 377 it was held as a matter of construction that 'permission' in what is now reg 123(1) envisaged permission being requested by one person from another and that a policeman could not therefore give himself permission. It was not contended that the exemption under what is now reg 123(2) (police vehicles) applied. Although the officer's vehicle was used for police purposes it could not be said that compliance with the regulation would hinder its use for police purposes.

## 6.81–4 Depositing mud and other matter on highways

Byelaws are in force in some areas prohibiting the dropping of mud from a vehicle upon the highway (see [1954] Crim LR 213). See Local Government Act 1972, s 238, for proof of byelaws.

It is an offence for a person without lawful authority or excuse to deposit any thing whatsoever whereby a user of the highway is injured or endangered (Highways Act 1980, s 161(1)). The prosecution must prove injury or danger caused by the matter deposited (*Gatland* v *Metropolitan Police Commissioner* [1968] 2 QB 279). It is also an offence for a person without lawful authority or excuse to allow any filth, dirt, lime or other offensive matter to run or flow on to a highway from adjoining premises (Highways Act 1980, s 161(3)).

There are further 'depositing' offences in s 148 of the Highways Act 1980. In *Perret Co Ltd* v *Newham LBC* [1981] RTR 502 it was held that no offence was committed under this section if the depositing was unintentional. It was suggested that the position might be different if a consistent practice of loading were adopted whereby material was likely to fall on the highway. The decision appears to cover the wording of s 161(1) also. For a case where depositing tubs of flowers in a London mews was held to be unreasonable and therefore without lawful excuse and contrary to s 148 see *Putnam* v *Colvin* [1984] RTR 150.

## Obstruction, Parking etc: Penalties

### 6.85 Generally

The penalty for obstruction under s 137 of the Highways Act 1980 is a fine of level 3; under s 28 of the Town Police Clauses Act 1847, a fine of level 3 or fourteen days' imprisonment; and under reg 122 of the Construction and Use Regulations, a fine of level 4.

The penalty for offences relating to parking places where charges are made under s 35(4), s 47(1) and Sched 7 of the Road Traffic Regulation Act 1984 is a fine of level 2. Illegal parking in a place reserved for disabled persons' vehicles under s 35(4) or 47(1) and Sched 7 is punishable with a fine of level 3, and improper use of a disabled person's badge and vehicle under s 117 with a fine of level 3.

The penalty for breach of a traffic regulation order under s 5(1) or 8(1) and Sched 7 of the Road Traffic Regulation Act 1984 is a fine of level 3.

The penalties for other parking offences considered in this section are as follows: parking on verges etc under s 36A or s 36B of the 1972 Act, level 3; abandoning vehicles under s 2(1) of the Refuse Disposal (Amenity) Act 1978, a fine of level 4 or 3 months' imprisonment or both (and see below as to removal charges); driving on footpaths etc under s 36 of the 1972 Act, level 3; driving on commons etc under s 193(4) of the Law of Property Act 1925 level 1; depositing builders' skips on a highway etc under s 139(1) and (3) of the Highway Act 1980, level 3; negligent opening of car doors under s 78 of the Highway Act 1835, level 1, or under reg 125 of the Construction and Use Regulations, level 4; leaving vehicles in a dangerous position under s 24 of the 1972 Act, level 3 (and see below as to endorsement etc); improperly parking at night under reg 123 of the Construction and Use Regulations, level 4; depositing mud etc on the highway under s 161(1) of the Highways Act 1980, level 3, under s 161(3) level 1, or under s 148, level 3.

Instead of prosecuting offenders for parking offences, s 145 and Sched 12 of the Road Traffic Regulation Act 1984 allows a fixed penalty to be imposed. The liability for payment of excess meter charges and offences for which fixed penalty notices have been issued is placed in the first instance on the owner of the vehicle. See 'Vehicle Owner Liability', 17.2.

Parking or driving on a cycle track under s 2(1) of the Cycle Track Act 1984 carries a maximum fine of level 3. This Act as such is not specified in Sched 12 and a cycle track is possibly not a road (see the definition of a road at 1.66).

The power to endorse and disqualify does not extend to obstruction and parking cases and offences under traffic regulation orders. It does extend to parking within the limits of a pedestrian crossing (see the section on 'Pedestrian Crossings'), and to leaving a vehicle in a dangerous position. In the latter case the court must endorse unless there are special reasons (see Chapter 21). The offences carry 3 penalty points. Disqualification (see Chapter 20) and disqualification until passing a driving test under s 93 of the 1972 Act may be ordered (see 20.32), and s 19 of the Transport Act 1981 (penalty points disqualification) applies (see 20.18–21).

The Magistrates' Association suggested penalties (see 18.1 and Appendix 3) for certain obstruction offences read:

Dangerous Position: £40
On zig-zags by Pedestrian Crossing: £20
Obstruction: £15
Clearway—stopping on: £40

It is submitted that magistrates, when deciding on the amount of the fine, should take into consideration whether the defendant has had the opportunity of paying a fixed penalty and, also, if the defendant has had to pay a removal fee (see below) after having had his vehicle towed away.

The endorsement code for an offence of leaving in a dangerous position is MS10.

### 6.86 Removal of illegally parked and abandoned vehicles

The power to remove illegally parked vehicles is given to the police by ss 99–102 of the Road Traffic Regulation Act 1984, and by the Removal and Disposal of Vehicles Regulations 1968 (SI 1968 No 43, as amended by SI 1978 No 1346, and SI 1982 No 1682 and other amending regulations now spent), and Sched 19 to the Local Government Act 1972. See also the Removal and Disposal of Vehicles (Loading Areas) Regulations 1978, SI 1978 No 1345 as amended by SI 1982 No 1696.

A schedule to the 1968 Regulations lists the enactments breach of which enables an offending vehicle to be removed, and includes virtually every statutory provision enabling orders to be made prohibiting waiting of motor vehicles. The powers of removal under s 99 include vehicles which have broken down, and vehicles causing obstruction, danger, potential danger (s 99(1)). Section 102(4) of the Road Traffic Regulation Act 1984 entitles the police or local authority to retain custody of the vehicle until the removal fee is paid. The fees are £47 where removal is from a motorway, £45 in the Metropolitan Police District and £43 elsewhere. A storage fee is also payable: £4 for each period or part period of twenty-four hours from noon on the day following the day on which the vehicle was removed. The fees as at the same date for removal from a loading area are £45 in the City of London and the Metropolitan Police District and £43 elsewhere, and the storage charge also £4. It was held that dismissal of proceedings for the contravention for which the vehicle was towed away was a bar to proceedings for recovery of the removal fee (*Metropolitan Police Commissioner* v *Meller* (1963) 107 SJ 381). *Quaere* in such circumstances whether the vehicle owner may recover a fee which he has paid in order to re-possess his vehicle.

A person convicted under s 2(1) of the Refuse Disposal (Amenity) Act

1978 may in addition to a penalty be ordered to pay the proper charges in respect of the removal of the vehicle under s 102 of the Road Traffic Regulation Act 1984 or under s 5 of the Refuse Disposal (Amenity) Act 1978.

# Chapter 7

# Accidents and Furnishing Information

## Accidents Involving Injury

### 7.1–5 Production of certificates: s 166

Under s 166(1) and (2) of the 1972 Act, where, owing to the presence of a motor vehicle (other than an invalid carriage: see further 1.5) on a road, an accident occurs involving personal injury to another person and the driver does not at the time produce his certificate of insurance to the police or to some person who has on reasonable grounds required its production, the driver shall, as soon as possible and in any case within twenty-four hours of the accident, report it to the police and thereupon produce his certificate, provided that he may within five days after the accident produce it at such police station as he specifies at the time of reporting. Note that the driver does not have to produce the certificate in person (as also under s 162(2): see 10.30).

In *Tremelling* v *Martin* [1971] RTR 196 the defendant produced his driving licence and certificate of insurance at a police station. The clerk was called to the telephone before the documents could be examined. The defendant did not wait and walked out of the station. Directing a conviction under both sections, the Divisional Court held that the purpose of producing driving licences was to enable the police to ascertain the name and address of the holder of the licence, the date of issue and the authority that issued it, and the purpose of s 162 was to enable a constable to inspect the certificate of insurance and see that it was a proper certificate. The case would appear to apply to s 166 also, because the object of the section appears to be similar to that of s 162.

The requirements under s 166, which only arise on an accident involving personal injury to another person, must be obeyed although the driver has given his name and address to some person reasonably requiring it under s 25, (see below). The section would not apply where the driver was quite unaware of the accident, or the injury (*Harding* v *Price* [1948] 1 All ER 283). In *Hampson* v *Powell* [1970] 1 All ER 929 a lorry driver was held not to be guilty under s 25 of failing to stop and failing to report an accident of which he was not aware, although he was convicted of careless driving as the evidence, although insufficient to show that he knew of the accident, was sufficient to show that he drove the vehicle without due care and attention. The section would seem to apply where a passenger was injured and it could be particularly important now that passenger liability is compulsorily insurable.

It would seem, following *Bulman* v *Bennett* [1974] RTR 1 (see 7.9), a case on s 25, that the driver does not have twenty-four hours to obey the section, he must do so 'as soon as possible'. (*Quaere* whether 'as soon as possible' in s 166 imposes a higher duty than 'as soon as reasonably practicable' in s 25. It would seem that it does.)

It is an offence under s 162 to fail to produce the certificate to a policeman at the time (subject to the same five days of grace as above), but no offence to fail to produce it to any other person.

If the driver has no certificate of insurance, he does not 'produce' one and so must report to the police.

Note that the 'driver' has the obligation, not the owner or anyone else, save so far as he may aid and abet the driver's failure.

Section 166 does not apply to drivers of trams and trolley vehicles operated under statutory powers (s 197(4)). Nor does it apply to Crown vehicles.

## Accidents to Persons, Animals, Vehicles or Property

### 7.6 Stopping and reporting: requirements of ss 25 and 164

Section 25(1) of the 1972 Act requires a driver to stop his vehicle if an accident has occurred owing to the presence of a motor vehicle on a road, in which *either* personal injury is caused to someone other than the driver of the vehicle, *or* damage is caused to a vehicle (excepting the defendant's own vehicle or a trailer drawn by the driver's vehicle), or to an animal (excepting an animal in the driver's vehicle or trailer), or to any property attached to land on which the road is situated or adjacent to the road. If so required by a person having reasonable grounds, the driver must give his own name and address, those of the owner of the vehicle and the identification marks of the vehicle (s 25(1)). If the driver (in such circumstances) does not give his name and address to any such person he must report the accident at a police station or to a constable as soon as reasonably practicable and, in any case, within twenty-four hours (s 25(2)).

It is also an offence under s 164(1) of the 1972 Act for a person alleged to have committed an offence of reckless or careless driving or cycling (ss 2, 3, 17 and 18 of the 1972 Act) to refuse, on being so required by any person having reasonable ground to do so, to give his name and address to that person, or to give a false name and address. The offence under s 164 does not require there to have been an accident. Section 164 applies to drivers of motor vehicles and riders of cycles. The person asking his name and address must have reasonable ground for so asking from the other person who is alleged to have committed reckless or careless driving or cycling.

Section 25 applies to the drivers of trams and trolley vehicles operated under statutory powers and to Crown drivers. The section casts no duties on the drivers or riders of vehicles which are not 'motor vehicles', as defined in

Chapter 1. (Compare this with the duty regarding damage to *other vehicles, motor or otherwise.*)

The obligations of s 25 arise only where there has been injury to a person or an animal (ie any horse, cattle, ass, mule, sheep, pig, goat or dog: see s 25(3)) or damage to another vehicle, motor vehicle or not, or to the road or roadside property as particularised in s 25(1). The words of the section make it clear that it does not apply where the only damage is to the motor vehicle concerned or its trailer or an animal therein or the only person injured is the driver himself. It applies where a passenger is injured. Note that the term 'animal' does not include cats or any other beast not mentioned in s 25 or birds. See 4.132 as to the meaning of 'cattle'.

A bicycle is a vehicle (*Ellis* v *Nott-Bower* (1896) 60 JP 760). Trams and trolley vehicles are also vehicles within the meaning of s 25 where damage is caused *to* them by a motor vehicle. Horse-drawn carts are, too. It may be that 'vehicle' in s 25 means one normally used on the carriageway as opposed to the footway. A metropolitan magistrate has held a barrow to be a 'carriage' ([1959] Jo Crim L 338). See also 210 LT News 201. A motorised invalid carriage is clearly a vehicle whether or not it is a motor vehicle as defined in the 1972 Act. Whether a pram or a child's fairy-cycle is a vehicle has not been decided; the case of *R* v *Mathias* (1861) 2 F & F 570, cited in some earlier editions of this book as to a pram not being a 'carriage', is not now put forward as an authority either way. Any wheeled vehicle, including a hand propelled invalid carriage, pram, doll's pram, or fairy-cycle, which is not within the 'de minimis' rule, however, appears to be within the dictionary definition of 'vehicle'. A wheel chair might be held to be a form of chair rather than a vehicle.

The section formerly applied only where there had been injury or damage to another vehicle or person or animal (as defined in s 25(3)), and if any other form of property, eg, a wall or lamp post was damaged, s 25 did not apply (*Pagett* v *Mayo* [1939] 2 All ER 362). The effect of *Pagett* v *Mayo* has been reversed by the inclusion of the words as to property in subs (1) by the Road Traffic Act 1974. Damage to property growing in, constructed on, fixed to or forming part of the land of the road or land adjacent thereto, now gives rise to the obligations contained in s 25. The words 'growing in' quite clearly bring damage to trees, crops and plants within the ambit of the section. The amendment does not include property not fixed, etc, on the road or roadside, and it would therefore appear that if the damage was, for example, only to the load of another vehicle, or to the clothing only of a pedestrian, he being unhurt, s 25 as amended would not apply. If a traffic sign or other roadside property is damaged, there will usually be no one to whom the motorist can reasonably be required to give his name and address, and in such a case he will therefore be under an obligation to report the accident to the police (see *Peek* v *Towle* at 7.9).

Section 25 applies only where the accident has been due to the presence of the defendant's motor vehicle 'on a road' within the meaning of s 196 (see 1.66). Unless it is a road to which the public have access it does not apply to accidents on a car park or private property. *Semble*, if only part of the defendant's vehicle is on a road, the section applies, eg where he is emerging from his private drive.

The driver is under the obligations imposed by s 25 even though the accident may have been caused entirely by the fault of someone else.

## 7.7 Knowledge of driver

It is the 'driver' who has the duties under s 25, not the owner or anyone else save so far as the latter may aid, abet, counsel or procure the driver's failure.

The requirement imposed by the provisions of s 25 only applies if the defendant knows that an accident has occurred (*Harding* v *Price* [1948] 1 All ER 283). The judges held in *Harding* v *Price* that there was a positive duty—something more than a mere prohibition—placed by the statute to report and the driver could not discharge that duty unless he had knowledge of the accident. When the case was decided 'knowledge' was thought to include wilfully shutting one's eyes to the obvious. This view is nowadays not put forward quite in this form: 'knowledge' refers also to the situation where the driver really knows that there has been an accident but deliberately chooses to put it out of his mind. Usually the prosecution can show either that the defendant actually knew of the accident or that he ought reasonably to have known of it, eg by there being a severe jolt or a loud crash at the time. Once the damage or injury has been proved, the burden of proof is on the defence to produce some evidence of the defendant's genuine unawareness of them. Unlike the original section in the Motor Act 1903, the current section does not require the prosecution to prove knowledge. In *Harding* the judges held, in view of this, that the absence of knowledge in the statute had the effect of shifting the burden of proof.

It is for the defendant to prove absence of knowledge. Where such a burden is placed on the defendant, the proof is on the balance of probabilities (*R* v *Carr-Briant* [1943] 2 All ER 156). If, after hearing all the evidence, the court is in doubt whether or not the defendant knew that he was involved, he should be acquitted.

The principle of *Harding* v *Price* was applied in *Hampson* v *Powell* [1970] 1 All ER 929, where convictions of a lorry driver were quashed for failing to stop and failing to report an accident. In this case it was held that the knowledge of the driver was a 'necessary ingredient' of the offence. No damage could be seen on the lorry; when the driver was seen by the police he admitted he was in the relevant area at the time but denied all knowledge of an accident.

Quarter sessions have held that a driver who was aware of the accident but was unaware of any injury to the victim, such belief being based on reasonable grounds, commits no offence if he fails to comply with s 25, eg where an apparently unhurt victim assures him that he is unhurt ([1955] Crim LR 317). A contrary view appears at 121 JP Jo 554. On a similarly worded Rhodesian statute, it was held that, where the driver is aware that he has been involved in an accident, ignorance that it had one of the consequences of injury or damage mentioned in the section will only be a defence if he establishes on a balance of probabilities that he believed honestly and on reasonable grounds that the accident was not one falling within the section (*R* v *Breingan* [1966] (3) SA 410). In this respect this decision corresponds with that in *Harding* v *Price* above.

## 7.8 Meaning of 'stop', 'driver', 'injury' and 'accident'

In *Lee* v *Knapp* [1966] 3 All ER 961 it was held that 'stop' in s 25(1) means stop and remain at the scene of the accident for such a time as in the prevailing circumstances, having regard in particular to the character of the road or place in which the accident happened, would provide a sufficient period to enable persons who had a right so to do, and reasonable ground for so doing, to require of the driver direct and personally the information which might be required under the section. It does not suffice if an employee or agent of the driver waits at the scene (ibid). It was also held in *Ward* v *Rawson* [1978] RTR 498 that to 'stop' means to remain near the vehicle for a sufficient period to allow a person having reasonable grounds for doing so to ask for the driver's name and address. (The defendant collided with a depot fence, inspected the damage, left his vehicle at the scene and ran off, not wanting to be breathalysed.) The driver does not have to wait indefinitely (*Norling* v *Woolacott* [1964] SASR 377: accident involving an unattended vehicle, no other people or houses near).

In *Jarman* v *Walsh* [1936] SASR 25, a case on an Australian statute requiring a driver to stop and, if required, give his name and address, it was held that a driver who had gone on for 300 yards and then returned to the scene of the accident had not complied with the statute. However, in *R* v *Criminal Injuries Board* [1981] RTR 122, a driver started to move away with the intention of leaving. The offence of failure to stop was held not yet to be complete.

Where the motor vehicle is stationary when the accident occurs, it is submitted that the driver must remain at the scene until he has ascertained or done the things required to be done when he stops (see the last paragraph and [1937] Jo Crim L 499), ie that 'stop' in s 25(1) means both 'bring to a stop' and 'remain stopped'.

There is nothing in the statute to require a person to go around knocking on doors or seeking by other means to discover whether there is anybody who might have the necessary right to ask the questions envisaged by the section; *Mutton* v *Bates (No 1)* [1984] RTR 256. This would be particularly true when the time as in that case is 2.30 am.

'Driver' in s 25 means the person who takes the vehicle out on the road; he remains the driver until he finishes the journey, although he may have stopped and switched off the engine some minutes before (*Jones* v *Prothero* [1952] 1 All ER 434—driver convicted for not reporting accident to cyclist knocked over by a car door opening suddenly; he was still in the car), see 1.51.

'Injury' has been held by a stipendiary magistrate to include shock, citing *Hay (or Bourhill)* v *Young* [1943] AC 92 (115 JP Jo 250). A hysterical and nervous condition can be 'actual bodily harm' (*R* v *Miller* [1954] All ER 529). In *Clements* v *Gill* [1953] SASR 25, an Australian case, a pedestrian was struck and thrown to the ground by a motor vehicle. Evidence was given that he was shaken and dazed, but there was no evidence of any actual physical injury. It was held that the evidence was insufficient to prove that injury had been caused to him.

For the meaning of the word 'accident', see 1.46.

## 7.9 Duty to exchange names or report

If the motorist for any reason has not given his name and address to any person who has reasonable grounds for requiring it, s 25(2) requires him to report the accident at a police station or to a police constable 'as soon as reasonably practicable and in any case within twenty-four hours'. Unlike s 25(1), s 25(2) only refers to the driver's name and address. 'As soon as reasonably practicable' was held to mean precisely what it says: a motorist who did not report the accident as soon as it was reasonably practicable for him to do so was held to have committed the offence even though he made admissions about the accident within twenty-four hours to a constable who came to interview him (*Bulman* v *Bennett* [1974] RTR 1). The additional words 'and in any case within twenty-four hours' do not qualify the obligation to report as soon as reasonably practicable and thus give a motorist the right to wait twenty-four hours before reporting; the words 'in any case' were held to be equivalent to 'without prejudice to the foregoing' (ibid). It is thus clear that (*a*) the motorist must report as soon as reasonably practicable (and this, it is submitted, is a matter of fact for the court to determine depending on the particular circumstances of each case) and (*b*) the motorist must in any event report it within twenty-four hours, seemingly, even if not reasonably practicable to do so within that time. Forbes J in *Mutton* v *Bates (No 1)* [1984] RTR 256 emphasised the difference between 'as soon as reasonably practicable' and 'as soon as reasonable'.

The suggestion that whether or not a motorist has reported an accident as soon as reasonably practicable' is a matter of fact for the court to determine depending on the particular circumstances of each case appears to have been followed by the court in *Britton* v *Loveday* [1981] Crim LR 49 where justices were upheld in dismissing a charge under s 25 in respect of a motorist who had failed to negotiate a bend and collided causing damage at 11 pm, who had left his address in his car at the scene, and who was interviewed at 8.30 am the following day by a police constable.

The test as to whether an offence is made out is not, 'Is it reasonable for the defendant to have reported the accident earlier?' but, as in the statute, 'Did the defendant report the accident "as soon as reasonably practicable"?' In *Bulman* v *Lakin* [1981] RTR 1 the defendant had had an accident at 1.10 am and at 11 am, after a police constable had fruitlessly called three times at the home of the defendant, called in and reported the accident at the police station. At the hearing of the charge of failing to report the accident the defendant made an unsworn statement but did not explain why he had not reported the accident earlier. The case was dismissed by the justices because they were of the opinion that it was not reasonable to expect the defendant to have reported the accident earlier. The Divisional Court held that the offence was made out. The justices had not asked themselves the right question: no reasonable tribunal would have done other than come to the conclusion, in the absence of an explanation to the contrary, that the defendant had not reported the accident as soon as was reasonably practicable.

It has also been held that if the driver refuses his name and address to a person reasonably requiring it, he commits an offence although he reports to the police within twenty-four hours (*Dawson* v *Winter* (1932) 49 TLR 128). If he does give his name and address, etc, to such a person, he need not report to the police (*Adair* v *Fleming* [1932] SC(J) 51; *Green* v *Dunn* [1953] 1 All ER 550), unless there has been personal injury and the insurance certificate has not been produced, so that s 166, applies.

It should be emphasised that if an accident occurs and the driver does not give his name and address, etc, because no one asks for it (eg because the driver was clearly not responsible for the accident) or because there is no one at the scene, or for any other reason, he must still report to the police (*Peek* v *Towle* [1945] 2 All ER 611).

In *R* v *Togo* [1966] (3) SA 695, a case on a like-worded Rhodesian statute, it was held that, if within twenty-four hours of its occurrence a driver becomes aware that he has been involved in an accident of the type specified in the section, it is still his duty to report to the police, even though he was unaware of the accident when it occurred; it might be, however, that it would be a defence if he had reasonable grounds for believing that the information given to him was not accurate.

The words 'owing to the presence of a motor vehicle on a road' were considered in *Quelch* v *Phipps* [1955] 2 All ER 302. It was held that there must be some direct causal connection between the vehicle and the occurrence of the accident and the section applied where a passenger jumped off a moving bus and hurt himself. The presence of the vehicle must be more than a mere *sine qua non* and an indirect connection is insufficient, eg a pedestrian stepping back to avoid a car and injuring another pedestrian. The section is not limited to collisions. Questions can arise as to how far the presence of a stationary car can be said to cause an accident; its presence probably does where a cyclist runs into but it might be otherwise if he swerved to avoid it and fell off his machine. See generally 108 SJ 249; often the driver will not have been in the car so that in that case there might be no duty on him.

It can be argued that the defendant driver's vehicle need not even have been involved in the accident if his driving has been the primary cause of collision between two other vehicles, if such accident would never have happened but for the defendant's own bad driving. In such a case the prosecutor would have to prove that the defendant knew both that there had been a collision and that injury or damage had been caused. On the other hand, it could be said that, if the collision of the pedestrians need not be reported (see above), nor need the collision of two other vehicles by a third driver whose conduct caused it.

There is a dictum by Avory J in *Dawson* v *Winter* (1932) 49 TLR 128 that it would not be reporting to the police if the defendant had told them of the incident only as a result of their coming to interview him during their investigations after he had left the scene, but in *Bulman* v *Bennett* above the Divisional Court did not on this ground criticise magistrates who had held that admissions about an accident by the defendant to a constable who had come to interview him constituted a report to a constable for the purpose of s 25(2).

In *Mutton* v *Bates (No 1)* [1984] RTR 256 the defendant informed a police constable as a friend and not in the capacity of a police constable. It was held that the justices were entitled to find that he did not report to a police constable.

The onus of proof that a driver failed to report to the police does not seem to lie on the police; it is a matter peculiarly within the driver's own knowledge whether he did so (see 2.87). Otherwise every constable from miles around would have to be called to say that the driver did not report to him.

The obligation under s 25(2) is to report 'at' a police station or 'to' a constable; this means that the motorist must report in person at a police station or personally make the report to a constable—telephoning a police station or police constable is insufficient (*Wisdom* v *Macdonald* [1982] RTR 186).

There might be circumstances in which the driver would be well advised to telephone if there were practical difficulties in attending in person. Although that would not fulfil the statutory obligations, it would bring the accident to the notice of the police and could be a relevant matter to be taken into account in deciding whether or not there had been a report as soon as reasonably practicable and in deciding whether or not to prosecute (ibid).

Sections 161 and 162 specifically empower a constable to require a motorist whom he has reasonable cause to believe was involved in an accident to produce his driving licence, insurance certificate, etc, and one of the purposes of these sections is seemingly to enable a policeman to require a motorist reporting an accident to produce these documents.

Forbes J however in *Mutton* v *Bates* was disposed to accept obiter that the object of s 25 was to obtain details for the other parties and had nothing to do with whatever powers the police might have to investigate possible infringements of proper driving procedures.

If either element of s 25(1) is missing, ie if a person fails to stop but later gives his particulars or if he stops but refuses those particulars, an offence is committed (*North* v *Gerrish* (1959) 123 JP 313).

### 7.10–15 One offence or two?

A person is guilty of an offence under s 25 of the 1972 Act if he fails to comply with either s 25(1) or s 25(2). He is guilty of two offences if he fails to comply with both (*Roper* v *Sullivan* [1978] RTR 181).

## Furnishing Information

### 7.16 Generally

The duty to give information as to the driver of a vehicle arises under s 168 of the 1972 Act, s 112 of the Road Traffic Regulation Act 1984 and s 27 of the Vehicles (Excise) Act 1971. There are also other instances when information may be required of owners and drivers, and these are discussed below, 7.18

and 7.19. As to the duty to state the ownership of a vehicle for fixed penalty offences and excess meter charges and the fixed penalty provisions in the Transport Act 1982 (not yet in force), see Chapter 17.

The Police and Criminal Evidence Act 1984, Part I when in force will give the police additional powers of search and carrying out road checks but not for minor motoring offences.

## 7.17 Driver alleged to be guilty of a specified offence

By s 168(2) of the 1972 Act, where the driver of a vehicle (whether a motor vehicle or not) is alleged to be guilty of an offence to which the section applies:

(*a*) the person keeping the vehicle shall give such information as to the identity of the driver as he may be required to give by or on behalf of a chief officer of police; and

(*b*) any other person shall if required as aforesaid give any information which it is in his power to give and which may lead to the identification of the driver.

As to whether a demand for information is made 'by or on behalf of' a chief officer of police, see *Record Tower Cranes Ltd* v *Gisbey*, *Nelms* v *Roe* and *Pamplin* v *Gorman* at the end of 7.17.

The section extends to any offence under the 1972 Act, other than offences under Part V (registration of driving instructors), ss 169–174 (forgery and fraudulent applications etc) and ss 15, 32, 45(7), 50(5), 53(4), 55(5), 56(3), 91, 119. It also extends to offences against any other enactment relating to the use of vehicles on roads and, by virtue of the 1974 Act, also extends to ss 36A and 36B of the Act (parking of vehicles on verges, footpaths and central reservations: see 6.73), in which case the local authority is empowered to make the requirement. See below as to s 168 extending to regulations.

In Scotland, s 168 extends to offences under s 175 (taking and driving away) also; it is submitted that, by virtue of the Interpretation Act 1978, s 17(2), it extends also to offences under s 12 of the Theft Act 1968 (taking conveyances) in England and Wales. *Quaere*, if s 168 extends to offences under s 12 in respect of conveyances which are vehicles but not motor vehicles; as s 12 extended the scope of s 175 to them, it is argued that it does (*Stevens* v *General Steam Navigation Co* [1903] 1 KB 890), so long as they are 'vehicles'.

Section 112 of the Road Traffic Regulation Act 1984 is in like terms to s 168 (although there are minor differences) and extends to offences under ss 1–111 of that Act, save those under s 35(7) (in England and Wales), ss 43, 52, 88(7), 104, 105 and 108, including s 108 as modified by s 109(2) and (3).

Neither s 112 of the 1984 Act nor ss 167 and 168 of the 1972 Act apply to persons and vehicles in the public service of the Crown.

Section 27 of the Vehicles (Excise) Act 1971 is also in like terms to s 168 and extends to offences under ss 8, 16(7) and 18(4). In relation to offences of using a vehicle in contravention of these sections, both the driver and the person using the vehicle shall be treated as the persons concerned whose identities are required to be given, and, where the offence alleged is keeping a vehicle, the person whose identity has to be given is the person keeping it. The persons who can demand information under s 27 are the chief officer of police or the Secretary of State for Transport.

Section 27 does not extend to Crown drivers.

The cases cited below with reference to s 168 presumably apply to s 167 and in principle also to s 112 of the 1984 Act and s 27 of the 1971 Act.

There are two types of case which can arise under s 168 (or indeed under s 27 of the 1971 Act or s 112 of the 1984 Act, above). The first and more usual situation is that once a good notice under the section has been served or sufficient requirement made, the person to whom the demand is made is then under the statutory obligation to give the information; once he is told of the fact that the vehicle in question was seen at a particular place at a particular time, the police do not have to prove the offence alleged or, indeed, any further information about the allegation (*Pulton* v *Leader* [1949] 2 All ER 747; *Jacob* v *Garland* [1974] RTR 40). If the person fails to give the information required he may only escape conviction if he can avail himself of the defence in s 168(3) if he is owner or if the other person referred to in s 168(2)(*b*), that it is not in his power to give the information. (The owner can properly be summoned under s 168(2)(*b*) as well as (*a*) (*Hodgson* v *Burn* (1966) 110 SJ 151).) The other type of case which can arise under s 168 is where the person from whom the information is demanded denies that the vehicle in question was at the place at the time alleged, and accordingly refuses to give the information required on the ground that it is impossible for him to do so as the vehicle was elsewhere at the time. In this case, the police are required to prove that the vehicle was at the place at the time specified in the notice (*Neal* v *Fior* [1968] 3 All ER 865; *Jacob* v *Garland*, above).

The question has been raised (see (1974) JP Jo 66, 137) as to the legality of a requirement under s 168 or s 112 or s 27, being made by post, and in particular if the requirement has been so made, whether the prosecution have to prove that the defendant has received the requirement which has been posted to him. The answer would seem to depend on whether s 7 of the Interpretation Act 1978 applies. If s 7 applies, the prosecution have only to show that the requirement was sent by post to the defendant's address because, by virtue of s 7, the defendant is deemed to have received it when it would have arrived in the normal course of post (provided that the letter is not subsequently returned to the sender as undelivered; *R* v *London County Quarter Sessions, ex parte Rossi* [1956] 1 All ER 670). Section 7 applies 'Where an Act . . . authorises or requires any document to be served by post, whether the expression "serve" or the expression "give" or "send" or other expression is used.' Although not one of the three sections referred to itself authorises or requires the demand for the requirement for information to be made by post, s 183 in the case of a requirement under s 168, s 114 of the 1984 Act in the case of a requirement under s 112, and s 32 of the 1971 Act in the case of a requirement made under s 27, all envisage requirements under the respective sections being made by post and further provide that a statement purporting to come from the accused admitting that he was the person driving, using or keeping the vehicle on the day in question is admissible in evidence of that fact. Proof of the posting of the requirement has to be given in each case by rules made under ss 144 and 145 of the Magistrates' Courts Act 1980. The previous equivalent section, which is referred to in s 183 and s 32, is s 15 of the Justices of the Peace Act 1949. Rule 67 of the Magistrates' Courts Rules 1981 is the relevant rule. It is also clear that a requirement under the sections cited can be in the form of a 'document'; it would be difficult to make a requirement sent by post in any other form. In *Pulton* v *Leader* above the request for information was in the form of a document.

In *Record Tower Cranes Ltd* v *Gisbey* [1969] 1 WLR 148, inquiring of only twelve out of twenty-five drivers was said not to show due diligence under s 168(3). It is not a condition precedent to the owner being required to give information that the driver should previously have refused his own name and address (*R* v *Hankey* (1905) 69 JP 219). The person who was the offending driver must give the required information if it is demanded under s 168(2)(*b*) and cannot claim the privilege of not incriminating himself (*Bingham* v *Bruce* [1962] 1 All ER 136). It would seem, similarly, that the keeper of the vehicle if he is also the driver likewise cannot claim the privilege of not incriminating himself when required to disclose who the driver was under s 168(2)(*a*).

The reference in s 168(2) to 'in his power to give' is in para (*b*) only, but by s 168(3) the person keeping the vehicle required under (*a*) is not guilty if he shows that he did not know and could not with reasonable diligence have ascertained who the driver was. The obligation under s 168(2)(*b*) to give any information 'which it is in his power to give' applies to a doctor who has the information as a result of a professional consultation. He cannot say that by reason of the ethics of the medical profession it is not within his power to give the required information (*Hunter* v *Mann* [1974] RTR 338). The court (per Lord Widgery CJ at p 345) cited with approval the *BMA Handbook* which states:

> A doctor should refrain from disclosing to a third party information which he has learnt professionally or indirectly in his professional relationship with a patient . . . subject to (the following exceptions) . . . where the information is required by law.

The court in *Hunter* accordingly upheld a conviction under s 168 of a doctor who had refused to disclose the identity of a man and a girl who had been treated by him following an accident in which a motor car which had been taken without the owner's consent had been involved. In *Hawkes* v *Hinckley* (noted at 120 JP Jo 642) the High Court held that the obligation to give information continues even after the person from whom it is required has himself been summoned for dangerous driving. The police may thus use s 168 to obtain information as to the identity of a driver at any time. The obligation imposed by s 168 on the person keeping the vehicle is a personal one and cannot be discharged by some other person, such as a solicitor, giving the information on his behalf (*Hodgson* v *Burn* (1966) 110 SJ 151). A person becomes owner of a vehicle on hire-purchase when he takes possession on the signing of the agreement; he must then answer questions under s 168 in respect of matters before that date, when he had in fact had possession of it (*Hateley* v *Greenough* [1962] Crim LR 329).

See *Ex parte Jefferson* (1966) *The Times*, 5 November, as to a person deliberately taking an inordinately long time to give information.

In the case of offences under the Road Traffic Regulation Act 1984, s 47, in relation to parking places, and s 35(4) (plying for hire on parking places), the power to require information may be exercised as well by the local authority, but must be in writing. Section 168(2) would generally extend to offences under regulations made under any provisions of the 1972 Act mentioned in s 168(1), eg the Pedestrian Crossing Regulations, the Construction and Use Regulations, etc (*Bingham* v *Bruce* [1962] 1 All ER 136; *Rathbone* v *Bundock* [1962] 2 All ER 257), but not to regulations made under any other enactment (*Rathbone* v *Bundock*, above). Section 112 of the 1984 Act would likewise extend to offences under orders and regulations made under that Act.

'Use' includes leaving a vehicle stationary (*Elliott* v *Grey* [1959] 3 All ER 733) (but see 'using' for the purposes of a requirement under s 27 of the 1971 Act, above).

It seems that the police can make more than one duly authorised demand, eg where a person says on Monday that he can ascertain by Friday who the driver was and fails to give the information when demanded again on Friday, he can be summoned for the Friday offence.

If a person duly required to give information under s 168, s 112 or s 27 knowingly gives false information, he seems to be guilty of an offence against the section because he has failed to give 'information which he is required to give' and which it is 'in his power to give'. He is likewise guilty if he pretends not to know the answer to the questions put.

Sections 168 and 112 apply where the 'driver' and to a certain extent riders of a vehicle are alleged to be guilty of an offence. *Semble*, it does not extend to inquiries as to offences by persons in other categories, eg to the supervisor of a learner. The extension to 'riders' in s 168 is only to riders of cycles which are not motor vehicles and in s 112 only to riders of bicycles and tricycles which are not motor vehicles and not multi-wheeled cycles to be seen at seaside resorts. It will not apply to other riders that are not mentioned in s 168.

*'By or on behalf of a chief officer of police'*

It seems that a constable may not use s 168 on his own initiative; he must be authorised by or on behalf of his chief constable and the prosecution should prove this (*Osgerby* v *Walden* [1967] Crim LR 307, where the silence of the defendant was held on the particular facts to amount to an admission as to this). Where information was demanded in writing on a form signed by a police sergeant and there were added after his signature the words 'on behalf of the Commissioner' this was held not to be proof that the sergeant had the necessary authority (*Record Tower Cranes Ltd* v *Gisbey* [1969] 1 WLR 148), but this case was distinguished in *Nelms* v *Roe* [1969] 3 All ER 1379, where evidence was given that the inspector who made the request was authorised to do so, by his sub-divisional police superintendent. Although it was held that the Commissioner of Police was not in the position of a Minister of the Crown who can act through an officer of the department of the Crown, the Commissioner of Police in entrusting the superintendence of the subdivision to the police superintendent impliedly authorised the superintendent to act on his behalf through a responsible officer in the sub-division. It was therefore held that the superintendent's delegation to the inspector of the power to make the request was done with the implied authority of the Commissioner of the Metropolitan Police. This principle would seem to apply also to the delegation by chief constables of provincial police forces to their divisional officers. In *Pamplin* v *Gorman* [1980] RTR 54, the notice was also signed by a police superintendent and it stated that he was so authorised by the chief officer of police for the county. The justices rejected the defence submission that the notice was invalid because the prosecution had not proved that the superintendent had been so authorised by the chief officer of police. Upholding the justices the Divisional Court held that the notice having been produced from an official source and having every appearance of authenticity, the justices could infer from the document itself in the absence of contrary evidence that the superintendent was so authorised. It has been held in Scotland that statements obtained by constables not authorised under s 168 may be inadmissible (*Foster* v *Farrell* [1963] SLT 182), but this decision was distinguished in *Miln* v *Cullen* [1967] SLT 35, on the question of admissibility in other proceedings of statements made. One should distinguish between the admissibility in other proceedings of statements made pursuant to requests purporting to be made under s 168 or s 112, whether intra vires or ultra vires the requesting constable, and the commission of an offence under those sections by refusing to answer. 'Chief officer of police' is now defined in Sched 8 to the Police Act 1964 as the Commissioner of the City or Metropolitan Police or the chief constable of a county, borough or combined force but does not, it seems, include the chief constable of a special force such as a Ministry of Defence Police Force or the British Transport Police. Compare *Westminster Coaching Services* v *Piddlesden* at 13.51 as to delegation by the chief officer of police on a differently worded section and also compare 'Authority to prosecute', 2.3.

### 7.18 Vehicle driven without insurance

It is the duty of the owner of a motor vehicle under penalty to give such information as he may be required by or on behalf of a chief officer of police to give for the purposes of determining whether the vehicle was or was not being driven in contravention of s 143 of the 1972 Act (no insurance), on any occasion when the driver was required to produce his certificate of insurance (1972 Act, s 167). 'Owner', in relation to a vehicle which is the subject of a hiring agreement, includes each party to the agreement (s 167(2)); and see 1.96.

### 7.19–25 Other instances

A person who refuses information or to give his name and address to the police is not guilty of obstructing the police (*Gelberg* v *Miller* [1961] 1 All ER 291), but it may be obstructing the police to give false information as to the identity of an offender (*R* v *Field* [1964] 3 All ER 269, at p 280).

Section 161 of the 1972 Act enables the police when requiring the driver to produce his driving licence to require him also in certain circumstances to state his date of birth (see 11.3). Likewise where a person is convicted of an endorsable offence, the court, unless his date of birth is known, is required to order the defendant to state his date of birth (s 104). Where a person has stated his date of birth either to a constable or to a court, the Secretary of State for Transport may serve a notice on the person requiring him to verify the date of birth (ss 104(5), 161(5)).

Section 162 of the 1972 Act also confers powers on constables, whether authorised by a superior officer or not, to require information as to drivers, owners and insurance in the case of accidents and suspected offences (see 11.3).

## Proceedings and Penalties

### 7.26 Penalties for failure to stop and report

The penalty for offences under s 166 or s 164(1) is a fine of level 3. Neither offence is endorsable nor is there power to imprison or disqualify or order penalty points. The offences are triable summarily only.

A person convicted under s 25 is on summary conviction subject to a maximum fine of level 5 (1972 Act, Sched 4, as amended). The defendant's licence must be endorsed on first or subsequent conviction under s 25 unless there are special reasons (see Chapter 21).

A useful example of what has been held to be capable of amounting to a special reason is contained in the unreported case of *Leeman* v *Walton* (judgment given on 8 October 1984). A bus driver pleaded guilty to failing to give his name and address. The bus was a corporation bus with a route service number and the driver had his identity disc in a prominent position attached to his uniform. The Divisional Court indicated that there was sufficient information available to be capable of amounting to a special reason for not endorsing. The driver had not sought to conceal his name, and his identity and the name and registration marks of the vehicle concerned were plainly exhibited and obviously intelligently recorded. The case was accordingly sent back to the justices to consider whether the special reason should be found to justify them in not endorsing. The court emphasised that no general rule was being laid down to this effect where the identification was obvious.

Despite the curious wording of Sched 7 to the Transport Act 1981, it is submitted that the number of penalty points for the offence of failing to stop and give particulars is 5–9 and failing to report not having given particulars 4–9. The same view is expressed in *The Magistrate*, February 1984 at p 31. As to variable points, see 19.23.

The defendant may be disqualified at the court's option and the Magistrates' Association's recommendation (see below) should be noted. Section 19 of the Transport Act 1981 (penalty points disqualification) applies to convictions under s 25 (see 20.18–21). The court may also order the defendant to be disqualified until he passes a test (s 93(7)) (see 20.32).

The endorsement offence codes for offences under s 25 are as follows:

| | |
|---|---|
| Failing to stop and/or give particulars after an accident | AC 10 |
| Failing to report the accident to the police | AC 20 |

The Magistrates' Association's suggested penalties are £125 for both failing to stop and failing to report (see 18.1 and Appendix 3). The Association recommends that courts should disqualify when both offences are involved. In practice courts seem not to disqualify for minor bumps where there are no aggravating factors, but in more serious cases the defendant (or his advocate) should appreciate that he may have to seek to dissuade the court from disqualifying.

### 7.27 Penalties for refusal to give information etc

It is submitted that refusal to give information is not a continuing offence and that the six months' limitation period starts with each demand (see generally 2.21). It is submitted also that an information for failing to give both name and address is not bad for duplicity (see 2.46).

A constable may not generally arrest a defendant for a refusal to give information where no breach of the peace arises or is about to arise. This was conceded by the Attorney-General and accepted by the five-member Divisional Court in *Gelberg* v *Miller* above where the arrest was in fact held to be for obstructing the highway under s 54 of the Metropolitan Police Act 1839 (a section which applies in the Metropolitan Police District only). The offence of wilful obstruction of the free passage of the highway contrary to s 137 of the Highways Act 1980 applies to the whole of England and Wales including London (see 6.67–9). Under s 137 there is a similar power of arrest without warrant exercisable by a constable who sees this offence being committed. In the *Gelberg* case the words of the constable when he said to the defendant that he was arresting him for refusing to give him his name and address were held to be superfluous.

If a driver gives a false name or address or other false information or otherwise behaves suspiciously he may find himself arrested by the constable for the suspected offence of having stolen a motor vehicle or having taken it without consent. The first is an arrestable offence and the second is deemed to be so. (See the Police and Criminal Evidence Act 1984 as to powers of arrest when in force.)

The penalty for an offence under s 167 of the 1972 Act is on level 4. Offences under s 168 of the 1972 Act, s 112 of the Road Traffic Regulation Act 1984, and s 27 of the Vehicles (Excise) Act 1971, carry a fine of level 3. There is no power to endorse or order penalty points or disqualify for any of these offences.

# Chapter 8

# Vehicle Offences

## Construction and Use

### 8.1 Generally

The Motor Vehicles (Construction and Use) Regulations 1978 (SI 1978 No 1017) are made under s 40 of the 1972 Act. They have been amended by SI 1978 Nos 1233, 1234, 1235, 1263, and 1317; 1979 Nos 138, 843 and 1062; 1980 Nos 139, 140, 287, 610, 880, 1166 and 1789; 1981 Nos 261, 697, 915, 1189, 1580, 1663 and 1688; 1982 Nos 1057, 1132, 1223, 1272, 1422, 1480 and 1576; 1983 Nos 112, 471 and 932; and 1984 Nos 195, 331, 386, 679, 813 and 1543.

The Pedal Cycles (Construction and Use) Regulations 1983 (SI 1983 No 1176) have also been made. The lighting regulations some of which are also made under s 40 and which deal with the fitting, maintenance and use of lamps etc are dealt with separately, see 8.76–96.

They are divided into two main parts; the part governing the construction, weight and equipment of motor vehicles and trailers, and the part governing the use on roads of motor vehicles and trailers. It seems that the fact that the brakes failed to work on one occasion does not prove that the braking system is improperly constructed contrary to Part II and in such a case a prosecution should be brought under reg 101 for bad maintenance (*Cole* v *Young* [1938] 4 All ER 39). Similarly, where the brakes do not comply with Part II but they are properly maintained, it is wrong to charge under reg 101 (*Unwin* v *Gayton* (1949) 93 SJ 72). A missing handbrake ratchet can be a defect of construction, as well as of maintenance (*Smith* v *Nugent* [1955] SLT (Sh) 60). A motor cyclist added 2ft 8in in extension pieces to his exhaust, causing danger. It was held that he should be convicted under reg 97(1) (*Reeve* v *Webb* [1973] RTR 130). This should be compared with the decision of a stipendiary magistrate that this regulation was aimed at maintenance and not construction so that a manufacturer's fitting on the bonnet was not within the regulation ([1957] Crim LR 562). In this case the magistrate was considering the original construction whereas the silencer had been altered. It may be that causing danger is in a category of its own. In a Scottish case, *Hamilton* v *Mackenzie* 1968 SLT 165 the defendant was charged with a breach of the 'construction' part of the regulations namely using a motor vehicle not provided with a readily visible brake vacuum reservoir warning device. The warning device had been provided originally and the lack of provision arose through a failure of maintenance. He had not been charged with contravening the appropriate maintenance regulations. The Sheriff Substitute acquitted, drawing a distinction between the construction and maintenance regulations respectively. The High Court of Justiciary directed a conviction. The argument would have been valid if the regulation had in fact used the word 'constructed' but 'provided' was a somewhat more general term not confined to the initial construction. It is necessary therefore to consider the exact wording of each regulation in the 'construction' part of the regulations.

The 'construction' part of the regulations is being gradually superseded by the system of type approval (see 8.6). It is essential therefore when any 'construction' regulation is in issue to check whether the type approval system applies instead of the construction regulation. For this purpose, reference should be made to regs 5 (voluntary type approval), 5A (compulsory type approval) and 5B (approval marks) of the 1978 Regulations. These regulations, however, are not necessarily conclusive (see 8.6). The position normally depends on the date of manufacture and date of first use.

Certain of the 'use' regulations depend on the 'construction' regulations. If the 'construction' regulation does not apply then the 'use' regulation will not apply either. A use or maintenance offence will sometimes be a contravention of the basic construction regulation and sometimes of the type approval or approval mark requirement (see for example regs 98 (speedometers) and 101 (brakes)). It is necessary for the prosecution to choose the correct provision and for the defence to ensure that they have done so. A practical test as to whether the vehicle is subject to type approval may be whether there is a type approval certificate.

The Construction and Use Regulations and the type approval schemes are considered below. Matters relating to particular regulations are then dealt with together with the penalties for all offences.

## 8.2–5 The Construction and Use Regulations

Regulation 3 contains the definitions, and definitions in the 1972 Act also apply where the regulations do not have a specific one. The case of *Wakeman* v *Catlow* [1977] RTR 174 is of importance where a court has to decide whether a vehicle comes within a specified class of vehicle. The defendant drove a jeep with two defective tyres. It was licensed under the Vehicles (Excise) Act 1971 as a 'land tractor' (see definition contained in reg 3(1)). A 'land tractor' is exempted from the requirements of reg 99 relating to defective tyres. The justices without considering the definition of 'land tractor' and in particular whether the jeep was used 'primarily for work on land' (reg 3(1)) dismissed the case. Sending the case back to the justices, the Divisional Court held that the nature of the excise licence alone is insufficient to establish the category of the vehicle and the onus of proof to show that a vehicle comes within an exempt category is on the defendant. Where the category of a vehicle depends not only on its physical characteristics but also on the use to which the vehicle is put, the defence must produce evidence to show that the vehicle was used for that purpose. It will be noted that many of the definitions contained in reg 3 require a vehicle to be used for a certain purpose, eg 'land tractor', 'industrial tractor', 'works trailer', 'works truck' and 'land locomotive'.

A living van is defined in reg 136 as a vehicle which is used primarily as living accommodation and which is not also used for the carriage of goods or burden which are not needed for the purpose of residence in the vehicle. For the interpretation of this the decision in *Plume* v *Suckling* [1977] RTR 271 may assist. A coach had been converted to carry six passengers, kitchen equipment and a stock car. The stock car was held not to be goods needed for the purpose of residence, but it is submitted that not every luxurious item of goods or burden would take the vehicle out of the definition.

As to 'roads', a judge in *Davidson* v *Adair* [1934] JC 37 did say obiter that the offence of quitting a vehicle without setting the brake under reg 124 could be committed on a common or public seashore; another judge, however, disagreed. Regulation 124 does not now mention 'quitting'.

The regulations and definitions are detailed and should always be carefully consulted. Offences under the regulations are generally for 'using' or 'causing' or 'permitting' use: see Chapter 1 as to these expressions. Of the cases there cited *Rushton* v *Martin* [1952] WN 258, *Austin (Leyton) Ltd* v *East* [1961] Crim LR 119 and *Magna Plant Ltd* v *Mitchell* (1966) 110 SJ 349, *Cornish* v *Ferry Masters Ltd* [1975] RTR 292 (all dangerous condition); *Prosser* v *Richings* (1936) 100 JP 390, *Churchill* v *Norris* (1938) 158 LT 255, *Morrison* v *Sinclair* [1937] SLT (Sh) 15, *Gifford* v *Whittaker* [1942] 1 All ER 604, *Windle* v *Dunning* [1968] 2 All ER 46, *Wurzal* v *Reader Bros Ltd* [1974] RTR 383, *Thurrock District Council* v *L A and A Pinch* [1974] RTR 269, and *Ross Hillman Ltd* v *Bond* [1974] RTR 279 (all overloading) *Adair* v *Donaldson* [1935] SLT 76, *Muir* v *Lawrence* [1951] SLT (Sh) 88, *James* v *Smee* [1954] 3 All ER 273, *Green* v *Burnett* [1954] 3 All ER 273, *Hutchings* v *Giles* [1955] Crim LR 784, *Clark* v *Hunter* [1956] SLT 188, *Hart* v *Bex* [1957] Crim LR 622, *Fransman* v *Sexton* (1965) *The Guardian*, 9 July, and *Hill & Sons (Bottley and Denmead) Ltd* v *Hampshire Chief Constable* [1971] Crim LR 538 (all brakes); and *Carmichael & Sons Ltd* v *Cottle* [1971] Crim LR 45 (tyres); *Garrett* v *Hooper* [1973] RTR 1 (silencer and tyres); *Balfour Beatty & Co Ltd* v *Grindley* [1974] Crim LR 120 (reflectors, lights, windscreen wiper, audible warning instrument) were on these regulations.

Some of the regulations refer to vehicles 'registered on or after' a certain date. Where this appeared in one such regulation (now reg 18) it was held to mean registered for the first time on or after that date (*Mackinnon* v *Peate* [1936] 2 All ER 240).

Regulation 4 contains exemptions for road rollers and vehicles going to a port for export; it also provides that certain regulations shall apply only to vehicles used on 'highways', a narrower term than 'road', see 1.66–8. It was held in *Borthwick* v *Vickers* [1973] RTR 390 that justices were entitled to use their own knowledge in deciding that a vehicle which contravened what is now reg 150 when travelling from one local works to another local works in their area necessarily had to make the journey by travelling on public roads. By reg 4(6) certain vehicles registered before the expiration of one year from the making of the regulations have certain exemptions for five years if complying with the previous regulations. Other exemptions in reg 4 are for vehicles in the service of a visiting force and for vehicles on test. Motor vehicles and trailers brought temporarily into Great Britain are also exempted. 'Temporarily' means 'casually' and does not include a trailer brought intermittently but regularly into this country (see *BRS* v *Wurzal* at 13.5). 'Works trucks' are exempted from some of the regulations, eg reg 29 (horns) and reg 66 (wings). A works truck is defined in reg 3 as one which is used in 'the immediate neighbourhood' of the premises. It was held that 'in the immediate neighbourhood' had to be construed with reference to the amount of user on the roads involved. Land adjacent or nearly adjacent to the main premises may not be in the 'immediate neighbourhood' if it nevertheless involves having to travel a considerable distance on a public road (*Hayes* v *Kingsworthy Foundry Co Ltd* [1971] Crim LR 239). This case was followed in *Lovett* v *Payne* [1980] RTR 103, a case of the nearest weighbridge. 'Nearest' was held not to be as the crow flies but the nearest suitable road route (ie suitable for the vehicle in question). Regulations 4(12) qualifies the case of *Wilkinson* v *Barrett* (1958) 122 JP 349 (see 1.21).

Regulation 4 confers other exemptions from some of the regulations for certain motor vehicles in addition to those mentioned. It may therefore be worthwhile to refer to reg 4 in an appropriate case.

The regulations apply only to wheeled vehicles, not being tram or trolley vehicles operated under statutory powers and additional obligations are imposed by the Public Service Vehicles (Conditions of Fitness, Equipment, Use and Certification) Regulations 1981 (SI 1981 257), as amended by the like-named amendment regulations (S1 1982 Nos 20, 1058 and 1482 and SI 1984 No 1763), and the Minibus (Conditions of Fitness, Equipment and Use) Regulations 1977 (SI 1977 No 2013, as amended by the like-named amendment regulations SI 1981 No 1599 and SI 1982 No 1484) (see further 13.45 and 13.56). Track-laying vehicles are subject to Motor Vehicles (Construction and Use) (Track Laying Vehicles) Regulations 1955 (SI 1955 No 990) as amended by SI 1957 Nos 439 and 972, SI 1959 Nos 2053 and 2231 and SI 1984 No 817 (and also SI 1984 No 1811, in force on 1 March 1985). Generally, the 1978 Regulations would seem to apply, with certain exceptions where some of the regulations apply only to roads which are highways (see reg 4(5)), only to motor vehicles and trailers while used on a road as defined in Chapter 1; strange results would flow if they applied to them off the road. See s 40(5) of the 1972 Act. The reason why the regulations do not apply to trams and trolley vehicles is that they were made under s 40 of the 1972 Act, which does not apply to such vehicles (s 198).

The regulations apply to Crown vehicles and drivers and (with the exceptions detailed in reg 4) to vehicles and drivers of visiting forces. There are certain exemptions for Crown vehicles of special types (see 8.34).

Failure to comply with the regulations is an offence (*Moss* v *Skirton* (1952) 116 JP Jo 351). The summons should indicate that it is contrary to s 40(5) of the 1972 Act and the particular regulation (*Simmons* v *Fowler* (1950) 48 LGR 623, discussed at 115 JP Jo 322). See generally Oke's *Magisterial Formulist*, and the forms there for the appropriate charge. The prohibition on 'use' (as opposed to permitting use) in s 40(5) is absolute in the sense that no mens rea, apart from user, need be shown unless a regulation is so worded as to show that the exercise of proper care and absence of knowledge are defences, as in the regulations on speedometers and excessive noise (*James* v *Smee*; *Green* v *Burnett* [1954] 3 All ER 273). Where, however, the charge is causing or permitting, this normally requires prior knowledge of the unlawful user on the part of the person causing or permitting (see *Ross Hillman Ltd* v *Bond* [1974] RTR 279 and other cases cited in 1.76–8). But where a regulation casts a duty only upon the vehicle-owner, it may be that use by another is not an offence (126 JP Jo 93), save so far as it is aiding and abetting.

As to the various provisions relating to weighbridges, ascertainment and transmission of weight, plated weights and defences to weight prosecutions, see 1.31–9. As to unnecessary obstruction (reg 122) see 6.67 and 6.68; as to opening car doors (reg 125) see 6.77; as to the use of lights in conditions of seriously reduced visibility see 8.91 and as to lights generally, see 8.76–96.

# Type Approval System

## 8.6 Vehicles subject to type approval

The construction of motor vehicles in Great Britain hitherto has been controlled by manufacturers being required to ensure that their vehicles are constructed in accordance with the Construction and Use Regulations. One result of the accession by the United Kingdom to the European Economic Community and the consequent acceptance and implementation of the EEC's common transport policy is that, in time, the construction of motor vehicles and their parts will be controlled by type approval schemes based on uniform conditions applying throughout the Community in accordance with EEC directives or regulations.

Whether a vehicle is subject to 'type approval' usually depends on the date of manufacture and the date of first use (which often means the first registration under the Vehicles (Excise) Acts). There is a time lag between EEC decisions being incorporated in the type approval regulations and in turn in the exemptions in the Construction and Use Regulations.

The law so far as it affects Great Britain is contained in ss 47–52 of the 1972 Act (as amended by s 10 of the Road Traffic Act 1974 and subject to the repeals in s 24(3) of and Sched 7 to that Act) and the regulations made thereunder. Using, or causing or permitting to be used on a road, a vehicle subject to the type approval requirements without a certificate of conformity is an offence against s 51(1) of the 1972 Act.

## 8.7 The optional EEC type approval scheme

The relevant regulations are, first, the Motor Vehicles (Type Approval) Regulations 1980 (SI 1980 No 1182), as amended by the like-named amendment regulations (SI 1982 Nos 7 and 1623), which apply to motor vehicles manufactured on or after 1 July 1973 with four or more wheels and so constructed as to be capable of exceeding a speed of 25 km/h on the level under their own power (reg 4). In addition the Agricultural or Forestry Tractors and Tractor Components (Type Approval) Regulations 1979 (SI 1979 No 221) as amended by SI 1981 No 669 and SI 1983 No 709 have been made and apply to every agricultural or forestry tractor manufactured on or after 1 August 1975 and to every component of such a tractor manufactured on or after 1 October 1978.

These regulations specify the Community directives relating to the design, construction, equipment and marking of vehicles or their parts for type approval. Regulation 5 provides for the issue of a type approval certificate by the Secretary of State and reg 7 for the issue by the manufacturer of a certificate of conformity to the type approval.

Where either a type approval certificate has been issued by the Secretary of State or a certificate of conformity by the manufacturer (see for example the Motor Vehicles (Type Approval) (EEC Manufacturers) Regulations 1981 (SI 1981 No 493)) reg 5 of the Motor Vehicles (Construction and Use) Regulations 1978 exempts from the regulations specified in the table the motor vehicle or trailer or its component part.

The following points may be emphasised. The application of the 1980 Regulations and reg 5 of the Motor Vehicles (Construction and Use) Regulations is not obligatory. The exemption therefore only exists where the type approval certificate or the certificate of conformity has been issued and these are optional provisions. The burden of proof of establishing the exemption is therefore on the defendant on the balance of probabilities (Magistrates' Courts Act 1980, s 101, and *R* v *Carr-Briant* [1943] 2 All ER 156). Under the 1980 Regulations, the type approval certificate is issued by the British Secretary of State. Regulation 5 of the 1978 Regulations also exempts motor vehicles, trailers and component parts manufactured abroad with either a type approval certificate from a member country or a certificate of conformity with such a foreign type approval certificate. By reg 5 the scheme applies to trailers.

## 8.8 The compulsory British type approval scheme

Where the type approval certificate applies, reg 5A of the 1978 Regulations exempts the motor vehicle or its component part from the construction and use regulations specified in the table.

The relevant regulations are the Motor Vehicles (Type Approval) (Great Britain) Regulations 1984 (SI 1984 No 981), as amended by the like-named amendment regulations (SI 1984 No 1401), and the Motor Vehicles (Type Approval for Goods Vehicles) (Great Britain) Regulations 1982 (SI 1982 No 1271) as amended by the like-named amendment regulations (SI 1982 Nos 697 and 1402). The 1984 Regulations make provision on a national basis for certain classes of motor vehicles and their components manufactured on or after 1 October 1977 to be compulsorily subject to conformity with type approval schemes. The main category to which the 1984 Regulations apply is (subject to reg 3(2)) every motor vehicle (and parts of such vehicles) which was manufactured on or after 1 October 1977 and first used on or after 1 August 1978 which is *either* constructed solely for the carriage of passengers and their effects *or* a dual purpose vehicle, and which is:

(*a*) adapted to carry not more than eight passengers (exclusive of the driver) and either has four or more wheels or has only three wheels and is of more than 1,000 kg gross weight, or
(*b*) has three wheels (not being a motor cycle with sidecar), falls below the specified maximum gross weight and falls within a specified design speed or engine capacity.

For the meaning of 'adapted', 'dual purpose vehicle' etc, see Chapter 1. Regulation 3(2) contains various exemptions including motor ambulances specially designed and constructed (but not adapted) as such (but see the 1981 Regulations below); motor caravans constructed or adapted for the purpose; certain imported vehicles, vehicles temporarily brought into Great Britain, visiting forces' vehicles, prototype vehicles not intended for general use on roads; certain test and demonstration vehicles; former exempt Crown vehicles; certain vehicles manufactured in Great Britain for export and do-it-yourself products.

The 1982 Goods Vehicles Regulations similarly provide that certain classes of motor vehicles and their components manufactured on or after 1 October 1982 or a later date as specified and first used on or after 1 April 1983, or six months after manufacture as the case may be, shall be compulsorily subject to conformity with type approval schemes. The main category to which the regulations apply is motor vehicles which have three or more wheels and are either goods vehicles, tractor units of articulated vehicles, or bi-purpose vehicles (reg 3(1)). A 'bi-purpose vehicle' means a vehicle constructed or adapted for the carriage of both goods and not more than eight passengers, not being a vehicle to which the 1984 Regulations apply nor a motor ambulance or a motor caravan which are also excluded separately (reg 2(1)). Regulation 3(2) contains a large number of exemptions. They include vehicles brought temporarily into Great Britain which comply with certain requirements and which display a registration mark mentioned in reg 5 of the Motor Vehicles (International Circulation) Regulations 1985 (SI 1985 No 610). The exemptions also include certain vehicles for export, visiting forces vehicles, vehicles formerly in the public service of the Crown, prototype vehicles not intended for general use on roads, motor tractors, light locomotives and heavy locomotives (see the definitions in Chapter 1); engineering plant, land tractors, pedestrian controlled vehicles, straddle carriers, works trucks and track laying vehicles, all as defined in reg 3(1) of the Motor Vehicles (Construction and Use) Regulations 1978; vehicles authorised for use on a road by arts 15, 17 or 18 of the Motor Vehicles (Authorisation of Special Types) General Order 1979; tower wagons, fire engines, road rollers, steam vehicles, snow ploughs, gritters and similar vehicles, two wheeled motor cycles with or without sidecars, electrically propelled vehicles, breakdown vehicles, do-it-yourself products not exceeding 1525 kg, motor ambulances and motor caravans. Finally the exemptions include individually imported vehicles with an unladen weight not exceeding 1525 kg subject to four conditions. The conditions include two which look to the past and two which look to the present. The latter two are that the vehicle is intended solely for personal use (as defined) in Great Britain, and that the individual importing the vehicle intends, *at the time when* the vehicle is imported, to remain in Great Britain for not less than twelve months from that time. Only the last condition specifies that the intention is that *at the time when* the vehicle is imported. Nevertheless it is submitted that by the use of the present tense 'is intended' the third condition relates to the intention at the time of importing and does not mean that the importer has to keep it in his family until Kingdom Come. If this were the meaning, the word 'intended' would be superfluous.

Section 51 of the 1972 Act makes it an offence to use, cause or permit to be used on a road (for the meaning of these words, see Chapter 1) a vehicle subject in whole or in part to type approval unless it appears from one or more certificates in force that the vehicle or its parts comply with the type approval. Type approval contraventions will be contrary to s 51. Under the scheme where the type approval certificate applies, reg 5A of the 1978 Regulations exempts the motor vehicle or its component part from the construction and use regulations specified in the table.

The following points may be emphasised. As stated, the scheme is compulsory. Presumably, therefore, proof of the type approval scheme and the certificate will be a matter for the prosecution to establish. At present the Regulations do not apply to trailers as such but only to motor vehicles and component parts. The scheme is limited to certificates issued by the Secretary of State backed up where appropriate by certificates of conformity.

Both the 1982 and the 1984 regulations prohibit the first issue of a vehicle excise licence in respect of a vehicle subject to type approval unless the application is accompanied by evidence showing that the vehicle conforms with the type approval requirements.

## 8.9 Approval marks

Vehicles showing designated approval marks are exempted by reg 5B from certain braking regulations. The Motor Vehicles (Designation of Approval Marks) Regulations 1979 (SI 1979 No 1088 as amended by SIs 1980 Nos 582 and 2027, 1981 Nos 126 and 1732, 1982 No 1479 and 1983 No 1602) have been made. These are based on EEC regulations, ie regulations prepared by the United Nations Economic Commission for Europe annexed to the Agreement of 20 March 1958 as amended (Cmnd 2535 and 3562) relating to conditions for approval for motor vehicles equipment and parts (see s 63 of the 1972 Act). By s 63(2) it is an offence under the Trade Descriptions Act 1968 to apply without authority any approval mark or a mark so nearly resembling one as to be calculated to deceive. See further under 'Brakes', 8.20.

## 8.10–15 Sale of vehicles and parts without required certificate

If a goods vehicle or parts are sold without the certificate of conformity or Secretary of State's approval certificate required by the compulsory type approval scheme being in force an offence is committed under s 62 of the 1972 Act. The person who supplies or offers to sell or supply or exposes for sale such goods vehicles or parts similarly will also commit an offence.

Section 62 exempts vehicles for export. It also exempts a person who had reasonable cause to believe that the vehicle (or the part when fitted) would not be used on a road in Great Britain or at least until it had been certified or that it would be used within the terms of prescribed exemptions.

## Specific Construction and Use Regulations

### 8.16 Land implements

Opinions as to land implements and crop sprayers appear at 125 JP Jo 314 and 341. 'Land implement' is defined in reg 3. An elevator capable by adaptation of being worked by belt and pulley from a tractor but designed to be run and driven by its own engine and having rubber wheels is not a land implement (*Hockin* v *Reed & Co (Torquay) Ltd* (1962) 60 LGR 203). A trailer, in this instance a Webb Masterspread, can fall within the definition of 'land implement' in reg 3 irrespective of the manner in which it is drawn and it can be within the exemptions given by the regulations whether or not it is for the time being used with a land locomotive or land tractor (*Amalgamated Roadstone Corporation* v *Bond* [1963] 1 All ER 682). Land tractors are specially dealt with by reg 6 and are exempted by it from certain of the regulations. A vehicle excise licence is insufficient evidence to show that a vehicle is a 'land tractor'. The defendant must show that the vehicle is used for the purpose specified in reg 3(1) (see *Wakeman* v *Catlow* at 1.12). A land implement under reg 3 does not include a machine used for scraping earth and carrying it from one place to another; it must be connected with agriculture and use with a land tractor is confined to farming and forestry land and does not cover engineering work on building sites (*Markham* v *Stacey* [1968] 3 All ER 758).

### 8.17 Overhang and overall length

A vehicle complies with the regulations as to overhang although the load projects beyond the permitted distance (*Marston Services* v *Police* (1934) 98 JP Jo 848), but there might be a prosecution for a dangerous load under reg 97 (see 8.22). Where an exhaust system protruded laterally from a car window conviction under s 97 was justified as the justices had found that there was a danger. This was despite the fact that a different offence would also have been committed because of the excessive projection. Under reg 97 the court has to find that there was a potential danger (or presumably, where appropriate, a nuisance) regardless of the extent of the projection (*O'Connell* v *Murphy* [1981] RTR 163). A hinged bridging section on the upper deck of a car transporter is not part of the overall length. The definition of 'overall length' in reg 3 has been amended to reverse the decision in *Corp* v *Toleman International Ltd* [1981] RTR 385. If a vehicle conforms with the regulations as to overhang when the tailboard is up, letting it down was held not to contravene them in this respect (*Andrews* v *Kershaw* [1951] 2 All ER 764), but see now the definition of 'overall length' in reg 3. Here again an offence might arise under reg 97. Note the reference to hoods and luggage racks in the definition of 'overhang' in reg 3. The term 'overhang' is explained at 115 JP Jo 254. The definition of 'overall length' in reg 3 now requires that account shall be taken of any device or any receptacle on or attached to the vehicle which increases its carrying capacity. *Andrews* v *Kershaw* was distinguished in *Guest Scottish Carriers Ltd* v *Trend* [1967] 3 All ER 52, where it was held that, when the tailboard of a van had been constructed in order to be used for increasing the van's carrying capacity, the overall length and the overhang should be measured with the tailboard let down. A conviction for using the van with overhang exceeding that permitted was upheld where it had been driven with the tailboard down and loaded with goods. By reg 3(1), 'overall length', a tailboard is not to be taken into account if it is let down to facilitate the carriage of loads which extend as far as the tailboard when upright or further, but not essential for their support.

In the proviso to reg 9(1) the word 'normally' has its ordinary meaning and is used in contradistinction to abnormal or exceptional; where a vehicle carried exceptionally long loads on forty-six journeys out of one hundred and seventy-seven, it was held that these forty-six journeys could not be said to be exceptional or abnormal (*Peak Trailer & Chassis Ltd* v *Jackson* [1967] 1 All ER 172). The exemption in the proviso did not therefore apply. An 'indivisible' load is not of 'exceptional' length if it would go in a vehicle of standard length (15 m) (*Cook* v *Briddon* [1975] Crim LR 466). The actual use of an articulated vehicle on the day in question is not the governing factor. In deciding whether the proviso to reg 9(1) applies the justices should consider whether (*a*) the vehicle is 'constructed' for the conveyance of indivisible loads of exceptional length and, if this is proved, then (*b*) whether the defendant can also show that the articulated vehicle was 'normally used' for this purpose (*Kingdom* v *Williams* [1975] RTR 333) (see also 8.35). As to 'constructed', see 1.12.

By reg 3, account should not be taken, in computing overall length (see para (iii) of the definition), of a receptacle constructed or adapted for the purpose of being lifted on or off vehicles with goods or burden contained therein and from time to time actually used for that purpose in the ordinary course of business. By the Special Types Order of 1979 and regs 139 and 140, where a vehicle carries long or wide loads or a combination of vehicles exceeds certain lengths or there are certain projections, an attendant must be carried, two clear days' notice to the police must be given and projections must be marked. In determining the period of two clear days, Sundays and certain public holidays are not to be counted. A movable cattle-container on an articulated vehicle does not make it a vehicle constructed to carry indivisible loads under reg 9(1) (*Fellside Transport* v *Hyde* (1962) unreported). See also *Patterson* v *Redpath Brothers Ltd* [1979] 2 All ER 108, to the same effect. In that case Griffiths J said that 'indivisible load' refers to the contents of the container and not the container itself.

In *Hawkins* v *Harold A Russett Ltd* [1983] 1 All ER 215 it was held, following *Patterson* v *Redpath Bros Ltd* that to determine overhang and overall length, the 'body' of the vehicle should be taken in account. It was immaterial that it was detachable. The exemption in reg 3 (para iii) did not apply (ibid). The court distinguished the expression 'body' from 'container'.

In the course of his judgment, O'Connor LJ said at p 218:

It is obvious that parts of a vehicle which are detachable do not cease to be parts of the vehicle, for example the wheels. The fact that the body of a vehicle is detachable does not justify referring to it as a 'container'. When overall length or overhang are in issue in a case such as the present, I think that the correct question to ask is: 'Is this vehicle fitted with a body?' The body of a vehicle does not cease to be a body because it can be detached with ease, laden or unladen and fitted to a sister chassis. This does not make the body 'a receptacle on or attached to the vehicle . . . ': it is part of the vehicle. On the facts of the present case as found by the justices, coupled with the sketch and photograph of the vehicle, the correct question can only receive one answer: 'This vehicle was fitted with a body.' It was not carrying a container; its body was loaded with jam etc; the overhang was excessive.

A case on the width of a vehicle (*Gwennap* v *Amphlett*) is discussed at 8.34.

## 8.18 Rear markings

Motor vehicles with a maximum gross weight exceeding 7,500 kg and trailers with a maximum gross weight exceeding 3,500 kg are required to display rear markings by virtue of the Motor Vehicles (Rear Markings) Regulations 1982 (SI 1982 No 430). See also the International Carriage of Dangerous Goods (Rear Markings of Motor Vehicles) Regulations 1975 (SI 1975 No 2111). Regulation 3 of the 1982 Regulations exempts certain vehicles. Regulation 4 prescribes which rear markings are fitted to which type of vehicle, while reg 6 and Parts I and II of the Schedule prescribe their size and colour. Part III of the Schedule details their position. Regulation 7 modifies Part III and enables rear markings to be fitted to the load of a vehicle instead when the load projects beyond the rear of the vehicle so as to obscure any rear markings which the vehicle might have. It is an offence not to maintain in a clean and efficient condition rear markings fitted under reg 4 (or reg 5) while the vehicle is in use on a road.

The International Carriage of Dangerous Goods (Rear Markings of Motor Vehicles) Regulations 1975 apply when the vehicle is carrying dangerous goods on a journey 'some part of which has taken place, or will take place, outside the United Kingdom'.

## 8.19 Speedometers

Regulation 18 requires a speedometer, as defined, to be fitted to every motor vehicle first used on or after 1 October 1937 except land tractors, invalid carriages, works trucks, motor cycles with engines not exceeding 100 cc, and certain other vehicles of low speed. In addition invalid carriages, works trucks and motor cycles with engines not exceeding 100 cc first used on or after 1 April 1984 must also be fitted with a speedometer. The speedometer must have a margin of accuracy of plus or minus 10 per cent when the speed is in excess of 10 mph. If a car has no speedometer but a revolution counter, it is doubtful if it would comply (*Sellwood* v *Butt* [1962] Crim LR 841), especially as, under the present regulation, the instrument must 'readily indicate the speed'.

The speedometer equipment of motor vehicles which complies with EEC Regulation 443/1975 have been brought within the Motor Vehicles (Type Approval) Regulations 1980 (see 8.7). Regulation 5 of the Motor Vehicles

(Construction and Use) Regulations 1978 exempts these speedometers from the construction requirements in reg 18.

Regulation 98 requires speedometers to be maintained which are fitted in accordance with reg 18(1) (construction requirements), which are exempted from reg 18 by reg 5 (optional type approval), or which have the marking specified in reg 18(2)(*g*) (certain approval marks). In fact (*g*) in reg 18 has subsequently been altered to (*f*), but the meaning is clear. The designated approval marks system, where applicable, replaces the normal construction requirement in reg 18. The exemption from the construction requirement also applies to both compulsory and voluntary tachograph vehicles.

There are two types of designated approval marks for speedometers: those for 'ordinary' speedometers and those for 'tachograph' (recording equipment) speedometers. Failure to maintain under reg 98 is an offence in respect of an 'ordinary' speedometer. It is also an offence under reg 98(1)(*d*) to fail to maintain a voluntary tachograph speedometer. Failure to maintain a compulsory tachograph speedometer is not an offence under reg 98 but an offence contrary to the amended s 97(1)(*a*) of the Transport Act 1968 where applicable. Reference should therefore be made to 14.46 and 14.50 as there are certain defences.

The exemption from the construction requirement only applies to tachograph equipment if the equipment complies with reg 18(3). Nevertheless it is submitted that a temporary defect in maintenance of a tachograph speedometer would not bring it, for the time being, within the construction requirements of reg 18(1) and the maintenance requirements consequent thereon (ie in the case of compulsory equipment the maintenance requirements not otherwise applicable and in the case of voluntary equipment different maintenance requirements). Any other conclusion could lead to a number of strange and unforeseen consequences (for instance while a vehicle was under repair) and the wording of reg 18 is not appropriate.

Regulation 98 requires the speedometer to be at all material times maintained in good working order and free from obstruction, but it is a defence that (*a*) the defect occurred in the course of a journey during which the contravention was detected or (*b*) at the time of detection steps had already been taken to have the defect remedied with all reasonable expedition. See the similar provisions in the Lighting Regulations at 8.86. The burden of proof on the defence is on the balance of probabilities (*R* v *Carr-Briant* [1943] 2 All ER 156). The wording of (*b*) is such that some step must have actually been taken. The regulation does not specify by whom the steps have to be taken (presumably it could be an employer or employee), nor their extent. It has been held by a magistrates' court that this defence includes a round journey but not the return journey from a fixed destination when the defect occurred in the course of the outward journey.

## 8.20 Brakes

See regs 13, 14, 14A, 50, 51, 55, 59, 64, 67, 71, 75, 76 and Sched 4 as to the brakes to be fitted. Regulation 5 (optional type approval) confers exemption from regs 13, 14, 14A, 51, 55, 59, 64, 71, 75 where there is a type approval certificate. Regulation 5A (compulsory type approval), where applicable, confers exemption from regs 13, 14 and 64 and, in some cases from reg 14A, where the first use is on or after the date specified and reg 5B confers certain exemptions where the vehicle bears a designated approval mark (see below). Regulations 101 and 101A relate to maintenance of brakes and are widely drawn so as to apply to all maintenance whether the construction is governed by the construction regulations, the type approval system or the approval mark system. It is advisable that prosecutors choose the right provision and defendants should ensure that they have done so.

In most cases each brake must be able to stop the vehicle in a reasonable distance under the most adverse conditions. For the Highway Code braking distance table, see inside cover. This table has been unaltered for a number of years. Nevertheless, it has been repeated in the present Highway Code and is still considered valid despite modern tyres and modern brakes. The commentary on the table has been expanded and now states:

> On a dry road, a good car with good brakes and tyres and an alert driver, will stop in the distances shown. Remember these are shortest stopping distances. Stopping distances increase greatly with wet and slippery roads, poor brakes and tyres, and tired drivers.

In *R* v *Chadwick* [1975] Crim LR 105 it was held that the table of stopping distances in the Highway Code was inadmissible as being hearsay unless there was a failure to observe a relevant provision of the Highway Code.

By reg 101 every part of the braking system and of the means of operation thereof must be maintained in good and efficient working order and properly adjusted. Regulation 101A is similarly worded save that the words 'means of operation' are omitted. The difference may result in the offence under reg 101 being wider than the offence under reg 101A. In *Kennett* v *British Airports Authority* [1975] Crim LR 106 justices who had dismissed a charge because the overall braking system of a car was efficient, were directed to convict the defendant because the disc braking on one wheel was badly worn. Justices on a charge of this nature should examine every part of the braking system as it applied to each wheel (ibid); but a conviction for bad maintenance under reg 101 cannot be sustained if a condition of bad maintenance of the brakes was 'probably' present prior to an accident. The degree of proof required to show that the vehicle was not so maintained as required by the regulation is proof beyond reasonable doubt (*Bailey* v *Rolfe* [1976] Crim LR 77). The regulation contains a number of other requirements. It seems that the fact that the brakes failed to work on one occasion does not prove that the braking system is improperly constructed contrary to Part II and in such a case a prosecution should be brought under reg 101 for bad maintenance (*Cole* v *Young* [1938] 4 All ER 39). Similarly, where the brakes do not comply with Part II but they are properly maintained, it is wrong to charge under reg 101 (*Unwin* v *Gayton* (1949) 93 SJ 72). A missing handbrake ratchet can be a defect of construction, as well as of maintenance (*Smith* v *Nugent* [1955] SLT (Sh) 60).

The method of calculating the number of wheels on which a braking system is deemed to operate under reg 59 was considered in *Langton* v *Johnson*

[1956] 3 All ER 474; see the relevant regulations now as to the inclusion of front wheels in calculating the wheels on which a braking system operates. The prosecution should prove that a trailer exceeds the specified unladen weight where its brakes are defective (*Muir* v *Lawrence* [1951] SLT (Sh) 88). A brake drum for the purposes of the regulations is part of the wheel and not of the braking system (reg 3(4)).

The obligation to maintain the brakes in good and efficient working order is an absolute one (*Green* v *Burnett* [1954] 3 All ER 273); it is not a defence that the defendant ensured that the brakes were regularly maintained or that he had done all he could to see his brakes were in order (*Hawkins* v *Holmes* [1974] RTR 436), otherwise the exemption from endorsement conferred in column 5 of Sched 4 would not be necessary (ibid) (see 8.46). All that a driver can assume after a car has been serviced by a garage is that it has been serviced. He cannot assume it is in good mechanical order; per Park J in *Haynes* v *Swain* [1975] RTR 40, at p 44. Cases on motorscooter brakes are at [1957] Crim LR 709 and [1965] Jo Crim L 155. It is suggested at the latter place that in the case of vehicles to which Sched 4 to the Construction and Use Regulations applies (viz, now, motor cycles, motor cars, heavy motor cars and goods vehicles not exceeding 1525 kg in unladen weight but not motor vehicles for more than eight seated passengers in addition to the driver, articulated vehicles, works trucks, pedestrian-controlled vehicles or vehicles to which reg 14A applies) the prosecutor must show both that the brakes are not in good and efficient working order and properly adjusted and also that they do not have the efficiency required by the relevant regulations. The case in question was decided by the former Chief Metropolitan Stipendiary Magistrate, Sir Kenneth Barraclough at Bow Street Magistrates' Court. But it may be that breach of either requirement suffices (cf *Butterworth* v *Shorthouse* at 8.24). Tests on stationary vehicles are also discussed.

The fact that brakes are inefficient does not have to be proved as a result of a test by an authorised examiner. In *Stoneley* v *Richardson* [1973] RTR 229 a constable, with the permission of the defendant, was able to push the defendant's car along the road with the handbrake fully applied; the justices were directed to convict even though the constable was not an authorised examiner. It is submitted that whether or not brakes are maintained in good and efficient working order is a simple question of fact, albeit in some cases technical evidence may be necessary. Normally, evidence improperly obtained is nevertheless admissible (see 2.89, in particular *R* v *Sang*). In *Stoneley* there was no suggestion that the evidence was improperly obtained, as the test was made with the defendant's consent.

Some of the older cases on brakes are collected at p 131 of the second edition of this book; they may be of some value in relation to 'vintage cars' as there are certain exemptions for vehicles registered many years ago (see reg 4(9)).

What is now s 41(2) of the 1972 Act provides that no provision in the regulations imposing or varying requirements in respect of the brakes with which a motor vehicle must be equipped shall be taken to relate to the construction of vehicles. The reason is explained in *Hansard*, 27 July 1960, cols 1734–1738.

Regulation 124 is not a regulation as to the condition of brakes but as to a failure to apply them: for this reason an offence under reg 124 is not endorsable (*Kenyon* v *Thorley* [1973] RTR 60). It is submitted that, for the same reason, offences under regs 126 and 127 as to the application of trailer brakes are not endorsable. See further 8.42.

*Designated approval marks*

Further important exemptions from the Motor Vehicles (Construction and Use) Regulations 1978 are conferred by reg 5B. This provides that the specified provisions of the 1978 Regulations are not to apply in respect of a vehicle which is legibly and indelibly marked in a conspicuous and readily accessible position with a marking designated and shown as an approved mark under the Motor Vehicles (Designation of Approval Marks) Regulations 1979 (SI 1979 No 1088, as amended by SI 1980 Nos 582 and 2027 and 1981 Nos 126 and 1732). The regulations specified are regs 13 (parking brakes), 14 (vacuum or pressure braking systems), 14A (further braking requirements), 51 (brakes on locomotives), 55 (brakes on motor tractors), 59 (brakes on heavy motor cars), 64 (brakes on motor cars), 67 (brakes on motor cycles), 75 (brakes on trailers) and 101 (maintenance). Brakes on motor vehicles or trailers not caught by reg 101 because of this are caught by reg 101A instead. These exemptions mark another step in the departure from the construction regulations.

Under s 63(2) of the 1972 Act any person who applies an approval mark without being authorised by the competent authority as defined in that section or applies a mark so nearly resembling an approval mark as to be calculated to deceive is guilty of an offence under the Trade Descriptions Act 1968. Under s 63(1) any markings designated by the Minister as approval marks by regulations are deemed to be a trade description for the purposes of the Trade Descriptions Act 1968 whether or not they fall within the definition of that expression in s 2 of that Act. It should be noted that in s 63 the definition 'motor vehicle' includes a trailer which has no motor!

Proceedings for defective brakes are most commonly taken under reg 101 or reg 101A. These are widely drawn so that they apply to the maintenance of motor vehicles and trailers subject to the regulations whether their construction is governed by the construction regulations, the type approval scheme or the approval mark system. It is essential that prosecutors choose the right provision, and defendants should ensure that they have done so.

## 8.21 Pedal cycles

The Pedal Cycles (Construction and Use) Regulations 1983 (SI 1983 No 1176) have been made under s 66 of the 1972 Act. They make separate provisions as to pedal cycles (including tricycles and other forms of pedal cycles) which are and are not respectively electrically assisted. For the definition of electrically assisted pedal cycles, see Chapter 1. The police are given powers of testing.

For electrically assisted pedal cycles the regulations require them to be fitted with a plate showing certain particulars, brakes as specified, a battery which does not leak and a device to control the operation of its motor. These brakes, battery and motor device and the pedals and motor must be in efficient working order. For ordinary pedal cycles the regulations refer only to brakes. An offence is committed if a person rides or causes or permits to be ridden on a road a pedal cycle in contravention of the regulations under s 178 of the 1972 Act. For 'causes' or 'permits' see 1.9. For 'rides' see 1.58. Magistrates have held parents liable under the similarly worded earlier regulations in respect of their children's cycles (99 SJ 602). The offence with regard to the maintenance of the motor appears harsh in that in the event of a breakdown it is not permitted to use the ordinary pedals to ride home without committing an offence.

Under s 66(5) it is an offence to sell, supply or offer to sell or supply a cycle in contravention of the regulations unless it is sold etc for export or in the belief that it would not be used on a road in Great Britain until it had been put in a condition complying with the regulations. The offence under s 66(5) is imposed by the 1983 Regulations in respect of brakes on electrically assisted pedal cycles and on and after 1 August 1984 on other pedal cycles unless it is a pedal cycle without a braking system specifically designed for off-road racing on enclosed tracks.

The regulations add the words 'for delivery' after supply. These words are not to be found in s 66(5) and it is not clear whether they add anything. The Pedal Bicycles (Safety) Regulations 1984 (SI 1984 No 145) have been made under s 1 of the Consumer Safety Act 1978 regarding the supply of bicycles.

## 8.22 Vehicle or load in dangerous condition

This offence arises under reg 97. As in any other construction and use regulation the defendant may either be charged with 'using' a vehicle in contravention of the regulations or 'causing or permitting' the vehicle to be used. In the former case it is an absolute offence and the driver and the employer of a vehicle being driven on the employer's business may both be convicted of 'using' even though the latter is unaware of the contravention (see Chapter 1 as to 'using', 'causing or permitting').

The different wording of subsections (1), (2) and (3) of s 97 should be carefully noted. The relevant words in these subsections read:

97(1): 'such that no danger is caused or is likely to be caused';
97(2): 'neither danger or nuisance is likely to be caused'; and
97(3): 'cause or be likely to cause danger or nuisance'.

Charges contrary to s 97(1) and (2) in effect contain a double negative and it may be misleading to try and simplify this by turning it round into a positive. Remote possibility of danger is not enough. Magistrates acquitted a defendant of using a mini without a front grille: the possibility of danger by a person touching the revolving fan on a transverse engine was considered to be unlikely. Defendants have, however, been convicted by magistrates in such circumstances when the fan was at the front. While these decisions are not binding, they are persuasive and illustrate the application of reg 97. Subsection (2) unlike the other subsections refers only to the situation where danger (or nuisance) is 'likely' to be caused. This distinction may be material as indicated below.

Subsections (2) and (3) (but not subs (1)) refer to 'nuisance'. In *St Albans Sand and Gravel Co Ltd* v *Minnis* [1981] RTR 231 it was held that an information alleging 'danger or nuisance' is not bad for duplicity. This decision gives rise to certain sentencing problems (see 8.44, below). This decision should be compared with that in a Scottish case where it was held that reg 97(1) creates three separate offences in respect of condition, of passengers and of load, and all three should not be charged in one information (*Dickson* v *Brown* [1959] SLT 207). The court in the *St Albans* case was apparently not referred to this case although they were referred to other cases on duplicity. The House of Lords in *R* v *Courtie* (1984) Crim App R 292 in a decision on a different statute implied that offences should be treated as separate where there was a different penalty. The summons should specify the defects in the parts and accessories (*Simmons* v *Fowler* (1950) 48 LGR 623), but need not specify whether the defects relate to the parts or to the accessories (see *Brindley* v *Willett* below).

Regulation 97 consists of three separate paragraphs (see *Dickson* v *Brown* above), and the prosecution should be careful to bring their case under the correct paragraph. Thus in *Leathley* v *Robson's Border Transport Ltd* [1976] RTR 503 an articulated lorry shed its load of bundles of paper while negotiating a bend. The defendants were charged under reg 97(1). The justices dismissed the case on the ground that there was no evidence to show that the weight distribution, etc of the load was not such that no danger was caused. In upholding the dismissal, the Divisional Court observed that on the face of it there would have been no defence if the charge had been brought under reg 97(2). See also the important case of *McDermott Movements Ltd* v *Horsfield* [1983] RTR 42 below. In *Turberville* v *Wyer*, *Bryn Motor Co Ltd* v *Wyer* [1977] RTR 29, justices were held to be entitled to apply what is now s 123 of the Magistrates' Courts Act 1980 in convicting the defendants of a breach of reg 97(2) even though the information might have been defective in that the load was described as being carried on a motor lorry instead of on the trailer of an articulated motor vehicle. It was also held that the justices were entitled to convict, in the absence of any explanation, once the driver had admitted that the load had fallen from the vehicle while he was driving it. In *Cornish* v *Ferry Masters Ltd* [1975] RTR 292 a drum fell off a lorry onto the road because the pallet upon which it was loaded collapsed due to some extraordinary, unexplained, inherent defect. The lorry's owners and driver were both charged with 'using' and the justices dismissed the charges against both defendants as both were neither at fault nor negligent. The High Court directed both to be convicted: the offence of 'using' is an absolute offence, the defendants' knowledge or lack of knowledge of the defect is irrelevant. The likelihood or otherwise of danger being caused was to be adjudged according to the factual circumstances as they were, regardless of the knowledge of the person using the vehicle (see also *Keyse* v *Sainsbury*, below). On the other hand where an employer is charged with 'permitting' a vehicle with an insecure load contrary to reg 97(2) the prosecution must prove that a director or 'brain' of the company knew of the contravention (*P Lowry & Sons Ltd* v *Wark* [1975] RTR 45, applying *Ross Hillman Ltd* v *Bond* at 1.77 and 1.78).

Where crates fall off a lorry when going round a sharp bend, an offence arises and the driver may be convicted though the crates were loaded by another person (*Gifford* v *Whittaker* [1942] 1 All ER 604). Where trees protruded 32 feet beyond the back of a trailer, an offence against reg 97 arose, and the proviso to reg 73 (as to trailers carrying indivisible loads) was no defence (*Cripps* v *Cooper* [1936] 2 All ER 48). There was an conviction under this regulation where the blades of a bulldozer being carried on a vehicle projected $3\frac{1}{2}$ feet beyond the offside of the vehicle; the blades being detachable, the bulldozer was not an 'indivisible' load (*Newstead* v *Hearn* (1950) 114 JP Jo 690). It was stated in *Andrews* v *Kershaw* [1951] 2 All ER 764, at p 768, that, if a large van was driven with the tailboard down, this might be an offence under reg 97. But evidence merely that many milk cans rattled on a lorry and made a great noise does not suffice to show that their loading or adjustment was faulty (*Re Scottish Farmers' Dairy Co* (1934) 98 JP Jo 848).

Regulation 97(1) is absolute in terms and the vehicle must at all times on the road be in such condition that no danger is caused or is likely to be caused to road users; if it is not in such condition, an offence arises even though the dangerous condition is due to a latent defect (*F Austin (Leyton) Ltd* v *East* [1961] Crim LR 119), and in *Keyse* v *Sainsbury* [1971] Crim LR 291 it was held that reg 65(1) was absolute. The fact that a defect was a latent defect and there was no negligence is a mitigating circumstance, however (*F Austin (Leyton) Ltd* v *East* above). The dangerous condition in reg 97(1) does not necessarily have to arise through lack of maintenance; where a motor-cyclist added extension pieces to his exhaust to a height of 2 ft 8 in causing danger in that passers-by could be burnt if they touched the exhaust or found the exhaust fumes directed at their faces, it was held that the motor cyclist should be convicted of an offence under reg 97(1) (*Reeve* v *Webb* [1973] RTR 130).

This case may throw some doubt on the decision of a stipendiary magistrate who has held that reg 97 is aimed at the maintenance of a vehicle, not its construction, so that a manufacturer's fitting on the top of the bonnet is not within reg 97 as being dangerous [1957] Crim LR 562. It may be material that in this case the court was considering the original construction whereas in *Reeve's* case the court was considering an alteration.

Regulation 97(1) creates three separate offences in respect of condition, of passengers and of load, and all three should not be charged in one information (*Dickson* v *Brown* [1959] SLT 207). The regulation applies to both the *number* of passengers and the *manner* in which they are carried. There is a difference in the sentencing between the two (see 8.42, below). So far as the *number* of passengers is concerned, reg 97(1) contains special provisions for public service vehicles.

Where an examiner found excessive play in the steering joint and pivot of the steering arm due to wear, causing one-third free play in the steering wheel, it was held that the charge was not improperly brought under reg 97 (dangerous condition) rather than under reg 102 (defective steering) (*Bason* v *Eayrs* [1958] Crim LR 397). Similarly, where an exhaust system protruded laterally from a car window a conviction under reg 97(1) was justified as the justices found there was a danger, despite the fact that a different offence would have been committed by reason of the excessive projection (*O'Connell* v *Murphy* [1981] RTR 163).

Regulation 97(1) refers to a motor vehicle, every trailer drawn thereby and all *parts* and *accessories* of such vehicles and trailers. In *Brindley* v *Willett* [1981] RTR 19, decided on the earlier regulations with like wording, it was held that a container was capable in law of being a part of a vehicle. (See also the other cases noted under 'Removable containers' in Chapter 1, 1.33.) It was immaterial that the container could not be bolted on as it should have been because it was warped. In the course of the judgment, Donaldson LJ observed that the prosecuting authority tied themselves to the proposition that the container was part of the vehicle. He said that he could see no reason why prosecuting authorities should make an advance election. There was no injustice to the accused provided the object in question was clearly specified.

In *Jenkins* v *Dean* (1933) 103 LJKB 250, an insurance case, a tow chain was held not to be part of the vehicle and a condition of the policy in respect of driving 'in an unsafe condition' was not breached by using a defective chain to tow another vehicle, and in *Keyse* v *Sainsbury*, above, a heavy weight of concrete and steel attached by two hooks to a steel bar at the back of a tractor were held not to be part of the tractor as such and the charge, which was so framed that it related solely to the condition of the tractor, was held to be rightly dismissed.

Even if parts and accessories are in good repair, they must also be in proper working order; where, for example, a tow bar was of good construction and in good repair but became uncoupled because someone failed to ensure it was properly engaged, the user of the vehicle was guilty under reg 97 (*O'Neill* v *Brown* [1961] 1 All ER 571).

Regulation 97(1) makes it an offence if the 'weight, distribution, packing and adjustment of the load' are dangerous; reg 97(2) provides that 'the load carried . . . shall at all times be so secured or be carried in such a position' that no danger is caused. It may be thought that 'securing' and 'carrying' a load are often akin to 'packing' and 'adjustment' and that it will be difficult to judge whether the offence is under reg 97(1) or reg 97(2). It is submitted that, where a load is not adequately tied by ropes or kept from falling overboard by other means, it is not 'secured' and that if it is placed on the edge of the vehicle or on top of it and is likely to bounce off, it is not 'carried in a [safe] position'. If it is packed in such a way that parts of it burst out of the packing and fall on the road or if it is distributed in such a way that heavier parts push other parts off the vehicle or if it is adjusted in such a way as to import a dangerous bias to one side, then reg 97(1) applies.

The above paragraph and submission were quoted with approval (from the 10th Edition of this book) in *McDermott Movements Ltd* v *Horsfield* [1983] RTR 42. In that case a load of tubular steel was too high and slipped. The prosecution was brought under s 97(1) as to the packing and adjustment. The Divisional Court held that the prosecution should have been brought under s 97(2). The load was properly adjusted and packed and it would not have been too high if it had been properly secured. It was not properly secured as required by s 97(2). The court also emphasised that under s 97(2) it is sufficient if the load or part of it moves—it need not be shed.

The *Oxford Dictionary* defines 'adjustment' as including 'settling, harmonising or properly disposing' and 'putting in proper order'. 'Packing' is defined as including 'the putting of things together compactly as for transport . . . the fitting (of a receptacle) with things so put in.' Reference, in cases of doubt, should also be made to *Leathley* v *Robson's Border Transport Ltd*, above. It would seem that if the load has been shed or partly shed or has moved, the prosecutors would usually be wise to prosecute under reg 97(2). *McDermott's* case demonstrates the importance of choosing the right paragraph.

An offence under reg 97(2) (insecure load, etc) and reg 97(3) (unsuitable use) is committed even if the insecure load or unsuitable use is likely to cause only nuisance and not danger. This difference from reg 97(1) should be carefully noted; the word 'nuisance' is not to be found in paragraph (1).

It should be noted that reg 97(2) requires a *likelihood* of danger or nuisance only (contrast reg 97(1)). Therefore one can have the rare situation that if danger is in fact caused but the load was so secured or in such a position that danger was *unlikely* to be caused, a prosecution under reg 97(2) might fail. In *Friend* v *Western British Services Ltd* [1976] RTR 103 a charge was dismissed because there was no requirement that the load should be secured and it was in such a position that no danger was likely to be caused. The load consisted of three coils of sheet steel weighing 17 tons, and due to an unexpected and unexplained phenomenon known as 'slow roll' the articulated lorry negotiating a roundabout shed the steel, causing danger. The dismissal of the charge under the former wording of reg 97(2) was upheld because the load was in such a position as to be unlikely to cause danger. It will be noted that the load is now required both to be secured 'if necessary by physical restraint other than its own weight' *and* to be in such a position that no danger is likely to be caused.

*Friend* v *Western British Road Services Ltd* above, was explained in *Dent* v *Coleman* [1978] RTR 1 as a defect not in the securing of the load or the fastening of the load but in the vehicle itself. In *Dent* v *Coleman* justices were directed to convict the defendant, who had been charged with using, contrary to reg 97, with an insecure load. The load consisted of three coils, one of which fell from the vehicle after its straps had come loose at the joints.

*Cornish* v *Ferry Masters Ltd*, above, was again applied, the court stating that the offence under reg 97 was an absolute offence as explained in that case.

Finally it should be noted that reg 97(2) has been widened to include the likelihood of danger or nuisance to property as well as persons.

Regulation 97(3) forbids a motor vehicle to be used for any purpose for which it is unsuitable so as to cause or be likely to cause danger. In *Hollis Brothers Ltd* v *Baily*, *Buttwell* v *Bailey* [1968] 1 WLR 663 a lorry's load was badly stacked, causing it to topple over; the conviction was set aside; the fact that the load was unsuitably stacked did not necessarily cause the vehicle to be unsuitable to carry that load. This case may be contrasted with *British Road Services* v *Owen* [1971] 2 All ER 999, in which a lorry was loaded with two forklifts which were too high to go under a footbridge, causing a collision. The load was properly secured and stable, and the lorry mechanically sound. The lorry was held to be unsuitable for the purpose, as when assessing the purpose for which a vehicle is to be used regard must be had to the nature and features of the route to be taken by that vehicle.

## 8.23 Attendants on trailers, drawing of trailers

Regulation 138 relates to attendants on trailers. It modifies the effect of s 34 of the 1972 Act and provides a long list of exemptions. As to s 34, see 1.25.

Restrictions under the Construction and Use Regulations on the number of trailers which may be drawn are also dealt with in Chapter 1, 1.24.

According to the headnote in *Union Cartage Co* v *Heamon* [1937] 1 All ER 538 the exemption for certain meat carrying trailers applies only when the trailer is actually carrying meat or, *semble*, returning empty from a journey to carry meat and not when it is carrying something else, such as tiles. This was the view of the magistrates, but the judgment in the High Court does not in fact refer to the point beyond saying that their decision was upheld, the judgment being on another point.

An offence contrary to reg 126 (driver or attendant to be in a position to operate trailer-brakes) does not appear to be endorsable (see 8.42).

## 8.24 Quitting vehicles etc

By reg 124 it is an offence for a person to cause or permit a motor vehicle to be on a road unattended by a person duly licensed to drive it unless the engine has been stopped and the brake set or it is a fire engine at work or a gas-driven vehicle or being used for police or ambulance purposes. A motorist who leaves a vehicle without setting the brake may also be convicted under s 24 of the 1972 Act (see 6.78) if the vehicle is on a slope so that it runs away and causes danger (*Maguire* v *Crouch* (1940) 104 JP 445). A motorist was charged with not stopping his engine and not setting the brake but the magistrates found that he had stopped the engine. He argued that the information was bad for duplicity and that reg 124 required both failures to be proved. The High Court upheld his conviction (*Butterworth* v *Shorthouse* (1956) 120 JP Jo 97). It is submitted at 119 JP Jo 262 that a person offends against this regulation if the vehicle has run on to the road from private land. See also *Davidson* v *Adair* [1934] JC 37, 8.2, and 122 JP 48.

For a car to be 'attended', there must be a person able to keep it under observation, see any attempt to interfere with it and have a reasonable prospect of preventing interference (*Starfire Diamond Rings Ltd* v *Angel* (1962) 106 SJ 854, followed in *Ingleton of Ilford Ltd* v *General Accident etc Co* [1967] 2 Lloyd's Rep 179, where a van was deemed unattended when the driver was in a place where he could not see it and had no reasonable prospect of being able to reach it in time). Donaldson LJ described the test as being whether there is a person 'in it or in close attendance on it' (*Bulman* v *Godbold* [1981] RTR 242). In *Attridge* v *Attwood* [1964] Crim LR 45 the defendant had left a taxi in the street and taken the ignition key with him; the taxi was in his view from the building nearby, where he was. His conviction, for leaving the taxi without someone proper to take care of it under the Town Police Clauses Act

1847, s 62, was upheld. On the terms of a policy, a vehicle was deemed to be 'not unattended' when the driver was in it, asleep (*Plaistow Transport Ltd* v *Graham* [1966] 1 Lloyd's Rep 639).

Regulation 124 is not a construction and use regulation as to the condition of brakes but as to their application and for this reason an offender against it cannot be disqualified nor have his licence endorsed (*Kenyon* v *Thorley* [1973] RTR 60). Similarly, it would seem that an offender against reg 126 (driver or attendant to be in a position to operate trailer brakes) or reg 127 (detached trailer to have one wheel braked or secured by chain) would also be exempt from disqualification or endorsement (see further 8.42).

Regulation 117 requires the engine to be stopped when the vehicle is stationary, so far as may be necessary for the prevention of noise; there are exceptions for examination, working for another purpose and gas-propelled vehicles.

**8.25 Tyres**

Using a vehicle with defective tyres means 'having the use of' (see *Eden* v *Mitchell*, 1.80). The 'use' is the use the vehicle is being put to at the time. It is not necessary to keep the tyre inflated so as to be fit for some possible or even probable future use (*Conner* v *Graham* [1981] RTR 291). Magistrates were held to be wrong when they took a tyre gauge with them when they retired and carried out a private test on a tyre. The magistrates were in breach of their duty to hear the whole case in open court (*R* v *Tiverton JJ* (1980) 144 JP 747). Where there is a question of whether a vehicle is exempt from the requirements of reg 107 by reason of it being a 'land tractor' the onus of showing that the vehicle comes within the exemption is upon the defendant (see *Wakeman* v *Catlow*, 1.12).

Regulation 107(1) specifies seven different types of defect in tyres in subparas (*a*)–(*g*). In *Saines* v *Woodhouse* [1970] 2 All ER 388 it was held that there must be a separate information in respect of each tyre which is alleged to contravene any of the subparagraphs. The justices had dismissed an information in respect of the rear offside tyre under one subparagraph after they had convicted the defendant in respect of the rear near-side tyre under a different subparagraph. Their reason was that reg 107(5) (which reproduces the wording of former regulations) required one information in respect of all the tyres of the vehicle. It is submitted that one information relating to a number of tyres under reg 107(5) is still valid. It is believed some police forces continue to charge under reg 107(5). It is submitted they may do so provided there is no charge in respect of any of the same tyres under reg 107(1). In *Goosey* v *Adams* [1972] Crim LR 49 it was held that, although close-coupled wheels are required by reg 3(6) to be treated as one wheel, this has no application to tyres, and that each tyre on a close-coupled wheel should be looked at in isolation to see whether it complies with what is now reg 107(1)(*g*).

Regulation 107(1)(*f*) creates an offence where the base of any groove which showed in the original tread pattern of the tyre is not clearly visible. This means that a bald patch where the base of the original groove in the tread pattern is no longer clearly visible is illegal. It follows that a bald inner or outer edge caused by a tracking defect will be illegal even though it does not extend to one-quarter of the breadth of the tread.

As any baldness in the tread pattern is caught by reg 107(1)(*f*), reg 107(1)(*g*) prohibits tyres which are not bald, but where the tread pattern is not of the required depth. Seemingly the fact that a tyre is partially bald would not preclude a prosecution being brought where the other requirements of this subparagraph are fulfilled. Regulation 107(1)(*g*) requires the grooves of the tread pattern of the tyre to have a depth of at least 1 mm throughout a continuous band measuring at least three-quarters of the breadth of the tread and round the entire outer circumference of the tyre. There is a special provision for tyres with a tread pattern covering only part of the tread. Where the original tread pattern of the tyre does not extend beyond three-quarters of the breadth of the tread, the base of any *groove* which showed in the original tread pattern must have a depth of at least 1 mm.

The entire outer circumference of the tyre means that part of the tyre normally in contact with the road surface; it does not include the outer walls and shoulder of a tyre which is not normally in contact with the road (*Coote* v *Parkin* [1977] RTR 61). See also the definition of breadth of tread below.

'Tread pattern', 'original tread pattern', 'breadth of tread', and 'grooves' are all defined in the regulations. Tread pattern includes both plain surfaces and grooves but it should be emphasised that tie bars and tread wear indicators (as defined) are excluded, and also features designed to wear out substantially before the rest of the pattern under normal conditions. Such tie bars and wear features are found particularly on goods vehicle and lorry tyres and have led to acquittals when it has been established that these were the only parts below the legal limits. 'Breadth of tread' means the breadth of that part of the tyre which can contact the road under normal conditions of use measured at 90 degrees to the peripheral line of the tread and 'grooves' means those which showed when the tyre was new or as recut.

'Contact the road under normal conditions' would not seem to include that part which only comes into contact on skidding or turning. This view is supported by *Sandford* v *Butcher* [1978] RTR 132 although that decision is outdated following revisions in the regulations.

In *Renouf* v *Franklin* [1971] RTR 489 a tyre had a V-shaped tear producing a triangular flap of rubber which could be lifted by the finger, exposing the tyre cord. A conviction under what is now reg 107(1)(*e*) was set aside, because for a tyre to have the 'ply or cord structure exposed' meant exposed to view. The word 'structure' no longer appears in the regulation but this does not appear to affect the decision. The court indicated that in such a case if the dimensions of the cut were sufficient subparagraph (*c*) would have been the appropriate sub-paragraph; on the other hand, if the tyre had a worn patch exposing the cords, sub-paragraph (*e*) would be appropriate.

Regulation 107(1)(*a*) deals with tyres generally but reg 108 prohibits the mixing of types of tyre whether on the same axle or different axles.

For a case where a lorry driver was held guilty of causing death by dangerous driving, and his employers guilty of aiding and abetting, when he knowingly drove a lorry with an unsafe tyre, see *R* v *Robert Millar (Contractors) Ltd*, 5.12.

Whether a tyre complies with the regulations is a question of fact; it does not matter that the constable who examined the tyre and gave evidence as to its condition is not an authorised examiner (*Phillips* v *Thomas* [1974] RTR 28, following *Stoneley* v *Richardson*, 8.20).

Informations were laid alleging that a tyre contravened what is now reg 107(1)(*c*), (*d*) and (*e*) of the 1978 Regulations. The informations referred to the tyre as the 'rear nearside tyre'. At the trial the police officer gave evidence that the tyre in question was the 'rear offside tyre'. The justices allowed an amendment to the informations notwithstanding that a fresh information would have been prohibited by reason of what is now s 127 of the Magistrates' Courts Act 1980. An application for an order prohibiting the justices from further hearing and adjudicating on the amended informations was dismissed by the Divisional Court. There was only one tyre involved, the defendants knew which it was and no injustice had been caused by its misdescription (*R* v *Sandwell JJ, ex parte West Midland Passenger Transport Board* [1979] Crim LR 56).

The Motor Vehicles Tyres (Safety) Regulations 1984 (SI 1984 No 1233) (operative on 1 January 1985) have been made under the Consumer Safety Act 1978. Subject to certain exceptions it is an offence to supply, offer to supply, agree to supply, expose for supply or possess for supply a tyre (other than a retread) designed for the specified motor passenger or dual purpose vehicles unless it complies with the requirements of reg 30 annexed to the Agreement concluded at Geneva on 20 March 1958 as amended (see Cmnd 2535 and Cmnd 3562) and is marked with an 'E' accordingly. The specified passenger or dual purpose vehicles are firstly those with four wheels or more and also three-wheelers with a maximum gross weight exceeding 1000 kg in either case adapted (see 1.12) to carry eight passengers or less exclusive of the driver; and secondly other three-wheelers under 1000 kg gross weight but over 255 kg unladen weight with either a design speed exceeding 40 km per hour or an engine over 50 cc. These three-wheelers do not include motor cycles with a sidecar. The most important exceptions are perhaps goods vehicle tyres, if appropriately coded, and tyres constructed solely for use on vehicles off roads and moulded by the manufacturer with words to indicate this.

It is similarly an offence to supply, etc a retread designed for a motor vehicle or trailer other than a motor cycle or trailer drawn thereby, unless it complies with and is marked with the appropriate BS specification. The only exception for new vehicles is where a person reasonably believes the tyre will not be used in the UK.

It will be noted that none of these regulations apply to motor bicycles and some unsafe tyres are used on motor bicycles on roads (see 'Knobbly tyres', below).

### 8.26 Knobbly tyres

A number of cases are being brought regarding knobbly tyres. These are special tyres used on scrambling motor bicycles. They are also found on bicycles used by farmers around their farms. The knobbly design is to give them a better grip over rough country.

These tyres are usually clearly marked 'not for Highway Use' or in a similar fashion. At speed the knobs will distort and the bicycle will become unstable. The tyres are not designed for use on roads because the adhesion of the rubber on the road is greatly reduced.

The charge usually brought regarding them is one contrary to reg 107(1)(*a*) namely that the 'tyre is unsuitable having regard to the use to which the motor vehicle or trailer is being put'.

Some magistrates' courts have convicted and some have acquitted. Some have taken the view that these tyres are completely unsuitable for use on roads. In other courts the defendant has emphasised the words 'having regard to the use to which the motor vehicle . . . is being put'. Evidence has been given that the motor cycle is being driven slowly and with extra care or for a short distance for access purposes.

## 8.27 Mirrors

By regs 23, 24 and 24A every passenger motor vehicle adapted to carry more than seven passengers, exclusive of the driver, and every goods and dual-purpose motor vehicle excluding locomotives and motor tractors, shall be equipped with at least two mirrors fitted as therein indicated to assist the driver, if he so desires, to become aware of traffic to the rear and on both sides rearwards. Most other motor vehicles (except pedestrian-controlled vehicles, certain older vehicles and motor vehicles drawing a trailer in which is an attendant who can clearly signal to the driver) shall be equipped with one internal or external mirror as specified to assist the driver, if he so desires, to become aware of traffic to the rear. The two mirrors on large passenger vehicles and goods and dual-purpose vehicles must show not merely traffic to the rear but on both sides rearwards; if the two mirrors are so adjusted that there is not a view on both sides rearwards, there may be an offence. Regulation 23(1)(*b*) makes special provision as to land tractors. Although the exceptional size of the load may for the time being obscure the driver's view in his mirror, there is no offence if the vehicle is in fact equipped with the mirror or mirrors required by reg 23 and he can see in them to the rear when the vehicle is carrying a normal load or is unloaded (*Mawdsley* v *Walter Cox (Transport) Ltd* [1965] 3 All ER 728).

Rear view mirrors are specified in reg 5 (optional type approval exemptions). Thus if the mirror complies with a certificate of type approval or a certificate of conformity, regs 23(3) and 24(5) are excluded (see 8.7 as to type approval).

## 8.28 Mascots

A manufacturer's fitting on a car has been held by a stipendiary magistrate not to be a 'mascot' within reg 142; the term means something supposed to bring luck ([1957] Crim LR 563). On this basis insignia would also be exempt, particularly where used for identification purposes. Presumably it is a question of fact when objects such as lions and unicorns cease to be exempt insignia and are regarded instead as lucky mascots.

A stipendiary magistrate has held that a manufacturer's fitting on the top of the bonnet is an item of construction. As reg 97 is aimed at maintenance, the fitting could not constitute an offence contrary to reg 97 as being dangerous [1957] Crim LR 562). See, however, the comments on this case in the section on offences of dangerous conditions, 8.22.

## 8.29 Wings

The *optional* type approval exemption (see 8.7) has now been extended to reg 66 (wings) by SI 1980 No 880, which applies to motor vehicles first used on or after 12 January 1979.

## 8.30 Emission of oil

The reference in reg 109 to the emission of oily substances, etc, covers not only the actual discharge but dripping which follows it (*Tidswell* v *Llewellyn* [1965] Crim LR 732).

## 8.31 Silencers, noise and warning instruments

Regulations 31 and 31A–E inclusive and 114, 116 and Sched 9 relate to noise and noise measurement; they are discussed in the *Police Review*, 14 June and 12 July 1968. Regulations 30, 116A, 116B and 116C relate to silencers and regs 29 and 118 to the use of audible warning instruments. Three toned horns, provided they do not sound similar to two toned horns (see definition in reg 3) which are limited to fire brigade, ambulance and police vehicles, etc, would appear not to offend against the regulations (but see now reg 29(2) which requires any instrument on a vehicle first used on or after 1 August 1973 to be continuous and uniform and not strident).

Use of two toned horns, gongs, bells, sirens, or instruments making similar sounds other than by users authorised in reg 29 is prohibited by reg 118(2).

The use of a warning instrument of a stationary vehicle is prohibited by reg 118(1) at any time other than times of danger due to another moving vehicle on or near the road. The use of a warning instrument is prohibited, even where there is danger, between 11.30 pm and 7 am in the case of a motor vehicle in motion on a restricted road. It would seem that a person can use his horn with impunity under reg 118 provided the vehicle is not on a road. Thus one can sound one's horn coming out of one's driveway up until one reaches the road. There are various exemptions to reg 118 for theft alarms, public service vehicles, authorised two toned horns and vehicles with goods for sale.

There is no offence of failing to maintain a warning instrument. Where a horn is defective, a prosecution is usually brought under reg 29. This refers to a motor vehicle being fitted with an instrument capable of giving audible and sufficient warning of its approach or position. The reasoning is not entirely satisfactory but it is based on the argument that the warning instrument must be both fitted and capable.

The most commonly brought silencer prosecutions are under regs 116A,

116B and 116C. All the offences refer to 'using', 'causing' or 'permitting' on a road. As to these expressions see Chapter 1. Regulation 116A refers expressly to an internal combustion engine and to the silencing system as 'the silencer expansion chamber or other contrivance'. See below as to the meaning of this. Exhaust gases must not escape without first passing through the silencing system. In effect for an offence to be committed there must be an escape before or from the silencing system so that all the gases do not pass through (reg 116A(*a*)). The silencing system must be in good and efficient working order (reg 116A(*c*)). The silencing system must not be altered or replaced with a resulting increase in noise so that the vehicle does not comply with reg 116B (reg 116A(*b*)). A vehicle to which regs 31, 31A, 31B, 31C or 31E applies or would apply but for reg 5 (optional type approval) must be fitted with parts to enable it to comply with those regulations or type approval requirements respectively (reg 116B).

Regulation 116C refers to motor cycles and mopeds (see Chapter 1, 1.6 *B* and *F* as these vehicles are defined more narrowly for this purpose than in other provisions) first used on or after 1 January 1985. The silencer which forms part of its exhaust system must be the original fitted when first used or have a clear BS or manufacturer's specification marking (reg 116C(1)). It is also an offence for any part of the exhaust system to be fitted marked with the words 'not for road use' or words to like effect (reg 116(12)). See, however, the definition of 'motor vehicle' in Chapter 1, 1.2, as to scrambling motorbikes etc. The distinction should be noted between the silencing system referred to in reg 116C(1) and the exhaust system covered by reg 116C(2). The conclusion to be drawn from the magistrates' decision described below is that reg 116C does not prohibit an alteration to parts of the exhaust system such as the tail pipe which are not part of the silencing system, providing there is no 'not for road use' or similar marking. The reference to marking appears to imply that there is nothing to prevent a person deleting the marking!

The optional type approval scheme may apply to warning instruments (see reg 5) thereby exempting them from reg 29(2) only (the continuous and not strident requirement). The optional schemes may apply to silencers similarly exempting them from regs 31, 31A, 31B, 31C and 31E (noise). Both the compulsory and optional schemes apply or may apply also to certain regulations regarding air pollution (see regs 5 and 5A). There may still be offences of failing to comply with the maintenance regulation requirements.

Although the decision is not binding, a magistrates' court has held that the tail pipe is not part of the silencing system but a means of conveying the gases after they have passed through the silencing system.

## 8.32 Petrol tanks

By reg 104 every motor vehicle shall at all times be so maintained that (*a*) the petrol tank is reasonably secure against it being damaged, and (*b*) petrol leakage from the tank is adequately prevented. The wording of this regulation appears to be absolute.

This regulation is unaffected by the fact that the optional type approval scheme (see 8.7) may apply to the construction of such tanks on motor vehicles or trailers, thereby exempting them from reg 19 (the construction regulation).

### 8.33 Sale of unroadworthy vehicles and parts

Section 60 of the 1972 Act makes it an offence to sell or supply or offer to sell or supply or expose for sale a motor vehicle or trailer for delivery in such a condition that its use on a road would be unlawful or, by regulations under s 40 of the Act as to brakes, steering or tyres or as to construction, weight or equipment or maintenance of vehicles, their parts and accessories in such a condition that danger is or is likely to be caused, or in such a condition as respects lighting equipment or reflectors or the maintenance thereof that there would be a breach of the obligatory lamps or reflectors laws on a road during the hours of darkness. It is also an offence to alter one so as to render its condition so that its use on a road would be unlawful under s 40 of the cited regulations.

An auctioneer does not offer to sell the goods auctioned, he invites those present to make offers to buy. Accordingly auctioneers of an unroadworthy vehicle which was driven away by the successful bidder cannot be convicted of an 'offer to sell' contrary to s 60 (*British Car Auctions Ltd* v *Wright* [1972] Crim LR 562: for criticism of the case see ibid, p 568). If the vehicle or trailer had been constructed and equipped in accordance with Part II of the Construction and Use Regulations, it was no offence to sell or supply it with defects which only indicated a failure to maintain it properly in breach of Part III of those regulations, unless it contravened a regulation as to the maintenance of brakes (see regs 101 and 101A), tyres (reg 107) or steering gear (reg 102). Section 11 of the 1974 Act has added to the regulations contravention of which gives rise to an offence under s 60, the regulation which requires vehicles, their parts and accessories to be maintained in such a condition that no danger is, or is likely to be caused (see reg 97(1)). This amendment reverses the effect of *Keyte* v *Dew* [1970] RTR 481 where it was held that construction, and the sale of a vehicle which was dangerous as a result of lack of maintenance was held not to contravene s 60. There are, however, other regulations as to maintenance, and no offence can arise under s 60 unless it can be shown that the vehicle contravenes the regulations specified in the section. Danger may be caused or likely to be caused as a result of the breach of other maintenance regulations (eg regs 98 (speedometer), 100 (windscreen), 106 (silencer), 109 (smoke)), but it is submitted that unless it can be shown that there is also a contravention of reg 97(1) or a contravention of the relevant regulations, no offence is committed under s 60. The amendment made by the 1974 Act follows almost word for word the relevant wording of reg 97(1). It may be noted that in *Bason* v *Eayrs* and *O'Connell* v *Murphy* at 8.22 convictions under reg 97 upheld where danger was shown even though the charge could have been under another regulation.

The liability of a seller under s 60 is absolute and, unless he has a statutory defence, he is guilty if he sells or supplies a vehicle in breach of it, whether or not he had guilty knowledge (*Sandford Motor Sales* v *Habgood* [1962] Crim LR

487). Section 60 extends to certain lighting equipment namely obligatory lamps and reflectors on motor vehicles and trailers. Obligatory lamps are defined in s 60(6). Other devices and markings mentioned in the Lighting Regulations, optional lamps and reflectors not legally required and items excluded by s 60(6) are not within the scope of s 60. Is it bad for duplicity to charge various breaches of the regulations in one information? Duplicity is discussed at 2.46. It may be argued that there is the single offence of selling etc an unroadworthy road vehicle and it would certainly be preferable if this were the case. Oke's *Magisterial Formulist* implies that separate informations should be used for each defect. A single information for a s 60(1) offence which included contraventions of two separate Construction and Use Regulations was accepted without comment in *Thornley* v *Clegg* [1982] RTR 405 but this particular point was not taken in that case.

Section 60(4) provides that a defendant shall not be convicted if he proves (presumably on a balance of probabilities): (*a*) that the vehicle or trailer was sold, supplied, etc, for export from Great Britain; or (*b*) that he had reasonable cause to believe that the vehicle or trailer would not be used on a road in Great Britain without it first being put into a roadworthy condition; or (*c*) that if the vehicle's or trailer's lighting equipment or reflectors are defective, the defendant had reasonable cause to believe that there would be no use on a road in Great Britain during darkness.

It is an offence under s 60A(1) for a person to fit or cause or permit a vehicle part to be fitted, if by reason of that part being fitted the use of the vehicle on a road would thereby constitute a contravention of or a failure to comply with *any* of the construction and use regulations. It is similarly an offence under s 60A(3) for a person to sell, supply, offer to sell or supply a vehicle part, or to cause or permit a vehicle part to be sold, supplied or offered for sale or supply when he has reasonable cause to believe it will be fitted to a motor vehicle so as to give rise to a contravention of or non-compliance with a construction and use regulation.

Subsections (2) and (4) of s 60A set out statutory defences to offences under s 60A(1) and (3) respectively. In each case it is for the defence to prove that the statutory defence exists, presumably on a balance of probabilities.

## 8.34 Special types of vehicles

The 1978 Construction and Use Regulations and the Construction and Use (Track Laying Vehicles) Regulations 1955 are qualified as to particular types of vehicles by the Motor Vehicles (Authorisation of Special Types) General Order 1979 (SI 1979 No 1198) as amended by SI 1981 No 1664. Part II of the Order relates to track-laying vehicles, naval, military, air force and aviation vehicles, vehicles used for saving life at sea, grass-cutting machines and hedge trimmers, pedestrian-controlled road maintenance vehicles, vehicles used for experiments or trials under s 283 of the Highways Act 1980, straddle carriers, land tractors for reaping and threshing, hay and straw binding and baling vehicles, vehicles for moving excavated materials, vehicles fitted with movable platforms and vehicles constructed for use abroad and new improved types of vehicle constructed for tests. Part III of the Order relates to abnormal and indivisible loads, engineering plant, and vehicles carrying wide loads. Notice to the police and highway and bridge authorities and to the Secretary of State for Transport must be given before a vehicle carrying an abnormal indivisible load or engineering plant exceeding certain widths and weights is used on roads and there are restrictions on speed and on such vehicles using or waiting on bridges. It should be noted that under the revised regulations Saturdays no longer count for the purpose of periods of notice (see art 3(1)). Attendants are required pursuant to art 24. Forms of notice to the police and to highway and bridge authorities are given in Sched 2 to the Order and notice is also required for certain other vehicles.

The Special Types Orders may give exemption for certain vehicles as to width, length, weight, etc provided certain conditions, eg notice to the police and highway authority, are fulfilled. A highway authority is empowered under art 28(2) of the Order to dispense with the requirements relating to the length of notice and as to the form of notice and as to the particulars given but has no power to dispense altogether with the giving of a notice (*George Cohen 600 Group Ltd* v *Hird* [1970] 2 All ER 650). Convictions under the Construction and Use Regulations were upheld even though the highway authority concerned (the GLC) apparently had never before required notices to be given nor prosecuted where notices had not been given. If the conditions are not fulfilled—notices, attendants, etc—an offence may arise under the general law as to those matters, eg reg 53 (as to width of tractors) of the Construction and Use Regulations, but no offence would arise under the Special Types Order (*Gwennap* v *Amphlett* [1957] 2 All ER 605) and it is submitted that it may be inappropriate to charge a breach of that Order at all, even if the speed limit laid down by any of the articles of the Special Types Order is exceeded. Certainly, s 40(5) of the 1972 Act does not apply in respect of the Order, for the Order is made under s 42 and s 40(5) creates offences under regulations 'under this section'. Nor does s 177 apply, it seems, as that relates to a contravention of 'regulations'.

Convictions under the relevant construction and use regulations were upheld in respect of use of vehicles of special types in *Sunter Bros Ltd* v *Arlidge*, *Siddle C Cook* v *Arlidge* and *Smith* v *North West Traffic Area Licensing Authority*, all below, and *George Cohen 600 Group Ltd* v *Hird*, above. In art 24 'vehicles' does not mean a combination of vehicles and covers a trailer (*Dixon* v *BRS* [1959] 1 All ER 449); this case related to attendants. And see *Siddle C Cook* v *Holden* [1962] 3 All ER 984 below. A motor tractor and combine harvester coupled together constitute two vehicles (*Gwennap* v *Amphlett*, above).

### 8.35–40 Abnormal indivisible load

The 1979 Order contains a minimum weight for an abnormal indivisible load (including the carrying vehicle) of 32,520 kg.

In deciding whether a load cannot without undue expense or risk of damage be divided into two or more loads and so is an abnormal indivisible load under the Special Types Order and exempt from weight and width restrictions, etc the only undue expense or risk of damage to which the court may have regard is that likely to be incurred in dividing the load; any additional expense or risk involved in carrying the load in two vehicles is irrelevant (*Sunder Bros Ltd* v *Arlidge* [1962] 1 WLR 199). The load in that case was two steel plates loaded on one vehicle for convenience. A like decision is *Siddle C Cook Ltd* v *Arlidge* [1962] 1 WLR 203, where the magistrates had found that a load of ten steel boxes could have been divided without undue expense or risk of damage. A vehicle carried a hopper, which was an abnormal indivisible load in the main, but valves, etc, had been detached from the hopper and left in the vehicle; the total weight exceeded that allowed by reg 87. It was held that the exemption for an abnormal load did not apply, as the hopper was divisible in respect of the valves, so that the carriage of the valves was not allowed; it was suggested that tarpaulins and plant battens might be allowed as being 'in connection with the carriage' of the load (*Crabtree* v *McKelvie & Co* (1964) 62 LGR 192). In *Smith* v *North-West Area Licensing Authority* [1974] RTR 236 it was similarly held that twelve separate prestressed concrete beams could not constitute an abnormal indivisible load; as the load was capable of being reduced into twelve separate beams, the company were accordingly rightly convicted of exceeding the plated train weight of the vehicle contrary to reg 150 (see also 8.17 and the decision in *Kingdom* v *Williams*).

In *Patterson* v *Redpath Brothers Ltd* [1979] 2 All ER 108, it was held that a container was not an indivisible load of exceptional length. The purpose of the container was to hold livestock and the livestock could have been separated and carried as two loads. Griffiths J said that 'indivisible load' refers to the contents of the container and not the container itself. Lord Widgery CJ said that it cannot have been the intention of the legislature to allow the provisions of the regulations to be circumvented merely by packing goods into a larger receptacle.

## Construction and Use: Penalties

### 8.41 Generally

An offence of breach of the 1978 Regulations under s 40(5) of the 1972 Act carries a fine of level 4 but a fine of level 5 in the case of an offence of using, or causing or permitting the use of, a *goods* vehicle or a vehicle adapted to carry more than eight passengers:

(*a*) so as to cause, or to be likely to cause, *danger* by the condition of the vehicles or its parts or accessories, the number of passengers carried by it, or the weight, distribution, packing or adjustment of its load; or

(*b*) in breach of a construction and use requirement as to brakes, steering-gear, tyres or any description of weight; or

(*c*) for any purpose for which it is so unsuitable as to cause or to be likely to cause *danger*.

The fine is also level 5 in the case of an offence of carrying on a *goods* vehicle only (the passenger provision is not repeated) a load which, by reason of its insecurity or position, is likely to cause *danger*. As to the meaning of 'goods vehicle' (which includes trailers) see Chapter 1. Where *nuisance* only, as opposed to danger, is alleged, it would seem that the maximum fine is a fine of level 4 only (see 8.44). Vehicles adapted to carry more than eight passengers will include some private vehicles and many minibuses. As to 'adapted' see 1.12. For whether 'passengers' includes the driver see 1.54. It is there submitted that it does not in the case of public service vehicles. The position for private vehicles is less certain but there seems to be a tendency to distinguish between drivers and passengers. There is a similar provision in s 44(1) of the 1972 Act (no test certificate). The passenger vehicle increased maximum fine does not apply to reg 97(2) (offences likely to cause danger by reason of insecurity or position of load). Endorsement, disqualification and penalty points may only be ordered in certain cases (see below). Like provisions apply to offences under the Track Laying Vehicles Regulations.

Using, or causing or permitting to be used on a road, a vehicle subject to type approval requirements without a certificate of conformity is punishable under s 51(1) of the 1972 Act. The offence is triable summarily, no endorsement may be ordered nor is it subject to imprisonment. The maximum fine is level 4.

As to brakes on pedal cycles and the various 'selling and supplying' etc offences, see 8.49 and 8.50.

### 8.42 Endorsement

Limited powers of endorsement and disqualification are given by Sched 4 to the 1972 Act. Endorsement must be ordered, unless there are 'special reasons' (see Chapter 21) or the defendant did not know *and* had no reason to suspect that an offence was being committed (see 8.46, below), for an offence under the regulations of using a motor vehicle or trailer or causing or permitting its use in the following circumstances:

(*a*) so as to cause or be likely to cause danger for the condition of the vehicle or its parts or accessories, the number of passengers carried by it, or the weight, distribution, packing or adjustment of its load;
(*b*) in breach of a requirement as to brakes, steering gear or tyres;
(*c*) for any purpose for which it is so unsuitable as to cause or be likely to cause danger.

The offence of carrying a load which, by reason of its insecurity or positon, is likely to cause danger similarly carries compulsory endorsement and discretionary disqualification subject to the same exemptions.

Regulation 97(1) falls under (*a*) above and regs 101, 101A, 102, 107 and 108 under (*b*). It also seems that regulations as to brakes and tyres in Part II come under (*b*). Offences under reg 97(1) as to 'weight, distribution, packing and adjustment of the load', as well as the other matters mentioned in reg 97(1), therefore carry compulsory endorsement. Offences under reg 97(2) as to 'security and position' of the load as stated also carry compulsory endorsement and discretionary disqualification. Offences contrary to reg 97(3) fall under (*c*) above and therefore carry compulsory endorsement and discretionary disqualification. In other words, only offences under regs 97(1) (other than as to 'manner' of carriage of passengers), 97(2), 97(3),

101, 101A, 102, 107 and 108 and under the regulations in Part II as to brakes and tyres carry endorsement, and it may not be ordered for any other offence under the regulations. Like considerations would apply in respect of offences under the Track Laying Vehicles Regulations.

An offence under reg 124 of leaving a vehicle unattended without setting the brake does not carry endorsement because it is not an offence as to use of the vehicle but as to the duties of the driver and also because it would be anomalous if this did carry endorsement while the offence under the same regulation of not stopping the engine did not (*Kenyon* v *Thorley* [1973] RTR 60) (see 8.24). For a similar reason it would appear that an offence contrary to reg 126 (driver, or attendant in a trailer to be in a position to operate a brake) or reg 127 (application of brake to wheel of detached trailer) is neither endorsable nor disqualifiable.

'Trailer' is defined by s 190(1) of the 1972 Act as a 'vehicle', so it is submitted that offences of use, etc of trailers in a dangerous condition, with defective brakes, etc attract compulsory endorsement and optional disqualification and penalty points. The draftsman of the consolidating 1972 Act apparently takes the same view. Column 5 of Sched 4, where it relates to offences contrary to s 40(5), refers to 'any motor vehicle or trailer'.

Paragraph (*a*) of column 4 of Sched 4 to the 1972 Act, for offences contrary to s 40(5), which indicates the offences of 'dangerous condition' for which endorsement may be ordered, does not mention the 'manner' in which passengers are carried and it is submitted that there is thus no power to endorse for an offence under reg 97(1) as to the manner of such carriage. Nor is there any power to endorse for offences of overloading a motor vehicle unless the charge is brought eg under reg 97(1), viz that the weight of the load was such as to cause or be likely to cause danger (see below).

## 8.43 Description of weight offences

The words 'description of weight' are to be found in column 4 (punishment) but not in columns 5 or 6 (disqualification and endorsement) of Sched 4 to the 1972 Act (as to the meaning of this, see 1.37). As indicated above, there is a higher maximum penalty for goods vehicles set out in column 4. In *Hudson* v *Bushrod* [1982] RTR 87 the defendants had been prosecuted under reg 97(1) in connection with a grossly overloaded goods vehicle. The Divisional Court upheld the decision of the justices that this was not an offence relating to a description of weight and congratulated them on their analysis of the provisions. The court drew attention to the absence of 'any description of weight' in columns 5 and 6. It follows that there is no power to endorse or disqualify or order penalty points for a description of weight offence but there may be power to do so for offences brought under reg 97, subject to the various exceptions discussed above and below.

## 8.44 Loads causing nuisance

Under reg 97(2) and (3) offences may be committed if the load or unsuitable use causes nuisance as well as danger. An information alleging both danger and nuisance is not bad for duplicity (*St Albans Sand and Gravel Co Ltd* v *Minnis* [1981] RTR 231). Despite this, however, it is submitted that where an offender is convicted under reg 97(2) or reg 97(3) and causes nuisance but no danger the court has no power to endorse or disqualify or order penalty points. The entries in paragraphs (*a*) and (*c*) of column 4 of Sched 4 to the 1972 Act for offences contrary to s 40(5) only refer to offences so as 'to cause or likely to cause danger'. The wording of this column is in very specific terms following closely the wording of reg 97 (see also *Hudson* v *Bushrod* above) and 'nuisance' is not included. The House of Lords in *R* v *Courtie* (1984) Crim App R 292 in a decision on a different statute implied that offences should be treated as separate when there was a different penalty. Many police forces still do not include danger and nuisance in one information, but if they do there may have to be a special finding for the purpose of endorsement as to which was committed. It would also seem that for the same reason, the maximum fine in respect of a goods vehicle where nuisance only is caused is a fine of level 4.

## 8.45 Penalty points

All endorsable offences under the Construction and Use Regulations carry 3 penalty points.

## 8.46 Exceptions from endorsement

By column 5 of the entry relating to s 40(5) contained in Part I of Sched 4 to the 1972 Act, where a person is convicted of the offences which carry compulsory endorsement under the Construction and Use Regulations, his licence shall not be endorsed if he proves (*semble*, on a balance of probabilities) that he did not know, and had no reasonable cause to suspect that the facts of the case were such that that offence would be committed. The effect of this is to exempt from endorsement, driving test and disqualification, including the penalty points disqualification (but not from conviction and fine), a driver who shows that he had taken out his vehicle in reliance on his foreman's or its owner's assurance that the brakes, steering, etc were in order or in reliance on the load being properly packed by his firm's loaders; likewise it will exempt an employer who sends out his drivers with properly maintained vehicles and proper instructions to take them off the road if defects appear but whose drivers disobey those instructions, so that the employer, though physically absent, is charged with using with defective brakes, etc. It may well exempt sons and daughters who drive their parents' cars on the assumption that they are in good running order.

It will be a question of fact in each case whether the defendant has any reasonable cause to suspect that there was anything wrong with the brakes, steering or tyres.

The provision will certainly exempt those who drive defective vehicles relying on the owner's assurance that they are in good condition and those who drive vehicles which have just come back from a check at a garage, provided that in these and the earlier cited cases they do not go on driving after the defect has become obvious or otherwise had no reasonable cause to suspect the defect to exist. The defendant's evidence will always be required and he must show not only that he did not know of the defect but also that he had no reasonable cause to suspect it. The test of reasonableness is, it is submitted, subjective; the test is not whether there is reasonable cause to suspect (that would be an objective test) but whether *he* has reasonable cause. The standard of knowledge expected of the driver of the Clapham omnibus will be higher than that of the man on it, when driving his own car, unless he is in the motor trade, but there must come a time when it is obvious to anyone that something is wrong. A motorist who genuinely believes his steering to be in order, having just had it repaired, but finds it fails in Piccadilly Circus, may claim the benefit of the exception if he stops at once but he cannot dodge the column if, knowing the defect, he continues to drive into Trafalgar Square. It will also exempt a lorry driver convicted of using the lorry with an insecure load which has been caused by a latent defect of which he neither knew nor could have known (eg situations such as arose in *Cornish* v *Ferry Masters Ltd* and *Keyse* v *Sainsbury* at 8.22).

Endorsement need not be ordered in any event if there are special reasons (see Chapter 21). This is discretionary and should be compared with the column 5 exemption from endorsement. Since the original column 5 provision which was contained in s 7 of the Road Traffic (Amendment) Act 1967 provided that, if a person proves that she did not know or have reasonable cause to suspect that an offence arose, 'he shall not be liable to be disqualified . . . nor shall particulars of his conviction be endorsed', it seemed that the court was forbidden to endorse or disqualify on such proof, even if it wished to do so. The 1972 Act now sets out the matter somewhat less clearly in columnar form but it would seem that the law is unchanged in this respect.

### 8.47 Disqualification

Disqualification for any period and a driving test may be ordered for any offence for which endorsement is obligatory but not for any other offence under the regulations. Section 19 of the Transport Act 1981 (penalty points disqualification, see 20.18–21) applies to all offences under the Construction and Use Regulations which are endorsable. The penalty points disqualification would not apply if the defendant proves that he had no reason to suspect that an offence would be committed (see 'Exceptions from endorsement', above).

### 8.48 Endorsement code

The endorsement codes for offences contrary to the Construction and Use Regulations are as follows:

| | |
|---|---|
| Using a vehicle with defective brakes | CU 10 |
| Causing or likely to cause danger by reason of use of unsuitable vehicle or using a vehicle with parts or accessories (excluding brakes, steering or tyres) in a dangerous condition | CU 20 |
| Using a vehicle with defective tyres | CU 30 |
| Using a vehicle with defective steering | CU 40 |

| | |
|---|---|
| Causing or likely to cause danger by reason of load or passengers | CU 50 |
| Undefined failure to comply with construction and use regulations | CU 60 |

## 8.49 Brakes on pedal cycles

The offence of riding, or causing or permitting to be ridden, a pedal cycle on the road in contravention of the Pedal Cycles (Construction and Use) Regulations is punishable under s 178 of the 1972 Act on summary conviction with a fine of level 3. Endorsement, disqualification and penalty points may not be ordered, even if the pedal cycle is an electrically assisted pedal cycle (see 1.9 and 8.21).

## 8.50 Selling etc unroadworthy vehicles and parts

Offences of selling, supplying etc motor vehicles and trailers in an unroadworthy condition under s 60, or without a certificate of conformity or type approval certificate under s 62, and for fitting or causing or permitting to be fitted parts which would render the vehicle unroadworthy under s 60A(1) are all punishable with a fine of level 5. The relevant part of Sched 4 to the 1972 Act was amended by Sched 3 to the Transport Act 1982. Sched 3 refers to the 'fitting and sale of defective or unsuitable vehicle parts'. Nevertheless it refers only to s 60A(1) and it follows therefore that the maximum fine for offences contrary to s 60A(3) (sale etc of such parts) is a fine of level 4. For the similar offence in relation to cycles under s 66(5) the penalty is a fine of level 3.The maximum fine under the Consumer Safety Act 1978, s 2 for supplying etc illegal tyres is a fine of level 5 or three months' imprisonment or both. It is triable only summarily. There are similar defences to those applicable for the sale of inadequate crash helmets (see 9.22). Endorsement, disqualification and penalty points may not be ordered for these offences.

## 8.51–60 Magistrates' Association's suggested penalties

The Magistrates' Association's suggested penalties for breach of the Construction and Use Regulations (see also 18.1 and Appendix 3) are as follows:

| | | |
|---|---|---|
| Brakes, faulty condition of: | | |
| Driver | £50 | Consider degree of responsibility |
| HGV owner | £125 | |
| Insecure load: | | |
| Non HGV owner/driver | £50 | |
| HGV driver | £200 | But consider degree of responsibility |
| HGV owner | £400 | |
| Overloading commercial vehicle or exceeding maximum axle weight: | | |
| HGV driver | £200 | |
| HGV owner | £400 | |

| Offence | Penalty | Note |
|---|---|---|
| (Suggested penalty refers to conviction on each charge. In addition to the suggestion for overloading add £20 per 1% of overload but always have regard to commercial gain and damage caused to roads.) | | |
| Steering, faulty condition of: | | |
| Driver | £50 | Consider degree of responsibility |
| HGV owner | £125 | |
| Tyres, faulty condition of: | | |
| Driver | £50 | Consider degree of responsibility |
| HGV owner | £125 | |
| (Suggested penalty refers to each tyre.) | | |
| Offences re number of passengers, dangerous condition of vehicle, weight distribution, packing and adjustment of load: | | |
| HGV driver | £50 | But consider degree of responsibility |
| HGV owner | £100 | |
| Goods vehicle, dangerously unsuitable use: | | |
| Driver | £60 | But consider degree of responsibility |
| HGV owner | £200 | |
| Other offences: | | |
| Driver | £15 | |
| HGV owner | £40 | |

# Test Certificates and Testing

## 8.61 Generally

Sections 43–46 of the 1972 Act contain provisions as to test certificates for vehicles, and ss 53–57, and the Road Traffic (Foreign Vehicles) Act 1972 as to the roadside testing of vehicles. These are discussed below, and the penalties for offences under these provisions will be found at the end of the section.

## 8.62 Test certificates

Sections 43 and 44 of the 1972 Act as extended by the Motor Vehicles (Tests) (Extension) Order 1982 (SI 1982 No 1550) require every motor vehicle first registered more than three years before the time at which it is being used on the road to pass a test under s 43. Motor vehicles used for the carriage of passengers and with more than eight seats excluding the driver's seat, taxis as defined and ambulances as specifically defined, must be tested after one year. This will apply to many minibuses. Section 44(2) and (3) ensure that vehicles manufactured abroad more than three years before their use on a road also require test certificates once they are brought into the United Kingdom and registered here. Sections 43 and 44 bind the Crown.

The Motor Vehicles (Tests) Regulations 1981 (SI 1981 No 1694) as amended by like-named 1982 and 1983 amendment regulations (SI 1982 Nos 783, 814, 1477 and 1715, 1983 Nos 1147 and 1434 and 1984 Nos 401, 727, 815 and 1126) apply and regulate the procedure, etc. There are exemptions from the operation of s 44 for inter alia locomotives, motor tractors, track laying vehicles, goods vehicles of an unladen weight exceeding 1,525 kg (other than dual-purpose vehicles and motor caravans), articulated vehicles (other than articulated buses), works trucks, pedestrian-controlled vehicles, invalids' vehicles of less than 306 kg (if a Department of Health and Social Security supplied invalid vehicle, one which does not exceed 510 kg), certain hackney carriages in London and some other towns, licensed private hire cars, vehicles for export or belonging to a visiting force or certain UK personnel, certain Northern Ireland vehicles, certain police vehicles, play buses and vehicles temporarily in Great Britain. Vehicles on certain small islands, electrically propelled goods vehicles with an unladen weight not exceeding 1,525 kg, and vehicles exempt from duty under s 7(1) of the Vehicles (Excise) Act 1971 (ie where minimal use of the road is established) are also exempt. There are further exemptions for the use of special types authorised under s 42, the use of vehicles imported into Great Britain driven to the importer's or driver's residence, the towing away of abandoned vehicles under the Refuse Disposal (Amenity) Act 1978, or illegally parked vehicles by the police or local authority under the Road Traffic Regulation Act 1984, or the detention or seizure of vehicles by the police or Customs and Excise. Motor traders may also use a vehicle under or after repair by them.

The major change effected by the 1981 Regulations is that public service vehicles are no longer exempt from tests. A person authorised by the Secretary of State may issue a temporary exemption certificate for up to three months for certain unexpected emergencies other than vehicle breakdowns or mechanical defects or non-delivery of spare parts, in the case of a public service vehicle adapted to carry more than eight passengers. The power to make this exemption is given by s 44(10A) of the 1972 Act. As to 'adapted' and 'passengers', see 1.12 and 1.59.

Section 44(2)(*b*) requires a vehicle manufactured more than three years ago and used on roads in the United Kingdom to have a test certificate whether or not it has been registered in Great Britain and whether or not it was manufactured in Great Britain. However, reg 6(xi) exempts vehicles from the requirement for a test certificate if they are temporarily in Great Britain and displaying a registration mark mentioned in reg 5 of the Motor Vehicles (International Circulation) Regulations 1971 (SI 1971 No 937). The exemption applies where less than twelve months have elapsed since the vehicle was last brought into Great Britain. Apart from the other exemptions for imported vehicles referred to above there are no other exemptions for imported vehicles and no reciprocal arrangements for recognising EEC or foreign tests.

The most common exemption relied on by defendants charged with using a vehicle without a certificate is that the vehicle was proceeding to or from a test (reg 6(2)(*a*)). It is sometimes argued by a defendant that he is exempted because he is taking his car to a testing station garage 'by previous arrangement' under reg 31(*a*)(i) even though he has not made a previous arrangement because the garage has advertised to the effect that tests can be given without prior notice. Where such an argument is put forward, many magistrates' courts have nevertheless convicted, taking the view that 'previous arrangement' requires the car owner to have previously contacted the testing station to confirm the test for his car.

Schedule 2 to the 1981 Test Regulations sets out the prescribed requirements for the testing of motor vehicles. The requirements are as to brakes, steering gear, certain lighting equipment and reflectors, stop lamps, tyres, seat belts and seat anchorages, direction indicators, windscreen wipers and washers, exhausts, horns, bodywork and suspension of the vehicle. There are additional requirements for public service vehicles (excluding community buses and certain school buses) (see Class VI in Sched 2). In addition, under s 43(7), as inserted by the Passenger and Goods Vehicles (Recording Equipment) Regulations 1981 (SI 1981 No 1692), tests may be prescribed where recording instruments (tachographs) are required to be installed. Such tests have so far been prescribed for public service vehicles (see Sched 2 to the 1981 Test Regulations). Test certificates under s 44 are issued annually but if a vehicle is re-tested within the last month of an existing test certificate s 44(9) allows the new test certificate to expire on the anniversary of the expiry of the old certificate.

Test certificates are obtainable only from 'authorised examiners' and other inspectors set out in s 43(3). Where a test certificate is refused the tester is required to issue a notification of refusal stating the grounds of refusal and a person aggrieved may appeal to the Secretary of State, who shall cause a further examination of the vehicle and either issue a test certificate or his own notice of refusal (s 43(4)).

A person who uses, or causes or permits a vehicle to be used without a test certificate commits an offence under s 44(1). No offence arises from mere failure to submit the vehicle to a test. It is use on the road which gives rise to an offence.

In a case at quarter sessions *Elliott* v *Grey* (see 1.79) was applied to a vehicle which was left in a cul-de-sac without rear wheels and a rear axle and the defendant's conviction of 'using' the vehicle without a test certificate was upheld, but in *Hewer* v *Cutler* [1974] RTR 155 it was held that a car parked on a road with disconnected gearbox linkage so that the car could be neither driven nor moved did not require a test certificate. *Elliott* v *Grey* was distinguished and it was doubted whether the test as to whether a car requires a test certificate is the same as the test to be applied in determining whether an insurance certificate is required. But in *Eden* v *Mitchell* [1975] RTR 425 *Hewer* v *Cutler* was explained as a case where the car had been completely immobilised and thus was incapable of being driven. Reversing the justices who had acquitted the defendant of 'using' a motor vehicle with defective tyres because he had said he had not intended to drive it, the court said that the true test that should be applied in the case of a stationary vehicle left on the highway was whether steps had been taken to make it impossible for a driver to drive the vehicle (see further as to the terms 'using', 'causing' or 'permitting' a vehicle to be used, Chapter 1).

Sections 169 and 171 (forging and issue of false documents, see Chapter 16) apply in respect of test certificates.

By s 162 (which extends to Crown drivers) test certificates must be produced to constables. It is no defence to a charge under s 162 that the driver would find it difficult if not impossible to obtain the test certificate from the owner (*Davey* v *Towle* [1973] RTR 326).

**8.63 Goods vehicles**

Unlike the testing of vehicles under ss 43 and 44, the testing and plating of goods vehicles under ss 45 and 46 is carried out by the Secretary of State for Transport at government testing stations. The relevant regulations are the Goods Vehicles (Plating and Testing) Regulations 1982 (SI 1982 No 1478 as amended by SI 1983 Nos 239 and 1800 and SI 1984 Nos 178, 816 and 1024). Under the regulations, after the first examination vehicles must be submitted for test annually. The complications regarding the dates by which these vehicles have to be first tested and plated are discussed in an article at (1983) 147 JPN 454. Schedule 2 to the regulations lists the vehicles which are exempt from the necessity of plating and test certificates. The exemption includes public service vehicles and hackney carriages (both as defined), dual-purpose vehicles, mobile cranes, breakdown vehicles, engineering plant, road construction vehicles, road rollers, asphalt or tar trailers, certain street cleaning vehicles, fire fighting vehicle, works trucks and trailers, snow ploughs, etc, living vans, hearses, land implements, land locomotives and land tractors, goods vehicles in the service of a visiting force, goods vehicles proceeding to a port for export, track laying vehicle, living vans with an unladen weight not exceeding 1,525 kg and police vehicles. Also included are tower wagons as defined in Sched 3 to the Vehicles (Excise) Act 1971. In *Anderson and Heeley Ltd* v *Paterson* [1975] RTR 248 a van fitted with an extensible high loader was held not to be a tower wagon as it could and did carry a load contrary to one of the requirements of the definition in Sched 3 to the 1971 Act. The exemption in Sched 2 does not extend to dual-purpose vehicles which are constructed or adapted to form part of an articulated vehicle unless otherwise exempt. The exemption for engineering plant extends to motor vehicles and trailers, which are not engineering plant, but are movable plant or equipment especially designed and constructed for the special purposes of engineering operations. They must presumably be both designed and constructed. The paragraph specifies that they must not be constructed primarily to carry a load. A scrap vehicle is not a disabled vehicle, so a goods vehicle used to transport a scrap vehicle is not a breakdown vehicle exempted by Sched 2 (*Gibson* v *Nutter* [1984] RTR 8). As to the meaning of 'breakdown', see 1.17.

Section 45(9), as inserted by the Passenger and Goods Vehicles (Recording Equipment) Regulations 1981 (SI 1981 No 1692), provides that tests may be prescribed where recording instruments (tachographs) are required to be installed. Such a test is now included in the annual test by SI 1981 No 1693.

Using a goods vehicle on a road, or causing or permitting it to be so used, without the necessary test certificate and using etc a goods vehicle without a plating certificate are offences under s 46(2) and (1) respectively. It is also an offence to use a goods vehicle on a road, or cause or permit it to be so used, with an alteration to the vehicle or equipment without the Secretary of State for Transport having been notified of the alteration as required by the regulations (s 46(3)). It is a defence to s 46(3) that the alteration was not specified in the relevant plating certificate (s 46(4)).

Section 169 applies in respect of goods vehicle test certificates and plating certificates, and s 170(2) applies to the supply of information or documents for the purposes of s 45 or s 46 (see Chapter 16).

The display of the Ministry plate issued under s 46(1) is governed by reg 148 of the Motor Vehicles (Construction and Use) Regulations. However, under that regulation the plate in the case of vehicles to which the Motor Vehicles (Type Approval for Goods Vehicles) (Great Britain) Regulations apply must be fixed fourteen days after issue. This is because the plate will be issued as part of the certification under these regulations and not as a result of the first examinations under s 45 and s 46.

## 8.64 Roadside tests

Section 53 of the 1972 Act enables an authorised examiner to make a roadside test of a motor vehicle as to its brakes, silencer, steering gear, tyres, emission of smoke or fumes and lighting equipment and reflectors and noise. 'Authorised examiner' for the purposes of this section may include both a constable appointed as such by his chief constable and a person appointed by the police authority for the purposes of this section acting under the directions of the chief constable. The driver may elect for the test to be deferred unless the constable thinks that the vehicle is so defective that the test should be carried out forthwith or that the vehicle has caused an accident (s 53(3)). The option extends to him only and not to the owner, nor need the examiner tell the driver of his option (*Brown* v *McIndoe* [1963] SLT 233). Failing to comply with the requirements of the section or obstructing an examiner is an offence.

Prosecution for contravention of a construction and use regulation as to tyres or brakes does not depend on whether the evidence as to the contravention has been obtained as a result of a test by an authorised examiner (*Stoneley* v *Richardson* [1973] RTR 229; *Phillips* v *Thomas* [1974] RTR 28). Similarly, production of a traffic examiner's authority is not a prerequisite of a conviction of being overweight contrary to reg 150 of the Construction and Use Regulations (*Wurzal* v *Reader Bros Ltd* [1974] RTR 383).

Section 54 contains the procedure for remedying defects discovered by the roadside test. It enables the examiner to give the owner (the person driving the vehicle can be required to state the name and address of the owner) a notice specifying the defect and requiring the owner to have the defect remedied. The owner is then required to give a certificate within twenty-eight days countersigned by an authorised tester that the defect no longer exists. Alternatively, the owner can make a declaration that he has sold or disposed of the vehicle to a person named in the declaration or that he no longer intends to use the vehicle on a road (s 54(3), (4)).

*Section 54 is not yet (1 February 1985) in force (see s 208)*. Failure to give the certificate or declaration within the specified time will be an offence, as will be failure by the driver to give the owner's name and address. It is submitted that an information for failing to give both name and address is not bad for duplicity (see 2.46).

Sections 56 and 57 contain parallel provisions relating to goods vehicles. Section 56 enables a goods vehicle examiner to inspect goods vehicles and to enter premises on which he has reason to believe that goods vehicles are kept. Section 57 enables the examiner to prohibit the driving of a goods vehicle which either is unfit for service or 'is likely to become unfit for service'. Such prohibition notices may either be immediate or delayed in their effect. Section 58 governs the procedure for removal of a goods vehicle prohibition order.

Obstructing a goods vehicle examiner is an offence under s 56(3). Driving a goods vehicle in contravention of a prohibition order or refusing to proceed to a place of inspection is an offence under s 57(9).

## 8.65–70 Foreign goods vehicles

The Road Traffic (Foreign Vehicles) Act 1972 gives additional powers to authorised examiners to issue prohibition orders in respect of foreign goods vehicles and foreign public service vehicles. The 1972 Act has been amended by the Road Transport (International Passenger Services) Regulations 1980 (SI 1980 No 1454), which is in turn amended by SI 1983 No 1025. Where the examiner exercises any function under s 8(1) of the Public Passenger Vehicles Act 1981 (entry and inspection of public service vehicle), s 99 of the Transport Act 1968 (inspection of drivers' records, etc), ss 53 and 56 of the 1972 Act (powers of testing etc) or s 160 of the 1972 Act (weighing of motor vehicles), he may issue a prohibition order should there by *any* contravention of any of the regulations or enactments in Sched 2 to the Act. Schedule 2 includes the whole of the Construction and Use Regulations, and certain requirements relating to lights on vehicles. The schedule also includes s 60 (operators' licences) and ss 96–98 of the Transport Act 1968 (drivers' hours and tachograph records), and regulations under s 91(1)(*c*) of the same Act (requiring plates and marks etc). The list of functions the exercise of which by an examiner confers on him the power to issue prohibition orders in respect of foreign goods vehicles now includes functions relating to the Passenger and Goods Vehicles (Recording Equipment) Regulations 1979 (SI 1979 No 1746) (see reg 3(9) of those regulations), and the list of contraventions in respect of which such prohibition orders may be issued includes the installation of recording equipment in, and the keeping of records of, goods and public service vehicles and the use of foreign public service vehicles in breach of reg 19 of the Road Transport (International Passenger Services) Regulations 1984, that is otherwise than under and in accordance with the authorisation or other document referred to in that regulation. A prohibition order may also be made if the driver obstructs the examiner.

Any person who drives a vehicle or causes or permits one to be driven in contravention of such a prohibition or does not comply with the direction made as a result of a prohibition order commits an offence (s 3(1)), and can be arrested by a constable without warrant (s 3(2)). The constable is also given powers of impounding a vehicle where he suspects an offence under s 3(1). He may authorise an appropriate person to remove the vehicle for that purpose (s 3(3)–(6)).

A foreign goods vehicle or foreign public service vehicle is one brought into the United Kingdom and not registered in the United Kingdom (s 7), and any vehicle not displaying a licence or trade plates issued under the Vehicles (Excise) Act 1971 shall be presumed unless the contrary be proved not to be registered in the United Kingdom (s 7(4)).

## Test Certificates: Penalties

### 8.71–5 Generally

Using, or causing or permitting a vehicle to be used, without a test certificate contrary to s 44(1), is punishable by a fine of level 3 save that the maximum penalty for s 44(1) offences in the case of a vehicle adapted to carry more than eight passengers is a fine of level 4. This will include some private vehicles and many minibuses. As to 'adapted' and whether 'passengers' includes the driver, see 1.12 and 1.59. It is submitted there that it does not in the case of public service vehicles. The position for private vehicles is less certain but there seems to be a tendency to distinguish between drivers and passengers. It is not punishable by imprisonment, nor may disqualification, endorsement or penalty points be ordered. The Magistrates' Association's suggested penalty is £20. For failing to produce the test certificate (s 162) the suggested penalty is £10 (see further 18.1 and Appendix 3).

Using a goods vehicle on a road, or causing or permitting it to be so used, without the necessary test certificate (s 46(2)) is subject to a fine of level 4 and using etc a goods vehicle without a plating certificate (s 46(1)) to a fine of level 3. Using etc a goods vehicle with an alteration not notified to the Secretary of State for Transport (s 46(3)) is punishable with a fine of level 3. None of the offences under s 46 carries endorsement or disqualification.

Offences of failing to comply with the requirements of s 53 or s 54 (when in force) or obstructing an examiner carrying out a test under those sections are all punishable with a fine of level 3. Driving a goods vehicle in contravention of a prohibition order under s 57 or refusing to proceed to a place of inspection is punishable with a fine of level 5, and any person who drives a vehicle or causes or permits one to be driven in contravention of a prohibition under s 3(1) of the Road Traffic (Foreign Vehicles) Act 1972 or does not comply with the direction made as a result of a prohibition order is liable on summary conviction to a fine of level 5. There is no power to order endorsement, disqualification or penalty points for any of these offences.

An offence against s 162 of the 1972 Act (production of certificates) is punishable with a fine of level 3.

## Lighting

### 8.76 The Road Vehicles Lighting Regulations

The law as to lighting of vehicles is contained in the Road Vehicles Lighting Regulations 1984 (SI 1984 No 812). They are made under s 40 of the

1972 Act in respect of all vehicles save cycles not being motor vehicles. The regulations in respect of cycles not being motor vehicles are made under s 66 of the 1972 Act. As to cycles not being motor vehicles, see 1.2, 1.8 and in particular 1.9. The regulations correspond with the Motor Vehicles (Construction and Use) Regulations also made under s 40 in that they are divided into equipment, maintenance and use.

What used to be called side lights are now more accurately called front position lamps. Headlamps are still so described and include main beam and dipped beam headlamps. In some places the regulations merely refer to headlamps and in other places specify main-beam or dipped-beam headlamps.

Dim-dip lighting devices provide for intermediate strength headlights for when a vehicle is about to start. They will only apply to motor vehicles with three or more wheels not being a motor bicycle with a sidecar, capable of exceeding 25 mph on the level and only to vehicles manufactured on or after 1 October 1986 and first used on or after 1 April 1987. It is important to note that under the regulations these dim-dip lights will not fulfil the headlamp requirements or the seriously reduced visibility in daytime requirements.

The term 'hours of darkness' in the regulations means the time between half an hour after sunset and half an hour before sunrise (reg 3(1)). 'Sunset' means sunset according to local, not Greenwich, time (*Gordon* v *Cann* (1899) 63 JP 324, and see 95 JP Jo 772 as to evidence to determine sunset and sunrise). 'Daytime hours' means hours other than hours of darkness as defined.

By s 60 of the 1972 Act it is an offence to sell or supply or expose for sale a motor vehicle which does not comply with the law's requirements as to lighting equipment and reflectors (see 8.33).

## 8.77 Application

The 1972 Act, s 40 and the regulations made under s 40 apply to vehicles of the Crown (s 188 of the 1972 Act) but see 2.8. Section 66 in theory also applies to Crown vehicles, but the offence section for s 66 is s 178 and this section does not apply to Crown vehicles (see s 188). The regulations therefore apply to Crown vehicles save that no offence is committed in respect of a cycle which is not a motor vehicle. Regulation 7 makes special provision as to vehicles of the home forces and of visiting forces. Section 40 and therefore the material regulations do not apply to trolley vehicles or trams.

## 8.78 Offences

Section 40 of the 1972 Act makes it an offence for any person to contravene or fail to comply with the regulations or to use or cause or permit to be used on a road a motor vehicle or trailer which does not comply. Section 178 makes it an offence if a person acts in contravention of or fails to comply with the regulations made under s 66. In fact the offences under the 1984 Regulations refer to *using*, *causing* or *permitting* the use on a *road* (for the meaning of these expressions see Chapter 1). An exception is reg 21(1)(*b*) (parked vehicles etc) which refers to 'allow to remain at rest, or cause or permit to be allowed to remain at rest, on a road'.

## 8.79 Exemptions from the 1984 Regulations

Nothing in the regulations requires any lamp or reflector to be fitted during daylight hours to a vehicle which does not have a front or rear position lamp, incomplete vehicles proceeding to a works for completion, pedal cycles, pedestrian controlled vehicles, horse drawn vehicles, vehicles drawn or propelled by hand or combat vehicles. Such vehicles are exempt from all such requirements during daylight. As to the meaning of daylight see above, 8.76. Horse drawn vehicles include vehicles drawn by any animal!

With regard to the exemption for vehicles not fitted with front or rear position lamps such a lamp is not to be treated as fitted if it is so painted over or masked that it is not capable of being immediately used or readily put to use, or if the lamp is an electric lamp which is not provided with any system of wiring by which it is or can readily be connected with a source of electricity. There is a difference between readily used and readily connected. A paper mask means that a lamp cannot be readily used, but merely a loose wire still means that the electricity can be readily connected.

There are also certain exemptions for invalid carriages, visiting vehicles, temporarily imported vehicles and vehicles proceeding to a port for export. Hand drawn or propelled vehicles are exempt if they are 800 mm or less wide including any load if used close to the near side or left-hand edge of the carriageway or to cross the road.

*Vehicles towing or being towed*

Basically rear lamps are only required for all drawing vehicles and front lamps etc for all trailers in the case of new vehicles that is motor vehicles first used on or after 1 April 1986 and pedal cycles or trailers manufactured on or after 1 October 1985. Trailers are exempt from stop lamps and indicators if one indicator at least on each side and the stop lamp(s) on the drawing vehicle are visible to an observer from 6 m behind the trailer whether loaded or not.

Broken-down vehicles are also exempt from fitting and maintenance of lamps reflectors or rear markings save that rear position lamps and rear reflectors must be fitted during the hours of darkness.

## 8.80 Fitting of lamps etc

Part II of the Regulations (regs 11–19) governs the fitting of lamps, reflectors, rear markings and devices. It is an offence to use, cause or permit to be used on a road a vehicle specified in Sched 1 not equipped with lamps, reflectors, rear markings and devices of the type specified in the Schedule and which comply with the described installation and performance requirements. From the wording it seems that there is a single offence of not having the vehicle equipped as required and the using, causing or permitting offences arise accordingly. See, however, 8.79 for the daylight exemption.

Column 2 of Sched 1 specifies the class of vehicle, column 3 the type of lamp etc required, column 4 where the relevant installation and performance requirements can be found and column 5 the exceptions.

The colour of light to be shown by lamps and reflectors is governed by reg 11, their movement by reg 12, restrictions on flashing lights by reg 13, and restrictions on the fitting of warning beacons, special warning lamps and similar devices by reg 15 and by reg 19 for additional side marker lamps for vehicles or combination of vehicles with an overall length (including any load) exceeding 18.3 m or in certain circumstances 12.2 m.

*Optional fittings*

It is an offence by reg 17 to use, cause or permit to be used on a road a vehicle fitted optionally with one of the seventeen specified lamps, reflectors, rear markings or devices unless it complies with the scheduled provisions.

## 8.81 Projecting trailers and projecting and overhanging loads

Regulation 18 governs projecting trailers and projecting and overhanging loads and reference should be made to the regulation for the full requirements.

It is an offence by reg 18 to use, cause or permit to be used on a road a vehicle during the hours of darkness or seriously reduced visibility in contravention of the requirements. In effect a sideways projection of more than 400 mm from the outermost part of the relevant position lamp has to be lit by an additional lamp or the original lamp moved. The projection may consist of a load or equipment or it may be a trailer without front lights projecting sideways more than 400 mm from the front position lamp on any proceeding vehicle. The same applies to a projection more than 1 m to the rear (more than 2 m in the case of agricultural vehicles and vehicles carrying fire escapes). The installation and performance requirements for rear position lamps do not apply to such rearward projection lamps.

If a vehicle carries a load or equipment which obscures any obligatory lamp reflector or rear marking the lamp etc must be moved or replaced by an additional lamp etc. This applies to stop lamps and indicators at all times and to other lamps etc during the hours of darkness and seriously reduced visibility.

In effect as seriously reduced visibility may occur at any time it will be necessary to provide for reg 18 to be complied with accordingly.

## 8.82 Headlamps—requirements

The specifications for headlamps are set out in Scheds 4 and 5. All vehicles must have two save solo motor bicycles, motor bicycle combinations, and certain old or small three-wheeler motor vehicles. (All these may have one only.) Certain old large passenger vehicles may have two main beam and one dipped beam headlamps. Pairs must be matched and must switch on or off simultaneously. The colour must be white or yellow. At first sight the intensity does not appear in all cases to be specified but this will be governed either in the specification or by the approval or BS mark.

## 8.83 Position lamps—requirements

The specifications for front position lamps are set out in Sched 2 and for rear position lamps in Sched 10. All vehicles must have two front position lamps save pedal cycles with less than four wheels and without a sidecar, solo motor bicycles, handcarts with an overall width (including any load) not exceeding 1250 mm and invalid carriages (all one lamp only). Motor cycle combinations with a headlamp on the motor cycle may have one front position lamp only on the sidecar. Apart from this and trailers manufactured before 1 October 1985, the two must form a pair, but on each front side. They must be white or if incorporated in a headlamp which is capable of emitting *only* a yellow light, yellow. In this context it may be argued that a headlamp with a yellow mask for a continental journey is not capable of emitting *only* a yellow light, so that the use of an incorporated front position lamp masked yellow is illegal in this country.

All vehicles must have two red rear position lamps save pedal cycles with less than four wheels and without a sidecar, solo motor bicycles, handcarts, trailers drawn by pedal cycles, trailers of 800 mm width or less drawn by motor bicycles including combinations (in this instance there is no reference to the width of the load) and certain old large passenger vehicles (all one position lamp only). Certain motor vehicles and trailers drawn by them which cannot comply with the full requirements as to position and angles of visibility must have four.

## 8.84 Rear registration plate lamps

As well as being included in these regulations, there is also the offence relating to the failure to illuminate the rear index plate. This is also an offence of using, causing or permitting. The offences under the two different sets of regulations are compared at 12.37.

## 8.85 Maintenance

Part III of the Regulations (regs 20–23) governs the maintenance and use of lamps, reflectors, rear markings and devices. Regulation 20 governs maintenance. It is an offence to use, cause or permit the use on a road of a vehicle if every front position lamp, rear position lamp, headlamp, rear registration plate lamp, side marker lamp, rear fog lamp, reflex reflector and rear markings required and every stop lamp and indicator fitted (required or not) is not in clean and good working order (reg 20(1)). As noted, the law applies additionally to optional stop lamps and indicators if fitted. From the wording it again seems that there is a single offence of not having the lamps etc as required, and using, causing or permitting offences arise accordingly.

## 8.86 Exemptions—maintenance

The main exemption from reg 20(1) is for a defective lamp or reflector fitted to a vehicle in use on a road during daytime hours if such lamp or reflector became defective during the journey in progress or if arrangements have been made to remedy the defect with all reasonable expedition (reg 20(4)). It must be necessary to have made some arrangements even if garages are closed or it is a Bank Holiday. Arrangements with a garage are not stipulated and presumably arrangements through a relative or an employer or employee might be sufficient. It may be reasonable expedition to await an insurance company's permission even though the company is not as prompt in replying as one would wish.

These exemptions are applicable during daytime and therefore during seriously reduced visibility but not during the hours of darkness even though the defect arose in the middle of nowhere in the course of the journey. It has been held by a magistrates' court in respect of the similarly worded speedometer exemption (see 8.19) that the defence would include a round journey, but not the return journey from a fixed destination when the defect occurred in the course of the outward journey.

There is an exemption in reg 20(4) from the maintenance of rear fog lamps on motor vehicles drawing trailers and on vehicles which are part of a combination of vehicles any part of which is not required to have rear fog lamps. There is also an exemption for lamps reflectors and rear markings during daytime hours fitted to combat vehicles (also reg 20(4))

## 8.87 Further maintenance offences

There is by reg 20(2) a separate offence in respect of hazard warning signals which only need be kept in good working order. There is a further offence by reg 20(3) for dipped beam headlamps, fog lamps and reversing lamps, including optional lamps. These must be so *maintained* that their aim will not cause undue dazzle or inconvenience to other persons using the road. Such other persons could in theory include passengers in the offending vehicle. This should be compared with the prohibition by reg 23 of *use* so as to cause undue dazzle or discomfort which applies to various lamps and devices, including both dipped-beam and main-beam headlamps. The reg 20(4) exemptions do not apply to contraventions of reg 20(2) or reg 20(3) and it is immaterial for example that the defect arose even during a daytime journey or arrangements had been made for repair.

*Exemptions*

Regulation 21(2), (3) and (4) provide wide exemptions for parked vehicles discussed separately below.

There is an exemption also for solo motor bicycles or pedal cycles being pushed along the left-hand edge of a carriageway and pedal cycles on the left-hand or nearside edge waiting to proceed (reg 21(3)(*a*) and (*b*)).

## 8.88 Headlamps—keeping lit during darkness or seriously reduced visibility

It is an offence by reg 22 to use, cause or permit to be used on a road a vehicle fitted with obligatory dipped-beam headlamps unless every such lamp is kept lit during the hours of darkness (except on roads restricted for the purpose of s 81 of the Road Traffic Regulation Act 1984 with street lamps *actually illuminated* not more than 200 yards apart (see further 6.28)) and in seriously reduced visibility.

As is noted below this cannot mean that the headlamp must be kept lit with the dipped beam and presumably the main beam may be used. Dim-dip lights do not satisfy reg 22.

*Exemptions*

The main exemption is for all parked vehicles. There are also exemptions for towed vehicles and snow plough vehicles.

By reg 23 it is an offence to use or cause or permit to be used on a road a vehicle with a headlamp dipped or main (*a*) so as to cause undue dazzle or discomfort to other road users or (*b*) when parked. Parked must mean something more than merely stationary—see reg 22 and in particular reg 22(2)(*e*).

### 8.89 Position lamps etc—keeping lit during darkness or seriously reduced visibility

By reg 21 it is an offence to use, cause or permit to be used on a road any vehicle during the hours of darkness or any vehicle which is in motion during daytime hours in seriously reduced visibility unless every front position lamp, rear position lamp, rear registration plate lamp and side marker lamp required is kept lit.

It is also an offence to allow or cause or permit a vehicle to remain at rest on a road during the hours of darkness unless these lamps are kept lit. For parking exemptions see below. As to 'during the hours of darkness' 'daytime hours', see 8.76 above.

Trailers by themselves must have front position lamps fitted and lit and a solo motor bicycle must have a front position lamp fitted and lit in these circumstances, even though not otherwise required for these vehicles. Similarly a motor cycle combination with a front position lamp on the sidecar must have a pair fitted and kept lit (reg 21(1)). From the wording it again seems that there are single offences of not having the various lamps lit and using, causing or permitting offences arise accordingly.

### 8.90 Exemptions for parked vehicles

Exemptions for parked vehicles from the need to illuminate position lamps, rear registration plate lamps and side marker lamps are contained in reg 21(2), (3) and (4). Parked vehicles are not required to display lights provided that the road in question is subject to a speed limit of 30 mph or lower. The exemption only applies if the vehicle is parked so that its left or near side is as close as may be, and parallel to, the edge of the carriageway and also no part of the vehicle is within 10 m of a carriageway junction, whether that junction is on the same side of the road as the parked vehicle or not. Where the street is one way only, the regulations allow the vehicle to be parked so that either its left or near side is as close as may be to the left edge of the carriageway or its right or offside is as close as may be to the right edge of the carriageway. The exemption from lights only applies to passenger vehicles constructed or adapted to carry not more than eight passengers exclusive of the driver, goods vehicles having an unladen weight not exceeding 1525 kg, invalid carriages, motorcycles and pedal cycles (or tricycles). Front and rear lights must be displayed if the vehicle has an overhanging or projecting load to which reg 18 applies. Lights also must be displayed on vehicles to which a trailer is attached.

The exemption for a parked vehicle only applies if no part of the vehicle is within 10 m of a junction. In *Bunting* v *Holt* [1977] RTR 373 it was held that the correct method of measuring was from point A to the parked car shown in the diagram below, and not point B. That case was under different regulations and the measurement was different, but the principle would seem to be the same.

KIRKGATE

A B

MANOR LANE

Regulation 21 allows an exempted vehicle to park without lights in a recognised parking place. Such places are:

(*a*) places set aside as parking places under an enactment or instrument;

(*b*) lay-bys indicated in accordance with Diagram 1010 in Sched 2 to the Traffic Signs Regulations and General Directions 1981 (SI 1981 No 859) (this diagram shows a longitudinal line to indicate the edge of the carriageway at a lay-by (or road junction although this is not material in this context));

(*c*) lay-bys where the surface is of a colour or texture which is different from that of the part of the carriageway of the road used primarily by through traffic; and

(*d*) lay-bys where the limits are marked out by a continuous (but not a dotted) strip of surface of a different colour or texture from that of the surface of the remainder of the carriageway of the road.

A vehicle is not exempted from showing lights if it is parked 'in a manner' which contravenes the provisions of an enactment or instrument relating to the parking place. The meaning of 'manner' in this context may give rise to argument. It is possible that parking for an excess period would not be a contravention of the manner of parking. The purpose presumably is that the vehicle should be visible without lights and should therefore be parked in the normal way. There would be a contravention of the Lighting Regulations if the vehicle were parked in a different way from that specified in the instrument.

The earlier regulations which allowed parking lights to be displayed on one side of the vehicle have been revoked. The effect of this is that where lights are required by the regulations to be displayed on a parked vehicle, that vehicle is required to display all four lights, front and rear.

The above exemptions for parked vehicles only apply to certain vehicles in an area of 30 mph or lower. They do not apply to lay-bys on other roads. There is, however, a general exemption in reg 21(3)(*c*) for all vehicles parked in an area outlined by lamps or traffic signs so as to prevent the presence of the vehicle its load or equipment being a danger to persons using the road. It is understood this is intended to cover illuminated lorry parks but the exemption is in wide terms and not restricted to lorries and the nature of the traffic sign is not specified.

Lay-bys on many roads are outlined by traffic signs and are planned to avoid danger by removing vehicles from the main carriageway. The wording of the exemption is wide enough to apply to them. The position may depend on the interpretation of 'outlined'. The *Concise Oxford Dictionary* indicates that 'outline' has a narrow meaning of enclosing lines and a wider meaning. The use of the expression outlined by lamps is in favour of the wider meaning and implies that circumference lines are not an essential feature.

It is an offence for the headlamp to be on when a vehicle is parked on a road (reg 23).

## 8.91 Seriously reduced visibility

The seriously reduced visibility offences together with the exemptions have been incorporated by the regulations in the reg 21 and reg 22 hours of darkness regulations.

It will be noted that there are two 'seriously reduced visibility' offences; use etc of vehicles with headlamps not lit as required by reg 22, and use etc of vehicles with position lamps, rear registration plate lamps and side marker lamps not lit as required by reg 21. Under reg 22 (headlamps) it is immaterial whether it is during daylight or darkness. Regulation 21 (other lamps) refers to vehicles *in motion* during *daytime*. It is therefore only possible to commit *both* offences during daytime and the reg 21 offence (other lamps) cannot be committed at night under the visibility limb. It is an offence in any event under the other limb of reg 21 not to have these other lamps lit at night. Regulation 21 (other lamps) is only breached when the vehicle is in motion but reg 22 (headlamps) may be breached when the vehicle is not moving but cannot be committed when the vehicle is parked (reg 22(2)(*e*)).

'Seriously reduced visibility' is not defined and seems to be essentially a question of fact. Examples will be fog, mist, snow storms, heavy rain storms, spray conditions, badly overcast weather. It is not restricted to poor weather conditions and might for instance include a poorly illuminated tunnel or a smoke cloud.

The previous regulations referred to poor visibility conditions. In *Swift* v *Spence* [1982] RTR 116 a case on the earlier regulations the Divisional Court accepted a finding of justices that visibility down to between 20 yards and 75 yards in icy fog amounted to poor visibility conditions. The justices considered that, having regard to the nose-to-tail line of very slow and frequently stationary traffic, failure to use headlights was, in the particular circumstances, not a hazard and acquitted. (The defendant's car had sidelights on.) The Divisional Court held that there ought to have been a conviction as there was 'no way under this regulation whereby it can be said that in some conditions there is an obligation to have sidelights on but not dipped headlights. It is dipped headlights or nothing.' It is submitted that while the decision is correct this statement may be misleading, as both the former and the present regulations permit either a main beam or a dipped beam on headlamps for this purpose.

In conditions of seriously reduced visibility the driver may use instead of his headlamps either two front fog lights so fitted that the outermost part of the illuminated area of each lamp in the pair is not more than 400 mm from the outer edge. One fog lamp may be used as an alternative to headlamps where only one headlamp is fitted or in the case of solo motor bicycles or motor bicycle combinations even though fitted with a pair of headlamps.

### 8.92 Fog lamps

The Road Vehicles (Rear Fog Lamps) Regulations 1978 (now revoked) made it compulsory for twin rear fog lamps or one fog lamp on the rear off side to be fitted to motor vehicles and trailers manufactured on or after 1 October 1979 and first used on or after 1 April 1980. There were certain exceptions. The position is continued under the present regulations.

A front or rear fog lamp may not be used etc on a vehicle on a road other than in conditions of seriously reduced visibility (as to this see 8.88, above) nor when a vehicle is parked, nor so as to cause undue dazzle or discomfort to other persons using the road. Any contravention will constitute offences under reg 23. It will be an offence therefore to use these fog lamps during daylight or darkness unless the exceptional visibility conditions exist. Presumably there will be no contravention in continuing to use them where the adverse visibility conditions exist but in a patchy form, providing there is no undue dazzle or discomfort.

### 8.93–5 Improper use of lamps etc

By reg 23 it is an offence to use cause or permit to be used on a road any vehicle on which a lamp hazard warning signal or warning beacon is used in a manner prohibited by table 3 of the regulation. In particular, in addition to the headlamps and fog lamps prohibitions already set out under these headings above, hazard warning signals may only be used to warn road users of temporary obstructions when the vehicle is at rest or in the case of large passenger vehicles to summon assistance. From this the practice of using such signals to indicate broken-down vehicles under tow seems to be illegal.

Reversing lamps may only be used etc for the purpose of reversing.

## Lighting: Proceedings and Penalties

### 8.96 Generally

The Road Vehicles Lighting Regulations 1984 are made under s 40 of the 1972 Act in respect of all vehicles save cycles not being motor vehicles and the maximum penalty for a contravention is a fine of level 4.

In respect of cycles not being motor vehicles the 1984 Regulations are made under s 66 of the 1972 Act and the maximum penalty for a contravention is a fine of level 3. As to the definition of cycles not being motor vehicles, see 1.8; this definition seems to include electrically assisted pedal cycles such as the Sinclair C5 car.

The maximum penalty for an offence under reg 19 of the Registration and Licensing Regulations (illumination of number plates) is a fine of level 3.

The Magistrates' Association's suggested penalty for driving without lights is £50. See further 18.1 and Appendix 3.

# Chapter 9

# Protection of Drivers and Passengers

## Seat Belts

### 9.1 Provision of seat belts

The vehicles which must be provided with seat belts and anchorage points are described in reg 17 of the Construction and Use Regulations. The regulation does not itself require any person to use a seat belt but is relevant for the seat belt provisions.

Regulation 102A of the Construction and Use Regulations deals with the maintenance of seat belts and anchorage points. Words used in reg 102A and defined in reg 17 have the same meaning. Paragraph 1 of reg 102A refers to the anchorages, fastenings, adjusting device and retracting mechanism (if any) of every such seat belt. This implies that all these are part of the seat belt. Note that there is a distinction between anchorages and anchorage points. The latter are specified separately in regs 17 and 102A.

There are two exceptions in para 5 of reg 102A—(*a*) where the requirement ceased to be complied with (ie the fault arose) after the start of the journey and (*b*) where steps have been taken for compliance with all reasonable expedition. As to the meaning of similarly worded defences for speedometers and lights, see 8.19 and 8.86. Here the word 'defence' is not used but it is submitted that it is nevertheless a qualification etc within the meaning of s 101 of the Magistrates' Courts Act 1980 so that the burden of proof remains on the defendant on the balance of probabilities.

Seat belts and anchorage points are exempt by reg 5 (optional type approval) from the provisions of reg 17 if they comply with a certificate of type approval or a certificate of conformity (see 8.7).

### 9.2 Wearing of seat belts

Sections 27 and 28 of the Transport Act 1981 inserted ss 33A (wearing of seat belts) and 33B (child restraints) in the 1972 Act. The Motor Vehicles (Wearing of Seat Belts) Regulations 1982 (SI 1982 No 1203) and the Motor Vehicles (Wearing of Seat Belts by Children) Regulations 1982 (SI 1982 No 1342) have been made thereunder. The provisions relating to children (s 33B) are dealt with separately below.

It is an offence under s 33A (applying reg 4 of the Seat Belt Regulations) to *drive* a specified motor vehicle without wearing a seat belt. It is also an offence under s 33A to *ride* in the *specified front seat* without wearing a seat belt. If that passenger seat is unoccupied it is also an offence under s 33A to *ride* in another forward facing seat alongside the driver without wearing a seat belt.

### 9.3 Aiding and abetting

Notwithstanding any enactment or rule of law (eg aiding and abetting) only the principal offender, ie the person actually breaking the seat belt law is to be guilty (s 33A(3)). If the driver and front seat passenger are both not wearing belts, both may be prosecuted as principals but cannot be prosecuted for aiding and abetting each other. If the front seat passenger is not wearing a belt, the driver cannot be prosecuted under s 33A if he himself is wearing a belt, but if the passenger is under fourteen the driver commits an offence under s 33B and a child of ten or more years of age can be prosecuted for aiding and abetting.

### 9.4 Specified motor vehicles

The motor vehicles are specified in reg 6 of the Seat Belt Regulations. They are vehicles required to have seat belts and anchorage points by reg 17 of the Construction and Use Regulations. They also *include* vehicles to which reg 17 would apply (providing they have seat belts and anchorage points) but for the fact that they are proceeding to a port for export, or have been brought temporarily into Great Britain by a person resident abroad, or are visiting forces vehicles, or are undergoing certain tests or are being used under a trade licence or are being driven from the premises of manufacturers to distributors or dealers or from them to purchasers etc. It should be emphasised that these are *inclusions* in the seat belt requirements and not *exclusions* from them.

### 9.5 Vehicles required to have seat belts and anchorage points

The vehicles required by reg 17 of the Construction and Use Regulations to have seat belts and anchorage points are:

(*a*) Passenger or dual-purpose motor cars (see 1.2 and 1.7) constructed or adapted to carry twelve or less passengers exclusive of the driver which were manufactured on or after 1 July 1964 and first registered on or after 1 January 1965.

(*b*) Goods vehicle motor cars other than dual-purpose vehicles manufactured on or after 1 September 1966 and first registered on or after 1 April 1967 which have an unladen weight not exceeding 1,525 kg or, in the case of such a goods vehicle motor car manufactured on or after 1 October 1979 or first used on or after 1 April 1980, which have a maximum gross weight not exceeding 3,500 kg. See reg 17(2)(*a*) for the full wording.

(*c*) Three-wheeler passenger and goods motor cycles (see 1.6*A*) (excluding motor cycles with sidecars) manufactured on or after 1 March 1970 and first used on or after 1 September 1970 which have an unladen weight exceeding 255 kg.

For the meaning of 'first used', see reg 3(2) of the Construction and Use Regulations.

Vehicles excepted from the requirement to have seat belts and anchorage points fitted are:

- A land tractor or an industrial tractor which is not in either case a motor tractor (reg 17(2)(*c*)).
- A motor tractor (reg 17(2)(*d*)).
- A works truck (reg 17(2)(*e*)).
- An electrically propelled goods vehicle (reg 17(2)(*f*)).
- A pedestrian-controlled vehicle (reg 17(2)(*g*)).
- A vehicle which has been used on roads outside Great Britain and has been imported into Great Britain (reg 17(2)(*h*)) and which is being driven straight home or from the home by previous arrangement to have the seat belts and anchorage points fitted.
- A vehicle which is incapable by reason of its construction of exceeding a speed of 16 miles per hour on the level under its own power (reg 17(2)(*i*)).
- A vehicle while it is being used under a trade licence within the meaning of the Vehicles (Excise) Act 1971 (reg 17(6)(*a*)(i)).
- A vehicle during certain initial journeys after leaving the premises of a manufacturer, distributor or dealer (proviso (*b*) to reg 17(6)(*a*)(ii)).
- A vehicle proceeding to port for export (reg 4(3)).
- A vehicle brought temporarily into this country by a person resident abroad (reg 4(7)).
- A vehicle which is exempt from car tax by virtue of para 7 or 8 of Sched 7 to the Finance Act 1972, or has been zero rated under reg 49 or 50 of the Value Added Tax (General) Regulations 1977 (reg 4(8)).
- A vehicle in the service of a visiting force or of a headquarters (reg 4(9)).
- A vehicle whilst being tested for an MOT certificate (reg 4(10)).

It must be emphasised however that as set out above, the seat belt law must be complied with in some of these cases if seat belts are in fact fitted.

## 9.6 Definitions

*'Seat belt'*

'Seat belt' is defined in reg 17(12) of the Construction and Use Regulations and this definition is adopted in reg 102A of those Regulations (maintenance of seat belts and anchorage points) and to some extent in the Motor Vehicles (Wearing of Seat Belts by Children) Regulations 1982 (9.10 below) but not directly in the Motor Vehicles (Wearing of Seat Belts) Regulations 1982 (see reg 7 of those regulations). The reason is presumably to require the wearing of belts of a wider description (but see below under the non-compliance exemptions).

*'Specified passenger seat'*

The 'specified passenger seat' has the same meaning as in reg 17(12) of the Construction and Use Regulations. Where there is one forward facing front seat alongside the driver's seat it is that seat. Where there is more than one such seat it is the one furthest from the driver. Where there is normally no such seat alongside, it is the foremost forward facing front passenger seat furthest from the driver's seat unless there is a fixed partition between it and the space in front alongside the driver's seat.

The definition may be particularly significant for minibuses where there is a middle front seat between what would be the specified passenger's seat and the driver's seat. A passenger in this seat need not wear a seat belt under the regulations if the specified passenger seat is occupied but must wear one if it is unoccupied.

## 9.7 General exemptions

There are a number of general exemptions in reg 5 of the Seat Belt Regulations including delivery persons, persons reversing, taxi etc drivers, police (and persons exercising similar responsibilities) on protection or on escort duty, firemen while donning operational equipment, for certain locked inertia reel belts and persons *riding* in vehicles under trade plates for the purpose of investigating or remedying mechanical faults.

The wording should be studied in each case. For instance the delivery exemption applies only to vehicles constructed or adapted (as to this see Chapter 1, 1.12) for the delivery or collection of goods or mail. It would not apply to a newsagent delivering papers or to someone collecting jumble in an ordinary car. It also only applies 'whilst engaged in making' (such) 'local rounds' and therefore would not seem to apply to a journey home where the round is some distance from the depot. It applies to persons using the vehicle and not merely the driver. The reversing exemption applies also to a supervisor and also covers a 'manoeuvre which includes reversing'. The taxi exemption only applies while the taxi is on hire business and the equivalent private hire vehicle exemption only when the vehicle is being used to carry a passenger for hire. Note the definitions of taxi and private hire vehicles. A taxi is by the Transport Act 1980, s 64(3), a vehicle licensed under s 37 of the Town Police Clauses Act 1847, s 6 of the Metropolitan Carriage Act 1869, s 270 of the Burgh Police (Scotland) Act 1892, or any similar local enactment. These statutes are in effect all statutes licensing vehicles to ply for hire.

## 9.8 Exemption on medical grounds

There is also an exemption in reg 5 for those holding a medical certificate as specified signed by a doctor to the effect that it is inadvisable on medical grounds for him to wear a seat belt. There has been some discussion about whether this applies to a person who is able to wear a seat belt when on but who cannot put the belt on or take it off. Clearly such a person can wear a seat belt just as an invalid can wear clothes in such circumstances. It is submitted, however, that a doctor may be justified in certifying that it would be inadvisable on medical grounds for such a person to wear a seat belt. From the wording the prosecution cannot go behind a medical certificate on the basis that there were no medical grounds for it to have been issued save conceivably by judicial review.

Following a police warning of prosecution, the medical certificate must be produced at the time to a constable or within five days to a specified police station if it is to provide a defence (s 33A(4)).

It is submitted that the wording does not require production in person of the certificate. (Compare the wording of ss 25, 161 and 162 of the 1972 Act discussed at 7.9 and 11.3.)

## 9.9 Non-compliance exemption

One of the exemptions in reg 5 is for seats where the seat belt does not comply with reg 102A of the Construction and Use Regulations (maintenance of seat belts and anchorage points). There is no such exemption where the anchorage point does not comply. Regulation 102A, by para 1, applies to reg 17 seat belts. Under reg 7 of the Seat Belt Regulations the seat belt law applies whether the seat belt is a Construction and Use seat belt (ie a reg 17/reg 102A seat belt) or not.

It seems that this non-compliance exemption is intended to apply *only* where there is non-compliance in accordance with reg 102A(5) (ie recent faults—see above). The failure to define seat belts in the Motor Vehicles (Wearing of Seat Belts) Regulations (see reg 7) (while there is a definition in the Motor Vehicles (Wearing of Seat Belts by Children) Regulations) seems to be deliberate so as to catch a wider category of belts. While the intention is clear, it is unfortunate that the exemption is so worded that it might be construed in general terms although, it is submitted, it cannot.

## 9.10 Wearing of seat belts by children

The Motor Vehicles (Wearing of Seat Belts by Children) Regulations 1982 (SI 1982 No 1342) have been made under s 33B. Under s 33B(1) and (2) it is an offence without reasonable excuse to drive a motor vehicle on a road when there is in the front of the vehicle a child under fourteen who is not wearing a seat belt or other child restraint in conformity with the regulations. Section 33B(1) only applies to vehicles specified in reg 6 of the Motor Vehicles (Wearing of Seat Belts) Regulations 1982 (see above).

The following differences should be emphasised between these provisions and the general wearing of seat belts provisions.

(1) This offence is under the Act and not the regulations.
(2) It is the driver who commits the offence.
(3) A person (unlike the general provisions) may be convicted of aiding and abetting. This could include the child in question providing he is at least ten.
(4) 'Seat belt' is partly defined (see above under the general provisions and the discussion there about the meaning of 'seat belt').
(5) There is the defence of 'reasonable excuse'. As to this a reference to 4.91*C* may help.
(6) The exemptions are different (see below).

The regulations apply to the same specified motor vehicle as under the general regulations (see above and reg 6 of those regulations).

### 9.11–20 Exemptions: children

There are similar exemptions on medical grounds for certain locked inertia reel belts and (providing there is not also a child restraint) where there is an adult seat belt (see the definition in the regulations) which does not comply with the requirements of reg 102A. See the comments on the general regulation exemptions as to these exemptions.

There is a further exemption where the child is occupying a forward facing seat alongside the driver's seat when every other seat including the specified passenger seat is occupied. 'Specified passenger seat' is as defined in reg 17 of the Construction and Use Regulations, see 9.6.

## Motor Cycle Helmets

### 9.21 Wearing of helmets

Section 32 of the 1972 Act empowers the Secretary of State to make regulations requiring persons driving or riding motor cycles of any class specified in the regulations to wear protective headgear, and by s 32(3) any person who drives or rides on a motor cycle in contravention of such regulation is guilty of an offence.

Regulations made under s 32 are the Motor Cycles (Protective Helmets) Regulations 1980 (SI 1980 No 1279) as amended by SI 1981 No 374.

The regulations limit the necessity of wearing protective headgear to persons riding or driving a motor *bi*cycle as defined in the regulations. A 'motor bicycle' is defined for the purpose of the regulations, by reg 4, as 'a two wheeled motor cycle, whether having a side-car attached thereto or not' (any wheels the centres of which in contact with the road surface are less than 460 mm apart to be counted as one wheel). The regulations do not apply to certain motor mowers which may otherwise come within the definition of 'motor bicycle' in the regulations (reg 4(2)(*a*)). As to the definition of 'motor cycle' generally, see 1.6.

It will be seen that protective headgear does not have to be worn while the driver is propelling the motor bicycle while on foot (reg 4(2)(*b*)). In *Crank* v *Brooks* [1980] RTR 441 Waller LJ said that if a person had been using a bicycle as a scooter by having one foot on the pedal and pushing herself along she would not have been a foot passenger. This referred to a pedal cycle. If the same principle were applied to a motor cycle such a person would presumably be riding on one. If so a helmet should be worn. Note that the exemption is for a driver or rider propelling on foot a motor *cycle* not a motor *bicycle*.

Regulation 4 requires every person driving 'or riding on' a motor bicycle to wear protective headgear. Thus both the driver and a pillion passenger are required to wear helmets. Persons riding 'in' a sidecar are exempt (for the meaning of sidecar, see 1.6*C*). As to 'riders', see 1.58.

The Motor Cycle Crash Helmets (Religious Exemption) Act 1976 inserted a new subsection (2A) to s 32 providing that a requirement imposed by regulations (whenever made) shall not apply to any follower of the Sikh religion while he is wearing a turban. The exemption is now contained in reg 4(2)(*c*) of the regulations.

The helmets required to be worn must either conform to one of the British Standards specified in reg 5 and the schedule, subject to any amendments to that standard at the date of manufacture, and be marked with the number of the British Standard and the certification mark of the British Standards Institution; or not only give a similar or greater degree of protection than a British Standard helmet but also be of a type manufactured for motor cyclists (reg 4(3)(*a*)). The regulations also provide that if the helmet is worn with a chin cup, it must be provided with an additional strap or other fastening under the jaw for securing the helmet (see reg 4(3)(*b*)).

The definition of protective headgear makes it clear that if the helmet is worn unfastened or improperly fastened, an offence is committed (reg 4(3)(*c*)).

Section 32 applies to vehicles and persons in the public service of the Crown.

### 9.22–5 Sale etc

It is an offence under s 33(2) for a person to sell, offer for sale, let on hire or offer to let on hire, a helmet for affording protection from injury in the event of accident for persons driving or riding on motor cycles if the helmet is either not of a type prescribed by the regulations (see above) or if of a type authorised by the regulations, it is sold or offered for sale, etc, subject to any conditions prohibited in the authorisation. By s 33(6) 'helmet' includes any head-dress. Topees together with hats worn at Ascot are thus included in the definition. A person may not be convicted if he proves (*semble* on the balance of probabilities) that the helmet was sold or offered for sale for export from Great Britain.

An offence under s 33(2) of selling etc an illegal helmet is committed even though the helmet is sold for off-road use only (*Losexis Ltd* v *Clarke* [1984] RTR 174).

A person charged with selling or offering for sale, etc, under s 33, a helmet which does not conform with a type set out in the regulations may himself summon the person actually responsible for the offence in the same proceedings by following the procedure set out for the purpose in Sched 1. Schedule 1 is almost identical to ss 100–103 of the Food Act 1984, and reference may usefully be made to the extensive case law upon these sections as set out in Stone's *Justices' Manual*. Paragraph 2(3) of Sched 1 gives the prosecutor the right to proceed directly against a person whose act or default gave rise to the offence and thus proceed in an appropriate case directly against the wholesaler or manufacturer instead of the retailer (see also s 100(3) of the Food Act 1984 in Stone's *Justices' Manual*).

Section 33 applies to vehicles and persons in the public service of the Crown.

## Motor Cycle Passengers

### 9.26–30 Carrying passengers

Section 16 of the 1972 Act makes it an offence to carry more than one passenger on a 'two wheeled motor cycle'. It is also an offence under the section to carry a passenger otherwise than sitting astride the cycle and on a proper seat securely fixed behind the driver's seat. Note that only the driver commits an offence under s 16 although any person carried in contravention of s 16 may be convicted of aiding and abetting. For definition of 'driver', see 1.52–6. For the meaning of 'carry', the definition of 'rider' at 1.58 may assist. It is submitted that 'carry' implies some movement from A to B.

Section 16 applies to vehicles and persons in the public service of the Crown (s 188).

## Penalties and Proceedings

### 9.31 Seat belts: ss 33A and 33B

Both s 33A and s 33B apply to the drivers and riders of Crown vehicles. See also 2.8.

The penalty for an offence under both s 33A and the regulations and under s 33B is a fine of level 2. There is no power to endorse, disqualify or order penalty points.

The Magistrates' Association's suggested penalty (see 18.1 and Appendix 3) is £15 in each case (this is the same as the suggested penalty for not wearing a motor cycle protective helmet, the maximum fine for which is also a fine of level 2).

### 9.32 Motor cycle helmets: s 32

The penalty for a first or subsequent offence under s 32 is a fine of level 2. For a first or subsequent offence under s 33 the maximum penalty is a fine of level 3. Both offences are triable summarily only and endorsement, disqualification, penalty points or imprisonment may not be ordered for either offence. The Magistrates' Association's suggested penalty for an offence under s 32 is £15 (see 18.1 and Appendix 3).

### 9.33 Motor cycle passengers: s 16

Offences under s 16 are triable summarily only and punishable with a maximum fine of level 3. The offence is obligatorily endorsable in the absence of 'special reasons' (see Chapter 21) and carries 1 penalty point. Disqualification may be ordered (see Chapter 20). The court has power to disqualify until the defendant passes a test under s 93(7) (see 20.32). Section 19 of the Transport Act 1981 (penalty points disqualification) applies (see 20.18–21).

# Chapter 10

# Insurance

### 10.1 Introduction

The principal offence relating to insurance of motor vehicles, using a motor vehicle without insurance, is contained in s 143(1) of the 1972 Act and is discussed in detail below. Other insurance offences of failing to produce insurance certificates and forgery etc of insurance certificates are in ss 162 and 169–171 of the 1972 Act and are discussed in Chapter 16. These latter offences apply also to other documents.

## Third Party Insurance Policies

### 10.2 Generally

Subject to exceptions, s 143(1) of the 1972 Act requires every person who uses, or causes or permits another person to use, a motor vehicle on a road to have a policy of insurance (or a security) in respect of third party risks in accordance with Part VI of that Act in relation to the user of the vehicle by the person using it. Section 145(2) prescribes the conditions with which such policies must comply, including a requirement that they be issued by authorised insurers.

It is, perhaps, worth emphasising that a person commits an offence contrary to s 143 of using etc a vehicle without insurance, notwithstanding the fact that a policy of insurance has been effected, if an insurance certificate in the prescribed form has not been first delivered to the assured (s 147(1): see 10.19). Section 147(2) makes a similar provision that, where security is given, such security is of no effect until a 'certificate of security' has first been given. The police do not always prosecute in such cases providing they are satisfied that the insured person would be regarded by the insurance company as being 'on risk', but they are entitled to do so.

By s 20 of the 1974 Act all authorised insurers (see s 145(2), above) in Great Britain were from 1 March 1975 required to be members of the Motor Insurers' Bureau.

For the special defence for employees using their employer's vehicle in ignorance of lack of cover see 'Special defence for employees', 10.25.

### 10.3 Nature of the insurance

The nature of the insurance required by s 143 is set out in s 145(3). The policy must insure the person or persons specified in respect of any liability which may be incurred in respect of the death of or bodily injury to any person caused by or arising out of the use of the vehicle on a road in Great Britain (s 145(3)(*a*)). There are two exceptions to s 143(3)(*a*) set out in s 145(4). In addition the policy must insure in respect of any liability arising out of the use of the vehicle and of any trailer, whether or not coupled, in the EEC member states other than Great Britain and Gibraltar, according to the law on compulsory insurance against civil liability in respect of the use of vehicles of that state (s 145(3)(*aa*)). The policy must also insure payments for emergency treatment (s 145(3)(*b*)).

Reading s 145(3) with s 143 it is clear that the use of only motor vehicles (and not trailers) in Great Britain has to be covered by law, whereas the use of both motor vehicles and trailers in other EEC member states is required to be covered by s 145(3)(*aa*). Obviously if a trailer is used with a motor vehicle it may be within the scope of the use of the motor vehicle.

The inter-relationship between s 143 and s 145(3) and the meaning of 'any person' in s 145(3) was considered in *Cooper* v *Motor Insurers' Bureau* [1985] 1 All ER 449 (CA) (a civil case). It was held that 'any person' did not in the context include the policy holder or the person the policy holder caused or permitted to use the vehicle. *K* permitted *C* to use a vehicle to test it. *K* was negligent in that the vehicle was defective. *C* was seriously injured. *C* was not a third party within the meaning of s 143 and s 145(3), and *K* did not have to be insured against risks to *C*.

Section 145(3) does not refer to damage to vehicles or property in Great Britain.

## 10.4 Social and business purposes

Policies often refer to use for social, domestic and pleasure purposes: this does not cover a trip by the proprietor of a business to negotiate a contract (*Wood* v *General etc Assurance Co* (1949) 65 TLR 53). A car lent to a friend for a pleasure trip, the friend paying the owner for the petrol in it, is being used for social and domestic purposes and is not 'hired' (*McCarthy* v *British Oak Insurance Co* [1938] 3 All ER 1). A policy limited to use 'in the assured's business' does not cover him when he and another member of his firm are using the car on their respective businesses (*Passmore* v *Vulcan etc Insurance Co* (1935) 52 TLR 193). But giving a lift out of courtesy to a person on business rounds is use for social purposes (ibid), and in *D H R Moody* (*Chemists*) v *Iron Trades Mutual Insurance Co* [1971] RTR 120 it was held that a council in trying to encourage contacts with a foreign town were using a car for a social purpose even if the driver, who was the clerk of the council, was fulfilling a duty to his employers by driving the car for that purpose. Carrying furniture, without payment, for a friend is use for 'social, domestic and pleasure purposes' (*Lee* v *Poole* [1954] Crim LR 942). Use of a tractor to convey household furniture of a newly engaged farm servant to the farm was not within a policy covering use 'solely for agricultural or forestry purposes including the haulage of articles required for agriculture' (*Agnew* v *Robertson* 1956 SLT (Sh) 90), a Scottish case). Carrying cattle food for cows is not use for domestic purposes though it might be otherwise if it was food for a pet dog or canary (*Whitehead* v *Unwins (York) Ltd* [1962] Crim LR 323). The court reserved its opinion whether lending a lorry to a person out of friendship would be for 'social' purposes even where the borrower's employee was driving. In *A-G (McCloskey)* v *East* (1964) 98 ILTN 33, a farmer loaded his vehicle with turf and was taking it to a neighbour to use as fuel; his policy permitted carriage of agricultural produce and it was held in Ireland that he was insured. If a car is insured in respect of use on the owner's business and that business is specified in the policy, use for another business which he also carries on would not be covered (*Jones* v *Welsh Insurance Co* [1937] 4 All ER 149). Where a car owner was insured for use in his business, specified as a builder's labourer, and used his car to carry swill in connection with his other business of pig farming, he was held covered on the facts as he was returning from his building work at the time (*Kelleher* v *Christopherson* (1957) 91 ILTR 191). Pig farming was said to be a business, not a hobby or amusement (ibid). When a car owner allowed the foreman of a garage, where his car had been left for certain work, to use the car on a condition and the foreman used it in breach of that condition, the insurers, on the terms of the policy, were held not liable (*Browning* v *Phoenix Assurance Co* [1960] 2 Lloyd's Rep 360).

## 10.5 Hire or reward; car sharing

Most standard form insurance policies specifically exclude, unless specifically included, the use of the insured's vehicle when it is used for hiring or for 'hire or reward'.

New subss (5), (6) and (7) have been inserted into s 148 of the 1972 Act by s 61 of the Transport Act 1980. Certain forms of car sharing must now be covered by an insurance policy issued to fulfil the requirements of s 145, even though passengers are carried at separate fares. Fares and separate fares have the same meaning as in the Public Passenger Vehicles Act 1981 (in relation to public service vehicles see 13.32). It is immaterial how the exclusion or restriction clauses in the policy or security are worded. The conditions which must be fulfilled are set out in s 148(6).

## 10.6 Employees and agents

Where a policy covered the assured 'or his paid driver' this was held to cover a driver who was driving for the assured and was paid as a driver, though not necessarily being paid by, or being in the general employment of the assured (*Bryan* v *Forrow* [1950] 1 All ER 294). An agent employed by the assured under a contract of service and using the car to try to sell it for him was held to be in his employment (*Burton* v *Road Transport etc Insurance Co* (1939) 63 Lloyd's Rep 253). Where an employee had the option of using his employer's vehicle to return from a job and was injured while so riding in it, this injury did not arise out of and in the course of his employment under a policy but he was nevertheless being carried on the vehicle by reason or in pursuance of his contract of employment (*McSteen* v *McCarthy* [1952] NI 33; cf the English workmen's compensation cases). A garage proprietor driving a lorry to the assured's premises after effecting repairs is not a person 'in the assured's employment' (*Lyons* v *May* [1948] 2 All ER 1062). If a policy covers employees, driving by one in an unauthorised manner, if within the scope of his employment, will normally be covered (*Marsh* v *Moores* [1949] 2 All ER 27). A garage proprietor with whom an owner has left his car is not in the owner's employment (*Lyons* v *May*, above).

A vehicle owner had frequent business deals with the defendant and one day asked him to drive the vehicle home and collect the owner next day to go on a business journey; the defendant deviated from the quickest way home to give a girl a lift. It was held that the defendant was in the owner's employment and was not on a frolic of his own in going 2½ miles more with the girl (*Ballance* v *Brown* [1955] Crim LR 384).

The principle in *Marsh* v *Moores* will not protect someone completely outside the scope of his employment. In *Sands* v *O'Connell* [1981] RTR 42, for the purpose of the relevant clause in the policy the hirer of a car and any person driving the vehicle was deemed to be in the employment of the policy holder (the hiring company) under a contract of service. One of the conditions of hire was that drivers had to be aged between 21 and 70. The hirer allowed a twenty-year-old girl to drive. It was held that she was not driving on the orders or with the permission of the hiring company. In view of her age the hirer was acting in a wholly unauthorised manner in allowing her to drive. Accordingly, since the policy did not extend to indemnify her she was rightly convicted of having no insurance.

## 10.7 Driving licence condition

A common form of policy allows driving, with the permission of the insured person, by any person 'who holds or has held a driving licence' and is not disqualified. Thus, if the driver has once held a driving licence, he will be covered even though it may have expired and even though it was only provisional. A driving licence would normally include a provisional driving licence (1972 Act, s 110(1)) and in *Rendlesham* v *Dunne* [1964] 1 Lloyd's Rep 192 it was held in a county court that the policy still covered use by a learner-driver although he was driving in breach of the terms of his provisional licence. It will depend on the terms of the policy whether he is covered if his licence extends to certain classes of motor vehicle and the insured vehicle is not in one of those classes. If a person who does not hold a licence commits an offence and the court lawfully orders his licence to be endorsed, a licence subsequently obtained by him is of no effect if he did not disclose particulars of the endorsement (s 101(6)). Consequently he might not be covered by a policy if it requires him 'to hold' a licence. In regard to policies which allow driving by a person 'who holds a driving licence', it is submitted that this includes a foreign driving licence, unless the terms of the policy make it clear that it does not. Persons are permitted to drive in Great Britain on foreign and international licences, and insurance companies must know that such people may well drive the insured vehicle with the policy holder's permission, particularly if he is himself a foreigner. Moreover, a policy will normally be construed against the insurer. In *Kinsey* v *Herts County Council* [1972] RTR 498, a sixteen-year-old was held not to 'hold' a driving licence which had been issued to him a month before his sixteenth birthday, to come into effect on his birthday. (The minimum age for driving the vehicle in question was raised to seventeen between the date of issue and his birthday.)

Where a person obtains insurance by concealing the fact that he is disqualified the insurance will nevertheless be valid for the purpose of s 143 until declared void (*Adams* v *Dunne* [1978] RTR 281, discussed at 10.18). It is suggested at (1980) 144 JP Jo 591 that a person who obtained such an insurance would nevertheless not be covered if the contract of insurance included a term requiring the person to be someone who 'is not disqualified for holding or obtaining a driving licence'.

A disqualified driver may still require insurance to cover the use of the vehicle on the road and its driving by someone else. He would be well advised to check the terms of the certificate and the policy and confirm the position with the insurance company. He will in any case be under a duty to disclose his disqualifications to the insurance company in view of the special nature of an insurance contract.

'Disqualified from holding or obtaining a driving licence' means 'disqualified by order of a court', and a person who has been refused renewal of a driving licence because he is mentally defective is not 'disqualified' within the meaning of the policy (*Edwards* v *Griffiths* [1953] 2 All ER 874). But a person is 'disqualified from holding a licence' if he is, under s 96 of the 1972 Act, prohibited from driving by reason of his age (*Mumford* v *Hardy* [1956] 1 All ER 337; *R* v *Saddleworth JJ* [1968] 1 All ER 1189).

Where a person is disqualified until he passes a test under s 93(7) it would appear that he does not become uninsured because s 98(3) allows him to take out a provisional licence.

## 10.8 Public authorities and other special cases

It seems that s 143 does not apply to Crown vehicles, because s 188 of the 1972 Act does not mention s 143, and Crown vehicles, it is gathered, are in fact not insured. But a Government employee who uses a Government vehicle for purposes other than the public service of the Crown without being insured offends against s 143 (*Salt* v *MacKnight* 1947 SC (J) 99). A metropolitan magistrate has held that a postman not employed to drive who drives a mail van on post office business without authority offends against s 143 ([1946] Jo Crim L 168). (Note, however, that the Post Office is in any event no longer a Department of the Crown.) Reference to s 144 shows that that section contains special exemptions for the vehicles of local and police authorities, for those of persons who have deposited £15,000 in the Supreme Court and for merchant navy salvage vehicles. Nor is insurance required for invalid carriages, or electrically assisted pedal cycles (including Sinclair C5 cycles), or for trams and trolley vehicles the use of which is authorised by special Act (ss 143(3) and 198), or for vehicles requisitioned by the Army or RAF (s 144(2)(*d*)). Section 143 does not apply to vehicles which are not mechanically propelled vehicles intended or adapted for use on roads, such as dumpers, or have ceased to be such vehicles. See further Chapter 1.

The use of motor vehicles of visiting forces (see 2.5) on duty need not be covered by insurance, but members of such forces, when off duty, must comply with s 143 (Visiting Forces and International Headquarters (Application of Law) Order 1965). The Motor Vehicles (International Motor Insurance Card) Regulations 1971 (SI 1971 No 792) as amended by SI 1977 No 895 relate to the insurance of vehicles brought here temporarily by visitors.

## 10.9 Void conditions

By s 148(2) of the 1972 Act, a condition in a policy that liability shall not arise or shall cease because of something done or omitted after the event giving rise to a claim is void, but a condition in a policy that pillion passengers should not be carried is valid and is not made void by s 148(2) if such a passenger is carried (*Bright* v *Ashfield* (1932) 96 JP 182). But see the next paragraph. Further, by s 148(1), so much of a third party policy as purports to restrict the insurance by reference to:

(*a*) the age or physical or mental condition of persons driving the vehicle; or
(*b*) the condition of the vehicle; or
(*c*) the number of persons that the vehicle carries; or
(*d*) the weight or physical characteristics of the goods that the vehicle carries; or
(*e*) the times at which or the areas within which the vehicle is used; or
(*f*) the horse power or cylinder capacity or value of the vehicle; or
(*g*) the carrying on the vehicle of any particular apparatus; or
(*h*) the carrying on the vehicle of any particular means of identification other than any means of identification required to be carried by or under the Vehicles (Excise) Act,

is of no effect as respects the liabilities to be covered by s 143 of the Act. A person holding a policy which contains a condition rendered void by s 148 and using the insured vehicle in breach of that condition only may therefore have a good defence to a prosecution under s 143 (but see a contrary opinion at 110 JP Jo 498) and, even if he has not, s 148 provides good grounds for arguing lenient treatment in cases to which it applies. Section 148(1)(*d*), relating to the physical characteristics of the goods carried, does not prevent the insurers limiting the policy to cover goods carried for the assured's business only (*Jones* v *Welsh Insurance Corpn* [1937] 4 All ER 149). A term in a policy that only steady and sober drivers should be employed is not one restricting it by reference to the physical or mental condition of persons driving the vehicle within s 148(1)(*a*) (*National Farmers' Insurance Society* v *Dawson* [1941] 2 KB 424).

*Quaere*, if a condition that a pillion passenger shall not be carried on a motor cycle or combination is rendered void by s 148(1) in that it is a condition 'as to the number of persons that the vehicle carries'. The importance of this condition has been increased in that passenger liability was made compulsorily insurable from December 1972. It is submitted that if a policy purports to exclude liability when a passenger is carried this may be held to be a void condition in that it restricts the number of persons carried if the vehicle is constructed or adapted to carry one or more passengers. On the other hand if a motor cycle does not, for example, have a pillion seat a condition in a policy that the motor cycle should not be adapted for the carriage of a passenger would appear to be lawful. This is because it would be a condition more as to the manner of carriage than as to the numbers carried.

A policy which prohibits the carrying of a load in excess of that for which the vehicle was constructed refers to the weight-load specified for lorries and vans and is not infringed by carrying excess passengers (*Houghton* v *Trafalgar Insurance Co* [1953] 2 All ER 1409). An overloaded vehicle can be in an 'unsafe and unroadworthy condition' within the meaning of an exception clause and this condition can be permanent or temporary (*Clarke* v *National Insurance and Guarantee Corporation* [1963] 3 All ER 375, CA). 'Maintaining a car in an efficient condition' generally means that it should be capable of doing what is normally and reasonably required of it (*McInnes* v *National Motor etc Union* [1963] 2 Lloyd's Rep 415). A policy required the insured to take all reasonable steps to maintain the vehicle in an efficient condition; this means in roadworthy condition. The tyres had no tread and this was obvious to anyone looking at them; it was held that the vehicle was not maintained in an efficient condition (*Conn* v *Westminster Motor Insurance Association Ltd* [1966] 1 Lloyd's Rep 407).

Under a somewhat similar Irish statute, a sidecar was held not to be 'equipment' of a motor cycle but part of the motor cycle itself (*Higgins* v *Feeney* (1954) 88 ILTR 152).

### 10.10–14 Trailers

Reading s 145(3) with s 143 it is clear that the use of only motor vehicles and not trailers in Great Britain has to be covered by law, whereas the use of both motor vehicles and trailers in other EEC member states is required to be covered by s 145(3)(*aa*). Obviously if a trailer is used with a motor vehicle it may be within the scope of the use of the motor vehicle.

A policy which excepts from cover any use while drawing more trailers than is permitted by law is avoided where the vehicle is so used, and the driver offends against s 143 (*Kerridge* v *Rush* [1952] 2 Lloyd's Rep 305). Use when drawing a trailer is an offence if the policy expressly does not cover use with a trailer (*Robb* v *M'Kechnie* 1936 SC(J) 25). But a policy which insures against the consequences of negligent driving is valid under s 143 although it may permit the vehicle to be used illegally by drawing laden trailers (*Leggate* v *Brown* [1950] 2 All ER 564). See also *Jenkins* v *Deane* at 1.21. A charge of using 'a motor vehicle and trailer' in breach of s 143 is bad; the reference to the trailer should be deleted (*Rogerson* v *Stephens* [1950] 2 All ER 144).

A motor vehicle which is being towed remains a motor vehicle and its use on the road must be covered by insurance (*Milstead* v *Sexton* [1964] Crim LR 474). See generally 1.21. A motor cycle sidecar is not a trailer (s 190(1)).

## Liability of Insurers

### 10.15 General conditions

The policy is the document which the court must consider and, where a policy clearly does not cover the risk, an offence is committed although the insurers may be willing, as an act of grace, to accept liability (*Egan* v *Bowler* (1939) 63 Lloyd's Rep 266, where it was also held that a letter from the insurers should be disregarded). But, where there was a question before magistrates whether a vehicle in its particular state was covered by the policy and evidence was given on behalf of the insurers that they regarded themselves as still liable on the policy, such being a reasonable interpretation thereof, the magistrates' dismissal of a charge under s 143 was not upset by the High Court (*Carnill* v *Rowland* [1953] 1 All ER 486). On the other hand, an offence will be committed where a policy does not cover a risk notwithstanding that the insurers accept liability on a mistaken view of the law (*Mumford* v *Hardy* [1956] 1 All ER 337). It is the policy of insurance that matters; if there is no insurance policy covering the use of the vehicle by the defendant, rights at law under contract, whether between the defendant and another or with the insurance company, cannot make good the deficiency of a policy (*Roberts* v *Warne* [1973] RTR 217).

While it may be desirable that the policy should be seen, it need not be seen if the court is satisfied that all the required information can be obtained from the certificate (*Borders* v *Swift* [1957] Crim LR 194). In *Leathley* v *Drummond* [1972] RTR 293 a case was remitted to the justices who had dismissed it on a submission of no case after only a certificate of insurance but no policy had been produced; it was for the defendants to prove that the use of the vehicle in question was covered by insurance (ibid). The policy overrides the certificate where there is inconsistency between the two (*Biddle* v *Johnston* 1965 109 SJ 395); not only cannot the certificate override the policy but the certificate itself is not a policy (*Roberts* v *Warne* above). In *Howey* v *Bradley* [1970] Crim LR 223 the Divisional Court left open the question whether, once a policy of insurance is produced which purports to cover the use of the vehicle, the burden is on the prosecution to show that the use of the vehicle is not within the uses covered by the policy.

Section 101 of the Magistrates' Courts Act 1980, it is submitted, has the effect of requiring the defendant to produce a certificate of insurance or policy to show that he was insured (see also *Williams* v *Russell* (1933) 97 JP 128; *Leathley* v *Drummond* above; and *Davey* v *Towle*, 10.29). Once he has done this, it would seem that it is for the prosecution to prove that that particular policy does not cover the defendant because of an exception clause in the policy.

Where a policy covers a named vehicle and 'any other vehicle not belonging to or hired by' the assured, the policy lapses on the sale of the named vehicle, unless rights of user of it are retained (*Boss* v *Kingston* [1963] 1 All ER 177; and see *Smith* v *Ralph* below). But a policy for third party risks only may not lapse on the sale of the vehicle, unless the terms of the policy show that it does (ibid). Many policies now make specific provision for the acquisition by the policy holder of a new car. The cases quoted above must be read subject to any such specific provision in the policy. See also *Tattersall* v *Drysdale* [1935] 2 KB 174 and *Rogerson* v *Scottish Automobile etc Insurance Co* (1931) 48 TLR 17, as to vehicles being used 'instead of' the insured car.

A car-hire firm held a policy which excluded publicans from driving hired cars. The defendant, who was a publican, completed the firm's form for hirer-driving insurance by giving his occupation as a printer. It was held that he was guilty of uninsured use in driving a car hired from the firm (*Evans* v *Lewis*[1964] Crim LR 472): there was no question of false representation being made to the insurance company by the publican; the policy was effected between the insurance company and the garage and therefore there was no question of s 149 applying.

Where the defendant has a policy covering the driving of any car by him, stipendiary magistrates have held that this covers driving of a car which he has illegally taken without the owner's consent (*The Times*, 25 May 1954 and 28 March 1961); at 124 JP Jo 109 quarter sessions apparently reached a like conclusion. In *Police* v *Bishop* [1956] Crim LR 569 a policy covering motor vehicles not belonging to the defendant was held to cover a vehicle which the defendant had taken without the owner's consent. But many policies cover only driving with the leave of the other car owner. See 125 JP Jo 108 where there is a useful article on taken motor vehicles, no insurance and joint enterprises.

Where cover has run out and the insurers give an extended cover note, the defendant must accept that cover note before he is validly insured under it and, if he is shown not to have relied on it, eg by later insuring with another company and never paying the first company, that cover note will not insure him (*Taylor* v *Allon* [1965] 1 All ER 557).

A cover note was issued at 6.30 pm on 25 March expressed to cover from 6.45 pm and later the policy was issued stating that the insurance commenced on 25 March. It was held that the insured was not covered at 6.05 pm on that day (*Smith* v *Alexander* [1965] 1 Lloyd's Rep 283).

The cover required by s 143 includes cover against intentional criminal acts (*Hardy* v *Motor Insurers' Bureau* [1964] 2 All ER 742 confirmed by the House of Lords in *Gardner* v *Moore* [1984] 1 All ER 1100).

A policy which covers persons driving a vehicle by the order, or with the permission, of the assured does not extend to a purchaser from him even though the purchase price has not been paid in full (*Peters* v *General etc Assurance Co* [1938] 2 All ER 267). Where the assured's business was taken over by a company in which she was the chief shareholder, a policy in her name did not insure the company's vehicles (*Levinger* v *Licences etc Insurance Co* (1936) 54 Lloyd's Rep 68). Permission to drive granted by the policy holder is not necessarily revoked by his death (*Kelly* v *Cornhill Insurance Co* [1964] 1 All ER 321) but permission to drive given by a policy holder cannot extend beyond the time when he ceases to have an insurable interest because he has sold the car (*Smith* v *Ralph* [1963] 2 Lloyd's Rep 439).

If a policy of insurance is in force covering the use of the vehicle, a policy covering the personal liability of the driver is not required (*Marsh* v *Moores* [1949] 2 All ER 27, a case which also deals with questions of driving within the scope of employment). An exceptions clause in a policy relating to persons who 'to the knowledge of the assured' were unlicensed means that the assured must have actually known that; the fact that the assured was reckless in not making inquiries does not mean that he actually had knowledge, and it was held that he was covered by the policy (*Ellis* v *Hinds* [1947] 1 All ER 337). A policy which did not cover driving by an unlicensed person was held to cover driving of a car by such a person where a licensed person sat by her and retained effective control (*Langman* v *Valentine* [1952] 2 All ER 803); it would be otherwise if the licensed person gave merely passive supervision (*Evans* v *Walkden* [1956] 3 All ER 64). The facts of these two cases are given at 1.51.

## 10.16 Meaning of 'use' generally

'Use' under s 143 means that there must be an element of controlling, managing or operating the vehicle as a vehicle: the term 'use' does not include the relationship of a passenger to a vehicle or part of it (*Brown* v *Roberts* [1963] 2 All ER 263).

A vehicle is in use on the road even when it is stationary and unattended, and it must be insured (*Elliott* v *Grey* [1959] 3 All ER 733, followed in *Adams* v *Evans* [1971] CLY 10361, a case at quarter sessions where the vehicle had no rear axle or rear wheels and was parked in a cul-de-sac).

An employer, whether or not in a vehicle as a passenger, would normally retain the control, management or operation of the vehicle when it was being used on his business with his permission and would therefore be using it for the purposes of s 143 as well as the driver. (For the special defence for employees, see 10.25.)

As to the meaning of 'use' generally and in particular as to the special position of employers, partners and hirers, see 1.79.

The distinction between 'use' and 'driving' was emphasised in *Samuelson* v *National Insurance and Guarantee Corporation Ltd* [1984] 3 All ER 107 (a civil case). The plaintiff was covered for the *use* of a vehicle whilst in the custody or control of a member of the motor trade for its upkeep and repair. He was not covered for *driving* by another person. It was held that he was not covered under the policy when the car was stolen whilst being *driven* by the motor trade repairer to buy spares.

## 10.17 Use by passengers

An owner (as well as an employer: see above) sitting by the driver would normally retain control of his vehicle and so would be a user under s 143 along with the driver. In *Carmichael & Sons* v *Cottle* [1971] RTR 11 it was suggested that the only person who could be said to 'use' a vehicle was either the driver or an employee when driven on the employer's business. This suggestion was followed in *Crawford* v *Haughton* [1972] RTR 125, where the court declined to extend the 'user' to include the owner of a car when it was driven by another at his request. In such cases he should be charged with 'causing' or 'permitting', which was said in *Carmichael's* case to provide for the offences of aiding and abetting or being an accessory (see 1.80). But where the owner was actually in his motor vehicle as a passenger, and the vehicle was driven for him by a friend, it was held that the owner was 'using' the vehicle (*Cobb* v *Williams* [1973] RTR 113).

Passengers engaged in a joint enterprise with the driver have been held to be using the vehicle under s 143. Passengers in a car who know that it is being used without insurance may be guilty under s 143 (*Ross* v *Rivenall*

[1959] 2 All ER 376, where there was evidence of all the car's occupants having been concerned together in unlawfully taking it) but not, it seems, if they are ignorant of the lack of cover and do not procure the use of the vehicle (*D* v *Parsons* [1960] 2 All ER 493 and other cases cited at 15.7).

In *Leathley* v *Tatton* [1980] RTR 21 it was held that a defendant who sat in the passenger seat of a vehicle to see how the vehicle performed with a view to purchase was 'using' it. The fact that a passenger in a motor vehicle runs away on seeing the police does not justify on its own the inference that he was knowingly helping the driver to commit the offence of no insurance, and a conviction of aiding and abetting the driver's uninsured use was set aside (*Smith* v *Baker* [1971] RTR 350).

Other than in these instances passengers who have no power of control over the driver will not be users under s 143 and, it is submitted, will not cause or permit his uninsured use merely by letting themselves be driven even if they know of the lack of insurance unless they have procured the making of the journey. For example, a passenger who said, 'I accede to your unsolicited invitation to drive me to London in your uninsured car' would not offend against s 143 or, in the absence of any form of procurement or assistance, cause or permit but he would cause or permit if he said to the driver, 'Please take me to London in your uninsured car.' It is appreciated that the number of persons who would use such language is probably small.

In *Fisher* v *Kearton* (1964) 108 SJ 258 it was held that a passenger, found drunk in the driving seat, was not a user under s 143 when a policy and the ignition keys were held by another person in the car.

In *Boldizer* v *Knight* [1981] RTR 136 the defendant was given a lift in a van. During the course of the drive he learned that it had been taken without the owner's consent. It was held that he should not be convicted of using the van without insurance; *aliter* if the taking had been a joint enterprise (cf *Ross* v *Rivenall* and *Leathley* v *Tatton* above). The defendant was, however, convicted of knowingly allowing himself to be carried contrary to s 12 of the Theft Act 1968. See also 15.7.

A person supervising a learner driver does not necessarily permit the driving. Where the learner was also the owner of the vehicle, the supervisor was not in a position to forbid the use of the vehicle to the owner (*Thompson* v *Lodwick* [1983] RTR 76). A conviction for permitting no insurance was quashed. While valuable, the test adopted in that case of forbidding the use is a negative one and may not therefore supply an answer in every case.

## 10.18 Policy obtained by misrepresentation

A policy obtained by a false and material representation remains valid so far as the criminal liability under s 143 is concerned, unless the insurers have taken steps to avoid it; it makes no difference whether it is void or voidable (*Durrant* v *MacLaren* [1956] Crim LR 632; [1956] 2 Lloyd's Rep 70). It had already been held that a voidable policy satisfied s 143 unless and until it was avoided (*Goodbarne* v *Buck* [1940] 1 All ER 613). In neither case, however, was reference made to *Guardian Assurance Co* v *Sutherland* [1939] 2 All ER 246, where it had been held that a policy obtained by a false and material representation insured no one and was not a policy within s 145(3). This conflict is discussed at [1965] Jo Crim L 81.

The most recent case of *Adams* v *Dunne* [1978] Crim LR 365 seems to have resolved the uncertainty in favour of validity. A defendant concealed the fact of his disqualification from an insurance company, who issued him a cover note. The justices dismissed a charge under s 143 of the 1972 Act of using the vehicle without insurance as no steps had been taken by the insurance company to void the cover note. Applying *Durrant* v *MacLaren*, the Divisional Court upheld the justices.

### 10.19–23 Certificates and policies

By s 147(1) of the 1972 Act, a policy is of no effect unless and until the insurer delivers to the assured a certificate in the prescribed form. For a conviction for using a vehicle contrary to s 143 because the certificate had not been delivered, see *Starkey* v *Hall* [1936] 2 All ER 18, a case on special facts. The Motor Vehicles (Third Party Risks) Regulations 1972 (SI 1972 No 1217) as amended by like-named amendment regulations (SI 1973 No 182 and SI 1974 Nos 792 and 2187) prescribe the forms of certificate. Form B in the schedule to the regulations is in such a form that the registered number of the vehicle does not have to be shown. By reg 10 every company issuing a policy or security is required to keep a record as to specified details of the policies and of any certificate issued therewith and all such companies are required without charge to furnish to the Secretary of State or any chief officer of police any particulars of such records. Regulation 13 requires an insurance company to issue on demand a fresh certificate to the loser if they are satisfied it has been lost or destroyed.

By s 158(1) 'policy of insurance' includes a cover note. Every such policy in the form of a cover note has to bear a certificate (Form C in the Schedule) that it satisfies the requirements of the relevant law in Great Britain (reg 5 (3) of the regulations above). A policy covering use of 'any farm implement or machine not constructed or adapted for the conveyance of goods' means 'any farm implement or farm machine' and does not cover a cement mixer, as that is not a farm machine (*J R M (Plant) Ltd* v *Hodgson* [1960] 1 Lloyd's Rep 538).

Sometimes different certificates are issued under one policy to cover different vehicles (eg where one is a sports car) even though it is now not uncommon for the vehicle not to be specified. It would be an offence to use such a certificate for the wrong vehicle with intent to deceive (see s 169 of the 1972 Act). These differences might well not be revealed by an examination of the policy or the certificates.

For the interrelationship between the policy and the certificate, see also 10.15.

## Absolute Liability

### 10.24 Generally

The offence under s 143 arises if a person 'uses' a motor vehicle on a road or 'causes' or 'permits' any other person to use it on a road while uninsured.

Subject to the special defence for employees, it was expressly held in *Tapsell* v *Maslen* [1967] Crim LR 53, following *Morris* v *Williams* (1952) 50 LGR 308 and *Lyons* v *May* [1948] 2 All ER 1062, that s 143 imposes an absolute prohibition on using an uninsured vehicle or causing or permitting it to be used on a road. A conviction must follow if it be shown that a defendant used it or caused or permitted its use, irrespective of whether he knew or not that the vehicle was uninsured (unless the special defence under s 143(2) of the 1972 Act (10.25) applies). But a person does not 'permit' a vehicle to be used uninsured if he allows another to use it only on the express condition that that person will first insure it. When the borrower used the vehicle without having insured it it was held that as he was using it without having insured the vehicle as required by the owner, he was using it without the owner's permission and thus the owner could not be convicted of 'permitting' (*Newbury* v *Davis* [1974] RTR 367). *Newbury* v *Davis* was followed in *Baugh* v *Crago* [1975] RTR 453. The defendant had a policy of insurance covering the use of his vehicle by any driver who was the holder of a driving licence. He permitted another person who did not hold a driving licence to use his vehicle, honestly believing that that person was the holder of a driving licence. The Divisional Court directed the justices to convict the defendant of the charge of 'permitting' the vehicle to be used without insurance. Honest and genuine belief that the vehicle was insured is no defence; it is only a defence if he had made it a prior condition of permission that the driver was the holder of a licence. *Lyons* v *May* and *Tapsell* v *Maslen*, above, were distinguished in *Newbury* v *Davis*, above, for the reason that in both those cases there was no question that the defendants had given permission for the respective vehicles to be used. The question in both those cases was as to whether it was also necessary to prove that the defendants knew there was no insurance covering the permitted use. *Sheldon Deliveries* v *Willis* [1972] RTR 217 was explained in support of the view that no one can be convicted of permitting a vehicle to be used unless that person has allowed the vehicle to be used. In *Sheldon*, a car delivery firm were held not to have permitted the uninsured use of a vehicle being delivered by them, when their delivery car driver had, contrary to instructions and unknown to the delivery company, driven the car on a Sunday for his own purposes and without the trade plates. It was held in *Sheldon* that the car delivery firm could not be convicted of permitting as they had no knowledge, actual or constructive, of the unauthorised use of the car. In *Newbury* v *Davis,* above, it was pointed out that a distinction must be drawn between lack of knowledge of the fact that a vehicle was being used as in *Sheldon* and lack of knowledge of the fact that when a vehicle was being used it was in contravention of s 143 because it was uninsured (*Lyons* v *May; Tapsell* v *Maslen*). In *British School of Motoring Ltd* v *Simms* [1971] 1 All ER 317 it was held to be an implied term of a contract between a driving school and a pupil that the vehicle provided by the school for the pupil to take the test should be insured. It is submitted that criminal liability under s 143 for 'permitting' would also attach. Any person using a vehicle in breach of s 143 offends against it, whether he be its owner or not (*Williamson* v *O'Keefe* [1947] 1 All ER 307), and in *Napthen* v *Place* [1970] RTR 248 it was held that ownership or proof of ownership of a vehicle was not essential to proof of an offence under s 143. The test is whether the prosecution can prove that the defendant 'used or permitted the use of it' (see 10.16). But it will be a defence if the employer is covered by his policy of insurance in respect of his employee's driving, even if the employee-driver himself is not covered because of his age (*Ellis Ltd* v *Hinds* [1947] 1 All ER 337). There is an article at 97 SJ 396. A person may 'permit' though he is not the owner (*Lloyd* v *Singleton* [1953] 1 All ER 291). On a charge of permitting the use of a car without insurance the defendant's counsel submitted that since the defendant was not the registered owner he could not be convicted of the offence. The prosecuting inspector referred to p 202 of the fifth edition of this textbook, where it was stated (above): 'A person may permit though he is not the owner,' citing *Lloyd* v *Singleton.* Counsel persuaded the justices that unless the inspector could produce *Lloyd* v *Singleton* they could not refer to this book. In remitting the case back to the justices for the hearing to be continued, Lord Parker stated: 'In my judgment that is wholly wrong. They are entitled to and should look at the textbook; and if they then feel in doubt they should, of their own motion, send for the authority and, if necessary, adjourn for it to be obtained' (*Boys* v *Blenkinsop* [1968] Crim LR 513).

A passenger who is ignorant of the lack of cover and does not procure the making of the journey should not be prosecuted (*D* v *Parsons* [1960] 2 All ER 493). See 10.17 as to 'use' by passengers.

### 10.25–8 Special defence for employees

Section 143(2) provides a special defence for employees using vehicles in ignorance of the lack of cover (see the wording of the provision itself). The burden of proof will be on the defendant on the balance of probabilities (*R* v *Carr-Briant* [1943] 2 All ER 156). The acquittal of an employee pursuant to s 143(2) does not prevent the conviction of his employer for causing or permitting under s 143(1) (*A-G* v *Downes* (1959) 93 ILTR 121), or, presumably, using the vehicle.

## Evidence and Procedure

### 10.29 Evidence

Notice to produce the policy is not required and evidence of its terms may be given by a policeman who saw the insurance certificate, if the defendant does not produce it in court (*Williams* v *Russell* (1933) 97 JP 128; *Machin* v *Ash* (1950) 94 SJ 705). The onus of proving possession of a policy is on the defendant once it is shown that he has used a motor vehicle on a road (*Philcox* v *Carberry* [1960] Crim LR 563, following *John* v *Humphreys* [1955] 1 All ER 793). In *Leathley* v *Drummond, Leathley* v *Irving* [1972] RTR 293 it was again affirmed that the onus is on the defendant, once it has been shown that a vehicle has been used on a road, to show that the use of the vehicle was covered by insurance. The onus is on the defendant to show that the vehicle's use in question was covered by an insurance policy, even though he is not the owner. A driver charged with using a vehicle without insurance must still show that the vehicle's use was insured even though, because he is not the owner, he might find it difficult to obtain the owner's certificate of insurance or insurance policy (*Davey* v *Towle* [1974] RTR 329). In *Howey* v *Bradley* [1970] Crim LR 223 the court left open the question of whether the onus is on the prosecution to prove that the use of a vehicle is not covered by an insurance policy which the defendant has produced. It is submitted that, once a defendant has produced a policy that prima facie shows the use of the vehicle by him to be insured, it is for the prosecution to prove that the particular use of that particular vehicle on the occasion of the charge was not covered by the terms of the policy.

### 10.30–3 Production of certificates

Section 162 of the 1972 Act makes provision for the production of insurance certificates to the police by drivers and suspected drivers and offenders. No offence is committed if the certificate is produced within five days at a named police station by the person concerned or on his behalf. Section 162(2) does not require production within five days in person by the person concerned. In *Tremelling* v *Martin* [1971] RTR 196 it was held that production for this purpose must be long enough to enable the police to inspect it and see that it is a proper certificate of insurance. The Motor Vehicles (International Motor Insurance Card) Regulations 1971 (SI 1971 No 792) as amended by SI 1977 No 895 apply this provision to such cards (reg 6 (1)). Section 162 also requires the giving of names and addresses of persons interrogated and vehicle owners. The term 'owner', in relation to a vehicle which is the subject of a hiring agreement, includes both parties to the agreement (s 162(4)).

## Proceedings and Penalties

### 10.34 Limitation of time

By s 180 proceedings may be brought for an offence under s 143 within six months from the date on which the offence came to the prosecutor's knowledge subject to an overall time-limit of three years from the commission of the offence. A certificate signed by or on behalf of the prosecutor as to when evidence of the offence came to his knowledge is conclusive evidence of that fact. A certificate purporting to be so signed shall be deemed to be so signed unless the contrary is proved. The offence can only be tried summarily.

### 10.35 Penalties

The penalty for an offence contrary to s 143 is a fine of level 4. The 1974 Act removed the power of magistrates to impose imprisonment for this offence.

Endorsement of the offender's driving licence must be ordered on his conviction under s 143 unless there are special reasons (see Chapter 21). The offence carries 4–8 penalty points. As to variable points, see 19.23

Disqualification for any period may at the court's option be ordered on a first or subsequent conviction under s 143. The court may also disqualify an offender until he passes a test (s 93(7)) (see 20.32).

Section 19 of the Transport Act 1981 (penalty points disqualification) applies to offences under s 143 (see 20.18–21).

Where there is deliberate uninsured use, an absolute or conditional discharge should be given only in exceptional circumstances (*Taylor* v *Saycell* [1950] 2 All ER 887). Where a defendant is placed on probation, or conditionally or absolutely discharged, his licence, in the absence of 'special reasons', is obliged to be endorsed and he may also be disqualified (1972 Act, s 102).

The endorsement code for an offence under s 143 is IN 10.

The Magistrates' Association's suggested penalty for the offence (see 18.1 and Appendix 3) is £125. The Association adds 'in fixing the fine regard should be had as to whether the offence was deliberate or inadvertent, whether the offender was misled or any other mitigating circumstances and whether the "user" or "permitter" was responsible for the offence. If deliberate, the offender should normally be disqualified or receive 7 or 8 penalty points. In any event the court must have regard to the amount of the insurance premium'. This comment represents a stronger attitude towards no insurance offences. Disqualification is not used in all courts as a matter of course for deliberate *first* offenders and for deliberate offenders the points seem to vary between 6–8 depending on the circumstances.

The penalty on conviction of an offence under s 162 is a fine of level 3. It is only triable summarily. The Magistrates' Association's suggested penalty (see 18.1 and Appendix 3) is £10.

# Chapter 11

# Driving Licences

## Provisions and Offences

### 11.1 Generally

Ordinary driving licences are dealt with by Part III of the 1972 Act, and driving licences for drivers of heavy goods vehicles (HGV licences) by Part IV of the Act. The Motor Vehicles (Driving Licences) Regulations 1981 (SI 1981 No 952 as amended by SI 1982 Nos 99, 230, 423 and 937, 1983 No 1662 and 1984 No 274) deal with ordinary driving licences, and HGV licences are regulated by the Heavy Goods Vehicles (Drivers' Licences) Regulations 1977 (SI 1977 No 1309) as amended by SI 1977 No 2174, 1978 No 669, 1980 Nos 1733 and 1821, 1981 Nos 631 and 1127, 1982 Nos 429 and 1174, 1983 No 1232 and 1984 No 98. Other regulations have also been made, relating to persons from abroad (see 11.16) and to other matters not within the scope of this book. Section 22(1) of the Public Passenger Vehicles Act 1981 relates to driving licences for public service vehicles.

Proceedings for breach of Part IV of the 1972 Act or of s 22(1) of the 1981 Act may, by s 123 of the 1972 Act and s 69 of the 1981 Act, be instituted only by the Director of Public Prosecutions or by a person authorised in that behalf by the traffic commissioners, a chief officer of police or a local authority (see 'Authority to prosecute', 2.3).

Part IV of the 1972 Act does apply to drivers in the service of the Crown (see s 188), but the licensing authority for the issue of HGV licences and their revocation or suspension is to be exercised in the case of army, navy or air force vehicles by the South East Area Traffic Commissioners (reg 25). By s 188(3), s 96 (restricting the driving of heavy vehicles by persons under twenty-one) shall not apply in respect of such vehicles to drivers in HM Forces or subject to the orders of HM Forces.

The legal requirements should be noted as to the physical fitness of drivers (see 'Disease or disability', 11.12) and that the passing of a test on automatic transmission cars only confers exemption for other classes of vehicles which also have automatic transmission (see Sched 3 to the regulations). It should also be noted (see 'Learner drivers', 11.7) that the holder of a 'full' licence does not need to take out a provisional licence in respect of certain vehicles for which he has not passed a test. A full licence confers provisional licence entitlement for certain vehicle classes not otherwise covered by the full licence. Reference should be made to the licence, to s 88 of the 1972 Act and to the regulations. A provisional licence holder may not drive a motor bicycle with an engine capacity exceeding 125 cc 'not being a vehicle having three wheels' (see 'Learner drivers', 11.7).

Driving permits issued by HM Forces are not driving licences (121 JP Jo 732). Permits issued by visiting forces may be valid as licences in respect of the holder but do not qualify him to be the 'qualified driver' to accompany a learner (*Urey* v *Lummis* [1962] 2 All ER 463). See further under 'Qualified drivers', 11.10, 'Drivers from abroad', 11.16, and 'Exchangeable driving licences', 11.17.

The provisions as to driving licences and the offences connected therewith are discussed below. The offence of driving whilst disqualified is considered separately afterwards, and proceedings and penalties for the offences will be found at the end of the chapter.

## 11.2 Renewal of licences and pending applications

Full licences were hitherto renewable every three years but are now granted or renewed until the holder attains the age of seventy (in the absence of any disease or disability; see 11.12). After seventy years of age the licence is renewable every three years. Applications for the grant of a licence may be received and dealt with at any time within two months before the date on which the grant is to take effect (reg 5 of the Driving Licence Regulations). 'Grant' includes grant by way of renewal (1972 Act, ss 88 and 89).

It is the duty of the licence holder to renew the licence on expiry and it is no excuse that no reminder has been sent to him (*Caldwell* v *Hague* (1914) 79 JP 152). A person is unlicensed if he has no licence at 11 am even though he takes one out later the same day (*Campbell* v *Strangeways* (1877) 42 JP 39; and cf *Wharton* v *Taylor* (1965) 109 SJ 475). There are no 'days of grace' for renewing driving licences. It was held in *Nattrass* v *Gibson* (1968) 112 SJ 866 that a vehicle is not licensed even if the cheque and application for a licence or renewal have been sent to the licensing authority so long as the licence has not been issued, but the position as to driving licences is now altered by virtue of s 84(4). The position may be summarised by saying that a person may drive notwithstanding he has not received his licence provided that a valid application for the grant or renewal of the licence has been received by the DVLC at Swansea except:

(*a*) where the application is for a first provisional licence (in which case the person concerned cannot drive until the licence is issued);

(*b*) where the application is to drive further classes of motor vehicle for which the existing licence carried no full or provisional licence entitlement (again, he cannot drive until the licence is issued);

(*c*) when the application for a full or provisional licence follows a lapse of ten years from the date of expiry of the previous licence or, if disqualified, the date of disqualification (see s 85(1)) (again, he cannot drive until the licence is issued);

(*d*) the applicant has in effect rendered himself ineligible to obtain a licence by stating on his application form that he is suffering from a relevant disability (s 87).

The scope of s 84(4) is extended by s 84(4A), inserted by s 29 of the Transport Act 1981, which allows the Secretary of State to make regulations extending the benefit of s 84(4) in similar circumstances to a person who has not previously held a licence to drive vehicles of the relevant class. The only regulations made under s 84(4A) have expired.

The exemption under s 84(4) is subject to certain conditions:

(*a*) the application must have been received by the Secretary of State; and
(*b*) the legal conditions under s 88(2) or (4) must have been complied with.

Where a person has been disqualified by the court he is (if such is the case) a person who 'has held and is entitled to obtain' a licence when the disqualification expires. It is submitted that by s 84(4) and the regulations thereunder such a disqualified person may drive immediately the disqualification expires providing the application has been received and the conditions are fulfilled.

An applicant who is only disqualified until he passes a test of competence to drive under s 93(7) may immediately apply for a provisional driving licence (see s 98(3)), and may therefore drive once the application has been received.

If the relevant conditions are not fulfilled a driver will commit the offence of driving without a licence because he will no longer be protected by s 84(4). In addition a person disqualified until a test is passed will commit the offence of driving whilst disqualified (see *Hunter* v *Coombs* [1962] 1 All ER 904).

## 11.3 Production of licences

See 19.36 as to production of licences to the court under s 101(4).

Section 89(3) requires a licence holder to surrender his driving licence forthwith to the Secretary of State for Transport on a change of name or address at the same time giving particulars of the change; if he fails to do so he is guilty of an offence. Under s 89(2) the Secretary of State may revoke a licence and require the holder by service of a notice to deliver it up where it was granted in error or there is an error or omission either in the licence particulars or in respect of any endorsement. On surrender of a licence under s 89(3) following a change of name and address or under s 89(2) because of an error or omission, the DVLC will then deliver a new and correct licence free of charge unless the error or omission under s 89(2) was attributable to the licence holder. In (1977) 141 JP Jo 77 the opinion is given that where a person has, following a change of name or address, surrendered his existing licence he has not applied for a new licence within the meaning of those words in s 101(4)and cannot avail himself of that defence should he be prosecuted under s 101 for not sending or producing his licence as required. See, however, 19.36 where reasons are given for considering this opinion to be wrong.

No offence is seemingly committed if a person fails to surrender a licence after service of a notice under s 89(2). As the licence may be revoked by service of the notice under s 89(2), the offender commits an offence under s 84 of driving without a licence should he drive after failing to comply with the notice.

Licences not produced pursuant to a requirement under s 101(4) of the 1972 Act are suspended and a person who fails to produce such a licence or to send it to the court after being so required commits an offence punishable by a fine of level 3 unless he satisfies the court that he has applied for a new licence and not received it (s 101(4)). The requirement to produce is a formal one and many courts make discreet enquiries as to whether there is a good reason for non-production before making the formal requirement leading to suspension. It is submitted that this is both reasonable and valid. If, after being required to produce the licence, he drives without having produced the licence to the court, he commits the offence of driving without a licence. In *R* v *Bogdal* [1982] RTR 395 a driver who produced to the police a licence he knew to be suspended under s 101(4) was convicted of using a driving licence with intent to deceive contrary to s 169(1) of the 1972 Act.

By virtue of s 101(6) an applicant for a driving licence who applies for or obtains a driving licence without giving particulars of an order of endorsement (unless he is entitled to have a licence issued free of the endorsement under s 101(7) because four or eleven years as the case may be have elapsed since the date of the endorsement (see 19.41)) commits an offence and any licence so obtained is of no effect. If such a person then drives, he can be convicted under s 84(1) of driving without holding a driving licence.

By s 161(1) of the 1972 Act the police may demand production of driving licences; this power extends to foreign and international driving permits and British Forces' driving licences (Motor Vehicles (International Circulation) Order 1975 (SI 1975 No 1208), Sched 3). Powers to seize revoked licences and to require the production of licences obtained by false statements are also given by s 161(2) and (3).

The power to require production of a driving licence under s 161(1) (or insurance or test certificates under s 162 which is in similar terms save as to personal production) applies s 161(1) to: (*a*) a person driving a motor vehicle on a road; (*b*) a person whom a constable has reasonable cause to believe was the driver of a motor vehicle involved in an accident; (*c*) a person whom the constable has reasonable cause to believe has committed an offence in relation to the use of the motor vehicle on a road; and (*d*) a person who is supervising a learner driver or whom the constable reasonably believed was supervising when an accident occurred or an offence was suspected. It will be noted that s 161(1)(*a*) and (*b*) are in similar terms to s 7(1) and (2) of the 1972 Act ('driving or attempting to drive') although closer still to those provisions before amendment, and in *Boyce* v *Absalom* [1974] RTR 248 the question arose for consideration as to whether a person who had ceased driving at the time of the constable's request could be validly required to produce his driving licence under s 161 or test or insurance certificate under s 162. Following *Edkins* v *Knowles* [1973] RTR 257 it was held that the test of the word 'driving' in s 161(1)(*a*) and s 162(1)(*a*) should be the same as in that case and as it was agreed that the defendant had ceased driving when the request was made, the dismissal of the charge was upheld. See also 'Continuing driving', 1.53. On the other hand where there was a suspicion of a traffic offence under s 161(1)(*c*), the test is whether there has been a continuous chain of events from the suspicion to the requirement, and the fact that the driving has then ceased is irrelevant. It would seem that where the requirement is based on suspicion of the vehicle having been involved in an accident under s 161(1)(*b*) the requirement (see 'Continuing driving', 1.53) may be made at any time.

Under s 161(3A), inserted by s 22 of the Transport Act 1981, where a person has been required under s 101(4) of the 1972 Act to produce a licence to the court and fails to do so, a constable may require him to produce it and, upon its being produced, may seize it and deliver it to the court. Under s 161(4) if 'a person required under the foregoing provisions of this section to produce a licence . . . to a constable' fails to do so, he commits an offence. Section 161(3A) fulfils the requirements of a 'foregoing provision'. Subsection 161(4), however, gives a further five days for production of the licence in person at a specified police station. Section 161(3A) is not clear as to whether one constable may seize on behalf of another. The section gives no right of entry to private property.

Where a driver fails to produce his licence to a constable and names a police station at which he wishes to produce it within five days under s 161(4), it is, it is submitted, unnecessary for the police to call any witnesses from that police station to show that he did not, for that is a fact peculiarly within his own knowledge; further, s 101 of the Magistrates' Courts Act 1980 applies. In *Tremelling* v *Martin* [1971] RTR 196 it was held that in order to avail himself of the defence of producing his licence at the police station, a person must produce it at a police station for a sufficient time for the constable to ascertain the matters set out in s 161(1), viz that person's name and address, the date of issue of the licence and the authority that issued it. The court also held that the similar proviso to s 162 as to the production of a certificate of insurance requires the defendant to produce the certificate of insurance for a sufficient time to enable the police to examine it.

A police constable, when he makes a requirement for production of a driving licence, may additionally under s 161 require the motorist to state his date of birth under any of the following circumstances: when he does not produce his licence forthwith, or where the constable has reason to suspect that the licence was not granted to the motorist, was granted in error or has been altered with intent to deceive (reg 24 of the Motor Vehicles (Driving Licences) Regulations 1981). A constable may also request the motorist to state his date of birth where the driver number on the licence has been altered, removed or defaced. Section 161(4) was amended by the Road Traffic Act 1974 to make it clear that the fact that a person produces a driving licence at the police station in five days is only a defence to a charge of not producing the licence, it is not a defence to a charge under the section of not stating his date of birth.

It may be that the time limit for an offence under s 161 or s 162 does not begin to run until the five days have expired. See 115 JP Jo 254 and 2.23.

In *Ex parte Jefferson* (1966) *The Times*, 5 November, the High Court declined to interfere with the conviction of a man who had spelt out the letters of his name one at a time and had taken an inordinate time in giving his name under s 161.

The driver must produce his licence 'in person' at the police station. He cannot, seemingly, avail himself of the defence if it is produced by someone else on his behalf. A constable may not be able to ascertain the name and address of the holder under s 161(1) if it is not produced in person and, following *Tremelling* v *Martin* above, this is the purpose of its production. Moreover s 161(4) may be contrasted with the parallel provisions as to production of a certificate of insurance contained in s 162(2) and s 166(2) as amended by the 1974 Act where, clearly, the sections allow the certificate of insurance to be produced by someone on behalf of the driver. Compare reporting an accident discussed at 7.9 and the seat belt medical certificate production discussed under seat belt offences, at 9.8.

Section 164(2) enables a constable to arrest without warrant a driver seen by him to commit an offence of careless or reckless driving (ss 2 and 3) unless the driver either gives his name and address or produces for examination his driving licence. It was said obiter in *Squires* v *Botwright* [1972] RTR 462 that the driver must have been asked for his name and address and for his driving licence and have failed to supply either for the constable to be able to arrest him under the section.

## 11.4 Driving without a licence

It is an offence under s 84(1) of the 1972 Act for a person to drive on a road a motor vehicle of any class if he does not hold a licence authorising him to drive a motor vehicle of that class. Note that s 84(1) requires not merely that a driver shall be licensed but that his licence extend to the type of vehicle he is driving. These types are grouped in Sched 3 to the Motor Vehicles (Driving Licences) Regulations 1981 and also appear on the licence itself. Section 84(3) exempts the second driver or steersman of vehicles with a speed limit of 5 mph. Where a licence at the time of issue allowed a person under twenty-one years to drive a motor vehicle not exceeding 2½ tons in weight and, on a re-issue, the law had been changed to allow persons under twenty-one years to drive 3-ton vehicles, it was held on the special facts that his licence was not extended to driving the heavier types (*White* v *Trainor* [1959] NI 147).

On a charge of driving without a driving licence, the prosecutor need in law prove only the act of driving a motor vehicle on a road and the defendant must prove he had the licence (*John* v *Humphreys* [1955] 1 All ER 793). In the Republic of Ireland it was held that there must be more evidence than the mere fact of driving (*A-G* (*McGowan*) v *Carville* (1961) 95 ILTR 41), but notwithstanding *A-G* v *Carville*, *John* v *Humphreys* is still good law and remains the English authority (*Tynan* v *Jones* [1975] RTR 465).

## 11.5 Employing an unlicensed driver

Section 84(2) of the 1972 Act as amended makes it an offence for a person to 'cause or permit another person' to drive without holding a licence. It is not clear whether the words 'cause or permit' require the prosecution to prove that an employer knew that his employee driver was unlicensed. The words 'cause or permit' in s 81 of the Act formerly in force seem to have been held to import strict liability (see ' "To cause", "to permit", "to use" ', 1.76–9). It would seem that an employer is under a duty to see that his employee driver has a current licence when he takes him into his employment and to take reasonable steps to ensure that the licence is renewed. Where, however, the employee driver has deliberately concealed the fact that he is unlicensed it would seem difficult to argue that the employer had then 'caused' or 'permitted' his employee to drive unlicensed. The better opinion would appear to be that the prosecution must prove that the employer knew that his employee was unlicensed. In *Ferrymasters Ltd* v *Adams* [1980] RTR 139 the employers were convicted of permitting their employee to drive unlicensed. Although they had checked that he had a driving licence when he was taken into their employment, they failed to adopt any system to check that their employee drivers renewed their licences. For this reason they were convicted by the justices. Upholding the justices, the Divisional Court held that the case was indistinguishable from *Baugh* v *Crago* (at 10.24). The ratio decidendi in *Ferrymasters* is inconsistent with other cases on 'causing' or 'permitting'. The commentator in [1980] Crim LR 187, 188 is rightly critical. Moreover, the words in s 84(2) of the 1972 Act, as amended, are not similar to those in s 143(1). There is no offence under s 84(2) of 'using'.

Aiding and abetting imports mens rea; an employer cannot be convicted of aiding and abetting his employee not to display 'L' plates and to drive unsupervised when the employer had no knowledge that the employee was a learner driver only and had not shut his eyes to the fact (*Stanton & Sons Ltd* v *Webber* (1972) 116 SJ 667).

## 11.6 Driving under age

The offence of driving under age contrary to s 4 of the 1972 Act disappeared with the repeal of that section by the Road Traffic (Drivers' Ages and Hours of Work) Act 1976. Section 96 of the 1972 Act as amended by the 1976 Act provides that a person is disqualified for holding or obtaining a licence to drive a motor vehicle if he is under the minimum age specified for a particular class of motor vehicle. In *R* v *Saddleworth JJ, ex parte Staples* [1968] 1 All ER 189 it was held that a person who drove while under age thus offended both against s 4 (driving under age) and against s 99 (driving while disqualified). With the repeal of s 4 it has therefore been suggested that a person who drives a motor vehicle below the minimum age may only be prosecuted under s 99 (see 11.23). It would seem, however, that a person who drives under age may alternatively be prosecuted under s 84 for the offence of driving while not being the holder of a driving licence. It is understood that police practice as to whether to prosecute an under-age driver under s 84 or s 99 varies between police forces. It would seem more appropriate to prosecute the under-age driver under s 99 because of the specific wording of s 96, but it would nevertheless appear that a conviction under s 84 is perfectly valid. *R* v *Saddleworth JJ*, above, was authority for the proposition that he should not be punished both under s 4 and under s 99. It is submitted that an under-age driver cannot be prosecuted under s 84 and s 99. The prosecutor in such a case should be required to make an election as to the charge upon which he wishes to proceed.

Section 96 sets out in tabular form the minimum ages for the driving of specified classes of motor vehicles. The table is to be read as amended by reg 4 of the Motor Vehicles (Driving Licences) Regulations.

## 11.7 Learner drivers

Part V of the 1972 Act (ss 126–142) provides for the registration of persons engaged in giving instruction in the driving of motor vehicles and for instruction for payment being given only by registered instructors. The sections require driving instructors to be registered and provide for the examination of persons applying to be registered. It is only the driving instruction given for money or money's worth that is controlled. Provided neither money nor money's worth is given, any unregistered person may give driving instruction, but free driving instruction given by someone engaged in the business of buying and selling motor cars shall be deemed to be for the payment of money if given in connection with the supply of a motor vehicle (s 126(2)). Exemption is given to police driving instructors giving instruction under the authority of a chief officer of police under arrangements made by him or a local authority.

As from 1 October 1982 provisional licences (apart from Group D) and most other licences last until the seventieth birthday and in this respect there is now no difference between full licences and provisional licences. After seventy years of age is reached they have to be renewed every three years.

Group D provisional licences (motor bicycles with or without sidecars) now normally run for two years. Save where the provisional licence was issued before 1 October 1982, Group D licences are not normally renewable within one year of expiry etc. There are special provisions for licences surrendered, revoked and exchanged and for short period licences granted on health grounds. During the gap year it would become necessary to rely on a different Group licence, eg one covering Group E (mopeds). If a person did not want the two-year period to run out and for instance was going abroad, he could surrender his licence and save the balance of the period. Similarly if a person is disqualified, the disqualification period would not count as his licence would be revoked. A disqualification until a test is passed is unlikely in such circumstances, but if such a person obtained the permitted provisional licence the period would start to run again. A person who drove a motor cycle in the gap year would commit the endorsable no-driving-licence offence (see s 84(1) and Sched 4). After the gap year expired the similar offence would not be endorsable if he displayed 'L' plates, because he would be entitled to a provisional licence. It is pointed out in an article at (1984) 148 JPN 212 that the one year rule will not affect the holder of a full licence who is treated as if a Group D provisional licence holder.

The effect of s 88(2)(*c*) of the 1972 Act as amended by s 23 of the Transport Act 1981 is to restrict motor cycle learner drivers to:

(*a*) mopeds (it is understood that all mopeds are likely to be within the (*b*) or (*c*) requirements below)

(*b*) learner motor cycles (see 1.6*E*)
(*c*) motor cycles first used before 1 January 1982 and not exceeding 125 cc (for 'first used' see reg 3(2))
(*d*) motor cycles having more than two wheels (this will include motor cycles with sidecars—see 1.6).

Subject to certain exceptions (for motor cycle licences over 125 cc) full and provisional licences are for certain groups treated as provisional licences for certain other groups. Reference should be made to the licence, to s 88 and to the regulations. It is submitted that this still may be the case even though a person is at first ineligible—for instance a sixteen year old who becomes seventeen will when seventeen have a provisional licence entitlement in respect of motor cars.

Subject to the statutory exceptions, a provisional licence holder (or the holder of a full licence who is driving a vehicle for which he has only a provisional licence entitlement and who is treated as a provisional licence holder for the vehicle in question) must when driving a vehicle covered by the provisional licence be under the supervision of a qualified driver and must ensure that the prescribed distinguishing mark is displayed on the vehicle; further, he may not (save in the case of agricultural tractors and articulated vehicles) use the vehicle to draw a trailer nor (in the case of a motor bicycle without a sidecar) may the vehicle carry any person other than a qualified driver (see reg 8 of the Motor Vehicles (Driving Licences) Regulations 1981 and 11.9). A driver from abroad who takes out a provisional licence may be exempt from these requirements (see *Heidak* v *Winnett* at 11.16).

A person who has never held a provisional licence or whose provisional licence has expired and who drives without supervision or 'L' plates commits only one offence, viz driving without a driving licence, contrary to s 84, but it is more serious because of his non-compliance with the conditions which would otherwise apply to him. Endorsement in such a case must be ordered (see 'Endorsement, disqualification and penalty points', 11.33). Only persons actually holding a current driving licence at the time of the offence can be charged under reg 8. A learner driver who drives a solo motor bicycle, without a sidecar, the engine capacity of which exceeds 125 cc does not offend against any of the Motor Vehicles (Driving Licences) Regulations; the effect of s 88(2)(*c*) is that he is only guilty of an offence contrary to s 84 of driving without a licence. Endorsement in such a case must also be ordered (see 11.33). The age for taking out a licence to drive motor cycles is seventeen save that it is sixteen for mopeds of up to 50 cc (see s 96 as amended).

## 11.8 Supervision of learner drivers

The supervisor's duties were considered in *Rubie* v *Faulkner* [1940] 1 All ER 285. It is his duty, when necessary, to do whatever can reasonably be expected to be done by a person supervising the acts of another to prevent that other from acting unskilfully or carelessly or in a manner likely to cause danger to others, and to this extent to participate in the driving. It would be a question of fact in each case whether the position and actions of the qualified driver were such that the learner was under his supervision. If the learner was not, he could be charged with driving when not under supervision and the supervisor with aiding and abetting him. A supervisor may also be convicted of aiding and abetting the learner driver to drive with excess blood-alcohol, contrary to s 6 of the 1972 Act. It is not a defence that he did not know that the defendant had consumed too much, because no one can know until his blood has been analysed. The justices were directed to convict the supervisor when the evidence was that the vehicle had been swerving from side to side, that it had hit the bank on three occasions, and that the supervisor had told the police that he and the learner driver had been out drinking together that evening (*Crampton* v *Fish* (1969) 113 SJ 1003). It was similarly held in *Carter* v *Richardson* [1974] RTR 314 that to convict a supervisor of aiding and abetting the learner driver to drive with an excess blood-alcohol level, it is sufficient for the justices to be satisfied that he knew the learner driver had an excessive amount of alcohol, even though he could not know the precise alcohol content of his blood.

As to careless driving by a learner driver, see 5.29, and in particular *McCrone* v *Riding* and *R* v *Preston*.

Regulation 8 allows a learner driver to drive a motor car unsupervised on an 'exempted island'.

It has been argued that a driving examiner has not the duties of a supervisor, and in *BSM Ltd* v *Simms and Another* [1971] RTR 190, a case of civil negligence, it was held that an examiner was not a driving instructor or a passenger supervising a learner driver. His duty is to examine the applicant and see if he passes the test. This means that sometimes he must not interfere in the driving in order to see if the applicant makes a mistake.

A supervisor who has ascertained that his pupil has a valid provisional licence and has warned him to renew it is not under a duty to see that the licence is valid every time they go out together (*Smith* v *Jenner* (1968) 112 SJ 52).

## 11.9 Learner drivers and unqualified passengers

A provisional licence holder cannot carry any passenger on a solo motor cycle other than a qualified driver. If he is driving a motor car, as defined in Chapter 1, whether a goods vehicle or a passenger vehicle, of an unladen weight between 410 kg and 3,050 kg, he must be accompanied by a qualified driver, and if the car is so constructed that there is no room for the supervisor, it must not be used by a learner driver. If he is driving a heavy motor car, a locomotive or a tractor (see Chapter 1) he should be under supervision unless the vehicle is made so as to accommodate the driver only. If he is driving a motor tricycle (ie not exceeding 410 kg in unladen weight) he should be accompanied by a qualified driver unless the vehicle is so constructed that there is no room for one; such a vehicle is not a 'motor bicycle' under reg 8(2)(*e*), as that means a two-wheeled machine, though it is a 'motor cycle' under s 198(4) (*Brown* v *Anderson* [1965] 2 All ER 1). The driver of a motor bicycle with a sidecar attached may carry an unqualified passenger. A flat tubular framework attached to a motor bicycle, with a wheel on an axle welded to that framework, is not a sidecar under reg 8(1)(*d*) (*Cox* v *Harrison*

[1968] 3 All ER 811), but such a structure attached to a motor bicycle may, it is submitted, enable a learner driver to drive a motor cycle with an engine exceeding 125 cc, since s 88(2)(*c*) only applies to motor cycles not being a vehicle having three wheels. It was said obiter in *Cox* v *Harrison* that a sidecar must be capable of carrying a passenger. In *Keen* v *Parker* [1976] RTR 213 the defendant rode a 500 cc motor bicycle with a tubular steel framework attached, designed for the carriage of goods. The framework was roadworthy with a properly sprung wheel. It was held that a roadworthy attachment for the carriage of goods was just as much a 'sidecar' as one designed for the carriage of a passenger. The obiter dictum of Ashworth J in *Cox* v *Harrison* above was disapproved. (A sidecar will be regarded as a trailer if it does not comply with conditions specified by regulation: see s 190(1) and reg 129 of the Construction and Use Regulations and generally, 'Sidecar', 1.6*C*.)

In *Vincent* v *Whitehead* [1966] 1 All ER 917, a learner driver was in a Mini car fitted with only one seat but the vehicle was designed with space for another seat, which could easily be added. It was held that the vehicle was constructed to carry more than one person and that the driver should have been accompanied by a qualified driver under reg 8(2)(*b*) of the Motor Vehicles (Driving Licences) Regulations 1981. The vehicle was not a 'motor car' but a 'motor tricycle' under s 198(4), being under 410 kg and having three wheels.

Note the special provisions as to small electric vehicles, road rollers and tandems.

*Aiding and abetting*

It is submitted that the mere presence of an unqualified person in a car or on the pillion of a motor bicycle driven by a provisional licence holder does not show that the former is guilty of aiding and abetting the latter's offence. As indicated at 1.86 there must be some knowledge of the illegality shown by the prosecutor. In *Stanton & Sons Ltd* v *Webber* (1972) 116 SJ 667 it was held that a limited company was rightly acquitted of aiding and abetting their employee, who only held a provisional licence, to drive without 'L' plates and without supervision of a full licence holder, when there was no evidence that the company knew of the absence of a full licence or that they had deliberately shut their eyes to that fact.

## 11.10 Qualified drivers

Qualified driver means the holder of a full driving licence under Part III of the 1972 Act authorising him to drive the vehicle in question (reg 8(5)). It follows that it is insufficient to be the holder of a provisional licence and a certificate of passing the relevant test. A conditional licence holder may supervise a learner driver provided the vehicle is one which the conditional licence holder may drive and provided the licence is limited only by reason of a leg disability (see reg 8(5)). The holder of a US Forces' driving permit is not a qualified driver under reg 8(5) for the purposes of supervising a learner (*Urey* v *Lummis* [1962] 2 All ER 463). British international driving permits provide no authority to drive in this country. Driving permits issued by HM

Forces are not driving licences (see 121 JP Jo 732). Non-residents temporarily in Great Britain may hold an international or local driving permit and be entitled to drive, but similarly this will not make them holders of Part III licences. See further 'Drivers from abroad', 11.16.

By reg 23 of the Motor Vehicle (Driving Licences) Regulations certain persons holding certain foreign and international driving permits and British Forces driving licences are to be treated as the holders of Part III driving licences for twelve months after they become resident in Great Britain for the purpose of s 84(1) and (2). These are merely no-driving-licence offence subsections and it is submitted that reg 23 as presently drafted is not wide enough for them to be treated as Part III licence holders generally so that they are drivers qualified to supervise learners. There is power to draft the regulations in wider terms (see s 84(5)) but this power has not as yet been exercised.

## 11.11 Miscellaneous offences

Sections 169 and 170 of the 1972 Act provide heavy penalties for forgery and fraudulent use of and fraudulent applications for driving licences (see Chapter 16 as to these sections).

Sections 161(3A) and 173 of the 1972 Act give to the police power to seize licences and other documents. These sections and s 169 extend to visitors' etc driving permits (Motor Vehicles (International Circulation) Order 1975, Sched 3).

## 11.12 Disease or disability

Section 90 of the 1972 Act gives a right of appeal against the refusal or revocation of a licence (under s 87) or a decision to grant a full licence for three years or less (under s 89(1)(*aa*)). These sections relate to the physical fitness of drivers. For the general provisions relating to epileptic, diabetic and disabled drivers, an article at (1983) 147 JP 515 may be helpful.

Regulation 22 of the Motor Vehicles (Driving Licences) Regulations 1981 sets out the diseases and disabilities justifying refusal of a licence: mental disorder or subnormality, epilepsy (but see below), sudden attacks of disabling giddiness or fainting (including liability to such attacks by reason of a heart condition or that a person has a heart pace-maker implanted in his body), and inability to read a number plate within the prescribed distance. Any one of the disabilities set out in reg 22 is described in s 87 of the 1972 Act as a 'relevant disability'. By s 87, a licence may be refused because of other diseases or physical disabilities which would make the applicant a source of danger to the public, eg deafness (*Woodward* v *Dykes* (1968) 112 SJ 787). Section 87(6) defines 'disability' as including a 'disease'.

As to revoking a licence because of physical unfitness, see s 87(5). A person who drives after his licence has been revoked by the Secretary of State for Transport under s 87(5) appears to commit only the offence of driving without a licence contrary to s 84; see *Ogilvie* v *O'Donnell* below. It does not appear that he commits the offence of driving whilst disqualified, since he is not disqualified either by order of a court or by age.

A person who is refused a licence because of defective eyesight which he had himself disclosed on his application form cannot appeal to a magistrates' court under s 90 (*R* v *Cumberland JJ, ex parte Hepworth* (1931) 95 JP 206). But, if a licence is refused because of information disclosed otherwise than on the form which the applicant has completed, eg from enquiries made by the authority, the applicant may appeal to the magistrates against refusal (*R* v *Cardiff JJ, ex parte Cardiff City Council* [1962] 1 All ER 751). He may likewise appeal against revocation under s 87(5) (ibid) or, save for certain disabilities, demand a test on revocation. Licensing of drivers is the responsibility of the Secretary of State for Transport. The regulations allow a licence to be revoked if a holder suffers from 'sudden attacks of disabling giddiness or fainting'. A person had attacks which allowed sufficient warning for her to stop and park the car; it was held that these, being attacks which came on unexpectedly, were 'sudden attacks' (*Swift* v *Norfolk CC* [1955] Crim LR 785).

A person had suffered from periodic epileptic fits, the last being about two years ago. He claimed that, so long as he continued to take the necessary drugs, the chance of another attack was practically eliminated. It was held that he should be refused a licence, for, so long as drugs were necessary to prevent the manifestation of the disease, the disease remained (*Devon County Council* v *Hawkins* [1967] 1 All ER 235), but by virtue of s 87(3)(*b*) an epileptic may now obtain a driving licence if he satisfies the following conditions prescribed by reg 22(2):

(*a*) he shall have been free from any epileptic attack during the period of two years immediately preceding the date when the licence is to have effect; or
(*b*) in the case of an applicant who has had such attacks whilst asleep during that period, he shall have had such attacks only whilst asleep during a period of at least three years immediately preceding the date when the licence is to have effect; and
(*c*) the driving of a vehicle by him in pursuance of the licence is not likely to be a source of danger to the public.

This redrafted epilepsy rule meets the difficulties encountered in *Secretary of State for Transport* v *Adams* [1982] RTR 369.

As to the duty of the court to notify the Secretary of State for Transport under s 92 of the 1972 Act where the defendant may suffer from a disease or disability, see 20.38. See 5.58 as to driving with defective eyesight.

Under s 87A if at any time a licence holder becomes aware that he is suffering from a 'relevant disability', a 'prospective disability', or that an existing disability has become more acute he must notify the Secretary of State for Transport of that fact unless the disability is one which the licence holder has not previously suffered and he has reasonable grounds for believing that it will not extend more than three months.

The Secretary of State may impose conditions to be attached to a driving licence restricting the classes or categories of vehicle which, in view of the licence holder's disability, he can properly drive. If the disabled driver drives a vehicle which is not within the class or category of vehicle to which his licence is restricted, he offends against s 84(1) (driving without a licence).

Section 196(2) of the Act provides that references in the Act to a class of vehicle shall be construed as references to a class defined by reference to any characteristics of the vehicle or to any other circumstances whatsoever. In *McKissoch* v *Rees-Davies* [1976] RTR 419, a licence was issued to a one-armed driver with a condition that the licence was restricted to 'a motor car with all controls correctly and conveniently operated without the use of the right arm'. The Divisional Court held that this condition, as worded, did not prevent the licence holder from driving an unadapted, standard model, car which had a central floor-mounted manual gear lever and central floor-mounted hand brake.

In *Ogilvie* v *O'Donnell* 1983 SCCR 257 a licence was issued to a driver without a right arm on condition that 'all the controls (including direction indicators and stop lights)' were 'so fitted that they can be correctly and conveniently operated despite loss of right arm'. The switches for the lights, windscreen wipers and washers were on the right-hand side. It was held that he was in breach of the condition in that they were controls which could not be correctly and conveniently operated. There had been a conviction under s 84(1) for no driving licence and the Scottish court accepted this without comment.

## 11.13 Appeal

Now that most licences normally last until the age of seventy and are not renewed periodically, increasing use is being made by the Secretary of State of the power to revoke licences by reason of disability. Consequently there is an increasing use of the right of appeal under s 90 of the 1972 Act. The procedure is by way of complaint in accordance with Part II of the Magistrates' Courts Act 1980.

Before a person may appeal under s 90 against the refusal or revocation of his licence to the magistrates' court acting for the petty sessions area in which he resides, he is required to be a 'person aggrieved'. It was held in *R* v *Cumberland JJ*, at 11.12, that the applicant could not be said to be a 'person aggrieved' where the disability which he himself disclosed on his application form was such that the authority had no choice but to refuse his application. The appellate court has no greater authority to grant a licence than has the Secretary of State for Transport. *R* v *Cumberland JJ* was followed in *R* v *Ipswich JJ, ex parte Robson* at 11.15. On appeal the magistrates' court is not entitled to entertain any question of the applicant's competence to drive if the examiner has declared that he failed the test (s 90(2)). It would seem that the burden of establishing that he is entitled to a licence or that the test was wrongfully conducted is on the appellant. He who asserts must prove. The DVLC is now keeping records of excess alcohol figures over 150 mg in 100 ml of blood and of the urine and breath specimen equivalents. The Secretary of State from 6 May 1983 may refuse to issue licences to offenders who have twice been convicted of two drink/drive offences in ten years in each of which the blood-alcohol level exceeded 200 mg of alcohol in blood (or the breath or urine equivalent) or two offences of refusing or where one is of refusing and the other is of over 200 mg of alcohol in the blood etc. (See further 4.125.)

## 11.14 Electrically assisted pedal cycles

An electrically assisted pedal cycle as defined (see 1.9) is not to be treated as a motor vehicle for the purposes of the 1972 and 1984 Acts. No driving licence is therefore required.

If a person under fourteen drives such a pedal cycle or if a person knowing or suspecting that another person is under the age of fourteen causes or permits him to drive such a pedal cycle, he commits an offence contrary to s 24(2) and (3) of the Transport Act 1981.

As to 'drives', 'pushing and driving', 'causes', and 'permits' see Chapter 1. 'Knowing' imports mens rea. The offence of dishonest handling contrary to s 22 of the Theft Act 1968 requires 'knowledge' or 'belief' and some of the cases on that section may assist. 'Suspect' is a lower 'standard' than 'believe'. See also 4.42*F* and 15.2.

## 11.15 Heavy goods vehicle licences

Heavy goods vehicle licences (HGV licences) are required for the driving of heavy goods vehicles (Part IV of the 1972 Act; Heavy Goods Vehicles (Drivers' Licences) Regulations 1977 (SI 1977 No 1309) as amended by SI 1977 No 2174, 1978 No 669, 1980 Nos 1733 and 1821, 1981 Nos 631 and 1127, 1982 Nos 429 and 1174 and 1984 Nos 98 and 1925).

'Heavy goods vehicle' is defined by s 124 of the 1972 Act, as amended by the Road Traffic (Drivers' Ages and Hours of Work) Act 1976, as follows:

'heavy goods vehicle' means any of the following vehicles—
(*a*) an articulated goods vehicle;
(*b*) a large goods vehicle, that is to say, a motor vehicle (not being an articulated goods vehicle) which is constructed or adapted to carry or to haul goods and the permissible maximum weight of which exceeds 7.5 tonnes.

'Articulated goods vehicle' and 'permissible maximum weight' have the same meanings as they have for the purposes of Part III of the Act (see s 110).

It is an offence under s 112 of the 1972 Act to drive a heavy goods vehicle or to cause or permit another person to drive a heavy goods vehicle unless the driver has a heavy goods vehicle driver's licence authorising him to drive goods vehicles of that class. The penalty is a fine of level 4 (1972 Act, s 112 (1) and (2) and Sched 4, as amended). Section 112(3) and (4) exempts steersmen of vehicles limited to 5 mph or less and some agricultural vehicles.

Provisional licences may be issued for drivers who have not passed an HGV licence test. Provisional licence holders can only drive if they comply with the conditions prescribed by reg 10, ie displaying HGV 'L' plates, driving only when under the supervision of the holder of a full HGV licence and not drawing a trailer (other than the trailer of an articulated vehicle). Failure to comply with a provisional licence condition is an offence under s 114(3) and punishable with a fine of level 3.

Proceedings for offences under s 11 or s 114 may only be instituted by or on behalf of the Director of Public Prosecutions, the traffic commissioners, the chief officer of police or the council of a county or county district (as to whether a police officer may be said to be authorised by the chief officer of police see *Nelms* v *Roe* and other cases referred to in 'By or on behalf of a chief officer of police', 7.17 in relation to s 168 of the 1972 Act and 'Authority to prosecute', 2.3). (As to proceedings instituted on behalf of a local authority see ss 222 and 223 of the Local Government Act 1972.)

The regulations (Sched 2) specify eight different classes of heavy goods vehicle drivers' licences.

It is an offence punishable with a fine of level 3 under s 114(4) to cause or permit a driver under twenty-one to drive a heavy goods vehicle in contravention of the prescribed conditions. An under twenty-one year old driver similarly offends against s 114(4) and may be similarly punished if he drives a heavy goods vehicle in contravention of the prescribed conditions.

HGV licences are additional to the ordinary driving licence. An HGV driver must have an ordinary licence as well as his HGV licence. Regulation 13 provides that where the holder is disqualified for holding or obtaining an ordinary driving licence he must notify, and deliver up his heavy goods vehicle driving licence to, the traffic commissioners, who will retain it until he is no longer under an order of disqualification.

The amendments in SI 1981 No 1127 enable a person who does not hold an ordinary driving licence but who is authorised to drive by virtue of s 84(4) of the 1972 Act (licence applied for or surrendered for correction of particulars, etc) or any corresponding Northern Ireland provision, to apply for an HGV licence, or to recover such a licence on expiry of a driving disqualification.

If the HGV driver is convicted of an offence which is ordinarily endorsable under s 101 of the Act of 1972 it is his ordinary driving licence which is required to be produced to the court for endorsement. Although the HGV licence has pages for 'endorsements' these pages are to record particulars of suspension or revocation of the HGV licence by the licensing authority. Under s 115(1) the licensing authority may revoke or suspend a licence holder if by reason of his conduct as a driver of a motor vehicle or by reason of physical disability the driver is not a fit person to hold a licence.

An applicant may appeal to the licensing authority to reconsider the refusal or failure to grant a licence or its suspension, revocation, etc (s 118). If still dissatisfied the applicant may appeal to the magistrates' court acting for the petty sessions area in which he resides (or in Scotland the sheriff's court).

It would appear that the burden of proof to show that he is entitled to hold a licence is on the appellant. He who asserts must prove (*semble*, on the balance of probabilities).

The magistrates' court has no greater power than the licensing authority and cannot grant on appeal an HGV licence which the licensing authority could not grant, nor may the applicant be a 'person aggrieved' if he has been deprived of something the licensing authority could not grant (*R* v *Ipswich JJ, ex parte Robson* [1971] 2 All ER 1395). A magistrates' court may determine whether a test for an HGV licence has been properly conducted in accordance with the regulations and, if it is found not to have been so conducted, the court may order the applicant to be allowed another test immediately without his having to wait the prescribed period of one month which he would otherwise have to wait before he took another test (s 117).

Where the applicant for an HGV licence who is at the date of the application the holder of such a licence (other than a provisional one) appeals under s 118 to a magistrates' court on the ground of refusal or failure to grant the licence, the existing licence continues in force until the appeal has been disposed of (s 118(4)). This is notwithstanding that the licence would otherwise have expired (ibid). It should be noted that the applicant must be the holder of a full licence at the date of application. It must not have expired before that date. This does not allow a continuation of the licence pending an appeal by case stated to the High Court (*Bennington* v *Peter*; *R* v *Swaffham JJ, ex parte Peter* (1984) *The Times*, 11 February). 'Disposal of' in s 118(4) means disposed of by the justices.

It is important that the justices apply the right test when considering such appeals. In *Bennington* v *Peter* above the case was remitted for rehearing because the regulations referred to 'likely' to cause his driving to be a source of danger to the public. The justices had not applied the correct test. 'Likely' in that context meant something more than a bare possibility but less than probable.

In the same case it was held that once the case was remitted for rehearing to the justices it again had not been disposed of. From the remission, therefore, s 118(4) operated to continue the licence in force until disposal by the justices.

As s 118(4) refers to appeals and s 118(1) does not, it is uncertain whether the continuation under s 118(4) applies to a reconsideration by the licensing authority under s 118(1). However, the reconsideration is probably sufficient in any event to reopen the application. There are provisions for the continuation of a licence pending the disposal of an application (see s 115(4)).

The licensing authority for HGV licences is the chairman of the traffic commissioners or his deputy (1972 Act, s 113).

## 11.16 Drivers from abroad

By reg 23(1) of the 1981 Driving Licence Regulations a person from abroad must within one year of becoming resident here take out a provisional driving licence if he wishes to drive, unless he has previously passed an official driving test here or has held a full licence here in the last ten years (s 85(1)).

Regulation 23(2)(*b*) makes it clear that the permit holder from abroad may not drive in the UK if he is under age even though his driving permit in his country of origin would have allowed him to drive.

Persons from Northern Ireland, the Isle of Man and the Channel Islands who have within the last ten years held the equivalent of full driving licences under their own countries' legislation are exempt from tests.

Under s 111 of the 1972 Act it is lawful for the holder of a Northern Ireland driving licence to drive in Great Britain a motor vehicle of any class which he is authorised by that licence to drive. Learner drivers are authorised to drive the specified vehicles and there is no reference in s 111 to compliance with any conditions. It seems therefore that no offence is committed in Great Britain by such a person who fails to comply with any learner driver conditions. See (1984) 148 JP Jo 736 where the same view is expressed.

A person who is resident outside the UK and is here temporarily is allowed by art 2 of the Motor Vehicles (International Circulation) Order 1975 (SI 1975 No 1208, as amended by SI 1980 No 1095 and SI 1985 No 459) to drive without a driving licence for twelve months from his last arrival here while his international driving licence or his foreign licence remains valid, and provided he is within the appropriate UK age limits. Article 12 refers to the 'date of the last entry into Great Britain'. For an example of a Brazilian temporarily in Great Britain who went on a two day trip to France to preserve his exemption, see a 'Question and Answer' at (1981) 145 JP Jo 47.

In *Flores* v *Scott* [1984] 1 WLR 690 a Mexican was in this country as a postgraduate student from 1980 and due to remain until 1985. A finding of fact by the Oxford justices and the Oxford Crown Court that he was resident in Great Britain and therefore in breach of the learner driver conditions was upheld. 'Temporarily in Great Britain' involved a presence for casual purposes as contrasted with regular habits of life.

Where a driver who was still exempt took out a provisional licence under the 1972 Act, he did not have to comply with the learner driver conditions because he could rely on his exemption (*Heidak* v *Winnett* [1981] RTR 445).

If he is disqualified for holding or obtaining a driving licence by an English court, his right to drive ceases.

Article 3 of the 1975 Order deals with visiting forces and their dependants.

Persons between the ages of eighteen and twenty may drive in certain circumstances even though they would otherwise be disqualified by being under twenty-one. Further, ss 169, 170 and 182 of the 1972 Act (forgery of documents etc, false statements and withholding material information, and admissibility of evidence) now apply to British international driving permits.

It would seem that a UK citizen cannot drive in the UK on an international driving permit issued to him, but it would seem that he may drive on his international driving permit outside the UK even if he is disqualified by an English court. Although the Secretary of State for Transport can do so, there is no provision requiring him to revoke the international driving permit; nor can it be said that an international driving permit is a licence issued under Part III of the 1972 Act.

### 11.17–22 Exchangeable driving licences

The Driving Licences (Community Driving Licence) Regulations 1982 (SI 1982 No 1555) give effect for Great Britain to art 8 of EEC Directive 80/1263 of 4 December 1980 on the introduction of a community driving licence. Such licences are national licences and should be distinguished from international driving permits. The plan is that ultimately community licences should be uniform and valid throughout all member states.

The 1972 Act has been amended by the Road Traffic (Driving Licences) Act 1983 to allow licences of other countries or territories to be exchanged as if they were community licences. The country or territory must be so designated by statutory instrument. See the Driving Licences (Exchangeable Licences) Order 1984 (SI 1984 No 672). To correspond, the 1983 Act has changed references in the 1972 Act from community licences where appropriate to exchangeable licences. An exchangeable licence by s 110(1) of the 1972 Act means a community licence or other designated exchangeable licence. The countries designated by the 1984 Order are Australia, Kenya, New Zealand, Norway, Singapore, Spain, Sweden, Switzerland and the Territory of Hong Kong. These are in addition to the licences of community countries.

Subject to satisfying the other requirements of Part III of the 1972 Act (eg age, physical fitness, not disqualified) a person may under s 85 of the 1972 Act exchange his exchangeable driving licence (other than a UK licence) for a corresponding British Part III licence if he has become normally resident in Great Britain (or, where the exchangeable licence is a community licence, the UK) but has not been so resident for more than a year. The right to exchange does not apply to learner exchangeable licences (see s 85(6)). It does not apply when the community licence has already been obtained by exchange for a non-community licence (see s 110(1)).

Section 85(6) specifies that for the purpose of this s 85 exchange application the exchangeable licence must be for the time being valid at the time of application. It must also be valid for the purpose of s 84(4) (ibid) which is to apply. This apparently means that the exchangeable licence must be valid at the time of the application for the Part III licence but the applicant may drive (even though the exchangeable licence expires in the meantime) under and subject to the s 84(4) conditions until the application is dealt with. For Part III renewals, by contrast, it is immaterial that the licence has already expired at the time of application providing the applicant *'has held'* such a licence (see s 84(4)).

Community licences also remain valid for one year after the holder becomes ordinarily resident in Great Britain (see reg 4 of the Driving Licences (Community Driving Licence) Regulations and reg 23(1) of the Motor Vehicles (Driving Licences) Regulations 1981). Exchangeable licences may also provide certain qualifications when HGV licences or PSV driver licences are sought.

The community licence provisions give effect to the decision of the EEC Court in *Choquet* [1979] 1 CMLR 535, concerning art 48 of the EEC Treaty which provided for freedom of movement of workers among member states. The application for the exchange must be made within the statutory period and an application outside was refused even though the applicant had been misled (*Farrall* v *Secretary of State for Transport* [1983] RTR 279).

## Driving While Disqualified

### 11.23 The offence: s 99

It is an offence under s 99(*a*) of the 1972 Act for a person who is disqualified by order of a court or by age to obtain a licence while he is disqualified. It is also an offence under s 99(*b*) to drive a motor vehicle on a road while he is disqualified by order of the court or by age. As to attempts to commit these offences, see 11.20.

As noted at 11.6, the offence of driving under age contrary to s 4 was abolished by the Road Traffic (Drivers' Ages and Hours of Work) Act 1976. A person under the minimum age for a specified class of vehicle is disqualified, by virtue of s 96, for holding or obtaining a licence for that class and, for this reason, if he drives such a vehicle he renders himself liable to prosecution under s 99. What is meant by 'disqualified for holding or obtaining a licence' was considered in two insurance policy cases (*Edwards* v *Griffiths* [1953] 2 All ER 874 and *Mumford* v *Hardy* [1956] 1 All ER 337) as well as in *R* v *Saddleworth JJ, ex parte Staples* [1968] 1 All ER 1189. In all these cases the court relied on the use of the word 'disqualified' in the Act. See now Part III of the 1972 Act which refers expressly to disqualified by an order of a court or disqualified as under age. In *Edwards* v *Griffiths* as explained in *Mumford* v *Hardy* a person who had been refused a driving licence because of his ill health was held nevertheless not to be disqualified.

It follows from these authorities that the practice at one stage adopted by some police authorities of prosecuting for driving whilst disqualified in other instances is wrong. Some police authorities have proposed prosecutions for driving whilst disqualified when a learner driver has driven a motor cycle of more than 125cc although prohibited by s 88(2)(*c*) of the 1972 Act from doing so. It follows that such a person is not disqualified and can therefore only be prosecuted for driving without a licence. Indeed he may be able to drive under an international permit or community licence. This interpretation is supported by Sched 7 to the Transport Act 1981 which provides penalty points only for driving whilst disqualified as under age and driving whilst disqualified 'by order of a court' and not for any other form of disqualification.

The offence of driving while disqualified is one of strict liability. It is no defence that the offender did not know of the disqualification; knowledge of the disqualification need not be proved (*Taylor* v *Kenyon* [1952] 2 All ER 726). In *R* v *Bowsher* [1973] RTR 202, the court upheld a conviction, following *Taylor* v *Kenyon*, where the defendant had had his licence returned to him in error by the licensing authority. In *R* v *Miller* [1975] RTR 479, it was held that the fact that the offender thought that the place on which he was driving was not a road could not provide a defence.

It will be noted that 'driving', as discussed in Chapter 1, must be proved. If the defendant is merely in charge, without any attempt at driving, there is no offence. The offence requires the vehicle to be driven 'on a road'. For the meaning of 'road' see Chapter 1.

A person disqualified under s 93(7) until he passes a test commits an offence under s 99 if after taking out a provisional licence he fails to comply with a provisional licence condition (*Scott* v *Jelfe* [1974] RTR 256). The wording of the provisions poses the problem which test or tests have to be passed to bring the disqualification to an end. The earlier driving licence will have been revoked. It is understood that following such a disqualification the DVLC will not issue a full licence covering any group unless the relevant test has been passed for that group.

In s 99 (and in all other sections of Part III), 'licence' means a licence to drive a motor vehicle granted under Part III (applicable only to England, Wales and Scotland).

A person from abroad who is disqualified under s 99 of the 1972 Act by a court in Great Britain may not drive here though he may hold a driving licence or permit of his own country; s 99 forbids driving while disqualified for holding or obtaining a 'licence' (which means a licence issued under Part III of the 1972 Act). A disqualified person may not, in Great Britain, drive on a road any motor vehicle (including a trolley vehicle) even though he may have joined HM Forces and have been issued with a service driving licence. He may drive outside Great Britain, eg Northern Ireland, the Isle of Man or the Channel Islands unless also prohibited by the laws of the foreign country.

Allowing a person who is known to be disqualified to drive can amount to aiding and abetting this offence (*Pope* v *Minton* [1954] Crim LR 711), but it is otherwise where the car owner allows a disqualified person to drive in ignorance of the disqualification and after making enquiries which a reasonable man should make (*Bateman* v *Evans* (1964) 108 SJ 522).

## 11.24 Applying for a licence whilst disqualified

Before a disqualified driver can drive after the period of his disqualification has expired he must apply for a driving licence, as his previous licence is treated as revoked by reason of the order of disqualification (s 98). If the formerly disqualified driver drives without a driving licence he commits an offence under s 84.

Section 99 of the 1972 Act replaced s 110 of the Act of 1960, as amended by the Act of 1962 and the Vehicles and Driving Licences Act 1969. This last Act abolished the offence of applying for a licence while disqualified. Presumably the reason was to allow a disqualified person, or a person under age, to make his application shortly before his disqualification ends or he becomes of age so that he can be sent the licence ready for use (see 11.25 below). A disqualified person who applies for a licence to be issued to operate during the currency of a disqualification may commit an offence under s 170 of the 1972 Act of knowingly making a false declaration to obtain a driving licence.

When a person has been disqualified by the court, he is nevertheless (if such is the case) a person who in the wording of s 84(4) of the 1972 Act 'has held and is entitled to obtain' a licence when the disqualification expires. It is submitted that by s 84(4) a disqualified person may drive immediately the disqualification expires providing the application has been received and the conditions are fulfilled.

A person only disqualified until he passes a test of competence to drive may immediately apply for a provisional licence (s 98(3)). He may therefore drive once the application has been received.

## 11.25 Obtaining a licence whilst disqualified

If a person disqualified for holding or obtaining a licence obtains a licence while so disqualified, he commits an offence (s 99(*a*) of the 1972 Act). This must be read in conjunction with the comments at 11.24. 'Licence' means a licence to drive a motor vehicle granted under Part III of the 1972 Act. Presumably 'licence' in this context means a current licence. Applications for the grant of a licence may be dealt with within two months before the date the licence is to take effect (Motor Vehicles (Driving Licences) Regulations 1981, reg 5). Licences are sometimes sent out in advance of the commencement date, particularly for young drivers close to the driving age. It is submitted that this does not constitute an offence under s 99(*a*).

Section 99(*a*) must be read in conjunction with s 97. By this a person is disqualified for obtaining a Part III licence for any motor vehicle class so long as he is the holder of another Part III licence for that class, whether it is suspended or not. The result of this is that it is possible to commit the s 99(*a*) offence of obtaining a licence whilst disqualified without, by driving, committing the offence of driving whilst disqualified, as the first licence is valid or only in suspense.

## 11.26 Disqualification quashed on appeal

It was held in *R* v *Lynn* [1971] RTR 369 that a person may still commit the offence of driving whilst disqualified even though the conviction imposing the disqualification is subsequently quashed on appeal. Presumably the same principle would apply to a person obtaining a licence whilst disqualified.

## 11.27 Power of arrest

A constable in uniform may arrest at any time a person driving or attempting to drive a motor vehicle whom he has reasonable cause to suspect of being disqualified (s 100). A civil claim for false imprisonment was rejected in *McCarrick* v *Oxford* [1983] RTR 17 on the ground that a constable acted reasonably in arresting an accused for driving whilst disqualified and in declining to go to his home to see a letter from the Crown Court suspending the disqualification pending appeal.

The power of arrest by a police constable is limited to a person 'driving or attempting to drive' whom the constable has reasonable cause to suspect of being disqualified. These words, 'driving or attempting to drive', in s 30 of the Road Safety Act 1967 (now s 100 of the 1972 Act) are identical with the words in s 2(1) of the Road Safety Act which were considered in *Pinner* v *Everett* [1969] 3 All ER 257. This fact was referred to by Lord Morris in his dissenting judgment in *Pinner* v *Everett* when he said: 'It would be irrational to suppose that an arrest under that section had to be while the car was in motion.' It is also clear from the judgment of the Court of Appeal in *R* v *Jones (E J M)* [1970] 1 All ER 209 that the doctrine of 'fresh pursuit' applies to an arrest under this section as it does to an arrest under s 2 (now s 7 of the 1972 Act). The scope of the drink/driving provisions in s 7 has been widened but in this context the comparison remains of value. See 'Continuing driving', 1.53.

Two points may be made. First, should s 100 come to be construed by the High Court, the words may not necessarily be construed in the same fashion as the majority judgments in *Pinner* v *Everett* because there is no alternative offence of being 'in charge' of a vehicle while a disqualified driver. Secondly, even assuming that the words 'driving or attempting to drive' are held to bear the same meaning as in s 7(1), a wrongful arrest cannot, it is submitted, affect a conviction for driving whilst disqualified contrary to s 99. An arrest is not an essential part of an offence under s 99 and the principle of *Scott* v *Baker* [1968] 2 All ER 993 cannot apply.

### 11.28–32 Attempts

Before the Criminal Attempts Act 1981, the rule was that there was no power to disqualify or endorse for attempting to drive while disqualified (*Bell* v *Ingham* [1968] 2 All ER 333). The offence is now under s 1 of the Criminal Attempts Act 1981 which adopts the procedural provisions (s 2) and the penalty of the principal offence. It is therefore submitted that the decision in *Bell* v *Ingham* no longer applies and that attempting to drive now carries compulsory endorsement and discretionary disqualification. There is no offence of attempting to drive without a driving licence. As to attempts, see further Chapter 1.

A disqualified motor cyclist pushed a motor cycle on a car park six yards to the entrance on to a public road, where he was about to ride it; although he could not be convicted of driving while disqualified, since the car park was not a road, he could be convicted of attempting to drive while disqualified (*Shaw* v *Knill* [1973] RTR 142).

There is no offence in s 99(*a*) of the 1972 Act of attempting to obtain a driving licence whilst disqualified: the principal offence is purely summary and the Criminal Attempts Act 1981 does not therefore apply.

## Penalties and Proceedings

### 11.33 General offences

Failure to sign a driving licence carries a fine of level 3. It is not a continuing offence (see 2.21). Failure to produce a driving licence or state date of birth under s 161 carries a fine of level 3 (1972 Act, Sched 4). Failure to produce a licence to a court under s 101(4) (or in the case of a Northern Ireland licence, s 111(2)) carries a fine of level 3 also (1972 Act, Sched 4, as amended). Failure to surrender a licence on change of address or name under s 89(3), failing to give information as to date of birth or sex when required by a court or the Secretary of State, contrary to s 104(4) and applying for or obtaining a licence without giving particulars of a current endorsement under s 101(6) all carry a maximum fine of level 3.

Driving without a licence or causing or permitting an unlicensed person to drive under s 84(1) and (2) carries a fine of level 3 (1972 Act, Sched 4, as amended). The suggested penalty for no driving licence by the Magistrates' Association is £10 except where it is endorsable (see below) when a penalty of £75 is suggested (see 18.1 and Appendix 3).

An offence under s 88(6) by a learner driver of disobeying the terms of his provisional licence carries a fine of level 3. The penalties suggested by the Magistrates' Association are £50 and consider disqualification for driving without supervision, £25 and consider disqualification for a motor cyclist carrying an unauthorised passenger and £15 for no 'L' plates (see 18.1 and Appendix 3). Despite the recommendation to consider disqualification first offenders are often not disqualified.

Failing to notify the Secretary of State for Transport under s 87A of a relevant or prospective disability without reasonable excuse is an offence under s 170(5A) and is punishable with a fine of level 3. No proceedings for an offence under s 170(5A) may be instituted except by the Secretary of State or by a constable with the approval of the Secretary of State. Section 180 applies (see 2.21).

The offence contrary to s 24(2) of the Transport Act 1981 (electrically assisted pedal cycles) is punishable by s 24(3) with a fine of level 3.

*Endorsement, disqualification and penalty points*

Endorsement, disqualification and penalty points may not be ordered for any of the above offences except: (1) an offence under s 84(1) committed by driving a motor vehicle in a case where either no licence authorising the driving of that vehicle could have been granted to the offender (eg an under-age driver or a learner driver riding a solo motor cycle with an engine exceeding 125 cc) or, if a provisional (but no other) licence to drive it could have been granted to him, the driving would not have complied with the conditions thereof; or (2) the offence of a learner driver failing to comply with a condition of his provisional licence or of a full licence holder likewise failing to comply with a provisional licence condition when the vehicle he drives is not covered by his full licence but, instead, confers a provisional licence entitlement. Thus, a person of any age who has not passed a test to drive the particular type of vehicle in use, or is not otherwise qualified to drive, is liable to disqualification if he drives unaccompanied by a competent driver or without 'L' plates. The holder of a provisional licence who drives unaccompanied or without 'L' plates may also be disqualified. A disqualification and endorsement was quashed where a person with a lapsed provisional driving licence drove complying with the learner driver conditions (*R* v *Reading JJ* [1982] RTR 30). *Semble*, endorsement must, and disqualification may be ordered if a provisional licence holder or a person who holds no licence and has not passed a test drives a solo motor bicycle with an engine of a cylinder capacity exceeding 125 cc. Endorsable driving licence offences all carry 2 penalty points.

The endorsement code for driving licence offences is as follows:

| | |
|---|---|
| Driving without a licence | LC10 |
| No 'L' plates | PL10 |
| Learner driver not accompanied by qualified driver | PL20 |
| Learner motor cyclist carrying a person not qualified | PL30 |
| Learner driver drawing a trailer | PL40 |

Endorsement under s 101 must be ordered for endorsable offences, as above, unless there are special reasons (see Chapter 21).

Disqualification may be imposed for any endorsable offence, as above, and s 19 of the Transport Act 1981 (the penalty points disqualification) applies to such offences (see 20.18–21). For 'mitigating circumstances' justifying a court not imposing the compulsory penalty points disqualification, see Chapter 21.

Endorsement, disqualification and penalty points may thus not be ordered for an offence of driving without a licence, full or provisional, if the offender has omitted to renew it, so long as that licence would have covered driving the class of motor vehicle which he was driving. Nor may they be ordered for a person who formerly held a full licence unless he has not taken out a licence for ten years from the expiry of his previous licence. (The effect of s 85(1) is that he would then only be entitled to take out a provisional licence, and he would then be liable to endorsement if he failed to comply with a provisional licence condition when driving.) Nor may they be ordered for causing or permitting an unlicensed driver to drive contrary to s 84(2) even though such orders are made in respect of the driver himself. In the case of an expired provisional licence, as stated, the driver must be accompanied by a competent driver and show 'L' plates to avoid liability to disqualification and endorsement. References above to learner drivers being accompanied should be applied with the necessary modifications to those riding motor bicycles. An order of disqualification until the passing of a driving test may be made for any of the above offences for which disqualification may be ordered. It would seem that a full licence holder, when relying on his provisional licence entitlement to drive a vehicle not covered by his full licence, will not only have his licence endorsed if he fails to comply with a provisional licence condition, but may also be ordered to be disqualified until he passes another test. The effect of such an order will be that his full licence is revoked, and that he has to take out a provisional licence for all groups.

### 11.34 Heavy goods vehicles licences

Failure to comply with certain of the Heavy Goods Vehicles (Drivers' Licences) Regulations is an offence punishable with a fine of level 3 (1972 Act, s 119(2), Sched 4, as amended by the 1974 Act), eg reg 3(3)—applying for an HGV licence when disqualified or suspended; reg 7—failing forthwith to sign the licence; reg 11(1)—failing to deliver up licence and notice of suspension or revocation; reg 13(1)—failing to notify and deliver HGV licence on disqualification of his Part III licence (see 11.15); reg 14(2)—failing to surrender HGV licence on its being found after a duplicate licence has been issued on its being lost; and reg 15—failure to produce an HGV licence to a police constable (this regulation is similar to s 161 of the 1972 Act in relation to Part III licences: see 11.3). Unlike proceedings for offences under s 112 or s 114(3) it would seem that anyone may institute proceedings under s 119(2) for failure to comply with a regulation.

### 11.35 Driving while disqualified

By s 180, proceedings for an offence under s 99 may be brought within a period of six months from the date on which sufficient evidence of the commission of the alleged offence came to the knowledge of the prosecutor, provided that no proceedings may be brought more than three years after the commission of the offence. As, however, an offence under s 99(*b*) (driving while disqualified) is an 'either way' offence under the Magistrates' Courts Act 1980, proceedings may now be instituted for this offence at any time (s 127).

As the offence under s 99(*a*) (obtaining a licence while disqualified) is purely summary, the defendant has no right of election for trial by jury. The offence of driving while disqualified under s 99(*b*) is an 'either way' offence for which the defendant has an absolute right of election for trial by jury. A defendant convicted of driving while disqualified by magistrates may be committed for sentence to the Crown Court if the magistrates consider their powers of punishment inadequate under s 38 of the Magistrates' Courts Act 1980. He may also be committed by the juvenile court to the Crown Court for a heavier sentence of youth custody under s 37 of the same Act.

A charge of driving while disqualified should not normally be tried along with another road traffic offence in view of the possible prejudice to the defendant (*R* v *Pomeroy* (1935) 25 Cr App R 147, as qualified at 2.39).

Proof of the order of disqualification may be by the endorsement (see s 101(1)), by a certified statement under s 182 or by certificate of conviction or extract from the magistrates' court register, with identification of the defendant (*Stone* v *Bastick* [1965] 3 All ER 713, where there was a certificate of quarter sessions to which the defendant had been committed for sentence and which had disqualified him, after conviction by magistrates). Only the offence for which he was disqualified should appear in the certificate or extract; if he was disqualified for more than one offence, it seems that only a conviction involving one of the current disqualifications should be shown (ibid). *Semble*, if there were consecutive disqualifications, it might be necessary to show more than one. If the defence are not disputing the disqualification, an admission under s 10 of the Criminal Justice Act 1967 can be used to avoid the magistrates or jury having to look at a certificate or extract which shows more than is necessary. It would also be possible to prove an order of disqualification by certificate under s 182 of the 1972 Act (see 2.80). In *Holland* v *Phipp* [1983] RTR 123 it was held that the justices were bound by a certified extract as to the duration of disqualification periods even though it showed an error of law on the face of it. The conviction for driving whilst disqualified after the end of the period shown on the certified extract was accordingly quashed.

The penalty for obtaining a licence while disqualified (s 99(*a*)) is a fine of level 3. Endorsement, disqualification, penalty points and a driving test cannot be ordered. The penalty for driving while disqualified (s 99(*b*)) is £2,000 or six months' imprisonment or both if tried summarily. When tried on indictment it is twelve months' imprisonment or a fine of unlimited amount or both. Magistrates' courts have power to make detention centre and youth custody orders where appropriate.

An order of endorsement must be made for the offence of driving whilst disqualified, unless there are special reasons. The offence carries 2 penalty points when the disqualification is by reason of age and 6 penalty points when the disqualification is by order of the court. An order of disqualification until the offender passes a driving test may be made (s 93(7)). Section 19 of the Transport Act 1981 (penalty points disqualification) applies (see 20.18–21) and the defendant must be disqualified in such a case unless there are 'mitigating circumstances' (see Chapter 21).

The Magistrates' Association suggests as a starting point a penalty of '£120 or detention centre or imprisonment: and consider disqualification for longer than existing disqualification' (see generally 18.1 and Appendix 3). This recommendation is only in respect of an offender who drives whilst disqualified *by order of a court.* No recommendation is made in respect of an offender disqualified *by reason of age.* The endorsement code BA 10 should be used for offenders disqualified by a court and BA 20 for offenders disqualified by reason of age.

*Disqualification*

It was said in *R* v *Phillips* (1955) 119 JP 499, that when disqualification and imprisonment are imposed together, the period of disqualification should be sufficiently long to ensure that the greater part of it will not have expired by the time the defendant is released from gaol, but it is suggested that regard should also be had to the danger of imposing long periods of disqualification, particularly if it is likely to cause the offender to drive while disqualified or is likely to hinder him in leading an honest life. A defendant sentenced to twelve months' imprisonment and disqualified for three years had the disqualification reduced to twelve months by the Court of Appeal on the ground that the period of imprisonment was the deterrent and he would face financial difficulties when leaving prison, strengthening the temptation to drive while disqualified (*R* v *Pashley* [1973] RTR 149).

Formerly the offence involved obligatory disqualification of at least twelve months which, like 'totting up' disqualifications, was required to be additional to any other period of disqualification whether imposed on that or any other occasion. This had the effect that a significant number of young men who ignored the law and persistently drove while disqualified in a short space of time found themselves disqualified for a considerable number of years. Moreover, as the periods of disqualification, although lengthy in total, were mostly of two years or less, it was not possible to apply for their removal. For this reason and following judicial criticism (see for example *R* v *Shirley* (1969) 113 SJ 721), the Road Traffic (Disqualification) Act 1970 was enacted. The effect of the amendment was to make any disqualification imposed for the offence of driving while disqualified no longer obligatory and, if imposed, no longer 'additional'. The amendments made by the 1970 Act have been incorporated in the provisions as to disqualification contained in the Road Traffic Act 1972. The effect is that a court is no longer obliged to impose any disqualification on conviction of the offence of driving while disqualified. All disqualifications must be concurrent. These provisions are mentioned because there may still be persons subject to these old consecutive disqualifications. The court may order an offender to be disqualified until he passes a test of competence to drive under s 93(7) of the 1972 Act (see 20.32).

Section 19 of the Transport Act 1981 (penalty points disqualification) applies to a person convicted under s 99(*b*), unless the court is satisfied having regard to all the circumstances that there are grounds for mitigating the normal consequences of the conviction. See 20.18–21 and for 'mitigating circumstances' see Chapter 21.

# Chapter 12

# Excise and Trade Licences

## Vehicle Excise Licences

### 12.1 Generally

The statute law as to vehicle excise licences is to be found in the Vehicles (Excise) Act 1971. It came into force on 1 April 1971, when the power to issue licences was transferred from county and county borough councils to the Department of the Environment. The functions of the Department of the Environment relating to motor taxation have since been transferred to the Department of Transport. The interpretation of the Vehicles (Excise) Act 1971 is complicated in that the practitioner will need to refer first to the main text of the Act and then to Sched 7 to the Act to see what transitional modifications are made. It was originally planned that the centralised computer at Swansea would be so developed that 'day-to-day' vehicle excise licences would be issued there. This is no longer envisaged and the transitional modifications will thus continue indefinitely or until vehicle excise duty is abolished. Sections 2 (commencement and duration of licences and rate of duty), 8–12, 14–20, 23–26 and 37 (liability to pay duty and issue, exhibition, exchange and registration, etc of licences) all have to be read in conjunction with Part I of Sched 7.

It was originally proposed that the vehicles excise duty should be abolished in favour of a petrol tax but this proposal was abandoned by the present administration, at least for the time being, although at the time of writing the possibility has been publicised again. Some form of registration and registration fee would still have been necessary.

Among the provisions of the Vehicles (Excise) Act 1971 not yet in force are the licensing of vehicles from day to day instead of month to month (s 2), continuous liability for duty unless the Secretary of State for Transport is first notified (s 10), the statutory enactments of 'days of grace' (ss 8(2), 12(5)) and the marking of vehicle engines and bodies (s 24). Section 13 (temporary fourteen-day licences) was brought into force on 1 January 1985 by SI 1984 No 1619.

It should, perhaps, be emphasised that the fact that a vehicle is taxed under the Vehicles (Excise) Act 1971 as a particular class of motor vehicle is not necessarily evidence that it is the same or a similar type of vehicle for the purpose of the 1972 Act, the Transport Act 1968 or the Road Traffic Regulation Act 1984 (see, eg, *Wakeman* v *Catlow*, 1.12).

The Act applies to Scotland but not to Northern Ireland.

By s 1 it is declared that the duties set out in Scheds 1 to 5 to the Act shall be charged in respect of mechanically propelled vehicles used or kept on public roads in Great Britain and paid upon a licence to be taken out by the person keeping the vehicle. These Schedules are regularly updated in the Finance Acts to take account of tax increases and inflation and the latest Finance Act should always be checked. The mechanically propelled vehicles mentioned in the Act include electrical, steam and gas driven vehicles as well as vehicles which run on petrol and diesel. Electrically propelled vehicles are, however, exempt (Finance Act 1980, s 4(4)). The Finance (No 2) Act 1975, s 5, exempts from duty tramcars used for the conveyance of passengers. See generally Chapter 1 as to the meaning of 'motor vehicle', but note that if a mechanically propelled vehicle is in fact used on a public road, duty will be chargeable, unless the Act itself exempts it, whether or not the vehicle is 'intended or adapted for use on a road'.

In so far as duty is chargeable in respect of the keeping of a vehicle on a road, the vehicle is chargeable with the like duty as on the occasion of the licence last issued or, if no licence has been issued, with the duty applicable under the relevant Schedule.

By the Customs and Excise Management Act 1979, s 102(2), a licence is void from the time it is granted if it is paid for by a cheque which is dishonoured.

The provisions of the Act and the offences contained therein are discussed below. The Road Vehicles (Registration and Licensing) Regulations 1971 (SI 1971 No 450) came into force simultaneously with the Vehicles (Excise) Act 1971. The provisions of these regulations are considered at the end of the section.

## 12.2 Vehicles kept or used on public roads

Practically all the offences under the Act and regulations are limited to matters arising on 'public roads', ie roads which are repairable at the public expense (s 38(1)), a definition narrower than that in the 1972 Act (see 1.66). A road which came into existence after 1835 will not normally be publicly repairable unless the procedure of Part IV of the Highways Act 1980 (or its statutory predecessor) has been followed (*Alsager UDC* v *Barratt* [1965] 2 QB 343) unless there is proof that it has become publicly repairable some other way, eg under the Private Street Works Act 1892 or the Public Health Act 1875. Some roads may be privately owned by the Highway Authority and be repaired by the Authority but in a private capacity.

It suffices in law for the prosecutor to show that the defendant used the vehicle on a public road; the defendant must show that it was licensed (*John* v *Humphreys* [1955] 1 All ER 793). It is submitted that where the defendant is charged with 'keeping' it is similarly sufficient for the prosecutor to prove that the defendant kept the vehicle on a public road and that it is then for the defendant to show that it was licensed.

Duty is chargeable on mechanically propelled vehicles kept or used on public roads, even though they are never driven (Vehicles (Excise) Act 1971, s 1(1)). A motor vehicle separated from the road surface by roller skates is nevertheless 'on' a road (*Holliday* v *Henry* [1974] RTR 101). A person 'keeps' a vehicle on a road if he causes it to be on a road when not in use, no matter how short the period may be (s 38(2), nullifying the effect of *Dudley* v *Holland* [1963] 3 All ER 732).

It is submitted, therefore, that the mere sight of a vehicle stationary and unattended on a public road is now sufficient evidence of its being kept there. Ownership or proof of ownership is not essential to proof of the offence of 'keeping' or 'using' (*Napthen* v *Place* [1970] Crim LR 474). It is a question of fact in each case whether the vehicle remains a 'mechanically propelled vehicle' (see Chapter 1); removal of most of its essential parts might cause it to cease to be, but a vehicle which resembles a car is presumed to be a mechanically propelled vehicle still, even though essential parts have been removed, if there is a possibility of their replacement in a reasonable time (see *Newberry* v *Simmonds*; *aliter* if there is no conceivable prospect of it being made mobile: see *Smart* v *Allan*). These and other cases are considered at 1.14. In *Binks* v *Department of the Environment* [1975] Crim LR 244, a vehicle without an engine was held to be mechanically propelled because it was the intention of the owner to make it mobile again. If it is shown that a motor vehicle has been used without an excise licence, the case must not be dismissed even though the breach of the law is highly technical and trivial and there are mitigating circumstances as well. The defendant must be found guilty but the penalty may properly be small in such a case (*Patterson* v *Helling* [1960] Crim LR 562). And see *Nattrass* v *Gibson* at 12.18 (no defence that cheque in post).

Where an employed driver is found using a vehicle on his employer's business and the proper duty has not been paid, generally the employer and not the driver should be summoned (*Carpenter* v *Campbell* [1953] 1 All ER 280). Applying *James & Son* v *Smee* (see 1.78) it was held that where an unlicensed vehicle is driven by an employee on his employer's business, the vehicle is 'used' by the employer even though the vehicle had been taken without the employer's knowledge or authority (*Richardson* v *Baker* [1976] RTR 56). Once it is shown that it is used on the employer's business, it is used on the employer's business for the purposes of s 8 of the Vehicles (Excise) Act 1971 (ibid).

See generally, as to using, 1.79.

If a vehicle is used on the road, there is a presumption that the use is by or on behalf of the registered owner and he may properly be summoned if the driver's identity is unknown (*Watson* v *Paterson* (1957) 121 JP Jo 336), though the person summoned may still show that he knew nothing of the use and so be not guilty. See the discussion on proof of ownership at 2.87.

## 12.3 Motor bicycles and three-wheeled vehicles

The duties in respect of motor cycles, motor scooters, motor bicycles, motor tricycles and vehicles, other than mowing machines, with more than three wheels neither constructed or adapted for use nor used for the carriage of a driver or passenger are specified in Sched 1; definitions are also in

Sched 1. Auto-assisted cycles are included. Electrically driven vehicles are exempt (Finance Act 1980, s 4(4)). The duty varies according to the cylinder capacity of the engine. Vehicles so chargeable with duty are not chargeable with duty under Sched 2 as hackney carriages or Sched 4 as goods vehicles. Part II of the Schedule is as substituted by the Finance Act 1984, Sched 2.

## 12.4 Hackney carriages

Schedule 2, as amended by the Finance (No 2) Act 1975, Sched 14, and the Finance Act 1984, Sched 2, relates to the duties on hackney carriages. Duty is calculated by seating capacity in accordance with reg 42 of the Road Vehicles (Registration and Licensing) Regulations 1971 (SI 1971 No 450). 'Hackney carriage' by s 38(1) means a mechanically propelled vehicle standing or plying for hire and includes any mechanically propelled vehicle let for hire by a person whose trade it is to sell mechanically propelled vehicles or to let mechanically propelled vehicles for hire, but a letting under a hire-purchase agreement is not treated as a letting for hire. To use a vehicle licensed for private use only as a hackney carriage renders the user liable to prosecution under s 18 if the hackney carriage rate is higher, and, conversely, use of a vehicle licensed as a hackney carriage for private purposes renders the user liable to prosecution also if the 'private rate' is higher. See 99 SJ 312 for a report of a successful prosecution of a taxi-driver who was giving a free lift to his family.

Cars hired out with or without a driver may be taxed under Sched 2 but, if so taxed, they must carry the hackney carriage plate under s 21 of the Act and reg 41 of and Sched 4 to the regulations. In fact, many firms lawfully tax their private hire cars at the higher 'private' rate under Sched 5 so that the plate need not be carried.

By para 3 of Part I of Sched 2, the 'private' rate may be chargeable under Sched 5 where a hackney carriage is partly used for private purposes; 'used for private purposes' means used otherwise than to carry passengers for hire or reward or on hire.

## 12.5 Tractors, agricultural vehicles etc

Schedule 3 specifies the rates of duty for vehicles dealt with in this paragraph. Schedule 3 applies to:

(*a*) locomotive ploughing engines, tractors, agricultural tractors and other agricultural engines which are not used on public roads for hauling any objects (with exceptions too numerous to detail here but mainly to do with farming);

(*b*) 'digging machines' and 'mobile cranes', ie vehicles designed, constructed and used for trench digging, shovelling and excavating and vehicles designed and constructed as mobile cranes, provided they are used on public roads only for work of excavating, etc (or, if cranes, for work on a site in the immediate vicinity), or for proceeding to and from the place of work, and carry or haul no load;

(*c*) 'works trucks';

(*d*) 'mowing machines';
(*e*) 'fishermen's tractors'; and
(*f*) 'haulage vehicles', ie vehicles not being ones already referred to, constructed and used on public roads for haulage solely, eg tractors, and not constructed and used to carry loads other than necessary for their own propulsion and equipment.

The Finance Act 1971, s 6, states, however, that a motor vehicle shall not be treated as a tractor within (*a*) above unless it was designed and constructed primarily for use otherwise than on roads and is incapable by reason of its construction of exceeding 25 mph on the level under its own power. The exemption under para 2(1)(*d*) for 'agricultural machines' for hauling articles required for a farm only applies if the vehicle is registered in the name of the owner or occupier of the farm or in the name of a contractor engaged by the owner or occupier. In *Bullen* v *Picking* [1974] RTR 46, a tractor hauling bricks for doing piping on and for the purposes of the farm was held to be within the exemption. Although the tractor was not registered in the contractor's name, because the tractor used was one which had been lent by the farmer to the contractor, it came within the first part of the exemption in that it was registered in the farmer's name and used for the purpose of hauling articles required for the farm. It is understood that certain drainage operators set aside haulage vehicles to carry equipment only for agricultural operations in order to bring them within the lower agricultural rate. Other vehicles are used to haul equipment for general drainage operations and therefore attract the higher rates.

In deciding whether a vehicle is an agricultural machine, no account shall be taken of certain uses of that vehicle on public roads in snow clearance. By Sched 4, para 11(*b*), an agricultural machine falling under (*a*) above is not chargeable as a goods vehicle by reason of the fact that it is constructed or adapted for use and used for the conveyance of farming or forestry implements fitted thereto for operation while so fitted. In *R* v *Berkshire County Council, ex parte Berkshire Lime Co (Childrey) Ltd* [1953] 2 All ER 779 it was said that the lower rate for class (*a*) above applies only so long as the vehicles mentioned in it are used for hauling and a vehicle consisting of a driver's cab mounted on a chassis on which was also imposed a large receptacle for holding lime was a goods vehicle chargeable under Sched 4 and not under Sched 3, because it carried goods, viz lime, although the vehicle was used in the business of spreading lime on agricultural land and was thus an agricultural engine. This case was decided prior to the operation of the exemption given by Sched 4, para 11(*b*), but it is doubtful if it is affected thereby. It is provided by Sched 3, para 2(2)(*a*), that references in Sched 3 to a farm include a market garden and there are further definitions relating to woodland and articles required for farm and forestry estates.

A tractor fitted with a winch, jib and anchor used for loading tree trunks on a trailer drawn by it, the tractor being incapable of carrying any goods, is constructed and used for haulage solely under Sched 3 and is not a goods vehicle under Sched 4 (*Worgan* v *Gloucestershire County Council* [1961] 2 All ER 301).

As to 'farmers' goods vehicles', see also 12.9.

As to whether mechanically propelled vehicles used in connection with road works are exempt from duty under s 4 as 'road construction vehicles' or are chargeable under Sched 3 as vehicles used for trench digging see 12.13 below.

In *London County Council* v *Hay's Wharf Cartage Co* [1953] 2 All ER 34, a Scammell heavy duty tractor, used for towing, was held, on the facts, to be a haulage vehicle and it did not become a goods vehicle merely because such things as tools, blocks and ballast were carried by it to render it more fit for haulage work. In *Brook* v *Friend* [1954] Crim LR 942, it was held that use of a farmer's tractor to haul a trailer loaded with bricks and a fireplace to one of his farmworkers' cottages was not within the exemption given by Sched 3, para 2(1)(*b*), for hauling 'articles required for the farm'. Nor is taking a pony to a show for exhibition (*Henderson* v *Robson* (1949) 113 JP 313). In *Thornton* v *Proudlock* (Queen's Bench Division, 1952, unreported) it was held that a tractor fitted with a transport box is a vehicle adapted for use for conveyance of goods or burden and in *A-G* (*Croke*) v *O'Sullivan* (1958) 92 ILTR 21 it was held that a tractor adapted to carry sacks by fitting a detachable wooden platform was 'hauling' goods, so as to attract the rate of duty for a goods vehicle. The effect of these cases is now qualified in Great Britain by Sched 4, para 12(2), which relates to removable appliances fitted at the front or back of agricultural tractors. Where a farmer was contractually bound to supply firewood to his employees, it was held that use of his tractor to haul it was use for agricultural purposes (*East Lothian County Council* v *Lambert* 1950 SLT (Sh) 41; this case cites two earlier English decisions which are to much the same effect as *Brook* v *Friend*, above; see also [1952] Jo Crim L 170, *Agnew* v *Robertson* and other cases at 1.81 and *Armitage* v *Mountain* at 12.9).

Schedule 4, para 12(7), relates to vehicles of this type with a double front wheel.

'Agriculture' in the Vehicles (Excise) Act seems to include chicken and livestock farming as well as cultivating the soil (*J M Knowles Ltd* v *Rand* [1962] 2 All ER 926).

Paragraph 5 of Part I of Sched 3 defines 'works truck' in similar terms to those contained in reg 3(1) of the Construction and Use Regulations (see 8.2), save that the vehicle must be a 'goods vehicle' as defined in Sched 4 and that the definition refers to 'the immediate vicinity' instead of 'the immediate neighbourhood'. 'Works truck' has the same meaning in Sched 4 (see para 15(1)). It was held in *Hayes* v *Kingsworthy Foundry Co Ltd* [1971] Crim LR 239 that a vehicle was not a 'works truck' within the meaning of the Construction and Use Regulations where the vehicle had to travel six-tenths of a mile along a road even though the two sites were very close together. 'Immediate neighbourhood' had to be measured by reference to the amount of user of the road involved, not in relation to the distance which the two sites are apart 'as the crow flies'. Similarly, a journey between two premises two miles apart by road was held not to be 'in the immediate neighbourhood' (*G Greaves & Son Ltd* v *Peam* [1972] RTR 146, applying *Hayes'* case, above).

A similar principle was followed in *Lovett* v *Payne* [1980] RTR 103, a case on the nearest weighbridge. 'Nearest' was held to be not as the crow flies but the nearest road route suitable for the vehicle in question.

## 12.6 Showmen's vehicles

There are special duty rates in Sched 3 for showmen's haulage vehicles and in Sched 4 for showmen's goods vehicles and such vehicles drawing trailers. 'Showman's vehicle' is defined in Sched 3 and has the same meaning in Sched 4. 'Showman's goods vehicle' is defined in Sched 4. A travelling commercial exhibition and sales point was held not to be a showman's goods vehicle in *R* v *Department of Transport, ex parte Lakeland Plastics (Windermere) Ltd* [1983] RTR 82: such a vehicle is a vehicle used in the entertainment industry. By virtue of the wording of the definition in Sched 4 'showman's vehicle' will be interpreted similarly. Again, in *Bowra* v *Dann Catering Co Ltd* [1982] RTR 120 a company which specialised in providing portable lavatories for travelling showmen was held (at p 125) not to be a 'travelling showman'. A conviction under s 18(1) and (4) of the 1971 Act for under payment of duty was directed.

Although the decision is not binding, a showman appeared before a magistrates' court after he had used a showman's vehicle to go to a show site for show business purposes. It was used for sleeping accommodation but not to provide a display on that occasion. The magistrates acquitted him holding that he was within the exemption. The vehicle was constructed to display novelties to be disposed of by lotteries. It was held in the same case to be a showman's goods vehicle.

## 12.7 Goods vehicles

The duties on goods vehicles are still based on unladen weight for goods vehicles of 1,525 kg or less unladen. This class is merged with private class vehicles in a new tax class of private/light goods and they are taxed at a flat rate. Many of the old cases have been retained in the text as they may still be of help to determine differences between private and goods use. They will usually no longer be of assistance for the types of vehicle in question because of the merger of private and light goods vehicles. Difficulties over the difference between private and goods are less likely to arise with larger vehicles. The duties on goods vehicles over 1,525 kg are now based on their plated gross weight or train weight, ie the weight of the vehicle together with the trailer or trailers. It will therefore be immaterial that the vehicle or trailer contains apparatus or machinery unless the vehicle is by it placed in a special category.

Schedule 4 relates to the duties on goods vehicles. It also refers to goods vehicles used for drawing trailers and to vehicles conveying a machine or contrivance only and no other load (not being chargeable under Sched 3). As to farmers' goods vehicles see 12.9 and showman's goods vehicles see 12.6. Schedule 4 refers, inter alia, to works trucks (which has the same meaning as in Sched 3), farmers' goods vehicles and showmen's goods vehicles and trailers.

There are exemptions in Sched 4, para 11; namely the goods vehicles set out in Sched 1: certain agricultural machine goods vehicles, mobile cranes, works trucks and fisherman's tractors and vehicles which, although constructed or adapted for use for the conveyance of goods or burden, are not so used for hire or reward or in connection with a trade or business.

'Goods vehicle', by para 15, means a mechanically propelled vehicle (including a tricycle weighing more than 425 kg unladen) constructed or adapted for use and used for the conveyance of goods or burden of any description, whether in the course of trade or otherwise. Thus, a private car, not constructed or adapted for the conveyance of goods, is still taxable at the private rate although it may carry goods in the course of trade (see *Taylor* v *Mead* [1961] 1 All ER 626 and generally the definitions of 'constructed' and 'adapted' in Chapter 1, 1.12).

Lord Parker CJ said in *Taylor* v *Mead* that 'constructed or adapted' in what is now para 15(1) meant 'originally constructed or where the structure is subsequently altered' and approved two earlier cases on the Customs and Inland Revenue Act 1888, s 4, holding that adapting meant some amount of alteration of the original construction. Making a small fitting or attachment involving the boring of holes for screws in the structure would not be altering the structure but fitting stronger springs and widening the wheels would be (ibid). See also *Thornton* v *Proudlock* at 12.5. The question whether an adaptation is such as to make a passenger vehicle into a goods vehicle is resolved by assuming that it had originally been constructed in its altered condition and then deciding whether as such it would be a passenger or goods vehicle; actual use is irrelevant (*Flower Freight Co* v *Hammond* [1962] 3 All ER 950). As to 'adapted' see 1.12.

Where the director of a firm of photographers carried photographic equipment in a shooting-brake on the firm's business, it was held that the vehicle was a goods vehicle and taxable accordingly; the exclusion provisions did not apply as it was used to carry goods or burden for a trade or business (*Taylor* v *Thompson* [1956] 1 All ER 352). A shooting-brake is now almost certain to be in the private/light goods category. Carriage of personal luggage or farm produce for the owner's own use would not attract the 'goods rate' duty. In *Armitage* v *Mountain* [1957] Crim LR 257, use of a farmer's goods vehicle to carry the furniture of a newly engaged farm-labourer as an act of kindness and not for payment was held not to be use for the farmer's trade or business. See also *R* v *Berkshire County Council, Worgan* v *Gloucestershire County Council* and *London County Council* v *Hay's Wharf Cartage Co* at 12.5. The term 'goods vehicle' in the 1972 Act is discussed at 13.7*C*. The term 'hire or reward' is discussed at 1.10 and see 13.7*A*.

By para 10 of Sched 4, a goods vehicle taxed at a lower rate than the 'private' rate must pay the private rate under Sched 5, if it is higher, when it is partly used for private purposes. This catches particularly vehicles taxed under Sched 4 when used for a family outing or other purpose not involving the carriage of goods for hire or reward or in the course of trade or business. In other words the private use takes it from the normal goods category to a category equivalent to the private category. 'Partly used for private purposes' means used partly otherwise than for the conveyance of goods or burden for hire or reward or for or in connection with a trade or business (para 10(3)). Partly private purposes does not, however, prevent a vehicle from being a farmer's goods vehicle.

In *James* v *Davies* [1952] 2 All ER 758 it was held that haulage by a Land Rover, itself empty, of a trailer laden with goods on the owner's business was a conveyance of the goods and that it mattered not that the towing vehicle carried no goods; duty was payable under both para 1(1) and 1(2) of Sched 4. The Land Rover was a vehicle constructed for the conveyance of both goods and passengers and was therefore itself within the definition of 'goods vehicle'. In *Pearson* v *Boyes* [1953] 1 All ER 492, however, an empty van towing an empty caravan was held not to be carrying goods or burden; the court pointed out that the Act seemed to differentiate between hauling and towing on the one hand and carriage on the other, and stressed that clear words imposing a higher rate of taxation must be used to authorise it. By s 18(6), if duty has been paid under Sched 4, higher duty is not payable on goods vehicles substantially used to carry loads if also used to carry employees of the owner of the loads.

'Tower wagons' attract a lower rate of duty (Sched 4, para 1(1)(*c*)). A 'tower wagon' is defined in para 15 of Part I of Sched 4 as a goods vehicle into which there is built any expanding or extensible contrivance for the erection, inspection, repair or maintenance of overhead structures or equipment provided that it is neither constructed nor adapted for use nor used for the conveyance of any load other than the extensible contrivance or articles used in connection therewith. A vehicle with such an extensible contrivance was held not to be a 'tower wagon' as it was being used for the conveyance of a load, namely, a pillar for a lamp standard (*Anderson & Heeley Ltd* v *Paterson* [1975] 1 All ER 523).

## 12.8 Trailers

There are increased rates of duty for goods vehicles 'drawing a trailer'. If a rigid goods vehicle exceeding 12 tonnes plated gross weight is used for drawing a trailer which has a plated gross weight exceeding 4 tonnes and when so drawn is used for the conveyance of goods or burden, a supplement is payable appropriate to the gross plated weight. Section 190(1) of the 1972 Act refers to a 'trailer' as a drawn vehicle. Although there are other differences between the Acts, in this respect the meanings seem to be similar.

By Sched 4, para 15(2), the term 'trailer' does not include grit-throwers not exceeding 5 cwt in weight, snow ploughs, certain road construction vehicles, trailers used solely to carry or produce gas for the propulsion of the towing vehicle, or farming implements not constructed or adapted for the conveyance of goods or burden of any description when drawn by a farmer's goods vehicle (as defined in Sched 4). The term 'trailer' has been held to include an empty poultry shed being drawn by a tractor (*Garner* v *Burr* [1950] 2 All ER 683) and a hut used as an office towed along the highway (*Horn* v *Dobson* 1933 SC(J) 1); for the purposes of Sched 4 (additional duty where trailer drawn), this duty is chargeable only when the drawing vehicle is a 'goods vehicle' as defined, above. There is a special rate of duty for tower wagons (see Sched 4, para 1(1)(*c*)).

A mechanically propelled vehicle can be both a 'mechanically propelled' vehicle and a trailer. There is nothing in the Vehicles (Excise) Act 1971 to exempt a mechanically propelled vehicle from taxation when it is being towed on a publicly repairable road. Where, therefore, a van was towed without its having been licensed, the justices were directed to convict the defendant even though the towing vehicle was itself licensed (*Cobb* v *Whorton* [1971] Crim LR 372). It is only if the vehicle is in such a condition that it can no longer be said to be mechanically propelled that no licence is needed (see meaning of 'mechanically propelled' at 1.14).

## 12.9 Farmers' goods vehicles

It should be noted that partly private use does not prevent a vehicle from being a farmer's goods vehicle (para 10(2)).

It is not use as a 'farmer's goods vehicle' as defined below to take furniture from a saleroom to the cottage of one of the farmer's employees (*M'Boyle* v *Hatton Estate Co* 1951 SLT (Sh) 101); see also *Agnew* v *Robertson* at 1.81. The term 'articles required for the purposes of the agricultural land' includes livestock and eggs as well as seeds, fertilisers and tools where a vehicle is being used by a chicken-farmer (*J M Knowles Ltd* v *Rand* [1962] 2 All ER 926). A different view prevailed in Northern Ireland (*Porter* v *Bloomer* [1957] NI 123, discussed at [1960] Jo Crim L 57). In *Armitage* v *Mountain* [1957] Crim LR 257, it was held that carrying furniture for a newly-engaged farm servant did not come within the uses for which a farmer's goods vehicle may lawfully be used as such, but on the facts higher duty was not payable. The term 'articles required for the purposes of the agricultural land which [the farmer] occupies' does not include the carriage of agricultural implements which have been sold by the farmer and are being taken to the purchaser (*MacMillan* v *Butter* 1963 SLT (Sh) 44). On an earlier statute it was held that a locomotive drawing to market some trolleys laden with farm produce was employed by the farmer 'for the purposes of his farm' (*London County Council* v *Lee* (1914) 78 JP 396). So where a locomotive was being used to take manure to a farm (*Cole Bros* v *Harrop* (1915) 79 JP 519).

The term 'farmer's goods vehicle' means a goods vehicle registered in the name of a person engaged in agriculture and used on public roads solely by him for the purpose of the conveyance of the produce of, or of articles required for the purposes of, the agricultural land which he occupies, and for no other purpose (Vehicles (Excise) Act 1971, Sched 4, para 15(1)). Thus, a vehicle licensed as a farmer's goods vehicle may not be used either simultaneously or separately for any purpose not caught by the definition just cited; if it is so used, and the unauthorised purpose is one which attracts a higher rate of duty, an offence arises under s 18(4). An example of an unauthorised use not attracting higher duty is *Armitage* v *Mountain*, above. In *Howard* v *Grass Products Ltd* [1972] RTR 552 a company agreed to cut a farmer's grass and remove it for dehydration. The work took three and a half days. The company's lorry which was used was registered as a farmer's goods vehicle. It was held that the vehicle was improperly registered and attracted a higher rate of duty as the 'occupier' for the purpose of para 15(1) meant a person in possession of agricultural land with some prospect of remaining in possession. The vehicle carried the produce of agricultural land but not of land of which the company was the 'occupier'. In *McKenzie* v *Griffiths Contractors (Agricultural) Ltd* [1976] RTR 140 the meaning of 'the produce of . . . the agricultural land which he occupies' as it appears in para 15(1) was considered. The character of the load should be taken into account. Straw from a farm used as bedding in racing stables, then sold as manure to a mushroom grower, was held to be the produce of the stables and no longer the produce of the farm as it had changed its character. The same principle was applied in *Cambrian Land Ltd* v *Allan* [1981] RTR 109 where animal carcasses were being taken from a slaughterhouse to a butcher after being produced on a farm. Certain exemptions also arise under s 18(7) for occasional carriage of another farmer's goods of small amount and without payment. There may also be special exemptions pursuant to s 18(8), which appears to relate to use of vehicles at harvest time. See also 'Tractors, agricultural vehicles etc', 12.5.

## 12.10 Private cars

The duties on mechanically propelled vehicles not caught by the other schedules are set out in Sched 5. It is under this provision that private cars fall to be taxed. See under 'Goods vehicles', 12.7, as to utility vehicles, shooting-brakes and Land Rovers. Light goods vehicles of 1,525 kg or less are taxed at a similar rate but under Sched 4. Cars not exceeding seven horsepower and first registered before 1947 pay less duty than the sum which all others pay per year.

## 12.11 Taxation of goods vehicles

A summary of the position may be helpful:

*Goods vehicles of 1,525 kg or less unladen*

These vehicles are taxed at a flat rate under Sched 4 whether used to carry goods or not and are merged together with private class vehicles in a new duty class (private/light goods) although technically light goods will be taxed under Sched 4 and private vehicles etc under Sched 5.

*Goods vehicles over 1,525 kg unladen weight*

These vehicles will be subject to duty according to their plated gross weight rather than unladen weight as before. In the case of tractor units (articulated vehicles) it will be the plated train or drawing weight (see Chapter 1, 1.31). Separate provisions apply depending on whether they are rigid vehicles or tractor units. 'Rigid vehicles' and 'tractor units' are defined in Sched 4, para 15(1).

(*a*) *Rigid vehicles* will be subject to duty according to the vehicle's gross weight recorded on its 'Ministry plate'. If this has not yet been issued—because it has not been tested or because it is not a compulsory type approval vehicle (see 1.35)—the taxable weight will be the maximum gross weight for use in Great Britain recorded on the manufacturer's plate. If the gross weight exceeds 12 tonnes duty will also depend upon the number of axles.

(*b*) *Rigid vehicles drawing trailers*. A rigid goods vehicle over 12 tonnes plated gross weight drawing a trailer which is being used for conveying goods or burden and which has a plated gross weight exceeding 4 tonnes will have to pay supplementary duty. The supplement will depend on the gross plated weight of the trailer. See further under 12.8 above.

(*c*) *Tractor units (articulated vehicles)*. (i) An articulated vehicle will be subject to duty as a combination according to the gross train weight for the tractor unit on its 'Ministry plate'. If this has not yet been issued (see above) the taxable weight will be the maximum train weight for use in Great Britain shown on the manufacturer's plate. When the gross train weight exceeds 12 tonnes the duty payable will also depend on the number of axles on the tractor unit and on the semi-trailer. (ii) Concessionary rates may apply for articulated lorries if operators undertake only to use the tractor unit with laden semi-trailers which have not less than two axles, or not less than three axles or in certain cases a single axled semi-trailer. A distinctive licence will be issued.

*Farmers and showmen*

Special rates for farmers' and showmen's goods vehicles continue to apply to all the categories.

*Vehicles subject to duty at a flat rate*

Goods vehicles exceeding 1,525 kg unladen which are:

(*a*) exempt from plating (eg dual purpose vehicles, tower wagons), or

(*b*) 'special types' vehicles, ie vehicles which do not comply with the Construction and Use Regulations but are specially authorised for road use under s 42 of the 1972 Act,

will fall into the Restricted HGV category. They will be charged at a flat rate of duty equal to the lowest rate on the gross weight scale. No supplement will be charged if a trailer is drawn (see Sched 4, para 5). Special rates for farmers' and showmen's goods vehicles will apply also where appropriate.

*Concessions which have ceased*

Duty concessions consisting of weight allowances deductible from the unladen, taxable weight of a vehicle, have automatically disappeared. The allowances for fixed equipment carried on vehicles which bear no other burden, for the built-in machinery of mobile concrete mixers, for containers, swap-bodies, towing attachments, gas containers and gas producing plant, have all also disappeared. See Sched 3, para 9 and also 12.12, below. Such machines or contrivances would be treated as laden and not taken into account in unladen weight cases, ie light goods vehicles of 1,525 kg or less.

## 12.12 Ascertainment of weight of vehicles

By para 15(1) 'unladen weight' in Sched 4 has the same meaning for goods vehicles as in s 194 of the 1972 Act. The Finance Act 1982 by s 5(6) amended s 38(4) of the 1971 Act to make it clear that while the 1971 Act definition of unladen weight (and Sched 6 in particular) continues to apply in other respects it does not apply to Sched 4 and in particular will not apply for the ascertainment of unladen weight in Sched 4.

Schedule 4, para 9 indicates the manner in which plated and laden weights are to be ascertained. Schedule 6 is not applicable. Any reference in Sched 4 (the Goods Vehicle Duties Schedule) to the plated gross weight of goods vehicle or trailer is a reference to the plated weight or manufacturer's plate (see Chapter 1, 1.35). The plated weight is that within the meaning of Part II of the 1972 Act, ie the maximum gross weight in Great Britain. The definition of plated train weight is similar. Plated weight will include a compulsory type approval certificate plate and any other plate such as a certificate of conformity plate having the same effect as a Ministry plate. See 1.35.

A vehicle with a detachable body is treated as being of the heavier weight unless it is re-weighed and re-registered (*Scott* v *Dickson* (1939) 83 SJ 317, a case on the Road Traffic Act). See generally as to 'weight', Chapter 1.

By Sched 9, para 3, if a vehicle is constructed or adapted (see 1.12) to carry a machine or contrivance and has neither a plated gross weight nor a plated train weight, the weight of the latter is treated as burden, even though it is built in as part of the vehicle. In effect this means that the machine or contrivance is not taken into account for light goods vehicles of 1,525 kg or less because the machine or contrivance will be treated as a load and not part of the unladen weight, but it will be taken into account indirectly for goods vehicles over 1,525 kg because the duty is for them based on the maximum gross weight.

Definitions are found in s 38 and the Schedules.

## 12.13 Exemptions from duty

The burden of proving that a vehicle is exempt lies upon the defendant (s 33, see 12.26, below).

Vehicles exempted from duty under s 4 of the Vehicles (Excise) Act include fire engines (whether kept by a public authority or any other person) (but see *Coote* v *Winfield* below), vehicles kept by a local authority for the purposes of their fire brigade service, ambulances for humans and animals (see further below), road rollers, vehicles used on tram lines (not being passenger-carrying trams), lifeboat haulage vehicles, vehicles not exceeding 10 cwt unladen specially adapted for invalids, road construction vehicles used or kept solely for the conveyance of road construction machinery which is built in or permanently attached to the vehicle and is used for no purpose other than the construction or repair of roads at the public expense, grit-throwing vehicles, tower wagons used by a street lighting authority or by a contractor with the authority (see definition in Sched 4 and *Anderson & Heeley Ltd* v *Paterson* at 12.7) and local authorities' watering vehicles. Vehicles made available by the Secretary of State to any person, body or local authority under s 23 or s 26 of the National Health Service Act 1977 and which are used accordingly are also exempted by s 4. By s 7(3) there is an exemption for snow-clearance vehicles. By s 7(1) the Secretary of State for Transport with the consent of the Treasury may exempt from duty when an application for a vehicle excise licence is made a vehicle intended to be used on public roads only in passing from land of the owner to other land of his and for distances not exceeding six miles in the aggregate in any week. Article 5 of the Motor Vehicles (International Circulation) Order 1975 (SI 1975 No 1208) relates to vehicles brought into the country by persons making only a temporary stay and to vehicles carrying foreign tourists. Vehicles used only at elections, without payment by the passengers, are also exempt (Representation of the People Act 1949, s 89), as are vehicles used by a public or local authority for civil defence purposes (Vehicles (Excise) Act 1971, s 7(4); Civil Defence Vehicles (Relief from Duty) Regulations 1953), and vehicles in the service of visiting forces (see 2.5) (Visiting Forces and International Headquarters (Application of Law) Order 1965). By s 6(1) (as substituted by the Finance Act 1972) exemption is also given for vehicles zero-rated for value added tax with a view to being taken abroad by an overseas resident, but duty is payable if they are not taken abroad.

In *Coote* v *Winfield* [1980] RTR 42 it was held that a 'fire engine' which had been modified so as to perform some other function and which could no longer be used for its original purpose had ceased to be a fire engine. Fire engines are exempt from duty but it is a question of fact and degree whether or not a vehicle is a fire engine.

Electrically propelled vehicles are exempt from duty by virtue of s 4(1)(*aa*) as added by the Finance Act 1980, s 4(4).

There is an exemption from vehicle excise duty for certain vehicles for disabled people under the Finance Act 1971, s 7, as amended and extended by subsequent Finance Acts. This exemption is not limited to vehicles which are 'invalid carriages'. Such persons should still obtain a 'nil' licence or an offence will be committed.

What is an ambulance is a question of fact (compare *Coote* v *Winfield*). It is submitted that an ambulance is a vehicle for conveying ill or wounded people whether sitting up or lying down.

There is a distinction between the speeding exemption (see 6.22) which clearly covers *any* vehicle being used for (police or) ambulance *purposes*, and the vehicles excise exemption which merely refers to 'ambulances'. It remains to be seen whether the vehicles excise exemption applies to any vehicle used as an ambulance or only a vehicle which is specially adapted as an ambulance; in other words, whether the distinction has any significance. *Coote* v *Winfield* does not help very much as it is the reverse situation except to confirm that the test is one of fact and degree but it is some indication that the use is material.

Tramcars carrying passengers are exempted by s 5 of the Finance (No 2) Act 1975. The only remaining public tram system is apparently the Blackpool system. Trams other than passenger trams are separately exempted as noted above.

By s 5 of the 1971 Act a vehicle is exempt from duty when proceeding to and from a previously arranged vehicle test either under s 43 (ordinary vehicles) or s 45 (goods vehicles subject to plated weights) of the 1972 Act, or to or from a place where a defect revealed by that test is by previous arrangement remedied. Section 5 only grants exemption where the vehicle is being used solely for the purpose of proceeding to and from the test or place of repair. This appears to prevent an impecunious holiday maker in London from arranging for his car carrying him and his family on holiday to Cornwall to be tested in Penzance and thus exempting the vehicle from being taxed.

Questions arise from time to time whether certain machinery used in connection with road works is exempt from duty under s 4 as a 'road construction vehicle' or is chargeable under Sched 3 as a vehicle used for trench digging or excavating. A vehicle carrying a built-in air compressor used only to supply power to pneumatic drills falls under Sched 3 as a trench digger and, *semble*, is not a road construction vehicle under s 4 (*NW Construction Co* v *Lancashire County Council*, a county court decision of 1939). In *Orr* v *Carmichael* 1941 SC(J) 27, a dumper used solely in connection with road construction was held to be exempt from duty as a road construction vehicle, as the law then stood. In *Cowan* v *Hale* [1966] NI 31 it was held, on a statute of Northern Ireland, in relation to a dumper fitted with a metal tipping skip, that the skip was road construction machinery, that, though capable of carrying loads nothing to do with road construction, the skip carried articles used for the purposes of road construction machinery and that the dumper was a road construction vehicle; it was said that the question of exemption from duty depends on the actual use of the vehicle and not on its obvious characteristics of function and design. The decision is criticised at [1966] Jo Crim L 210. In *McCrone* v *J & L Rigby (Wigan) Ltd* (1952) 50 LGR 115, however, a dumper and an excavator were both held to be chargeable under Sched 3, but the decision proceeded partly on the view that the vehicle owners had not discharged the burden of proof cast on them by s 33 of the Act to show that the dumper was used 'for no purpose other than the construction of roads'. It was also held that the excavator was specifically taxable under Sched 3, which refers to vehicles used for trench digging or any kind of excavating or shovelling work. The legal position as to dumpers still remains unsettled and the two cases should be carefully studied when any point arises. They are discussed at 119 JP Jo 458. See also 1.15.

## 12.14 Duration of licences

By s 2(1) of the Act licences for any vehicle may be taken out for a period of twelve months and licences of a shorter duration may be taken out for certain other vehicles. As amended by the Vehicles Licences (Duration and Rate of Duty) Order 1980 (SI 1980 No 1183) s 2(1) provides that excise licences may run for six months from the beginning of the month for which application is made (instead of four) for vehicles for which the annual rate of duty exceeds £18. The six-monthly rate is one half of the annual rate plus 10 per cent. Seven-day licences are available for certain goods vehicles authorised to be used under s 42(1) of the 1972 Act. In respect of six-month and seven-day licences, fractions of 5p are to be regarded as 5p if they exceed 2·5p and otherwise are to be disregarded. By s 13, now in force, a temporary fourteen-day licence or licences may be issued pending the issue of the full six months or one-year licence.

## 12.15 Days of grace for renewal

It is the practice to allow fourteen days grace for renewal of excise licences (but not trade licences). It should be remembered that this applies only following *expiration* of tax; it does not apply when the vehicle is first put on the road or put back on the road after being laid up without tax. Strictly it is only on condition that renewal is obtained in the fourteen days. If a licence is not taken out after they have passed it is proper to charge unlicensed use during the period (*Sly* v *Randall* (1916) 80 JP 199). Section 8(2) gives statutory effect to the fourteen days of grace and refers to the application being duly made while the expired tax was in force, but this subsection has not been brought into force. However, it is not uncommon practice to give effect to the spirit of a relieving statute when it has been passed but not brought into force.

## 12.16 Failing to display licence

By s 12(4) of the 1971 Act, the excise licence shall be fixed to and exhibited on the vehicle in the manner prescribed by the regulations. It is an offence under s 12(4) to fail to exhibit a licence whether a licence is in force for the vehicle or not. If there is no licence for the vehicle, the user may be prosecuted and incur the excise penalty under s 8 for using the vehicle without a licence and may also be fined for the offence of not exhibiting a licence under s 12(4) (*Pilgram* v *Dean* [1974] RTR 299). It may also be noted that the offence of failing to display a vehicle's excise licence may be dealt with by means of a fixed penalty under Sched 12 of the Road Traffic Regulation Act 1984 or the Transport Act 1982 fixed penalty provisions when in force. Failure to pay the fixed penalty not only makes the offender liable to prosecution but other proceedings may ensue, if, as is usually the case, the 'vehicle owner liability' provisions are used (see 'Vehicle owner liability', 17.2). When subs (5) comes into force it will be a defence to a charge under s 12(4) if (*a*) application has been made for renewal of an existing licence and (*b*) the old licence is displayed, and (*c*) no more than fourteen days have elapsed since the previous licence has expired. The only existing defence is the limited defence set out in the proviso to reg 16(1) of the 1971 regulations.

A New Zealand regulation reads: 'No person shall permit a motor vehicle to be on a road . . . unless there is carried on the vehicle a current warrant of fitness.' A car exhibited the necessary warrant on the windscreen and the owner left the car for a short time; when he returned, he found that a trespasser had removed the warrant and that a traffic-offence notice had been stuck to the windscreen. It was held, after reference to 10 Halsbury (3rd ed) 272, and to Russell on *Crime* (11th ed) 25, that the owner was not guilty as the omission to carry the warrant was not within his conduct, knowledge or control (*Kilbride* v *Lake* [1962] NZLR 590).

This New Zealand case was considered in *Strowger* v *John* [1974] RTR 124. It was held that the offence under s 12(4) was absolute and no mens rea was required. A motorist left his car locked and while away the plastic holder containing the licence fell from the windscreen out of sight on to the floor of the car; the justices were directed to convict the motorist in that the car and its accessories were at all times under his control (ibid). *Kilbride* was distinguished because in *Kilbride* the removal of the licence was totally unexplained—it had disappeared from the car. Lord Widgery CJ in *Strowger*, at p 130, specifically reserved for future consideration whether a driver would have a defence to a charge under s 12(4) if the car is broken into and the licence stolen.

An offence under s 12(4) is punishable by a fine of level 3. For an explanation as to how the penalty is arrived at, see 12.39. Where the failure to exhibit is without fault or blame on the part of the defendant an absolute discharge may be the appropriate penalty. In *Strowger* v *John*, above, the Divisional Court remitted the case back to the recorder of the Crown Court to enable him to give '(with a clear lack of discouragement) the opportunity of imposing an absolute discharge as the only possible penalty'.

Trade licences for motor traders are dealt with under s 16 of the 1971 Act and Part V of the Road Vehicles (Registration and Licensing) Regulations 1971.

### 12.17 Under-payment of duty

By s 18(1) it is provided that, where a licence has been taken out in respect of a vehicle at a certain rate and the vehicle is at any time used on a public road in an altered condition or in a manner or for a purpose which brings it within or which, if it was used solely in that condition or in that manner or for that purpose, would bring it within a class or description of vehicle to which a higher rate of duty is applicable, duty at that higher rate shall become chargeable. By s 18(4), where by virtue of such user a higher rate of duty becomes chargeable and duty at the higher rate was not paid before the vehicle was used on a public road, the person so using the vehicle shall be liable to whichever is the greater of the following penalties, viz:

(*a*) an excise penalty of a fine of level 3; or
(*b*) an excise penalty of an amount equal to five times the difference between the duty actually paid and the amount of duty at that higher rate (calculated, *semble*, at the annual rate: see 12.18).

A magistrates' court may, however, mitigate the penalty to such extent as it thinks fit (Magistrates' Courts Act 1980, s 34). The burden of proof as to user is not laid on the defendant in proceedings under s 18, since s 33 of the Act does not apply to them. But see s 154 of the Customs and Excise Management Act 1979, at 12.26.

Section 18(2) makes provision as to the payment of extra duty when, because of a change of use, a licence has to be exchanged.

By s 18(5), duty at a higher rate applicable to vehicles of some other class or description shall not become chargeable by reason of such user of a vehicle as is mentioned in s 18(1), unless the vehicle as so used while the licence at the lower rate is in force complies with all the conditions which must be satisfied in order to bring it into the other class. In *Payne* v *Allcock* (1932) 96 JP 283, it was held that use of a private car of the ordinary passenger type to convey goods in the course of trade attracted the 'goods' duty, but this decision no longer applies since s 18(5) requires the vehicle to satisfy all the conditions which would bring it into the other class before it becomes taxable at the higher rate for that other class; a private car does not satisfy the condition in Sched 4, para 15(1), that it is a goods vehicle constructed or adapted for use for conveying goods (cf *Flower Freight Co* v *Hammond* [1962] 3 All ER, at p 952, letter G).

Where boards were fitted to the side of a lorry to enable it to carry more coal, this was held to be use in an altered condition, attracting more duty (*Lowe* v *Stone* [1948] 2 All ER 1076). See also *Blaikie* v *Morrison* at 1.32, and *Bowra* v *Dann Catering Co Ltd* at 12.6, a prosecution under s 18(1) and (4).

The liability to prosecution under s 18 for a use not covered by the licence and to pay higher duty for it arises where the duty payable in respect of that other use is higher than the proper duty actually paid in respect of that vehicle. If the duty is the same or less, no offence is committed.

By s 18(6) and (7) there are special exemptions for goods vehicles used to carry employees, provided such vehicles are mainly used to convey goods, and for farmers' goods vehicles used occasionally to carry small amounts of agricultural goods, without payment, for other agriculturists at the same time as they carry agricultural goods for the owner. Section 18(8) also gives exemptions for farmers' goods vehicles in circumstances specified by statutory instruments; these instruments, if issued, generally relate to harvesting. See 12.9 as to such vehicles.

The goods vehicles taxation system may lead to prosecutions for underpayment of duty. Set out below are possible examples.

(*a*) Using a goods vehicle over 1,525 kg for the carriage of goods for hire, reward or in connection with a trade or business without paying the appropriate goods rate.
(NB Vehicles under 1,525 kg may be used to carry goods for hire, reward or in connection with a trade or business without paying any extra excise duty.)

(*b*) Using a vehicle with fewer axles than the number for which the licence was issued.

(*c*) Using a vehicle at a gross weight exceeding that for which the licence was issued.

(*d*) Taking out a licence for a vehicle at a lower duty weight than the gross weight requires and then using it accordingly.

(*e*) Using a rigid goods vehicle over 12 tonnes gross weight to tow a laden trailer over 4 tonnes gross weight without paying the appropriate trailer supplement.

The time limit for proceedings under s 18 is six months from the date when the offence comes to the knowledge of the authorised prosecutor, subject to an overriding time limit of three years from the commission of the offence (see s 28 at 12.29). A prosecution may be instituted only by the Secretary of State for Transport or by a constable with his approval (ibid).

Previously there was no provision for a court to order payment of additional back duty in cases prosecuted for under-licensing under s 18(4) of the Vehicles (Excise) Act 1971. The Finance Act 1982 has amended this section to require a court to order the appropriate additional back duty to be paid following a conviction under this section, which applies to all motor vehicles. The amount to be paid will vary according to the case type:

(i) in cases where the vehicle has been replated after the current licence was taken out the back duty liability starts from the date on which the vehicle was replated at the higher weight and ends with the date of the offence;
(ii) in other cases back duty liability starts from the date on which the current licence was taken out and ends with the date of the offence.

The summary and examples given in 12.25 as to payment of back duty may assist.

By s 30, under-payments of duty may be recovered by the Secretary of State for Transport (*semble*, in the county court), provided that the action is begun before the expiration of the twelve months beginning with the end of the period in respect of which the licence was taken out. A similar time limit applies to proceedings by a vehicle owner who has overpaid duty.

## 12.18 Using or keeping a vehicle on a public road without a licence

It is provided that a person who uses or keeps on a public road a vehicle for which a licence is not in force, shall be liable:
(1) to whichever is the greater of the following penalties, viz:
(*a*) an excise penalty of a fine of level 3; or
(*b*) an excise penalty equal to five times the amount of duty chargeable (s 8); and
(2) to back-duty (s 9: see 12.24 below),
unless the vehicle is exempt from duty under the Act or any other enactment.

Proceedings under s 8 may be brought within six months of the offence coming to the knowledge of the prosecutor, subject to an overriding time limit of three years from the date of the offence. Proceedings may only be brought by the Secretary of State for Transport or a constable with his approval (see s 28, 12.29).

The Magistrates' Association's recommended penalty for an offence under s 8 is 'Actual duty lost plus fine of approximately twice that amount' (see generally 18.1 and Appendix 3).

Because the punishment for non-payment is expressed as a penalty and not as a fine imposed as a punishment for an offence, the various provisions of the Customs and Excise Acts apply where they have not been expressly excluded. (See in particular 12.31 below.) It should be remembered that, although rarely exercised, under s 147(3) of the Customs and Excise Management Act 1979 the prosecutor has a right of appeal to the Crown Court against any decision of a magistrates' court in proceedings for an offence to which that Act applies.

It may be relevant that the defendant has been given the opportunity to pay a mitigated penalty and has either not availed himself of the opportunity or has declined it wishing instead to mitigate the offence before a magistrates' court or to plead not guilty (see 12.30 below).

If use without payment of duty is established, the defendant must be found guilty, however trivial the case (see *Patterson* v *Helling* at 12.2). Ownership or proof of ownership of the vehicle is not essential to proof of the offence of 'keeping' or 'using' (*Napthen* v *Place* [1970] Crim LR 474). It is no defence that a cheque has been posted to the licensing authority prior to the use of the vehicle on the road (*Nattrass* v *Gibson* (1968) 112 SJ 866), but s 8(2), when no longer modified by Sched 7, will alter this.

Section 16(7) imposes like penalties on a holder of a trade licence or licences who uses on a public road at any one time a greater number of vehicles than he is authorised to use by virtue of that or those licences. The same time limit applies under s 28.

A licence is void from the time it is granted if it is paid for by a cheque which is dishonoured (Customs and Excise Management Act 1979, s 102(2)).

Section 8 refers to a person using, etc, a vehicle 'for which a licence is not in force'. A licence is, presumably, 'in force' as soon as it is issued or granted. The time at which a licence is issued or granted is not the time at which it is received but the time at which it is granted by or on behalf of the Secretary of State for Transport. The tax disc will usually be stamped with the date of issue.

The maximum penalty under s 8(1)(*b*) is calculated as five times the annual rate of duty applicable to the vehicle at the date of the offence and, in the case of a continuing offence, the offence shall be deemed to have been committed on the date or latest date to which the conviction relates (ss 8(3)(*b*), 16(7)). Where, in the case of a vehicle kept on a road, the rate of duty at the date of the offence differs from the annual rate by which the vehicle was chargeable, viz that applicable at the date of issue of its last licence, the duty shall be calculated at the latter rate (ibid). It would seem that s 8(3)(*b*) nullifies the decision in *Holland* v *Perry* [1952] 2 All ER 720 in that the maximum penalty is five times the annual rate of duty or a fine of level 3, whichever is the greater. Any duty actually paid by the defendant would seem not to alter the maximum penalty; only the amount of any back-duty payable under s 9 would be affected (see below). Where a licence has not been taken out at all, the defendant cannot plead that he would have licensed the car for a shorter period and that the quintuple duty should be calculated for that period only (*Holland* v *Perry*, above).

The court may mitigate the penalty to whatever extent it wishes and is no longer limited to an amount not less than a quarter of the duty (Customs and Excise Management Act 1979, s 150).

The burden of proof as to user, etc, is thrown on the defendant by s 33 (12.26) in proceedings under s 8.

Fourteen days of grace are, in practice, allowed for the renewal of licences (other than trade licences) providing the earlier licence has expired immediately before (see 12.15) but, if a licence is not taken out after they have passed, it is proper to charge unlicensed use during them (*Sly* v *Randall* (1916) 80 JP 199). It is the duty of the licence holder to renew it when it expires and it is no defence that he has not been given a reminder by the authorities (*Caldwell* v *Hague* (1914) 79 JP 152).

A person who is detected using an unlicensed vehicle on a public road at any time commits an offence and cannot plead as a defence that he took out a licence five minutes later (*Campbell* v *Strangeways* (1877) 42 JP 39; *Wharton* v *Taylor* (1965) 109 SJ 475), nor that a cheque had been posted to the licensing authority before the vehicle was used on the road (*Nattrass* v *Gibson* (1968) 112 SJ 866).

In *Flack* v *Church* (1918) 82 JP 59, it was held that the fact that in a particular year a person had been convicted of keeping a dog without a licence did not prevent a further conviction for keeping the same dog without a licence on another day later in the same year. Liability under taxing statutes can sometimes be strict. In *Strutt* v *Clift* (1911) 74 JP 471, a master sent his servant out in a carriage on lawful business; the servant used it for a frolic of his own in an unlawful way which attracted higher duty. The master was held liable. In *Stone* v *Horton* (1949) 113 JP Jo 674, an owner was likewise held liable under what is now the Vehicles (Excise) Act where he had hired or lent the car to a customer. On the other hand, it was held in *Abercromby* v *Morris* (1932) 96 JP 392, that an owner who lends his car to a friend for a period, on the understanding that the friend will renew the licence, is not liable for unauthorised use by the friend on expiry of the licence. And see *Dove* v *Tarvin* and *Carmichael & Sons Ltd* v *Cottle*, cases on the Construction and Use Regulations, and other cases at 1.79.

## 12.19 Effect of failure to transfer licence

If a licensed vehicle is transferred by the holder of the licence to another person without the licence being handed over at the same time, any use of that vehicle on a public road is deemed by s 8(3)(*a*) of the Act to be an unlicensed use. *Quaere*, if the vehicle becomes re-licensed, as it were, once the licence has been delivered; it is arguable on the wording of s 8(3)(*a*) that it still remains unlicensed, especially from the omission of 'and until' after 'unless'. On the other hand, this subsection imposes a taxing burden in making duty payable possibly twice and it can be said that only clear words can justify such an interpretation against the transferee.

## 12.20–3 Miscellaneous offences

*Registration marks*

By s 21 hackney carriages are required to exhibit distinctive signs showing that they are hackney carriages and their seating capacity, in the form indicated in Part VI of the regulations. These signs must be exhibited in addition to any signs of a *different* kind required by a local Act or byelaw (*Eccles* v *Kirke* [1949] 1 All ER 428).

By s 22(1) it is provided that, if a mark or sign required by s 19 or s 21 is not fixed to the vehicle as required, the *driver* of the vehicle or, if it is not being driven, the person keeping the vehicle, shall be liable to a fine of level 3. It shall be a defence that the defendant had no reasonable opportunity of registering the vehicle and that it was being driven for the purpose of being registered.

By s 22(2), if any mark or sign fixed on a vehicle pursuant to s 19 or s 21 is in any way obscured or allowed to become not easily distinguishable, the *driver* or, if it is not being driven, the person keeping the vehicle, shall be liable to the penalties just mentioned but it shall be a defence that he took all steps reasonably practicable to prevent it being obscured or rendered not easily distinguishable. On a somewhat similarly worded provision in earlier legislation it was held in *Printz* v *Sewell* (1912) 76 JP 295 that this defence could be invoked where the charge was failing to illuminate the rear number-plate, so that its numbers and letters were not easily distinguishable. Of course, this defence would not apply in charges under the Road Traffic Act for not having a rear light (see 8.86), even though the same light might serve both as a rear light and to illuminate the number plate, so the defendant could properly be convicted on the one charge and acquitted on the other.

*Information as to user*

By s 27 owners and other persons are required, under penalty of a fine of level 3, to furnish information to the police or licensing authority as to the identity of users of a vehicle, where it is alleged that a vehicle has been used etc in contravention of s 8, s 16(7) or s 18(4). This and the similar provision in s 168 of the 1972 Act are discussed at 7.16–19. Any person may prosecute under s 27(1) and the time limit is six months. Information may be demanded under s 18 in writing (s 32).

## Excise Licences: Proceedings and Penalties

### 12.24 Payment of back-duty

By s 9 of the Vehicles (Excise) Act 1971, where a person convicted of an offence of using or keeping an unlicensed vehicle is the person by whom that vehicle was kept at the time of the offence, the court shall order him to pay, in addition to any penalty, back-duty calculated in accordance with s 9(2)–(4); this provision applies also where the defendant is put on probation or discharged absolutely or conditionally (see s 9(5)). The amount of back-duty is, subject to s 9(3), an amount equal to one-twelfth of the annual rate of duty for each calendar month or part of a calendar month in the relevant period. 'The relevant period', by s 9(2), is one ending with the date of the offence and beginning:

(*a*) if the defendant has before that date notified the licensing authority of his acquisition of the vehicle, with the date of receipt of that notification or, if later, with the expiry of the licence last in force for the vehicle, or

(*b*) in any other case, with the expiry of the licence last in force for the vehicle before the date of the offence or, if there has not at any time before that date been a licence in force for the vehicle, with the date on which the vehicle was first kept by that person.

By a proviso to s 9(2), if a person has been previously ordered to pay back-duty for the same vehicle, the relevant period begins with the month following that in which the first offence was committed.

By s 9(3), where the defendant proves (*semble*, on balance of probabilities and not beyond reasonable doubt) that (*a*) throughout any month or part of a month in the relevant period the vehicle was not kept by him, or was neither used nor kept by him on a public road, or was not chargeable with duty, or (*b*) that he has paid duty in respect of the vehicle for any such month or part, whether or not on a licence, the amount payable under s 9(2) shall be calculated as if that month or part were not comprised in the relevant period.

Note that s 9 applies only to the person convicted under s 8 and only if he was the person by whom the vehicle was kept at the time of the offence. Thus, if *A*'s son uses *A*'s unlicensed car, the son cannot, on conviction under s 8, be made to pay back-duty under s 9 of the Act of 1971. If *A* has been convicted of aiding and abetting his son's unlicensed use, *A* has, it is submitted, been himself 'convicted of an offence' under s 8; s 44 of the Magistrates' Courts Act 1980 says that an aider and abettor is 'guilty of the like offence'. Then *A* must be ordered to pay back-duty.

Home Office circular 158/1967, of 29 August 1967, and the *Justices' Clerk*, April 1968, p 74, give guidance as to s 9.

See s 6(1) (as substituted by the Finance Act 1972) as to back-duty on vehicles zero rated for VAT because they are to be taken abroad, and then becoming chargeable with duty because not taken abroad.

Section 31 of the Act enables evidence of prescribed matters to be given by the production of a document authenticated by a person authorised in that behalf by the Secretary of State for Transport (see 2.80).

Details in respect of vehicle excise licences are held in the centralised computer at Swansea, and evidence of the existence or non-existence of such a licence may therefore be established in this way.

## 12.25 Summary as to proceedings for payment of back-duty etc

The provisions of s 9 as to back-duty apply only where there is a conviction under s 8 of the Vehicles (Excise) Act for using or keeping an unlicensed vehicle on a public road; if the conviction is under s 16 (trade licences), the Act does not apply in respect of back-duty; in these circumstances back-duty is recoverable as a civil debt. With regard to s 18 (alteration of use of vehicle) there are in s 18A separate back-duty provisions. See 12.17.

If, however, there is a conviction (including an order of absolute or conditional discharge or probation) under s 8, the court has a discretion as to the amount of the fine or penalty but must order the full back-duty, however great the financial hardship to the defendant and however impecunious he is, unless the defendant can show that for some or all of the relevant period he was not the keeper of the vehicle or that it was not used or kept on a public road or chargeable with duty or that the relevant back-duty has in fact been paid.

The effect of s 85(2) of the Magistrates' Courts Act 1980 is that, although a court after non-payment of a fine or enquiring into the offender's means may ordinarily remit the whole or part of a fine because of a change in his circumstances, this power of remission cannot be exercised either in respect of orders for the payment of back-duty under s 9 or in respect of any penalties imposed under s 8 or s 18(4) as these do not come within the definition of 'fine' in s 85(2) (see also 12.31). Courts sometimes achieve the same result by ordering one day's detention in default of the fine, costs and back-duty.

The statement of facts normally indicates the amount of back-duty claimed and the Department of Transport should know when any was last paid. A defendant who seeks to prove that he was not the keeper during any part of the relevant period should adduce evidence to that effect; the then owner of the vehicle may give evidence as to this but is in danger of incriminating himself both for not notifying the change and for not paying duty. Or the defendant may give and call evidence that the vehicle was not used or kept on a public road during the period before the offence or some of that period; members of his household or neighbours can often help on this point.

The defendant may also show that he has paid duty for the relevant period or some of it and in that case the period is calculated as if the month or part of a month for which he has paid were not comprised in the relevant period (s 9(3)). Or it may be shown that he has already been ordered to pay back-duty for the same vehicle on a previous conviction, in which case the back-duty now payable by him begins to run with the month following the previous conviction. The defendant may, possibly, appeal to the Crown Court against the amount ordered (see further on this point, 22.6).

*Examples*

Some examples may assist:

(1) *A* commits the offence of using a motor vehicle on a public road on 18 March 1985. The licence ran out on 31 December 1983 and *A* calls no evidence to suggest that the vehicle was not on a public road during 1984–85. In addition to the fine, the amount of which is at the magistrates' discretion, he must be ordered to pay full back-duty for the twelve months of 1984 and three months of 1985. The duty to be claimed, by s 9(4), is the annual rate applicable to it at the beginning of each month, or part.

(2) The same facts but *A* notified the licensing authority that he had become the owner on 22 June 1984. Then he is liable to pay back-duty only for the months commencing 1 June 1984. It seems on the wording of s 9(2)(*a*) that it is only notification by the person convicted that counts; a notification by the previous owner does not. Notification must be before the offence, not the conviction.

(3) The same facts but *A* proves in court that on 31 December 1983 he put the car in his garage and the car was first put on the road a week before 18 March 1985, the day of the offence. He pays back-duty for March 1985 only. *Quaere*, if he first got the car out on 18 March; by s 9(2) the relevant period is one 'ending with the date of the offence'. Does that period 'end' at 00.01 hours on 18 March or at 23.59 hours on that day? It is suggested that the construction against the Revenue should be adopted both because a taxing statue is so construed and because there is ambiguity, so that no back-duty for March is payable. The licensing authority can always obtain the March duty by other means.

(4) The same facts but *A* shows that he has in fact paid the back-duty before he came to court, eg, he had sent a cheque off to the DVLC a fortnight before he came to court. Then no back-duty is orderable by the court; if he paid only part of the back-duty, the court should order payment of the part unpaid. *A* can also prove that the vehicle was exempt from duty in the relevant period or part of it.

(5) *B*'s last licence expired on 30 June 1984; he commits the offence of using his car on a public road on 21 March 1985, and is later convicted of it at Oxford. He proves to the Oxford court that he was convicted of a like offence committed at Cambridge in January 1985 and that the Cambridge court ordered him to pay back-duty for July to December 1984 and for January 1985. The Oxford court should order him to pay back-duty for February and March 1985 under the proviso to s 9(2).

In all the above cases the court should order a fine or absolute or conditional discharge in addition to the back-duty. By s 9(4) a vehicle is deemed to have belonged to the same duty-class throughout, unless otherwise proved; the prosecution may elect to treat it as being in the class in which it was when a licence was last taken out.

A defence under s 9(3)(*b*) arises only if the defendant paid the back-duty prior to the hearing. If someone else paid it, it is arguable that there is no back-duty 'appropriate to the vehicle' under s 9(2).

Where a false statement was knowingly made in one jurisdiction in an application for a licence and it was sent by post to the licensing authority in another jurisdiction, it was held in Scotland that the *locus* for the offence could only be where it was received (*Gibb* v *Hill* [1948] Jo Crim L 185). In England, however, it would seem that there could be a prosecution in either place, provided the form was received by the licensing authority (now the Secretary of State for Transport) (*R* v *Burdett* (1820) 4 B & Ald 95; *Grimble* v *Preston* (1914) 78 JP 72; Magistrates' Courts Act 1980, s 3(2)). Under the regulations various offences arise of failing to notify change of ownership; it is submitted that such defaulters can be prosecuted either where they are when they make default or where the offices which should be notified are, but it is understood that the Department of Transport have recommended that proceedings should be taken in the place where the offender resides.

The general rules as to venue set out at 2.16–20 supplement the above provisions.

## 12.26 Burden of proof

By s 33 it is provided that if, in proceedings under s 26(2) (false declarations on applications for licences and false information on change of registration), under s 8 (using and keeping vehicles without a licence) or under s 16(7) (using excess vehicles under trade licence), any question arises:

(*a*) as to the number of vehicles used, or
(*b*) as to the character, weight, horse-power or cylinder capacity of any vehicle, or
(*c*) as to the number of persons for which a vehicle has seating capacity, or
(*d*) as to the purpose for which any vehicle has been used,

the burden of proof in respect of the matter in question shall lie on the defendant. The section was discussed in *McCrone* v *J & L Rigby (Wigan) Ltd* (1952) 50 LGR 115, and it should be noted that it applies only to proceedings under s 8, s 16(7) or s 26(2); in summary proceedings under other sections, eg s 18, the normal rule as to the burden of proof applies. Generally, a defendant must prove facts peculiarly within his own knowledge, eg that he has a licence (*John* v *Humphreys* [1955] 1 All ER 793), and by s 101 of the Magistrates' Courts Act 1980 any exception, exemption, proviso, excuse or qualification for a defendant should be proved by him and need not be negatived by the prosecution in opening. The defendant's burden under s 33 may be discharged by evidence for the defence or by precise admissions made by the witnesses for the prosecution (*McCrone* v *Rigby*, above) and would seem to be less than that on a prosecutor generally to prove a criminal charge; he may satisfy the court of the probability of what he alleges (*R* v *Carr-Briant* [1943] 2 All ER 156).

By the Customs and Excise Management Act 1979, s 154, where in any proceedings relating to excise any question arises as to whether duty has been paid on any goods or as to whether any goods or other things whatsoever are of the description or nature alleged in the information, the burden of proof lies on the defendant.

## 12.27 Who may prosecute and authorisation to do so

Section 2 of the Magistrates' Courts Act 1980, granting magistrates' courts jurisdiction to try summary offences, is an overriding provision and confers jurisdiction on a magistrates' court to try an offence under s 8 of the Vehicles (Excise) Act 1971 committed by a 'privileged tinner' who claimed trial by a county court which had inherited the jurisdiction of the Stannaries Court (*R* v *East Powder Justices, ex parte Lampshire* (1979) 123 SJ 49).

Summary proceedings for an offence under s 8, s 11(2), s 16(7), or s 18(4) of the Vehicles (Excise) Act 1971 or under any regulations made under that Act may be instituted in England and Wales by the Secretary of State for Transport or a constable (severally referred to as 'the authorised prosecutor') within six months from the date on which sufficient evidence (in the opinion of the authorised prosecutor) came to his knowledge to warrant the proceedings (s 28(1)). No such proceedings may be instituted more than three years after the commission of the offence (s 28(1)). Proceedings under ss 8, 16(7) and 18(4) may only be instituted in England and Wales by the authorised prosecutor; and no such proceedings may be instituted by a constable except with the approval of the Secretary of State (s 28(2)). As to 'Authority to prosecute', see 2.3.

If the information is laid by an official and not by a constable and it alleges that the proceedings are instituted by that official on behalf of the Secretary of State, it seems that this is sufficient proof that they are so instituted unless the contrary is proved (*Dyer* v *Tulley* (1894) 58 JP 656; Customs and Excise Management Act 1979, s 148). The magistrates' clerk or justice issuing a summons to a constable should satisfy himself by the production of the certificate under s 28(2) that the proceedings are brought by the constable with the approval of the Secretary of State. There is no need for the prosecutor to take any further step to prove authorisation in open court unless the defence object that it has not been proved. Such objection by the defence should be taken before the close of the prosecution's case, and if objection is made the prosecution should be given the opportunity to prove the consent (*Price* v *Humphries* [1958] 2 All ER 725); if necessary, an adjournment can properly be granted. It is submitted that as the matter is of a technical or formal nature, the adjournment should be granted almost as a matter of course (see, for example, *Royal* v *Prescott-Clarke* [1966] 2 All ER 366). Where an information is laid by an officer who has not been generally or specially authorised to take those proceedings, an authorisation given after the laying of the information would not, it seems, validate the proceedings; furthermore from the wording of s 28(3)(*b*) it would seem that the Secretary of State for Transport does not have power to give subsequent approval to a constable who has already instituted proceedings.

### 12.28 Venue

Section 28A of the Customs and Excise Management Act 1979 appears to apply to offences under the Vehicles (Excise) Act and regulations made thereunder. Consequently, proceedings may also be taken where the offender resides or is found or in any part of England in cases where the offence was committed in England (similarly in Scotland: see [1958] Jo Crim L 269) as well as where the offence was committed. The view is, however, held in some authoritative circles that s 148 applies only to offences which are 'excise offences', ie where payment of duty is in issue, and not, eg, to failing to illuminate a number plate or to display an excise licence. This view is based on s 3(2) of the Vehicles (Excise) Act, which applies the Customs and Excise Act in relation to 'duties of excise' and punishments and penalties in connection therewith. See *M'Millan* v *Grant* 1924 JC 13.

By far the majority of cases under s 8 are brought under the procedure set out in the Magistrates' Courts Act 1980, by which a defendant may plead guilty by post. Section 34 of the Vehicles (Excise) Act adapts the procedure to allow the prosecutor to serve with the summons a notice stating that, in the event of the defendant being convicted, he will be required to pay the amount of back-duty specified in the notice unless he states that it is inappropriate. If he pleads guilty and does not state that the amount is inappropriate s 34 requires the court to order payment of the back-duty. Frequently, defendants delete on the form the wrong alternative, leaving the other alternative: 'I do not wish to challenge the accuracy of the amount alleged to be due . . .', and then proceed to write as mitigating circumstances a statement that the vehicle has only just been purchased, that the vehicle has been kept in the garage or some other statement showing that the amount of back-duty is inappropriate. It is submitted that the court can and should adjourn such cases to give the defendant an opportunity of disputing the back-duty. Section 34, it is submitted, only requires the court to order payment of back-duty where the defendant unequivocally accepts the amount of back-duty or does not answer at all regarding the back-duty.

### 12.29 Limitation

Offences of failure to notify change of ownership are not continuing offences (see 12.36).

It should be noted that the special time limit in s 28 only applies to the particular offences specified in s 28 together with any offence under regulations made in pursuance of the Act. The period of six months runs from the date of the discovery of the offence although the overriding limit of three years runs from the date of the commission of the offence. The extended time limit given by s 28 is now otiose so far as prosecutions under s 26(1) or (2) are concerned. The offence under s 26(1) or (2) is an 'either way' offence and there is no time limit under s 127 of the Magistrates' Courts Act 1980 for 'either way' offences.

It may also be noted that a certificate of the authorised prosecutor shall be conclusive evidence of the date of discovery of the offence by him and the approval of the institution of proceedings by the Secretary of State for Transport. This may be contrasted with the signature of the certificate, which is deemed to be signed on behalf of the Secretary of State 'unless the contrary is proved'.

A right of appeal by the prosecutor to the Crown Court is given by the Customs and Excise Management Act 1979, s 147(3); *quaere* whether this applies only to 'excise duties' (see above under 'Venue').

In *R* v *Godstone JJ, ex parte Secretary of State for the Environment* [1974] Crim LR 110 it was held that a summons which did not bear the date upon which the information was laid was not ineffectual. It is only where there is some question as to whether the information was laid in time that it is material. It is submitted that if there is any question whether the information was laid in time, it is the duty of the prosecution to give proof of the date of laying of the information because an information for a purely summary offence laid out of time renders the proceedings a nullity.

## 12.30 Mitigated penalties

The Secretary of State for Transport is, by s 3 of the Vehicles (Excise) Act 1971, given the same powers of mitigation and remission of penalty as are possessed by the Commissioners of Customs and Excise in respect of customs offences.

The power conferred by s 3(3) to offer a mitigated penalty is used by the Secretary of State in a very large number of cases under s 8 of using a vehicle without an excise licence. The offender is sent a letter offering him the opportunity of paying a mitigated penalty within fourteen days if he would like to avoid being prosecuted. This procedure is used only where the vehicle has been unlicensed for less than six months (three months in London) and also where the offender is not being prosecuted for other offences committed on the same occasion.

The mitigated penalty is calculated by the formula of: Back duty lost × $1\frac{1}{2}$ + £10, eg where the tax for a car is two months overdue the mitigated penalty is £34.99: £100 (annual car tax) × 2 (months)/12 (months) × $1\frac{1}{2}$ + £10.

If the offender does not pay within fourteen days he is prosecuted either by the Department of Transport or by an authorised policeman. Magistrates have been advised by the Association of the procedure (see *The Magistrate*, August 1979).

The power to offer a mitigated penalty applies only 'with respect to the duty of excise chargeable under this Act and the excise licences provided for thereby' (s 3(3)). It would seem therefore to apply only to excise penalties and not to fines for summary offences under the Act, eg s 12(4). In *Pilgram* v *Dean* at 12.16 the court laid stress on the fact that an offence under s 8 attracted an excise penalty and an offence under s 12(4) was punishable by a fine.

It is submitted that it may be proper for a court to be informed after the conviction of the amount of the mitigated penalty offered to a defendant by the prosecution.

### 12.31–5 Remission of fine or penalty

By reason of the definition of 'fine' contained in s 85(2) of the Magistrates' Courts Act 1980, on an enquiry into a defendant's means after non-payment of a fine where there has been a change in the defendant's circumstances magistrates may remit the whole or part of a fine imposed under s 12(4) (failure to exhibit a licence), s 26(1) and s 26(2) (false declarations, forgery and fraudulent use of licences), s 22 (failure to display number plates), s 27 (failure to give information) and s 37 (breach of regulations), but magistrates may not do so in respect of any penalties imposed under s 8 (no excise licence), s 18(4) (using a vehicle without paying a higher rate of duty), any order for payment of back-duty under ss 9 or 18A and any penalty under s 16(7) (trade licence offences) (see 12.46–9).

It may be worthwhile to note that the distinction between an 'offence' punishable with a fine and a contravention punishable with a 'penalty' generally (but see the Vehicles (Excise) Act 1971, s 28(5)) means that the Customs and Excise Management Act 1979 applies to the latter but probably not to the former. It should be remembered that under s 147(3) of the Customs and Excise Management Act 1979 the prosecutor has a right of appeal to the Crown Court against any decision of a magistrates' court in proceedings for an offence to which that Act applies.

## Excise Licences: Registration

### 12.36 Registration and licensing

The relevant regulations are the Road Vehicles (Registration and Licensing) Regulations 1971 (SI 1971 No 450), as amended by SIs 1971 No 1285, 1972 No 1865, 1975 Nos 1089 and 1342, 1976 Nos 1680 and 2089, 1977 No 230, 1978 No 1536, 1981 No 366, 1982 No 1802, 1983 No 1248 and 1984 No 814).

The 1971 Regulations define 'works truck' as in reg 3 of the Construction and Use Regulations; Sched 3 to the Act is similar but uses the word 'vicinity' instead of 'neighbourhood' (see 8.2 and 12.5).

By reg 3(1) of the 1971 regulations 'owner' means in relation to a vehicle the person by whom it is kept. By reg 16 the licence in force shall be fixed to and exhibited on the vehicle at all times while it is kept or used on a public road (see *Pilgram* v *Dean* and *Strowger* v *John* at 12.16 and in particular *Elliott* v

*Grey* as to 'use' when stationary at 1.79, and as to 'keeping' see s 38(2) at 12.2). The only defence at present to a charge of failing to exhibit a licence, contrary to s 12 (until s 12(5) is brought into force), is contained in the proviso to reg 16(1), which allows an applicant at a post office to detach the licence in order to apply for a new licence, and allows the new licence to be displayed in place of the old licence even though the new licence may not be in force. The manner and place of exhibition are also prescribed. Regulation 7 forbids alteration of a licence or exhibition of a faded or altered licence or document which could be mistaken for a licence (it will be noted that an offence contrary to reg 7 appears to be absolute; the regulation may be contrasted with s 26 (see Chapter 16) which makes it an offence to use, etc, a licence 'fraudulently'). Other regulations relate to the production of registration books (reg 8(2)) and to the duty of vendors and purchasers of motor vehicles to notify the registration authority of the sale and of changes of address and of alterations to the vehicle (regs 10–15). Many of these duties are cast on 'the owner' and a summons alleging an offence by the owner under these regulations, committed after he had ceased to be owner, is bad, although he has omitted to notify the change of ownership and the vehicle is still registered in his name (*Spain* v *Johns* (1950) 48 LGR 532). Of course, by reg 12(1) he committed an offence as 'the previous owner' by failing to report the change. Failure to notify the registration authority is not a continuing offence and time runs from a day or two after the change of ownership (*A & C McLennan* (*Blairgowrie*) *Ltd* v *MacMillan* 1964 SLT 2) but the special time limit of s 28 applies (see 12.29). See s 8(3)(*a*) at 12.19 as to the effect of non-delivery of the licence on transfer.

Regulations 17–22 and Scheds 2 and 3 relate to the exhibition and position of registration marks; the figures and letters must be white, silver or light grey, indelible and on a black surface, save where translucent; or where the plate is constructed of reflex reflecting material the letters and figures must be black, and the front number must have a white reflex reflecting background and the rear a yellow reflex reflecting background. It is submitted that these paragraphs (paras 6, 7 and 8 of Part II of Sched 2) do not prohibit a vehicle first registered prior to 1 January 1973 from displaying a white plate in front and a black one at the rear or a black plate in front and a yellow one at the rear; otherwise there would be the absurd result that, while a vehicle with black plates front and rear would be legal, one with a white plate in front and a black at the rear (or a black in front and a yellow at the rear) would not, notwithstanding that the white and yellow plates are easier to see than the black and consequently the vehicle would be safer than one with two black plates. All vehicles required to display number plates, other than the exceptions specified in the Schedule, are required by para 5A to display the new type reflex number plates if the vehicle was registered on or after 1 January 1973. Schedule 3 makes special provision as to the position and visibility of registration marks on vehicles registered before 1 October 1938. It should be noted that Sched 3, para 14 as to illumination has been revoked. The Vehicles (Excise) Act 1971, s 22, applies to all vehicles; it provides certain defences in respect of obscured, unfixed or unlit marks.

Part VI and Sched 4 prescribe the additional marks to be displayed by hackney carriages and the method of computing their seating capacity; Part IV relates to vehicles exempt from duty, and requires certain declarations to be made in respect of them, and Part VII indicates the method of calculating horse-power, cylinder capacity and unladen weight.

Regulation 45 empowers the Secretary of State for Transport to require a certificate of weight of a vehicle or to have the vehicle made available for weighing.

## 12.37 Rear number plate lamps

The fitting, maintenance, keeping lit and use of rear registration plate lamps is governed by the Road Vehicles Lighting Regulations 1984 (SI 1984 No 812). See 8.84. There is also an offence under reg 19(1) as amended of using, causing or permitting to be used (see Chapter 1) on a road during the hours of darkness any motor vehicles unless every letter and number of the rear index plate of the rearmost vehicle is illuminated so as to be easily legible as specified in the absence of fog. This does not apply to works trucks and vehicles not required to be fitted with a rear index plate. The 1984 Regulations concentrate on the lamps themselves and the 1971 Regulations concentrate on the provision of illumination. Nevertheless there is some overlap and the penalties are different. The 1984 Regulations also apply in seriously reduced visibility, but reg 19(1) only applies during the hours of darkness. Where there is in effect only one failure it is submitted that two convictions should not be recorded—see 5.49.

The defence in s 22 (see above) applies to reg 19(1) offences only. The case of *Printz* v *Sewell* at 12.20 was a case on an unlit mark under the former reg 19 and would seem still to be applicable. The offence under reg 19, like the Lighting Regulations offences but unlike many of the offences under the 1971 Regulations, applies on any road and not merely a public road.

## 12.38 'Computerised' and other figures on number plates

Although very detailed, neither the Vehicles (Excise) Act nor the regulations specify the type of figures. A number of vehicles now display 'computer type' numerals. Probably when the regulations were drafted no one considered the possibility of anything but normal figures. There seems to be nothing which expressly renders 'computer type' figures illegal. Regulation 18(3), however, states that the registration mark 'shall be fixed and displayed . . . so that in normal daylight the letters and figures are easily legible from every part of the relevant area'. There is a letter on the subject at 142 JP 746. The opinion is tentatively advanced that if '5' can be mistaken for 'S' or vice versa the letters cannot be said to be 'easily legible'. If a number may be mistaken for a letter it cannot be said to be 'legible' which means 'clear enough to be deciphered'. It would seem therefore that an offence under reg 18(3) may be committed.

The regulations refer to letters and figures. Roman numerals are based on letters and not figures. A magistrates' court has convicted a man who showed his registration numbers in Roman numeral letters. While the decision is not binding it would seem that the figures should be shown in figures and not letters. The purpose of the regulation is that number plates should be easily read.

### 12.39–45 Penalty

The Vehicles (Excise) Act 1971 provides that, in effect, a breach of the regulations is punishable with a maximum fine of £20. Section 31 of the Criminal Law Act 1977 provides that, where certain penalties have not been increased since the end of 1948, they shall be increased by that Act. By s 31(9) this increase applies to 'an enactment passed before 1 January 1949 or an enactment passed on or after that date which (whether directly or, through successive re-enactments, indirectly) re-enacts with or without modification an enactment passed before that date'. The Vehicles (Excise) Acts have been re-enacted several times, but s 12 of the Roads Act 1920 seems to be in similar form to the relevant regulation provisions of the 1971 Act. This seems to mean that the maximum penalty has been increased by the 1977 Act and subsequent amendments to a fine of level 3. If the 1977 Act did not increase the penalty the new maximum is a fine of level 1.

There is no power to endorse, disqualify or order penalty points.

## Trade Licences

### 12.46 Generally

A motor trader or vehicle tester may, on payment of the appropriate rate of duty, apply to the Secretary of State for Transport for a trade licence under the Vehicles (Excise) Act 1971, s 16. A motor trader may apply for a licence to cover all mechanically propelled vehicles which are from time to time temporarily in his possession in the course of his business as a motor trader and all recovery vehicles kept by him for the purpose of dealing with disabled vehicles (s 16(1)(i)). A vehicle tester may apply for a licence to cover all mechanically propelled vehicles which are from time to time submitted to him for testing in the course of his business as a vehicle tester (s 16(1)(ii)). A motor trader who is a manufacturer of mechanically propelled vehicles may apply for a licence to cover all vehicles kept and used by him wholly and solely for purposes of conducting research and development in the course of his business as a manufacturer (s 16(1)(iii)). Restrictions on the use and purposes to which the vehicles may be put are contained in the proviso to s 16(1) and in s 16(3).

Days of grace are not allowed for the purpose of renewing trade licences.

The Road Vehicles (Registration and Licensing) Regulations 1971, Part V, have been made under s 16 to prescribe the conditions subject to which trade licences are issued and the purposes for which the holder of a trade licence may use a vehicle under the licence. Regulation 28 relates to applications for trade licences, reg 29 prescribes twenty-eight days as the period for requesting review of a decision refusing a trade licence, reg 30 requires the holder to notify the Secretary of State for Transport of any change in the name or address of his business and in such a case also to forward his trade licence for amendment, reg 31 prescribes the issue and replacement of trade plates, and reg 32 forbids the alteration or mutilation of trade plates or the exhibition of anything which might be mistaken for a trade plate. Regulation 33 relates to the exhibition of trade plates and licences, reg 34 restricts the use of trade plates and licences, regs 35–37 prescribe the conditions for which a vehicle may be used under a trade licence, regs 38 and 39 prohibit the conveyance of goods on vehicles used under a trade licence and reg 40 prohibits the carriage of passengers on such vehicles.

## 12.47 Improper use of vehicles under a trade licence

It is an offence under s 16(7) of the Vehicles (Excise) Act 1971 for a person holding a trade licence or licences issued under s 16 and the regulations to use on a public road by virtue of that licence or those licences (i) a greater number of vehicles at any one time than he is authorised to use under the licence(s); or (ii) any vehicle for any purpose other than such purposes as may have been prescribed by regulations made under s 16(2). It is also an offence if he uses the licence(s) for the purpose of keeping on a road a vehicle which is not being used on that road.

It will be seen that in effect s 16(7) creates three different offences.

For the meaning of 'using' and 'keeping', see the definition of 'use' in Chapter 1 and also 12.2.

*A 'Public road'*

The offences under s 16(7)(i) and (ii) are only committed if the vehicle is on a public road. This is also true of most offences under the regulations. For the meaning of 'public road' see the comments on vehicle excise licence offences at 12.2. It will be noted that the term 'public road' is not used in relation to the third offence under s 16(7). The effect of this is that it is an offence to use a trade licence to keep a vehicle on a 'road' (see 1.66–71) when the vehicle is not being used.

*B 'Holder of a trade licence'*

The offences under s 16(7) can be committed only by the holder of a trade licence. A non-licence holder may be convicted as an aider and abettor but mens rea will be required. The regulations should be studied carefully as some apply only to the holder of a licence and others apply generally (see *Waugh* v *Paterson* (1924) 68 SJ 52).

*C 'Prescribed business purposes'*

The vehicle must be used for a business purpose or an offence is committed. Under the former regulations a holder was allowed to use a trade licence not only for a 'business purpose', which was defined in identical terms to those now set out in reg 35(1)(*a*) and (*b*), but also for any additional purpose as long as it was used at the same time for a 'business purpose'. This was found difficult to control and the present regulations, instead of allowing the purposes to be unspecified, specify the purposes in detail in reg 35(4)(*a*)–(*l*).

Although at first sight it appears that an offence is committed under reg 35(4), it is submitted that a defendant should be charged under s 16(7)(ii), since the purpose of reg 35 is to define and delimit s 16(7)(ii) in accordance with s 16(2). In any case s 18 of the Interpretation Act 1978 prevents two convictions for the same offence under two separate Acts and the same principle would presumably apply.

The cases on the pre-1970 regulations are generally of little use on the present regulations. Although most of them turned on the question of 'business purpose', they are now of little help because the present regulations only allow trade plates to be used for one of the specific business purposes set out in reg 35(4)(*a*)–(*l*) or reg 36.

One case on 'business purpose' under the former regulations may be helpful by way of example. In *Murphy* v *Brown* [1970] Crim LR 234 the defendant was the holder of trade plates issued for use in his business as a repairer and dealer in motor vehicles. He bartered a vehicle for a pony and towed the pony to pony rides in a trailer, making use of the trade plates. It was held that the process was unauthorised and the defendant was guilty. The use must be in connection with the defendant's business (in this case as repairer or dealer). It was not sufficient that the use was in general connected with the business (ibid).

By way of contrast a magistrates' court has held that the temporary use by a motor trader of a towing vehicle and trailer with trade plates to draw a large model moon rocket was for the purpose of his business. The moon rocket was being delivered for a temporary forecourt display and advertisement was held to be an essential ingredient of the modern business. There appears to be nothing in reg 35(4)(*a*)–(*l*) which would allow such a piece of equipment to be conveyed in a carnival on trade plates but the use of a showroom model on trade plates in a carnival might be held to be a test or trial for the benefit of a prospective purchaser.

In the pre-1970 regulations the term 'prospective purchaser' included a possible purchaser (*Helson* v *Barnard* 1922 SLT 40), and this decision would appear to apply to reg 35(4)(*c*) of the 1971 Regulations.

As indicated, the business purposes are specified and an offence is committed if the vehicle is used for any other purpose, business or otherwise. It is immaterial that the vehicle is also being used for a specified business purpose.

*D 'Vehicles temporarily in his possession'*

It should be noted that, except for recovery vehicles and vehicles used by motor manufacturers under reg 36 solely for the purpose of research and development, a vehicle may not be used under trade plates unless it is temporarily in the possession of the motor trader (reg 35(3)). A motor trader who carries on the business of collecting and delivering vehicles may legitimately use trade plates for this purpose (see reg 35(4)(*g*)–(*k*)), but where part of the business of the motor trader was to collect and deliver trailers from one factory where they were partly assembled to another factory where the trailers were completed, a magistrates' court has held that the motor trader could not use trade plates on the vehicles which towed the trailers unless the towing vehicles as well as the trailers were temporarily in the possession of the motor trader. Regulation 35(2), which requires the towing vehicle and trailer to be treated as one vehicle, could not be construed in such a way that the towing vehicle could therefore be said to be temporarily in the possession of the motor trader merely because the trailer was.

*E 'Recovery vehicles', 'workshops'*

As to 'recovery vehicles' see 1.17. Regulation 35(4)(*h*) allows a trade licence to be used for a vehicle proceeding to or returning from a workshop in which a body or a special type of equipment or accessory is to be or has been fitted to it or in which it is to be or has been painted or repaired. In *Bowers* v *Worthington* [1982] RTR 400 a vehicle was used under trade plates to carry six container bases. Each in turn was to be built up on the vehicle in question in the workshop. It was held that the purpose was not that of having the bases fitted to the particular vehicle and the use was not covered by the trade plates. There would be a breach of reg 38(1)(*d*) ('relevant purpose'). Ormrod LJ at p 404 said that, looking at reg 35(4)(*h*) in its context, what was contemplated was a vehicle being taken to a workshop to be fitted, more or less permanently, with either a body or some special type of equipment. It could not mean the vehicle standing as a kind of dummy.

## 12.48 Display of trade plates

By reg 33 trade plates must be fixed and displayed so that they comply with reg 18 (display) and reg 19 (illumination) as if they were registration marks. Under reg 18 the display must be 'on both the front and the back of the vehicle'. From this it seems that trade plates lodged on the front dashboard or the rear shelf would be held not to be displayed on the front or the back. This is borne out by the reference to reg 19.

## 12.49–55 Offences under the regulations

The restriction on the use of trade plates and trade licences by persons other than licence holders in reg 34, the restriction on the conveyance of goods and burdens in regs 38 and 39 and the widely drawn restrictions on the carriage of passengers in reg 40 should be particularly noted.

Regulation 34 prohibits the loan of trade plates to a friend unless the friend drives the vehicle and it is being used for the licence holder. The restrictions on use in reg 35 should be borne in mind. An independent contractor or a hirer may similarly drive in accordance with reg 34 providing the use is that of the licence holder.

Regulation 34 should be compared with reg 40 (restriction on the carriage of passengers), where the term 'employee' is used. Regulation 40 will normally preclude the carriage of hitch-hikers, spouses, children and friends as passengers.

## Trade Licences: Proceedings and Penalties

### 12.56 Generally

The penalty under s 16(7) is a fine of level 3 or five times the actual duty, whichever is the greater (for calculation of the penalty see 12.18). The penalty for a breach of the regulations is also a fine of level 3 (Vehicles (Excise) Act 1971, s 37(3)(*b*) as modified by Sched 7). For a discussion of how the penalty of a fine of level 3 is arrived at, see 12.39.

A vehicle bearing trade plates for which their use is unlawful will usually not have a current vehicles excise licence. In such a case a prosecution under s 8 may be brought, particularly if the user was not the holder of the trade plates.

Offences may be tried by magistrates only. Any person may prosecute for an offence under the regulations. For offences under s 16(7) the time limit is six months from the discovery of the offence by the prosecutor, subject to an overriding time limit of three years from the date of the offence and only the Secretary of State for Transport or a constable with his approval may prosecute (see 12.27).

Magistrates cannot remit payment wholly or partly of a penalty under s 16(7) on a means enquiry under s 44 of the Criminal Justice Act 1967, as the penalty is not a 'fine': *aliter* a fine for breach of the regulations (see 12.31). The special time limit under s 28 applies to breach of the regulations.

Because the punishment under s 16(7) is expressed as a 'penalty' and not as an 'offence' punishable with a fine, the various provisions of the Customs and Excise Acts apply where they have not been expressly excluded (see s 28(5) of the 1971 Act and also 12.31).

There is no power to endorse, disqualify or order penalty points.

As to the prosecutor's right of appeal to the Crown Court, see 12.29.

# Chapter 13

# Goods and Passenger Vehicles

## Goods Vehicle Operators' Licences

### 13.1 Generally

The licensing of a goods vehicle for the carriage of goods for hire or reward or for or in connection with a trade or business comes under Part V of the Transport Act 1968. Substantial changes have been made regarding goods vehicle operators' licences: see the Transport Act 1982, s 52, Sched 4, Sched 5, para 6 and Sched 6 (so far as it relates to the Transport Act 1968) which came into force on 1 June 1984. See also the Goods Vehicles (Operators' Licences) (Qualifications and Fees) Regulations 1984 (SI 1984 No 176), in force on the same date.

### 13.2 Licensing requirements

An operator's licence is required under s 60 from the area chairman of the Traffic Commissioners (see s 59) for the use on a road of a goods vehicle for the carriage of goods (*a*) for hire or reward, or (*b*) for or in connection with any trade or business carried on by the applicant. The regulations under which operators' licences are obtained are the Goods Vehicles (Operators' Licences) (Qualifications and Fees) Regulations 1984 (SI 1984 No 176).

Later sections of Part V indicate the procedure for applying for an operator's licence.

Provision is made by s 85 of the Act and reg 32 of and Sched 4 to the regulations as to operators' licences in respect of holding companies and subsidiaries.

Part V of the Act is not applied to vehicles of the Crown or of visiting forces.

The definitions section for the purposes of Part V is s 92; the latter part of s 92(1) applies definitions in the Road Traffic Act 1960, eg 'road', 'light locomotive' and so on. Section 92 is supplemented by the definitions in the regulations (reg 11(1)).

Schedule 10 to the Act applies provisions of the Road Traffic Act 1960 as to powers of vehicle examiners, duty to give information as to driver's identity, forging, altering, using etc with intent to deceive, false statements and calculation of weight, certificates and diplomas of qualification for the purposes of Part V of the Act.

## 13.3 Types of licence

The 1984 Regulations implement, in relation to Great Britain, EEC Council Directives 74/561 of 12 November 1974 (OJ No L 308/18), (admission to the occupation of road haulage operator in national and international transport operations) and 77/796 of 12 December 1977 (OJ No L 334/37) (mutual recognition of diplomas, certificates and other qualifications). Under the Regulations, operators' licences under Part V of the Transport Act 1968 are divided into two classes:

*Standard operators' licences*

Under these goods vehicles may be used either for hire or reward as well as for or in connection with a trade or business carried on by the holder of the licence. The types of licence are further divided into two in that they may cover the carriage of goods for hire or reward on both international and national transport operations (sometimes called international standard operators' licences) or may cover such carriage on national transport operations only (sometimes called national standard operators' licences).

*Restricted operators' licences*

Under these goods vehicles may only be used for or in connection with a trade or business carried on by the holder of the licence.

In general the provisions of Part V of the 1968 Act so far as in force continue to apply to both types of operator's licence, but by the Qualifications Regulations the provisions are made more stringent with regard to the repute, financial standing and professional competence of applicants for standard operators' licences, or one of the partners, or their transport managers as appropriate. As with the Part V provisions, there are special arrangements for holding companies and subsidiaries under the regulations.

## 13.4 Professional competence

New entrants to the industry have to qualify as to good repute, appropriate financial standing and professional competence (reg 5 and Sched 6). In determining good repute, the licensing authority must have regard to relevant convictions of the individual applicant, company, company officers, employees and agents and their conduct generally. They have to obtain from a body approved by the Secretary of State for Transport a certificate as to their skills in certain subjects specified in the annex to the Council directive, or obtain some other certificate of competence, diploma or other qualification approved for the purpose by the Secretary of State, if they are to meet the requirements prescribed for the holder of a standard operator's licence or for his partner or transport manager(s) (Qualifications Regulations, reg 5 and Sched 6). Only an individual will be regarded as professionally competent in this way (Sched 6(3)). Regulation 5(3) requires one partner of a partnership which applies for a standard operator's licence to be professionally competent and to 'be responsible for the operation of the vehicles used under the licence'. This requirement does not, however, necessarily involve the professionally competent partner spending a substantial proportion of his working time discharging that responsibility; see *Baker and Baker* (1984) Appeal 1983 No U 19, Transport Tribunal (overruling the licensing authority on that point). It is sufficient (even if the professionally competent partner has another, full-time, job) if he spends enough time on it to carry out the work satisfactorily.

## 13.5 Exemptions

By s 60 (2) an operator's licence is not required in cases specified in the regulations or for the use of a 'small goods vehicle'. 'Small goods vehicle' is defined in s 60 (4) as being, in the case of a lone vehicle without a trailer, one with a plated (ie laden) weight of 3.5 tonnes or less or, if it has no plated weight, with an unladen weight of 1,525 kg or less; see s 60 (4) as to the term 'relevant plated weight' and also as to the definition of 'small goods vehicle' in relation to an articulated vehicle or a goods vehicle linked with a trailer or trailers. Basically for the 3.5 tonnes or 1,525 kg limits to apply the aggregate weight of all the vehicles and trailers in a vehicle combination must be below that limit (excluding any small trailer) but for articulated vehicles only the aggregate weight of the combination (ie the drawing vehicle and superimposed trailer) must be below that limit, and other drawn trailers are not taken into account. Under reg 3 and para 24 of Sched 1, a vehicle first used before 1 January 1977 which has an unladen weight not exceeding 1,525 kg, and for which the maximum gross weight on the Construction and Use Regulations exceeds 3.5 tonnes but does not exceed three and a half tons, is exempt from the requirement of an operator's licence.

Regulation 34 of the regulations, together with Sched 5, exempts twenty-seven classes of vehicle from the necessity of obtaining operators' licences. These include dual-purpose vehicles (as defined in reg 3 (1) of the Construction and Use Regulations), public service vehicles, hackney carriages, road-cleansing vehicles, vehicles used for police, fire brigade or ambulance purposes, showmen's goods vehicles and trailers drawn thereby and vehicles used for the purposes of funerals. In this context 'showman's goods vehicle' means a vehicle registered under the Vehicles (Excise) Act 1971 in the name of a person following the business of a travelling showman and used solely by him for the purposes of his business and no other (Sched 1, para 24 and reg 3(1)). Clearly use for private purposes would not mean that an operator's licence would be required. See further 'Showmen's vehicles' at 12.6; in *Bowra* v *Dann Catering Co Ltd* noted there convictions for both no operator's licence and under payment of vehicle excise duty were directed.

One of the exemptions in Sched 1 is for vehicles fitted with a machine, appliance, apparatus or other contrivance which is a permanent or essentially permanent fixture, provided that the only goods carried on the vehicle are such as are required for use in connection with it or the running of the vehicle.

In *North West Traffic Area Licensing Authority* v *Post Office* [1982] RTR 304, the Post Office used a goods vehicle with a machine for drilling telephone pole holes. The justices found that the vehicle carried in addition goods for erecting the poles, a kettle and the poles themselves. The Divisional Court directed a conviction. The telegraph poles were not for use in connection with the machine but for the operation in which the machine was going to be used. They were not therefore within the exemption proviso and an operator's licence was required. The court made no comment about the kettle.

The decision was followed in *British Gypsum Ltd* v *Corner* [1982] RTR 308. There the vehicle carried a water bowser and pipes for use in connection with a drill. An operator's licence was required as the drill was mounted on another vehicle.

The Goods Vehicles (Operators' Licences) (Temporary Use in Great Britain) Regulations 1980 (SI 1980 No 637), as amended by SI 1981 Nos 37 and 527, 1983 No 1832 and 1984 Nos 179 and 1835, modify the relevant sections of the Transport Act in respect of foreign and Northern Ireland goods vehicles. Regulation 3 defines a 'foreign goods vehicle' as a goods vehicle:

(*a*) which has been brought temporarily into Great Britain and does not remain in Great Britain for more than three months; and
(*b*) which is engaged in carrying goods by road on a journey, some part of which has taken place, or will take place, outside the United Kingdom; and
(*c*) which is not used at any time during the said journey for the carriage of goods loaded at one place in the United Kingdom and delivered at another place in the United Kingdom.

The word 'temporarily' was construed as 'casually'. If the vehicle is brought regularly, although intermittently, into Great Britain it is not 'temporarily' in Great Britain (*BRS* v *Wurzal* [1971] 3 All ER 480). The regulations make special provision for Northern Ireland or foreign goods vehicles used for the carriage of goods in the EEC, Austrian, Belgian, Bulgarian, Channel Islands, Cypriot, Czechoslovakian, Danish, Dutch, Finnish, French, German (both East and West), Greek, Hungarian, Italian, Jordanian, Luxembourg, Manx, Norwegian, Polish, Portuguese, Rumanian, Spanish, Swedish, Swiss, Turkish and Yugoslavian goods vehicles by dispensing with the need for them to have operators' licences, substituting a requirement in certain circumstances for the carrying of other permits or documents, and modifying (as set out in various schedules to the regulations) s 60 of the Transport Act 1968. The regulations also provide (see reg 34 (2) and Sched 5, Part II) for alterations to the 1984 Regulations in relation to foreign goods vehicles temporarily in Great Britain and fulfilling the terms of the definition and make special provisions for the Irish Republic.

## 13.6 Authorised vehicles

The vehicles which are authorised to be used under an operator's licence are specified in s 61(1) of the Act. Section 61(2) restricts the authorisation of vehicles to vehicles whose operating centres are for the time being within the area of the licensing authority by whom the licence was granted (or outside that area if the operating centres have not been there for a period of more than three months).

Note that by s 61(5) a motor vehicle can be specified in only one licence. *Semble*, if two licences are issued for one vehicle, the second one may be void and any conditions attached to the second one issued in point of time may be void also, so that it may not be an offence to fail to comply with a condition of the second one.

The licensing authority under the earlier (1960) Act could lawfully specify the type as well as the number of trailers to be used under an A licence and specify a particular trailer by the maker's number (*Arthur Sanderson* (*Great Broughton*) *Ltd* v *Vickers* (1964) 108 SJ 425). Under s 61 of the Transport Act 1968 the licensing authority can now specify different types of motor vehicles or trailers and specify the maximum numbers for each type.

## 13.7 Using a goods vehicle without an operator's licence

Section 60, subject to exceptions, requires any user of a goods vehicle (other than a small goods vehicle or a vehicle in a specified class) on a road for the carriage of goods for hire or reward or for or in connection with any trade or business carried on by him to hold an operator's licence. A person who uses a vehicle in contravention of the section commits an offence (s 60(5)).

### A *'Goods vehicle'*

Only goods vehicles, ie vehicles and trailers constructed or adapted to carry goods, need licences under the Transport Act. By s 92(1) and (5) goods-carrying trailers are included and trams and trolley-vehicles operated under statutory powers excluded.

A van adapted for the carriage of passengers and used only to carry samples to the owner's place of business was held not to be a goods vehicle in *Tait* v *Odhams Press* (1937) 26 Traff Cas 80, where certain exempting regulations were also in point. Where a passenger vehicle has been altered to carry goods, the test whether the vehicle is a goods or passenger one is whether it would, if it had been constructed in its altered condition, still be regarded as a vehicle used to carry passengers and their effects (*Flower Freight Co* v *Hammond* [1962] 3 All ER 950, further discussed at 1.12). Passengers' effects are not goods (ibid). A shooting-brake or other utility vehicle would be within the Act if used to carry goods for reward or in connection with a trade or business (cf *Taylor* v *Thompson* [1956] 1 All ER 352), but many will be exempt as being under 1,525 kg (s 60 (4) (*a*)). The term 'goods vehicle' includes a van used only for carrying a window cleaner's ladders, rags and buckets, as these are goods (*Clarke* v *Cherry* [1953] 1 All ER 267). A decision of magistrates that a car adapted to carry dresses hung on rails at the back was not adapted to carry goods was upheld in *Taylor* v *Mead* [1961] 1 All ER 626. It is submitted that, as in s 92 the term 'adapted' is contrasted with 'constructed', the former means 'altered physically so as to make fit for the purpose' (*Maddox* v *Storer* [1962] 1 All ER 831) (see further Chapter 1 and in particular the definitions of 'adapted' and 'constructed' at 1.12).

An essential ingredient of the offence of using a vehicle without an operator's licence under s 60 of the Transport Act 1968 is that the vehicle is carrying goods at the relevant time (*Robertson* v *Crew* [1977] RTR 141).

*B 'Use'*

Note that an offence under s 60 can only be committed by a person who 'uses' in contravention of s 60; any person who is not a 'user' can be charged only with aiding and abetting use. By s 92 (2) the driver, if he is the owner or is in possession under a hire-purchase agreement, etc, and in any other case the person whose servant or agent the driver is, is deemed to be the user; normally therefore an employed driver should not be charged under s 60 and the High Court said in *Carpenter* v *Campbell* [1953] 1 All ER 280 that, where it is the employer's duty to get the licence, the driver should not be prosecuted. For a case in which an employment agency who introduced drivers to haulage companies were held not to be the employers of the drivers and thus could not be prosecuted by virtue of s 92 (2) when a client haulage company had no operator's licence, see *Alderton* v *Richard Burgon Associates Ltd* [1974] RTR 422. And see 1.79 as to the meaning of 'use'.

It is very doubtful whether a lorry returning from a place where it has carried goods for hire or reward or going to a place where it will carry goods for hire or reward can be said at such times to be used on the road for carriage of goods for hire or reward (per Lord Parker CJ in *Roberts* v *Morris* [1965] Crim LR 46). By the definition in s 92 of the Transport Act 1968, 'authorised vehicle' means one authorised to be used under an operator's licence whether or not it is for the time being in use for a purpose for which an operator's licence is required and whether or not it is specified therein as so authorised.

*C 'Hire or reward'*

The leading case on the meaning of 'hire or reward' is *Albert* v *Motor Insurers' Bureau* [1971] 2 All ER 1345. This was not a case on an operator's licence but on s 203(4) of the Road Traffic Act 1960, which exempted a driver of a motor vehicle from being required to insure against passenger liability provided the passengers were not carried for 'hire or reward'. The House of Lords disapproved *Coward* v *Motor Insurers' Bureau* [1962] 1 All ER 531, where it was held that 'hire or reward' meant a monetary reward legally recoverable under a contract express or implied, and held that the test as to whether a vehicle was being used for 'hire or reward' was whether there had been a systematic carrying of passengers for reward which went beyond the bounds of mere social kindness. It was immaterial that no contractual relationship was intended. The words 'hire or reward' must be read disjunctively.

A garage proprietor who used a converted bus only for the purpose of transporting a stock car to stock car race meetings where it competed for modest prizes was acquitted of using the converted bus without an operator's licence for goods vehicles, contrary to s 60 (use of vehicle for hire or reward or in connection with a trade or business) (*Stirk* v *McKenna* [1984] RTR 330). It was conceded that in the light of *Customs and Excise Commissioners* v *Lord Fisher* [1981] 2 All ER 147 and *Blakemore* v *Bellamy* [1983] RTR 303, neither competing for prize money nor the receipt of money from sponsorship was sufficient to constitute a connection with a trade or business for the purpose of s 60.

A defendant trained horses for reward and it was his duty to see that they reached the racecourses; he carried a horse to a race meeting in an unlicensed vehicle. It was at the owner's discretion whether he paid the defendant for the transport and in fact he was not paid. The defendant was held not guilty under a corresponding Irish statute (*A-G* v *Brogan* (1953) 87 ILTR 181). A company owning a vehicle with a C licence agreed for an expected reward to arrange for the transport of goods from London to Northumberland; a vehicle belonging to another firm, with an A licence, was to take them from East London to Northumberland but the company's vehicle took them from North London to the starting point. A metropolitan magistrate held this journey to be part of the whole journey for arranging which the company was being paid and convicted the company of carrying goods without an A or B licence ([1954] Jo Crim L 219). Where a vehicle was used at a standard charge to empty a septic tank and dumped the effluent emptied from the tank on farmland some distance away, it was held that the effluent was 'goods' and that it was a carriage for reward (*Sweetway Sanitary Cleansers Ltd* v *Bradley* [1961] 2 All ER 821).

A C licence allowed the holder to use the vehicles for or in connection with any trade or business carried on by him but not for carrying goods for hire or reward. The vehicles were used to remove surplus excavated earth at an agreed price from a building site for the builders (third parties). The vehicle owner paid someone else to tip it. It was held that, as a large part of the payment was for the carriage of the rubbish, the vehicles were used to carry goods for reward, it being immaterial that the property in the earth passed to the vehicle owners when it was loaded (*Spittle* v *Thames Grit and Aggregates Ltd* [1937] 4 All ER 101). This case was distinguished by a metropolitan magistrate in *Metropolitan Traffic Commissioner* v *Alexander Thomson & Co* [1952] Jo Crim L 194, where the vehicle owners were themselves also the contractors who did the work of laying cables as well as removing the surplus earth.He held that this was not carrying goods for hire or reward requiring a B licence but was use in connection with the company's trade or business and was covered by their C licence. The prosecution did not appeal by case stated.

A firm of sand and gravel merchants excavating those materials from a pit were required by a planning condition to fill up the parts excavated. To do this, they took rubbish from a building site, the builder paying them 8s 6d per cubic yard of rubbish. The House of Lords held that, by virtue of s 164(5)(*a*) of the Road Traffic Act 1960, the rubbish was being used in the course of the sand merchant's business and was not being carried for reward (*Hammond* v *Hall and Ham River Ltd* [1965] 2 All ER 811, overruling *Corbett* v *Barham* [1965] 1 WLR 187).

A lorry owner went from *C* to *B* in Ireland to borrow some planks. The plank owner agreed to lend them but said they were at *F* and asked the lorry owner, when bringing them to *C*, to take some scaffolding for him at the same time. The lorry owner, when charged with carrying the scaffolding 'for reward', pleaded that he did so merely to oblige and he was found not guilty (*A-G* (*Holland*) v *Hurley* [1960] Jo Crim L 59, where conflicting views are discussed). In *Stewart* v *McFadyen* 1958 SLT (Sh) 7 it was held that a licence to carry building materials included granite chips for road making, as being road building materials. A stipendiary magistrate acquitted a coal merchant who had loaded his vehicle with scrap iron to see if it was likely in the future to be fit for use for carrying coal ([1958] Crim LR 693).

An incorporated society, consisting of miners at one colliery, delivering coal to one of its members at a charge to be deducted from his wages, uses the vehicle for hire or reward; *aliter* where it is an unincorporated society delivering to a member (*Wurzal* v *Houghton Main Home Delivery Service Ltd* [1936] 2 All ER 311).

Other cases on use in the course of the licence holder's business, carrying goods for process or treatment, use in agriculture and farmers' goods vehicles appear in the fifth edition of this book.

## 13.8 Conditions attached to licences

By s 66(1) conditions as to notifying certain matters may be attached to an operator's licence. Section 66(2) makes it an offence for any person to contravene any condition attached under s 66 to a licence of which he is the holder.

The conditions which a licensing authoritv may attach under s 66(1) may require the holder to inform him:

(*a*) of any change, of a kind specified in the conditions, in the organisation, management or ownership of the trade or business in the course of which the authorised vehicles are used;

(*b*) where the holder of a licence is a company, of any change, or of any change of a kind so specified, in the persons holding shares in the company;

(*c*) of any other event of a kind so specified affecting the holder of the licence which is relevant to the exercise of any powers of the authority in relation to the licence.

Under reg 7 of the Goods Vehicle Operators (Qualifications) Regulations 1984 it is obligatory on the licensing authority on the grant of a standard operator's licence to attach conditions requiring the licence holder to inform the authority of any such event as is referred to in the conditions set out in s 66(1) above as modified by reg 7(1). By the modifications it is necessary to notify any event which could affect the holder of the licence satisfying the requirements of good repute, appropriate financial standing and professional competence and to notify any similar event affecting the transport manager (save as to appropriate financial standing). In the case of the transport manager the reference to professional competence is to anything relied on by him to satisfy that requirement. The notification must be within twenty-eight days of the event.

The duty only refers to the licence holder and only concerns events affecting him and the transport manager and not other directors or employees, unless the happening is such as to reflect on the holder or transport manager himself. The duty on the face of it extends to the notification of convictions for dishonesty and relevant road traffic and transport convictions.

The appropriate licensing authority is the authority appropriate to any standard operator's licence granted to the holder concerned.

In the case of a company, it is not necessary for the holder to notify a shareholding change unless the control of the company passes. The exact meaning of a change in control is defined for this purpose by reg 7(4) and s 69(11) of the 1968 Act.

A reg 7 condition is to be treated as a s 66 condition and an offence may be committed accordingly (reg 7(2)).

Note that by s 61(5) a motor vehicle can be specified in only one licence. *Semble*, if two licences are issued for one vehicle, the second one may be void and any conditions attached to the second one issued in point of time may be void also, so that it may not be an offence to fail to comply with a condition of the second one.

An offence under s 66 can be committed only by the holder of an operator's licence or by a person who aids and abets him, as indicated at 13.*7B*. Some knowledge of the fact that the condition is being breached or possibly a wilful shutting of eyes to it is generally needed to prove aiding and abetting. As the licence holder will almost always know of the matters to be notified, when they arise, it seems unnecessary to discuss whether his liability is absolute or not; see 2.21 as to whether this would be a continuing offence.

Save under ss 69C (control on environmental grounds) and 66 (see above), no express power to attach conditions to an operator's licence is conferred.

### 13.9–15 Operating centres and environmental control

Part V of the 1984 Regulations sets out the provisions for operating centres. Their control on environmental grounds is governed by ss 69A–G inclusive. A person who uses (see 1.79) a place as an operating centre for authorised vehicles under an operator's licence which is not specified in the licence commits an offence which carries a maximum fine of level 4 (s 69A). It is necessary to advertise applications in the period twenty-one days before the date of application or twenty-one days after (s 69E). There is provision for objections. There is power to attach conditions on environmental grounds (s 69C and reg 21).

## Goods Vehicle Operators' Licences: Proceedings and Penalties

### 13.16–20 Generally

The following offences carry a maximum fine of level 4: use of a goods vehicle contrary to s 60 of the Transport Act 1968 without an operator's licence (s 60(5)); breach of the condition of an operator's licence (s 66(2)), including a breach of the condition of a standard operator's licence (s 66(2) and reg 7(2) of the 1984 Regulations) and the breach of an environmental condition (s 69C).

Section 69 of the 1968 Act empowers the licensing authority to revoke, suspend or curtail an operator's licence. Where an operator's licence is revoked, the operator may be disqualified from holding or obtaining an operator's licence. Any operator's licence obtained by a disqualified person in breach of the disqualification is of no effect and a person who applies for or who obtains a licence in breach of an order of disqualification commits an offence punishable on summary conviction by a fine of level 3 (s 69(5)).

A person who, under a standard operator's licence which covers national transport operations only, uses a goods vehicle for carrying goods for hire or reward on international transport operations contrary to reg 33(2) and a person who under a restricted licence uses a goods vehicle for hire or reward contrary to reg 33(3) are in each case liable to a maximum fine of £500.

The effect of s 40 of the Criminal Justice Act 1982 is merely to permit relevant increases under the subordinate legislation, and not to effect them. This view of the law is believed to be shared by the Home Office. Assuming this to be so the maximum fines under regs 33(2) and (3) will not automatically be increased when fine levels are increased. This should be contrasted with the regulations where the offence is specified to be under the relevant section of the Transport Act 1968 so that level increases will apply.

A person who contravenes or fails to comply with a provision of regs 25(3), 25(4), 27, 28, 29(1), 30(1), 30(2), 30(3) or 32(6) of the Goods Vehicles (Operators' Licences) Regulations commits an offence contrary to s 91(6) of the 1968 Act and is liable to a maximum fine of level 1.

The time limit for all the above offences is six months. The court has no power to endorse or disqualify or to revoke, suspend or curtail the operator's licence.

## Public Service Vehicle Licensing

### 13.21–5 Generally

The law as to the operation of public service vehicles (PSVs) is contained in the Public Passenger Vehicles Act 1981. The provisions as to PSV operators' licences and discs are in Part II of the 1981 Act. This system is similar to that for goods vehicle operators' licences. Note that a Transport Bill which may affect the position is now (1 April 1985) before Parliament.

Apart from s 25(2), the 1981 Act extends to Scotland.

The following sections deal with the definition and classification of PSVs, the licensing and fitness requirements relating thereto and the offences arising thereunder. Special types of services exempted from these requirements or subject to special provisions are considered at 13.34, 13.44, 13.56–8. The conduct of drivers, conductors and passengers on PSVs is considered at the end of this chapter, 13.61–5.

## PSVs: Definition and Classification

### 13.26 'Public service vehicle'

Section 1(1) of the 1981 Act defines a 'public service vehicle' for the purposes of the Act as a motor vehicle (other than a tramcar) which:

(*a*) if adapted to carry more than eight passengers, is used for carrying passengers for hire or reward; or (*b*) if not so adapted, is used for carrying passengers for hire or reward at separate fares in the course of a business of carrying passengers.

A vehicle is used for this purpose if it is being so used or if it has been so used and that use has not been permanently discontinued (s 1(2)).

Public service vehicles are classified as either stage, express or contract carriages. Stage and express carriages are carriages at separate fares; contract carriages are not (see below). It follows that s 1(1)(*a*) relates to all these but s 1(1)(*b*) relates only to stage and express carriages.

## 13.27 Stage, express and contract carriages

### A *'Stage carriage'*

A 'stage carriage' is defined by s 2(1)(*a*) of the Act as a public service vehicle being used in the operation of a local service, and a 'local service' by s 2(2)(*a*) as a passenger service at separate fares which is not an express service. The meaning of 'stage carriage' in s 2 was considered in *R* v *Traffic Commissioners, ex parte Licensed Taxi Drivers' Association Ltd* [1984] RTR 197. The service was to be provided on demand and the precise route and termination points could not be specified. The service was nevertheless held to be a 'stage carriage' service.

### B *'Express carriage'*

An 'express carriage' is defined by s 2(1)(*b*) as a public service vehicle being used in the operation of an express service, and by s 2(2)(*b*), 'express service' means a passenger service at separate fares where the conditions in s 2 (3) are satisfied. These conditions are that:

(*a*) save in the case of an emergency, every passenger travels between places which are 30 miles or more apart, measured in a straight line, or either one of which is 30 miles or more, measured in a straight line, from some point on the route between those two places; and

(*b*) the service is an excursion or tour, or a service notified as prescribed to the traffic commissioners for the area in which the starting point is situated.

The 30-mile qualification is so worded as to include not only journeys of 30 miles or more between two points, but also what may be described as roundabout services, tours or excursions of that length: although stops may be less than 30 miles apart, passengers must in effect travel at least 30 miles save in an emergency. The definition no longer refers to the amount of the fare; the distinction is now based on the length of the passenger journey. Where part of a passenger service at separate fares qualifies, that part will be an express service and the rest will be treated as a separate local service (s 2 (4)). It will be noted that this is not optional if the requirements are fulfilled.

### C *'Contract carriage'*

A 'contract carriage' is defined by s 2(1)(*c*) as a public service vehicle being used to carry passengers otherwise than at separate fares. However, a vehicle adapted for the carriage of eight or fewer passengers which is used as what would otherwise be a contract carriage does not fall within the definition of a public service vehicle (see s 1(1)) and therefore is not a contract carriage. No road service licence is required for a contract carriage service.

The difference between a stage carriage and an express carriage depends on the length of the journey and no longer on the minimum fare. An express carriage is where the passenger journey is of 30 miles or more. The definition in s 1 means that a stage carriage is an ordinary bus picking up and setting down passengers along a local route, eg the bus along the Strand, and an express carriage is a bus on a regular service, eg from Exeter to London, picking up passengers from towns on the way but, for instance, not stopping for the last 30 miles.

Stage and express carriages are those in which passengers each pay separate fares, though not necessarily to the vehicle owner; a contract carriage is one hired by one person or body, the cost falling entirely on the hirer, eg a football club hiring a coach for the football team where the club meets the whole cost of the hire, or a philanthropist hiring a motor coach to give a free outing to the blind. Where the head of a family hires a taxi for the family and pays the whole cost, this would be in the nature of a contract carriage, but normally the vehicle will be adapted for eight or fewer passengers.

As to certain PSVs not treated as such (s 1(3)) and certain stage and express carriages treated as contract carriages (s 2(5)), see 13.34 and 13.35.

### 13.28 'Used for carrying passengers'

This expression is used in both limbs of s 1(1). It is pointed out at (1981) JP Jo 145 107 that the definition does not say habitually or normally used. It is suggested there that where a mechanic was road testing a coach it was not being used as a public service vehicle and therefore was not to be classified as such. It seems that this conclusion, however desirable, is not in accordance with the extended definition in s 1(2) set out above ('has been used' . . . 'and that use has not been permanently discontinued'). The arguments are set out at (1981) 145 JP 107 and 352. See also 1.79 as to the meaning of 'use' and also compare *Roberts* v *Morris* [1965] Crim LR 46 noted at 13.7*B*.

### 13.29 'Adapted'

'Adapted' is discussed at 1.12. The cases on the meaning of 'adapted' in s 117(1) of the Road Traffic Act 1960 would seem still to be relevant to the definition of 'public service vehicle' in s 1(1) of the 1981 Act.

Whether a vehicle is 'adapted' is a question of fact. *Westacott* v *Centaur* [1981] RTR 182 noted at 1.12 was a case relating to public services vehicles. In that case four out of eleven seats on a minibus were rendered unusable: two double seats had been placed upside down to block four seats off. A finding of fact by the justices that the minibus was not adapted to fill the additional seats and that therefore the vehicle was not a public service vehicle was upheld.

The word 'adapted', according to the judgment in *Traffic Commissioners for South Wales Traffic Area* v *Snape* [1977] Crim LR 427, must, however, be read in conjunction with reg 28(1)(*b*) of the Public Service Vehicles (Conditions of Fitness, Equipment, Use and Certification) Regulations 1981 (SI 1981 No

257) which provides that 'a length of at least 400 mm measured horizontally along the front of each seat shall be allowed for the accommodation of a seated passenger'. The folding arms of continuous seats are to be ignored. This case was in fact decided on an earlier similarly worded regulation which referred to 1 ft 4 in in place of 400 mm. It was held following *Wurzal* v *Addison* (see 1.12) that as the vehicle was used for hire or reward and no factor other than the length of the seats was relevant in the case and the minibus had three seats together with a bench 7 ft 4 in long, it was thus suitable and, therefore, 'adapted' as a public service vehicle.

### 13.30 'More than eight passengers'

A crucial element of the definition of 'public service vehicle' in s 1(1) is the number of passengers for which the vehicle is adapted. The specified number of passengers is nine as the section refers to 'more than eight'. The criterion in s 1(1)(*a*) is whether the vehicle is adapted to carry nine or more passengers, not the number in fact carried.

Whether the driver should be counted among the passengers is not clear. In Parts I and III of Sched 1 to the 1981 Act 'driver' is contrasted with 'passenger'. The problem is one which arises under a number of statutory provisions and the question is discussed with the relevant cases at 1.59. For the purpose of s 1(1)(*a*) and (3) and Sched 1, Parts I, II and III, it is submitted that eight persons plus the driver may be carried before the limit is reached: ie the driver is not to be regarded as a passenger.

### 13.31 'Hire or reward'

The expression 'hire or reward' is found in both s 1(1)(*a*) and s 1(1)(*b*) and also in Sched 1. Its meaning is discussed at 13.7*C*. Here the meaning is extended by s 1(5) which provides as follows:

> (5) For the purposes of this section, section 3 and Schedule 1—
> (*a*) a vehicle is to be treated as carrying passengers for hire or reward if payment is made for, or for matters which include, the carrying of passengers, irrespective of the person to whom the payment is made and, in the case of a transaction effected by or on behalf of a member of any association of persons (whether incorporated or not) on the one hand and the association or another member thereof on the other hand, notwithstanding any rule of law as to such transactions;
> (*b*) a payment made for the carrying of a passenger shall be treated as a fare notwithstanding that it is made in consideration of other matters in addition to the journey and irrespective of the person by or to whom it is made;
> (*c*) a payment shall be treated as made for the carrying of a passenger if made in consideration of a person's being given a right to be carried, whether for one or more journeys and whether or not the right is exercised.

Paragraphs (*a*), (*b*), and (*c*) of s 1(5) are in like terms to s 118(3)(*a*), (*b*) and (*c*) of the Road Traffic Act 1960. Section 118(3)(*d*) which is not reproduced in the 1981 Act used to catch within the meaning of 'hire or reward' the carriage of passengers for hire or reward otherwise than in the course of a business of carrying passengers. This is no longer necessarily the case.

A group of parents acquired a minibus jointly which carried more than eight passengers. They ran it as a joint enterprise without profit to take their children to school. They took it in turns to drive. No fares were collected and each met his own expenses. There was no question of hire or reward in the normal sense. The question was whether there was a reward within the extended definition of s 1(5)(*a*). The parents argued that it was a joint enterprise and on the facts there was no payment for matters which included the carrying of passengers, between one member of the group and another. The police and the traffic commissioners decided not to prosecute. In view of the wording of s 1(5)(*a*), however, the position cannot be regarded as settled.

### 13.32 'Separate fares'

The expression 'separate fares' appears in s 1(1)(*b*) and also in s 2(1)(*c*) and (2)(*a*) and (*b*) (definitions of 'stage', 'express' and 'contract' carriages). The cases as to the meaning of 'separate fares' which follow were decided on the old law and the 1960 Act (now repealed). What is now 1(5) of the 1981 Act makes more stringent provision as to the payment of separate fares. The cases should be read in the light of it.

A bus proprietor hired a bus out to a football club and it stood in a street awaiting any passengers who might come along; there was no question of a private party. Each passenger paid a separate fare, which went to the club secretary. It was held to be used as a stage carriage, as what is now s 1(5) makes it immaterial to whom the fares are paid (*Osborne* v *Richards* (1932) 96 JP 377). A railway company ran excursions to a certain station, where the defendants' buses met the passengers and conveyed them to a chocolate factory, the railway company receiving an inclusive fare from each excursionist; the railway company afterwards paid to the defendants a sum exceeding 1s for each passenger carried in the buses. It was held that the buses were express carriages, it being immaterial, in view of what is now s 1(5), that the excursionists paid nothing to the defendants (*Birmingham etc Omnibus Co* v *Nelson* (1932) 96 JP 385). Where a company hired a bus to take employees to work and the employees made payments to the company, this was held to be carriage at separate fares requiring a road service licence for an express carriage although the passengers paid nothing themselves to the owner of the bus (*Wurzal* v *Wilson* [1965] 1 All ER 26). 'Separate fares' simply means payments for carriage by individual passengers and it is immaterial whether there is a firm arrangement as to the amount of payment or a tariff of payments (*Aitken* v *Hamilton* 1964 SLT 25). Tips unsolicited by the driver were held on the facts not to be separate fares (*McLean* v *Fearn* 1954 SLT (Sh) 37). Coaches hired from the defendants by a stadium proprietor picked up casual passengers at several points and took them to the stadium; the passengers paid nothing for their rides and were free not to go into the stadium, if they wished, the charge for admission being the same for them as for anyone else. It was held that the coaches were stage, not contract carriages, as the passengers were carried in consideration of separate payments made by them to the stadium proprietor and were thus caught by what is now s 1(5) (*Westminster Coaching Services* v *Piddlesden* (1933) 97 JP 185). A lorry owner who used his lorry to carry other people's goods to market and also carried as passengers the people whose goods were in the lorry was held to be running an express carriage although he contended that the payments were for carriage of the goods only (*Drew* v *Dingle* (1934) 98 JP 1). Public advertisement of a trip can convert what would otherwise be a trip for which a licence is unnecessary, under Sched 1 to the 1981 Act, into one requiring a licence under s 134 (*Evans* v *Dell* [1937] 1 All ER 349; and see *Goldsmith* v *Deakin* (1933) 98 JP 4). A car owner regularly drove three fellow-employees to work at a factory and back; the expenses of oil and petrol were shared by each paying 5s per week. It was held that the friends were carried in consideration of separate payments and the vehicle was an express carriage (*East Midlands etc Commissioners* v *Tyler* [1938] 3 All ER 39). A club hired a taxi to take members to work regularly and each member made separate payments, covering both transport charges and other purposes; it was held that, under s 118(3)(*d*), these were separate fares (*Hawthorn* v *Knight* 1962 SLT 69).

Where a hirer of a minibus agreed to pay to its owner 7s per day to take her and her fellow workers to work, however many were carried, and she herself collected separate fares from the other passengers, it was held that, under what is now s 1(5), there was a payment of separate fares and the owner was guilty of use as an express carriage without a public service vehicle licence (*Wurzal* v *Addison* [1965] 1 All ER 20). An arrangement was made whereby 15p was paid for each journey during the week by each of seven passengers going to a factory. If a regular passenger could not travel on a particular day that passenger would have to pay for that day but her place could be taken free of charge by a fellow workmate. At the end of the week all the money was collected by the passenger sitting nearest the driver and paid over to him. It was contended by the defendant, who owned and operated the vehicle, that it was not an express carriage because he received the same amount of money each week and did not separately charge the passengers. Following *Wurzel* v *Addison* it was held that under what is now s 1(5)(*b*) there was a payment of separate fares and thus the defendant should be convicted of operating an express carriage without a licence (*Vickers* v *Bowman* [1976] RTR 165). In this last case the vehicle might now presumably be within s 1(1)(*b*) of the 1981 Act (not adapted for more than eight passengers and not used in the course of a passenger carrying business). If so it would not now be a public service vehicle. The principle, however, remains.

### 13.33 'In the course of a business of carrying passengers'

The expression 'in the course of a business of carrying passengers' is found in s 1(1)(*b*) and also in s 1(3) (certain vehicles fulfilling the conditions of Parts I, II and III of Sched 1 not to be treated as public service vehicles). The expression does not include, for the purposes of s 1, passenger journeys for separate fares where the total running costs (including depreciation and general wear) are not exceeded and the fare arrangements were made before the journey began (s 1(4)). This subsection seems designed to exempt works buses and similar non-profit-making journeys in vehicles adapted for eight passengers or less. As the word 'including' indicates that the list of running costs given is not exhaustive, it is submitted that a 'safety margin' or 'windfall' profit would not necessarily therefore turn the venture into a business.

It should be noted that s (1)(*b*) and (3) only relate to vehicles adapted for eight or less passengers. Where a vehicle is adapted for more than eight passengers, it will be caught by s 1(1)(*a*) and the test will be merely 'hire or reward', as extended by s 1(5).

### 13.34 Certain PSVs not treated as such

A public service vehicle carrying passengers at separate fares in the course of a business of carrying passengers, but doing so in circumstances where the conditions of Parts I, II or III of Sched 1 are fulfilled shall be treated as not being a public service vehicle unless it is adapted to carry more than eight passengers (s 1(3)).

The conditions in Parts I and III may be summarised by saying that, in general, vehicles which would otherwise be public service vehicles by reason of s 1(1)(*b*) will not be public service vehicles if they are adapted to carry eight passengers or less and the journey is not organised by the driver or owner or person making the vehicle available or receiving any remuneration in respect of the arrangements. The journey must also be made without previous advertisement to the public. Under Part I the service may be advertised where, in England and Wales, the Greater London Council or a county council, or, in Scotland, a regional or islands council, have approved the arrangements as designed to meet the social and welfare needs of one or more communities. Otherwise the only advertisements permitted are those which, by virtue of the supplemental provisions of Part IV, are not regarded as advertisements. Several announcements taken together can constitute an advertisement (*Poole* v *Ibbotson* (1949) 113 JP 466).

A bus hired to take people back after a dance went to their various homes; it was held that this was not a 'journey to a particular destination' under what is now para 7 (in Part III) of Sched 1 (*Clark* v *Dundee Council* 1957 SLT 306).

The condition in Part II is that each of the passengers making the journey must have been outside Great Britain at the time of concluding his arrangements to make the journey.

### 13.35–40 Certain stage and express carriages treated as contract carriages

Where the conditions of Part II or Part III of Sched 1 (see above) are fulfilled a public service vehicle is treated as a contract carriage and not as a stage or express carriage even though carrying passengers at separate fares (s 2(5)).

## PSV Licensing and Fitness Requirements

### 13.41 PSV operators' licences

The licensing requirements as to PSVs apply to PSVs as defined at 13.26 and are subject to the relaxations and exemptions discussed below.

PSV operators' licences are required for operators of all PSVs whether stage, express or contract carriages (s 12(1)). It is an offence to use a vehicle on a road (as to 'use' and 'road', see Chapter 1) as a stage, express or contract carriage without such an operator's licence. The offence is only committed by the operator of the vehicle, but another person may be guilty of aiding and abetting him. See further 'Offences' below.

A PSV operators' licence may be held by an individual, a company or a partnership. The 1981 Act is modified in certain respects as far as partnerships are concerned (see the Operation of Public Service Vehicles (Partnership) Regulations 1981 (SI 1981 No 259)).

A PSV operator's licence is obtained from the traffic commissioners for the area where the operating centre, or one of the operating centres, is situated (s 12(2)).

The licence may be of one of two kinds: a standard licence or a restricted licence (s 13(1)). The provisions are somewhat similar to those requiring standard and restricted operators' licences for goods vehicles (see 13.3).

A standard licence authorises the use of any public service vehicle for both international and national transport operations or national transport operations only.

A restricted licence authorises the use (whether in national or international operations) of public service vehicles:

(*a*) not adapted to carry more than eight passengers; and

(*b*) not adapted to carry more than sixteen passengers when used:

- (i) otherwise than in the course of a business of carrying passengers (and this includes local and public authority passenger vehicles unless used for the authority PSV undertaking); or
- (ii) by a person whose main occupation is not the operation of public service vehicles adapted to carry more than eight passengers (s 13(3) and (4)).

It is difficult to envisage much use of the provision (*b*)(i), but provision (*b*)(ii) may be of some use to an operator running services with comparatively small vehicles as a sideline or by way of reserve.

Under ss 14 and 17 the traffic commissioner may refuse, suspend or revoke a PSV operator's licence.

It is obligatory for the traffic commissioners to attach condition(s) specifying the maximum number of vehicles which may be used under a licence (s 16(1)) and they have a discretion to attach further conditions for restricting or regulating the use of vehicles under the licence being conditions of any prescribed description (s 16(3)). Contravention of such a condition is an offence (s 16(7)), but only by the holder of the licence. Another person may be guilty of aiding and abetting him. See further 'Offences' below.

Where a vehicle is being used where a PSV operator's licence is required, a PSV operator's disc must be fixed and exhibited on the vehicle as prescribed (s 18(1)). The Public Service Vehicles (Operators' Licences) Regulations 1981 (SI 1981 No 258) prescribe the manner in which operators' discs are to be fixed and exhibited (reg 7), and provide for the production of licences and discs for examination (reg 11). Contravention of s 18(1) is an offence (s 18(4)), but it can only be committed by the operator of the vehicle. See further 'Offences' below. It is an offence under s 65 to forge, alter, use etc such a disc with intent to deceive (see Chapter 16).

Applicants for PSV operators' licences and the holders of such licences are obliged to give the traffic commissioners certain information regarding relevant convictions (s 19) and as to vehicles (s 20), and the traffic commissioners may require certain information themselves. The applicant and any one who aids or abets him commits an offence if he fails to comply (ss 19(5) and 20(4)).

A person who under s 20(3) supplies information which he knows to be false or does not believe to be true commits a more serious offence (s 20(5)). For the s 68 defence available, see 13.47.

## 13.42 PSV drivers' licences

Drivers of all PSVs require PSV drivers' licences (s 22(1)), and it is an offence to drive or employ a person to drive a PSV on a road (defined in Chapter 1) without one (s 22(9)). See further 'Offences' below. Notwithstanding s 1(1) of the 1981 Act, 'public service vehicle' in ss 22–26 means a stage, express or contract carriage (ibid).

A PSV driver's licence is obtained from the traffic commissioners for the traffic area in which the driver resides (s 22(2)).

There are powers to suspend or revoke such licences on grounds of conduct or physical disability (s 22(5)). There are also certain rights of appeal to magistrates' courts and sheriff's courts (see s 23). The proceedings will be by way of complaint.

## 13.43 Road service licences

In a report entitled 'Buses' (Cmnd 9300) the Government indicated its intention to abolish road service licences and to transfer PSV operator licensing to the licensing authorities for goods vehicle operators' licences from which appeals would be to the Transport Tribunal. A Transport Bill dealing with this is now (1 April 1985) before Parliament. At present road service licences are required only for stage carriage services (s 30(1)). (This should, however, be read subject to s 23 of the Transport (London) Act 1969 which is due to be repealed by the London Regional Transport Act 1984 when brought into force and is also subject to s 45 of that Act which is now in force.) However, road service licences are not required for stage carriage services within or in certain circumstances partly outside designated trial areas in Great Britain outside Greater London (see ss 38–41, in particular s 39 of the 1981 Act). The Bus Services in Trial Areas Regulations 1981 (SI 1981 No 269) as amended by SI 1981 No 886 have been made under these provisions. Certain parts of Devon have been designated a trial area by the Devon Trial Area Order 1982 (SI 1982 No 1243). If a stage carriage is provided without a road service licence where one is required, the operator of the service or anyone who aids or abets him commits an offence under s 30(6). See also 13.46.

A road service licence must be obtained from the traffic commissioners for any area in which the service is to be provided unless no passengers are to be taken up or set down in that area (s 30(2)). Subject to this, separate licences must be obtained for separate areas (s 30(4)).

A road service licence is of no effect if the holder does not also hold a public service vehicle operator's licence which has not been suspended (s 30(4)). However, a PSV operator's licence is not necessary where the road service licence is held by a local education authority or a Scottish education authority, or for a community bus service (s 30(5)), or for certain excursions and tours where the licence is granted under s 35 (s 35(2)). It is submitted that this must be the effect of s 35(2) despite its rather complicated wording.

The traffic commissioners may attach conditions to road service licences under ss 32 and 33. If there is a breach of a condition attached to such a licence, the holder of the licence or an aider or abettor commits an offence (s 30(7)). See further 'Offences' below.

See also the Public Service Vehicles (Road Service Licences and Express Services) Regulations 1980 (SI 1980 No 1354) as amended by SI 1981 No 264.

## 13.44 Relaxations and exemptions

There has been an increasing tendency to relax the laws relating to public service vehicles and in particular for small and rural operations. The Passenger Vehicles (Experimental Areas) Act 1977 enables local authorities in respect of areas designated by order under the Act to relax the normal public service vehicle requirements. By the Passenger Vehicles (Experimental Areas) Designation (Extension) Order 1983 (SI 1983 No 917) Sedburgh, Dent and Garsdale in Cumbria remain designated an experimental area for two years from 3 August 1983.

The experimental area for the parishes in North Yorkshire had its period extended by SI 1983 No 1453 for two years from 5 November 1983. There was a similar extension for Mid and East Devon by SI 1984 No 204 for two years from 26 March 1984.

Under s 46 of the 1981 Act education authorities may use school buses, when being used to provide free school transport, to carry also fare paying passengers. They may also use school buses belonging to the authority, when not being used to provide free school transport, to provide local stage carriage services. In both cases no PSV driver's licence or PSV operator's licence is required where the school bus belongs to the authority.

As to exemptions in relation to services by certain educational and other bodies under s 42 permits and as to community bus services under s 45, see below. There are also special provisions relating to foreign PSVs, and British PSVs on international journeys (see below). Other exemptions are noted above in the context of requirements to which they relate.

*Examples*

It may be helpful to explain the PSV licensing requirements by examples. As to eight or more passengers, see 1.59. It is submitted there that the driver is excluded, making the demarcation point nine seats or less (including the driver's seat) and ten seats or more.

Smith owns an eight-seater car and carries on business as a taxi proprietor. Smith will not require either a PSV operator's licence or a road service licence for any use as a contract carriage, or for any use which falls within s 37 and the subsequent sections of the Town Police Clauses Act 1847 or Parts I, II or III of Sched 1 to the 1981 Act although separate fares are paid by his passengers. He will not require a road service licence for an express service in any event. If he takes not more than eight passengers on any journey at separate fares and does not previously advertise the journey save as permitted and otherwise complies with Part I or III he is exempt from both licences. But if he takes two or more passengers at separate fares and advertises other than as permitted or otherwise fails to comply with Part I or III, he will require both licences. Again, if he carries overseas visitors on any journey at separate fares he will not require either licence if each passenger was outside Great Britain (ie England, Wales and Scotland but not the Channel Islands or the Isle of Man) at the time of concluding the arrangements for the journey (Part II of Sched 1).

Jones similarly owns an eight-seater car and takes passengers on similar journeys for separate fares. He does not carry the passengers in the course of a passenger-carrying business. He will be exempt from both licences (s 2(1)(*b*)) and Sched 1 will not concern him.

Brown owns a 24-seater motor coach. For use as a stage carriage, as an express carriage or as a contract carriage he will require a PSV operator's licence under s 12. He will normally require a road service licence under s 30 in addition whenever passengers are carried at separate fares as a stage carriage service but not as an express carriage service. He will not require a road service licence for a contract carriage service.

Robinson owns a twelve-seater minibus. He does not have a s 42 permit (formerly known as a minibus permit) and is not operating a community bus service. He carries passengers for payment. He will be in exactly the same position as Brown. This will be so even if the 'hire or reward' or the 'payment' is merely implied within the terms of s 1(5)(*a*), (*b*) or (*c*). In some circumstances, however, Robinson may be eligible for a *restricted* PSV operator's licence or to be authorised for a community service bus.

If Brown or Robinson fulfils the conditions of Parts II (overseas visitors) or Part III of Sched 1 the service will be treated as contract carriage and there will be no question of them requiring a road service licence.

If the conditions of any Part of Sched 1 applicable to the journeys of the vehicles of Smith, Brown or Robinson are not complied with, a licence under s 12 and/or s 30 of the Act as appropriate may become necessary and an offence may arise. An offence might be committed in respect of a Part I or III trip if it were publicly advertised.

### 13.45 Fitness of PSVs

A PSV operator's licence can only be granted for a vehicle adapted for eight or more passengers if a certificate of initial fitness is in force in accordance with s 6(1) of the 1981 Act. Alternatively, by s 6(1) there may be a type approval certificate under s 10 of the 1981 Act, or an equivalent type approval certificate under s 47 of the Road Traffic Act 1972. An offence under s 6(2) is committed by the operator of the vehicle if a vehicle is used in contravention of s 6(1). See further 'Offences' below.

The fitness requirements are specified in Part II of the Public Service Vehicles (Conditions of Fitness, Equipment, Use and Certification) Regulations 1981 (SI 1981 No 257) as amended by SI 1982 Nos 20, 1058 and 1482 and 1984 No 1763. The requirements of these regulations are additional to those of the Construction and Use Regulations. Part II (fitness) only applies to vehicles adapted to carry eight or more passengers (reg 3(1)). Part IV (use) does not apply to Crown vehicles or vehicles in the service of a visiting force or of a headquarters (reg 4).

There is power under s 9 to prohibit the driving of unfit PSVs. Under the Public Service Vehicles (Exemption from Prohibitions) Regulations 1981 (SI 1981 No 262) the prohibition does not apply for the purpose of certain tests. A person who knowingly drives a vehicle in contravention of such a prohibition or causes or permits (see Chapter 1) such a vehicle to be driven commits an offence (s 9(9)). See further 'Offences' below.

## 13.46 Offences

The principal offences under the 1981 Act have been referred to in context above. However, in each case the relevant section should be closely consulted as to the persons who may be liable and the defences available. These and other matters are discussed below.

Section 12(5) (no PSV operator's licence) refers to a vehicle being 'used' and s 30(6) (no road service licence) to a service being 'provided'. The previous equivalent sections were differently worded and many of the earlier cases are therefore no longer applicable. The liability now seems to be absolute without any need for a guilty intent. See below, however, for defences available.

As to 'using' see 1.79. A person may 'use' through his agent or employee. He will, however, not normally be 'using' if the vehicle is hired to another.

'Provided' is a new expression in this context and must be given its ordinary and natural meaning (cf *Brutus* v *Cozens* [1973] AC 854). It is submitted that an operator of a stage carriage service will be absolutely liable under s 30 (6) if he provides the service without a road service licence, but not (save as an aider or abettor) if someone else does. He will not therefore be liable if he does not provide the service himself but hires it out to someone else who does. See, however, below for certain modifications as to hirings with regard to the meaning of 'operator of a vehicle'.

By s 65 of the Transport Act 1947 (now repealed) a road service licence was not required for a service provided under a scheme by the British Transport Commission or its agent; where the Commission itself hired a bus and gave all the directions as to its movements, it was held to provide the transport itself (*Railway Executive* v *Henson* (1949) 113 JP 333).

If an employee disobeys a term of his master's road service licence, eg by diverting from the authorised route, the master may be liable for a breach of what is now s 30 (*G Newton Ltd* v *Smith* [1962] 2 All ER 19). In that case, the charge was failure to comply with a condition of the licence and it was held that what is now s 30(7) imposes on a master liability for a failure by him or his servant to comply with the conditions of the licence, provided the driver acted wilfully or negligently. The case was, however, decided on s 134 of the 1960 Act which was differently worded.

In *Carpenter* v *Campbell* [1953] 1 All ER 280 it was stated that where it is an employer's duty to obtain a licence and he fails to do so, the driver should not be prosecuted. Many prosecutions are now restricted to specified defendants in any event, but it is possible that a prosecution might be considered against a driver for aiding and abetting where it can be established that he is aware of the lack of a licence.

Under the old law there was no liability when a trip was made illegal by the action, unknown to the defendant, of a person not subject to his control (*Reynolds* v *Austin* [1951] 1 All ER 606). See below as to the defences available in any event.

Where an offence is committed by a company under Part II or Part III of the 1981 Act, certain responsible officers of the company will also be liable to prosecution (s 74).

Section 1(5) of the 1981 Act makes special provisions as to arrangements between a society and its members or between members for transport being deemed a carriage for hire or reward; otherwise, a member of an unincorporated society could be said to be using his own vehicle if the society owned it. The principle laid down in *Wurzal* v *Houghton Main Home Delivery Service Ltd* at 13.7*C* therefore seems inapplicable.

If a condition imposed by the commissioners is ultra vires, its breach is no offence (*Ellis* v *Dubowski* (1921) 85 JP 230).

Many of the regulations provide that no PSV operator's licence, PSV driver's licence or road service licence need be held if certain requirements are fulfilled. If these requirements are not fulfilled and if no other offence is substituted it is submitted that the appropriate no licence offence is committed.

Section 65 provides for offences of forgery and misuse of documents etc. By s 65(3) as amended by s 12 of the Forgery and Counterfeiting Act 1981 'forges' means 'makes a false document or other thing in order that it may be used as genuine'. This is a different and simpler definition from that used in the Forgery and Counterfeiting Act itself. Section 66 provides for offences in relation to false statements to obtain licences etc. Sections 65 and 66 are worded similarly to ss 169 and 170 of the 1972 Act, and reference to Chapter 16 where these sections are discussed may be helpful.

Section 67 provides for offences for breach of regulations made under the Act, other than under s 44 (services by certain educational and other bodies: see 13.56).

*'Operator of the vehicle'; 'operator of the service'*

Certain offences are committed only by the 'operator of the vehicle', eg s 12 (5) (no PSV operator's licence). Certain other offences can only be committed by the 'operator of the service', eg s 30(1) and (6) (no road service licence).

The 'operator of the vehicle' for the purposes of the 1981 Act means (s 81(1)):

(*a*) the driver, if he owns the vehicle; and

(*b*) in any other case, the person for whom the driver works (whether under a contract of employment or any other description of contract personally to do work).

This seems to be wide enough to include a self employed person who hires himself out.

This definition may be modified in the case of hiring arrangements: for a modification in the case of hiring between holders of PSV operators' licences see the PSV (Operators' Licences) Regulations 1981, reg 16. Under these regulations the hirer is still regarded as the operator of the vehicle if under the hiring the hirer is not entitled to keep the vehicle in his possession for a total period of more than fourteen days (reg 16(i)). There must be a gap of at least fourteen days between such hirings to the same hirer (reg 16(ii)). The purpose of this is presumably to prevent long-term arrangements being disguised by short breaks, but there seems to be nothing to prevent a hiring of a different vehicle to the same hirer for fourteen-day periods. The reference in reg 16(i) and (ii) is to the vehicle. The disc of the person making the hiring must be displayed when required. If this is not done, reg 16 ceases to apply and seemingly the hirer will be operating the vehicle without a PSV operator's licence.

Under s 81(2) the 'operator of a stage or express carriage service' for the purposes of the Act is the person or each of the persons providing the service. The reference to 'each' implies that the liability is joint and several so that *each* may be liable. For these purposes the 'operator of a vehicle' (see above) being used as a stage or express carriage shall be taken to be 'providing' (see the use of this word in s 30) the service unless he proves that the service is or forms part of a service provided not by himself but by one or more other persons. The burden is therefore placed on the operator of the vehicle in these circumstances to prove on the balance of probabilities that he is not providing the service.

**13.47–50 Defences**

Defences contained in s 68 are available for many of the offences under the 1981 Act.

The defence of reasonable excuse in s 68(1) is available for offences contrary to ss 19(5), 20(4), 24(2) and (3), 25(3), 26(2), 33(7), 40(6), 67 and 70(3) and so much of s 22(9) as relates to contravention of s 22(1)(*a*).

The defence in s 68(3) that the defendant took all reasonable precautions and exercised all due diligence to avoid the commission of any offence under that provision is available for offences contrary to ss 6(2), 9(9), 12(5), 16(7), 18(4), 26(2), 27(2) and 30(6) and (7) and so much of s 22(9) as relates to contravention of s 22(1)(*b*). The most important of these are s 12(5) (no PSV operator's licence) and s 30(6) and (7) (no road service licence and breach of condition of road service licence). For the meaning of 'all due diligence' see 14.63 and for 'reasonable excuse' compare 4.91*C* and 14.51.

The defences will be judged on the balance of probabilities and it will be for the defendant to establish them.

## PSV Licensing: Proceedings and Penalties

### 13.51–5 Generally

By s 69 of the 1981 Act proceedings for an offence under s 12 (PSV operators' licences) or s 30 (road service licences) or any other provisions in Part II or III of the Act or any regulations made thereunder shall not in England be instituted except by or on behalf of the Director of Public Prosecutions or by a person authorised in that behalf by commissioners of a traffic area, a chief officer of police or the council of a county or county district. This does not apply to regulations under s 25 (conduct of passengers) or s 26 (control of number of passengers). There is also a partial exception under s 27 (operators' returns).

Where a police sergeant laid an information which was signed by an Assistant Commissioner of the Metropolitan Police and by a superintendent and the Commissioner had given a general authorisation in writing to prosecute, it was held in *Westminster Coaching Services* v *Piddlesden* (1933) 97 JP 185, that the sergeant had authority to take proceedings under what is now s 69. Contrast *Record Tower Cranes* v *Gisbey* and *Nelms* v *Roe* in 7.17, 'By or on behalf of a chief officer of police' and see generally 'Authority to prosecute', 2.3. There is an article on authority to prosecute at (1984) 148 JP 521 which discusses the difficult wording in s 69.

As to evidence by certificate, see s 71, and as to proof of a driver's identity, see s 72.

The penalty for offences under s 12(5) (PSV operators' licences) and s 22(9) (PSV drivers' licences) is a fine of level 4. The penalty for offences under s 30(6) or (7) (road service licences) is a fine of level 3. The penalty under s 16(7) (breach of PSV operator's licence conditions), s 18(4) (fixing and exhibiting operators' discs), ss 19(5) and 20(4) (failing to give information to traffic commissioners) is a fine of level 3. The penalty under s 20(5) (false information) is a fine of level 4. Breach of s 66 (false statements to obtain licences) carries a maximum fine of level 4. Breaches of regulations under the 1981 Act (other than s 44) carry a penalty of a fine of level 2 where no other penalty is specified (s 67). Offences contrary to s 6(2) (no certificate of fitness) carry a maximum fine of level 4. The penalty under s 9(9) (contravention of prohibitions as to unfit vehicle) is a fine of level 5. All these offences are triable by magistrates only.

The offence contrary to s 65 is an 'either way' offence triable in accordance with ss 18–23 of the Magistrates' Courts Act 1980. The maximum penalty on indictment is two years' imprisonment or an unlimited fine or both, and on summary conviction, £2,000.

There is no power in the court to endorse a driving licence or disqualify the defendant or order penalty points.

## PSV Licensing: Miscellaneous Provisions

### 13.56 Services by certain educational and other bodies

Certain vehicles used by educational and other bodies are exempted by ss 42–44 of the Public Passenger Vehicles Act 1981 from the PSV licensing requirements of the Act even though passengers are carried for hire or reward. Section 42 permits must be held instead. Before the provisions were extended to large passenger-carrying vehicles, these were known as minibus permits and some of the applicable regulations still refer to minibus permits. 'Hire or reward' in ss 42–44 has the same meaning as in s 1(5) of the Act (s 42(7)).

Sections 42–44 apply to vehicles which:

(*a*) come within the definition of a small or large passenger-carrying vehicle;
(*b*) are specified in a s 42 permit;
(*c*) are not used for the carriage of members of the public at large;
(*d*) are not used with a view to profit;
(*e*) are used by the body to whom the permit is granted; and
(*f*) are used in accordance with the conditions of the permit.

By s 42(7) a 'small passenger-carrying vehicle' is a vehicle which is adapted to carry more than eight but not more than sixteen passengers, and a 'large passenger-carrying vehicle' is a vehicle adapted to carry more than sixteen passengers. As to 'passengers', see 1.59.

So long as conditions (*a*)–(*f*) above are satisfied, s 12(1) (PSV operators' licences), s 22 (PSV drivers' licences) and s 30 (road service licences) and s 23(2) of the Transport (London) Act 1969 (restrictions on provision of London bus services) will not apply to the driving or use of a large passenger-carrying vehicle used for carrying passengers for hire or reward, although the vehicle will still be a public service vehicle (s 42(2)). Section 23(2) is due to be repealed by the London Regional Transport Act 1984 when in force. So long as the same conditions are satisfied small passenger-carrying vehicles will not be treated as being public service vehicles (s 42(1)).

Under s 42(3), s 42 permits may be issued in respect of small passenger-carrying vehicles by the traffic commissioners for the traffic area in which the vehicle concerned is ordinarily kept to any body appearing to them to be concerned with education, religion, social welfare or other activities for the benefit of the community. Section 42 permits may also be granted in respect of either small or large passenger-carrying vehicles used by a body designated by the Minibus (Designated Bodies) Order 1980 (SI 1980 No 1356) as amended by SI 1981 No 1037. In this instance the permits are not issued by the traffic commissioners but by the designated body either to itself or to another body as specified in the order.

Under s 43(5) there is power to grant a permit to a named individual on behalf of the body. Under s 43(2) there are powers to impose conditions and under s 43(3) there are certain powers to vary or revoke a permit.

Under the Minibus (Permits) Regulations 1977 (SI 1977 No 1708) as amended by SI 1978 No 1931 and 1980 No 1357 every authorised minibus shall carry a disc and a driver's notice setting out the conditions which have been imposed. Under reg 6 every driver must be the holder of a full licence granted by s 88 of the 1972 Act and be over twenty-one. A person whose application for renewal has been received in accordance with s 84(4) of the 1972 Act is to be treated as the holder of a full licence. These regulations define a 'minibus' as either a small or a large passenger-carrying vehicle.

The Minibus (Conditions of Fitness, Equipment and Use) Regulations 1977 (SI 1977 No 2103 as amended by SI 1980 No 142, SI 1981 No 1599 and SI 1982 No 1484) have been made. Under these regulations 'minibus' means a small passenger-carrying vehicle (reg 2).

*Offences*

There is no offence provided for a breach of s 42 itself. In the case of small passenger-carrying vehicles the effect is that if there is a breach of the s 42(1) conditions, the vehicle will be treated as a public service vehicle so that there may be an offence accordingly. In the case of large passenger-carrying vehicles, if there is a similar breach of the s 42(1) conditions the exemptions (see s 42(2)) from ss 12(1), 22 and 30 of the 1981 Act and s 23(2) of the Transport (London) Act 1969 will cease to apply so that there may be an offence accordingly. Section 23(2) is due to be repealed as noted above.

The various regulations now have effect as if made under s 44. Section 44 provides no offence and is expressly excluded in s 67 which provides for breach of regulations under the 1981 Act. It is submitted that a breach of the regulations will not necessarily be such as to take the vehicle outside the definition of a small or large passenger-carrying vehicle and therefore outside the protection of s 42.

The Minibus (Conditions of Fitness, Equipment and Use) Regulations 1977 (as amended) are treated as if made under s 44 of the 1981 Act and s 40(1) and (3) of the 1972 Act. The maximum penalty in Sched 4 to the latter Act is a fine of level 5 or level 4 depending on the circumstances. See the penalty provisions under the section on the Construction and Use Regulations, 8.41–60. Certain offences (brakes and steering) carry endorsement and discretionary disqualification. These offences will carry 3 penalty points. A defendant will escape endorsement if he proves that he did not know and had no reasonable cause to suspect that the facts of the case were such that the offence would be committed (see 8.46).

### 13.57 Community bus services

Section 45 of the 1981 Act provides for the authorisation of community bus services.

The traffic commissioners may grant a road service licence under Part III of the Act for use as a stage carriage so as to provide a community bus service.

The licence may be authorised by the commissioners so that it covers the use of the bus as a contract or express carriage or both, subject to such restrictions (if any) as the commissioners think fit to impose (s 45(3)). They must be satisfied that the authorisation is reasonable in all the circumstances with a view to the financial support of such a service (ibid).

The service must be provided by a body of persons (whether corporate or unincorporate) who are concerned for the social and welfare needs of one or more communities (s 45(8)). The wording of this seems to preclude an application by an individual person. Section 6 of the Interpretation Act 1978 provides that the plural includes the singular unless the contrary intention is shown. An individual cannot be a body of persons and it seems therefore that there is a contrary intention. The service must also be non-profit-making (s 45(8)).

There are special provisions relating to applications in respect of services to be provided wholly or partly in the Greater London area (see s 45(5)).

Section 45(2) specifies the conditions which must be attached to the road service licence for community bus services.

The vehicles must be only those adapted to carry at least eight and at most sixteen passengers (s 45(2)(*a*)). The meaning of 'adapted' and the question of whether 'passengers' includes the driver is discussed in Chapter 1.

Volunteer drivers must be used (s 45(2)(*b*)(i)). 'Volunteer' is defined in s 45(8). The driver is entitled to reasonable expenses. In addition he may be paid for loss of earnings incurred in making himself available to drive in exceptional circumstances.

The use of an authorised community bus service means that a PSV operator's licence need not be held and the driver need not hold a PSV driver's licence. If the driver does not hold such a licence he must comply with the prescribed conditions. These are contained in the Community Bus Regulations 1978 (SI 1978 No 1313), as amended by SI 1980 Nos 144 and 1358 (see Part V). Prescribed conditions of fitness must be fulfilled (s 45(2)(*c*); see Part II of the regulations). A community bus service disc must be displayed (s 45(2)(*d*); and reg 36). It follows that the Public Service Vehicles (Conditions of Fitness, Equipment, Use and Certification) Regulations 1981 as amended will not apply unless a PSV operator's licence is in fact held.

The requirements in s 44 of the 1972 Act as to test certificates apply to a vehicle used in providing a community bus service if no PSV operator's licence is in force in respect of the vehicle. The amendment to this effect to the 1972 Act was made by s 5(10) of the Transport Act 1978. There is power to prescribe exemptions but none have been so prescribed specifically relating to community bus services. Such vehicles are, however, placed in a less stringently defined category (see the Motor Vehicles (Tests) Regulations 1981, reg 5).

*Offences*

No offence is expressly provided for a breach of s 45. If the use is outside the terms of the licence, the vehicle may be a public service vehicle so that there may be an offence contrary to s 12(5) (no PSV operator's licence) or s 22(9) (no PSV driver's licence).

Section 45(6) provides that if there is a breach of a condition contained in s 45(2)(*a*)–(*d*), s 30(7) (breach of conditions attached to road service licence) shall apply and an offence will be committed accordingly.

The Community Bus Regulations 1978 have effect not only under the 1981

Act but also under s 40(1) and (3) of the 1972 Act. If a breach of the regulations is charged under the 1981 Act, the penalty section is s 67 and the maximum fine is of level 2. For the defence of reasonable excuse available for offences under s 67, see s 68 and 13.47. If a breach of any of the regulations is charged as an offence contrary to s 40 of the 1972 Act, the maximum penalty is a fine of level 5 or level 4 depending on the circumstances. See the penalty provisions under the section on the Construction and Use Regulations, 8.41–60. Certain offences (brakes and steering) carry endorsement and discretionary disqualification and 3 penalty points. A defendant will escape endorsement if he proves that he did not know and had no reasonable cause to suspect that the facts of the case were such that the offence would be committed (see 8.46).

### 13.58–60 International passenger services

British vehicles on international passenger journeys, such journeys by vehicles from EEC member countries and certain journeys by passenger vehicles from third countries are controlled by the Road Transport (International Passenger Services) Regulations 1984 (SI 1984 No 748). These regulations are to be treated as made under s 60 of the Public Passenger Vehicles Act 1981 and s 40 of the 1972 Act. They extensively modify the 1981 Act in relation to public service vehicles on international journeys and, as they are complicated, reference should be made to the specific regulations. The regulations refer to EEC Regulations 117/66, 1016/68 and 516 and 517/72.

Part II of the regulations (regs 4–6) provide for vehicles registered in the United Kingdom; Part III (regs 7–12) for vehicles registered abroad. The regulations do not make provision for vehicles registered in Northern Ireland when used in Great Britain on services running between Northern Ireland and Great Britain but not outside the United Kingdom. Provision for them is made in the Road Transport (Northern Ireland Passenger Services) Regulations 1980 (SI 1980 No 1460).

The Public Service Vehicles (Conditions of Fitness, Equipment, Use and Certification) Regulations 1981, as amended, do not apply to non-British vehicles (to which Part III of the 1984 Regulations applies instead), or to vehicles registered in Northern Ireland (to which Part II applies instead).

Where appropriate British vehicles must comply with British law as well.

By reg 2 of the 1984 Regulations 'public service vehicle' has the same meaning as in s 1 of the 1981 Act.

The 1984 Regulations refer to 'Community regulated' services and to 'regular' and 'shuttle' services. 'Community regulated' services are those to which EEC Regulation 117/66 applies. These are services by a vehicle which is registered in a member state; which is, in construction and equipment, suitable for carrying more than nine persons (specifically including the driver) and intended for that purpose; whose place of departure is in an EEC member state; and whose destination is in the territory of the same or another member state (reg 2 and art 4(1) of EEC Regulation 117/66).

Community regulated services may be 'regular', 'special regular' or 'shuttle' services. The nature of a 'regular' service is itself explanatory and is defined in art 1 of EEC Regulation 117/66. The same article defines a 'special regular' service as a service for a special category of persons such as workers or school-children. A 'shuttle' service is defined by art 2 as a service whereby by repeated outward and return journeys previously formed groups of passengers are carried from a single place of departure to a single destination. Subject to certain exceptions, each group must travel together, must not be taken up or set down during the journey and the first return and the last outward journey must be made unladen.

*PSVs registered in Great Britain*

Regulation 4 provides that where a public service vehicle, registered in Great Britain or Northern Ireland, is being used for the Community regulated carriage of passengers on regular, special regular, shuttle or worker services, providing the vehicle is used in accordance with the applicable requirement of the Council Regulations (see reg 2 and Sched 1), no road service licence under s 30 of the 1981 Act is required. If there is a breach of the Council Regulations it would seem that the offence of providing a stage carriage service without a road service licence may be committed by the operator of the service and any person aiding and abetting him (see s 30 of the 1981 Act). Regulation 4 also provides that, in addition, s 6 (certificate of initial fitness), s 12 (PSV operators' licences), s 18 (exhibition of operators' discs) and s 22 (PSV drivers' licences) do not apply to vehicles registered in Northern Ireland on such journeys through Great Britain.

In respect of PSVs registered in Great Britain or Northern Ireland, used for non-Community regulated international carriage of passengers on regular, special regular or shuttle services, reg 5 provides that s 30 of the 1981 Act shall apply as substituted by that regulation. The substituted s 30(1) provides that no person shall cause or permit such a public service vehicle to be used on a road for the international carriage of passengers unless there is in force in relation to the use of the vehicle and is carried on the vehicle an international passenger transport authorisation. Note that the words 'cause or permit' do not appear in the original s 30(1). A certifying officer or a public service vehicle examiner may at any time, on production if so required of his authority, require the operator or driver to produce and permit him to inspect and copy the authorisation, and there are certain powers to stop and detain the vehicle for that purpose (s 30(2) as substituted). A person who, without reasonable excuse, contravenes the substituted s 30(1) or fails to comply with a requirement of a certifying officer or public service vehicle examiner, or wilfully obstructs such officer or examiner in the exercise of his powers under s 30(2), will be guilty of an offence. Regulation 5 also provides that, in addition, ss 6, 12 and 18 (PSV operators' licences etc) and s 22 (PSV drivers' licences) do not apply to vehicles registered in Northern Ireland on such journeys through Great Britain. But presumably if the appropriate authorisation is not in force, the offence of not having the s 12 or s 22 licences will be committed.

In respect of occasional services by vehicles registered in Great Britain or Northern Ireland being used for the international carriage of passengers by road (which are Community regulated by paras 1(*a*), (*b*) and (*c*) of EEC Regulation 117/66, art 3 or regulated by the Agreement on the International Carriage of Passengers by Road by means of Occasional Coach and Bus Services (ASOR) or otherwise are public service vehicles or services as described in art 3), reg 6 substitutes a new section for s 30 of the 1980 Act. The substituted s 30(1) provides that no person shall cause or permit a vehicle to be used on a road for the international carriage of passengers unless (*a*) in relation to such use of the vehicle a passenger waybill (required by arts 2, 3 and 4 and Annex 2 of Commission Regulation 1016/68) is completed by the person by whom or on whose behalf the vehicle is used and the top copy carried on the vehicle; and (*b*) the vehicle is used on the service in accordance with the waybill. In ASOR regulated cases the requirements of arts 7, 8 and 9 and Annex to ASOR (the similar completion and carrying of the top copy of a waybill) must be fulfilled and the vehicle used accordingly. As to ASOR see Volume 2, Section D. The substituted s 30(2) and (3) give certifying officers and PSV examiners various powers. Under the substituted s 30(4) a person who (*a*) without reasonable excuse contravenes the substituted s 30(1), or (*b*) without reasonable excuse fails to comply with a requirement of an officer or examiner or wilfully obstructs an officer or examiner in the exercise of his powers under s 30(2) or (3) is guilty of an offence. Regulation 6 also provides that, in addition, ss 6, 12 and 18 (PSV operators' licences etc) and s 22 (PSV drivers' licences) do not apply to vehicles registered in Northern Ireland on such journeys through Great Britain.

*PSVs registered abroad*

No public service vehicle operator's licence, road service licence or PSV driver's licence is needed in Britain in respect of regular, special regular, shuttle, worker or occasional services in the following instances:

(*a*) certain temporary visits to Britain of three months or less by public service vehicles which are for nine or less passengers (specifically including the driver) (reg 7);

(*b*) Community regulated regular, shuttle and worker services, providing the use is in accordance with the appropriate Council or Commission Regulations (reg 8);

(*c*) non-Community regulated regular and shuttle services, providing the vehicle is used by or on behalf of a person who is authorised as appropriate in the country of registration (reg 9);

(*d*) certain Community regulated occasional services under art 3(1)(*a*), (*b*) or (*c*) and certain ASOR occasional services under art 2(1)(*a*), (*b*) or (*c*) (subject to the requirements as to waybills) (reg 10);

(*e*) certain non-Community regulated occasional services, described in art 3(1)(*a*), (*b*) or (*c*), by vehicles registered in ECMT States excluding EEC and ASOR states for temporary visits of three months or less, provided the vehicle is used by or on behalf of a person who is authorised as appropriate in the country of registration (reg 11);

(*f*) certain occasional services of whatever kind (ie under art 3(1)(*a*), (*b*) or (*c*)) by vehicles not registered in an EEC member state or a country not otherwise mentioned above for temporary visits of three months or less (subject to the same proviso) (reg 12).

In cases (*c*), (*d*) (in certain circumstances), (*e*) and (*f*) a new s 12 is also substituted by Sched 2 of the regulations. Under this section a person who causes or permits such a public service vehicle to be used on a road for the international carriage of passengers without an international passenger transport authorisation in force and carried on the vehicle commits an offence. In case (*e*) (in certain circumstances) a slightly different s 12 is substituted. In this case the document which must be carried on the vehicle is one issued by the competent authority of the country in which the vehicle is registered and it must be in the form set out in Sched 3 to the regulations and duly completed.

*Further requirements*

Regulations 15–18 contain provisions as to authorisations, certificates, waybills etc.

It is an offence contrary to reg 19(1) if a person without reasonable excuse uses a vehicle for the Community regulated carriage of passengers by road, or causes or permits such a vehicle to be used to provide regular, special regular, shuttle, or worker services, without or not in accordance with the appropriate authorisation or without the appropriate certificate for worker services. He commits an offence contrary to reg 19(2) if without reasonable excuse he uses a vehicle for the Community regulated or ASOR regulated carriage of passengers by road or causes or permits a vehicle to be so used to provide occasional services when there is not duly and correctly completed for the vehicle a passenger waybill or when the top copy of the waybill is not kept on the vehicle as required.

A person commits an offence contrary to reg 20 who (*a*) without reasonable excuse contravenes or fails to comply with a requirement imposed by or under regs 15(4) or (5), 16(2)(*a*), 17(1) or (2) or 18(4) or (5), or by or under any provision of ASOR or the Council or Commission regulations referred to in any of these provisions; or (*b*) obstructs an examiner in the exercise of his powers under regs 16(2), 17(1) or (2) or 18(5) or (6) or under any provision of ASOR or the Council or Commission regulations referred to in any of these provisions.

*Penalties*

The penalty for a breach of reg 19 is a fine of level 3. The penalty for a breach of regs 15(4) or (5), 16(2)(*a*), 17(1) or (2), 18(4) or (5) or (relating to the obstruction of examiners) regs 16(2), 17(1) or (2) and 18(5) or (6) of the Road Transport (International Passenger Services) Regulations 1984—or the regulations referred to in any of them—is a fine of level 3 also (reg 20). The regulations have effect as if made under the 1981 Act and under s 67 of that Act the penalty regarding the remaining regulations is a fine of level 2.

Section 65 of the 1981 Act (forgery etc of licences and documents) is applied by reg 21 of the regulations to authorisations, certificates and other documents required by the Council or Commission regulations or the 1980 Regulations. The offence contrary to s 65 is an either way offence triable in accordance with ss 18–23 of the Magistrates' Courts Act 1980. The maximum penalty on indictment is two years' imprisonment or an unlimited fine or both and the maximum penalty on summary conviction is £2,000. See further 13.46 and Chapter 16.

## Conduct on Public Service Vehicles

### 13.61 Generally

The behaviour of drivers, conductors and passengers on public service vehicles (other than trams) is regulated by the Public Service Vehicles (Conduct of Drivers, Conductors and Passengers) Regulations 1936 (SR & O 1936 No 619) as amended by SIs 1975 No 461 and 1980 No 915. These regulations are deemed to have been made pursuant to ss 24 and 25 of the Public Passenger Vehicles Act 1981. The Stage Carriages Act 1832, which formerly applied to trams and trolley vehicles, was repealed by the Statute Law (Repeals) Act 1981, save that it still applies to the Blackpool Tramway system, the only remaining tramway system in the country.

Definitions are in reg 2 of the 1936 Regulations. 'Driver' means a person licensed to act as such. In a case noted at 120 JP Jo 110 magistrates dismissed a case where it was not proved that a conductor was licensed. Although conductors no longer need to be licensed, the same principle would appear to apply to drivers.

'Disorderly conduct' is not defined but includes something less aggressive than a breach of the peace (*Campbell* v *Adair* 1945 SLT 135).

For cases on the term 'passengers' including intending passengers, see [1952] Jo Crim L 102, and 116 JP Jo 280. As to 'entering' and 'alighting', see [1952] Jo Crim L 116.

### 13.62 Conduct of drivers and conductors

Regulations 4–8 of the 1936 Regulations deal with the conduct of drivers and conductors.

In *Reid* v *MacNicol* 1958 SLT 42, the driver of a bus was charged with failing to take precautions for the safety of passengers entering it contrary to reg 4(*c*) in that he did not halt at a bus stop and a person stumbled on boarding the bus. It was held that the regulations only imposed a duty towards persons entitled to enter the bus and no person was entitled to enter a moving bus.

In *Askew* v *Bowtell* [1947] 1 All ER 883, a tram conductor was charged with endangering the safety of a passenger by negligence contrary to the Stage Carriages Act 1832, s 48. The conductor was on top of the tram as it approached a compulsory stop and the driver slowed to a speed of 1 mph. A lady began to get off when the driver accelerated and she was thrown. The conductor was unaware that she wished to alight. It was held that the conductor was entitled to assume that the driver would stop at the compulsory stop and that passengers would not alight before the tram halted; the conductor was therefore not guilty of negligence. It was also said that, if the tram had stopped, it would be his duty to see that passengers were safely off and on before it started again. This Act has been repealed but the case may still be of assistance in interpreting the regulations.

Civil cases on the duties of conductors are *Mottram* v *S Lancs Transport Co* [1942] 2 All ER 452, *Davies* v *Liverpool Corporation* [1949] All ER 175, *Prescott* v *Lancashire United Transport Co* [1953] 1 All ER 288 and *Wingrove CB* v *Scottish Omnibus Ltd* 1965 SLTN 55. Other cases are in Bingham's *Motor Claims Cases*.

For a case where the justices' finding of fact that the prosecutor had not proved that a defendant coach driver had failed to take all reasonable precautions to ensure the safety of his passengers contrary to reg 4 was upheld, see *Edwards* v *Rigby* [1980] RTR 353.

A conductor should not open the door for passengers to alight until the vehicle has stopped (*Nicholson* v *Goddard* [1954] Crim LR 474, a prosecution). Where a Mrs Entwistle fell off a bus and the conductress was charged with failing to take reasonable precautions for the safety of the passengers contrary to reg 4(*c*), it was held that whether 'reasonable precautions' had been taken was a question of fact for the court and it was immaterial that the regulations do not define them (*Marshall* v *Clark* 1958 SLT 19).

The 1936 regulations are not intended to deal with traffic offences by a driver, eg where he has driven without reasonable consideration for his passengers (*Pawley* v *Wharldall* [1965] 2 All ER 757).

Regulation 4(*e*) as amended requires the driver or conductor when acting as such to give particulars of his name and the name and address of his employer and, if the driver, his PSV operator's licence when requested by a police constable or other person having reasonable cause.

## 13.63 Conduct of passengers

Regulations 9–12 of the 1936 Regulations deal with the conduct of passengers.

The provisions of reg 11 as to non-payment of fares were drafted to avoid the difficulty raised by the decision in *LPTB* v *Sumner* (1935) 99 JP 387. For the railway ticket fraud cases see Stone, Part IV: Railways. When in force the London Regional Transport Act 1984, ss 54–58, will provide for penalty fares in place of conviction.

Under regulation 11 where a passenger uses or attempts to use a ticket which has been altered or defaced it is not necessary for the prosecution to prove that he did so with intent to avoid payment of a fare. Nor does the prosecution have to prove an intent to avoid payment of a fare where an expired period or season ticket is produced; nor where a passenger leaves or attempts to leave the bus without having paid the fare. In the latter two cases the prosecution are instead simply required to show that the passenger so acted without reasonable excuse. Where a passenger travels beyond the distance for which he has paid a fare, he may be required to pay the additional fare or leave the public service vehicle.

The legal position as to boarding buses between stops is discussed at 119 JP Jo 98. The decision of a metropolitan stipendiary magistrate is noted there to the effect that a bus was available to the public and could be boarded anywhere en route when it was standing in a street. This will be subject to any byelaw or provision or order to the contrary. The decisions of magistrates' courts are not binding but this decision is supported in the article. Another magistrates' court has held that it is not entering a bus when the person is on the platform. In such circumstances the person was found to have already entered. A metropolitan magistrate has held that it is not obstructing a conductor under the regulations to board a bus ahead of one's place in the queue and to refuse to alight when the conductor tells one to get back in the queue ([1961] Jo Crim L 9). It might be that the passenger would be guilty of conducting himself in a disorderly manner or of unreasonably impeding other passengers seeking to enter the bus under reg 9 or under local byelaws directed against disorderly conduct or, in an extreme case, of a breach of the peace.

### 13.64 Carrying capacity

The number of passengers to be carried in a public service vehicle is regulated by the Public Service Vehicles and Trolley Vehicles (Carrying Capacity) Regulations 1984 (SI 1984 No 1406) made under ss 26 and 60 of the 1981 Act. Special provision is made as to children. A bus owner, who had appointed a young and inexperienced conductor and had not provided for adequate inspection, was convicted of aiding and abetting the conductor to allow overcrowding, although the owner was not present on the bus at the material time (*Gough* v *Rees* (1930) 94 JP 53). The offences under the regulations include driving, causing or permitting to be driven on a road a vehicle with seated passengers in excess of the number specified. There is a similar offence regarding standing passengers. There are also prohibitions against standing in certain places including the upper deck and the steps leading to it. Any person may prosecute under them.

### 13.65–70 Lost property

Lost property on public service vehicles is subject to the Public Service Vehicles (Lost Property) Regulations 1978 (SI 1978 No 1684). Schedule 2 contains a scale of charges for lost items. The regulations do not apply to London Transport, as to which see the London Transport (Lost Property) Regulations 1971 (SI 1971 No 2125), as amended by SI 1978 No 1791.

## Conduct on PSVs: Proceedings and Penalties

### 13.71 Generally

Proceedings for an offence by a passenger may be instituted by any person, but those for an offence by a driver, inspector or conductor only by a person mentioned in s 69 of the 1981 Act (see 13.51 and 'Authority to prosecute', 2.3), so far as the regulations are concerned. Offences under the regulations may be prosecuted within six months (*Orr* v *Strathern* 1929 SC (J) 30).

Because of increasingly violent and disorderly behaviour on public service vehicles, particularly at night, by s 25(2) a constable who with reasonable cause suspects a person of contravening or failing to comply with a provision of the regulations having effect by virtue of what is now s 25 of the 1981 Act (ie the 1936 regulations in so far as they relate to passengers), or of byelaws made under the Tramways Act 1870, may require that person to give his name and address. The constable may then arrest him if that person:

(*a*) refuses to give his name and address to the constable; or

(*b*) gives a name and address to the constable but does not answer to the satisfaction of the constable questions put to him by the constable for the purpose of ascertaining whether the name and address are correct.

Subsection (2) of s 25 will be repealed by Sched 7, Part 1 to the Police and Criminal Evidence Act 1984 when in force, and will be replaced by the general power of arrest without warrant under s 25(1) of that Act.

The Act does not apply to Scotland and Northern Ireland.

The penalty for offences contrary to s 24(2) of the 1981 Act is a fine of level 2 in respect of offending inspectors, drivers or conductors. Particulars of the conviction may be endorsed on the PSV licence of an offending driver. The penalty for failing to produce the licence within a reasonable time under s 24(3) is a fine of level 3. The penalty for offending passengers under s 25(3) is a fine of level 3. The penalty under the Carrying Capacity Regulations is under two different sections depending on the circumstances (s 26—control of number of passengers) and s 67 (other regulations) but the maximum penalty is the same—a fine of level 2 in each case. In view of s 31 of the Criminal Law Act 1977 the maximum penalty under the Stage Carriages Act 1832 is a fine of level 1. All such offences are triable by magistrates only.

There is no power to disqualify from driving or to endorse a driving licence or order penalty points.

As to the defence of reasonable excuse under s 68(1) of the 1981 Act, which is available for offences contrary to ss 24(2) and (3), 25 and 26, see 13.47.

# Chapter 14

# Drivers' Hours and Records

## Introduction

### 14.1 Generally

British law as to drivers' laws and records is governed primarily by Part VI of the Transport Act 1968. The purpose of the law is set out in s 95(1) of the Act. This states:

> This Part of this Act shall have effect with a view to securing the observance of proper hours or periods of work by persons engaged in the carriage of passengers or goods by road and thereby protecting the public against the risks which arise in cases where the drivers of motor vehicles are suffering from fatigue.

The legal requirements for drivers' hours and conditions of work and the keeping of records are complicated, and in particular complicated by the application of the Community rules. The recommended approach is to apply a process of elimination. Firstly, it must be ascertained whether the vehicle in question is subject to Part VI of the Transport Act. If it is, the classification of the particular journey or work must then be established. There are four classes of journeys or work:

(*a*) international journeys or work;
(*b*) national journeys or work;
(*c*) domestic journeys or work; and
(*d*) 'mixed' driving, ie journeys or work falling partly in one of the above classes and partly in another.

### 14.2 Application

Part VI of the Transport Act 1968, by s 95(2), applies to:

(*a*) passenger vehicles, ie:
   (i) public service vehicles; and
   (ii) motor vehicles (other than public service vehicles) constructed or adapted to carry more than twelve passengers;
(*b*) goods vehicles, ie:
   (i) heavy locomotives, light locomotives, motor tractors and any motor vehicle so constructed that a trailer may by partial super-imposition be attached to the vehicle in such a manner as to

cause a substantial part of the weight of the trailer to be borne by the vehicle; and

(ii) motor vehicles (except those mentioned in para (*a*)) constructed or adapted to carry goods other than the effects of passengers.

It is not clear whether 'more than twelve passengers' includes the driver among the twelve, but it is submitted that it does not (see 'Passenger', 1.59).

The application of Part VI to the Crown, military, police and fire brigade vehicles is indicated in s 102. See also 'The Crown', 2.8.

Finally it may be relevant whether the use is for private purposes or a commercial operation.

All these matters are discussed in greater detail below.

## 14.3 National and international journeys

National and international journeys or work are subject to EEC Regulation 543/69 as to hours and conditions of work of crew members, and to the tachograph provisions as to records. There are certain total or partial *exemptions* but despite this the classification of national or international journeys or work still applies. There are also *exceptions* from the EEC regulation and from the tachograph provisions. These exceptions are contained in art 4 of the EEC regulation and are also exceptions from the compulsory tachograph provisions (art 5 of EEC Regulation 1463/70: the tachograph regulation).

The art 4 exceptions are classified as domestic journeys or work, and are discussed at 14.4.

The nature of international journeys or work is self evident. (As to non-EEC international journeys, see the AETR agreement, discussed at 14.25.) It should be noted that the AETR agreement and not primarily the EEC regulations also cover *EEC journeys* which take place in part through a third country. The AETR agreement is apparently enforced through EEC Regulation 543/69.

International journeys or work include that part of the journey which takes place in this country (quoted and confirmed as correct in *Paterson* v *Richardson* [1982] RTR 49). The Divisional Court in *Paterson* also quoted as persuasive authority for the meaning of an international operation an EEC Commission opinion of 16 May 1974 addressed to the Irish Government. The intention of the Irish Government had been to draft regulations basing the journey on the driver, rather than on the vehicle plus the load and driver. The opinion stated:

The Irish Government's interpretation of the term 'international transport operations' which appears in article 19(2) of Council Regulation (EEC) No 543/69 is, admittedly, not defined in the Regulation, but this is because it is generally considered to be self-explanatory. The Community has always understood international transport to be all transport between the beginning of a journey and the destination. What the transport world generally considers international transport to be appears clearly from the following definitions taken from two high-level international agreements:

General agreement on the economic regulation of international road transport, 17 March 1954 . . .: 'International goods transport is transport carried out by means of a vehicle employed in the transport of goods, the point of departure and the destination being located in two different countries.'

European agreement concerning the work of crews of vehicle engaged in international road transport (AETR) of 1 July 1970: 'For the purposes of the present Agreement the expression "international road transport" means road transport which involves the crossing of at least one frontier.'

In *Paterson* v *Richardson* the driver drove a vehicle to the docks at Dover. Another driver drove the vehicle on to the continent. It was held that the first driver was engaged in an international transport operation.

In *Paterson* the vehicle left the country. The Department of Transport has expressed the view in a booklet on tachographs published by HMSO that this is necessary and that therefore merely taking a load to the docks and unloading it for shipment is not an international journey or work. While this view is not authoritative, it is submitted that it is correct (cf the EEC opinion quoted in *Paterson* and the definition of 'carriage by road' at 14.10).

The Department of Transport booklet points out that the definition is different in the Drivers' Hours (Harmonisation with Community Rules) Regulations 1978. In these regulations 'international journeys or work'are defined as 'those Community regulated journeys or work which are undertaken in connection with international transport operations and to which the Community rules apply in unmodified form'. There is no reference to crossing frontiers or passing to a different country. Despite this it is submitted that the definition must mean that international transport operations have the same meaning in the Harmonisation Regulations as in the EEC regulation, because the EEC regulation would have applied in unmodified form to them and them alone. These particular modification provisions are now spent but the principle remains. The point is of importance for drivers making dock journeys because of the different provisions in the Harmonisation Regulations for national and international transport operations respectively and because there are exemptions from the Community rules for certain national operations. It is submitted therefore that a dock journey where the vehicle is not transported abroad is a national transport operation.

National journeys or work are those national operations which are not excepted from the EEC regulation by art 4.

## 14.4 Domestic journeys

Domestic journeys or work are those which are outside the scope of the EEC regulation. The exceptions from EEC Regulation 543/69 as amended (which therefore primarily become domestic journeys or work) are set out in art 4 of that regulation. The most important exception is in art 4, para 2, namely 'vehicles used for the carriage of goods, the permissible maximum weight of which, including any trailer or semi-trailer, does not exceed 3.5 metric tons'. The 'permissible maximum weight' means the maximum authorised combined operating weight (art 1(7)).

One of the exceptions in art 4 (see para 9) is for 'specialised breakdown vehicles'. As a working description a 'specialised breakdown vehicle' should be regarded as a vehicle which is specially built or adapted, and kept, for the purpose of going to the assistance of a broken-down vehicle and which, generally, has the capability, for this purpose, of raising a broken-down vehicle (wholly or partially) with a view to its recovery either by conveyance on, or by towing behind, the breakdown vehicle; *Universal Salvage Ltd* v *Boothby* [1984] RTR 289. The EEC regulation and the British statutory instruments had different origins and were not necessarily to be interpreted in the same way although in fact a like result was reached (ibid) (see 1.17). In that case it was held that a vehicle used to collect broken-down vehicles from garages was in effect a transporter and not a breakdown vehicle.

Domestic journeys or work are still covered by the United Kingdom provisions, in particular Part VI of the Transport Act 1968 (see the definition in the Drivers' Hours (Harmonisation with Community Rules) Regulations 1978 (SI 1978 No 1157)). Where records are concerned, the relevant provisions are the Drivers' Hours (Keeping of Records) Regulations 1976. Hours and conditions of work are covered by the domestic drivers' hours code. This code is defined by s 96(13) of the Transport Act 1968, and means the provisions of s 96(1)–(6) inclusive, modified as appropriate. Section 96(13) was added by s 2 of the Road Traffic (Drivers' Ages and Hours of Work) Act 1976. Although they remain in force, these United Kingdom provisions will now only apply, in their original form, in comparatively rare instances, so far as drivers are concerned.

## 14.5 EEC law: summary

As a result of the United Kingdom's accession to the Treaty of Rome and the consequent enactment of the European Communities Act 1972, the law relating to drivers' hours and records in respect of both British and foreign vehicles has undergone substantial alteration.

Under the European Communities Act 1972, EEC regulations have a direct and binding effect on United Kingdom law save and so far as they are expressly excluded or modified (see s 2). The EEC regulations may be implemented by statutory instrument or Order in Council (s 2(2)). The penalty for breach is to be provided by the member countries (but see Sched 2 for certain maximum limitations). Action may be taken against a member country in the European Court for failing to give effect to such regulations. For example, in the *Commission of the European Communities* v *UK* [1979] RTR 321 the European Court of Justice on the application of the Commission declared that the United Kingdom had failed to fulfil its obligations under the EEC Treaty by not implementing the EEC tachograph regulation as required. The United Kingdom was ordered to bear the costs of the hearing.

Article 74 of the Treaty of Rome requires member countries to work towards a common transport policy and art 75 is directed towards the establishment of common rules for international transport. Substantial progress had been made towards harmonisation at the time of the United Kingdom's accession, and the European Communities Act 1972 accordingly amended the relevant provisions of the Transport Act 1968.

The major and striking result is that, as will be seen, the majority of journeys in this country, whether the vehicles be registered in this country or in the EEC, will be governed by EEC Regulation 543/69 as amended so far as a crew member's driving hours are concerned and by the tachograph provisions (which incorporate and to some extent directly apply EEC Regulation 1463/70 as amended) so far as the keeping of records is concerned. EEC Regulation 543/69 has been amended by Regulations 514/72 and 515/72 (both of 28 February 1972) and 2827/77 and 2829/77 (both of 12 December 1977).

Reference may also be necessary to the European agreement concerning the work of crews of vehicles engaged in international transport (the AETR Agreement) where foreign vehicles are operating in the United Kingdom and where United Kingdom vehicles set out in the United Kingdom on a journey to, or return from, a country which is subject to the AETR agreement but which is not an EEC country. This agreement is summarised at 14.25.

## 14.6 International haulage permits

The provisions relating to international haulage permits are unaffected by EEC law: see the International Road Haulage Permits Act 1975 and the Goods Vehicles (International Road Haulage Permits) Regulations 1975 (SI 1975 No 2234) made thereunder.

Under s 1 of the Act it is an offence to use a goods vehicle or trailer on an international journey as prescribed by the regulations without an international haulage permit. Using a goods vehicle in contravention of s 1 is punishable summarily with a fine of level 4. Section 1(2) requires the permit to be produced to a goods vehicle examiner. Obstructing a vehicle examiner is summarily punishable with a fine of level 3. Under the regulations an international journey for which a permit is required to be carried is restricted to journeys to or through Austria, France, West Germany or Italy. The wording of the regulations and the Act are such that the international journey commences as soon as the journey starts. An offence may thus be committed before the vehicle leaves the United Kingdom and while passing through the UK. The 1975 Act has amended ss 169, 170 and 173 of the 1972 Act to include international permits within their ambit. See further Chapter 16.

## 14.7 International carriage of perishable foodstuffs

The provisions as to the international carriage of perishable foodstuffs is also not affected by EEC law. The International Carriage of Perishable Foodstuffs Act 1976 as amended by the International Carriage of Perishable Foodstuffs Act 1976 (Amendment) Order 1983 (SI 1983 No 1123) provides for issue of a certificate of compliance in respect of transport equipment for such carriage based either on an examination or on type approval. Alternatively a certification plate may provide evidence of compliance. The International Carriage of Perishable Foodstuffs Regulations 1979 (SI 1979 No 415), as amended by SI 1981 No 521, are in operation.

'Transport equipment' is as prescribed by the ATP agreement on the International Carriage of Perishable Foodstuffs and the Special Equipment to be used for Such Carriage as concluded in Geneva on 1 September 1970 (Cmnd 8272).

Designation marks are to be affixed (reg 24).

## 14.8 Conveyance of dangerous substances

The Dangerous Substances (Conveyance by Road in Road Tankers and Tank Containers) Regulations 1981 (SI 1981 No 1059) as amended by the Classification, Packaging and Labelling of Dangerous Substances Regulations 1984 (SI 1984 No 1244) have been made.

These regulations replace earlier regulations including a number of regulations relating to specific substances. Radioactive substances are still dealt with separately. The new regulations apply to any dangerous substance on the approved list and also to any dangerous substance having the specified dangerous characteristics. Offences are not limited to road journeys and breaches may occur from the commencement of loading to the final cleansing (see reg 3(2)).

The regulations are made under the Health and Safety at Work etc Act 1974. The offences are 'either way' offences and the maximum penalty for a contravention is a fine of £2,000 on summary conviction and a fine on indictment (s 33 of the 1974 Act).

There are certain exceptions in reg 3. In particular there is an exception if the vehicle is engaged in an international transport operation within the meaning of the European Agreement concerning the international carriage of dangerous goods by road (ADR) unless under the Agreement it is governed by national legislation. The vehicle must comply instead with the conditions in Annexes A and B to that Agreement and be certified as complying with it.

Where a defendant is summoned for a breach of the regulations, he has a defence if he can prove that he took all reasonable precautions and exercised all due diligence to avoid the commission of the particular offence (reg 24). For the procedure, reference should also be made to the 1974 Act which contains a number of special provisions. See also the procedure at 14.63.

The most familiar provision of the regulations is the requirement for hazard warning panels and labels with signs indicating the type of danger. The regulations make special reference to petrol. In addition to labelling there are a number of other requirements designed to reduce the risk of danger.

## 14.9 EEC law: historical development

EEC Regulation 543/69 was originally implemented for records on *international journeys* only by the Drivers' Hours (Passenger and Goods Vehicles) (Keeping of Records) (International Rules) Regulations 1973 (SI 1973 No 380), which were subsequently replaced by the Drivers' Hours (Keeping of Records) Regulations 1976 (SI 1976 No 1447). The 1976 Regulations revoked and replaced all the former regulations. These regulations now have only a limited effect as the EEC regulation was then applied directly to international journeys. The EEC regulation was subsequently applied also to records on *national journeys*. This was brought about by the Road Traffic

(Drivers' Ages and Hours of Work) Act 1976 by the substitution 'applicable Community rules' for 'international rules' in Part VI of the Transport Act 1968.

So far as drivers' hours are concerned the EEC regulation again originally applied only to *international journeys*, but similarly now applies to *both international and national journeys* subject in each case to certain modifications and exceptions under the Drivers' Hours (Harmonisation with Community Rules) Regulations 1978 (SI 1978 No 1157).

Contraventions of EEC Regulation 543/69 as amended (the applicable Community rules) as to hours of work etc on both international and national journeys are punishable under s 96(11A) of the Transport Act 1968 as amended by the 1976 Act.

Finally the tachograph rules were brought into force fully from 1 January 1982 to govern the keeping of records. The tachograph rules are contained in ss 97, 97A and 97B of the 1968 Act and in the Passenger and Goods Vehicles (Recording Equipment) Regulations 1979 (SI 1979 No 1746). These statutory rules incorporate and to some extent make directly applicable the EEC tachograph regulation (EEC Regulation 1463/70 as amended). Article 5 of this regulation makes it clear that the tachograph rules replace art 14 of EEC Regulation 543/69 (record books). A tachograph is now a compulsory requirement for virtually every transport operation subject to EEC Regulation 543/69 (drivers' hours and rest periods) (see s 97(6) and art 3 of EEC Regulation 1463/70). The only exemption is for vehicles used for the carriage of passengers on regular services on routes exceeding 50 km. Crew members of such services did not previously and do not now have to keep records but had and still have to comply with art 15 of EEC Regulation 543/69 (service timetables and duty rosters) if no tachograph is fitted.

## 14.10 EEC law: definitions

Some basic definitions in art 1 of the EEC Regulation 543/69 differ from those in the 1972 Act and the Road Traffic Regulation Act 1984, eg 'vehicle' and 'trailer'. The same definitions apply in EEC Regulation 1463/70 (the tachograph regulation) (see art 2 of that regulation).

'Motor vehicle' under art 1(2) means any mechanically self-propelled vehicle circulating on the road (other than rails), and normally used for carrying passengers or goods. The interrelationship of 'carriage by road' and 'motor vehicle' in art 1 was considered in *British Gypsum Ltd* v *Corner* [1982] RTR 308. It was held that the words 'on the road' were not to be added by implication to the last part. In *British Gypsum* the lorry was normally used for carrying goods and it was immaterial that it was not normally used on roads. It did circulate on a road and was therefore within the EEC definition. In interpreting 'normally used' the court followed *Peak Trailer & Chassis Ltd* v *Jackson* [1967] 1 All ER 172 noted at 8.17.

'Crew member' is defined in art 1 as meaning the driver, driver's mate and conductor. 'Driver' in this context means 'any person who drives the vehicle, even for a short period, or who is carried in the vehicle in order to be available for driving if necessary'. The offences in s 96(11A) (hours and rest periods), s 97, s 97A and s 97B (tachograph offences) and s 98(4) (offences in respect of the former EEC-regulated manual, ie non-tachograph, records and records under the AETR agreement (see 14.25)), are not restricted to drivers, but extend to crew members also. They should be contrasted with the s 96 provisions as to hours and rest periods which apply to drivers only. Section 96(11A) offences are expressly restricted to offences in Great Britain; ss 97 and 98(4) do not contain a similar restriction. There is a wide jurisdiction given by s 103(7) (see 14.70). The question was raised (but not answered) in *Pearson* v *Rutterford* [1982] RTR 54 whether an HGV driving instructor was a crew member.

References in Part VI of the 1968 Act to a person 'driving' a vehicle are references to 'his being at the driving controls of the vehicle for the purpose of controlling its movement, whether it is in motion or is stationary with the engine running' (s 103(3)). Contrast the wider definition in art 1 of EEC Regulation 543/69 of the 'driver' crew member.

The meanings of terms which provide exceptions or exemptions are discussed under the particular exception or exemption. Examples are the meaning of 'local road tests', 'animal carcases', 'specialised vehicles', and 'door-to-door selling' and 'local market' (for all see 14.21). For 'specialised breakdown vehicles' excepted by Art 4(9) of EEC Regulation 543/69, see *Universal Salvage Ltd* v *Boothby* at 1.17 and 14.4.

The time recorded is the time which agrees with the official time in the country of registration of the vehicle (art 17(2) of the tachograph regulation). Tachographs should not therefore be adjusted on the continent to show continental time and a time allowance may have to be made for foreign vehicles in Great Britain.

The tachograph regulation refers to 'employers' but both EEC Regulation 543/69 and the AETR agreement refer to 'undertakings'. The meaning of 'undertaking' was considered by the European Court in *Auditeur du Travail* v *Du Tour* [1978] RTR 186. It was held that responsibility rested with the undertaking rather than the agency so far as compliance with art 14(7) and (8) of EEC Regulation 543/69 was concerned. There is no reason why the decision should not be of more general application. Compare *Alcock* v *Griston Ltd* at 14.63.

'Carriage by road' is defined as 'any journey by road of a vehicle whether laden or not used for the carriage of passengers or goods' (art 1(1)). As stated, this also applies to the tachograph regulation (art 2 of that regulation).

## 14.11–16 'Carriage by road'—private use of goods and passenger vehicles

There is a conflict over whether the EEC rules (including the tachograph regulation) apply to the private use of a goods or passenger vehicle or only to a commercial operation. The definition of 'carriage by road' (see 14.10) does not distinguish between the two. There is no contrast between business and private use and no reference to hire or reward. There is a conflict between this and the narrower definition of 'on duty' in s 103(4). 'On duty' is one of the expressions used in s 96(11A). See also the decision in *Carter* v *Walton* (1984) *The Times*, 28 May, at 14.39. At first sight the wider definition ('carriage by road') is not restricted by ss 96(11A) and 103(4). Section 96(11A) is in this respect in general terms ('applicable Community rules as to periods of driving, or distance driven or periods on or off duty') while the Community rule is specific ('carriage by road' etc). The inference is that if the journey is subject to the EEC regulations the purpose is immaterial.

The Secretary of State for Transport has expressed the view that neither EEC Regulation 543/69 nor the tachograph regulation applies to privately owned and driven goods or passenger vehicles. The written answer is in *Hansard* 20 July 1981: written answers, col 38–39.

*Tachographs (Minibuses)*

Mr Newens asked the Secretary of State for Transport if he will take steps to exempt minibuses with over 10 permanent seats owned by local education authorities and used for educational trips or visits to Europe from European Economic Community tachograph regulations; and if he will make a statement.

Mr Kenneth Clarke [*pursuant to his reply*, 17 July 1981]: There is no specific exemption for educational vehicles from the tachograph or drivers' hours regulations. My right hon. friend has no further power to exempt classes of vehicles from them. However, it is strongly arguable that the regulations do not apply to privately owned and driven vehicles. It is very unlikely that any such vehicle would be prosecuted in this country or that any attempted prosecution would be successful. It is for the courts to interpret the law in any borderline case, however, and I cannot bind the prosecuting authorities or the courts in this or any other EEC country. I understand that the European Commission may shortly be undertaking a review of these regulations and Her Majesty's Government will continue to press for clarification of their terms.

A letter dated 19 August 1981 from the Department of Transport commenting on the Parliamentary Answer has been produced in court. The relevant extracts from the letter are as follows, with emphasis added:

2 You will appreciate that (the Parliamentary Answer) goes a long way towards reversing the view we have previously expressed that, specific exemptions apart, all passenger-carrying vehicles with more than 15 seats overall on domestic journeys (and 9 seats on international journeys) and all goods vehicles over 3.5 tonnes permissible maximum weight were subject to the EEC Regulations 543/69 and 1463/70. Mr Clarke's statement is based upon an opinion from the Attorney-General that the best view, in the absence of decided cases, is that the EEC Regulations, being primarily directed to the harmonisation of conditions of competition among professionals within the Community, *do not extend to operations which are entirely non-commercial. We understand that, if approached by a Police Force, the Director of Public Prosecutions would advise against prosecution in a case involving driving for non-commercial purposes.*

3 The answer . . . is clear in so far as it relates to privately owned and driven vehicles; different considerations may or may not apply to private driving by professional drivers and to the various other permutations of use. We hope in due course to be able to elaborate on these aspects. Mr Clarke has however made it clear that he regards vehicles owned and used by scout groups, youth clubs, angling societies, jazz bands, charities and the like as being entirely non-commercial (provided of course that they are not carrying passengers for hire or reward) and some uses of school-owned vehicles may also be regarded in this light. There will of course be problems of definition and borderline cases but we have no doubt that enforcement staff are fully

occupied by commercial operations and will wish to concentrate their efforts on those operations. You will know that in the longer term Ministers wish to see clarification of the EEC Regulations through the Community's legislative processes, and Commission officials have now said that a review of the relevant legislation will begin shortly. We cannot expect early results from this review but we hope that clearer legislation will result; as with other Community law, all depends on the collective agreement of the ten Member States.

4 PT2 and RF2 are continuing to advise those going abroad on a private journey that it is prudent to have a tachograph fitted since other Member States may take a different view of the law. We are considering what modifications may be needed to leaflets and guides on the subject.

5 The European Commission is aware of these developments and, whereas we had anticipated a hostile reaction, those responsible for directing policy in this area have tended to support the view that a Regulation aimed at harmonising competition and improving social conditions for employees is nothing to do with the non-commercial sector.

If this view is correct it is difficult to see why in law any distinction should be drawn for the private use by a commercial driver of his own goods or passenger vehicle for his private journey home. The legislation makes no such distinction expressly. It is understood that some commercial drivers are using *each other's* vehicles for their private journeys between depot and home in order to try to comply with the spirit of the recommendations and to avoid legal challenges.

In conclusion therefore it seems that until the law is clarified, the Department of Transport is not recommending prosecutions for vehicles when they are being used for non-commercial purposes. The decision in *Carter* v *Walton* (1984) *The Times*, 28 May gives some support to this view (see 14.39).

## Drivers' Hours

### 14.17–20 Generally

The main provisions as to drivers' hours and conditions of work so far as national and international journeys or work (defined at 14.3) are concerned are contained in arts 6–13 and 14a of EEC Regulation 543/69 as amended and (in appropriate contexts) in s 96 of the Transport Act 1968. The provisions of s 96 are discussed at 14.22.

The EEC regulation applies in full to both national and international journeys.

Domestic journeys or work are excepted from the regulation by art 4 (see the definition at 14.4). Section 96 in an earlier form applies to domestic journeys or work. These subsections (1)–(6) of s 96 are known as the domestic drivers' hours code and are discussed at 14.22. As well as applying in an *unmodified* form to *domestic* journeys or work and *modified* as appropriate to *mixed* journeys or work, s 96 also applies in a yet *differently modified* form to *national* journeys or work, but in the latter case *only so far as hours of duty are concerned* (as to on and off duty and whether the required breaks are part of the duty periods see 14.39 and in particular *Carter* v *Walton*). Section 96 basically applies to drivers only, although others may aid and abet or cause or permit offences (see s 96(11)). Contrast the applicable Community rules which apply to drivers or crew members (see s 96(11A)).

The EEC regulation applies to all goods and passenger vehicles, subject to the exceptions and exemptions stated therein and also subject to Part VI of the 1968 Act, in particular s 95(2) which specifies the vehicles to which Part VI of the Act applies. Section 96 applies to public service vehicles, passenger vehicles constructed to carry more than twelve passengers and goods vehicles, all as defined in s 95(2) which relates to drivers' records and tachographs as well as to drivers' hours. The application of these sections to Crown, military, police and fire brigade vehicles is indicated in s 102.

The EEC regulation will normally apply not only to British vehicles on national and international journeys or work but also to vehicles from other EEC countries on any international journey in Great Britain. Journeys to, from or through a third country (ie a non-EEC country) are, however, subject to the European Agreement concerning the Work of Crews of Vehicles Engaged in International Road Transport (the AETR agreement), discussed at 14.25, whether or not the third country is a party to the AETR agreement and whether or not the journey is to, from or through an EEC country. The AETR agreement is apparently enforceable through EEC Regulation 543/69; see 14.25.

Definitions are to be found in s 103 of the 1968 Act and in art 1 of the EEC regulation. It should be noted that the EEC regulation definitions do not always correspond and reference should be made where appropriate to the regulation. (See also 14.3 and 14.10.)

The offences of breach of the EEC regulation and the domestic drivers' hours code are set out in s 96(11A) and (11) respectively and are considered at 14.39. Various other offences relating to the inspection of records and other documents under s 99 are considered at 14.70.

## Drivers' Hours: Goods Vehicles

### 14.21 National and international journeys

The provisions of EEC Regulation 543/69 as regards hours and rest periods for drivers of *goods* vehicles on national and international journeys or work are summarised in Table 1. (As to *passenger* vehicles see 14.31–4.) The first column shows the original position under s 96 of the Transport Act 1968 which applied prior to 1 January 1978 and which still applies to domestic journeys or work. The second column shows the position under the EEC regulation as from 1 January 1981. The relevant articles for national and international journeys or work are arts 7 and 8 (driving periods) and 11, 11a and 12 (rest periods).

It will be noted that there are special restrictions for drivers of large vehicles etc, ie vehicles over 20 tonnes or vehicles with more than one trailer or semi-trailer. Article 7 restricts the daily driving period so that it cannot be extended beyond eight hours and art 8 provides that the permitted rest

**Table 1**
**Goods vehicles: hours and rest periods**

*(For the transitional period between 1.1.78 and 31.12.80 see 10th ed, p 480.)*

| *Nature of provision* | *Domestic journeys or work as at present and the position generally prior to 1.1.78* | *National and international journeys or work as from 1.1.81* |
|---|---|---|
| *Continuous driving period* | 5½ hours *working* period (s 96(2)) | 4 hours (art 7) |
| *Daily driving period* | 10 hours (s 96(1)) | 8 hours (art 7) (or 9 hours for drivers of other than large vehicles etc* twice in one week, but this must be compensated). |
| *Rest breaks* | 30 mins (s 96(2)) | Period of at least 30 mins after maximum permitted continuous period of driving, but may be 2 × 20 mins or 3 × 15 mins instead (art 8). This does not apply to drivers of large vehicles etc.* Such a driver must take at least a 1-hour break after the first maximum period of driving. This may be replaced by two 30-min breaks providing the maximum period is not exceeded (art 8). |
| *Weekly driving limit* | — | 48 hours (art 7) |
| *Fortnightly driving limit* | — | 92 hours (art 7) |
| *Daily rest period* | 11 hours (s 96(4)) | Normally 11 hours but may be reduced to 9 hours not more than twice a week when taken at the crew/vehicle base *or* may be reduced to 8 hours twice a week when taken away from crew/vehicle base (art 11). |
| *Weekly rest period* | 24 hours (s 96(6)) | 29 consecutive hours plus daily rest period immediately before or after (art 12(1)). But may be reduced to not less than 24 hours if a rest period equivalent to the reduction is granted during the same week (art 12). Any consecutive 7 days must include a rest period. |
| *Daily hours of duty limit (spread over)* | 11 hours (s 96(3)(*a*))<br>12½ hours (s 96(3)(*b*)) | These are not expressly covered by the EEC regulation. Part VI of the Transport Act 1968 as modified will continue to apply in certain circumstances. See the Drivers' Hours (Harmonisation with Community Rules) Regulations 1978. |
| *Weekly hours of duty limit* | 60 hours (s 96(5)) | |

* 'Large vehicles etc' means combination over 20 tonnes or motor vehicles or tractors with more than one trailer or semi-trailer.

breaks may not be reduced below thirty minutes although this is possible for other vehicles. These restrictions are incorporated in Table 1.

There are special provisions as to daily rest periods in arts 11 and 11a for vehicles with two drivers, vehicles with bunks and vehicles transported by ferry or train. For vehicles with two drivers and no bunk the daily rest period must be ten consecutive hours in the previous twenty-seven. For vehicles with two drivers and a bunk the daily rest period is eight consecutive hours in the previous thirty. For journeys by ferry or transportation by train the daily rest period can be divided into not more than two parts. The working period must be as short as possible and may on no account exceed one hour before embarkation or after disembarkation. Customs formalities are regarded as part of the embarkation or disembarkation procedure and not as part of the hour. The part of the daily rest period taken on land may be taken before or after the daily rest period taken on board, in other words before the commencement or after the conclusion of the carriage by boat or train. During both portions the crew member must have access to a bunk or couchette. It would not be sufficient in these circumstances of a divided daily rest period with part taken on land for a couchette to be provided for the boat or train only. Where there is such an interruption the permissible total of the two periods must be increased by two hours. The purpose of these special provisions is apparently to allow a short period of preparatory work of up to one hour to be carried out either prior to going on board or after leaving.

*Definitions*

Article 1 contains definitions. The principal definitions are discussed at 14.10. The 'week' is the continental period of seven consecutive days. There is some uncertainty as to whether this is the case in respect of the hours of duty for drivers on national operations alone (see further 14.17). 'Driver' includes any person carried to be available for driving. As to on and off duty and whether the required breaks are part of the duty periods, see 14.39 and in particular *Carter* v *Walton*. 'Daily rest period' does not include any period on standby duty. It must be an uninterrupted period of at least eight hours (but see art 11).

The weekly rest period must adjoin a daily rest period which must immediately precede or must immediately follow it. However, the weekly rest period and the daily rest period may be in different weeks, although it follows obviously that the two weeks must be contiguous.

*Exceptions and exemptions*

The journeys or work excepted by art 4 of EEC Regulation 543/69 are domestic journeys or work (see 14.4) and are altogether outside the scope of the Community rules.

Article 14a of EEC Regulation 543/69 allows member countries to grant exemptions in respect of *national* but not international transport, and the Community Road Transport Rules (Exemptions) Regulations 1978 (SI 1978 No 1158, as amended by SI 1980 Nos 266 and 2018 and SI 1981 No 1855) achieve this.

There is a general exemption from the EEC regulation for national operations involving the use of vehicles constructed and equipped to carry not more than fifteen persons, including the driver, the use of vehicles undergoing local road tests for the purposes of repair or maintenance, for the transport of live animals from farms to local markets or vice versa or for the transport of animal carcases or waste not intended for human consumption (reg 3). Specialised vehicles used at local markets, for door-to-door selling, for mobile banking, exchange or savings transactions, for the purposes of worship, for the lending of books, records or cassettes, or for cultural events or mobile exhibitions are also exempt (reg 4). There are also certain limited exemptions relating to the transportation of milk.

The local road test exemption applies not to vehicles undergoing tests but to the *use* of vehicles undergoing tests. This could mean use while undergoing or use for the purpose of undergoing. It is submitted that the exemption would include a vehicle being taken to or being returned from a test. This interpretation is supported by the reference to repairs and maintenance; the exemption might well be impossible to operate if a narrower interpretation were adopted. For 'local market', see *DPP* v *Sidney Hackett Ltd* (1985) *The Times*, 15 April.

The leading case on the meaning of 'specialised vehicles' is *R* v *Thomas Scott and Sons (Bakers) Ltd* [1984] RTR 337. This is a decision of the European Court following a reference by the House of Lords. The European Court held that 'specialised' referred to the vehicle and was intended to cover exclusively vehicles whose construction, fitments or other permanent characteristics guaranteed that they were used primarily for the operation in question. This conclusion was applied by the court to those specialised for door-to-door selling, mobile banking or the trading of books or records, but there is no reason why the same principle should not be applied to the other named operations such as cultural events and mobile exhibitions. The court indicated that modification of the vehicle was insufficient. It is submitted that a modification to provide a permanent characteristic could be sufficient.

The vehicle in question in the case had been specially adapted for the transport of bread and cakes by means of plastic interlocking trays held by clips moved up and down by metal rods fitted to the side of the vehicle. It did not have a specialised engine such as that normally used in a milk float where door-to-door selling required constant stopping and starting, nor was it so arranged as to enable the potential customer to inspect within the vehicle the goods offered for sale. It was not so constructed or adapted as to render the constant loading and unloading envisaged in the concept of door-to-door sales particularly more convenient to the salesman. It had been held not to be a specialised vehicle (see the earlier report at [1983] RTR 369).

The earlier cases have to be reconsidered in the light of this decision but they may still be of some assistance. In a Scottish case, *Stewart* v *Richmond* 1983 SLT 62 the High Court of Justiciary held that a flat-bottomed lorry used for coal deliveries was not specialised in any respect. For an instance where a specially constructed and adapted coal lorry was held to be 'specialised', see *Re British Fuel Co Ltd* noted at [1983] Crim LR 747. In another Scottish case *Struthers (Lochwinnoch) Ltd* v *Tudhope* 1982 SLT 393 the vehicle had been provided with a platform designed to carry only soft drinks and was held to be specialised.

As to 'door-to-door selling' the court stated that it did not matter whether the selling was to individuals, to wholesalers or to other customers provided that the activity of selling was characterised by frequent stops. It could consist of calls on potential wholesale customers, such as shops, works canteens, old people's homes or supermarkets providing that the activity of selling is characterised by frequent stops by the specialised vehicles. In *Struthers (Lochwinnoch) Ltd* v *Tudhope* above on the day in question delivery and collection was being made of a whole load and this was held not to be door-to-door selling. The court considered it important to examine the nature of the transport operation and not whether the vehicle was commonly used for door-to-door selling.

Many door-to-door transactions consist of taking an express or implied order for a future week coupled with delivery under a previous order, eg a mik round or the delivery of bread and other foods. In the *British Fuel Co Ltd* case above it was stated that door-to-door selling did not cease to be so because the commodity had been pre-ordered. This was a Crown Court decision on appeal from a magistrates' court and is not binding. However, in the judgment of the lower court in *Oxford* v *Thomas Scott and Sons Bakery Ltd* [1983] RTR 369 a distinction was drawn between a delivery vehicle and a sales vehicle. It is submitted on the authority of this remark in *Oxford* v *Thomas Scott and Sons Bakery Ltd* that deliveries to order made previously at the door would be within the expression 'door-to-door' selling. It would not include delivering goods door-to-door against sales not made door-to-door but made beforehand by different means. (As to the location of a sale see the notes to s 160 of the Licensing Act 1964 in Paterson's *Licensing Acts*.)

'Animal carcases' in reg 3 are to be construed along with waste not intended for human consumption, that is not intended for food or drink (*Paterson* v *W Weddell & Co Ltd* [1984] 2 CMLR 540). Accordingly animal carcases intended for food are not within the exemption which only applies to items such as hides and skins for tanning and waste such as offal and items for pet food.

A horse box is a specialised vehicle and it has been suggested that the use of a horse box to attend a gymkhana or even a hunt would be attendance at a 'cultural event'. The exemption for specialised vehicles for cultural events or 'mobile exhibitions' was not considered in *Bowra* v *Dann Catering Ltd* at 12.6. Nevertheless, the decision is justified on the facts (portable lavatories being conveyed to a public house under renovation). A conviction under EEC Regulation 543/69 was directed, as the circus and fun-fair equipment exception in art 4 did not apply. What is a cultural event is a matter of taste and could apply to the specialised props vehicles of both the English National Opera and a pop star with his entourage.

There is no exemption for dumper trucks or works trucks as such if they are otherwise subject to the EEC regulation but they may be exempt under reg 2.

There is a partial exemption in reg 2 in respect of operations carried out within a radius of 50 km (31¼ miles) from the place where the vehicle is based (including municipalities the centre of which is situated within that radius). These last words, which are printed in brackets in reg 2, are not in brackets in art 14a. The effect seems to be, therefore, that operations are also exempt which are carried out within a municipality the centre of which is situated within the radius of 50 km even though parts of the municipality are outside that radius.

The partial exemption in reg 2 exempts such operations from art 7(1) (continuous driving periods) and art 8 (breaks in driving periods), provided that there is a break of thirty minutes at the end of the first four-hour period of continuous driving. This break may be replaced by two fifteen-minute breaks. As regards the transport of harvest produce only a daily rest period of ten consecutive hours (cf art 11(1)) need be observed. The harvest exemption must not apply for more than thirty days in any year and the lost periods must be made good by an addition to the weekly rest period.

Article 13a of the EEC regulation provides partial exemptions in cases of emergency. This exemption applies to both national and international operations. The exemptions are from art 7(2) (daily driving period); art 7(4) (weekly and fortnightly driving periods) and art 11 (daily rest periods). The emergency must be in case of danger, in circumstances outside the driver's control, to render assistance, or as a result of a breakdown; and action that departs from the specified provisions is permitted to the extent necessary to ensure the safety of persons, of the vehicle or of its load, and to enable the driver to reach a suitable stopping place or, according to circumstances, the end of his journey. It is necessary first to establish the specified emergency and then to see if the breach is justified both on the safety ground and to enable the driver to reach a suitable stopping place or his destination as appropriate. The emergency action must not jeopardise road safety. The driver must indicate the nature and reasons for the breach on the record sheet of the tachograph equipment.

Although the above transport operations may be exempt, it must be stressed that such operations still remain subject to the EEC regulation. These *exemptions* should be compared with the *exceptions* (see 14.4) which take the transport operations in question altogether outside the scope of the EEC regulation so that they become domestic journeys or work.

The exemptions discussed above may be compared with the exemptions for drivers on domestic journeys or work contained in the Drivers' Hours (Goods Vehicles) (Exemptions) Regulations 1978 as amended (see 14.61).

It seems that the exemptions from the EEC regulation apply whether or not the tachograph is being correctly operated (see 14.52 and 14.53).

Regulation 2 of the Drivers' Hours (Harmonisation with Community Rules) Regulations 1978 states that s 96(1)–(9) of the Transport Act 1968 (see 14.22) shall not apply to the Community regulated (ie national or international) journeys or work of a driver of a passenger vehicle or goods vehicle. This is, however, qualified by reg 3 as to goods and passenger vehicles and by regs 4 and 5 as to goods vehicles (see below under 'National journeys only', 14.23 and 'Mixed journeys', 14.24).

*International journeys: mixed journeys*

EEC Regulation 543/69 applies to international journeys or work. It basically deals with driving periods and rest periods rather than duty periods. Section 96 of the Transport Act 1968 (see 14.22) does not apply (Harmonisation Regulations, reg 2). It follows that the Drivers' Hours (Goods Vehicles) (Exemptions) Regulations 1978 have no relevance. The Harmonisation Regulations provide, as to international journeys or work, that if in any period of seven days at the beginning of which a person has undertaken international journeys or work:

(*a*) that person also undertakes national journeys or work, the domestic rules will not, during that period, apply to the national journeys or work (regs 2 and 4(1));

(*b*) that person also undertakes domestic journeys or work, the domestic rules will during that period apply to those journeys or work without the limits on duty (ie as to the working day and the working week) (reg 5), but, in so far as the domestic rules do apply, the time spent on the international journeys or work (and the national journeys or work, if relevant) must be taken into account in applying the limits imposed by the domestic rules (reg 3).

## 14.22 Domestic journeys

EEC Regulation 543/69 does not apply to domestic journeys or work. These are journeys or work which are excepted by art 4 from the terms of the EEC regulation and to which Part VI of the Transport Act 1968 applies instead. This definition of domestic journeys or work is in reg 1(3) of the Drivers' Hours (Harmonisation with Community Rules) Regulations 1978.

The provisions of s 96 will continue to apply in their entirety to journeys or work excepted from the EEC regulation unless there is an exception from the requirements of s 96 also. It must be emphasised that s 96 only applies in a form not modified by the above-mentioned Harmonisation Regulations where the driver undertakes domestic journeys or work alone, or domestic journeys or work and international journeys or work where the international visit has not taken place in the preceding seven days. Section 96(1)–(6) is known as the domestic drivers' hours code (s 96(13)). Section 96(13) was added by s 2 of the Road Traffic (Drivers' Ages and Hours of Work) Act 1976. Section 96 is basically but not completely (see s 96(1)) a code of working hours for drivers rather than a code of driving hours.

The definition of 'working day' in s 103(1) of the 1968 Act applies in its original form. In particular it is still brought to an end only by a daily rest period of eleven hours or, where permitted, 9½ hours. The definition of 'working week' in s 103(1) is also in its original form (ie from midnight Saturday to midnight Saturday). The definition of 'working week' is modified for certain limited purposes where various forms of driving are mixed (see 14.24). Section 103(4) explains references to a driver being on duty, so that he is deemed to be on duty for purposes other than driving when engaged in the course of his employment by his employer; there is special provision as to owner-drivers. See also 14.39 and in particular *Carter* v *Walton*.

Orders have been made under s 96(12) modifying s 96 in respect of both goods vehicles and passenger vehicles. The order relating to goods vehicles is the Drivers' Hours (Goods Vehicles) (Modifications) Order 1970 (SI 1970 No 257), as amended by SI 1971 No 818. The effect of the modification is that drivers of light vans (not exceeding 3½ tons plated weight or 30 cwt unplated) or dual purpose vehicles used for professional purposes (doctors, dentists, midwives, nurses or vets) or for services of maintenance, repair, installation, cleaning or fitting, or by commercial travellers, or by employees of the AA or RAC, RASC or by a person carrying on for himself or for his employer the business of cinematography (motion pictures), radio or television broadcasting are exempted from all the provisions of s 96 other than the requirement in s 96(1) not to drive for more than ten hours a day. A day is midnight to midnight. The weights in the regulations have not yet been changed to correspond with the metric weights in s 103(6) of the 1968 Act. The order also modifies the text of s 96(9).

Exemptions for drivers of goods vehicles for various purposes are set out in the Drivers' Hours (Goods Vehicles) (Exemptions) Regulations 1978 (SI 1978 No 1364) as amended by the like-named Amendment Regulations (SI 1982 No 1554). The purposes include an 'emergency' (Part I of the schedule), and 'emergencies' are defined as events which cause or are likely to cause danger to the life or health of a human being or an animal, serious interruption to public water, gas, electricity, drainage, telecommunication or postal services, serious interruption in the use of roads, railways or airports, or serious damage to property so as to necessitate the taking of immediate action. The other exemptions relate to cases of special need which are set out in Part II of the schedule. They include the handling of Christmas mail, the carriage of perishable food in holiday periods, the carriage of animals, fish and agricultural produce and requirements, newspapers, building and engineering materials, furniture removal and shopfittings, explosives, radioactive substances, ships' stores and exceptional loads accompanied by the police. The 1978 regulations added an exemption for the case of special need in relation to the carriage of goods by sea ferry. Reference in each case must be made to the schedule as to the extent of the exemption and the circumstances which confer the exemption. The 1978 Exemption Regulations refer to 'on duty' so that the principle in *Carter* v *Walton* (see 14.39) may apply to exclude 'rest breaks' in the calculation of the overall period.

Note s 96(9) as to drivers engaged in agricultural, forestry, quarrying or road construction operations. The section applies to empty vehicles of the types specified in s 95 as well as to loaded ones, seemingly, even when on joyrides.

## 14.23 National journeys only

By reg 4 of the Harmonisation Regulations certain of the provisions of s 96 are applied in a modified form to national journeys or work. This is not merely a provision to solve the problems of mixed driving but a provision which applies whether or not the national journeys or work are intermingled with domestic journeys or work. Regulation 4 does not apply when in any seven consecutive days' period the driver at the beginning of it undertakes international journeys or work (see reg 4(1) above).

Subject to this proviso as to international journeys, the relevant provisions of s 96 are applied by reg 4 to national journeys or work where the driver performs such journeys or work only, or such journeys or work and domestic journeys or work, or such journeys or work and international journeys or work.

By reg 4 the following subsections of s 96 apply: s 96(2) (rest breaks from work); s 96(3) (length of working day); s 96(5) (length of working week) and s 96(7), (8) and (9) in so far as they provide for modification of or exemption from these subsections. It should be emphasised that these are limitations of periods of working duty and not merely limitations of driving duty.

In addition, certain of the exemptions in the Drivers' Hours (Goods Vehicles) (Exemptions) Regulations 1978 (SI 1978 No 1364) also apply (see 14.22). These are exemptions from s 96(2), (3) and (5) in the case of an emergency and from s 96(3) and (5) in the case of a 'special need' as defined (see 14.22 and the reference to *Carter* v *Walton*). The exemptions are subject to certain conditions and reference should be made to the regulations. EEC Regulation 543/69 must still be complied with (reg 3(4)), although the EEC regulation also contains provisions for emergencies (see art 13a). So far as the special need exemption is concerned account must also be taken of domestic journeys or work (reg 3(3)).

Regulation 4 modifies s 96(2) (rest breaks from work) and s 96(3) (length of working day) so as to take account of art 11 of the EEC regulation (daily rest period). Section 96 is also modified by the Drivers' Hours (Goods Vehicles) (Modifications) Order 1970 (SI 1970 No 257) as amended by SI 1971 No 818. Section 96, as modified by reg 4 and the 1970 Order, and so far as applicable to national journeys or work, reads as follows:

(1) *[Inapplicable.]*

(2) Subject to the provisions of this section, if on any working day a driver has been on duty for a period of, or for periods amounting in the aggregate to, five and a half hours and—

(*a*) during that period, or during or between any of those periods, the driver has not had—
  (i) one interval of not less than half an hour, or
  (ii) two intervals of not less than 20 minutes each, or
  (iii) three intervals of not less than 15 minutes each,
  in which he was able to obtain rest and refreshment; and

(*b*) the end of that period, or of the last of those periods, does not mark the end of that working day,

he shall at the end of that period, or of the last of those periods, have such an interval as aforesaid of not less than half an hour, but that interval may be reduced to—

(A) 20 minutes where during the period, or during or between any of the periods, mentioned above the driver has had one interval of at least 20 minutes in which he was able to obtain rest and refreshment, or

(B) 15 minutes where during that period, or during or between any of those periods, he has had two such intervals of at least 15 minutes each.

(3) Subject to the provisions of this section, the working day of a driver—

(*a*) except where paragraph (*b*) or (*c*) of this subsection applies, shall not exceed eleven hours;

(*b*) if during that day he is off duty for a period which is, or periods which taken together are, not less than the time by which his working day exceeds eleven hours, shall not exceed twelve and a half hours;

(*c*) where the vehicle of which he is driver is one manned by two drivers—
  (i) shall, in a case where the vehicle has no bunk enabling crew members who are not performing any activity to lie down comfortably, not exceed

17 hours if during that working day that driver is for a period of, or for periods amounting in the aggregate to, at least 6 hours not required to perform any activity in connection with the operation of the vehicle, and

(ii) shall, in a case where the vehicle has such a bunk as aforesaid, not exceed 22 hours if during that working day that driver is for a period of, or for periods amounting in the aggregate to, at least 11 hours not required to perform any activity in connection with the operation of the vehicle.

(4) *[Inapplicable.]*

(5) Subject to the provisions of this section a driver shall not be on duty in any working week for periods amounting in the aggregate to more than sixty hours.

(6) *[Inapplicable.]*

(7) If in the case of the working week of any driver the following requirement is satisfied, that is to say, that, in each of the periods of twenty-four hours beginning at midnight which make up that week, the driver does not drive a vehicle to which this Part of this Act applies for a period of, or periods amounting in the aggregate to, more than four hours, the foregoing provisions of this section shall not apply to him that week, except that the provisions of subsections (1), (2) and (3) shall nevertheless have effect in relation to the whole of any working day falling partly in that week and partly in a working week in the case of which that requirement is not satisfied.

(8) If on any working day a driver does not drive any vehicle to which this Part of this Act applies—

(*a*) subsections (2) and (3) of this section shall not apply to that day, and

(*b*) the period or periods of duty attributable to that day for the purposes of subsection (5) of this section shall, if amounting to more than eleven hours, be treated as amounting to eleven hours only.

(9) For the purposes of subsections (1) and (7) of this section no account shall be taken of any time spent driving a vehicle elsewhere than on a road if the vehicle is being so driven in the course of operations of agriculture or forestry, of quarrying or of carrying out any work in the construction, reconstruction, alteration, extension or maintenance of, or of a part of, a building, or of any other fixed works of construction or civil engineering (including works for the construction, improvement or maintenance of a road) and, for the purposes of this exemption, where the vehicle is being driven on, or on a part of, a road in the course of carrying out any work for the improvement or maintenance of, or of that part of, that road, it shall be treated as if it were being driven elsewhere than on a road.

Regulation 2 only refers to s 96(1)–(9) inclusive. Section 96(10) onwards are therefore unaffected by the Harmonisation Regulations and these subsections still apply to national journeys or work.

Vehicles over 20 tonnes and vehicles drawing more than one trailer or semi-trailer (see art 6) are subject to s 96(2) in its form unmodified by reg 4.

As to on and off duty and whether the required breaks are part of the duty periods see 14.39 and in particular *Carter* v *Walton.*

The definition of 'working day' for the purpose of s 96(2), (3), (7) and (8) in s 103(1) is amended by reg 4(3) in respect of national journeys or work as follows:

'Working day', in relation to any driver, means—

(*a*) any period during which he is on duty and which does not fall to be aggregated with any other such period by virtue of paragraph (*b*) of this definition; and

(*b*) where a period during which he is on duty is not followed by an interval for rest of not less than eleven hours or, where permitted by Article 11(1), (3) or (4) of Council Regulation (EEC) No 543/69 (daily rest) or by section 96(4) of this Act as amended by Regulation 4(6) of the Drivers' Hours (Harmonisation with Community Rules) Regulations 1978, of not less than ten, nine or, as the case may be, eight hours, the aggregate of that period and each successive such period until there is such an interval as aforesaid, together with any interval or intervals between periods so aggregated.

Although this definition does not apply for the purposes of s 96(5) and (9), this will not normally make any material difference.

'Working week', with effect from 1 January 1979, apparently means any period of seven consecutive days. This allowed for the introduction of the continental seven-day rolling week concept. This altered definition does not apply for the purpose of s 96(9) (exemption for agriculture and forestry etc) but this does not appear to be material. The altered definition is effected by reg 4(8). The provision in s 103(5) whereby the traffic commissioners etc can substitute a different 'weekend' is as a result no longer needed and is to be inapplicable (reg 4(8)). For an alternative view that the original Saturday midnight to Saturday midnight working week definition in s 103(1) and the provision in s 103(5) still apply to purely national operations, see (1981) 145 JP Jo 8 and (1982) 146 JP Jo 68.

## 14.24 Mixed journeys

The Harmonisation Regulations make special provision for mixed driving, that is, where drivers perform journeys or work which are partly international, partly national and partly domestic. These special provisions are contained in regs 3, 4 and 5, and for mixed driving therefore the requirements of s 96 of the Transport Act 1968 continue to be material for both national and international journeys or work. The purpose is to prevent drivers on domestic journeys or work from escaping the restrictions by interposing national or international journeys or work.

*Domestic journeys or work to take into account national and international journeys or work*

Regulation 3 of the Harmonisation Regulations 1978 provides that periods spent on national or international journeys or work are to count towards the periods specified under the domestic rules in s 96(1)–(9) (periods of driving or duty or length of working day) for goods vehicle drivers performing domestic journeys or work.

*Domestic journeys or work mixed with international journeys or work (whether or not national journeys or work are also undertaken)*

Where a driver in addition to domestic journeys or work also undertakes international journeys or work (whether or not he also undertakes national journeys or work), s 96 will continue to apply to the domestic journeys or work and the periods will be extended to include the national and international journeys or work in accordance with reg 3. However, s 96 only applies in a modified form and s 103 (the definition section) is also modified. This is effected by reg 5. The reg 5 modifications apply during any period of seven consecutive days at the beginning of which the international journeys or work are undertaken (reg 5(1)).

There is no liability for contravening the provisions of s 96 in the course of the Community regulated journeys or work (ie journeys or work subject to the EEC regulation) but the periods of the latter must be taken into account (reg 3) for the purpose of determining whether there is any contravention of s 96 in respect of the domestic journeys or work.

The whole of s 96 will continue to apply to such domestic journeys or work but, because of the link with international journeys, subject to the following alterations:

(*a*) the limits on duty for the working day (s 96(3)) and the working week (s 96(5)) are excluded;

(*b*) s 96(2) (rest periods), (4) (daily rest period) and (6) (weekly rest period) are modified by reg 5; and

(*c*) s 96(2) as modified is amended so as to apply the limit to driving instead of duty.

The definition of 'working day' in s 103(1) is modified in the same way as it is modified by reg 4. The definition of 'working week' in s 103(1) is amended so as to apply the seven-day continental rolling week. Presumably the exclusion (para (*a*) above) of s 96(3) and (5) (the limits on duty for the working day and the working week) is to facilitate the international journeys. The modifications in s 96(2), (4) and (6) are again the same as the modifications effected by reg 4. It is important to note that the explanatory note in the Harmonisation Regulations is misleading in that it refers to the other modifications and amendments but omits to refer to the modification of s 96(2), although this is clearly set out in reg 5(3).

These amendments preserve, in relation to the international crew members who mix in domestic journeys or work, the substance of the modifications of Part VI of the Transport Act 1968 provided for in the Drivers' Hours (Passenger and Goods Vehicles) (International Rules) Regulations 1973, revoked by reg 1(2) of the Harmonisation Regulations 1978.

Section 96 is also modified by the Drivers' Hours (Goods Vehicles) (Modifications) Order 1970 (SI 1970 No 257) as amended by SI 1971 No 818.

Because of the complicated nature of the provisions, s 96, as modified by reg 5 and the 1970 Order, and so far as applicable to mixed domestic and international journeys or work, is set out below:

(1) Subject to the provisions of this section, a driver shall not on any working day drive a vehicle or vehicles to which this Part of this Act applies for periods amounting in the aggregate to more than ten hours.

(2) Subject to the provisions of this section, if on any working day a driver has been driving for a period of, or for periods amounting in the aggregate to, five and a half hours and—

(*a*) during that period, or during or between any of those periods, the driver has not had—

(i) one interval of not less than half an hour, or

(ii) two intervals of not less than 20 minutes each, or
(iii) three intervals of not less than 15 minutes each,
in which he was able to obtain rest and refreshment; and

(*b*) the end of that period, or of the last of those periods, does not mark the end of that working day,

he shall at the end of that period, or of the last of those periods, have such an interval as aforesaid of not less than half an hour, but that interval may be reduced to—

(A) 20 minutes where during the period, or during or between any of the periods, mentioned above the driver has had one interval of at least 20 minutes in which he was able to obtain rest and refreshment, or

(B) 15 minutes where during that period, or during or between any of those periods, he has had two such intervals of at least 15 minutes each.

(3) *[Inapplicable.]*

(4) Subject to the provisions of this section, there shall be, between any two successive working days of a driver, an interval for rest which—

(*a*) subject to paragraphs (*b*) and (*c*) of this subsection, shall not be of less than eleven hours;

(*b*) may be reduced to nine hours not more than twice in any working week when such rest is taken at the place where the driver or the vehicle is based, or to eight hours not more than twice in any working week when such rest is taken elsewhere than at that place; and

(*c*) where the vehicle is manned by two drivers—

(i) may, if the vehicle has no bunk enabling crew members who are not performing any activity to lie down comfortably, be reduced to ten hours during the 27 hour period preceding any time when the driver is on duty, or

(ii) may, if the vehicle has such a bunk as aforesaid, be reduced to eight hours during the 30 hour period preceding any time when the driver is on duty;

and for the purposes of this Part of this Act a period of time shall not be treated, in the case of an employee-driver, as not being an interval for rest by reason only that he may be called upon to report for duty if required.

(5) *[Inapplicable.]*

(6) Subject to the provisions of this section, there shall be, in the case of each working week of a driver, a period of not less than twenty-four hours for which he is off duty, being a period which is either immediately preceded or followed by such an interval for rest as is mentioned in subsection (4) above (as that subsection is amended by Regulation 4(6) of the Drivers' Hours (Harmonisation with Community Rules) Regulations 1978).

(7) If in the case of the working week of any driver the following requirement is satisfied, that is to say, that, in each of the periods of twenty-four hours beginning at midnight which make up that week, the driver does not drive a vehicle to which this Part of this Act applies for a period of, or periods amounting in the aggregate to, more than four hours, the foregoing provisions of this section shall not apply to him in that week, except that the provisions of subsections (1), (2) and (3) shall nevertheless have effect in relation to the whole of any working day falling partly in that week and partly in a working week in the case of which that requirement is not satisfied.

(8) If on any working day a driver does not drive any vehicle to which this Part of this Act applies—

(*a*) subsections (2) and (3) of this section shall not apply to that day, and (*b*) the period or periods of duty attributable to that day for the purposes of subsection (5) of this section shall, if amounting to more than eleven hours, be treated as amounting to eleven hours only.

(9) For the purposes of subsections (1) and (7) of this section no account shall be taken of any time spent driving a vehicle elsewhere than on a road if the vehicle is being so driven in the course of operations of agriculture or forestry, of quarrying or of carrying out any work in the construction, reconstruction, alteration, extension or maintenance of, or of a part of, a building, or of any other fixed works of construction or civil engineering (including works for the construction, improvement or maintenance of a road) and, for the purposes of this exemption, where the vehicle is being driven on, or on a part of, a road in the course of carrying out any work for the improvement or maintenance of, or of that part of, that road, it shall be treated as if it were being driven elsewhere than on a road.

The wording of the remaining subsections of s 96 is not altered by the Harmonisation Regulations, with the result that these subsections remain applicable.

As to on and off duty and whether the required breaks are part of the duty periods see 14.39 and in particular *Carter* v *Walton*.

For the purpose of the domestic journeys or work of a driver performing mixed driving of the type under consideration (ie in the course of a consecutive seven-day period at the beginning of which international journeys or work were undertaken), the definitions of 'working day' and 'working week' in s 103(1) are amended by reg 5(3) and (6).

'Working day', in relation to any driver, means—

(*a*) any period during which he is on duty and which does not fall to be aggregated with any other such period by virtue of paragraph (*b*) of this definition; and

(*b*) where a period during which he is on duty is not followed by an interval for rest of not less than eleven hours or, where permitted by Article 11(1), (3) or (4) of Council Regulation (EEC) No 543/69 (daily rest) or by section 96(4) of this Act as amended by Regulation 4(6) of the Drivers' Hours (Harmonisation with Community Rules) Regulations 1978, of not less than ten, nine or, as the case may be, eight hours, the aggregate of that period and each successive such period until there is such an interval as aforesaid, together with any interval or intervals between periods so aggregated;

'Working week' means any period of seven consecutive days.

The provision in s 103(5) whereby the traffic commissioners etc can substitute a different 'weekend' is no longer needed and is inapplicable (reg 5(6)).

*Domestic journeys or work mixed with national journeys or work*

In this case s 96 applies in its entirety but is modified by reg 4 of the Harmonisation Regulations. Regulation 4 contains no definition of when domestic journeys or work are to be regarded as mixed with national journeys or work. Compare the precise definition in reg 5(1). The position seems to be that as soon as a driver undertakes national journeys or work in addition to domestic journeys or work the modifications of reg 4 apply. Time spent on national journeys or work must be taken into account (reg 3).

Regulation 4 modifies s 96(2) (rest breaks from work) and s 96(3) (length of working day) so as to take account of art 11 of the EEC Regulation 543/69 (daily rest period). Section 96(4) (daily rest period), s 96(6) (weekly rest period) and the definition of 'working day' in s 103(1) are also modified to take account of art 11. In addition, where the driver is engaged in mixed domestic and national operations, reg 4 amended from 1 January 1979, for such domestic journeys or work, the definition of 'working week' in s 103(1) to substitute the continental rolling week of seven consecutive days.

Section 96 is also modified by the Drivers' Hours (Goods Vehicles) (Modifications) Order 1970 (SI 1970 No 257) as amended by SI 1971 No 818.

Section 96, as modified by reg 4 and the 1970 Order, and so far as applicable to domestic journeys or work where the driver also undertakes national journeys or work, reads as follows:

(1) Subject to the provisions of this section, a driver shall not on any working day drive a vehicle or vehicles to which this Part of this Act applies for periods amounting in the aggregate to more than ten hours.

(2) Subject to the provisions of this section, if on any working day a driver has been on duty for a period of, or for periods amounting in the aggregate to, five and a half hours and—

(*a*) during that period, or during or between any of those periods, the driver has not had—
 (i) one interval of not less than half an hour, or
 (ii) two intervals of not less than 20 minutes each, or
 (iii) three intervals of not less than 15 minutes each,
 in which he was able to obtain rest and refreshment; and

(*b*) the end of that period, or of the last of those periods, does not mark the end of that working day,

he shall at the end of that period, or of the last of those periods, have such an interval as aforesaid of not less than half an hour, but that interval may be reduced to—

(A) 20 minutes where during the period, or during or between any of the periods, mentioned above the driver has had one interval of at least 20 minutes in which he was able to obtain rest and refreshment, or

(B) 15 minutes where during that period, or during or between any of those periods, he has had two such intervals of at least 15 minutes each.

(3) Subject to the provisions of this section, the working day of a driver—

(*a*) except where paragraph (*b*) or (*c*) of this subsection applies, shall not exceed eleven hours;

(*b*) if during that day he is off duty for a period which is, or periods which taken together are, not less than the time by which his working day exceeds eleven hours, shall not exceed twelve and a half hours;

(*c*) where the vehicle of which he is driver is one manned by two drivers—
 (i) shall, in a case where the vehicle has no bunk enabling crew members who are not performing any activity to lie down comfortably, not exceed 17 hours if during that working day that driver is for a period of, or for periods amounting in the aggregate to, at least 6 hours not required to perform any activity in connection with the operation of the vehicle, and
 (ii) shall, in a case where the vehicle has such a bunk as aforesaid, not exceed 22 hours if during that working day that driver is for a period of, or for periods amounting in the aggregate to, at least 11 hours not required to perform any activity in connection with the operation of the vehicle.

(4) Subject to the provisions of this section, there shall be, between any two successive working days of a driver, an interval for rest which—

(*a*) subject to paragraphs (*b*) and (*c*) of this subsection, shall not be of less than eleven hours;

(*b*) may be reduced to nine hours not more than twice in any working week when such rest is taken at the place where the driver or the vehicle is based, or to eight hours not more than twice in any working week when such rest is taken elsewhere than at that place; and

(*c*) where the vehicle is manned by two drivers—

(i) may, if the vehicle has no bunk enabling crew members who are not performing any activity to lie down comfortably, be reduced to ten hours during the 27 hour period preceding any time when the driver is on duty, or

(ii) may, if the vehicle has such a bunk as aforesaid, be reduced to eight hours during the 30 hour period preceding any time when the driver is on duty.

(5) Subject to the provisions of this section a driver shall not be on duty in any working week for periods amounting in the aggregate to more than sixty hours.

(6) Subject to the provisions of this section, there shall be, in the case of each working week of a driver, a period of not less than twenty-four hours for which he is off duty, being a period which is either immediately preceded or followed by such an interval for rest as is mentioned in subsection (4) above (as that subsection is amended by Regulation 4(6) of the Drivers' Hours (Harmonisation with Community Rules) Regulations 1978).

(7) If in the case of the working week of any driver the following requirement is satisfied, that is to say, that, in each of the periods of twenty-four hours beginning at midnight which make up that week, the driver does not drive a vehicle to which this Part of this Act applies for a period of, or periods amounting in the aggregate to, more than four hours, the foregoing provisions of this section shall not apply to him in that week, except that the provisions of subsections (1), (2) and (3) shall nevertheless have effect in relation to the whole of any working day falling partly in that week and partly in a working week in the case of which that requirement is not satisfied.

(8) If on any working day a driver does not drive any vehicle to which this Part of this Act applies—

(*a*) subsections (2) and (3) of this section shall not apply to that day, and

(*b*) the period or periods of duty attributable to that day for the purposes of subsection (5) of this section shall, if amounting to more than eleven hours, be treated as amounting to eleven hours only.

(9) For the purposes of subsections (1) and (7) of this section no account shall be taken of any time spent driving a vehicle elsewhere than on a road if the vehicle is being so driven in the course of operations of agriculture or forestry, of quarrying or of carrying out any work in the construction, reconstruction, alteration, extension or maintenance of, or of a part of, a building, or of any other fixed works of construction or civil engineering (including works for the construction, improvement or maintenance of a road) and, for the purposes of this exemption, where the vehicle is being driven on, or on a part of, a road in the course of carrying out any work for the improvement or maintenance of, or of that part of, that road, it shall be treated as if it were being driven elsewhere than on a road.

The wording of the remaining subsections of s 96 is not altered by the Harmonisation Regulations, and these subsections are still applicable.

However, vehicles over 20 tonnes and vehicles drawing more than one trailer or semi-trailer are subject to s 96(2) in its form unmodified by reg 4.

As to on and off duty and whether the required breaks are part of the duty periods see 14.39 and in particular *Carter* v *Walton*.

The 'working day' for the purpose of s 96(1)–(9) inclusive is defined in s 103(1) as amended by reg 4(3) of the Harmonisation Regulations as follows:

> 'Working day', in relation to any driver, means—
>
> (*a*) any period during which he is on duty and which does not fall to be aggregated with any other such period by virtue of paragraph (*b*) of this definition; and
>
> (*b*) where a period during which he is on duty is not followed by an interval for rest of not less than eleven hours or, where permitted by Article 11(1), (3) or (4) of Council Regulation (EEC) No 543/69 (daily rest) or by section 96(4) of this Act as amended by Regulation 4(6) of the Drivers' Hours (Harmonisation with Community Rules) Regulations 1978, of not less than ten, nine or, as the case may be, eight hours, the aggregate of that period and each successive such period until there is such an interval as aforesaid, together with any interval or intervals between periods so aggregated.

'Working week' means any period of seven consecutive days; this is to provide for the introduction of the continental seven-day rolling week concept. The provision in s 103(5) whereby the Traffic Commissioners etc can substitute a different 'weekend' is no longer needed as a result and is to be inapplicable (reg 4(8)). There is here no uncertainty over the interpretation of reg 4(8) (cf the position as to national journeys under 'Domestic journeys or work mixed with international journeys or work (whether or not national journeys or work are also undertaken)').

*Goods vehicles and passenger vehicles*

Where a person on any working day or in any working week drives or carries out work in connection with both passenger and goods vehicles, he is not to be treated for the purposes of the domestic rules as a goods vehicle driver unless at least half the time he spends with the passenger and goods vehicles is spent with the goods vehicles (Harmonisation Regulations, reg 5(7)).

## 14.25–30 The AETR agreement

The member states of the EEC have ratified or acceded to the European Agreement concerning the Work of Crews of Vehicles Engaged in International Road Transport (AETR) (Cmnd 7401). The United Kingdom ratified the agreement on 17 February 1978. The agreement did not become operative for the UK immediately on ratification but is now operative. The agreement becomes operative for a country 180 days after it deposits its instrument of ratification or accession (art 16(5)). Apart from the member states of the EEC, contracting countries to the AETR agreement currently are Austria, Czechoslovakia, the German Democratic Republic, Norway, Portugal, the Soviet Union, Spain, Sweden and Yugoslavia. It is understood that further countries are in the process of acceding to the agreement. As will be seen below, however, its effect is not limited to these countries.

*Provisions*

The requirements under the agreement are broadly the same as under EEC Regulation 543/69 as amended, except that there is no provision for time spent on ferry boats or on trains. There are, however, differences of substance. Some definitions are different: a continuous driving period may in certain circumstances be extended to four and a half hours; the weekly rest period is twenty-four hours instead of twenty-nine hours and conductors need not keep record books. The most important difference is that the AETR agreement does not refer to the tachograph.

Every driver and driver's mate must therefore have and keep up an individual control record book conforming to the model in the annex to EEC Regulation 543/69 (AETR agreement, art 12). A different but similar control book may be approved by the EEC Commission for drivers of foreign vehicles from countries which are not member states and not parties to the AETR agreement. The requirement does not extend to conductors. 'Driver' and 'driver's mate' are defined in art 1. They must produce the individual control book whenever required to do so by any of the control authorities (art 12(1)). Undertakings must keep a register of the individual books which must show the name of each driver or driver's mate to whom a book is issued, his signature in the margin, the number of the book, its date of issue and the date of the last daily sheet completed, before final return (art 12(4)). The used control books and register must be produced at the request of any control authority. All completed individual books must be kept by the undertaking for at least one year (art 12(5)). Instead there may be voluntary reliance on the use of a tachograph (see 14.53). As to the meaning of an 'undertaking', see *Auditeur du Travail* v *Dufour* at 14.63 (a decision of the European Court).

*Application*

Article 2 of the AETR agreement provides that the agreement shall apply to the territory of each contracting party to all international road transport by any vehicle registered in the territory of the said contracting party or in the territory of any other contracting party. There are certain exceptions which differ from the EEC regulation exceptions. In particular the AETR agreement need not be applied to national transport operations.

The AETR agreement applies in theory to international road transport (art 2). This must, however, be read subject to the EEC regulation which itself covers international road transport within the EEC and specifies in art 2 the limited international road transport operations to which the AETR agreement is to apply. The application is much wider than might at first be thought.

The second part of art 2 provides that as from 1 January 1978 the AETR agreement 'shall apply to international road transport operations to and/or from third countries which are contracting parties to that agreement, or in transit through such countries, for the whole of the journey where such operations are effected by vehicles registered in a member state or contracting party'. This part of the article also provides that the AETR agreement shall apply to 'transport operations to and/or from a third country effected by vehicles registered in a third country which is not a contracting party to the agreement' in respect of 'any journey made within the Community'. In effect, therefore, the AETR agreement applies to these third country transport operations. In particular it will be noted that it applies to operations to and/or from a third country which is *not a contracting party* to the agreement. A 'third country' is a country that is not an EEC member state.

*Enforcement*

The AETR agreement has not been directly enforced by United Kingdom legislation. A spokesman for the Department of Transport has stated that the Department regards the AETR agreement as being enforceable under s 96(11A) and s 98(4) of the Transport Act 1968 in the same way as the EEC regulation is enforceable. This is based on a belief that art 2 of the EEC regulation has incorporated the AETR agreement by reference. This link is rather tenuous, especially as ss 96 and 98 refer to 'applicable Community rules' and the AETR is not a Community rule but an international agreement or rule in a wider sense. EEC countries are only contracted to it on an individual basis.

The incorporation by reference propounded by the Department of Transport is achieved as follows. The effect of art 2 of the EEC regulation is to disapply it to certain AETR journeys (see above) and to substitute the AETR agreement instead. Article 19(3) of the EEC regulation states that the regulation 'shall apply to all transport operations covered by Article 2'. Article 2 is in wide terms and, as shown above, includes the third country transport operations (including AETR and non-AETR operations) specified therein. Contraventions of the AETR rules are thereby contraventions of ss 96(11A) and 98(4).

The penalties for breach of these sections are set out at 14.40 and 14.71.

## Drivers' Hours: Passenger Vehicles

### 14.31 Generally

The provisions of EEC Regulation 543/69 as regards the hours and conditions for drivers of passenger vehicles on national and international journeys or work are summarised in Table 2. The first column shows the original position under s 96 of the Transport Act 1968 which applied prior to January 1978 and which still applies to domestic journeys or work. The second column shows the position under the EEC regulation as from 1 January 1981. In every case, as to on and off duty and whether the required breaks are part of the duty periods see 14.39 and in particular *Carter* v *Walton*.

### 14.32 National and international journeys

Both the national and international journeys or work of drivers and other crew members of passenger vehicles are governed by EEC Regulation 543/69 as amended. Article 4 of the EEC regulation sets out the *exceptions* to the regulation. They include carriage by certain passenger vehicles. These exceptions are completely outside the EEC regulation and are known as domestic journeys or work. Part VI of the Transport Act 1968, and in particular s 96 as modified, continues to apply to them.

**Table 2**
**Passenger vehicles: hours and rest periods**

*(For the transitional period between 1.1.78 and 31.12.80 see 10th ed, p 498.)*

| *Nature of provision* | *Domestic journeys or work as at present and the position generally prior to 1.1.78* | *National and international journeys or work as from 1.1.81* |
|---|---|---|
| *Continuous driving period* | 5½ hours *working* period (s 96(2)) (but see s 96(2) as modified for certain variations) | 4 hours (art 7) |
| *Daily driving period* | 10 hours (s 96(1)) | 8 hours (or 9 hours for drivers of other than large combinations twice in one week but this must be compensated) (art 7). |
| *Rest breaks* | 30 mins (s 96(2)) | Period of at least 30 mins after maximum permitted continuous period of driving but may be 2 × 20 mins or 3 × 15 mins instead (art 8). |
| *Weekly driving limit* | — | 48 hours (art 7) |
| *Fortnightly driving limit* | — | 92 hours (art 7) |
| *Daily rest period* | 10 consecutive hours during the 24-hour period preceding working time, but may be reduced to 8½ hours three times a week (s 96(4)). | 11 consecutive hours but may be reduced to 10 hours twice a week and 9 hours twice a week if there is a scheduled uninterrupted break of 4 hours or 2 × 2 hours.<br>Alternative—10 consecutive hours without reduction (art 11 (2)). |
| *Weekly rest period* | 24 hours per fortnight from Sat midnight to Sat midnight not necessarily preceded or followed by a daily rest period (s 96(6)). | 29 consecutive hours plus daily rest period immediately before or after (art 12(1)). But may be reduced to not less than 24 hours if a rest period equivalent to the reduction is granted during the same week (art 12). Any consecutive 7 days must include a rest period. |
| *Daily hours of duty limit (spread over)* | 16 hours (s 96(3)) | These are not expressly covered by the EEC regulation and are *not* applied to passenger vehicles by the Drivers' Hours (Harmonisation with Community Rules) Regulations 1978. Part VI of the Transport Act 1968 as modified will continue to apply. |
| *Weekly hours of duty limit* | — | |

Certain of the exemptions in the Community Road Transport Rules (Exemptions) Regulations 1978 (SI 1978 No 1158) for national operations apply to passenger vehicles as well as goods vehicles. The exemptions are for the use of vehicles constructed and equipped to carry not more than fifteen persons, including the driver, and the use of vehicles undergoing local road tests for the purposes of repair or maintenance (reg 3(3)). As to local road tests see 'Exceptions and exemptions', 14.21. Although exempt from the EEC regulation so far as national operations are concerned, they will still be services within the EEC regulation definition and subject to the rules for international operations.

In general the rest periods are set out in the chart. During the summer period between 1 April and 30 September the weekly rest period for crew members of vehicles used for the carriage of passengers on international journeys may be replaced by a rest period of not less than sixty consecutive hours to be taken at the end of a fortnight. This rest period must be immediately preceded or followed by a daily rest period. The EEC regulation has certain special provisions as to the daily rest period in relation to transportation by ferry boat or train. These have been described in the section on goods vehicles at 14.21, and the same provisions apply to passenger vehicles.

'Crew member' includes the driver's mate and the conductor (art 1; see also 14.10).

### 14.33 Domestic journeys

Domestic journeys or work by passenger vehicle drivers are still governed by s 96 in an extensively modified form unless otherwise exempt. The modifications were effected by the Drivers' Hours (Passengers and Goods Vehicles) (Modifications) Order 1971 (SI 1971 No 818).

The definition of 'working day' in s 103 is also modified in relation to passenger vehicles by the substitution of 'ten hours' for 'eleven hours' and 'eight and a half hours' for 'nine and a half hours' in respect of the rest periods which conclude a working day.

There are certain exemptions, in particular for certain emergencies (see the Drivers' Hours (Passenger Vehicles) (Exemptions) Regulations 1970 (SI 1970 No 145) as amended by the like-named SI 1970 No 649).

### 14.34–8 Mixed journeys

Under the Drivers' Hours (Harmonisation with Community Rules) Regulations 1978 (SI 1978 No 1157), reg 3, where the driver of a passenger vehicle engages in mixed driving or work, the periods spent on national or international journeys or work are to count towards the periods specified under the domestic rules in s 96(1)–(9) (periods of driving or duty or length of working day) for passenger drivers performing domestic journeys or work. This applies similarly to goods vehicles.

Where a person on any working day or in any working week drives or carries out work in connection with both passenger and goods vehicles, he is not to be treated for the purposes of the domestic rules as a goods vehicle driver unless at least half the time he spends with passenger and goods vehicles is spent with goods vehicles (regs 4(9) and (10) and 5(7)).

## Drivers' Hours: Penalties and Proceedings

### 14.39 Offences and proceedings; driving and duty periods

Criminal liability for a breach of the applicable Community rules for international or national transport is cast by s 96(11A) on any driver or crew member and any other person, being the offender's employer or a person to whose orders that offender was subject, who caused or permitted the contravention. See also the decision in *Coggins* noted below. The breach must be of a rule as to periods of driving, or distances driven, or periods on or off duty. Criminal liability is limited to offences in Great Britain (see s 96(11A)), although periods of driving or work abroad may be taken into account.

Payments to wage-earning crew members are prohibited by art 12a of EEC Regulation 543/69, even in the form of bonuses or wage supplements, if they relate to distances travelled and/or the amount of goods carried, unless these payments are of such a kind as not to endanger road safety. See 'Liability of employers for staff defaults', 14.62.

Criminal liability under s 96 or for breach of the domestic drivers' code is similarly cast by s 96(11) on the driver and on any other person, being that driver's employer or a person to whose orders that driver was subject, who caused or permitted the contravention. Consequently a transport manager might be liable for causing or permitting. 'Permitting' in s 96(11) requires proof of knowledge; despite the defence it is not an absolute offence (*Licensing Authority for Goods Vehicles in Metropolitan Traffic Area* v *Coggins* (1985) *The Times*, 28 February). Aiding and abetting can also be charged. Cases on causing and permitting will be found in Chapter 1: see in particular *Sidcup Building Estates* v *Sidery; Forsyth* v *Phillips; Gray's Haulage Co Ltd* v *Arnold*; and *Dixon Bool Transport Ltd* v *Forsyth*.

In *Knowles Transport Ltd* v *Russell* [1975] RTR 87 knowledge of the irregularities was held to be an essential requisite before an employer could be said to have 'caused' or 'permitted' contravention of the regulations. Where the defendant is a corporation, such guilty knowledge must be imputed to a 'responsible officer' of the corporation, ie 'one whose duty included some measure of control of the company's business' (per Melford Stevenson J at p 93). Two checking clerks could have detected the excessive hours worked by the company's drivers when they checked the drivers' time sheets and calculated their wages, but as there was no evidence that the matter was brought to the attention of a responsible officer of the company or that any matter came to his notice which should have put him on enquiry, the company's conviction was set aside.

In *P Foster (Haulage) Ltd* v *Roberts* [1978] 2 All ER 751 a solicitor entered a plea of guilty on behalf of the company to forty-eight offences under s 96 of the Transport Act 1968 of permitting its drivers to work excessive hours. The solicitor was under the mistaken impression that the offence was an absolute offence and that lack of knowledge provided no defence. The solicitor informed the magistrates' court accordingly. The magistrates made their own enquiries and were satisfied that the company must have known the true position. The Divisional Court held that this was an unequivocal plea of guilty. However, if the plea had been equivocal the justices would have been called upon to intervene even though the defendant was represented.

The defence under s 96(11)(i) as to unavoidable delay applies to all types of journeys or work (see also s 96(11B)(*a*) which stipulates this) and to any person, driver or not.

In *Whitby* v *Stead* [1975] RTR 169, a driver was delayed for an hour while attempting to deliver some goods and again delayed while helping in an accident to other vehicles. He was charged with exceeding the working day of fourteen hours and driving for a period exceeding ten hours, because by s 103(1)(*b*) his two periods of driving became aggregated, since they were not separated by an interval of rest of at least eleven hours. The justices acquitted because of unavoidable delay under s 96(11)(i). The Divisional Court directed a conviction because the problems caused to the defendant by the delays could have been avoided by the defendant starting his second period of driving later. The defence of unavoidable delay is not available to excuse a failure to have an interval of eleven hours rest (ibid).

In *Green* v *Harrison* [1979] RTR 483 a minibus driver took a party to York races and back. He was delayed on the outward journey by a puncture to his vehicle. On the return journey several hours were spent in a cafe and leisure centre and as a result the round trip took more than the permitted sixteen hours. The justices concluded that the puncture had caused an unavoidable delay and dismissed the case. The Divisional Court directed the justices to convict. Neill J said that 'the circumstances which caused the delay on the outward part of the journey did not lead to delay "in the completion of the journey" and indeed had nothing to do with the return journey at all'. The defence under s 96(11)(ii) or s 96(11B)(*b*) applies to all types of journeys or work and applies to employers, transport managers and other directing staff. In such a case the defendant must show not only that he was unaware that a driver had been driving otherwise than in his employment with the defendant's firm but also that the defendant could not reasonably have become aware of that fact. This suggests that employers and transport managers may have some duty to instruct their drivers to report to them if the drivers have been driving outside their employment. It seems to be no defence under s 96(11) or (11A) (assuming a defence is not available under s 96(11)(ii) or (11B)(*b*)) if the driver had been on duty in his employer's business for an excessive period even though directly against his master's orders: the master should supervise properly, but it may be a defence if he did supervise properly and his orders were still disobeyed unknown to him (*Gray's Haulage Co Ltd* v *Arnold* at 1.78). Some of the cases are concerned with driving and some with duty and rest periods. Clearly, different criteria may apply. As stated in *Carter* v *Walton* below the question must be one of fact in each case.

Where a driver is engaged in canvassing and delivering during a journey, this was held under the old law to be time spent in driving (*M'Callum* v *Adair* 1937 SC (J) 114) and clearly is time on duty under s 96 of the Transport Act (see s 103(4)(*a*)). As, by s 103(4), time spent on other 'employment under the person who is his employer' is time spent on duty, as is time spent in the employment as a driver, cases such as *Jesner* v *Waugh* 1936 JC 47 (time spent by driver at the depot awaiting orders), *Wells* v *Sidney* [1939] 3 All ER 54 (watching his lorry being unloaded) and *Parkinson* v *Axon* [1951] 2 All ER 647 (working on a different job, sorting parcels) are probably no longer of authority, where the driver is working or acting for the employer who employs him as a driver. Subject to the comments below, it may be that time spent on work for another employer does not count and, since questions may arise as to who is the employer, eg where there are several subcontractors on a site, the common law cases as to who is the employer may be of relevance.

The phrase 'on duty' appears in s 96(11A) as well as in the domestic drivers' hours code. The restrictive definition of 'on duty' in s 103(4) should be compared with the definition of 'carriage by road' in art 1 of EEC Regulation 543/96. In *Carter* v *Walton* (1984) *The Times*, 28 May, it was said that whether statutory breaks for rest and recreation of 30 minutes, whether paid or unpaid, should be considered 'off duty' breaks and be deducted in arriving at the length of a working day for the purpose of section 96(3)(*a*) of the 1968 Act was a question of fact in each case. The court allowed an appeal against the defendant's conviction for exceeding working hours. Watkins LJ said that there was nothing in the relevant legislation or EEC regulations which led to the conclusion that the whole of the legislation assumed that when a driver was taking a statutory break he was still on duty. If that was the implication some provision would appear in the Act that that was the effect of a driver taking a break. A driver might be on a break away from his lorry without being under any duty to his employer. Although it applies to s 96(3)(*a*) the principle cannot apply to s 96(3)(*b*) because off duty periods are by the wording clearly included in s 96(3)(*b*). In other words the break may have to be excluded from the s 96(3)(*a*) 11 hours, but must be included in the s 96(3)(*b*) 12½ hours. It is a question of fact in every case as to whether a lorry driver who took statutory breaks was off duty (*Carter* v *Walton* above). The cases below should be read subject to this so far as s 96(11)) and s 96(11A) are concerned.

It was held in *Beer* v *Fairclough* (1937) 101 JP 157 on the old law that provided employers allowed their driver proper time for resting they did not have to see that he actually spent it in resting and they committed no offence if he did not, but it might be otherwise if he had, to their knowledge, to spend part of his rest-period in travelling to the place at which he had orders to resume work. This rule is not expressly reversed by s 96, but s 96(11)(*b*) and s 96(11B)(*b*) suggest that an employer or transport manager might be liable if a driver had been working for someone else to the defendant's knowledge and would therefore be driving for the defendant for an excessive period or would not have enough rest. See also *Pearson* v *Rutterford* below.

A driver, after driving a goods vehicle for the maximum permitted period, used his employers' car to get home; sometimes he drove it and sometimes he was a passenger in it, but his employers gave him a genuine option to stay overnight at the place where he left his goods vehicle. It was held that, in view of this option, he had been given his rest period and no offence was committed if he chose to use the car (*Witchell* v *Abbott* [1966] 2 All ER 657, at p 659), but this case was distinguished in *Potter* v *Gorbould* [1969] 3 All ER 828. The defendant was allowed by his employer, when he had finished his normal day's work, to earn overtime by cutting up scrap in his employer's scrapyard if he wished. As a result the defendant had less than the period for rest required. It was held that, as what was being done was not purely for the benefit of the driver but equally for the benefit of the employer and he was bound by the terms of his employment to obey the employer's directions and it was within the general terms of his employment, it could not be held that he had been given his period of rest.

A driver for employer *A* also worked as an HGV driving instructor on behalf of employer *B*. This was to the knowledge of employer *A*. The court held that the work for employer *B* should be regarded as a period of attendance at work so far as employer *A* was concerned and not put down as a daily rest period. The driver should have been convicted of keeping false records contrary to s 99(5) and of failing to take the daily rest periods required by art 11 of the EEC regulation (*Pearson* v *Rutterford* [1982] RTR 54). (The question was also raised but not answered whether an HGV driving instructor was a crew member.)

Where a driver worked for a number of periods which in the aggregate exceeded eleven hours, an offence was held to have been committed, though each separate period was separated from the next by an interval of at least thirty minutes (*Cook* v *Plumpton* (1935) 99 JP 308). Daily rest periods are now defined for the purposes of the EEC regulation in art 1 and the regulation also specifies various times for driving periods and breaks. The principle in *Carter* v *Walton* is therefore more likely to arise when considering s 96 and the modifications to s 96 by the Drivers' Hours (Harmonisation with Community Rules) Regulations 1978 in relation to on duty hours.

Where the driver's records show that he was working for a particular period and that period exceeds the permitted period of work, there is a prima facie case against him and against his employers for permitting him to work excessive hours; he or his employers must show that he was in fact resting or off duty (*Smith* v *All-Wheel Drive Co Ltd* (1962) *The Guardian*, 12 February). The magistrates should not infer that it was unlikely that he was working without such evidence (ibid).

The records of the driver's hours are admissible against his employer in a charge under s 96 (s 98(5)). They appear to be admissible anyhow at common law against the driver himself and possibly against the transport manager, if the court holds that the latter has the duty of seeing that his firm's drivers obey the requirements of s 96. Under s 97B similarly tachograph entries are admissible and in Scotland are sufficient evidence. Under s 97B also any entries made thereon for the purposes of arts 17(2) or (3) or 18(2) (temporary records) of the EEC tachograph regulation may be admitted in evidence. If the manager is charged with aiding and abetting the employer, it could be argued that, by s 44 of the Magistrates' Courts Act 1980, the manager is 'guilty of the like offence', so that evidence admissible against the employer is likewise admissible against the manager; on the other hand, there are cases every day where evidence against one defendant is not admissible against another. Certainly, if the manager is charged as the principal offender, it can be said that, as against him, the driver's records are hearsay and not admissible. The prosecutor might be wise to call the driver to give oral evidence or submit his written evidence under s 9 of the Criminal Justice Act 1967, the driver refreshing his memory from his records (*R* v *Bryant* at 2.79). Relevant cases are *Beer* v *Clench* and *Adair* v *Craighouse & Co* at 14.70; also *Hogg* v *Burnet* at 14.70 as to a vehicle number on a record identifying it. An indictable charge of conspiracy to contravene s 96 may properly be brought (*R* v *Blamires Transport Services Ltd* [1963] 3 All ER 170).

### 14.40–5 Penalties

The penalty for breach of s 96(11) or (11A) for contravening the hours is a fine of level 4. Offences can be tried by magistrates only. There is no power to endorse, disqualify or order penalty points.

By s 103(7) proceedings may be brought not only in the court normally having jurisdiction but also in any other court having jurisdiction in accordance with s 103(7). Section 96(11A), however, refers only to offences in Great Britain.

The licensing authorities are empowered to revoke, suspend or curtail an operator's licence if a goods vehicle driver has been convicted under Part VI of the Act (s 69(4)(*c*)).

## Drivers' Records

### 14.46–9 Generally

The provisions relating to the installation and use of recording equipment ('tachographs') are contained in ss 97, 97A and 97B of the Transport Act 1968, as substituted for the original s 97 by the Passenger and Goods Vehicle (Recording Equipment) Regulations 1979 (SI 1979 No 1746), and in those regulations. Like-named 1981 regulations have been made relating to test certificates (see 8.62). These statutory rules incorporate and to some extent make directly applicable EEC Regulation 1463/70 as amended (the tachograph regulation).

A tachograph is a cable-fed combination of a speedometer, an odometer and a twenty-four hour clock. The expression used in the statutory provisions and the EEC regulation is 'recording equipment' but 'tachograph' is the commonly used name.

The tachograph provisions became fully applicable for national and international transport operations (defined at 14.3) from 1 January 1982. Domestic journeys or work excepted from EEC Regulation 543/69 by art 4 of that regulation are also excepted from the tachograph regulation by art 3(1). (See the definition of domestic journeys or work at 14.4.) They are subject to s 98 of the 1968 Act and the Drivers' Hours (Keeping of Records) Regulations 1976 (SI 1976 No 1447) as amended, made thereunder.

The tachograph provisions apply to all the vehicles specified in s 95(2) subject to the exceptions and exemptions set out at 14.50. Section 98 and the 1976 Regulations apply to such vehicles on domestic operations and also to certain responsibilities of employers (see 14.60–3). The application of these sections to Crown, military, police and fire brigade vehicles is indicated in s 102.

Tachographs may also be used voluntarily on vehicles which are excepted or exempted from the tachograph provisions (see 14.53).

Where 'conforming' tachographs are used hand-written records need not be kept (see 14.52).

Definitions are contained in s 103 of the 1968 Act and art 1 of EEC Regulation 543/69 (applied by art 2 of the tachograph regulation).

Contraventions of the tachograph provisions and the regulations as to domestic journeys are offences under ss 97(1) and 97A(1) and (2) and s 98(4) respectively. These are discussed under 'Offences and proceedings', 14.70, which also deals with various other offences relating to the inspection of records and other documents under s 99.

## Drivers' Records: Tachographs

### 14.50 Goods vehicles on national and international journeys

The provisions of the EEC tachograph regulation as amended, as applied by ss 97, 97A and 97B of the Transport Act 1968, are considered below. (As to passenger vehicles, see also 14.65. For a general introduction, see 14.1–16.) The offences for breach of the regulation and penalties are considered at 14.70–1.

*Definitions*

Article 2 provides that for the purposes of the tachograph regulation the definitions in art 1 of EEC Regulations 543/69 (driver's hours and rest periods) shall apply. For the definitions in art 1, see 14.10. Any expression in the tachograph regulation which is also used in s 97, s 97A or s 97B of the 1968 Act has the same meaning in the Act as in the regulation (s 97(6)).

The time recorded on a tachograph is the time which agrees with the official time in the country of registration of the vehicle (art 17(2)). Tachographs should not therefore be adjusted on the continent to show continental time and time allowance may have to be made for foreign vehicles in Great Britain.

The first part of Annex I defines, for the purpose of the annex, 'recording equipment', 'record sheet', the 'constant' of the recording equipment, the 'characteristic coefficient' of the vehicle and the 'effective circumference' of the wheel tyres. The definition of 'recording equipment' is differently worded from the definition in s 97(7) for the purposes of Part VI of the 1968 Act. In ss 97(7) and 103(1)(*b*) it means 'equipment for recording information as to the use of a vehicle'. In Annex I it is defined as equipment 'intended for installation in road vehicles to show and record automatically or semi-automatically details of the movement of those vehicles and of certain working periods of their crews'.

*Provisions*

The EEC tachograph regulation is EEC Regulation 1463/70 as amended by Regulations 1787/73 and 2828/77. It is not directly applied in the way EEC Regulation 543/69 (driver's hours and records) is. The application is only in so far as specified by the 1979 Recording Equipment Regulations, but most of the EEC regulation is specified directly or indirectly. One exception is the requirement in art 4 that all vehicles used for carrying dangerous goods must have operating tachographs. This provision has not been specifically enforced in the United Kingdom. Many such vehicles (but not all) will be otherwise subject to the compulsory tachograph requirements. The parts of the regulation which are specifically applied, and contraventions of which therefore constitute an offence are, by s 97(1) as substituted by the Passenger and Goods Vehicles (Recording Equipment) (Amendment) Regulations 1984 (SI 1984 No 144), the using, causing or permitting to be used (as to these expressions see Chapter 1) a vehicle to which the tachograph provisions apply without recording equipment (*a*) which has been installed in accordance with the regulation (see in particular Annex I), (*b*) which complies with Annex I (requirements for construction, testing, installation and inspection) and Annex II (approval mark and certificate), and (*c*) is being used as provided by arts 15–17. One purpose of the substitution seems to have been to combine items (*a*), (*b*) and (*c*) into a single offence. It is submitted that it is still possible to charge them separately if so desired. See 'Duplicity', 2.46.

The other parts of the tachograph regulation which are applied and are material are as follows:

(i) Art 18(2) is relevant for the defence in s 97(3)(*b*), which relates to keeping temporary records when the recording equipment breaks down;

(ii) Art 3 contains certain exemptions; and

(iii) Any expression used in s 97, s 97A or s 97B which is also used in the regulation has the same meaning as in that regulation (s 97(6)).

By Part III of Annex I a tachograph must include visual instruments showing the distance travelled, the speed and the time, instruments for recording the distance travelled, speed and time and a marking device showing on the record sheet each opening of the case containing that sheet. A common form of tachograph record consists of a waxed circular disc placed on a rod and marked by three styli, one stylus showing automatically the distance by a line going to and fro, one similarly showing the speed and one manually set by means of a 'mode key' showing the current activity of the driver. This form of tachograph record is, however, not obligatory and Annex I makes it clear that the recording sheet may be in the form of a strip as well as a disc.

Part II of Annex I provides that the tachograph must be capable of recording the following activities:

(*a*) driving time;

(*b*) periods of work or attendance at work; and

(*c*) breaks from work and daily rest periods.

Where there are two crew members, a separate tachograph must show these three separate activities for each.

Regulation 4 of the 1979 Regulations as amended by the like-named (Amendment) Regulations (SI 1984 No 144) provides for the approval of fitters and workshops for installation and repair and the nomination of bodies for carrying out checks and inspections. The inspection of the equipment must be every two years and the inspection as to maximum tolerances must be every six years. Apart from transitional arrangements these dates begin with the date shown on the installation plaque. These inspections are in accordance with requirements in Annex I. The offence is created by s 97 which requires the recording equipment to comply with Annex I. If the equipment has not been inspected as required can it be said not to comply? It is submitted that an offence is created although the wording is rather tenuous.

Article 15 stipulates that the employer and the crew members are responsible for seeing that the equipment functions correctly and that the seals remain intact. Article 16(1) provides that the employer shall issue a sufficient number of record sheets to crew members and that the sheets must be of an approved model, and art 16(2) that the employer must retain record sheets for a period of at least one year after their use. The sheets for each crew member must be produced or handed over at the request of any authorised inspecting officer. Article 17 contains the detailed obligations of crew members. In particular, crew members must see that the tachograph is kept running continuously and that driving times, other periods of work and of attendance at work and breaks from work and rest periods are recorded (art 17(2)). Each crew member must enter his surname and first name on beginning to use the sheet, the date and place where such use begins and where it ends and the registration number and odometer reading of each vehicle at the start of the first journey and the end of the last journey recorded on the sheet and on a change of vehicle and the time of such a change (art 17(3)). Crew members on British national transport operations must retain the sheets for production for a period of two days (art 17(5) as adjusted by reg 5 of the Passenger and Goods Vehicles (Recording Equipment) Regulations 1979). On international journeys the period is still seven days.

From the wording of the EEC regulation it seems that the tachograph sheets are personal to the crew members rather than to the vehicle. Under s 97A(1)(*a*) it is an offence for an employed crew member to fail without reasonable excuse to return any record sheet which relates to him to his employer within twenty-one days of completing it. Where he has two employers he must notify each of the name and address of the other (s 97A(1)(*b*)).

Record books need not be kept where a tachograph is used. Section 98(2A) as substituted by reg 3 of the 1979 Regulations provides that where s 97(1)(*b*) (use of tachograph) applies to a vehicle, the regulations under s 98 regarding the driving of a vehicle (in particular as to record books) cease to apply. See further 14.52.

The requirement in art 6 of EEC Regulation 543/69 that drivers of certain large vehicles etc must carry a second driver or shall be relieved by a second driver after 450 km (281¼ miles) is no longer applicable; now a tachograph must be used in accordance with the tachograph regulation. The right to use a simplified record book under Part IV of the 1976 Regulations has similarly ceased (see art 14a(1)(*b*)).

As the tachograph records the speed of the vehicle, the record can be used as evidence in a speeding prosecution by either the prosecution or the defence. It may also be material evidence for other prosecutions, eg reckless or careless driving.

Under the Passenger and Goods Vehicles (Recording Equipment) Regulations 1981 (SI 1981 No 1692) new ss 43(7) and 45(5)(9A) were inserted in the 1972 Act. These provide that, where a tachograph is required, the test requirements of ordinary motor vehicles and goods vehicles (see 8.62) may include a test that the tachograph is installed and the seals are fixed. Such tests are now obligatory for public service vehicles other than certain community and school buses. They are also required for goods vehicles.

*Exceptions and exemptions*

(1) Article 3(2) of the tachograph regulation allows member countries to make certain *exemptions* in respect of national transport operations. Under regs 3 and 4 of the Community Road Transport Rules (Exemptions) Regulations 1978 (SI 1978 No 1158), as amended by SIs 1980 Nos 266 and 2018 and 1981 No 1855, the following are exempt:

(*a*) vehicles constructed and equipped to carry not more than fifteen persons, including the driver;
(*b*) vehicles undergoing local road tests for the purposes of repairs or maintenance;
(*c*) vehicles used for the transport of live animals from farms to local markets or vice versa, or for the transport of animal carcases or waste not intended for human consumption; and
(*d*) specialised vehicles used at local markets, for door-to-door selling, for mobile banking, exchange or savings transactions, for the purposes of worship, for the lending of books, records or cassettes or for cultural events or mobile exhibitions.

For the meaning of 'specialised vehicles', 'animal carcases', 'cultural events' and other expressions see 14.21.

Under the same regulations these vehicles are also exempt from the requirements of EEC Regulation 543/69 as amended (drivers' ages, records and hours and conditions of work).

(2) Tachographs need not be installed or used in passenger vehicles on regular services where the route exceeds 50 km (31¼ miles) (art 3(1)). These remain national transport operations. Service timetables and duty rosters must be drawn up and carried for such operations (EEC Regulation 543/69, art 15). Each crew member assigned to such a regular service must carry an extract from the duty roster and a copy of the service timetable. Article 15 contains certain further requirements as to the roster.

Record books need not be kept (see art 14(1) of the 1969 Regulation, which excludes regular services).

(3) Tachographs need not be installed or used in the vehicles referred to in art 4 of EEC Regulation 543/69 (art 3(1)). The journeys or work *excepted* by art 4 (see 'Domestic journeys', 14.4) are altogether outside the scope of the Community rules.

The AETR agreement makes no reference to tachographs.

The references in s 99 of the Transport Act 1968 to records include tachograph records (s 99 as amended by reg 3 of the 1979 Regulations). As to this and the penalties for contravening s 97 and s 97A see 14.70–1.

*Defences*

Article 5 refers to tachographs which 'conform' to the provisions of Annexes I and II to the tachograph regulation. Where an obligatory tachograph has been installed but for one reason or another does not conform to Annex I or II is there an offence under s 97(1)? Section 97(3) of the 1968 Act provides that a person shall not be convicted under s 97(1) (installation of conforming tachographs and their use) if the tachograph installed is not in working order if he proves that approved repairs were not reasonably practicable and that the requirements of art 18(2) were being obeyed. Article 18(2) requires that where the tachograph is unserviceable or operating defectively, temporary records must be kept instead.

The failure to keep temporary records under art 18(2) or otherwise to comply with the tachograph regulation will mean that the defence in s 97(3) cannot be made out. Compare the defence under s 98(4A), discussed at 14.52, relating to the voluntary use of tachographs, and compare also the exception in s 98(2A), discussed below, which covers the interrelationship between the tachograph and the 1976 Regulations but does not refer to applicable Community rules such as art 14.

## 14.51 Liability of employers for staff defaults

An employer may be liable generally for using or causing or permitting to be used a vehicle to which s 97 of the 1968 Act applies where the tachograph is not installed and used as specified (s 97(1)). (For 'using', 'causing' and 'permitting' see 1.76–9.) Clearly the employer may be vicariously liable where an employee is using the vehicle without a tachograph being installed as required. The question is whether he can be vicariously liable where the employee is using the vehicle without using the tachograph as required. This is something which is very often completely outside the control of the employer. Nevertheless, it seems that the wording is wide enough to make him vicariously liable (cf the other examples under 'To use' at 1.79).

As an example of the absolute nature of the using offence, a stipendiary magistrate has convicted a limited company for using a vehicle without a tachograph sheet inserted. The transport manager had orally warned the driver, given him a written warning and sacked him for the offence. The comment of the transport manager in court was: 'He's a young man who simply will never learn he's got to do as he's told; he will always go his own sweet way.' The manager's comments out of court have not been quoted. The company received an absolute discharge. The defence in s 98(4) does not apply as this was a contravention not of s 98(4) but s 97 and the defence in s 98(4) only applies to employers 'liable to be convicted under this subsection'.

The responsibilities of an employer under arts 15 and 16 have already been described at 14.50.

An employer commits an offence who fails without reasonable excuse to secure that employee crew members comply with s 97A(1)(*a*), ie failing without reasonable excuse to return any record sheet relating to the employee to the employer within twenty-one days of completing it (s 97A(2)). As to the meaning of 'without reasonable excuse', compare 4.91*C* and 13.47.

It seems that the liabilities of an employer under the Drivers' Hours (Keeping of Records) Regulations 1976 have now ceased in the case of international and national transport operations because the requirement to keep records under EEC Regulation 543/69 has ceased. The liabilities in respect of such operations will now be under the tachograph rules. See below and 14.60, and as to the AETR agreement see 14.25. For the liability in respect of domestic journeys or work and generally see also the following pages.

An employer may be convicted of aiding and abetting an employee or of conspiracy to contravene a Part VI offence (see *R* v *Blamires Transport Services Ltd* [1963] 3 All ER 170).

### 14.52 Tachograph records replacing hand-written records

Where a person is a crew member of a vehicle using a 'conforming' tachograph, the requirements of art 14 (individual hand-written control books) and of art 15 (timetables and duty rosters) of EEC Regulation 543/69 cease to apply (art 5 of the tachograph regulation). The wording is such that it is immaterial whether the use is compulsory or voluntary. (As to voluntary use, see 14.53.)

Section 98(2A) of the Transport Act 1968 states that regulations under this section (ie the Drivers' Hours (Keeping of Records) Regulations 1976) are not to apply as respects the driving of a vehicle 'to which Section 97 of this Act [the tachograph provisions] applies and in relation to which subsection (1)(*b*) of that section has come into force'. It is clear from this that for the purpose of s 98(2A) it is immaterial that the tachograph is not installed as required or does not conform. The wording of s 98(2A) is such that only the vehicles subject to the tachograph rules, ie where the tachograph is compulsory, are excluded from being subject to the 1976 Regulations (cf the wording of art 5 noted above). Section 98(2A) refers to the 'driving' of a compulsory tachograph vehicle. There is no suggestion that any other applicable Community rules such as art 14 of EEC Regulation 543/69 are to be applied instead where the tachograph rules do not apply. At first sight therefore the 1976 Regulations continue to apply to employers with compulsory tachograph vehicles as they are not 'driving'. However, as has been noted above, art 5 exempts compulsory tachograph crew members from arts 14 (hand-written individual control books) and 15 (timetables and duty rosters). In these circumstances it seems that there is nothing left for employers of compulsory tachograph vehicle crew members to comply with under the 1976 Regulations. Similarly, there will be nothing for them to comply with when there is an exemption from keeping records. Where the tachograph breaks down and the required alternative temporary written records are not kept instead, then the requirements of the 1976 Regulations for employers are not resurrected so far as the driving is concerned. The temporary record is not an individual control book under EEC Regulation 543/69 and as specified in the 1976 Regulations (see reg 3(1)), but a record sheet as specified under EEC Regulation 1463/70, and the employer's liability will therefore be under that regulation and under s 97, 97A and 97B of the 1968 Act as noted at 14.50 (see in particular 'Defences').

## 14.53 Voluntary use of the tachograph

Drivers of vehicles excepted or exempt from the compulsory tachograph requirements may instead rely on a tachograph as a voluntary alternative to keeping manual records if the vehicle is suitably equipped. In fact all the transport operations exempt from the compulsory tachograph rules are in effect also exempt from keeping records (see the exemptions set out at 14.50). The voluntary use of a tachograph will therefore only be appropriate for a vehicle within the classification of domestic journeys or work or within the AETR provisions (see 14.25). The AETR agreement makes no reference to the tachograph.

Section 98(4A) of the 1968 Act, as inserted by the Passenger and Goods Vehicles (Recording Equipment) Regulations 1979, provides that, in effect, a person may rely on the tachograph rules instead of keeping manual records, and if so, no offence will be committed under s 98(4) (failing to keep records etc). The burden of establishing this rests on the defendant on the balance of probabilities. Section 98(4) relates to manual record contraventions whether under the applicable Community rules (including the AETR agreement) or regulations made under s 98 (ie the Drivers' Hours (Keeping of Records) Regulations 1976). There is therefore a complete exemption from s 98(4) records offences for drivers, drivers' mates and employers relying voluntarily on a tachograph in this way.

The wording of s 98(4A) is such that if a person is relying on the voluntary use of a tachograph and the tachograph breaks down, the standard tachograph defences will apply to him also. If, however, he is unable to establish the tachograph defence, there will be (per s 98(4A)) a contravention of s 98(4).

Section 98(4A) is curiously worded in that it refers to proving 'there would have been no contravention of the provisions of this Part of this Act so far as they relate to the use of such vehicles'. In fact the only 'use' offences under Part VI are the s 97(1) tachograph 'use' etc offences. If a person is using a tachograph on a purely voluntary basis and not instead of keeping records then it is submitted the legal tachograph rules cannot bind him.

## 14.54–9 Passenger vehicles

Basically the same rules and regulations apply to passenger vehcles as to goods vehicles. Section 95(2) of the 1968 Act applies the provisions to *all* public service vehicles and other motor vehicles constructed and adapted to carry more than twelve passengers. It is not clear whether this includes the driver, but it is submitted that it does not (see 'Passenger', 1.59). However, art 4 of EEC Regulation 543/69 which also applies to the tachograph regulation (see art 3 of that regulation) excepts vehicles (ie public service vehicles) which in construction and equipment are suitable for carrying not more than nine persons including the driver and are intended for that purpose. Also excepted are passenger vehicles on regular services not exceeding 50 km ($31\frac{1}{4}$ miles). These become primarily subject to the domestic journeys or work rules and therefore subject to the records requirements of the Drivers' Hours (Keeping of Records) Regulations 1976.

A tachograph need not be installed or used in passenger vehicles on regular services exceeding 50 km (31¼ miles). These remain subject to the Community rules, but hand-written records need not be kept for regular services (see EEC Regulation 543/69, art 14(1)). Timetables and rosters must be prepared etc (see art 15 ibid).

The national operations exemptions include the use of vehicles which are constructed and equipped to carry not more than fifteen persons including the driver. It seems that the occasional use of such a vehicle with more than fifteen persons may not affect the exemption providing the vehicle has only fifteen seats. This exemption should be compared with the exception for passenger vehicles used for domestic journeys or work (see 14.4). One of these items is worded 'vehicles which in construction and equipment are suitable for carrying not more than nine persons including the driver and are intended for that purpose'. Regular use with an excessive number of passengers may be evidence of the appropriate intent. Drivers of vehicles carrying out domestic journeys or work have to keep records in accordance with the 1976 Regulations.

## Drivers' Records: Manual Records

### 14.60 Generally

The Drivers' Hours (Keeping of Records) Regulations 1976 (SI 1976 No 1447) are made under s 98 of the Transport Act 1968 and have been amended by SIs 1978 Nos 1878 and 1938. They apply in the following instances:

(1) They govern the records to be kept by goods vehicle *drivers* carrying out domestic journeys or work. 'Goods vehicle driver' includes drivers who also drive passenger vehicles (see reg 5(2)). This is subject to the exemption under reg 12. These provisions are in Part II of the 1976 Regulations.

(2) They govern the *employer's* responsibility generally (including *owner-drivers*) for the keeping of records for goods and passenger vehicles subject to the domestic drivers' hours code (see Part II).

(3) They govern, in theory, the *employer's* responsibility generally (including owner-drivers) for the keeping of records for goods and passenger vehicles subject to EEC Regulation 543/69 (see Part III). However, tachographs are now normally compulsory in such vehicles (see s 97(6) of the Transport Act 1968 and art 3 of the tachograph regulations), and records need no longer be kept (see 14.51). Where such vehicles are exempt from the tachograph rules they are also exempt from the keeping of records under art 14 of the drivers' hours regulation. As there are no records to be kept it seems that the provisions of Part III (and Parts IV and V also) are now otiose.

### 14.61 Domestic journeys

Domestic journeys or work are defined at 14.4. Goods and passenger vehicle drivers in this category still have to carry and complete records in accordance with Part II of the 1976 Regulations unless they are otherwise exempt (see reg 12 discussed below). The continental form of control book is the form of record also prescribed by the 1976 Regulations. The provisions apply equally to goods and passenger vehicles as defined in s 95(2) of the Transport Act 1968 and to employee-drivers and owner-drivers as defined in s 95(3).

Regulation 12(1) exempts vehicles which do not require an operator's licence (see below) or which if Crown vehicles would be exempt. The exemption does not apply if the driver also drives a non-exempt vehicle during any period of twenty-four hours commencing at midnight. Reg 12(2) exempts also where the driver does not drive for more than four hours nor outside a radius of 25 miles from the vehicle's operating centre.

*Provisions of the regulations*

Regulation 5 is perhaps the most important; it requires the driver to record and the employer of an employee driver to cause him to record in his record book the information required. Regulation 12 exempts drivers from keeping records in specified circumstances (see above).

Regulation 8(4) requires an employee driver to detach the duplicate record sheet from the book on completion and within seven days deliver it to the issuing employer. It was held under the former regulations that an employer should not be convicted of aiding and abetting a breach by his driver unless the employer knowingly encouraged such a breach in some way (*Cassady* v *Reg Morris (Transport) Ltd* [1975] Crim LR 398). Regulation 8(4)(*a*) of the 1976 regulations provides that the employer must cause the driver (within seven days) to deliver the duplicate sheet and within seven days of receipt the employer must examine and sign it. While the *Cassady* case is still good law, charges of aiding and abetting will now be rarely brought against employers in view of the introduction of the provisions in reg 8(4)(*a*).

Regulation 10(4) requires employers to 'preserve . . . intact' a driver's record book for one year. Under earlier regulations an employer issued a book to one employee who duly completed the required records on the first five pages and then returned it to his employer, who then reissued it to another driver, who used it and produced it to a police officer when stopped. It was held in *Blakey Transport* v *Casebourne* [1975] RTR 221 that the employer did not preserve the book intact in accordance with what is now reg 10 by reissuing the book to another employee for use by him; nor in such a case is it a 'new' book as is required by what is now reg 6 (*Cassady* v *Ward & Smith Ltd* [1975] Crim LR 399). However, a used record book may be reissued to a different driver so that he can use the remaining daily sheets and weekly reports (*Lackenby* v *Browns of Wem Ltd* [1980] RTR 363). The prosecution in *Lackenby* was for a breach of reg 5 of the 1976 Regulations. Griffiths J pointed out that in neither the Transport Act nor the EEC regulation is there any specific requirement that the book should be issued in an unused condition. *Cassady* v *Ward & Smith Ltd* relates to reg 6 and Griffiths J was not prepared to read a similar obligation into reg 5. He added that he could see a powerful argument for construing 'new' as 'another' in the context of reg 6. This dictum must cast some doubt on this aspect of the decision in *Cassady*. The record book in *Lackenby* should not have been issued, but should have been kept for twelve months in accordance with reg 10. Griffiths J pointed out that as it was issued in breach of reg 10, it was not issued in conformity with the regulations as required by reg 5. This point was never taken or argued before the justices and was therefore ignored in reaching a decision.

*Cases under the old law*

The cases which follow were decided on the 1960 Act and regulations thereunder and may still be of relevance. A fitter was employed to do running repairs to vehicles broken down in the highway; it was held that, when he drove to that work, he was a part-time driver and should keep records (*Mackie* v *MacLeod* 1956 SLT 116). In *Gross Cash Registers Ltd* v *Vogt* [1965] 3 All ER 832 a salesman was free to do his travelling in any way he chose—on foot, by bus or in the firm's van; if he used the van, he was allowed to drive it and did so; it was held that, when he drove it in the course of his employment, he was a part-time driver and should keep records.

Under the old regulations, no licence holder needed to keep records in respect of driving by him of a licensed vehicle on journeys which were in no way connected with any trade or business carried on by him, and there was no duty to keep records outside the scope of an employed driver's work. The court should ask itself whether the driver was working in an irregular and unauthorised manner or was acting wholly outside the scope of his employment. In the latter case the employer was not liable for not keeping records (*Jack Motors Ltd* v *Fazackerly* [1962] Crim LR 486). See *Flatman* v *Poole* [1937] 1 All ER 495, *Manley* v *Dobson* [1949] 2 All ER 578, *Leach* v *Cooper* (1950) 48 LGR 526, and *Fillingham* v *Hall* (1935) unreported, on p 305 of the fifth edition of this book, as to exemptions in respect of agricultural user of vehicles. It is proper to charge a defendant, where appropriate, with 'failing to keep or to cause to be kept' the necessary records in one information (*Field* v *Hopkinson* (1944) 108 JP 21). Compare 'comply' and 'cause to comply' in reg 5.

## 14.62 Simplified records for goods vehicles on national journeys

There were provisions for the keeping of simplified records in Part IV of the 1976 Regulations, but they are no longer applicable. In the words of the heading of Part IV they governed 'cases where the Community rules with regard to drivers' hours apply but where the specific requirements of those rules as to record books do not apply'.

Simplified records were permitted to be used by drivers of British vehicles used for national transport within a radius of 50 km (31¼ miles) from where the vehicle was based including the municipality the centre of which was situated within that radius, providing the time spent in driving in the course of any day did not exceed four hours. Article 14a(1)(*b*) makes it clear that now the installation of a tachograph is compulsory, this provision for simplified records has come to an end.

## 14.63 Liability of employers for staff defaults

The hours and conditions of work of *drivers and* (where applicable) *other crew members* are governed mainly by the Community rules. The tachograph rules (see 14.50) govern for the most part the keeping of records, particularly for national and international journeys or work, and affect *drivers, crew members and employers*. The employer's liability for breaches of the tachograph rules is dealt with at 14.51. An employer may be convicted of aiding and abetting an employee in breach of these rules or conspiracy to contravene them (see *R* v *Blamires Transport Services Ltd* [1963] 3 All ER 170). In respect of domestic journeys or work the duties and responsibilities of *employers* are still governed by the Drivers' Hours (Keeping of Records) Regulations 1976 (Part II). Part II relates to the employers of British goods and passenger vehicle drivers where the Community rules *do not* apply (that is, employers of drivers subject to the domestic drivers' hours code). For the extent of Part II see 14.60.

'Employer' for the purposes of Part VI of the 1968 Act is defined by s 103(1) of the Act as meaning, in relation to an employee-driver, the employer of that driver in the employment by virtue of which that driver is an employee driver. Interpreting this subsection, Kilner Brown J said in *Alcock* v *GC Griston Ltd* [1981] RTR 34: 'It is perfectly plain having regard to the definition of employer that whilst he was driving for the firm which required him to drive he was an employee driver in relation to that firm.' The company obtained the part-time services of a driver from an employment agency which continued to pay his wages. He failed to keep records as required by art 14(1) of EEC Regulation 543/69 and Part VI of the 1968 Act. The Divisional Court held that the company was his employer and had been wrongly acquitted by the justices.

The meaning of 'undertaking' was considered by the European Court in *Auditeur du Travail* v *Dufour* [1978] RTR 186. In that case an employment agency supplied a driver to a transport undertaking. It was held that the responsibility rested with the undertaking rather than the agency so far as compliance with art 14(7) and (8) was concerned.

Article 12(*a*) prohibits payments to wage-earning crew members, even in the form of bonuses or wage supplements, related to distances travelled and/or the amount of goods carried, unless these payments are of such a kind as not to endanger road safety. If enforceable at all this would presumably be enforceable under s 96(11A) of the 1968 Act. However, although in wide terms, it is not clear that s 96(11A) is wide enough to cover this provision. Defendants would no doubt put forward the defence in the last part of the article although it is likely that bonuses or like payments related to distances would endanger road safety by encouraging speeding and inducing fatigue. Similarly bonuses or like payments as to the amount carried would be likely to endanger road safety by encouraging overloading. The exemptions from EEC Regulation 543/69 would apply (see 14.50).

Under the old regulations it had been held that a guilty intent was not a necessary ingredient in the offence of not causing a true record to be kept and employers were convicted where a driver had made an incorrect entry, although the employer had had no chance to check it. Employers were also convicted where a driver had made an entry, which proved to be correct, in advance. However, the employer of a driver engaged in domestic journeys or work or subject to the AETR agreement now has the defence in the proviso to s 98(4), that he had given proper instructions to his employees and checked from time to time; the onus is on the employer and the prosecution do not have to disprove this in advance. Compare the absolute responsibility of employers for user tachograph offences contrary to s 97(1) discussed at 14.51.

This defence applies to domestic drivers' hours code records. The tachograph has, however, largely supplanted s 98(4) records offences save for domestic journeys or work and for AETR international journeys (see 14.25). Presumably the defence is on the balance of probabilities and the burden is on the defence (see s 101 of the Magistrates' Courts Act 1980). It is for the court to say, after hearing the employer, whether he has given 'proper' instructions and taken 'reasonable steps' from time to time. Under the previous law it was a defence if an employer had been able to show 'due diligence' in seeing that the law had been complied with.

The expression 'due diligence' still appears in ss 100–103 of the Food Act 1984, in s 24 of the Trade Descriptions Act 1968 and in other statutes. The meaning of the expression does not seem to be very different from the words used in s 98(4). The leading case on the meaning of 'due diligence' in s 24 etc is *Tesco Supermarkets* v *Nattrass* [1971] 2 All ER 127. In the case of a large-scale organisation the owner, whether it be a limited company or an individual, cannot personally supervise the activities of all his servants, and it would be consistent with the taking of reasonable precautions and the exercise of all due diligence to institute an effective system to prevent the commission of offences under which superior servants were instructed to supervise inferior servants whose acts might otherwise lead to the commission of an offence. It is submitted that the approach to the problem posed under the Trade Descriptions Act shown by the House of Lords in *Tesco* is of relevance in considering whether a defence under s 98(4) is made out. It is submitted that whether the employer has given 'proper' instructions and taken 'reasonable steps' is essentially a question of fact and degree.

### 14.64 The AETR agreement

The AETR agreement makes no reference to the tachograph and provides instead for manual records. As noted at 14.25 the AETR rules are apparently to be treated as applicable Community rules. A contravention of the AETR requirement for manual records will therefore be an offence relating to the requirement as to books, records or documents contrary to s 98(4) of the 1968 Act, and the defence in s 98(4) as noted at 14.63 will apply accordingly.

It was held in *Oxford* v *Spencer* [1983] RTR 63 that the model individual control book was not part of the annex to EEC Regulation 543/69. The annex is specifically incorporated in that regulation. The model was held to be merely attached to the annex. It was not therefore an offence under the regulation to fail to comply with the instructions in the model (and in particular the instruction to complete name, date of birth and address). Although the case concerned EEC Regulation 543/69 art 14 (failing to keep records), the AETR agreement is in similar terms. The principal application of the decision would seem therefore now to be to the AETR agreement.

## 14.65–9 Passenger vehicles

The records requirements for passenger vehicles are set out in Table 3.

**Table 3**
**Passenger vehicles: tachographs and records**

| *Class of transport operation* | *Class of vehicle* | *Records requirements* |
|---|---|---|
| *International journeys or work* | PSVs for 10 or more passengers including the driver (s 95(2) and art 4(1) of EEC Reg 543/69). | Tachograph required (art 4(1) of EEC Reg 1463/70 and s 97 (1)). No timetables or duty rosters required (art 5 of EEC Reg 1463/70). |
| | Other passenger vehicles for more than 13 passengers including the driver (s 95(2)). | |
| *National journeys or work* | All passenger vehicles (including PSVs) for 16 or more passengers including the driver (see Community Transport Rules (Exemptions) Regulations 1978). | Tachograph required (art 3 and s 97(1)). No timetables or duty rosters required (art 5). |
| | Above vehicles on regular services exceeding 50 km | No tachograph required (art 3). Timetables and duty rosters required (art 15 of EEC Reg 543/69). |
| | PSVs for from 10 to 15 passengers including the driver (s 95(2) and art 4(1)). | No tachograph, records, timetables or duty rosters required (Community Transport Rules (Exemptions) Regulations 1978). |
| | All passenger vehicles (other than PSVs) for 14 or 15 passengers including the driver (s 95(2) and art 4(1)). | No tachograph, records, timetables or duty rosters required (Community Transport Rules (Exemptions) Regulations 1978). |
| | All PSVs and other passenger vehicles for 14 or more passengers including the driver on regular services of 50 km or less (s 95(2) and art 4(3)). | |
| *Domestic journeys or work* | All PSVs for 9 passengers or less including the driver (s 95(2) and art 4(1)). | No tachograph required (art 4). Drivers' Hours (Keeping of Records) Regulations 1976 apply. |
| — | Passenger vehicles (other than PSVs) for 13 passengers or less including the driver (s 95(2)). | No tachograph, records, timetables or rosters required (outside Part VI: see s 95(2)). |

Notes 1. A tachograph may be used on a voluntary basis to replace record keeping.
2. This chart must be read subject to other exceptions or exemptions where applicable.
3. As to passengers 'including the driver' for the purposes of s 95(2), see further 1.59. In all the other provisions mentioned the inclusion of the driver is specified.
4. See 14.11 as to whether the tachograph requirements apply to non-commercial use.

Reference should also be made where necessary to the interrelationship of the tachograph and hand-written records at 14.52. It is submitted there that the responsibility of employers under Parts III, IV and V of the 1976

Regulations has ceased. There may also be voluntary reliance on the tachograph (see 14.53).

## Drivers' Records: Penalties and Proceedings

### 14.70 Offences and proceedings

Under s 97(1) it is an offence to use, cause or permit to be used a vehicle to which the tachograph provisions apply without recording equipment:

(*a*) which has been installed in accordance with the regulation,
(*b*) which complies with Annexes I and II, and
(*c*) is being used as provided by arts 15–17.

One purpose of the change by the 1984 Regulations already noted seems to have been to combine items (*a*), (*b*) and (*c*) into a single offence. It is submitted that it is still possible to charge them separately if so desired. See 'Duplicity', 2.46. As to 'using', 'causing' and 'permitting', see 1.76–9.

Section 97(2), (3) and (4) provide defences where:

(*a*) a vehicle is proceeding to a place where the recording equipment is to be fitted in accordance with the EEC regulation requirements (s 97(2));
(*b*) in the case of defective recording equipment, it had not become reasonably practicable for the equipment to be repaired by an approved fitter or workshop *and* the requirements of art 18(2) (temporary records) were being complied with (s 97(3));
(*c*) in the case of broken seals, breaking or removal could not have been avoided *and* it had not become reasonably practicable for the seal to be replaced by an approved fitter or workshop *and* in all other respects the equipment was being used as provided by arts 15–17 (s 97(4)).

Both the wording of the statute and the sense imply that (*b*) and (*c*) respectively are cumulative. In other words the defendant must prove *both* limbs of (*b*) above before that defence applies and the three limbs of (*c*) above before that defence applies. In each case the burden of proof will be on the defendant on the balance of probabilities. It will be for the prosecution to show that the vehicle is one for which a tachograph must be installed or used as the case may be. The defendant may also be able to rely on one of the exemptions (see 14.50) or the defences at 14.51.

It is an offence under s 98(4) for a person to contravene the Drivers' Hours (Keeping of Records) Regulations 1976. There are defences in the proviso to s 98(4) and in s 98(4A). These are discussed at 14.63 and 14.53 respectively.

A traffic examiner or police officer is empowered under the Transport Act 1968, s 99(1), to require the production for inspection of various documents to which the Act or regulations made under the Act refer. He is given power under s 99(2) and (3) to enter vehicles and premises in the course of his duties and he may detain a vehicle. Any person who fails to comply with a requirement under s 99(1) or who obstructs an officer in the course of his duties under s 99(2) or (3) commits an offence (s 99(4)). Any person who knowingly falsifies tachograph entries under s 97 or entries kept for the purposes of regulations under s 98 or under applicable Community rules is guilty of an offence (s 99(5)). Doubts are expressed at (1982) 146 JP Jo 186 as to whether certain parts of s 99 (including parts of s 99(2)(*b*) and (3)) have come into force. It is submitted that the better view is that these subsections were merely, to some extent, kept 'on ice' and came fully into force with s 99(2)(*a*).

Records are admissible in evidence against the employers, whether on charges under s 98 or otherwise (*Beer* v *Clench* [1936] 1 All ER 449; *Adair* v *Craighouse & Co* 1937 SLT 499). When the number of a vehicle appears in the record, that may suffice to identify that vehicle (*Hogg* v *Burnet* 1938 SC (J) 160). Such records were not made admissible previously by any statute but are now made specifically so by s 98(5), when entered by an employee-driver, in proceedings under Part VI against his employer whether for contravening EEC Regulation 543/69 or the 1976 Regulations. Under s 97B similarly tachograph entries are admissible and in Scotland are sufficient evidence. Under s 97 also any entries made thereon for the purposes of arts 17(2) or 17(3) or 18(2) of the EEC tachograph regulation may also be admitted in evidence. It is submitted that these provisions do not cut down the admissibility of such records generally under the cases just cited.

Section 103(7) of the Transport Act 1968 was substituted by s 3 of the Road Traffic (Drivers' Ages and Hours of Work) Act 1976. The amendment overrules the decision in *R* v *Hitchin JJ, ex parte Hilton* [1974] RTR 380. It extends the jurisdiction of the courts with very wide terms. Prosecutors have suggested that the wording is such as to enable prosecutions to be brought in Great Britain for offences committed on the continent when the defendant has been found in this country. It should be noted, however, that s 96(11A) specifies that contraventions of applicable Community rules caught by that subsection must be in Great Britain. Sections 97(1) and 98(4) are not so limited. It should be noted that s 103(7) relates to *any* offence under Part VI of the Transport Act 1968, whether relating to the observance of hours or the keeping of records or any other provision in Part VI.

An indictable charge at common law of conspiracy to contravene these provisions may properly be brought (*R* v *Blamires Transport Services Ltd* [1963] 3 All ER 170). In that case a haulage company's conviction on indictment of conspiring with the company's drivers to make false records under the 1960 Act was upheld on appeal.

### 14.71 Penalties

Offences contrary to s 97(1) (installation and use of tachographs) are punishable with a maximum fine of level 4. There is a similar maximum fine for contravention of s 97A (employees failing to return record sheets to employers and employers failing to receive these, in each case without reasonable excuse). The venue for proceedings includes any court having jurisdiction in accordance with s 103(7) (see 14.70). There is no power to endorse, disqualify or order penalty points.

The Magistrates' Association's suggested penalty for no tachograph or for the tachograph not being used as required is £100 (see 18.1 and Appendix 3).

Contraventions of the regulations as to domestic journeys and contravention of EEC Regulation 543/69 as amended as to records on AETR journeys are punishable under s 98(4) on a first or subsequent conviction with a maximum fine of level 4.

Offences contrary to s 99(1), (2) and (3) are punishable with a maximum fine of level 3 (s 99(4)).

The falsification offences under s 99(5) are 'either way' offences triable in accordance with ss 18–23 of the Magistrates' Courts Act 1980. The defendant can insist on trial by jury. On summary conviction there is a maximum fine of £2,000 and on indictment the maximum penalty is two years' imprisonment or unlimited fine or both. There is no time limit as this is an 'either way' offence (s 127 of the 1980 Act).

The licensing authorities are empowered to revoke, suspend or curtail an operator's licence if the goods vehicle licence holder or his driver has been convicted under Part VI of the Act (s 69(4)(*c*)).

# Chapter 15

# Theft, Taking Conveyances and Criminal Damage

## 15.1 Generally

This chapter deals with the offences of theft and taking conveyances in ss 1 and 12 of the Theft Act 1968. Thereafter the related offences of interfering with vehicles (s 9 of the Criminal Attempts Act 1981), tampering with and getting on vehicles (ss 29 and 30 of the 1972 Act), and criminal damage (s 1 of the Criminal Damage Act 1971) are considered.

## Theft and Taking Conveyances

## 15.2 The offences: ss 1 and 12

As to theft generally, see the standard textbooks.

The offence of taking a conveyance without consent is to be found in s 12 of the Theft Act 1968. A person commits an offence under s 12 who, without having the consent of the owner or other lawful authority, takes any conveyance (as defined in subs (7)) for his own or another's use *or* who, knowing that any such conveyance has been taken without such authority, drives it or allows himself to be carried in or on it.

The provisions of s 12 do not apply to Scotland, where s 175 of the 1972 Act applies. This section is a re-enactment, almost word for word, of s 217 of the Road Traffic Act 1960 as amended by s 44 of the Road Traffic Act 1962. The section relates to motor vehicles only. Some of the cases cited below were on s 217 of the 1960 Act.

Section 12 was primarily designed to deal with people who took cars for 'joy rides' and then abandoned them, thus escaping a charge of theft on the ground that there was no intention permanently to deprive the owner of it.

A person who enters a building as a trespasser with intent to take a conveyance does not commit burglary under s 9 of the Theft Act because offences under s 12 are not comprised in s 9(1) or (2). By s 25(5) of the Theft Act 1968, the offence of having an article for use in connection with theft is, however, specifically applied to offences under s 12(1); a person who had with him (otherwise than at his place of abode) a set of car-keys or a car-park attendant's uniform with a view to facilitating an offence under s 12 would be guilty—see s 25(3) as to burden of proof. This does not apply to persons equipped to take pedal cycles.

Belief by a defendant to a charge under s 12 that he had lawful authority or would have had the owner's consent had the owner known of his action and the circumstances of it constitutes a statutory 'defence' to the charge: see s 12(6) discussed at 15.5, although in fact where the issue is raised the onus is on the prosecution to establish lack of belief on the criminal standard of proof.

The belief of the accused that he had authority need not be reasonable and the onus is not on him to prove it; the offence is complete if the defendant 'takes' not 'takes and drives away' the conveyance (see *R* v *Bogacki and Others*, *R* v *Pearce* and *R* v *Bow* below, and also, in relation to employee-drivers, *McKnight* v *Davies* at 15.8).

The section extends to ships, rubber dinghies, aircraft, vehicles whether mechanically propelled or not, eg carts, trams, trolley vehicles, railway rolling-stock, and, as indicated in s 12(5), cycles; the *Concise Oxford Dictionary* defines 'cycle' as including a bicycle, tricycle or similar machine. The definition of 'conveyance' in s 12(7) suggests that there is no offence if a person takes a remotely-controlled aircraft or vehicle (see *R* v *Roberts* at 15.6). The conveyance must be constructed or adapted for the carriage of a person or persons, so that a goods trailer, milkfloat or porter's trolley or hand-barrow is not covered. Presumably, the presence of a seat for the driver shows that a conveyance is constructed for the carriage of 'a person'; otherwise it would not be an offence to take a lorry. It is submitted that an excavator or bulldozer which has a seat for the driver is constructed or adapted for the carriage of a person and so is a conveyance under s 12. In *R* v *Bow*, below, it was said that the vehicle must be used as a means of transport.

A horse is not a 'conveyance' (*Neal* v *Gribble* [1978] RTR 409). Moreover, even if a horse could be said to be a conveyance, which it is not, it cannot be said to be 'adapted' for the conveyance of the rider by the putting of a bridle on it: a bridle, halter or saddle does not 'adapt' the horse but simply makes it easier to ride (ibid).

In *R* v *Bogacki and Others* [1973] RTR 384 it was held that 'take' as expressed in s 12 of the Theft Act was not equivalent to 'use', nor could it consist of a mere assumption of possession adverse to the rights of the true owner; to constitute the offence of taking there must be an unauthorised taking possession or control of the conveyance adverse to the rights of the true owner or person otherwise entitled to such possession or control coupled with some movement of the conveyance no matter how small. *Bogacki* was followed and applied in *R* v *Miller* [1976] Crim LR 147, where it was held that the charge of allowing oneself to be carried requires movement of the conveyance while carried.

*Bogacki* was further considered in *R* v *Bow* [1977] RTR 6 where it was held that for a vehicle to be taken for 'his or another's use', the vehicle had to be used as a conveyance, namely, as a means of transport. The vehicle in *Bow* was a gamekeeper's Land Rover obstructing the poachers' escape route. One of the poachers entered the Land Rover and coasted it down hill, without using the engine, for two hundred yards. The conviction under s 12 was affirmed as the Land Rover was in fact used as a conveyance. It was, however, said that pushing an obstructing vehicle out of the way for a yard or two would not involve the use of the vehicle as a conveyance and that the facts involved in the removal of an obstructing vehicle must be examined in each case (ibid, at p 11c).

The need to take as a conveyance was again emphasised in *R* v *Stokes* [1983] RTR 59. In that case the car belonged to a former girl friend. The car was pushed around the corner as a practical joke. It was held following the decision in *Bow* that 'use' involved use as a conveyance and the defendant was acquitted. It is submitted that the intent to use it as a conveyance is sufficient, providing it is moved (compare *R* v *Pearce* below) without anyone actually travelling in it. On the other hand in *Bow* the Land Rover was in fact used as a conveyance even though the purpose of the poacher was not to be conveyed but to remove an obstruction. Although it is not a binding decision further support for the view that the taking must be for use as a conveyance may be derived from the direction to the jury in *R* v *Dunn and Derby* [1984] Crim LR 367. A motor bicycle had been taken and wheeled 40 yards to look at it by a porch light but not for use as a conveyance. An acquittal was directed.

Accidentally putting a foot on the accelerator of an automatic drive vehicle which had the engine running with the result that the vehicle drove all over the road, is not 'taking' for the purpose of s 12 (*Blayney* v *Knight* [1975] Crim LR 237). The construction placed on 'drive' in s 12(7) does not mean that the movement of the conveyance has to be in the element in which the conveyance is designed to travel; thus, in *R* v *Pearce* [1973] Crim LR 321 a defendant's conviction was upheld for taking an inflatable rubber dinghy from a life-boat depot, and putting it on a trailer which he then drove away.

*R* v *Miller* was applied in *R* v *Diggin* [1981] RTR 83. A defendant allowed himself to be carried in a vehicle taken without the owner's consent by his brother and a Mr Zubal. Because of drink and because the vehicle was of the same year and manufacture as one he knew was owned by Mr Zubal, he thought he was in that vehicle. The car stopped at a motorway service area, and before the car could move off, the police approached. The defendant asserted that only then did he realise the vehicle had been taken without consent. The Court of Appeal held that, for the offence under s 12 of allowing oneself to be carried knowing it to have been taken without authority, there must have been some movement of the vehicle after the defendant had knowledge of its unlawful taking.

Although not otherwise adverted to, it should be noted that the second part of s 12(1) and (5) of the Theft Act refers to 'knowing' that the conveyance or pedal cycle has been taken without authority. There has been no reported decision adverting to the contrast between s 12 and s 22 of the Theft Act, namely that the mens rea on a charge of handling stolen goods under s 22 is stated as 'knowing or believing' the goods to be stolen, whereas the mens rea in s 12 is stated as 'knowing' only. It would seem that the prosecution under s 12 has to prove knowledge of the unauthorised taking of the vehicle; belief would seem to be insufficient. An article on the mental element in s 12 offences appears at [1980] Crim LR 609.

*The difference between theft (s 1) and taking a conveyance (s 12)*

Sometimes a person who takes a car or motor-vessel is accused of stealing the petrol also but it is submitted that he should not be punished for both offences (see [1968] Crim LR 282; *R* v *Burnham JJ* at 2.49; and 'Two offences from one incident' at 5.49). On summary trial the punishment is the same anyhow. A person charged under s 12 may still, it is submitted, be convicted even if the facts show that he is guilty of theft because he dishonestly took the conveyance with the intention of permanently depriving the owner of it. It was held to be no defence to the previous offence of driving or allowing oneself to be carried, when not a party to the original taking, that the defendant knew that the vehicle had been *stolen* and not just taken (*Tolley* v *Giddings* [1964] 1 All ER 201).

While a jury may convict a defendant charged with theft of taking under s 12 (s 12(4)), a magistrates' court cannot do so unless he has been additionally charged in the alternative.

One distinction between theft and taking is that the offence of theft is required to be dishonestly committed and requires proof of mens rea; an offence under s 12(1) does not require proof of an intention to commit it, but it does require knowledge and mens rea in this respect (see *R* v *Diggin* above). On the other hand s 12(1) requires the vehicle to be physically moved (*R* v *Bogacki* above), and the offence of theft is complete once the vehicle has been dishonestly appropriated; 'appropriation' does not require the vehicle to be physically moved. It is necessary to prove intent to use as a conveyance or actual use for conveyance (see *R* v *Stokes* and *R* v *Pearce* above). This is not essential to establish theft. An offence of theft also requires proof on the part of the defendant of an intention permanently to deprive the owner of the vehicle; under s 12 no such intention is required.

## 15.3 Pedal cycles

Section 12(1) does not apply to pedal cycles even though they are conveyances. Section 12(5) creates the separate offence of taking a pedal cycle without consent. The wording is similar to s 12(1) save that the reference is to riding instead of driving or allowing oneself to be carried etc. The maximum penalties are less severe. As to riding, see 1.58. The expression is wide enough to include a passenger, whether carried legally or illegally. The defence in s 12(6) of belief in lawful authority or owner's consent applies to s 12(5) offences as does, it is submitted, the law generally relating to the taking of conveyances and movement of pedal cycles only for the purpose of conveyance. The s 25 offence of going equipped applies by s 25(5) to s 12(1) offences, but not to pedal cycles.

Where a person takes an auto-assisted pedal cycle, the question arises whether he should be charged with taking a conveyance under s 12(1) or with taking a pedal cycle under s 12(5). The position has become more relevant with the introduction of electrically assisted pedal cycles such as the Sinclair C5 (see 1.9) which can be lawfully ridden by persons as young as fourteen and which are not classified as motor vehicles for the purposes of the 1972 Act and the Road Traffic Regulation Act 1984. This non-classification does not apply to the 1968 Act which refers to 'conveyances'; 'motor vehicle' is not an expression used in s 12. Many of the earlier cases, such as *Floyd* v

*Bush* [1953] 1 WLR 242, were for taking and driving away a *motor vehicle* under the 1960 Act where the test was different.

Section 12(5) states specifically that s 12(1) shall not apply to pedal cycles and the issue is not whether the vehicle is a motor vehicle but whether it is a pedal cycle. If a s 12(5) charge is used it will be for the prosecution to establish to the criminal standard of proof that it is a pedal cycle. If a s 12(1) charge is used, the pedal cycle provision would seem to be an exception, so that under the Magistrates' Courts Act 1980, s 101, the onus of proof is on the defendant to establish that it is a pedal cycle and that the s 12(1) offence does not therefore apply.

The standard of proof will be on the balance of probabilities (*R* v *Carr-Briant* [1943] 2 All ER 156). Whether a vehicle is a pedal cycle is a question of fact. Most auto-assisted motor vehicles (including electrically assisted pedal cycles) are not really designed to be driven extensively with pedals although they are capable of being propelled by them. Nevertheless it is submitted that they are also pedal cycles (as for example is indicated by the expression electrically assisted pedal cycles) and that prosecutions should be under s 12(5) and not s 12(1). Penal provisions should be construed strictly.

## 15.4 Consent of owner

If the owner's consent were obtained by intimidation seemingly this would not be 'consent' under s 12 (*R* v *Hogdon* [1962] Crim LR 563). In *R* v *Peart* [1970] 2 All ER 823 it was held that consent of the owner as to the use of the car by another was not vitiated by the fact that the defendant obtained the owner's consent by falsely pretending that he needed the car to go to Alnwick when in fact he went to Burnley instead. The court held that when s 12 was enacted there was no intention by Parliament to create a new offence of taking conveyances by false pretences. If therefore the owner's consent is obtained by means of a false pretence either as to the destination or purpose of the journey, no offence under s 12 appears to be committed. The court, however, reserved for a future occasion the legal position where the consent of the owner was obtained by a fundamental misrepresentation, as for example where *B* pretended to the owner that he was *C*.

This was partly answered by the important case of *Whittaker* v *Campbell* [1983] 3 All ER 582, which held, following *R* v *Peart*, that fraud did not vitiate consent. The defendants had used another's driving licence to hire a car, representing that one of them was that person. It is immaterial that *B* thought *C* was someone else such as a famous film star as in *Lewis* v *Averay* [1971] 3 All ER 907 referred to in the *Whittaker* case. The position should be compared with *R* v *Phipps*, *R* v *McGill* [1970] RTR 209, a case under the 1960 Act where *M* obtained permission to borrow the car to go to the railway station. He did not return and used it next day to go to Hastings. It was held that, since he had once failed to return the car, his use was unlawful unless he reasonably believed that the owner in the circumstances would have given his consent if asked. It seems that if the defendant in *Peart* had in fact gone to Alnwick and then on to Burnley he would be guilty in accordance with *Phipps*. For further criticism of *Peart* see [1970] Crim LR 480. It should also be noted that *Phipps* was followed and applied in *McKnight* v *Davies* (see 15.8). The distinction between a person obtaining permission to use a vehicle for a limited purpose and going beyond that purpose and therefore being held guilty of an offence under s 217 or s 12 (*Phipps*) and a person obtaining permission for a different purpose from the one he actually used it for (*Peart*) is a fine one. *Peart* was cited in argument to the court in *McKnight* v *Davies* but there is no mention of it in the judgment. (*Phipps*, contrary to the statement in the judgment of *McKnight* v *Davies* [1974] RTR 4, at p 7G, was a case under s 217 of the Act of 1960, not s 12 of the Theft Act.)

*Evidence*

It was held in a Crown Court case, *R* v *Ronald Francis* [1982] Crim LR 694, applying *R* v *Hulbert* (1979) 69 Cr App R 243, (a receiving case contrary to s 22 of the Theft Act 1968) that the fact that the defendant had said that his companion the driver of the car had told him that he had 'nicked it' was not evidence upon which the prosecution could rely to prove that the car had been taken without consent. The comment may be evidence to show the defendant's state of mind. Neither that nor the surrounding circumstances were such that the jury could properly infer that the owner had not, as a matter of fact, consented.

## 15.5 Defences: belief of lawful authority or owner's consent (s 12(6))

Unlike the former offence in England and Wales, and the present offence in Scotland under s 175 of the 1972 Act, the onus of proving that the accused did not believe under s 12(6) that he had lawful authority to take the conveyance or that he would have had the owner's consent if the latter knew of his doing it and the circumstances of it is on the prosecution.

Section 12(1) and (5) refer to the owner's consent or *other* lawful authority. Section 12(6) refers to lawful authority *or* the owner's consent. This distinction may imply that there may be a valid belief in the owner's consent even though there is an unlawful element.

It was held in *R* v *McPherson* [1973] RTR 157 that if an issue arises as to whether a defendant under s 12(6) had a belief of lawful authority, etc the onus is on the prosecution to prove that the defendant had no such authority or consent. On the other hand the prosecution do not have to prove a specific intent on the part of the defendant to take the vehicle (ibid). Thus where the defendant was drunk (but not so drunk as to raise the defence of insanity) a judge was entitled to direct the jury that self-induced drunkenness was no defence, and that, unless an issue under s 12(6) was raised, the only matters that the jury had to be satisfied about were (*a*) that the vehicle was taken by the defendant and (*b*) that it was without the owner's consent.

Magistrates' courts have acquitted where it has been established that the defendant mistook the vehicle believing it to be his own on the basis that as it was his own he believed he had lawful authority. There is a well known story of a junior barrister who drove off from a golf club in a Mini belonging to a senior judge. The judge's Mini was identical to his own. There was another incident where a person took a police vehicle after dark and parked it in his garage leaving behind his own similar white Ford Escort. No prosecution followed.

The statute does not apparently require the defendant's belief under s 12 (6) that he had lawful authority or consent to be reasonable. The very absurdity of some factors for the belief can show that he did not really hold it, but it need not be reasonable. A follower of an obscure religion might have some literally fantastic belief but, if the prosecution do not disprove that he had such a belief, it seems to be a defence. It is a question of fact even though the defendant has no driving licence and no insurance (*R* v *Clotworthy* [1981] Crim LR 501). Magistrates acquitted a defendant who took a car in the belief that the owner, a friend, would have consented; the owner testified that, while normally he would have consented, he would not have done so on that occasion as the fanbelt was broken ([1968] Jo Crim L 3). Moving a motor vehicle simply for one's own convenience, eg because it is blocking a doorway, is not normally an offence under s 12 (*Shimmell* v *Fisher* [1951] 2 All ER 672; see also *R* v *Bow* at 15.2).

## 15.6 'Driving away'

In *Shimmell* v *Fisher* [1951] 2 All ER 627 three men approached a parked lorry and the hand brake was released; two of the men pushed it and the third held the steering wheel and they tried unsuccessfully to start the engine. On a charge under s 217 of the Road Traffic Act 1960 of taking and driving away the lorry, it was held that 'driving away' meant causing the vehicle to move from the place where it was standing and that a vehicle could be said to be driven if one man pushed and another steered. It is submitted that under s 12 all three would be joint offenders engaged in a common purpose and should be convicted if they intended to use it as a means of transport (see *R* v *Bow* at 15.2). But merely releasing the brake of a lorry, so that it ran downhill driverless, is not taking and driving away (*R* v *Roberts* [1964] 2 All ER 541). It can be argued that letting a vehicle run downhill unattended or a vessel drift away unmanned is likewise not 'taking' it under s 12 and that there should be some measure of control by the accused over it. The case of *R* v *Roberts*, however, turned partly on the question whether what the defendant did was 'driving away' and it was suggested in the judgment of Lord Parker CJ that this might be taking. The taking, by s 12 (1), must be for 'the use of' the defendant or another; letting a vehicle run away is hardly for anyone's use, and it would now seem from *R* v *Bow* (see 15.2) that the unauthorised possession or control of the conveyance for purposes of transport is the essential element in such cases. Letting a vehicle run downhill or a boat downstream unattended would not constitute transport, but otherwise if the offender was in the driving seat or on the boat.

## 15.7 Passengers

In *R* v *Baldessare* (1930) 22 Cr App R 70, two persons engaged in a common purpose were both held guilty of criminal negligence in driving though only one drove. Passengers are, it seems, aiders, abettors, counsellors and procurers of the offence by the driver if they all act together in taking the car, and they can all properly be convicted along with him. The matter is put beyond doubt by the second part of s 12(1), which extends to a person who, 'knowing that any conveyance has been taken without [the owner's consent or other lawful] authority, drives it or allows himself to be carried in or on it'. Where any such driver or passenger was not a party to the original taking and the charge is contrary to this second part of s 12(1) (knowingly etc), the prosecution must prove that the driver or passenger knew that the vehicle had been taken without consent or other lawful authority. The passenger must also be carried in the conveyance while it is in motion (*R* v *Miller* and *R* v *Diggin* at 15.2). There is a clear case to answer against passengers as well as against the driver where a car is found at 2 am without petrol and the passengers give an unsatisfactory explanation to the police of the reason for their presence in the car (*Ross* v *Rivenall* [1959] 2 All ER 376) but Donovan J (as he then was) doubted if mere presence in a car as a passenger, without any suspicious circumstances, was enough (ibid). It does not matter whether the driver or a passenger took the car, so long as they were acting in concert, or even if they had it from another person (*R* v *Richardson* [1958] Crim LR 480), but to convict a passenger of taking there must be some evidence to show that each accused was a party to the taking or knew of the unlawful taking; entering a car after it has been taken, without evidence that the passenger was a party to or knew of the taking, is not enough (*R* v *Stally* [1959] 3 All ER 814).

In *Boldizer* v *Knight* [1980] Crim LR 653 the defendant was given a lift in a van. During the course of the drive he learned that it had been taken without the owner's consent. It was held that he should not be convicted of using the van without insurance; *aliter* if the taking had been a joint enterprise (cf *Ross* v *Rivenall* above). The defendant was, however, convicted of knowingly allowing himself to be carried contrary to s 12 of the Theft Act 1968. (See also under Chapter 10, 'Insurance'.) Compare *R* v *Diggin* at 15.2, where the passenger also did not learn that the vehicle had been taken without consent until after the beginning of the journey. Here there was no evidence of movement or of being carried after the discovery and an acquittal was directed.

It is wrong to convict a juvenile under fourteen of taking a vehicle merely because he took an active part in the taking of the vehicle by another; in the case of a child it is necessary to show that he knew that he was doing something wrong (*C (a minor)* v *Hume* [1979] Crim LR 328). If evidence is produced to show that a passenger was a party to the taking, it need not be shown that he was present at the taking (ibid). It was said in *R* v *Pearce* [1961] Crim LR 122 that it was not correct to say that there was a new taking and driving away every time the car was moved. Convictions were quashed where there was no evidence to show that a passenger was concerned in the original taking (*D* v *Parsons* [1960] 2 All ER 493; *A* v *Bundy* (1960) 125 JP 89), but see now the express reference in s 12 (1) to knowledge that a conveyance has been taken without authority. A person not a party to the taking who, knowing that a motor vehicle has been *stolen*, drives or travels in it commits an offence (*Tolley* v *Giddings* [1964] 1 All ER 201).

## 15.8 Employees and hirers

It was held that a van driver, in lawful possession of his employer's van, who drove it on a frolic of his own, committed no offence in *Mowe* v *Perraton*

[1952] 1 All ER 423. It would be otherwise if he had put the vehicle back into his employer's possession, eg by leaving it in the employer's garage, and then took it out of such possession without leave. The reason for the decision was that an employee, being in lawful possession of his employer's vehicle whilst on duty, cannot 'take' what he already has, but this reasoning was inconsistent with *R* v *Phipps*, *R* v *McGill* [1970] RTR 209, and the latter case was followed in preference to *Mowe* v *Perraton* in *McKnight* v *Davies*, below.

In *R* v *Wibberley* [1965] 3 All ER 718, the defendant, a truckdriver, was supposed to return the truck to his employer's premises at the end of the day's work but, instead, he took it home and parked it outside his house for two hours. He then drove it away for a purpose of his own. The employers would not have objected to him parking outside his house for the night and taking the truck to work next morning. His conviction for taking it for his own purposes, after he had parked it, was upheld, as he had no authority to use it, after parking it outside his home, until the next day's work began. There was a distinction between deviation from employment during working hours, when he still intended to carry out his instructions to drive the vehicle to his employer's premises, and taking it after working hours with no such intention and after an interruption in time.

In *McKnight* v *Davies* [1974] RTR 4 a lorry driver returning to his employer's depot struck a low bridge with the roof of his lorry. He was not permitted to use the lorry for his own purposes, but, being scared on seeing the damage to the lorry's roof, he drove to a public house and had a drink, then drove three men to their homes and returned to the centre of the city, had a drink at another public house and drove home leaving his lorry nearby, in all driving 30 miles in excess of his proper delivery route. *R* v *Wibberley*, above, and *R* v *Phipps* [1970] RTR 209 were followed in preference to *Mowe* v *Perraton*, which was held to be inconsistent in particular with *Phipps*. (In *Phipps* it was held that where a defendant had been given permission to take and use a vehicle for a limited purpose, and thereafter used it for another purpose, he was guilty of the offence; see also 15.4.) The court went on in *McKnight* v *Davies* to consider to what extent the unauthorised use by an employee of his employer's vehicle could in law amount to a 'taking' for the purposes of s 12. Not every brief unauthorised diversion from his proper route would necessarily involve a 'taking' for use (ibid, p 8); if, however, he returned the vehicle and parked it for the night and drove off on an unauthorised errand (as in *R* v *Wibberley*) that would be a sufficient 'taking' (ibid). It was suggested that to constitute a 'taking' of the vehicle during his working day or while he had authority to use the vehicle, he must have appropriated it in a manner which repudiated his employer's true rights. In other words he had altered the character of his control over the vehicle so that he no longer held it as employee but assumed possession of it in the legal sense. In the opinion of the court, the defendant 'took' the vehicle not when he first went to a public house, but when he left it to drive the three men home.

A person who takes away a conveyance on hire-purchase with the hirer's consent but without the consent of the dealer or finance company which owns it does not offend against s 12 because, by s 12(7)(*b*), 'owner', in relation to a vehicle which is the subject of a hiring agreement or hire-purchase agreement, means the person in possession of the vehicle under that agreement (*R* v *Tolhurst* [1962] Crim LR 489).

### 15.9–15 Attempts

See 'Attempt' at 1.91 and the cases at 4.26 as to attempting to drive. The definition of 'attempt' offences is now to be found in the Criminal Attempts Act 1981, and the cases below must be read in the light of that Act, and the definition contained therein, although they may well still be of assistance.

In *R* v *Cook* [1964] Crim LR 56 it was held that a man who was found in the front seat of a car fiddling with the ignition, the dashboard being lit, and who later said that, if not caught, in another minute he would have got away with the car, could properly be convicted of an attempt to take it. In *R* v *Bogacki and Others* (see 15.2) the defendants acting in concert entered a bus with the intention of driving it away; one of them turned the engine over with the starter, but the engine never started and the bus did not move; their conviction of attempting to take the bus was quashed because the jury were wrongly directed as to the meaning of the word 'take', but it is clear from the judgment of the Court of Appeal that if the jury had been properly directed there was ample evidence to constitute an attempt. The act of endeavouring to open a car door is capable of amounting to an attempt to take and drive it away without authority; in deciding if such an equivocal act does amount to an attempt, the court should take into consideration any evidence of the defendant's actual intention, including any statement made by him (*Jones* v *Brooks* (1968) *The Times*, 26 June).

A person charged with attempting to commit an offence can be convicted of the attempt even though in law he committed the full offence. In *Webley* v *Buxton* [1977] Crim LR 160 the defendant, who had been charged with attempting to take a motor cycle without the owner's consent, was seen astride the motor cycle with his hands on the handlebars and using his feet to push it eight feet across a pavement towards a motorway. The magistrates convicted him as charged, ie attempting to commit the offence, even though they were satisfied he had committed the full offence. It was held by the Divisional Court that the justices were entitled to do so. It is submitted that this decision is unaffected by the Criminal Attempts Act 1981.

As to the offences with which a defendant may be charged where the offences under s 1 or s 12 are incomplete, see 'Interfering with vehicles', 15.26 and 'Tampering with vehicles', 15.27.

## Theft and Taking Conveyances: Proceedings and Penalties

### 15.16 Generally

Offences of theft and unlawful taking under s 1 and s 12(1) and any attempt to commit them are 'either way' offences triable at the Crown Court and may be tried by magistrates pursuant to ss 18–23 of the Magistrates' Courts Act 1980. The defendant must consent to any summary trial and accordingly may insist on trial by jury. In *R* v *Wakefield JJ, ex parte Butterworth* [1970] Crim LR 102 a solicitor consented on behalf of his client to summary trial on a charge under s 12 and added 'and he pleads guilty' before the court could ask for the plea. As the court did not *ask* the plea (Magistrates' Courts Act 1980, s 9) the case was sent back to the justices for the court to ask the plea. Taking a pedal cycle etc is a summary offence only (s 12(5)). There is no offence under s 1 of the Criminal Attempts Act 1981 of attempting to commit a purely summary offence such as this.

If the accused, being of the age of seventeen or over, has a firearm or imitation firearm in his possession when committing an offence under s 1 or under s 12(1) of the Theft Act or attempting such an offence, or uses one with intent to resist arrest, he must be sent for trial at the Crown Court (Firearms Act 1968, Sched 6, Part II, para 3; Theft Act 1968, Sched 2). This provision does not apply where a pedal cycle etc is taken.

It is submitted that a vehicle taken in breach of s 12 is not stolen goods so that a person who dishonestly receives one which he knows to have been so taken is not guilty of handling under s 22 of the Theft Act.

Where an offence under s 1 or s 12 is committed, attempted, abetted or procured by a member of a visiting force (see 2.5) in respect of a conveyance which belongs to that force or to a member, or dependant of a member, of that force, he may not be tried by a British civil court, save where the visiting force consents (Visiting Forces Act 1952, s 3). 'Dependant' does not include a person who is a British citizen or ordinarily resident here.

Offences and attempts to commit offences under s 1 or s 12(1) would be an 'unlawful purpose' within s 4 of the Vagrancy Act 1824 relating to persons found in certain buildings or enclosed places, and this applies in respect of taking pedal cycles also. This part of s 4 has not been repealed.

## 15.17 Arrest

The offences under ss 1 and 12 are 'arrestable offences' within the meaning of the Criminal Law Act 1967 (s 12(3) of the 1968 Act). This subsection and also the Criminal Law Act 1967, s 2, will be repealed by Sched 7, Part 1, to the Police and Criminal Evidence Act 1984 when in force and will be replaced by the specific power of arrest for s 12(1) and s 25(1) offences and also for arrestable offences in general such as theft and robbery contained in s 24 of that Act. Section 2(2) of the Criminal Law Act 1967 provides that any person may arrest without warrant anyone whom he with reasonable cause suspects to be in the act of committing such an offence; by s 2(4) a constable who with reasonable cause suspects that the offence has been committed may arrest without warrant anyone reasonably suspected by him of an offence under s 12(1) or of an attempt to commit it, and by s 2(5) a constable may arrest without warrant anyone reasonably suspected by him of being about to commit such an offence. These powers of arrest do not apply to persons taking pedal cycles, because taking a pedal cycle only is not an 'arrestable offence'.

## 15.18 Penalties

The penalty on summary conviction under s 1 (theft), s 12(1) (taking) or s 25 (going equipped for stealing or for taking a conveyance), or for an attempt to commit any such offence is a fine of £2,000 or six months' imprisonment, or both. Community service and other powers dependent on imprisonment may be used. A person convicted of taking a pedal cycle etc (s 12(5)) may be fined on level 3 but not sent to prison or detention or committed for sentence. On indictment the penalty is a fine of unlimited amount or three years' imprisonment or both for an offence under s 12(1) or s 25 or ten years or an unlimited fine or both for theft.

A person found guilty under s 1, s 12(1) or s 25 by magistrates may be committed to the Crown Court for heavier sentence under s 38 of the Magistrates' Courts Act 1980. He may, if of the relevant age, be so committed for a heavier sentence of youth custody under s 37 of that Act. Magistrates should not order disqualification and endorsement before committing for sentence (see the Criminal Justice Act 1967, s 56, and 20.33) but leave that to the Crown Court; they may order an interim disqualification (see 20.33).

If under the age of seventeen, an offender under s 12(1) may be sentenced to youth custody (15–16 years old) or a detention centre (14–16 years old) or community service (16 years old if a community service scheme is in operation in the area) by a juvenile court (if convicted by a magistrates' court he must be remitted to the juvenile court for sentence if these are thought appropriate; this applies if he was under seventeen at the time proceedings were commenced (see 2.4), even if he has subsequently attained that age); if he has attained the age of seventeen, magistrates may sentence him to youth custody or detention as appropriate.

See further 'Committals for sentence', 2.57 and 20.33.

Compensation may be ordered, on conviction of any offence in respect of personal injury, loss or damage resulting from that offence, of up to £2,000 if convicted by magistrates or of an unlimited amount if convicted on indictment (Powers of Criminal Courts Act 1973, s 35, as amended by Magistrates' Courts Act 1980, s 40). The court is required to have regard to an offender's means, so far as they are known, in fixing the amount of compensation (s 35(4)). No application by or on behalf of the loser is necessary. When making an order the court is to give preference to compensation over a fine although it may impose a fine as well. Compensation is to be of such an amount as the court considers appropriate, having regard to any evidence and to any representations that are made by or on behalf of the accused or the prosecution.

Although ordinarily no compensation is payable in respect of injury, loss or damage which results from a road accident (s 35(3)), if the offence is under the Theft Act and the property is recovered any damage occurring to the property while out of the owner's possession shall be treated as resulting from the Theft Act offence no matter who caused the damage or how it occurred (s 35(2)). Thus if a person is convicted of stealing or taking a vehicle, driving it knowing it to have been taken, or allowing himself to be carried on or in it under the Theft Act and it is damaged, whether in a road accident or any other way, that person can be ordered to pay compensation for that damage (but compensation cannot be ordered in respect of damage to any other vehicle damaged in an accident with the vehicle taken by the offender (see 18.24)). Compensation may be awarded not only in respect of an offence for which the defendant is convicted but also an offence taken into consideration (in such a case a magistrates' court is still limited to a maximum sum of £2,000 for each offence for which the offender is *convicted* (see further 18.24)).

In *R* v *Donovan* [1982] RTR 126 the defendant hired a car for two days but kept it for some two and a half months. He was ordered to pay £1,388 compensation based on loss of use. The compensation order was quashed by the Court of Appeal. Eveleigh LJ said that:

> The amount of such damages is notoriously open to argument, and this case is therefore not one of the kind for which a compensation order is designed. A compensation order is designed for the simple, straightforward case where the amount of the compensation can be readily and easily ascertained.

## 15.19 Endorsement and disqualification

On conviction under s 1 or s 12 in respect of a motor vehicle and also for an offence under s 25 committed with reference to the theft or taking of motor vehicles, the defendant's driving licence must be endorsed unless there are special reasons (see Chapter 21). The offence carries 8 penalty points. On conviction the defendant may be disqualified at the court's option for any period and a driving test may be ordered (1972 Act, s 93 (2) and (7)) (see 21.32). By virtue of s 4 of the Criminal Attempts Act 1981 attempts carry the penalty of the full offence where no other penalty is specified. Attempts to commit these offences therefore carry the same penalties.

These provisions as to endorsement, disqualification and penalty points apply to anyone convicted under s 1 or s 12 as well as to drivers, provided in all cases the offence was in respect of a motor vehicle. It is appropriate to disqualify the passenger as well as the driver in a joint venture (*R* v *Reed* [1975] RTR 313; *R* v *Saunders* [1975] RTR 315). It was said by the Court of Appeal in *R* v *Earle* [1976] RTR 33, at p 36E, that the object of giving a court the discretionary power of disqualification for taking vehicles without consent was to ensure that vehicles may not be used for criminal offences. One other reason might be to punish joyriders.

Section 19 of the Transport Act 1981 (penalty points disqualification: see 20.18–21) applies to offences and attempts to commit offences under s 1, s 12 and s 25 where committed in respect of motor vehicles.

It seems that a person convicted of burglary or robbery involving theft of a motor vehicle is liable to obligatory endorsement and optional disqualification. Paragraph 1 of Sched 4, Part III, to the 1972 Act does not specify a section of the Theft Act and refers simply to 'stealing or attempting to steal'. Contrast ibid, paras 2 and 3.

The endorsement codes for offences under the Theft Act or s 175 (see below) are as follows:

| | |
|---|---|
| Taking and driving away without consent or attempting to do so (s 175: Scotland only) | UT 10 |
| Stealing or attempting to steal a motor vehicle | UT 20 |

| | |
|---|---|
| Going equipped for stealing or taking a motor vehicle | UT 30 |
| Taking or attempting to take a motor vehicle or allowing oneself to be carried knowing it to be unlawfully taken, etc | UT 40 |

The Magistrates' Association's suggested penalties for offences under s 12 in respect of motor vehicles read: 'Taking vehicle without consent: £150. Consider custodial sentence. Carried in taken vehicle: £100' (see further 18.1 and Appendix 3).

### 15.20–5 Scotland

The punishment under s 175 of the 1972 Act is three months' imprisonment or a fine of £50 on summary conviction. There is no power to fine *and* imprison on summary conviction. On indictment the maximum is an unlimited fine or twelve months' imprisonment or both. The offence or attempted offence under s 175 carries compulsory endorsement and optional disqualification and driving test and the liability to compulsory disqualification under s 19 of the Transport Act 1981 (see 20.18–21).

## Other Related Offences

### 15.26 Interfering with vehicles

Where a potential offender is caught before he has done anything amounting to the complete offence or an attempt under s 1 or s 12 of the Theft Act 1968, he may be charged with interfering with a vehicle contrary to s 9 of the Criminal Attempts Act 1981. A person commits the offence if he interferes with a motor vehicle or trailer or with anything carried in or on a motor vehicle or trailer with the intention to commit, by himself or some other person, the offence of:

(*a*) theft of the motor vehicle or trailer or part of it;
(*b*) theft of anything carried in or on the motor vehicle or trailer; [or]
(*c*) an offence under s 12(1) . . . (taking and driving away without consent).

The reference to taking and driving away is a strange reference to the law before it was changed by the Theft Act 1968. Presumably it is a general reference to s 12(1) offences and the obsolete reference is therefore immaterial. The concept of 'taking and driving away' still applies in Scotland (see 15.20) but the 1981 Act (apart from a minor reference to service personnel) does not apply to Scotland. Presumably the reference to s 12(1) therefore includes the offences of driving or allowing oneself to be carried etc. Unlike s 12(1) in offence (*c*) above, s 1 is not specified in offence (*a*) or (*b*). By reason of the wording of s 9 of the 1981 Act, 'theft' will seemingly include burglary and robbery.

The offence does not apply to s 12(5) (pedal cycles). Nor does it apply to other forms of conveyance such as a yacht, whereas s 12(1) does. As to the nature of a pedal cycle see 1.8 and 15.3. An electrically assisted pedal cycle is not a motor vehicle under the 1972 Act (see Chapter 1) and is therefore not a motor vehicle for the purposes of s 9(2)(*a*) or (*b*). It might be a trailer although this is unlikely. Other auto-assisted cycles are motor vehicles and therefore within s 9(2)(*a*) and (*b*), but as noted at 15.3 all pedal cycles are not within s 12(1) and therefore not within s 9(2)(*c*).

If it is shown that a person intended that one of the specified offences should be committed, it is immaterial that it cannot be shown which it was (s 9(2)). It is not therefore necessary for the prosecutor to select which specified offence providing he alleges the intention that an offence specified in s 9 (2) shall be committed. Nevertheless, it is submitted that if the prosecutor does select, and if both the prosecutor and the defendant base their cases on that selection, it may be wrong to convict on a completely different basis. Up to a point it may be possible to amend (see 2.45).

'Motor vehicle' and 'trailer', by s 9(5), have the meanings assigned to them by s 190(1) of the 1972 Act (see Chapter 1). 'Trailer' under s 190(1) means a vehicle drawn by a motor vehicle. It is doubtful whether a trailer can be said to be so 'drawn' if it has been detached, particularly if the detachment is for a substantial period of time. It is submitted therefore that the offence is not committed where the trailer has been detached and left for unloading, eg in a dock or factory yard. A poultry shed can be a trailer and an office hut also (*Garner* v *Burr*; *Horn* v *Dobson*, both noted 1.21), but it is hardly likely that this offence extends to interfering with a poultry shed in the middle of a field in order to steal the chickens in the shed.

The offence extends to interfering with anything carried in or on the motor vehicle or trailer. The intent to commit the specified offence must, however, still be established (s 9(1)). This includes the theft of the 'motor vehicle or trailer or part of it'. It is not clear whether 'part of it' refers to part of the motor vehicle as well as part of the trailer but it is submitted that it does (eg the theft of a car wheel). It also includes the theft of anything carried in or on the motor vehicle or trailer.

Merely looking into vehicles is not interfering with them (*Reynolds and Warren* v *Metropolitan Police* [1982] Crim LR 831). It clearly may be supportive evidence if there is evidence of interference. It was said in the same case that merely touching car door handles did not amount to interference. It might have been different if the defendants had been seen to apply pressure. The decision was that of a Crown Court hearing an appeal from Acton Magistrates' Court. The decision is not satisfactory, in that the members of the court seem to have had different reasons for acquittal, and is not binding. The commentary in the Criminal Law Review is rightly critical and it is submitted that touching car doors in this way is capable of constituting interference.

While in many cases it will be desirable for the prosecution to show more than one act of interference, a single act seems sufficient in law under s 9.

A constable may arrest without warrant anyone who is or whom he with reasonable cause suspects to be guilty of the offence, but see the Police and Criminal Evidence Act when in force.

The maximum penalty for an offence against s 9 is a fine of level 4 or three months' imprisonment or both. It is triable only summarily. There is no power to order disqualification or endorsement or penalty points.

## 15.27 Tampering with vehicles; getting on vehicles

Where a potential offender is caught before he has done anything amounting to the complete offence or an attempt under s 1 or s 12 of the Theft Act 1968 and a charge of interference cannot be established or is not thought appropriate, he may instead, if the facts warrant, be charged under s 29 of the 1972 Act with getting on a motor vehicle or tampering with the brake or other part of its mechanism without lawful authority or reasonable cause. It is submitted that, as the brake alone is mentioned and no other category of equipment, the *ejusdem generis* rule is excluded and 'other part of its mechanism' includes parts nothing to do with the brakes. This offence arises only if the vehicle is on a road or on a parking place *provided by a local authority*. It is submitted that the term 'local authority' includes parish councils as well as county and district councils and London boroughs (cf Local Government Act 1972, s 270). It seems that it need not be a parking place open to the public; if a local authority provides a parking place for its employees' cars, that is within s 29. Car parks provided by Government departments and public utility boards are not within s 29.

It is also an offence under s 30(1) for a person otherwise than with lawful authority or with reasonable cause to take or retain hold of or get on to a motor vehicle or trailer while in motion on a road for the purpose of being carried. An offence can only be committed under s 30(1) if the person got on or took or retained hold of the vehicle while it was in motion on a road. If it was stationary and a motor vehicle, he may be charged under s 29, if appropriate. Section 29 refers only to motor vehicles, not trailers. Section 30(1) and (2) refer to trailers as well. The trailer must be drawn by a motor vehicle (1972 Act, s 190(1)). 'For the purpose of being carried' (s 30(1)) should be compared with the offence in s 30(2) of taking or retaining hold of a motor vehicle or trailer while in motion on a road 'for the purpose of being drawn'. There is no reference to lawful authority or reasonable cause in s 30(2).

The penalty under s 29 is a fine of level 3 and under s 30, of level 1. Disqualification and endorsement may not be ordered for these offences.

## 15.28–32 Criminal damage

The taker of a car without authority may damage it in order to drive it away; he may also damage it while in his possession. Apart from the liability to be sued civilly for the damage, what is the criminal liability of such people? By s 1(1) of the Criminal Damage Act 1971 it is an offence either intentionally or recklessly to destroy or damage property and by s 1(2) it is an aggravated offence if there is an intention of endangering life or recklessness as to whether someone else's life would be endangered.

The offence under s 1(1) is committed if the defendant either had an intention to destroy or damage property or was reckless as to whether the property would be destroyed or damaged. It should be noted that the intention relates to the destruction or damage not of the particular property intended to be damaged but of any property belonging to another, and therefore the fact that the defendant may not have intended to damage or destroy the particular property that was in fact destroyed is not a defence. The prosecution only has to prove either an intention to destroy or damage property of another or that the defendant was reckless in that regard. It would therefore appear that a person who drives recklessly and damages or destroys another vehicle could theoretically be charged with and convicted of an offence under s 1(1), but Parliament presumably did not intend reckless drivers to be charged under the Criminal Damage Act 1971 rather than s 2 of the 1972 Act. However, there are obvious examples where the police may well wish to use the Criminal Damage Act; where, for example, the thief or joyrider damages the car to break into it in order to drive it away. It might also be used, it would seem, in cases where s 2 of the 1972 Act cannot apply because the vehicle has not been driven on a road as defined in the 1972 Act, or the vehicle is not a motor vehicle. As to proof of recklessness, see *Metropolitan Police Commissioner* v *Caldwell* at 5.3. The meaning of the first limb of the definition of recklessness used in the *Caldwell* case was further considered in *R* v *Miller* [1983] 1 All ER 978 (HL) and *Elliott* v *C* [1983] 2 All ER 1005 (CA). The 'obvious risk' in the first limb means that the risk is one which must have been obvious to a reasonably prudent man and not necessarily to the particular defendant if he or she had given thought to it.

It would seem from *R* v *Smith (DR)* [1974] 1 All ER 632 that a person who honestly believes, whether it is a justifiable belief or not, that the property he damages is his own, cannot be convicted under the Criminal Damage Act 1971. But as long as it is property belonging to another, the identity of the person is irrelevant (*Pike* v *Morrison* [1981] Crim LR 492).

'Property' includes any property of a tangible nature, real or personal (s 10), but not the flowers, fruit or foliage of a plant growing wild on any land.

## Other Related Offences: Proceedings and Penalties

### 15.33 Generally

For penalties for offences under s 9 of the Criminal Attempts Act 1981 and ss 29 and 30 of the 1972 Act see 15.26 and 15.27 respectively.

As for s 1(1) and (2) of the Criminal Damage Act 1971, where there is a reliance in the alternative on specific intent and recklessness, it was said in *R* v *Hardie* [1984] 3 All ER 848 (CA) that the alternatives should be made the subject of separate counts for the jury. The extent to which this practice is applicable to magistrates' courts and is adopted there remains to be seen.

Subject to certain exceptions, if the amount of damage does not exceed £400, the offence under s 1(1) is triable only summarily and the penalty is £1,000 and/or three months' imprisonment. If the amount of damage exceeds £400 the offence is an 'either way' offence; the offender has a right of election for trial by jury and if he consents to summary trial is subject to a maximum penalty of £2,000 and/or six months' imprisonment. If the value of the damage cannot be ascertained, the offence remains an 'either way' offence but if the defendant then consents to summary trial the penalty to which he is subject on summary conviction is the same as if it were a summary offence, ie £1,000 and/or three months' imprisonment (ss 22 and 33 of the Magistrates'

Courts Act 1980). Arson is triable either way regardless of the amount of the damage.

There is also a right of election where, even if the value of the damage does not exceed £400 (*R* v *St Helens JJ, ex parte McClorie* (1983) 147 JP 456), the offence appears to the court to constitute or form part of a series of two or more offences of the same or similar character (Magistrates' Courts Act 1980, s 22(7)). There are a number of authorities as to the meaning of the words, not all of which are easy to reconcile.

In *R* v *Hatfield JJ, ex parte Castle* [1980] 3 All ER 510 it was held that for offences to be of the same or similar character:

(*a*) they must bear a similarity of fact and law;
(*b*) one of the essential characteristics of similarity in law that must be present is that the other offence or offences are also triable either way;
(*c*) the offences must form part of a series of two or more offences.

For a discussion of this and other cases see the commentary at [1980] Crim LR 580.

In *R* v *Leicester JJ, ex parte Lord* [1980] Crim LR 581 it was held that, provided there was sufficient nexus, offences could be of the same or similar character even if under differing sections of different Acts.

In *R* v *Tottenham JJ, ex parte Tibble* (1981) 145 JP 269 in the Divisional Court, the Lord Chief Justice, Lord Lane, resolved the dilemma after considering the various cases by following the decision in the *Hatfield* case. It is submitted therefore that principles (*a*), (*b*) and (*c*) above should be applied.

The mode of trial procedure for criminal damage is set out in ss 22 and 23 of the Magistrates' Courts Act 1980 and the penalties in ss 32 and 33. Schedule 2 of that Act applies the same principles to aiding, abetting, inciting and attempting.

In *R* v *Canterbury and St Augustine JJ, ex parte Klisiak; R* v *Ramsgate JJ, ex parte Warren* [1981] 3 All ER 129 it was held that where a court was directed by s 22(1) to consider whether the value exceeded £400 'having regard to any representations made by the prosecutor and the accused', 'representations' meant something less than evidence. Justices could at their discretion hear evidence but were not bound to do so.

Even though justices are required to deal with the offence as if it were a summary offence if the value does not exceed £400, it remains an indictable offence for other purposes. Thus a certificate of costs of prosecution or defence may be granted out of public funds.

The offence under s 1(2) (destroying or damaging property either intending another's life to be endangered or reckless in that regard) can only be tried on indictment, the maximum punishment being life imprisonment.

There is no power to order disqualification, endorsement or penalty points for either offence.

Under s 35 of the Powers of Criminal Courts Act 1973, as amended by s 40 of the Magistrates' Courts Act 1980, compensation up to £2,000 may be ordered to be paid by the defendant to the person whose property was damaged. The court has power to award compensation of its own motion under s 35 and its power to do so does not depend on an application by the loser. No compensation is payable under the Act in respect of loss or damage due to an accident arising out of the presence of a motor vehicle on a road (s 35(3)) unless it is as a result of an offence under the Theft Act 1968 (see 18.24). Compensation was accordingly refused in *M* v *Oxford* [1981] RTR 246 despite a conviction for criminal damage when a lorry was driven into a wall.

# Chapter 16

# Forgery, Fraudulent Use and False Statements

## 16.1 Introduction

This chapter deals with forgery and fraudulent use under the Vehicles (Excise) Act 1971, with the obtaining of a pecuniary advantage by deception (s 16 of the Theft Act 1968), and with forgery and fraudulent applications under the 1972 Act.

## Forgery and Fraudulent Use

### 16.2 Generally

It is an offence under s 26(1) of the Vehicles (Excise) Act 1971 for a person to *forge* or *fraudulently* alter, use, lend or allow to be used a number plate, trade plate, licence or registration document. It is an 'either way' offence punishable summarily with a fine of £2,000, or on indictment with an unlimited fine or two years' imprisonment or both.

*R* v *Manners-Astley* [1967] 3 All ER 899 and the other earlier cases about the meaning of 'fraudulently' were overturned by the House of Lords in *R* v *Terry* [1984] 1 All ER 65. It is not necessary for the prosecution to prove an intent to avoid payment; it is sufficient to prove that the defendant's purpose was to deceive a person responsible for a public duty and that the intended means of achieving this purpose was dishonest.

The cases noted below on the meaning of 'forge' are unaffected.

The word 'forge' as it appears in s 26(1) is not there defined, but it is comprehensively defined in s 1 of the Forgery and Counterfeiting Act 1981 as 'making a false instrument with the intent . . . to induce somebody to accept it as genuine and by reason of so accepting it to do or not to do some act to his own or any other person's prejudice'. It will be noted that this differs from the simplified definition provided by s 12 of the same Act for s 169(3) of the 1972 Act and s 65(3) of the Public Passenger Vehicles Act 1981. The position is further complicated by the gloss on the interpretation of s 1 of the Forgery and Counterfeiting Act 1981 in ss 8–10 of that Act. In *Clifford* v *Bloom* [1977] Crim LR 485 'forge' within the meaning of s 26 was considered. It was defined as the making of a false document or a mark on a number plate with the intention that it should be regarded as genuine. The defendant had altered the number plates from YYR 798H to YYR 798K. His conviction was upheld. Although the number plate did not tell a lie about itself, it could not be treated in isolation. For the purposes of s 26 the mark, the plate to which it should be fixed and the motor vehicle were to be treated and regarded as a whole (ibid).

*Clifford* v *Bloom* was followed in *R* v *Clayton* (1980) 72 Cr App R 135 where a disabled driver entitled to a vehicle licence exempt from duty altered his tax disc and number plates from GWK 923N to GWK 923R. His conviction under s 26(1) of forging the tax disc was upheld: an intention to deceive was sufficient for the purposes of s 26. The court made use of the definition of forgery in s 1 of the Forgery Act 1913 in reaching its decision. It was pointed out in the judgment that there was a tendency to approach these cases as if there was a hard and fast dividing line between intent to defraud and intent to deceive. The truth was that they overlapped and ran into each other. Section 26(1) refers separately to 'forges' and 'fraudulently'. In view of the changed definition in s 1 of the Forgery and Counterfeiting Act 1981, these cases may now carry less weight.

The term 'licence' in the section is not defined but in *Taylor* v *Emmerson* (1962) 106 SJ 552 it was held to include an expired licence. Compare *Aziz* v *Knightsbridge Gaming and Catering Services and Supplies Ltd* (1982) *The Times*, 6 July where an instrument drawn on a fictitious bank was nevertheless held to be a cheque.

### 16.3–7 False declarations

It is an offence under s 26(2) of the Vehicles (Excise) Act 1971 if a person, in connection with an application for an excise licence, makes a declaration which to his knowledge is false or, in any material respect, misleading. It is an 'either way' offence punishable summarily with a fine of £2,000, or on indictment with an unlimited fine or two years' imprisonment or both.

The onus of proving the truth of his declaration is cast on the defendant by s 33 to the extent set out therein (see 12.22). As s 26 requires that the declaration be false or misleading 'to the knowledge' of the declarant, such knowledge must be shown, subject to s 33, and it does not suffice to convict merely on proof of the falsity; *R* v *Cummerson*, at 16.15, is not applicable. A defendant who signed an application form completed by his daughter and failed to read it and thus notice that it contained a false declaration was not guilty of making a declaration which to his knowledge was false (*Bloomfield* v *Williams* [1970] Crim LR 292). It was said obiter by Donaldson J that if someone signs an application he impliedly says that he knows what is in the particulars and he must be guilty of making a declaration which to his knowledge is misleading (another offence under the subsection) if he has not bothered to check. With respect, it is submitted that 'knowledge' is the same for the offence of making a false declaration as it is for making a declaration 'in any material respect misleading'. 'Knowledge' in this context means either actual knowledge or second degree knowledge 'where a man deliberately shuts his eyes to information which he fears will give him knowledge he does not wish to acquire' (per Devlin J in *Roper* v *Taylor's Central Garages* (*Exeter*) *Ltd* [1951] 2 TLR 284, at p 288, referred to in *Bloomfield* v *Williams* [1970] Crim LR 292).

The declaration on the application form in *Bloomfield* v *Williams* used words to the effect that 'I declare that all the information I have given in this application is correct'. The present declaration on the application form has been expanded and contains the words 'I declare that I have checked the information given in this application and that to the best of my knowledge it is correct'. With such a declaration the defendant in *Bloomfield* might well have been convicted.

Section 26 (2) extends to applications for trade licences.

Persons applying for licences must do so on the appropriate form as prescribed by the Road Vehicles (Excise) (Prescribed Particulars) Regulations 1972 (SI 1972 No 850), as amended by SI 1975 No 1341.

## Obtaining a Pecuniary Advantage

### 16.8–12 Generally

It is an offence under s 16 of the Theft Act 1968 to obtain a pecuniary advantage by deception. The police occasionally prosecute defendants under s 16 who attempt to evade payment of vehicle excise duty by displaying notices such as 'tax applied for' on windscreens.

In *Smith* v *Koumourou* [1979] RTR 355, the defendant had had his vehicle excise tax disc seized by the police in April 1976 because it was suspected not to relate to his vehicle. He was issued with an undated receipt for the licence on a police memorandum form. Some eighteen months later in October 1977 his vehicle was seen with the police memorandum displayed on the vehicle's windscreen. The justices dismissed a prosecution under s 16 of the Theft Act on the grounds that the display of the police memorandum was calculated only to deceive a member of the police and to avoid prosecution and was not evidence of evasion of vehicle excise duty. Directing the justices to proceed with the case, the Divisional Court cited with approval the words of Lord Reid in *R* v *Turner* [1974] AC 357 at p 365H where he said 'An obligation is evaded if by some contrivance the debtor avoids or gets out of fulfilling or performing his obligation.' In *Smith* v *Koumourou* the Divisional Court held that there must be some causal connection between the deception and the obligation to pay and on the facts of the case held that they afforded 'the clearest possible causal connection'.

Section 16 of the Theft Act is an 'either way' offence punishable summarily by a fine of £2,000 and/or six months' imprisonment.

## Forgery and Fraudulent Applications

### 16.13 Generally

Sections 169, 170 and 171 of the 1972 Act respectively penalise a person who, (1) with intent to deceive, forges or alters or uses or lends or allows the use of a document or thing or makes or has in his possession a document so closely resembling a certificate as to be calculated to deceive, or (2) makes a false statement or withholds any material information for the purpose of obtaining such a certificate, or (3) issues one knowing it to be false in a material particular.

## 16.14 Forgery

'Forges' in s 169 means making a false document or other thing in order that it may be used as genuine (s 169(3) as amended by the Forgery and Counterfeiting Act 1981).

Under ss 1 and 3 of the 1981 Act forgery carries no ingredient of dishonesty (*R* v *Campbell (Mary)* (1984) *The Times*, 31 July; *Horsey* v *Hutchings* (1984) *The Times*, 8 November). The same would seem to be true for s 169. Compare the offence under s 65 of the Public Passenger Vehicles Act 1981 of forging, altering, using etc a PSV operator's disc with intent to deceive.

Section 169 applies to certificates of insurance, test certificates, plating certificates, certificates of conformity, driving test certificates, international road haulage permits, British international driving permits and other documents, which are set out or referred to in s 169(2).

Under s 169(1)(*a*) of the 1972 Act it is an offence for a person to use, with intent to deceive, a document to which the section applies. Alternatively it is an offence under s 169(1)(*b*) for a person with intent to deceive to have in his possession any document '. . . so closely resembling a document . . .' to which the section applies as to be calculated to deceive. In *Holloway* v *Brown* [1978] RTR 537 the defendant used a forged international permit and was convicted by justices of an offence under s 169(1)(*a*). The conviction was set aside because, as the document was forged, it could not be said to be 'a document . . . to which this section applies'. Per curiam, the justices could have convicted the defendant, applying s 123 of the Magistrates' Courts Act 1980, of an offence under s 169(1)(*b*). *Holloway* v *Brown* was distinguished in *R* v *Pilditch* [1981] RTR 303. A Ministry of Transport test certificate form which had been stolen and which bore a false stamp and had been completed by someone other than an authorised vehicle examiner was nevertheless held to be a test certificate and therefore 'a document . . . to which this section applies'. It was further held that the statute had to be construed so as to give a sensible and unstrained meaning to all the words, including the word 'forges'. In *Pilditch*, however, the document was nevertheless a true original and although the decision in *Holloway* v *Brown* may now be regarded as doubtful, it has still not been overruled. See also on this point the *Aziz* decision noted at 16.2.

The case of *R* v *Cleghorn* [1938] 3 All ER 398 is sometimes cited as showing that a certificate of insurance which was once valid but has ceased to be so because of the cancellation of a policy is a document so closely resembling a certificate as to be calculated to deceive. 'Calculated to deceive' seems to mean 'likely to deceive' as well as 'intended to deceive' (82 JP Jo 447, and see Stroud's *Judicial Dictionary*). In *R* v *Davison* [1972] 1 WLR 1540 'calculated to deceive' in the House to House Collections Act 1939 was held to mean 'likely to deceive'. An expired certificate would still seem to be a certificate under s 169 (cf *Taylor* v *Emerson* (1962) 106 SJ 552). Under a similarly worded provision in another context, it was held that, on a charge of possessing documents resembling clothing coupons with intent to deceive, it sufficed if the prosecutor established the intent to deceive and he was not also put to proof that the defendant knew of the falsity of the documents (*R* v *Greenberg*[1942] 2 All ER 344), but the defendant may set up the defence that he acted in good faith (*Brend* v *Wood* (1946) 110 JP 317).

## 16.15 False statements etc

The documents to which s 170 applies are set out in that section.

The question is posed in (1976) 140 JP 270 whether a person may be convicted under s 170 of making a false statement for the obtaining of a certificate of insurance, if, in answer to the question whether he has been convicted of an offence for which an order of endorsement has been made, he states that he has not been so convicted on the ground that the conviction has become 'spent' as a result of the operation of the Rehabilitation of Offenders Act 1974. Whether an endorsement is a disability within the meaning of that Act is discussed in an article at (1980) 144 JP Jo 542. It is submitted that the opinion set out in (1976) 140 JP 270 is correct, viz an order of endorsement is a 'disability' and thus only becomes 'spent' when it may be lawfully removed from a driving licence (ie four or eleven years as the case may be). (See 19.41 as to the periods of the effect of endorsements.) If therefore the endorsement is 'spent' because four or eleven years have elapsed, a person may safely reply 'no' to the question as to whether he has been convicted as a result of which an order of endorsement has been made, as such an order of endorsement is 'spent' by virtue of the Rehabilitation of Offenders Act 1974. *Aliter* of course if the order of endorsement is still of effect.

It is immaterial, in a charge under s 170 of making a false statement, that no gain accrued to the defendant from it (*Jones* v *Meatyard* [1939] 1 All ER 140). The offence under s 170(6) of making a false statement for the purpose of obtaining the issue of a certificate of insurance is an absolute offence and consciousness by the defendant of the statement's falsity need not be shown, so long as it was false; the offence of withholding material information for the same purpose may, however, predicate a conscious withholding on his part (*R* v *Cummerson* [1968] 2 All ER 863). It is doubtful how far, if at all, the Criminal Justice Act 1967, s 8 (proof of criminal intent), applies a subjective test as to what a defendant intended or foresaw in these cases.

A person who commonly uses a name other than his proper name may be guilty of an offence if in completing a proposal form for insurance he uses the adopted name and does not reveal his real one (*Clark* v *Chalmers* 1961 SLT 325). It might be otherwise if he had lawfully changed his name (ibid). On a charge against a car owner of making a false declaration that a car had not been used within a particular period, it was held not sufficient for the prosecutor to show that some unidentified person was seen to use it within the period and rely on the presumption that a car is being used by its owner (*A-G (Connor)* v *Shorten* (1959) 93 ILTR 168).

## 16.16 Issue of false documents

Section 171 applies to the documents referred to in that section.

On a charge under s 171 of issuing a certificate which is to the knowledge of the defendant false, the prosecutor must show not only that it was false but also that the defendant knew it to be so (*Ocean Accident etc Co* v *Cole* (1932) 96 JP 191).

## 16.17 Test certificates

Sections 169 and 171 (forging and issue of false documents) apply in respect of test certificates. In *R* v *Pilditch* a test certificate form which bore a false rubber stamp and the signature of a person who was not an authorised examiner was nevertheless held to be a test certificate. The material date for deciding if a test certificate is false in a material particular contrary to s 171 is the date of issue, even though the examination may have taken place earlier (*R* v *Evans* [1964] 3 All ER 2666; see also reg 15(1)). A test certificate which has been backdated is false in a material particular (*Murphy* v *Griffiths* [1967] 1 All ER 424).

Under a s 171 prosecution it is necessary to prove that the defendant knew that the certificate was going to be issued false in a material particular. In *Essondon Engineering Co Ltd* v *Maile* [1982] RTR 260, a certificate was issued by an employee while the sole director was away on holiday. The court reviewed the authorities on whether the knowledge of the employee could be imputed to the company—see further 'Proof generally', 2.87.

## 16.18 Driving licences

A false answer on the application form for a driving licence is an offence whether or not the question asked is intra vires (*Woodward* v *Dykes* (1968) 112 SJ 787). These sections extend to badges of, and applications to become, approved driving instructors. Use of a licence with intent to deceive means use in connection with driving or attempted driving and not merely sending it for renewal (ibid) but this decision of quarter sessions is respectfully doubted as putting too narrow a meaning of 'use'. See also *R* v *Howe* at 1.79. For a case of conspiracy by impersonation at a driving test see *R* v *Potter* [1958] 2 All ER 51. The term 'licence' would include an expired licence (*Taylor* v *Emerson* (1962) 106 SJ 552) and possibly a forged licence—see the *Aziz* decision at 16.2.

In *R* v *Bogdal* [1982] RTR 395 (CA) it was held that there was insufficient nexus between a charge of using a driving licence with intent to deceive contrary to s 169 and a dangerous driving charge committed on different occasions but in the same car. The two charges were in the circumstances not a 'series of offences of a similar character' within the meaning of r 9 of the 1971 Indictment Rules. The deception charge evidence prejudiced the dangerous driving charge. The judge should have ordered the severance of the counts and the conviction for dangerous driving was quashed. In *Bogdal* the defendant had produced a driving licence to the police which he knew had been suspended under s 101(4) of the 1972 Act pending its production for the court. The conviction for using a driving licence with intent to deceive was upheld.

## 16.19 Proceedings and penalties

Offences under s 169 are 'either way' offences triable in accordance with ss 18–23 of the Magistrates' Courts Act 1980.

An extended time limit, ie within six months from the time when the offence came to the prosecutor's knowledge but not more than three years from its commission, is provided by the 1972 Act, s 180 for s 169, s 170(1) and s 171. There is no time limit for 'either way' offences under s 169 (Magistrates' Courts Act 1980, s 127) but the limit given in s 180 applies to cases under ss 170(1) and (6) and 171. See *R* v *McCardle* and *R* v *Howe* at 1.79 as to 'use'. In the light of these cases it may be preferable to charge under s 169(1)(*b*) (possession etc: see above) where there is doubt as to the use.

By s 173 power of seizure of documents contravening ss 169–171 is given to the police.

The penalty under s 169 is a fine only of £2,000 on summary conviction, but on indictment an unlimited fine or two years' imprisonment or both may be imposed. The penalty under s 170(1) (false statement in connection with licence etc) or s 170(6) (false statement to obtain insurance certificate) or under s 171 (issuing false insurance certificates) is a fine only of level 4. Sections 170 and 171 offences cannot be tried on indictment. Disqualification, endorsement and penalty points may not be ordered for any of these offences.

A person convicted under s 169(1) by a magistrates' court may be committed for sentence if the magistrates' court considers its power of punishment is inadequate (see 'Committals for Sentence', 2.57). As the offence cannot be punished summarily by imprisonment, it would seem that magistrates may commit him for sentence if they consider the offender should be sent to prison even for a short period or even where a suspended prison sentence, community service order or other order dependent on the power to imprison is considered appropriate. In *R* v *Melbourne* [1980] Crim LR 510 it was held that since the defendant had been convicted summarily of such an offence (an offence under the Trade Descriptions Act 1968, s 14), he could not be said to have been convicted of an offence punishable with imprisonment as was required by ss 23 and 24 of the Powers of Criminal Courts Act 1973 (power to activate suspended sentences).

# Chapter 17

# Fixed Penalties

## 17.1 Introduction

The fixed penalty system was brought into being by the Road Traffic and Roads Improvements Act 1960. Its application was originally confined to parking offences and lighting offences in respect of a stationary vehicle. The number of offences to which the fixed penalty procedure could apply was considerably increased when s 80 of the Road Traffic Regulation Act 1967 was enacted. As a result of difficulties experienced in the collection of fixed penalties and excess meter charges the vehicle owner liability provisions of ss 1–5 of the Road Traffic Act 1974 were introduced. The relevant parts of the 1967 and 1974 Acts have recently been re-enacted without any substantial amendments as ss 107–111 of, and Scheds 7, 8 and 12 to, the Road Traffic Regulation Act 1984. With the exception of Sched 8, para 3 (which defines the statutory statement of facts to be used in unpaid excess charge cases) these provisions were brought into force on 26 September 1984.

The Report of the Inter-Departmental Committee on Road Traffic Law (HMSO 1981) drew attention to a number of deficiencies in the present system and suggested several improvements which might be made. The principal problems were identified as the inconsistent use of fixed penalties, the failure to enforce a large proportion of the tickets issued, the procedural difficulties of the owner liability provisions of the Road Traffic Act 1974 (now the Road Traffic Regulation Act 1984, Sched 12, paras 5 and 6, ss 107–111, and Sched 8) and the costliness of their enforcement. It was with the intention of eradicating such problems that Part III of the Transport Act 1982 was enacted.

Those parts of the new provisions which relate to Scotland were brought into force when the Procurator Fiscal and Fixed Penalty Scheme came into effect on 30 June 1983. So far as England and Wales are concerned, the Home Secretary has indicated (Home Office Circular No 45/1984) that the new provisions (with the probable exception of s 39 which contains provisions for notification of court and date of trial) will be brought into force no later than April 1986.

It may be assumed that any references hereafter to the fixed penalty system, either as existing or as proposed, will appertain to England and Wales.

# Scope of the Fixed Penalty System

## 17.2 The existing provisions

The fixed penalty system is a system enabling a person to avoid prosecution for certain offences by payment of a fixed penalty (now £10: Fixed Penalty (Increase) Order 1982 (SI 1982 No 137)). Although Sched 12, para 4(1) of the 1984 Act provides that the fixed penalty shall be one half the maximum penalty for the offence or £10, whichever is the less, the maximum penalty for all the offences is now at least £20 and therefore the fixed penalty is £10 in every case.

Schedule 12, para 2(2) lays down offences to which the fixed penalty procedure may apply. It includes virtually all parking offences including non-payment of parking charges, being on a road during darkness without lights, failing to display vehicle excise licence discs and construction and use offences which do not carry endorsement, and certain prescribed route offences. The Secretary of State, however, specifically excluded (by virtue of the Fixed Penalty (Offences) Order 1960 (SI 1960 No 1599)) from the operation of the system any offence committed in respect of a vehicle obstructing a road, together with any offence of leaving a vehicle in a dangerous position (s 16 of the 1972 Act). On 1 December 1984 no order had yet been made applying the fixed penalty system to any breach of a construction and use regulation.

The system extends to the whole of England and Wales (Fixed Penalty (Areas) England and Wales Order 1970) (SI 1970 No 1194).

The prescribed notice may be given by a constable to a person whom he has reason to believe may have committed an offence to which the system applies (Sched 12, para 3(1)). Where a constable finds a vehicle in respect of which he has reason to believe an offence may have been committed, the prescribed notice may be affixed to the windscreen and if so notice shall be deemed to be given to the person liable for the offence (Sched 12, para 3(4)). A traffic warden may exercise the power of a constable under Sched 12, para 3(6) of the 1984 Act and Functions of Traffic Wardens Order 1970 (SI 1970 No 1958).

The form of the notice is prescribed by the Fixed Penalty (Procedure) Regulations 1977 (SI 1977 No 1711). Regulation 4 of the 1977 Regulations allows a form 'to the like effect' to that in the regulation to be used.

Where payment of the fixed penalty is made before the expiration of the twenty-one days following the date of the notice or before the proceedings are begun, whichever is the later, no person is liable to be convicted of the offence in respect of which the notice is given (Sched 12, para 3(1)). (As to when proceedings may be said to have begun see 'When "proceedings are begun" ', 2.4.)

In any proceedings for the offence, a certificate purporting to be signed by the clerk to the justices as to whether the fixed penalty has been paid by a date specified in the certificate shall be sufficient evidence of the facts stated unless the contrary is proved (Sched 12, para 4(4)).

By reg 6(1) of the 1977 Regulations, a person when making the fixed penalty payment is either required to forward the fixed penalty notice or specify its serial number. If, as a result of failing to include the notice or giving its number, the clerk is unable to identify the relevant notice, the clerk shall return the remittance.

It is an offence punishable by a fine of level 2 for a person (other than the person in charge of the vehicle or with his authority) to remove or interfere with a fixed penalty notice affixed to a vehicle under Sched 12, para 3(5) (Sched 7).

Where proceedings are taken for the offence in respect of which the fixed penalty notice was issued, it is now permissible to give evidence that the fixed penalty was issued. The provision in s 80 of the 1967 Act (the surviving parts of which are now Scheds 12 and 7 to the 1984 Act) forbidding such evidence was repealed by the Road Traffic Act 1974.

*Vehicle owner liability*

Sections 1–5 of the Road Traffic Act 1974 were enacted to deal with the situation caused by the increasing proportion of excess meter charges and fixed penalties found to be uncollectable, particularly in London. These sections, together with Sched 1 to the Act, have been reenacted by ss 107–111 of, and Scheds 8 and 12 to, the 1984 Act. The solution adopted by the 1974 Act was to fix the liability for the payment of the excess meter charge or fixed penalty in the first instance on the owner of the vehicle. The following is a brief summary and an attempted explanation of the provisions as reenacted in the 1984 Act.

Where an excess meter charge or fixed penalty is unpaid, the police or local authority will serve a notice under Sched 12, para 5(6) or s 108(1) on the registered owner of the vehicle. The forms of notices are prescribed by the Road Traffic (Owner Liability) Regulations 1975 (SI 1975 No 324). Regulation 3 requires the forms to be as contained in Sched 1 to the Regulations 'or forms to the like effect'. Experience has indicated that owing to the complicated nature of the forms many defendants misunderstand what is required and the Central Ticket Office of the Metropolitan Police have simplified the forms relying on the provision referred to above in reg 3. The notice requires the person served, unless the fixed penalty or excess meter charge is paid by him or any other person, to send to the police or local authority who served the notice a statement as to the ownership of the vehicle at the relevant time, ie at the time the offence giving rise to the fixed penalty was committed or the vehicle was left at the parking meter (see definitions of 'relevant time' in Sched 12, para 1·1(1)). The requirements as to 'the statement of ownership' are set out in Sched 12, para 9(1) to the Act in respect of fixed penalties and Sched 8, para 1 for excess charges. The 'owner' is the person by whom the vehicle was kept at the relevant time and for the purposes of Sched 12 to and ss 107–110 of the 1984 Act is presumed to be the registered owner (s 111(3)) but by virtue of s 111(4) it is open to the defence and prosecution notwithstanding this presumption to prove that the vehicle was in fact kept by some person other than the registered owner at the particular time. The statement of ownership is required to be signed by the person furnishing it and if he admits he was the owner the statement can be used by the prosecutor to prove his ownership (s 110(4)) and in accordance with the presumption contained in Sched 12, para 5(2) or s 107(2) he may be prosecuted in respect of the fixed penalty offence or excess meter charge. If, on the other hand, he was not the owner at the relevant time, he is required, in so far as the information is in his possession, to give the name and address of the person from whom he bought or to whom he sold the vehicle as the case may be, together with the date of sale or purchase. If he states that he was not the owner then the presumption that he was the driver under Sched 12, para 5(2) or s 107(2) no longer applies (Sched 12, para 5(4) and s 107(4)).

The person served with a notice under Sched 12, para 5(6) or s 108(1) can also serve with the statement as to ownership 'a statement of facts' as set out in Sched 12, para 9(3) for fixed penalties and Sched 8, para 3 (not yet in force) for excess charges giving the name and address of the driver at the relevant time. The advantage from the owner's point of view of serving such a notice is that, provided the statement of facts is countersigned by the driver, the police or local authority can then proceed to prosecute the driver. If the driver is convicted, the original person served with the notice under Sched 12, para 5(6) or s 108(1) then escapes any further liability for an offence under Sched 12, para 6(2) or s 108(2) (see Sched 12, para 6(5)(*a*) or s 108(4)(*b*)). (It should be noted that it is only if the driver is *convicted* that the person served with the original notice escapes liability; if the driver goes abroad or cannot be found or for any other reason escapes conviction, the person served with the notice remains liable.) 'Driver' is defined by s 111(2).

If the person served with a notice under Sched 12, para 5(6) or s 108(1) fails without reasonable excuse to furnish a statement of ownership he commits an offence under Sched 12, para 6(2) and Sched 7 or s 108(2) and Sched 7 punishable summarily unless the fixed penalty or excess meter charge is paid within the appropriate period, ie, fourteen days from service of the notice or such longer period as is specified in the notice. This is so even if the person served was not the owner of the vehicle at the relevant time or, seemingly, had never been the owner (*Hedges* v *Wray* [1977] RTR 433). It was held that the statute does not require the police to show that they had reasonable grounds for suspecting the recipient of the notice to be the owner of the vehicle. However, notwithstanding the fact that the fixed penalty or excess meter charge is not paid within this time limit, a person served with a notice can still escape liability under Sched 12, para 6(2) or s 108(2) if the amount due is paid before proceedings under Sched 12, para 6(2) or s 108(2) are 'commenced' against him (Sched 12, para 6(4) and s 10(4)(*a*)). The Act is silent as to the exact moment of time when it can be said proceedings are commenced (see 'When "proceedings are begun" ', 2.4). Where a person is convicted under Sched 12, para 6(2) or s 108(2) this discharges any liability for the excess meter charge or for the offence for which the fixed penalty was incurred (Sched 12, para 6(5)(*b*) and s 108(4)(*c*)).

The presumption under Sched 12, para 5(2), or s 107(2) that the owner was the driver does not apply if it is proved that the vehicle was in the possession of some other person without the accused's consent or that the accused was not the owner of the vehicle at the relevant time and had a reasonable excuse for not complying with the notice served on him under Sched 12, para 5(6) or s 108(1) (see Sched 12, para 5(5) and s 107(5)).

Where in response to a notice under Sched 12, para 5(6) or s 108(1) a person furnishes a statement which is false in a material particular and does so recklessly or knowing it to be false he is liable to proceedings under Sched 12, para 6(3) and Sched 7 or s 108(3) and Sched 7. It would appear that 'a statement' in Sched 12, para 6(3) or s 108(3) includes a statutory statement as to ownership, a statement of facts as to the driver of the vehicle under Sched 12, para 9(3) and a statement as to the hiring of the vehicle under Sched 12, para 9(2). Subject to an overall time limit of three years, proceedings under Sched 12, para 6(3) and Sched 7 or s 108(3) and Sched 7 for an offence in England and Wales may be commenced within six months of the date upon which evidence sufficient to warrant the bringing of proceedings comes to the notice of the prosecutor (s 110(1) and (3)). Subsections (1) and (3) of s 110 are in almost identical terms to s 180 of the Act of 1972 (see 2.21).

*Car-hire firms*

Section 109 of the 1984 Act deals with vehicles hired out under a 'hiring agreement' by 'a vehicle-hire' firm. A 'hiring agreement' does not include hire-purchase agreements. It is an agreement containing the particulars prescribed by the Road Traffic (Owner Liability) Regulations 1975; and a 'vehicle-hire firm' is defined as 'any person engaged in hiring vehicles in the course of a business' (s 109(7)). The effect of s 109 is that where a vehicle is hired out by a car-hire firm the car-hire firm escapes all liability under the vehicle owner provisions as soon as the firm produces to the police or local authority a signed statement as prescribed by the regulations that the vehicle concerned was hired under a hiring agreement, together with copies of the hiring agreement and of a 'statement of liability' signed by the hirer. (The 'statement of liability' is a statement signed by the hirer acknowledging that he will be liable in respect of any excess meter charges and fixed penalties during the currency of his hiring agreement.) By virtue of s 109(4) a person authorised by the local authority or police may, at any reasonable time within 6 months after the service on the vehicle-hire firm of a notice under Sched 12, para 5(6) or s 108(1), inspect the originals of the hiring agreement and statement of liability signed by the hirer, and if the documents are not produced, the firm becomes liable as not having complied with the notice under Sched 12, para 5(6) or s 108(1).

Where a statement under s 109 together with copies of the hiring agreement and the hirer's statement of liability have been furnished by the vehicle-hire firm, the vehicle owner provisions of Sched 12, paras 5, 6 or ss 107, 108 then operate as if references to the owner of the vehicle referred to the hirer. The hirer, when in turn served with a notice under Sched 12, para 5(6) or s 108(1), is then under a duty to serve a statutory statement of hiring under Sched 12, para 9(2) for fixed penalties or Sched 8, para 2 for excess charges. This statutory statement (which should not be confused with a statement under s 109 by the vehicle-hire firm) requires him to state whether at the relevant time the vehicle was let to him under the hiring agreement and, if not, the date when he returned the vehicle to the vehicle-hire firm. The regulations require the statement under s 109 of the hiring of the vehicle to give the full name and address.

Regulation 4 of and Sched 2 to the Owner Liability Regulations (SI 1975 No 324) require the statement of hiring given by the vehicle-hire firm under s 109 to contain the registration number and make of the vehicle and of any other vehicle substituted during the currency of a hiring agreement together with the times and dates of any change of vehicle, the commencement and expiry of the hiring and the commencement and expiry of any extension of the hiring. The statement of liability signed by the hirer is required to contain the full name, date of birth and permanent address of the hirer, his address at the time of hiring if different, together with the driving licence number, its issuing authority and its date of expiry.

*Service of notices*

Service of notices is dealt with by s 111(5) and (6). It should be noted that s 7 of the Interpretation Act 1978 applies. The effect of s 7 is that the service of any notice is deemed to have been effected when it would have arrived in the ordinary course of post. It would seem that by virtue of these provisions the prosecution can prove an offence under Sched 12, para 6(2) and Sched 7 or s 108(2) and Sched 7 by giving evidence that a notice under Sched 12, para 5(6) or s 108(1) has been posted and has not been returned, that no statutory statement of ownership has been furnished and that the excess meter charge or fixed penalty has not been paid. (For a brief discussion of s 7 see 7.17.)

However, an offence under Sched 12, para 6(2) and Sched 7 or s 108(2) and Sched 7 of failing to supply a statutory statement of ownership is only committed if committed 'without reasonable excuse'. It would clearly be a reasonable excuse if the defendant had not received the notice. For this reason most police forces or local authorities serve the notices by recorded delivery.

*Penalties*

Offences under the Road Traffic Regulation Act 1984, Sched 12, para 6(2) and Sched 7, and s 108(2) and Sched 7 of failing to furnish a statutory statement of ownership are punishable by magistrates only and with a fine of level 3. Offences under Sched 12, para 6(3) and Sched 7 and s 108(3) and Sched 7 are punishable by magistrates only and with a fine of level 5. There is no power to endorse or disqualify.

A conviction under Sched 12, para 6(2) and Sched 7 or s 108(2) and Sched 7 discharges the liability of any person for the offence specified in the notice or the excess meter charge offence.

The Magistrates' Association recommends a penalty of £20 for an offence under Sched 12, para 6(2) and Sched 7 or s 108(2) and Sched 7 (see 18.1 and Appendix 3).

### 17.3–5 The new provisions

The Government has stated that the extended system of fixed penalties embodied in Part III of the Transport Act 1982 will be brought into force no later than 30 April 1986. Apart from increasing the number of offences which may be dealt with by way of fixed penalty, the Act provides that, with certain safeguards, an unpaid fixed penalty may be treated as though it were a fine imposed on conviction and collected under the normal court enforcement procedures. The motorist's lack of response to the notice(s) served upon him raises the presumption of his guilt. The result of his inertia will be a 'conviction' without benefit of due process of law. Radical though this departure from accepted principles of justice may appear at first sight, in reality the safeguards enshrined in the Act should be sufficient to ensure the protection of the innocent.

## Definitions

Some of the terms of art employed by the Transport Act 1982 ('the Act') are already familiar as a result of their use in existing fixed penalty legislation; others are new. For the avoidance of doubt, the most important terms are set out below as they appear in the new Act.

### 17.6 'Fixed penalty'

Section 29(3) of the Act provides that the 'fixed penalty' for a fixed penalty offence shall be the amount appropriate in accordance with s 29(4) (£20 for an offence involving obligatory endorsement, £10 in any other case) or one half of the maximum fine which the offence carries, whichever is the less. Since none of the offences listed in Sched 1 to the Act as fixed penalty offences is punishable on summary conviction by a maximum fine of less than £40 or £20 as appropriate, the fixed penalty becomes £20 if the offence is endorsable, £10 if it is not. Section 29(5) enables the Secretary of State to vary the appropriate amount by order.

### 17.7 'Fixed penalty notice'

Section 27(8) defines 'fixed penalty notice' as a notice offering the opportunity of the discharge of any liability to conviction of the offence to which the notice relates by payment of a fixed penalty.

### 17.8 'Suspended enforcement period'

Section 29(1) provides that proceedings shall not be brought against any person for the offence to which a fixed penalty notice relates until the end of the 'suspended enforcement period'; that is to say, the period of twenty-one days following the date of the notice or such longer period (if any) as may be specified in the notice.

## 17.9 Owner

Section 49(2) provides that for the purposes of Part III of the Act the owner of a vehicle shall be taken to be the person by whom the vehicle is kept. It is further provided that for the purposes of determining ownership in the course of proceedings brought under s 31 of the Act (effect where fixed penalty notice is affixed to a vehicle) it shall be presumed that the owner was the registered keeper of the vehicle at the material time. Section 49(3) provides that notwithstanding the above presumption it shall be open to the defence to prove that the registered keeper was not the person by whom the vehicle was kept at the relevant time, and to the prosecution to prove that it was kept by some other person at that time.

## 17.10 'Notice to owner'

Section 31(1), (2) and (3), provides that where a fixed penalty notice has been affixed to a vehicle and the fixed penalty has not been paid within the suspended enforcement period, and no person has given notice requesting a hearing in respect of the offence, a 'notice to owner' may be served by the police upon any person who appears to be the owner of the vehicle. The notice must:

(*a*) give particulars of the alleged offence and of the fixed penalty concerned;

(*b*) state the period allowed for response to the notice (twenty-one days or longer if so specified);

(*c*) indicate that if the fixed penalty is not paid before the end of that period, the person on whom the notice is served is asked to furnish before the end of that period to the police a 'statutory statement of ownership'.

## 17.11 'Statutory statement of ownership'

Part 1 of Schedule 3 to the Act provides that for the purposes of Part III of the Act, a 'statutory statement of ownership' is a statement on an official form signed by the person furnishing it and stating whether he was the owner of the vehicle at the time of the alleged offence and, if he was not the owner of the vehicle at that time, whether:

(*a*) he was never the owner; or

(*b*) he ceased to be the owner before, or became the owner after, that time;

and in a case within paragraph (*b*) above, stating, if the information is in his possession, the name and address of the person to whom, and the date on which, he disposed of the vehicle, or similar particulars of the person from whom, and the date on which, he acquired it.

## 17.12–15 'Statutory statement of facts'

Part II of Schedule 3 to the Act provides that a 'statutory statement of facts' is a statement on an official form, signed by the person furnishing it, to the effect that the person furnishing it was not the driver of the vehicle at the time of the alleged offence, and further stating the name and address (at the time when the statement is furnished) of the person who was the driver of the vehicle at the time of the alleged offence.

## New Fixed Penalty Procedure: An Outline

It should be noted at the outset that the procedure to be followed varies in accordance with the circumstances in which the fixed penalty notice was issued. The object of this introductory section is to set out a brief and, it is hoped, manageable guide to the new system. Later sections will deal in greater detail with its procedural elements.

As an aid to rapid familiarisation, terms whose definitions are contained in the previous section will make their first appearance in *this* section in italic script.

### 17.16 Person present

A constable in uniform who has reason to believe a fixed penalty offence is being or has been committed may give the person concerned a *fixed penalty notice* (s 27(1)).

If the offence is endorsable, the constable can only give a fixed penalty notice to a person if:

(*a*) the person produces a driving licence;
(*b*) the penalty points to be incurred for the offence will not bring the total on the licence to 12 or more; and
(*c*) the person surrenders his licence to the constable (s 27(3)).

If the offence is endorsable and the person concerned is travelling without his licence, the constable may give him a notice to be produced within five days together with the driving licence at a police station of the person's choice (in England and Wales)(s 28(1)).

If the person concerned produces both notice and licence at the specified police station within the five days allowed to him, and if:

(*a*) the penalty points to be incurred for the offence will not bring the total on the licence to 12 or more; and
(*b*) the person surrenders his licence to the police;

he *shall* be given a fixed penalty notice (s 28(2)).

If the fixed penalty is paid before the end of the *suspended enforcement period* no proceedings may be brought against any person in respect of the offence concerned (s 33(5)).

In the case of an endorsable offence, where the fixed penalty is paid before the end of the suspended enforcement period the fixed penalty clerk must endorse the licence and return it to its holder (s 34(4)).

If, before the end of the suspended enforcement period, the recipient of the fixed penalty notice gives notice requesting a hearing in respect of the offence concerned his case may be tried summarily in due course (s 30(2)).

If, by the end of the suspended enforcement period, the recipient has not given notice requesting a court hearing, and the fixed penalty has not been paid, the police may, by means of a certificate, register a sum equal to the fixed penalty plus one half of the amount of that penalty for enforcement against the recipient as a fine (s 30(3)).

The registration certificate must be sent by the police to the justices' clerk for the petty sessional division (in England and Wales) in which the defaulter appears to reside (s 36(4)).

The justices' clerk must register the sum for enforcement as a fine (or pass the certificate on to the appropriate justices' clerk if the defaulter appears to reside in another petty sessional division) (s 36(6), (7)). The justices' clerk who registers the sum for enforcement must send notice of the registration to the defaulter (s 36(8)).

If the offence concerned is endorsable, the justices' clerk who registers the sum for enforcement must notify the fixed penalty clerk of the registration. On being so notified, the fixed penalty clerk must endorse the licence and return it to its holder. If the fixed penalty clerk is himself the clerk who registers the sum for enforcement he must endorse and return the licence upon registration of the sum (s 34(5)).

The registered sum is enforceable in all respects as if it were a fine imposed by the registering court on the conviction of the defaulter on the date of registration (s 36(10)).

The recipient of a notice of registration may within twenty-one days of receipt of that notice make and serve a statutory declaration to the effect that:

(*a*) he was not the person to whom the fixed penalty notice was given; or
(*b*) before the end of the suspended enforcement period he gave notice requesting a hearing (s 37(1),(2)).

In broad terms, such a declaration invalidates both the registration and any licence endorsement which may have taken place, and in case (*b*) above also serves as a notice requesting a hearing in respect of the alleged offence.

## 17.17 Stationary vehicle

A constable who has reason to believe that a non-endorsable fixed penalty offence is being or has been committed in respect of a stationary vehicle may affix a fixed penalty notice to that vehicle (s 27(2),(4)).

If the fixed penalty is paid before the end of the suspended enforcement period no proceedings may be brought against any person in respect of the offence concerned (s 33(5)).

If before the end of the suspended enforcement period any person gives notice requesting a hearing and states in that notice that he was the driver at the time of the alleged offence, his case may be tried summarily in due course (s 31(3)).

Where the fixed penalty has not been paid before the end of the suspended enforcement period and no person has in that time requested a hearing in accordance with s 31(3) above, the police may serve a *notice to owner* upon the person who appears to be the owner of the vehicle (s 31(2)). The procedure which follows the service of such a notice varies in accordance with the nature of the response (if any) elicited by that notice.

### 17.18 Nil response

If there is *no response whatsoever* within the time allowed by the notice to owner, and the fixed penalty remains unpaid, the police may register a sum equal to the fixed penalty plus 50 per cent thereof for enforcement as a fine against the person on whom the notice was served (s 32(2)). The procedure for registration is the same as that for a non-endorsable offence where the fixed penalty notice has been given to a 'person present' (17.16). The recipient of a notice of registration is similarly protected by the power to make a statutory declaration of a specified kind (s 37(1),(3)). The statutory declaration provisions of the Act are discussed in detail later in this chapter (17.52–4).

### 17.19 Person served requests hearing

If the person on whom the notice to owner was served gives notice requesting a hearing in respect of the offence concerned within the period allowed for response to the notice, proceedings may be brought against him in due course (ss 31(6), 32(1)). For the purposes of instituting and conducting such proceedings it is to be conclusively presumed (subject to the exception immediately below) that the person on whom the notice to owner was served was the driver of the vehicle at the time of the alleged offence (s 31(7)).

Section 31(8) provides that the above presumption will not apply if it is proved that at the time of the alleged offence the vehicle was in the possession of some other person without the consent of the accused.

### 17.20 Person served not the owner

A person on whom a notice to owner is served will escape liability for the offence concerned if he was *not* the owner of the vehicle at the time of the alleged offence and he furnishes a *statutory statement of ownership* to that effect within the time allowed for response to the notice (s 31(5)).

### 17.21–5 Person served not the driver

If the person on whom a notice to owner is served was not the driver at the time of the alleged offence, and the person purporting to be the driver wishes to have a court hearing, the person served may furnish within the time allowed for response to the notice both a statutory statement of ownership and a *statutory statement of facts* identifying the driver at the time of the alleged offence. The latter document has effect as a notice by the driver requesting a hearing in respect of the offence concerned (s 32(3)).

## Schedule of Fixed Penalty Offences

### 17.26 Description of offences

Section 27(5) of the Act provides that subject to any limitation or exception mentioned in the 'description of offence' column of the Schedule, any offence in respect of a vehicle committed or punishable under an enactment specified in column 1 of Sched 1 to the Act is a fixed penalty offence.

Section 27(6) provides that an offence under an enactment so specified is *not* a fixed penalty offence if it is committed by *causing or permitting* a vehicle to be used in contravention of any statutory provision, restriction or prohibition. It would seem, therefore, that whilst the driver of a vehicle being used, for example, in breach of a construction and use regulation may take advantage of the convenience and relative inexpensiveness of a fixed penalty, a permissive owner or employer may not. There would appear to be nothing (other, perhaps, than a sense of equity) to prevent the latter person being prosecuted in the normal way. It is to be hoped, however, that where any question of causing or permitting an offence arises, the constable concerned will use the discretion vested in him by the Act and report the offence(s) disclosed for prosecution rather than offer or issue a fixed penalty notice. Similarly, although the Act does not specifically exclude the offence of aiding, abetting, counselling or procuring the commission by another person of a summary offence, and notwithstanding the fact that an aider and abettor may be charged with, and convicted of, the principal offence, it is submitted that the better course would be for both principal and accessory to be reported for prosecution.

Although ss 27 and 28 of the Act (which deal with the issue of fixed penalty notices at the roadside and subsequently at a police station) refer to 'fixed penalty offence' in the singular, applying the Interpretation Act 1978, s 6, there would appear to be no reason why more than one notice should not be issued at the same time if more than one fixed penalty offence is being or has been concurrently committed. (For a discussion of the procedure to be followed where some endorsable offences have been dealt with by fixed penalty and others have been prosecuted in the 'normal' way, see 17.61.)

In the table of fixed penalty offences set out below, 'E' in the endorsement column means that the offence is subject to obligatory endorsement, and 'E*' means that the offence is endorsable if committed in the circumstances described in Sched 4 of the 1972 Act.

It is to be noted that the Secretary of State may by order provide for offences to become, or (as the case may be) to cease to be, fixed penalty offences (s 29(2)).

The amount of the fixed penalty is £20 in the case of an endorsable offence and £10 in any other case (s 29(4)). The amount(s) may be varied by the Secretary of State by order (s 29(5)).

## 17.27–30 Table of fixed penalty offences

| *Section* | *Offence* | *Endorsement* | *Penalty points* |
|---|---|---|---|
| RTRA 1984 | | | |
| s 5(1), Sched 7 | Using vehicle in contravention of traffic regulation order outside Greater London | — | — |
| s 8(1), Sched 7 | Breach of traffic regulation order in Greater London | — | — |

| Section | Offence | Endorsement | Penalty points |
|---|---|---|---|
| s 11 | Breach of experimental traffic order | — | — |
| s 13, Sched 7 | Breach of experimental traffic scheme regulations in Greater London | — | — |
| s 16(1) | Using vehicle in contravention of temporary prohibition or restriction of traffic in case of execution of works, etc | — | — |
| s 17(4), Sched 7 | Wrongful use of special road (motorway offences) | E* | 3 |
| s 18(3), Sched 7 | Using vehicle in contravention of provision for one-way traffic on trunk road | — | — |
| s 20(5), Sched 7 | Driving vehicle in contravention of order prohibiting or restricting driving vehicles on certain classes of roads | — | — |
| s 25(5), Sched 7 | Breach of pedestrian crossing regulations, except an offence in respect of a moving motor vehicle | E* | 3 |
| s 29(3), Sched 7 | Using vehicle in contravention of street playground order outside Greater London | E* | 2 |
| s 30(5), Sched 7 | Using vehicle in contravention of street playground order in Greater London | E* | 2 |
| s 35(4), Sched 7 | Breach of order regulating use etc of local authority parking place, but only where offence committed in relation to parking place on road | — | — |
| s 47(1), Sched 7 | Breach of parking place designation order and other offences committed in relation to a designated parking place, *except* offence of failing to pay an excess charge within the meaning of s 46 of the 1984 Act | — | — |
| s 53(5), Sched 7 | Using vehicle in contravention of parking place designation order having effect under RTRA 1984, s 53(1)(*a*) (inclusion of certain traffic regulation provisions, eg directions for proceeding or waiting and loading restrictions) | — | — |
| s 53(6), Sched 7 | Breach of parking place designation order having effect under RTRA 1984, s 53(1)(*b*) (use of any part of a road for parking without charge) | — | — |
| s 88(7), Sched 7 | Driving vehicle in contravention of minimum speed limit order under RTRA 1984, s 88(1) | — | — |
| s 89(1), Sched 7 | Speeding offences | E | 3 |
| V(E)A 1971 | | | |
| s 12(4) | Using or keeping vehicle on public road without exhibiting excise licence in prescribed manner | — | — |
| s 22(1) | Driving or keeping vehicle without required registration mark or hackney carriage sign | — | — |
| s 22(2) | Driving or keeping vehicle with registration mark or hackney carriage sign obscured, etc | — | — |
| RTA 1972 | | | |
| s 16 | Carrying *more* than one passenger on motor-cycle or carrying *one* such in an unlawful position | E | 1 |

| Section | Offence | Endorsement | Penalty points |
|---|---|---|---|
| s 22 | Failure to comply with traffic directions or signs | E* | 3 |
| s 24 | Leaving vehicle in dangerous position | E* | 3 |
| s 32(3) | Breach of regulations relating to protective headgear for motor cycle drivers and passengers | — | — |
| s 33A(3) | Breach of regulations requiring wearing of seat belts | — | — |
| s 33B(2) | Breach of restriction on carrying children in the front of vehicles | — | — |
| s 36 | Driving vehicle elsewhere than on a road | — | — |
| s 36A(1) | Parking heavy commercial vehicle on verge or footway | — | — |
| s 36B(1) | Parking vehicle *other than* heavy commercial vehicle on verge or footway | — | — |
| s 40(5)(*a*) | Breach of construction and use regulations | E* | 3 |
| s 40(5)(*b*) | Using on road motor vehicle or trailer which does not comply with construction and use regulations | E* | 3 |
| s 81(1) | Contravention of RTA 1972, ss 68–79, or regulations made thereunder (requirements as to lights, reflectors etc) | — | — |
| s 84(1) | Driving without requisite licence | E* | 2 |
| s 88(6) | Breach of provisional licence conditions | E | 2 |
| s 159 | Failure to stop when required by constable in uniform | — | — |
| Greater London Council (General Powers) Act 1974 | | | |
| s 15 | Parking vehicle on footways, verges etc | — | — |
| Highways Act 1980 | | | |
| s 137 | Obstructing highways (by means of vehicle) | — | — |

# Fixed Penalty Notice

## 17.31 Issue of a fixed penalty notice

*Driver present; offence endorsable*

A police constable in uniform who has reason to believe that an endorsable fixed penalty offence is being or has been committed may, provided that certain requirements are fulfilled, give the person concerned a fixed penalty notice. The requirements are that:

(*a*) the person concerned produces his driving licence for inspection;

(*b*) the constable is satisfied that the addition of the appropriate number of penalty points for the offence concerned will not bring the total of points on the licence to 12 or more and thus render the holder liable to disqualification under s 19(2) of the Transport Act 1981;

(*c*) the person concerned surrenders his driving licence to the constable (s 27(1), (3)).

It is to be noted that the term 'constable' in the context of an endorsable offence cannot include a traffic warden (s 49(11)).

If the constable makes a mistake in calculating the total number of penalty points which will appear on the licence as a result of the fixed penalty endorsement, and the driver is in fact liable to a penalty points disqualification, s 41 of the Act enables the fixed penalty clerk to retrieve the situation (from the prosecution's point of view) by sending the licence unendorsed to the police. A 'normal' prosecution may subsequently be embarked upon. (The available methods of rectifying mistakes are discussed at 17.51–5.)

If by chance the driver is travelling without his licence, the constable may give him a notice to be produced together with his driving licence within five days at a police station of his choice in England and Wales. Upon doing so, provided that the points to be added for the offence concerned will not bring the total on the licence to 12 or more, and provided that he surrenders his licence to the police, he *shall* be given a fixed penalty notice (s 28(1), (2)). The constable at the police station is not left with any discretion as to whether or not to invoke the fixed penalty procedure; provided that the requirements of s 28(2) are met, he *must* issue a fixed penalty notice. In effect, the decision as to whether or not the offence should be dealt with as a fixed penalty offence will already have been taken by the officer who detected it.

The holder of the licence who surrenders it either at the roadside or at a police station must be given a receipt for it (s 35(1)). This initial receipt will be valid for one month (beginning with the date of issue) or such longer period as may be prescribed (s 35(3)(*a*)). A new receipt may be obtained on request from the fixed penalty clerk to whom the licence will have been sent by the police (ss 35(2) and 34(3)). Such a receipt will be valid for as long as specified therein by the fixed penalty clerk (s 35(3)(*b*)).

Subsections (4), (5) and (6) of s 35 of the Act provide defences respectively to charges under s 101(4) of the 1972 Act (failure to produce licence to court for endorsement), s 103(2) of the 1972 Act (failure to produce licence to court making order for interim disqualification) and s 161(4) of the 1972 Act (failure to produce licence to constable). In order to avail himself of any such defence the person concerned must produce a current receipt for the licence in the manner in which the licence itself was required to be produced and must subsequently produce the licence 'immediately on its return'. It is submitted that in this context 'immediately' means 'as soon as is reasonably practicable'.

Section 35(7) of the Act provides that a person who has surrendered his licence on receipt of a fixed penalty notice shall not be taken to be in breach of any duty under ss 87 or 89 of the 1972 Act (revocation on disability etc) to deliver his licence forthwith to the Secretary of State if he delivers the licence immediately on its return.

*Driver present; offence not endorsable*

A police constable in uniform who has reason to believe that a non-endorsable fixed penalty offence is being or has been committed may give the person concerned a fixed penalty notice (s 27(1)). A traffic warden may be authorised to perform this function by an order made under the Road Traffic Regulation Act 1984, s 95(5).

*Driver absent*

Where a police constable (or traffic warden if authorised by order under the Road Traffic Regulation Act 1984, s 95(5)) comes upon a stationary vehicle and has reason to believe that a non-endorsable fixed penalty offence is being or has been committed in respect of it, he may affix to that vehicle a fixed penalty notice (s 27(2)).

The fixed penalty procedure cannot be used in the absence of the driver if the offence concerned is an endorsable one (s 27(4)) since the constable will have no way of ascertaining whether or not the offender is liable to fall foul of the totting-up provisions of the Transport Act 1981, s 19. Difficulties may conceivably arise in respect of, for example, construction and use offences which become endorsable if the conditions as to their commission set out in Sched 4 to the 1972 Act are satisfied. There would not appear to be any machinery within the Act for correcting the error if a fixed penalty notice is issued in the mistaken belief that the offence concerned is not endorsable.

Section 29(7) provides that it is an offence for a notice affixed to a vehicle as above to be removed or interfered with except by or under the authority of the driver or person in charge of the vehicle, or the person liable for the offence in question. It is punishable on summary conviction by a maximum fine of level 2.

## 17.32 Contents of a fixed penalty notice

A fixed penalty notice must give such particulars of the circumstances alleged to constitute the offence to which it relates as are necessary for giving reasonable information about the alleged offence, and must specify the suspended enforcement period in respect of the offence, the amount of the fixed penalty and the justices' clerk to whom and the address at which the fixed penalty may be paid (s 29(6)). It must also specify the manner in which notice may be given requesting a court hearing in respect of the offence. The form of such a notice (and that of the 'provisional fixed penalty notice' to be issued under s 28(1) to a driver travelling without his licence where an endorsable fixed penalty offence is alleged to have been committed) will in due course be prescribed by the Secretary of State in the exercise of his powers under s 49(1)(*a*). It is understood (from Home Office Circular No 45/1984) that two visually distinct forms will be developed for use respectively in 'driver present' and 'driver absent' cases.

## 17.33–5 Notification of court and date of trial

Section 39, which provides an optional additional procedure for notification of court and date of trial, is not expected to come into force at the same time as the rest of Part III of the Act. In order to operate effectively it will require a computerised link between police and court in each area. The section will be brought into force at a later, and as yet indeterminate, date and its procedures will almost certainly be subjected to trials in a selected area or areas before being introduced nationally.

The section provides that when a 'person present' is given a fixed penalty notice he may also be given written notification of the magistrates' court by which and the date on which he will be tried if he gives notice requesting a hearing in respect of the offence. If he does request a hearing in the manner specified in the fixed penalty notice, s 39(2) and (3) provide that for the purposes of any proceedings in respect of the alleged offence, the fixed penalty notice is to be treated as if it were an information duly laid in accordance with the Magistrates' Courts Act 1980, s 1, and the written notification is to be regarded as a summons duly issued upon that information. It is also to be noted that the provisions of the Magistrates' Courts Act 1980, s 14 (proceedings invalid where accused did not know of them) do not apply to the recipient of a notification of court and date of trial.

## Suspended Enforcement Period

### 17.36 Provisions of s 29(1)

Section 29(1) provides that proceedings shall not be brought against any person for the offence to which a fixed penalty notice relates until the end of the 'suspended enforcement period'; that is to say, the period of twenty-one days following the date of the notice or such longer period (if any) as may be specified in the notice.

Payment of the fixed penalty before the end of the suspended enforcement period is an absolute bar to proceedings being brought against any person in respect of the offence concerned (s 32(5)). If the offence for which the fixed penalty has been paid is endorsable, the fixed penalty clerk must endorse the licence and return it to its holder (s 34(4)).

Payment may be made (without prejudice to payment by any other method, eg in person) by post to the fixed penalty clerk specified in the fixed penalty notice and, in the absence of proof to the contrary, shall be deemed to have been made at the time at which the letter concerned would be delivered in the ordinary course of post (s 33(3)). In any proceedings for the offence, a certificate purporting to be signed by the fixed penalty clerk, stating whether or not payment of a fixed penalty was received by a date specified in the certificate, or stating that a letter containing an amount sent by post in payment of a fixed penalty was marked as posted on a specified date, shall be evidence of the facts stated (s 33(4)).

### 17.37 Requests for court hearings

*Driver present*

Where a fixed penalty notice has been given to an alleged offender, no proceedings shall be brought against the recipient for the offence concerned unless before the end of the suspended enforcement period he has requested a hearing in the manner specified in the notice (s 30(2)).

*Driver absent*

Where a fixed penalty notice has been affixed to a stationary (and presumably unoccupied) vehicle, the 'notice to owner' procedure (see 17.46 below) may not be embarked upon if before the end of the suspended enforcement period any person has requested a hearing in the manner specified in the notice and has further stated in his notice that he was the driver of the vehicle at the time of the alleged offence (s 31(2), (3)).

## 17.38–45 Events subsequent to the suspended enforcement period

*The consequences of inertia*

It is to be expected that in at least a proportion of cases the suspended enforcement period will expire without either payment being made or a court hearing being requested. The procedure to be followed in such circumstances depends upon the method by which the fixed penalty notice was issued.

*Driver present*

If by the end of the suspended enforcement period the recipient of a fixed penalty has not given notice requesting a court hearing, and the fixed penalty has not been paid, a sum equal to the fixed penalty plus one half of the amount of that penalty may be registered for enforcement against the recipient as a fine (s 30(3)).

The procedure for registration is governed by s 36. The chief officer of police may issue a certificate in respect of any sum payable in default (ie the fixed penalty plus 50 per cent thereof) for enforcement against the defaulter as a fine (s 36(2)). Having issued such a certificate (known as a registration certificate), he must cause it to be sent to the clerk to the justices for the petty sessions area in which the defaulter appears to reside (s 36(4)). The certificate must, inter alia, give particulars of the offence to which the fixed penalty relates and state the name and last known address of the defaulter and the amount of the sum payable in default (s 36(5)). With regard to a body corporate, the place where that body resides shall be either that body's registered or principal office, or the address which, with respect to the vehicle concerned, appears in the record kept under the Vehicles (Excise) Act 1971 as that body's address (s 36(9)). Provided that the defaulter does indeed reside within his petty sessions area, the clerk to the justices who receives the registration certificate must register the sum concerned for enforcement as a fine in his court by entering it in the court register (s 36(6)). If by chance the defaulter resides in another petty sessions area, he may send the certificate without registering it to the clerk to the justices in whose area the defaulter appears to him to reside. Assuming that he correctly locates the area in which the defaulter lives, the recipient clerk will be responsible for registering and enforcing the sum payable (s 36(7)).

The clerk who registers the sum payable in default for enforcement as a fine must thereupon give notice of the registration to the defaulter, specifying inter alia the amount payable and the particulars of the offence contained in the registration certificate forwarded by the police (s 36(8)).

Once registered, the sum payable in default is enforceable in all respects as if it were a fine imposed by the registering court on the conviction of the defaulter on the date of registration (s 36(10)).

In the case of an endorsable fixed penalty offence, the justices' clerk who registers the sum for enforcement is under a duty to notify the fixed penalty clerk of the registration. Upon receipt of such notification the fixed penalty clerk must endorse the relevant particulars upon the licence and return it to the licence holder. If the fixed penalty clerk is himself the clerk who registers the sum for enforcement as a fine, he must endorse and return the licence upon registration of that sum (s 34(5)).

*Driver absent; notice affixed to vehicle*

If by the end of the suspended enforcement period the fixed penalty has not been paid, and no person has given notice requesting a court hearing in respect of the offence, a notice to owner may be served by or on behalf of the chief officer of police upon any person who appears to him (or his authorised officer) to be the owner of the vehicle (s 31(2)). It is provided by s 49(2) that the owner of a vehicle shall be taken to be the person by whom the vehicle is kept. It is further provided that, for the purposes of determining ownership in proceedings for the offence concerned, it shall be presumed that the owner was the registered keeper of the vehicle at the material time.

Section 49(3) provides that notwithstanding the above presumption it shall be open to the defence to prove that the registered keeper was not the person by whom the vehicle was kept at the relevant time, and to the prosecution to prove that the vehicle was kept by some other person at that time. The notice to owner must give particulars of the alleged offence and of the fixed penalty concerned, must state the period allowed for response (twenty-one days or such longer period as may be specified therein), and must indicate that, if the fixed penalty is not paid before the end of that period, the person served is asked to furnish to the police a statutory statement of ownership (s 31(4)). It must also indicate that the person on whom it is served may, within the period allowed for response, either:

(*a*) give due notice requesting a hearing in respect of the offence; or

(*b*) if he was not the driver at the time of the alleged offence, and the person purporting to be the driver wishes to give notice requesting a hearing, furnish together with a statutory statement of ownership a statutory statement of facts identifying the actual driver (s 32(3)).

In order to preserve their right subsequently to bring proceedings in respect of the offence against the person served, if that person requests a hearing within the time allowed for response, the police must ensure that the notice is served before the end of the period of six months beginning with the day on which the fixed penalty notice was affixed to the vehicle (s 31(6)).

## Service of Notice

### 17.46–50 Procedure following service of notice to owner

The procedure which follows the service of a notice to owner is governed by the nature of the response (if any) which the notice produces.

*Payment during the period allowed for response*

It is provided by s 33(6) that payment of the fixed penalty before the end of the period allowed for response to a notice to owner is an absolute bar to proceedings being brought against any person identified as the driver of the vehicle in a statutory statement of facts furnished in response to that notice. Proceedings against the person properly served with a notice to owner may only be brought if he has requested a hearing in due time and form (s 32(1)) and the fixed penalty has not been paid before the end of the period allowed for response to the notice (s 31(6)(*b*)); it is clear, therefore, that payment during the time allowed for response is also an absolute bar to proceedings against the person served with the notice to owner.

*Nil response*

If the notice to owner provokes nothing in the way of a response within the time it allows for response, and if the fixed penalty remains unpaid, the police may issue a certificate in respect of the sum payable in default (ie the amount of the fixed penalty plus 50 per cent thereof) for enforcement against the person on whom the notice to owner was served, as a fine (s 32(2)). The procedure for registration is similar to that which applies in the case of a non-endorsable offence where the fixed penalty notice was given to a driver who was present at the time (see 'Driver present', 17.38). Once such a sum has been registered for enforcement as a fine against the person on whom the notice to owner was served, no proceedings may be brought against any other person in respect of that offence (s 32(6)).

*Person served requests a hearing*

If the person on whom the notice to owner was served gives notice requesting a hearing in respect of the offence concerned in the manner indicated, and within the time allowed, by the notice to owner, proceedings may be brought against him in due course (s 31(6), s 32(1)). It is to be noted that in order to commence proceedings the police must lay an information within twelve months of the time the offence was committed (s 49(13)).

For the purposes of instituting proceedings against the person on whom the notice to owner was served, and in the course of any proceedings so brought, it shall be presumed (subject to the exception in s 31(8) discussed immediately below) that the person on whom the notice to owner was served was the driver of the vehicle at the time of the alleged offence, and the acts or omissions of the driver will be imputed to him (s 31(7)). Section 31(8) provides that the above presumption will not apply if it is proved that, at the time of the alleged offence, the vehicle was in the possession of some other person without the consent of the accused.

*Person served not the owner*

A person on whom a notice to owner is served will not be liable for the offence concerned if he was *not* the owner of the vehicle at the time of the alleged offence and he furnishes a statutory statement of ownership to that effect within the time allowed for response to the notice (s 31(5)). A statutory statement of ownership is a statement on an official form signed by the person furnishing it and stating whether he was the owner of the vehicle at the time of the alleged offence and, if he was not the owner of the vehicle at that time, whether:

(*a*) he was never the owner; or

(*b*) he ceased to be the owner before, or became the owner after, that time;

and in a case within paragraph (*b*) above, stating, if the information is in his possession, the name and address of the person to whom, and the date on which, he disposed of the vehicle, or similar particulars of the person from whom, and the date on which, he acquired it (Sched 3, para 1(1)).

*Person served not the driver*

If the person on whom a notice to owner is served was not the driver at the time of the alleged offence, and the person purporting to be the driver wishes to give notice requesting a court hearing, the person served may furnish within the time allowed for response to the notice both a statutory statement of ownership and a statutory statement of facts identifying the driver at the time of the alleged offence. The latter document, provided it is countersigned by the purported driver, has effect as a notice given by the driver requesting a hearing in respect of the offence concerned (s 32(3), Sched 3 para 3(2)). This, incidentally, is the only means by which proceedings in respect of the offence concerned can be brought against any person other than the person served with the notice to owner (s 32(4)).

If the person served with a notice to owner furnishes a statutory statement of facts as described above, any notice requesting a hearing which he may purport to give on his own account shall be of no effect. In addition, a sum in default may not be registered against him unless no summons in respect of the offence in question is served on the purported driver within the two months immediately following the end of the period allowed for response to the notice to owner (s 32(5)).

The police would appear to be under no duty to serve a summons upon the purported driver, although common sense and equity suggest that they should at least attempt to do so. If they fail (or neglect) so to do, they may proceed at the end of the two months' period to issue a certificate of registration of a sum payable in default for enforcement as a fine against the person served with the notice to owner.

*False statements in response to notices to owner*

In order to discourage unlawful attempts to escape liability for the consequences of a fixed penalty offence, s 46(1) provides that any person who in response to a notice to owner furnishes a statement which is false in a material particular, and does so recklessly or knowing it to be false, commits an offence punishable on summary conviction by a maximum fine of level 5. Subject to an overall time limit of three years from the date of commission of the offence, proceedings may be brought within six months from the date on which evidence, sufficient in the opinion of the prosecutor to warrant the proceedings, came to his knowledge (s 46(2)).

## Rectification of Mistakes

### 17.51 Driver liable to penalty points disqualification

It will be recalled that one of the conditions which must be fulfilled before a constable may issue a fixed penalty notice for an endorsable offence is that the penalty points to be added for the offence concerned will not bring the total number of points on the licence of the driver concerned to twelve or more and thus render him liable to disqualification under the Transport Act 1981, s 19(2). It is inevitable that from time to time miscalculations of points will be made and fixed penalty notices will be issued when they should not have been. In such circumstances all is not necessarily lost for the prosecution, provided that the fixed penalty clerk spots the mistake.

Section 41 provides that having discovered on inspecting the licence sent to him by the police that the holder thereof would be liable to a penalty points disqualification if the penalty points for the fixed penalty offence were added to those already endorsed upon it, the fixed penalty clerk may not endorse the licence but must instead send it to the police (s 41(1), (2)). Proceedings may thereafter be brought for the offence concerned, provided that those proceedings are commenced within six months of the date on which the fixed penalty notice was erroneously issued (s 41(3)). If proceedings are commenced, the fixed penalty notice is treated in all respects as if it had never been issued, and any action previously taken in respect of it (eg registration and enforcement) is regarded as void (s 41(4)).

There is no provision in the Act, however, for rectification of a mistake made in the opposite direction, as it were. A police officer at the roadside may conclude erroneously from an inspection of the licence that an offender would be liable to a penalty points disqualification and hence will feel obliged not to issue a fixed penalty notice.

A police officer subsequently inspecting a licence at a police station in a case where a 'provisional' fixed penalty notice has been issued by another officer at the roadside may similarly err. In each case it is to be presumed that the offender will be reported for prosecution in the normal way. It is submitted that the fact that the offender has mistakenly been denied the opportunity to discharge his liability for the offence by payment of a fixed penalty amounts to a mitigating factor which the court ought properly to consider when passing sentence.

### 17.52 Statutory declarations

It is inevitable with procedures as complicated as those to be introduced by the new Act that from time to time matters will go awry. Identities will be mistaken, documents will go astray, and errors may not be discovered until a notice of registration of a sum payable in default is served upon an alleged offender, or proceedings to enforce that sum are taken against him. Sections 37 and 38 of the Act are intended to provide adequate safeguards for the innocent victims of such mistakes. The machinery of the sections is modelled upon the statutory declaration provisions of the Magistrates' Courts Act 1980, s 14. It is designed to cater for any of three sets of circumstances in which an error has occurred. The first of these is where the operation of the fixed penalty procedure has failed (for whatever reason) to advise a person before registration of his liability to pay a fixed penalty. The second is where registration has taken place despite the driver's request for a court hearing in respect of the offence. The third is where due to impersonation (possibly accompanied by the fraudulent use of a driving licence) the wrong person has been made liable to a fixed penalty and the error has not been detected until receipt of a registration certificate.

As will be seen in due course, the nature and content of a statutory declaration made under s 37 vary in accordance with the manner in which the fixed penalty notice concerned was issued. Certain aspects of the procedure, however, are common to all cases.

The declaration must be made and served within twenty-one days of receipt of a notice of registration upon the clerk of the court which issued that notice (ss 37(1)(*b*) and 38(7)). It may be delivered to him, left at his office or sent to him by registered or recorded delivery post (s 38(4)). There is provision for the court (which for this purpose may consist of a single justice) to accept late service in circumstances where it would be unreasonable to expect service within the normal time limit (s 38(5)). In order to cater for cases where the notice of registration does not find its target, s 38(7) provides that a person shall be taken as receiving notice of registration when he receives notice either of the registration as such or of any enforcement proceedings in respect of the sum registered.

### 17.53 Procedure where fixed penalty notice given to offender

In this case the declaration must state either:

(*a*) that the declarant was not the person to whom the relevant fixed penalty notice was given; or

(*b*) that he gave notice requesting a court hearing in the time allowed and the manner prescribed by the notice

(s 37(2)).

In case (*a*) above, the effect of the declaration is to render void the fixed penalty notice, the registration and any enforcement proceedings already taken (s 37(4)). In such a case, where the actual recipient of the fixed penalty notice has surrendered the declarant's driving licence, any endorsement of that licence which may have been made will also be void (s 37(5)).

In case (*b*) above, the registration, any enforcement proceedings already taken and any endorsement of the declarant's driving licence will be made void, and the declarant will be treated as if he had given notice requesting a hearing in respect of the offence (s 37(6)). For the purposes of subsequent proceedings for that offence, the six months time limit for the initiation of proceedings for summary offences (Magistrates' Courts Act 1980, s 127(1)) runs from the date on which the declaration was served rather than the date of commission of the alleged offence (s 38(3)).

### 17.54 Procedure where fixed penalty notice affixed to stationary vehicle

In this case the declaration must state either:

(*a*) that the declarant did not know of the fixed penalty or any notice issued in respect of it until he received the notice of registration; or

(*b*) that he was not the owner of the vehicle at the time of the alleged offence and that he has a reasonable excuse for failing to comply with the relevant notice to owner; or

(*c*) that he gave notice requesting a court hearing in the time allowed and the manner prescribed by the notice to owner

(s 37(3)).

In cases (*a*) and (*b*) above, the relevant notice to owner, the registration and any enforcement proceedings already taken will be void, but without prejudice in case (*a*) to the service on the declarant of a further notice to owner (irrespective of whether the original notice to owner was properly served) (s 37(7)).

In case (*c*) above, no proceedings may be brought for enforcing payment of the sum registered for a period of twenty-one days following the date of the declaration; if during that period a fresh notice to owner is served, enforcement proceedings will be further suspended until the end of the period allowed for response to that notice (s 37(8)). If no such notice is served, or if a notice is served and the recipient supplies a new statutory statement of ownership as requested, the registration and any enforcement proceedings already taken will be void, and the case will be treated (after certain amounts of time have passed) as one in which the declarant has asked for a court hearing in respect of the alleged offence (s 37(9)). In a case where no new notice to owner has been served, the time which must elapse is twenty-one days following the date of the declaration; in a case where a new statutory statement of ownership has been furnished, it is twenty-one days following the time when the statement was furnished (s 37(10)). It is to be noted that the in the event of non-compliance with a new notice to owner served as above, the original registration and any associated enforcement proceedings do not become void; in such a case, enforcement may get under way again after the time allowed for response to the notice has expired.

### 17.55–60 Protection from unauthorised actions

The provisions of ss 37 and 38 described above do not in any way prejudice any other rights of redress a person may have as a result of the invalidity of any action purportedly taken in pursuance of the fixed penalty procedure but not in fact authorised by the Act (s 38(8)).

## Miscellaneous Provisions

### 17.61 Treatment of other offences committed on the same occasion

It may very well arise in practice that whereas one, or possibly more than one, endorsable offence is dealt with by way of fixed penalty, other and possibly more serious offences may be reported for prosecution in the normal way. It is more than likely, for example, that a driver travelling without his driving licence (or, for that matter his insurance certificate) will be issued with a Form HO/RT/1 requiring production of any missing documents at the same time as he is given a 'substantive' or 'provisional' fixed penalty notice for any concurrently committed fixed penalty offence. In such circumstances he may find himself liable both to a fixed penalty and to a summary prosecution.

Section 44 provides that where a person is convicted of an endorsable offence, and the court is satisfied that his driving licence has been or is liable to be endorsed without a court hearing by a fixed penalty clerk in respect of an offence committed on the same occasion, the appropriate number of penalty points for the offence of which he is convicted shall be treated for the purposes of the Transport Act 1981, s 19 as *reduced* by the number of points required to be endorsed in respect of the 'connected' fixed penalty offence.

## 17.62–70 Special provisions for hired vehicles

In order to protect car hire firms from some of the indiscretions of their customers, s 45 makes provision for dealing with the problems of fixed penalty notices affixed to hired vehicles.

It applies to hiring, but not hire-purchase, agreements which provide for a fixed period of hire of less than six months (whether or not that period is extendable by agreement) (s 45(7)). In any case where a hire firm is served with a notice to owner, the firm concerned may escape liability for a fixed penalty offence if at the time of the alleged offence the vehicle concerned was let to another under a qualifying hiring agreement, and if within the time allowed for response to the notice it serves certain documents upon the police (s 45(1)). These documents are as follows:

(*a*) a statement signed by or on behalf of the firm to the effect that the vehicle was hired under a hiring agreement at the time of the alleged offence;
(*b*) a copy of the hiring agreement; and
(*c*) a copy of a statement of liability signed by the hirer under that agreement indicating his acceptance of liability as the 'owner' of the vehicle for fixed penalty offences committed during the currency of the hiring agreement (s 45(2), (3)).

It is to be noted that the police may, at any reasonable time within six months of service of the notice to owner, require the firm to produce the originals of the hiring agreement and statement of liability in question (s 45(5)). Such production would obviously be necessary if any question arises as to the authenticity of the copy documents originally produced in response to the notice to owner. Failure to produce the original documents when so required results in the firm losing the protection of s 45 and becoming liable in the same way as a person who has been served with a notice to owner and has failed to furnish the statutory statement of ownership in response to it.

In normal circumstances, however, the copy documents will suffice, and s 45(4) provides that where such documents have been served the default procedure appropriate in the case of a fixed penalty notice affixed to a stationary vehicle will apply as if reference to 'owner of vehicle' and 'statutory statement of ownership' were references to 'hirer' and 'statutory statement of hiring' respectively.

## Operation of the Fixed Penalty System

### 17.71–5 Conclusions and anticipated problems

Time alone will tell how well the new fixed penalty procedures will work in practice. One of the bugbears of the old system was a considerable degree of inconsistency in the use made of it from area to area. In an attempt to introduce a measure of consistency and conformity in the use to be made of the new system throughout England and Wales, the Secretary of State will be obliged by s 51 to issue guidance to chief officers of police throughout the jurisdiction in respect of the operation of Part III of the Act, with the objective, so far as possible, of working towards uniformity.

Another area of concern in the operation of the new system is the strain and potential points of breakdown inherent in the complexity of its procedures. The sheer volume of paperwork which must be handled is a daunting one. With at least ten categories of official notice, to say nothing of driving licences, to be processed, it is inevitable that some documents will go astray. To take but one trivial example, the driver who elects to produce his provisional fixed penalty notice at a police station in Ashford, Newcastle, Newport or St Ives may unwittingly be the source of some confusion. An overall impression of the complexity of the system may be gleaned from the 'flow charts' which appear at 17.76.

One source of potential difficulty to fixed penalty clerks, police and public alike is the problem of late payments, most particularly in the case of a fixed penalty notice affixed to a stationary vehicle. The opportunity to pay the fixed penalty lapses at the end of the suspended enforcement period, but is revived when the notice to owner is issued. In the possibly protracted fallow period between these two events, the fixed penalty clerk has no authority to receive a payment. It is clearly unfortunate that in such circumstances the police will be obliged to embark upon the costly and time-consuming 'notice to owner' procedure even if the offender attempts, albeit belatedly, to pay the fixed penalty, but given the way in which the Act has been drafted, no obvious solution is at hand.

## Flow Charts

### 17.76 Explanation and key

The flow charts set out on the next few pages are designed to illustrate in simple terms the procedure to be followed in the cases of 'driver present' fixed penalty offences (endorsable and non-endorsable) and 'stationary vehicle' non-endorsable offences where the fixed penalty notice has been affixed to the vehicle in question.

The symbols used are as follows:

= A question

= An instruction, item of information or procedural step

= An outcome

The abbreviations used are as follows:

DL = driving licence
FP = fixed penalty
FPC = fixed penalty clerk
FPN = fixed penalty notice
SEP = suspended enforcement period
SSoF = statutory statement of facts

**17.77 'Driver present'—endorsable offence**

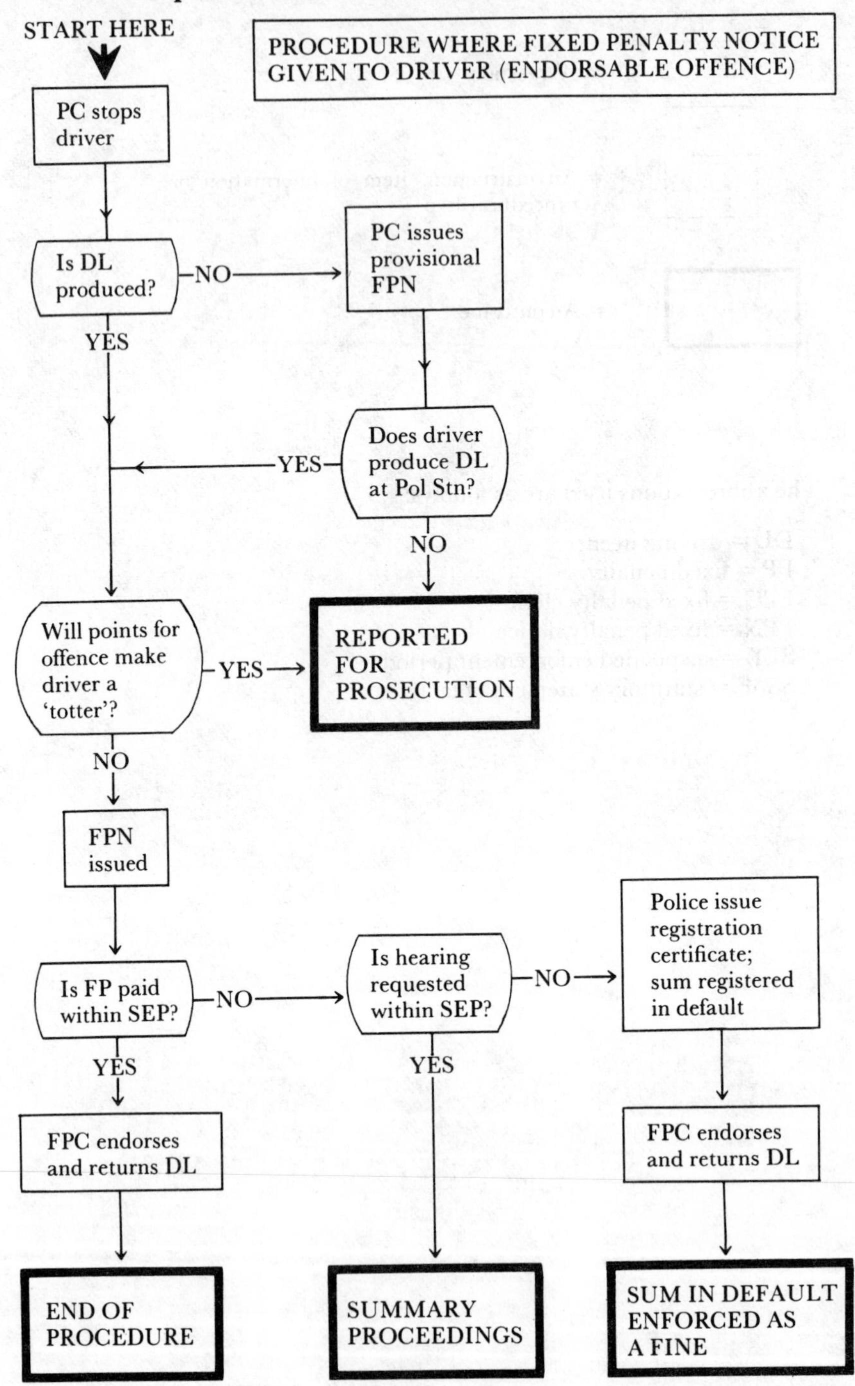
START HERE
PROCEDURE WHERE FIXED PENALTY NOTICE GIVEN TO DRIVER (ENDORSABLE OFFENCE)
PC stops driver
Is DL produced?
NO
PC issues provisional FPN
YES
Does driver produce DL at Pol Stn?
YES
NO
Will points for offence make driver a 'totter'?
YES
REPORTED FOR PROSECUTION
NO
FPN issued
Is FP paid within SEP?
NO
Is hearing requested within SEP?
NO
Police issue registration certificate; sum registered in default
YES
YES
FPC endorses and returns DL
FPC endorses and returns DL
END OF PROCEDURE
SUMMARY PROCEEDINGS
SUM IN DEFAULT ENFORCED AS A FINE

**17.78 'Driver present'—non-endorsable offence**

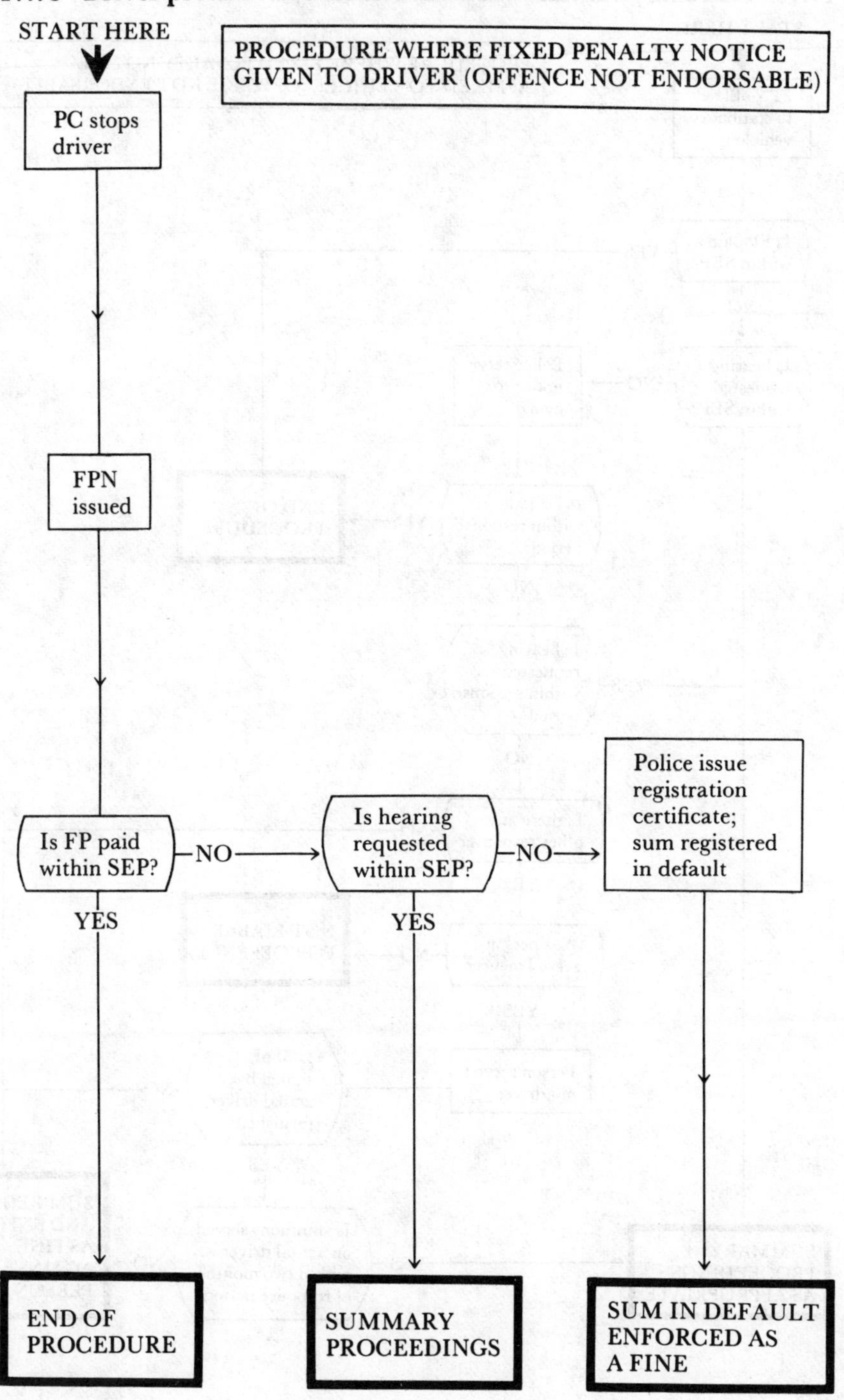

## 17.79 'Stationary vehicle'—non-endorsable offence

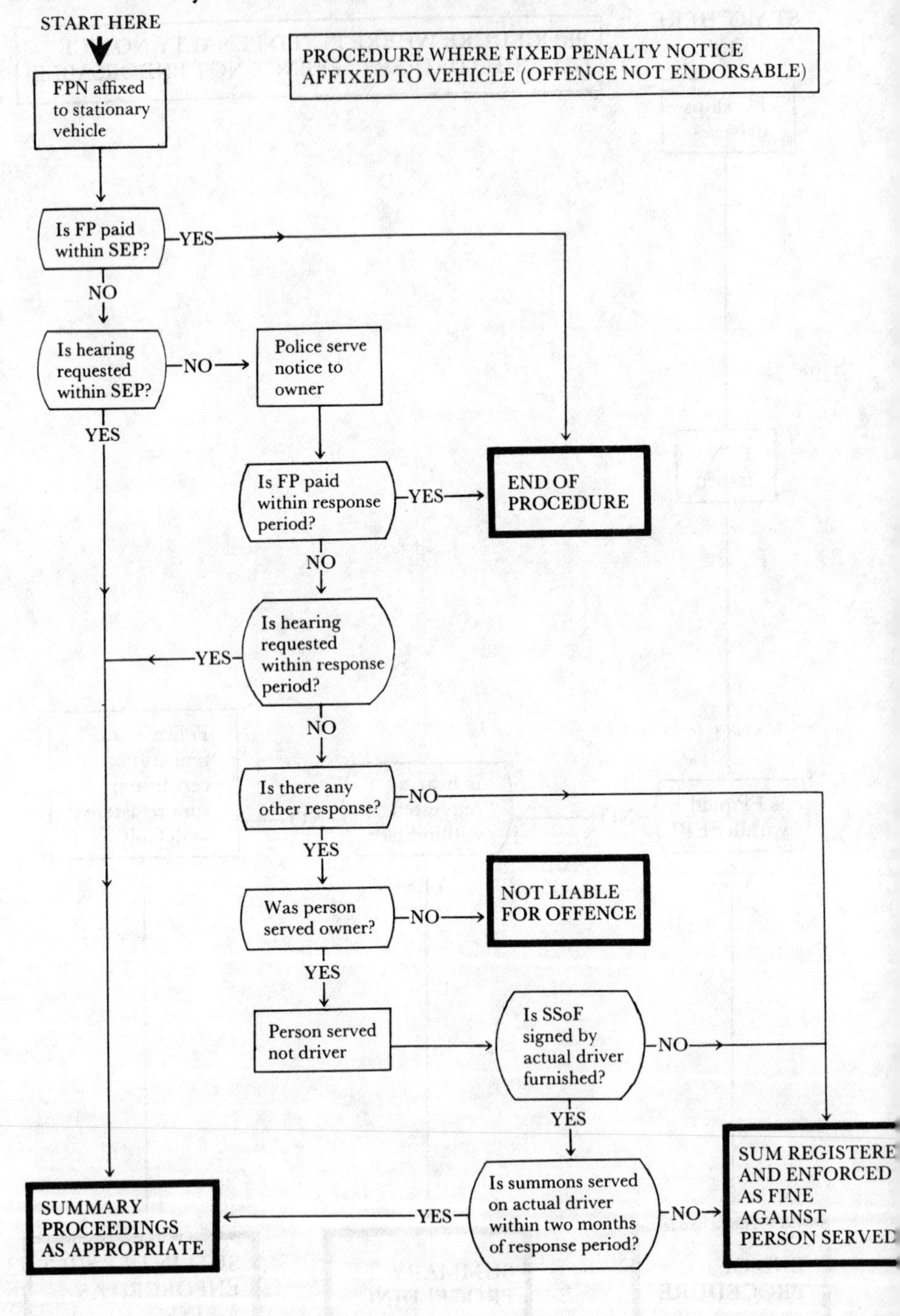

Chapter 18

# Custodial and Other Penalties

## Assessing Penalties

### 18.1–5 The Magistrates' Association's suggested penalties

The Magistrates' Association for a number of years has circulated among benches suggestions for assessing penalties for more common road traffic offences. At one stage the list was confidential, but it has now been made public. The current edition (May 1985) is set out in Appendix 3.

As in previous editions, it is emphasised that the suggested figures are not a tariff. The purpose of the suggestions is to secure uniformity of approach, not uniformity of penalty. The suggestions make it clear that it is a misuse of the folder if the principles set out in the introduction are not followed, viz that each case must be judicially assessed in accordance with the circumstances of the particular offence and of the offender.

The suggestions are approved in principle by the Lord Chancellor and Lord Chief Justice. The Court of Appeal in *R* v *Simpson* [1981] Crim LR 649 had regard to the Magistrates' Association's suggested penalty of £60 for careless driving when reducing a fine of £200 to £100. Similarly, in *R* v *St Albans CC, ex parte Cinnamond* [1981] RTR 145 the suggested penalty of £60 and no disqualification 'for an average case' was referred to when reducing a disqualification for eighteen months to six. Perhaps most significantly of all in *R* v *Krawek* [1985] RTR 1 the Court of Appeal, in reducing a fine of £350 to £250 for careless driving, emphasised the introduction to the suggestions when it states that the list is not a tariff, that the seriousness of offences varies widely, and that the suggested figures represent a broad consensus of view on appropriate penalties for 'average' offences committed by first offenders of average means.

## Fines

### 18.6 Generally

The Criminal Justice Act 1982 assimilated all maximum summary fines into five levels. By s 143 of the Magistrates' Courts Act 1980 the Home Secretary is given power by Order to alter the levels if it appears to him that there has been a change in the value of money. By Order each of the levels in respect of offences committed on or after 1 May 1984 was doubled. The scale is as follows:

| *Level on the scale* | *Original maximum* | *Maximum on or after 1/5/84* |
|---|---|---|
| 1 | £25 | £50 |
| 2 | £50 | £100 |
| 3 | £200 | £400 |
| 4 | £500 | £1,000 |
| 5 | £1,000 | £2,000 |

The maximum fines for 'either way' offences tried summarily are similarly doubled from £1,000 to £2,000 for offences committed on or after 1 May 1984.

In fixing the amount of the fine a magistrates' court is required to take into consideration among other things the means of the offender so far as they are known to the court (Magistrates' Courts Act 1980, s 35). The opinion is given in Stone, with which the editors of this work concur, that a court cannot claim to have regard to the means of the offender merely by ordering payment by instalments over a long period of time.

Enforcement of payment of fines imposed by magistrates is dealt with by Part III of the Magistrates' Courts Act 1980 as amended by the Criminal Justice Act 1982. An offender cannot be committed to prison by a magistrates' court for non-payment of a fine unless a means enquiry has subsequently been held in his presence, but exceptions to this rule are where he is at the time of his conviction serving imprisonment or detention or is at that time sentenced to imprisonment or detention for an offence, or appears to have enough money to pay the fine immediately or appears to be unlikely to stay long enough at a place of abode in Great Britain or Northern Ireland to enable payment to be enforced by other methods. Section 86 of the Magistrates' Courts Act 1980 enables a magistrates' court to order a defendant to appear in court at a specified later date if he has not paid his fine by then. If on the means enquiry the only evidence is that the defendant has never had the money to pay, he cannot be imprisoned for non-payment (*R* v *Woking JJ, ex parte Johnstone* [1942] 2 All ER 179), but it is otherwise if the magistrates are the same at both hearings and there was evidence of means at the first hearing (*R* v *Dunne, ex parte Sinnatt* [1943] 2 All ER 222). A defendant may be searched in court and money found used for his fine. Schedule 4 to the Magistrates' Courts Act indicates the calculation of reduction in imprisonment for part payment of fines and the periods of imprisonment in default of payment. Note the special provisions as to excise penalties; note also that the power of remission at a means enquiry under s 85 of the Act does not apply to excise penalties nor to orders for payment of back duty (see 12.31), nor to any sum other than a fine, eg compensation, forfeiture or pecuniary penalty.

Magistrates have power to mitigate a pecuniary penalty for any road traffic offence, including excise licence ones, however many the previous convictions (Magistrates' Courts Act 1980, s 34), unless the statute otherwise provides.

As to the fixed penalty procedure for certain offences, see Chapter 17.

As to mitigated penalties offered by the Department of Transport see 12.30.

Where a penalty in excess of the permitted maximum is imposed, the High Court need not quash the penalty altogether but may substitute the proper penalty (Administration of Justice Act 1960, s 16).

### 18.7–10 Fines, costs and compensation imposed on juveniles

By virtue of s 55 of the Children and Young Persons Act 1933 as amended by the Criminal Justice Act 1982 and s 3(6) of the Children and Young Persons Act 1969 also amended by the Criminal Justice Act 1982 parents or guardians shall be required to pay the fines or compensation imposed on a juvenile, unless either the court considers it unreasonable for the parent or guardian to be required to do so or the parent or guardian cannot be found. The court cannot order the parent or guardian to pay the fine etc unless the parent or guardian has been given the opportunity of being heard by the court or having been required to attend the hearing has failed to do so. Notwithstanding the maximum fine levels for particular offences committed by non-juveniles, there is an overriding maximum fine level of £100 in respect of offences committed by children (ten to thirteen years of age) and an overall fine level of £400 in respect of young offenders (fourteen to sixteen).

## Imprisonment and Other Custodial Sentences

### 18.11 Statutory restrictions on imposition of custodial sentences

Section 20 and s 20A of the Powers of Criminal Courts Act 1973 provide that a person who has never previously been sent to prison may not be sent to prison unless the court considers no other course appropriate. Before coming to such a conclusion the court shall obtain and consider a social enquiry report unless the court considers it unnecessary to obtain such a report. The court shall state its reason why it considers no other course is appropriate other than imprisonment and also state the reason why no social enquiry report is necessary if none has been obtained. (If the court is a magistrates' court such reasons must be entered in the register.) These statutory restrictions also apply to a sentence of imprisonment which is wholly or partly suspended. Persons who have been sentenced to detention or committed to prison for contempt and persons who have been given a suspended prison sentence which has not been put into operation have not 'previously been sent to prison' within the meaning of s 20.

Section 21 of the Powers of Criminal Courts Act 1973 forbids a court to sentence an offender to prison, unless:

(*a*) he is legally represented; or

(*b*) he has been offered and has refused or failed to apply for legal aid; or

(*c*) he has applied for legal aid and has been refused legal aid on the grounds that he had adequate means; or (*d*) he has been previously sentenced to immediate imprisonment, borstal training or detention as the case may be.

A sentence passed in breach of s 20 is a sentence not authorised by law (*R* v *Birmingham JJ, ex parte Wyatt* [1975] 3 All ER 897).

## 18.12 Young offenders and juveniles

The Criminal Justice Act 1982 abolished imprisonment in respect of any person under twenty-one. Borstal orders were also abolished. The Act provided that offenders may instead be sentenced to terms of youth custody or detention. A sentence of youth custody shall, subject to exceptions set out in the Criminal Justice Act 1982, be more than four months and detention be not less than twenty-one days or more than four months.

Sections 1–3 of the Criminal Justice Act 1982 impose restrictions on courts passing sentences of youth custody or detention and may be broadly summarised as follows:

Before imposing an order of youth custody or detention the court must—

(*a*) ensure that the offender is legally represented (unless after being told of his right to legal aid he refused or failed to apply or his legal aid was refused on financial grounds); and

(*b*) obtain and consider a social enquiry report (unless this is considered unnecessary); and

(*c*) be of the opinion that no other course other than detention or youth custody is appropriate for one or more of the following reasons:

 (i) the offender appears to the court unwilling or unable to respond to non-custodial penalties; or

 (ii) a custodial sentence is necessary for the protection of the public; or

 (iii) the offence is so serious that a non-custodial sentence cannot be justified.

Courts are required to state in open court the reasons for their opinion that no course other than detention or youth custody is appropriate, and if no social enquiry report was considered necessary the reason why it was considered unnecessary.

## 18.13 Suspended sentences

Sentences of imprisonment of two years or less may be suspended for a minimum period of one year and a maximum of two years (Powers of Criminal Courts Act 1973, s 22(1)). A court shall not impose a suspended sentence unless the court is of the opinion that a sentence of immediate imprisonment would have been appropriate in the absence of any power to suspend it (s 22(2)). A suspended sentence should not be passed if a probation order for another offence is made on the same occasion, nor should one be passed on the same occasion as one of immediate imprisonment is passed for another offence, nor should the period of a suspended sentence be made consecutive to a term which the accused is already serving. Where, however, the suspended sentence for a single offence is for more than six months, the court may make a suspended sentence supervision order for a period not exceeding the period for which the sentence of imprisonment is suspended (Powers of Criminal Courts Act 1973, s 26). If the offender is convicted of an offence in Great Britain punishable with imprisonment committed during the operational period of his suspended sentence, it must be put into effect for the full term unless it would be unjust to do so, in which case the court may pass a shorter term than that originally suspended or extend the operational period for up to two years from the date of variation or make no order (s 23).

If the offence is punishable by fine *or* imprisonment the punishment must be either a fine or sentence of imprisonment, but where the offence is punishable by fine or imprisonment or both, both may be imposed. This applies also in the case of a suspended sentence of imprisonment and fine (*R* v *Leigh* (1969) 113 SJ 897).

## 18.14 Partially suspended sentences

Section 47 of the Criminal Law Act 1977 as amended by the Criminal Justice Act 1982 allows a court partially to suspend a sentence of not less than six months and not more than two years. The part to be held in suspense may be not less than one-quarter of the sentence term and the part to be served shall be no less than twenty-eight days. The court may not impose a partially suspended sentence unless a fully suspended sentence is inappropriate. General guidance to the courts on the proper use of partially suspended sentences was given by the Court of Appeal in *R* v *Clarke (Linda)* now reported at [1982] 3 All ER 232. The Lord Chief Justice in that case emphasised that the court should first consider whether a custodial sentence was really necessary and, if it was, whether a community service order could be imposed or the sentence could be wholly suspended. If immediate imprisonment was thought to be unavoidable the court should consider what the shortest sentence could be. If imprisonment was necessary and a very short sentence was not enough and it was inappropriate to suspend it in full, then partial suspension should be ordered but not in such a way as to increase the length of the sentence overall.

## 18.15 Detention in police cells etc

Section 134 of the Magistrates' Courts Act 1980, as amended by the Criminal Justice Act 1982, enables a magistrates' court to sentence an offender convicted of an imprisonable offence to be detained for up to four days in police cells or other premises approved by the Home Secretary as suitable for detention under the section. It would seem that the statutory restrictions on the imposition of imprisonment, youth custody or detention centre orders do not apply to an order under s 134. It would, however, seem impracticable, if not illegal, for a magistrates' court to make an order under s 134 unless there are cells or other premises approved by the Home Secretary in the court's area. Certain magistrates' courts, notably in Essex, have used s 134 in respect of offences under ss 5 and 6 of the Road Traffic Act 1972.

Section 135 of the Magistrates' Courts Act 1980 similarly allows a court to order an offender found guilty of an offence carrying imprisonment to be detained in the courthouse or at any police station until such hour as the court may direct being not later than 8 pm.

### 18.16–20 Deferment of sentence

Section 1 of the Powers of Criminal Courts Act 1973 as amended by the Criminal Justice Act 1982 allows a court to defer passing sentence for a period of up to six months after the date on which the deferment is announced by the court for the purpose of enabling the court in determining the sentence to have regard to the defendant's conduct during the period of deferment, including the making of reparation for his offence. The court can only defer sentence if the defendant consents (s 1(3)); the consent must be obtained from the defendant personally (*R* v *Gilbey* [1975] Crim LR 352); moreover the court must be satisfied, having regard to the nature of the offence and the character and circumstances of the offender, that it would be in the interests of justice to defer sentence. It would not seem normally appropriate for a court to defer sentence for an obligatorily disqualifiable offence, because the main penalty, that of disqualification, could not be altered after any deferment; the disqualification is mandatory unless 'special reasons' exist and such special reasons are limited to the offence and cannot include 'the character and circumstances of the defendant' or 'his conduct during the period of deferment' (see s 1). It is bad practice and contrary to the statute to impose an order of disqualification and then defer sentence (*R* v *Fairhead* [1975] Crim LR 351).

The power of a court to pass sentence when the sentence has been deferred now extends to committing the offender to the Crown Court for sentence (s 1(8) as amended by the Criminal Justice Act 1982).

If sentence is deferred and the offender is subsequently convicted of another offence during the period of deferment, the court which convicts him of the new offence may also sentence him in respect of the offence for which sentence was deferred (save that a magistrates' court cannot subsequently sentence an offender in respect of an offence for which a Crown Court deferred sentence) (s 1(4A), as amended by the Criminal Law Act 1977). In considering the sentence of an offender after deferment, the Court of Appeal will normally look at two matters: first how the offender had behaved during the period of deferment, and secondly whether the sentence imposed was excessive having regard to the actual offence (*R* v *Smith* [1977] Crim LR 234).

## Non-Custodial Sentences

### 18.21 Probation orders

A probation order may be made for a period not less than six months nor more than three years. While on probation the offender will be under the supervision of a probation officer and must comply with the conditions of the probation order. Before making a probation order the court is required to explain the effect of the probation order in ordinary language and the offender must express his willingness to comply with its requirements.

A probation order or an order of absolute or conditional discharge is deemed not to be a conviction except for the purpose of the proceedings for which the order is made (Powers of Criminal Courts Act 1973, s 13). This has the effect that if a person is placed on probation for an offence committed during the period of a suspended prison sentence the court cannot put the suspended sentence into operation (*R* v *Tarry* [1970] 2 QB 560).

A fine may not be imposed for an offence for which a probation order is made but an order for compensation or costs may be coupled with a probation order. Section 102 of the 1972 Act requires a court to disqualify and endorse for an obligatorily disqualifiable offence and to endorse with a discretion to disqualify for an offence for which the court are obliged to endorse.

An offender who fails to comply with a condition of the probation order may be fined up to £400 or sentenced in respect of the original offence for which he was placed on probation. He may also be sentenced for the original offence if he commits an offence during the probation period.

A court may substitute an order of conditional discharge for a probation order on application.

## 18.22 Absolute or conditional discharge

Where a court thinks it inexpedient to inflict punishment and a probation order is inappropriate, the offender may be given an absolute discharge or a conditional discharge. The only condition that may be attached to a conditional discharge is that the offender may not commit a further offence during the period of the order which may be fixed up to a maximum of three years. If he does he may be sentenced for the original offence as if he had just been convicted of the original offence.

An order for compensation or costs may be coupled with an order for conditional or absolute discharge. Section 102 of the 1972 Act requires a court to disqualify and endorse for an obligatorily disqualifiable offence and to endorse with a discretion to disqualify for any offence for which the court are obliged to endorse.

A court may not impose a fine and an order of conditional discharge for one offence (*R* v *McClelland* [1951] 1 All ER 557). An offence for which an offender is given an absolute or conditional discharge is deemed to be a conviction only for the purposes of the proceedings for which the conditional or absolute discharge was made (Powers of Criminal Courts Act 1973, s 13) and it would seem that a court may not put into operation a suspended prison sentence for an offence committed during the period of the suspended sentence for which he is given an absolute or conditional discharge (see *R* v *Tarry* at 18.21 above).

Before making an order of conditional discharge the court is required to explain the effect of an order of conditional discharge in ordinary language: for this reason it would appear that an order of conditional discharge cannot be made in a defendant's absence.

## 18.23 Community service orders

Sections 14–17 of the Powers of Criminal Courts Act 1973 deal with the making of a community service order.

A person aged sixteen or over convicted of an offence punishable with imprisonment may be ordered to perform within a period of a year unpaid work in service of the community for not less than 40 nor more than 240 hours (120 hours in the case of a sixteen year old). The court cannot make a community service order unless:

(*a*) the offender consents; and

(*b*) a scheme for community service exists in the petty sessional division in which the offender resides, or will reside; and

(*c*) the court is satisfied after considering a probation officer's report that the offender is a suitable person for such an order; and

(*d*) that provision can be made for him to perform community service.

A community service order cannot be combined with any other sentence for the same offence, eg a fine (*R* v *Carnwell* [1978] Crim LR 60), nor is it appropriate to combine a community service order with a suspended prison sentence imposed on the same occasion (*R* v *Starie* [1979] Crim LR 751). However, by s 14(8) the court is empowered in addition to make orders as to costs, compensation, deprivation of property used in connection with the offence and restitution (but not seemingly any power of forfeiture). Section 14(8) also empowers the court when making a community service order to disqualify the offender either under the Road Traffic Act or s 44 of the Powers of Criminal Courts Act 1973 (see 20.31). Although the power of endorsement is not specifically included in s 14(8), it is submitted that where an offender is sentenced to community service in respect of an endorsable offence, the court must make an order of endorsement whether or not he is disqualified.

If the offender is shown to be in breach of the requirements of the community service order, he may either be fined up to £400 or dealt with in any manner as if he had been convicted of the offence and the community service order had not been made.

It is possible to make one community service order consecutive to another, but it is highly desirable that the maximum total of 240 hours should not be exceeded (*R* v *Evans* [1977] Crim LR 230).

## 18.24 Compensation

Compensation of up to £2,000 by a magistrates' court (unlimited for a Crown Court) may be ordered under s 35 of the Powers of Criminal Courts Act 1973 to be paid by any person convicted of an offence.

Where a person has inadequate means to pay what would otherwise be the appropriate fine together with the appropriate amount of compensation, the court is required to give preference to the order of compensation (s 35(4A)). Moreover an order of compensation is a sentence in its own right; s 35 as amended by the Criminal Justice Act 1982 allows a court to make an order of compensation instead of dealing with the offender in any other way.

Compensation is not limited to any damage which has been incurred but includes compensation for any personal injury, loss or damage resulting from the offence for which the offender was convicted or any other offence taken into consideration by the court. In deciding how much compensation to award, the court is required to have regard to the defendant's means. No application for compensation need be made by the loser to the court; the court may award compensation on its own motion. In the case of an offence under the Theft Act 1968 where the property in question is recovered, any damage which occurred while it was out of the owner's possession shall be treated as having resulted from the offence, howsoever and by whomsoever the damage was caused (s 35(2)).

No compensation may be ordered in respect of loss suffered by the dependants of a person in consequence of his death, nor may compensation be ordered in respect of 'injury, loss or damage due to an accident arising out of the presence of a motor vehicle on a road' (s 35(3)). The offence for which the defendant is convicted is (except where it is under the Theft Act: see below) irrelevant. If the damage etc is due to an 'accident arising out of the presence of a vehicle on a road', no compensation is payable (s 35(3)). In *M (a minor) and another* v *Oxford* [1981] RTR 246 an order of compensation made by justices following the defendants' conviction under s 1 of the Criminal Damage Act 1971 was quashed. It should also be noted that the accident does not have to be on the road, it merely has to arise out of the presence of a motor vehicle on the road. The following remarks of Bridge J in *Redman* v *Taylor* [1975] Crim LR 348 were quoted with approval in *M (a minor) and another* v *Oxford* above:

> Any accident resulting from such driving on a road as resulted in the vehicle running off the road and then colliding with some stationary object was clearly an accident which occurred 'owing to the presence of a motor vehicle on a road' within section 8(2) [of the 1972 Act] notwithstanding that the vehicle was off the road before the impact occurred.

(It will be observed that s 8(2) of the 1972 Act and s 35(3) of the 1973 Act are in similar terms.) Compensation may be awarded, notwithstanding s 35(3), where the offence is under the Theft Act 1968. The effect is that if a vehicle has been taken without the owner's consent or has been stolen, the thief or person convicted under s 12 may be ordered to pay compensation in respect of any damage to the owner's vehicle, including damage that has occurred in respect of a road accident before the vehicle was recovered; but a court has no power to award compensation in respect of damage to any other vehicle than the loser's. Thus where a defendant took and drove away a Morris without the owner's consent and collided with two other cars, it was held that compensation could only be ordered in respect of the Morris (which was the subject of the charge under s 12(1) of the Theft Act 1968) and that the court had no jurisdiction to make an order of compensation in respect of the damage to the other two cars because of the terms of s 35(3) (*Quigley* v *Stokes* [1977] RTR 333).

Although compensation can legally be awarded to the Department of Transport in respect of excise offences, it is submitted that courts should not use their discretionary power to award compensation under s 35 for such regulatory offences.

Compensation can be ordered to be paid jointly and severally by co-defendants, but in view of the difficulties which ensue as to accountability and enforcement, such an order should not be made (*R* v *Grundy* [1974] 1 All ER 292). Nor should compensation be ordered unless the claim is simple and straightforward (*R* v *Daly* [1974] 1 All ER 290), nor if the amount ordered would take a number of years to repay (ibid). Compensation should not be ordered in respect of costs for a parallel civil claim (*Hammertons Cars Ltd* v *Redbridge LBC* [1974] Crim LR 241).

The effect of a compensation order on a subsequent award in civil proceedings is dealt with in s 38. A compensation order made by magistrates is suspended until the time has elapsed for notice of appeal (twenty-one days) and if notice of appeal is given until the appeal is determined (s 36). Stone proffers the opinion that s 36 does not preclude a court accepting payment within the period of suspension or even ordering it to be paid within that time. The suspension does, however, preclude a court enforcing payment or paying any money received to the person entitled to the compensation.

Magistrates may not order compensation on committing a person to the Crown Court for sentence (*R* v *Blackpool JJ, ex parte Charlson* [1972] 3 All ER 854; *R* v *Brogan* (1975) *The Times*, 6 February).

Compensation may be awarded for any offence taken into consideration (s 35(1)). An offender placed on probation, or given an absolute or conditional discharge, may be ordered to pay compensation (s 12(4)); similarly an offender ordered to perform community service may also be ordered to pay compensation (s 14(8)).

### 18.25–30 Forfeiture of property used for criminal purposes

The power of forfeiture of property under s 43 is frequently used in respect of motor vehicles used for criminal purposes, since 'property' must clearly include a motor vehicle. Where an order is made under s 43 the offender is deprived of all right to the property and it is required to be taken into police possession (if not already in their possession) (s 43(3)). By s 43(4) and (5) a person claiming ownership may apply under the Police (Property) Act 1897 within six months of the order but cannot succeed in his application unless he satisfies the magistrates' court that either he did not consent to the offender having possession or he did not know and had no reason to suspect that it would be used for criminal purposes.

An order under s 43 may only be made if the offence is one punishable on indictment with imprisonment for a term of two years or more. This definition includes 'either way' offences dealt with in this book. The court, whether it is the Crown Court or a magistrates' court, must be satisfied that the property was in his possession or under his control at the time of his apprehension (ie either physical possession or an entitlement to an immediate right to possession): for this reason an order was quashed where the car was detained by the police at the time of the offence but the offender was not arrested until some days later (*R* v *Hinde* [1977] RTR 328).

An order should only be made if the property was used for the purpose of committing or facilitating the commission of the offence (s 43(1)(*a*)), or intended to be used by that person for that purpose (s 43(1)(*b*)). For this reason an order of deprivation of a motor car was quashed in *R* v *Lucas* [1976] RTR 235. An order was set aside on appeal in respect of a motor car used to convey the appellant and co-accused from the scene of a robbery on the grounds that the robbery was committed on the spur of the moment and the order of forfeiture of a £1600 motor car was too heavy an additional punishment (*R* v *Miele* (Note) [1976] RTR 238). In *R* v *Tavernor* (Note) [1976] RTR 242 a defendant was ordered to be deprived of a car used to transport drugs in a burglary; the order was quashed as the car was bought out of compensation moneys for physical injuries and it would be too heavy an additional penalty to deprive him of the car which he had still to use as a means of transport because of his injuries. On the other hand, although the power of forfeiture is an additional penalty, the legislature intended it to be such and where a car was used as an integral part of an offence of handling stolen property ('the reason why the thieves had come to him, was because he had a motor car suitable for transferring the goods'), the order depriving the handler of the £250 Jaguar was upheld (*R* v *Lidster* [1976] RTR 240).

Like compensation orders, orders requiring forfeiture should only be made in simple, uncomplicated cases. Difficulties arise where the defendant does not have individual ownership of the property. Accordingly, an order was quashed in respect of a tipper lorry which was owned jointly by the defendant with his business partner (*R* v *Troth* [1980] RTR 389). An order cannot be made to secure the payment of fines and compensation by the offender (*R* v *Kingston upon Hull JJ, ex parte Hartung* [1981] Crim LR 42). In *R* v *Thiebeault* [1983] Crim LR 102 an order under s 43 in respect of a motor vehicle was upheld but following *R* v *Kingston upon Hull JJ* the further order that the proceeds from the sale of the motor vehicle should be distributed to the defendant's victims was quashed.

Where an order is made under s 43 depriving a defendant of his rights in respect of a motor vehicle, the proper course for a third party who claims in respect of it is to apply to the magistrates' court under s 1(1) of the Police (Property) Act 1897 within six months of the order being made (see s 43(4)). In *R* v *Chester JJ, ex parte Smith* [1978] RTR 373, justices were compelled by order of mandamus to hear such an application.

## Costs

### 18.31 Generally

Costs can be awarded against the defendant, when he has been found guilty, or against the prosecutor, when the case has been dismissed, on conclusion of a trial of a summary offence in a magistrates' court (Costs in Criminal Cases Act 1973, s 2). The amount must be specified by the court and, where the defendant is under seventeen, the amount of costs awarded against him must not exceed the amount of the fine (ibid). By s 1, examining justices who discharge a defendant instead of committing him for trial may give him his costs out of central funds but may award costs against the prosecutor himself, on refusal to commit for trial, only if of opinion that the charge was not made in good faith (s 2(4)). The prosecutor may appeal if ordered to pay more than £25 under s 2(4) (s 2(5)). A magistrates' court dealing summarily with an 'either way' offence (eg taking a motor vehicle) may order payment of the prosecution's costs out of central funds and should normally do so in the absence of a special reason to the contrary. A defendant may be ordered to pay the whole or part of the prosecution's costs and a certificate for payment of the costs may be granted either for the balance or, if the defendant is given time to pay them, pending payment by th defendant. Witnesses' costs as ascertained by the justices' clerk will also be paid out of central funds, but there is no power to order payment of witnesses' costs out of central funds in respect of summary cases. In summary cases, costs may only be ordered to be paid by a convicted defendant to the prosecutor or by the prosecutor to an acquitted defendant (s 2), although if an interpreter is needed because of the defendant's lack of knowledge of English, the interpreter's costs must be paid out of central funds even if the defendant is convicted (Administration of Justice Act 1973, s 17).

Costs may be ordered to be paid by the prosecutor to a defendant where proceedings are withdrawn (s 12) and the prosecutor has no right of appeal against an order under s 12 (*R* v *The Crown Court at Lewes, ex parte Rogers* [1974] 1 All ER 589). Where an order is made for costs out of central funds, the amount should be ascertained out of court by the justices' clerk (*R* v *Chertsey JJ* [1974] 1 All ER 156), but the final ascertainment of the costs must be the decision of the justices themselves: they have no power to delegate their powers to the clerk. It is submitted that, once a court has decided to make an award of costs, there is no further discretion to award part of the costs only (see *R* v *Bow Street Magistrate, ex parte Palmer* (1969) 113 SJ 735).

A Practice Note as to the award of costs in criminal cases in magistrates' courts was issued by the Lord Chief Justice on 25 November 1982 (*The Times*, 27 November). It reads as follows:

Under section 1 of the Costs in Criminal Cases Act 1973 a magistrates' court dealing summarily with an indictable offence and dismissing the information, or inquiring into any offence as examining justices and determining not to commit the accused for trial, may order the payment out of central funds of the costs of the defence. A similar power exists under Section 12(1) of the Act where an information is not proceeded with.

Whether to make such an award is a matter in the unfettered discretion of the court in the light of the circumstances of each particular case.

It should be accepted as normal practice that such an award be made unless there are positive reasons for making a different order. Examples of such reasons are:

(*a*) Where the prosecution has acted spitefully or has instituted or continued proceedings without reasonable cause the defendant's costs should be paid by the prosecutor under section 2 of the Act. If there is any doubt whether payment will be forthcoming from the prosecutor the position of the defendant should be protected by making an order for costs from central funds in his favour as well.

(*b*) Where the defendant's own conduct has brought suspicion on himself and has misled the prosecution into thinking that the case against him is stronger than it is the defendant can be left to pay his own costs.

(*c*) Where there is ample evidence to support a conviction but the defendant is acquitted on a technicality which has no merit. Here again the defendant can be left to pay his own costs.

(*d*) Where the defendant is acquitted on one charge but convicted on another. Here the court should make whatever order seems just having regard to the relative importance of the two charges and the conduct of the parties generally.

In *R* v *Burt, ex parte Presburg* [1960] 1 QB 625, an award of two guineas to the prosecution on conviction was upheld, although there had been no legal representation and a constable, who lost no pay, was the witness and prosecutor. In *Palastanga* v *Salmon* [1962] Crim LR 334, it was said obiter that a party who brings about an adjourned hearing for a technical point should pay the costs, but it is submitted that this can only be ordered if he loses the case, since s 2 contains no provision for awarding costs against a successful party.

The power to award costs against a defendant is restricted to the costs of his prosecution and conviction; he cannot be ordered to pay costs relating to the trial of his co-accused (*R* v *Gould* [1965] Crim LR 547). When deciding to order the defendant to pay costs, his financial circumstances are a relevant consideration (*R* v *Wright* [1977] Crim LR 236).

Any criminal court may order a legally aided defendant to pay all or part of the prosecutor's costs, if convicted.

Save where a point of law allowing appeal to the High Court arises or s 2 (5) applies there is no appeal against a magistrates' order for costs alone by either party but, in view of the power of the Crown Court to vary a sentence on appeal by a defendant, an appeal against a sentence, not being an order for probation or conditional discharge, might result in the costs ordered being reduced (Magistrates' Courts Act 1980, s 108).

Particulars as to costs no longer have to be stated in the particulars of a conviction endorsed on a person's licence (Magistrates' Courts Rules 1981, r 32).

## 18.32 Administrative costs

The practice has grown up of many magistrates' courts ordering, as a matter of routine, defendants to pay a fixed sum of costs to the police when convicted of summary offences. The only legal basis of this practice is *R* v *Burt* at 18.31, above where the prosecution had to call evidence as a result of the defendant's inaction.

It is submitted that it is an inappropriate exercise of the court's discretion to award the police administrative costs where it is exercised as a matter of routine in cases where a defendant has pleaded guilty in writing. Indeed, some courts have agreed with prosecuting authorities the amount of costs that will be awarded for pleas of guilty by post. It is submitted that such an agreement might be considered an improper fetter on the court's discretion.

### 18.33 Costs on appeal

Note that a defendant successfully appealing to the Crown Court against sentence will not normally be entitled to an order against the police for his costs in bringing the appeal if the prosecution have limited their part in the hearing of the appeal to a simple recital of the facts, there being no question of the offence being trivial or being a case which should never have been brought, or of the prosecutor contributing to the fines being held excessive (*R* v *Lewes Crown Court, ex parte Castle* [1980] RTR 381). See further Chapter 22.

### 18.34 Costs on indictment

A defendant convicted at the Crown Court may be ordered to pay the whole or part of the prosecution costs (Costs in Criminal Cases Act 1973, s 4 (1)(*a*)).

It is desirable and important that the court of trial should either order a particular quantified sum or order costs to be paid 'not in excess of' a particular and quantified sum' (*R* v *Newlove* [1978] RTR 150; *R* v *Hier* (1976) 62 Cr App R 233).

### 18.35 Costs on acquittal

A Practice Direction has been issued in respect of costs of defendants who are acquitted at the Crown Court ([1981] 3 All ER 703). It reads as follows:

1. The principal power of the Crown Court to order the payment of the costs of an acquitted defendant either out of central funds under s 3 of the Costs in Criminal Cases Act 1973 or by the prosecutor under s 4 of that Act is limited to those cases in which the accused is acquitted on all counts in the indictment.
2. There is a subsidiary and unrestricted power under s 5 of the Indictments Act 1915 to order the prosecutor or the defendant to pay any costs incurred as a result of an amendment to or the severance of any indictment.
3. The exercise of those powers is in the unfettered discretion of the court in the light of the circumstances of each particular case.
4. It should be accepted as normal practice that an order should normally be made for the payment of the costs of an acquitted defendant out of central funds under s 3 of the 1973 Act unless there are positive reasons for making a different order. Examples of such reasons are: (*a*) where the prosecution has acted spitefully or has instituted or continued proceedings without reasonable cause, the defendant's costs should be paid by the prosecutor under s 4 of the 1973 Act; (*b*) where the defendant's own conduct has brought suspicion on himself and has misled the prosecution into thinking that the case against him is stronger than it is, the defendant can be left to pay his own costs; (*c*) where there is ample evidence to support a conviction but the defendant is acquitted on a technicality which has no merit, here again the defendant can be left to pay his own costs.
5. This Practice Direction is to take effect from 16 November 1981.

Where a defendant has elected trial in respect of an 'either way' offence for which summary trial would have been more appropriate he must take the consequences of his having to pay the prosecution costs at the Crown Court if the Crown Court thinks he is in a position to pay the costs (*R* v *Boyesen* [1982] Crim LR 596).

# Chapter 19

# Endorsement and Penalty Points

## Endorsement

### 19.1 Summary

The principles of endorsement contained in the 1972 Act and the Transport Act 1981 are summarised below; their detailed application is discussed in the subsequent sections of this chapter.

(1) Unless an offence is one which is described in Schedule 4 to the 1972 Act and shown there to involve 'obligatory endorsement' (an 'endorsable' offence) a court has no power to order the endorsement of the offender's licence.

(2) Every endorsable offence carries penalty points and, on conviction, unless the offender is disqualified, the licence must be endorsed with the appropriate number of penalty points.

(3) A court may only refrain from endorsing the offender's licence on conviction if:

(*a*) 'special reasons' for not doing so are found by the court (see Chapter 21); or

(*b*) the offence is in respect of a contravention of the Construction and Use Regulations and the defendant is able to show that he did not know and had no reasonable cause to suspect that the facts of the case were such that an offence would be committed (see 8.46).

(4) Where a licence is ordered to be endorsed, particulars of the endorsement are recorded on the licence and are also recorded (following notification by the court) centrally at the Driver and Vehicles Licensing Centre (DVLC) at Swansea.

(5) Endorsable offences are divided into two classes: those involving obligatory disqualification (an 'obligatorily disqualifiable offence', eg causing death by reckless driving, driving with excess alcohol, etc); and the remainder, for which the court has a discretion whether to disqualify.

### 19.2 Table of endorsable offences

The following table sets out all the endorsable offences, their penalty points values, and whether or not they are obligatorily disqualifiable.

| *Offence* | *Legislative provision* | *Number of penalty points* | *Disqualification* |
|---|---|---|---|
| Manslaughter (or in Scotland culpable homicide) by driver of a motor vehicle | (common law) | 4[1] | Obligatory |
| | *1972 Act* | | |
| Causing death by reckless driving | s 1 | 4[1] | Obligatory |
| Reckless driving when previously convicted of an offence under s 1 or s 2 in previous 3 years (see 5.74) | s 2 | 4[1] | Obligatory |
| Other reckless driving offences | s 2 | 10 | Discretionary |
| Careless or inconsiderate driving | s 3 | 2–5 | Discretionary |
| Driving or attempting to drive when unfit through drink or drugs | s 5(1) | 4[1] | Obligatory |
| Being in charge when unfit through drink or drugs | s 5(2) | 10 | Discretionary |
| Driving or attempting to drive with excess alcohol | s 6(1)(*a*) | 4[1] | Obligatory |
| In charge with excess alcohol | s 6(1)(*b*) | 10 | Discretionary |
| Failing or refusing to provide breath for preliminary test | s 7(4) | 4 | Discretionary |
| Failing or refusing to provide specimens for analysis when driving or attempting to drive | s 8(7) | 4[1] | Obligatory |
| Failing or refusing to provide specimens for analysis when not driving or attempting to drive | s 8(7) | 10 | Discretionary |
| Motor racing or speed trials on highway | s 14 | 4[1] | Obligatory |
| Carrying passenger on motor cycle other than astride and on a seat | s 16 | 1 | Discretionary |
| Failing to comply with traffic directions or signals in respect of motor vehicle[2] | s 22 | 3 | Discretionary |
| Leaving motor vehicle in dangerous position | s 24 | 3 | Discretionary |
| Failing to stop after accident | s 25 | 5–9 | Discretionary |
| Failing to give particulars or report accident | s 25 | 4–9 | Discretionary |
| Contravention of certain Construction and Use Regulations[3] | s 40(5) | 3 | Discretionary |
| Driving without a licence[4] | s 84(1) | 2 | Discretionary |
| Failing to comply with provisional licence conditions | s 88(6) | 2 | Discretionary |
| Driving with uncorrected defective eyesight | s 91(1) | 2 | Discretionary |
| Refusing eyesight test | s 91(2) | 2 | Discretionary |
| Driving while disqualified by court order | s 99(*b*) | 6 | Discretionary |
| Driving while disqualified by reason of age | s 99(*b*) | 2 | Discretionary |
| Using motor vehicle whilst uninsured | s 143 | 4–8 | Discretionary |
| Taking etc a motor vehicle in Scotland without authority | s 175 | 8 | Discretionary |

| *Offence* | *Legislative provision* | *Number of penalty points* | *Disqualification* |
|---|---|---|---|
| | *Theft Act 1968* | | |
| Stealing or attempting to steal a motor vehicle | | 8 | Discretionary |
| Taking or attempting to take etc a motor vehicle without authority | s 12 | 8 | Discretionary |
| Going equipped for stealing or for taking motor vehicles | s 25 | 8 | Discretionary |
| | *RTR Act 1984* | | |
| Motorway offences[5] | s 17(4) | 3 | Discretionary |
| Pedestrian crossing offence in respect of motor vehicle | s 25 | 3 | Discretionary |
| School crossing patrol offence in respect of motor vehicle | s 28 | 3 | Discretionary |
| Street playground offence in respect of motor vehicle | ss 29, 30 | 2 | Discretionary |
| Speeding offences | s 89 | 3 | Discretionary |
| | *1972 Act* | | |
| Aiding and abetting etc an obligatory disqualifiable offence | s 93(6) | 10 | Discretionary |
| Aiding or abetting etc an endorsable offence | (see 19.10) | | |
| Attempting to commit an endorsable offence | (see 19.9) | | |

[1] No penalty points may be imposed when the offender is disqualified; see 19.25.
[2] Certain traffic signs only; see 6.18.
[3] As which Construction and Use Regulations involve endorsement, see 8.42.
[4] As to when the offence is endorsable, see 11.33.
[5] As to when motorway offences are endorsable, see 6.40.

## 19.3 Requirement to endorse

Section 101(1) of the 1972 Act requires a court to order the defendant's driving licence to be endorsed with particulars of the conviction whenever he is convicted of an offence carrying obligatory endorsement and with particulars of the disqualification also if he is ordered to be disqualified from driving as well, unless:

(*a*) there are special reasons justifying non-endorsement (see Chapter 21); or

(*b*) the Mental Health Act 1983, s 37(3), applies; or

(*c*) the offence was under the Construction and Use Regulations as to brakes, steering, tyres, dangerous condition or load etc and the court finds that he did not know and had no reasonable cause to suspect that the facts were such that an offence would be committed (see 8.46).

Any special reasons under head (*a*) above for not endorsing or disqualifying should be stated in open court and, in the case of a magistrates' court, entered on the court register (1972 Act, s 105(1)); the finding is valid, however, if they are not stated aloud (*Brown* v *Dyerson* [1969] 1 QB 45).

If the defendant is placed on probation or discharged absolutely or conditionally in England or Wales, his licence must be endorsed unless there are special reasons (1972 Act, s 102(1)).

The phrasing of s 101 is such that 'any' licence of which the defendant is the holder is required to be endorsed. The court is required to make such an order (in the absence of 'special reasons') whether or not the defendant actually has a licence. A 'licence' in the context of s 101 means a licence issued under Part III of the Road Traffic Act 1972 (s 110), and a court cannot therefore actually endorse particulars of a conviction on an international driving permit, a foreign licence, a driving permit issued under the Visiting Forces Act 1952, or a heavy goods vehicle licence. Although holders of foreign driving licences and driving permits will not have their licences or permits actually endorsed, any order of endorsement counts towards a penalty points disqualification. Moreover, should a British driving licence be taken out in the future, the applicant will have to disclose any previous orders of endorsement; and the endorsements will be entered on the British licence unless it is outside the period after which the endorsement may be removed (see 19.41). A Northern Ireland driving licence cannot be endorsed by a court in England or Wales.

It used to be thought that a fine or imprisonment or other order should always accompany endorsement. However, in *Bell* v *Ingham* [1962] 2 All ER 333 it was said obiter that endorsement can truly be described as 'part of the penalty'. This statement, taken with *R* v *Bignell* (1967) 111 SJ 773 (that there need be no penalty when disqualification is ordered), suggests that endorsement on its own may be ordered as the sole penalty. While a court on convicting should normally proceed to judgment, it is not clear whether there is precise authority that the 'judgment' must include a custodial sentence or a fine or probation or absolute or conditional discharge; convictions followed by recognisances only (which the relevant statutes allowed) were held to be valid in *R* v *Miles* (1890) 24 QBD 423 and *R* v *Blaby* [1894] 2 QB 170. It is submitted, however, that endorsement should not be ordered on its own as the sole penalty. As was said in *Bell* v *Ingham* above, it is 'part of' the penalty; the court in the absence of special reasons is obliged to order endorsement if it is an obligatorily endorsable offence. Moreover, by r 32 of the Magistrates' Courts Rules 1981, particulars of the sentence of the court are required to be included, and it is difficult to regard as a sentence an order under s 101 that particulars of the conviction, which must include the sentence, are to be endorsed on the licence. It is submitted, to avoid these problems and such circular arguments, that the court should order an absolute discharge where the court considers an endorsement by itself is sufficient punishment.

Where a court orders endorsement, the particulars to be endorsed include the name of the court, the date of the offence, the date of the conviction and (where different) the date on which sentence is passed, particulars of the offence and particulars of the sentence (including the number of penalty points and the period of any disqualification); but not, any longer, particulars relating to any order for costs.

### 19.4 Omission to order endorsement

If the chairman omits to say 'licence endorsed' on a conviction where there are no special reasons, the prosecutor can seek mandamus from the High Court to require endorsement. See 2.44 suggesting that a decision once announced cannot be altered; but a distinction should be drawn between altering a decision after it has been pronounced and omitting to pronounce an order which the court intended to make. Moreover if the magistrates' court does not make an order of endorsement it is required to state its reasons for not doing so in open court (s 105(1) of the 1972 Act). If the omission is caused by a slip of the tongue there can be no doubt, it is submitted, that the court may repair the omission (see for example *R* v *Newcastle-upon-Tyne JJ, ex parte Swales* [1972] RTR 57). Section 142(1) of the Magistrates' Courts Act 1980 allows a magistrates' court to vary a sentence or other order made by it when dealing with an offender. This power seems sufficiently wide to include the power to order endorsement which was originally omitted and which the court was obliged to make by virtue of s 101 of the 1972 Act. An order under s 142(1) of the 1980 Act must, however, be made within twenty-eight days beginning with the day on which the sentence was imposed or order made and must be made by a court constituted in the same manner as the original court (or where the court consisted of three or more justices by a majority of those justices) (s 142(3)). (Care must be taken to calculate the twenty-eight-day period. As the date upon which the mistake was made has to be included in the twenty-eight-day period, a court giving a mistaken sentence on 1 March cannot purport to rectify the mistake on 29 March: the latest date for doing so is 28 March.)

### 19.5 Endorsement as evidence

Particulars of any conviction, disqualification, or penalty points, endorsed on a driving licence which is produced on conviction of an endorsable offence are prima facie evidence of such particulars (s 101(1)). Endorsement of a licence is especially important as it is only convictions to be endorsed that count as the 'qualifying' ones leading to obligatory disqualification under s 19 of the Transport Act 1981. A court after conviction is bound to require its production (see s 101(4), as amended) and are entitled to take into consideration particulars of any convictions endorsed upon it (see s 101(4A)).

### 19.6 Notification of endorsement

By s 105(2) of the 1972 Act, the court ordering endorsement must notify the Department at the central licensing department at the DVLC, Swansea. The notification to the central licensing department is in code form and the endorsement of licences issued from Swansea is in the same code (see Appendix 2). The court may either notify the DVLC and send the driving licence back to the defendant after endorsement, or send the licence itself after endorsement to the DVLC (s 105(2) as substituted by para 14 of Sched 9 to the Transport Act 1981). If disqualification is ordered, the court must send the licence to the DVLC. Courts are also required to notify particulars of the motorist's sex and date of birth, in addition to the other particulars prescribed. The court when making an order of endorsement is required to order the defendant to state in writing his sex and date of birth, if not already known. If a person knowingly fails to comply with such an order he is guilty of a summary offence punishable with a fine of level 3 on the standard scale (s 104(4)). Where a person has stated his date of birth to a court, the Secretary of State can require him to produce evidence to verify that date of birth, and where he has changed his name, his name at the date of his birth. Non-compliance with the Secretary of State's order is similarly punishable (s 104(5)). (It may be remarked that the subsection places adopted persons in a difficulty. An adopted person usually knows only the names given to him on adoption. Presumably the Secretary of State would be content with production of the adoption certificate.)

To enable particulars of the conviction to be recorded on the central computer at Swansea by the Driving and Vehicles Licensing Centre (DVLC) courts are required to notify many of the particulars in code form. Particulars are endorsed on the licences in the same form.

The endorsement and sentence code is set out in Appendix 2 at the end of this volume.

## 19.7 Committal for sentence

Where a magistrates' court commits a defendant to the Crown Court for sentence the magistrates' court may disqualify him until he is dealt with at the Crown Court. The magistrates' court has no power of endorsement if they do so (see 20.33).

## 19.8 Deferment of sentence

It is submitted that, where sentence is deferred in respect of an obligatorily endorsable offence, the endorsement should only be ordered when the sentence is imposed following the deferment; it should not be ordered at the time of conviction. Any order of endorsement must include particulars of the sentence as well as particulars of conviction. An order of deferment is not a sentence, it is an order that sentence be deferred.

## 19.9 Attempts

The 1972 Act gives no power to endorse for an attempt to commit an endorsable offence save for:

(*a*) attempting to drive when unfit through drink or drugs or with more than the permitted amount of alcohol in the blood;

(*b*) refusing evidential specimens under s 8 (7) of the 1972 Act when attempting to drive at the relevant time; or

(*c*) attempting to steal or take without authority a motor vehicle.

In these excepted cases the 1972 Act gives express power to endorse for the attempt. Otherwise, for attempting to drive while disqualified or attempting to commit any other offence specified in Parts I, II and III of Sched 4 to the 1972 Act, there was no power to endorse (*Bell* v *Ingham* [1968] 2 All ER 333), (but see the Criminal Attempts Act 1981, below).

For a case in which a court disqualified a person convicted of an attempt to take and drive away a motor vehicle prior to s 12 of the Theft Act 1968, see *R* v *Cockermouth JJ* [1971] Crim LR 287, where an order of certiorari was granted to quash the original order of disqualification and also another order of disqualification which was made as a result of his conviction for driving during the first period of disqualification.

Although *Bell* v *Ingham* above remains authority for the proposition that unless the 1972 Act gives express power to endorse and disqualify for an attempt there is no such power, it would now seem that by virtue of the Criminal Attempts Act 1981 (which came into effect on 27 August 1981) where the attempted offence is an indictable offence or an 'either way' offence the person convicted of attempting to commit the offence is now liable to exactly the same penalties as if he had been convicted of the actual offence. Section 4(1)(*b*) of the 1981 Act provides that if the offence is indictable a defendant convicted on indictment under s 1 of attempting to commit an offence shall be liable to 'any' penalty to which he would have been liable if convicted on indictment of the offence which he attempted to commit. Section 4(1)(*c*) similarly provides that a person summarily convicted under s 1 of an attempt to commit an offence is liable on summary conviction to 'any' penalty to which he would have been liable on summary conviction of the 'either way' offence. Section 1 does not apply to offences triable only summarily.

It would seem, therefore, that a person convicted of an attempt to commit an indictable or 'either way' offence incurs obligatory or discretionary disqualification and obligatory endorsement to exactly the same extent as if he had actually committed the offence. Thus courts may disqualify and must endorse for convictions under s 1 of the 1981 Act for attempts to commit the following offences:

(*a*) reckless driving if committed otherwise than within three years of a previous conviction under s 1 or s 2;

(*b*) driving whilst disqualified;

(*c*) being equipped for stealing etc committed with reference to the theft or taking of a motor vehicle;

and are obliged to disqualify and endorse in respect of attempts to commit the following offences:

(*d*) manslaughter, or in Scotland culpable homicide, by the driver of a motor vehicle;

(*e*) causing death by reckless driving;

(*f*) reckless driving when committed within 3 years of a previous s 1 or s 2 offence; and (*g*) motor racing.

A defendant charged with attempting to commit an offence may be convicted of the attempt although the magistrates' court are satisfied he had committed the full offence (*Webley* v *Buxton* [1977] Crim LR 607). It would seem that if an offender is charged with attempting to commit an offence for which the attempt is not endorsable he will escape endorsement even if the justices are satisfied he committed the full offence because he may be convicted of the offence charged, viz an attempt.

Where an attempt is endorsable, the offender will have his licence endorsed in accordance with the endorsement code as if he had been convicted of the full offence and will incur the appropriate number of penalty points for the full offence.

## 19.10–20 Aiders and abettors

A person convicted of aiding, abetting, counselling and procuring an offence is, by s 44 of the Magistrates' Courts Act 1980, 'guilty of the like offence' and is thus liable to the same penalties as the principal offender. An aider or abettor who aids or abets an endorsable offence must therefore have his licence endorsed and may be disqualified. If not disqualified, his licence will be endorsed with the same number of penalty points as if he had been convicted of the principal offence; but if the offence is obligatorily disqualifiable, an aider and abettor of that offence is not liable to obligatory disqualification, but will incur 10 penalty points if not disqualified (s 93(6)). But he is liable, like a principal offender, to an obligatory disqualification under s 19 of the Transport Act 1981 if the offence for which he is an aider or abettor is an endorsable offence and brings the total number of penalty points to 12 or more. The only effect of s 93(6) of the 1972 Act is that if the principal offence is an obligatory disqualifiable offence, an aider or abettor is not liable to obligatory disqualification for the offence itself, but he is still liable to obligatory endorsement. It was held in *Ullah* v *Luckhurst* [1977] Crim LR 295 that s 93(6) did not exempt an aider or abettor from the former 'totting up' provisions of s 93(3). Similarly, if a person has a previous conviction for aiding and abetting a drink/driving offence and is subsequently convicted of a drink/driving offence he is liable to the minimum period of three years' disqualification under s 93(4) (*Makeham* v *Donaldson* [1981] Crim LR 570).

If endorsement of the driving licence of an aider and abettor is required, then it may be avoided if 'special reasons' are found (see Chapter 21) or the provisions as to certain offences under the Construction and Use Regulations apply (see 8.46).

The endorsement code (see Appendix 2) provides that an aider and abettor of an endorsable offence is distinguished in that the last numeral 0 of the code is replaced by 2. For a person convicted of inciting an offence, the 0 is changed to 6. Thus a conviction of taking a conveyance without authority is shown as UT 40, one of aiding and abetting such an offence as UT 42 and one of inciting such an offence as UT 46. The 0 is changed to 4 in respect of a person convicted of 'causing or permitting'.

As to attempts, see 19.9 above.

# Penalty Points

## 19.21 Summary

The penalty points system is contained in s 19 of and Sched 7 to the Transport Act 1981. These statutory provisions largely follow the recommendations of the *Report of the Inter-Departmental Working Party on Road Traffic Law* (HMSO 1981). They are summarised below, as is the endorsement of penalty points; penalty points disqualification is discussed at 20.18. The penalty points system was brought into force on 1 November 1982.

*Endorsement*

A person convicted of any existing endorsable offence in addition to the previous particulars has endorsed on his licence the number of penalty points allocated to the offence unless there are 'special reasons' for not endorsing his licence.

*Number of points to be endorsed*

The number of penalty points for most offences is usually a fixed number but for four offences the number of points has to be decided by the court within the range indicated: careless or inconsiderate driving (2–5); failing to stop after an accident (5–9); failing to give particulars or report an accident (4–9); and using etc without insurance (4–8). The number of penalty points for each offence is set out in the table at the head of this chapter and in Sched 7 to the Transport Act 1981 (as amended).

Where a person is convicted of a number of offences committed on the same occasion, the number of penalty points to be imposed is the number of points in respect of the offence which incurs the highest number of points.

Where the court disqualifies the offender the court may not impose any penalty points.

*Disqualification*

A person is liable to disqualification if he incurs a total of 12 relevant points. Relevant points are points incurred in respect of offences *committed* within a period of three years, other than offences which are 'wiped off' as a result of a previous disqualification.

*'Wiping the slate clean'*

The points system does not derogate in any way from the courts' existing discretionary or obligatory powers of disqualification, but *any* order of disqualification (other than an interim order of disqualification on committal to the Crown Court, an order of disqualification where a vehicle was used for the commission of a crime and an order as a result of s 21 of the Transport Act 1981) has the effect of 'wiping the slate clean', ie removing all existing penalty points from the licence.

*Period of disqualification*

The minimum period of disqualification is six months, but is increased to one year if the defendant has been previously disqualified within three years immediately preceding the commission of the latest offence in respect of which penalty points have been taken into account. If there are two such orders of disqualification the period is two years. Unlike 'totting up' disqualifications, a penalty points disqualification is not consecutive to any other order of disqualification. Where a person is convicted on the same occasion of more than one offence not more than one disqualification under s 19(2) may be imposed.

*Transitional provisions*

An endorsement imposed before 1 November 1982 counts as 3 points.

*Crown servants*

Section 30(2) of the Transport Act 1981 which governs the interpretation of the penalty points provisions has been amended by para 25 of Sched 5 to the Transport Act 1982 to make it quite clear that the penalty points system applies to vehicles and persons in the public service of the Crown (as to vehicles and persons in the service of the Crown generally see 2.8).

## 19.22 Number of points to be endorsed

A court is required to endorse the number of penalty points set out in Sched 7 unless the court either finds 'special reasons' for not endorsing or disqualifies the offender. Where 'special reasons' are found the court cannot impose a lesser number of points: it must either endorse the appropriate number of points or decide, because of 'special reasons', not to endorse at all. The court's power or duty to disqualify for the offence is unaffected by the penalty points system. The court remains under exactly the same duty to disqualify as before in respect of an offence involving obligatory disqualification. Similarly, the points system in no way alters the discretionary power of disqualification in respect of any endorsable offence. Once a person is disqualified, whatever the type of disqualification, the 'slate is wiped clean', ie he starts again with a licence free from penalty points once the disqualification is ended (see 20.23).

Schedule 7 sets out either a fixed number or a variable number of points for each offence. The penalty points for each offence are indicated in the table at 19.2 and also in Chapters 4 to 16 where the penalties for each offence are discussed.

## 19.23 Variable points

Where a variable number of points is ascribed to an offence (careless or inconsiderate driving (2–5); failing to stop after an accident (5–9); failing to give particulars or report an accident (4–9); and using, or causing or permitting use of, an uninsured motor vehicle (4–8)), problems both of sentencing and practice arise. The fundamental question as to sentencing is the criteria by which a court should decide the number of penalty points. Should a court have regard primarily to the facts of the offence in fixing the number of points or should it take into account the previous motoring record of the offender? The Inter-Departmental Committee (see 19.21) intended the criteria to be the circumstances of the offence or such number of points 'as may seem appropriate to the court having regard to the evidence' (Annex G, para 2, of the committee's report). The Transport Bill as originally introduced contained a fixed number of points for all offences, but as a result of amendments by both Houses variable points were introduced because of the opinion expressed that the gravity of these particular offences varied so much. Although neither *Hansard*, nor the report of the committee under which a Bill was based, can be used in the interpretation of an Act of Parliament, it is submitted that the Act requires a court to have regard primarily to the gravity of the offence in deciding the appropriate number of points. The record of the offender, it is submitted, is of little relevance. Parliament intended, it is submitted, the previous convictions of an offender to be dealt with by the accumulation of penalty points and consequent risk of disqualification under s 19(2). What is most relevant, it is submitted, in deciding the number of points is the gravity or otherwise of the facts of the offence. For example, in careless driving cases the primary criterion is the degree of carelessness; was it on the one hand a case of momentary inattention, or did the offender deliberately take a risk? In insurance cases, did the offender deliberately use the car knowing it to be uninsured, or did he have an insurance policy but was ignorant of the fact that its terms did not cover the particular use on the day in question?

Difficulties in practice will arise if courts sentence an offender for a variable points offence and fix the number of penalty points in the absence of the offender. It is submitted that in many cases the court can only accurately determine the number of penalty points in the presence of the defendant. Because the criterion, it is submitted, for fixing the number of points is the gravity of the offence, the court may have difficulty in properly assessing the appropriate number of points simply on consideration of the prosecution's statement of facts and what is written in mitigation by the defendant. Whether or not the plea of guilty by post procedure has been adopted, it is submitted that in any event a court should sentence an offender for a variable number of penalty points offence in his absence only if it is satisfied it can adequately decide the right number of points in his absence. Although there is no statutory requirement on the court to adjourn to give the offender an opportunity to attend where the court is intending to impose a high number of points, it is submitted that a court should do so. Advocates will similarly no doubt advise offenders that the opportunity should be taken for the defendant to appear in order that the court may be adequately addressed in mitigation of the offence in order to avoid a high number of points. Offences of no insurance, failing to stop and failing to report accidents, and (to a slightly less extent) careless or inconsiderate driving are in any event comparatively serious motoring offences and ones for which, it is submitted, the court should normally require the presence of the offender.

It is stated that a court should have regard primarily to the gravity of the offence in deciding the appropriate number of points in respect of a variable points offence. Some commentators have gone so far as to suggest that this is the only criterion and for this reason a court should not look at the licence before deciding the number of points.

This, it is submitted, is wrong. Not only does s 101 of the 1972 Act implicitly require the court to look at the driving licence before sentencing the defendant, but the gravity of an offence can also be affected by a previous conviction of a *similar* offence. It may be relevant to know whether the defendant has previously been convicted of another case of careless or inconsiderate driving, for example. Otherwise previous convictions of endorsable offences which are different from the instant offence will usually be of little relevance in deciding the appropriate number of points. Moreover a court should be careful not to give the impression, when it hears of the number of penalty points already on a licence, that it is increasing the number of points in order to be able to impose a penalty points disqualification, or, on the other hand, decreasing the number of points it would otherwise impose in order to avoid having to impose a penalty points disqualification.

## 19.24 Fixed points offences

Some of the fixed points offences deserve specific comment.

The offence of driving without a licence will incur 2 penalty points only if the offence is endorsable. The offence is endorsable if the offender was driving a class of vehicle which he was not entitled to drive or, if he was entitled only to a provisional licence, he offended against a provisional licence condition (see further 11.4).

The offence of driving while disqualified contrary to s 99(*b*) of the 1972 Act itself shows no distinction between a person who drives while disqualified by order of a court and one who drives when he is disqualified from obtaining a licence because he is too young. Schedule 7, however, distinguishes between the two offenders: the former incurs 6 points and the latter 2.

The new drink/driving provisions were not brought into force until 6 May 1983; for this reason Sched 7 to the Transport Act 1981 was amended by para 26 of Sched 5 to the Transport Act 1982 so that references in Sched 7 to the 1981 Act to ss 6(1)(*b*), 7(4) and 8(7) should instead refer to ss 6(2), 8(3) and 9(3), respectively, in respect of drink/driving offences committed between 1 November 1982 and 6 May 1983. It should be noted, however, that despite this amendment, courts had no power to impose 4 penalty points for the offence under the former s 8(3) of refusing a preliminary breath test because the offence of refusing a preliminary breath test contrary to s 8(3) was not endorsable.

The offence of failing to comply with traffic signs or directions is in some cases endorsable and in others not. Failing to comply with the directions of a traffic warden is now expressly made endorsable by virtue of the amendment contained in para 22 of Sched 9 to the 1981 Act and the offender will thus incur penalty points. Although the Inter-Departmental Committee (see 19.21) recommended a review of the Traffic Signs Regulations, at the time of writing no such review has taken place. Contravention of some traffic signs involves endorsement; contravention of others does not. If the offence is not endorsable, then no penalty points are incurred (for a list of traffic signs contravention of which involve endorsement, see 6.18).

It will be noted that para 1 of Part II of Sched 4 to the 1972 Act requires the convicting court to order endorsement for 'stealing or attempting to steal a motor vehicle'. It is submitted that the omission of any reference to any particular section of the Theft Act 1968 is deliberate and that an offender is required to have his licence endorsed with 8 penalty points if he is convicted of burglary or robbery involving the theft or attempted theft of a motor vehicle.

Paragraph 3 of Part III of Sched 4 allows disqualification and requires endorsement with 8 penalty points if a person, when not at his place of abode, has with him any article for use in the course of or in connection with any theft or taking of motor vehicles, eg a set of duplicate ignition keys. The power to disqualify and endorse seems to be confined to cases where the offender was equipped to steal or take a motor vehicle itself (including theft of a motor vehicle by burglary or robbery) and not to extend to cases where he was equipped only to steal from the car. *Semble*, evidence as to his intentions should be sought after he has been found or pleaded guilty, if not otherwise apparent.

It may also be noted that this offence, like the other offences in the Theft Act 1968 involving obligatory endorsement, contains no requirement that the offence was committed on a road or highway. Section 12 makes it an offence to 'take' the motor vehicle; there is no requirement that it be driven on a road. Theft of a motor vehicle merely requires a dishonest appropriation; the offence of theft under the Theft Act 1968 no longer requires asportation, although the offence under s 12 of taking does (see further 15.2).

A person may be convicted of refusing to supply a specimen for analysis even when he was neither driving or attempting to drive nor in charge of a motor vehicle. On conviction his licence must be endorsed with 10 penalty points or he may be disqualified (see 4.91).

## 19.25 Penalty points for obligatorily disqualifiable offences

Where a person is disqualified, whether for an obligatorily disqualifiable offence or otherwise, the court may not impose penalty points (s 19(1)). Part 1 of Sched 7 to the Transport Act 1981 fixes the number of penalty points at 4 for any obligatorily disqualifiable offence. If, therefore, 'special reasons' are found for not disqualifying for the obligatorily disqualifiable offence the courts are obliged to impose 4 penalty points. Because 'special reasons' are narrowly defined (see Chapter 21) a court, if it thinks it unjust to impose 4 penalty points, may in such circumstances consider whether the facts constituting the reason for not disqualifying are also sufficient to constitute 'special reasons' for not endorsing.

Although a court may not impose the 4 penalty points if the offender is disqualified for the offence, the 4 points are still required to be taken into account in accordance with s 19(3)(*a*). The effect of this is that, if the offender already has 8 penalty points or more in respect of offences committed within the three-year period, the court is obliged to consider a penalty points disqualification under s 19 in addition to the disqualification for the offence itself. Any such disqualification must, however, be concurrent with the disqualification for the offence itself.

## 19.26 Offences committed on the same occasion

If a person is convicted of two or more offences committed on the same occasion the number of penalty points to be endorsed 'shall be the number or highest number that would be endorsed on a conviction of one of the offences' (s 19(1)). At first sight the phrase 'the number or highest number' seems confusing and might appear to allow a court to take the absurd course of arbitrarily selecting the number of any one of the various offences committed on the same occasion whether that offence has the highest points or not. It is, however, submitted that the correct interpretation of the phrase is that the court is required to impose the number of points for any one of those offences if all those offences have the same number, or if the offences have differing numbers of points, the court is required to impose the number appropriate to the offence which has the highest number of penalty points. It should be remembered that in many instances all the offences committed will incur the same number of points. Moreover, it cannot have been Parliament's intention to allow a court to impose a lower number of points simply because the offender has committed another offence on the same occasion, which, by definition, is the more serious.

A further difficulty of interpretation occurs where one of the offences has a variable number of points. Should the court automatically impose the highest number of points within the range of points for that offence if that offence is committed on the same occasion as other offences? For example, if a person commits the offence of failing to comply with a provisional licence condition and on the same occasion also drives while uninsured, should the court automatically impose 8 points (the highest number of points for the insurance offence)? It is submitted that the court is not required to do so. The proper approach for a court is first to consider the circumstances of the variable points offence and then decide the appropriate number of points for that offence and if the number so decided is then the highest of the offences, that is the number that should be endorsed.

It should be noted that s 19(1) of the Transport Act 1981 refers to offences which 'were committed on the same occasion'. This phrase should be contrasted with the corresponding provision in respect of 'totting up' which refers to the offender having 'been *convicted* on not less than two occasions'. The phrase in s 93(3) of the 1972 Act has often been interpreted as meaning the same occasion of *conviction*. If an offender was convicted on the same occasion of a number of offences committed on differing dates, the court would normally have treated all the offences as one occasion for 'totting up' purposes if the offender was simultaneously convicted by the court on the same day. This should be contrasted with s 19(1) of the Transport Act 1981. The section requires the offences to be *committed* on the same occasion. It is clear that offences committed on differing dates will not have been committed on the same occasion (unless, perhaps, the occasion was spread over midnight). It is also clear that the court may be required to add up points if the offences were committed on separate occasions even if committed on the same day (eg speeding on the way to work in the morning and speeding home after work). Whether offences are committed on the same occasion is a question of fact: the offences do not have to be committed simultaneously, they can be committed one after another, but they must be linked in some way so that it can be said that all were committed on the same occasion. This seems to have been the approach adopted by the court in *Johnson* v *Finbow* [1983] 1 WLR 879 where it was held that a motorist who failed to stop after an accident, contrary to s 25(1) of the 1972 Act, and who subsequently failed to report that accident to the police contrary to s 25(2) of the 1972 Act was to be treated as having committed both offences on the same occasion because their commission arose from the same accident. In *Johnston* v *Over* (1984) *The Times*, 13 July, 1 RTLB 51, it was held by the Divisional Court that where two vehicles were used by the defendant for stripping parts from one vehicle to repair the other and the defendant was not insured for either vehicle, the two offences of using the vehicles without insurance were committed on the same occasion for the purpose of endorsing penalty points.

### 19.27–35 Transitional provisions

Where an offence was committed before the appointed day for the penalty points system (1 November 1982) but sentence was imposed after that day, the court was held to be obliged to endorse the appropriate number of penalty points for the offence (*Porter* v *Manning* (1984) *The Times*, 23, 24 March, 1 RTLB 27).

Where the defendant was sentenced before 1 November an order of endorsement counts as 3 penalty points unless a disqualification was imposed on that or any subsequent occasion (s 19(7)(*a*)). In *King* v *Luongo* (1984) *The Times*, 10 March, 1 RTLB 27, it was held that where an offender was convicted on the same occasion by the same court in respect of a number of offences committed on different dates, all those offences together only counted as 3 points.

## Procedure on Conviction

### 19.36–40 Production of driving licence for endorsement

Section 101(4) of the 1972 Act was amended by the Road Traffic Act 1974 to make clear beyond doubt the power of the courts to call for the licence following conviction of an obligatorily endorsable offence in order to discover what previous convictions are endorsed on the licence. The position, therefore, is that a person prosecuted for an offence involving obligatory endorsement must deliver his driving licence to the court or send it by registered or recorded delivery post or produce it at the hearing. If he is not convicted of the offence, he commits no offence if he has not sent or produced his licence to the court. If he is convicted of the offence, the court must require the licence to be produced to it and, if the court does not know his date of birth, must also require him to state his date of birth (s 104(1)). Under the former law (s 111(5) of the 1960 Act), the court could order production of the licence within five days or more; s 101, however, appears to allow no suspension of the requirement for production of the licence and, if it has not been sent or is not produced on conviction for an endorsable offence, it is suspended from the time of the making of the order for production. Under s 101(3A) of the 1972 Act where a person has been required under s 101(4) to produce his licence to the court and has failed to do so a constable may require him to produce it and upon it being produced may seize it and deliver it to the court. It would appear that if a defendant fails to produce the licence to the constable after being so required he commits an offence under s 101(4) unless he subsequently produces it at a police station of his choice within five days of the requirement.

Section 101(4A) in England and Wales and s 101(8) in Scotland make it clear beyond any doubt that the court is entitled to look at any endorsement on the licence and take it into account in determining sentence. In *Dyson* v *Ellison* [1975] Crim LR 48 (a case on s 101 before its amendment by the 1974 Act) it was held that the court should call for the licence after conviction in order to look at the licence to see if any convictions were endorsed upon it.

A court is entitled to adjourn after conviction under s 10(3) of the Magistrates' Courts Act 1980 and may quite properly do so for the production of the licence. Where a court does so adjourn it should not be for a period of longer than four weeks at a time (*R* v *Talgarth JJ, ex parte Bithell* [1974] RTR 546). Moreover s 10(3) requires that the court shall not have sentenced or dealt with the defendant on the first occasion; where the court fined the defendant in his absence and then adjourned under s 10(3) and disqualified him on the adjourned hearing, the disqualification was set aside on the ground that the magistrates had acted in excess of their jurisdiction (ibid). If a court is minded to adjourn, it should adjourn the whole question of sentencing and disposal and deal with the whole of the sentencing process at the adjourned hearing (ibid). But in *R* v *Manchester JJ, ex parte Miley* (1977) unreported, 16 February, it was held that s 10(3) was directory and not mandatory; a sentence will not be quashed because it was passed after an adjournment of more than four weeks in breach of s 10(3) (ibid).

On a conviction for an endorsable offence being announced, the court should look at the defendant's licence, if it has been sent to the clerk or the defendant voluntarily produces it, before deciding whether to endorse and disqualify; if the defendant is present and will not produce it voluntarily, an order for its production must be pronounced and then an offence arises under s 101(4) if it is not produced. If the defendant has not got it with him or he has not sent it, the court may adjourn so that it may be inspected at the adjourned hearing to see if there are previous convictions; on non-production, the court should order it to be produced and adjourn for not more than four weeks. During this period the police may make enquiries of the DVLC at Swansea and prove previous endorsements under s 182 of the Act (see 2.80), and may require the defendant to produce the licence and seize it under s 101(3A) (see below).

The above provisions as to production of a driving licence to the court appear to apply to Northern Irish driving licences (1972 Act, s 111(1)), but not to international driving licences, visiting forces' driver's permits or foreign domestic driving licences (Motor Vehicles (International Circulation) Order 1975) unless disqualification is ordered.

If the court has not received the offender's driving licence when the order for production is made, he is liable by s 101(4) to a fine of level 3 on the standard scale and his driving licence is suspended and of no effect until it is produced to the court. An offender who drives a motor vehicle on a road after conviction and prior to the production of the licence appears to offend against s 84 of the 1972 Act (driving without a licence) in addition to being liable to a fine under s 101(4), but not, it is thought, under s 99 for driving whilst disqualified. (Section 101(4) only 'suspends' the licence; the holder is not disqualified for 'holding or obtaining a licence'.) In certain circumstances, however, the defendant may be prosecuted for using a licence with intent to deceive, contrary to s 169. The Court of Appeal held the defendant to be 'clearly guilty' of this offence in *R* v *Bogdal* [1982] RTR 395 when he had been required under s 101(4) to produce a licence within seven days and within this period had been seen driving by a constable who had thereupon stopped him and asked for his licence which was then produced as a valid licence.

In any prosecution for disobedience to s 101(4) or under s 84 (as a result of the suspension of the licence for non-production to the court), presumably the prosecution must prove that the defendant was aware that he had been summoned for the offence. In proving that the defendant had received the summons, the Interpretation Act 1978, s 7, provides that a properly addressed letter is deemed to have been received, unless the contrary is proved, when it would be delivered in the ordinary course of post. Posting may be proved by the certificate endorsed on the duplicate summons. Rule 67(2) of the Magistrates' Courts Rules 1981 specifically allows proof of the posting, etc, by such a certificate 'in any proceedings before a magistrates' court'. Must the prosecution prove that the defendant had been informed that his licence was required for production? Although most summonses refer to his duty to produce it, the duty does not arise until he is convicted and an order for its production is made, and the prosecutor would be wise to prove that notice to produce it after conviction was duly given to the defendant, though, as disqualification is deemed effective as soon as it was ordered by the court (*Taylor* v *Kenyon* [1952] 2 All ER 726), the making of the order for production alone might suffice where the defendant claimed never to have been told of it. The duty to produce falls on 'the holder of a licence' (see s 101(4)); if he does not hold one or his licence expired before the conviction without prior production, seemingly he commits no offence of non-production. It will be seen from the text of s 101(4) (in Volume 2) that an offender is not guilty of an offence under the section nor is his licence suspended if his failure to produce the licence is caused by the fact that 'he has applied for a new licence and has not received it'; nor if he produces a receipt for his driving licence when it has been surrendered on receipt of a fixed penalty notice under s 27(1) or s 28(2) of the Transport Act 1982 (not yet in force in England and Wales), provided that he produces the licence to the court 'immediately on its return' (see s 36(4) of the 1982 Act).

Where the name or address on a licence holder ceases to be correct, the licence is required by s 89(3) of the Act forthwith to surrender the licence and furnish particulars of the alteration. On surrender of the licence, the

Secretary of State for Transport may then furnish the person who has surrendered his licence with 'a new licence' (s 89(4)). The opinion is given in a 'Practical Point' in (1977) 141 JP Jo 74, that a surrender for a new licence under s 89(3) as described does not amount, in law, to an application for a new licence for the purposes of s 101(4) and that, therefore, a person who complies with s 89(3) and does not receive his new licence back in time to produce it to court commits an offence under s 101(4) and, if he drives, is guilty of the offence of driving without a licence. It is submitted that although it is possible to argue that this might technically be a possible interpretation of the relevant statutory provisions, this interpretation of s 101(4) and s 89(3) is wrong. Both s 89(4) and s 101(4) refer to a 'new licence', and the purpose of the defence to s 101(4) is to prevent the conviction of a person who genuinely cannot produce his licence because he is awaiting a new licence.

If the offender is not at the time of his conviction the holder of a driving licence (*semble*, a current one), he must by s 101(6) disclose particulars of the endorsement ordered when he next applies for the grant or renewal of his licence. Further, a licence granted or renewed without such disclosure is of no effect and a person who drives on a licence so obtained offends against s 84 (driving without a licence) and, if he had never previously held a licence, he may not be covered by a policy of insurance in breach of s 143. If a defendant charged under s 101(6) or s 84 as mentioned above claims he never received the summons for the original endorsable offence, he may not be guilty but, if he had had the summons, but particulars of the order for endorsement had not been sent to him, it may be that the non-sending would not be a defence (cf *Taylor* v *Kenyon* [1952] 2 All ER 726).

The court cannot require the production of a driving licence to inspect it for endorsements if the offender is convicted of an offence which does not carry endorsement.

## Removal of Endorsement

### 19.41 Application for removal of endorsement

Once an endorsement ceases to be effective, the licence holder is entitled to apply to the DVLC for a new licence free from the endorsement on payment of the prescribed fee and on the surrender of the subsisting licence (s 101(7) as substituted by para 12 of Sched 9 of the Transport Act 1981).

The periods are laid down by s 101(7A) (as added by para 12 of Sched 9 to the Transport Act 1981) as follows:

(*a*) if an order is made for the disqualification of the offender, until four years have elapsed since the *conviction*;

(*b*) if no order of disqualification is made, until either four years have elapsed since the *commission* of the offence or an order of disqualification is made;

(*c*) if the offence is causing death by reckless driving or reckless driving, the endorsement in any event must remain effective until four years have elapsed since the *conviction* of the offence; and

(*d*) if the offence is driving or attempting to drive while unfit (s 5(1)) or driving or attempting to drive with excess alcohol (s 6(1)(*a*) or the former s 6(1)) or refusing to provide evidential specimens of breath, blood or urine (s 8(7) or the former s 9(3)) while driving or attempting to drive, until eleven years have elapsed after the *conviction* (a close analysis of the former s 101(7) or the present s 101(7A) leads to the conclusion that the period of eleven years applies to any conviction for these offences even if a disqualification was not imposed for 'special reasons').

# Chapter 20

# Disqualification

## General Principles

### 20.1 Summary

The principles of disqualification contained in the 1972 Act are summarised below; their detailed application is discussed in the subsequent sections of this chapter.

*Obligatory orders of disqualification*

(1) A court is obliged to disqualify an offender for at least twelve months when he is convicted of an 'obligatorily disqualifiable offence' (see 20.16) unless the court is able to find 'special reasons' (see Chapter 21) for not doing so.

(2) A court is obliged to disqualify an offender for at least six months when he is convicted of offences totalling 12 or more penalty points (see 20.18) unless the court is able to find 'mitigating circumstances' for not doing so (see Chapter 21).

*Discretionary orders of disqualification*

(1) A court may disqualify for any endorsable offence (but cannot do so in respect of a non-endorsable offence).

(2) The Crown Court may disqualify under s 44 of the Powers of Criminal Courts Act 1973 where a motor vehicle has been used for crime in respect of *any* indictable offence punishable with imprisonment of two years or more (see 20.31).

(3) Any court may disqualify an offender until he passes a test of competence to drive on convicting him of any endorsable offence (see 20.32).

(4) A magistrates' court may disqualify an offender who has been convicted of an endorsable offence when committing him for sentence to the Crown Court (see 20.33).

*Period and commencement of disqualification*

All orders of disqualification commence immediately and cannot be postponed (except when suspended pending the hearing of an appeal; see 22.3) and cannot be made consecutive to any other order of disqualification.

*Escaping disqualification by deception*

Where a court is deceived regarding any circumstances that were or might have been taken into account in deciding whether or for how long to disqualify an offender when dealing with him for an endorsable offence, then if the deception constituted or was due to an offence committed by that person, on conviction of that offence the court have the same powers and duties regarding an order of disqualification as the original court, but must take into account any order made on his conviction of the original endorsable offence (see 20.37).

*Notification of disease or disability*

A court must notify the Secretary of State for Transport if an offender suffers from any prescribed disease or disability which may render his driving a source of danger to the public (see 20.38).

*Removal of disqualification*

Application may be made to the court for the removal of any order of disqualification for a period of more than two years (see 20.41).

## 20.2 Scope and effect of disqualification

A person may be disqualified without any other sentence, such as a fine, being passed on him for the offence (*R* v *Bignell* (1968) 52 Cr App R 10), but Brian Harris in *The Criminal Jurisdiction of Magistrates*, states that an order of disqualification is not a sentence but merely an order ancillary to sentence, his argument being expanded in an article at 131 JP Jo 677. *R* v *Surrey Quarter Sessions, ex parte Commissioner of Police* [1963] 1 QB 990, which is to the contrary, was not cited to the court in *Bignell* but it is nevertheless considered that unless and until *Bignell* is reconsidered by the Court of Appeal it may be relied on. It is, however, submitted that if a court does not wish to impose any penalty other than disqualification, it is proper to make an order of absolute discharge.

A person who holds a foreign driving licence, an international driving licence or a visting forces' driving permit is, if disqualified by a court in Great Britain, forbidden to drive on roads in Great Britain even though his foreign licence is still valid (Motor Vehicles (International Circulation) Order 1975 (SI 1975 No 1208), art 2(4)); moreover s 99 (*b*) forbids a person to drive when disqualified for holding or obtaining a licence issued under the 1972 Act.

The effect of a disqualification is that the defendant may not drive in Great Britain a motor vehicle of any type on a road which is a highway or to which the public have access (see 1.66) during the period of disqualification, but he may drive on private land or on places which are not 'roads'. If a disqualified farmer drives straight across the highway on a tractor from one field to another he commits an offence, though the brevity of the journey and lack of any other vehicles when he crosses might possibly be a 'special reason' (see *Coombs* v *Kehoe* and other cases at 'Shortness of distance driven', 21.8). A British disqualification does not forbid driving abroad but the driver must comply with the foreign law as to licences.

There is now no power to limit disqualification to the type of vehicle in use at the time of the offence. If disqualification is imposed, the defendant is disqualified from driving all types of motor vehicle and for all purposes.

'Disqualified' in a policy was held to mean 'disqualified by order of the court' and not to cover the case of a person who had been refused renewal of his driving licence because of mental deficiency (*Edwards* v *Griffiths* [1953] 2 All ER 874). The offence of driving under age was put an end to by the Road Traffic (Drivers' Ages and Hours of Work) Act 1976. Section 96 of the 1972 Act provides that a person is disqualified for holding or obtaining a licence to drive a motor vehicle if he is under the minimum age specified for the particular class of motor vehicle. An under-age driver may thus be prosecuted for driving while disqualified. Some police forces instead prosecute under-age drivers for driving without holding a driving licence.

Where the holder of a licence is disqualified by order of a court, the licence shall be treated as having been revoked from the beginning of the period of disqualification or, if suspended, from the day on which the suspension ceases (s 98, as amended). One effect is that, before an offender may drive after a period of disqualification has ceased, he must apply for a new driving licence. If he drives after the period of disqualification without doing so he commits the offence of driving without holding a licence contrary to s 84 of the Act.

## 20.3 Undertaking not to drive

Sometimes a defendant will give an undertaking to the court that he will not drive again, and the court may refrain from disqualifying in reliance on this undertaking. Should he then drive again, 'vows, etcetera, deriding', the books on criminal law do not mention such a breach as being the crime of contempt, but breaches of an undertaking to the courts in general are mentioned in 9 *Halsbury's Laws* (4th ed) 44 as being contempts. It is suggested that, in such a case, the matter should be reported to the Director of Public Prosecutions.

If the defendant has surrendered his licence, after having given such an undertaking, he may be prosecuted for driving without a licence because, having given up his licence to the Department of Transport, he is no longer the holder of it.

## 20.4 Period and commencement of disqualification

Every order of disqualification must commence from the moment the order is pronounced; it cannot be ordered to run consecutively to any other order of disqualification or to an order of imprisonment (*R* v *Meese* [1973] RTR 400; *R* v *Higgins* [1973] RTR 216; *R* v *Bain* [1974] RTR 213; *R* v *Graham*, below).

The former order of disqualification for 'totting up' under s 93(3) of the 1972 Act was required to be consecutive or additional to any other order of disqualification. Its successor (the 'penalty points' disqualification under s 19 of the Transport Act 1981) must, by contrast, commence like any other order of disqualification from the moment the order is made.

The usual minimum periods in the absence of 'special reasons' are six months for a penalty points disqualification and twelve months for an obligatorily disqualifiable offence. These periods and when the minimum periods are increased are discussed at 20.17 and 20.21, respectively.

In all cases disqualifications should be for a specified period and not for an indefinite one (*R* v *Fowler* [1937] 2 All ER 380). Offences for which disqualification is a proper penalty should not be taken into consideration when sentence is being passed for a different offence (*R* v *Collins* [1947] 1 All ER 147), but it is permissible to take into consideration another offence of a similar kind (*R* v *Jones* [1970] 3 All ER 815). Disqualification is effective as soon as it is ordered by the court (*Taylor* v *Kenyon* [1952] 2 All ER 726) and a disqualification expressed to run from the day of release from prison is void (*R* v *Graham* [1955] Crim LR 319). When it is imposed along with imprisonment, the period of disqualification should not be so short that most of it will have expired on release from prison (*R* v *Phillips* (1955) 119 JP 499) but in *R* v *Pashley* [1973] RTR 149 a defendant sentenced to twelve months' imprisonment and disqualified for three years had the disqualification reduced to twelve months on the ground that the imprisonment was the deterrent and he would face financial difficulties when leaving prison, strengthening the temptation to drive while disqualified. It is submitted that the correct sentencing policy is not to impose a very lengthy period of disqualification unless the defendant's driving record shows that the public needs to be protected against his being allowed to drive. In *R* v *McLaughlin* [1978] RTR 452 the Court of Appeal, after observing that very long peiods of disqualification may be said to be counter-productive, upheld a twenty-year period of disqualification where the defendant had a drink problem, did not recognise that he had a problem, and had previous convictions and where in the opinion of the court there was a serious risk that he would injure or kill someone if allowed to drive.

Unless its minimum period be limited by statute, the disqualification can be for such period, long or short, as the court orders. It should nevertheless be borne in mind that an order of disqualification, no matter how short, revokes a driving licence (s 98 of the 1972 Act as amended by the 1974 Act). The effect is that a motorist who has been disqualified may not drive after the end of the period of disqualification unless he has applied for a new licence. If he has not applied and drives after his disqualification has ended he commits the offence of driving without a driving licence. Obligatory orders of disqualification have minimum periods, but no maximum periods; but if a period less than the statutory minimum is imposed, the High Court may substitute the period allowed by law (Administration of Justice Act 1960, s 16).

The court should decide on the period of disqualification which is appropriate to the facts of the case; it is wrong for the court in pronouncing sentence to advert to the fact that the defendant after the appropriate period can apply for restoration of his licence under s 95 (*R* v *Lobley* [1974] RTR 550). Disqualification for life was upheld in *R* v *Wallace* [1955] NI 137 and in *R* v *Tunde-Olarinde* [1967] 2 All ER 491, but the policy of the Court of Appeal is increasingly to discourage disqualification for life or for very long periods, particularly where the offender is young. Thus in *R* v *Ward* [1971] Crim LR 665, a 'bad case of dangerous driving' by a person sentenced to borstal, disqualification was varied from life to five years. Likewise in *R* v *Lee* [1971] Crim LR 177 a disqualification for another young man sentenced to borstal was reduced from ten to three years. Indeed in *R* v *North* [1971] RTR 366 (applied in *R* v *Ward* above) it was said that 'unless there were unusual circumstances a disqualification for life is wrong in principle'. The danger of imposing long consecutive periods of disqualification was, of course, recognised by Parliament itself when enacting the Road Traffic (Disqualification) Act 1970 (repealed by and incorporated in the 1972 Act: see in particular para 7 of Sched 10 to the Act), which removed the offence of driving while disqualified from the list of offences involving obligatory disqualification and allowed persons who had been disqualified for 'additional' periods for that offence to apply for their removal (see 20.44). In the 'guideline' sentencing case of *R* v *Boswell* (see 5.88) the Court of Appeal drew a distinction (in relation to cases of causing death by reckless driving and reckless driving) between offences such as driving while disqualified where no bad driving may be involved and offences of causing death by reckless driving and reckless driving which, by definition, entail bad or wicked driving for which long periods of disqualification are usually appropriate.

Disqualification starts to run on the day on which the order of disqualification is made, even though that day is later than the day of conviction, eg because there has been an adjournment (see below). The day on which the order is made counts as one full day of the period of disqualification and the defendant may not drive from the moment when the court pronounces the order; someone else must drive his vehicle away from the court unless notice of appeal in writing is given and the court suspends the disqualification. Thus, a disqualification for twelve months imposed on the afternoon of 1 January will expire at midnight on 31 December. If an unlawful period of disqualification has been imposed and the High Court substitutes the correct period, that runs from the date of the magistrates' original decision, unless the High Court otherwise orders (Administration of Justice Act 1960, s 16). Time during which the disqualification was suspended is disregarded (Road Traffic Act 1972, s 94(4)). There is no power to disqualify from the driving of any type of vehicle other than a motor vehicle or trolley vehicle.

### 20.5–15 Attempts

Whether there is power or a duty on a court to disqualify depends on whether an attempt to commit the offence is itself endorsable. This is discussed at 19.9.

## Obligatory Disqualifications

### 20.16 Obligatory disqualification

On conviction for an offence involving obligatory disqualification (see the table at 19.2), the offender must (save as mentioned below) be disqualified for holding or obtaining a licence to drive a motor vehicle for not less than twelve months (1972 Act, s 93(1)). See 20.17 below as to the three-year compulsory disqualification for committing within ten years of a previous conviction a second drink/driving offence. The requirements of s 93(1) apply on first or subsequent conviction, save that for reckless driving under s 2 it applies only on commission of a second or subsequent offence if the date of the offence (not conviction) is within three years of the date of a previous conviction under s 1 or s 2. *Semble*, under s 102(2) of the 1972 Act, if a defendant in England or Wales was put on probation or absolutely or conditionally discharged, this counts as a conviction, if it was endorsed.

There cannot be a disqualification in the defendant's absence unless the case has been adjourned to give him an opportunity to be present and he has been warned in the notice of adjournment of the intention to disqualify (s 11(4) of the Magistrates' Courts Act 1980).

The court may only refrain from imposing the twelve-month or three-year disqualification for any offence involving obligatory disqualification or impose a shorter period of disqualification:

(*a*) if there are special reasons (see Chapter 21), when the court may either not disqualify at all or disqualify for less than twelve months (s 93(1)) (or for less than three years on a second 'drink' conviction);

(*b*) if the offenders are aiders and abettors, counsellers or procurers of an obligatorily disqualifiable offence, when they need not be disqualified (s 93(6) but otherwise incur 10 penalty points (see 19.10)).

(*c*) where, under the Mental Health Act 1983, s 37(3), the court is satisfied as to the offence and makes a guardianship or hospital order 'without convicting him', when, presumably, there can be no disqualification or endorsement at all as there is no 'conviction'.

A person ordered to perform community service must also be disqualified if sentenced for an obligatorily disqualifiable offence (s 14(8) of the Powers of Criminal Courts Act 1973).

The effect of an obligatory disqualification is that the defendant has removed from his licence all previous penalty points (see 20.20). The disqualification counts, however, as a disqualification for the purpose of any increase in the minimum period of a penalty points disqualification (see 20.21).

In England and Wales, he must be disqualified, unless there are special reasons, on the making of an order for probation or absolute or conditional discharge for an offence for which disqualification is obligatory (Road Traffic Act 1972, s 102(1); *Owen* v *Imes* [1972] RTR 489).

The disqualification imposed under s 93(1) must be imposed even if the court is obliged also to impose a penalty points disqualification.

The court may at its discretion disqualify for a longer period than the obligatory period of twelve months or three years.

Any order of disqualification, whether it be discretionary or obligatory, must run from the moment it is pronounced (*R* v *Higgins* [1973] RTR 216; *R* v *Bain* [1973] RTR 213); likewise, it seems, a penalty points disqualification or, indeed, any other order of disqualification. Thus where a defendant was disqualified for two and a half years on one count of causing death by dangerous driving and two and a half years on another count of driving with excess blood-alcohol, the order of the trial judge that the two periods of disqualification should run consecutively was set aside by the Court of Appeal, who ordered them to run concurrently (*R* v *Meese* [1973] RTR 400). Where an offender was liable to both an order of obligatory disqualification for an offence and an order of disqualification for penalty points, the Court of Appeal made one order of disqualification only in *R* v *Elliott* (*R* v *Boswell* etc [1984] 1 WLR 1047, 1 RTLB 45).

Where the court does not disqualify in a case under s 93(1) or disqualifies for a shorter period, the 'special reasons' must be stated in open court and, if a magistrates' court or, in Scotland, a court of summary jurisdiction, entered in the register (1972 Act, s 105(1)), but failure to state them aloud does not invalidate the decision (*Brown* v *Dyerson* [1968] 3 All ER 39).

## 20.17 Second conviction for drink/driving etc offences

A previous conviction in the ten years preceding the commission of a second such offence for driving or attempted driving when unfit through drink or drugs, for driving or attempted driving with alcohol concentration above the prescribed limit or for refusing to give a specimen for analysis or a laboratory test when the accused had been driving or attempting to drive at the relevant time brings a three-year minimum obligatory disqualification on subsequent conviction for any one of those three offences (1972 Act, s 93(4)). Consequently a person convicted in 1985 of driving with excess blood-alcohol must be disqualified for three years if within the ten years prior to the date of the commission of the offence for which he was convicted in 1985 he had been *convicted* of driving a motor vehicle contrary to s 6 of the Road Traffic Act 1960 (driving whilst unfit), or s 1 of the Road Safety Act 1967 (excess blood-alcohol), or refusing to supply a specimen of blood or urine when at the relevant time he was driving a motor vehicle. It should be noted that the ten-year period is calculated from the date of *commission* of the second offence back to the date of *conviction* of the earlier offence. An offender just within the ten-year period cannot therefore avoid his liability to a three-year disqualification by obtaining an adjournment. These provisions do not apply where the conviction is for being in charge or refusing to supply a specimen while in charge at the relevant time, but do apply where the previous conviction was for aiding or abetting a drink/driving offence (*Makeham* v *Donaldson* [1981] RTR 511). It should also be noted that offenders convicted of attempting to drive are liable to three years' disqualification whether the first or second offence (or both) was only attempting to drive.

See further 4.124.

## 20.18 Summary of penalty points disqualification

The penalty points system came into operation on 1 November 1982. Every endorsable offence attracts a fixed or variable number of penalty points. The number of points to be imposed for the particular offences is set out in the table at 19.2 and discussed in detail at 19.21–7. The system is set out in s 19 of and Sched 7 to the Transport Act 1981 (as amended).

Unlike the former 'totting up' disqualification under s 93(3) of the 1972 Act, a penalty points disqualification is not additional or consecutive to any other order of disqualification. Like any other type of disqualification, unless suspended pending the hearing of an appeal, it takes effect from the moment it is made and cannot be postponed to take effect at a later date or to be made consecutive to any other order of disqualification. Again unlike the former order of 'totting up' disqualification under s 93(3), where an offender is dealt with on the same occasion by a court in respect of a number of endorsable offences, the court is required to make only one order of penalty points disqualification (see 20.21).

Again unlike the former order of disqualification for totting up under s 93(3), where an offender appears before the court for one or more offences which were not *committed* on the same occasion, each of the offences committed on different occasions incurs the imposition of penalty points (see 19.26).

Where a penalty points disqualification is imposed the court (as with any other order of disqualification) is required to notify the DVLC. The code used for a penalty points disqualification is TT99.

A penalty points disqualification (like most other orders of disqualification) removes from the defendant's licence any previous penalty points (see 20.20) and counts as a disqualification for the purpose of increasing the period of a subsequent penalty points disqualification (see 20.21).

A court is obliged to impose the minimum period of a penalty points disqualification unless 'having regard to all the circumstances there are grounds for mitigating the normal consequences of the conviction'. Certain mitigating circumstances which were previously possible when a defendant sought to escape a 'totting up' disqualification are now, however, specifically excluded (see Chapter 21).

A court is required (in the absence of 'mitigating circumstances'; see Chapter 21) to impose a penalty points disqualification under s 19 of the Transport Act 1981 when an offender is convicted of any endorsable offence when the number of penalty points for that offence and others which have to be taken into account under s 19(3) amount to twelve or more.

## 20.19 Penalty points required to be taken into account

The points required to be taken into account under s 19(3) are:

(*a*) the points that would be imposed on the occasion of the present conviction; and

(*b*) any points that were on a previous occasion ordered to be endorsed, except that:

  (i) no points will be taken into account if since that occasion and before conviction the offender has been disqualified (see 20.20); and

  (ii) points will not be added to each other where any of the offences in respect of which points were imposed was committed more than three years before another.

These rules at first sight seem complicated and it may assist if a number of examples of their operation are given. (In these examples it is assumed that all the offences took place after s 19 was brought into operation.)

*Example 1*

| *Offence* | *Date of offence* | *Sentence* |
|---|---|---|
| Tyre | 1.1.83 | 3 points |
| Careless driving | 1.7.83 | 5 points |
| No insurance | 1.9.84 | 3 points |
| Speeding | 1.12.85 | (instant offence) |

In this example the court is required to consider disqualifying as soon as he has been convicted of all the offences. It will be noted that all the offences took place within three years of each other and he was not disqualified for any of them.

*Example 2*

| *Offence* | *Date of offence* | *Sentence* | *Date of conviction* |
|---|---|---|---|
| Tyre | 1.1.83 | 3 points | 2.4.83 |
| Careless driving | 1.7.83 | 5 points | 4.9.83 |
| No insurance | 1.9.84 | Disqualified 6 months | 2.11.84 |
| Speeding | 1.12.85 | (instant offence) | |

In this case it will be noted that the court is not obliged to disqualify: although all the offences were committed within three years of each other, the disqualification imposed on 2 November 1984 'wiped the slate clean' (see 20.20).

*Example 3*

| *Offence* | *Date of offence* | *Sentence* | *Date of conviction* |
|---|---|---|---|
| Tyre | 1.1.83 | 3 points | 4.3.83 |
| Careless driving | 1.7.83 | 5 points | 12.9.83 |
| No insurance | 1.8.83 | Disqualified 1 month | 1.9.83 |
| Taking and driving away | 1.12.85 | (instant offence) | |

In this case the court is obliged to consider disqualifying because despite the defendant being disqualified for the insurance offence the careless driving points were not 'wiped clean' because they were imposed after the conviction and disqualification for the insurance offence (the offence of taking and driving away incurs 8 points).

*Example 4*

| *Offence* | *Date of offence* | *Sentence* | *Date of conviction* |
|---|---|---|---|
| Reckless driving | 1.1.83 | 10 points | 1.4.83 |
| Reckless driving | 2.1.86 | (instant offence) | |

In this instance the court is not obliged to impose a penalty points disqualification but is obliged to consider disqualifying for the offence because although the dates of commission of the offences are more than three years apart, the second reckless driving offence was committed within three years of the conviction of the earlier offence and thus becomes an obligatorily disqualifiable offence (see 5.74).

*Example 5*

| *Offence* | *Date of offence* | *Sentence* | *Date of conviction* |
|---|---|---|---|
| Tyre | 1.1.83 | 3 points | 1.4.83 |
| Careless driving | 1.7.83 | | (10.10.84) |
| No insurance | 1.9.84 | 7 points | 1.10.84 |

It would seem that where an endorsable offence committed before another is dealt with after a later offence was dealt with, the court is usually required under s 19(3) to take into account the number of points imposed in respect of the later offence when the court comes to deal with the earlier offence. Assuming the sentence for careless driving is dealt with on 10.10.84, the court is then obliged to consider a penalty points disqualification.

*Example 6*

| *Offence* | *Date of offence* | *Sentence* | *Date of conviction* |
|---|---|---|---|
| Tyre | 1.1.82 | 3 points | 1.9.82 |
| Speeding | 1.4.82 | 3 points | 1.12.82 |
| No insurance | 30.3.84 | (6) points | (1.12.85) |
| Careless driving | 2.3.85 | 2 points | 1.10.85 |

Where, however, the earliest offence and the latest offence are more than three years apart and the offence for which the court is sentencing the offender took place between the dates of the earliest offence and the latest offence, the points for the earliest offence and the latest offence cannot both be included in the total computation. In such a case some commentators suggest the wording of the proviso to s 19(3) requires the court not to take into account the points in respect of both offences.

In this example the court have fixed 6 as the appropriate number of points to be imposed in respect of the insurance offence being dealt with on 1.12.85. It is submitted that the court is obliged to impose a penalty points disqualification.

Some commentators have argued that a strict interpretation of the proviso to s 19(3) requires the court to ignore the points for the earliest offence and only take into account the points of the latest offence. This seems to be wrong. The proviso only requires them not to be added to each other. It may nevertheless be argued that s 19(3) should be interpreted in the same way as s 19(4) where the relevant periods are much more clearly expressed. This would involve interpreting the words 'the other' at the conclusion of s 19(3) as meaning 'the other or others'. The Interpretation Act 1978 requires the singular to include the plural unless the context otherwise requires. If this latter interpretation is correct it will result in a defendant in an example similar to that given being able to avoid a penalty points disqualification by virtue of his having committed a subsequent offence. This cannot have been the intention of Parliament.

## 20.20 'Wiping the slate clean'

The effect of s 19(3)(*b*) seems to be that as soon as a disqualification is ordered points imposed before an order of disqualification no longer count towards any future possible disqualification. It should be noted that it would seem that if a person commits two offences on different occasions and the earlier offence is dealt after the later offence, the defendant's licence is not wiped clean if the court convicts and disqualifies for the later offence before the earlier offence has been dealt with (see Example 3 above).

It must also be noted that *any* disqualification under s 19(2) or s 93 of the 1972 Act wipes the slate clean. The only disqualifications which do not have this effect are those under s 103 of the 1972 Act (interim disqualification on committal to the Crown Court), s 44 of the Powers of Criminal Courts Act 1973 (disqualification by the Crown Court where vehicle used for commission of offence) (see 20.31) and a disqualification under s 21 of the Transport Act 1981 (see 20.37). Not only does any type of disqualification wipe the slate clean (including a disqualification under s 93(7): until a person passes a test of competence to drive), but any period of disqualification suffices, no matter how short.

Section 19(3) states that penalty points for an offence must be added to penalty points for another if the former offence was committed 'more than three years' before the other. It would seem therefore that if the earlier offence was committed on 1 January 1983 and the later offence on 1 January 1986, the court is not required to consider disqualification because although the earlier offence was committed three years before the later offence, it was committed 'more than' three years before the other (as to earlier offences being dealt with later than subsequent offences, see Examples 5 and 6 above).

**20.21–9 Period of disqualification**

The statutory period of a penalty points disqualification is a *minimum* period of six months. Unlike the former 'totting up' disqualification (which by s 9(5) of the 1972 Act was required to be 'additional'), it is concurrent with any other period of disqualification and, it would seem, like any order of obligatory disqualification under s 91(1) or discretionary disqualification under s 92(2) cannot be ordered to be consecutive (*R* v *Higgins* [1973] RTR 216; *R* v *Bain* [1974] RTR 213). It is submitted that the absence of a specific statutory provision allowing or requiring a penalty points disqualification to be made consecutive was deliberate and that, as in other orders of disqualification, a penalty points disqualification must commence from the moment it is pronounced. The only circumstances where this is not the case is where an order is suspended pending an appeal (see 22.3).

It will also be noted that s 19(4) refers to six months as the 'minimum period'. There seems no distinction between the 'minimum period' of six months in s 19(4) and the period of 'at least' six months in s 93(3). The Inter-Departmental Committee (see 19.21) envisaged (Annex G, para 8, of the committee's report) that a court when imposing a discretionary or obligatory disqualification should, in determining the period of disqualification, have regard to any penalty points already incurred. No express statutory provision to this effect has been made (other than s 19(5): see below) but it is submitted that a court, when determining a period of disqualification, should take into account the amount of points that will be wiped clean and the extent to which the penalty points would be exceeded if he were not disqualified. The period under s 19(2) is a minimum period and should not become the tariff period, it is submitted.

Section 19(4) provides that the minimum period shall be twelve months if there has been a previous disqualification imposed within the three years immediately preceding the latest offence in respect of which penalty points are to be taken into account. The subsection further provides that the minimum period shall be two years if there have been two such previous disqualifications. It seems clear from a reading of the subsection (particularly when one refers to s 19(9)) that the word 'disqualification' in s 19(4) refers not only to a previous penalty points disqualification under s 19(2), but also to any type of disqualification including, it seems, one imposed under s 21 of the Transport Act 1981 (see 20.34). Thus an offender who was disqualified for an offence and at the same time disqualified under s 19(2) is liable to a minimum period of two years' disqualification should he be liable to be disqualified again under s 19(2) within the three-year period. Like the period in s 19(3) (see above) the period of three years referred to in s 19(4) would seem to include the last day and exclude the first day.

Section 19(5) requires a court, when an offender is convicted on the same occasion of more than one offence involving discretionary or obligatory disqualification, to take into account in determining the period of disqualification 'all the offences'. The subsection further states that no more than one order under s 19(2) shall be made, but for the purposes of appeal the order shall be treated as being made on the conviction of each of the offences. As already stated, although no express statutory provision has been made (other than s 19(5)) requiring a court when determining a period of disqualification to have regard to the number of points already imposed, it is submitted that, by reason of the 'wiping the slate clean' provisions and the fact that the period under s 19(2) is expressed as a 'minimum' period, a court should, whenever imposing a discretionary, obligatory or penalty points disqualification, have regard to the number, if any, of penalty points that will be wiped off by reason of the disqualification and also the number of points which the offender would incur but for the disqualification. A court must distinguish one offender from another and do justice as between offenders. It is submitted therefore that where, for example, an offender who already has 10 or 11 points is then convicted of, for example, reckless driving (which itself carries 10 points), he normally should be disqualified for a longer period than an offender who commits offences the total points value of which only just reaches 12.

## Discretionary Disqualifications

### 20.30 Exercise of discretionary power

It should be noted that the offences for which the court has a discretionary power of disqualification under s 93(2) are all those offences for which endorsement is obligatory but which do not involve obligatory disqualification under s 93(1) (see the table at 19.2). It is entirely a matter for the court whether or not to order disqualification, and, if so, for how long in a case where the court has a discretion to disqualify, subject to these qualifications:

(1) In England and Wales an offender may be disqualified at the court's discretion on making an order for probation or absolute or conditional discharge (Road Traffic Act 1972, s 102).

(2) A person who has pleaded guilty in writing under s 12 of the Magistrates' Courts Act 1980 may not be disqualified in his absence unless he has been given the opportunity of attending at an adjourned hearing (see s 11(4) of the 1980 Act. The notification of the adjourned hearing must indicate the reason for the adjournment, ie that the magistrates are considering disqualification (*R* v *Mason* [1965] 2 All ER 308; s 11(4)). Disqualification may be ordered in his absence if he has been duly notified and does not attend. The same rule was held to apply in 'totting up' cases under s 93(3) (*R* v *Llandrindod Wells JJ, ex parte Gibson* (1968) 112 SJ 218) and, no doubt, applies to all other types of disqualification as s 11(4) of the 1980 Act is general in its terms.

Where the procedure of the 1980 Act for a plea of guilty in his absence has not been used for the first hearing but the defendant has been summoned and fails to attend he may not be disqualified in his absence at that first hearing, but the case should be adjourned to give him the opportunity of attending and the notice of adjournment given to him should give the reason for the adjournment (1980 Act, s 11(4)). Any disqualification imposed in a defendant's absence in breach of what is now s 11(4) of the 1980 Act is invalid notwithstanding that the disqualification was mandatory and that the defendant knew that he might be disqualified (*R* v *Bishop's Stortford JJ, ex parte Shields* (1968) 113 SJ 124). If he fails to attend at the adjourned hearing he may then be disqualified. An absent defendant represented by counsel or solicitor is deemed not to be absent (1980 Act, s 122).

(3) An aider and abettor of an offence involving obligatory or discretionary disqualification may be disqualified, but the court is not obliged to do so (s 93(6); *Ullah* v *Luckhurst* [1977] Crim LR 295). As to persons convicted of attempts, see 20.5.

(4) Where the Mental Health Act 1983, s 37(3), applies, disqualification may not be ordered.

(5) Where the defendant has been convicted of a Construction and Use Regulation offence as to dangerous condition, dangerously unsuitable use, insecure load, or brakes, steering or tyres etc (see 8.46), he may not be disqualified if he did not know and had no reasonable cause to suspect that the facts of the case were such that that offence would be committed (1972 Act, Sched 4, Part I, offences contrary to s 40(5), column 5).

(6) The whole of the sentence, including any order of disqualification, should normally be imposed on the same occasion (*R* v *Talgarth JJ, ex parte Bithell* [1973] RTR 546; *R* v *Fairhead* [1975] Crim LR 351), but a Crown Court was able to adjourn a question of disqualification for possible 'totting up' disqualification when neither the defendant's licence nor details of previous endorsements were available. Under these circumstances the Crown

Court might have sentenced immediately and postponed the question of disqualification (*R* v *Annesly* [1976] RTR 150).

(7) A discretionary order of disqualification, no matter how short, like any other type of disqualification (subject to three exceptions) has the effect of wiping off the offender's licence all previous penalty points (see 20.20).

## 20.31 Disqualification where vehicle used for crime

The Criminal Justice Act 1972 introduced two new orders where motor vehicles are used for the purposes of crime. The first was an order entitling a court to deprive the offender of his property rights in a motor vehicle which had been used for the purposes of a crime. (This power is described at 18.25.) The second is a power of disqualification for driving or holding or obtaining a driving licence. This power of disqualification is now contained in s 44 of the Powers of Criminal Courts Act 1973 (see Volume 2). The power can only be exercised by the Crown Court and applies only where a person is convicted on indictment of an offence punishable on indictment with imprisonment for a term of two years or more or, having been convicted of such an offence, is committed to the Crown Court for sentence by a magistrates' court under s 35 of the Magistrates' Courts Act 1980.

The court is under a duty to require the person disqualified to produce his licence to the court. If he does not do so he commits an offence under s 101(4) of the 1972 Act (see 19.36) of failing to produce a licence (s 44(3) of the Powers of Criminal Courts Act 1973). An order of disqualification under the section may be removed, like any other disqualification, under s 95 of the 1972 Act (s 44(3); for s 95 see 20.41). It would seem that an order under s 44 may be suspended pending the hearing of an appeal under s 94(2) of the 1972 Act, as s 94(2) does not seem to be limited to an order of disqualification made under the Act. The order of disqualification in *R* v *Ackers* [1977] RTR 661 was suspended by a single judge pending the hearing of the appeal by the full Court of Appeal.

The court cannot order the licence to be endorsed, because the power of endorsement only applies to the offences referred to in s 101(1) of the 1972 Act. For this reason a conviction of an offence for which the defendant is disqualified under s 44 does not count as a conviction for the purpose of a penalty points disqualification under s 19 of the Transport Act 1981. Neither does such a disqualification wipe the offender's licence clean (see 20.20) nor count as a disqualification so that the minimum period of a penalty points disqualification is increased (s 19(9) of the Transport Act 1981).

The court is obliged to send notice of the disqualification (code NE) to the Department of Transport (s 105 of the 1972 Act).

It will be noted that the motor vehicle does not have to be actually used in the course of the crime; it merely has to have been used for the purposes of committing or facilitating the offence. Note also the very wide definition of 'facilitating' in s 43(2) of the Powers of Criminal Courts Act 1973. Moreover the offender does not have to be the person driving the vehicle; the only requirement is that the person be convicted of an offence in respect of which the motor vehicle was used.

An offender allowed himself to be carried as a passenger in a motor vehicle to ten separate banks, at each of which he drew £30 on a stolen cheque. While he was in the bank, an accomplice in the car prepared a duplicate cheque-book for use at the next bank to be visited. It was held that the motor vehicle was used by the defendant for the purpose of facilitating the commission of offences (*R* v *Mathews* [1975] RTR 32).

Although the section is in very wide terms, the provision seems primarily designed to enable the courts to disqualify 'the motor man', the driver of the getaway car, in a serious crime such as a wages snatch or bank robbery. In *Mathews* above the Court of Appeal, although holding that the trial judge was legally entitled to disqualify the offender, allowed his appeal against the sentence of disqualification, since the vehicle was not used as a getaway car. Moreover, as the offender was sentenced to prison for five years, it was unnecessary and undesirable that he should have the additional penalty of disqualification when he was released, which could hinder him in earning an honest living. On the other hand, where an offender was paid £50 to drive a vehicle containing carpets worth £33,000 stolen from a warehouse, his disqualification for two and a half years, together with an order under s 43 depriving him of the car, were upheld (*R* v *Brown (Edward)* [1975] RTR 36*n*). In *R* v *Thomas (Derek)* [1975] RTR 38*n* a disqualification of six years was reduced to five; the defendant was sent to prison for five years for driving another man to a car park to steal jewellery worth £20,000 from the boot of a parked car belonging to a jeweller. In *R* v *Ackers* [1977] RTR 66 the appellant had used his heavy goods vehicle licence for the purpose of hiring a van and lorry to enable stolen tyres to be disposed of. He was disqualified under s 44 for twelve months. The order of disqualification was upheld on appeal because the use of the appellant's licence by him was an integral part of the offences.

There is no power to make an order of disqualification under s 44 of the Powers of Criminal Courts Act 1973 for the offence of conspiracy to steal (*R* v *Riley* [1984] RTR 159, 1 RTLB 35).

## 20.32 Disqualification pending passing a driving test

By s 93(7) of the 1972 Act the court convicting the driver of a motor vehicle of any endorsable offence (see table at 19.2) may order him to be disqualified until he passes a driving test, whether or not he has previously passed one. Such an order cannot be made for any other road traffic or other type of offence. The order may take effect immediately or on the expiration of a period of complete disqualification if the court also orders the latter. Where the order takes effect immediately, the offender may drive as soon as he obtains a provisional licence (s 98(3)) but, of course, must comply with the conditions of a provisional licence. If a person is disqualified for a period and also disqualified until he passes a driving test, he cannot take out a provisional licence until the period of ordinary disqualification has elapsed.

A person who has been disqualified from driving until he has passed the test offends against s 99 (driving while disqualified) if he drives after having taken out a provisional licence and fails to comply with a provisional licence condition (eg not displaying 'L' plates, driving while not accompanied by a qualified driver, etc) (*Scott* v *Jelfe* [1974] RTR 256); but the law is different in Northern Ireland (*McGimpsey* v *Carlin* [1968] Jo Crim L 221, showing the resident magistrate's decision to have been upheld by the Court of Appeal). Such a disqualification expires as soon as evidence of passing the test is produced to the licensing authority (s 93(7)).

The effect of the above provisions is that, if Jehu is disqualified from driving for twelve months on 1 July 1985 and further disqualified until he passes a driving test, he is disqualified from that moment and may not drive at all until 1 July 1986. On and from 1 July 1986 (provided he takes out a provisional licence) he may drive only as a learner driver, ie with 'L' plates and accompanied in a car by a duly qualified person, until he passes the test.

Section 93(7) is not a punitive section (see *R* v *Donnelly* and *R* v *Banks* below). An order of disqualification until the passing of a test should not be imposed as part of the penalty for the offence. Nor, it seems, can a court impose a condition that the applicant take and pass a driving test when considering an application for removal of disqualification under s 95 or para 7 of Sched 10 to the 1972 Act (*R* v *Bentham* [1982] RTR 375). The power to disqualify under s 93(7) should be used where the offender is aged, infirm or inexperienced and where the circumstances of the offence or the offender are such that it is in the public interest that the offender pass a driving test before he again drives on a full licence. It may also be used where the offender is inexperienced and the length of ordinary disqualification is such that he should be required to pass a test before he obtains a full licence. In general, the less experience the driver has had and the longer the period of the disqualification, the more important it is that an order under s 93(7) should also be made (*R* v *Guilfoyle* below).

In *R* v *Donnelly* [1975] 1 WLR 390 the defendant, aged fifty-two, pleaded guilty to driving with 229 mg of alcohol in 100 ml of blood. An order under s 93(7) was removed on appeal, as such an order should not be imposed as a punishment and there was no reason to question the defendant's driving competence. The Court of Appeal approved the reasoning of quarter sessions in *Ashworth* v *Johnson*; *Charlesworth* v *Johnson* [1959] Crim LR 735, where it was said that the powers of a court under s 6(3) of the 1934 Act (now s 93(7)) should be used in respect of persons who are growing old or infirm or who show in the circumstances of the offence some kind of incompetence which requires looking into. Similarly in *R* v *Banks (John)* [1978] RTR 535 it was again held that an order under s 93(7) should not be imposed as a punishment and that such an order is designed for cases of age or infirmity or where the circumstances of the offence were such that the defendant was not a competent driver.

A court should not impose an order under s 93(7) where the offender is not incompetent but instead suffers from a disease or disability rendering his driving a danger to the public. In such a case the court should notify the Secretary of State for Transport under s 92 of the 1972 Act (*Hughes* v *Challes* [1984] RTR 283, 1 RTLB 51, where the defendant was convicted of reckless driving during an episode of hypomania due to manic depressive psychosis but who was otherwise perfectly competent to drive) (as to s 92 see 20.38).

In *R* v *Guilfoyle* [1973] RTR 272 a nineteen-year-old lorry driver was disqualified for three years and also disqualified until he passed a test, for causing death by dangerous driving. The Court of Appeal reduced the disqualification to twelve months but upheld the order that he should pass a test before obtaining a full licence. An interruption of twelve months in his driving career was substantial for one of his length of experience. In general the longer the period of disqualification the more important it is that there should be a driving test before the driver obtains a full licence (ibid). In *R* v *Lobley* [1974] RTR 550 a nineteen-year-old driver who pleaded guilty to causing death by dangerous driving had his disqualification of four years reduced to two, but the Court of Appeal upheld the order that he should pass a test before driving on a full licence. The facts of the case were such that the court had doubts as to his ability and qualifications for driving. In *R* v *Heslop* [1978] RTR 441 the Court of Appeal, in reducing a period of disqualification for causing death by dangerous driving from ten years to two years, imposed additionally an order that the driver should be disqualified until he passed a test, in view of his lack of experience and to ensure that he did not again drive until he passed a test. Similarly in *R* v *Raynor* [1982] RTR 286 a disqualification for causing death by reckless driving was reduced from seven to three years by the Court of Appeal but an order under s 93(7) on the nineteen-year-old defendant was added.

The disqualification until the test is passed cannot be removed under s 95 of the 1972 Act; the person must pass the test (s 95(5)). Section 95(5) does not prevent a person who was disqualified for five years and who was also disqualified until he passed a test from applying for the removal of the five-year disqualification (*R* v *Nuttall* [1971] RTR 279). The two orders are separable. When a term of disqualification expires or is removed under s 95 or para 7 of Sched 10, the applicant may then take out a provisional licence and on passing the test may obtain a full licence.

There is no endorsement code for an order disqualifying an offender pending passing a test. Instead the court notifies the DVLC of the order on form D20.

### 20.33–6 Disqualification on committal for sentence

By s 56 of the Criminal Justice Act 1967, where a magistrates' court commits an offender to the Crown Court for sentence under s 38 of the Magistrates' Courts Act 1980 the Crown Court may or shall disqualify him and shall order endorsement of his licence, as required, whether or not a custodial sentence is imposed. By s 103(1) of the 1972 Act, a magistrates' court committing for sentence, in custody or on bail, may order the defendant to be disqualified, if he has been convicted of an endorsable offence, until the Crown Court deals with him; by s 103(5) any period of disqualification imposed by the Crown Court on any such person committed for sentence shall be treated as reduced by any period he was disqualified by reason only of an order made under s 103(1), but such latter period shall not be taken into account for the purpose of reducing more than one other period of disqualification.

The provisions above and in the next paragraph extend to committal to the Crown Court for offences occurring during the currency of a probation or conditional discharge order, offences committed while on parole (s 62 of the Criminal Justice Act 1967), offences committed during a suspended sentence (s 24 of the Powers of Criminal Courts Act 1973) and offenders committed for sentence under the Vagrancy Act 1824.

A court may not impose an interim order of disqualification on committal for trial. Section 103 only allows an order to be made where the offender has been committed for sentence. On committal for trial the offender, by definition, will not have been convicted. It is possible to make it a condition of bail that a defendant does not drive, but such a condition may only be imposed if necessary for one of the reasons set out in the Bail Act 1976 and where it would not cause injustice.

By s 56(1), where a magistrates' court has convicted a person of an offence or offences which carry compulsory or optional disqualification, whether a summary offence or one triable summarily or on indictment, and commits him to the Crown Court for another offence under s 38 of the Magistrates' Courts Act 1980 or under the powers mentioned in the last paragraph, the magistrates may commit him in respect of the first-mentioned offences also, notwithstanding that they are not triable on indictment. By s 56(5), the Crown Court may deal with him for such offence or offences in any way in which the magistrates could have dealt with him and, in particular, may disqualify and endorse. Thus if *A* is convicted by magistrates of stealing a car, driving it carelessly and using it without insurance and the magistrates commit him for sentence for the first of those offences under s 38 of the Magistrates' Courts Act 1980, they may also, by s 56(1), commit him to the Crown Court for the other two offences also, so that the Crown Court may fix the total amount of disqualification and will not be hampered by any decision of the magistrates as to disqualification. The effect of s 56(5) and s 56(6) is that magistrates have no power to sentence or otherwise deal with him (other than by interim disqualification); the magistrates' powers and duties are vested in the Crown Court which in an appropriate case may be required to disqualify the offender (*R* v *O'Connor* [1976] RTR 414).

This power of committal of summary, etc, offences, which anyhow arises only after the magistrates have convicted, does not extend to committals *for trial*; if a person is charged with causing death by reckless driving and with a drink/driving offence, the magistrates should commit for trial on the first charge and not hear and convict in respect of the second offence until the Crown Court has dealt with the other.

Magistrates may by s 103(1) of the 1972 Act disqualify for a summary offence so committed for sentence until it is dealt with by the Crown Court.

These powers under s 56(1) of the Criminal Justice Act 1967 of committing summary, etc, offences for sentence extend to summary offences punishable with imprisonment as well as to those for which disqualification may or must be ordered.

An order of disqualification under s 103 does not wipe off any penalty points on the offender's licence (see 20.20), nor does it count as an order of disqualification so as to increase the minimum period of a penalty points disqualification (see 20.21) (s 19(9) of the Transport Act 1981).

The defendant must produce his licence to the magistrates' court on conviction and if he does not do so is guilty of an offence (s 103(2)). The magistrates' court shall send the licence to the Crown Court.

## Miscellaneous Matters

### 20.37 Escaping disqualification by deception

Section 21 of the Transport Act 1981 provides that where a court was deceived regarding any circumstances that were or might have been taken into account in deciding whether or for how long to disqualify an offender when dealing with him in respect of an endorsable offence and the deception constituted or was due to an offence committed by him, then if he is convicted of that offence the court shall have the same power and duties of disqualification as the original court. The court must take into account any order of a disqualification by the original court.

It remains to be seen how much this provision will be used by the courts. It may be noted, however, that where a court has been deceived and as a result the offender escaped an obligatory disqualification, whether it is under the penalty points system or 'totting up' provisions, or in respect of an obligatorily disqualifiable offence, the court subsequently dealing with the offender is under the same obligation to consider disqualifying the offender as the original court, except in so far as the original court disqualified him on the earlier occasion. An offender may, for example, obtain a duplicate licence free from endorsement relating to a previous drink/driving offence in order to produce it when subsequently convicted of another drink/driving offence. If he is then disqualified for only one year and subsequently convicted for knowingly making a false statement in obtaining the duplicate driving licence (under s 170), the court convicting him is then under an obligation to disqualify him for at least two years (ie the obligatory three years less the twelve-month disqualification originally imposed).

It should be noted that the prosecution may not have to prove that the offender deceived the court, only that the court was deceived due to the offence committed by the defendant.

Where a court disqualifies an offender under s 21 the court is under an obligation to notify the Secretary of State of the order of disqualification (s 105(2) of the 1972 Act), and as the court 'shall have the same powers and duties regarding an order of disqualification as had the court which dealt with him for the endorsable offence' it would seem that the court should endorse the offender's licence and notify the DVLC as if the court had originally disqualified the offender. As, however, it is not a disqualification 'under s 19(2) of the Transport Act 1981 or s 93 of the 1972 Act' it would seem that any previous penalty points are not wiped off by the disqualifications (see s 19(3)(*b*)). It would seem, however, to count as a disqualification for the purpose of increasing the minimum period of disqualification of a subsequent penalty points disqualification because s 19(9) of the Transport Act 1981 states that only disqualifications under s 103 of the 1972 Act and s 44 of the Powers of Criminal Courts Act 1973 do not count for this purpose.

## 20.38–40 Notification of disease or disability

Section 92 of the 1972 Act requires a court to notify the Secretary of State for Transport if in any proceedings committed in respect of a motor vehicle it appears to the court that the accused may be suffering from any relevant disability or prospective disability within the meaning of s 87 of the Act.

The section requires the court to notify the Secretary of State in such manner and containing such particulars as are required, and for the notification to be sent to such address as the Secretary of State may determine. No such determination has yet been made.

It should be noted that a court has no discretion whether to notify the Secretary of State or not. The terms of the section are such that once it 'appears' to the court that the accused *may* be suffering from a notifiable disability the court must send notification to the Secretary of State. It does not appear necessary for the accused always to be convicted. The offence may be committed but because of the defendant's notifiable disease or disability he may not be guilty of the offence, eg the defendant suffered unknowingly from blackouts and drove in a state of automatism. In such a case the defendant may be acquitted but it is submitted that the court is required to notify under s 92.

'Relevant disability' for the purposes of s 87 is any disability or disease likely to cause the driving of a vehicle by the person concerned to be a source of danger to the public together with any 'prescribed' disability. The 'prescribed' disabilities are those prescribed by reg 22 of the Driving Licences Regulations 1981 (SI 1981 No 952, as amended by SI 1982 No 423). These include epilepsy, severe subnormality, mental deficiency, sudden attacks of disabling giddiness or fainting and inability to pass the eyesight test (see 11.12). A 'prospective' disability is one which while not a relevant disability is one which because of its intermittent or progressive nature may become in the course of time a relevant disability.

A court should not disqualify an offender until he passes a test of competence to drive under s 93(7) where the defendant is competent but suffers from a disease or disability. In such a case the court should notify the Secretary of State under s 92 (*Hughes* v *Challes* [1984] RTR 283, 1 RTLB 51, where a defendant was convicted of reckless driving during an episode of hypomania due to manic-depressive psychosis but was otherwise competent to drive).

When notified under s 92 the Secretary of State will make enquiries and if satisfied that the defendant is suffering from a relevant disability may either revoke the licence outright or substitute a licence subject to conditions depending on the nature or extent of the disease or disability. Where the offender is subject to a prospective disability the Secretary of State will revoke the licence and may grant a licence of limited duration.

Although alcoholism is not a prescribed disability, it would appear unarguable that alcoholism is a disease or disability likely to cause the driving of a motor vehicle by the person concerned to be a source of danger to the public. What is the duty of the court when informed by the defendant's solicitor while speaking in mitigation of a drink/driving offence that his client 'has a drink problem'? In *R* v *Chichester JJ, ex parte Crouch* (1981) JP Jo 702 it was held that while in such a case justices could properly take notice of something said in mitigation, the fact that he 'had a drink problem' and the present case was his first conviction was insufficient to justify a court making a notification under s 92. It is submitted that the Divisional Court in this case may have overlooked the fact that s 92 is mandatory in its terms. Once it 'appears' to a court that a defendant 'may' be suffering from a relevant disability or disease, s 92 states that a court 'shall' notify the Secretary of State. The purpose of s 92 is to enable the Secretary of State to enquire whether the person concerned is, or is not, suffering from the disease or disability. Moreover, it should be noted that the Secretary of State will not automatically re-issue a driving licence to a 'high risk offender' (see 4.125).

An authorised insurer (ie a company empowered to issue insurance policies for the use of motor vehicles under s 145 of the 1972 Act) is required to notify the Secretary of State under s 92(2)) if he refuses to issue a motor insurance policy on the grounds that the health of the proposer is unsatisfactory or on grounds which include that ground.

## Removal of Disqualification

### 20.41 Application for removal

By s 95 of the 1972 Act a person disqualified may apply for removal of his disqualification:

(*a*) if the disqualification is for less than four years, when two years from the date on which it was imposed have expired;

(*b*) if the disqualification is for less than ten years but not less than four years, when half the period of disqualification has expired;

(*c*) in any other cases, ie ten years or more or for 'life', when five years have expired from the date of disqualification.

Thus, a person disqualified for two years or less cannot apply at all for removal of his disqualification; his only course is to appeal to the Crown Court in the hope of a reduction of the period. This limitation was modified, however, in respect of 'additional' periods of disqualification imposed for the offence of driving while disqualified (see 20.44) and by s 20 of the Transport Act 1981 it is now provided that, where a period of disqualification was imposed in addition to any other period or periods of disqualification, it must be treated for the purpose of s 95 of the 1972 Act as one continuous period of disqualification (see 20.43).

An offender disqualified for three years or more because of a second drink/driving offence may nevertheless apply under s 95 (*Damer* v *Davison* [1976] RTR 44). Lord Widgery CJ observed, however, at p 94:

I would only add that justices . . . may if they think fit regard a mandatory disqualification as one which they are somewhat less ready to remove than a discretionary disqualification.

An order of disqualification under s 24 of the Criminal Justice Act 1972 or s 44 of the Powers of Criminal Courts Act 1973 (disqualification for using a vehicle for criminal purposes (see 20.31)) may, seemingly, be removed under s 95 (but is, of course, subject to the time limits set out above).

There is no power to remove a disqualification imposed under s 93(7) of the 1972 Act, ie a disqualification until a driving test is passed (see 20.32). Section 95 of the 1972 Act does not apply to such a disqualification (s 95(5)). In *R* v *Nuttall* [1971] RTR 279 the applicant was disqualified for five years for the offence of causing death by dangerous driving and also disqualified until he passed a test of competence to drive. In view of s 95(5) some doubt had been expressed whether the five years' disqualification could be removed in view of the additional order of disqualification pending a test. Bridge J, in hearing the case, considered the matter, held that he had power to do so and granted the application on its merits.

## 20.42 Procedure for removal

If the application is refused, another application may not be entertained until three months thereafter (s 95(3)). Rule 101 of the Magistrates' Courts Rules 1981 requires an application to a magistrates' court under s 95 to be made by way of complaint and for a summons to be issued to the chief officer of police to show cause why an order shall not be made. 'Chief officer of police' would seem to be the Chief Constable or in the Metropolitan area, the Commissioner. Can a complaint be made for the issue of a summons before the relevant period under s 95 has elapsed? It is submitted it can, provided that the date upon which the summons is returnable is after the period has expired. Section 95 only prohibits application being made to the court before the period has expired. The complaint for the summons is made to a justice of the peace or justice's clerk for a summons to be issued and is a matter of procedure not of substance. The application is made when heard.

The court may, if it thinks proper having regard to the applicant's character, his conduct subsequent to his conviction, the nature of the offence and any other circumstances of the case, remove the disqualification. The magistrates' clerk on the granting of an application notifies the Department of Transport of the removal of the disqualification.

Where the disqualification was imposed by a Crown Court, the application should be made to the location of the Crown Court where it was originally made (if it was made by assizes or quarter sessions, to the location of the Crown Court which is most convenient to the place where the order was made) (*Practice Direction* [1971] 1 WLR 1535, para 11, given by the Lord Chief Justice with the concurrence of the Lord Chancellor). Where the disqualification was imposed by the Crown Court, the applicant should get in touch with the Crown Court offices at the location specified in the *Practice Direction* (see above). It is said at 111 JP Jo 699 that, where a juvenile court has disqualified a young person, any application to remove the disqualification should be made to the juvenile court, although the defendant may have since become an adult.

If a disqualification is 'for life', it is submitted that five years must elapse before the first application to remove can be made.

It is submitted that a magistrate or justices' clerk cannot refuse to issue a summons for removal of a disqualification, whatever he may think of the applicant's chances, provided the application is not less than three months after any previous one and not before the expiry of the period after which the applicant may first apply (see above); the reason for this view is that r 101 of the Magistrates' Courts Rules 1981 says that the magistrates 'shall' issue a summons to the police, thus taking away the normal discretion whether or not to issue one.

The application need not be heard by the same judge or justices as imposed disqualification, so long as the same court hears it, but, where a disqualification period is varied on appeal to the Crown Court, it seems that the magistrates' court can hear an application to remove (*The Times*, 4 February 1931; [1956] Crim LR 41; for a contrary view see [1955] Crim LR 767 and [1956] Crim LR 110). It is submitted that the correct view is that given at 121 JP Jo 819, viz that in view of the latter part of s 110 of the Magistrates' Courts Act 1980, declaring that a decision of quarter sessions on appeal has effect as if it is made by the magistrates' court, it should be the magistrates' court which hears an application to remove a disqualification imposed or confirmed by quarter sessions on appeal. The Courts Act 1971 (see now the Supreme Court Act 1981) made no difference to the legal position save to substitute the Crown Court for quarter sessions. However, in *Sherrard* v *Woods* [1958] NI 13, where a like Northern Irish statute was under consideration, it was said that, while the magistrates' court was the proper tribunal to remove a disqualification imposed there and upheld by sessions on appeal without alteration, it might be otherwise if the magistrates' order had been varied or sessions had imposed a disqualification and the magistrates had not. No doubt the magistrates can obtain leave by letter from the Crown Court to deal with the application if in doubt as to their powers; see generally 120 JP Jo 294 and 374. There is no appeal from a refusal to remove the disqualification or against a removal save in either case to the High Court on a point of law. The applicant may be ordered to pay costs, whether successful or not (s 95(4)), and by the Magistrates' Courts Act 1980, s 64, the person opposing removal may be ordered to pay costs if the disqualification is removed (see the Magistrates' Courts Rules 1981, r 101, declaring such applications to be by complaint and making the police, in effect, the respondent).

It seems that, in computing the time after which a person may apply for removal of a disqualification, any time after the conviction during which it was suspended or he was not disqualified shall be disregarded.

It seems that the court must either remove the disqualification altogether or refuse the application altogether; a disqualification cannot be varied under s 95 (*R* v *Cottrell (No 2)* [1956] 1 All ER 751), but a court may remove the disqualification 'from such date as may be specified in the order' (s 95(1)). There seems nothing to prevent a court, therefore, granting the application for removal to come into effect, say, in one year's time from the date of the hearing of the application. A person was disqualified in April 1954 for three years. In May 1955 the court removed the disqualification as from April 1956. He applied in August 1955 for its immediate removal. It was held that the magistrates were not estopped by their May decision from hearing the August application (*R* v *Manchester JJ, ex parte Gaynor* [1956] 1 All ER 610).

There is no power when considering an application under para 7 of Sched 10 to the 1972 Act (see 20.44) to impose a condition that the applicant should pass a driving test (*R* v *Bentham* [1982] RTR 357). It would seem that there is no such power either for a court to do so when considering an application under s 95.

Where a licence is restored under s 95 the court is required to endorse particulars of the order on any licence previously held by the applicant (s 95(4)), except where the order of disqualification which is removed is an order under s 44 of the Powers of Criminal Courts Act 1973 (disqualification for using a vehicle for criminal purposes; see 20.31). The court is obliged to notify the Department of Transport of an order under s 95 (whether it is an ordinary order of disqualification or one under s 44, above).

### 20.43 Removal of consecutive disqualifications

In *R* v *Lambeth Metropolitan Magistrate, ex parte Everett* [1967] 3 All ER 648, it was held that a defendant who had been disqualified for three years plus three years consecutive on the same day and applied for removal of the second disqualification three and one quarter years after it had been imposed and when it had been effective for only three months must wait until two years had elapsed from the date on which the second disqualification began to run, viz, five years from the date it was imposed.

The effect of the decision in *R* v *Lambeth Metropolitan Magistrate, ex parte Everett* has been reversed by s 20 of the Transport Act 1981. This provides that for the purpose of determining whether an application may be made under s 95 in respect of any additional period of disqualification, the periods will be treated as one continuous period of disqualification. It seems clear from the wording of s 20 that an application may be made under s 95 even though the periods of disqualification were imposed before s 20 was brought into force (1 November 1982). If it were not so, s 20 would be wholly nugatory because s 93(5), which is the only provision allowing a period of disqualification to be additional to another, was itself repealed by the Transport Act 1981.

It may be difficult to decide to which court application should be made when the orders of disqualification have been made by different courts. It would seem that as the orders are to be treated as one continuous period of disqualification the application might be made to the court which imposed the current order of disqualification but unfortunately there is no provision in s 20 (as there was in the Road Traffic (Disqualification) Act 1970) enabling the defendant to apply to one court only. It would seem advisable in such a situation for the applicant to enquire of the other court or courts if objection would be raised if his application for the total period were heard by the court under whose order he is currently disqualified. If objection is raised, he may then be forced to apply to the other court or courts successively.

If the subsequent consecutive orders have been imposed as a result of an incorrect original order of disqualification, the court will normally remove all the orders of disqualification either by certiorari or allowing an appeal out of time. Thus in *R* v *Middleton &c JJ, ex parte Collins* [1970] 1 QB 216 in excess of jurisdiction a defendant was initially disqualified for a year. He drove during that first year, for which he was disqualified for a further five years. He again drove and was disqualified for yet another five years. All the convictions and disqualifications were set aside. Similarly in *R* v *Lambert* [1974] RTR 244 the Court of Appeal quashed a conviction for driving while disqualified in respect of periods of disqualification which were wrongly ordered to run consecutively; the court also refused to apply s 11(3) of the Criminal Appeal Act 1968 to substitute lawful orders of disqualification disqualifying him for the same period.

## 20.44 Removal of disqualifications for driving while disqualified (for orders made before 15 July 1970)

Section 2 of the Road Traffic (Disqualification) Act 1970 allowed persons disqualified for 'additional' periods of disqualification for the offence of driving while disqualified to apply for their removal. Section 2 was repealed and replaced by para 7 of Sched 10 to the 1972 Act.

Until 1970 a person who was convicted of driving while disqualified was required to be additionally disqualified for at least twelve months. Such 'additional' disqualification was consecutive to any other period of disqualification whether imposed on that or any other occasion. 'Car mad' young men who were addicted to driving thus could and did accumulate lengthy periods of disqualification and the purpose of the Act was to help the rehabilitation of such young men who wished to settle down and earn an honest living and to whom the possession of a driving licence would be a help in doing so. There is thought to be only a small number of offenders who remain so disqualified, and practitioners wishing to advise anyone seeking to remove such an order of disqualification are referred to the ninth edition of this work.

There is no power when hearing an application under para 7 of Sched 10 to impose an additional requirement to pass a driving test (*R* v *Bentham* [1982] RTR 357).

Chapter 21

# Special Reasons and Mitigating Circumstances

## 21.1 Introduction

In chapters 19 and 20, the offences carrying obligatory endorsement or disqualification were described in detail. The first part of this chapter is concerned with the reasons upon which a court may refrain from disqualifying in respect of an obligatorily disqualifiable offence or to refrain from endorsing in respect of an endorsable offence. The reasons are commonly referred to as 'special reasons'.

Advocates should be careful to distinguish between 'special reasons' for not disqualifying or endorsing, and the circumstances in which a court, under a very much wider discretion, may refrain from disqualifying when considering a penalty points disqualification. The latter are usually referred to as 'mitigating circumstances' and are dealt with at 21.21–31.

It is important to remember that neither 'special reasons' nor 'mitigating circumstances' automatically enable the defendant to escape disqualification or endorsement. Where 'special reasons' or 'mitigating circumstances' are found it merely means that the court has a discretion to disqualify the offender for a lesser period or not at all; the court is not bound to exercise its discretion and in an appropriate case will not do so. Indeed in *Vaughan* v *Duff* [1984] RTR 376 it was said (per Robert Goff LJ at p 381J following Lord Widgery CJ in *Taylor* v *Rajan* [1974] RTR 304, an 'emergency' case) 'the exercise of the discretion [of special reasons] should only be exercised in clear and compelling circumstances'. This should be contrasted with the provision made for defendants convicted of offences under the Construction and Use Regulations. If such a defendant proves that he did not know and had no reasonable cause to suspect that the facts of the case were such that an offence would be committed, the court cannot order endorsement or disqualification (see 8.46).

'Special reasons' cannot be found to impose a lesser number of penalty points for an endorsable offence. If, however, special reasons are found for not endorsing the licence then there is no power to endorse the licence with penalty points.

## Special Reasons

### 21.2–5 Definition and criteria

As to practice and procedure see 21.16.

Hitherto the great majority of cases on 'special reasons' have been in respect of offences involving obligatory disqualification. With the advent of the penalty points system the importance of avoiding penalty points may encourage advocates to seek to persuade courts of 'special reasons' for not endorsing because if no order of endorsement is made, no penalty points are incurred. It may be particularly important for 'special reasons' to be found by a court for refraining also from ordering endorsement where 'special reasons' have already been found enabling an offender to escape disqualification in respect of an obligatorily disqualifiable offence. If the offender has already incurred 8 penalty points, in such a case although the offender will have escaped disqualification for the offence, the court will be obliged to impose a penalty points disqualification if an order of endorsement is made (see 19.25).

Where special reasons are found for not endorsing in respect of an offence for which penalty points are incurred, the court may decide either that the special reasons are sufficient not to order endorsement, or that the reasons are insufficient, in which case the appropriate number of points must also be endorsed. A court cannot find special reasons for not imposing a lesser number of points than those set out in Sched 7: it must either endorse the appropriate number of penalty points or decide because of special reasons not to endorse at all.

The phrase 'special reasons' is not statutorily defined. But in *R* v *Crossen* [1939] 1 NI 106, the King's Bench Division of Northern Ireland held:

> A 'special reason' within the exception is one which is special to the facts of the particular case, that is special to the facts which constitute the offence. It is, in other words, a mitigating or extenuating circumstance, not amounting in law to a defence to the charge, yet directly connected with the commission of the offence and one which the court ought properly to take into consideration when imposing punishment. A circumstance peculiar to the offender as distinguished from the offence is not a 'special reason' within the exception.

This passage was approved by Lord Goddard in *Whittall* v *Kirby* [1946] 2 All ER 552, and it remains the basic definition of the phrase. In *R* v *Wickens* (1958) 42 Cr App R 236 four minimum 'criteria' were laid down: to amount to a 'special reason' a matter must:

(*a*) be a mitigating or extenuating circumstance;
(*b*) not amount in law to a defence to the charge;
(*c*) be directly connected with the commission of the offence; and
(*d*) be one which the court ought properly to take into consideration when imposing sentence.

In Scotland, the courts have adopted the same approach (see *Adair* v *Munn* 1940 SC (J) 69).

Curiously, in none of these cases was the court's attention apparently drawn to s 11(3) of the Road Traffic Act 1930 which entitled the court to refrain from disqualifying 'having regard to the lapse of time since the date of the previous or last previous conviction, or for any *other* special reason'. Whether or not full consideration of all the contexts in which the phrase 'special reasons' (or indeed 'special circumstances', a phrase which has been held to have an identical meaning) appeared in the various Road Traffic Acts prior to the Road Traffic Act 1960 would have produced the same judicial opinion is now academic. In *R* v *Steel* (1968) 52 Cr App R 510, it was said that it was too late to challenge the decision in *Whittall* v *Kirby*. And in *R* v *Anderson* [1972] Crim LR 245 the Court of Appeal expressly declined to redefine 'special reasons', and stated that *Whittall* v *Kirby* remained good law and should be followed.

But the application of *Whittall* v *Kirby* causes considerable difficulties in practice. The triviality of an offence could appear to meet all four criteria. Indeed in Scotland, the High Court of Justiciary held that a very minor degree of blameworthiness on the part of a defendant convicted of driving without due care and attention could amount to a special reason: see *Smith* v *Henderson* 1950 SC (J) 48. It was there suggested that the mischief at which the provisions relating to endorsement and disqualification were aimed was the element of danger to the public, and that where that element was absent, special reasons could be found.

In *Reay* v *Young* [1949] 1 All ER 1102, Lord Goddard applied a similar test when upholding a finding of special reasons where an uninsured driver merely held the wheel of a car for a distance of 150 yards on an open moorland road on which 'there was no traffic'. Again, in *James* v *Hall* [1968] Crim LR 507, a finding of special reasons was upheld where a driver, whose blood-alcohol level was above the prescribed limit, drove his car a few yards off the road into a friend's driveway (but see 21.8).

However, in *Nicholson* v *Brown* [1974] RTR 177, Lord Widgery, disapproving *Smith* v *Henderson*, said:

> I would not accept the proposition that if a man is guilty of driving without due care and attention, he can be excused endorsement of his licence on the basis of special reasons merely because it was not a bad case, or merely because the degree of blameworthiness was slight. I think that the line must be drawn firmly at guilt or innocence in those cases. If the defendant is guilty, then the consequences of endorsement of the licence must follow, unless there is some special reason properly to be treated as such, not such a matter as that the offence was not a serious one.

In *Delaroy-Hall* v *Tadman* [1969] 2 QB 208, Lord Parker declined to find special reasons where the analysis of a defendant's blood-alcohol level showed that he was only just above the prescribed limit. In doing so, he stated that there may be some overriding reason to be found in the legislation constituting the offence, which precludes a court from considering as a special reason something which at first sight might appear to fall within the principle of *Whittall* v *Kirby*.

In *Marks* v *West Midlands Police* [1981] RTR 471 it was held that while a special reason could never be constituted by the fact that the breach of the law was small, the minor nature of the offence could not be totally ignored: the lack of an intention to commit an offence had to be weighed against the problem faced by the defendant. In that case the defendant exceeded a motorway speed limit of 70 mph by 10 mph. He was worried by his blind, incontinent, eighty-year-old passenger becoming ill and was thereby not aware of exceeding the limit, being anxious to reach the nearest motorway service area.

These decisions cannot easily be reconciled into a coherent set of principles which can be applied to future circumstances. There is, undoubtedly, a strong public policy element in the decisions. But so long as *Nicholson* v *Brown* remains good law, the principle often appears to be that a special reason has to be found outside the facts which constitute the mischief of the offence itself.

Because of the difficulty in practice of identifying what the court will accept as a special reason, the most useful approach is by analogy with previous decisions. Set out below are a number of examples first under a general heading and then divided by reference to the offence in question.

## Examples of Special Reasons

### 21.6 Generally

The following are capable of amounting to special reasons:

The fact that the defendant drove for a short distance and in circumstances such that he was unlikely to be brought into contact with other road users: *Reay* v *Young* (above), *James* v *Hall* ([1968] Crim LR 507, 21.8 below) as qualified by *R* v *Mullarkey* [1970] Crim LR 406 and *Coombs* v *Kehoe* [1972] RTR 224 (see 'Shortness of distance driven', 21.8 below).

The fact that the defendant unintentionally committed the offence or was misled, without negligence, into committing it: see below under 'Insurance', 'Drink/Driving' and 'Speed limits'. (21.7, 21.8 and 21.11.)

The fact that the defendant committed the offence whilst coping with a true emergency: see below under 'Insurance', 'Drink/driving', 'Reckless and careless driving' and 'Speed limits'.

The following have been held *not* to be capable of amounting to special reasons:

The fact that the defendant is of good character, has a good driving record, or that he, his family or employees, will suffer personal, financial or other hardship, however severe: *Whittall* v *Kirby* (see 21.2).

The fact that the defendant is a doctor, or has some other employment of benefit to the public, for the proper discharge of which a licence ,is important or vital: *Gordon* v *Smith* [1971] Crim LR 173; *Holroyd* v *Berry* [1973] RTR 145.

The fact that, as a condition of bail prior to trial, the defendant was not permitted to drive: *R* v *Kwame* [1975] RTR 106. Such a condition is lawful, but could produce injustice of which a court should be made aware whenever it considers imposing this condition. The defendant's redress in the event of the condition being imposed is to apply to a High Court judge in chambers for a variation of the conditions of bail.

The fact, by itself, that the offence was trivial (see *Nicholson* v *Brown*, *Delaroy-Hall* v *Tadman* and *Marks* v *West Midlands Police* at 21.2 above).

## 21.7 Insurance

Prior to 1965, disqualification or at one time, imprisonment was obligatory for using a motor vehicle without insurance, or causing or permitting such use. A substantial number of early decisions on the application of *Whittall* v *Kirby* are in respect of convictions for this offence.

There are numerous examples of cases in which the court has held that the defendant was misled into committing the offence, and that this was capable of amounting to a special reason, eg:

A garage proprietor applied for full cover, but was issued with a named-driver policy without the difference being pointed out to him by the insurance company: *Labrum* v *Williamson* [1947] 1 All ER 824.

The owner of a lorry requested the proprietor of the garage at which it was repaired to drive it to his premises, assuming that the garage proprietor would, as in normal commercial circumstances he should, have been covered by his own insurance. He was not, and did not inform the owner: *Lyons* v *May* [1948] 2 All ER 1062.

An employer told his employee to take a vehicle onto the road. It was reasonable for the employee to assume that he would be insured: *Blows* v *Chapman* [1947] 2 All ER 576. (The employee would now have a defence under s 143(2) of the 1972 Act: see 10.25.)

A perusal of the words of the policy by a layman would suggest that the use of the vehicle was covered by the policy: *Boss* v *Kingston* [1963] 1 All ER 177 and *Carlton* v *Garrity* [1964] Crim LR 146.

But the defendant must show that he was in some way misled. An honest, but groundless, belief that the policy covered a particular use cannot amount to a special reason: *Rennison* v *Knowler* [1947] 1 All ER 302.

Although in *Reay* v *Young* (at 21.2) the shortness of a journey was held, in the particular circumstances, to be capable of amounting to a special reason, the facts were unusual; and its application is likely to be rare in practice: see *Milliner* v *Thorne* [1972] Crim LR 245. In *Gott* v *Chisholm* (1950) 114 JP Jo 212, the court refused to find special reasons where an unskilled, unsupervised driver drove only a short distance, but caused an accident in the process.

The defendant's ignorance of the law cannot be a special reason: *Swell* v *McKechnie* [1956] Crim LR 423. Nor is the fact that the defendant made several attempts to obtain a policy, was not conversant with insurance practice and was not deliberately or intentionally trying to evade the law: *Surtees* v *Benewith* [1954] 3 All ER 261.

## 21.8 Drink/driving

The circumstances which have been held to be capable of amounting to special reasons can be divided into three groups:

(1) those explaining how the defendant became unfit to drive, or had excess alcohol in his body;
(2) those explaining why the defendant drove in such a condition; and
(3) miscellaneous circumstances relating to the offence.

A clear distinction must be drawn between the cases involving charges under s 5 of the Act (unfitness to drive) and those involving charges under s 6 of the Act (having excess alcohol). In the latter, Parliament has set a clear dividing line between guilt and innocence, and an obligatory penalty in the event of guilt. There is no room for arguing special reasons simply because the blood-alcohol level is marginally too high (*Delaroy-Hall* v *Tadman* at 21.2) or because the defendant's driving ability was in no way impaired (*R* v *Jackson* [1969] 2 All ER 453) or because the defendant's ability to drive was impaired, not by the alcohol even though over the limit, but by disease or drugs (*R* v *Scott* [1969] 2 All ER 450 and *Goldsmith* v *Laver* (1970) 134 JP Jo 310) but there is room for arguing that when the blood-alcohol level is below the limit, special reasons can be found for refusing to supply laboratory specimens (see *White (Arvin)* v *Metropolitan Police Commissioner* in 'Miscellaneous circumstances' below).

Where a defendant is liable to a minimum three-year period of disqualification because of a previous drink/driving conviction by virtue of s 93(4), a court can only take into account special reasons which relate to the commission of the later offence (*Bolliston* v *Gibbons* (1984) *The Times*, 31 March).

*Explanations for being unfit: charges under s 5*

A defendant took a drug to soothe pain from an injured leg not knowing that this would make him more susceptible to the effects of alcohol. With reluctance, the court was prepared to hold that this could amount to special reasons: *Chapman* v *O'Hagan* [1949] 2 All ER 690. In *R* v *Wickens* (1958) 42 Cr App R 236, a defendant, who did not know that he was a diabetic, drank beer which, but for his illness, would not have affected his driving. This was held to be capable of amounting to a special reason. In *R* v *Holt* [1962] Crim LR 565, a defendant took Amytol tablets prescribed by a doctor who had failed to warn him of the effects of even a small quantity of alcohol; the full Court of Criminal Appeal held that this was capable of amounting to a special reason. It falls within the general proposition set out above that special reasons can be found where a defendant has been misled into committing an offence.

In *Brewer* v *Metropolitan Police Commissioner* [1969] 1 All ER 513, the defendant had absorbed fumes from a vat which made him unfit to drive after consuming a small quantity of alcohol. Quarter sessions found that he did not know, but ought to have known, that he had absorbed these fumes. The Divisional Court held that this was capable of amounting to a special reason.

It is not a special reason that the defendant's unfitness to drive has been contributed to by a lack of food: *Archer* v *Woodward* [1959] Crim LR 461. Nor is it a special reason that the defendant took the drugs which caused him to be unfit in an attempt at suicide: *Bullen* v *Keay* [1974] RTR 559.

For mistakes as to the nature of the drink consumed, see below.

*Explanations for having excess alcohol in the body: charges under s 6*

In complete distinction to *R* v *Wickens* and *R* v *Holt* above, special reasons cannot be found where the defendant has been affected by an illness or a drug of the effect of which he had no knowledge: see *R* v *Scott* and *Goldsmith* v *Laver* above.

But special reasons have been found where the defendant did not know the nature of what he was drinking. The two types of situation in which this can arise are:

(*a*) when the defendant does not know that he is drinking alcohol at all; and

(*b*) where the defendant knows that he is drinking alcohol, but has been deceived or misled as to the nature of the drink.

It cannot be a special reason for a defendant to say simply that he was mistaken as to the amount of alcohol that he had drunk. In *Newnham* v *Trigg* [1970] RTR 107, the defendant had been given whisky in bed by his wife, but by reason of his cold, could not tell how much he had drunk. It was held that ignorance of the exact quantity of drink cannot be a special reason, whereas a mistake as to the quality might be.

It will usually be difficult for a defendant to establish that he did not know that he had been drinking alcohol at all; but clearly, if he can, this would be a special reason: see Lord Parker in *Newnham* v *Trigg*, above.

The court is more often concerned with the defendant who alleges either that his drink was 'laced', or that he was in some other way deceived as to its strength.

In *Pugsley* v *Hunter* [1973] RTR 284 it was held, following *R* v *Shippam* [1971] Crim LR 434, that where a defendant can establish that:

(*a*) his drink was 'laced';

(*b*) he did not know or suspect that his drink was 'laced'; and

(*c*) if his drink had not been 'laced' the alcohol level in his blood would not have exceeded the prescribed limit,

the court could be entitled to find special reasons, but that the defendant must establish head (*c*) with medical or scientific evidence unless it is obvious to a layman that the added drink explains the excess. No medical evidence was called for by the Bridport justices where special reasons were found because the defendant, whose blood-alcohol level was 81 mg, had been taking cough medicine which unknown to him contained alcohol.

In *Williams* v *Neale* [1971] Crim LR 598, the same approach was adopted where the defendant was charged with driving when unfit. He had drunk a fruit cup which, without his knowledge, had been 'laced' with brandy. The burden of establishing that the added drink resulted in impairment is less onerous than that required to establish that the blood-alcohol level would have been below the limit.

However it should, perhaps, be emphasised that even if special reasons have been established, the court must go on to consider whether or not to exercise its discretion in the defendant's favour. If the blood-alcohol level is high, or the impairment substantial, the court is bound to take into consideration the fact that whatever excuse the defendant may have had for drinking in the first place, he may have no proper excuse for driving or continuing to drive when he must or should have realised that he was affected by drink (*R* v *Newton* (*David*) [1974] RTR 451).

In *Alexander* v *Latter* [1972] Crim LR 646, the Divisional Court upheld a finding that where a defendant was offered diabetic lager by a barman as an alternative to ordinary lager without being informed that it was twice as strong, this could amount to a special reason. But this case must be read with *Adams* v *Bradley* [1975] Crim LR 168 where a defendant drank strong lager without realising its strength, and the court declined to find special reasons. The distinction was found in the fact that in *Alexander* v *Latter* the defendant was misled by the barman, whereas in *Adams* v *Bradley* the defendant made no enquiries about the strength of the lager. The distinction between *Alexander* v *Latter* and *Adams* v *Bradley* was again adverted to in the case of *R* v *Krebbs* [1977] RTR 406. The Court of Appeal found special reasons for not disqualifying where the defendant had initially been given Harp Lager to drink but unknowingly was subsequently supplied with Lowenbraü, which was double the strength. In *Adams* v *Bradley* the mistake of the defendant as to the alcoholic strength of the beverage could not be said to have been induced by the action of a third party.

In *R* v *Messom* [1973] RTR 140, the Court of Appeal considered that special reasons existed where a defendant, having asked for a large ginger ale topped up with a small whisky, was in fact given a small ginger ale topped up with a large brandy. It is suggested that this is an example of a case where the defendant was misled.

*Emergency*

In *Brown* v *Dyerson* [1969] 1 QB 45, it was stated that a sudden medical emergency could justify driving so as to be capable of amounting to a special reason. Whilst approving this principle, the courts have not yet been faced with facts which they are prepared to say fall within it.

While the High Court have been willing to recognise that an emergency is capable of amounting to a special reason, in every case so far reported the High Court have emphasised that before an emergency can constitute a special reason, the defendant must first show that there was no alternative but for him to drive and that he had explored every reasonable alternative before driving. The emergency must be real, not nebulous, nor manufactured. It is not a sufficient emergency if it can be shown that the defendant should have anticipated the emergency arising.

In *R* v *Baines* [1970] Crim LR 590, the defendant drove to rescue his partner's frail, ailing and elderly mother stranded at night without petrol. It was held that he had not explored other avenues of rescue; and therefore it could not be said that the emergency necessitated his driving.

In *Evans* v *Bray* [1977] RTR 24, the defendant was telephoned by his wife, who was away on a holiday, saying that she had forgotten tablets she required to control her blood pressure. The defendant, who had been drinking, drove over to her taking the tablets. The Divisional Court held that special reasons had not been established. He had not telephoned any of the emergency services. The question was not whether his action was understandable, but whether the defendant had no alternative but to drive as a result of the emergency.

The same principle applies when the emergency is non-medical. In *Jacobs* v *Reed* [1974] RTR 87 where the defendant had been drinking at the airport awaiting a flight, when telephoned as a matter of emergency by his wife to say that their daughter had failed to turn up at school, as a result of which he drove home without considering alternative methods of transport.

It is not an emergency that the defendant was a detective constable engaged on undercover operations which involved visiting licensed premises in plain clothes and had been given a £2 per day drinking allowance (*Vaughan* v *Duff* [1984] RTR 376).

In *Park* v *Hicks* [1979] RTR 259 the defendant had driven his wife away from a party where there was a disturbance. The justices held it to be a special reason for not disqualifying that his wife had had a brain haemorrhage and the disturbance had created a sudden medical emergency, namely a danger of a recurrence of a brain haemorrhage. Allowing an appeal from the justices' finding, the Divisional Court held that the evidence was too nebulous; unless full details of the special reasons relied on were given, a court could not exercise its discretion under s 93(1) of the Road Traffic Act 1972.

In *Powell* v *Gliha* [1979] RTR 126 it was held not to be a special reason for a wife to drive her paraplegic husband home in order that he might use a specially fitted lavatory. She and her husband had gone to a silver wedding anniversary party thirty miles from home and she was irresponsible in not having anticipated that her husband would need lavatory facilities while away from home.

Generally it cannot be an excuse amounting to a special reason for a doctor, ambulanceman or other member of emergency services to say that he was called out in an emergency; for to him it is routine. However, there may be circumstances in which he could properly say that he had no reasonable expectation of being summoned (for example, where he was off duty and not on call, but a disaster required all available manpower, or, in the case of a doctor, where full and proper arrangements for covering emergencies had been made but for some unforeseen reason his services were essential). In this type of event it should be open to him to say that there are special reasons.

*Shortness of distance driven*

The shortness of the distance driven is capable of amounting to a special reason particularly where the defendant has only driven his car at the request of a third party. It cannot, however, amount to a special reason unless the shortness of the actual distance driven by the defendant is such that he is unlikely to be brought into contact with other road users and danger would be unlikely to arise.

In *James* v *Hall* [1968] Crim LR 507, the shortness of the distance driven by the defendant was held to be capable of amounting to a special reason. This was followed in *R* v *Agnew* [1969] Crim LR 152 where a passenger was asked by the owner to move the car a matter of six feet.

But the courts have been anxious to restrict any principle which may be gleaned from these cases to situations where the defendant is unlikely to be brought into contact with other road users and where, if this did happen, danger would be unlikely. In *Coombs* v *Kehoe* [1972] RTR 224, justices were directed to disqualify a lorry driver who had driven 200 yards through a busy street, colliding with cars as he attempted to park. And in *R* v *Mullarkey* [1970] Crim LR 406, the fact that a defendant drove 400 yards after midnight in winter when there was little traffic about was held not to amount to a special reason.

Where a defendant, the worse for drink, but not intending to drive home, mistakenly and genuinely believed that he was being requested by a police constable to move his car a short distance, and did so, the court held that these were special reasons (*R* v *McIntyre* [1976] RTR 330). However, account has to be taken not only of the driving which has taken place at the constable's request, but also of the defendant's previous voluntary act of driving which preceded it. In *De Munthe* v *Stewart* [1982] RTR 27 a constable saw the defendant park his car and walk away and asked him to move it as it was causing an obstruction. After the defendant had reparked, but before he had ceased to drive, the constable suspected he had excess alcohol and asked for a specimen of breath. The court held there was no special reason for not disqualifying.

*Miscellaneous circumstances*

In *R* v *Anderson* [1972] RTR 113, the defendant was informed that he was not going to be prosecuted. As a result he destroyed the sample of blood which had been given to him for analysis. The prosecution analysis was 81 mg. The Court of Appeal held that he had been deprived of a possible defence, particularly bearing in mind the finding of the prosecution analyst and that there were special reasons therefore for not disqualifying, but stated that the facts in the case were very unusual ('it is difficult to think that the facts of this case could ever be repeated . . . or indeed that the conclusion of this court . . . could ever be a precedent in any other case' (per Roskill LJ at p 117F)). In *Doyle* v *Leroux* [1981] RTR 438 the defendant's blood analysis was 168 mg. He kept his sample for over a fortnight in his refrigerator but destroyed it on receiving a letter from the police stating that he would not be prosecuted. The Crown Court disqualified him holding that these facts could not amount to special reasons. The Court of Appeal upheld the Crown Court's decision, holding that although *R* v *Anderson* above established that such a defence could be, in law, a special reason, in this instance it was not such as would, or should, have led the Crown Court not to impose the normal disqualification. In *Harding* v *Oliver* [1973] RTR 497, it was held that the loss of the defendant's sample could not itself amount to a special reason and in *Lodwick* v *Brow* [1984] RTR 394 (where the defendant had no recollection because of post traumatic amnesia of giving a specimen of blood or being offered a sample at hospital and when he knew about the sample some time after leaving hospital could not trace it) it was held that, following *Harding* v *Oliver*, the loss of the sample specimen could not be a special reason which related to the offence, because the taking of the specimen took place after the offence had been completed. It was also held that the decision in *Doyle* v *Leroux* that the loss of a specimen could amount to a special reason was decided *per incuriam* in view of the fact that *Harding* v *Oliver* was not cited to it.

Where a defendant has been convicted under the former s 9 of failing to provide a sample of blood or urine for analysis, it has been held that there is no room for special reasons based on the circumstances in which he refuses. If special reasons exist the defendant will have a reasonable excuse for refusing and if he has a reasonable excuse he should not be convicted. If the reason why he refused to supply a laboratory specimen does not amount to a reasonable excuse there cannot exist a special reason for not disqualifying (*Scobie* v *Graham* [1970] Crim LR 589, *Hockin* v *Weston* (1971) 115 SJ 675, *R* v *Hogan* [1976] Crim LR 319 and *Brown* v *Ridge* [1979] RTR 136), but in *White (Arvin)* v *Metropolitan Police Commissioner* [1984] Crim LR 687 it was held to be a 'special reason' for reducing to twelve months the minimum three-year period for a second drink/driving offence in a case of refusing to supply two specimens of breath, contrary to s 8(7) of the Act, that he duly provided a first sample, which was below the prescribed limit namely 27 microgrammes.

It is not a special reason to avoid disqualification for the defendant to have consumed alcohol after an accident when convicted of refusing to supply a specimen of blood or urine for laboratory testing, even though if he had consented he would have had a defence to a charge under the former s 6 (1) (*Courtman* v *Masterson* [1978] RTR 457).

The special reason proffered for failing to supply a specimen of blood or urine must relate to the failure to provide the specimen and not the circumstances in which the driver came to be driving in the first place (*Anderton* v *Anderton* [1977] RTR 424).

## 21.9 Reckless and careless driving

In England and Wales, ,the triviality of the offence by itself cannot amount to a special reason (see 21.2; see also *Nicholson* v *Brown* ibid). In Scotland, *Smith* v *Henderson* (see 21.2) may still be followed, a fact which will produce an undesirable difference of view in two parts of the United Kingdom over the same statutory provision.

The fact that the defendant was dealing with an emergency is capable of amounting to a special reason. In *R* v *Lundt-Smith* [1964] 3 All ER 225, an ambulance driver conveying an urgent case to hospital crossed traffic lights at red, having, he thought, ensured that it was safe to do so. In fact, a motor cyclist was approaching and there was a collision in which the motor cyclist was killed. Although the ambulance driver pleaded guilty to the offence of causing death by dangerous driving, the judge found that the facts were capable of amounting to special reasons, absolutely discharged the driver, and did not disqualify him. Similarly, in *Wood* v *Richards* [1977] Crim LR 295, the conviction by magistrates of a police officer, who was responding to an emergency call, of driving without due care and attention was upheld; no special exception or standard was to be applied for police officers. The magistrates' finding of special reasons in the case for not endorsing was approved.

## 21.10 Traffic signs, pedestrian crossings, school crossings

Unless on public policy grounds the decisions in *Nicholson* v *Brown* and *Delaroy-Hall* v *Tadman* at 21.2 are to be restricted to the particular offences with which they were concerned: the triviality of the infringement will not amount of itself to a special reason. If the submission is simply that the defendant passed, for example, a red stop light extremely slowly, it will not be possible to point to any facts, other than those which constitute proof of the offence, as special reasons and therefore none could be found. However, if the offence was committed in circumstances where no danger was either caused or was likely to have been caused, particularly if the red lights had remained at red for an inordinate period and there was justification for a belief that these had jammed, those circumstances might be capable of amounting to special reasons on the same principle that the court applied in *James* v *Hall* and *R* v *Agnew*, 'Shortness of distance driven', 21.8. In those cases, the shortness of the distance driven by drivers who were over the blood-alcohol limit was held to be capable, in very restricted circumstances, of amounting to a special reason. The words 'capable of' must be emphasised. The Divisional Court is clearly concerned to restrict the ambit of special reasons. But, in principle, it would seem wrong to endorse the licence of a driver who, approaching a red traffic light in circumstances where he has ample visibility in both directions well before the junction, determines to proceed across when no danger or inconvenience could conceivably be caused in so doing.

The fact that the defendant was dealing with an emergency can amount to a special reason (see *R* v *Lundt-Smith* above).

If a defendant has been misled by the actions of a police officer, or pedestrian or school crossing patrol, this could also be capable of amounting to a special reason. The fact that a defendant was without fault in failing to accord precedence to a pedestrian on a pedestrian crossing might also be so capable. It is an absolute offence: the facts showing that the defendant was without fault would therefore be facts other than those constituting proof of the offence.

## 21.11 Speed limits

Special reasons can be found where the defendant exceeded a speed limit by reason of an emergency (see Lord Goddard in *Whittall* v *Kirby* at 21.2). In *Police Prosecutor* v *Humphreys* [1970] Crim LR 234, the Divisional Court refused to intervene when magistrates found special reasons in the fact that the defendant was a solicitor's articled clerk hurrying to quarter sessions to instruct counsel, having been delayed en route, in order that he should not hold up the business of the court.

While the fact that the 70 mph motorway speed limit is only exceeded by 10 mph cannot by itself amount to a special reason, the fact that the limit was unintentionally exceeded can be (*Marks* v *West Midland Police* at 21.2).

It is not a special reason that a road subject to a limit of 30 mph was often mistakenly thought to be subject to one of 40 mph, nor that the defendant was the last of a line of vehicles driving at the same speed in such an area: *Jones* v *Nicks* [1977] RTR 72. Ignorance of the fact that a 30 mph area is normally created by a system of street lights placed not more than 200 yards apart, and therefore a failure to appreciate, in such an area, that there was such a limit cannot be a special reason. Street lights are readily visible whether at night or day and a motorist should be alerted by them to the existence of the limit: *Walker* v *Rawlinson* [1976] RTR 94. However, where a motorist came from a 40 mph area to a 30 mph area and genuinely thought he was still in a 40 mph area because there was no 30 mph sign when leaving the 40 mph area, it was held that this could amount to a special reason (*Burgess* v *West* [1982] RTR 269).

## 21.12 Accidents

Where the failure to report an accident was as a result of an emergency, or because the defendant was misled, for example where both parties are apparently agreed that the incident is too trivial to be reported, then special reasons could be found, it is submitted.

It is also an offence under s 25(1) for a driver involved in an accident to fail to give his name and address and also the name and address of the owners of the bus to a person who had reasonable grounds for so requiring. A bus driver had a slight impact with a car which had pulled out very suddenly in front of the bus. The driver of the car got out and asked the bus driver for his name and address (he was wearing his bus driver's identity disk in a prominent position on his uniform) which he omitted to give. The justices on his pleading guilty endorsed his licence with 6 penalty points holding that the fact that there were other means of identification available to the lady car driver did not relieve the bus driver of his responsibility and found no special reasons for not endorsing his licence. The Divisional Court disagreed and held that on the very special facts of the case there was material which could constitute special reasons and remitted the case back to the justices but also said (per Croom-Johnson J) 'We wish to make it clear we are laying down no general rule which applies to all cases where the identification of the driver is obvious' (*Leeman* v *Walton* (1984) Divisional Court, unreported, 8 October.)

## 21.13–15 Construction and Use Regulations

The entries relating to s 40(5) in columns 5 and 6 of Part I of Sched 4 to the 1972 Act provide that where a person is convicted of an offence under the Motor Vehicles (Construction and Use) Regulations or like regulations applying to track-laying vehicles, being an offence for which endorsement or disqualification is obligatory, the court *cannot* order endorsement or disqualification or a driving test if he establishes that he did not know and had no reason to suspect that the facts were such that an offence had been committed. This provision was first enacted in the Road Traffic (Amendment) Act 1967, s 7. All cases relating to special reasons in respect of such offences prior to 1968 must therefore be read with this new provision in mind. It is intended to deal with the cases where, for example, an innocent employee or partner has been convicted; and, unlike special reasons, it does not simply give to the court a discretion to mitigate the normal consequences, but precludes the court from imposing them if the relevant facts are established. It will assist not only the innocent employee or partner, but also the employee who is without fault, the private car owner who has relied on his garage, even the member of the family who uses the family car reasonably believing it to be free of any defects. See further 8.46.

It is obviously sensible for any employer who owns vehicles driven by employees to form a limited company to run the business. Otherwise he will be at risk of endorsement on his own licence in respect of defects in those vehicles, and therefore of disqualification under the 'totting up' provisions. Even though the provision referred to above provides some protection for him, it may not always be easy to satisfy a court that his maintenance and supervision have been adequate to establish that he was free of fault.

## Special Reasons: Practice and Procedure

### 21.16–20 Onus of proof etc

The onus of proof of establishing special reasons is on the defendant (*Jones* v *English* [1951] 2 All ER 853). The standard of proof is the balance of probabilities (*Pugsley* v *Hunter* [1973] RTR 284). Special reasons must be supported by evidence, and not mere assertion by advocates (*Jones* v *English* above, *Brown* v *Dyerson* [1968] 3 All ER 39, *R* v *Lundt-Smith* [1964] 2 QB 147 and *McClean* v *Cork* [1968] Crim LR 507).

Admissions made by the prosecution under s 10 of the Criminal Justice Act 1967 would suffice in theory. But the court should always examine the facts as thoroughly as it can; and admissions may not always be a satisfactory form of proof.

Once the court has found special reasons to exist it is then not bound not to disqualify or endorse, it merely means that the court has a discretion not to disqualify for the minimum period or not to endorse. Having found special reasons the court should then decide whether to exercise its discretion (*R* v *Newton (David)* [1974] RTR 451, where it was held that if the blood-alcohol level is high or the impairment substantial the court is bound to take into account the fact that, whatever excuse the defendant may have had for drinking in the first place, he may have no proper excuse for driving or continuing to drive when he must or should have realised that he was affected by drink).

It was said by Lord Widgery CJ in *Taylor* v *Rajan* [1974] RTR 304, an 'emergency' case, that the discretion where special reasons are found should only be exercised in clear and compelling circumstances, that in deciding whether to exercise their discretion the justices should have regard to the way in which the car was driven, and that they should have regard to the defendant's level of alcohol. 'If the alcohol content exceeds 100 milligrammes per 100 millilitres of blood the justices should rarely if ever exercise their discretion in favour of the defendant driver' (per Lord Widgery at 310F). Applying *Taylor* v *Rajan* it was held in *Vaughan* v *Duff* [1984] RTR 376 that justices should be directed to disqualify where the defendant (who was a detective constable on an undercover operation which involved visiting public houses for which he was paid £2 a day drinking allowance) was so drunk that he drove straight into a lamp-post without any vehicle being involved and when breathalysed had a reading of 100 microgrammes, nearly three times the permitted limit.

Whether facts are, or are not, capable of amounting to special reasons is a matter of law, not of fact. Justices are well advised to consult their clerk and hear from the defence and the prosecution before deciding that special reasons exist. In *Barnes* v *Gevaux* [1981] RTR 236 justices decided that the special circumstances of a careless driving offence amounted to a special reason for not endorsing the licence. The justices declined to state the special reasons or, at the clerk's suggestion, hear any submission from the prosecution and the defence. The Divisional Court held the justices to be wrong: although s 105(1) is directory not mandatory, the justices should have allowed both the prosecutor and the defence to make submissions on the matter. It is well within the prosecutor's field 'to bring to the justices' attention the jurisdictional limitations which exist on their power to decide whether to disqualify or to refrain from endorsing in a case which would otherwise be mandatory' (per Donaldson LJ at p 241)).

The evidence upon which the court acts must be admissible evidence, not hearsay: *Flewitt* v *Horvath* (1972) 136 JP Jo 164. Where it is suggested that the defendant's drink was 'laced', medical or other expert evidence should be adduced to show that, but for the added drink, the defendant would not have been over the limit, unless this would be obvious to the layman: *Pugsley* v *Hunter* [1973] RTR 284, 21.8 above. If the defendant is intending to argue that special reasons exist by reason of the fact that his drink was 'laced', he should inform the prosecution in sufficient time before the hearing for the police to make enquiries: ibid.

If the court finds special reasons established, the reason must be stated in open court and, if in a magistrates' court, also entered in the court register: Road Traffic Act 1972, s 105. This requirement is directory and not mandatory and failure to comply is not of itself a ground of appeal by the prosecutor (*Brown* v *Dyerson* [1968] 3 All ER 39), but not where the justices refused to specify the special reasons (*Barnes* v *Gevaux* [1981] RTR 236).

## Mitigating Circumstances

### 21.21–5 Penalty points disqualification

The *Report of the Inter-Departmental Committee on Road Traffic Law* (HMSO 1981) decided that the grounds on which courts may refrain from disqualifying should be restricted in view of the fact that, unlike the 'totting up' system, the new penalty points system discriminates according to the seriousness of the offence. The committee recommended that a person liable to be disqualified under the penalty points system should be allowed to put forward mitigating circumstances in the same way as for 'totting up', but recommended that none of the following circumstances should be allowed to be taken into account:

(*a*) any that are alleged to make the offence or any of the offences not a serious one;
(*b*) hardship, other than exceptional hardship; and
(*c*) any circumstances taken into account by a court when the offender escaped disqualification or was disqualified for less than the minimum

period on a previous occasion when he was liable to be disqualified under s 19(2) or s 93(3) of the 1972 Act.

These recommendations were accepted by the government and are embodied in s 19 of the Transport Act 1981. One other useful and practical recommendation of the committee was either overlooked or rejected. This was that where mitigating circumstances were to be put forward advance notice should be given in order that there may be an opportunity for them to be challenged.

The general statutory formula which enables a court not to disqualify or to disqualify for a period less than the minimum period in s 19(2) of the Transport Act 1981 is identical with the former words in s 93(3) and is *unless the court is satisfied, having regard to all the circumstances, that there are grounds for mitigating the normal consequences of the conviction.*

It should be noted that analysis of the words of s 19(2) seems to show the following two propositions:

(1) It is for the court to be satisfied that there are mitigating circumstances before the court can exercise its discretion not to disqualify for at least six months. It is suggested that the question the court might ask itself is 'Are the mitigating circumstances sufficient to justify us in not disqualifying the offender for not less than six months?' *not* 'Ought the offender to be disqualified?'

(2) Mitigating circumstances must be found if the court disqualifies for *less than six months*. Obviously the mitigating circumstances must be much greater to justify the court not disqualifying at all rather than merely reducing the period of disqualification. The more the period of disqualification is reduced, the greater should be the mitigating circumstances.

In *Lambie* v *Woodage* [1972] 2 All ER 462 the House of Lords held that the purpose of s 93(3) was to deal with the man who does not commit serious offences and that the subsection is aimed at the person who commits comparatively trivial offences frequently. It was held by the House of Lords in *Lambie* v *Woodage* that evidence that the previous convictions were for trivial offences was admissible. *Lambie* v *Woodage* does not apply to mitigating circumstances for the purposes of s 19(2) of the Transport Act 1981. One of the grounds now specifically excluded from consideration by a court is 'any circumstances that are alleged to make the offence or any of the offences not a serious one' (s 19(6)(*a*)) (see below).

It was said in *Baker* v *Cole* [1971] 3 All ER 680n that anything which amounts to a special reason can be taken into account by the court under s 93(3) and so can reasons special to the offender as well as those special to the offence, for the wording is intended to catch circumstances wider than those which constitute special reasons.

In *R* v *Thomas* [1984] Crim LR 49 the appellant aged twenty-five was convicted of two offences of driving while disqualified. He was disqualified for two years, the judge being bound by s 19(4)(*b*) to impose a mandatory disqualification of two years by reason of previous orders of disqualification. It was held that the general sentencing policy of not imposing a long term of disqualification on a persistent motoring offender who is sentenced to a term of imprisonment was a 'ground for mitigating the normal consequences of conviction' and the Court of Appeal reduced the disqualification to twelve months.

## Mitigating Circumstances: Excluded Grounds

### 21.26 Circumstances alleged to make the offence not serious

Section 19(6)(*a*) of the 1981 Act excludes 'any circumstances that are alleged to make the offence or any of the offences not a serious one'. The effect of this exclusion seems clear: an advocate cannot avoid a penalty points disqualification by alleging that the particular offence or any of the offences do not justify the penalty points which have been imposed or would be imposed but for the disqualification. The exclusion seems to refer both to the instant offence or offences which brings the number of penalty points up to 12 and also to the offences for which previous penalty points were incurred. It is also clear that this exclusion does not prevent the advocate putting forward 'special reasons' for not endorsing the offender's licence on the ground that the offence or offences are not serious. (As already explained, if 'special reasons' for not endorsing an offender's licence are found, no penalty points are incurred.) Indeed, the effect of the exclusion is to force the advocate who wishes to avoid disqualification for his client because of the nature of the offence to confine his advocacy to 'special reasons' for not endorsing in accordance with s 101(2) of the 1972 Act. Although triviality of the offence is not itself a 'special reason' for not endorsing (see *Nichols* v *Brown* at 21.2), 'special reasons' relate necessarily to the offence and not the offender (see 21.2). The effect of this exclusion is to nullify the effect of *Lambie* v *Woodage* above.

### 21.27 Hardship other than exceptional hardship

The exclusion of 'hardship, other than exceptional hardship' is contained in s 19(6)(*b*). Almost every order of disqualification entails hardship for the person disqualified. It will be for the courts to interpret this phrase. For hardship to be 'exceptional' it must be more than is normally suffered. Loss of employment, for example, undoubtedly causes hardship, and many offenders lose their jobs if disqualified, but whether loss of employment amounts to 'exceptional hardship' to the offender is a matter of fact and degree to be determined in each case.

It seems clear that the word 'hardship' is not confined to the hardship that the disqualification will cause to the offender: often hardship will be caused to persons other than the offender who are wholly innocent and will suffer hardship if the offender is disqualified (see for example *Cornwall* v *Cole* [1976] Crim LR 519). It is submitted that a court may properly take more notice of hardship where it is caused either to the public or to the offender's employer, employees or family, and, depending on the degree of hardship, hardship to persons other than the offender may more readily be regarded as 'exceptional hardship' than hardship to the offender himself. The offender's family or employees are innocent; the defendant himself, by definition, is not.

Because of the way s 19 is drafted, there appear to be two instances where courts may be prepared to find that the drafting of the section has caused 'exceptional' hardship. The first is where the offender has committed a number of offences and for some reason a court has disqualified the offender for a later offence before an earlier offence was dealt with. In such a case the penalty points for the offence will not be 'wiped clean' (see 20.20). If the offender subsequently becomes liable to another penalty points disqualification as a result of the additional penalty points for the earlier offence, it is submitted that this might amount to 'exceptional hardship', provided the defendant can show he was not responsible for the delay in the earlier offence being dealt with.

The other instance where the drafting of the section can result in exceptional hardship is where the offender was disqualified under both ss 19(2) and 93 on the same occasion and subsequently reaches 12 penalty points. In such a case, even if the disqualification were for the same offence and imposed on the same occasion and he had no previous penalty points, the minimum disqualification period is two years. For example, if the offender is disqualified for one month for an offence of careless driving and on the same occasion is also disqualified until he passes a test of competence to drive, s 19(4) requires him to be disqualified for at least two years if he subsequently incurs 12 penalty points within three years. In such a case a court may be able to regard this as amounting to 'exceptional hardship' and disqualify him for less than the minimum of two years (but not, it is submitted, for less than twelve months).

The phrase 'exceptional hardship' in s 3(2) of the Matrimonial Causes Act 1973 (which enabled a petitioner to obtain leave to present a petition for divorce within three years of marriage) was considered by the House of Lords in *Fay* v *Fay* [1982] 2 All ER 922. Although many of the considerations adverted to in the case are irrelevant for the purpose of considering the meaning of 'hardship, other than exceptional hardship' in a criminal statute, it is submitted that the approach to the problem as set out in the speech of Lord Scarman (who gave the only reasoned speech) is helpful to a court considering whether exceptional hardship exists for the purpose of s 19(6)(*b*) of the Transport Act 1981. The speech of Lord Scarman appears to show (*a*) that in choosing the imprecise concept of 'exceptional hardship' Parliament deliberately intended that what is or is not 'exceptional hardship' should be a matter of fact for the judge at first instance to decide by making his own subjective value judgment, (*b*) that it would be wrong for an appellate court to attempt to define the concepts of 'exceptional hardship' with any precision or to attempt to lay down guidelines as to how the concepts should be applied and (*c*) that the decision of the judge at first instance should be treated as final unless it can be shown to be clearly wrong.

It is submitted that this approach is one which may be broadly applied by a criminal court in considering whether 'exceptional hardship' exists.

The first consideration is that s 19(6)(*b*) requires the defendant to satisfy the court on the balance of probabilities that exceptional hardship other than ordinary hardship exists. The burden of establishing exceptional hardship is on the defendant. The court must disqualify the offender for the minimum period unless the court is satisfied exceptional hardship exists.

The second consideration is that what is exceptional hardship is a question of fact to be judged by the court on evidence. All that can be said with certainty is that the hardship must be something 'out of the ordinary' (per Connor LJ cited with approval by Lord Scarman at p 926G). While the court in *Fay* v *Fay* was dealing with past as well as present and future suffering, a court in applying s 19(6)(*a*) is of necessity considering future suffering only. Nevertheless the principle stressed in *Fay* v *Fay* that there must be evidence of the degree of the circumstances relied on to show the character of the hardship to be exceptional seems to be equally applicable to a criminal court in deciding whether exceptional hardship exists.

The third consideration, namely that the Appeal Court will only intervene if the inferior court is clearly in the wrong, is no doubt correct when there is an appeal on law by way of case stated from the magistrates' court to the Divisional Court. It does not seem to apply so cogently, however, to an appeal against sentence from the magistrates' court to the Crown Court which is by way of rehearing of the facts.

### 21.28–30 Any circumstances previously taken into account

The exclusion regarding circumstances previously taken into account is set out in s 19(6)(*c*) and s 19(7)(*b*). Circumstances which were taken into account on an earlier occasion either for not disqualifying or for disqualifying for a lesser period of disqualification than the minimum are excluded by s 19(6)(*c*). In addition, any circumstances similarly taken into account in respect of a 'totting up' disqualification under s 93(3) are also excluded by s 19(7)(*b*).

Oddly, the period during which circumstances are excluded differs between s 19(4) and s 19(7). Section 19(4) provides that the minimum period of disqualification is increased to twelve months (or two years if more than one) if a previous disqualification was imposed 'within the three years immediately preceding the commission of the latest offence'. The period for excluding circumstances under s 19(7) previously taken into account is 'within three years immediately preceding the conviction'. This difference could be slightly unfortunate. The effect is to encourage an unscrupulous offender in an appropriate case to endeavour to delay his conviction for an offence for which he will again be liable to a s 19(2) disqualification in order to try and get outside the three-year period and put forward similar circumstances put forward on the previous occasion.

The main difficulty, however, in the operation of s 19(7)(*c*) is to decide whether or not circumstances put forward were put forward on the previous occasion. Although a court is required to state the grounds for not disqualifying and, if it is a magistrates' court, to enter the grounds in the register (1972 Act, s 105(1)), it often may be difficult to ascertain all the circumstances taken into account earlier. Even if an extract from the court register of the previous occasion is available, the full circumstances will rarely be disclosed in the register. It is likely that, for this reason, most courts will insist in future on the circumstances being more fully set out. It would not be improper for the prosecution similarly to keep a record of the circumstances where an offender is not disqualified or is disqualified for less than the minimum period.

It is submitted that the evidential onus is on the defendant to show that the circumstances being put forward on a second occasion differ from those put forward and accepted by the court on the first occasion.

## Mitigating Circumstances: Practice and Procedure

### 21.31 Onus of proof etc

As in the case of 'special reasons' it is submitted that the onus of proof in establishing 'mitigating circumstances' is on the defendant (see *Jones* v *English* and *Pugsley* v *Hunter* at 21.16). Similarly where the facts relied on depend on evidence from the defendant, the defendant should be called to give evidence of those facts.

If the court finds mitigating circumstances established they must be stated in open court and if in a magistrates' court entered in the court register (the Road Traffic Act 1972, s 105). It is particularly important now that s 105 be fully complied with in that once mitigating circumstances are found they may not be put forward again (see above). It was held in *Brown* v *Dyson* [1968] 3 All ER 39 that the requirement in s 105 is directory, not mandatory, and failure to comply with it is not appealable (*aliter* if the justices refuse to specify them (*Barnes* v *Gevaux* [1981] RTR 236)).

# Chapter 22

# Appeals

*'It is constantly said (although I am not sure that it is sufficiently remembered) that the function of a court of appeal is to exercise its powers when it is satisfied that the judgment below was wrong, not merely because it is not satisfied that the judgment was right.'*
(Lord Goddard CJ in *Stepney Borough Council* v *Joffe* [1949] 1 KB, at pp 602, 603, quoted with approval by Edmund Davies LJ in *Sagnata Ltd* v *Norwich Corporation* [1971] 2 QB 614.)

## Introduction

### 22.1 Rights of appeal

Appeals from magistrates' courts lie to the Crown Court by the defendant against conviction or sentence or both and to the High Court by the defendant or prosecutor against conviction or dismissal and, to a limited extent, sentence. The appeal to the High Court will be heard by a Divisional Court of the Queen's Bench Division.

As to suspension of an order of disqualification pending the hearing of the appeal, see 22.3, below.

### 22.2 Appeals generally

Where a sentence or order of a magistrates' court is clearly wrong or has been made or imposed as a result of an obvious error, a defendant should be immediately advised to ask the court to rectify the mistake under s 142 of the Magistrates' Courts Act 1980. Unfortunately the power under s 142 can only be exercised within twenty-eight days of the sentence or order (for computation of the time limit and s 142 generally see 2.44). There appears to be no reason why notice of appeal to the Crown Court or notice to state a case should not be lodged at the same time. The procedure under s 142 will usually be considerably speedier and much less expensive than an appeal either to the Crown Court or the Divisional Court.

A defendant's advisers should carefully consider the position where he wishes to appeal against conviction. If his case is strong on law and facts, the case will end completely if the Crown Court allows his appeal on the facts. If, however, the Crown Court decides the appeal in his favour on a point of law only, this gives to the prosecution the right to appeal to the High Court from the decision of the Crown Court, with consequent delay and further expense.

Also, though a defendant can on an appeal to the Crown Court call additional witnesses or refrain from calling witnesses who were unhelpful before the magistrates, the prosecution can do the same in order to bolster up weaknesses in their own case. *Quaere* whether an appellant may appeal to the Crown Court and seek certiorari simultaneously.

If the defendant's case rests on law only, appeal by case stated may at first sight appear to be the better course. Where the possible success of the appeal will depend largely on the facts as found by the magistrates, the appeal may have to be abandoned if, when the case is finally agreed, the facts as stated leave little room for argument on a point of law. Moreover, if a recognisance to prosecute the appeal to the High Court has been entered into, there is danger of its forfeiture, and, more important still, once a notice to state a case has been given any right of appeal to the Crown Court ceases (Magistrates' Courts Act 1980, s 111(4)). The right of appeal to the Crown Court ceases even if the application to state a case is subsequently abandoned (*R* v *Winchester Crown Court, ex parte Lewington* [1982] Crim LR 664).

If there is a danger of time limits for giving notices expiring or having expired it should also be borne in mind that, while the time limit for giving notice to state a case to a magistrates' court cannot be extended, leave to appeal out of time to the Crown Court is usually readily granted. Moreover the time limit of twenty-one days which applies when asking the Crown Court to state a case can, unlike the notice to a magistrates' court for a case stated, be extended by the Crown Court (Crown Court Rules 1982, r 26(14)).

## 22.3–5 Suspension of disqualification pending appeal

By s 94(1) of the 1972 Act, a person who by virtue of an order of a magistrates' court is disqualified from driving may appeal against the order in the same way as against a conviction, and the court may, if it thinks fit, pending the appeal, suspend the operation of the order. The wording suggests that the disqualification may be suspended only if there is an appeal against the order of disqualification; a defendant wishing to appeal against his conviction should presumably include an appeal against the order of disqualification also in his notice of appeal and later abandon it if he fears that the Crown Court may increase the period of disqualification.

There is an appeal, with the leave of the Court of Appeal, Criminal Division, to that court against an order of disqualification imposed by a Crown Court whether on conviction on indictment there or on dealing with a person committed for sentence (Criminal Appeal Act 1968, ss 9, 10(3), 11(1) and 50(1), as amended by the Courts Act 1971). The time for appealing is twenty-eight days but it may be extended with the Court of Appeal's leave. The Criminal Appeal Rules 1968 contain no provision automatically suspending a disqualification pending an appeal, as the revoked 1908 Rules did (but see below).

Although it would appear from a reading of ss 94(2) and 94A(2) that the Crown Court may suspend its own order of disqualification, the circumstances must be rare in practice in which it would be either proper or appropriate for application for suspension to be made to the Crown Court rather than to the Court of Appeal. It is submitted that an application to suspend any order of disqualification can only be made when there is an appeal pending or, in the case of a conviction by the Crown Court, when application has been made for leave to appeal. An appeal or application for leave to appeal can only be pending once notice in the appropriate form is served on the Registrar of the Court of Appeal in accordance with r 2 of the Criminal Appeal Rules 1968. Once notice has been so served, a single judge of the Court of Appeal has power to suspend the order of disqualification (Criminal Appeal Act 1968, s 31(2A)), and where he refuses an application, the applicant is entitled to have the application determined by the Court of Appeal (Criminal Appeal Act 1968, s 31(3)).

In Scotland, there is an appeal against a disqualification ordered by any court and the latter court may suspend it pending the appeal.

Until 1975 only the court which disqualified the offender could suspend the disqualification, but by virtue of ss 94A and 94B of the 1972 Act appellate courts can suspend an order of disqualification imposed by the court of first instance. These sections were inserted in the 1972 Act by Sched 3 to the 1974 Act and enable all appellate courts other than the House of Lords to suspend an order of disqualification pending appeal. It is submitted that because an appeal to the Crown Court can only be commenced by giving notice in writing (see r 7 of the Crown Court Rules 1982) a court should not suspend an order of disqualification pending appeal until such notice has first been given. A Crown Court may suspend an order of disqualification pending the hearing of an appeal from a magistrates' court (s 94A(2)); the High Court may do so on appeal by way of case stated from a magistrates' court or Crown Court (s 94A(4)), or on application for certiorari or for leave to make such an application (s 94A(2)); the Court of Appeal may do so on appeal or application for leave to appeal (s 94A(5)). Similar powers apply to Scottish appellate courts (s 94B). The Court of Appeal or the Divisional Court may suspend an order of disqualification on appeal, or after application has been made for leave to appeal to the House of Lords (s 94A(3)). Disqualification must be endorsed on any licence held or to be held by the defendant (1972 Act, s 101) (except an order of disqualification under s 44 of the Powers of Criminal Courts Act 1973 (see 20.31)).

Disqualification is not suspended by notice of appeal alone (*Kidner* v *Daniels* (1910) 74 JP 127); there must be an application to suspend it. There seems to be no appeal against refusal to suspend but if the court of first instance has refused to suspend, application may be made to the appellate court and, seemingly, vice versa. A power to suspend also exists where the appeal is from the magistrates to the High Court. On suspending an order of disqualification pending appeal, the court suspending the order must notify the Department of Transport (ss 94(3A), 94A(7) and 94B(3) of the 1972 Act as amended by Scheds 3 and 6 to the 1974 Act). The power to suspend an order of disqualification pending appeal applies to an order of disqualification for use of a vehicle for crime (see 20.31).

By s 94(4) of the 1972 Act in calculating the period for which a person is disqualified, by conviction or order, any time after conviction during which the disqualification was suspended or he was not disqualified shall be disregarded. Thus, if Jehu is convicted of driving under the influence of drink on 1 July 1985 and disqualified from driving for a year but immediately appeals and has the disqualification suspended the same day until the appeal is heard, the period of disqualification will run from the hearing of the appeal. If the Crown Court affirm the disqualification on 1 October 1985, he will be disqualified from then until the first moment of 1 October 1986. Again, if Toad is convicted of a second offence of reckless driving on 1 August 1985 and the magistrates omit to disqualify and the High Court, on appeal by the prosecutor, directs on 4 December 1985 that he be disqualified for a year, his disqualification will run from then until the first moment of 4 December 1986.

Days during which disqualification runs prior to suspension should be subtracted from the period running from the date of the appeal. Thus if Jehu was disqualified on 1 July 1985 for twelve months and appeals to the Crown Court who on 1 August suspend the disqualification pending hearing the appeal and on 10 October hear and dismiss Jehu's appeal, Jehu then again becomes disqualified on 10 October and remains disqualified until 10 September 1986.

Where an appeal is abandoned it would seem that an order of disqualification which is suspended pending the appeal will again come into effect as soon as the appeal is abandoned.

Any licence held by a person who is disqualified is revoked and where the disqualification is suspended pending appeal the licence is treated as revoked on the day on which the disqualification ceases to be suspended (the 1972 Act, s 98).

# Crown Court

## 22.6 Scope of right and procedure

Appeals to the Crown Court from magistrates' courts are now regulated by ss 108–110 of the Magistrates' Courts Act 1980, rr 6–11 of the Crown Court Rules 1982, and rr 74 and 75 of the Magistrates' Courts Rules 1981. Appeal may be against conviction or sentence or both but appeal may not be brought against conviction if the defendant unequivocally pleaded guilty. The Courts Act 1971 and the Crown Court Rules substituted the Crown Court as the appellate court in place of quarter sessions. The notice of appeal must be in writing and has to be given to the magistrates' clerk and to the other party. (In third party proceedings notice has to be given to all the parties concerned.) It has to be given within twenty-one days of the day on which the court's decision was given; r 7(3) of the Crown Court Rules 1982 provides that such day shall, where there was an adjournment after conviction, be the day on which the court sentences or otherwise deals with the offender. Such day is excluded in computing the twenty-one days. Where, however, the magistrates' court defers sentence, notice of appeal against conviction has to be given within twenty-one days of the date upon which the court deferred sentence. The notice of appeal to the Crown Court from a conviction by a magistrates' court must state whether the appeal is against conviction or sentence or both and, unless his appeal is under the General Rate Act or certain licensing or housing Acts set out in Part III of the rules (none of which is the subject of this book), need not state the ground of appeal.

Rule 7(5) of the 1982 Rules allows the Crown Court to extend the time for giving notice of appeal and r 7(6) requires the application for extension of time to be given in writing specifying the grounds of the application. It would also seem that the Crown Court has an inherent jurisdiction to reinstate an appeal (*Hagon* v *Croydon LBC* [1976] Crim LR 632). A form of notice of appeal is in Stone; the magistrates' clerk notifies the Crown Court of it.

Appeal lies against sentence only; 'sentence' includes any order made on conviction by the magistrates, not being a probation order, an order of conditional discharge, an order for payment of costs or 'an order made in pursuance of any enactment under which the court has no discretion as to the making of the order or as to its terms' (Magistrates' Courts Act 1980, s 108(3)(*d*)). An obligatory disqualification under s 93(1) or (3) of the 1972 Act or s 19(2) of the Transport Act 1981, it is submitted, comes within this definition and it is for this reason that statutory provision was made (s 94(1)) specifically allowing an appeal to be made against such orders in the same manner as against a conviction. Section 94(1) is similarly specifically amended to allow appeals against disqualification under s 19 of the Transport Act 1981 for penalty points. A discretionary order of disqualification under s 93(2) is appealable (*R* v *Surrey Quarter Sessions, ex parte Commissioner of Police of the Metropolis* (1962) 126 JP 269) but, it is submitted, neither an endorsement nor an order for the payment of back duty under s 9 of the Vehicles (Excise) Act 1971 may be appealable as both types of order appear to come within the definition under s 108(3)(*d*), above. There is a right of appeal in respect of the number of penalty points endorsed where the offence is one in which the court has a discretion as to the number of points to be imposed. Section 108(3)(*d*) only prohibits an appeal against sentence where the court has no discretion as to the order 'on its terms'. *Quaere* however as to whether 'special reasons' gives a court discretion for the purpose of s 108. If it does not, why did Parliament enact s 94(1) and its amendment (see above)? However, if an appeal is lodged against sentence generally, it would seem to be open to the Crown Court in considering sentence to review an order of endorsement or as to back duty.

Whether or not the appeal is against the whole of the decision, the Crown Court may increase or lessen the sentence provided the punishment is one which the magistrates' court might have awarded (Supreme Court Act 1981, s 48(4), (5)). The same period of notice applies whether the appeal is against conviction, sentence or other order, and the other side and the magistrates' clerk must be notified. The notices may be sent in all cases by registered letter or recorded delivery. A notice of appeal arising out of a conviction must state whether the appeal is against sentence or conviction or both (Crown Court Rules, r 7(3)).

Where the appellant is in custody, the magistrates' court may fix the amount of the recognisance, with or without sureties, for his appearance at the appeal and such recognisances may be entered into before any magistrates, magistrates' clerk or officer in charge of a police station, or the prison governor. On this being done, he should be released. Appeal lies to the High Court against refusal to admit to bail and against a condition of bail (Criminal Justice Act 1948, s 37; Criminal Justice Act 1967, s 22), but s 81(1)(*b*) of the Supreme Court Act 1981 now gives power to the Crown Court to grant bail to any person who has appealed to the Crown Court.

If the defendant pleads guilty and the plea is unequivocal, there is no appeal to the Crown Court against conviction, but if the plea is equivocal, the case may be remitted by the Crown Court for hearing of a plea of not guilty. But a Crown Court has no jurisdiction to remit a case for rehearing on a plea of not guilty unless it has first made proper enquiries into the circumstances surrounding the guilty plea and has satisfied itself that the plea was equivocal (*R* v *Manchester Crown Court, ex parte Anderton* [1980] Crim LR 303). (See also 2.48 as to equivocal pleas.)

It is the duty of the magistrates' clerk to send to the Crown Court the notice of appeal, a statement of the decision from which the appeal is brought, and notification of the last or usual place of abode of the parties. Most justices' clerks will supply a copy of any notes taken to either side on request.

No recognisance is required for the appellant to prosecute an appeal to the Crown Court.

There is no appeal by the prosecutor to the Crown Court in road traffic prosecutions, unless there be one in an excise prosecution (Customs and Excise Management Act 1979, s 147(3)).

The view is advanced at 112 JP Jo 284 that endorsement should be carried out immediately on conviction even though an appeal is pending. There is certainly no statutory provision allowing endorsement to be suspended pending an appeal as there is with a disqualification; nor is there any power for the court to remove an endorsement after lapse of time. The Secretary of State was advised in 1905 that where an endorsement had been ordered under the Motor Car Act 1903 'it is open to justices to refuse to defer endorsement on the ground that the defendant announces an intention to appeal'. It would seem that this 1905 opinion may still apply today.

An appeal against conviction is a rehearing, and either side may call additional witnesses or refrain from calling witnesses called before the justices. The Crown Court may confirm, reverse or vary the justices' decision or remit it to them with their opinion, and exercise any power which the magistrates could have exercised. The Crown Court may not have regard to evidence given before the magistrates but not before it (*Bishop* v *Hosier* (1962) *The Guardian*, 11 October). The Crown Court has no power to amend an information on appeal (*Garfield* v *Maddocks* [1973] 2 All ER 303). The prosecution call their evidence first and then the defence theirs.

Where a person convicted or sentenced by a magistrates' court desires to appeal to the Crown Court, either court may order that legal aid be given to him and to the other party (Legal Aid Act 1974, s 28(5)). A legal aid order for proceedings before a magistrates' court automatically confers authority on the solicitor to advise the defendant whether there are reasonable grounds for appeal either to the Crown Court or to the High Court by way of case stated (Legal Aid Act 1974, s 30(5)). It is submitted that if he wishes to appeal, it is proper for the court considering an application for legal aid to cover the costs of his appeal to enquire from the solicitor who acted before the magistrates' court as to whether he advised that there were reasonable grounds for appeal.

Costs may be awarded against the unsuccessful party to the appeal; the amount may either be fixed by the appellate court or ascertained by taxation. But on a successful appeal against sentence costs should not be awarded against the police unless the original case was so trivial that it should never have been brought or the police have taken a part in the appeal beyond laying the facts before the Crown Court (*David* v *Commissioner of Police of the Metropolis* [1962] 1 All ER 491). This case was approved and applied in *R* v *Lewes Crown Court, ex parte Castle* [1980] RTR 381. A motorist had appealed in respect of various offences for which the justices had fined him a total of £500. In relation to the appeal against conviction for one offence the prosecutor indicated he would not oppose it and in relation to the appeal against sentence in respect of the remaining offences the prosecutor limited himself to informing the Crown Court of the facts. The fines were reduced to a total of £69 and, under r 10(2) of the Crown Court Rules 1971, the Crown Court ordered the prosecutor to pay the motorist's costs estimated at £150. The order for costs was set aside by order of certiorari. There was no question of the offences being trivial; nor was the case one which should never have been brought; nor had the prosecutor contributed to the fines being excessive: his part in the appeal had been limited to informing the Crown Court of the facts.

Where the appeal is against conviction or sentence the Crown Court may increase or lessen the sentence, provided that the punishment is one which the magistrates' court might have awarded (Supreme Court Act 1981, s 48(4)). The powers of the Crown Court contained in s 48 apply whether or not the appeal is against the whole of the magistrates' court's decision (s 48(5)) and by section 48(2)(*c*) the Crown Court may make 'such other order in the matter as the court thinks just, and by such order exercise any power which the [magistrates' court] might have exercised'. In *Killington* v *Butcher* [1979] Crim LR 458 it was held that what is now s 48(2)(*c*) entitled the Crown Court, on allowing an appeal against a conviction by a magistrates' court for an offence contrary to s 2 of the Road Traffic Act 1972, to prefer a charge of careless driving in accordance with Sched 4, Part IV, para 4, to the 1972 Act.

The Court of Appeal in reducing a nineteen year old's disqualification from seven to three years additionally disqualified him under s 93(7) on the grounds that he was not sufficiently competent to drive (see *R* v *Raynor*, 20.32). It is submitted that the Crown Court also has power to do so when hearing an appeal from a magistrates' court as the Crown Court has power to 'exercise any power that the magistrates could have exercised' (s 48(2)(*c*) of the Supreme Court Act 1981).

Either party to the appeal to the Crown Court may, if dissatisfied with the determination of the court as being erroneous in point of law, apply to have a case stated by the Crown Court for the opinion of the Divisional Court

(Supreme Court Act 1981, s 28). The application must be made in writing to the Crown Court within twenty-one days of the decision but the Crown Court may extend the time for making application to state a case (Crown Court Rules 1982, r 6). Legal aid will be available to either side under Part I of the Legal Aid Act 1974. Appeal will lie from the Divisional Court, with leave, to the House of Lords (Administration of Justice Act 1960, s 1), provided that the Divisional Court certifies that a point of law of general public importance is involved.

Once notice of appeal has been given the appellate court, as well as the court of first instance, may suspend an order of disqualification pending appeal (see 22.3).

## 22.7 Offences heard at the same time

The procedure as to appeal and suspension pending appeal (see 22.3) is the same as for an appeal against any other obligatory disqualification with one qualification. This is caused by the fact that by virtue of s 19(5) of the Transport Act 1981 not more than one order of disqualification under s 19(2) may be imposed where an offender is convicted on the same occasion of more than one offence. Section 19(5)(*c*) accordingly provides that for the purpose of any appeal any disqualification under s 19(2) will be treated as an order made on the conviction of each of the offences.

Where, however, there are a number of endorsable offences committed on the same occasion and no disqualification is imposed there is no provision similar to s 19(5)(*c*). Doubt has accordingly arisen, therefore, as to the correct legal position where a defendant who is convicted of a number of offences committed on the same occasion appeals only in respect of the offence meriting the highest number of penalty points and is successful in his appeal. A defendant, for example, is convicted of reckless driving, no 'L' plates and driving not under supervision. He will then incur 10 penalty points in total. He appeals successfully against conviction in respect of the reckless driving offence. What is then the penalty points position in respect of the 'L' plate and driving unsupervised offences? A number of commentators have stated that in such a situation the successful appellant has avoided any penalty points in respect of those offences. This argument is based on the premise that where a person is convicted of a number of offences committed on the same occasion, only the offence bearing the highest number of penalty points is endorsed with penalty points. It is submitted that this may be an incorrect interpretation of the proviso to s 19(1) and that a better interpretation is that all the offences committed on the same occasion bear the same number of points. It should be noted that the proviso to s 19(1) does not state that the court shall only impose penalty points in respect of the one offence bearing the number or highest number that would be endorsed; instead it states '. . . the number of penalty points to be endorsed in respect of *those of them* that were committed on the same occasion shall be the number or highest number that *would* be endorsed on a conviction of one of those offences' (italics supplied). It is submitted that this wording makes it clear that all the offences committed on the same occasion bear the same number of penalty points. In order to avoid doubt as to the number of penalty points remaining it is suggested that a defendant who wishes to appeal against conviction for one only of a number of offences committed on the same occasion should appeal against sentence in respect of the remaining offences. This would then enable the Crown Court to impose the correct number of penalty points should the defendant be successful in his appeal against conviction of one of them.

### 22.8–15 Abandonment of appeal

An appellant may abandon his appeal by giving notice not later than the third day before the hearing fixed for the appeal. To do so the notice must be given to the magistrates' clerk and the other party to the appeal, with a copy to the appropriate officer of the Crown Court. For the purposes of determining whether notice of abandonment was given in time any Saturday, Sunday and any day which is, or is to be observed as, a bank holiday shall be disregarded (Crown Court Rules 1982, r 9).

If notice has not been given in time, the Crown Court may give leave to abandon the appeal. Alternatively a Crown Court may simply leave the appeal in the list and on the day listed simply dismiss the appeal. If any period of disqualification has been suspended pending appeal, the period of disqualification will commence to run as soon as the appeal is abandoned. If notice to abandon is not given in time, it would seem that the period of disqualification runs from any date upon which leave to abandon is given, or if no such leave has been given, upon dismissal of the appeal. Once a valid notice of abandonment has been given, the Crown Court cannot hear an appeal (*R* v *Essex Quarter Sessions, ex parte Larkin* [1961] 3 All ER 930). Where notice of abandonment has been given, the other party may apply to the magistrates' court to order the appellant to pay his just and reasonable costs incurred in connection with the appeal before he received notice (Magistrates' Courts Act 1980, s 190(1)).

Where the appeal is abandoned or dismissed, the magistrates' court may issue process for enforcing their original decision (ss 109 and 110 of the Magistrates' Courts Act 1980). It would seem that if the licence has not been surrendered on abandonment or dismissal of the appeal, the magistrates' court has the power and duty to obtain the licence under ss 109 and 110 for the purpose of endorsement and sending to the Secretary of State. Any licence held by a person who is disqualified is treated as revoked; where the disqualification is suspended pending an appeal, the licence is treated as revoked on the day on which the disqualification ceases to be suspended (1972 Act, s 98).

## High Court

### 22.16 Cases stated

Either side may appeal to the High Court from a decision of a magistrates' court on the ground that it is wrong in law or in excess of jurisdiction (Magistrates' Courts Act 1980, s 111; Magistrates' Courts Rules 1981, rr 76–81;

RSC Ords 56, 57). Written notice has to be given to the magistrates' clerk requiring the magistrates to state a case for the opinion of the High Court. It has to be given within twenty-one days from, and excluding, the day on which the justices finally disposed of the matter. The time for giving notice cannot be extended (*Michael* v *Gowland* [1977] 2 All ER 328). Sundays are included in the computation of the period (*Peacock* v *R* (1858) 22 JP 403).

Rules 76–81 of the Magistrates' Courts Rules 1981 replace rr 65–68 of the 1968 Rules which were amended in 1975 in order to reduce the delays in cases reaching the Divisional Court. Rule 77(1) places on the justices' clerk the responsibility for delivering the first draft of the case to the parties concerned. The intention is thereby to place on the justices' clerk the responsibility for preparing the initial draft unless the justices wish to assume the responsibility themselves. A detailed timetable is prescribed by the new rules. A period of twenty-one days is allowed for delivery by the justices' clerk of the first draft to the parties (r 77(4)), a further period of twenty-one days is allowed for the parties to make representations after receiving the case and a final period of twenty-one days for the case to be settled by the court after having received the parties' observations. It was held in *Parsons* v *FW Woolworth & Co Ltd* (1980) 124 SJ 775 that what is now r 77(1) is directory not mandatory. Rule 79 enables those time limits to be extended but if there is a delay a written statement of the reasons for it must accompany the final case. Rule 76 requires the applicant to identify the point of law upon which the opinion of the High Court is sought or, where the point of law is that there was insufficient evidence to support the decision, r 76(2) provides that the application must identify the particular finding of fact which cannot be supported by the evidence. If the notice does not state the point of law it is a nullity, and the Divisional Court will not allow such a defective notice to be amended if the amendment is itself out of time (see (1980) 144 JP 303). But in *Robinson* v *Whittle* (1980) 124 SJ 807 it was held that the requirement in r 76(1) to state the point is directory not mandatory (the case referred to in 144 JP 303 was not, apparently, brought to the court's attention: *Robinson* is to be preferred, it is submitted).

Justices are entitled, unless the application is by the Attorney-General, to refuse to state a case on the ground that the application is frivolous and if the applicant so requires shall give him a certificate to that effect (s 111(5)). In an appeal to the Court of Appeal the question for the court was whether the appeal was 'frivolous or vexatious'. The Court of Appeal held that the word frivolous in s 20 of the Criminal Appeal Act 1968 could not be intended to mean only foolish or silly, but must mean that the ground of appeal was one that could not possibly succeed on argument (*R* v *Taylor* [1979] Crim LR 649). It is submitted that 'frivolous' in s 111(5) should be similarly interpreted.

Where justices refuse to state a case, the High Court on application by the person who applied for a case to be stated may by order of mandamus require a case to be stated (s 111(6)).

Hitherto the High Court has not been prepared to hear argument on any point not raised before the magistrates' court. As the point of law is now required to be stated in the application, it may well be that the High Court will not be prepared to hear or consider any argument on any other point of law (other than a point of jurisdiction) unless it arises on the face of the facts stated in the case or upon a point of law which no evidence could alter. It was said in *Whitehead* v *Haines* [1964] 2 All ER 530 that on an appeal by case stated the High Court should entertain and determine a point of pure law open, on the facts found in the case, to an appellant convicted on a criminal charge, if that point of law was one which, if sound, might afford him a defence, notwithstanding that the point was not raised prior to his conviction.

Generally, the appellant must argue his point on the facts as found by the justices and indicated in their case. But the decisions of magistrates that certain acts did amount to obstruction and that other facts did not amount to dangerous driving were upset by the High Court in *Gill* v *Carson* (1917) 81 JP 250 and *Bracegirdle* v *Oxley* [1947] 1 All ER 126 respectively. The High Court can confirm, reverse or vary the magistrates' determination and can send back the case for further hearing with the High Court's ruling. The Divisional Court will not usually interfere with findings of fact by magistrates unless there was no evidence to support those findings or they were such that no reasonable magistrates, giving themselves proper directions and applying the proper considerations, could reach them. *Bracegirdle's* case, above, was an example of a successful appeal by the prosecutor against the dismissal of a dangerous driving charge.

An appellant in custody has the same right to apply for bail and to appeal against its refusal as he has on an appeal to the Crown Court (see above). The appellant, whether prosecutor or defendant, is usually required to enter into a recognisance to prosecute the appeal before the High Court and to submit to judgment.

Appeals by the prosecution against sentence on a point of law are sometimes brought where an order of conditional discharge, for example, has been made and it is considered there has been an improper exercise of that power in view of the seriousness of the charge (*Gardner* v *James* [1948] 2 All ER 1069). They are frequently brought by prosecutors contesting a finding of special reasons. Costs may be, but are not always, awarded to a successful respondent (Summary Jurisdiction Act 1857, s 6); they can include the appellant's costs before the magistrates (*Turner* v *Owen* [1955] 3 All ER 565).

Where the appellant abandons his appeal by way of case stated, there appears to be no statutory provision enabling the other party to obtain the costs incurred as a result. If, however, he has entered into a recognisance to prosecute his appeal, such recognisance can be forfeited. Although a forfeited recognisance is payable to the Crown and not to the respondent, it may be wise for a respondent, if he suspects that a case stated may be withdrawn by the appellant, to insist on a recognisance being entered into by the appellant. If this is done it is suggested that if the appellant wishes to withdraw his appeal the respondent should be able to request payment of his reasonable costs by the appellant or forfeit the appellant's recognisance. The conditions of an appellant's recognisance under s 114 of the Magistrates' Courts Act 1980 are to prosecute his appeal without delay, to submit to the judgment of the High Court and to pay any costs that the court may award.

Legal aid may be granted to either side, as with other High Court proceedings, under the Legal Aid Act 1974, Part I.

A legal aid order for proceedings before a magistrates' court includes the cost of a solicitor's assistance in making application for a case to be stated (Legal Aid Act 1974, s 30(5)).

Examining justices have no power to state a case (*Dewing* v *Cumming* [1971] RTR 295, where the defendant elected trial on indictment on a charge under s 1(1) of the Road Safety Act 1967 (now s 6 of the 1972 Act), and the justices had found that there was no case to commit for trial). In the event of an unreasonable refusal to commit for trial, the prosecution can, if the facts warrant, apply to a judge of the High Court for a voluntary bill of indictment under the Administration of Justice (Miscellaneous Provisions) Act 1933, s 2. Where a defendant has been discharged, fresh committal proceedings may be brought against him (*R* v *Manchester City Magistrates' Court, ex parte Snelson* [1977] Crim LR 423).

Appeal by either side will lie from the Divisional Court, with leave, to the House of Lords (Administration of Justice Act 1960, s 1), provided the Divisional Court certifies that a point of law of general public importance is involved.

The Divisional Court may suspend an order of disqualification pending hearing of an appeal by way of case stated, or on application for leave to apply for a writ of certiorari (see 22.3).

In accordance with *Practice Note* [1974] 3 All ER 528 an 'expedited hearing list' is maintained of prerogative writs and appeals by way of case stated which involve sentences of imprisonment, disqualification for driving or possession of property. The main purpose is to dispose of short and simple cases quickly. Any party may apply to be placed on the list and the court of its own motion may place a case on the list.

## 22.17–20 Application for judicial review

The textbooks will show the occasions for which an application by way of judicial review for orders of certiorari, mandamus and prohibition are appropriate. Where the error is obvious or undisputed, the situation can be rectified by an order under s 142 of the Magistrates' Courts Act 1980 provided that the magistrates' court can exercise its power within twenty-eight days. In *R* v *Wells Street JJ, ex parte Collett* [1981] RTR 272 (see below) it was said that the unsuccessful applicant for certiorari should have made application under s 142. Per Ormrod LJ at p 278H: 'It would be wrong, in my judgment, to allow the remedy of certiorari to be used to make good a delay of that kind in taking advantage of the statutory protection of section 142.'

The House of Lords has held that the remedy of judicial review is concerned not so much with the decision of which the review is sought but with the fairness of the decision-making process (*R* v *Chief Constable of N Wales Police, ex parte Evans* [1982] 3 All ER 141).

A motorist and a woman gave perjured evidence to the Crown Court at the hearing of an appeal against conviction for not displaying 'L' plates and driving with excess blood-alcohol, as a result of which convictions were set aside by the Crown Court. It was held that the Divisional Court had power on a hearing by way of judicial review to quash the decision of the Crown Court on appeal and thus restore the original conviction (*R* v *Wolverhampton Crown Court, ex parte Crofts* [1983] RTR 389).

*R* v *Wolverhampton Crown Court* was followed in *Weight* v *Mackay* (1984) Cr App R 324 where it was held that certiorari also lay to quash a decision of the Crown Court allowing an appeal not only where the Crown Court's decision had been obtained by fraud but also where the Crown Court had failed to comply with the rules of natural justice.

Costs on certiorari to remedy a mistake made by the magistrates should not be granted against them unless they have been guilty of deliberate misconduct (*R* v *Amersham JJ* (1964) 108 SJ 841). It was held that an order of certiorari cannot be used to quash a decision in order to introduce fresh evidence; but in *R* v *Leyland JJ, ex parte Hawthorns* [1979] RTR 109 it was held that an order of certiorari could be made to quash a conviction by a magistrates' court on the grounds that there had been a denial of natural justice because the defendant had not been notified by the prosecution of the existence of witnesses known to the prosecution but whom the prosecution did not intend to call. In *R* v *Wells St JJ, ex parte Collett* above certiorari was refused where the defendant neither appealed to the Crown Court nor applied to the magistrates' court under what is now s 142 of the Magistrates' Courts Act 1980 and where it was not established there had been any fault on the part of the prosecution. In that case the defendant sold her car and subsequently was served with a request to serve a statutory statement of ownership under s 1(6) of the Road Traffic Act 1974. She was charged with failing to supply a statement and subsequently convicted in her absence. She sought certiorari on the ground she had posted a statement and had written saying that she had done so after receiving the summons.

An order of certiorari may be granted if the decision of the inferior tribunal was 'harsh and oppressive' (*R* v *St Albans JJ, ex parte Cinnamond* [1980] RTR 139), or, to put it another way, the sentence is 'so far outside the normal discretionary limits as to enable the court to say that its imposition must involve an error of law of some description, even if it may not be apparent at once what is the precise nature of that error' (per Donaldson LJ at p 144E). The applicant had been convicted by justices of driving with excess alcohol and of careless driving and was disqualified for a total of two years of which twenty-one months related to the excess alcohol charge. He appealed to St Albans Crown Court where the conviction for excess alcohol was quashed on technical grounds, but the sentence on the careless driving was varied from an order of disqualification of three months only for 'totting up' to a disqualification of eighteen months for the offence plus the consecutive period of three months for 'totting up'. An order of certiorari was granted and the disqualifications set aside, the court substituting an order of six months' disqualification for the offence and three months for 'totting up'.

It should be noted that an applicant in Scotland can similarly appeal by way of case stated under the Summary Jurisdiction (Scotland) Act 1954 where the court will similarly intervene if satisfied the sentence is 'harsh and oppressive' (*Fleming* v *MacDonald* 1958 JC 1).

An applicant is entitled to go to the Divisional Court from the Crown Court either by requiring the Crown Court to state a case under s 28 of the Supreme Court Act 1981 or by applying by way of judicial review for an order of mandamus, prohibition or certiorari under s 29. It was held in *R* v *Ipswich Crown Court, ex parte Baldwin* [1981] 1 All ER 596 that the applicant may bring whichever proceeding is the more convenient in the circumstances, but where there is difficulty in obtaining the facts, the proper way to go to the Divisional Court is by way of case stated.

## Royal Pardon

### 22.21 Free pardon and remission of penalties

It sometimes happens that a defendant is convicted of an offence and afterwards a decision of the High Court in another case shows that his conviction was wrong. In such circumstances he should be advised to apply to the Home Office for a royal pardon. If the defendant pleaded guilty on a mistake of fact (believing, for example, that he was uninsured as his own policy did not cover him but subsequently finding that the car owner's policy covers him) he can apply to the Home Office for a *remission* under the Sovereign's royal prerogative. This has the effect of commanding the magistrates to remit the penalty imposed (Remission of Penalties Act 1859, s 1).

# Appendices

# Appendix 1

# Drink/Driving

See generally Chapter 4, Drink/Driving Offences. For evidential breath test devices, see 4.76, and 4.74 for blood or urine option experiment.

## Alcohol concentrations

### Conversion of breath-alcohol (μg/100 ml) to blood/urine-alcohol (mg/100 ml)

| | *Alcohol/* | | | *Alcohol/* | |
|---|---|---|---|---|---|
| *Breath* | *Blood* | *Urine* | *Breath* | *Blood* | *Urine* |
| 26 | 60 | 80 | 74 | 170 | 227 |
| 27 | 62 | 83 | 76 | 175 | 234 |
| 28 | 64 | 86 | 78 | 180 | 240 |
| 29 | 67 | 89 | 80 | 185 | 247 |
| 30 | 69 | 92 | 83 | 190 | 254 |
| 31 | 71 | 95 | 85 | 195 | 260 |
| 32 | 74 | 98 | 87 | 200 | 267 |
| 33 | 76 | 101 | 89 | 205 | 274 |
| 34 | 78 | 104 | 91 | 210 | 280 |
| 35 | 80 | 107 | 94 | 215 | 287 |
| 37 | 85 | 113 | 96 | 220 | 294 |
| 39 | 90 | 120 | 98 | 225 | 300 |
| 41 | 95 | 127 | 100 | 230 | 307 |
| 43 | 100 | 133 | 102 | 235 | 314 |
| 45 | 105 | 140 | 105 | 240 | 321 |
| 48 | 110 | 147 | 107 | 245 | 327 |
| 50 | 115 | 153 | 109 | 250 | 334 |
| 52 | 120 | 160 | 111 | 255 | 341 |
| 54 | 125 | 167 | 113 | 260 | 347 |
| 56 | 130 | 173 | 115 | 265 | 354 |
| 59 | 135 | 180 | 118 | 270 | 361 |
| 61 | 140 | 187 | 120 | 275 | 367 |
| 63 | 145 | 193 | 122 | 280 | 374 |
| 65 | 150 | 200 | 124 | 285 | 381 |
| 67 | 155 | 207 | 126 | 290 | 387 |
| 70 | 160 | 214 | 129 | 295 | 394 |
| 72 | 165 | 220 | 131 | 300 | 401 |

To convert breath-alcohol readings outside of these figures, multiply breath-alcohol result by 2.3 and round to the nearest whole number to obtain the equivalent blood-alcohol reading; multiply by 3.06 for urine-alcohol reading.

## Camic Breath Analyser

### Operational Instructions

Check that the analyser and simulator units are both switched on. If the analyser has been switched off for any reason allow a 30 minute warm up period to elapse before taking any breath test.

TO START TEST, SIMPLY PRESS TEST BUTTON.

The instrument will now calibrate itself and after approximately one minute the green 'blow now' lamp will come on requesting the subject to blow.

A CONTINUOUS breath of at least six seconds is required to provide an accurate sample and bring on the 'stop blow' lamp.

The subject has a total of 3 minutes to provide a correct sample. The subject may make as many attempts as necessary to provide a six second continuous sample.

If, after providing a correct breath sample, the subject attempts to suck the gas back out of the breath pipe, the instrument will sense this and immediately reset and print out 'Breath Invalid'.

After the first breath test has been completed the instrument will request a second breath sample exactly as before.

After the second breath test the instrument will again check its calibration and if accurate then the results will be printed out, together with the date and time of test.

## Blood or urine option experiment (16/4/84)

On 26 March 1984 the Home Secretary announced that, from 16 April to 15 October 1984, motorists whose lower breath-alcohol readings exceed 50 μg on the Lion Intoximeter or Camic Analyser may choose to provide a sample of blood or urine. The sample will be analysed and the motorist can use it to challenge the accuracy of the breath test machine. As will be noted, the scheme is experimental and is not based on statute: the police will continue to rely on the printout to prove their case; and the defendant will merely be provided with an official analysis of the sample of blood or urine provided by him to use it to dispute the accuracy of the breath printout.

The circular makes it clear that the defendant will not have an option to provide blood or urine; the option is merely to provide a sample of blood or urine, and (as in the case of the statutory option where the reading is 50 μg or less), the police will decide whether he is to provide blood or urine.

If, because of the lapse of time between the time the motorist provides the breath specimen and the time he provides the sample of blood or a second specimen of urine, the subsequent official analysis is below the prescribed limit, the police will not prosecute. If, however, the certificate of analysis is above the prescribed limit, the defendant can attempt to challenge the accuracy of the Lion Intoximeter or Camic Analyser printout by production of the certificate. This will be difficult. Two points, in particular, should be made.

Firstly, the courts when faced with such a challenge will presumably follow the line of reasoning set out in *R* v *Coomaraswamy* [1976] RTR 21 where it was held that the question of fact to be determined by the court under the former law was whether or not the prosecution has established that the defendant's blood-alcohol level exceeded the limit and that the prosecution do not have to prove a particular figure; dicta to different effect in *R* v *Boswell* [1974] RTR 273 were not approved. *R* v *Coomaraswamy* was again followed and applied in *Thomas* v *Henderson* [1983] RTR 293 where it was similarly held that the prosecution only have to prove that the defendant's blood-alcohol was above the prescribed limit, the prosecution do not have to prove a specific figure.

The second and more important observation is that unless the giving of the blood sample or second specimen of urine for analysis took place very shortly after the time of the breath test, the defendant will have to prove with some degree of precision the rate at which his body eliminated alcohol between the time of the printout and the time he provided the blood specimen or second specimen of urine. (Advocates should make careful note of time: the time of the sample of blood or urine will be recorded as British Summer Time (if in force) while the printout is recorded as Greenwich Mean Time.)

It will be noted that the table of changes in body fluid set out below (an annex to the Home Office circular) is based on the assumption, inter alia, that the average metabolic rate of alcohol destruction by the body is 15 mg per 100 ml per hour in the blood or 6.5 $\mu$g per 100 ml per hour in the breath. These figures are only averages: the mean elimination rate is 11–21 mg per hour, and even this spectrum of variability is subject to significant numbers of individual clearance rates which extend or trail the average by factors of 2 to 4 or even, in some extremes, 8.

It should be also noted that the defendant who wishes to challenge the printout by means of the subsequent certificate of analysis of blood or urine will have to take into the calculations the fact that the certificate of analysis will be 6 mg below the proper figure if below 100 mg or 6 per cent if above 100 mg (see Note on Annex to the Home Office Circular). The circular does not make it clear whether the defendant who decides to provide a specimen of blood or urine will be offered a sample for independent analysis.

As the scheme is purely non-statutory, it would seem that a defendant cannot plead as a special reason that he was unable to provide a sample of blood or urine, nor of course, will he be guilty of the offence of failing to provide a specimen of blood or urine for analysis as he will already have provided a specimen of breath for analysis. It is also clear for the same reason that the defendant must provide two specimens of breath before he can have the option to provide blood or urine. He will not be able to argue as a reasonable excuse for failing to provide a breath specimen for analysis that he was willing to provide blood or urine.

It was held in *Anderton* v *Lythgoe* (1984) *The Times*, 31 October that justices have a discretion to exclude the intoximeter 'printout' as evidence and dismiss the charge if the motorist was not informed by the police of his statutory option under s 8(6). It is thought doubtful whether justices have a similar discretion if the motorist is not informed of this non-statutory option, first because it is a wholly non-statutory scheme and secondly because by definition the breath-alcohol level will be above 50 $\mu$g and thus it will be all the more unlikely that the defendant is below the prescribed level.

The Home Office Circular reads as follows:

### 1 Temporary extension of blood or urine option on a non-statutory basis

1 The purpose of this letter is to draw attention to certain advice that has been given to chief officers of police following a review of the operation of the evidential breath testing procedures contained in the Road Traffic Act 1972, as amended by section 25 of, and Schedule 8 to, the Transport Act 1981 (see HO Circular 41/1983), in

the light of allegations which have been made about breath testing machines as a reliable source of evidence in drink drive cases.

2 Preparatory to their introduction the Lion Intoximeter 3000 and the Camic Breath Analyser were subjected to field trials which proved their general accuracy as devices for measuring the amount of alcohol in the breath by comparing their results with blood samples. Since then a further survey has been undertaken by the Forensic Science Service. A report of this survey has recently been produced and is available separately from the Home Office Central Research Establishment, Aldermaston, Reading, Berks. It shows that in the 620 cases examined, blood samples confirmed the accuracy of the results shown by the breath testing machines. After the necessary allowance was made for alcohol eliminated from the body naturally during the lapse of time between the taking of the breath and blood samples there was no case in which the result of the blood test pointed to an inaccurate instrument.

3 The Secretary of State is nevertheless conscious of the importance of maintaining public confidence in the machines if the benefits which have been derived from them are to continue. It was therefore announced on 26 March that for a period of six months, beginning at 00.01 BST on 16 April 1984, anyone who gives a breath test result which is over the present option limit of 50 microgrammes per hundred millilitres of breath would have the option of a blood/urine test. The assistance of police forces has therefore been requested in putting into effect arrangements whereby for that trial period the option of a blood/urine test is extended on a non-statutory basis, as a matter of administrative practice, to persons whose breath alcohol reading on the machine is over 50 microgrammes.

*Police procedure*

4 The arrangements which have been suggested to the police for operation of this non-statutory option are as follows. Subjects whose breath test readings show a level of about 50 microgrammes should be told that they may, if they wish, provide a sample of blood or urine. It should be made clear that they need not do so unless they wish to. It should also be explained that the subject may take part of the blood or urine sample away for analysis, and that a copy of the Forensic Science Service certificate of analysis will in any event be sent to them.

5 It has been suggested that where a person opts for a non-statutory blood/urine test in addition to the breath test result, the choice as between blood or urine should lie with the police, as is now the case within the statutory option range—the same safeguards being applied as to medical advice in a particular case where a specimen of blood cannot or should not be taken.

6 It is expected that in these cases the prosecution will proceed on the basis of the breath test printout as happens at present in cases over 50 microgrammes. The difference will be that the defendant will have available to him the certificate of analysis of the blood/urine sample and he will be free to apply to introduce this as evidence at his trial if he wishes to do so. The police have been advised that where this option is exercised a decision as to whether to proceed with prosecution should take account of the results of both tests. If the analysis of blood/urine is, by virtue of the lapse of time between the breath test and the taking of the blood/urine sample, under the prescribed limit it will normally be considered fair to the defendant not to proceed with the prosecution. A table of equivalent breath and blood/alcohol levels showing standard rates of elimination of alcohol over time is attached at Annex A to this circular.

7 Cases arising before the start of the operation of the non-statutory option at 00.01 BST on 16 April should continue to be dealt with as at present. (As the machines use GMT, the starting time as it appears on the printout will be 23.01 on 15 April.) The reason for delaying the operative date to 16 April is so that the necessary police prep-

arations can be made for operating the new system uniformly and to allow magistrates' courts to be informed of the procedures which the police will adopt.

*Costs*

8 The taking of all blood samples will be done at public expense. However the police have been advised that there is nothing in these arrangements which is intended to preclude the prosecution from applying to the courts for an order as to costs where it is considered appropriate.

*Monitoring*

9 The results of all cases where the blood/urine option is exercised, whether within the existing statutory option range or under these non-statutory arrangements, will be closely monitored by the Forensic Science Service over the 6 month period and a report of the results will be published. Professor Sir William Paton, CBE, DM, FRS, FRCP, Professor of Pharmacology at Oxford University, has been appointed to conduct an independent scrutiny of these monitoring arrangements and a critical examination and assessment of the report which will flow from them.

## Annex A

### Table of metabolic losses for breath and blood analyses with time

| *Breath (μg%)*<br>*Blood (mg%)* | *15 min* | *30 min* | *45 min* | *60 min* | *75 min* | *90 min* |
|---|---|---|---|---|---|---|
| 35 | 33 | 31 | 30 | 28 | 26 | 25 |
| 80 | 76 | 72 | 68 | 65 | 61 | 57 |
| 40 | 38 | 36 | 35 | 33 | 31 | 30 |
| 92 | 88 | 84 | 80 | 77 | 73 | 69 |
| 45 | 43 | 41 | 40 | 38 | 36 | 35 |
| 103 | 99 | 95 | 91 | 88 | 84 | 80 |
| 50 | 48 | 46 | 45 | 43 | 41 | 40 |
| 115 | 111 | 107 | 103 | 100 | 96 | 92 |
| 55 | 53 | 51 | 50 | 48 | 46 | 45 |
| 126 | 122 | 118 | 114 | 111 | 107 | 103 |
| 60 | 58 | 56 | 55 | 53 | 51 | 50 |
| 138 | 134 | 130 | 126 | 123 | 119 | 115 |
| 65 | 63 | 61 | 60 | 58 | 56 | 55 |
| 149 | 145 | 141 | 137 | 137 | 130 | 126 |
| 70 | 68 | 66 | 65 | 63 | 61 | 60 |
| 161 | 157 | 153 | 149 | 146 | 142 | 138 |
| 75 | 73 | 71 | 70 | 68 | 66 | 65 |
| 172 | 168 | 164 | 160 | 157 | 153 | 149 |
| 80 | 78 | 76 | 75 | 73 | 71 | 70 |
| 184 | 180 | 176 | 172 | 169 | 165 | 161 |
| 85 | 83 | 81 | 80 | 78 | 76 | 75 |
| 195 | 191 | 187 | 183 | 180 | 176 | 172 |
| 90 | 88 | 86 | 85 | 83 | 81 | 80 |
| 207 | 203 | 199 | 195 | 192 | 188 | 184 |

| *Breath (μg%)*<br>*Blood (mg%)* | *15 min* | *30 min* | *45 min* | *60 min* | *75 min* | *90 min* |
|---|---|---|---|---|---|---|
| 95 | 93 | 91 | 90 | 88 | 86 | 85 |
| 218 | 214 | 210 | 206 | 203 | 199 | 195 |
| 100 | 98 | 96 | 95 | 93 | 91 | 90 |
| 230 | 226 | 222 | 218 | 215 | 211 | 207 |
| 105 | 103 | 101 | 100 | 98 | 96 | 95 |
| 241 | 237 | 233 | 229 | 226 | 222 | 218 |
| 110 | 108 | 106 | 105 | 103 | 101 | 100 |
| 253 | 249 | 245 | 241 | 238 | 234 | 230 |
| 115 | 113 | 111 | 110 | 108 | 106 | 105 |
| 264 | 260 | 256 | 252 | 249 | 245 | 241 |
| 120 | 118 | 116 | 115 | 113 | 111 | 110 |
| 276 | 272 | 268 | 264 | 261 | 257 | 253 |
| 125 | 123 | 121 | 120 | 118 | 116 | 115 |
| 287 | 283 | 279 | 275 | 272 | 268 | 264 |
| 130 | 128 | 126 | 125 | 123 | 121 | 120 |
| 299 | 295 | 291 | 287 | 284 | 280 | 276 |
| 135 | 133 | 131 | 130 | 128 | 126 | 125 |
| 310 | 306 | 302 | 298 | 295 | 291 | 287 |
| 140 | 138 | 136 | 135 | 133 | 131 | 130 |
| 322 | 318 | 314 | 310 | 307 | 303 | 299 |
| 145 | 143 | 141 | 140 | 138 | 136 | 135 |
| 333 | 329 | 325 | 321 | 318 | 314 | 310 |
| 150 | 148 | 146 | 145 | 143 | 141 | 140 |
| 345 | 341 | 337 | 333 | 330 | 326 | 322 |
| 155 | 153 | 151 | 150 | 148 | 146 | 145 |
| 356 | 352 | 348 | 344 | 341 | 337 | 333 |
| 160 | 158 | 156 | 155 | 153 | 151 | 150 |
| 368 | 364 | 360 | 356 | 353 | 349 | 345 |
| 165 | 163 | 161 | 160 | 158 | 156 | 155 |
| 379 | 375 | 371 | 367 | 364 | 360 | 356 |
| 170 | 168 | 166 | 165 | 163 | 161 | 160 |
| 391 | 387 | 383 | 379 | 376 | 372 | 368 |
| 175 | 173 | 171 | 170 | 168 | 166 | 165 |
| 402 | 398 | 394 | 390 | 387 | 383 | 379 |

This table has been drawn up to aid persons who wish to compare breath and blood analysis, when the samples have been taken at different times.

When compiling the table, the following assumptions were made:

(a) The subject has fully absorbed all of the alcohol consumed into his bloodstream.

(b) The average metabolic rate of alcohol destruction by the body is 15 mg/100ml/hour in the blood, and 6.5 μg/100 ml/hour in the breath.[1]

(c) The blood/breath ratio is 2300:1.[2]

Each pair of numbers shows equivalent breath and blood concentrations, and each row is calculated to show how these values will decrease with the elapse of time in steps of 15 minutes.

For example, after 60 minutes have elapsed, a breath concentration of 70 μg/100 ml will, on average, drop to 63 μg/100 ml, and the corresponding blood concentration of 161 mg/100 ml will drop to 146 mg/100 ml.

Note. As a routine practice the Forensic Science laboratories make an allowance for analytical variation, by deducting 6 milligrammes from the blood analysis below 100 milligrammes per 100 millilitres, and 6% above this level, *before* they issue the certificate of analysis under the Road Traffic Act 1972. This table gives unadjusted figures. Thus the table shows that if a breath analysis of 50 μg/100 ml is obtained, the blood concentration at that time would be, on average, 115 mg/100 ml. A certificate of analysis of a blood sample taken an hour after this breath sample would, in a case of exact correspondence, show an alcohol concentration in the blood of not less than 94 mg /100 ml (94 mg + 6 mg FSS allowance + 15 mg for time lapse = 115 mg.) Results will not always agree as exactly as this, due to variation in the metabolic rate and/or the blood/breath ratio between individuals.

*References*

1 Walls HJ, Brownlie AR (1970) *Drink, Drugs and Driving* Sweet and Maxwell, London.

2 Isaacs MDJ, Emerson VJ *et al* (1980) *8th International Conference on Alcohol, Drugs and Traffic Safety* Stockholm, p 442.

# Lion Intoximeter 3000

## Operator Instruction Card

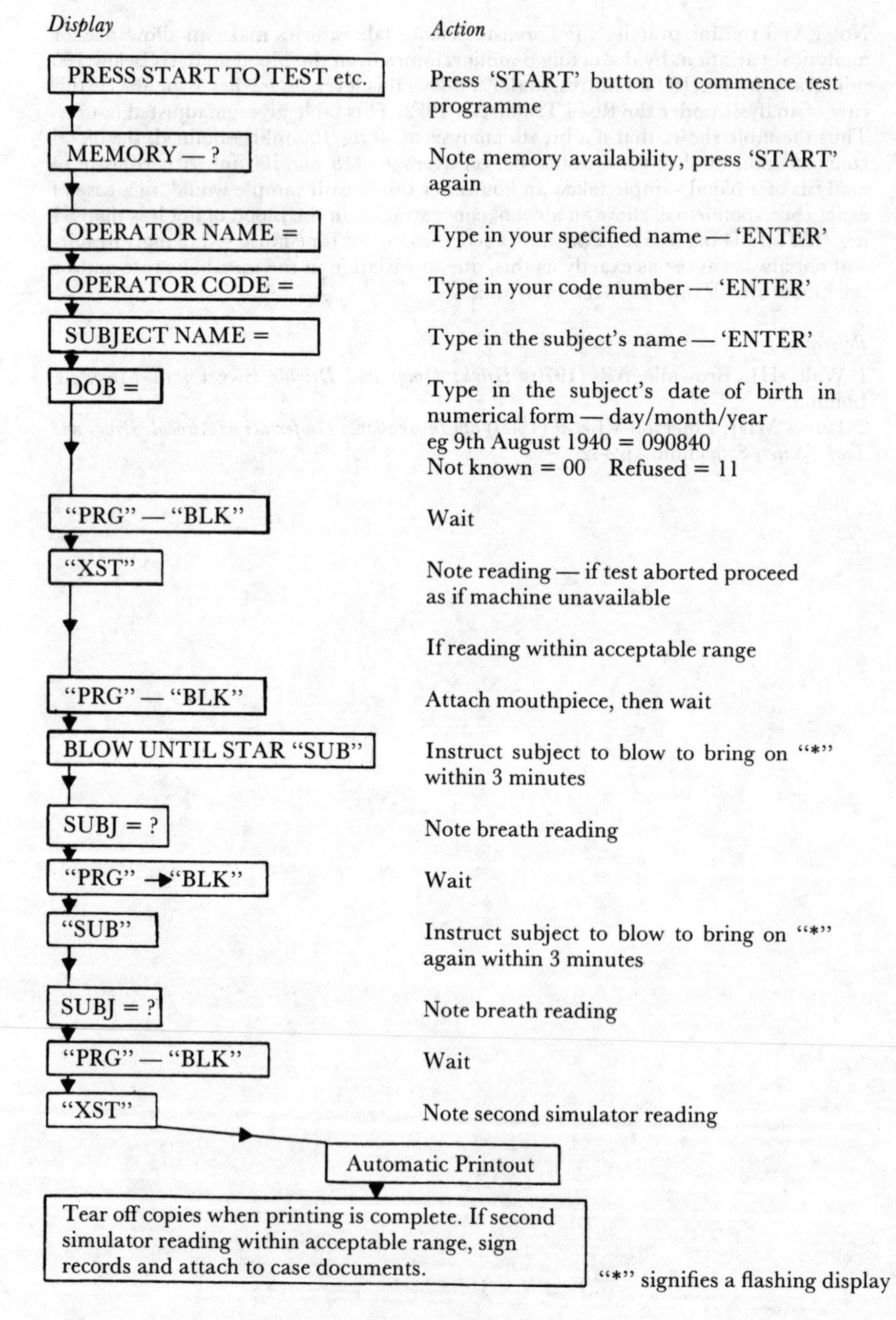
*Display*
*Action*
PRESS START TO TEST etc.
Press 'START' button to commence test programme
MEMORY — ?
Note memory availability, press 'START' again
OPERATOR NAME =
Type in your specified name — 'ENTER'
OPERATOR CODE =
Type in your code number — 'ENTER'
SUBJECT NAME =
Type in the subject's name — 'ENTER'
DOB =
Type in the subject's date of birth in numerical form — day/month/year
eg 9th August 1940 = 090840
Not known = 00 Refused = 11
"PRG" — "BLK"
Wait
"XST"
Note reading — if test aborted proceed as if machine unavailable
If reading within acceptable range
"PRG" — "BLK"
Attach mouthpiece, then wait
BLOW UNTIL STAR "SUB"
Instruct subject to blow to bring on "*" within 3 minutes
SUBJ = ?
Note breath reading
"PRG" → "BLK"
Wait
"SUB"
Instruct subject to blow to bring on "*" again within 3 minutes
SUBJ = ?
Note breath reading
"PRG" — "BLK"
Wait
"XST"
Note second simulator reading
Automatic Printout
Tear off copies when printing is complete. If second simulator reading within acceptable range, sign records and attach to case documents.
"*" signifies a flashing display

## Sample Printouts

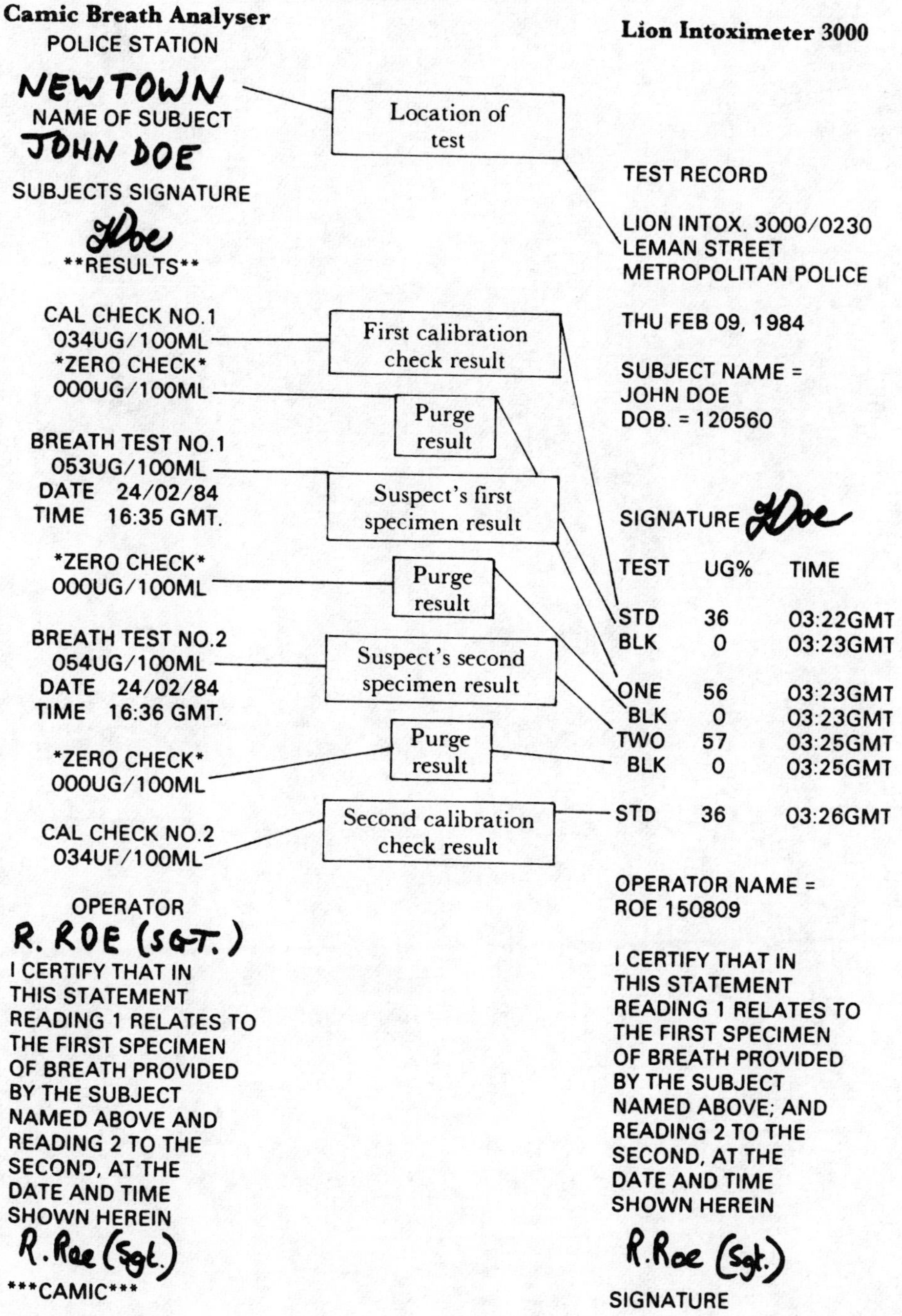

### Camic Breath Analyser

POLICE STATION
NEWTOWN
NAME OF SUBJECT
JOHN DOE
SUBJECTS SIGNATURE
J Doe
**RESULTS**

CAL CHECK NO.1
034UG/100ML — First calibration check result
*ZERO CHECK*
000UG/100ML — Purge result

BREATH TEST NO.1
053UG/100ML — Suspect's first specimen result
DATE 24/02/84
TIME 16:35 GMT.

*ZERO CHECK*
000UG/100ML — Purge result

BREATH TEST NO.2
054UG/100ML — Suspect's second specimen result
DATE 24/02/84
TIME 16:36 GMT.

*ZERO CHECK*
000UG/100ML — Purge result

CAL CHECK NO.2
034UF/100ML — Second calibration check result

OPERATOR
R. ROE (SGT.)
I CERTIFY THAT IN THIS STATEMENT READING 1 RELATES TO THE FIRST SPECIMEN OF BREATH PROVIDED BY THE SUBJECT NAMED ABOVE AND READING 2 TO THE SECOND, AT THE DATE AND TIME SHOWN HEREIN
R. Roe (Sgt.)
***CAMIC***

### Lion Intoximeter 3000

TEST RECORD

LION INTOX. 3000/0230
LEMAN STREET — Location of test
METROPOLITAN POLICE

THU FEB 09, 1984

SUBJECT NAME =
JOHN DOE
DOB. = 120560

SIGNATURE J Doe

| TEST | UG% | TIME |
|---|---|---|
| STD | 36 | 03:22GMT |
| BLK | 0 | 03:23GMT |
| ONE | 56 | 03:23GMT |
| BLK | 0 | 03:23GMT |
| TWO | 57 | 03:25GMT |
| BLK | 0 | 03:25GMT |
| STD | 36 | 03:26GMT |

(STD = First/Second calibration check result; BLK = Purge result; ONE = Suspect's first specimen result; TWO = Suspect's second specimen result)

OPERATOR NAME =
ROE 150809

I CERTIFY THAT IN THIS STATEMENT READING 1 RELATES TO THE FIRST SPECIMEN OF BREATH PROVIDED BY THE SUBJECT NAMED ABOVE; AND READING 2 TO THE SECOND, AT THE DATE AND TIME SHOWN HEREIN

R. Roe (Sgt.)
SIGNATURE

## Appendix 2

# Endorsement and Sentence Codes

The information in the codes sent out below is derived from Chapter 4 of and Appendix I to the publication *Endorsement of Driving Licences and Preparation of Notifications by Court of Orders for Endorsement*, issued by the Driver and Vehicle Licensing Centre, Swansea (Home Office circular 85/1982). The publication has been amended: see Home Office circulars 16/1983 and 45/1983.

## Endorsable Offences Code and Penalty Points

### (Appendix I)

†indicates obligatory disqualification except for special reason when 4 points imposed

| *Code* | *Offences* | *Penalty points* |
|---|---|---|
| | *Offences in relation to accidents* | |
| AC10 | Failing to stop after an accident | 5–9 |
| AC20 | Failing to give particulars or to report an accident within 24 hours | 4–9 |
| AC30 | Undefined Accident Offence | 4–9 |
| | *Offences of driving while disqualified* | |
| BA10 | Driving while disqualified by order of Court | 6 |
| BA20 | Driving whilst disqualified as under age | 2 |
| BA30 | Attempting to drive while disqualified by order of Court | 6 |
| | *Careless driving offences* | |
| CD10 | Driving without due care and attention | 2–5 |
| CD20 | Driving without reasonable consideration for other road users | 2–5 |
| CD30 | Driving without due care and attention or without reasonable consideration for other road users (primarily for use by Scottish Courts) | 2–5 |
| | *Construction and use offences (vehicles or parts dangerous)* | |
| CU10 | Using a vehicle with defective brakes | 3 |
| CU20 | Causing or likely to cause danger by reason of use of unsuitable vehicle or using a vehicle with parts or accessories (excluding brakes, steering or tyres) in a dangerous condition | 3 |

| *Code* | *Offences* | *Penalty points* |
|---|---|---|
| CU30 | Using a vehicle with defective tyres | 3 |
| CU40 | Using a vehicle with defective steering | 3 |
| CU50 | Causing or likely to cause danger by reason of load or passengers | 3 |
| CU60 | Undefined failure to comply with construction and use regulations | 3 |
| | *Reckless driving offences* | |
| DD30 | Reckless driving | 10 |
| DD60 | Manslaughter or, in Scotland, culpable homicide while driving a motor vehicle | † |
| DD70 | Causing death by reckless driving | † |
| | *Drink or drugs offences* | |
| DR10 | Driving or attempting to drive with alcohol concentration above limit | † |
| DR20 | Driving or attempting to drive when unfit through drink or drugs | † |
| DR30 | Driving or attempting to drive then refusing to provide a specimen for analysis | † |
| DR40 | In charge of a vehicle with alcohol concentration above limit | 10 |
| DR50 | In charge of a vehicle when unfit through drink or drugs | 10 |
| DR60 | Failure to provide a specimen for analysis in circumstances other than driving or attempting to drive | 10 |
| DR70 | Failing to provide specimen for breath test | 4 |
| | *Insurance offences* | |
| IN10 | Using a vehicle uninsured against third-party risks | 4–8 |
| | *Licence offences* | |
| LC10 | Driving without a licence | 2 |
| | *Miscellaneous offences* | |
| MS10 | Leaving vehicle in a dangerous position | 3 |
| MS20 | Unlawful pillion riding | 1 |
| MS30 | Playstreet offence | 2 |
| MS40* | Driving with uncorrected defective eyesight or refusing to submit to a test of eyesight | |
| MS50 | Motor racing on the highway | † |
| MS60 | Offences not covered by other codes | as appropriate |
| MS70 | Driving with uncorrected defective eyesight | 2 |
| MS80 | Refusing to submit to an eyesight test | 2 |
| | *Motorway offences* | |
| MW10 | Contravention of special roads regulations (excluding speed limits) | 3 |

*following the introduction of MS70 and MS80 the offence code MS40 can no longer be used but will continue to appear on existing licences for some time.

| *Code* | *Offences* | *Penalty points* |
|---|---|---|
| | *Non-endorsable offence* | |
| NE99 | A disqualification under Section 24 of the Criminal Justice Act 1972 | |
| | *Pedestrian crossing offences* | |
| PC10 | Undefined contravention of pedestrian crossing regulations (primarily for use by Scottish courts) | 3 |
| PC20 | Contravention of pedestrian crossing regulations with moving vehicle | 3 |
| PC30 | Contravention of pedestrian crossing regulations with stationary vehicle | 3 |
| | *Provisional licence offences* | |
| PL10 | Driving without L-plates | 2 |
| PL20 | Not accompanied by a qualified person | 2 |
| PL30 | Carrying a person not qualified | 2 |
| PL40 | Drawing an unauthorised trailer | 2 |
| PL50 | Undefined failure to comply with the conditions of a provisional licence | 2 |
| | *Speed limits offences* | |
| SP10 | Exceeding goods vehicle speed limit | 3 |
| SP20 | Exceeding speed limit for type of vehicle (excluding goods/passenger vehicles) | 3 |
| SP30 | Exceeding statutory speed limit on a public road | 3 |
| SP40 | Exceeding passenger vehicle speed limit | 3 |
| SP50 | Exceeding speed limit on a motorway | 3 |
| SP60 | Undefined speed limit offence | 3 |
| | *Traffic directions and signs offences* | |
| TS10 | Failing to comply with traffic light signals | 3 |
| TS20 | Failing to comply with double white lines | 3 |
| TS30 | Failing to comply with a 'stop' sign | 3 |
| TS40 | Failing to comply with directions of a constable or traffic warden | 3 |
| TS50 | Failing to comply with a traffic sign (excluding stop signs, traffic lights or double white lines) | 3 |
| TS60 | Failure to comply with a school crossing patrol sign | 3 |
| TS70 | Undefined failure to comply with a traffic direction or sign | 3 |
| | *Offences of theft or unauthorised taking* | |
| UT10 | Taking and driving away a vehicle without consent or an attempt thereat (in England and Wales prior to Theft Act 1968 only). Driving a vehicle knowing it to have been taken without consent; allowing oneself to be carried in or on a vehicle knowing it to have been taken without consent. (Primarily for use by Scottish Courts) | 8 |
| UT20 | Stealing or attempting to steal a motor vehicle | 8 |
| UT30 | Going equipped for stealing or taking a motor vehicle | 8 |

| Code | Offences | Penalty points |
|---|---|---|
| UT40 | Taking or attempting to take a vehicle without consent. Driving or attempting to drive a vehicle knowing it to have been taken without consent. Allowing oneself to be carried in or on a vehicle knowing it to have been taken without consent | 8 |
| | *Special code* | |
| TT99 | ONLY to be used to indicate a disqualification under the penalty points procedures ie where the number of penalty points totals 12 or more—including any penalty points 'taken into account', but not endorsed because a driver has been disqualified. *NB* When using this code, a date of conviction must always be shown on the licence. | |
| | *Aiding and/or abetting and/or counselling and/or procuring* Offences as coded above but with zero changed to 2 eg UT10 becomes UT12. | |
| | *Causing or permitting* Offences as coded above but with zero changed to 4 eg PL10 becomes PL14. | |
| | *Inciting* Offences as coded above but with zero changed to 6 eg DD30 becomes DD36. | |
| | *Obsolete special code* | |
| XX99 | To signify a disqualification under the old 'totting up' procedure. Following the introduction of the penalty points scheme this code can no longer be used but will continue to appear on existing licences for some time. | |

## Sentence Code

(Chapter 4)

In the case of sentences other than fines or disqualification, the nature of the sentence is indicated on the driving licence by the following code which provides the first character of the endorsement:

| | |
|---|---|
| A | Imprisonment |
| B | Detention in a place specified by the Secretary of State |
| C | Suspended sentence of imprisonment |
| D | Suspended sentence supervision order |
| E | Conditional discharge |
| F | Bound over |
| G | Probation |
| H | Supervision order |
| J | Absolute discharge |
| K | Attendance centre |

L Detention centre
M Community service order
N Cumulative sentence (Scottish courts only)
P Youth custody sentence
Q Parent or guardian order
R Borstal
S Compensation order
T Hospital or guardianship order
U Admonition (Scottish courts only)
V Young offenders' institution (Scottish courts only)
W Care order
X Total period of partially suspended prison sentence ie period sentence served + period sentence suspended

If the first character of the endorsement is A,B,C,D,E,F,G,H,K,L,P,R,U,V or X, two digits and a character follow the initial character, indicating the duration of the sentence in hours, days, weeks, months or years (ie H,D,W,M or Y, respectively). For example, 18 months' imprisonment would be indicated by the code A 18 M. If no period is specified, the initial character is followed by three zeros.

If the first character of the endorsement is H, J,N,Q,S,T or W, three zeros follow the initial character. For example, absolute discharge would be indicated by the code J 000.

If the first character of the endorsement is M (community service order), three digits follow the initial character, indicating the number of hours' service (the letter H is not used). For example, 40 hours' community service would be indicated by the code M 040, 240 hours' by M 240.

If the first character of the endorsement is C (suspended prison sentence), two digits and a character follow the initial character, indicating the period the prison sentence has been suspended. For example, one month's prison suspended for one year would be indicated by A 01 M followed by C 01 Y.

If the first character of the endorsement is X (partially suspended prison sentence), the code is similar. Two digits and a character follow the initial character, indicating the period of prison sentence actually served. For example, four months' imprisonment with one month to be served would be indicated by A 04 M followed by X 01 M.

## Appendix 3

# Suggestions for Assessing Penalties

The following *Suggestions for Traffic Offence Penalties* were published by the Magistrates' Association in May 1985 superseding the eighth edition of April 1983.

## How to Use the 'Suggestions'

This folder, approved in principle by the Lord Chancellor and Lord Chief Justice, is designed to help courts in assessing their penalties to achieve a consistency of approach throughout England and Wales. It cannot be emphasized too strongly that THE LIST IS NOT A TARIFF. The list provides a suggested figure which the court might wish to increase or decrease in their discussion as to the proper penalty in each case. The responsibility for the sentence is that of the bench in each particular case and the penalty in each case must be judicially assessed in accordance with the circumstances of the particular offence and of the offender.

The circumstances include the gravity of the particular offence and sometimes its prevalence; the record of the offender; the means of the offender (as required by Statute); whether the offence was committed deliberately or inadvertently; and of the different impact of disqualification on different offenders bearing in mind the number of penalty points incurred **and that a sentence of disqualification deletes these**. When fixing the amount of the fine where an order of disqualification is also made, it should be remembered that the disqualification will frequently itself entail a very heavy financial burden.

The level of penalties for traffic offences must not become out of proportion compared to the level of fines for other common criminal offences such as thefts from shops and assaults.

The seriousness of offences varies widely, especially in cases of careless driving, and many road traffic offences are more hazardous when speeds are higher. Experience has proved that drinking and driving offences account for very many accidents, injuries and deaths. The Court of Appeal has consistently upheld higher penalties for offenders with higher blood alcohol, and it is suggested that fines and especially periods of disqualification should reflect this.

These figures represent a broad consensus of view on appropriate penalties for 'average' offences committed by first offenders of average means. But there may be good reasons for local variations. Average rates of pay are much higher in some areas than in others, so it is consistent that average fines should vary too. A column has been left for the bench 'norm' which it is hoped each bench will review after consulting neighbouring benches and giving full weight to these considered suggestions.

*The Multiple Offender*

Where on one occasion an offender is convicted of a large number of offences it is suggested that the court can initially decide upon the maximum total amount of the fines which it is appropriate to impose, having regard to the offender's financial circumstances even though this total may prove to be considerably less than the sum which would result from adding together all the suggested penalties involved.

Geoffrey Norman
*Secretary*
*The Magistrates' Association*

*Ninth Edition*
*May 1985*

IMPORTANT

These suggestions may be reproduced for the use of benches provided [this preface] is included.

**THIS LIST IS NOT A TARIFF and these Suggestions are to be used only in conjunction with the front page**

## Suggestions for Courts' Assessment of Penalties for Main Traffic Offences

The maximum standard levels are at present: Level 1— £50
Level 2— £100
Level 3— £400
Level 4—£1,000
Level 5—£2,000

D – Must disqualify at least 12 months (unless special reasons) and endorse. (If disqualifying for a lengthy period, or if driving skill suspect, consider disqualifying until test passed.)

E – Must endorse (unless special reasons) and may disqualify.

The maximum penalties for 'goods vehicles' also apply to 'vehicles adapted to carry more than eight passengers'. (See offences 7, 21, 22, 23, 33, 40 and 41.)

| *Offence* | *Points* | *Maximum Penalty* | *Suggestion* | *Bench 'Norm'* |
|---|---|---|---|---|
| ACCIDENT | | | | |
| 1. Failing to stop | 5–9 | Level 5 E | £125 } should disqualify when both offences involved | |
| 2. Failing to report to police | 4–9 | Level 5 E | £125 } | |
| ALCOHOL | | | | |
| 80 mg blood = 35 $\mu$g breath = 107 mg urine | | | | |
| 3. Drunken driving or driving with excess alcohol | (4) | Level 5 D and/or 6 months prison | £200 D 12 months but—<br>Blood / Breath / Urine<br>18 months: over 150 mg / 66 $\mu$g / 200 mg<br>2 years: over 200 mg / 88 $\mu$g / 267 mg<br>3 years: over 250 mg / 110 $\mu$g / 333 mg | |

| *Offence* | *Points* | *Maximum Penalty* | *Suggestion* | *Bench 'Norm'* |
|---|---|---|---|---|
| 4. Refusing evidential specimen (driving) | (4) | Level 5 D and/or 6 months prison | £200 D 18 months | |
| 5. In charge drunk or with excess alcohol or refusing evidential specimen | 10 | Level 4 E and/or 3 months prison | £100 | |
| 6. Refusing roadside breath test | 4 | Level 3 E | £50 | |
| BRAKES | | | | |
| 7. Faulty condition of | 3 | Level 4 E but for goods vehicle: Level 5 E | £50 Driver<br>£125 HGV Owner | } Consider degree of responsibility |
| DISQUALIFIED | | | | |
| 8. (a) By court order | 6 | Level 5 E and/or 6 months prison | Consider custodial penalty | |
| (b) By age | 2 | Level 5 E and/or 6 months prison | £50 | |
| DOCUMENTS | | | | |
| 9. Failing to produce | – | Level 3 | £10 | |
| DOUBLE WHITE LINES | | | | |
| 10. Failing to comply with system | 3 | Level 3 E | £50 and consider disqualification | |
| DRIVING | | | | |
| 11. Reckless | 10 | Level 5 E and/or 6 months prison | £300 and consider disqualification | |
| 12. Careless or inconsiderate | 2–5 | Level 4 E | £60 but always consider degree of carelessness | |

| Offence | Penalty points | Level / endorsement | Suggested fine |
|---|---|---|---|
| **HELMET** | | | |
| 13. No safety helmet | – | Level 2 | £15 |
| **INSURANCE** | | | |
| 14. No insurance | 4–8 | Level 4 E | £125 |

In fixing the fine regard should be had as to whether the offence was deliberate or inadvertent, whether the offender was misled or any other mitigating circumstances and whether the 'user' or 'permitter' was responsible for the offence. If deliberate the offender should normally be disqualified or receive 7 or 8 penalty points. In any event the court must have regard to the amount of the insurance premium.

| Offence | Penalty points | Level / endorsement | Suggested fine |
|---|---|---|---|
| **LEARNER DRIVER** | | | |
| 15. Unsupervised in car | 2 | Level 3 E | £50 } and consider disqualification |
| 16. Motor cyclist with unqualified passenger | 2 | Level 3 E | £25 } and consider disqualification |
| 17. No L plates | 2 | Level 3 E | £15 |
| **LICENCE** | | | |
| 18. No driving licence | 2 (if endorsable) | Level 3 in some cases E | £75 if endorsable: £10 otherwise |
| 19. No excise licence | – | Level 3 or 5 times annual duty | Actual duty lost plus fine of approximately twice that amount (adjourn if in any doubt as to back duty). |
| **LIGHTS** | | | |
| 20. Driving without lights | – | Level 4 | £50 |

| Offence | Points | Maximum Penalty | Suggestion | Bench 'Norm' |
|---|---|---|---|---|
| **LOAD** | | | | |
| 21. Insecure load | 3 | Level 4 E but for goods vehicles: Level 5 E | £50 Non HGV Owner/Driver<br>£200 HGV Driver<br>£400 HGV Owner | but consider degree of responsibility |
| 22. Overloading commercial vehicle or exceeding maximum axle weight | – | Level 5 | £200 HGV Driver<br>£400 HGV Owner<br>Suggested penalty refers to conviction on each charge.<br>In addition to the suggestion for overloading add £20 per 1% of overload but always have regard to commercial gain and damage to roads. | |
| 23. Offences re number of passengers, dangerous condition of vehicle weight distribution, packing and adjustment of load | 3 | Level 4 E but for goods vehicles: Level 5 E | £100<br>£50 HGV Driver<br>£100 HGV Owner | but consider degree of responsibility |
| **PARKING** | | | | |
| 24. Dangerous position | 3 | Level 3 E | £40 | |
| 25. On zig-zags by pedestrian crossing | 3 | Level 3 E | £20 | |
| 26. Obstruction | – | Level 3* | £15 | |
| 27. Not supplying statement of ownership | – | Level 3 | £20 | |
| 28. Stopping on Clearway | – | Level 3 | £40 | |

*Level 4 if contrary to the Construction and Use Regulations.

| | | | |
|---|---|---|---|
| PEDESTRIAN OR SCHOOL CROSSING | | | |
| 29. Offences other than parking | 3 | Level 3 E | £40 and consider disqualification |
| SEAT BELTS | | | |
| 30. Not wearing | – | Level 2 | £15 |
| 31. Driving with child not wearing | – | Level 2 | £15 |
| SPEEDING | | | |
| 32. Exceeding speed limit | 3 | Level 3 E | £2.00 per mph over any limit. More for heavy vehicles. Consider disqualification if 30 mph over limit. |
| STEERING | | | |
| 33. Faulty condition of steering | 3 | Level 4 E but for goods vehicles: Level 5 E | £50 Driver / £125 HGV Owner } consider degree of responsibilty |
| TACHOGRAPH | | | |
| 34. No tachograph or not used as required | – | Level 4 | £100 |
| TAKEN VEHICLES | | | |
| 35. Taking vehicles without consent | 8 | Level 5 E and/or 6 months prison | £150 Consider custodial sentence |
| 36. Carried in taken vehicle | 8 | Level 5 E and/or 6 months prison | £100 |

| *Offence* | *Points* | *Maximum Penalty* | *Suggestion* | *Bench 'Norm'* |
|---|---|---|---|---|
| TEST CERTIFICATE | | | | |
| 37. No test certificate | – | Level 3 but for vehicles adapted to carry more than 8 passengers: Level 4 | £20 | |
| TRAFFIC LIGHTS | | | | |
| 38. Failing to comply with | 3 | Level 3 E | £40 | |
| TRAFFIC OR POLICE SIGNS | | | | |
| 39. Failing to comply with (except lights or double white lines) | 3 | Level 3 (power to disqualify, endorse, test in some cases only) | £40 (Endorse where required) | |
| TYRES | | | | |
| 40. Faulty condition | 3 | Level 4 E but for goods vehicles: Level 5 E | £50 Driver<br>£125 HGV Owner<br>} Consider degree of responsibility<br>Suggested penalty refers to each tyre | |
| VEHICLE OFFENCES under the Construction and Use Regulations not shown elsewhere. | | | | |
| 41. Goods vehicle, dangerously unsuitable use | 3 | Level 5 E | £60 Driver<br>£200 HGV Owner | |
| 42. Other offences | – | Level 4 | £15 Driver<br>£40 HGV Owner<br>} (41–42) but consider degree of responsibility | |

## Motorway Offences

| *Offence* | *Points* | *Maximum Penalty* | *Suggestion* | *Bench 'Norm'* |
|---|---|---|---|---|
| DRIVING | | | | |
| 43. Driving in reverse | 3 | Level 4 E | £150 On main motorway<br>£40 On sliproad | |
| 44. Driving in wrong direction | 3 | Level 4 E | £200 On main motorway<br>£50 On sliproad | Consider disqualification |
| 45. Driving off carriageway | 3 | Level 4 E | £75 On central reservation<br>£50 On hard shoulder or verge | |
| 46. Driving on slip road against 'No entry' sign | 3 | Level 4 E | £40 | |
| 47. Making U-turn | 3 | Level 4 E | £150 Consider disqualification | |
| LEARNERS | | | | |
| 48. Learner driver or excluded vehicle | 3 | Level 4 E | £75 | |
| SPEEDING | | | | |
| 49. Exceeding speed limit | 3 | Level 4 E* | £2.00 per mph over limit. More for HGVs and PSVs. Consider disqualification if 30 mph over limit | |
| STOPPING | | | | |
| 50. Stopping on hard shoulder | – | Level 4 | £40 On main motorway<br>£20 On sliproad | |

*Level 3 E in respect of goods and other vehicles subject to lower limit.

| *Offence* | *Points* | *Maximum Penalty* | *Suggestion* | *Bench 'Norm'* |
|---|---|---|---|---|
| THIRD LANE | | | | |
| 51. Vehicle over 7.5 tonnes or drawing trailer in third lane | 3 | Level 4 E | £75 | |
| WALKING | | | | |
| 52. Walking on motorway | – | Level 4 | £40 On main motorway or sliproad<br>£20 On hard shoulder or verge | |

# Index

## Table of Braking Distances

*(taken, by permission, from the Highway Code)*

### Stopping distances—in feet

| *mph* | *Thinking distance* | *Braking distance* | *Overall stopping distance* |
|---|---|---|---|
| 20 | 20 | 20 | 40 |
| 30 | 30 | 45 | 75 |
| 40 | 40 | 80 | 120 |
| 50 | 50 | 125 | 175 |
| 60 | 60 | 180 | 240 |
| 70 | 70 | 245 | 315 |

On a dry road, a good car with good brakes and tyres and an alert driver, will stop in the distances shown. Remember these are shortest stopping distances. Stopping distances increase greatly with wet and slippery roads, poor brakes and tyres, and tired drivers.

(For use of the Highway Code and table, see 2.90 and *R* v *Chadwick* at 5.46.)

### Conversion Table

| *Miles per hour* | *Feet per second (to nearest foot)* |
|---|---|
| 20 | 29 |
| 30 | 44 |
| 40 | 59 |
| 50 | 73 |
| 60 | 88 |
| 70 | 103 |
| 80 | 117 |

### Metric Equivalents

| *km* | *miles/km* | *miles* |
|---|---|---|
| 16.093 | 10 | 6.214 |
| 32.185 | 20 | 12.428 |
| 48.278 | 30 | 18.642 |
| 64.371 | 40 | 24.856 |
| 80.463 | 50 | 31.070 |
| 96.556 | 60 | 37.284 |
| 112.649 | 70 | 43.498 |
| 128.742 | 80 | 49.712 |
| 144.834 | 90 | 55.926 |
| 160.927 | 100 | 62.140 |
| 177.020 | 110 | 68.354 |
| 193.112 | 120 | 74.568 |

1 mm = 0.03937 in    1 in = 25.4 mm
1 m = 1.0936 yd = 3.2808 ft = 39.37 in
1 kg = 2.205 lb    1 lb = 0.454 kg
1 tonne = 1,000 kg = 2,204.6 lb
(1 ton = 20 cwt = 2,240 lb)

## Standard Scale Fines

| Level on the standard scale | Original maximum | Amount on or after 1 May 1984 |
|---|---|---|
| 1 | £25 | £50 |
| 2 | £50 | £100 |
| 3 | £200 | £400 |
| 4 | £500 | £1,000 |
| 5 | £1,000 | £2,000 |

See note on standard scale fines at pp 701–2.